Effective Practice in Health, Social Care and Criminal Justice

Second edition

n or before

v

Effective Practice in Health, Social Care and Criminal Justice
A Partnership Approach

Second edition

Edited by
Ros Carnwell and Julian Buchanan

 Open University Press

Open University Press
McGraw-Hill Education
McGraw-Hill House
Shoppenhangers Road
Maidenhead
Berkshire
England
SL6 2QL

email: enquiries@openup.co.uk
world wide web: www.openup.co.uk

and Two Penn Plaza, New York, NY 10121—2289, USA

A catalogue record of this book is available from the British Library

ISBN-10: 0-33-522911-5 (pb) 0-33-522912-3 (hb)
ISBN-13: 978-0-33-5339116 (pb) 978-0-33-5229123 (hb)

Typeset by Kerrypress, Luton, Bedfordshire
Printed and bound in the UK by Bell and Bain Ltd, Glasgow

The *McGraw·Hill* Companies

Contents

Notes on the contributors   vii
Foreword by Walid El Ansari   xiii
Preface   xv

Part I: The context of partnerships   1

1   The concepts of partnership and collaboration   3
Ros Carnwell and Alex Carson
2   The impact of the digital age on partnership and collaboration   22
Ros Carnwell and Julian Buchanan
3   Promoting inclusive partnership working   31
Joy Merrell
4   Ethical issues of working in partnership   47
Althea Allison

Part II: Partnerships in practice   63

5.   Inter-professional communication in child protection   65
Brian Corby with Frances Young and Stella Coleman
6.   Working in partnership to support people with mental health difficulties   80
Adrian Jones
7.   Working across the interface of formal and informal care of older people   96
Pat Chambers and Judith Phillips
8.   Understanding and misunderstanding problem drug use: working together   111
Julian Buchanan
9.   Addressing homelessness through effective partnership working   130
Emma Wincup
10.   Problem drug use and safeguarding children: partnership and practice issues   143
Julian Buchanan with Brian Corby
11.   Tackling behavioural problems in the classroom using a student assistance programme.   160
Ros Carnwell, Sally Ann Baker and Carl Wassell

12. Not behind closed doors: working in partnership against
    domestic violence   177
    Liz Blyth and Sobia Shaw
13. Working with Gypsy Travellers: a partnership approach   195
    Angela Roberts
14. Effective partnerships to assist mentally disordered offenders   209
    Virginia Minogue
15. Partnership approaches to working with people with HIV   228
    Ruth Wilson

Part III: Learning from partnerships   **249**

16. On the receiving end: reflections from a service user   251
    Amir Minhas
17. Evaluating partnerships   263
    Ros Carnwell
18. Learning from partnerships: themes and issues   281
    Ros Carnwell and Julian Buchanan
19. Developing best practice in partnership   288
    Julian Buchanan and Ros Carnwell

References   295
index   337

Notes on contributors

Dr Althea Allison is Senior Manager for the West Midlands North Comprehensive Local Research Network (CLRN). Althea has previously worked for the National Research Ethics Service (NRES) as Manager for the Office for Research Ethics Committees (OREC), for Thames Valley, Hampshire and the Isle of Wight, and undertook a part-time secondment as Deputy Director of Operations. Althea has also worked as a lecturer in health and social care at the University of Reading where her research area was grounded in ethics and professional practice. She began her professional life as a registered mental health nurse, and previous professional roles have included working as a mental health nurse both in hospitals and in the community. She has also taught and supervised community nurses. Her work has been published in refereed journals, presented at international conferences and she has contributed a chapter in *Ethical Issues in Cognitive Behaviour Therapy* in *Cognitive Behaviour Therapy: An Introduction to Theory and Practice* (Ballière Tindall, 1996) edited by Sue Marshall and John Turnbull.

Sally-Ann Baker is a senior lecturer in the Centre for Health and Community Research at the Glyndŵr University, Wrexham. She has a background in psychology and is research active, having been involved in a range of research projects within health, social care and education. More recently, these have focused on the evaluation of community development and health promotion initiatives. She has an interest in research methods and increasing research capacity. She teaches and advises novice researchers on research methods and is a member of an NHS Trust Internal Review Panel and the Research Ethics Committee of North East Wales Institute.

Liz Blyth has worked in leadership, management and operational roles in health and social care, community development, neighbourhood renewal, and culture and sport for almost 20 years, with experience in both the voluntary and statutory sectors. She currently works as Cultural Strategy and Improvement Manager at Leicester City Council during a time of significant culture-led regeneration in the city, and she is also seconded part-time as a sub-regional champion for the Cultural Improvement Partnership East Midlands. Prior to this she worked for five years for Coventry City Council as Coordinator for the Coventry Domestic Violence Partnership, a multi-agency forum developing Coventry's strategic response to domestic abuse. Liz has a diploma in youth and community work and a Master's in management, organization and change from Loughborough University.

Professor Julian Buchanan is a founder member of the Social Inclusion Research Unit at Glyndŵr University, Wrexham. He has over 25 years' experience in the drugs field as a practitioner, lecturer and researcher. In the mid-1980s, as a drugs specialist with the Merseyside Probation Service, he developed a 'risk reduction' approach, and was instrumental in establishing one of the largest multi-agency community drugs teams in the UK. His research interests include problem drug use, drug policy and practice, social exclusion, discrimination and marginalized people. He has published in a wide range of journals including: *Social Work Education, Child and Family Social Work, Practice, Journal of Social Work in Mental Health, Drugs: Education, Prevention, Policy, Probation Journal*, and *British Journal of Community Justice and Criminal Justice Studies*. He is currently on the editorial board of the *Open Addiction Journal, Probation Journal, British Journal of Community Justice*, and Specialist Assessor for the *International Journal of Drug Policy*.

Professor Ros Carnwell is Director of the Centre for Health and Community Research and Glyndŵr University, Wrexham, where she manages funded projects, mainly in primary/community care settings. She has a professional background in health visiting, and has taught and researched at a number of universities including, Keele University, Manchester Metropolitan University, University of Wolverhampton and the Open University. Her research interests include: developing nursing roles in primary care, evaluation of health and social care provision, and educational research.

Dr Alex Carson is Reader in Nursing Studies and Head of School of Health, Social Care and Sport and Exercise Sciences at Glyndŵr University, Wrexham. After a number of years as a practitioner in acute surgery, Alex has worked in education for 20 years. His main teaching interests have been in health care ethics. He has a doctorate in sociology from Edinburgh University and has been developing new teaching and research methods, using a narrative-based approach. He has published in nursing and medical journals.

Dr Pat Chambers is a senior lecturer in social work within the School of Criminology, Education, Sociology and Social Work at Keele University. Her research interests lie primarily within social gerontology and social work. She has a specific interest in the development of research skills and knowledge among social work practitioners and is an active participant in the Making Research Count initiative at Keele University and the Academic Representative on the Research Advisory Panel for Staffordshire County Council Social Care and Health Directorate. Prior to her career in higher education, Pat worked in a variety of voluntary and statutory agencies. She continues her link with the voluntary sector as a trustee of Age Concern Cheshire.

Stella Coleman is a senior lecturer in the Department of Social Work at University of Central Lancashire, teaching in childcare and inter-professional working on qualifying and post-qualifying programmes. A qualified social worker, she worked for many years within children and families social work and retains strong links with practice issues in the area of child protection / safeguarding children.

Professor Brian Corby was at the Social Work Studies Department at the University of Central Lancashire. His research interests were in the field of safeguarding children and child care social work, with particular emphasis on assessment, interprofessional communication and service users' views. He published widely in these fields and was author of *Child Abuse: Towards a Knowledge Base*, (3rd edn) published by Open University Press (2006). Sadly Brian died on 19 January 2007 after a long struggle with myeloma.

Walid El Ansari is Chair of Public Health at the University of Gloucestershire. His background is in clinical medicine and paediatrics after which he moved to public and family health. Walid has completed DFID commissioned public health work in Malawi, and has been an advisor with WHO Geneva where he has also co-authored two WHO reports for the Organization. Walid has been an invited member of the Network of Innovators. Observatory on Chronic Conditions, WHO Geneva; a member on NICE programme development committee for community engagement charged with the development of the national guidelines for the UK; is currently appointed to the European Court of Auditors of the European Parliament, involved in evaluating 250 European funded health promotion projects that operate on partnership and networking principles. Walid is a co-investigator on the National Institute of Health grant, examining and producing the national guidelines on multi-professional team working in health and social care in the UK. He has been a visiting scholar with the School of Public Health at UCLA; has contributed to the work of the Forum on Microbial Threats, Board on Global Health, Institute of Medicine of the National Academies in Washington, DC; and collaborated with colleagues from the New York Academy of Medicine. Research interests include community development and involvement in health and the interactions between stakeholders involved in health alliances and partnerships.

Dr Adrian Jones is a nurse consultant and Head of Mental Health Nursing at the North East Wales NHS Trust. He has worked for 20 years in mental health services as both a manager and clinician. Adrian has published extensively on nurse prescribing, care pathways and medication management. His main areas for research are different forms of prescriptive authority and medication. He has a PhD from City University in mental health nursing. Adrian has published widely in nursing and medical journals and has spoken at a range of peer reviewed national and international conferences.

Professor Joy Merrell is Professor of Public Health Nursing at the School of Health Science, Swansea University. Her clinical background is in public health nursing. Joy's research interests include the participation of volunteers and the public in primary health care, accessibility of services especially for minority ethnic groups, evaluating health promotion initiatives particularly for older people and public health nursing. She has conducted several national reviews of community and public health nursing for the Welsh Assembly Government. She Chairs the West Wales Region of the Wales Equality and Diversity in Health and Social Care Research and Support Service (WEDHS) and is a core member of the Older People and Ageing Research and Development Network (OPAN). She has published on partnership working in various health and social care journals.

Amir Minhas has written in the capacity of a service user. As a wheelchair user he has a lifetime experience of needing external consideration and support to negotiate the practical and social difficulties faced by people with limited mobility. Amir also has considerable experience as a service provider. He is a qualified probation officer who works for the Merseyside Probation Trust. He has worked for the Probation Service for more than ten years and has experience in most of the various roles including specialist PSR writer (Racially Motivated Offenders), and the full range of pre- and post-release and community supervision functions. Amir has acheived a Master's degree (social work) and a Diploma in Social Work, and is currently a member of the *Probation Journal* editorial board. He enjoys a stable, committed relationship and is step-father to his partner's three teenage/early adulthood children.

Dr Virginia Minogue works in the NHS as Head of the West Yorkshire Mental Health Research and Development Consortium. Her particular areas of interest are service user and carer involvement in research and service development and planning, partnership working and mentally disordered offenders. She works particularly closely with service users and carers and has published papers in this area as well as a training package. She was previously a senior lecturer in community justice at Sheffield University. Prior to this she worked for a number of years in the Probation Service as a manager, researcher, Family Court Welfare Officer and probation officer. She is currently Chair of the Editorial Board for the journal *Mental Health and Learning Disabilities Research and Practice*. She is also Chair of a voluntary sector mental health organisation that offers support, housing and employment services to adults with mental health problems and their carers.

Professor Judith Phillips is Professor of Gerontology and Social Work at Swansea University and director of the Older People and Ageing Research and Development Network (OPAN Cymru) in Wales. Her research interests are in social work and social care, and include carers in employment, housing and retirement communities, family and kinship networks, carework and older offenders. She is Series Editor for *Ageing and the Lifecourse* (Policy Press) and is President of the British Society of Gerontology.

Angela Roberts is a qualified nurse and health visitor. She currently works as a strategic commissioning manager for Wrexham Local health Board and as Health Visitor Project Lead for the Welsh Assembly Government-funded Inequalities in Health Initiative: Redressing the Balance. Angela has worked for over 12 years with Gypsies and Travellers. Angela has presented at many local national and international conferences on the needs of this vulnerable group.

Sobia Shaw is the Chief Executive of Panahghar Asian Women's Organisation, a voluntary charitable organization that has for nearly 30 years provided services to women and children experiencing domestic violence. Sobia has spent over 20 years working in the field of health and social care, community development, training, equality and diversity, and research and development. Her first research paper looking at equality and employment among Muslim women was published by the Department of Employment when she was 22 years old. Since then she has worked for London and Warwick Universities, the Health Department and Panahghar. Sobia was a founder member of the Coventry Domestic Violence and Abuse Partnership. She was instrumental in the design and delivery of many of its initiatives during her 13 years as Vice Chair, securing funding for the Partnership's activities, including the appointment of the Coordinator post, services for African Caribbean women, research into children's issues including child contact, and a perpetrators programme. She has presented a range of papers and represented the Partnership and Panahghar at local and national conferences on issues around domestic violence, including forced marriages and honour crimes, BME communities, equality and diversity, and community development. She has recently been invited to sit on a Hate Crimes Scrutiny Panel for the West Midlands Crown Prosecution Service looking at domestic violence issues.

Carl Wassell is a freelance consultant and trainer in Sussex, where his current contracts involve evaluating the Student Assistance Programme (SAP) run by Kirklees local authority and delivering training to school staff in Cumbria and Merseyside. After developing services for people with HIV/AIDS in London and Brighton, Carl joined the Society of Saint Francis as a novice brother in 1989 to test a vocation to the religious life. He later qualified in occupational therapy and worked in acute adult psychiatry. Carl met Cheryl Watkins, author of the SAP, in 1998 and, inspired by her work, negotiated with Wrexham Local Education Authority to pilot SAP in a secondary school in Wrexham, and subsequently to coordinate an authority-wide SAP. The Wrexham SAP has won a Welsh Secondary School Award, been written about in Welsh Assembly Government and Estyn good practice guidance documents to schools, and there have been four papers published in a peer reviewed journal.

Ruth Wilson has worked as the Community Mental Health Nurse Specialist for HIV/AIDS based within the Palliative Care Directorate of Berkshire West Primary Care Trust since 1997. She is responsible for the mental health assessment, treatment and care of people infected and affected with HIV in Berkshire, working as part of the multi-disciplinary team within the local HIV service. She researched the 'Lived experience of taking highly active antiretroviral therapy as the treatment for HIV' for her MA and ongoing research interests include the effects of being diagnosed HIV positive during pregnancy and the ongoing stigma, fear and isolation that often accompanies HIV diagnosis and its impact on adherence to treatment.

Dr Emma Wincup is a senior lecturer in criminology and criminal justice at the University of Leeds, School of Law. She is also Deputy Director of the Centre for Criminal Justice Studies. Prior to joining the University of Leeds in 2005, Emma held lecturing posts at the University of Kent (2000–04) and Cardiff University (1997–2000). In 1998 she spent six months on secondment to the National Assembly for Wales to develop their drug policy. Emma's research interests coalesce around crime and social exclusion. She has conducted a range of research projects relating to housing and homelessness. These include studies of young homeless people and problem substance use, hostel provision for offenders and the housing needs of female offenders. Most recently she completed two evaluations of resettlement programmes for prisoners. Emma has published on a wide range of criminological and criminal justice topics. She is currently working on a second edition of *Criminology* for Oxford University Press and has recently published a second edition of *Doing Research on Crime and Justice*, also for Oxford University Press. Emma is currently co-editor of the *Journal of Social Policy*, published by Cambridge University Press.

Frances Young is a senior lecturer in the Department of Social Work at University of Central Lancashire where she teaches child care on the qualifying and post-qualifying programmes. Prior to this she worked in local authorities social work specializing in the areas of fostering and adoption. She retains practice and research interests in both these areas.

Foreword

(by Walid El Ansari, Chair of Public Health, University of Gloucestershire)

The landscape of health and social care is changing. At the heart of the change is growing awareness among policy makers, health and social care practitioners, service users and their carers of the need for effectively integrated services. But such integration is confronted by multi-faceted challenges. For instance, synergy requires concerted thinking and activities from partners at the macro level of policy, meso levels of health and social care organization and delivery, in addition to the micro levels of the user's family and other community linkages. Consequently, in the UK, a body of legislations and policy documents highlights a duty to develop collaborative working arrangements for health and social care service delivery. The same is true for criminal justice.

In everyday practice this translates to multi-agency partnerships. The aspiration is a service that holistically addresses the health, social, legal and psychological aspects of any case, empowers individual users and is supportive to carers. This in turn requires a threefold solid understanding of the 'science' of working together; the 'art' of effective partnership working in a digital age; and the frequently forgotten issue of the internalization of the 'learning' that is generated so that new effective practices become embedded into the participating organizations, which will in turn ensure both the viability and durability of the effort.

This second edition of the book addresses the 'science' of the partnership approach. It offers a dissection of the theoretical context and concepts of partnership and collaboration. It examines the ethical issues that require attention when working in partnership and the consequences of actions and omissions within the context of professional relationships. It explores the factors that promote inclusive partnership working, and provides in-depth insights into the multiple challenges that are encountered when evaluating partnerships in order that information gained can be useful in enhancing the relationships between professional and community stakeholders.

The book also addresses the 'art' of partnering. It searches the intricate fabrics of effective practice in a range of settings that are characterized by their high need for inter-disciplinary thinking and actions. The authors offer many rich 'on the ground' accounts of the challenges with suggestions for a way forward for child protection and safeguarding children, care for older people and people with mental health difficulties, and problem drug use. It also contributes practice perspectives in relation to joint working for mentally disordered offenders and people with HIV, victims of domestic violence, the homeless and Gypsy Travellers. The case studies illustrate the importance of understanding the different ideological perspectives when multi-agency groups work together, the cultural differences of the client populations and disadvantaged communities that are the priority groups, as well as the prerequisites for user and public participation in planning and service delivery.

The book additionally attends to the importance of the 'learning' that is required for better collaboration and a more effective partnership approach. Many organizations sometimes have a very short-lived 'memory'. Hence, the vivid reflections of a physically disabled service user illustrate a rich understanding of what a relevant service should offer. The themes and issues that are involved in the learning process similarly remind us of the many interlacing and delicate issues that require attention when partnering in order to function as an effective team. The features, characteristics and key principles that underpin best practice when developing partnerships also mean that structures, roles and function, and boundaries of agencies require a more fluid, adaptable approach to facilitate working alongside other agencies.

Partnerships remain the prominent governance strategy for the planning and delivery of health, social care and criminal justice interventions in the coming years. Practitioners will need to be connected with the constant developments of the 'science', the 'art', and the 'learning' of partnership working. This book offers a strong contribution to the long haul journey this strategy will entail.

Preface

This book is essentially about effective practice, recognizing that today the needs of a client/patient/service user can rarely be met by one single agency or using one single method of intervention. The book recognizes the realities of practice intervention in the twenty-first century welfare state where collaboration, working together and partnership between various statutory, voluntary and independent organizations are essential elements of any packages of care. This second edition of the book has been completely revised to reflect the constantly changing nature of policy and practice in the human services. The book includes new chapters and the additional feature of recommended websites.

The book is presented in three parts covering the theory and practice of partnership, with the main emphasis being on effective practice. It draws authors from different disciplines of health, the voluntary sector, probation service, hospitals and social services, as well as providing a mix of academics and practitioners. Importantly, the book also includes a service user perspective.

The emphasis on practice is reflected in all three parts of the book, although it is most prominent in Part II. Hence, the book is not an academic exploration of the meaning of partnership, although the chapters in Part I do not duck this issue. The first two chapters explore the theoretical context within which partnership takes place, such as what is meant by partnership, and how partnership work has changed as a result of the digital age. The second two chapters, while being theoretical in nature, draw on practical examples to explore the challenges of addressing social inclusion as ethical issues raised by partnership work.

Part II, the main section of the book, examines the role and impact of agencies working together to provide services for a range of key client groups and social issues where a partnership approach is seen as particularly appropriate. The focus of Part II, however, is not only on providing services for key client groups but also on working in partnership with client groups as well as with other agencies. Client groups covered within Part II are: children in need of protection; people with mental health difficulties; older people and their carers; drug users; people who are homeless; children and young people with behavioural difficulties; victims of domestic violence; the travelling community; mentally disordered offenders; and people who have HIV/AIDS. The chapters in Part II are written in an accessible style by authors who are able to draw upon considerable expertise, knowledge and skills in their particular field. At the beginning of each chapter is a set of bullet points indicating what the chapter will address. Chapters also include case studies, where possible, to help make the links between theory and practice. At the end of each chapter is a short list of key questions to stimulate further discussion. A list of useful websites is also provided.

The book will be of particular interest to practitioners and students working in settings where partnership work, joined-up thinking and seamless service provision are becoming embedded within mainstream practice due to legislation and policy directive. The book will, therefore, have equal appeal to students, practitioners and managers in health, social and community services, and/or criminal justice settings.

Some of the issues or client groups may not at first appear relevant to some readers who work with a different client group. However, each chapter provides valuable real life examples, expertise and insight into the strengths, struggles and dilemmas of working together with other agencies, as well as with service users, towards establishing a partnership approach to practice. Lessons can be learnt from understanding and reflecting upon the issues others have faced, the ways in which they have overcome them and the models of partnership that have emerged.

In the final section, Part III, the first chapter is a reminder of what the provision of services is all about. In this chapter, Amir Minhas provides a sensitively written personal reflection on his own experience of being dependent upon such services. The second chapter in Part III explores methods used to evaluate partnership work. In the final two chapters we reflect on the examples of partnership work throughout the book and review the case studies. We then draw out the lessons of partnership working, identify reoccurring issues, and offer 14 principles for best practice. In contrast to the drift towards technocratic and rigidly prescribed practice in accordance with policy practice directives, the drive towards partnership work is much more 'organic' and fluid by nature, and requires different skills that are not easily acquired. However, this book provides the important contextual analysis of partnership, and a thorough examination of the strengths, weaknesses and issues arising from working in partnership with a diverse range of client groups.

Ros Carnwell and Julian Buchanan

May 2008

Part I:

The context of partnerships

1 The concepts of partnership and collaboration

Ros Carnwell and Alex Carson

This chapter will:

- Examine key concepts that will be referred to throughout the book, such as working together, partnership and collaboration.
- Use a concept analysis framework to analyse and explore key concepts and outline their distinguishing features.
- Highlight similarities and differences between the concept of collaboration and the concept of partnership and contextualize these differences within the current health and social policy agenda.
- Discuss the implications of partnership and collaboration for effective working together and how they are understood and operationalized by professionals from different agencies.

Collaboration, partnership and working together: the use of language

Within health and social care literature, there are many references to the need for health and social care agencies to 'work together' more effectively in 'partnership' and in 'collaboration'. A recent example can be found in the Department of Health's (DoH 2007d) policy for tackling health inequalities, which requires local service providers to work in partnership to address the wider determinants of health such as poverty, employment, poor housing and poor educational attainment with primary care trusts and local authorities being the key partners, leading and driving change locally.

Partnership and collaboration are often used inter-changeably, sometimes within the same paragraph or even sentence. Much use of the terminology is policy driven, giving way to the use of terms such as 'joined-up thinking' and 'joined-up working'; for example, *Every Child Matters* (DfES 2004: 9) states that progress in improving educational achievement for children and young people in care and in improving their health has been possible through better joint working.

As a preliminary, we think it worthwhile to broadly distinguish between what something is (a partnership), and what one does (collaborate or to work together in a joined-up way). This chapter will initially distinguish what different models of partnership are in current use and then go on to look at the way these different partnerships actually work. One thing that emerges from this discussion is the way that theory (what a partnership is) and practice (what it does) can often drift apart. Sometimes partnership may be nothing more than rhetoric or an end in itself, with little evidence that partners are genuinely working together. Equally, it is possible for different agencies to work collaboratively together without any formal partnerships being in place. It is important, therefore, to tease out the relationships between these concepts so that we can be clear about how effective they are in practice. However, before doing this, we want to say something about the current philosophical and policy context in which these definitions and arrangements have begun to be developed.

Partnerships: philosophy and policy

We live in what many commentators refer to as a post-modern world (Lyotard 1992). Philosophically or theoretically, post-modernism is a critique of the older 'modern' forms of social health and welfare, the 'one size fits all' policy that characterized the post-war creation of universal health and welfare provision. Lyotard argues that these huge national schemes or 'grand narratives' have failed to help the people they were created to help. He cites the examples of poor housing and poverty as social problems that have increased rather than diminished in the last 50 years. Lyotard sees these attempts at social amelioration as more about helping the system rather than the people who need the help. This critique of large scale attempts to solve people's problems has been reinforced by critiques outlining the disempowering effects of professional solutions to social problems. Beginning in Britain in the 1980s, both the system and the professionals within the system have been seen as disempowering for clients and receivers of services, with terms used such as the 'nanny state' or the 'disabling state'. Currently these critiques have resulted in an increasing emphasis on service user or 'consumer' choice. Health and social care services have been encouraged to allow consumers to become more involved and to have more of a say in the design and provision of services. Part of the reason for this refocusing on service users as active consumers rather than passive recipients of services may simply be that health and social problems have become more complex and multi-dimensional and that the older more static models of welfare have outlived their usefulness. In the past, the Department of Health has focused on 'health' issues, while social services departments have reacted to the rise in 'social' problems. This is increasingly seen as too simplistic a way of tackling more difficult and intractable problems. There is, for example, undoubtedly a close relationship between illness and poverty.

It is in the context of putting service users at the centre of health, social care and criminal justice, that partnerships have become more necessary. Service user problems, which may be complex and requiring input from a number of services, are more important in designing services than the traditional, centralizing distinctions between, for example, social workers and community nurses, or between social workers and criminal justice workers. A community may have a need or problem that is peculiar to that particular area. For instance, Bournemouth may be more in need of specialized care for older people than are other areas. A service user with a health problem might need a particular package of care that was previously provided by both the NHS and social services. In the new way of working, both health and social care might join up to provide a seamless 'one stop shop', which meets service users' needs. People's needs may change over time and place and so partnerships may be formed to respond to particular problems.

However, while most people would agree that clients should participate and be involved in the choices that affect their lives, two more practical implications need to be sketched out. While both are closely related, the more important consequence of this shift to a 'problem oriented' approach to health and social care is the inevitability of the disappearance of discrete professions such as nursing and social work. With the emphasis of social care and health changing to meeting local needs through local solutions, the rationale for a generic training might disappear. Moreover, professional 'expertise' is often viewed with suspicion. It is reasonable to suggest that current models of partnership, which are organized around current professional identities, will give way in the long-term to 'problem specific' professions. Within this book there are numerous examples of problem specific professionals focusing upon specialisms as diverse as Gypsy Travellers, victims of domestic violence and drug abusers, to name but a few, but what is evident from their writing is that they can demonstrate explicit examples of working in partnership. Moreover, as Merrell points out in Chapter 3, partnership should not just involve professionals, but should also involve people from disadvantaged groups. It is important that this changing political context provides a background for our current ideas of what partnerships are and what they do. In the next section, we will examine what partnership models are currently in use in health and social care, using Walker and Avant's (1995) concept analysis framework. The process of conducting a concept analysis is useful in that it can clarify the meaning of a single concept (Cahill 1996). Using a concept analysis framework and drawing on examples within the rest of the book, this chapter will therefore:

- define partnership and collaboration
- explore attributes of the concepts
- identify 'model', 'related' and 'contrary' cases of the two concepts
- discuss the antecedents to and consequences of the concepts

Partnerships and collaboration: what are they?

Using Walker and Avant's (1995) concept analysis framework first requires us to seek as many definitions of the terms as possible, including dictionary definitions and definitions used within the literature.

The concept of partnership

Looking at definitions of 'partnership' and 'collaboration' reveals some interesting similarities and differences between them. Dictionary definitions of the term 'partnership' are in Box 1.1 and Table 1.1 (towards the end of the chapter). We have also added web-based definitions to those offered by dictionaries.

Box 1.1   Definitions of partnership

Collins English Dictionary (1991):

- Equal commitment
- The state of being a partner

The Concise Oxford Dictionary (1992):

- To be one of a pair on the same side in a game
- A person who shares or takes part with another, especially in a business firm with shared risks and profits

Web definitions:

- A type of business entity in which partners share with each other the profits or losses of the business undertaking in which all have invested'. See: en.wikipedia.org/wiki/Partnership (2007)
- 'A contract between two or more persons who agree to pool talent and money and share profits or losses'. See: wordnet.princeton.edu/perl/webwn (2007)

What is evident from the definitions is the notion of sharing and agreement, with particular emphasis on business. Despite the availability of definitions, however, Taylor and Le Riche (2006) in a literature review, found conceptual confusion about partnership to be rife in the theoretical and empirical literatures and argue that the concept is loosely defined and expressed through multiple terminologies.

The reference to business partnerships is interesting given the recent trends in health and social care. Use of the term 'partnership' in health and social care settings is strongly influenced by policy, and policy changes quickly. Thus, because terms like 'partnership' are closely allied to policy they can change across time and place as the context changes. For this reason, it is also useful to consider an alternative concept analysis framework (Rodgers 2000), which takes into account the 'context' of the concept. This is illustrated by Gallant et al. (2002), who describe how partnership has changed over the past five decades. First, there was an emphasis on an equitable, just and free society enshrined within the International Declaration of Human Rights (United Nations 1948). Thirty years later, the World Health Organisation (WHO/

UNICEF 1978) stated that citizens should be enabled to become more self-reliant and take control over their own health. Finally, by the end of the twentieth Century, writers such as Frankel (1994) were commenting on how a better educated and informed public have begun to challenge the quality of services provided and are searching for more meaningful interactions with service providers. This change in policy is poignantly reflected in Minhas's personal account in Chapter 16 of this book, which traces his experiences of accessing health, social and educational services during the past 40 years.

This need for partnerships between service providers is reflected in policies emerging at the end of the last century, when community development (NHS Executive 1998) and joint employment, education and deployment of staff (DoH 1999a), were viewed as necessary to solve local problems in partnership with statutory agencies and meet the needs of the local population. Since then, partnerships between professionals and clients have also been emphasized. For example, *Building on the Best* (DoH 2003b), states that 'people want to work in partnership with clinicians, to draw upon the essential knowledge, skills and experience of healthcare professionals, but they also want to be able to contribute their own knowledge about their condition and their own perspective on what matters most to them' (DoH 2003b: 40). Indeed Greenall (2006) found that patients placed more emphasis on the need to be valued as a partner in the therapeutic relationship with the team (particularly the physician) than they did the issue of use of technology and distribution of staffing and funding. Further emphasis has also been placed on partnerships between agencies; *Choosing health*, for example, states that effective local partnerships, in which local government and NHS work towards a common purpose, are key to its success. Furthermore, as a result of *Choosing Health*, community collaboratives have been set up to support action through local partnerships.

It is clear then that current policy emphasizes a 'three-way partnership' between health and social care providers and service users, in which there is joint agreement about what services should be provided and by whom, with joint employment, community development and teamwork seen as means of breaking down existing professional barriers and responding to local needs. What the above definitions and rhetoric therefore implies is that of a partnership as a *shared commitment, where all partners have a right and an obligation to participate and will be affected equally by the benefits and disadvantages arising from the partnership*. What a commitment amounts to may vary from one context to another. In the next section, we will trace the limits of what a commitment could amount to. In addition, talk of rights and obligations implies that all parties in a partnership must work to high ethical standards. In effect, this has implications for collaborative working, as this would be substantively defined in ethical terms. This is discussed in Chapter 4 in terms of the moral obligations placed on professionals when they work together and the fiduciary relationship, which characterizes the features of a client–professional relationship in which both parties are responsible and their judgements are given consideration.

The concept of collaboration

Dictionary definitions of 'collaboration' are in Box 1.2 and Table 1.1 (which is located towards the end of this chapter).

Box 1.2 Dictionary definitions of collaboration

The Concise Oxford Dictionary (1992):

- Cooperate traitorously with an enemy
- Work jointly

Web definitions:

- The process by which people/organizations work together to accomplish a common mission. See: wind.uwyo.edu/sig/definition.asp
- A social skill involving working together with two or more persons. See: www.dpi.state.nc.us/curriculum/artsed/scos/music/mglossary

---

Table 1.1 Attributes, antecedents and consequences of partnership and collaboration

	Partnership	**Collaboration**
Defining attributes	Trust and confidence in accountability	Trust and respect in collaborators
	Respect for specialist expertise	Joint venture
	Joint working	Team work
	Teamwork	Intellectual and cooperative endeavor
	Blurring of professional boundaries	Knowledge and expertise more important than role or title
	Members of partnerships share the same vested interests	Participation in planning and decision making
	Appropriate governance structures	Nonhierarchical relationship
		Sharing of expertise
		Willingness to work together towards an agreed purpose
		Partnership

	Partnership	**Collaboration**
	Common goals Transparent lines of communication within and between partner agencies Agreement about the objectives Reciprocity Empathy	Inter-dependency Highly connected network Low expectation of reciprocation
Antecedents	Individual, local and national initiatives Commitment to shared vision about joint venture Willingness to sign up to creating a relationship that will support vision Value cooperation and respect what other partners bring to the relationship.	Educational preparation, maturity and experience to ensure readiness Understanding and acceptance of role and expertise Confidence in ability and recognition of disciplinary boundaries Effective communication, respect for and understanding of other's roles Sharing of knowledge, values, responsibility, visions and outcomes. Trust in collaborators. Nonhierarchical organization with individual autonomy Willingness to participate in formal, structured joint working to the extent that they do not rely on reciprocation in order to ensure that each contributes to the shared vision
Consequences: *Benefits*	Social exclusion tackled more effectively through multi-disciplinary action Less repetition of service provision from different organisations Less dilution of activities by agencies Less chance of agencies producing services that are counterproductive to each other	More effective use of staff due to cooperation rather than competition Demystification of healthcare due to bridging of gaps between fragmented service provision Sustained energy Cross-pollination of ideas Sharing of effort and ultimately sharing of organizational structure

	Partnership	**Collaboration**
Barriers:	Complexity of relationships. Representativeness of wider public Tokenism and excessive influence of vocal groups Desire of individuals not to be involved in making decisions about their care Threat to confidentiality. Role boundary conflicts Inter-professional differences of perspective Threats to professional identity	

These two very different dictionary definitions perhaps reflect the change of emphasis in health and social care over recent decades. Hence, the *context* of the concept (Rodgers 2000) is as important for understanding the concept of collaboration as it is for understanding the concept of partnership. During the 1980s there was considerable suspicion between the health and social care professions, to the extent that working together would have been regarded as problematic. However, recent policy reforms have encouraged different professional groups to break down barriers and to work together collaboratively. It is these changes that have given way to the development of more formal partnerships. It is interesting that a common language of 'working together' and 'breaking down barriers' draws together the two concepts of partnership and collaboration. The close proximity of definitions relating to these two concepts is also reflected in Henneman et al.'s (1995: 104) definition of collaboration as being frequently 'equated with a bond, union or partnership, characterised by mutual goals and commitments'.

More recently, the rhetoric around partnership and collaboration is beginning to give way to alternative terms, such as 'working together', as seen in the contemporary web definitions of collaboration, with their emphasis on social skills required to work together towards a common goal. In fact, Burke (2001) cites Service Level Agreements (SLAs) as an example of how different agencies have been encouraged to *work together* by the government, thus drawing up SLAs lasting three to ten years, which should be based on health improvement programmes.

Exploring the attributes of partnership and collaboration

Walker and Avant (1995) propose that once definitions and uses have been identified, the defining attributes of the concept should be explored (see Table 1.1). These attributes are found in the literature, and help to differentiate between similar concepts. In this case, this process will help to differentiate between the concepts of 'partnership' (who we are) and 'collaboration' (what we do).

Attributes of partnership

Within the literature, there is much reference to the characteristics of partnership. Characteristics referred to include: trust; the need for partners to share the same vested interest; the need for appropriate governance structures (Gannon-Leary et al. 2006); the need for respect; common goals and agreed objectives and transparent lines of communication between partners; blurring of professional boundaries, teamwork and joint working (Robinson and Cottrel, 2005). While much of the literature considers partnerships between professionals, Bidmead and Cowley (2005) conducted a concept analysis of partnership with health visiting clients and arrived at 11 attributes of partnership: genuine and trusting relationship; honest and open communication and listening; praise and encouragement; reciprocity; empathy; sharing and respect for the others' expertise; working together with negotiation of goals, plans and boundaries; participation and involvement; support and advocacy; information giving; and enabling choice and equity. It seems evident then, that partnership between professionals and clients includes some additional attributes not normally associated with partnership between professionals such as praise and encouragement, support and advocacy, and enabling choice and equity.

Defining attributes can therefore be summarized as follows:

- Trust and confidence in accountability
- Respect for specialist expertise
- Joint working
- Teamwork
- Blurring of professional boundaries
- Members of partnerships share the same vested interests
- Appropriate governance structures
- Common goals
- Transparent lines of communication within and between partner agencies
- Agreement about objectives
- Reciprocity
- Empathy

We can see that the trust and respect evident between partners has a substantive ethical content. What this amounts to is that partners really need to have a shared identity. As Robinson and Cottrel's (2005) research shows, role convergence can occur in multi-disciplinary partnerships in which members become affiliated to the team rather than to different agencies. However, as Robinson and Cottrel point out, while this has advantages for teamwork, it can cause concern over threats to specialist identity.

This may mean the gradual erosion of current professional identities in favour of new, more problem orientated professional partnerships or even, professions. The potential threat to professional identity may lead to a reluctance to collaborate, as it could be perceived as threatening existing professional boundaries or failing to develop a particular profession (Masterson 2002). Indeed, one could argue that an ideal partnership would be practically impossible, as partnerships need at least two clearly identifiable partners. In the long-term this may happen but at this transitional stage in health and social care provision, partnerships may represent a staging post. Trade union reform in recent years has seen the amalgamation of smaller unions who initially formed partnerships with other similarly related unions. While starting off as partners, these reconstituted unions such as UNISON took on a new single identity. Over time the sense that this union was a partnership of smaller unions has been forgotten. Therefore there are limits to what can really be called a partnership. There must be some tension in all partnerships between different partners' identities and all partners' commitment to a shared identity. What determines differences between partnership models is less a shared commitment and more the nature of each partnership's commitment. Types of partnership can be differentiated by the type of commitment they undertake, which we summarize as follows.

Project partnership

These are partnerships that are time limited for the duration of a particular project. A partnership between the police and other road safety organizations to lower the speed limit will end when their project is successful. Equally, when two companies sign a joint contract to manufacture a particular product, the partnership ends when production ceases. In Chapter 13, for example, a multi-agency 'project partnership' funded by the Welsh Assembly Government is described, which aimed to redress the inequality of access to health care experienced by the Traveller population in North East Wales. Arguably, once the funding ceases and the aims have been achieved, then the partnership could cease to exist.

Problem oriented partnerships

These are partnerships that are formed to meet specific problems. Examples of this might include Neighbourhood Watch schemes or substance abuse teams. These partnerships arise in response to a publicly identified problem and remain as long as the problem persists. These can be subject to changing definitions of what the 'problem' really is. Chapter 14, for example, discusses a partnership group established in Leeds to develop a strategic multi-agency approach to provide services for mentally disordered offenders. It can be defined as a problem orientated partnership because it arose from a recognition that people with mental health problems who offend were not always dealt with appropriately, and a belief that a partnership response was the most effective way of addressing the issues.

Ideological partnerships

These types of partnerships arise from a shared outlook or point of view. They are similar in many ways to problem oriented partnerships, but they also possess a certain viewpoint that they are convinced is the correct way of seeing things. A case in point is abortion in which various organizations, ideologically aligned, form a 'pro-life' and a 'pro-choice' partnership. In addition, various anti-war and peace partnerships are ideologically driven. As with problem oriented partnerships, ideology can change and develop. For instance, Amnesty International or Christian Aid have evolved into more overt political partnerships as the ideological context has widened. Within this book, this type of partnership is illustrated in the Coventry Domestic Violence Partnership, established in the 1980s as a focus group to advise planners and commissioners in health and social care about service gaps and priorities (see Chapter 12). Although the impetus for the partnership came from the voluntary sector in collaboration with the police and 'safer cities' community safety workers, it has since developed into a strong and dynamic multi-agency partnership with a wide remit across the spectrum of public and community services. Although, as suggested above, this could be described as a problem oriented partnership, its long-term dynamic nature is suggestive of an ideological partnership.

Ethical partnerships

These share a number of features with the above but they also have a sense of 'mission' and have an overtly ethical agenda, that seeks to promote a particular way of life. They tend to be democratic and reflective and are as equally focused on the means as the end. While most partnerships have codes of ethics or ethical procedures, ethical partnerships have a substantive ethical content in their mission and practice.

The above types of partnerships are inclusive; indeed some partnerships might have all of the above types within it. For instance, it would be reasonable to conclude that health and social care partnerships are ethical partnerships since they aim at helping people. However, they may also work successfully but be ideologically distinct. Social services, for example, may favour a 'social model' approach, while the health care system may favour a more 'medicalized' approach. Project partnerships may take a problem oriented approach to their work at the behest of one of the partners. Service users may want particular problems solved and demand that service providers address ongoing issues rather than focusing on the big picture.

Gallant et al. (2002) also suggest that partnership attributes include *structure* and *process* phenomenon. The *structure* involves partners in two phases in their relationship – initiating and working phases (Courtney et al. 1996). During the initiating phase, they negotiate responsibilities and actions, while during the working phase they evaluate their progress towards the goal of partnership. The structure might also include identification of suitable partners. Most literature relating to partnership identifies partnership arrangements between certain groups, including both service providers and service users. An example of this is Roberts' (2002) study, which found that older people welcome advice concerning their discharge from hospital and during the period following discharge, although some preferred decisions to be made for them. Roberts used Arnstein's ladder of citizen participation (discussed further in Chapter 3) to analyse the findings, with notions of 'partnership', 'relationship', 'communication' and 'paternalism' being discussed. As will be seen in the chapters of this book, however, involving vulnerable people in partnership can be difficult, when there is still so much work to do in developing multi-agency partnerships. As can be seen in Chapter 14, for example, 'involving service users in forensic mental health poses a challenge because some individuals present a significant risk and are difficult to engage and treat'.

Key to the *process* of partnership is the involvement of partners in power sharing and negotiation (Gallant et al. 2002). In partnerships between health and social care agencies, this process might involve considerable negotiation in order to arrive at a shared understanding of roles and responsibilities across multi-disciplinary boundaries, as well as the relinquishing of power relationships. Equally in partnerships between clients and professionals, this same process of negotiation and relinquishing of professional power will take place. However, this can be difficult in practice, particularly if professional codes of practice and legal frameworks work against it. In addition, there are safety issues that, while they might help the effective management of a partnership, may restrict the scope of practice. While it might be practically better for a social worker to assess clients' health needs, professionally it might be difficult for a nurse to give care solely on the basis of this assessment. Professional rules may insist on nurses carrying out their own assessments.

Attributes of collaboration

The defining attributes of collaboration include that 'two or more individuals must be involved in a joint venture, typically one of an intellectual nature in which participants willingly participate in planning and decision making' (Henneman et al. 1995: 104). Henneman et al. further argue that individuals consider themselves to be members of a team working towards a common goal, sharing their expertise and responsibility for the outcome. Fundamentally, the relationship between collaborators is nonhierarchical, and shared power is based on knowledge and expertise, rather than role or title (Henneman et al. 1995). Similarly, Hudson et al. (1998) emphasize joint working as a key characteristic of collaboration, and add that trust and respect for partners means that they are willing to participate in formal, structured joint working, including joint assessments, planning, service delivery and commissioning. Interestingly, Hudson et al. (1998) place collaboration on a continuum from isolation (in which there is an absence of joint activity) through to integration (in which separate identities are no longer significant and the creation of unitary organization may be possible) (see Figure 1.1).

More recently, in a literature review of collaboration, D'Amour et al. (2005) found that certain concepts were mentioned repeatedly in the definitions of collaboration, which included: sharing, partnership, and interdependency.

The defining attributes of collaboration can therefore be summarized as follows:

- Intellectual and cooperative endeavor
- Knowledge and expertise more important than role or title
- Joint venture
- Team working
- Participation in planning and decision making

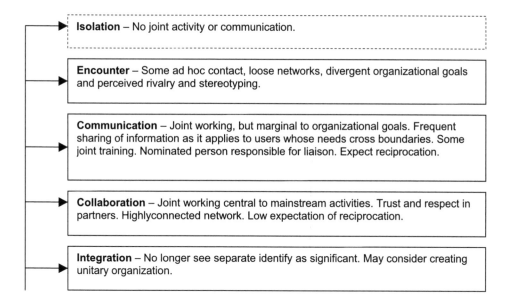

Figure 1.1 Characteristics of collaboration
Source: Hudson et al. 1998

- Nonhierarchical relationship
- Sharing of expertise
- Willingness to work together towards an agreed purpose
- Trust and respect in collaborators
- Partnership
- Inter-dependency
- Highly connected network
- Low expectation of reciprocation

As in the concept of partnership, the involvement of the public is central to working collaboratively. Stewart and Reutter (2001) exemplify this, citing evidence from three studies in which peers and professionals collaborated as co-leaders and partners in 21 support groups. The three studies were: survivors of myocardial infarction and their spouses; parents of children with chronic conditions; and older women with disabilities. These three studies, however, are all contextualized around chronic illness, which might not be universally applicable. The current consensus of opinion, for example, is that clients with chronic illnesses have more insight into their conditions than professionals do. Indeed, it is significant that many examples cited in the literature deal with chronic problems such as social care, disabilities and mental health.

Identifying 'model', 'related' and 'contrary' cases of partnership and collaboration

Having refined the concepts through identifying their defining attributes, the next stage of analysing concepts is to identify a 'model' case, a 'related' case and a 'contrary' case (Walker and Avant 1995). A model case includes all the stated attributes of the concept and is so called because there is no doubt that it represents the concept. Clifford (2003) suggests the model case of 'partnership' between education and service providers would be people (or organizations) willing to join with a partner, together with a shared vision and commitment to making the partnership work. Clifford also remarks that collaborative arrangements would be set up to demonstrate a willingness to share in successes and failures. An example of a model case can also be seen in the Partnerships for Carers in Suffolk (Chapter 7). This could be described as a model case because each partner 'signed up' for the Charter for Carers in Suffolk, and furthermore, each of the partners is committed to implementing an action plan. However, to be certain that this was a model case we would need to have more intimate insights into the initiative and compare its characteristics with the defining attributes listed above to see if they were all present.

A model case of collaboration would occur if a social services department joined with a local NHS trust to identify training needs of their staff, and used knowledge and expertise from both partners to produce shared training. If they also had mutual respect and trust, with strong networks, together with joint working, planning and service delivery, this would be a good example of a model case. In this instance, it seems that collaboration is a means of making 'partnership' work. That is, 'collaboration', the verb, is what we do when we engage successfully in a 'partnership', partnership being the noun. Considering Hudson et al.'s (1998) continuum in more detail, there would be few examples of 'isolation' in health and social care agencies, as this would suggest that they never met, wrote to or talked to each other. 'Encounters' in health and social care agencies would imply infrequent, ad hoc, inter-professional contact, characterized by rivalry and stereotyping. While it may be assumed that in modern health and social care agencies, such 'encounters' would be rare, professionals do stereotype other professional groups and make assumptions about what they expect from them, which can limit the effectiveness of collaboration. This can be seen in Chapter 8, when a person's drug problem can be interpreted very differently by different agencies with different treatment options proposed as a consequence. Stereotyping can also exist when dealing with homelessness, when, as discussed in Chapter 9, social services staff are frequently perceived by the voluntary sector as being aloof, unapproachable and not fulfilling their statutory responsibilities. They in turn complain that voluntary sector staff do not understand the limits of those responsibilities and fail to appreciate what they can take on within the parameters of their departments and their scarce resources. Modern health and social care agencies are arguably in transition from communication to collaboration. However, the high degree of trust and low expectation of reciprocation within collaboration might suggest that many health and social care agencies still have considerable progress to make.

Identifying a related case of these terms (Walker and Avant 1995) is a little more difficult, as this requires a similar (but different) instance of partnership or collaboration to be identified. A related case for 'partnership' could be an 'associate partner', as this implies a connection between two organizations or people, but the link would be quite loose and might imply that one of the organisations or people was subordinate to the other. An example of this would be an associate director, who would normally act as deputy to the director. At the level of patient/client partnership, Cahill (1996) presents a concept analysis of *patient participation* and suggests that patient *partnership* is a related case for this concept, along with patient *collaboration* and patient *involvement.* She views patient involvement and collaboration as being at the bottom of a pyramid. Slightly higher up the pyramid is patient participation, while at the top is partnership, this being the goal to which all practitioners should aspire. This suggests then that as people become more involved, they begin to collaborate with each other and through this process of collaboration a greater sense of involvement transpires. This sense of involvement can ultimately result in sufficient trust, respect and willingness on the part of different parties for partnership to develop (see Figure 1.2).

Figure 1.2 A continuum of involvement

A related case of 'collaboration' could be an 'alliance' in which organizations share some understanding, but may lack the joint working arrangements required to be collaborators.

Identifying a 'contrary' case is even more difficult, for the contrary case must have characteristics that illustrate that it is not representative of the concept, although similarities may be present. A contrary case of 'partnership' would be when two organizations or people convey the impression of being partners when in fact the characteristics they display do not resemble those of a true partnership. We see examples of this with many professional sports personalities. Some professional footballers are accused of not being a 'team player' and some nurses and social workers are accused of the same thing when they do 'their own thing'.

A contrary case of collaboration could be seen in organizations that communicate (Hudson et al. 1998) with each other, but only as far as they need to in order to deliver services across organizational boundaries. Frequent liaison may give the impression of collaboration when in fact the expectation of reciprocation may reveal a different state of affairs. This is currently the norm in many areas, where services communicate on a case by case basis. An example of this can be seen in child protection work in which the child protection system is complex with a bewildering overlap of occupational boundaries and the added complication of disadvantaged and transient families (Chapter 5). With such complexity it is not surprising that collaborative working between different professional groups is difficult. Another example is illustrated in mental health work in which psychiatric team members complain that they are not on the same level as other members of the team, or that they use a different professional language compared to other team members, which enables them to shore up a separate professional identity (Hamilton et al. 2004; see also Chapter 6).

Antecedents and consequences of partnership and collaboration

Walker and Avant (1995) also suggest that concepts have antecedents and consequences, some examples of which can be seen in Table 1.1. Antecedents are events that happen prior to the concept occurring, while consequences follow the occurrence of the concept. According to Walker and Avant, exploring antecedents and consequences enables us to refine the attributes of the concept. So, for partnerships to occur in health and social care, certain events must happen first. These might include local directives, individual initiatives and social policy changes; and they can occur at all levels in the organization and may spring up in response to individual, local or national perceptions. Doran (2001), for instance, traces the route from policy to practice in the proposed integration of district nursing services with social services to provide a seamless care in the community. Another example of policy antecedents is the legislation concerning paedophilia, which arose from a bereaved mother's suffering as a result of her daughter's murder. Partnerships between parents with autistic children and research centres grew out a 'perceived' increase in cases of autism. In many ways, their antecedents define partnerships. In response to antecedents, for 'partnership' to occur, there must be two sides who are committed to a shared vision about the joint venture, and there must be two or more people who are willing to sign up to creating a relationship that will support this (Clifford 2003). Furthermore, partners must respect what other partners bring to the relationship (Labonte 1994).

According to Henneman et al. (1995), antecedents to collaboration include a number of personnel and environmental factors (see Table 1.1). Personnel factors include: sufficient educational preparation, maturity and experience to ensure readiness to engage in collaboration; clear understanding and acceptance of their role and expertise; confidence in ability and recognition of disciplinary boundaries; effective communication, respect for and understanding of others' roles; sharing of knowledge, values, responsibility, visions and outcomes; and trust in collaborators. Environmental factors include: a nonhierarchical organization in which individuals can act autonomously and in which reward systems recognize group rather than individual achievements. Furthermore, they must be willing to participate in formal, structured joint working to the extent that they do not rely on reciprocation in order to ensure that each contributes to the shared vision (Hudson et al. 1998).

The consequences of 'partnership' can result in benefits, but there are also some barriers to working in partnership. The main benefits of working in partnership are that multi-faceted problems, such as social exclusion, can be tackled more effectively through multi-disciplinary action (Peckham and Exworthy 2003). For example, partnership working can reduce repetition of service provision from different organizations. It can also ensure that services are not withdrawn by one service because of the mistaken belief that another organization is providing them. Another consequence of partnership is that it can prevent dilution of activities by agencies as they each try to deliver services independently of each other. Finally, it can reduce the possibility of different agencies producing services that are counterproductive to each other.

Barriers to working in partnership have also been reported in the literature. Barriers can exist at a healthcare system level or at the individual client level. The English healthcare system, for example, creates barriers between health and social care, partly through government guidance reinforcing dominance of the biomedical model, but also through quasi-markets in healthcare, which also sustain the health- and social care divide (McMurray 2006). Another barrier at the healthcare system level is the complexity of relationships due to the greater interplay between those involved in the partnership (Gallant et al. 2002), an example of this being collaboration to protect children as discussed above in relation to Corby et al.'s chapter. At the individual level, Burke (2001) cautions that there is some scepticism about the partnership approach with respect to a number of factors, including how much particular individuals can be representative of the wider public; concern that public participation can lead to both tokenism and to excessive influence of vocal groups, and the possibility that individuals might not wish to be involved in making decisions about their care.

Secker and Hill (2001) also report a number of barriers arising in mental health services. One important barrier was a reluctance to share information about clients due to confidentiality, which, if breached, could result in staff dealing with unanticipated responses from clients with inadequate knowledge and support. This could also be a problem when partnership involves the joint use or joint commissioning of premises in rural areas, where even the simple act of going into a particular building may be witnessed by others and may lead to particular assumptions about what is going on. Working with people who are HIV positive is one example of this, as they may be reluctant to fill in prescriptions in their home neighbourhood and often hide or relabel medications to maintain secrecy within the home (see Chapter 15).

Role boundary conflicts and tensions between agencies were also reported as barriers in Secker and Hill's (2001) study, such that both learning disability nurses and the police service felt that they were 'dumped on' by mental health services. Such boundary conflicts were reported to arise partly from inadequate resourcing of mental health services, as well as misunderstanding of agency roles, often resulting in unrealistic expectations. Other barriers to partnership included inter-professional differences of perspective (such as those arising from the medical model and the more holistic social model) and differences in approach to risk. As a number of authors have suggested, as multi-disciplinary working gains momentum and professional roles converge, the more professional identities are threatened (Robinson and Cottrel 2005), to the extent that professionals will either be reluctant to collaborate (Masterson 2002) or will use their own professional language in furtherance of their separate identity (Hamilton et al. 2004).

The consequences of *collaboration* can also be explained in terms of benefits and barriers. The benefits of collaboration include: more effective use of staff as they utilise their skills cooperatively rather than competitively (Henneman et al. 1995), demystification of health care with the bridging of gaps between fragmented service provision, sustained energy, cross-pollination of ideas, sharing of effort and ultimately sharing of organizational structure (El Ansari and Phillips 2001). There are also a number of barriers to closer collaboration. These may include a fear that individual professions may be threatened as work becomes more problem focused (Billingsley and Lang 2002). Brown et al. (2000) suggest that a lack of managerial direction and the encouragement of a more generic way of working can prevent closer collaboration across professional boundaries. In collaboration between service providers and service users, service users may be reluctant to assume an equal part in partnerships. Roberts' (2002) study of older people on discharge showed that some preferred service providers to make decisions for them. However, this may reflect older people's perspectives on the relationship between professionals and patients. Likewise, as indicated in Chapter 9, homeless clients may have their own preferences about which needs should be addressed first, and problems can arise if the priorities of clients are at odds with the priorities of staff.

A summary of the defining attributes, antecedents and consequences of partnership and collaboration is presented in Table 1.1

As indicated in Table 1.1 there are a number of similarities between the concepts of partnership and collaboration. Within their defining attributes each share traits of trust and respect for partners, joint working and teamwork. The main shared antecedent is a willingness to participate; while the main shared consequence is increased effectiveness of staff resources.

The final stage in Walker and Avant's (1995) concept analysis framework is to identify empirical referents to the concept. These provide examples of the concept in practice, so that the concept can be measured and validated in order to demonstrate that it does actually exist. For example, observing procedures, processes and the behaviour of people within organizations would show evidence of partnership and collaboration. A partnership, for example, might be legally binding with a written contract detailing the obligations of each partner. A collaboration could be evidenced by written procedures for joint working. These could then be checked through observation and/or participation to establish the extent of collaboration. Throughout this chapter there are many examples of how partnership and collaboration are played out in the behaviour of personnel and all of these can provide evidence that partnership and collaboration really do exist.

Conclusion

This chapter has explored and analysed the concepts of partnership and collaboration. Partnerships, collaboration and working together need to be seen as new solutions to 'new' problems. It may be the case that the current situation reflects both a negative view of the paternalistic state with its grand narratives of fairness and equality, and a more positive view that wants to put the client at the centre of things.

Whatever the reason, and we suspect that both have played their part, partnerships and collaboration are likely to grow rather than diminish. Evidence discussed above suggests that, despite the potential barriers to partnership and collaboration, they are worthwhile pursuits. Moreover, policy directives are creating the imperative for organizations to work together. However, the evidence for the effectiveness of partnerships and collaborative care arrangements are less clear (El Ansari and Phillips 2001).

This may indicate that the current view is more that partnerships and collaboration are good in themselves, rather than more effective at solving problems. However, there is no doubt that client problems are more complex and require new ways of working. Part of the reason for the paucity of evidence about their effectiveness may be that they need time to be integrated with existing provision. In addition, if partnerships and collaboration are going to be the future ways of working together, old forms of professional education and training need to be reviewed. The problem with new innovative ways of working may be that they are working within the old context, where professions were discrete entities with their own body of knowledge. So while the policy context is changing to encourage collaboration and partnerships, professional regulation has been slow to catch up. In addition, many clients and potential clients still prefer the old ways of working and may be reluctant to become too involved in their care. What seems clear, however, is that certain problems will, by their nature, be more amenable to a partnership or collaborative approach.

Questions for further discussion

1 What attributes of partnership and collaboration have you found in health and social care settings evidence?
2 What benefits (if any) of partnership and collaboration do you think exist in health and social care settings?
3 How can the barriers to partnership and collaboration be overcome?

2 The impact of the digital age on partnership and collaboration

Ros Carnwell and Julian Buchanan

This chapter will:

- Outline the development of digital information in recent years.
- Summarize the benefits and drawbacks.
- Explore the impact upon service provider and service user.
- Outline the opportunities for improvement networking and communication.

The use of electronic information technology: benefits and limitations

Computer-based information systems are increasingly used by individuals and organizations throughout the world to store, look after, process, translate, send out and access information. The arrival of the digital age has had a global impact upon work and leisure patterns across the world. Information technology has increasingly been incorporated within the human services, replacing old forms of data collections, storage and retrieval and creating new possibilities and opportunities for electronic databases and communication. Anaraki et al. (2003) describes how electronic patient records and access to electronic information are now the cornerstones of delivery of modern primary care, facilitating the delivery of effective evidence-based patient care, providing needs driven health care, assisting research and improving quality of services.

A study by Adams et al. (2004) suggested that the 'health information journey' could be divided into three broad stages: the initiation of an information requirement; information facilitation; and contextual interpretation. During the first of these stages – initiation of an information requirement – an almost limitless amount of broad ranged and indepth information available on the World Wide Web including resources sites such as NHS Direct (2008) is used by patients to learn about health conditions (Hart et al. 2003; Adams et al. 2004). The Internet is able to provide immediate access to up to date global evidence-based information. In a survey of 733 doctors (Potts and Wyatt 2002), the participants estimated that around 2 percent of patients had accessed health material on the Internet during the past month, and given the increasing access to the Internet in recent years and growing familiarity with the use of search engines such as Google (2008) one would not be surprised if this figure was now much higher and continuing on an upward trend.

Patients' use of the Internet can be either 'active' or 'passive' (Adams et al. 2005). Active information is defined as a proactive engagement with the Internet to seek out particular information or a response to a specific complaint or issue, while passive information is the more general access to topical news reports, which might be relevant to the patient. Typically, patients then bring such information to consultations with healthcare professionals so they become better informed, and its use can affect decisions about health or healthcare (Jacobson 2007). In this way the use of the Internet can result in both benefits and limitations for service users and practitioners. The advantages and disadvantages of the Internet can be seen in relation to several facets of health and social care practice: quality and interpretation of information; access to the Internet; IT competence; and relationships between service users and practitioners.

Quality and interpretation of information

There are two main contexts in which electronic information is used in the human services. The first is at the organizational level as a means of storing, retrieving and sharing information, which can provide opportunities for sharing across agency and service boundaries. The second is at the level of the World Wide Web, in which service users and practitioners access information of different levels of complexity which can be shared in different ways, thus also creating opportunities for partnerships between service users and practitioners, between different service users, between different practitioners and services, and across different geographical areas nationally and internationally.

As practitioners and service users both use the Internet, the quality of information must be suited to users with different types of need and different levels of competence in terms of access to IT as well as in relation to understanding of information. Furthermore, as the Internet is used across health, social care and criminal justice sectors and, therefore, has the potential for gathering and sharing of information electronically across different services, the need for accuracy in information is then paramount. The perception of accuracy of Internet information seems variable and in some cases unreliable (Adams et al. 2005). In Rhodes' (2003) study of eight councils, for example, 72 percent of respondents were confident of the accuracy of the information available to them, although some staff were concerned about the value of user databases, especially the accuracy of the data held, due to data bases not always being kept up to date. By comparison, Potts and Wyatt's (2002) questionnaire survey of 733 doctors suggested that participants did not consider the general quality of health information particularly reliable, although the benefits for patients was considered to outweigh the problems.

Eysenbach and Jadad (2001) also raise concerns regarding a possible lack of credibility of authorship on some websites, which they suggest can result in misinformation. Moreover, misinformation can be further compounded by misinterpretation of information, which can result in self-mistreatment and misdiagnosis (Wyatt 2002). As Adams et al.'s (2004) study reveals, there is a growing risk that even high quality reliable information can be misinterpreted by consumers with regard to their personal experiences and needs. They cite an example of a health information manager recalling how a patient who had experienced a miscarriage retrieved information from the Internet and misunderstood medical terminology so that she thought someone had aborted her baby, and became very distressed as a result. Rapidly improved access to the electronic information exchange, online discussion, Internet databases and powerful global search engines have to some degree shifted power and knowledge from the 'expert' professional and made it accessible to the service user. The consequences of this are still being unravelled.

Of clear importance to patients within both Adams et al. (2004 and 2005) studies was the quality and trustworthiness of the information and its providers. Furthermore, as Adams et al. (2004) point out, during the second and third categories of the health information journey, information facilitation and contextual interpretation are paramount. This requires supporting service users to interpret information according to their individual needs. Digital resource designers, therefore, need to recognize that patients may be unclear about their information requirements and instead may be driven by vague fears, which can lead to specific 'personalised questions with loaded personal attributes and emotional repercussions that are hard to answer simplistically' (Adams et al. 2004: 5). Adams et al. (2004) are critical of some systems designed to support patients in interpretation and contextualization of information. NHS Direct callcentres, for example, have ambiguous roles in the facilitation of information, which, together with poor handover to other bodies means that patients' 'information journeys' are often disjointed. Similarly, according to Adams et al. (2004) digital resources fail to contextualize information within the 'information journey' resulting in a lack of coordination. Although some digital resources do provide these distinct functions, they are often hidden within the interface design and as such are not evident as a key information requirement which should be quickly apparent to the user.

Considerations for improvements to the quality of information differ according to context – either organizational or World Wide Web. At the organizational level, Rhodes' (2003) study identified a range of good practices, including Data Improvement Days in North Lincolnshire designed to improve data in areas of known weakness; and a project to address data accuracy in Gloucestershire. Councils used various ways to ensure the information used was accurate, although these could be patchy and reactive, with better performing councils being most systematic and promoting the importance of accurate and prompt recording. Cheshire council, for example, conducted regular audits and systematic validation at team level as well as generating missing data reports.

At the service user level in relation to the World Wide Web, patients need to access a wide variety of high quality health information outside the doctor–patient consultation (Adams et al. 2004). Increasingly patients can now access a wealth of knowledge and expertise via dedicated websites (such as Epilepsy Action, MIND, Drugscope, Women's Aid), which act as service user support groups and/or pressure groups. These groups sometimes also provide online discussion forums so that people can network with others who may have similar shared interests and experiences. As patients/service users now have access to vast amounts of information available through the Internet, interpretation and contextualization of this information needs to be increased. 'Digital health resource providers are on the verge of realising their huge potential or dropping into the depths of damaging possibilities, and the burden of this responsibility must not be taken lightly' (Adams et al. 2004: 6).

Access to the Internet

In order for practitioners and the public to use information from the Internet, they must first have access to it. This includes having access to a physical location where Internet facilities are installed, and having the technical ability and knowledge to access relevant sites. Problems with each of these can create barriers to using the Internet. For example, although access to the Internet is increasing, approximately 43 percent of households in Great Britain did not have access to the Internet from home between January and April 2006 (Office of National Statistics 2008). This is similar to the United States, in which half of the adult population did not have Internet access in 2002. Modern information technology tends to be the province of youth and, significantly, those not online tend to be less educated, older and living in rural areas (Horrigan 2007).

Practitioners working in the human services also have variable access to the Internet at their place of work. Adams et al. (2005), for example, in a study of health professionals, callcentre staff and patients in London hospitals and primary care trusts, found barriers to Internet access resulting from physical location of the technology within communal workplaces, especially for those with lower status. In addition, systems were poorly designed, with poor support resulting in many staff perceiving informatics systems as complex and inappropriate for their needs (Adams et al. 2005: 5). In another study, Anaraki et al. (2003) found that primary care staff in prisons in the southeast region of England did not have access to either the Internet or electronic clinical records, and almost all clinical data was recorded on paper. Rhodes' (2003) inspection of eight councils also revealed variable access. Although managers had good access to the Internet, practitioners were less fortunate, with large numbers of staff sharing computers and computers being located in separate rooms to workers' desks. Rhodes (2003) found that, while most councils had made their sites accessible to people with visual impairments, other disabilities were not catered for. Furthermore, websites tended to be promotional rather than interactive, with limited opportunity for users and carers to actively organize their own care.

Other barriers also exist to limit access to the Internet. Of particular importance to the human services and especially those working in the criminal justice system is concern regarding the potential breach of security, as well as issues of data security and a culture of low priority given to health in prisons (Anaraki et al. 2003). Issues of data security also seem to limit access of social services departments as, according to Rhodes (2003: 32) 'Remote access to the user database was rare for anyone other than the Emergency Duty Team and even for some Emergency Duty Teams this could be limited'. Councils are, however, responding to the modernization agenda by offering access to services over extended hours, outside usual office opening. It will be important for social services to make available to staff operating these extended hours, up to date information on the people served and ways of updating records of their involvement.

IT competence

Even when the practitioners and the public have access to the Internet, their competence in its use and their interpretation of information gained from the Internet varies immensely. Rhodes' (2003) found that the use of ICT in local authorities was restricted by practitioners' competence. Furthermore, study of both patients and practitioners (Hart et al. 2003) found that most participants were not very IT literate in relation to searching for health information on the web and many asked other people to access information on their behalf. Hart et al.'s study also found that practitioners were more aware of their lack of skills than were patients, although time constraints and lack of convenient Internet access prevented practitioners from tackling their lack of competence. Many participants (both patients and practitioners), though, were embarrassed about not being 'Internet savvy'.

Even when successful in searching the Internet, the outcomes of these searches are variable, with many patients being unable to find anything useful, some searching being haphazard (Adams et al. 2005) and many other patients being unable to understand medical information even when the information is accurate and useful (Eysenbach and Jadad 2001). Facilitation of information is therefore important, and involves exploring patients' requirements and providing information. Many callers to NHS Direct, for example, require information facilitation support even if they have direct Internet access (Adams et al. 2005).

Closing the gap between service users and practitioners

Use of the Internet by patients can have considerable impact on their relationship with practitioners. Patients' health behaviours are more informed (Adams et al. 2004) and patients are more knowledgeable (Helft et al. 2003), so that having accessed information prior to a consultation they have the opportunity to reflect on and reconsider preferences prior to discussions with health professionals. They are therefore (Gerber and Eiser 2001) more capable of actively engaging in decision making (Woolf et al. 2005). This trend represents a shift during the past ten years, from a model in which patients receive diagnosis and treatment without question to a model of proactive engagement on the part of the patient (Jacobson 2007). Jacobson (2007: 3) goes on to argue that 'the Internet mediates power relations between physicians and patients', thus 'altering the way each experiences the clinical encounter'. Physicians too recognize the need for patients to participate as partners in interpreting medical information and selecting treatment options (Eysenbach and Jadad 2001), thus making consultations more effective (Potts and Wyatt 2002, Adams et al. 2004) as more time can be spent on discussions necessary to arrive at a clinical decision (Gerber and Eiser 2001) and creating a more equitable partnership between patient and doctor (Adams et al. 2004).

These subtle changes have resulted in debates about the potentially empowering effect of the Internet on the physician–patient or worker–service-user relationship (Jacobson 2007). Patient empowerment refers to a patient role in which the power is redistributed between physician and patient to the extent that patients take more control when interacting with healthcare professionals (Roberts 1999). Empowerment exists both in terms of the sharing of knowledge, values and power within the patient–provider interaction, and also in the form of personal transformation on the part of the patient (Aujoulat et al. 2006). Underlying this sharing and transformation of knowledge and power is an assumption that, although patients want to be more informed about healthcare options (Jacobson 2007), they may prefer to leave certain decisions to professionals because of the cost and time involved in researching treatments, together with the emotions involved in making complex health decisions (Woolf et al. 2005). Indeed, some patients, even when informed by gaining information from the Internet, have been found to be reticent in discussing this information with a physician, as they were reluctant to challenge the doctor's expertise (Henwood et al. 2003) or because they were aware of the negative reactions they may trigger from physicians (Kivits 2006).

Despite the obvious advantages of the Internet in empowering patients, the advantages of the Internet can be both positive and negative (Hart et al. 2003) and there is much written about the disadvantages of the Internet with regard to the patient–practitioner relationship. Helft et al. (2003), for example, found that physicians referred to the anxiety and false hopes generated by patients searching for information online resulting in the physician having to 're-educate the patient'. It has also been reported that information from the Internet can cause patients to misdiagnose themselves or be misinformed about their condition, on the basis of 'wrong' information, or it can erode patients' trust in medical authority, causing them to challenge the doctor's expertise (Potts and Wyatt 2002; Hart et al. 2003; Adams et al. 2004). Such findings might explain the reported extended length of physician consultations (Helft et al. 2003), due to the need to for the patient and physician to sift through and evaluate the information (Potts and Wyatt 2002). Other reported problems include patients taking advice from sites which did not concur with medical opinion; and the propensity of the Internet to feed the anxieties of patients with hypochondria; and to feed patients' desire for unavailable treatments (Potts and Wyatt 2002). It is perhaps for these reasons that patients are usually not given information about Internet sites from practitioners (Hart et al. 2003), which possibly perpetuates a finding from Hart et al.'s study that most patients would go to a known healthcare practitioner to discuss a health issue, rather than use any other source, including those to be found on the Internet.

Partnership

The Internet can be a useful channel for research and good practice guidance, which should encourage practitioners to improve their casework decision making (Rhodes 2003). In terms of using the Internet to work in collaboration with other agencies, Rhodes explains that partnership work was hampered by technical barriers, such as progress in information sharing between major partners and social services, due to a lack of infrastructure to support the exchange of information across organizational boundaries. In addition, the use of electronic communications with providers of social care services was not well developed. According to Rhodes (2003) simply sharing access to what already existed was enough to improve things for individuals, and, where access to PCs for practitioners was adequate, direct inputting helped generate a greater sense of responsibility for the quality of data in the system and was quicker and more efficient. One example that would improve communication of information, cited by Rhodes (2003: 43), was Leicester City Council, who were placing their children's procedures on the council intranet. 'The procedures were supported by good practice examples and specimen documents and letters'.

Improvements could also be made in relation to patients' use and interpretation of information from the Internet. As a result of the changing partnership between patients and health practitioners, Jacobson (2007) identifies a potential for an expanding role for librarians and information specialists working in medical settings. Such librarians would need training in clinical or evidence-based medicine, as suggested by Homan and McGowan (2002). Informationists could help patients and families understand medical jargon, and work individually with each patient to assess their information needs in the context of a particular illness or diagnosis. This type of service could be delivered directly to patients by attaching articles or web printouts to patient charts, or through an 'information prescription form', filled out by a nurse or physician and compiled, summarized or given value-added features by a librarian (Calabretta 2002). These functions would complement the clinical librarian's role within the physical library by providing outreach services to patients who might be inclined to do research on the Internet instead of visiting the hospital library.

Another role for librarians is as educators, helping patients and families make sense of the vast amounts of Internet health information and informing consumers about the risks associated with inappropriate information and self-diagnosis. Working in patient libraries in health centres or hospitals, librarians acting as 'evidence educators' (Homan and McGowan 2002: 82) could educate the public on how to appraise, synthesize and compare medical research within an evidence-based framework. Librarians could also work with hospital website developers on portals designed to assist patients and practitioners in evaluating the quality of medical and health information on the Internet.

The Internet as a community

The use of Internet services across the health, social care and criminal justice sectors will inevitably continue to expand and improve. Not only is it better equipping and empowering patients with information: 'Integrating technology with communities and their practices, and exploiting the skills of information intermediaries, produced increased perceptions of user and group empowerment' (Adams et al. 2005: 8), the Internet is also making it easier for agencies to work together by enabling different agencies to become more informed of what other agencies and organization have to offer. While improved access to information can facilitate improved collaboration between agencies, it also has the potential to assist staff to challenge the decision or judgement of another individual or organization, whereas in the past they may have felt uncertain or disempowered by a lack of knowledge. The breadth and quality of information available via the Internet can facilitate more informed debate and communication, which potentially could result in improved multi-agency communication and accountability.

While the Internet has demonstrated its vast potential for information storage and retrieval it is increasingly also being used as a means of electronic communication and social networking. A range of different mediums are available usually free of charge, see Box 2.1.

Box 2.1 Internet Communication Tools

- email – such as Hotmail (www.hotmail.co.uk)
- live chat – such as Google Talk (www.google.com/talk/)
- video conferencing – such as Windows Live Messenger (www.mesenger.us/uk)
- internet voice calls – such as Skype (www.skype.com)
- social networking sites – such as Facebook (www.facebook.com)
- WebBlogs – such as (www.wordpress.com/)

These various forms of communication on the Internet have made synchronous and asynchronous communication between individuals and organizations faster, more convenient and cheaper; while social networking websites allow the creation of customisable online communities for people with shared interests. The flexibility and scope is endless, for example over 800 people have joined a Facebook community for people with dyslexia (Facebook 2008). Social networking sites can also be used effectively as pressure groups as illustrated by the campaign against HSBC bank after thousands of students joined the online community and threatening to boycott the bank unless the bank agreed to stop charging interest on student overdrafts – the campaign succeeded (BBC 2008). Another good example of the use of the Internet to communicate is the creation of a WebBlog by the Chief Constable of North Wales to be better in touch with the general public (North Wales Police Community Portal 2008). In addition to social networking sites and WebBlogs, dedicated discussion forums, such as the SANE discussion board (SANE 2008), provide a forum for support and information exchange for people suffering from, or helping those with, mental health difficulties. Global discussion forums exist on a wide variety of topics and are a rapidly growing form of self-help, but as already discussed the reliability and quality of information is largely only regulated by the members of the forum.

Conclusion

Information technology has made extensive resources and information available to homes throughout the world on virtually every subject possible. While this presents great opportunities it also raises issues such as equal access to this wealth of knowledge; the reliability and responsible use of the information; and concern regarding the ability of users to search, sift and distil the information available appropriately. Even accurate and reliable information maybe be problematic, as it may require a degree of technical or professional competence to avoid misunderstanding. Some information on the Internet may be biased or incorrect as most websites are not regulated. This could result in people who are seeking help arriving at the wrong conclusion about their situation/condition due to misleading information or advice. However, access to global knowledge and expertise has the potential to empower patients and service users and could result in greater accountability being expected from organizations by the people they serve. As previously discussed, improved access to information could facilitate improvement in partnership work between agencies as they develop a clearer understanding of each other's role and function.

The improved and constantly changing scope for communication, debate, information and networking on the Internet has opened up new avenues for interaction no longer bound by geographical limitations and time constraints. The Internet has successfully brought people together from across the UK, and indeed across the globe, who have similar or shared interests. It has created virtual communities which can provide new opportunities for support groups, user groups, discussion groups, problem solving debates, idea exchanges, etc. Creative and appropriate use of these possibilities in the health, social care and criminal justice sectors in the UK can help cement partnerships and improve their effectiveness, but at the time of writing agencies and organisations have been somewhat slow to properly exploit this opportunity.

Questions for further discussion

1 What measures can be taken to ensure the Internet improves access to information for all?
2 The Internet allows service users to gain detailed expert advice and information – is this a good thing or a bad thing?
3 How could online communities or networks be used to assist service delivery?

3 Promoting inclusive partnership working

Joy Merrell

The chapter will:

- Highlight the importance of effective partnership working for people from marginalized and disadvantaged groups.
- Outline the social and political context of partnership working.
- Explore partnership working specifically in respect of patient and public involvement.
- Consider strategies for enhancing the involvement of people from disadvantaged groups in decision making about health and social care.
- Discuss the challenges for partnership working in rural areas.

The organization, delivery and quality of health and social services impacts on the lives of everyone living in Britain. However, some groups of people, because they have multiple and complex health and social care needs, are more reliant on these services and often need to use multiple services. When services do not work well together in a joined-up way this poses significant problems for the most vulnerable and disadvantaged in our society. In this chapter I outline the importance of effective partnership working for people from disadvantaged groups and briefly explore the social and political context of partnership working. Models of participation and partnership working are then considered before the discussion focuses specifically on partnership working with service users and patients from disadvantaged groups. If the potential benefits of partnership working are to be realized then there is a need for cultural change at the level of the individual health and social care practitioner and at the organizational level, in other words within health and social care services. People from disadvantaged groups also need to be willing and able to participate in partnership working with practitioners and public bodies. Throughout the discussion strategies and resources for facilitating and evaluating the involvement of people from disadvantaged groups in decision making about health and social care are presented. Finally, I explore issues in respect of partnership working in rural areas. There is a perception that disadvantaged areas are predominantly urban, but deprivation within rural areas is often not fully recognized or taken into account. People living in rural areas do not have equality of access to health and social care services, and for people from disadvantaged groups the difficulties are compounded.

Disadvantaged groups

So who do we mean when referring to people from disadvantaged groups? As Steel (2004) suggests the range of individuals and groups who may be considered as vulnerable, disadvantaged or marginalized by service providers and practitioners is extensive but includes for example, people living with disabilities and chronic conditions, excluded older people, Black and minority ethnic (BME) groups; Gypsies and Travellers, homeless people, people living in poverty, and some people living in rural areas (SEU 2005). It is acknowledged that some individuals from these groups would not consider themselves as vulnerable or marginalized at all, and indeed as Steel (2004: 1) identifies, Travellers, for example, 'may see the NHS as hard to reach and marginal to their culture'.

In 2001 there were 4.6 million people from minority ethnic groups residing in the UK (ONS 2001). While 40 percent of the UK population live in the 88 most deprived districts of the UK this figure rises to 70 percent of all people from minority ethnic groups (SEU 2001). People of Pakistani, Bangladeshi, Black Caribbean and Black African descent are most likely to experience socio-economic and health disadvantage (SEU 2005). For example, Bangladeshi women report the poorest health status of any ethnic group, with 41 percent reporting their health as fair or poor compared with 32 percent of white women (Nazroo 1997).

By 2020, 20 percent of the population in England and Wales will be aged over 65 (ONS 2006). Older people tend to report higher levels of chronic and longstanding illness. For example, in 2003, 65 percent of people aged 65–74 and 64 percent of people aged 75 and over reported experiencing longstanding illness (ONS 2003). According to the Family Resources Survey as cited by the Social Exclusion Unit (2005) there are 5.9 million disabled people of working age in Britain, who are more likely to be unemployed than nondisabled adults (DWP 2004) and more likely to be living in poverty (DWP 2003). The relationship between socio-economic disadvantage and health has long been well established (Townsend et al.1988a, Acheson 1998) and it is known that people from disadvantaged groups have a higher incidence of ill health, poorer life expectancy and are less likely to receive or benefit from health and social care services (Benzeval et al. 1995, Nazroo 1997, Lazenbatt et al. 1999, Social Trends 2007).

Tackling social exclusion has been a priority for the Labour government since coming to power in 1997. Social exclusion is defined as:

> a short-hand term for what can happen when people or areas have a combination of linked problems, such as unemployment, discrimination, poor skills, low incomes, poor housing, high crime and family breakdown it is an extreme consequence of what happens when people don't get a fair deal throughout their lives, often because of disadvantage they face at birth. Since

this disadvantage can be transmitted from one generation to the next, it is important to consider social exclusion within the context of wider social inequality'

(SEU 2004: 14)

In seeking to address the disadvantage experienced by some groups within society and tackle discrimination, equality legislation has been extended over the last few years (SEU 2004, 2005). Public sector bodies including health and social care organizations are currently required by law to promote equality of opportunity and good relations between people from different ethnic groups. From December 2006, the new Disability Discrimination Act 2005 requires public sector bodies to promote equality of opportunity for disabled people in all aspects of their work and in service delivery. The Equality Act 2006 proposes a similar duty for public authorities relating to gender as well as establishing the Commission for Equality and Human Rights, which combines the functions of the three existing equality commissions (the Equal Opportunities Commission; the Commission for Racial Equality; and the Disability Rights Commission). The new Commission for Equality and Human Rights was established in October 2007. In addition, the Employment Equality (Age) Regula-tions 2006 outlaws age discrimination in the workplace and in vocational training, while the Equality Act (Sexual Orientation) Regulations 2007 prohibits discrimination on the grounds of sexual orientation outside the workplace.

It can be seen therefore that a raft of discrimination laws has been passed to tackle discrimination. Recently a review of all the discrimination laws in the UK has been undertaken with a view to developing a single equality bill, which will bring together and simplify the existing major pieces of discrimination law to make it clearer, more consistent and coherent (Department for Communities and Local Government 2007). The recommendations of the review are out for consultation, but it is proposed to replace the three different duties relating to race, disability and gender equality with a single new overarching duty on public authorities which will also take into account the need to promote good relations. The single duty may also encompass one or more of the new protected grounds such as age and sexual orientation. The aim is to focus on the outcomes that the new integrated duty must achieve ensuring that public authorities have acted to:

- address disadvantage
- ensure respect for the equal worth of different groups and foster good relations within and between groups
- accommodate difference and promote shared values
- promote equal participation.

(Department for Communities and Local Government 2007: 23)

However, as the Social Exclusion Unit (SEU 2005: 65) acknowledge, while these public duties are an *'important framework for promoting equality across the public sector in themselves they are no guarantee that equality will be achieved'*. In 2004 the Audit Commission found that one in six ethnic minority people said they had experienced racial discrimination, abuse or harassment, and despite the race equality duty being in effect for three years progress by public services had been 'slow' and 'sporadic' (Audit Commission 2004). In the report *Disabled for Life* four-fifths of disabled people reported feeling there was either 'a lot' of or 'a little' prejudice against disabled people in Britain (DWP 2002).

The Social Exclusion Unit report, (SEU 2005) *Improving Services, Improving Lives*, identified a number of changes needed to make services accessible and effective for meeting the needs of disadvantaged individuals. The issues identified were subsumed under six themes which included: improved information and communication; improved interactions with frontline staff; building personal capacity; joining-up services and the role of the voluntary and community sector (SEU 2005: 7). The latter are viewed as being particularly important as this sector often provides services directly to these groups, or acts as a bridge or intermediary between disadvantaged groups and the statutory sector. Joining-up services or partnership working is viewed as a key aspect of improving service provision for disadvantaged groups.

Partnership working: the policy context

Since the Labour party came to power in 1997 the concept of partnership working has been a central tenet of health and social care policy in Britain (Dowling et al. 2004). While partnership working had been advocated prior to this date, the 1999 Health Act and Local Government Act 2000 placed a statutory duty on health and local authorities to work together in partnership. Partnership working therefore has become a statutory duty rather than a voluntary option in respect of health and social care provision. Even where partnership working is not a statutory duty, it is often a requirement in order to achieve performance indicators or secure funding to develop new services or research grants, and therefore there are incentives to work together. Partnership working features prominently in the national service frameworks for mental health (DoH 1999; WAG 2002), older people (DoH 2001; WAG 2006), and children and young people (DoH and DES 2004, WAG 2005) in England and Wales. It is viewed as being central to the provision of high quality, responsive and equitable services for all, but particularly for disadvantaged groups. Partnership working has therefore been promoted by the government as a means for overcoming the fragmented and disjointed services previously provided by health and social care agencies which often left patients falling between these services: 'when people have complex needs spanning both health and social care good quality services are sacrificed for sterile arguments about boundaries it places the needs of the organisation above the needs of the people they are there to serve. It is poor organisation, poor practice, poor use of taxpayers – it is unacceptable' (Department of Health 1998: 3).

The rationale underpinning partnership working is that there will be added value from agencies and practitioners working together. The benefits of partnership working which pervade the literature include reduced duplication and overlap of services, improvement in the performance of service providers, more flexible, responsive services and improved outcomes for the public, patients and their carers

(Peckham and Exworthy 2003, SEU 2005). However, the review of the literature by Dowling et al. (2004) into the impact of partnership working in health and social care identified that evidence to support partnership working as being effective in terms of improvements for clients and their carers is cost-effective is sparse. Research to date has primarily focused on process rather than on outcomes measures. It is acknowledged that designing studies which can isolate and attribute partnership working to improved outcomes for service users is challenging (Dowling et al. 2004) and may take longer, as it may take several years before some improved user outcomes are evident. However, if practice is to be informed by evidence-based policy then there is an urgent need to address this deficit in respect of the effectiveness of partnership working in health and social care. Let us now consider discourses and models of participation and partnership working.

Discourses and models of participation and partnership working

Although now somewhat dated, Arnstein's (1969) classic analysis of citizen participation still has relevance today (Figure 3.1). She likened citizen participation to an eight-rung ladder with each rung of the ladder representing a degree of citizen power in influencing planning and policy making.

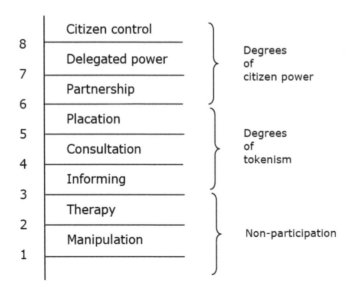

Figure 3.1 Arnstein's ladder of citizen participation
Source: Arnstein 1969

The bottom two rungs of the ladder (manipulation and therapy) constituted nonparticipation and were perceived as being more to do with public relations than participation. The next three rungs of the ladder (informing, consulting and placating) constituted degrees of tokenism. Public bodies engaged with citizen participation because of a political requirement or other incentives to do so (e.g. condition of a funding body), but decision making powers remain vested with the public bodies. The next rung 'partnership' constituted a situation where power is distributed between citizens and public bodies and responsibilities are shared, (i.e. joint committees). Citizens share in the decision making and can influence outcomes. The final two rungs 'delegated power' and 'citizen control' depicted decision making and control being vested with citizens.

The extent to which partnership working in health and social services has led to power sharing between users and service providers as represented in Arnstein's ladder is questionable. Research by Barnes et al. (2007) as part of the ESRC Democracy and Participation programme involved in-depth analysis of 17 examples of public involvement across a range of policy contexts (including health and social care services) in two English cities. Analysis of the case studies identified that although public participation had enabled citizens to gain a better understanding of decision making processes, promoted greater understanding and respect of others' perspectives and improved communication with public bodies, there was limited evidence of change in service delivery or challenging of professional expertise. Thus the authors concluded that these new ways of engaging the public have had little impact on challenging professional and institutional power (Barnes et al. 2007).

Based on the empirical data Barnes et al. (2007) identified three types of what they term institutions by which they mean the rules and norms that facilitate or impede the process of engagement between people and public bodies. These are 'institutions as sources of support, institutions as sites of challenge and opportunity and institutions as prisons' (p.189).

Institutions as sources of support

Within this type institutional norms and rules supported marginalized voices to be heard, people were empowered, their experiences were respected and valued as sources of expertise. This situation was mainly found in case studies which had their origins in voluntary or community organizations and who were led by people experienced in political action. A key factor was that these groups maintained their own values and norms and remained separate from the public bodies they were seeking to influence. As they engaged with public bodies there was the potential risk of cooptation where the public bodies' norms and values take over those of the voluntary or community organization and their capacity to challenge or influence decision making was diminished.

Institutions as sites of challenge and opportunity

Within this type there were opportunities for the public to participate and the potential to challenge public bodies, but in practice Barnes et al. (2007) found that public bodies managed to retain and expand their power. Power remained vested with the public bodies or practitioners who decided the rules and norms of the engagement, with whom they engaged (i.e. often with those they already know and with whom they have developed close relationships who will not 'rock the boat'), to set the agenda as to what is open for debate and the power to decide whether or not to take account of the views expressed. There was some evidence that through their closer engagement with practitioners or public body representatives, which promoted greater understanding of the constraints in practice, that people negotiated and modified their claims.

Institutions as prisons

In this instance public bodies go through the motions of public participation because there is a requirement to do so but the public are viewed as passive observers or even troublemakers. Within this type the rules and norms may be so entrenched that they 'effectively imprisoned officials and the public alike' (Barnes et al. 2007: 192).

The analysis by Barnes et al. (2007) identifies a contradiction in that through the process of public participation and partnership working, and dependent upon the norms and rules of engagement, there is the risk that local people or the public may have less capacity to challenge and influence outcomes because they are drawn into the field of institutional power. Failure on the part of practitioners or public bodies to take full account of the public's view and where needed take action may lead to disaffected citizens who are unwilling to participate in the future. If public participation is to be sustained then institutions and practitioners need to change (Barnes et al. 2007).

Partnership working can operate at several levels, at national level between government departments, at strategic level between public bodies and at the micro level or interface between practitioners and between practitioners, patients and their carers. It can not be assumed that if partnership working is operating at one level that it is necessarily working at another. Within the following discussion I have focused on developing effective partnerships with service users, patients and the public, particularly from disadvantaged groups. It is acknowledged that other stakeholders are involved in developing effective partnerships but as Beresford and Branfield (2006: 442) have identified service users have historically been 'left out of the equation'. If more inclusive partnerships are to be developed then there is a need to promote the involvement of service users, patients and the public.

Partnership working and patient and public involvement

While the concept of patient and public involvement and participation in the design, delivery and evaluation of health services has been a feature of government policy for the last 30 years since *Patients First* (DHSS 1979), policies particularly over the last decade (for example *Our Health, Our Care, Our Say*, DoH 2006, *Choosing Health*, DoH 2004, *The NHS Plan*, DoH 2000 have strengthened this focus in the UK (Milewa et al.

2002) and it is also gaining international importance (e.g Institute of Medicine 2001). Patients and their carers are no longer perceived as being 'passive recipients' of services, but as being at the centre of health and social services and the ultimate arbiters of service quality. There is therefore an increasing expectation and require- ment that practitioners and public bodies work in partnership with patients and carers and promote their involvement in decision making about their care. The *Health and Social Care Act 2001* (GB Parliament 2001) introduced a statutory duty to ensure public and patient involvement. By promoting the participation of marginalized and disadvantaged groups there is an expectation that this will lead to more responsive services and improved outcomes in terms of improved health and well being. Ultimately the government aim is that this will facilitate reducing health inequalities and social exclusion (SEU 2005). However, in order for the potential of partnership working to be realized patients and their carers need to be willing and able to participate, and practitioners and public bodies need to be willing to address the power relationships and institutional inertia (Barnes et al. 2007). Despite a plethora of government policies it is of concern that a series of external assessments have continued to highlight the lack of progress being made towards public and patient involvement (CHI 2003, CHI 2004), which it could be argued is central to partnership working.

Changing the culture of public bodies and practitioners to promote partnership working with service users

The findings from the Barnes et al. study (2007) indicate that there needs to be a change in the culture of decision making bodies including health and social service providers if partnership working with service users and local communities is to be enhanced. Andrews et al. (2006) have developed guidance for local authorities to promote effective citizenship and community empowerment. While these guidelines have been developed for local authorities they may be applied to a range of public bodies including the health sector. They emphasize the need for more evidence in respect of the *quality* of public involvement and whether public involvement is becoming more inclusive, which goes beyond simple headcounts in order to gain an understanding of what people learn from their involvement and how that impacts on their lives and their communities (Andrews et al. 2006). Additionally further evidence is required of what public bodies and practitioners learn from public involvement and how this impacts on decision making and outcomes. There has been little research to date on how services are influenced by patient and public involvement. Public bodies and practitioners need to consider how effectiveness in patient and public involve- ment could be assessed. This is not straightforward as there may be a number of intended purposes of public and patient involvement against which effectiveness could be measured. However, Box 3.1 identifies some examples of the kinds of changes you may wish to measure as proposed by the Community Care Needs Assessment Project. This is not an exhaustive list and you may wish to explore other measures of effectiveness which link to the specific purpose of patient and public involvement in your own practice or organisation.

Box 3.1 How could effectiveness in user involvement be evaluated?

Measuring change:

1   Within participants themselves (service users becoming more confident, practitioners feeling less fearful).
2   Within the nature of the relationships between the participants (is there a more equal distribution of power?).
3   In attitudes and working practices.
4   In efficiency (the best result that can be obtained from the resources. Thus (used), for example, by providing the services that make a difference to people's lives.
5   In effectiveness (services that do what they were intended to) measured in terms of service users' quality of life.

(CCNAP 2001: 48)

A fundamental aspect of effective partnership working is mutual understanding and trust. The Social Exclusion Unit (SEU 2005) proposes that staff training in respect of partnership working should be delivered by people from disadvantaged groups as this would provide opportunities for staff to improve their understanding of disadvantaged people's experiences and needs through first hand contact. There is evidence within the health service that, for example, there is not a consistent approach to disability or equality training (SEU 2005). Findings from a scoping study to explore the feasibility of a health and social care research network for Black and minority ethnic groups (BME) in Wales (Saltus et al. 2005) involving 142 staff and service users from across a range of statutory and voluntary sectors, identified the need to enhance health and social care practitioners' knowledge through training and raising awareness of BME issues, in order to develop cultural competency (individual as well as organizational). Respondents viewed staff training as a priority, and that time allocated for these activities needed to be protected. A lack of understanding of other cultures can lead to the stereotyping of minority ethnic groups, which results in differential practice being delivered (Davies and Bath, 2001; Burr, 2002). As Steel has commented in relation to involving vulnerable and marginalized people in health and social care research that: 'Whether overt or covert, institutional or individual, the attitudes of others generally have a strong effect on a vulnerable individual and can therefore be fundamentally empowering or disempowering' (2004: 6).

Inevitably there is an imbalance of power between practitioners and patients, particularly patients from disadvantaged groups. Practitioners represent agencies that have statutory powers and duties, have specialized knowledge and control of resources. The aim of working in partnership and involving patients and carers from disadvantaged groups should be to empower them, but in order for this to occur practitioners have to relinquish power, which can be challenging.

Practitioners and public bodies may lack the knowledge, confidence, skill and resources to involve people from disadvantaged groups in service design, delivery, evaluation and research. While there is no one way or a prescriptive list for how to involve disadvantaged groups there are some excellent resources available. Guidance by Steel (2004) specifically relates to involving vulnerable and marginalized people in health and social care research, while the comprehensive guide developed by the Community Care Needs Assessment Project (2001) entitled *Asking the Experts: A Guide To Involving People In Shaping Health And Social Care Services* assimilates relevant research evidence and practical experience of involving people, focusing on community care settings.

The onus is not just on practitioners and senior managers to embrace partnership working and engage and involve people from disadvantaged groups in decision making. Organizational structures and processes also need to change and adapt. It is important that public bodies have a clear strategy for working in partnership with patients and the public, and particularly with individuals from disadvantaged groups, which is viewed as integral to the organizations' work. While resources are required to ensure service user involvement, it is also the case that resources may be saved for example by reducing complaints and reducing the need to rectify expensive mistakes (Audit Commission 2000). In order to avoid tokenism clear expectations as to what users can expect from their involvement with public bodies needs to be agreed. Some user groups have taken control in this area and developed their own rules of engagement. Box 3.2 presents a contract developed by Swindon People First (for people with learning difficulties) as cited by CCNAP (2001) for organizations seeking their involvement.

Box 3.2 Swindon People First contract

If you want People First to be on your committee you must agree these things to make it OK for us:

1. We should have a voice to say what we want.
2. You need to listen to us and give us time to talk.
3. We won't come to your committee just so it looks good.
4. You need to let us know why you want us on the committee.
5. You need to tell us what we will get out of being on your committee.
6. You have got to make minutes and agendas on tape if we want them.
7. The committee should pay for a supporter.
8. Everyone on the committee needs to be trained to know how to involve us.
9. The committee has to use words we understand.
10. We must be able to stop meetings if we need you to say something again or explain it.
11. Everyone should have their expenses paid.
12. If the rest of the committee get paid then we should too.

(CCNAP 2001: 30)

To enable people from disadvantaged groups to work in partnership with practitioners and public bodies often requires them to make adjustments, as for some they are embarking on a new activity which requires appropriate preparation and support.

Building capacity for partnership working with disadvantaged groups

The development and expansion of patient and public participation poses important challenges for health and social service providers if they are to ensure that this opportunity is available to all, including people from disadvantaged groups. Engaging with public bodies and health professionals can be intimidating even for those who are familiar with how organizations are managed, so a level of personal effectiveness or 'capacity' may be required if patients are to benefit from the opportunities which participation may provide.

Evidence suggests that voluntary and community organizations are more effective than public bodies in building personal capacity and empowering marginalized groups. Voluntary and community organizations have the flexibility to be more responsive to the needs of service users and the capacity to build service users' trust (SEU 2005). Building up trust and the confidence to participate with practitioners and public bodies can be long term, particularly if people have had a previous poor experience in previous engagements (SEU 2005).

Appropriate training and support needs to be provided if people are to be able to engage fully with practitioners and public bodies. The following are training needs identified by service users from an evaluation of a national evaluation project:

- Assertiveness and 'speaking up' courses
- Disability equality training
- Equal opportunities training
- Confidence building courses run by service user trainers
- Guidance on decision making structures within public bodies
- Training in committee procedures and negotiating skills
- Information about what has and hasn't worked in other areas
- Legal issues and rights under community care and other legislation

(JRF 1999)

However, each person is an individual and a sensitive assessment of an individual's needs is required to ensure that they can fully participate and that if this opportunity is to be available to all, then specific requirements may need to be provided, such as provision of interpreters.

Partnership working between statutory providers and the voluntary sector can enhance access to groups who are considered 'hard to reach'. For example, social workers in Caerphilly reported improved access to families and uptake of services when they worked together with community workers, and came under the auspices of Sure Start rather than Social Services (Williams et al. 2002). Sure Start workers were trusted within the community and acted as intermediaries in enabling disadvantaged families to access the resources and facilities to meet their needs.

Volunteering has been shown to provide many benefits in terms of extending social networks, building confidence and esteem, improving knowledge and skills and enabling access to further education and employment (Davis Smith 1998). Some of the most disadvantaged groups such as refugees and people seeking asylum can benefit from volunteering opportunities established through partnership working between mainstream services and refugee organizations (Wilson and Lewis 2006). Lack of awareness among organizations recruiting volunteers and among refugees and people seeking asylum that volunteering is a legal and worthwhile option has meant that opportunities are being missed for mainstream organizations to benefit from a more diverse and inclusive service, and for individuals to develop their personal capacity in terms of learning English, building self-esteem and confidence, engaging with mainstream services, and integrating into the community. A key motivation for refugees and asylum seekers to volunteer is to gain employment. While the latter are not allowed to undertake paid work unless they are granted leave to remain in the country, it is important that volunteering offers experiences and quality placements which enable those eligible and seeking work to improve their employment opportunities.

The Volunteering and Asylum Project (Wilson and Lewis 2006) involving case studies with ten organizations across the UK, identified that the key to effective and sustained partnerships was the involvement of an intermediary organization, which brought together organizations seeking volunteers and those people seeking asylum. Intermediary organizations were located within the refugee sector, adult education college, work placement agencies and volunteer development centres, but all volunteering and support organizations are potential intermediaries. The role of the volunteer coordinator was seen as key in promoting diversity and inclusion through volunteering (Wilson and Lewis 2006).

However, it should be acknowledged that while the voluntary and community organizations have an important role to play in improving access to disadvantaged groups and building personal capacity, not everyone is a member of a voluntary group and resources may need to be expended in the use of outreach or link workers, who have been shown to be effective, to promote the involvement of people who do not join voluntary or community groups (JRF 1999). Seeking to promote the involvement of vulnerable and disadvantaged groups in decision making about health and social care is, however, the business of everyone, from the directors of public bodies to individual practitioners.

An example of an innovative approach to identifying the needs of rural communities is the study of long term care needs of older people living in the most isolated communities of Gwynedd conducted by the Rural North Wales Initiative for the Development of Support for Older People (RuralWIDe) (Burholt et al. 2007) (see Box 3.3).

Box 3.3: Example of working in partnership with older people in a rural area

Gwynedd located in the North West of Wales is similar to many rural areas in Wales and to several rural areas in England in having a higher proportion of older residents (NaW 2002). RuralWIDe is a partnership between The Centre for Social Policy Research and Development at the University of Wales Bangor, Age Concern Gwynedd a Mon and older volunteers residing in Gwynedd. This was a participatory research project which involved older people living in the rural communities participating as co-researchers in all aspects of the study from design to dissemination. A specific objective was to improve partnership working between Age Concern Gwynedd a Mon, university researchers, the Local Authority and other voluntary organizations to improve service planning for older people in remote rural areas. Additionally, to build the research capacity of Age Concern staff and volunteers to use and conduct research to promote the planning of services 'for older people by older people' (Burholt et al. 2007: 4). A key feature of this study therefore was to empower older people through the provision of appropriate training and support to enhance their level of participation and involvement in their own communities and to ensure that they had a voice which was respected and valued. Recommendations from the study are being used to inform future planning of services for older people in Gwynedd.

This project demonstrates the commitment of all stakeholders to the involvement and empowerment of older people in decision making about their long term care needs in a rural community. Finally, I wish to explore issues in respect of partnership working in rural areas. There is a perception that disadvantaged areas are predominantly urban, but deprivation within rural areas is often not fully recognized or taken into account.

Partnership working in rural areas

A key issue as Pugh (2005) reports is the 'invisibility of rural problems' as policy makers and service providers fail to recognize the existence of social problems in rural areas. This is partly attributed to idealized notions of rural life and associated assumptions of self-sufficiency, homogeneity and community cohesion.

Rural populations are not homogenous or indeed static. Rural communities comprise those who have resided within the area for most of their lives and those who move into the area often following retirement (Burholt et al. 2007). There are major differences between rural areas, such as the population needs and services required for a remote island compared with a rural community which has good communication links with an urban area (Craig and Manthorpe 2000). Rural areas often include transient populations such as tourists, migrant and seasonal workers and Travellers, which make it difficult to plan services for a fluctuating population. It may also be more difficult to identify areas of deprivation in rural areas as traditional indices of deprivation such as those by Jarman (1983) and Townsend et al. (1988b) include, for example, car ownership as a measure of affluence, but this is a necessity not a luxury for rural dwellers. For those who are on low incomes the cost of running a car is an additional drain on their limited resources. Of rural settlements 29 percent have no bus service at all and 50 percent of rural households live more than a 13-minute walk away from a bus stop (SEU 2005). The accessibility and availability of transport therefore has a significant impact on the uptake of health and social services (SEU 2005; Burholt et al. 2007). Utilization rates of some services and in particular preventative health services may be poor (SEU 2005). As a result of the increased distance and difficulty in accessing services disadvantaged people living in rural areas often present for treatment of health problems at a later stage when diseases are more advanced and outcomes are often poorer (Deaville 2001).

Other barriers to health and social service uptake in small rural communities include fears that confidentiality will be breached, a culture of self-reliance, lack of anonymity and fear of stigma, especially in relation to use of mental health services (Boulanger et al. 1999), sexual health services (Swindlehurst 2003) and adult literacy services (SEU 2005).

There may be insufficient numbers to support services such as schools, nurseries and general practice surgeries in small rural areas and less provision of specialist services, which limits choice. Due to the geographical dispersion of the population and the increased travelling time involved it is more expensive to provide services in rural areas. People living in rural areas therefore do not have equality of access to services and for people from disadvantaged groups the difficulties are compounded. So having explored the particular challenges for disadvantaged groups of living in rural communities, what are the implications for partnership working?

Craig and Manthorpe (2000) in their survey of social care provision in rural authorities throughout the UK identified that joint working was undeveloped, that there was an over dependence on the voluntary sector especially in respect of provision for people with particular needs such as those with learning disabilities and that residents' and users' views and priorities in terms of service provision were rarely being heard. Despite identifying a number of initiatives in rural areas there has been a lack of evaluation and dissemination of good practice and therefore these initiatives have had little impact on policy development (Craig and Manthorpe 2000). The authors identified that development in respect of rural health services seemed to be more developed but that these were not always well integrated with local authority initiatives (Craig and Manthorpe 2000).

In respect of partnership working by health services in rural areas, findings from a consultation survey (Swindlehurst 2003) of 60 rural primary care trusts (PCTs) in England, (66 percent response rate, n=40) and interviews with a range of health professionals in three PCTs, identified that 95 percent were working in partnership with local government and had formed local strategic partnerships. Local strategic partnerships are umbrella partnerships which bring together all the different sectors, public, private, voluntary and community and service users within a locality to improve governance and quality of service provision. ninety percent were working with the voluntary sector and between 55–65 percent were working with businesses and local transport providers (Swindlehurst 2003). The majority of PCTs who responded were therefore involved in partnership working to some extent, although the nature and scope of these partnerships are unknown.

As Pugh (2005) acknowledges, while the benefits and challenges of partnership working in rural areas are similar to those in urban areas, there are additional considerations which need to be taken into account. As a result of the dispersed nature of the population in rural areas and fewer opportunities to utilize other services and venues such as schools to locate services, the cost of service delivery tends to be higher. This may act as an incentive for statutory and voluntary bodies to work together. However, there are costs involved in establishing partnership working, which often are not recognized by funding bodies (Merrell et al. 2005). Smaller agencies such as voluntary groups may not have the resources in terms of personnel or funding to fully support partnership working. On a practical level they may have insufficient staff cover to enable regular attendance at partnership meetings. Their participation may involve subsidizing or absorbing the costs associated with establishing partnership working (Williams et al. 2002). An evaluation of the Sure Start programme in Caerphilly involving 11 partners working collaboratively, identified that costs for administering the partnership had been underestimated and while the larger statutory bodies could absorb such costs, this was a strain on the funds of smaller voluntary organizations within the partnership (Williams et al. 2002). Additionally projects delivered though voluntary organizations are often supported by short term funding, which may militate against the additional lead in time which has been identified as being required in the development of effective partnerships in rural areas (Edwards et al. 1999).

Due to an often reduced number of staff working in rural areas, health and social care practitioners may have not have the expertise, skills or knowledge to meet the needs of some disadvantaged groups, such as Black and minority ethnic groups, or the complexity of needs which, for example, a disabled person from a minority ethnic group may present. Rural dwellers tend to complain less about service provision than their urban counterparts, and those least likely to complain are people from disadvantaged groups (SEU 2004). There therefore may be less pressure, for example, for cultural appropriate services, and less expertise available in a rural community to advise or directly provide services (Pugh 2005). Limited research to date has explored service provision for Black and minority ethnic groups in rural areas and their views of the services provided.

Despite the extent of rural areas in the UK, the majority of health and social care practitioners receive no specific training on rural issues (Pugh 2005) and there has been limited research to establish what training and development models are used by practitioners and volunteers and what works in practice (Craig and Manthorpe 2000). It can not be assumed that models of practice and service delivery developed for urban areas will be appropriate, relevant and effective for rural areas and ensure that the needs of all rural dwellers, but particularly those from disadvantaged groups are addressed.

Rural proofing, a concept developed by the Countryside Agency following the government's white paper *Our countryside: The Future – A Fair Deal for Rural England* (DETR 2000) is a process for assessing the impact of policies on rural areas to ensure that the needs of rural dwellers are considered (Swindlehurst 2003). It is a mandatory requirement for all government departments to rural proof all policies and its use is encouraged at all levels. The Commission for Rural Communities (2008) has developed a checklist for agencies to assist the process of rural proofing.

Rural proofing is not specifically aimed at the service delivery level. However, regional and local policy developments can be influenced by the process of rural proofing through the Regional Rural Affairs Forums (Swindlehurst 2003). A toolkit for primary care organization to rural proof health services has been developed by the Institute for Rural Health and the Countryside Agency and is available online (IRH 2008). This resource if widely implemented will assist in ensuring that health services are rurally sensitive and that inequities in accessing healthcare by rural dwellers do not persist.

Conclusion

There is a clear policy imperative to promote partnership working and public and patient involvement in health and social care. It is acknowledged that promoting the involvement of marginalized and disadvantaged groups is challenging and that there is a need for cultural change at the individual and organizational level if this is to be achieved. Service users, patients and carers may also feel reticent about the concept of partnership working because of previous poor experiences and the fact that there is much rhetoric but, in practice, limited action in terms of changes to service provision and delivery. It would seem that there is much more to be done if partnership working is to be inclusive and involve service users, patients and carers from disadvantaged groups in decision making about the design, delivery and evaluation of health and social care services. There is also a need for more research into, for example, the effectiveness of partnership working, especially in terms of patient outcomes; the extent to which patient and public involvement is inclusive, and how decision making and services are influenced by patient and public involvement.

Questions for further discussion

1   What strategies could an organization adopt to enhance the involvement of disadvantaged and marginalized groups in decision making?
2   What measures could be put in place to assess the impact of user involvement on decision making?
3   What issues might arise if there is a shift in the balance of power towards meaningful service user involvement?

4 Ethical issues of working in partnership

Althea Allison

This chapter will:

- Discuss the ethical and moral issues that may arise in relation to inter-professional working.
- Provide an explanation of ethical frameworks and moral codes, in order that an understanding of these differing frameworks may facilitate the discernment of 'right' decisions.
- Consider the consequences of actions and omissions within the context of professional relationships.
- Consider values and principles specific to practice and to the individual, as well as the theoretical frameworks that need to be applied within the context of practice to have any value for the professional.

All professional groups, whether working in isolation or in fully integrated teams, face challenges in the delivery of their particular skills and services. These challenges may be located in many different areas including:

- Increased consumer expectations, evolving cultural boundaries, advances in technology, political and legal norms
- Government policy initiatives and changes
- Financial considerations
- Social mores

(Soothill et al. 1995).

This list is clearly not presented as a definitive catalogue of potential challenges, but serves to offer an insight into the complex contextual influences which may come to bear on the reality of professional practice. Moreover, the broad category influences noted by Soothill et al. over a decade ago, have continued to gain in breadth and momentum. Take, for example, government initiatives to further integrate the training and preparation of professional groups in health and social care in order to achieve the vision of an interprofessional workforce (DoH 2007b). Of fundamental importance to the focus of this chapter is a common element running through all the categories listed above. Within every category cited, there are ethical and moral considerations linked to the challenges faced.

Professional groups have a specific remit within society in that they meet particular needs within society, needs which pertain specifically to that professional body (Burkhardt and Nathaniel 2002). When one assumes the role of a professional, one takes on certain role specific duties in the usual course of events, those that advance and preserve the special good(s) which the profession aims to provide. Generally speaking, each professional group has a defined contribution to make that is not shared by others. Bayles (1989) argues that each professional group has its own particular special 'good', its own specific contribution to make. The resulting profession specific duties impose obligations upon the professional that do not normally apply to everyone else, for example, a doctor is obligated to heal, a lawyer to advance legal justice, a social worker to enhance the well being of people within their social contexts, a teacher to promote knowledge and facilitate learning, nurses to promote health and care for the sick and dying. It would appear then, that each professional group has some particular service that it provides, some 'good' that others need or want. Arguably, the more professional a job, the greater the responsibilities and obligations that go with it.

An obvious starting point for the individual professional is being clear about the raison d'être or the professional purpose of the group to which they claim membership. While the specific responsibilities may change, influenced by context and development as a professional group, the purpose of the profession does not. This chapter will, therefore, address the following issues:

- Approaches to ethics
- Partnership working and the context of inter-professional practice
- Working together: the fiduciary relationship

Approaches to ethics

Before considering the different approaches to ethics, it is first necessary to distinguish between ethics and morals. There are misapprehensions surrounding the words *ethics* and *morals* embodied in the, sometimes inter-changeable, use of the words adopted in various writings in health and social care. 'Ethics' offers a formal process for applying moral philosophy and provides a framework for discerning logical and consistent decisions concerned with questions of how one *ought* to behave in a given situation (Burkhardt and Nathaniel 2002). The word 'morals' has, in a colloquial sense, been narrowed to become synonymous with considerations of sexual behaviour, while problems associated with issues other than sexual behaviour are more often referred to using the word *ethics*. In effect then, *ethics* and *morals* can refer to two different areas of ordinary morality (Downie and Telfer 1980). Perhaps the most important issue here is not whether certain acts or judgements are ethical or unethical, but *why* they are deemed to be so. Moral judgement presupposes the moral argument for the case that if something is right or wrong, it will be so for a reason (Fletcher and Holt 1995).

Consider the case study in Box 4.1:

Box 4.1 A case study of multi-disciplinary ethical care

A GP cares for a family with many health and social care problems. They have five children; the father is a heavy drinker and known to be violent, and the mother suffers from a psychotic illness which is controlled by medication. The mother does not like taking her medication but is visited regularly by the community psychiatric nurse (CPN) who monitors her care. During her last admission to hospital, the psychiatrist made it clear that if she did not cooperate with taking her oral medication, then he would have to think about prescribing her medication via an intramuscular route. The social worker assigned to the family is most concerned about their youngest child, aged two and half years, who appears not to be thriving physically and has delayed speech patterns, and there is a worry that the child is at risk. She would like to place the child in a day nursery but is faced with a lack of resources. The health visitor to the family has known the mother very well over a great number of years and has developed a very trusting relationship with her. Recently, the mother confided in her that she wanted to stop taking her medication because it made her too lethargic to do anything with her life and was making her fat. She said she wanted to 'be like she used to be' and added that she had been considering telling her husband to go because she was fed up with his behaviour.

Although it might seem that the psychiatrist was being coercive in making the mother comply with her medication, psychotic illness is devastating for the individual and for those who love and care for them. Hospital admissions can be traumatic for the individual and, in this case, disruptive to the family, particularly the youngest child. The CPN is acting ethically within their professional role in monitoring the medication and progress of the mother but, arguably, there is an element of social control here, which is not primarily in the client's best interest. The health visitor is faced with possibly damaging a trusting relationship, built up over years, if she reports what she knows, and is in the unenviable position of considering whether to breech a confidence. The social worker, who sees a way to support the mother and the child, is thwarted by a lack of nursery places. Resource allocation issues are ever present in health and social care. Deciding whose needs are most pressing is both daunting and fraught with ethical considerations. Ultimately, the GP carries the responsibility for the family's health related needs in the community.

Questions:

- Is it in the best interest of all concerned to make sure the mother remains well and within the family or to keep her on medication that she is not happy with, in effect using her as a means to an end?

- Whose frame of reference is being used to decide best interest?
- What personal qualities within the professional are demanded?

Moral philosophy and ethical theories can be useful, therefore, in helping professionals to determine 'right' actions. Moreover, the purpose of moral philosophy and ethics, according to Norman (1983), is an attempt to arrive at an understanding of the nature of human values, of how we ought to live and of what constitutes right conduct. If the pursuit of moral philosophy and ethical theory is to bring greater understanding and insight to practice, a clearer view of the propositions offered by major schools of philosophical thought is required.

The main schools of philosophical thought are utilitarianism, deontology and virtue ethics, as discussed below.

Utilitarianism

Utilitarianism, sometimes referred to as 'consequentialism', can be broadly presented as an approach which seeks to maximize the greatest happiness of the greatest number. This conceptual notion forms the basis of all utilitarian theories of ethics. Arguably, it is quite an attractive morality involving a straightforward idea of maximizing happiness and minimizing misery. Utilitarian approaches promote the moral theory, which proposes that 'right action' is that which brings about the greatest utility or usefulness, allowing that no action is, in itself, either good or bad, but rather it is the associated outcomes that carry moral significance. Central concepts of utilitarianism are 'good' and 'evil' – happiness equating to good and unhappiness equating to evil (Husted and Husted 1991). Although the concept of promoting happiness alone may be criticized as a simplistic notion, utilitarians hold that the only elements that make actions good or bad are the outcomes that can be ascribed to them (Burkardt and Nathaniel 2002). In other words, the 'right' decision is judged by the consequences which result from that decision.

Deontology

The word 'deontology' emanates from the Greek word 'deon', meaning duty. Deontological theories may also be referred to as duty-based theories and provide a very different framework for assessing ethical questions. Ethical action, within the deontological tradition, is based on 'doing one's duty'. Central concepts within this approach are the notions of 'right' and 'wrong'. The moral agent has a duty to do what is 'right' and to refrain from doing what is 'wrong'. Right action, therefore, consists of doing one's duty, while failing to do one's duty is wrong (Husted and Husted 1991).

The deontological approach is often represented by the exhortation not to treat people as a means to an end but as a means in themselves. This underpinning tenet is based on the belief that people have intrinsic moral worth that prevents them being used as a means to an end. Actions within this approach are governed by the rule that actions decided upon must be able to be applied without fear or favour to all humans. There is also recognition within this approach that there are prima facie and absolute principles which we *know* should guide our actions. Examples might include duties of fidelity (keeping promises, not acting deceitfully) and duties of beneficence.[1]

The absolute requirement to respect the autonomy and dignity of the person is of utmost importance within this approach, leading to the imperative to treat each individual 'as an end in themselves', not merely as a means for arbitrary use by others. In contrast to the utilitarian school, the rightness or wrongness of an act, then, depends upon the nature of the act, rather than the consequences.

Virtue ethics

The concept of virtue ethics, also referred to as character ethics, presents a challenge to deontological and utilitarian theories. Virtue ethics has experienced a revival in fortune and has re-emerged as an influential framework for examining moral behaviour (Pence 1993). The central tenet of virtue ethics is derived from the view that an individual moral agent will choose particular actions based upon a certain degree of innate moral virtue. This approach appeals to the virtues held within the person (e.g. trustworthiness, honesty, integrity, fidelity, compassion and courage). An important point to remember is that virtue is closely associated to motive. An action can be right without being virtuous, but an action can be virtuous only if performed from the right state of mind. For example, a nurse can perform an asceptic procedure technique absolutely correctly but do so without compassion or care for the patient.

Deontological and utilitarian theories ascribe to the view that ethics provides guidelines to action based on the question, 'What morally ought one to do?' Virtue ethics, however, does not start from this question, but rather start from the premise that the basic function of morality is the moral character of persons. The question then becomes not, 'What should one do?' but rather, 'What kind of person should one be?' (Burkhardt and Nathaniel 2002).

Behaving ethically and behaving morally are, therefore, different and both terms are frequently used by health and social care professionals when referring to 'professional' behaviour. 'You can't do that, it's immoral', is not an unusual proclamation on the part of caring professionals. Equally, those working in health and social care take pride in their ethical behaviour, which is enshrined in codes of conduct that they are required to follow. However, different codes of behaviour and understanding of ethical and moral rules held by different professional groups have important implications for partnership working.

Partnership working and the context of inter-professional practice

The notion of working in partnership was established into the NHS ideology in the 1997 Department of Health document, *The New NHS*. Indeed, inter-agency working and collaboration between professional groups, notably between health and social care, was established as a 'duty of care'. The notion of partnership has continued to gain strength and is now central to NHS ideology and purpose. Indeed, McLaughlin (2004) has argued that partnership provides a 'core theme' within social policy areas as diverse as health- and social care, urban regeneration, education, crime and biotechnology (p. 103). While working boundaries between professional groups may become less defined and user perspectives are given greater credence (Biggs 2000), ideological boundaries do not necessarily change by dictat. It remains questionable as to whether different professional groups are able to make the ideological shift. As Morrison (2007) observes, experience shows how delicate achieving collaborative working can be, a major reason being that individuals need both the skill and a positive mindset towards working together.

The modernization agenda inherent in the policy changes alluded to requires a fundamental culture shift and attitude change by all professional groups at all levels. Fish and Coles (1998) point out that professionals cannot continue to work in isolation from other professional groups. The complexity of contemporary health and social care provision is such that the full range of professional groups must work together as a team. Partnership potentially expands access to resources by virtue of sharing knowledge and expertise. It also promotes cross-fertilization of approaches to intervention. Partnership also highlights the limitations of single agency working in dealing with complex human problems. Surely this provides an argument for the rationalization of resources, to avoid waste of scarce resources and to maximize the good from resources available. In practice, however, working together as a team is more easily said than done, as Ashwell (2003) has noted in particular relation to health and social care collaborators. Clashes of professional culture, objectives and ways of dealing with the client groups have yet to be fully overcome.

The context of care delivery has been influenced by changes in the philosophical underpinnings informing political policies and the myriad policy and legislative changes which have emanated as a result. These include:

- The financial position of the national economy continuing to fuel the quest for cost-effectiveness
- Continuing technological and scientific advances in health care
- The voice and influence of professional bodies and
- The demands of stakeholders, including patients and carers

A surfeit of government policies provides an indication of these changes within the NHS, two in particular encapsulating the changing ideology: *The New NHS: Modern, Dependable* (DoH 1997b) and *The NHS Plan* (DoH 2000f). These policies aim to place consumers at the centre of health care provision and include arrangements for more stringent mechanisms for maintaining accountability in professional practice and for monitoring resources. Those professionals working in the public service in particular have witnessed unprecedented changes to the way in which they have been expected to provide their services. A fundamental shift in philosophical emphasis is evidenced in the increasing empowerment of consumers of services offered within the public services. Consumers, in response, have become more questioning and articulate in relation to professional expertise and the quality of services offered. Changes in societal expectations have also contributed to an increased emphasis on partnership and respect for individual responsibility in client–professional relationships.

So what do these changes mean for the professional in the delivery of their services and expertise? What ethical issues arise in this situation? In the main, professional groups would argue that a central core of the way they work is to make certain that client interests are served as a primary consideration. Professional codes of ethics generally reflect this philosophy, focusing on obligations to individual clients. It is highly likely that individual practitioners from different professional persuasions would believe that they try, in all conscience, to do a good job. To imply otherwise could be considered vaguely insulting. However, health and social care professionals may be faced with very complex situations which call for expertise outside of their normal sphere of practice, resulting in a demand for collaboration and pooling of expertise that locates the client as being central to the exercise rather than being peripheral to it. This inevitably means having sufficient insight to know when one is at the limits of one's professional expertise and can be open to working with other professional groups for the good of the client. This can be seen in the case study in Box 4.2.

Box 4.2 A case study of multi-professional working

Sally, a social worker of many years' experience, received a referral following a telephone report from a member of the general public that they thought a child in the street where they lived was being 'neglected'. The child, who was thought to be under school age, wandered in the street, looked uncared for and asked neighbours for food and drink. There were believed to be three other children of school age but the eldest child, aged about 10, was frequently seen looking after the youngest child.

On visiting the house, the mother, a single parent living on state benefits, appeared to be withdrawn, had difficulty in responding to Sally's questions and the house was dirty, cluttered and cold. When asked about the report that her daughter had been begging for food and drinks from neighbours, the mother just curled up on the couch and closed her eyes.

The potential for many agencies to become involved in this scenario is obvious and, depending on who in the scenario is seen as the client, might include professionals from health, social care and education at the very least. More specialist sections of each of those broad professional groups may also be engaged, including mental health workers, child and family social care workers, and educational psychologists. Of course here lies one of the first problems: professional groups may see their primary obligations not only as being of a different nature but also to establish different priorities. One may prioritize the mother, another may prioritize the child, another the whole family as a unit. One may see it as an emergency, another as a situation that needs intervention but not an immediate threat. Taking the deontological view, then, different professionals will have different views about for whom they should 'do their duty', while taking the utilitarian stance, it is evident that whatever action the professional takes there will be consequences, some of which may be in competition. However, while the individual professional assesses the possible contribution they may make to a given situation, what remains true for all groups is that they have obligations to their clients emanating from the privileged position they hold.

Obligations to whom?

In the discussion above, it was stated that professional codes of ethics generally focus on obligations to individual clients. Within any client–professional relationship, there are certain moral obligations that are imposed by virtue of the relationship. A professional relationship differs from a social relationship in a number of fundamental ways. In a professional relationship, there is an expectation that the needs of the client will form the focus of the relationship and that the professional will be vigilant to those needs, given that clients will generally become clients because they have a need for which the expertise of the professional is required (Allison 1996). As individuals in our own daily lives, we each will make decisions about our personal circumstances, for example, how we may conduct our relationships, through to a decision about whether we avoid paying the fare on public transport. We have, if you like, personal frameworks and moral codes by which we live our lives. Within the professional role we inhabit, personal criteria may not be enough. In the context of practice, other considerations fall into the equation, not least the privileged position held by any professional group. Sometimes, the laws and customs of a particular society will determine the scope of moral obligations to be assumed by individuals in that society (Gillon 1986). Possible conflicts between obligations to clients and third parties are also an important consideration in teamworking. Responsibilities of truthfulness, nonmaleficence[2] and fairness are implicated here, as indicated in the examples in Box 4.3.

Box 4.3 The ethics of protecting third parties

There is a duty incumbent on professionals to protect third parties from danger. For example, a physician may have good reason to believe that a particular medical condition may present a danger to others, as in the case of a train driver who starts to suffer from unpredictable blackouts. Physicians clearly have a responsibility to provide care and treatment for the client, but there is also an obligation to third parties who may be injured. Truthfulness is a basic expectation that a client can expect from a professional, but what about third parties?

There are certainly examples of physicians and nurses being asked by relatives to withhold information about potentially fatal illnesses from a patient and vice versa. However, a terminally ill patient may be denied support and practical help that would support their independence if social service colleagues

> were not allowed to know the diagnosis. Fairness and truthfulness often combine in forming a dilemma for professionals. Consider the professional who is asked to support an application for rehousing, but is expected to exaggerate the circumstances so that a higher priority is assigned.

There are several groups to whom professionals can reasonably be expected to owe an obligation including:

- Patients/clients
- Patient's/client's relatives
- Fellow professionals
- Employers
- The general public
- Themselves and their dependents

Of course it would be exceedingly difficult to serve all these stakeholders in equal measure. When a situation presents itself where conflicting demands are being made, the question is raised of where one's first obligation lies. Arguably, professionals enter a contract with society when they take on a professional mantle. In effect, they agree to provide a specialist service and in return society grants a monopoly around that service. The argument for professional obligations to third parties is located in the role of professions conferred by society (Burkhardt and Nathaniel 2002). The danger in viewing the professional as having a responsibility to society that may outweigh the responsibility to the client is that it relieves the client of responsibility for themselves. How might the professional reconcile these competing demands? Let us consider the notion of what Bayles (1989) described as the fiduciary relationship.

Working together: the fiduciary relationship

When a client and professional come together, they do so as one human being to another. In essence, they meet as equals, except that a client is generally involved with a professional because the professional has superior knowledge, expertise and gate-keeping abilities that the client does not have. This, therefore, shifts the relationship into more of a dependent one. Bayles (1989) recognized the need for a concept that acknowledged the special contribution of the professional within a client–professional relationship, but also one that allowed the client to retain significant authority and responsibility in the decision making. He utilized the notion of the fiduciary relationship, a concept used in legal relationships to characterize the features of a client–professional relationship. In a fiduciary relationship, both parties are responsible and their judgements are given consideration. However, because the professional is in a more advantageous position because of their special knowledge and expertise, Bayles (1989) emphasises the special obligation of the professional to be worthy of client trust in a fiduciary relationship. The notion of trust implied in such a relationship is one that accomplishes the outcomes for which the professional has been appointed and which meets the client's needs. Trustworthy professionals, he argues, will demonstrate several virtues within their character. These are listed in Box 4.4:

Box 4.4 Professional virtues as identified by Bayles (1989)

- Honesty
- Candour
- Competence
- Diligence
- Loyalty
- Fairness
- Discretion

Although these attributes are offered as a group of virtues that a trustworthy professional can be expected to possess, Bayles (1989) goes further than this, offering that the obligations implied and explicit in these characteristics may be regarded as 'norms of conduct' for the professional practitioner. The possession of these virtues in caring professionals in their relationships with clients might also help to explain the revival of *virtue ethics*.

It would be easy to discard Bayles's list of desirable virtues as only being relevant to the client–professional relationship but what about the other working relationships a professional must engage in? Professional–professional relationships pose particular challenges, especially when considering virtues of candour, loyalty and honesty, as do professional–nonprofessional relationships with charities and voluntary groups in this time of increasing collaboration. Do the same values and guides to conduct apply? In order to place trust in another person, one must have confidence in them, to be secure that they will act in a particular manner. This is just as true of client–professional relationships as it is of professional–professional relationships. Dalley's (1993) notion of tribalism describes the development of a cultural ideology, which may lead to an inflated notion of superiority about one's own organization, resulting in a lack of respect and trust in another organization with the consequence that there is unlikely to be a willingness to collaborate, even where it is indicated for the good of the client. The sharing of information, expertise and active collaboration in this context is unlikely to be undertaken with confidence. The result of such poor communication between professional groups not only makes us question the possession of ethical virtues discussed above but is also unlikely to promote client centred care. In considering professional relationships with other professionals, think about the example in Box 4.5:

Box 4.5 Behaving ethically in professional life

As a student nurse, I was given a poem to read by a tutor, which was said to have been written by a patient in a long stay mental hospital. I cannot do justice to the rhyme and language after all these years but the gist of the message was this: next time you are engaged in a case conference discussing the future of someone else, and you think you are the professional with the most important contribution to make, then think of this image. Imagine a bucket of water filled nearly to the top. Put your hand in and swirl it around until you make a hole in the centre of the water and take note of the impression you have made. Then take your hand out and watch again. The water will subside and eventually it will still, as if no one had ever touched it.

The point of this illustration is that the motivation for 'swirling the water' should not be about self-aggrandisement. Neither should it be short lived with little to show for it.

It is in the nature of working with other human beings, then, that professionals face ethical and moral challenges in relation to client care. It is not difficult to find issues in any profession that involve the application of general (i.e. nonprofessional specific) moral rules and values, such as telling the truth, respecting privacy, keeping promises. Just as in everyday life, many such 'professional' issues are easily resolved without sophisticated analysis, while others are messy and awkward. Some seemingly minor questions do not have unambiguous answers, such as prioritizing where to spend one's professional time and in what proportion. Equally, complex situations may offer more than one alternative strategy for dealing with them, with pros and cons to endorse or eliminate support for competing solutions depending on the gains and losses from a particular perspective.

Box 4.6 Issues for consideration

Think again about the case study in Box 4.1. The complex problems within this family could be addressed in a number of ways with competing priorities, concerns and financial implications depending on which professional is making the assessment of needs. Does the health visitor work with the mother to teach her how to improve her child's language development? Does the social worker recommend a registered child minder in the absence of a nursery place? Does the community psychiatric nurse devise a care plan that will increase the mother's ability to be assertive and confident using a cognitive behaviour therapy programme with a view to reducing her medication in line with the mother's wishes? Is anyone going to work with the father? More importantly, what ethical concerns are there if the mother is the 'glue' keeping this family unit together? Do the interventions offered seek to maintain the status quo, or challenge it? How will the individual autonomy[3] of family members be respected and supported? Whose frame of reference will be adopted in deciding whether planned interventions will be beneficent? How will the principle of justice[4] be utilized in deciding the type and amount of resources available to this family?

Client oriented and professional liaison relationships are not the only trusting relationships in which professionals may engage. A professional is also engaged in a trusting relationship with their employer. Clearly, the obligations imposed in the employer/employee relationship are similar to those contained in the client professional relationship. Arguably, professionals who are 'self-employed', can be expected to embrace the relevant responsibilities and duties inferred in Bayles's taxonomy of professional virtues listed in Box 4.4. Indeed, one might argue that when one is self-employed, one's client may also become one's employer and as such a greater obligation may be imposed. Certainly, diligence would be a significant requirement in this circumstance. Bayles's (1989) professional virtues are helpful in understanding these wide ranging responsibilities in the context of inter-professional working.

Honesty

A professional should not be dishonest with a client. This quite obviously includes not telling lies or stealing from a client. There are of course less obvious methods of being dishonest with clients. Stealing time from a client is one example. It could be easy to find a justification to spend time with likeable characters who appear to be appreciative of one's efforts as opposed to spending time with someone who is less responsive or lives in unpleasant surroundings. From an interprofessional perspective, denying a client referral for an assessment by another professional because of personal prejudice or 'baggage' about other professional groups is a theft. In other words, deliberately failing to provide access to a service involves dishonesty.

Just as a client can be robbed of respect, lack of respect between professionals can happen too. Where relationships lack respect and value for the expertise possessed by a fellow professional, the client loses out.

Candour

If honesty includes not telling lies, candour carries with it the obligation to offer information. While working in partnership with clients involves sharing information and negotiating aspects of interventions with professional colleagues, this would imply volunteering information in the client's interest. If professional groups are to collaborate in the best interest of their clients, sharing information is arguably a key component. However, professionals often avoid sharing information in order to preserve client confidentiality. Notwithstanding this, the setting of ground rules within a client–professional relationship can make it possible to work in an inter-professional scenario without abusing client privilege (Allison and Ewens 1998).

Competence

There is an ethical obligation on professionals to maintain competence in their area of expertise. Keeping abreast of changes in practice is implicated here. Some professional groups make this requirement explicit, in that evidence of professional development is required for continuous registration on the professional register. Whereas honesty with clients has been cited earlier as a desirable characteristic in a professional relationship, honesty with oneself is also indicated here. Recognizing the limits to one's expertise and competence requires vigilance from all professionals, regardless of how long they may have been doing the job. In inter-professional settings, it is not comfortable to feel ill at ease or unskilled. One might fear losing a professional reputation and be tempted to persevere regardless. Recognizing one's limitations is an essential requirement of the professional in developing self-awareness and determining their own level of competence. It is also the mechanism for developing sufficient confidence to recognize when other professional expertise is required and consequently making it possible to work more closely in inter-professional groups without losing face.

Diligence

Diligence refers to commitment and is closely aligned with competence. To be diligent in one's work implies that the professional attempts to provide competent care, complemented with a commitment to the well being of the client. Irvine et al. (2002) notes that the '(re)discovery of the whole patient' during the 1970s, provided the forum to reassess the inter-relationship between the many new medical specialists, allied technologies and professions (p. 200). This refocusing of how the patient may be viewed established a different way of considering client need. In particular, this included the recognition that patients/clients grapple with difficulties so complex that it would be almost impossible for single agencies acting alone to address them. Increasing credence was also given to recognizing that clients might experience both medical and social needs at one and the same time. Clearly, the implication for all professional groups is that to be a diligent worker, there is a need to pool expertise in the interest of clients.

Loyalty

To display loyalty implies a faithfulness and commitment to duty within the client–professional relationship. However, the client does not have total call on the allegiance of the professional. The professional also has a responsibility to third parties including employers, fellow professionals and themselves. Sometimes, clients may make demands on the professional for a loyalty that would be misplaced. Sharing the burden of difficult and complex cases within an inter-professional setting is an advantage that is likely to be recognized by frontline workers.

    Unfair expectations of loyalty may also emanate from employers and/or fellow team members. The potential 'whistleblower', for example, is faced with competing loyalties and responsibilities in a situation where it is inevitable that some individuals will suffer harm either by breaking silence or by condemning others to continued harm through lack of action.

Fairness

Fairness relates directly to the principle of justice. It requires the professional to work without discriminating against people on the grounds of race, religion, ethnic origin or gender. Again, these are recognized aspects of conducting oneself in a fair manner. However, there are subtle ways of practising discriminatory behaviour. For all professionals, but especially those working with vulnerable groups, fairness is particularly important. It is essential for professionals to be alert to internal obstructions to working in a respectful and egalitarian manner. Such obstructions might include value judgements and attributions about whether a client is 'deserving'.

Discretion

While most professionals feel comfortable with an understanding of what it means to keep confidences, to be discrete may not be so widely grasped. As Bayles (1989) indicates, discretion, perhaps, is not so well recognized. Discretion encapsulates both a broader understanding of the concept of confidentiality and a broad consideration of privacy.

Clients come from all walks of life. Some may be citizens with very regular lives, others may be very much outside those societal norms. It can be very tempting to comment on the circumstances of the lives of clients. Often, however, encapsulated in those throwaway comments lie 'telling' value judgements. The two case studies in Box 4.7 illustrate this point.

Box 4.7 Case studies illustrating lack of discretion

Having completed a community assessment following a referral of a person who was believed to be depressed, the professional undertaking the assessment returned to the place of work and announced to the rest of the team that if they lived in a house that resembled the setting of a BBC play, they would not find anything to be depressed about.

In a very poor area of an inner city, a health professional returned to the health centre following a home visit. The health worker met with the supervisor in supervision. The preliminary part of the feedback from the visit to the client involved the lengthy and graphic description of the poor standard of hygiene in the house. The description was accompanied by strong nonverbal indicators that the poor state of the home environment was experienced as quite shocking to the professional conducting the visit. It was clear that the assessment had included a value judgement about the levels of cleanliness within the house.

Even if it were feasible to assume that all professionals possess the virtues presented in the section above, given the complexities of practice already referred to, it would not necessarily follow that the obligations inferred would or could be honoured. While the context in which team working takes place is important, the individual within a team can seriously affect the ability of the team to function as a team.

An individual practitioner brings with them a personal perspective on teamwork and collaborative working which will profoundly affect the motivation to engage in teamwork, ascribing different values and meaning towards the concept of teamworking. Consequently, this will affect the way in which teamworking may or may not develop. If a member of the team values hierarchy, for example, where leadership is linked to status and power, interactions with others in the team and the respect and value for the perspective brought by other team members may be viewed less favourably.

Conclusion

The ethical implications of working in partnership are complex. This is partly because working within an ethical framework creates personal tensions for individual professionals when attempting to balance potentially competing responsibilities. These tensions are then compounded when working with other professionals either from the same or from other agencies. This chapter has introduced the reader to ethical dilemmas arising in interprofessonal practice and suggested the use of Bayles's (1989) concept of the fiduciary relationship as a guide to practice in reconciling the best way to meet the needs of the client within an interprofessional environment. The increased benefit to the client of combining resources when faced with dealing with complex human problems cannot be ignored and, consequently, brings to bear a clear ethical requirement on the professional to collaborate in the interests of the client.

Questions for further discussion

1 Given that human problems are diverse and complex, what moral arguments can there be for not pooling interprofessional expertise in the interest of clients?
2 How far does continuing to engage in 'tribalism' and lack of respect for fellow professionals suggest a lack of virtuous character traits in the individual practitioner?
3 When professional groups fail to work together, to what extent is the duty of care to clients being compromised?

Notes

1 Beneficence – one of the four major ethical principles, which carries the obligation 'to do good'.

2   Non-maleficence – one of the four major ethical principles which carries the obligation to 'avoid doing harm'
3   Autonomy – from the Greek language meaning 'auto-rule' is one of four major ethical principles recognized as a central ethical concept.
4   The principle of justice – one the four major ethical principles, often interpreted as fairness and desert (what is deserved).

Part II

Partnerships in practice

5 Inter-professional communication in child protection

Brian Corby[1] with Frances Young and Stella Coleman

This chapter will:

- Exemplify professional errors in safeguarding children by drawing on the Laming Inquiry into the death of Victoria Climbie.
- Review central government developments of safeguarding procedures following the Laming Inquiry.
- Highlight potential consequences arising from these developments and consider implications for interprofessional communication.
- Examine issues arising in interprofessional communication and suggest pointers for improvements.

Since the first of the modern day inquiries into child abuse deaths, that of Maria Colwell (DHSS 1974), to that of Victoria Climbie (Laming 2003), one of the key problems associated with safeguarding children has been seen to be inadequate communication and cooperation between the various professionals involved (see DoH 1991; Corby et al. 1998, 2001). Between these two landmarks, almost all inquiries and published reviews have, with the advantage of hindsight, looked back at the situations in which child deaths have occurred and highlighted missed opportunities by social workers, NSPCC workers, police, health visitors, nurses, paediatricians, teachers, probation officers and housing officials to pass on information to each other which, if pooled together, and accurately assessed, could have heightened concern and perhaps have led to protective intervention before a child died. This was most graphically demonstrated in two Part 8 reviews carried out by the Bridge Child Care Consultancy, which were subsequently made publicly available, one into the death of a girl named Sukina in the county of Avon (Bridge 1991), and the second into the death by neglect of a child named Paul in the London borough of Islington

The authors of these reports, using the material found in the case files of key involved agencies (health, social services and education), showed how the cumulative information in these documents painted a far more worrying picture than that provided by examination of one agency's files only. The inference is that, had all agencies been privy to and shared the details of each other's records, they would probably have acted sooner to safeguard the children in question.

The Victoria Climbie inquiry

The Victoria Climbie inquiry (Laming 2003) points to similar conclusions. In the short time in which Victoria was involved with health, housing and social work agencies (she died only ten months after coming to live in England), there were several occasions where the sharing of information between professionals could have led them to have been more concerned about her safety. The most glaring example of this was when she was brought to North Middlesex Hospital on 24 July 1999 with scalds to her head and face. Doctors there were told by her aunt that Victoria had scabies and that she had poured hot water over herself in order to relieve the itching. This, of course, was a highly dubious explanation, made even more suspect by the fact that there had been a five-hour delay between the time of the alleged incident and Victoria being brought into the hospital. Indeed, the doctors who examined her were rightly concerned and, in accordance with agreed procedures, the matter was communicated to the social services department in which the child was resident. As all this took place on a Saturday, it was referred on to the emergency duty social services team, who in turn passed it on to the relevant district office on the following Monday. A strategy meeting was held on the subsequent Wednesday. It was attended by a hospital social worker and police and social services personnel, and a decision was reached that there was a need for protective measures of intervention. However, the degree of concern was still not a strong one, and it was suggested in the inquiry that the hospital social worker might not have sufficiently emphasized the concerns of the hospital staff because she did not attend ward meetings and, therefore, had not had direct contact with them. One of the hospital staff who was particularly concerned was the consultant paediatrician who had examined Victoria. She was adamant at the inquiry that she had expressed her views robustly, but social services department social workers did not think this was the case. It is notable that her communications were by letter and there was no face-to-face meeting with social services department personnel. Nurses in the hospital witnessed worrying changes in Victoria's behaviour when visited by her aunt on the ward, but did not communicate their concerns sufficiently strongly to other professionals. In addition to this, no one had collected information about Victoria's previous contacts with other hospitals, social services departments and the police. The net outcome was that Victoria was returned to the care of her aunt and that she was viewed as a child in need of help and support rather than as one who was either being abused or at risk of being abused. This particular incident highlights many of the reasons why communication in safeguarding children can go wrong, as indicated in Box 5.1.

What is evident from this box is that failure of communication between professionals was one of the main reasons why Victoria was not protected from abuse.

Box 5.1 What went wrong for Victoria Climbie?

1   There was a wide range of people from differing professions involved in the case, and as is well known the more people that are involved in

> a communication chain, the greater the likelihood of the original message being altered in the process.
>
> 2   There was little face-to-face contact between the key professionals, with a good deal of communication depending on letters and messages being passed on by third parties, which again is likely to influence the integrity of the original message.
>
> 3   Some professionals (e.g. the nurses on the ward) did not realize the significance of their observations and, therefore, did not ensure that they were communicated.
>
> 4   There were difficulties in gathering and collating past information sufficiently quickly to influence current decision making.

Certainly had there been better communication in this case, it is likely that the pooled concerns would have aroused greater suspicion and, possibly, Victoria could have been properly safeguarded at this time. For a detailed account of these events see chapter 10 of the Climbie inquiry (Laming 2003 paras. 10.1–10.163, pp. 255–78).

Communication in context

Of course, communication is not the only issue in safeguarding children cases. There are many other factors that have a part to play in making this area of work problematic. Lack of adequate resources is a key issue. An audit of health, police and social services arrangements for safeguarding children following on from the Climbie inquiry (CHI 2003b) found that there was a high level of unallocated registered child protection cases in several areas. Another key factor is that the quality of staff involved in safeguarding children work, in terms of knowledge and experience, is very mixed. In particular, inter-professional training seemed to have been very variable over the past decade, according to the post-Climbie audit just referred to. Also the child protection system is a complex one with a wide range of health, welfare and police personnel involved, and in some parts of the country, particularly in large urban areas like inner London, there is a bewildering overlap of occupational boundaries and the added complication of disadvantaged and transient families. Furthermore, policy developments since the mid-1990s have made the task of safeguarding children even more uncertain, in that they have required social workers to be more careful about pursuing investigations and more focused on the needs for family support (Dartington Social Research Unit 1995; Spratt 2001; Corby 2003). Bearing these contextual factors in mind, however, this chapter will single out interprofessional communication for examination.

It is not easy to come to a clear assessment of where we are now in terms of interprofessional communication in safeguarding children. In some ways, there have been considerable improvements. For instance, the level of awareness of child abuse is much higher than it was 20 years ago. Also the systems now in place to aid professional communication are more fully developed. Any analysis of the development of the child protection system will conclude that it has become far more complex over time. The procedures for responding to child protection cases today are labyrinthine compared with those in the 1970s. There are a whole host of guidelines, assessment frameworks and procedures across all the agencies involved. Area Child Protection Committees – Local Safeguarding Children Boards since 2006 – have taken on a wider range of responsibilities over time, including the conduct of serious case reviews in cases where children die or are seriously harmed as a result of child abuse. A major consequence of this is that at frontline worker level, the demands of the systems result in the likelihood of less face-to-face contact with service users.

The extent and range of cases coming into the child protection system has mushroomed over time. It now deals with physical abuse and neglect, emotional abuse and neglect, organized abuse, institutional abuse, child prostitution, young sex offenders, sexual exploitation of children through pornography, child trafficking, abuse on the Internet and bullying (DoH 1999) – a far cry from the single focus on battered children in the 1960s (Kempe et al. 1962). Resourcing this 'industry' has proved problematic. Throughout the late 1980s and 1990s there have been regular reports of unallocated cases on child protection registers, echoed, as we have seen, in the post-Climbie audits. Social services departments in the 1990s were criticized for allocating the bulk of their community child care resources to child protection cases and for not providing services and support for children and families in more general need of help. Training of professionals has also been variable, and, as has already been noted, has not been sufficiently inter-professional.

Breaking down the barriers between professionals has not been achieved as well as it might have been. While the failure to communicate, evidenced in the Climbie inquiry, may be a worst-case scenario there are as post-Climbie audits attest (CHI 2003b), similar situations (in terms of type) in many other parts of the country. The issue of the political and cultural context in which child abuse and safeguarding takes place while not directly related to day-to-day practice, is important in the long-term. The present Labour government has made a strong commitment to reducing child poverty and this commitment is reflected in its policy towards safeguarding children. However, it has been much more ambivalent in relation to the issue of parental corporal punishment, which many child protection professionals consider to be crucial to the goal of reducing the incidence of child abuse (see Freeman 1999).

The current situation

The Laming Inquiry resulted in 108 recommendations for changes in organization and practice of the child protection system the majority of which, along with many recommendations arising from the *Joint Chief Inspectors' Report Safeguarding Children* (House of Commons 2003b), clearly informed *Every Child Matters* (House of Commons 2003a) and subsequent legislation and guidance, including the Children Act 2004, Working Together (DoH 2006b) and the recent consultation document *Staying Safe* (Department for Children, School and Families 2007).

The government has introduced these measures to bring about its vision of services for children and their families based on a number of key principles:

- Meeting the needs of all children
- Meeting needs through child focused policy and services
- Prevention through increased take up of universal services
- Increased provision of services by voluntary organizations and local community groups
- Early intervention in cases of additional need
- Service user participation in planning services

These key principles aimed to safeguard and promote the welfare of all children, and to impress upon professionals and the wider public a strong commitment and responsibility for child welfare. Within a relatively short period of time, a number of potentially far reaching changes, shaped by these principles were set in train. These changes reflected a shift of ethos and culture, encapsulated in the title of the Scottish Executive's (2002) report: 'It's everyone's job to see I'm all right'. Achieving such a culture change amounts to a transformation of services and it is too early to assess how successful they will be. Earlier attempts at refocusing social services from their child protection investigative approach to a broader 'children in need' perspective was slow in bringing change. Social services struggled with the contextual problems of child poverty, increased demand from other agencies and the public, and the broader struggle to promote a needs focus within a climate preoccupied by risk aversion and blame cultures.

The duty and expectation for various agencies involved in safeguarding children to work together is long standing: set out in Sections 7(9)(10) and (11) of the 1989 Children Act, which stress that where a local authority is carrying out an inquiry into suspected child abuse, it is the duty of other local authorities and of the local education, housing and health authorities to assist with the inquiries if called on to do so, by providing information or advice. It is broadly accepted that child protection concerns override confidentiality issues. At the time of Victoria's death, the agency with primary responsibility in the field of child protection was the social services department. A key change has been the bifurcation of local authority social services into Children and Adult Services. Despite the focus on inter-professional working, Children Services social workers remain central to child protection.

Social work remained central to child protection, but the responsibility and accountability for safeguarding is located across all organizations who work with children, young people, their families and carers. It remains important for there to be key personnel with ultimate responsibility for dealing with abused and disadvantaged children. However, a major worry for social workers in social services departments is one of resources, in terms of person power, to handle the number of assessments required (see Corby et al. 2002). Yet a further concern is that spreading the focus across families in need as well as across safeguarding children, may mean more serious cases slipping through the child protection net. This may well have played a part in the Climbie case – for the most part she (and her family) were seen to be 'in need' rather than at risk of serious abuse.

There will now be a brief review of the key changes followed by a discussion of the implications for interprofessional communication.

Every Child Matters

Every Child Matters (ECM) House of Commons (2003a) is the overarching strategy for promoting and safeguarding the welfare of all children encapsulating in the five outcomes:

1. Being healthy.
2. Staying safe.
3. Enjoying and achieving.
4. Making a positive contribution.
5. Achieving economic well-being.

All services working with children, young people and their families across all sectors are expected to adopt these priority outcomes and show how, within their policies, planning and service development they are meeting them. While the Government have been proactive in tightening accountability for safeguarding children, they have stopped short of legislating against the parental right to administer corporal punishment to their children. This amounts to a mixed message in the context of violence against children and is at odds with many European countries.

The Children Act 2004

This legislation set out new tiers of accountability from top to bottom of the safeguarding system and this was clearly needed. As the Laming report demonstrated, accountability for a specific child was often diffuse, unclear or absent in the many agencies that had contact with Victoria Climbie.

Section 10 and 11 of the Act set out duties of care and cooperation among the agencies as shown in Box 5.2 below

---

Box 5.2   Children Act 2004 duties of care and cooperation

Senior management commitment to importance of mission

- A clear statement of agency's responsibilities towards children – available for all staff
- Clear line of accountability for work on safeguarding and promoting
- Service development that takes account of need to safeguard and promote and informed (*where appropriate*) by views of children and families
- Training on safeguarding and promoting for all staff working with, or in contact with, children and families
- Safe recruitment procedures in place
- Effective inter-agency working to safeguard and promote
- Effective information sharing

At a national level, Children's Services were brought together with education services in the summer of 2003, and the resulting government ministry, named the Department for Children, Schools and Families (DCSF) since 2007 has cabinet representation, a voice at national government level and a wide remit for child welfare issues. There has now been the appointment of an independent children's commissioner for England to protect the rights of all children and young people, with the remit of ensuring that all national and local government policy takes account of their best interests. It remains to be seen whether this role will be more than window dressing for Government's broad vision of *'progressive universalism'* (Treasury 2005) and a child focused society.

At local government level, all local authorities must now appoint a director of children's services and designate a lead councillor for children's services. In this way, it is intended that local accountability will be firmly entrenched with no possibility for slippage between officers and elected councillors – again, a feature of Laming's findings. Also at a local level, the area child protection committees have been replaced by local safeguarding children boards (LSCBs) which, unlike their predecessors, have a statutory footing, requiring all the main statutory agencies to work together to provide and maintain LSCBs, and actively work together with any other organization working with children and their families in the local area. In the recent Priority Review of LSCBs progress (DfES 2007) LCSBs were described as 'the single most important mechanism for ensuring that the welfare and wellbeing of children and young people is thought through and reflected in service planning' (p. 3). Their primary functions of safeguarding and promoting the welfare of children as set out in s. 14 (10) of the Children Act 2004 are to:

- Coordinate the work by the staff and agencies represented on the board
- Ensure the effectiveness of that work

While the remit of LSCBs reflects the wider government vision of prevention with the expectation that they will promote proactive development of services for children and their families, the Priority Review has made it clear that this aspect should not take precedence over what amounts to a quality assurance function in relation to the child protection needs of children. This is welcomed, as it is a worrying possibility that children currently in need of protection may slip through the net as a range of agencies adjust to the cultural shift and the attendant reconfigurations that are a consequence of widespread policy change. LSCBs have the lead responsibility for promoting interprofessional training in safeguarding children and for reviewing all child deaths and serious child injury incidents. The partnership approach to child protection, exemplified in LSCBs is also reflected in the approach to integrated service development at the front line.

Integrated children's services

This represents the government's longstanding emphasis on 'joined-up' thinking and working. There is no blueprint but there is an expectation that local variations will reflect particular local circumstances. Children's trusts are clear examples of joined-up services and take many different forms reflecting local diversity and decision making. Joint commissioning of services is seen as key to generating the range of services deemed necessary in the Children and Young Person's Plans (CYPP) and this will bring together a range of public, voluntary and private sector bodies. Local children's services are required to produce, in conjunction with their partners, CYPP the outcomes they want to achieve for children in their locality. These outcomes will become performance indicators against which local authorities and other public sector services will be judged.

Some local authorities have developed new teams bringing together staff from a range of professions, working with children and their families where there are concerns about significant harm (Children's Act 1989: S47). Others are focusing on provision of information and ease of access to a wide range of services in the interests of prevention and early interventions. Bringing together a range of professionals in integrated children's teams or deploying a mix of professionals in a range of service settings, such as for example children's centres and extended schools is expected to bring two broad benefits: accessibility and destigmatizing of services.

In addition bringing together professionals, on a routine daily basis, seems likely to reduce the kinds of miscommunications discussed earlier, as for example, reliance on written communiqués, third party transference of information, delayed or lost contacts and the heightened tensions which may mask information when cases are at crisis point. But processes of communication are highly complex and a number of factors can be seen to have an impact on communications between professionals, including status, perceptions of professional role, professional socialization and differences between knowledge and skills bases.

Common Assessment Framework (CAF)

It is recommended that all agencies use a unified assessment form for the evaluation of children's needs, to replace the proliferation of separate methods currently existing. The Common Assessment Framework (CAF), like the Integrated Children's System, is intended to ensure that all the information and any concerns about specific children is collected, recorded and collated in such a way that all the main agencies can have access and see the whole picture. Key to the usefulness of these changes is the development of the appropriate technology and the training of staff. While this won't necessarily deal with the interpretation and understanding of information, it will ensure a common basis of information for decision making where children are identified as having additional needs.

Box 5.3 *Key points of CAF*

- CAF enables any agency to undertake assessment where there are concerns or indications that the health / development of a child / young person known to them is not progressing appropriately in line with 5 core outcomes

---

- CAF constitutes:
  1   A clear framework to be used by all local agencies directing what information should be gathered and from where.
  2   A standard format for recording information about children assessed, how stored and how to be accessed.

- Guidance on development of C and IT systems to facilitate recording and communicating information
- Development of a common vocabulary to describe need and record achievements and progress
- Development of a role designated, the lead professional who acts:
  1   As a single point of contact that the child or young person and their family can trust, and who is able to support them in making choices and in navigating their way through the system.
  2   Ensures that they get appropriate interventions when needed, which are well planned, regularly reviewed and effectively delivered.
  3   Reduces overlap and inconsistency from other practitioners.

(ECM 2008)

Integrated Children's System (ICS)

Alongside the move to bring children's services together, a system of electronic information sharing has been developed. Whereas, previously, different agencies have maintained separate and often widely differing approaches to recording and mainte-nance of information about children and their families, they are now required to operate a shared electronic system. The introduction of the Integrated Children System (ICS) has been heralded as key to the problem of inter-agency communica-tion. The pooling of information is seen a critical to effective safeguarding (see Box 5.1: point 4, above) although as yet it is too early to assess how effective ICS will be in practice.

Issues for inter-professional communication

Five key factors have acted as barriers to inter-professional communication, as indicated in Figure 5.1. The plethora of change, reviewed above, demonstrates the government's determination to improve the well-being and safety of all children. While some moves are clearly to be welcomed, for example the embedding of accountability throughout the system and the placing LSCBs on a statutory footing, the question remains whether these changes will facilitate inter-professional commu-nication and reduce the numbers of children suffering avoidable harm.

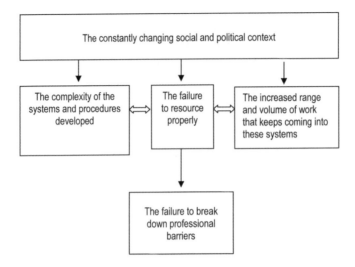

Figure 5.1 Barriers to professional communication

Increased system complexity

Underlying integrated services is the assumption that bringing professionals together will result in a more accessible, seamless and more effective service for children and their families. It would however be a mistake to underestimate the resulting complexity for agencies and professionals who are required to develop and deliver this integration. For example, the range of agencies, groups and staff who now have responsibilities for safeguarding children has expanded enormously. While this holds the promise of increasing awareness of children and their needs and of developing a wider range of resources it also adds to the overall complexity of the system. Among the consequences are that inter-professional communication has now to be achieved among a wider number of participants, including staff from long recognized professions and those from newer occupations, volunteers, community representatives and service users – children, young people and their families.

Problems of communication in professional practice are well documented (Reder et al. 1993, Dale et al. 2002, Laming 2003) and the issues identified are both practical and interpersonal: 'The major problems ... could be characterized as more psychological than practical, since they concerned how professionals thought about the case, processed information available to them and interacted with other informants" (Reder and Duncan 2003: 83).

The welcome move towards service user participation in planning and developing services presents additional challenges for professionals and agencies. In the context of safeguarding, parents and carers are rightly acknowledged as playing a pivotal role. The difficulties of developing real and effective partnerships have been well evidenced. Some professionals, for example health visitors, have worried that a child protection agenda undermines what they have seen as their traditional roles and remit and prove damaging to the trusting relationships they have built with parents. Similar concerns have been expressed by drug and alcohol workers whose interventions require considerably longer time scales than those deemed appropriate by social workers focused on the needs of individual children for stability.

Breaking down professional barriers to inter-professional communication.

Barriers to effective communication are well known within traditional professional groups, whose training and professional and occupational socialisation inculcates a professional identity and predisposes them to distinctive perspectives and approaches. A paediatrician giving evidence to the Victoria Climbie Inquiry stated 'I cannot account for the way people interpreted what I said. It was not the way I would have like it to have been interpreted.' (Laming 2003: 9)

This telling comment summarizes a central issue of communication and is a stark reminder that perceptions are filtered through our professional identity and personal values. The professional cultures of health workers, doctors and social workers are very different (Barr 1997) and although over time there has been more convergence in this respect and improved communication (Cooper et al. 2001), as the Climbie Inquiry has shown, it is an area which needs constantly working at. Pietroni (1992) argued that 'it is not only the language subsets [used by health and social care professionals] that separate us, but the mode of thought that is made possible by the different languages' (cited in Williams 2002: 53).

Power and status are often enmeshed with professional identity, and in particular, perceptions of one profession's status relative others. Again, the increased range of participants gives scope for an increase in failures of communication influenced by perceived status differentials. Power differentials can result in a significant barrier to communication and their impact can be even more profound on service users. The various issues of communications with service users, have been well documented and include lack of information to enable informed decision making (Danso et al. 2003), unreasonable professional expectations that service users speak 'managerial language' (Crawford et al. 2003) and the inappropriateness of traditional participation methods (Begum 2006). While much progress has been made on establishing the principle of service user participation, it still presents a challenge to traditional professional modes of thinking and operating (Carr 2004).

Further barriers arise in connection with role and remit of people involved. Unlike teams of social workers, who focus almost exclusively on deprived families where children are either in need or at risk, other professional such as health workers, teachers, police, have a wide range of responsibilities for meeting the needs of children. Some professionals, such as teachers, might argue that child protection is not their core business and indeed many will rarely work with a child at risk of significant harm. In such circumstances, it is hard to develop expertise and knowledge of procedures and to maintain vigilance. One way of developing expertise among health professionals has been the appointment of specialists with a training function within their own agency and a liaison/communication function with children's services, for example designated teacher role for reporting child protection concerns. This model also operates within other professional settings.

Interprofessional training is frequently recommended as the solution to problems of interprofessional communication and it clearly has a role to play but as the system has struggled previously with far fewer professional groups having responsibilities it can be seen that the task is now enormous with the increased range of participants to be involved.

Inter-professional training

This seeks to bring staff together from a range of agencies and settings, in order to disseminate knowledge and provide learning opportunities for inter-professional interaction away from the practice setting. Bringing people together enables professionals to put names to faces, learn about each other's roles, remit and agency practice and the increasing requirement for inter-professional training is to be welcomed. However it is not enough to think that this alone will result in optimal inter-professional communication. The process of communication is an equally crucial factor and the evidence base around complexities of communication process in child protection is growing.

Training opportunities need to be provided on a regular basis rather than merely in response to a crisis. Local safeguarding children boards (LSCB) have a duty to deliver and direct inter-professional, multi-disciplinary child protection training. This should break down the silo mentalities attached to the idea that individual professionals need to have safeguarding training opportunities tailored exclusively to their profession. Providing opportunities for staff from differing professional backgrounds to come together may lead to positive outcomes as each develops awareness of different agencies with different perspectives. Professionals need to have a good working knowledge of policy and procedures; however equally important is an understanding of the processes of communication and the barriers to it, such as stereotyping.

The establishment of children workforce development councils (www.cwdcouncil.org.uk/) has developed a common core skills and knowledge base for all children's services workers, which includes the period of initial qualification. The extent to which this can be rolled out among relevant professionals remains dependent upon the willingness and ownership of professionals.

Conclusion

In this concluding section, consideration will be given to the measures introduced post-Climbie in order to improve working together between agencies in safeguarding children, the publication of *Every Child Matters* (House of Commons 2003a) and *Working Together to Safeguard Children* (DfES 2006), and a plethora of guidelines about safeguarding children.

Many of the recommendations of these reports are at policy and systems levels, and there is a strong emphasis on 'progressive universalism' aimed at prevention and early intervention, as a means of reducing the need for child protection interventions. At national government level we have seen the merging of children's education and children's social services and the establishment of strategic arrangements at a local authority level, for example children's trusts. While there is some regional variation, the requirement is for local services to reflect local need and to achieve this through joint commissioning and front line service integration. The implementation of local safeguarding children boards has strengthened responsibilities for promoting interprofessional cooperation through training and dissemination of information about best practice thus differing from their predecessors in that there is now a duty to care and cooperate for the designated agencies (Children Act 2004). The Children's service is charged with the publication of children and young people's plans, mapping needs and service provision and clearly defining their strategies for meeting the five outcomes of Every Child Matters. They are required to do this in conjunction with relevant public sector, third sector agencies, and local communities informed by children, young people, their families and carers. At the frontline level developments include electronic health and social care records, giving key professionals common access to data held about children. The Common Assessment Framework seeks to unify the assessment processes across agencies with particular attention to the development of a common vocabulary and agreed definitions. Key to the usefulness of these changes is the development of the appropriate technology and the training of staff to use it.

It is clear, therefore, that the concerns raised by the Climbie inquiry have been given serious consideration by central government. The issue may well be, however, whether all these systemic and technological changes will have any significant impact on cooperation between agencies at the cutting edge. As already noted, the child protection system at present suffers from being over burdened, leading to crisis intervention and potentially more problematic relationships with service users. Such a climate is not conducive to effective and productive relationships and communication with other professionals and service users.

The most significant hurdle to be overcome in interprofessional communication is cultural. Professional socialisation is directed toward membership of a distinct agency involving role definition and approaches to working. If integrated approaches are to work, there will be a requirement for staff, across a whole range of disciplines, to be flexible and adaptable.

There are several ways of developing better working together relationships at the front-line level, which are crucial to the process of safeguarding children. Some are in the process of implementation:

1   The need for joint training for professionals to establish a common purpose and sympathetic evaluation and understanding of each other's roles. An ideal place to start would be in initial professional qualifying courses.

2   The effectiveness of inter-professional, specialist child protection teams, which have no common blueprint, needs careful evaluation to enable evidence for best practice to be disseminated.

3   In this context, perhaps it is time to question whether the orthodoxy of a generic approach to social work qualifying training should give way to specialist child care social work courses where a significant part of the early curriculum would be shared across a number of professional courses thereby embedding inter-professionality.

4   The need for positive regular contact between professionals in the form of inter-professional discussions about policy and practice at a general rather than crisis level. These developments could take many forms, for example monthly lunch time forums to raise and discuss local issues relevant to safeguarding children in their area.

5   Secondments between agencies might facilitate better communication and better understanding of different roles. It might also go some way to promoting respect across the professions breaking down entrenched stereotypes.

The biggest barrier to developments of this kind is that they are time-consuming and costly, and could be seen as an unaffordable luxury. However, time spent in reflection and careful discussion with others about cases is, in our view, not wasted. Returning to the Climbie inquiry, one gets a sense of decisions being made quickly, assessments being carried out on the hoof and follow-up work not being done because staff were busy moving on to the next problem at 'breakneck speed'. There is need for more careful consideration of issues and for a more questioning, critical approach to the work of safeguarding children (see Munro 2002). To achieve these goals, in addition to time, there is also a need to retain good quality and experienced practitioners at the front line. Measures of this kind are every bit as important as the development of sophisticated tracking systems – indeed they are crucial to their effective use.

Questions for further discussion

1   What strategies can professionals use to ensure a clear focus on children and their safety?

2   Besides the issue of cost, what other resource issues are barriers to inter-professional working?

3   What are the major challenges in overcoming cultural barriers across professional groups?

4   What practical steps could be taken to overcome these barriers at local level?

Useful websites

- Every Child Matters: www.everychildmatters.gov.uk This website is intended to be a working resource for providing current policy, guidance, practice tools and useful links for day to day practice for UK professionals working with children, young people, their families and carers.

- Department for Children, Schools and Families: www.dcsf.gov.uk This is the government department with overall responsibility for local authority children's services provides a range of policy, guidance and useful links for practitioners, children, families and carers.
- Joint website of the General Social Care Council (GSCC) the General Teaching Council for England (GTC) and the Nursing and Midwifery Council (NMC): www.nmc.org.uk/interprof was set up in 2007 as part of a joint initiative to produce a statement of shared values to underpin interprofessional work with children, young people and their families. Given the move to integrated working in child protection and given that differences in values have sometimes been identified as factors impeding effective interprofessional working, it would be worthwhile all children's services professionals visiting this site to take part in the consultation.

Note

1 The original chapter in the first edition of this book was sole authored by Brian Corby who sadly died in January 2007. Brian was a good friend and ex-colleague. He was held in high esteem for his depth of knowledge in child protection and was also much appreciated for his approachable, unassuming and good natured disposition. This chapter has been revised and updated by two of his colleagues from the University of Central Lancashire (Julian Buchanan).

6   Working in partnership to support people with mental health difficulties

Adrian Jones

This chapter will:

- Consider teams and team working in adult mental health services.
- Discuss the current context of multi-disciplinary teamwork.
- Explore various models of care and their implications for teamwork.
- Explore occupational culture, team identity, and leadership and the tensions that exist in teams as a result of these factors.

Managing diseases requires skilled practitioners. It is inconceivable for one professional group to possess the skills and knowledge to treat the full range of disorders. This is why modern psychiatric services have a multitude of teams. Each team brings with it expectations for staff to take on new roles and responsibilities. Understanding how mental health professionals work together is fundamental for collaborative working.

Mental health and social care policy has sought to map out the different types of teams and how they should work. We have also seen the growth of care pathways and managed care networks to help structure health and social care (DoH 1998b; Jones 2001). Great attention has been paid to how professions work together and the benefits teamwork brings to patient care but also in terms of how working roles can be expanded to take on different tasks. The challenge is to introduce these new roles and new ways of working into multi-disciplinary teams (MDTs) (DoH 2004g).

The focus of this chapter will be to consider teams and team working in adult mental health services. The diagnostic and treatment area of adult mental health is so vast but the chapter will consider the various specialist teams that have been set up over the years. In particular, the chapter will discuss the various tensions that exist and get played out in teams and include occupational culture, theoretical framework or model of care and team identity and leadership. All impact on how teams function in the modern world.

Strategic and political context

Ever since the asylum, health workers have worked within a team. However, it was the demise of the asylum that witnessed the development of community teams (Leff et al. 2000). We have seen the early growth of community mental health teams in the 1980s, assertive outreach teams and early intervention teams post-2000. We have also seen an enlightenment period of growth and development for acute inpatient psychiatry (DoH 2002, Clarke 2004) and its integration with home treatment teams (DoH and CSIP 2007a, b).

Key features that have supported the multitude of teams and how they work are system changes in the way mental health services interlock and collaborate. From 1997 to the present day, we have robust policy implementation guidance which stipulates how teams should work, what patients should be seen and how relationships should play out in care packages (DoH 1999b, 2004e). Without exception all sets of guidance emphasize the value of multi-disciplinary teamworking (DoH 1998b, 2007e, f).

The UK National Health Service has seen rapid reform with major investment to fund different ways of working in mental health services (DoH 2002, 2004e). The underbelly to this investment and modernization is the development of specialized teams and specialist workers. The history of this development shows that pockets of innovation do occur within teams when specialized teams are set up, for example home treatment, but in the absence of a strategic approach, they often fail (DoH and CSIP 2007a). This can be damaging for collaborative team working with other teams. Considerations in this chapter point towards clear linkage of all teams within the whole system of care. The challenge is to help clinicians that work in teams to see beyond the outer limits of their own team and to accept that their team works within the whole system and can be connected; the conclusion being that specialist teams are not collaborative when they are isolated and disconnected.

Who leads teams?

A question that is mulled over in many teams is who controls or leads the team. It is so important that the team leader is able to display leadership and lead the team so that patients can receive the best quality of care. However, the role of the team leader is fraught with difficulties ranging from lack of leadership style, content and influence, right down to being unable to guide the team to meet organizational objectives.

Starting off, let us consider the composition of adult teams. It is rare for health professions to work in isolation from their colleagues and from other professional groups. Health and social care staff for the most part work harmoniously in teams, which for mental health, are comprised of psychiatrists, nurses, occupational therapists (OT), social workers and psychologists. In addition, teams also have a variety of students and support staff. Teams co-exist alongside one another either in hospital or community environments. They are inter-connected into a system of care. This has been popularly described as whole systems working. The team aim is to work together to accomplish care and treatment goals.

However, we know that based on particular theoretical perspectives of the professional group, coupled with individual opinions and anecdotal ways of working, common goals may be a fictional aspiration of the team. Clinicians jealously guard professional integrity (Beattie 1995). Team members may communicate this using negative connotation to describe patients such as 'he's a malingerer', 'he should be discharged by the team'. The role of the team manager may have to play the role of 'peace maker' to ensure the malignant views of team members towards the patient and other staff members do not lead to poor health outcomes or dissatisfaction with the service. At times it is the views of malignant team members that control the team as opposed to the team leader.

One cannot assume that all team members are necessarily equal to or below the team leader role. Teams have staff that have been trained and belong to professional organisations, like nurses and OTs. Team members may also be unqualified or junior members of staff who carry out routine tasks that have been delegated down to them by the team manager. Cott (1998) arrived at an interesting observation in her study of MDTs working in long term care teams where 'direct care' team members would have lesser involvement in team decisions than higher qualified staff. On this basis, any perceived equality of team membership is compromised. However, there are instances where certain members of unqualified staff end up running the team through the shear force of their personality and their ability to influence decisions and team members.

The role of the medical profession in teams is an interesting concept when considered against who leads the team. Medicine is traditionally occupied by men who come from a higher socio-economic class, have obviously studied for long periods of time and have acquired expert knowledge on care and treatment of the various diseases in healthcare. Nursing on the other hand, along with other health and social care professions are dominated by women and who come from a lower socio-economic division. Even a superficial analysis of this situation displays a gender imbalance. If one were to apply sociological principles of gender control then the male members of the team would come to dominate the female members of the team (Turner 1987). So doctors come to dominate health and social care staff. Now this is a simplistic explanation, but one which resonates and fuels tension about who leads teams and one that cannot be airbrushed away.

All professions have a stated hierarchy which is recognized by remuneration and job titles. With hierarchy comes assumed power and control over people that are subservient to a higher paid worker. We have situations where professions try and have managerial power over other professional groups. The most frequent example is the team leader in mental health teams who may come from a nursing, social work or occupational therapy background. However, we also have psychiatrists who are part of teams and who may 'play the game' in being subservient to the team manager. In no way are they accountable to that team manager for their practice.

There is no simple answer as to who leads the team. Each team may have a team manager but other professions or clinicians may lead the team by being the most dominant or forthright in their views. This leads us on to why conflict occurs within the team.

So why does conflict occur within teams?

Many studies have investigated the numerous problems of teams and these have helped to shape policy and lead to ways to improve team functioning (Mason et al. 2002). Issues that have been raised by team members include being stressed through excessive case loads (Kipping and Hickey 1998). Occupational class has also been raised as a stress factor. OTs report more stress than other professional groups working in mental health teams (Rees and Smith 1991). A later study also reaffirmed these findings but added that OTs and social workers experienced stress due to 'professional self-doubt' (Lloyd et al. 2005). This may help to explain why mental health workers need to understand the particular 'lens' or view point employed by the range of professions within teams so that dissonance can be reduced.

The study of the way mental health teams work has interested researchers and policy planners for the last 30 years. Effective teams (where people work together in a MDT) have often been associated with effective care (Onyett 2003; Burns and Lloyd 2004). Policy documents lament the need for collaborative team working to reduce system failures and minimising duplication within services (DoH 2007e, f). It has been demonstrated that patient care improves when professions work together or collaborate, as opposed to working in isolated silos (Zwarenstein and Reeves 2006). One example is the positive effect of different disciplines working together to improve prescribing decisions compared to disciplines working in isolation from each other (Schmidt et al. 1998). Other examples are the effects of team working on delivering patient engagement with services and this being more superior to individual case management arrangements (Burns and Lloyd 2004).

When we want to illustrate team work it is best to describe how teams work in the real world as opposed to class room examples (Stark et al. 2002). Throughout this chapter, real live examples will be discussed that highlight some of the quintessential aspects of adult mental health team work. A simple example of this may be found in hospital psychiatry. In policy terms, hospital teams and community teams have as their goal to only keep patients in hospital for the shortest amount of time so they can go home. This seems a simple ideal but the reality is an inconsistent thresholds for admission and discharges (Warner and Hoadley 2004). It is in the interests of the community teams to have patients in hospital if they are in any way difficult to engage or perceived to be high risk. It is in the interests of the hospital staff to discharge patients when the goals for admission and continued treatment are unclear (Jones and Bowles 2005). Each set of teams pit their knowledge and expertise to argue why the patient should remain in hospital and why the patient should be discharged. Ultimately the team and system is out of balance and team tensions arise.

Well, teams and team members as we have referred to before have different ways of looking at the world and this may place different values on healthcare, as indicated in Box 6.1:

Box 6. 1 Case study

Jack has suffered from schizophrenia for five years. Three years ago he ceased to be able to work as a council worker and his mental health has continued to

---

deteriorate. Following an initial hospital admission for six weeks he has been seen regularly by a psychiatrist, a clinical nurse specialist and a social worker. Jack has been difficult to engage in a community care plan for the last two years. The emphasis of these three professionals has differed considerably during this period. The social worker, for example, has been working with Jack recently to try to engage him in vocational work, rather than deciding the right psychotropic treatment. The psychiatrist and clinical nurse specialist, on the other hand, have both focused on ensuring concordance with medication.

There is, however, a compromise, offered by the assertive community treatment team approach. This approach:

- Recognizes that some patients are treatment resistant and in a sense the disease model has failed to cure them
- Emphasizes social and psychological approaches and how the patient can manage their illness and achieve quality of life
- Requires the team to engage the patient in psychotherapeutic approaches with less emphasis placed on medication, albeit recognizing that medication is essential in preventing relapse

As can be seen from Box 6.1, different teams place different emphasis on different approaches and if certain members of the team were to be employed in those settings that had a conflict with those values then ultimately team conflict will arise. Power, dominance and control arise constantly within teams (Davies 2000). Coffey and Jenkins (2002) looked at how forensic nurses perceived their role within the team. A feature of this study was how 'psychiatrists allowed collaboration and team working' and if a view from the forensic nurse would be sought in the team discussion. Nursing staff experienced a sense of being undervalued within the team to which an opinion from the forensic nurse would be sought. However, what are the barriers to team working? An interesting study sought to uncover the tensions underlying teamwork. Three main barriers were identified by a small sample of 19 nurses. These included how members of the team viewed the nature of team work. The second revolved around the types of skills team members possessed and the third, the perceived dominance of the medical profession in influencing decision making (Atwal and Caldwell 2006).

The unintended and tragic consequences of conflict and misunderstandings within teams on patient care has been studied and reported on through many external homicide and suicide enquiries (Appleby et al. 1997; DoH 2006a). Most often, the patient falls through the net of service provision because teams fail to pass on information or understand the responsibilities of clinicians or teams. Teams, as opposed to individuals fail to deliver care as required. There are other examples where teams within systems of care shift 'risky' or difficult patients around the system as a way of managing worker anxiety or organizational anxiety (Bowles and Jones 2005).

Some members of the team complain that they are not on the same level as other members of the team or they use a different language compared to other team members. Evidence already supports the case that psychiatrists, nurses and social workers use a form of discourse that supports a shoring up of professional identity but also a separate identity (Hamilton et al. 2004). This dichotomy may be played out between the psychiatrists and nurses. Nurses may complain that their level of knowledge is inferior to that of psychiatrists because their depth of knowledge of diseases and systems is limited to mental health (Jones 2006b). Psychiatrists tend to 'think systems' (Jones 2008) and to formulate a diagnosis based on a history and standardised mental state examination (Gelder et al. 2004).

Use of a common method to classify diseases may help to ease communication and so promote team functioning from one team member to another (Tempest and Mcintyre 2006). In mental health teams, the International Classification of Diseases-10 would serve this purpose (Cooper 1994). Herein lies the rub. Team members may be uncomfortable adopting the language and spirit of ICD classification due to its negative connotations with the medical model. Lanceley et al. (2007) concluded in their study of decision making in cancer MDT meetings that 'air time' is dominated by professions that can relate to a diagnostic discourse and this limited the influence of disciplines from a psychosocial background.

Team conflict may occur through how professions may see themselves alongside other professions. One common alliance is between nurses and psychiatrists. Nursing has historically been placed in the hierarchy of carrying out tasks in the asylums of latter years under the instruction of psychiatrists (Brindlecombe 2005). However, there is a symbiotic relationship between psychiatrists and nurses where both cannot exist without each other. If one were removed from the relationship, the process of healthcare would tumble. The same can be said for social work and other health and social care professionals. The entwinement of different ways of looking at the world and the needs of the patient are intricately woven into the fabric of healthcare. When one strand of that fabric is loose or missing then the rich tapestry of teamwork falls apart.

The way the team functions is therefore critical to the outcomes of care. But what makes for a successful team? Notwithstanding the different make up of teams, a number of factors come through as indicated in Box 6.2:

Box 6.2 Attributes of a successful team

Attributes of a success team can be categorized as follows:

- Avoidance of role conflict – Wrapped up with team functioning is how professions see themselves and others in the team. Role conflict can lead to teams being a difficult place to work (Burns and Lloyd 2004).
- Facilitation of communication through team meetings – Effective team working also requires opportunity for clinicians to communicate their view to other team members within team meetings (Liberman et al. 2001).
- Opportunities to collaborate in providing patient care – Underpinning team work is how well clinicians are able to discuss and

---

> collaborate. Various structures are created by teams in order for them to discuss patient care, the most obvious being team meetings and ward rounds.

One way to understand what clinicians do is for their interventions to be placed upon a care pathway. Care pathways attempt to define the patient journey according to the diagnosis and expected treatment outcomes (Andolina 1995). A study has been completed to look at how teams work together in defining what they did for people with schizophrenia (Jones 2006a). Important factors for clinicians in how they work together were the tensions in describing standardized care and what that actually means. Clinicians cherish the clinician–patient relationship. They hold it as sacrosanct and something which is fundamental to their ways of working.

Psychiatrists believe that the relationship they have with patients is so deep and important that patient care would suffer if other clinicians like nurses were to take on tasks akin to the medical model like prescribing medication or the right to discharge patients from hospital. Psychiatrists use the argument of deepseated relationships with patients as a reason for why different systems of care cannot be instituted. An example is home treatment teams admitting and discharging patients without the catchment area psychiatrist having control over the process.

The qualitative study carried out by Jones (2006a) discovered that teams, far from being harmonious and accepting of other people's roles and interventions, were in fact infested with the culture of conflict. For example, some clinicians wanted to freely enter into a debate into what people did and to 'let the sparks fly and open up a degree of competition'. By this, clinicians wanted to openly challenge what each other did. They saw it as an opportunity to compare what they did against their own evidence base and against what others did. Clinicians used stated policy imperatives such as 'value for money', 'efficiency' and 'effectiveness' as their drivers to challenge intervention. Another feature of the study revolved around confidence in role. If clinicians feel confident in what they do, it then makes them feel as though they have a special purpose within the team and this special purpose places them on a higher hierarchy compared to other clinicians.

The practical realities of the Mental Health Act (MHA) illustrate this point very well. Mental health nurses are essential for the running of psychiatric wards in terms of application of the MHA in the form of Section 5(4) 'emergency holding powers' and also in the administration of medicines for patients detained under the MHA. Psychiatrists are equally essential given that they also apply the MHA, take on responsible medical officer and prescribe medication. OTs do neither of these two tasks and therefore could be seen as less important in the team. This example alone serves to underline the various tensions that lie under the crust of what are said to be collaborative teams and how important some tasks are seen to be. Latest developments with the reform of the MHA will see certain types of mental health nurses being clinical supervisors for patients detained under the Act (DoH 2007e). We are also seeing a growth in the number of nurses who have trained to be a nurse prescriber and the challenge this brings to the ethos of team working (Jones 2006b).

When clinicians feel a sense of confidence in their role then it displaces those members of the team that are possibly more peripheral to the delivery of care. It leads these members of the team to feel as though they are being 'scape-goated' and has a sense of vulnerability (Hummelvoll and Severinsson 2001). A reaction to these two elements is to be defensive. We often see elements of professions being defensive in our everyday teams today. For example, within systems of care, barriers are placed up that are passed off in common parlance such as referral forms, waiting lists, and separate professional notes on patients. These all demonstrate a level of defensiveness. However, they are also ways to control the professional input of team members for the sake of harmonious team working. This way of working also supports a protectionist mentality whereby clinicians protect their scope of practice and are resistive to others carrying out interventions that traditionally come under their remit.

What has been suggested in the preceding paragraphs is that teams approach patient care from their own professional silo with an intention to protect their professional boundaries. The reality is somewhat different, however. Differences between what clinicians do are small and there is a great deal of scope to make roles plural and this has been developed by the NHS and the sponsored bodies into developing core generic skills for mental health workers (Hope 2004). However, professions are notoriously defensive about what they do. This is not helped by professional training and the socialization process which supports separation and an elitist mentality within specialties (Pietroni 1992).

Models seen within the multi-disciplinary team (MDT)

MDT working is influenced by organizational, structural and professional paradigms. The model adopted by the team or the system of care will have an impact on how the teams function. The multitude of professions that make up teams has been described. We now need to look at the model of care that is followed within teams. A strange occurrence that happens in teams is that clinicians report that they, or a member of the team, are following a medical model or a social model. They are often pitted against each other in sometimes negative ways where one model is seen as the perpetrator to some evil act that is played upon the patients' care and treatment. We also hear the word 'eclectic' in that clinicians follow an eclectic model of care as though it is a model that has attributes of all different models. However, in looking at team work it is helpful to consider each of the major models that are played out in our teams today, as presented in Table 6. 1.

Table 6.1 Assumptions and characteristics of models of care

Model	Assumptions/ origins	Main characteristics
The medical model	When people have a mental illness, its origin arises from within the body, i.e. a disease. Thus, one has to find the origins for that defect and for the defect to be fixed (Tyrer and Steinberg 2005).	Scientific breakthroughs: • Abnormal physiology of the brain (e.g. magnetic resonance imaging studies have found enlarged ventricle volumes in the brains of people with schizophrenia (Steen *et al.* 2006) • Evidence that developing schizophrenia increases if the foetus is exposed to a virus in the second trimester (O'Reilly 1994) • Increased phosphor-lipid changes in the white matter regions of brains in people with obsessive compulsive disorder (Kitamura et al. 2006) • The dopamine hypothesis assumes that people with schizophrenia have excess dopamine or disturbance in the dopamine neurons in the temporal limbic pathways of the brain compared to people without schizophrenia (Reynolds 1989)
Cognitive and psychodynamic model	Emerged from the work of Freud and Erickson (Nye 1986).	Now have: • Members of teams engaging in specialised psychodynamic practices • Drama therapy and art therapy • Focus on pattern of emotion Therapist's role is to identify and bring to consciousness what the patient is thinking and behaving in certain situations (Nye 1986). Psychodynamic model requires a large degree of interpretation and analysis with a co-therapist or supervisor on what certain behaviours and thoughts mean to the patient.
Social model	Recent policy documents that raise awareness of the importance of social inclusion for patients	Self-explanatory theory for the emergence of mental health problems in society. Mental disorder affected by life events or social deprivation (relationship breakdown, loss of employment or bereavement).

Model	Assumptions/ origins	Main characteristics
	(Office of the Deputy Prime Minister 2004a; DoH 2006b).	Social factors as predictors for service utilization (Thornicroft 1991). The government has spearheaded a campaign to remove the boundaries for people with mental illness in gaining employment and improved living conditions (DoH and CSIP 2007b).

In the examples given in Table 6.1 one can clearly see how a pathological basis for mental illness has brought about mainstream treatment of mental illness using drugs. The disease model has been championed by *medicine*. However, medicine has chartered the development of professions like nursing, physiotherapy and psychology. But, it is the ramifications of this historical and contemporary influence that is important for team functioning. The medical profession is influential within the team and psychiatrists tend to rely on their diagnostic skills in setting the direction of travel for care and treatment. This tends to alienate other professional groups and shores up professional resentment. However, this is not helped by the perceived attitudes of doctors. For example, there is the early work of Miles (1977) and Harold (1977) in their descriptions of psychiatrists. A common factor in both of these studies was the superior attitude that these medical professions held about themselves in relation to other members of the team, particularly nurses. People who offer criticism of the medical model may do so out of resentment and subservience to it given their relationship with psychiatrists.

By comparison, within the *cognitive psychodynamic approach* we find family therapy, where team members attempt to discover and help remove stress patterns in the family life of patients (Tarrier et al. 1999). There have been lots of examples where mental health teams have engaged in completing the training for family work (Brooker 2001). Implementation deficit has been repeatedly found across adult mental health services most often due to problems for staff to access supervision. Research has also been carried out to find out what needs to happen to ensure family work takes place; for example sufficient time given to the family work worker to see patients (Farhall and Cotton 2002). However, psychological approaches like cognitive and family therapy have been successfully adopted, if not implemented, as 'shared' interventions by all but the most 'disciplinary pure' members of teams.

Despite the adoption of such approaches, however, the *social model* is most pervasive in our teams today. There have been many theories put forward that integrate the biological and social factors as explanatory models for schizophrenia. The stress vulnerability model being one example that has helped to shape the training and work carried out by mental health workers in teams over the last 20 years (Zubin and Spring 1977). The stress-vulnerability model makes clear the importance of life events and the adverse reaction on the person's mental illness. We know that people with depression and anxiety experience symptoms that arise prior to a full blown relapse of their illness, otherwise known as the prodrome state

(Murphy et al. 1989). Boardman et al. (1997) noted that prodrome and admission to hospital is affected by social factors like family stress, the burden of caring for other relatives and employment difficulties.

One must examine the role that society places in terms of labelling people to be mentally ill and the devastating consequences that people experience when they have been labelled as being 'depressed' or having 'schizophrenia'. There will be inevitable change in the person in terms how they react to that diagnostic label and the consequences for them within society. The social model tries to determine societal norms in what acceptable behaviour is and what is deviant and therefore, what can be defined as mental illness (Tyrer and Steinberg 2005). The challenge however for teams is to make sure clinicians are able to embrace aspects of the social model and for its core values to be part of the team ethos as this is not always the case in psychiatric teams (Bertram and Stickley 2005).

Influence of models upon teamwork

It is perfectly acceptable for clinicians to hold different interpretations of each of the models described above. The beauty of team work is that people have different views on the cause, treatment and outcome of mental illness. Clinicians adopt a view depending on their orientation towards science. Nurses and doctors who prefer biological explanations are more likely to find resonance with the medical model. Social workers and OTs may find the social model offers greater theoretical and practical relevance for their work (Beresford 2004).

Team work also finds clinicians who do not profess to use any such model but to describe their approach as being eclectic (Tyrer and Steinberg 2005). This is probably true because very rarely do patients fall into single, explanatory models of practice. Patients do not simply present with a disease in isolation from their social and psychodynamic contexts. However, it is important to actually identify and to be clear on some of the guiding models that underpin team work. Conflict arises when clinicians are negative and condescending about alternative suggestions for managing patient care.

Each clinician will want to place an emphasis on their model of practice to explain what is going on with the patient. The aim would be to work in harmony so that a treatment plan can be agreed. Conflict may emerge due to the emphasis placed on one particular model over another. This is where clinicians like medicine and possibly nursing, which has a close association to medicine, may end up being more dominant in the discussion compared to other members of the team.

Another thing we can say about models in teamwork is that some particular models may work best in some types of teams rather than others. For example, there is a group of people who do not respond adequately to psychiatric treatment and have a diagnosis like treatment resistant schizophrenia and persistent mood disorders. They are high users of services and they are usually managed by an assertive community treatment team approach (DoH 1999b). They are on medication but they have distressing symptoms that need to be managed by other behavioural and social means. Rating scales have been developed to capture deficits in social functioning and are integral to everyday practice (Birchwood et al. 1990). It is readily acknowledged that this client group is susceptible to poor standards of housing, as well as significant stress within families and their environment (DoH 1999b). The social model applies very well to this type of client group because practitioners are more likely to correctly interpret signs of further mental distress due to toxic environmental stimuli and to respond accordingly.

Teams that work closely with disorders like anorexia nervosa may well find resonance with psychodynamic approaches (Lyttle 1986). It would be unhelpful if teams were to treat anorexia nervosa as a disease which can be cured and managed by simply restricting diet or increasing calorie intake when the person's body mass index reaches a critical stage. Although this may be a necessary stage in the patient's condition, they may respond more favourably to a psychodynamic approach and to nurses and doctors that believe in this model of care.

By outlining these different models, it helps to explain how mental health teams can use these models in their practice but how tensions can develop when one clinician advocates a certain model over another. Each model will have a certain power differential where the occupational class of the clinician advocating the model may well be perceived as having more power in the team than others.

What can be done to improve team collaboration?

Whole systems working

Within adult mental health services, attempts have been made to improve morale within acute psychiatric unit teams by shoring up team identity and control over work patterns. Innovative projects such as refocusing (Bowles and Dodds 2002; Bowles et al. 2002) have looked at how ward staff, as part of a team approach, set 'early wins' to change the system of care in hospitals. Although no clear evidence of effect on patient care has been published, anecdotal accounts support the approach. Other examples have looked at training whole teams in delivering interventions. A notable example is team-based learning on risk management (Sharkey and Sharples 2003).

Collaborative teams assume that the constituent aspects of the team are joined together and are in balance (Onyett 2003). However, the reality may be somewhat different (Hannigan 1999). More often, team members struggle to identify their own team identity, let alone that of other teams within the whole system (Garcia 2006). Teams fail to pass on information about patient care from one part of the service to another as the patient passes through the ever increasing numbers of boundaries (Kennedy and Griffiths 2001).

One study has looked at how members of an acute psychiatric team (hospital and Community Mental Health teams) viewed their understanding of team work within the whole system (Bowles and Jones 2005). Key features of this study indicated that clinicians were not clear about the range of teams that made up adult mental health services and what their purpose was. They argued for teams to have a clear specification outlining what the team did and how the team linked in with other teams in the whole system of care. In essence, clinicians were unclear on the role of teams and at times described a sense of confusion.

Ways to bring about clear team identity for staff included whole team training events and an explicit warming up of the networks that exist between teams. This included shadowing opportunities and staff swaps. Stark et al. (2002) supports the conclusions by Bowles and Jones in suggesting that understanding team work does not arise by esoteric classroom discussion. Rather it happens by identifying and dissecting real every day cases of MDT conflict and seeking to understand them within the context in which they arise.

Producing a team profile may help to understand the learning and development of teams. The National Service Framework for England identified a number of teams within adult mental health services like community mental health teams, assertive community treatment teams and crisis resolution home treatment teams (DoH 1999b). Although perceived as rather prescriptive at the time, it did serve other helpful functions like spelling out team attributes, skills of team members and the types of patients to be served by the team.

Changing the practice of MDT working is affected by the particular political context of the day (Mccallin 2001). Particular to the UK, the control of risk and containment associated with the mentally ill in society was a factor leading to the growth of specialised teams. However, as we have seen when teams fail to collaborate or work well together or when they are unclear about their own and other team's role and function then risks will still arise. For teams to carry on being a positive force for good, it is necessary for periodic overview of how teams are functioning and whether they are meeting the objectives set by the organisation.

Effective team working requires time to iron out differences. A particular challenge for clinicians is to make time available both in the team development but also in the day to day working of the team. Use of away days and whole systems training and refocusing projects have been discussed as ways to bring about greater team collaboration. Perhaps the simplistic but most important task is to help clinicians to understand the function, location and composition of the myriad teams in the system and how their own team relates to it on a day by day basis.

Changing roles

Over the last 20 years we have witnessed a revolution in what all professions do within adult mental health services. Nurses now diagnose and prescribe medication (DoH 2007f) while social workers have moved away from a model of only carrying out social care. Support workers are employed to carry out direct social care activities. Social workers, like nurses, now deliver broad case management responsibilities like symptom tracking, medication management and supporting patients to gain employment and better housing. The shifts are driven by a whole range of factors including service user need, economic necessity and an explicit professional agenda where the 'skills escalator' impacts on all clinicians. The only certainty is that professions are constantly on the change as team identity and purpose meet the ever changing needs of the consumer.

The Department of Health has put forward a framework for teams to embrace new ways of working and new roles called 'Creating Capable Teams' (CCT) (DoH 2007e). The emphasis is on workforce redesign and supporting teams to modernize their approach. Similar to the refocusing model, it is team members themselves that identify the means and ways to deliver health care. CCT is seen as a whole systems approach where each team in the system is worked with to modernize and embrace new ways of working. A team that is reviewed by the CCT process should have clear team identify and sense of purpose: essential attributes for a successful team.

Sitting alongside CCT is the new ways of working programme run by the DoH (2007f). The aim of this policy initiative is to enable clinicians to work in teams and to be more flexible in what interventions they deliver to patients. The concept of 'distributed responsibility' has been put forward. This is where the members of the team share responsibility for patient care. In order for teams to collaborate in this way, some clinicians will need to give up jurisdiction over certain interventions or control over patient care, while other clinicians will need to 'raise their game' to take on new skills. The process of changing roles will both be a provocateur to team strife as well as delivering on some of the opportunities for team collaboration.

Collaborative education

There have been studies that advocate team training or interprofessional education (Barnes et al. 2000; Barr et al. 2005). Inter-professional education has helped teams to collaborate and appreciate the efforts of various team members. Important to consider is the diversity of clinicians that work within teams and how to effectively engage staff members when delivering collaborative education (Fielding et al. 2002). Reeves and Freeth (2006) describe a project where team members working in a community mental health team were encouraged to reflect on the contributions made by individual professions within the team. Interventions to bring this about included interactive games and group discussions on role and function. Following the intervention, respondents acknowledged a greater clarity about the roles of team members. However, attempts to implement plans to bring about greater collaborative working had not been implemented. Reasons noted were the lack of investment by medical staff in the initiative and the lack of managerial support. The study indicates that simply providing training without managerial support is likely to be ineffective.

Debate will continue on the generalist–specialist tension and how collaborative education seeks to support core generic skills across a pool of professional workers. Other examples of collaborative education have reported improvements in the core skills of assessment, communication and networking (Parsons and Barker 2000) and spectacularly successful has been the Thorn based teaching on working with people who have schizophrenia (Rolls et al. 2002).

Clinical supervision

Clinical supervision is a common method to support, train and develop team members to deliver mental health care (Grant and Townend 2007). Collaborative working will be helped along by sharing some of the clinical issues and problems within a MDT supervision context. There is some evidence for this way of working. For example, Townend (2005) reports a study of 170 psychotherapists and nurses. Respondents were able to share experiences and the forum provided opportunities for interdisciplinary learning and development. Clinical supervision can also serve a useful function to mop up institutional anxiety that builds up within teams in the management of patient care. For staff from different disciplines to share worries and concerns about managing patients seems more likely to shore up collaborative working than bottling up the unspoken thoughts and views that take place in teams today.

Clinical supervision can also support the broad application of cognitive approaches like family work. The acceptance of family work as a legitimate intervention across the full range of multi-discipline members is unique. However, the opportunity for collaborative working using family work may be lost if clinicians are not given access to individual and group supervision (Brooker et al. 2003). To help address this deficit, Mairs and Arkle (2007) suggest that generic family work training courses include training in the delivery of family work supervision.

Conclusion

This chapter has identified factors that contribute to and hinder collaborative team working. The political context has indicated that teams of people work best to bring about patient outcomes and government reports have indicated willingness for this to continue. Understanding how teams operate beyond the rhetoric of a policy is important. Simply expecting teams to 'get on with it' leaves a lot to chance and this should be avoided. What is important is to continually evaluate the effectiveness of team members and teams in delivering health care outcomes (Jefferies and Chan 2004),

In order for teams to work collaboratively they need to get the basics right. The key success factors are clear leadership by a team manager, a clear strategic role of the team in the whole system and ongoing monitoring of team functioning to ensure it is fit for purpose and achieving the goals that it has been set. In order to get the basics right, health and social care systems must invest commitment and resources. Team training, education and professional awareness have been reviewed as a way to make teams work in balance. They all offer merit and should be judged accordingly to the particular difficulties and challenges of the team.

The considerations within this chapter illustrate the inter-play between the factors that go on to make successful teams. Organizational leadership and steering teams to be effective are important but the reality is probably more complex. Successful teams are made up of groups of individuals that have different ways of viewing the world and the patient. Obviously, the success of the team, and how well they collaborate, must also be seen in how teams relate to patients (Barker and Walker 2000). People who work in teams need to understand the complexity that this adds into team working. That is why making improvements in team working cannot be viewed as a mechanical and sterile intervention. Lots of factors interplay and the success of the intervention cannot be brought down to this simple explanation.

Questions for discussion

1 What are the prevailing models of care in mental health in your experience?
2 How might these different models of care impact on teamwork?
3 What do you think are the likely areas of conflict within teams and what do you think might be the causes of these?
4 What attributes do you think make for:
  - a successful team?
  - an unsuccessful team?

Useful websites

- *MIND:* www.mind.org.uk/ is a leading mental health charity in England and Wales that seek to create a better life for people who experience mental distress.
- *The Mental Health Foundation:* www.mhf.org.uk/ is a leading UK charity that provides information, carries out research, campaigns and works to improve services for anyone affected by mental health problems.
- *Rethink:* www.rethink.org is a leading national mental health membership charity that works to help everyone affected by severe mental illness recover a better quality of life.

7 Working across the interface of formal and informal care of older people

Pat Chambers and Judith Phillips

This chapter will:

- Explore the extent to which older people and carers of older people are able to work in meaningful partnerships with the private, voluntary and independent sectors of health and social care.
- Discuss the social policy and legal context of 'caring' in defining 'who' carers are, 'what' we know about the way in which they receive services and the diversity of the caring experience.
- Analyse 'models' that have been developed to explain the relationship between carers and service providers and explore their potential for developing relationships with a multiplicity of service providers that are rooted in partnership.

In this chapter we draw on the general literature on informal care and, more specifically, on research that one of us undertook with 'working' carers of older adults, that is, those carers who are in full or part time paid employment as well as undertaking unpaid, so-called informal care of an older relative (Phillips et al. 2002). We suggest a way of working that acknowledges the complexities of the experience of being a carer of an older person and identify some key issues for good practice in 'working together'. Although the focus in this chapter is on the interface of formal and informal care of older people, it is essential to acknowledge that older people themselves are integral to any service development. Indeed, a significant strand of current social policy emphasises that the needs and aspirations of older people and active support of their involvement, alongside those of carers, is fundamental to the success of any relationships with formal services. The National Service Framework for older people (DoH, 2001b) underpins the government's national strategy for older people and subsequent policy has focused attention on key objectives which seek to create improved, flexible, integrated and 'person centred' services for older people (DoH, 2004f, 2005a, 2006b; Audit Commission 2004b). Indeed, a 'preventative' policy agenda that encompasses independence, well-being, quality of life, choice, autonomy and dignity has been extolled across the UK (see for example Welsh Assembly Government 2007) However, it is also necessary to acknowledge that the other major strand of government social policy in relation to old age, the imperative for local authorities to operate within a 'managerialist' agenda (budgetary constraints, more restrictive eligibility criteria, persistent re-organization of services, externally derived performance criteria and so on) also directly impacts on the lives of older people and their carers, presenting major challenges to the provision and delivery of integrated social and healthcare services and notions of partnership. We therefore conclude our chapter with a note of caution.

Social and legal context of caring

In order to better understand the current situation, let us briefly consider the way in which the social and legal context of caring has developed. During the 1970s the idea of care being undertaken by the community instead of just care in the community (Bayley 1973) came to underlie much of the thinking about community care. Increasing public and governmental disquiet about the spiralling welfare costs of a rising elderly population further fuelled the debate about 'who' was going to provide the bulk of care, and with the advent of the 1979 Conservative government committed to the reduction of the overall costs of welfare and the development of a mixed economy of care (Bernard and Phillips 1998), 'informal care' (that is, care provided by family and friends), became an explicit component of social care provision enshrined in The NHS and Community Care Act (DoH 1990). The care provided by 'informal carers' was acknowledged as a vital resource which, depending on the outcome of a 'needs led' assessment of the person being cared for, would be partnered by the 'formal' sector of care: local authority social services departments; private agencies; and the voluntary sector. Indeed, throughout the last decade of the twentieth century, the increasing reference to carers in public policy documents has been striking. The Carers (Recognition and Services) Act (DoH 1995b) gave carers access to a 'carer's assessment subsequent to an assessment having been carried out on the person being cared for' and was hailed as a further acknowledgement of the government's commitment to partnership.

A significant milestone in the recognition of carers as potential 'partners in care' was the publication, in 1999, of *The National Strategy for Carers* (DoH 1999d) that for the first time identified the need for a legislative framework for practical support to be provided directly to carers. More importantly, this was followed, in 2000, by The Carers and Disabled Children Act (DoH 2000e), which gives carers a right to ask for an assessment in their own right, and the inclusion in the National Service Framework for Mental Health of a standard specifically relating to carers: Standard 6 – Caring about Carers (DoH 1999b). Carers' needs were also acknowledged in the *National Service Framework for Older People* (DoH 2001b). Early in 2007, the government announced its intention to pro-actively engage carers in a timely review of the *National Strategy for Carers*; this review is currently being undertaken (DoH 2008). We will argue later in this chapter that these recent initiatives have important implications for partnership working.

The government's commitment to partnership, however, is a recent development, with carers often being invisible in policy and taken for granted for many years. It was only when feminist writers in the 1980s (Finch and Groves 1983; Ungerson 1987; Lewis and Meredith 1988) challenged the gendered and unequal nature of caring that their voice became heard. Furthermore the explosion of research on caring in the 1990s (see, for example, Parker 1990; Twigg 1992; Twigg and Aitken 1994; Phillips 1994), alongside the activities of the carer lobby led by the Carers National Association (now Carers UK) and the work of the King's Fund Informal Carers Unit, demonstrated that the reality of 'partnership' was often different. 'Informal' care often superseded the 'formal' contribution, carers' assessments were patchy, limited to those carers providing a substantial amount of care on a regular basis, and there was no guarantee of services. The Social Services Inspectorate (SSI) carried out an inspection of local authority support for carers in 1996 and produced a highly critical report: *A Matter of Chance for Carers* (SSI 1996). The inspectors found that support for carers was dependent on where carers lived and who they were in contact with, rather than on what they needed. They praised carers' groups and acknowledged that support for carers of older people was better developed than support for other groups, particularly those carers who supported people with mental ill health.

Since the SSI report a number of policy and research initiatives have sought to grapple with the place of 'informal care' or 'family care' (Nolan et al. 1996) within overall social care provision and to extend the way in which partnerships between formal and informal care might be forged. In particular, there have been a number of detailed explorations of what informal care is about, the nature of caring relationships, who undertakes care and what are the problems encountered in the delivery of care (see, for example, Nolan et al. 1996, 2001; Brechin et al. 1998), the experience of 'juggling' work and care (Phillips et al. 2002), older people and caring (Carers UK and Sheffield Hallam University 2005a), caring and pensioner poverty (Carers UK and Sheffield Hallam University 2005b), and more recently: access to information (Carers UK 2006) and the financial impact of caring (Carers UK 2007). However just under ten years ago now, and we would argue still relevant, Banks (1999) urged caution suggesting that despite the prominence of carers in policy and research, carers' concerns were still not embedded in mainstream thinking; partnership was far from being a reality. One reason for this, we argue, is that 'partnership' implies a level of equality between the partners, which may not be the case if people or organizations are merely 'working together'. While the impact of carers (and service users) has grown significantly over the last 20 years, carers are still relatively powerless when compared to service providers. Reasons for this have included:

- Stereotyping of carers as a homogenous group
- The myriad health and social care services provision within the statutory, voluntary and private sectors
- Paternalism of health and social care professions
- Resource constraints and increasingly 'moveable' eligibility criteria
- The costs of caring

- Multiplicity of potential partnerships

(Twigg and Aitken 1994; Nolan et al. 1996; Brown et al. 2001; Ray and Chambers 2007)

According to the 2001 census (Office of National Statistics) there are 5.2 million carers in England and Wales, a million of whom provide care for more than 50 hours a week. Over 225,000 people providing more than 50 hours unpaid care per week state that they are 'not in good health' themselves and more than half of the people providing this much care are over the age of 55; it is at these ages that the 'not good health' is highest. The age group where the largest proportion provides care is in the fifties: more than one in five of people aged 50–9 are providing some unpaid care. This confirms the findings from *The National Strategy for Carers* (DoH 1999d) that the likelihood of becoming a carer increases with age, with the peak age being 45–64. Many carers in this age group are working either full or part time. For example in 1999, 2.7 million people combined work with informal care for another adult (DoH 1999a). *The National Strategy for Carers* also notes that nine out of ten carers care for a relative, of whom two out of ten care for a partner or spouse and four out of ten care for parents. One half of all carers look after someone over 75.

Once we move away from the numbers of carers, and start to identify and describe both 'who' does care and 'what' is their experience, our task becomes difficult. As we noted earlier in this chapter, the 1980s saw a burgeoning of feminist literature which highlighted the gendered nature of caring (Finch and Groves 1983; Ungerson 1987; Lewis and Meredith 1988). However, most commentators now acknowledge that while it is true that more women than men are carers, the picture is much more complex. Carers are a diverse group of people in terms of age, marital status, gender, ethnicity, sexuality, disability, education, health, household composition, family, income, employment status and, of course, in terms of willingness, capacity and expertise to care. Indeed some carers share care with other family members, while others are sole carers. Some are more politicized than others and feel able to claim both the title and identity of 'carer', whereas others reject it in favour of their status or relationship as relative: daughter, wife, husband, etc. (see, for example, Henderson 2001). This may also be the preferred emphasis of the person being 'cared for'. The relationship that they have with the person they care for will be individual and located in their shared biography and relationships over the life course (Nolan et al. 1996; Brechin et al. 1998), and will inevitably be influenced by the views and expectations of others, including other family members. That caring relationship will, in turn, develop its own history, of which a relationship with formal services may be an increasingly substantial component. Furthermore, carers differ in both the quantity and the type of care that they offer. Some carers undertake the regular physical labour of personal care and supporting domestic tasks, either living with or near to the person they care for, whereas others may 'care at a distance', offering emotional support, organizing and overseeing care services. Indeed, carers differ in the amount of support they want and receive from formal services and perhaps more importantly, in the relationships they develop with a variety of service providers, for example, local volunteer support groups.

While it is impossible to do justice in a chapter such as this to the multiplicity of caring experiences, the examples in Box 7.1 of women caring for their mothers, serve to illustrate the diversity of the caring experience.

Box 7.1 Three examples of women caring for their mothers

When my mother left mental hospital I was told to accept what she had become. She just sat staring at the wall. I have worked hard to rehabilitate her and though this has cost me a great deal both mentally and physically, I have a great deal of satisfaction seeing that my efforts have been worthwhile and have proved the medical profession wrong

(cited in Nolan *et al.* 1996: 93).

There was this terrific pressure because the (paid) carer would leave at say 4 p.m. and I needed to be there shortly afterwards. If I was late ... then I had to telephone my mum's neighbours and let them know I would be late. I would stay with mum, give her tea, chat, help with continence, shower, undress and help her to bed and read to her etc., then go home and start studying or spend some time with my partner. We had a bizarre existence and it was extremely stressful and pressurised ... the possibility of giving up work was very much on my mind as I didn't know how I could continue to cope with no end in sight, and also my family, especially my grandfather, was very critical of me trying to continue with my career ... At times, I was accused of neglecting mum and did feel that I was not doing a good job. Others were critical of a 'stranger' looking after her when it should have been me ...

(Mia, cited in Phillips 2000: 47–50)

The constant juggling put stresses and strains on them all (Ursula, two sisters and brother, all of whom had multiple demands with their own jobs and families). Despite the support of the team Ursula worked with, and of her manager who was very good, Ursula became ill herself. She had to have a few weeks off work but still kept going to her mother's. One of her sisters also lost her job due to the inflexibility and demands of the children's home where she worked ... Towards the end, Ursula says, 'We were all so stressed. We were tired and there was friction in the family. That sounds petty but that's how it gets. But we managed to keep it together ... there was no sort of fighting in front of her or anything [but] there was tension'. Looking back, Ursula feels angry about the responsibilities she had to take on, the travelling she had to do, the work and social things she missed out on.

('Ursula Vine: the reluctant worker', cited in Phillips et al. 2002: 35)

Indeed, it would be fair to say that the differences between carers may well outweigh their commonalities and any attempts by service providers to develop partnerships have to recognize and work with both uniqueness and diversity.

There are clearly both costs and benefits to being a carer. Early feminist literature, in an attempt to emphasize the physical labour of caring and demonstrate that the 'personal is political' (Ungerson 1987), tended to emphasize the 'burden' of caring for women. Carers UK, in its literature, has emphasized the physical, emotional and financial costs of caring for all carers. The third example in Box 7.1 taken from recent research with working carers, exemplifies some of these costs. Ursula's description of a family under stress is not uncommon and we would argue that the costs of caring can be major barriers to partnership working. It is difficult for a carer to consider herself to be an equal partner with formal services when she is constantly juggling many roles and trying to maintain some control over her whole life, not just the care giving component. This is not to suggest that carers are passive 'victims'. To the contrary, as Nolan et al. (1996: 79) remind us: 'Far from being a passive and largely reactive group, carers are characterised by being pro-active and purposeful in bringing a range of methods to bear on the difficulties they face'. Carers, they argue have to learn, if they did not know already, how to be resourceful in relation to finding relevant information, seeking help from formal services and seeking out a confidante. For some carers, this is an empowering experience which enables them to work side by side with formal services but for others these coping responses result in stress and exhaustion that contribute instead to an increasing sense of powerlessness and isolation.

Nonetheless, there is increasing evidence that some carers find care giving to be a satisfying and rewarding experience. Nolan et al. (1996), for example, while noting the embryonic nature of literature on the rewards of care giving compared to the burgeoning literature on burden and stress, highlight the reciprocal nature of care giving, the potential to develop relationships and the subjective meaning of care for both the care giver and the cared for person. The continuation of ongoing loving relationships, the capacity to 'give back', doing a good job and gaining satisfaction, are some of the benefits cited by daughters who cared for their mothers, in research carried out by Lewis and Meredith (1988). More recently, Karen, a 46-year-old part time district nurse has looked after her 72-year-old mother since her father died of cancer some five years ago. She says:

> What goes round comes round. You're cared for, you care and you're cared for. That's how it is ... Only do it if you want to. If it's not something that you want to do – not everybody can do it – then don't do it. Find another way round it. There are good care homes and because someone is in a care home, it doesn't mean that the family doesn't care – it means they can't care.

(Cited in Phillips et al. 2002: 23)

Karen is a working carer who is supported by a range of informal and formal networks and services. She clearly feels that she has some control over her decision to care, and has a sense of empowerment and satisfaction that is derived from that control. As we have demonstrated in previous examples, not all carers are in such a position.

The National Strategy for Carers (DoH 1999d) sought, through consultation with a multiplicity of stakeholders, to document these diverse experiences of caring and put forward a realistic strategy for carers that would make working in partnership a reality rather than a pipedream for all carers. The document identified that in order to care effectively, carers need a partnership with service providers, which is based on respect and recognition of carers' expertise. This must be accompanied by: accessible, relevant and comprehensible information; recognition both as individuals and as a collective; a multi-agency approach which incorporated health, housing and employment as well as social care; and transparency in relation to policy and practice. So often, by focusing on the negative burden of caring, 'partnership' with statutory service places carers in a deficit role. Instead, *The National Strategy for Carers* (DoH 1999d) recognized that carers are service users, service providers and above all, citizens. As such, carers have the right to expect:

- Freedom to live a life of their own, including spending time with family and friends outside of caring responsibilities or remaining in work
- Maintenance of their own health and wellbeing
- Confidence in the standard and reliability of services
- To share caring responsibilities with service providers and feel that the person they care for is respected; this includes practical and emotional support that contributes to their well being and knowing that assistance will be available in a crisis

(DoH 1999d: 24)

In addition, those carers who work or care at a distance may need the following: time off from work in a crisis; the use of a telephone to arrange care/check arrangements; help from the local carers' centre; particular support from statutory services in their relative's area. In summary, in order to achieve partnership: 'Carers need caring for. Most of them need high quality, reliable and responsive support from statutory or voluntary services. Many need help from their employer. Carers have many of the same needs as the rest of the population ... carers have less opportunity to get what they need.' (DoH 1999d: 83).

The National Strategy for Carers (DoH 1999d), and more recently 'Independence, Well-being and Choice' (Department of Health 2005a), stressed the importance of involving carers in discussions about care delivery, in planning care and in providing feedback on services and initiatives. Furthermore, and significantly, it also highlighted the urgency for legislation to enable local councils with social services responsibilities to provide services direct to carers. Along with the Government's previous initiatives to support carers in their caring role (Health Improvement Programmes; requirement for consultation in Joint Investment Plans, NHS surveys of patients and carers; Patient Partnership Strategy; consultations with carers' organizations; and the active development of carers' support groups), it provided impetus for *The Carers and Disabled Children Act* (DoH 2000e). The Act, which came into force on 1 April 2001, gives local councils the power to supply certain services to carers following assessment. There is also, as indicated earlier in this chapter, a new right to a carer's assessment, even where the person cared for has refused an assessment for, or the provision of, community care services. Disappointingly, a survey undertaken by Crossroads for carers (Carers UK, 2005c), found that many carers were not informed of their right to an assessment, and in those instances where an assessment had been undertaken, there was little evidence of either contingency planning or updating.

Resultant good practice guidelines issued by the Department of Health have highlighted the need for carers' employment to be a main factor in assessment. This is clearly significant, given the increasing numbers of carers of older people who are also in paid employment. The needs of working carers have also been addressed by other government departments. For example, the 1999 Employment Relations Act gave employees the right to unpaid 'reasonable' time off to deal with unexpected or sudden situations relating to those that they care for. The Department for Education and Employment subsequently launched the Employers for Work–Life Balance Initiative, encouraging organizations to make a commitment to support carers in the workforce and the *Work–Life Balance Campaign*, which sought to encourage employers to develop more flexible working practices (DTI 2002). However, according to Phillips et al. (2002: 2) existing family friendly schemes are still primarily designed for working parents of young children and most current schemes rarely address the needs of employees who care for older or disabled adults. The *Carers (Equal Opportunities) Act* (DoH 2004d), which came into force in England and Wales in 2005, may go some way towards redressing this imbalance but it is still too early to ascertain its full impact. More recently, Watson et al. (2006) have suggested that the Human Rights Act (1998) gives carers for the first time the potential to claim 'hard rights' should they wish to do so. Moreover: 'the Act's framework of balancing rights, just as importantly, gives service providers an opportunity to recognize carers' humanity and treat them as equal partners in a situation.' (Watson et al. 2006: 25).

Understanding the experience of carers

A number of initiatives, therefore, have sought to raise the profile of carers, and develop partnerships between carers and those who provide formal services at both macro level and micro level. First, at the macro level of 'community' or 'workplace', there is the potential for partnerships to develop in relation to planning and provision of services. A carer, either as an individual or as a member of a carers' organization may, for example, be invited onto a working party to develop new initiatives or may be consulted about the development of an ongoing service. At this level, the carer is a representative, the 'voice' of carers. Given the diversity of carers and experiences identified earlier, this, of course, can be problematic, and the potential and effectiveness of such partnerships weakened if that diversity is neither acknowledged nor incorporated into service delivery. What is missing from a lot of the discussion surrounding these initiatives, however, is not just a lack of recognition of the reality of that diversity but also a lack of clarity concerning the differential power imbalance between the formal and the informal sectors of care: carers do not have access to the power and resources available to the formal sectors, and as such may find themselves at a constant disadvantage. There may, however, be unantici-pated consequences of recent policy and practice, according to Leece (2003: 27). She suggests that the increasing 'commodification' of care inherent in health and social care policy in recent years and, we would argue, especially in relation to caring relationships, may cause a shift in this balance of power, with informal carers reassessing their position and demanding payment, better support or indeed refusing to continue providing care for their relatives.

At a micro level, carers are personally at the interface of formal and informal service provision but in an ambiguous position. As service users, there is potential for partnership development with formal service providers in their own right, through community care processes of carer assessment and care delivery. For those carers who are also in paid employment there is, in addition, a need to develop collaborative working arrangements with their employers. As service providers that potential development will be via the person they are caring for, who will also be subject to community care processes. It is well documented, however, that community care processes have the potential to either empower or further disempower carers and service users, who find themselves dependent on the skills, values and practice of individual workers and local systems and resources (see, for example, Hughes 1997; Oliver and Sapey 1999). Within that caring relationship, a carer may be working in partnership with the person they care for, may be acting as advocate for that person or may even find that they are in conflict with that person. What emerges is a very complex web of relationships, which itself may be a barrier to developing partnership with formal service providers.

So, given the barriers to partnership working identified so far, to what extent does the social and legal context that is being developed enable carers to develop real partnerships with service providers? A number of 'models' have been put forward that have attempted to conceptualize the differential relationships that carers have with the health and social care sector. These models have sought to both better understand and inform practice and, for the purposes of the current discussion, enable us to analyse the potential for partnership and collaboration. We will focus here on two approaches.

First, Twigg and Aitken (1994) suggested a framework that sought to explore the way in which service providers respond to carers. They contended that service agencies and professionals, generally lacking an explicit rationale for work with carers, tended to adopt instead one of four implicit models (see Table 7.1).

Table 7.1 Four models of carers

	Carers as resources	**Carers as co-workers**	**Carers as co-clients**	**Superseded carer**
Definition of carer	Very wide.	Wide.	Narrow.	'Relatives'.
Focus of interest	Disabled person.	Disabled person with some recognition of the carer.	Carer.	Recognized but in relation to both carer and disabled person.
Conflict of interest	Ignored.	Partially recognized.	Recognized fully but only one way.	Recognized but in relation to carer and disabled person.

	Carers as resources	**Carers as co-workers**	**Carers as co-clients**	**Superseded carer**
Aim	Care maximization and minimization of substitution.	Highest quality of care for the disabled person. Wellbeing of carer as a means to this.	Wellbeing of the carer.	Wellbeing of carer and independence for the disabled person but seen as separate.

Source: Twigg and Aitkin (1994: 13).

Each of the 'models' reflects a different relationship that formal service providers adopt, often unwittingly, with carers. According to Twigg and Aitken (1994: 12), 'carers as resource' reflects the predominant reality of social care, embodied in the *NHS and Community Care Act* (DoH 1990). Care provided by carers is a 'given' against which agencies operate: it is 'freely available' with no 'cost' attached to it; and there seems to be an assumption by both service providers and the wider public that informal care is preferable with the social care system only needing to step in when informal care support is unavailable. The 'cared for' person is the focus of intervention and the concern with carer welfare is marginal. The primary focus of agency intervention is that of maintenance. Alternatively, 'carers as co-workers' are jointly involved in the enterprise of care. Ideally, the divisions of formal and informal care are transcended in this joint enterprise and partnership is achieved. The reality of the differing worlds of formal and informal care, with potentially diverse values and expectations, means that this rarely happens (Twigg and Aitken 1994: 14). The primary aim of the formal care system is to assist 'carers as co-workers' to carry on caring. In the model of 'carers as co-clients' the aim of the service system is primarily to support those carers who are most stressed and heavily burdened. Carers are regarded as clients and the focus of attention is on the carer and their needs, sometimes at the expense of the cared for person.

Finally, 'the superseded carer': here the aim is to replace current informal care relationships either in the interests of the person being cared for or, in some cases, to enable a person to give up caring. This model is often employed with parent carers of disabled adults, as a way of developing independence for the 'cared for' person. Twigg and Aitken (1994) argue that these models are ideal types of response and that no one agency draws exclusively on one model. However, they go on to suggest that there is evidence that different models are stressed at different levels of organizations. For example, those workers with social work training tend to be more comfortable with the 'co-worker' model, whereas managerial staff find more favour with 'carers as resources'. There would also appear to be differences in emphasis between socially and medically oriented practitioners, with a tendency by medical staff to view carers as: 'an unquestioned background resource' (Twigg and Aitken 1994: 15). It would seem then that the potential for partnership is heavily dependent not only on the model of carer that is adopted, but also on 'who' in an organization is involved in assessment, including the professional orientation of that person. Increasing multiplicity of service providers, drawn from the voluntary and private sectors whose workers have varying degrees of training, as well as an increasing variety of health and social service providers, adds even greater complexity and possibility of variation in practice.

A second approach is that of Nolan et al. (1996). While acknowledging that the 'models' advocated by Twigg and Aitken might be appropriate in describing given circumstances, Nolan et al. (1996) suggest that none of the models is adequate as a basis for intervention across the interface of formal and informal care because they fail to really reflect ideals of empowerment, partnership and choice. Moreover, they contend that underpinning Twigg and Aitken's framework is the principle that all parties (formal and informal care providers) bring something of value to an encounter and share views in moving towards a common goal (Nolan et al. 1996; Brown et al. 2001:30). The literature, they go on to argue, suggests that this is often not the case, and that professionals, family carers and, importantly, older people themselves, frequently have differing and not necessarily complementary goals and sources of knowledge. Furthermore, what is needed is a working model that reflects more adequately the goals of partnership and empowerment inherent in policy and practice guidelines and recognizes the power differentials of formal service provision and family care.

This critique has led them to develop such a model, 'carers as experts', that can be used as a basis for assessment and intervention (Nolan et al. 1996). The model incorporates a number of basic assumptions. First, important though the problems of caring are, a full understanding of carers' needs will not solely be achieved via assessment of the 'difficulties' of caring but instead must be grounded in knowledge of the expertise that is derived from a 'caring career'. This might include, for example, past and present relationships, rewards of caring, coping skills and resources. Second, assessment must incorporate the subjective experience of the carer, and the carer's willingness and/or capacity to care. Third, a life course approach to 'caring'is adopted, which acknowledges temporality, that is 'the changing demands of care and the way in which skills and expertise change over time' (Brown et al. 2001: 31). And finally, if carers are conceptualized as 'experts', then it becomes possible to help them attain further competence, skills, resources, etc., enabling them to provide quality care without detriment to their own health.

The National Strategy for Carers (DoH 1999d) also recognized the importance of carers' expertise and recommended the following strategies to support partnership:

- Active monitoring and provision of information by GPs and primary health care teams who are in touch with carers
- Training to 'care' course to be developed in consultation with carers: practical skills such as lifting and handling; stress management; 'taking care of yourself'
- Carers' breaks
- Carers' support services and carers' centres, which incorporate information and advice, emotional support and befriending schemes

We would concur with the basic assumptions of this model of 'carers as experts'. Indeed, without recognition of such expertise, partnership may well be impossible.

Developing good practice

Arising from the discussion thus far, we now seek to identify key issues for practice in order to maximize meaningful partnerships across the interface of formal and informal care. At a micro level, it is clearly crucial for service providers to acknowledge both power differentials and temporality. Not all carers will experience the same sense of powerlessness and not all carers will be at the same stage in their 'caring career'. As we have previously acknowledged, many carers will also be differentially engaged in full or part time paid work. Carers' assessments must be routinely offered (Carers UK 2005) and carers must be encouraged to participate. In order to promote collaboration, a life course perspective, which is grounded in an understanding of the diversity of carers and the multiplicity of caring experiences, must be adopted during assessment and the provision of support must be appropriate to the stage of 'caring career' that the carer has reached. The subjective experience of the carer must be accounted for alongside the more objective criteria such as 'hours spent caring', and the 'burden' of caring must not be assumed. Indeed, an exploration of the positive aspects of caring and the recognition of carer expertise will be more conducive to developing a partnership, and less likely to pathologize either the carer or the cared for person. Such an approach is advocated by Askham (1998), who suggests a broad definition of support for carers which includes any action that helps carers to: take up or decide not to take up a care-giving role; continue in the care giving role; or end the care giving role. She stresses a variety of possible interventions: training and preparation for caring; information; emotional support; instrumental help. We would argue that this requires a framework for assessment, grounded in the recommendations of *The National Strategy for Carers* (DoH 1999d) and the rights outlined in The Carers and Disabled Children Act (DoH 2000e), that takes account of differences, acknowledges power, is sensitive to dynamics of care and is able to collect relevant information. In addition, the person carrying out the assessment must have understanding and knowledge of the diversity of caring experiences and must be able to adopt a person centred, life course approach to understanding caring relationships.

For interventions to be successful, then, the carer must be valued as a whole person, a citizen with a multiplicity of roles and responsibilities. This will require of service providers both flexibility and an understanding of what is or is not acceptable or appropriate at a particular time. Ongoing recognition of the temporal nature of caring, and the way in which needs and support will inevitably change, is essential. A 'one off' assessment will clearly not suffice. Instead, service providers must be prepared to build evaluation and reassessment into partnership arrangements. The entire collaborative enterprise must be underpinned by anti-discriminatory practice (Burke and Harrison 2002; Dalrymple and Burke 2006), attention to the human rights of both carers and those who are cared for, and relevant information must be shared with all those involved in the delivery of a care package.

At a macro level, it is recognized that support for carers in the area where they live works best when a range of local organizations work in partnership to maintain and develop a community service to carers. This might include a range of organizations: social services; housing; transport; education; health trusts; general practitioners; employers; volunteer bureaux; benefits; carers' groups (DoH 1999d: 68). It must also include private and voluntary agencies that are at the forefront of service delivery. These must be more than 'talking shops' and the commitment to partnership needs to be developed and regularly reviewed, perhaps through the development of shared policy and practice guidelines. One example of a local partnership is the Partnerships for Carers in Suffolk. This comprises Suffolk Carers, a number of local authorities' social services and education departments, the health authority, voluntary organizations, NHS trusts and Primary Care Groups. Each partner has 'signed up' for the Charter for Carers in Suffolk, which emphasizes the following: carers' right to recognition; choice, information; appropriate practical help; assistance towards the financial costs of caring; and coordinated services. Furthermore, each of the partners is committed to implementing an action plan.

Communication, information and recognition are crucial to developing and maintaining partnership. Formal care services must work together with individual carers and their organizations, to develop appropriate and accessible systems that recognize carers' needs. There are a number of examples of good practice of innovative systems in different parts of the United Kingdom. For example, Newcastle City NHS Trust has appointed a nurse specialist in carer support to work with carers and educate professionals. A GP carers' project in York and Selby has developed a range of initiatives to provide carers with information and support; these include, carer messages on prescriptions, the use of notices to identify carers and carer designated notice boards. Other initiatives have included: handbooks for carers (Cambridgeshire), a free phone, designated carers' line and carers' packs (Rhondda Cynon Taff Social Services Department (DoH 1999d).

Partnership arrangements with employers are an effective way of supporting working carers of older people and can benefit both carer support services and employers themselves (DoH 1999d: 69). In the organizations they studied, an NHS Trust and a social services department (Phillips et al. 2002), they were able to identify a number of 'family friendly' policies. These included: extended leave; short term leave; time off in lieu; shorter week and reduced hours; flexitime; job share; eldercare information; dependent leave; special leave; and counselling. However, the authors were critical that the way in which these policies were translated into practice was heavily dependent on managerial discretion and support, knowledge of staff and the subcultures of the organization. There are interesting parallels here with the way in which carers in general report their experience of formal services: so often, despite policies for partnership being in place, their experience is dependent on the way in which they interact with a particular health or social worker, and the way in which organizational systems and constraints help or hinder (Twigg and Aitken 1994; DoH 1999d; Carers Association Southern Staffordshire, discussion with one of the authors 2003). It is vital that training for those who work with carers is provided, both in the workplace and the community, in order that policy is translated into practice. Disappointingly, Phillips et al. (2002) also found that partnership arrangements between public, private and voluntary agencies to support working carers of older people were virtually nonexistent. We endorse their advocacy for such developments at a local level and argue for a pooling of knowledge about working carers and joint initiatives between employers from public, voluntary and private sectors, in order to develop effective partnership arrangements.

Conclusion

In this chapter our focus has been to explore the extent to which carers of older people are able to work in meaningful partnership with formal care services. We have recognized both the potential and some of the challenges inherent in that journey. Considerable progress has been made in both policy and practice but we live in ever changing times. As a recent CSCI review of social services activity and provision (CSCI 2006) has evidenced, the tendency for councils to respond to the highest level of eligibility within Fair Access to Care Services has reduced the overall level of provision provided by the formal care sector. Services now go to fewer people, the consequences of which include fewer older people receiving any form of services and the 'preventative agenda' becomes increasingly undermined (see Ray and Chambers, 2007). Once older people and their carers start to feel uncertain about the support that might be available to them and lose confidence in the formal sector, so the power differentials between the formal and informal sectors of care become greater. Importantly for our discussion, the extent to which older people, their carers and formal services are then able to develop meaningful partnerships becomes ever more challenging: trust and mutual respect are vital to such partnerships. We started our chapter with an emphasis on older people, and we have made reference to older people in the course of the text. However, our focus has been on carers and the context of caring. Inevitably in a chapter of this size we have been unable to pay much attention to the 'cared for' person and what has been described as the politics of care (Brechin et al. 1998; Priestley 1998, 1999). We wish, therefore, to end with a note of caution. Any attempt to develop partnerships with carers must not be at the expense of further disempowering the cared for person. Partnerships with carers must, therefore, encompass relationships of care that seek to enable, empower and promote the independence of the cared-for person. This will inevitably add further complexity to an already complex web of relationships between the formal and the informal sectors of care. Cooperation, understanding and a commitment to working together must, therefore, be the starting point to any relationship between formal care services, carers and the cared for person, with partnership as the goal to strive for.

Questions for further discussion

1   How might you begin to develop a partnership with a carer during a carer's assessment? What would this depend on?
2   Highlight the dilemmas for carers in caring at long distances.
3   How would you reconcile the needs of carers with the needs of the 'cared for 'person in developing a partnership across the interface of formal and informal care?

Useful websites

- *Carers UK:* www.carersuk.org is the voice of carers. Carers provide unpaid care by looking after an ill, frail or disabled family member, friend or partner.
- *Age Concern:* www.ageconcern.org.uk seeks to promote the well being of all older people and to help make later life a fulfilling and enjoyable experience.
- *Help the Aged:* www.helptheaged.org.uk is an international charity fighting to free disadvantaged older people from poverty, isolation and neglect.

8 Understanding and misunderstanding problem drug use: working together

Julian Buchanan

This chapter will:

- Outline the legal and policy context of drug taking in the UK.
- Explore nature and use of legal and illegal drug taking.
- Introduce the reader to the legal, social, psychological and physical aspects of problem drug use.
- Outline general approaches to working with people who develop problems with drugs.
- Explore the context and issues regarding partnership practice with problem drug users.

The legal policy context

In the UK the terms drug user, addict, problem drug user, or substance misuser invariably refer to people who use drugs, which under criminal law have been categorised as 'controlled substances'. The Misuse of Drug Act 1971 grades these different drugs Class A, B and C to reflect their apparent dangerousness, the Act also indicates the maximum court sanctions for anyone caught in possession or supplying one of these controlled substances. Those who possess or supply controlled drugs risk severe penalties:

- *Class A drugs* include ecstasy, LSD, heroin, cocaine, crack, magic mushrooms and amphetamines (which is normally a Class B drug but becomes a Class A drug if prepared for injection). If caught in possession the maximum penalty is up to seven years in prison. If caught dealing (or passing the drug onto another person) the maximum penalty is up to life in prison.
- *Class B drugs* includes amphetamines, DF118s, codeine and Ritalin. If caught in possession the maximum penalty is up to five years in prison. If caught dealing (or passing the drug onto another person) the maximum penalty is up to 14 years in prison.

- *Class C drugs* includes cannabis, Benzodiazapines, Ketamine, GHB (Gamma hydroxybutyrate). If caught in possession the maximum penalty is up to two years in prison. If caught dealing (or passing the drug onto another person) the maximum penalty is up to 14 years in prison.

The Misuse of Drugs Act (MDA) 1971 has remained the cornerstone of UK drug policy despite being almost 40 years old. Various minor amendments have been introduced over the decades, in particular the reclassification of cannabis from Class B to C in January 2004. Although this change has been met with widespread support from experts in the field (most notably the Advisory Council on the Misuse of Drugs) there is constant political pressure to reverse this decision as politicians and organisations seek popular support by appearing to 'get tough on drugs'. In addition to the maximum sentences prescribed in the MDA 1971 a range of additional sentencing options were incorporated under various Acts – such as the Crime and Disorder Act in 1998 which resulted in the launch of the USA styled Drug Treatment and Testing Orders. The Drugs Act of 2005 – perhaps the most significant Act to follow the MDA 1971 – provided new powers for the police on arrest (rather than on charge), to drug test people suspected to be drug using offenders. This Act provided power to require any person who tests positive for a Class A substance to be assessed by a drugs specialist. If the person arrested is believed to have swallowed an illegal substance to avoid detection the Act gives the police powers to remand the person in police custody for up to 192 hours so that the evidence can be recovered. In addition, if the person arrested refuses without good cause, to consent to an intimate body search, X-ray or ultrasound scan (to detect the presence of drugs) the Act allows the court or jury to draw an adverse inference. The Act also amends the 1998 Crime and Disorder Act by introducing a new civil *Intervention Order* requiring adults whose anti-social behaviour is believed to be drug related to attend drug counselling as part of an Anti-Social Behaviour Order (ASBO). This Act is one of many tough new legislative attempts to tackle drugs in the UK.

In 1998 the appointment of a Drug Tsar (Sir Keith Hellawell) saw the launch of an ambitious ten year drug strategy that identified a range of quantifiable targets for the reduction in drug use and drug harm. Four years later the post of 'Drug Tsar' was phased out, targets amended and the UK drugs strategy updated (Home Office 2002). More recently new ten year strategies have been launched: in England the *Drugs: Protecting Families and Communities* (HM Government 2008), and in Wales *Working Together to Reduce Harm* (Welsh Assembly Government 2008) which is at the time of writing inviting consultation. Differences in approach to drug policy/practice are beginning to emerge in the different countries that comprise the United Kingdom, for example the Welsh strategy focuses upon harm reduction from substance misuse that includes alcohol, whereas the English drug strategy doesn't include legal drugs. Despite various changes to legislation, new police measures, more coercive treatment options and new policy directives the use of illegal drugs remain a pressing problem in the UK:

> The United Kingdom has the highest level of dependent drug use and among the highest levels of recreational drug use in Europe. The drug problem

steadily worsened over the last quarter of the twentieth century: the number of dependent heroin users increased from around 5,000 in 1975 to a current estimated 281,000 in England and over 50,000 in Scotland. Since the turn of the millennium, drug trends have shown signs of stabilisation, albeit at historically high levels

(Reuter and Stevens 2007: 1)

The legal illegal divide

The focus upon controlled drugs encourages a reductionist framework which over-simplifies the complexity of twenty-first century recreational drug taking. It risks promoting a misguiding belief that illegal drug use is fundamentally different to legal drug use. This division reinforces a false distinction between the recreational use of legal substances (such as alcohol, tobacco and caffeine) which are portrayed as safe, respectable, clean and legal. Whereas, those who take illegal substances are referred to as 'addicts' and 'junkies' who use drugs which are portrayed as dirty, shameful, unsafe and criminal. This dominant reductionist conceptualisation of recreational drug use is illustrated in the *Drug Divide*:

Figure 8.1 The drug divide

It is easy in these narrow and potentially misleading terms to think of the drug user as the 'other' – someone not like us, someone who risks taking 'dangerous' controlled substances and poses a threat to family, friends and society. This approach to drug use could have a significant and detrimental impact upon agency and inter-agency policy and practice with illegal drug users.

Hard as it may seem to appreciate, we all take drugs and we are all drug users. Historic records indicate that drugs have been taken for thousands of years, for example, the Book of Genesis chapter 9 v. 21 written over 3000 years ago records that Noah was badly intoxicated on alcohol. We may find it easier to acknowledge our regular use of drugs for medicinal purposes (such as antibiotics, painkillers and indigestion tablets) – but most of us actually take drugs regularly for pleasure simply because like illegal drug users we enjoy the impact drugs have on us. However, we find it hard to see ourselves as 'drug users' as it carries negative and stigmatised connotations normally ascribed to the 'other'.

Throughout the day the stimulant drug caffeine which is found in tea, coffee, soft drinks, chocolate is widely consumed. Regular times of the day are set aside for tea breaks or coffee breaks. Caffeine is also present in larger quantities in particular drinks such as espresso or Red Bull. These drinks are usually specifically taken for the stimulant 'rush' or 'hit' of alertness or energy. Another popular everyday drug is the depressant drug alcohol which is taken on a regular basis to relax, unwind, 'loosen up' or celebrate an occasion. Some people enjoy a relaxing cigarette, although interestingly this stimulant drug, now less popular among the middle classes, is rapidly attracting public scorn and disapproval not dissimilar to that ascribed to illicit drugs.

The risks posed by drugs

These legal drugs (caffeine, alcohol and tobacco) are seen in society as somehow less problematic, less risky and less dangerous. The people who use legally acceptable drugs (which are to some extent also culturally and commercially promoted drugs) don't tend to see themselves as drug users or 'addicts'. This is not surprising because these drugs are legal, can be bought and used freely (albeit with some restrictions), and possession or supply doesn't risk serious criminal sanctions. Being legal helps to prevent a number of additional risks which arise when drugs are made illegal and driven underground, for example someone using a drug that has been made illegal:

1   Has no idea of the strength of the drug – it could be so strong it could result in risk of overdose or death.
2   Has no guarantee about the purity or indeed content of the drug – it could be contaminated or even mixed with toxic ingredients that could cause serious harm even death.
3   Has to buy the drug 'underground' – exposing the person to the vagaries of a potentially dangerous criminal underworld.
4   Buying, using and sharing illegal drugs puts the person at risk of serious criminal sanctions such as a community sentence with a drug rehabilitation requirement or even imprisonment.
5   A person using an illegal drug risks acquiring a criminal record for a drugs offence – which could have lifelong consequences upon employment prospects, opportunities for world travel and housing.
6   Has to use the drug in secret. For some people this may mean using in an isolated location which could be potentially dangerous especially when intoxicated – such as a condemned building, under a railway bridge, a canal etc.
7   Has to hide the use of illegal drugs making it more difficult to manage and harder to seek help, support or advice if a problem arises.

Ironically, criminalisation of drugs can cause greater risks than those posed by the drugs themselves. However, despite the additional safety benefits afforded by the legal status given to tobacco and alcohol, the risks posed by these legal substances suggest they must be regarded as potentially dangerous and life threatening drugs. The health related problems caused by tobacco use cost the NHS around £1.7 billion every year (Healthcare Commission 2007). In the UK tobacco kills around 120,000 people every year (DoH 2003a). Alcohol is a toxic drug that can damage the major organs of the body (Rehm et al 2004). In 2006, alcohol killed 8,758 people in the UK – a number that has been rising steadily since 1991 when there were just over 4,000 alcohol deaths (National Statistics 2008). In terms of crime 44 percent of all violent offences are carried out by an offender who was under the influence of alcohol (Home Office 2006).

The received wisdom that controlled drugs are dangerous but that alcohol and tobacco are somehow in a different category and are not *really* drugs is ill-informed. The separation and distinctions made between legal and illegal drugs are false (although as already highlighted illegality does in itself create an additional range of negative consequences). The bifurcation process that separates legal drugs as somehow safe and respectable, and presents illegal drugs as inherently threatening, dangerous and toxic is confusing, contradictory and misleading.

A scientifically based league table of the harms was published by a government advisory committee (House of Commons Science and Technology Select Committee 2006) that reviewed drug legislation and was later published in *The Lancet* (Nutt et al, 2007) looked at the harms posed by 20 of the most widely used legal and illegal drugs (see Figure 8.2). The assessment of harm was based upon advice from a group of independent experts including psychiatrists, chemists and drug specialists working in the drugs field. They gave ratings for physical harm, psychological harm, and social harm – the higher the overall score the greater the risk of harm. This somewhat simplified league table of harm which also indicates whether the drug has been classified A, B or C (Figure 8.2) indicates clearly that it would be wrong to assume that legal drugs carry fewer risks than their illegal counterparts, and wrong to imagine that the classification of drugs provides a good indication of the degree of risk posed.

The drug on the far left of the table in first place (heroin) was assessed as posing greatest risk whereas the drug on the right of the table (khat) that came twentieth on the list posed the least risk of harm. Interestingly, alcohol appears fifth in the league table of harm and tobacco ninth – this is some way ahead of a number of Class A drugs, ecstasy for example which is eighteenth in the table. There are also contradictions between drug classifications in that two Class B drugs (barbiturates and benzodiazepines) appear in the top half of the table whereas three Class A drugs appear in the bottom half of the table. Given these discrepancies and the risks and dangers posed by legal and illegal drugs the tendency to bifurcate drugs into a *Drug Divide* (Figure 8.1) should be replaced by the *Continuum of Risk* (Figure 8.3) which recognizes that virtually everyone is a drug user and that all drugs (legal and illegal) carry some degree of risk.

The level of risk posed by a particular drug cannot be so easily assessed by examining the graph in Figure 8.2; the risks will vary from person to person. While

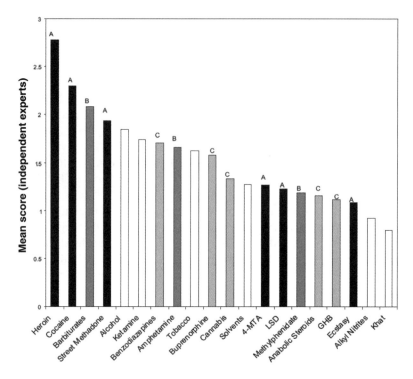

Figure 8.2 Risk of harm
Source: House of Commons Science and Technology Committee (2006: Ev. 114).

each drug has unique characteristics and risks, the overall risk of harm cannot simply be dependent upon the nature of the particular drug. The risks posed will also depend upon a wide range of other factors such as: the frequency of use; the method of administration; the strength of the drug; the financial means of the user; when, why, where and how the drug is used – so while one person's use of cannabis may pose minimal risk, another person's use of cannabis may pose high risk. All drug taking presents a degree of risk and some legal drugs will pose greater risk than some illegal drugs. It is argued then that rather than consider legal drugs as safer and illegal drugs more harmful, and rather than assess drugs according to a hierarchical table of risk posed by different drugs, there is a need for a comprehensive individual assessments to be made for each person according to the nature and context of the drug taking and this is best placed upon a broad continuum of risk (see Figure 8.3) which is applicable for all.

Recreational drug use and perceived problems

When working with drug users it should be remembered then that virtually everyone uses drugs, and all drug taking presents some risk. Illegality as indicated earlier increases risk significantly. The motivations for using illegal drugs are largely the same

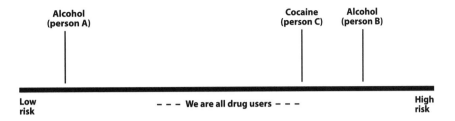

Figure 8.3 The continuum of risk

as the motivation for using legal drugs – a pleasurable habit, to be social, to relax and generally enjoy the effect of the drug. However, a small proportion of people who use drugs (legal and illegal substances) develop serious drug problems (UNODC 2007). The vast majority of drug users are recreational users who use drugs in a controlled manner without incurring significant social, psychological and/or physical problems to themselves or others around them. In contrast the minority who develop problems sometimes referred to as 'problem drug users' become socially, psychologically and/or physically dependent and this lack of control tends to have a detrimental impact upon their social, psychological and/or physical well being, and is likely to have a negative impact upon those around them.

The recreational drug of choice for those over 35-year-old is highly likely to be caffeine, alcohol or possibly tobacco, whereas given the widespread use of illicit drugs the preferred recreational drug of choice for those under 25-years-old could be an illicit drug. Table 8.1 extracted from the findings of the 2002/03 British Crime Survey illustrates how only one in fifty 35–59 year-olds had used an illicit drug in the past month compared to around one in six of 16–24 year-olds (Condon and Smith 2003).

Table 8.1 Illicit drug use by age

Percentage used an illicit drug:	16–24-year-olds	25–34-year-olds	35–59-year-olds
Last year	28%	17%	5%
Last month	18%	11%	2%

It would be foolish to conclude from the British Crime Survey figures in Table 8.1 that one in six young adults who have used an illicit drug in the past month have a drug problem. Taking illicit drugs does not inevitably lead to the development of an illicit drug problem; in the same way that taking alcohol does not necessarily lead to an alcohol problem. A survey involving over 10,000 secondary schools in the UK found that almost one in four 15-year-olds had taken an illegal substance in the past month, and over one in three in the past year (NatCen 2003). Clearly there is a considerable amount of experimental or recreational use of illicit drugs among the younger sections of society. While to some degree the way they use drugs may present low risk, there is a conundrum in that anyone who uses any illegal drug faces considerable wider consequences largely caused by criminalization as listed above (p. 114).

The differing experiences and exposure to illicit drugs between young adults and the older population could result in a generation gap that might make it difficult for middle aged sections of society (often in positions of power and authority) to appreciate the changing attitudes and patterns of behaviour in respect of drugs of choice. In addition, conflicting information and misinformation regarding the perceived risks and dangers of illegal drugs only adds to the levels of ignorance. The *gateway theory* suggests that people who start using 'soft' illicit drugs on a recreational basis such as cannabis inevitably progress to hard drugs (such as heroin or crack cocaine) and become out of control problem drug users (ACMD 2002). Every year a significant proportion of young people admit to using illicit drugs, however, there is little evidence to suggest these young people are likely to move on to lose control and become problem drug users, so the gateway theory seems misguided.

Some commentators (Parker et al. 1998) have suggested that exposure and recreational use of illegal drugs has become a normalized adolescent activity. It is clear that a growing number of people are using illicit drugs with an estimated 1.6 million young people using an illicit drug every year (Condon and Smith 2003). This high prevalence raises practical and ethical issues criminalising large numbers of recreational drug users who are otherwise law abiding citizens. In addition to recreational users who take drugs for pleasure there is growing use of illegal drugs as a form of self-medication in an attempt to alleviate the symptoms of a range of conditions such as anxiety disorders, serious mental health problems, epilepsy and multiple sclerosis (MS). Unlike recreational users, self-medicating illicit drug users cover a wide cross section of ages. Many MS sufferers claim to have found benefits using cannabis (Chong et al. 2006), however, the medical benefits of cannabis have yet to be proven. People who suffer with debilitating diseases and injuries and use illegal drugs such as cannabis for pain relief risk intervention from the law enforcement agencies and ultimately could face imprisonment (see for example Mark Gibson and his wife Lezley who suffers with MS (http://tinyurl.com/yq7wgu) or Patricia Tabram who takes cannabis for pain relief (http://tinyurl.com/5z36d).

Problem drug use

Clearly not all people who use illicit drugs are 'otherwise law abiding', a minority of illicit drug users develop drug problems and get involved in other drug related criminal activity. The concern that drug users were responsible for a considerable amount of crime in 2003 resulted in a robust and well funded UK government Drugs Interventions Programme (DIP) which introduced coercive measures to get 'drug using offenders out of crime and into treatment'. There is clearly some connection between drug use and crime, however, for most recreational drug users there is no direct causal link between drug taking and crime, and no suggestion they are committing crime to pay for their drugs, some may commit crime but the two acts are not necessarily linked (UKDPC 2008). The drugs–crime relationship is not as straightforward as is sometimes presented. Alex Stevens (2007) casts doubt on the apparent causal relationship between crime and drugs which he says is overexaggerated in scale and precision, he argues there are wider political issues involved to better understand the drugs/crime connection. Buchanan and Young (2000a) suggest that any analysis must incorporate an appreciation of the co-existing factors of crime, drug taking and social and economic deprivation. What is clear is that a distinction needs to be made between the recreational drug user and the problem drug user, and most concern and support needs to be directed towards the latter. Despite this, UK drug policy continues to focus more broadly on all illegal drugs and all illegal drug users, and attempts continue to be made to progress the criminalisation of drug policy as a recent speech by the Drugs Minister illustrates:

> We all face significant challenges in dealing with illegal drugs and drug related crime. This Government is in no doubt that tackling drug misuse is a key priority. The costs to society are enormous. Not only because of the huge impact of drug-related crime ... but also because of the damage drugs do to the health of individuals and the way they undermine society and family life.

> (Coaker 2008: 1)

While coercive treatment attached to court orders requiring regular drug testing and monitoring may be seen by some as an appropriate measure for problem drug use (although the jury is still out), arguably it is neither justified nor appropriate for the vast majority who use illicit drugs in a recreational manner. The distinction between the recreational drug user and the problem drug user is an important one as it focuses upon the pattern and manner of drug use rather than making assumptions simply based upon the particular drug or drugs used. Policy and practice which fails to distinguish the risks posed by different drugs and sees all illegal drugs as an inherent danger to society will lose the credibility, respect and confidence from drug users seeking help who are likely to be disappointed by the levels of ignorance.

It is the problem drug user that is most likely to come to the attention of the health visitor, the midwife, the nurse, the social worker, probation worker or volunteer, most recreational drug users are quite able to keep their use of drug use hidden and under control. Problematic drug users have lost control of their drug habit and often present difficulties and challenges. Much has been made of the link between drug use and crime. Crime might be one of many symptoms of problematic drug use, but more important causal connections can be made between social exclusion and problem drug use (Buchanan and Young 2000b, Buchanan 2004). What is significant is that a high proportion of problem drug users endure serious difficulties and problems *before* they even begin taking drugs. In her editorial for a special edition of *Drugs: Education Prevention and Policy Journal* which examined the drugs crime nexus Susanne MacGregor felt that 'throbbing throughout [the article was] the underlying theme of the impact of deindustrialisation and the rise of the consumer market society which has created a class of losers and discarded youth who continue to provide new recruits to the ranks of problematic drug misusers' (2000: 315). It could be argued that for many problem drug users illicit drug use is not the major difficulty they faced in life. Perversely, a drug dominated lifestyle can be to some extent a solution that, besides all the risks, stresses and problems it brings – is able to offer the person activity, routine, purpose, structure, belonging, graft, excitement and rewards. These are aspects of everyday life that many problem drug users would otherwise struggle to legitimately find in society given their limited resources. This is illustrated in the seven days a week 52 weeks of the year daily cycle which illustrates just how busy and demanding each day can be for a problem drug user:

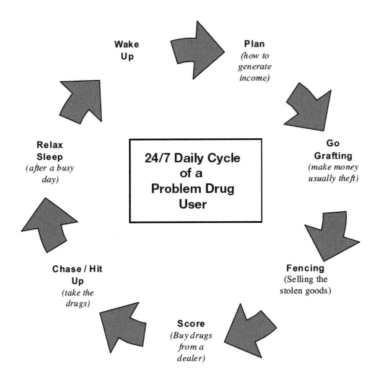

Figure 8.4 The 24/7 daily cycle
Source: Buchanan (2006: 56).

These aspects of daily life have otherwise largely been denied to the majority of problem drug users (even before they started taking drugs), many of whom have had unsettled or abused childhoods, were in care, excluded from school, developed learning difficulties, struggled to achieve qualifications, have limited or no employment experience, live in poor housing, etc. Not surprisingly given this background disadvantaged problem drug users often lack the personal resources and social capital to engage with the demands and responsibilities of independent adult life. Opportunities for them to 'make a living' and access the consumer benefits (paraded widely through multi-media advertising) are extremely limited at best. The highly competitive capitalist environment has increasingly less need for the unqualified, unskilled/semi-skilled manual worker, and what work is available is often low paid with uncertain hours and an uncertain future. After decades of unstable, unsatisfactory and uncertain employment opportunities alternative illegal (and sometime lucrative) economies have developed within many deprived communities – managing and running a complex illicit drugs business being particular popular. For some of the *'class of losers and discarded youth'* this entrepreneurial pathway may seem worth considering given the lack of credible and legitimate alternatives available.

The complex nature of problem drug use

Dominant thinking in relation to problem drug use emphasizes the physical/health related aspects of problem drug use, the legal aspects in terms of criminal activity and the trouble caused to communities and the psychological cravings and need to get 'another fix'. However, it is important to appreciate the often overlooked social context of problem drug use. Efforts to help the person become drug free sometimes fail to address the deep seated underlying social and personal needs and the considerable difficulties overcoming discrimination. Unless the social aspects of problem drug use are tackled relapse will be almost inevitable. There are then, four components to problem drug use:

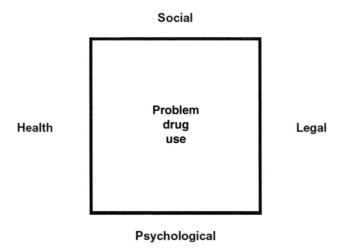

Figure 8.5 Understanding problem drug use
Source: Buchanan (2004: 391).

It is not easy for agencies and individuals to work together because the nature and cause of problem drug use is contested, as is the most effective treatment and policy response. This poses difficulties for multi-agency partnership work, yet working together is essential if a person is going to receive the broad range of help they need. Few would dispute that the four aspects of problem drug use (health, social, legal and psychological) are all key components that help understand the multi-faceted nature of the problem. What is disputed is the importance and emphasis that should be given to each of these different aspects. To illustrate this each component will be explored separately, although the different components do not reflect the particular philosophy of any particular agency's work. Rather it is intended to illustrate the different ways of seeing and interpreting 'the drug problem' use and how this can lead to different responses:

Seeing problem drug use as a health issue

This approach focuses upon the health and well being of the person and reducing the risks they pose to the health and well being of others. Some may regard problem drug use as a physical addiction, a biological dependence or even a genetically determined outcome. The problem drug user might be seen as someone who has a disease or illness who needs treatment so they can be cured (this is sometimes referred to as the medical model). Within this approach some hold the view that the only way an 'addict' can receive help is for them to become totally drug free, and unless they become drug free they have little or no capacity to think logically and clearly about their future, therefore, ongoing continued drug use (controlled or maintained) cannot be tolerated. This approach is embraced in abstentionists' models to drugs who seek to get the drug user drug free and clean – for example the 12 step model Alcoholics Anonymous AA and Narcotics Anonymous NA.

The focus of intervention is often upon health education and the reduction of infections and contagious diseases (such as HIV and Hepatitis A, B and C). This may be achieved by literature and health promotional material concerning the risks of drugs, but it could also pragmatically involve the provision of clean legal substitute drugs (such as methadone), the provision of needles or indeed showing drug users how to inject more safely. This pragmatic approach which tolerates and supports the drug user during ongoing drug use in order to reduce risks and harm to themselves or others is widely referred to as 'harm reduction' (see the UK Harm Reduction Alliance website at: www.ukhra.org).

Those who adopt an abstentionist approach to drug problems sometimes find they have philosophical and practice difficulties working with people who take a harm reduction approach (and vice versa). Attitudes towards needle exchange schemes and methadone maintenance prescribing often highlight the philosophical differences between harm reduction and abstinence approaches.

Seeing problem drug use as a social issue

The social aspect of problem drug use sees drug taking as one of many choices or risks that are taken by young people today, all part of the risk society they occupy. Some might regard illicit drug use as a normal recreational activity whereas others may see it as deviant behaviour belonging to a subcultural group. Either way drug taking is seen as a social phenomenon, a choice influenced by factors such as: advertising; perceptions of pleasure; availability; choice; peer pressure; boredom; hedonism; and social networks. Drug taking is seen largely as a rational social action rather than a biological drive, psychological need or illness.

Those who take drugs but go on to develop drug problems tend to be those with limited social skills, education, qualifications and social capital. For this group the all-consuming drug centred life can become their central focus of life. Problem drug use is seen as an escape or response to marginalisation, poverty and disadvantage. Furthermore, some would argue the drug problem has been exacerbated by an ill informed drug policy which promotes the 'war on drug users' and creates a criminal underground. Those adopting this critical approach – more often voluntary and user groups such as Transform (see the Transform Drug Policy Foundation at: www.tdp-f.org.uk) rather than statutory agencies – may emphasise the importance of down grading or decriminalizing drugs. They highlight the importance of human rights and tackling the discrimination which has hindered recovery and made it difficult for recovering drug users to gain equal access to education, housing, employment and local amenities. What is important in the social perspective is to give recovering drug users something to do, somewhere to live and help them to reintegrate and feel accepted and valued.

Seeing problem drug use as a legal issue

An enforcement approach sees all illicit drug use as a major criminal problem that is damaging and undermining society, and the main focus is upon protecting society. Possession and/or supply of any illegal drug are serious criminal offences that should carry the risk of imprisonment. Illegal drug use is seen as the cause of considerable drug related crime in terms of the sale and distribution of drugs, the management and security of the drugs industry and in terms of acquisitive crime committed to generate sufficient finances to fund an expensive drug habit. The considerable investment from the government funded Drugs Interventions Programme has locked the criminal justice system and treatment agencies together in an attempt to require problem drug users to move out of crime and into treatment. This carrot and stick approach means that problem drug users caught up in the criminal justice system will be coerced into carefully supervised 'treatment' which is monitored by court orders with conditions of drug testing and regular court reviews. Failure to respond to treatment could result in further court sanctions including imprisonment.

The legal approach is primarily concerned to eradicate illegal drug use from society, protect the community from drug users and drug dealers and get people off drugs (abstinence). The emphasis upon regular monitoring and drug testing encourages the focus upon the physical aspects of problematic drug use rather than appreciating the lifestyle or social context. A positive drug test is only able to indicate whether drugs have been taken (not how, when, where, why or the frequency).

Seeing problem drug use as a psychological issue

Psychological approaches to problem drug use emphasise the habitual nature of drug taking as a pattern of learnt behaviour in which the person's thinking, expectations, and behaviours are affected. The business of drug taking becomes a ritualized pattern of behaviour which is repeated so frequently in certain times, places and circumstances that the person can easily be psychologically 'triggered' to crave and use drugs. Once triggered perhaps by the sight of silver foil, perhaps by seeing a ten pound note, or being with certain people – craving 'kicks in'. The problem drug user then feels they have 'no choice' but to get drugs. Patterns of habitual behaviour can trigger relapse long after the person has been drug free.

Two dominant and useful psychological approaches in the drugs field have been motivational interviewing (Miller and Rollnick 2002) and the cycle of change (Prochaska et al. 1994). These approaches emphasise the need for the client/patient to exercise choice, regain control, to decide what they want to do and these approaches recognize the different stages of a drug habit to enable workers to more appropriately engage, understand and empower problem drug users to regain control of their thinking and behaviour.

Partnership and practice

All four aspects (physical, social, legal and psychological) have an important contribution in understanding the complex nature and context of problem drug use. However, particular agencies and individuals will tend to promote one aspect at the expense of another depending upon their philosophical viewpoint and understanding of problem drug use. This is explored further in the following case study:

Box 8.1 Case study: Peter

Peter is 25 years old and has a long standing drugs problem mainly injecting heroin. He's been using drugs regularly since he was 16 years old. He doesn't blame anyone but himself. However, his social history reveals that he had little or no contact with his father who left home when Peter was a toddler. Peter was born and brought up in deprived inner city area where housing stock was largely owned by the council. Shops and amenities were poor, educational achievement low and unemployment high. The area had a reputation for crime, violence and anti-social behaviour. Peter lived there with his mother (who suffered with depression) and his two older sisters until he was 19.

At primary/junior school Peter had no particular problems and recalls getting looked after by his older sisters. He started struggling academically aged 12 at the local secondary school and says he 'fell into a bad crowd'. Life at home was also difficult at that time because his mother met her second husband who would often be drunk and abusive towards Peter. Due to the difficulties at home, his poor school attendance and difficult behaviour he was taken into care and 'looked after' by the local social services department. He lived for 18 months in a residential home. He returned home aged 14 but felt that life at home was just as bad as before – he didn't get on with his step-dad and both sisters had left home.

Unhappy at school, he hardly attended. Instead he used to wander the streets with other lads who were 'bunking' school. They would spend their time drinking alcohol and what Peter described as 'fooling around'. When 15 years old, after a series of shoplifting offences, handling stolen goods and criminal damage he was eventually sent to a young offenders institution (YOI) for 12 months. While there he was assessed by an educational psychologist who said he had dyslexia and she was hardly surprised he didn't feel he fitted into school. Also while at YOI he was introduced to 'hard' drugs although he admits that he had previously used tobacco and cannabis but didn't particularly like either.

Upon his return home with no qualifications and little education Peter tried to find a job. After 12 months of temporary short term labouring jobs which Peter describes as 'moronic' he drifted back into alcohol binge drinking and started using heroin. Within 9 months his pattern of life had changed rapidly and he was soon busy everyday 'grafting' to generate income to feed his drug habit. His crimes eventually caught up with him and he was sentenced to 18 months imprisonment. Released aged 19 he lived for a short while at his mother's home, before leaving when things 'got bad'.

For the past six years Peter has been unemployed (apart from short lived casual labouring jobs), he's lived at various friends' houses and hostels, has been using heroin along with whatever drugs he could find, he's overdosed and been in hospital twice and done a further prison sentence. He is up in court again this time for attempted burglary of a local warehouse and has presented himself at the local drug partnership wanting help. Following assessment the different agencies involved in the partnership take a different view of his problem and offer different solutions.

While there should be no stereotype ascribed to any particular agency or worker the following responses to Peter's situation illustrate the different ways problem drug use can be interpreted and how a wide range of different treatment options may be proposed:

1   *The criminal justice worker* sees the crime committed by Peter and the risk to the community as the main priority to tackle. She wants Peter to be placed on a Community Order with a Drug Rehabilitation Requirement so that Peter can begin a supervised detox to become drug free over a four week period. To ensure this happens she wants Peter to be regularly tested and monitored for all illicit drugs. She says he's a high risk to society and argues it's time Peter accepted responsibility for his actions. Failure to cooperate would result in Peter being brought back before the court.

2   *The health worker* is uneasy with the coercive nature of this proposal and fears that Peter is being 'set up to fail' by forcing him to change when he might not be ready or able to change. As an alternative the health worker proposes Peter should be offered a daily supervised oral methadone reduction programme with a view to him becoming drug free within six months.

This would prevent 'leakage' of the methadone into the wider community and through regular contact would enable health staff to inform Peter of the health risks of drug addiction.

3 *The social worker* with a degree in psychology believes that it'll probably take Peter years to break the pattern of learnt behaviour and that the main focus of work should be developing his self esteem and cognitive behavioural insights of his egocentric drug dominated lifestyle. He agrees that Peter should become drug free but unless Peter is given intensive therapy he'll soon relapse and be back on drugs. He argues for immediate hospital detoxification followed by 12 months at a Therapeutic Residential Community for recovering drug addicts so that Peter can get help to rebuild his identity and learn to live and relate to others.

4 *The drug counsellor* (also an ex-user) argues that Peter needs time, space, support and help. She argues that he has 'loads of problems' and that drugs are just one of them. She argues that Peter is heavily dependent upon the drugs, the drug lifestyle and the needle habit. She thinks he should be offered injectable methadone ampoules and that the dosage must be high enough so that he doesn't crave heroin. She argues that he should not be 'weaned' off the drug but kept stable on the same dosage until he says he is ready and able to start reducing his intake. During this period of maintained substitute prescribing the drug counsellor says it will be important for all agencies to work together to help Peter occupy his time, understand more about the nature of problem drug use, how it affects him and others, improve his health and begin to rebuild his life.

The four different responses illustrate some of the barriers and difficulties that agencies and individuals face when trying to work collaboratively to assist people with drug problems. Despite these challenges the need for good collaboration and the provision of a broad range of services able to address the medical, social, psychological and legal aspects of drug dependency are crucial for any successful intervention. In England different agencies come together in partnership for Drug and Alcohol Action Teams (DAAT) or Drug Action Teams (DAT) whereas in Wales they are Substance Misuse Action Teams (SMAT). These partnerships may include representatives from the health authority, the council, police, probation, social services, education and youth services as well as the voluntary sector. The partnerships are responsible for delivering the national drug strategy at a local level and are expected to work closely with the Crime and Disorder Reduction Partnerships (CDRPs) or Community Safety Partnerships (CSP).

The challenge that faces these partnerships is to establish a genuine partnership that goes beyond a public relations exercise and actually makes a difference in the community. Good partnerships will also include a number of different user representations (who should be remunerated for their attendance and participation) so that the voice and perspective of the different drug user groups are properly 'heard'. The partner agencies need to work together towards an agreed shared philosophy to respond to local need and local context to tackle problematic drug use. Although agencies may have a different focus and possibly a different language to describe the client/patient/service user, they each need to acknowledge and respect the contribution of the other partner agencies. Effective multi-agency partnership should make accessing and coordinating services easier, avoid duplication, help identify gaps in service and disseminate best practice. This is no easy task. Recent research in respect of piloted Dedicated Drugs Courts (DDCs) where different agencies have been brought together to tackle drug related crime recognized the difficulties of partnership work:

> The criminal justice and drug treatment systems have a set of goals (rehabilitation, punishment, protection of the public and so on) that can, at worst, be in direct conflict with each other. The DDC model provides a framework for agencies to find a common path through these agendas, even if it is a complicated one requiring constant negotiation
>
> (Matrix Knowledge Group 2008: vii)

Good partnerships will need good channels for open and honest communication to clarify philosophy, policy and practice and when necessary allowing scope for negotiation and re-negotiation. Clearly this can be a time consuming task and one that gets easier once good relationships and trust have been established, but good partnerships will often take years to grow and mature and this requires some stability of personnel and agencies – if it is to happen.

One example is the DAWN partnership, which was established in 2000. DAWN is an umbrella organization that brings a wide range of agencies together (CAIS Ltd, NACRO, The Duke of Edinburgh's Award, The Prince's Trust, SOVA, Shelter, Working Links, Altcourse Prison, North Wales Probation Service and North Wales Local Health Boards across North Wales and beyond) to develop 'joined-up' services that are supported by shared satellite venues from existing partnership facilities. The partnership unites agencies who embrace a shared vision to tackle social exclusion by providing an accessible, rapid and seamless service that bridges the gap from exclusion to mainstream further education, training and employment for hard to reach client groups (Senior et al. 2007). By being in partnership agencies not only become more familiar with services available from other agencies but agencies can more easily refer so that a client/patient from one agency gains easy access to a wide range of agencies. The DAWN partnership seeks to function as a federal structure with a shared vision to provide a 'one stop shop' that offers clients a seamless service. Together the partnership is able to provide: help with social problems; help to move towards qualifications and employability; assistance in dealing with addiction; help to reduce offending behaviour; welfare advice and information; social support and mentoring; social skills, confidence building and self-esteem; counselling and group work activities; individual packages of care and help towards positive lifestyle changes.

Conclusion

A partnership approach to problem drug use is not easy because illegal drugs use is a highly contested area: what do we mean by drugs? What constitutes a drug? Why do people take drugs? Is taking drugs normal? What are the risks and dangers posed by different drugs? How do we make sense of legal drugs? Why do some people develop drug problems? How do we understand addiction? Is harm reduction the way forward? Should we force people to have treatment? What treatment works? These are just some of the issues that have been highlighted in this chapter that need 'thinking through' in order to engage more effectively and appropriately with people who have developed problems with drugs and indeed with other agencies and individuals. The confusion and uncertainty is hardly surprising given the general levels of ignorance surrounding legal and illegal drugs and exacerbated by the politicization of the issue. Despite these challenges there are many examples of good practice throughout the UK where agencies and individuals work collaboratively together to help assist people who have unfortunately developed a drug problem.

Questions for further discussion

1   Should we see legal drug problems differently to illegal drug problems? Why?
2   To what extent do you think problem drug use is a social, legal, medical or psychological matter?
3   In the case study above why do you think Peter took drugs in the first instance, and why do you think he takes them now?
4   What approach and intervention do you think might help Peter?

Useful websites

- *DrugScope*: www.drugscope.org.uk/ is a leading independent centre of expertise on drugs. The site provides authoritative drug information to reduce drug related risk and encourage a more informed appreciation of drug related issues.
- *Black Poppy*: www.blackpoppy.org.uk/ is a nonprofit making, user run organization that creates and produces the drug user's health and lifestyle magazine, *Black Poppy*. The website contains some of the key articles from the magazine as well as additional news, health and lifestyle information.
- *Wired*: www.wiredinitiative.com/ is best known for the development of its excellent electronic news portal Daily Dose, as well as the magazine *Drink and Drugs News*. The web site also contains personal stories, project profiles, community-based research, film and music engagement projects.
- *SMMGP (Substance Misuse Management in General Practice)*: www.smmgp.org.uk/ is a developing network to support GPs and other members of the primary healthcare team who work with substance misuse in the UK.

9 Addressing homelessness through effective partnership working

Emma Wincup

This chapter will:

- Explore the nature and extent of homelessness in England and the current policy context.
- Examine the key issues and difficulties facing professionals and volunteers working with homeless people.
- Identify best practice.
- Consider the issues surrounding effective partnership working.

This chapter considers the housing and related needs of homeless people in England and explores the challenges faced by those who work with this group. Its focus is on England, although the legislation referred to in the chapter is also applicable to Wales. Within one short chapter it is not possible to analyse homelessness across the UK or to examine the issue in an international comparative way. However, the basic argument advanced in this chapter – that a partnership approach is essential to meet the housing and related needs of homeless people – is applicable to policy and practice in other countries.

There is no universal definition of homelessness (see Lund 2006 for a discussion of the contested nature of the term). For many members of the public, homelessness is equated with rooflessness or rough sleeping, arguably the most visible face of homelessness. In contrast, charities campaigning to eradicate homelessness adopt a more inclusive definition that takes account of a wider range of unacceptable housing circumstances including temporary accommodation (for example, living in a hostel or a bed and breakfast); accommodation which is permanent but inadequate (for example, without basic facilities such as hot water or heating); or accommodation that could be considered inappropriate (for example, living with a violent partner). Following Hutson and Liddiard (1994), a useful approach is to consider homelessness as a continuum of housing need ranging from those situations which almost everyone would describe as homelessness (for example, rough sleeping) through to more contentious circumstances that only some commentators would describe as homeless (for example, staying temporarily with family or friends). This chapter will note that many of those identified by academics or homelessness charities as homeless do not fit the category of 'statutory homelessness' used by local authorities to determine who is entitled to access their stock of temporary and permanent accommodation. To be defined as statutory homeless, individuals need to demonstrate that they are legally homeless (i.e. because there is no accommodation that they are entitled to occupy or they have accommodation but it is not reasonable for them to continue to occupy this accommodation) and they must fall into one of the 'priority need' categories (listed in Box 9.1). They must also demonstrate that they have a local connection with the area in which they wish to be accommodated and have not made themselves intentionally homeless. Those who do not meet the criteria for inclusion as 'statutory homeless' do not qualify for housing assistance from local authorities and instead must look to the private or voluntary sector for help. These sectors do not offer accommodation to all and also specify criteria which homeless people must meet. The implications of these exclusionary criteria for homeless people are discussed later in this chapter.

It is not possible to provide a clear figure on the number of homeless people living in England. Local authorities have responsibility for collecting data on homelessness but focus predominantly on those accepted as statutory homeless. In addition since 1998, they have provided estimates of the number of rough sleepers. Rough sleepers can be defined by as people who sleep in the open air (such as on the streets or in doorways, parks or bus shelters) or in buildings or other places not designed for habitation (such as barns, sheds, car parks, cars, derelict boats, stations or 'bashes'[1]). In June 2007, it was estimated that there was 498 rough sleepers in England and approximately half of these were concentrated in London (Communities and Local Government 2007a). Estimates of the number of rough sleepers are a source of political controversy and the government has been accused of manipulating the numbers to downplay the scale of the problem (see Wyner 2005; Lund 2006). At the very least, charities working with homeless people suggest that they underestimate the scale of the problem. For example, Crisis (2006), a charity which works with and for homeless people, holds an Open Christmas event for homeless people each year. In 2005, 547 people who attended the event stated they were sleeping rough, which raises serious doubts about the accuracy of government figures suggesting less than 500 people sleep rough in England.

This debate aside, as others have noted (Watson and Austerberry 1986; Hutson and Liddiard 1994) when homelessness is equated with rooflessness the scale of the problem can appear relatively small. Adopting a broader definition and examining statistics on statutory homelessness reveals that the problem is significantly larger. For the period June to September 2007, almost 83,000 households in England were in temporary accommodation including bed and breakfast accommodation, hostels, women's refuges and self-contained accommodation owned by the local authority or registered social landlords or leased to them (Communities and Local Government 2007b). Between October 2006 and September 2007 data published by Communities and Local Government recorded that approximately 67,000 households were accepted as homeless (Communities and Local Government 2006, 2007b, c, d.). The majority of acceptance relate to families: since 1997 the percentage of acceptances who were households that included dependent children or an expectant mother has ranged between 60 and 70 per cent (Communities and Local Government 2007c). Consequently, it is difficult to estimate the number of single homeless people. Crisis estimates that there are around 380,000 single homeless people in Britain (Crisis 2006) and it is important to note that very few of these people will be included in local authority statistics.

Recent policy developments

Lack of space precludes a detailed analysis of the evolution of policies to tackle homelessness (see Lund 2006 for a recent overview). Instead here we will consider, albeit briefly, policy developments over the past decade which have emphasized the importance of partnership working.

When New Labour came to power in 1997 one of its key policy agendas was tackling social exclusion. The government established a Social Exclusion Unit in 1998, now reconstituted as a Social Exclusion Task Force, premised on the belief that a cross-departmental approach is essential to help those most in need. Shortly after the inception of the Social Exclusion Unit it published *Rough Sleeping* (SEU 1998). One of its recommendations was the established of a Rough Sleepers Unit. Established in 1999 under the direction of the 'Homelessness Tsar' Louise Casey, it produced a strategy on rough sleeping (Rough Sleepers Unit 1999) with the ambitious target of reducing the number of people sleeping rough by at least two-thirds by 2002. The strategy promised to offer 'a radical new approach to helping vulnerable rough sleepers off the streets, rebuilding the lives of former rough sleepers and preventing new rough sleepers of tomorrow' (Rough Sleepers Unit 2000: 4), It advocated a 'constructive partnership approach' (Rough Sleepers Unit 1999: 4) because it recognized 'the complexity of need'; (p. 5) and the fragmented nature of service provision. One proposal for change focused on supporting rough sleepers most in need such as those with mental health problems and problem drug and alcohol users.

In 2001 a Homelessness Directorate (since 2004, a Homelessness and Housing Support Directorate with a wider remit) was established in the Office of the Deputy Prime Minister (now Communities and Local Government). The Bed and Breakfast Unit, established in 2001 to reverse the growing number of homeless households placed in such accommodation, and the Rough Sleepers Unit were absorbed into this directorate shortly afterwards. A key aspect of the work of the directorate was to implement the Homelessness Act 2002. For Lund (2006), the Act is an example of New Labour's rights/obligations agenda in that it combined a more liberal approach to helping homeless people with 'behavioural conditions' to the rules governing the allocation of social housing. Consequently, as we will discuss later in this chapter, for some of the most needy homeless people, it removed certain barriers to accessing accommodation but erected others. The Act required each local authority housing department, in conjunction with social services, other statutory agencies and voluntary organisations, to review its homelessness problem and develop a local strategy for tackling homelessness.

In 2003, the directorate launched its plans for tackling homelessness. The title of the report – *More than a Roof* – reflected its understanding that 'simply putting a roof over someone's head does not always solve his or her homelessness' (ODPM 2003: 2). It emphasized the importance of 'joined-up' working at government level and at local authority level and the need for effective partnerships. Two years later, a strategy to tackle homelessness was published entitled *'Sustainable Communities: Settled Homes; Changing Lives'* (ODPM 2005). This aims to halve the number of households in temporary local authority accommodation by 2010 through a twin-track approach of preventing homelessness and increasing access to settled homes. Potentially this target could encourage local authorities to focus their efforts on tackling homelessness among those they need to provide temporary accommodation for to the detriment of other homeless people.

Given the interconnections between homelessness and other aspects of social exclusion, a wide range of government policies could impact upon the lives of homeless people. It is beyond the scope of the chapter to consider them all but one in particular, Supporting People, is worth highlighting. Launched in 2003, Supporting People is a single programme which draws together housing-related support services to help homeless people, among others, to improve or maintain their ability to live independently. Partnership is judged to be 'paramount' (ODPM 2004c: 6) to the programme.

For the remainder of this chapter we will focus on three key issues facing service providers. While they are closely interrelated, for the purposes of this chapter each issue is discussed in turn.

Accommodating housing and related needs

In the first edition of this volume Wyner (2005) emphasized that only a minority of homeless people had needs which were confined to housing and the vast majority had multiple and complex needs. Homelessness Link, a national membership organization for frontline homelessness agencies in England, regularly conducts surveys of its members in order to identify the prevalence of multiple needs. Its members include a wide range of agencies providing services to homeless people ranging from the provision of accommodation through to information and advice: consequently, their experiences are diverse. However, it is possible to identify some commonality within their responses to their latest membership survey (Homeless Link 2006). For instance almost all the agencies (94%) who responded said that they worked with people with multiple needs and on average estimated that approximately three-fifths (58%) of their client group presented with multiple needs.

The needs presented by homeless people may be distinct from the reasons given for why they became homeless in the first place because some needs arise from their experience of homelessness. Carlen (1996) warns that examining the characteristics of homeless people and arguing that these are the causes of their homelessness runs the risk of developing teleological explanations. For service providers questions of cause and effect are less relevant. Instead, they have to tackle what Fountain and Howes (2002: 17) refer to as the 'thorny issue' of prioritizing certain needs over others. Interviewees with service providers also revealed that a further challenge was that clients may have their own preferences about which needs should be addressed first and problems can arise if the priorities of clients are at odds with the priorities of staff. Similarly, Wincup et al. (2003) found that a minority of young homeless problem drug users reported that service providers wanted them to tackle their drug use before they could find stable accommodation while most young homeless problem drug users did not see their drug use as barrier to accessing accommodation and argued that having accommodation was a prerequisite for reducing their drug use. Fountain and Howes (2002) also identified a further dilemma of service providers prioritising certain clients above others.

We have noted above that homeless people typically have needs which extend far beyond their lack of access to appropriate accommodation. There is some consensus in the academic literature that rough sleepers have the most entrenched needs (Crane and Warnes 2001; Fountain and Howes 2002) and these include difficulties related to problem drug and alcohol use and poor mental health. These additional needs can make it even more difficult to access suitable accommodation because they are either excluded from existing provision or it does not meet their needs. This issue is discussed further in the next section of this chapter.

Barriers to accessing housing

Professionals and volunteers seeking to help homeless people to access accommodation often find it difficult to access provision for a range of reasons. First, the availability of social housing is limited and in order to access it individuals must fulfil certain eligibility requirements and not meet others. Second, alternative provision, mostly offered by voluntary sector agencies, is almost always only available to certain categories of homeless people and sometimes they have to be willing to accept conditions attached to their period of residence. Consequently certain groups of homeless people find it particularly difficult to access accommodation. Finally, homeless people face multiple barriers in their attempts to access housing in the private rented sector. Each of these issues is discussed in turn.

As we noted at the beginning of this chapter, for the majority of people who can be regarded as homeless the only support they are entitled to receive from local authorities is advice. To qualify for further support such as the provision of temporary accommodation, they must have nowhere currently to stay, be assessed as in 'priority need' group (see Box 9.1) and have a connection with the local authority area.

Box 9.1   'Priority need' groups

- Pregnant women
- Individuals with dependent children
- Vulnerable individuals (due to age, mental illness, learning or physical disability)

- Individuals who become homeless following an emergency (for example, due to a fire or flood)
- 16 and 17 year olds with the exception of those 'in care'*
- Care leavers aged 18–20*
- Vulnerable individuals due to time spent in care, the armed forces or prison*
- Vulnerable as a result of having to leave home through violence or the threat of violence* (previously only specified domestic violence)

* only since the Homelessness Act 2002.

At the same time, applicants must not fit the criteria of 'intentionally homeless' and be able to meet the behaviour condition specified in the Homelessness Act 2002. Applicants can be treated as ineligible for housing if they (or a member of their household), have been found guilty of 'unacceptable behaviour' serious enough to make them unsuitable as a tenant. Examples could include a history of rent arrears, anti-social behaviour or drug offences. Additionally in order to retain any accommodation provided, homeless people need to ensure that they are 'good' tenants through prompt payment of rent and adhering to any rules or regulations. They also need to take steps to ensure that they do not fall foul of anti-social behaviour legislation which local authorities can now use to take any against 'problem' tenants.

Consequently, few homeless people are entitled to assistance with housing and instead often turn to the voluntary sector for support. As Wyner (2005) outlines, there is a long-established tradition of voluntary sector agencies working with homeless people but also a history of antagonism between the voluntary and statutory sectors. Fuelled in part by housing allocation policies, the voluntary sector perceive the statutory sector to be unsupportive and who fail to fulfil responsibilities while the response of the statutory sector is to remark that voluntary sector organizations fail to understand the limits of their responsibilities and what can be achieved realistically in a climate of scarce resources (see also Roche 2004 for a discussion of how partnership working between the voluntary and statutory sector needs to overcome entrenched working practices and cultures).

The provision offered by the voluntary sector is also governed by the application of inclusionary and exclusionary criteria. Drawing upon but extending Carlen's (1996) typology it is possible to map out the different forms they might take

1. *Definitional exclusions*: some provision is aimed specifically at particular groups of homeless people and thus others are excluded. For example, providers may specify a particular age group, restrict provision to either males or females or only admit homeless people with a particular need, for example, a 'wet' shelter for problem drinkers.
2. *Status exclusions*: some provision is only offered to homeless people of a particular status. For example, providers may restrict entry only to single homeless people rather than couples or families.
3. *Behavioural exclusions*: service providers often exclude a range of homeless people based upon their past or current behaviour. These might include

problem drug or alcohol use, sex offences, violence, arson, nonpayment of rent and behaviours leading to exclusion from the same service or similar services.

4. *Conditional exclusions*: organisations may only be willing to accept homeless people who are willing to accept certain conditions. For example, foyers offer accommodation to young and single homeless people but only if they are already engaged or about to engage in employment, education and training (Foyer 2008). A further example is Emmaus (2008) which offers accommodation to women and men willing to sign off benefits and work in one of their 'communities'.

It would be wrong to give the impression that restricting provision to particular groups of homeless people is in itself problematic. On the contrary, studies have found that reserving provision for particular groups of homeless people can encourage greater take up of services. For example, Wincup et al. (2003) found that young homeless people expressed a strong preference for dedicated young people's services and were reluctant to use mixed age provision. Part of the difficulty is that provision for homeless people has developed in an ad hoc uncoordinated manner and consequently, there is a risk that some homeless people find it impossible to access any form of accommodation because they are repeatedly defined as 'ineligible'. This group is likely to comprise of those with the greatest level of housing and related needs. In order to meet their housing needs, homeless people need to navigate their way through a complex array of bureaucratic procedures. They find themselves subject repeatedly to assessment procedures which require them to fulfil some criteria and not others. They may also find that organizations which can provide support for some of their needs (for example, relating to poor mental health) exclude them because of other needs (for example, relating to problem drug use).

Homeless people often have little choice but to attempt to seek housing from local authorities or voluntary sector agencies because there are multiple barriers to accessing accommodation through the private rented sector. These include financial barriers such as being unable to afford advance payments such as a 'bond', a month's rent in advance and letting agency fees, plus status barriers because they are unemployed or claiming housing benefit. Letting agencies typically vet applicants by requesting personal, employment and financial references or performing 'credit' and 'identity' checks and many homeless people are unable to comply with these requirements. Some groups of homeless people face particular barriers; for example, young people aged under 25 are only entitled to receive housing benefit equivalent to the cost of a 'single room'.

If homeless people are able to find accommodation, often their situation remains precarious. They are usually subject to rules and regulations and sometimes particular conditions which they may find difficult to abide by. Levels of eviction are high among homeless people: Fountain and Howes' (2002) study of rough sleepers found that almost two-fifths had been excluded in the past year while Wincup et al.'s (2003) study of young homeless people revealed that that almost one-quarter (23%) had been excluded from accommodation in the year prior to being interviewed.

Dilemmas over the most appropriate form of service provision

Earlier in this chapter we noted that Homeless Link's (2006) survey of agencies working with homeless people found a high level of prevalence of multiple need. The survey also explored agencies' responses to these needs. A common response to accommodate these needs was to form partnerships with different agencies who could offer specialist support. Most commonly (84% of agencies) this involved working with a statutory agency, typically to provide primary health care and mental health services. Additionally, approximately three-fifths (59%) of agencies had established a partnership with a voluntary sector agency; for example, to offer treatment for problem drug and/or alcohol users. Homeless agencies offered these services 'in-house' to provide easy access for their clients of homelessness services. In other words, partners offered 'outreach' services, taking them to potential clients rather than expecting them to access their services in the usual manner.

Agencies reported that using specialist support services allowed their own staff to concentrate on more generic issues such as providing 'advice around resettlement, move-on, benefits, finances, debt and life skills training' (Homeless Link 2006: 2). Evidently there is scope to develop further partnerships here to provide additional support for particular challenging cases: for example, Citizens Advice could provide support relating to benefits, finances and debts.

Effectively, many respondents to the Homeless Link survey were operating a 'one stop shop' model of service delivery. At its most basic this can involve little more than agencies being physically located in the same building. A more developed approach involves employing generic advisors who are trained to assist with the range of needs clients are likely to present with. These advisors can make specialist referrals if they are unable to deal with the matter personally. It has a number of advantages, particularly if implementation of the model involves more than agencies being physically located together. Working together creates a synergy which provides a more effective and appropriate response to meet the range of needs presented by clients – it also avoids duplication of effort. An example of this approach is provided in Box 9.2.

Box 9.2 Youth Advice Centre (YAC), Hove

Run by the YMCA, YAC aims to provide a safe space for young people aged 13–25 which allows them to access impartial advice and information on a wide range of issues. In addition to providing housing advice, it offers support relating to education, training and employment and health issues, particularly sexual health. It provides these services through working in partnership with other agencies; for example, Connexions and the local primary care trust. The YAC combines the 'one stop shop' approach with an 'outreach model of service delivery, taking their services to young people as well as operating from their own office.

See www.hoveymca.org.uk/ for further details.

Developing partnerships with agencies who can offer specialist support provides a solution to the dilemma about whether services for homeless people should be generalist or specialist. Fountain and Howes' (2002) study revealed that the service providers interviewed favoured a needs-led rather than a service-led approach which allowed generic housing workers to assess homeless people and direct them to specialist services. However, they warned that funding structures made it difficult to facilitate such joint working.

In particular, there has been a debate about the development of specialist GP services for homeless people. A number of studies from both a GP's perspective (Lester et al. 2002) and a homeless person's perspective (for example, Wincup et al. 2003) have found evidence that homeless people find it difficult to access the healthcare they need. Of particular concern are the findings that homeless people experience discrimination which is felt most acutely by those with the greatest level of need such as problem drug users. One response to overcome the barriers to accessing healthcare experienced by homeless people is the establishment of specialist general practitioners, which either operate from their own surgeries or work in a peripatetic manner taking their services to agencies homeless people are already accessing; for example, day centres and hostels (see Wright et al. 2004 for an overview of this debate). They provide a range of general primary care services and often provide specialist services such as drug treatment. To develop specialist GP services partnerships must be established between primary care trusts and homelessness agencies. Box 9.3 provides an example of specialist provision. While these services provided the most appropriate care for homeless people, they are controversial because they can have the unintended consequence of restricting further homeless people's access to mainstream health services, contributing to the further marginalisation of this group.

Box 9.3 The NFA (No Fixed Abode) Health Centre for Homeless People (Leeds)

Managed by Leeds primary care trust (PCT), this centre provides personal medical services to single homeless people in Leeds. It comprises of a multi-disciplinary team which provides support and treatment for problem drug and alcohol users and individuals with mental health problems. It receives funding from the PCT which is supplemented by funding from Safer Leeds (a crime and disorder reduction partnership) to allow it to deliver drug services. It also conducts research on health and homelessness. Staff at the centre emphasize the importance of working with 'users' of their services and therefore sought to canvas their views on how this might be best facilitated, resulting in the introduction of a suggestion box (Wright et al. 2004).

These partnerships provide an example of how previously antagonistic relationships between health care providers and voluntary sector agencies working with the homeless can be transformed. As Wyner (2005) notes, the shift away from institutional care to community care in the early 1990s created particular difficulties as voluntary sector agencies found themselves accommodating people with mental health problems with few resources available to meet their needs.

While taking services such as GPs to homeless people is often viewed as good practice, it is based on the assumption that homeless people are willing to use homelesssness services. In the first edition of this volume, Wyner (2005: 126) noted that some homeless people are 'reluctant to engage with agencies offering help, wary of formal professional settings and may find it difficult to keep appointments'. Research on homeless people has identified a range of actual and perceived barriers relating to access to homelessness services. Studies by Fountain and Howes (2002) and Wincup et al. (2003) revealed a range of barriers, especially relating to the behaviour of other service users (for example, drug or alcohol use and violence) and lack of awareness of services available. Overcoming the first barrier is challenging and one solution is to provide specialist provision for groups whose presence is a deterrent to others. Although this was not the main reason for their development, there are already examples of such provision for alcohol users in the form of 'wet' shelters (which allow alcohol to tbe consumed on the premises) and hostels although establishing these in the face of local opposition can be challenging. Equivalent provision for problem drug users is not available although a number of countries have pioneered the use of drug consumption rooms where problem drug users can consume drugs but also 'hang around' (Joseph Rowntree Foundation 2006). An alternative approach is to develop specialist provision for groups who are particularly reluctant to access services; for example, women and young people.

Working together

In this chapter we have argued that that working with many homeless people involves more than providing access to a roof over their heads: it also means making available support which addresses other needs they may have which should improve their ability to obtain and retain accommodation. Given the multiplicity of needs of many homeless people and their diverse nature, partnership working is an essential ingredient of working effectively with homeless people.

Homeless Link (2007) proposes that there are four key types of partnership in the homelessness field. This typology is useful for identifying the opportunities which exist for agencies from both the voluntary and statutory sectors to come together to develop effective partnerships. First, there are 'service delivery' partnerships involving frontline staff networks aimed at improving on the ground service delivery through coordination of the work of two or more agencies. Second, there are 'learning and best practice' partnerships involving similar agencies in a town or city or region coming together to share best practice and to provide peer support and learning. Wincup et al.'s (2003) study of youth homelessness uncovered a variant of this with staff from homelessness agencies involved in delivering training courses to other agencies who came into contact with homeless people. Third, there are 'influencing and strategic' partnerships whose responsibilities relate to funding and strategic development. Fourth, there are 'consortia' partnerships when voluntary sector agencies form networks to lobby or to bid for public funding to deliver contracted-out services.

While this typology is useful it fails to appreciate partnerships may also arise as a consequence of efforts to tackle other social problems. For example, the national action plan for reducing re-offending (Home Office 2004a) describes seven pathways for reducing re-offending: the first is accommodation. Its action plan for identifying the housing needs of offenders, increasing the number of offenders released with a known address, providing housing advice and developing an accommodation strategy makes explicit that 'joined-up' working will be required at a national, regional and local level. Such developments make explicit the importance of coordination between partnerships as well as within them.

During the past decade there have been important developments at a national level which have encouraged influencing and strategic partnerships to develop. The Homelessness Act 2002 provided the impetus for local authorities to establish homelessness forums to design and deliver homelessness strategies. For Roche (2004), key partners include a range of local authority departments (housing, asylum teams, homeless units, social services), other public sector agencies (primary care trusts, mental health teams, substance misuse teams, police, child support, education and training) and partnerships (Drug Action Team), voluntary agencies (Citizens Advice, agencies working with asylum seekers and organizations running hostels and day centres for homeless people) and the private sector (bed and breakfast accommodation, housing trusts). The more obvious additions to this list include youth offending teams, probation areas and a wide range of voluntary sector agencies working with clients with housing needs (for example, victims of domestic violence). Despite these encouraging aspirations and developments, practice remains inconsistent and there is scope to develop these partnerships further as Shelter, a housing and homelessness charity note: 'While there are many examples of good practice around the country, there is a clear need to develop and build on these to effectively engage all agencies involved in the development of strategies' (Shelter 2007).

One impetus for developing these would be to give these partnerships a statutory basis. In contrast to the response to other 'social problems' such as crime or drug use, there is no homelessness equivalent to crime and disorder reduction partnerships or drug action teams. Without this status, such partnerships can 'lack teeth' and barriers to effective partnership working such as disagreements over funding and responsibilities can be difficult to overcome.

While these partnerships are important they tend to focus upon strategic planning rather than the realities of service delivery where joint working is necessary to ensure that efforts are coordinated. At this level, practices such as the introduction of standardized assessments, common referral forms and information sharing protocols plus the clarification of responsibilities can transform the quality of service provided to clients. It is, of course, essential that the efforts of influencing strategic partnerships and service delivery partnerships are coordinated. One example of how partnerships at different levels can work together to maximize their impact can be found in Box 9.4. It describes efforts to address homelessness among people leaving prison, a group who often have acute housing needs (see Maguire and Nolan 2007). More generally, the protocol has other aspirations to aid the resettlement of prisoners and promote community safety.

Box 9.4 Housing and Returning Prisoners (HARP) protocol

Developed in Tyne and Wear, it brought together statutory and voluntary sector housing providers with prisons and probation areas to create a common approach to planning for the housing of returning prisoners. It offers a framework to reduce homelessness among people returning from custody. It aims to develop a culture of understanding, effective forward planning and communication to ensure that statutory and organization responsibilities are met and staff time is deployed in an efficient and effective manner. In order to achieve this the protocol outlines the process to be followed from pre-custody through to post-release and specifies who has responsibility for the task. It also includes model letters for liaising with housing providers, contact details for key individuals in the region, an information sharing protocol and a common referral form.

Further information can be found at:
http://noms.justice.gov.uk/news-publications-events/publications/strategy/harp-protocol

---

The protocol discussed above was informed by the available evidence on the housing needs of prisoners. For example, a survey conducted in 2003 of almost 2000 prisoners in the last three weeks of their sentence found that one-fifth were homeless or living in temporary accommodation prior to their imprisonment and just under one-third did not have any accommodation to go to upon release (Niven and Stewart 2005). Partnership working is most effective when informed by evidence about the nature and extent of a problem. Box 9.5 provides an example of good practice when planning what accommodation should be made available for female offenders. The same approach could be followed for developing accommodation strategies for different groups with housing needs. It details how the first step in the process was to conduct a 'needs analysis' in order to ensure that future service development was appropriate and a review of the evidence-base to establish best practice. This process also helped to identify the key partners who should be involved in strategic developments and service delivery.

Box 9.5 Developing an accommodation strategy for female offenders

In 2004 the East of England region of the National Probation Service commissioned research on the housing needs of female offenders (Wincup and Norvell 2004). It analysed data collected by probation officers using Offender Assessment System (OASys), a tool used to identify criminogenic needs (i.e. needs judged to be linked to criminal behaviour). The research revealed that approximately two-fifths of women on their caseload were assessed as having 'accommodation' as a criminogenic need. In addition, it also identified that sizeable proportions of those with accommodation needs also had needs related to 'emotional well-being' (30%), 'education, training and employability' (29%) and 'alcohol misuse' (18%). The research concluded that accommodating female offenders requires more than providing access to a roof over their head and emphasized the importance of partnership working. Given the identified needs of female offenders the key players should include primary care and mental health trusts, Jobcentre Plus, Connexions, drug and alcohol action Teams and a wide range of voluntary sector agencies.

The research allowed the East of England region to establish a strategic partnership which included partners who *needed* to be involved rather than those they thought *should* be involved. It made explicit the need for supported accommodation for the significant minority of female offenders with multiple needs.

To summarize, working together effectively to tackle homelessness requires a commitment to evidence-based policy and practice and coordination between partnerships at all levels and between the range of partnerships that identify addressing homelessness as one of their goals.

Conclusion

This chapter has highlighted the lack of a coordinated strategy to tackle the housing and related needs of homeless people, the complexity of need among those who are homeless, and the range of barriers, conditions and exclusions that make accessing services particularly difficult. If more people in severe housing need are to access accommodation then statutory, voluntary and private agencies will need to work together. However, whatever form partnership working takes it is important to recognize that effective partnership working is not inevitable when agencies come together. As Newburn (1999) notes the literature on this approach is full of examples of mishap and failure. Others have noted that multi-agency initiatives fail to appreciate existing conflicts between agencies or the potential for further conflict to arise (Coles et al. 2004). Partnership working is neither an end in itself nor a panacea for dealing with challenges that homelessness presents. It does, however, offer the greatest potential for supporting some of the most socially excluded individuals in society.

Questions for further discussion

Based upon your reading of this chapter and further research complete the following exercises.

1   Explore what you consider to be homelessness, and what behaviours or circumstances you think should exclude people from receiving temporary and permanent accommodation.

2 Produce a list of recommendations for the Communities and Local Government Department on how the government might improve provision for homeless people.

3 Put together a good practice guidance document for service providers working with homeless people.

Useful websites

- *Crisis*: www.crisis.org.uk a homelessness charity.
- *Homelessness Link*: www.homeless.org.uk an umbrella organization which brings together frontline homelessness services.
- *Shelter*: www.england.shelter.org.uk/home/index.cfm a housing and homelessness charity. Follow the links to separate sites for Wales, Scotland and Northern Ireland.

Note

1 A temporary 'home' made out of materials such as tin or cardboard.

10 Problem drug use and safeguarding children: partnership and practice issues

Julian Buchanan with Brian Corby[1]

This chapter will:

- Explore the social context in which 'problem drug users' and 'inadequate parents' are constructed.
- Outline key issues and difficulties involved in working with problem drug users whose children are considered to be at risk of abuse or neglect.
- Draw on research carried out with social workers, health visitors, drugs clinic workers and parents to examine the barriers of working together to assess children's needs where parents misuse drugs.
- Explore strategies for better partnership approaches.

Problems with drugs

Professionals working with drug misusing parents must grapple with two taboo issues that are fraught with fear and risk – problem drug use and child neglect. The combination of the two issues heightens fear for the worker and brings considerable stigma to the client. Illicit drug using parents (as opposed alcohol using parents) are seen as social outcasts who bring disgrace to their family and neighbourhood. The disparity in the reaction to illegal drug use seems a little incongruous given the serious criminal, social and medical problems caused by the misuse of alcohol and tobacco.

In Western society, alcohol and tobacco are deeply embedded within cultural expressions of celebration, pleasure and leisure. These legal drugs also pose serious social, psychological and physiological risk to individuals, their families and the wider community. In the UK 120,000 people die prematurely as a result of tobacco use (losing an average of 14 years of life), and the health related problems tobacco causes cost the NHS up to £1.7 billion every year (Commission for Healthcare Audit and Inspection 2007). In England and Wales the damage caused by alcohol to health, crime and lost days at work costs around £20 billion per year (DoH 2007c). In terms of risk to children, the US Institute of Medicine (1996) asserts that alcohol causes more damage to the developing foetus than any other substance (including marijuana, heroin and cocaine), and the irreversible effects of Foetal Alcohol Syndrome is claimed to now affect one baby in every 500 born in the UK (see Feotal Alcohol Syndrome Aware UK at: www.fasaware.co.uk/pics/FASleafleta4.pdf).

Curiously, excessive use of alcohol in the UK has long been seen as a fitting and appropriate way of 'celebrating' a special occasion or event. This cultural norm is largely perceived as perfectly reasonable. However, imagine the reaction to a person who passed an important exam being encouraged to go out and 'celebrate' by taking ecstasy (a Class A drug). In contrast to alcohol such a suggestion is seen as dangerous, deviant and highly irresponsible. Yet in terms of risk, it could be argued that alcohol is a more dangerous drug (House of Commons Science and Technology Select Committee 2006). The distinctions made between legal and illegal drugs, and the classification of illicit drugs (A, B and C) under the Misuse of Drugs Act 1971 are a poor guide to the actual risks posed by different drugs. It is important that professionals who work with drug misusing parents are well informed about drugs and are able to objectively assess behaviour and parental capability, rather than gather evidence to support assumptions which have been reached through the 'tinted lenses' of ignorance, prejudice and fear.

Successive British Crime Surveys (BCS) indicate that over the past 30 years there has been a significant growth in the percentage of the population using illicit drugs (although more recently this has finally begun to plateau), however, the UK now has the highest proportion of problem drug users across Europe (Reuter and Stevens 2007). There are an estimated 332,000 problem drug users in England alone (HM Government 2008). Drugs have become a common feature of life in the UK, most young people have contact with drugs, and many young people have direct experience as drug users. The most popular drug remains cannabis. Around 34 percent of the UK adult population have used an illicit drug and this figure rises to over 50 percent for those in their mid-20s (Roe and Man 2006). Given the extent of illicit drug use, particularly among young adults, inevitably significant numbers of young parents will be illicit drug users; however, it is an important to make distinctions between experimental drug users, recreational users and problem drug users, with most concern towards the latter.

The majority of problem drug users have a history of multiple disadvantage before the onset of a drug problem, with a high number having: experiences of being 'looked after' as children; few or no qualifications; a record of criminal activity and/or anti-social behaviour; poor family support; and patterns of chronic unemployment (Buchanan and Young 2000a; SEU 2002; Buchanan 2004). Drug taking for this group could be understood as a symptomatic response to long standing social inequalities and personal difficulties and many problem drug users end up in prison. The steep rise in the UK prison population correlates with the steep rise in drug use. In the early 1980s, there were around 43,000 people held in prison and by April 2008, this had risen to 82,000. Prisons are becoming dumping grounds for people with drug problems and poor mental health. The female prison population is growing rapidly, many of whom are sole carers for their children. The Corston inquiry found that 58 percent of women in prison had used drugs daily in the six months before prison, and 75 percent of women prisoners had taken an illicit drug in those six months (Corston 2007). This evidence concurs with research by the Social Exclusion Unit into the social circumstances of prisoners in England and Wales, which found that:

> Many prisoners have experienced a lifetime of social exclusion. Compared with the general population, prisoners are thirteen times as likely to have been in care as a child, thirteen times as likely to be unemployed, ten times as likely to have been a regular truant, two and a half times as likely to have had a family member convicted of a criminal offence, six times as likely to have been a young father, and fifteen times as likely to be HIV positive. Many prisoners' basic skills are very poor. 80 percent have the writing skills, 65 percent the numeracy skills and 50 per cent the reading skills at or below the level of an 11-year-old child. 60 to 70 percent of prisoners were using drugs before imprisonment. Over 70 percent suffer from at least two mental disorders. And 20 percent of male and 37 percent of female sentenced prisoners have attempted suicide in the past.

> (SEU 2002: 6)

Drug policies that declare a 'war on drugs' in effect declare a 'war on drug users' (Buchanan and Young 2000b). Problem drug users – portrayed as the 'enemy within' – are then further excluded and become easy targets for discrimination and blame within their community. This 'otherness' ascribed to problem drug users leads to further isolation from families, the community and wider society making relapse more likely and reintegration less likely. Given this hostility towards problem drug users it is easy to understand how statutory agencies shift their focus away from rehabilitation, care or social inclusion of problem drug users, and instead concentrate efforts upon the assessment of risk, monitoring and the protection of others. When children are involved, the need to protect becomes paramount. In a climate of fear concerning drug misuse and child neglect it is easy to understand how agencies might concentrate upon identifying negative risk factors rather than identifying positive resilience factors. Paradoxically, the best interests of the child may be better served by a more balanced appreciation of positive factors that promote resilience alongside the negative factors that place the child at risk. With an unbalanced preoccupation upon the latter it could be wrongly assumed that any parent who uses an illegal drug places their child at risk, and agencies involved with drug using parents may be tempted to play safe by adopting a zero tolerance approach to illicit drugs taking.

The problem of misunderstanding and ignorance regarding the nature, context and risk of illicit drug use inevitably impacts upon the relationships between the worker and the client, as well as between the different agencies. A drug using parent could be involved with a variety of agencies and individuals, each having a different attitude and understanding of the risks posed by illicit drug use. A pregnant drug using parent could be discussing her drug habit with her GP, midwife, social worker, community psychiatric nurse (from the drugs team), health visitor, probation officer, drug counsellor (from the voluntary organization) and housing support worker – each worker/agency could be giving different messages about how best to tackle drugs, what changes they expect, what risks are posed to the parent and what the risks are to the unborn child. Getting these professionals to work collaboratively in partnership to provide the most effective service is not easy.

Child protection

Social attitudes have also had a major influence on work done with children and families where there are concerns about abuse and/or neglect, though in a somewhat different way to that in the drugs field. While it is clear that society has little sympathy for adults who ill treat their children, perhaps even greater criticism has been levelled at professionals who have 'failed' to ensure their protection. This has been a consistent issue from the time of the Maria Colwell inquiry (DHSS 1974) right up to the present day. Social workers have borne the brunt of this criticism, but it should be noted that other professional workers have also been included. What has particularly exercised many public inquiries into child deaths by abuse has been the failure of all the professions and agencies with responsibilities in the child protection field to collaborate and communicate effectively. Although formal systems have been set up to improve this aspect of child protection work, nevertheless the findings of inquiries and serious case reviews have consistently pointed to poor information sharing and role confusion as key factors in events leading up to the child deaths they have been looking into (Corby et al. 1998). More recently, in the Victoria Climbie inquiry (Laming 2003), there has been extensive criticism of those responsible for managing child protection agencies for failing to ensure that front line workers are properly overseen and supervized in their activities.

A key consequence of this critical atmosphere has been to promote among child protection professionals a defensive mentality about their work, resulting in greater emphasis being placed on procedures and processes. Research conducted in the 1990s concluded that childcare workers were overfocused on child protection issues and that child protection agencies were targeting all their resources on cases where risks of child abuse were deemed to exist (Dartington Social Research Unit 1995). As a consequence, the much larger number of families where children were in need received less attention and services than they warranted. This analysis led to a policy shift placing greater emphasis on the need to support families with a view to preventing abuse. There is still much ambivalence about how to get the balance right between working to support families while at the same time remaining vigilant to the possibilities of abuse (Corby 2003). Another key factor emerging from the Dartington research was the fact that many parents saw child protection workers as officious and unhelpful in the way in which they dealt with them. There has been relatively little change in perception on the part of parents as to the roles and purposes of statutory social work intervention – they are still seen by many as people with authority to protect children by removing them from parents and placing them in care (Parrot et al. 2006).

Drugs misuse and child protection

The causal connection between drug misuse and child protection remains a contested one (as will be seen from our empirical study). Until relatively recently, little was written on this subject, however there is now a good range of research into the lives of parents who misuse substances and the impact on their children and families. What is still lacking is a range of research on: the views of children of drug using parents, particularly in respect of impact, resilience factors and service needs; their views on existing service provision; the perspectives, role and impact of fathers and siblings; service needs; service provision; mental health; rurality, and ethnicity (Bancroft el al. 2004, Templeton et al. 2006).

While social workers are dealing with many more drug using parents than ever before, there has been little serious estimation of overall numbers. The Advisory Council on the Misuse of Drugs (ACMD) estimates that between 250,000 and 350,000 children have at least one parent with a serious drug problem, and on average, parental problem substance use was identified as a feature in 24 per cent of cases of children on the child protection register (ACMD 2003). The ACMD's authoritative report identified 48 recommendations that cut across drugs, children's health and criminal justice sectors, and address a broad range of issues. They established a working group to monitor progress in respect of these recommendations and in 2007 the ACMD reviewed progress and concluded that while some development has been made overall it was patchy with some significant variations between the four countries that make up the United Kingdom. The report was concerned to note 'there is no requirement in the UK for Safeguarding/Child Protection Units or Services to routinely record and monitor the extent of parental substance misuse as a significant contributory factor in referrals for case conferences and child protection registrations' (ACMD 2007: 33).

Despite the extent of drug use among families at risk, clear guidance about how to assess the nature, extent and type of parental substance misuse as a child protection issue remains limited. The ACMD reports (2003, 2007) offer a thorough examination of the nature, extent and response to the problem, but in terms of safeguarding children, much has been left to the judgement and interpretation of workers in the field. There are some useful publications. The Department of Health publication (Cleaver et al. 1999) helpfully highlighted research findings about the links between child neglect, drug and alcohol misuse and mental illness, emphasizing the risks to children. Jo Tunnard (2002) provided an informative overview to distil the key messages from a wide range of research in the drugs and child protection field. The Scottish Executive has produced a number of helpful reports including *Good Practice Guidance for working with Children and Families affected by Substance Misuse* (Scottish Executive 2006) which provides useful policy and practice guidelines for working with children and families affected by problem drug use, while *Looking Beyond Risk* provides an informative scoping study examining research in parental substance misuse (Templeton et al. 2006). There are also some helpful texts on practice with drug using parents (Harbin and Murphy 2000; Klee et al. 2001, Kroll and Taylor 2003, Barnard 2006). There are also a few detailed research accounts describing intervention and support for drug using parents where children are at risk (see Klee et al. 1998; Forrester 2000; and Straussner and Fewell 2006). However, the amount of researched information about inter-professional issues, while extensive in the child protection field generally (see Birchall and Hallett 1995; Corby 2001), remains somewhat limited in relation to the combined issues of drug misuse and child protection.

A major conundrum is how to support both the parent and the child while keeping the family together. This is particularly difficult when the parent is struggling with a drug problem and continuing with patterns of drug related behaviour that make the child vulnerable. Marina Barnard's research study highlights the difficulties and dilemmas this places upon carers and relatives, with many in her study expressing concern that supporting the parents could create a dilemma by inadvertently facilitating ongoing drug use (Barnard 2003: 296). Brynna Kroll suggests that a shift of focus towards the child is needed, in order to develop a better understanding of the impact of parental drug misuse. She advocates the importance of interviewing the children of drug using parents: 'Communication between professionals needs to be made open and the child's perspective needs to be brought more firmly into the entire assessment process so that workers can gain a sense of what children's lives are really like' (Kroll 2004: 138). The importance of listening to children has been further emphasized by the ACMD (2007). This challenge of juggling with the distinctively different needs of the parent to that of the child illustrates the complexity of engaging with the combined and inter-related issues of drugs and child protection. It not only raises issues regarding the focus of intervention but also about the balance held between a surveillance approach that seeks to identify risk behaviours, or a rehabilitative approach that seeks to identify and cultivate positive factors that promote resilience.

Inter-professional issues

Across the UK Drug Action Teams (DATs) or similar bodies have been established at local authority or health authority level with the explicit purpose of enabling services to work together in partnership to tackle drugs/substance misuse. However, when drugs become combined with child protection concerns the range of agencies broadens further and may also include:

- The National Probation Service, who supervise offenders on court orders and can make proposals in presentence reports for a range of sentencing options including Drug Rehabilitation Requirement as part of a Community Order
- The Social Services Department who have a statutory responsibility to protect children from abuse and neglect. They can provide a range of services including social workers, family support workers and family centre workers who may provide day care, residential care, home care support or foster care
- The National Health Service who have a responsibility to oversee all substitute prescribing services and provide health promotional advice and

treatment for drug users. Within the NHS there is a range of health professions who will come into contact with drug-using parents – GPs, Drug Dependency Services, drug action team workers, midwives, health visitors, community psychiatric nurses and nursing staff involved in inpatient detoxification facilities

- Education and careers advice services, which include school teachers, learning mentors, Connexions advisers, and youth and community workers who provide drug and alcohol information and support with further education and employment
- The enforcement agencies such as the Crown Prosecution Service (CPS), Courts, Police, Customs & Excise who are concerned to uphold and enforce the rule of law
- A diverse range of national and regional voluntary, independent and private organisations such as NACRO, Shelter, CAIS, Addaction, Princes Trust, NCH

While attempts have been made to draw these agencies together through DATs, Area Child Protection Committees (ACPCs) now renamed local Safeguarding Children Boards (SCB), policy and practices between the different agencies in respect of problem drug use and child protection too often remain parochial, uncoordinated and something of a postcode lottery (Best et al. 2008).

Professionals from different agencies are not immune from prevailing negative stereotypes, but in this difficult field of work professionals need to be careful not to embrace such prejudice as Jo Tunnard emphasizes: 'practitioners and policy makers need to be vigilant about the biases they bring to their work' (2002: 43). As already noted, problem drug users experience stigma and isolation from the wider population. This is intensified in the case of drug using parents and even more so for drug using mothers, who are seen to be failing their maternal responsibilities ascribed by narrowly defined gender stereotypes. An inappropriate response from agency staff could damage the relationship between the organisation and the client, and ultimately this could place the child more at risk if cooperation, trust and honest dialogue between the drug using parent and the agency break down. Holding the balance between supporting the parent and protecting the child from neglect or harm is not easy: 'Many drug misusing parents are already consumed with guilt about the effect their drug use may be having on their child, and it is important to maintain a non-judgmental approach while being firm and precise about the limits of adequate child care' (Keen and Alison 2001: 299).

An open relationship with drug using parents that seeks to appreciate and understand *their* experience of the world from *their* background and *their* context will yield a more accurate assessment of the situation. Indeed professionals whose key role is to work with the parents will not be able to do their job effectively without getting alongside drug using parents and developing some degree of empathy. This may not always be easy for those professionals whose primary role is to protect and care for the child. As we have seen, child protection social workers have experienced considerable criticism for not being sufficiently authoritative and proactive in intervening in risk situations. It would be surprising if those concerned with protecting children did not therefore, think and act defensively in the case of children whose parents are misusing drugs. On the other hand, it could be argued that agencies should have a professional commitment to respect the dignity of each client regardless of their behaviour, and this should involve a commitment to listen, to understand, and as far as possible to be non judgemental in their approach. Hence, there is a range of complex and at times competing and conflicting values and attitudes those professionals must bring, not only to their work with drug using parents, but also to their involvement with other agencies in multi agency partnerships.

Working with drug using parents

In our qualitative small scale research study (Bates et al. 1999), we asked professionals from three different agencies involved in working with drug using parents on Merseyside about their value positions in relation to drug misuse and child protection issues. We carried out semi structured interviews with 11 specialist drug workers from a Drug Dependency Unit, 15 child protection social workers based in three field teams and one based at a maternity hospital, and 15 community-based health visitors. We also interviewed ten known drug using parents who had been subject to child protection investigations to ascertain their perceptions of how professionals viewed and responded to them. Key themes emerging from this study are: attitudes and values; knowledge base; roles and boundaries; inter-professional collaboration and training; and the perspectives from drug using parents.

Attitudes and values

The DDU workers were the most experienced of the professional groups we interviewed in relation to working in the drugs field. Their main commitment was to work with the drugs users themselves in a positive and rehabilitative way in order to reduce the harm arising from illicit drug dependence. Most of the drug workers seemed to have sympathy for the parents they worked with and a strong awareness of the stigma attached to parents who use drugs: 'Drug using parents have to live with stigma. Society considers them very low down the ladder. A lot of work needs to be done to help them get their confidence back. Drug users are made to feel they are bad parents from the outset.' Many of the drug workers felt that other professionals by comparison tended to be more judgemental. In particular, they felt that social services department workers' narrow concerns with child protection could, at times, result in negatively stereotyping drug using parents: '(they) should be looking at the specific issue of concern rather than the fact that someone uses drugs.'

Several of the Drugs Dependency workers commented that parents who used drugs were capable of being responsible parents: 'if drug use is managed properly, i.e. taking place privately and the after effects don't interfere with child care, then the parents can't be considered a poor role model.' In contrast, most social workers were convinced that parental drug misuse was bound to impact negatively upon children, largely because of the lifestyle and poverty that dependence on an illicit drug created.

Some, however, held views similar to DDU workers: 'I do not like making a judgement on families just because they use drugs. Every family is different. The risk is not necessarily greater.'

Nine of the 15 health visitors felt that drug using parents were poor role models for their children. One health visitor was clearly appalled by her experiences and felt strongly about the issue: 'I would strongly agree that they are poor role models. It is the psychology of evil – the violence the children have to witness – the comings and goings that goes on.' There were some clear differences between the three agencies in relation to values and attitudes, reflecting to some degree their different roles in dealing with drug misuse and child protection. DDU workers were overall more optimistic about the potential of drug using parents to care reasonably for their children, reflecting the fact that they work mainly with and on behalf of parents. Social workers, on the other hand, were more circumspect, probably because of their focus on the needs of the child. Health visitors were overall the least positive about drug using parents, possibly reflecting their focus on the child, being referrers on behalf of at risk children, and their lack of sustained contact with drug-using parents. While these attitudinal differences between professions have significant implications for partnership work, it should be noted that there was encouragingly a good deal of common ground.

Knowledge base

Not surprisingly, the DDU workers in our study had the most detailed and informed knowledge about the impact of drugs and this was recognized among the other agencies: 'people from the DDU are well informed, well organized and usually very good to talk to when working with drug using families.' This level of competence in respect of drugs led DDU workers to be more considered and less likely to panic about situations where children were involved. From their point of view, other professions tended to overreact as a result of their lack of knowledge: 'Some midwives told parents that methadone leads to deformed babies, or your baby will withdraw, or if it sneezes five times, we will need to take it to hospital.' On the other hand, some drug workers had limited knowledge of child protection matters. As one drugs worker put it: 'Some drug agencies can be quite blasé. If we are not careful, we can become overconfident about drug users' capability of parenting'.

The situation was almost reversed for social workers, who had considerable knowledge about child protection but more limited knowledge about drug misuse. While several social workers had received some training about drug misuse, most felt that it was inadequate given the extent of drug taking among their client group: 'I don't think the department supports us enough in training. Most of my experience comes from working with families where drug use is involved.' Social workers, however, felt that lack of knowledge of child care and child protection issues was a weakness for some drugs dependency workers: 'Drugs agencies tend to put their clients' interests first before that of the clients' children, which is fair enough to a certain extent unless those children are at risk. I feel that they need more knowledge as to what degree of neglect is acceptable.'

Only two of the 15 health visitors in this study had received specific drugs training, although most had received some child protection training. As a whole, health visitors felt they had less expert knowledge than professional workers from the other two agencies, in that they were neither drugs nor child protection specialists. In some ways, they saw their generalist approach as being more balanced than that of the other two agencies: '(DDU workers) are still not keyed up to looking at issues of child care. They are looking at issues of drugs and not at the wider family.' Social workers were seen by health visitors to have too high a threshold of concern about child protection and, therefore, did not respond sufficiently to what health visitors considered to be 'worrying' cases. The variations in knowledge combined with the different roles and focus of their job, meant that drug workers, social workers and health visitors had different perceptions regarding what they understood to be acceptable and unacceptable behaviour from drug misusing parents.

Roles and boundaries

As can be seen from the two preceding sections, the roles and responsibilities of the different agencies seem to play an important part in shaping the values, attitudes and views of the workers. In this section, the roles of the three sets of agency workers interviewed in our study are considered in more detail. DDU workers, who were concerned more directly with the needs of the adults using drugs, estimated that less than a quarter of their work involved parents with families. Their attention focused on helping problematic drug users to stabilize their habit with substitute drugs (reduction or maintenance), reduce health and social harms, and support them once they had become stable. In this respect, parental care of children was not their main focus of attention and they felt that drug misuse did not necessarily put children at risk: 'The only problem with drug users is what they have to do to get drugs. Most are decent families just like any other person.' DDU workers did recognize their responsibility to protect children and some were critical of drug counselling and support agencies for being too adult focused and not being sufficiently aware of the need to protect children: 'Some voluntary agencies [don't take child protection seriously they] ... seem to think "confidentiality" is paramount.'

The commitment to respect confidentiality of information between the worker and client cannot be allowed to become paramount in all circumstances. The complex task of engaging with social problems requires the worker to understand when other values, such as the rights of a child, or the rights of others, override a commitment to maintain confidentiality with the client. Several of the social workers interviewed had a fair amount of experience of working with drug using parents and, despite their primary child protection concern, saw that their allegiances were to the whole family not just the child. Health visitors saw their allegiances as being most closely with the children, more so than did the social workers. They were more likely for instance, to be critical of drugs workers for failing to take into account the needs of children in the families with which they were working: 'Drugs workers ... [they] do not see risk as they tend to look at their client and not the child.'

Interprofessional collaboration and training

Given these clear differences between the agencies, we were interested to explore what each of the professional groups felt about working in partnership. All felt that multi-agency collaboration and training was important for different reasons. DDU workers generally felt that health workers (including health visitors) were ill informed and ill trained in relation to illegal drug use. They felt that many workers in these professions and some social workers, were not sufficiently discerning in the way in which they worked with drug using parents. They welcomed more informal methods of collaboration with other professionals as a means to improve this situation, and Core Group meetings for the key professionals responsible for ongoing work with families were seen as more effective than child protection conferences. The need for all agencies to operate along shared, agreed guidelines was stated as important by the DDU workers. In particular, the emphasis given to confidentiality was seen as a thorny issue, which needed greater clarification and consistency in application.

Social workers shared many of these views. They too felt that health workers needed to be better informed and more realistic in their attitudes to drug using parents. Many social workers commented on the lack of good communication across all agencies with particular criticism of drugs workers, GPs, health visitors, school teachers and the police. The impression gained was that communication and collaboration was something of a lottery. Another concern raised was the fact that in the absence of clear policy practice guidelines in respect of drug misuse and parenting, an individual worker's views about illicit drug taking could result in an overly negative assessment of a family situation: 'Sometimes you are working with drug users and you come across a health visitor or a doctor who really does have a problem with drugs. This is also the case with some social workers. You can't work together when some people have their own personal agendas.'

Many of the social workers felt that specialized drug training was essential to improving the situation and that this should be carried out jointly on an inter-professional basis with all the key agencies represented. This level of exchange may also address the need to improve knowledge and understanding across the different agencies of each other's roles and responsibilities. Training concerning child protection may also benefit from being interprofessional, as most of the health visitors had concerns about the lack of attention to child protection by DDU workers:

> Drug agencies are adult-centred and keying their service to the needs of the individual who is an older person and not necessarily looking at issues around whether they are or are not involved with families. I think that in Liverpool it has become enlightened that they should seek information but they are still not keyed up at looking at issues of child care. They are looking at issues of drugs and not at the wider family.

Several of the health visitors considered that they were not properly informed of what was happening in cases where there were concerns about drug misuse and child care. They considered that some drugs agencies' preoccupation with confidentiality was a barrier to communication. Health visitors felt marginalized by the other professionals, particularly GPs, who, in their view, were not sufficiently aware of the potential risks to children that drugs present. They considered that social workers were too crisis oriented and failed to give sufficient attention to health visitor referrals for families in need of preventive intervention. Most of the health visitors felt dissatisfied with the quality of inter-professional work:

> No one seems to understand each other's professional role. There is a long way to go. When I was first health visiting we used to make social contact with all the social workers, so you used to know who they were and they used to know who you were. You could pick up a telephone and it was much easier to make a referral. Now that we are coming out of clinics and we are all separate, I think it is a negative move – you don't know each other.

Health visitors, like social workers, felt that matters could only be improved by a much greater emphasis on joint training. The following case study (based upon a real life case) illustrates the potential issues that can arise and how they could be resolved by greater multi-agency partnership practice.

Box 10.1 Case study: Michelle

The probation service, social services, the education authority and the health service each had specialist workers with a remit to specialize in substance misuse. However, each had different perspectives, philosophies and language to understand and describe the drug problem: 'addicts', 'users', patients, clients, service users. Some agencies saw methadone as a dangerous drug only to be prescribed as a last resort on a four-week reducing programme; others believed methadone maintenance should be freely available. Some felt that 'addicts should be left to hit rock bottom' before any help should be given. It became apparent that clients were seen by a number of agencies with limited coordination or exchange of information, and were being given conflicting advice and information. The drug specialists from the different agencies got together, and after almost 18 months of careful planning and preparation exploring different philosophies, policies, practices, terminology and understanding more about each others different roles, they united together by locating their staff into a single centrally located building to form a specialist drugs team for the borough.

When Michelle, who was six months pregnant and dependent upon street heroin, came to the newly-created team for help, she was extremely anxious and fearful of having her child taken from her once it was born. However, the partnership approach meant that with Michelle's permission, the CPN was able to ring her GP, explain the situation and immediately arrange a methadone maintenance prescription. The social services drug counsellor was able to speak to the social worker at the local hospital to explore the likely outcome and the need for hospital support, and the probation officer was able to clarify the situation with a colleague who was supervising Michelle on a two-year Drug Rehabilitation Requirement following an offence of theft from a local shop.

Throughout the pregnancy a rather relieved Michelle was stable taking 35mls of methadone linctus daily, she didn't use street drugs and kept all her

---

appointments. Just after the birth of the baby a case conference was held. The mood of the conference was somewhat negative towards drug using mothers and it was suggested by one of medical staff that: (a) Michelle should immediately be placed on a four-week methadone reduction programme to become drug free, (b) the baby placed on the at risk register, and (c) arrangements made to systematically monitor her child care capabilities. However, specialist members of the drugs team representing two different agencies were able to argue against this pressurizing strategy, which they believed was in danger of asking too much of Michelle and 'setting her up to fail'. After some heated debate the decision was eventually made to keep the baby in hospital for an extra three days to monitor possible withdrawal symptoms, not to make any immediate demands to reduce Michelle's current levels of substitute prescribing, and to allow informal support from the drugs team to continue. There was not felt to be sufficient concern to warrant placing Michelle's baby on the at risk register.

Had it not been for the authoritative intervention supported by expert knowledge and understanding from the recently established specialist multi-agency drug team representatives who spoke at the conference, the outcome of the case and the ultimate future care of the baby could have been very different.

Perspectives from drug-using parents

Drug using parents confronted by professionals who have a duty to protect children (including an authority to instigate the removal of children from parents) understandably feel anxious and this can result in some difficult encounters:

> I lied to social services and told them that I didn't know nothing about it, because the vibes I was getting from the situation was that H. could be whisked away into care.

> I said you're not getting your hands on this one ... what I don't agree with is that the baby's not even born yet and as soon as it's born, even if it's born in the night, these have got to phone child protection to let them know I've had the baby so that it can go on the at risk register straight from birth. Now I don't think that's right. I think you should be given a chance like, a couple of months, six weeks' trial, to see whether the baby does need to go on the at risk register or whatever. Know what I mean?

Clearly, health and social care workers have to be prepared for this type of resistance. Parents who are subject to child protection investigations are sometimes antagonistic and resentful, particularly drug using parents who consider interventions are too often based upon judgemental attitudes about drug taking, rather than on the way they care for their children. The parents who had attended child protection conferences felt intimidated and threatened by the process. Here are three separate responses:

I didn't like it … it was scary. It was very intimidating. I was sitting there and everybody was looking at me as if I couldn't look after my own children … and I felt so annoyed.

Worse than a court … you haven't got a jury. It was scary.

It was awful … it was awful … we just ended up screaming at them, giving them all loads of abuse, verbal abuse, and walking out. I was in tears … it was awful.

However, drug using parents were not generally dismissive of agency staff. They were critical of those who they believed were patronizing and excluded them from an open dialogue, whereas many parents spoke highly of those staff that dealt with the process of monitoring and social control in a manner that was open and honest, yet retained respect and dignity for the parent as well as the child. 'Some are better than others. That last one I had – Derek – he was brilliant. He always used to tell us up front. The last time everything was done behind your back'. Am important message here is that, it is not so much what is done, but how it is done that matters. This is further supported by a research study that centred exclusively on the views of drug using clients about agencies: 'judgemental attitudes are also criticised by service users and it is clear that the type of service and the way people are treated is more important than the model of treatment' (Jones et al. 2004: 36).

Conclusion

It is important to reiterate that holding the balance and working effectively and constructively in the field of drug misuse and child protection is not an easy task, and it is made more difficult by the high media profile given to both issues. Most people in society avoid contact with drug misusers and parents who ill treat or neglect their children. Policies and practices for dealing with drug using parents reflect and augment this concern and distancing. Illegal drug misuse is seen as dangerous and threatening, and tolerance towards or help for drug users is not high on the political agenda. In the child protection field there have been some key shifts in approaches. Since the mid-1990s, there has been greater emphasis placed on responding more supportively to families where children are seen to be in need or at risk of neglect or ill treatment with a view to prevention. However, social workers and other child protection professionals have adapted slowly to these changes (see Corby 2003), while at the same time social workers face constant reminders of the dangers of not being proactive enough when confronted by risk situations (see Laming 2003). In a climate such as this not only are professionals put on the defensive but so are the local community, family and service users. It is hardly surprising then, that drug using parents tend to avoid contact and open dialogue with child protection agencies or professionals. Drug using parents might be willing to work more openly and cooperatively with professionals if low threshold intervention was offered in a sympathetic, helpful and supportive manner (Buchanan and Young 2001). Trust, honesty and genuine communication not only depend upon the client – but also depend upon the attitudes, values and responses of professional workers.

The importance of achieving positive interprofessional collaboration to deliver high quality, early intervention and shared care to all drug using parents is widely recognized (Keen and Alison 2001, Templeton et al. 2006) though it is not so straightforward to achieve. Child protection work generally has long struggled to establish high quality interprofessional communication and collaboration. With the added ingredient of drug misuse collaboration becomes even more problematic. However, the ACMD (2003, 2007) argues strongly for partnership work and in particular for effective joint working across children and adult services 'children can experience improvements in their lives and those of their families, when the complexity of "Hidden Harm" is grasped and co-ordinated responses between and across adults' and children's services are developed and put into practice' (ACMD 2007: 12). Coordinated practice between agencies is not easy when there are limited policy/practice guidelines for effective practice with drug using parents. Key issues are:

1 The wide variations in knowledge between professions and, in some cases, within professions about what constitutes drug misuse and what constitutes unacceptable risk patterns of behaviour.
2 The lack of shared values and attitudes about drug use and misuse between and within professions.
3 The conflict in respect of the focus and priority of the different professionals – some aligning themselves with supporting the drug using parent, while others align themselves with protecting the child.
4 The lack of shared training and opportunities for developing shared interprofessional understanding.
5 The lack of guidance and shared understanding regarding what constitutes acceptable and unacceptable risk behaviour.

There is also much work needed to achieve greater consistency of approach among the different professions, and indeed across the UK. Establishing ongoing interprofessional training will help to address some of these issues. Another tool for achieving consistency between professions is that of secondment across agencies to appoint specialist practitioners. Areas of sufficient size could consider the example illustrated in the case study by setting up specialist inter-professional teams with remits for developing interprofessional policy/practice guidelines and working with drug misusing parents: 'Developments of this nature cannot succeed without positive liaison between different disciplines and between adult and children's services ... There are examples of good practice along these lines developed in the UK. One offered parents misusing drugs a one-stop shop' (Tunnard 2002: 40).

Our interviews with drug using parents (in the Merseyside study) all of whom had had contact with drugs workers and child protection professionals are highly instructive. It was notable that style and approach (rather than the actual decisions made) were seen by parents as the key factors in their acceptance or rejection of professional intervention. They emphasized: (a) the importance of professional consistency; (b) the importance of open and honest communication; (c) the need for workers to be comfortable with the issue of drugs; and (d) the need to be viewed realistically and not harshly or negatively. To achieve a consistency between professionals from the same agency as well as between different agencies will require professionals to work closely, collaboratively and openly together. It is clear there is considerable work to be done:

> At present, we have a patchwork of response based on the preferences and value systems of individual commissioners, service managers and workers. While good practice may shine brightly in some services and even in some DATs and regions, murky gloom pervades other areas, where we have no idea how many children live with drug-using parents – and far less what their needs are or what services do to address these needs.

(Best el al. 2008: 14)

Questions for further discussion

1 To what extent do you think is a parent who regularly uses illicit drugs a poor role model?
2 What specific drug related behaviours would you identify in relation to child protection as posing 'low' risk and what specific drug related behaviours would you consider pose a 'high' risk?
3 What practical steps can be taken to help agencies work closely together?
4 What issues arise if a worker attempts to support both the drug using parent and the child?

Useful websites:

- *DrugScope*: www.drugscope.org.uk/ is a leading independent centre of expertise on drugs. The site provides authoritative drug information to reduce drug related risk and encourage a more informed appreciation of drug related issues.
- *Every Child Matters: Change for Children* is a new approach to the well being of children and young people from birth to age 19 led by the UK government: www.everychildmatters.gov.uk/lscb
- *Adfam*: www.adfam.org.uk/index.php is a leading national UK-based organization working with and for families affected by drugs and alcohol.

Note

1 The original chapter in the first edition of this book was written with Brian Corby who sadly died in January 2007. Brian was a good friend and

ex-colleague. He was held in high esteem for his depth of knowledge in child protection and was also much appreciated for his approachable, unassuming and good natured disposition (Julian Buchanan).

11 Tackling behavioural problems in the classroom using a student assistance programme[1]

Ros Carnwell, Sally-Ann Baker and Carl Wassell

This chapter will:

- Outline the importance of multi agency collaboration in the development of children's services
- Discuss the problems and issues which become barriers to learning
- Outline the Student Assistance Programme approach;
- Provide case studies to illustrate how SAP has been implemented in English and Welsh Schools

---

Johnny is eleven years old. He and two older siblings lived with their mum after her divorce when Johnny was three years old. Contact with dad since then has been, at best, sporadic.

As far back as he can remember his mum has been in and out of hospital with mental health, alcohol and drug related problems. Two years ago mum's partner abducted and terrorised the family for a week. The ordeal ended when the man accidentally shot himself: the children were first hand witnesses.

Johnny always appeared to thrive at school. Teachers only became worried when he became silent, withdrawn and started missing classes. No-one knew about his life at home until he approached the school social worker to ask why his mum picked the wrong boyfriends. Six months later Johnny's mum died by overdosing on her medication: he found her body. Johnny and his siblings now live with their paternal grandmother ...[2]

(Peatfield 1998)

In her article, Peatfield (1998) articulates the problems for children like Johnny, saying:

Which of the many possible agencies – social services, education welfare, child and adolescent mental health, the voluntary sector – is going to help

Johnny either on its own or jointly, or, will Johnny fall through the gap between agency priorities?... Managing that tricky boundary across agencies can be great when you get results, but when it does not work the outcome for children can be a source of shame to us all.

(Peatfield 1998: 8)

As childhood becomes more pressured and children are at more risk, an increasing number of pupils in British schools experience serious personal and social difficulties. Society is fragmented, fewer children live in traditional nuclear families, increased mobility has eroded the support traditionally afforded by the community, and pressures on parents to work all impact on the child. Children are also exposed to a number of difficulties, including poverty; a lack of appropriate role models; inadequate parental supervision or support; and exposure to 'inappropriate ways of being' through 'electronic media'; and negative peer group pressure. While peer groups are important in childhood, they can lead to a weakening of adult supervision and a loss of respect and children and young people can be led through such pressure to act in inappropriate ways, such as engaging in criminal activity violence, bullying, and substance misuse (Weare 2000; Primary Review 2007). It is natural then that troubles children experience will be brought to school, where they will be reflected in their behaviour (Watkins 1999). Watkins (1994) cites one classroom teacher's description of the problem, as: 'My students bring their dysfunctional home life to school, they bring their fear, their rage, their loneliness and feelings of shame and worthlessness. Sometimes there is no way to reach them and school has no meaning'

(Watkins 1994: 8)

Poor emotional and mental health impacts on learning, and is relatively common in the school age population. Almost 20 percent are diagnosed with either a psychiatric disorder (10%), or suffer an emotional, conduct or hyperkinetic disorder (8.7%) (Green et al. 2005). Moreover, a social gradient is evident, with more children from disadvantaged backgrounds being at increased risk (Green et al. 2005, Ford et al. 2007) and those in care having the highest risk of psychiatric morbidity (McCann et al. 1996; Green et al. 2005; Ford et al. 2007). Gender differences are also apparent, psychiatric disorders are more common in boys whereas girls appear more likely to be at risk of emotional problems, especially in their teenage years (Green et al. 2005). The impact of these challenges on schools is clearly evident as troubled pupils have poorer school attendance (Green et al. 2005) are more likely to be excluded from schools (Parsons and Castle 1998; Evans and Lunt 2002; DfES 2004) and fail to achieve. All of these factors are associated with social exclusion, and an increased likelihood of criminal behaviour (Hallam and Castle 2000).

It is increasingly recognized that children's services are failing to meet the health needs of children and young people and that mental and emotional health is the responsibility of all and not just the responsibility of health services but also of schools (e.g. NHS Health Advisory Service 1995, National Assembly for Wales 2001). In order to tackle this issue, the World Health Organisation launched the 'Global School Health Initiative' to 'strengthen [school health programmes]... at the local, regional, national and global levels' (WHO 1995: 1).

In the UK, a range of legislation and policies have been put in place which give further impetus to considerations of emotional health of children and young people. These include the Children Act (2004), *Every Child Matters* (DfES 2004) the *Children's Plan* (DCFS 2007a) the *National Service Frameworks for Children, Young people and maternity services* (DoH 2004a, WAG 2006) and public service agreements (HM Government 2007). These advocate cooperative working between statutory and nonstatutory organizations at both the macro and micro levels to overhaul and improve services, making them more integrated, child centred and responsive to needs. Consistent with this, Child and Adolescent Mental Health Services will be reviewed in 2008, in order to identify more effective ways of working (DCSF 2007a).

This changing climate signifies an imperative for schools to identify tools, strategies, and programmes that enhance the safety and success of all children and the adults who serve them. Because young people are legally required to attend school, schools have a duty to provide a safe, secure and peaceful environment in which learning can occur and promote welfare (Section 175 of Education Act 2000). Achieving this end requires that every local authority, the NHS and each individual school develop approaches to address these issues (Children Act 2004) and 'by 2011 all schools will offer access to extended services which may include health or therapy service on site' (HM Government 2007). Furthermore, a whole school initiative such as SEAL (Social and Emotional Aspects of Learning) provides 'a comprehensive approach to promoting social and emotional skills for all who learn and work in schools' (DCSF 2007b: 1).

Schools, however, have become increasingly target driven and this can result in a lack of recognition that pupils will struggle to meet the academic goals set for them if their emotional and social needs are not considered. Such considerations are perceived by some as 'yet another demand' (p. 6) on already pressured professionals and not sufficiently recognized as a facilitator to pupil and school success (Weare 2000). Cleary, a significant shift in ways of thinking is needed to enable children and young people to safely negotiate the societal, family and academic pressures placed on them. It seems logical that the creation of safe and supportive schools must involve partnership working between pupils, teachers, administrators, parents, police officers, mental health professionals, business and community leaders, and an array of youth-serving professionals from the local community. The development of such approaches is not limited to the school alone, but must take place in partnership with the community. In achieving this aim *The Children's Plan* outlines 'a new role for schools [in England] as the centre of their communities, and more effective links between schools, the NHS and other children's services so that together they can engage parents and tackle all the barriers to the learning, health and happiness of every child' (DCSF 2007a: 2).

Employing a whole school approach and tackling the underlying issues which affect emotional well being within the school and community setting can benefit children and young people academically and help equip them with the emotional and social skills needed for life (Weare 2000). Moreover, school-based interventions can also offer greater access to care and support than the more traditional approaches to delivering health and preventative services to children and adolescents (Wagner et al. 2004). One such intervention, popular in the United States, is the Student Assistance Program (SAP) (Wagner et al. 2004).

Student Assistance Programmes (SAPs)

The Student Assistance Program (SAP) was designed for everyone in American educational communities from Kindergarten to University who had emotional health problems or exhibited high risk behaviours, such as substance abuse, or who were experiencing stresses such as poverty, family breakdown or loss. The main aim of SAP is to prevent adverse consequences of these problems becoming a barrier to learning and full participation in society. SAP first involves primary prevention through identifying, assessing and referring those whose individual and family problems seriously impact on them. Once referred, SAP then provides early intervention in the form of learning activities and support groups. Included in the SAP approach is support for parents and families in the wider community.

In the United States, the Texas SAP Initiative (2008) describes the programme as one of the most effective school-based prevention and early intervention strategies and they are reported by Watkins (2008) as being effective in areas such as drug and alcohol abuse, teenage pregnancy, violence, attendance and self-esteem.

The design of SAPs varies considerably in terms of philosophy and delivery, with some models using school personnel, others using trained service providers and others combining both school and community agency staff to deliver assessment and intervention services on site (Wagner et al. 2004). The SAP discussed here was devised 23 years ago in the USA by Cheryl Watkins (Executive Director, Student Assistance Training International). Her work in the American public school system gave rise to federal legislation enabling this approach to develop in state schools in all 50 United States and 30 other countries around the world. SAP is universal in its appeal and has been successfully adapted to meet the needs of a wide array of cultures.

Watkins' Student Assistance Program

Watkins' SAP follows that previously described (Wagner et al. 2004), where a combination of school and community agency staff are trained together to provide both assessment and intervention on the school site. Crucial to this model is the idea that in some way, the school system, which may be very efficient at handling the bureaucracy of education, becomes increasingly unable to provide help to pupils (and sometimes staff) who are struggling with their high risk behaviours. Anderson (1987) suggests that school systems can resemble dysfunctional family life. Becoming aware of this and the need to recover functional ways of being is the aim of Watkins:

> Let's create a healthy school family where kids are cherished ... let's create a healthy school family where we respect kids and care for kids and care for each other. Let's be that healthy family for these kids. We've [adults] got to heal ourselves, we can't just send the kids [to outsiders] for help

> (Personal communication by Watkins 2007).

Watkins' model has been adopted by a number of Local Education Authorities (LEA) in England and Wales. It comprises 12 components (Figure 11.1) and provides a process by which SAP can be implemented across a whole LEA. However, partnership and collaboration are key to the success of SAP, as putting a SAP into place requires agencies to work across previously respected boundaries in partnership with each other. This requires considerable time and commitment by all involved: SAP is not a short term solution. Each of the components will be described in more detail before presenting the experiences of three Local Education Authority areas (Caerphilly, Kirklees and Wrexham).

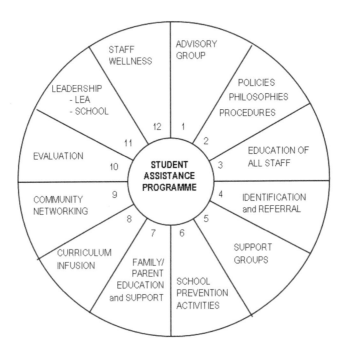

Figure 11.1 Watkins' (1999: A-2). SAP model
Source: Reproduced with kind permission of Cheryl Watkins © Chemical Awareness Training Institute Inc. 2001

Formation of a County advisory group

The first step in developing a SAP is to form an advisory group. The purpose of this is to involve the community in planning, implementation and evaluation of SAP. Members of the group are drawn from the LEA, and local schools and community agencies. This group works in partnership to develop policies, procedures and philosophy of the SAP which reflect the local context (component 2). As a result, there are local differences in how SAP has been implemented.

Staff education and training

Once policies are in place, multi-agency staff education is instigated; because successful implementation requires collaboration between staff they are trained in the principles of SAP and how it will operate in their context. In addition, SAP facilitators are recruited and trained to deliver the support group component which provides the main intervention of the programme. Training is delivered by an approved team and comprises a three-day training course, normally 'in-house' recruited to access advanced training in specialist topic these will be described in the following paragraphs. In addition to learning about SAP, the course gives participants an opportunity to experience, first hand, what it is like to be in a support group from both the perspective of facilitator and member. Having had this experience, newly trained facilitators become aware of the power of the support group process. In addition to the 'basic group' training, further training is available in a range of specialist topics (Appendix 11.1).

Identification and referral

Once facilitators have been trained, strategies are put in place to enable identification and referral of young people who would benefit from attending a SAP support group. Although each school/agency has to have its own system, the roles and responsibilities of individuals involved are clearly articulated and communicated across the partnership. Commonly, school staff, pupils, parents and other agencies can initiate a referral.

Support Groups

Within SAP the key intervention consists of support groups (normally of eight weeks duration), which take place during the school day. Sessions are run by trained facilitators and guided by a script which facilitates the exploration of topics such as sharing, grief and loss, divorce, school transition, anger and bullying.

As indicated in Figure 11.2, support groups focus on providing a sense of safety and trust through healthy interactions. This requires an appropriate environment in which trained facilitators enable children to form a bond between themselves and the other children so that life struggles can be shared. To remove power relationships the use of first names is required. In many cases, children express feelings for the first time in Group, and therefore effective use of words is often the first step in grasping previously unspoken feelings. Children are encouraged to use 'I' messages (I think, I need, I feel) in order to help them to understand the connection between feelings and behaviour, and are discouraged from speaking for other members in the group. This process then enhances mental health and well being by enabling each child to find their own words to describe their own experience; and as children struggle to find the most appropriate words to describe their feelings, they reflect upon their thoughts and behaviours in order to find meaning.

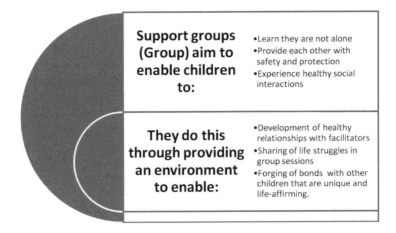

Figure 11.2   The aim of support groups and how they are achieved
Source: Watkins 1985

Through this process of articulating thoughts and meaning, children learn to emphasise and to reciprocate in their interactions with each other so that a caring relationship naturally develops. Jointly working on one person's difficulties then influences everyone else's in the group, and the various interactions trigger perceptions, attitudes and behaviours that have proved to be problematic in day-to-day life. This process of working through interactions that mirror everyday life within Group thus provides opportunities for feedback and to experiment with alternative ways of responding to situations. The reinforcement that children provide each other is a powerful means of changing behavioural patterns as peer group influences on behaviour can be much stronger than other influences. Confidentiality is key to the group process, the only exception being disclosure of child protection issues.

Prevention activities

In the spirit of a whole school approach, additional prevention activities are put in place, such as relaxation workshops, mentoring schemes, and peer education. The purpose of these is to enhance self-esteem in pupils and to enable them to develop and practice healthy living skills that will in turn affect the whole child and help create a more positive school environment.

Parental and community education

School is only one part of a child's life, thus partnerships are also built with parents, carers and the outside community. In order to promote parental involvement, schools sponsor education classes, parent facilitator training and support groups for parents. However, developing partnerships with parents, carers and families, especially those who would most benefit from participation, can be difficult in the early days of implementation as parents may have had a difficult time in school, and may be struggling with relationship breakdown, poverty and social exclusion, all of which can act as barriers to engagement with services.

Curriculum infusion

Integrating SAP across the school is further achieved through curriculum infusion. This is a prevention curriculum that is aligned with other curriculum initiatives such as the SEAL (DCSF 2007b). Infusion involves tackling issues such as: risks surrounding the use of tobacco, alcohol and other drugs, as well as the promotion of emotional and mental well being through the whole curriculum. It seeks to enhance problem solving, decision making and communication skills by building self awareness and self-esteem.

Community Networking

The child's wellbeing is of primary importance in SAP, thus SAP coordinators and facilitators develop links with partnership agencies to enable children in need to access services. In the USA, federal policy means that SAP is embedded within the community and cross-agency working means that links with government agencies, behavioural health agencies and other services are in place to develop total community wellness and promote future partnership working. Further collaborations with other agencies can be built such as: neighbourhood coalitions to fight drug abuse, gangs, violence and crime; networking with feeder schools; criminal justice; business partnerships – local Chamber of Commerce; drug free workplaces; and drug free school zones.

Programme evaluation

As with all initiatives, evaluation is needed to track progress and assess effectiveness of the SAP. A set of evaluation tools are included in the SAP, which enables schools to track progress and to report back to the 'Advisory Group' as well as the wider partnership.

Programme leadership and administration

For SAP to be implemented effectively there should be a Local Authority level coordinator and school/campus coordinator to provide leadership and administration at the county and school level. The coordinators link to external partnership agencies and facilitate implementation of the programme, thus ensuring that the SAP adheres to local policies and procedures.

Staff wellness

As adults are vital role models to children and young people, their health and well-being is also paramount. In Watkins' SAP, an understanding of the importance of staff wellness is encapsulated in a philosophy that recognizes the need for adults to have access to support and services. Activities suggested include the provision of staff support groups; staff retreats; coordination of employee and student assistance programme referrals and resources; support for staff to attend community services; and team building and staff rejuvenation.

The Student Assistance Programme in England and Wales

A number of LEAs in the England and Wales have adopted SAP. In England, the SAP has been adopted in Winchester, Basingstoke, Reading, Andover, Woking, Surrey, and Kirklees. In Wales it as been adopted in Caerphilly Borough and Wrexham. In addition, SAP is beginning to cascade into other areas. To illustrate how SAP has been implemented in practice three case study examples are provided: Kirklees, Caerphilly and Wrexham. These will be described in more detail in the following sections

In Kirklees, the SAP was introduced in 2005 as SAFE (Support Available For Everyone) (Kirklees ed net), with training of 30 delegates representing departments such as Child and Adolescent Mental Health Services and primary care trusts, the police, Looked After Children, Education Psychology, Ethnic Minority Groups and school improvement officers. Successes since the introduction of the course include the completion of a whole school exercise, with numerous schools groups supporting children and young people from all four key stages, plus successful parent support group work.

In Caerphilly Borough, the priority is for training of school-based staff and SAP has been implemented in 12 of 13 Comprehensive Schools and 30 of 84 Primary Schools. A part time coordinator has been appointed and multi professionals that have been trained include youth workers, school health nurses, educational welfare officers, educational behaviour support, social workers, school councillors, school youth mentors, community liaison police officers, head teachers, heads of years, and classroom support workers.

A case study of SAP implementation and evaluation: the Wrexham experience

In Wrexham, a full time coordinator is employed and Watkins' (1985) SAP process has been customized to meet the needs of eight of Wrexham's nine secondary schools and an increasing number of primary schools. Of the 12 components of Watkins' (1985) model, Wrexham LEA has implemented support groups, staff training, school prevention activities and evaluation. Also under development are curriculum infusion and staff wellness initiatives.

Support groups

Student support groups have promoted emotional, social and behavioural change on a range of issues from drug and alcohol use, family breakdown, bereavement, transitional pupil progress and more recently with students who have speech and language difficulties. Another important issue being addressed by the primary sector is supporting pupils who live with addicted parents. A key intervention strategy of SAP is the student support group. Each year, in eight of Wrexham's nine secondary schools, many pupils participate in support groups where they find the information and support necessary to sustain them through times of emotional pain and pressure as they attempt to survive their life circumstances. Box 11.2 provides a selection of the comments made by students in response to attending Group.

Box 11.1 Pupils' comments about attending group

- I found Group useful and it helped me a lot. The only thing I was worried about was the confidentiality issue. But nothing was said out of Group by other pupils
- The support group helped a lot and now I know how to deal with different situations
- Support group was great. I felt really comfortable being there after a few days. It has really helped me take a positive and happy attitude to life
- I felt comfortable coming to Group. It helped me get closer to friends. Since I started coming to Group I've let more barriers down more than in 14 years
- It was helpful and I'm more aware of my feelings now I have talked about them with other people
- Very good to listen to other people and to be listened to
- The support group has helped me to open up
- It has helped me to achieve more e.g. more confidence, not scared to have a go at things
- Insight group really did promote insight
- I thought it was very helpful to talk to people who understand what you're going through
- It has calmed me down but there could be an anger management group
- When I come to school I feel safer than I did because I know I can always come to Group if I need to
- I really enjoyed working with the teachers because they were more like friends than teachers. I really enjoyed it!!
- I feel much better about myself and know how to deal with problems, much easier than before. I also enjoyed getting to know the teachers as friends
- Built lasting, trusting relationships
- It helps me be more aware of the feelings I have

- I don't think I lose my temper as much as I did before Group
- I have learned to get higher confidence because of SAP members

Staff training

In Wrexham although the priority for training is for school-based staff, other groups have also been trained, and recipients include youth workers, school nurses, educational welfare officers, educational behaviour support, social workers, school councillors, school youth mentors, community liaison police officers, head teachers, heads of years, class room teachers and classroom support workers. The SAP training has been described as 'life changing' and 'exhausting' as the selection of quotes in Box 11.2 illustrates.

Box 11.2 Comments made participants following the 3 day training course

- No one could prepare themselves or know what to expect from this course – it changes your whole outlook on life
- I find the group sessions to be excellent, just the sort of practical work which is sadly lacking in most training activities
- A very positive, powerful experience. I believe all teachers would benefit from attending this workshop – it helps you understand the problems faced by youngsters in our care
- It has given me skills to identify children in need and ways to follow up their behaviours in a positive, worthwhile way
- I have personally gained a better awareness into the problems young people and adults experience
- I learned to be patient and to look beyond what we see in a person
- An insight into life – a reminder that we all take varying paths in life – and that we all need people
- It changes your life and allows you to see yourself and others in a new way – also to realise how important it is to help our children so they can learn
- It was a wonderful workshop that put me in touch with myself and why I do the work I do
- Made me realise the feelings that go on in pupils' minds and made me look at myself and others a bit deeper
- Having very little experience of the issues faced by our pupils I have gained an inspiring insight during the past three days
- It enables teachers to respect the 'whole' of our pupils' needs, not just the academic
- It has helped me with direction in my role as Personal Social Education Coordinator

---

School prevention activities

In Wrexham, the School prevention activities have been developed in line with expressed needs of students and have focused, in particular, on healthy living skills such as self-esteem, stress management and relaxation training, positive thinking, addictions and bullying. These subjects have been explored in experiential workshops and support groups where students and staff are, together, encouraged to bring their subjective experiences to bear on the issues under debate. The sessions provide emotionally safe spaces for all participants to deal with concerns in an open and direct manner and can provide opportunities for staff and students to re-appraise their relationships and to learn from one another. The workshops can be challenging and emotive, and feedback is consistently positive from both staff and students. There are plans to develop more activities in other areas along similar lines.

Curriculum infusion

Curriculum infusion is another area under development in Wrexham secondary schools that concentrates on making personal health and social education (PHSE) more responsive to staff and student concerns. In one school, following a campus wide consultation about PHSE, the existing curriculum was reworked to take into account the developmental milestones of students as they transfer to key stage 3 (11–14 years) and beyond. Staff concerns about PHSE were addressed through inset training (Postgraduate Professional Development run by the Teacher Training Agency) designed for year group tutors consisting mostly of structured time for reflection. In addition to these sessions, a whole school 'renewal' process has been undertaken along with an official launch of the new curriculum. Two years on, PHSE at this particular high school, is a strong and relevant tier of learning for the students.

In other secondary schools, PHSE sessions have been delivered on 'health' days utilizing experiential workshops (described earlier). Many students have self-referred into the SAP process following participation in these PHSE sessions: self-referral is a core aim of the SAP process.

Staff wellness

A development of critical importance is a growing interest among teachers and other school staff about their own wellness. A central element of the SAP ethos recognizes that it is adults who set the emotional tone of the organizations in which children learn, therefore, adult emotional and psychological health is imperative if good role modelling is to take place. Much of the interest in staff wellness has arisen from schools where SAP is strong and teachers have seen the benefits to students who have engaged in the SAP process.

Evaluation of SAP in Wrexham

In addition to self-evaluation, an independent evaluation of SAP was undertaken in Wrexham (Carnwell and Baker 2005a, 2007) which used focus group interviews of students, facilitators and head teachers to find out how effective SAP had been in changing students' behaviour and to consider wider implications of 'Group' in terms of its effects on peers, teachers and family members.

The results revealed important lessons for partnerships, both between students and between students and teacher/facilitators. These can be described as building partnerships through relationships, boundaries in transition, and sustaining partnerships

Building partnerships through relationships

In order to develop successful relationships, students learned techniques to help them to express feelings towards one another. As facilitators explained, although at first 'students could not explain a feeling … some were able to explain how they felt before the end' and in the words of one student 'you've got an hour to cope with seeing people crying … upset and … angry'.

Building relationships also required trust to be developed and students learned to trust people whom they had not previously trusted and began to see teachers in a different light and to respect them more, partly because, in the view of students, teacher/facilitators had learned to handle them better because they understood why they got upset. Equally, facilitators felt privileged to work with students in Group as 'they let you in'.

Boundaries in transition

Building partnerships through the development of relationships also results in changes in boundaries, one of which was the use of facilitators' first names during group sessions. Both students and facilitators were uncomfortable with this at first. However, students came 'to realize that they are teachers and when you go out of Group your attitude has to change'.

Other uncomfortable boundaries for students were those that existed around previously established relationships, which resulted in students feeling uneasy about sharing feelings with certain people or talking 'to people you don't want to talk to'. As one student said: 'it's difficult telling someone about things for the first time … Your voice gets all croaky and you know you're going to cry, so it's nerve racking … but after that it's easy'. Equally, it was difficult discussing subjects they had no experience of, such as divorce, as 'it's asking you to talk about something you've not had any experience of; it's difficult to find language to describe it'.

An important boundary transition took place when, in order to overcome awkward silences, facilitators shared personal experiences with students to encourage them to speak. This was contentious among facilitators as there was debate about what professionals should share with students. Taking on the different role was also difficult for facilitators because in the facilitator role 'it's not your place to say "pack it in" when they misbehave', neither can they 'cut across them when they are saying something, even if it seems inappropriate'.

Further boundary transitions had to take place for teachers as they stepped from being a Group facilitator to the classroom, which could be emotionally draining. As one facilitator said: 'I've seen a [facilitator] … say to another member of staff "just give me a hug, I just need a hug to deal with what I've just heard in that room" … They might then … go straight in to teach another class.

Sustaining partnerships

Partnerships between students, staff and ultimately the wider community requires sustained effort in terms of building relationships and overcoming challenges arising from shifting boundaries. As participants pointed out, facilitators need special qualities. Moreover, students and teachers indicated the necessity for teachers to be trained. If teachers are used as facilitators, this leaves teaching gaps, which may result in increases in class sizes elsewhere. This might in turn threaten the educational standards across the school.

For head teachers, prioritizing one 'good thing' over another is difficult when expectations in schools continue to increase and when there is a lack of funding in schools generally. As the head teachers interviewed pointed out, SAPs are needed due to the high incidence of mental health problems in young people. One head teacher suggested that Group: 'Should be a core subject; unless we get the emotional literacy of students, which is an important part of the School's core curriculum, we are not going to be able to teach these students who have huge …problems that impact on them in such devastating ways'. Using Group to improve emotional literacy is a long term commitment though. Restricting attendance to a series of eight weeks can be problematic and improvements in behaviour may not be sustained in the long term. As one facilitator indicated: 'Expectations are raised but then not sustained in the long term. One child had been a great success from attending Group but was not allowed to continue and the child's behaviour has now deteriorated.

Facilitators also explained how one student kept asking when Group was re-commencing because the student perceived that 'behaviour was suffering as SAP had helped keep [the student] on the straight and narrow'. There is also scope for multi-disciplinary partnerships to develop, so that other professionals, such as counsellors, could be trained as facilitators, particularly as 'using a stranger for a confidential matter could be advantageous'.

A case study of SAP implementation and evaluation – the Kirklees experience

Using Watkins' Student Assistance Programme model Kirklees has introduced the concept of support to schools and their communities under the banner of their SAFE

(Support Available For Everyone) programme. This is a recommended element of the Kirklees Behaviour Improvement Programme (Kirklees Ednet 2008).

In Kirklees, the impact of the SAP courses has identified and supported children and people in need. For some adults, life changing decisions have been made and implemented, while for some youngsters the outcomes have resulted in improved attendance at school, with resultant potential for improved attainment and ultimately improved life chances. The structure of group work is one of the main strengths of this approach, with everyone being valued regardless of the characteristics that impact on their behaviour; everyone is encouraged to value their peers both within and without the process. Of particular note has been the benefits arising from the opportunity to talk and be listened to, which have enhanced the life skills and equipped resilient children, young people and adults with the skills to best focus and share their resilience. The other strong advantage of the SAFE project has been the partnership working, with professionals now being more familiar with each other's constraints and pressures. Schools also have access to different types of support, such as from nonschool staff from a variety of agencies, who come into schools to support school staff and children. Similarly, a multi-agency approach in the management of the project overseeing all aspects of SAFE in Kirklees has raised the profile of the success of multi-agency working. The fundamental support for behaviour improvement programmes is multi-agency working and none is better exemplified than the multi-agency approach to SAFE in Kirklees. Barnsley Local Authority began the training process in 2006, and has started developing SAP in their school system after seeing the successes in Kirklees.

A case study of SAP implementation and evaluation – the Caerphilly experience

In Caerphilly Borough, the Student Assistance Programme is being piloted in four Caerphilly schools, with the hope of rolling this out to further schools. The most successful part of the programme is that of youth mentors in schools who are running Group, although there are many examples of good practice. One comprehensive school involved is an all-boy's school, in which Group is being run three or four times a week and the boys are queuing up. This school has around 20 staff trained to deliver support groups, including the head master, classroom support staff, as well as an education welfare officer and educational psychologist. Another comprehensive school is planning to run seven groups and has invited young carers staff to be trained and to run Group. A further comprehensive school has taken on the Crisis Intervention model as well as running three Groups a week. SAP is now beginning to spread through Wales. Monmouthshire has four comprehensive schools that are running Group and some primary mental health workers in Aberystwyth have recently completed the training. Some comprehensive schools have been inspected by ESTYN (Her Majesty's Chief Inspector of Education and Training in Wales), and have achieved high marks due to their use of SAP.

The programme is also very popular with primary schools, with the LEA focusing on getting as many schools on board as possible within the funding period.

There are, however, a few schools that are not using SAP properly. They are not involving teaching staff and are resistant to change their approach.

Conclusion

In the UK, Student Assistance Programmes are beginning to gain recognition as a powerful means by which to achieve a number of targets set by current policy, these are:

- Multi-agency cooperation through a shared training process which unites professionals around a number of common goals
- Partnerships between adults and children
- Partnerships between children and their peers

More importantly, they provide a mechanism to improve the mental health, well being and resilience in children and young people which considers their needs and context. Inter-group, inter-agency and cross-agency partnership working however is the key to successful delivery and the creation of links which will benefit the child within the community setting, enabling them to cope with and conquer adverse life experiences. To achieve this, however, requires a considerable mind shift in adults about their own health and emotional well being, and a recognition that educating children is not just about curriculum delivery but also a recognition that pupils are individuals with emotional needs, who have a right to a healthy and happy childhood if they are to achieve their future potential.

Question for further discussion

1   To what extent are the emotional health and well being of staff and users considered within your experience?
2   Considering that partnership working is key to the implementation of a SAP, which agencies would you consider working with to facilitate a SAP?
3   What additional benefits and or difficulties could you anticipate in developing a SAP?

Useful websites

- *Kirklees Ednet*: www.kirklees-ednet.org.uk/subjects/eic/behaviour/ SAFE.htm This website describes the SAP model as model as developed and supported by Cheryl Watkins of student assistance training international. Kirklees have introduced the concept of support to schools and their communities under the banner of their SAFE – Support Available For Everyone – programme.

- *Social and Emotional Aspects of Learning (SEAL)*: www.bandapilot.org.uk/secondary/ This website introduces Social and Emotional Aspects of Learning for secondary schools (Secondary SEAL). This is a whole school approach to promoting social and emotional skills which involves all members of the school and all aspects of school life.
- *Excellence and Enjoyment: social and emotional aspects of learning*: www.bandapilot.org.uk/primary/ This website provides a resource for Social and Emotional Aspects of Learning (SEAL) for primary schools, key stages 1 and 2.

Notes

1   Our thanks to Ian Dutton, BIP coordinator Kirklees and Julian Edwards Primary Mental Health Worker, Caerphilly for providing case studies of their experience. We are also grateful to Cheryl Watkins for her advice on this chapter.
2   Based on a real life case study, details have been changed and pseudonyms used to protect identity.

12 Not behind closed doors: working in partnership against domestic violence

Liz Blyth and Sobia Shaw

This chapter will:

- Discuss the nature and extent of domestic violence and the implications for service providers.
- Explore the context of multi-agency work on domestic violence and explain why effective collaboration and coordination is important.
- Examine some of the challenges, obstacles and opportunities created by working in partnership across the boundaries of statutory, voluntary and community organizations.
- Draw on research and experience of multi-agency partnership work on domestic violence to provide examples of good practice.

This chapter examines some of the issues, obstacles and opportunities created by working in partnership to challenge domestic violence. It is based on research carried out for a Master's dissertation, as well as practical experience of working in a multi-agency context. One of the authors worked as domestic violence coordinator with a multi-agency partnership in Coventry, and the other is chief executive of Panahghar Asian women's domestic violence services in Coventry and Leicester and a founder member of the multi-agency partnership in Coventry. Their combined professional experience has emphasized the importance of working in partnership when seeking to challenge complex societal problems such as abuse. Domestic violence is a complex issue, which creates complex problems for individuals, service providers and communities. No single agency is able to successfully respond to this complexity alone and therefore real 'joined-up' working between the statutory, voluntary and community sectors is essential. The chapter explores some of the key issues for partnership work on domestic violence, using practical examples to illustrate that analysis.

Domestic violence: the social and political context

In Britain, over the last two decades, there has been a significant societal shift in the public perception of domestic violence as a private, family matter to be excused, ignored, dismissed or even ridiculed. The view that what goes on behind closed doors is somehow outside the usual boundaries of acceptable behaviour, and indeed beyond the scope of legal jurisdiction, is finally being challenged. Domestic violence is the subject of increasing public concern and condemnation and there is a much greater understanding of the nature of abuse and its serious, long lasting consequences.

This increased level of awareness is largely due to the determined efforts of refuges (safe houses) and other women's organizations that have forced the issue of domestic violence from the margins to the mainstream. Since the first refuges were set up in the 1970s, the Women's Aid Federation of England and Wales (WAFE) has developed a network of over 500 local services providing refuge, advocacy, help lines, drop-in and outreach services (WAFE 2006). Working alongside academics and practitioners, Women's Aid has been the key driver in ensuring increased coordination through multi-agency fora, as well as successfully lobbying for a number of significant changes to legislation in order to protect women and children and bring perpetrators to justice. Public awareness has also increased as women have found the courage to tell their stories, celebrities have spoken out about their personal experiences, and cinema and television, in particular the 'soaps', have made many more people aware of the realities of abuse.

In the UK, domestic violence did not receive national attention until the Labour government came to power in 1997. As the number of women MPs increased so did the effectiveness of their advocacy for women's issues, and gradually domestic violence was forced up the political agenda. In 1995, and 2000 the Home Office issued inter-agency guidance, in 1996 the Family Law Act was passed providing new protection, and in 1999 the domestic violence and abuse awareness campaign 'Break the Chain' was launched. This was closely followed by the publication of *'Living without Fear: An Integrated Approach to Tackling Violence against Women'* (Women's Unit 1999), which set out the government's strategic intentions to:

- Reduce and prevent crimes of violence against women
- Provide timely support and protection
- Bring perpetrators to justice
- See effective multi-agency partnership throughout England and Wales

The 1998 Crime and Disorder Act placed a statutory duty on 'responsible authorities' to tackle crime and disorder, initially defining the police and local authorities as responsible and later extending this to fire authorities and primary care trusts. A key component of the legislation was the requirement to set up crime and disorder partnerships in each local authority area, which were tasked with auditing the nature and extent of crime and disorder in their area, including domestic violence, and take action accordingly. Most importantly they were required to plan and act together, across the agencies, to tackle issues at the local level.

In 2003 the Inter-Ministerial Group on Domestic Violence was established leading to the publication of *'Safety and Justice: The Government's proposals on Domestic Violence'* with wide consultation with local refuges, WAFE, Imkaan (the National Umbrella Organisation for Asian Women's Refuges), Domestic Violence Fora, statutory agencies and survivors and victims of abuse. *'Safety and Justice'* focused on three priorities: prevention, protection and justice, and support. It set out changes to legislation as well as improvements across a wide range of agencies, including a new 24 hour free-phone helpline, £32 million investment in new refuge places, a series of good practice guides in relation to health, children's services and criminal justice, guidance on 'information sharing' among practitioners, and the roll out of perpetrator programmes in the Probation Service (Home Office 2005b).

The consultation carried out for *'Safety and Justice'* informed the Domestic Violence Crime and Victims Act 2004; the first serious piece of legislation addressing domestic violence in over 30 years. The Act introduced new powers for the police, new courts to deal with offenders, and strengthened the rights of victims and witnesses of domestic violence offering them more support and protection. A year later, the Home Office launched a 'National Domestic Violence Plan aimed at all those working in domestic violence, and reporting on progress to date. More recently the government has been consulting on the establishment of homicide review panels. These panels will require agencies that may have known about or suspected domestic violence to look into the background and learn lessons for the future in the same way that Section 8 inquiries are carried out when a child dies.

It is clear that the government is determined to ensure better joint working between criminal justice agencies to make sure they provide better services to victims and witnesses, bring more offenders to justice and at the same time increase public confidence in the criminal justice service. It is perhaps within the criminal justice system that the most innovative initiatives have been introduced with pilot projects for specialist domestic violence courts, Multi Agency Risk Assessment Conferences (MARACs), the perpetrator programmes delivered through the probation service, and independent domestic violence advocates (IDVAs) who will work in Specialist Domestic Violence Courts.

Domestic violence: the nature and extent of abuse

Domestic violence is the everyday life experience of many thousands of women and children. According to the British Crime Survey, domestic violence accounts for 16 percent of all violent crime (Home Office, 2007a). Research by Stanko (2000) found that in the UK the police received a call every 60 seconds and that an incident of domestic violence took place every six to 20 seconds. According to the Home Office, approximately two women each week are killed by a current or former partner (Home Office 2007a). WAFE's annual survey for 2004/05 found that 19,000 women and 24,000 children had been provided with refuge in one year, and 196,000 women and 129,000 children were supported through refuge, outreach, advocacy and support services (WAFE 2006). It is estimated that domestic violence costs £5.7 billion each year in England and Wales, calculated as the cost of providing criminal justice, healthcare and other services as well as the associated loss in economic output (Walby 2004).

Domestic violence is not just a major concern in the UK, it is an international issue. It is the main cause of morbidity for women worldwide, greater than cancer, war and motor vehicle accidents (Home Office 2007c). Women and girls are exploited through abuse in the family, sexual violence, trafficking and prostitution but with the courage of women speaking out across the world there is a growing recognition and commitment to ending the violence. The United Nations have adopted a declaration on the elimination of all forms of violence against women. As former UN Secretary General, Kofi Annan said: 'Violence against women is ... perhaps the most shameful human rights violation and it is perhaps the most pervasive. It knows no boundaries of geography, culture or wealth. As long as it continues, we cannot claim to be making real progress towards equality, development and peace' (Kofi Annan cited in amnesty.org.uk 2007).

Research and practical experience have shown that domestic violence can affect anyone, regardless of gender, ethnicity, race, sexuality, age, marital status, disability or lifestyle. However, the majority of abuse is perpetrated by men against women, usually by a partner or ex-partner. Although men do experience abuse from their female partners, they are less likely to be physically injured, frightened or upset by the experience and less likely to be subjected to a repeat pattern of abuse (Mirrlees-Black 1998). Domestic violence may also be perpetrated by another adult with whom there is a close relationship, for example a brother, son, carer or extended family member. Abuse does also take place in same sex relationships, an area that is only recently beginning to be addressed in service provision and where lesbians and gay men can find their traumatic experiences exacerbated by stereotyping, misunderstanding and homophobia.

Domestic violence is a complex issue. It is bound up with society's norms and values, myths and stereotypes, gender roles and relationships. It is linked to identity and autonomy in intimate relationships and the misuse of power and control. According to the Home Office (2008) it can take a number of forms. Some are physical, such as assault, indecent assult, rape or marital rape and damaging property. Others are non-physical, such as criticism, belittling, isolation, control of finances, threats and harassment. It also includes denying physical freedom or medical care, forced marriage, female genital mutilation, prostitution and trafficking. In the most extreme forms it leads to homicide. For indeed a key issue for professionals is that domestic violence usually escalates over time and that the risks increase at the point of separation (DoH 2005b). However, the most important point in understanding domestic violence is, as Hester et al. (1998) noted, to listen to the accounts of survivors, as only from these can we really begin to understand how domestic violence feels, what it involves and what the implications are.

Domestic violence: the links with other forms of abuse

The links between domestic violence and child abuse are well documented and children living with domestic violence have been found to be at risk of psychological and physical harm (Mullender 1996; Hendessi 1997; Hester et al. 1998). In Coventry, in a seven month period in 2006/07, the police recorded 1600 incidents of domestic violence with 2700 children involved (45 percent of the children were under 5 years old). In 2005, Coventry Area Child Protection Committee (ACPC) reported that domestic violence had been a feature in 47 percent of case conferences in the previous year; of these 20 percent involved domestic violence alone, while a further 16% involved both domestic violence and alcohol abuse, 7 percent involved domestic violence and drug abuse and 4 percent involved domestic violence, alcohol abuse and drug abuse (Coventry ACPC 2005).

National research has suggested that up to two-thirds of children on a child protection register live with domestic violence (Moxon 1999). We also know that recorded incidents are the tip of the iceberg as many incidents go unreported, unrecorded and are not prosecuted (BMA 1998).

Developing effective measures to safeguard children has improved greatly over the last few years, with the renewed focus on keeping children safe from harm enshrined in the Every Child Matters policy framework (Department for Education and Skills (2004). Safeguarding Children's Boards are required to ensure representation from Domestic Violence Partnerships, and the Home Office has issued guidance on *Tackling Domestic Violence: Providing Support for Children who have Witnessed Domestic Violence* (Home Office 2004). Multi-agency Risk Assessment Conferences (MARACs) screen for the level of risk in domestic violence cases, in order to identify those at greatest risk of serious harm. In Coventry a new initiative has been introduced to assess the level of risk for children living with domestic violence independently to the adult victim.

The link between domestic violence and pregnancy is now better understood, with studies finding that violence begins or escalates during pregnancy (Bewley and Gibbs 2002). Indeed there is evidence that around 30 per cent of domestic violence starts during or just after pregnancy (Lewis 2002). The Confidential Enquiry into Maternal Deaths first raised the impact of domestic violence on pregnant women in its 1994–96 report. This later became the subject of a specific chapter in the report covering 1997–99 when eight deaths were attributed directly to domestic violence (Lewis 2002). The effects of domestic violence during pregnancy have been found to include miscarriage, stillbirth, low birth weight or premature labour, as well as depression, alcohol or drug misuse and suicide (Berenson et al. 1994 and Lewis 2001, both cited in Bewley and Gibbs 2002). There is an increasing recognition that health care workers are in a unique position to identify and respond to domestic violence. For example, midwives and health visitors usually visit women in their homes a number of times, and have opportunities to build a rapport while assessing their client's health and well being, as well as being well placed to assess relationship dynamics. Women who experience domestic violence may pay several visits to a General Practitioner, perhaps presenting with depression or repeated injuries. In addition, Accident and Emergency staff come into contact with women in crisis when they have been seriously injured by abuse.

Although there is still a good deal of misunderstanding, reticence, embarrassment or disbelief about domestic violence, there has also been considerable progress in providing the evidence that underpins the case for a better response. This has resulted in the Department of Health, Royal College of Obstetricians and Gynaecologists, Royal College of Midwives, the British Medical Association and other professional bodies issuing guidance and training materials on domestic violence and establishing an advisory group of representatives from the Royal Colleges. In 2004 the

Home Office issued *Tackling Domestic Violence: The Role of Health Professionals* and in 2005 the Department of Health revised and reissued *Domestic Violence: A Resource Manual for Health Care Professionals* which promotes networking and information sharing among professionals. In 2006 the two government departments collaborated to publish a *Domestic Violence Training Manual for Health Professionals*. However, there is still a long way to go before policy is matched by consistent responses on the ground; national guidance is important but it has to lead to *local* policies, procedures and most importantly *training* for staff, in order to be truly effective.

In many ways the reticence of public bodies to consider domestic violence as core business echoes the difficulties faced in the last 20 years in forcing the issue of child abuse out into the open. Families are expected to be places of safety, love and respect and yet in some families trust is betrayed by the closest family members. Generally in society there is a belief that what takes place at home is a family matter, and that it is private business and not for public concern. The challenge for services dealing with the reality of abuse in all its forms is to challenge assumptions about the boundaries of acceptable behaviour and protect adults and children where home is no longer a place of safety.

In Coventry the domestic violence services available in the voluntary sector include a specialist refuge for Asian women and a support service for African-Caribbean women. The Asian women's project developed out of a grassroots response to violence against women and responds to a high number of incidents of abuse by other family members, attempted suicide, as well as forced marriage and abduction of young women. These issues present a challenge to statutory and voluntary sector services, which have not yet fully grasped the complex cultural contexts of domestic violence. There has been a great deal of research about domestic violence but most studies have focused on white heterosexual relationships (Hester et al. 1998) and most services have developed from this perspective. Women with disabilities may also face additional obstacles in getting the help and support they need, especially if the violence is from their carer. Reporting and escaping violence is difficult enough but many services are simply not sensitive to the needs of individual women. Inadequate interpretation and translation services, poor physical access, lack of cultural under-standing or fear of making things worse often compound the physical and emotional isolation women experience when seeking help.

A significant number of women who arrive in the UK to join spouses find themselves trapped by their abusers and the system. They do not have the same rights as other victims until they receive 'leave to remain' in the UK, which in turn depends on the Home Office being satisfied that the couple have been together for two years, that the woman is being financially supported by her spouse and that she has not made any claims on the state. Women in this situation have little option but to endure the abuse. With 'no recourse to public funds', they have no access to legal services, health services, housing, welfare benefits or social services if they leave a violent partner or family members. Concerted lobbying by women's organizations has resulted in some concessions from the Home Office including guidance to local authorities on funding women in fear of violence with insecure immigration status.

Asian women's refuges have been dealing with forced marriages as part of domestic violence for the past 30 years, and have lobbied government to make a clear distinction between 'arranged' and 'forced' marriage, the latter being a marriage where one or more of the parties do not consent and which has been conducted under *duress*, which can involve anything from emotional pressure to physical violence, and honour crimes and killings. In 2005 the Forced Marriage Unit was established in government to deal with casework, develop policy, coordinate interventions, and provide signposting and support for victims and professionals.

The issues faced by black and minority ethnic women, disabled women, women with drug and alcohol dependencies, and lesbians and gay men, need to be explored by professionals if public services are to be accessible to all and not compound experiences of oppression and abuse. In summary, there is increased understanding among people working with abuse that where one form of abuse is identified professionals should be looking for other forms; indeed it is important that people do not 'think in boxes' but understand the overlap between different forms of abuse. This is essential not just in understanding the child protection implications in families but also the connection with the abuse of vulnerable adults – an inter-relationship that began to be addressed in the Department of Health's *No Secrets* guidance on adult abuse (DoH 2000c) which is mandatory for local authorities to implement. There is a degree of overlap between domestic violence and the abuse of vulnerable adults, for example in Coventry recent figures found that 22 percent of vulnerable adult abuse was domestic violence related, and in 80 percent of these cases the perpetrator was a family member, while in 20 percent it was a partner.

It is perhaps important to note that domestic violence also challenges professionals on a personal level, because the patterns of abuse and examples of abusive behaviour, particularly controlling, manipulative and undermining behaviour, may not be so far removed from the dynamics of the intimate relationships of some professionals. Indeed, the high level of prevalence of domestic violence in society suggests that in any sizeable staff group or organization there are likely to be both perpetrators and survivors of domestic violence, and for this reason it is important that organizations develop good policies to deal with domestic violence as it affects staff, as well as in relation to clients. A summary of the main issues discussed above is presented in Box 12.1.

Box 12.1 Domestic violence: in summary

- Domestic violence can affect any adult in an intimate family-type relationship, although the majority of serious and repeated abuse is perpetrated by men against their female partners or ex-partners
- Most studies suggest that one in four women will experience domestic violence at some point in their lives
- In the UK two women every week are killed as a result of domestic violence
- An incident of domestic violence takes place every six to twenty seconds

- Domestic violence accounts for 16 percent of all reported violent crime
- Domestic violence often begins or escalates during or just after pregnancy
- Risks increase at the point of separation, e.g. when the relationship breaks down
- Individuals from minority or excluded groups and those who have additional needs can face additional barriers in getting help
- Children who witness domestic violence are at risk of physical and psychological harm
- There a strong correlation between domestic violence and other forms of abuse, e.g. child abuse, the abuse of vulnerable adults

Domestic violence: the importance of partnership work

Domestic violence is a complex issue that causes complex problems in people's lives, and no single organization can respond effectively on its own. Effective partnership work is needed to share resources and information and to build the momentum to challenge the attitudes that dismiss, ignore or perpetuate violence and abuse in our society. In the past, statutory organizations have lagged behind in recognizing the social, financial and individual costs of not taking domestic violence seriously. While there was a recognition that it was a cross-cutting issue it was everybody's business but nobody's responsibility. However in the last few years there has been a huge momentum with domestic violence positioned firmly in the statutory arena through multi-agency crime and disorder partnerships. Tackling crime and disorder has become a major priority, and crime disorder partnerships have to take action to address domestic violence.

Concern about lack of funding for refuge and other support services is no longer voiced by the voluntary sector and women's groups alone. Professionals in statutory organizations, who rely on these essential services, have also been concerned about the shortfall and successful lobbying of government has led to millions of pounds of investment to tackle the problem in the last few years. As domestic violence is pushed up the agenda, and public awareness raised, more women come forward for help; an increase of 60 percent over three years was recorded by Women's Aid (WAFE 2006). Similarly, once professionals are sensitive to the possibility of domestic violence, they begin to look beyond their client's presenting issues to the possibility of domestic violence as an underlying factor. This, in turn, leads to an increase in referrals to refuges and domestic violence projects. One of the dilemmas in domestic violence work is that when awareness is raised, and people feel safe enough to come forward, professionals need to be able to respond with confidence. It is important to be able to provide up-to-date information about local support services, know where to get advice from other professionals, and most importantly to give a supportive, believing response. Being part of a domestic violence forum can help organizations to do this by sharing information about services, providing access to training, establishing referral mechanisms between agencies and sharing expertise, for example, by assisting with the development of domestic violence policies and procedures.

There are over 200 domestic violence fora in the UK (Hague 2000), many established by the police in collaboration with refuges, women groups and the voluntary sector in response to guidance from the Home Office or under the 1998 Crime and Disorder Act. Where dynamic local domestic violence fora already existed before the 1998 Act, as in Coventry, the challenge has been slightly different to places where no forum existed. The only national study of inter-agency responses to domestic violence was carried out in 1996 (Hague et al. 1996). The researchers found considerable variation in multi-agency fora with no easily distinguishable model or approach. They concluded that multi-agency fora offered considerable opportunities for effective coordination but there was a danger that they could be used as a smokescreen for inactivity or as a 'talking shop' with little actual change in practical responses.

Partnership: the Coventry response

Coventry Domestic Violence Partnership was established in the 1980s as a focus group to advise planners and commissioners in health and social care about service gaps and priorities. The impetus for the Coventry Partnership came from refuges and the voluntary sector in collaboration with the police and 'safer cities' community safety workers. Since then it has developed into a strong and dynamic multi-agency partnership with a wide remit across the spectrum of public and community services. At the time of this research, it was a closed group consisting of representatives from statutory and voluntary organizations whose core business partly or wholly involved domestic violence. This included the police, probation, magistrates, Crown Prosecution Service, social services, primary care trust, education, area child protection committee, Panahghar, Haven and other voluntary organizations such as Victim Support and Relate. The partnership had a statutory sector chairperson with the vice chair role shared between the managers of Coventry's three specialist domestic violence services, one supporting Asian women, one for African-Caribbean women and a generic refuge all of which were provided by the voluntary sector. This balance of power between the voluntary and statutory sectors as well as addressing equality and diversity was perceived to have been one of the reasons for the partnership's success. While the statutory organizations, such as police, probation and social services, were powerful in structural terms, the voluntary sector women's organizations represented the voices of survivors of domestic violence and ensured the partnership remained focused on work that made a real difference to their lives. In terms of accountability, the partnership was accountable to its membership and reported to the local crime and disorder partnership.

An increasingly common role in partnership work is that of a coordinator. Research has found that this is an important factor in successful partnership, requiring the skills to operate across service boundaries, build bridges between different interest groups, broker difference and build consensus (Webb 1991). The role of a domestic violence coordinator is to 'oil the wheels' of partnership: facilitating communication; building bridges; networking; keeping a strategic overview; and being a catalyst for action. Importantly, in Coventry this post was supported by excellent administrative staff who helped with organization and communication – vital tasks in keeping 20 organizations on board in the partnership, as well as engaging wider stakeholders in the city.

One of most effective mechanisms for partnership development in Coventry involved improvements to structure and processes within the partnership. Some of these were implemented as a result of research asking members to reflect on their experiences of the partnership and their organization's role within it. Partnership meetings moved from a time frame of monthly to quarterly meetings and were supplemented by task groups meeting more regularly. Each task group was charged with implementing part of the annual work programme drawn from priorities identified in the city's Multi-agency Strategy on Domestic Violence (Coventry Domestic Violence Focus Group 2000). Task groups were chaired by different members of the partnership according to expertise (e.g. health, children, perpetrators, diversity) and additional members were co-opted from a wide network of organizations. One of the conditions for membership of the partnership was that each member was expected to be active in at least one task group. This helped to ensure the partnership did not become a talking shop or allow organizations to 'tick the box' on domestic violence by sending a representative without a real commitment to improving services. Another significant factor was the introduction of a mentoring system, through which new members were assigned a 'buddy' to brief them about the work, explain the context of current initiatives and support them in working out how best to take forward the agenda in their own organization.

The partnership was organized in a way intended to build ownership and commitment among the representatives and their organizations. It was a closed group to avoid the difficulties of attendance changing from one meeting to the next, and numbers were restricted to around 20 members to ensure everyone had an opportunity to contribute. Organizations who had less of a key role in domestic violence work and who expressed a desire to join were encouraged to become members of task groups, and to take part in the 'City Forum on Domestic Violence' – an annual conference for anyone with an interest in the issues in the city. The process of developing a multi-agency strategy on domestic violence was also an inclusive one with organizations consulted on strategic priorities and encouraged to develop their own practical action plans. Monitoring and evaluation mechanisms were put in place to celebrate the achievements of member organizations and to hold them to account, for example, through the production of an annual report on progress in implementing the multi-agency strategy.

One of the key roles for the partnership was building momentum among communities, professionals, the media and civic leaders to create a city where violence, whatever its form, would not be tolerated. The Coventry experience showed that to get domestic violence on people's agendas it was important to do two things: to give a voice to the experiences of survivors in order for people to understand the very personal impact of abuse, and to make the social and economic case for putting a stop to the continued escalation of violence in all its forms, from school bullying to rape and sexual abuse. The partnership had a clear communications strategy and held regular seminars and conferences, published information on the Internet and worked closely with the media. The Coventry experience is encapsulated in the case study in box 12.2.

Box 12.2 Case study: Sandeep and Jasbir

Sandeep and Jasbir married in the Punjab in 2004 and came to England in 2006, where they lived with his parents in London. Even before the birth of their son in January 2005 her husband physically abused her. In 2006 the family was thrown out of the house by Sandeep's in-laws and they came to live in Coventry. Sandeep and her son, Aaron, were referred to a refuge in April 2006, by which time Aaron had been placed on the child protection register. Sandeep had been helped by a sympathetic neighbour to claim Child Benefit and Income Support as she was a British citizen. She was first referred to the refuge by social services in an emergency situation after reporting another violent incident, and it was decided that both she and her son would not be safe remaining in the marital home.

The refuge arranged for her to see a doctor who examined her because of the bruises to her body. The police took a statement and photos and referred the case to the Multi-agency Risk Assessment Conference. After the police had visited, Sandeep asked to see a social worker to discuss returning home. She was advised that her son would be at risk if she did so. She was upset by this as she wanted to return home. While in the refuge, Sandeep's brother-in-law offered to adopt her son so that she and her husband could be reunited and the 'shame' upon the family name could be redressed, but social services advised that this was not feasible. Instead she agreed to return to the family home provided her husband left first and the refuge arranged for her to see a solicitor to get an injunction order against her husband, requiring him to leave the marital home. Thus after several months Sandeep and Aaron left the refuge and returned home.

By this time, and after being cautioned by the police, Jasbir had agreed to attend a perpetrators programme because of his abusive behaviour. He also agreed that any contact with his son would be supervised at all times and Social Services agreed to facilitate this. Once back in her own home Sandeep continued to receive emotional support from the refuge through their outreach service. The refuge provided advocacy to help her through the legal system, helped her to arrange appointments and accompanied her when required. She went on social outings with the refuge and attended women's support groups to help her build up her self-confidence and to interact with other women who had been, or were still in a similar situation to herself, which made her feel less isolated.

Sandeep's social worker and health visitor continued to monitor the situation and assess Aaron to ensure all his developmental needs were met. The refuge assisted Sandeep to access her local Sure Start centre for child care and 'play and stay' sessions. While Aaron was being looked after Sandeep attended computer classes at a nearby training centre and also received individual counselling sessions to help her deal with the domestic violence she had experienced. She made good progress and eventually she and her husband divorced. Sandeep remarried several years later to a man she met through a friend and is very happy in her new relationship.

Partnership: the Coventry priorities

Detailed priorities are set out in Coventry's Multi-agency Strategy on Domestic Violence for the four key service areas of:

1   Emergency and support.
2   Children.
3   Prevention.
4   Justice.

In addition to these, the key priorities for the partnership as a whole are set out in Box 12.3.

Box 12.3   Key priorities

- Secure *political* commitment from civic leaders, chief officers and senior managers in key organizations, e.g. health, social care, probation services, etc.
- Secure *strategic* commitment by ensuring that domestic violence is addressed in relevant strategies and plans
- Raise awareness among staff in statutory, voluntary and private sector organizations.
- Improve coordination between services
- Improve the quality of existing services and responses
- Identify unmet need and develop new services and responses
- Share good practice
- Raise awareness with the public

The partnership gained a regional and national profile for its work, with recognition by the Home Office for its model of partnership (Home Office 2000). Group members regularly provided support and consultancy for new and emerging partnerships. They succeeded in getting domestic violence accepted as a political priority in the city, including the establishment by elected members of a city council advisory panel on domestic violence. In 2002 the Lord Mayor chose the domestic violence partnership children's projects as the beneficiaries of the Lord Mayor's Appeal. The high level of support among civic leaders and decision makers in the city led to additional resources for direct services and enabled the partnership to negotiate change in the statutory partner organizations. It has also ensured that when new strategic initiatives came on board, domestic violence was recognized and addressed, for example, through the Children's Fund or Neighbourhood Renewal.

The partnership led on a number of key policy and practice developments, underpinned by research. Being able to make the case for service development based on local research and data was one of the most significant factors in getting the large statutory organizations, such as health and social services, on board and begin to mainstream domestic violence into their work. The *Voices of Children* research (Hendessi 1997) carried out in the early years of the partnership led to a whole range of initiatives aimed at supporting children living with domestic violence, including funding for children's workers in refuges, a new school-based children's counselling service and a much greater understanding about the close correlation between domestic violence and child abuse. This, in turn, led to the development of inter-agency guidance on domestic violence by the Area Child Protection Committee, which challenged the old notions in social work of 'problem families' and the value-laden judgement of women's 'failure to protect' their children. Instead the emphasis was on prevention, intervening earlier to protect women and their children, and taking steps to hold perpetrators accountable for their actions.

Members of the partnership also worked with individual organizations to develop policies and practice guidance on domestic violence, a very important step in translating research and national policy into local good practice. These included guidance for the local authority, police, area child protection committee, supported housing organizations and the primary care trust. The process of developing guidance in partnership rather than in isolation was also significant. It provided the opportunity for a group of workers from different agencies to come together, explore the dilemmas and difficulties for a particular organization, build on existing good practice, and develop a policy that would not only work in that organizational context but which would be coordinated across the agencies. The members of the partnership found that this brought benefits in other areas of work, for example, in dealing more generally with policing or homelessness issues, and that the relationships forged by working together around domestic violence helped establish more effective coordination across the board.

The development of an active partnership with the University of Warwick enabled practitioners to benefit from the knowledge and expertise of leading academics in the domestic violence field in the School of Health and Social Studies, and for members of the faculty to benefit from close contact with projects on the ground. The University of Warwick and the Coventry domestic violence partnership worked on a number of projects together including: the *Research into Practice* initiative developing knowledge in Health and Social Services, and focusing on mental health and domestic violence; a Home Office funded research project into work with nonconvicted perpetrators of abuse; and local research into child protection and domestic violence.

The *Research into Practice* collaboration helped pull together the research evidence on the links between domestic violence and mental health difficulties, and then ran a series of workshops for health and social care professionals to disseminate this knowledge and identify appropriate responses. A similar project was undertaken by the Coventry domestic violence partnership with the Coventry Lesbian and Gay Policing Forum (established to assist the police in combating hate crime). This led to a regional seminar on the impact and implications of domestic violence for lesbian, gay, bisexual and transgender men and women, and the opportunity to disseminate information on this little known area of abuse.

In 2002 the Coventry domestic violence partnership received funding for a three-year training project and initiated a programme of joint training across organizations, an essential step in giving frontline staff the tools and confidence to be able to respond to domestic violence sensitively and appropriately. This led to a much more strategic approach to training, some of it generic, and some bespoke, utilizing the expertise of the Asian women's refuge or mental health professionals, or those working in drug and alcohol abuse. Part of the legacy of the project was a training video *Scars of a Quiet Denial* to support the training package.

In 2004 a new structure for the partnership was introduced to align it with the community safety partnership, and encompassing the Domestic Violence and Abuse Partnership Board and three main delivery groups: support services, justice, and prevention and early intervention, thus echoing the broad areas of the government's 2005 Domestic Violence Safety and Justice paper. In 2005/06 a new three-year strategy was produced with a broadening of terminology to include abuse. The coordinator's post was also resited from Social Services to the community safety team.

There are now over 70 members of the Coventry domestic violence and abuse Partnership representing 30 different agencies from the voluntary, statutory and private sectors. The board and each delivery group meet bi-monthly and delivery groups are responsible for creating an annual action plan to deliver their strategic priorities from the overarching strategy. The action plans are outcome and output focused, and meet national domestic violence performance indicators and targets as well as local performance indicators. The delivery groups include short term working groups formed for particular tasks. The overall responsibility for the delivery of the strategy is held by the Board, who measures performance against the action plans and supports the membership by seeking to ensure any emerging issues are responded to and resolved. The power sharing roles of chair and vice chairs have disappeared leaving a single statutory sector chair, a position held by the local authority. Additionally long term steering groups are in place, namely the training project steering group and the communications working group.

Partnership: productivity or procrastination?

Partnership is very much in the spirit of the time, with new initiatives springing up throughout public services. Eradicating bureaucratic and outdated professional boundaries and establishing 'seamless' services is a clear ambition of the government's modernization agenda. In recent years, crime and disorder partnerships, drug action teams and health partnership boards have all been established to improve service coordination and provide a more effective response across organizations. However, the fundamental point that government guidance and local strategies often gloss over is that partnership work is difficult. There are differences in organizational culture, terminology, practice, operational priorities and training, to say nothing of the lack of co-terminous service boundaries, for example, between health services and the police. Each partner regards the other with a degree of professional scepticism and sometimes with downright distrust. Different interests, priorities and practices in multi-agency groups make collaborative working difficult. It has been argued that trust between organizations can only be developed if based on an appreciation of divergent interests and views (Webb 1991). Practical experience suggests that providing opportunities to explore different ideological perspectives is as important as establishing common ground. Researchers have noted that one way to overcome mistrust is to take small steps early on rather than immediately set ambitious partnership goals (Webb 1991). This certainly reflects current thinking in regeneration and neighbourhood renewal where 'early wins' have been found to be very important in new and distrusting partnerships, for example, by running community clean-up campaigns, or replacing run down play equipment in neighbourhood parks. The sense of achievement gained by working together to achieve small goals can provide the momentum for tackling more difficult, longer-term problems.

Difficulties also arise in partnerships because of the multiple organizational structures that group members come from and the fact that each representative has a different reporting arrangement and a different level of decision making power within their own organization (Iles and Auluck 1990). Unless decision making and reporting back processes are clearly established, partnerships can be frustrated by their members' lack of authority, and their inability to make the decisions and agreements necessary to move the work forward.

In terms of the Coventry domestic violence partnership, recognizing partnership dynamics in organizations' vested interests, conflicting priorities, different professional practices and competition over scarce resources has been important. The partnership has found that, for partnerships to work effectively, it is important to establish certain agreements (see Box 12.4).

Box 12.4 Making partnership work

The following factors help to ensure productive partnership:

- Establishing shared values
- Setting common goals
- Finding champions
- Clarity of structure
- Clarity in roles and responsibilities
- Agreed work programme carried out through task groups
- Focus on outcomes – i.e. what difference will it make to service users

Individual members of the partnership have also identified factors to help them participate more effectively in a multi-agency context. These include the need for management commitment in their own agencies, clarity of mechanisms for communication and decision taking in their own agencies, establishment of personal and organizational goals, and opportunities to profile the work of their own agencies.

Partnership work: the future

Although there has been considerable progress in responding to domestic violence in a joined-up way, there is no room for complacency. In Coventry since this chapter was first written there has been a great deal of change in the landscape of work to tackle domestic violence work at both the national and local level. Changes in key personnel and a political impetus for local authorities to push the government domestic violence agenda, plus the promise of extra funding, have meant that statutory sector partners have exerted more control over the mechanisms of partnership. As a result the balance of power between statutory and voluntary sector partners has shifted, and some of the spirit of cooperation and collaboration has ebbed away. Structural changes have meant the sharing of power between the statutory sector and the voluntary sector women's organizations has been undermined, with women's organizations again needing to exert their right for a place at the table. Coventry's experience of this shift of power is not unique, the positioning of domestic violence as a priority for the statutory agencies has meant that across the UK the voluntary and community sector has struggled to keep an equal voice. In many places domestic violence fora have simply been subsumed into the crime and disorder partnership, but in Coventry the domestic violence partnership remained as a separate body with lead responsibility to ensure that domestic violence remained high profile and firmly positioned on the agenda of the relevant partnerships and strategies in the city. A more centralized model has not been without its advantages including a higher degree of ownership from the key statutory organizations, a sharper focus on key priorities and of course more resources to improve the quality of services.

A key challenge is the need for more robust data to enable agencies to measure the true extent of domestic violence and to design services accordingly. This is linked to establishing systems to share information between organizations and the development of joint protocols to improve responses to individual service users, with a Home Office toolkit for practitioners on how to do this safely (Home Office 2007d). Most importantly, there are examples in the UK of joint service delivery on domestic violence, including multi-disciplinary teams with co-located staff and joint budgets. Co-located staff can help break down barriers between organizations but most importantly well trained, well informed staff, who understand their roles and that of other agencies who work together to find the best solutions possible, are essential in providing an effective response to domestic violence. The Coventry experience has highlighted many practices that could be described as 'good practice', which are identified in box 12.5.

Box 12.5 Good practice checklist

- Take on board messages from government guidance, e.g. Department of Health, Home Office
- Develop good practice guidelines
- Establish links with the local domestic violence forum and Crime and Disorder Partnership
- Discuss issues about domestic violence with colleagues
- Organize training
- Consider routine questioning
- Display information about domestic violence support services
- Keep careful records
- Listen and respect service users

Conclusion

Domestic violence is set in a cultural context that has traditionally condoned, ignored or diminished the seriousness of violence and abuse perpetrated in intimate relationships. Until recently, women have typically been expected to keep quiet about their experiences of abuse, been blamed for provoking violence or conversely criticized for 'putting up' with violence. There is no doubt that considerable progress has been made in raising the profile of domestic violence and its impact on individuals, families and communities. It is safe to say that the days when brutal and systematic abuse were dismissed as 'just a domestic' by the police and other public bodies are finally over – but there is still a long way to go before victims and survivors of abuse, and their children, get all the help and support they need.

Domestic violence is a complex issue and no single organization has overall responsibility for providing the services that protect and support those affected. Therefore, effective partnership work is essential. As this chapter has demonstrated, a multi-agency partnership can draw on the strengths and resources of different agencies, work together to raise public awareness, challenge the attitudes that perpetuate violence and abuse, and ensure effective services are in place to deal with domestic violence. The challenge ahead is to create a society where violence of any sort is no longer the everyday life experience of many thousands of women and children. Until that situation changes, it is imperative that the services work together to protect and support women and children, and to bring perpetrators to justice.

Questions for further discussion

1   According to the evidence, which groups in society are most vulnerable to domestic violence?

2 What aspects of the Coventry experience of partnership could you apply to your practice?

3 In your experience how successful are organizations in achieving the items listed in the 'good practice' checklist?

Useful websites

- *Women's Aid*: www.womensaid.org.uk is a key UK charity working to end domestic violence against women and children
- *Hidden Hurt*: www.hiddenhurt.co.uk is a UK-based Abuse Information and Support Site
- *Refuge*: www.refuge.org.uk offers a range of services for to increases women's choices and gives them access to professional support whatever their situation

13 Working with Gypsy Travellers: a partnership approach

Angela Roberts

This chapter will:

- Explore the origins of Gypsy Travellers.
- Assess the impact of the legal system upon Gypsy Travellers.
- Discuss the cultural identity of this community.
- Identify one project and its multi-agency approach to addressing the health needs and problems of access to services for this socially excluded group.
- Explore the potential for utilising this model as a basis for working with other vulnerable groups.

Throughout this chapter I will identify the theories of origin purported by the many Gypsiologists who have studied groups of Gypsies and Travellers throughout the centuries and across the nations. In order to explicate the problems faced by these much-maligned groups of people, I will look at some of the attitudes and stereotypes underpinning the legal reform used to assimilate or exclude Gypsy Travellers. Readers will begin to understand the impact of history, prejudice and politics on their culture, social well being and health. A multi-agency approach to assisting this group to access appropriate primary and secondary health care will be described and proposed as one model which may create good partnership working and good practice.

The origins of Gypsy Travellers

Wibberley (1986) defined Travellers as a nomadic people who sold the products of seasonal work. Other contemporary definitions allude to the ethnicity of those descendants of Irish Travellers and Romanies who continue to live by the cultural norms of that society (Okely 1983). Many generalizations are available about the origins of Gypsy Travellers; some lead from a need to romanticize this group and this is exemplified in songs about 'raggle-taggle' Gypsies and the freedom of roaming. Additionally, there are stories about those who can cast curses, read the future from crystal balls and predict life chances and happenings from a palm reading or with tarot cards, and it is true that many Gypsies previously made their living from such pursuits. In order to hold such abilities there is a need to look the part, hence the image conjured up is one of a man with swarthy good looks, slick black hair and a brightly coloured neckerchief. The women in this myth are good looking, slim, flamboyant, dark skinned and surrounded by children. For many Gypsy Travellers this is only the stuff of legend and story telling, since a good number of Gypsies and Travellers are fair skinned and fair or red haired.

There are many groups who refer to themselves as Gypsy Travellers and these include Eastern European and Mediterranean Gypsies and Roma, English Gypsies said to be of Roma origin, Scottish, Welsh and Irish Travellers; and New Age Travellers. For the purpose of this chapter, I will not address the issues surrounding New Age Travellers as these differ vastly from the other groups.

It is said that Gypsies living in Britain can be traced back to the sixteenth century. There are historical accounts of these first recordings of Gypsies being mistaken for and named as Egyptians. Okely (1983) gives a good account of the many and varied categories and representations that she found in her social anthropological study of *The Traveller Gypsies*. In the study she describes the plethora of explanations of the component groups, their ascendancy, their Romanic and secret languages and the differences and similarities between the hundred or so groups of nomadic peoples across the world. Theories include one of Indian descent, which was first postulated in the nineteenth century (Smith 1880, as cited by Okely 1983). There is evidence to suggest that many Indian entertainers and craftsmen moved continents to escape slavery and became the first recorded nomads to be known as Gypsies, or more correctly Roma, initially inhabiting what is now modern Greece and Turkey (Kenrick 1998).

Although official national figures on the size of the Traveller and Gypsy population do not exist, estimates have been made of the broader definition of amounts of Travelling peoples including English, Welsh and Scottish Gypsies, Irish Travellers, New/New Age Travellers, Roma, fairground Travellers and boat dwellers (bargees), with such estimates varying between 2–300,000 (Morris 1996). In some rural parts of the UK, Gypsies and Travellers make up the largest ethnic minority in the region. More recent estimates suggest that there are around 300,000 Gypsies and Travellers in Britain, of which there are 63,000 Romany Gypsies and 19,000 Irish Travellers (Race Equality West Midlands 2005).

Historically there has been legislation dating back to the sixteenth century that outlawed Gypsies and Travellers. Initially much confusion arose from the descriptions given of early nomadic peoples in this country and it was generally thought that their dark skin was due to them originating from Egypt. Early laws passed referred to them as 'outlandish people calling themselves Egyptians', and during the reign of Philip and Mary (1553–58) the law made it a felony punishable by death to reside in this country as an Egyptian, unless you agreed to enter into service and give up the travelling lifestyle (Morris 1996). Effectively many of these laws aimed to make the travelling lifestyle illegal. An example of this type of legislation is the Housing of the Working Classes Act 1885, which placed controls on 'nuisances in tents and vans' (Hawes and Perez 1996).

Romany (Gypsy) history

It is thought that the origins of the Romany Gypsy lie in India where, as nomads, they were entertainers and craftsmen and there is historical evidence to suggest that as early as AD 855 persecutions began in Syria. Movement of Roma probably began around the thirteenth century when recordings took place of Romany shoemakers residing in Greece. Roma arrived in Europe in 1445. Twelve thousand people who 'looked like Egyptians', were transported from Bulgaria for slave labour and in 1471 the first anti-Gypsy law was passed in Lucerne Switzerland (see the Patrin Timeline in Kenrick 1998).

Kenrick (1998) states that throughout the sixteenth century further anti-Gypsy laws were passed across Europe including in Germany, Spain and Italy. Throughout medieval times Roma Gypsies were thought to be traitors to Christianity and were accused of witchcraft, child kidnapping and banditry. The first recordings of Gypsies in the UK are in Scotland in 1505 – this group are thought to have travelled from Spain – the first recording of Gypsies in Wales is in 1579. During the sixteenth century there are numerous recordings of Gypsies being banished and deported from many European states and countries. In 1541 Scotland passed its first anti-Gypsy law. Around the same time Edward VI of England introduced branding and enslavement for Gypsies. In 1560 the Swedish Lutheran Church issued an edict to its priests forbidding the christening of Gypsy children or Christian burial of their dead. Later that century, Spain forbade the wearing of distinctive gitanos dress, punished those who travelled in groups of more than two, condemning them to a period of up to 18 years in the galleys and later altered legislation to death for all nomads. Similar legislation existed in England at the same time. In the early seventeenth century, Spanish gitanos were forbidden to trade in horses and vigilante groups were permitted by law to pursue gitanos. Sweden introduced harsh anti-Gypsy laws in 1637 and any Gypsy men not complying with expulsion orders were to hang (Kenrick 1998).

Throughout Europe, between 1600 and 1800, anti-Gypsy laws were beginning to take a hold. Indeed punishment for pursuing a nomadic lifestyle and speaking Romany included: flogging, branding, banishment, deportation, shooting, mutilation, forced labour, whipping and hanging. In Germany, Gypsy children under the age of 10 could even be forcibly removed from their families to be brought up by Christian families. During the eighteenth century authorities throughout Europe made further attempts to deal with Gypsies. These included forced public work, incarceration in poor houses, being pressed into service or into factory work, sentencing to the galleys and many other attempts at banishment, reform or assimilation (Kenrick 1998).

It is apparent that Gypsy history is one of constant prejudice, hatred and harassment. Hunted down like animals, prohibited from speaking their own language, constantly moved on or incarcerated, Gypsies have a historical right to be wary of Gajos or Georgios (the name given to non-Gypsies) who clearly do not believe that being a nomadic Gypsy is a legitimate way of life.

Effects of recent legislation

In 1960 the Caravan Site and Control of Development Act effectively disbarred willing private landowners from providing temporary or permanent sites. This was followed by the 1968 Caravan Sites Act, which placed a duty on local authorities in England and Wales to provide static sites for Gypsies. This law was often not enacted and faced enormous opposition from the general public. The main impact of these laws is two-fold; first, they send clear messages that a nomadic lifestyle is not acceptable in the UK and, second, they attempt to assimilate nomadic peoples into the settled population by making travelling illegal and enforcing a working life.

In addition, legislation further establishes static sites provision, sending messages to local authorities that Gypsy Travellers should be contained. Latest legislation, under the jurisdiction of the Criminal Justice and Public Order Act in 1994 initiated by a conservative government, seemingly exorcised by the need to contain 'raves' and large groupings of New Age travellers, had the effect of removing the duty to provide sites and gave police forces increased powers of eviction. Despite the fact that this law was unpopular and contested by both the Country Landowners Association and the Association of Chief Police Officers it has been used repeatedly to prevent unauthorized camping by Gypsy Travellers. We can see from the aforementioned examples that the law has been used to assimilate this minority group and curtail the nomadic lifestyle.

Local authorities have responded to legal requirements by closing many traditional stopping places and green lane camping areas and providing legal encampments on council owned and managed sites instead. In doing so, they have incited local prejudice. Those country landowners who would willingly have allowed small Gypsy Traveller encampments on their land have been prohibited from doing so, and since Gypsies were first recorded in Britain, they have been moved on without stopping rights or provision.

More recently the Race Relations Amendment Act 2000 gave Gypsies and Irish Travellers ethnic status (CRE 2000). This means that they have the entitlements of nomenclature as shown in capitalization of the first letters of Gypsy and Traveller and are afforded the protection of the law, in the same way as other ethnic minorities. This law is often broken. How many times have you seen signs saying 'travelling people are not welcome here'? Are we shocked by those words and how would it be if the same signs read 'Blacks not welcome here' or 'Jews not welcome here'?

How does the Human Rights Act 1998 impact upon Gypsy Travellers? The two articles of the European Convention on Human Rights, enacted in the UK in 2000, which relate to the plight of Gypsy Travellers, are Article 8 and 14 (see Table 13.1).

Table 13.1 The European Human Rights Act 1998 as it applies to Gypsy Travellers

Article	Application to Gypsy Travellers
Article 8 refers to the right to respect for private and family life, home and correspondence.	Article 8 should, therefore, enable Gypsy travellers to determine their own family way of life, in so far as it does not cause a problem of national security, public safety, economic well-being or disorder and crime to others.
Article 14 prohibits discrimination on any ground such as sex, race, colour, language, religion, opinion, national or social origin, association with a national minority, property, birth or other status.	Article 14 has limitations in that it does not apply to indirect discrimination and where discrimination occurs between private individuals and organizations. In such cases, the complainants must seek redress through pre-existing Acts of Parliament, such as the British Race Relation Act 1976.

The latter requirements of Article 8, referred to in Table 13.1 are limitations to Article 8.1 seen in Article 8.2. In respect of planning application from Gypsy travellers wishing to reside on their own land this set of laws clearly expects that Town Councils should take the view that unless Article 8.2 is applicable then the requirements of Article 8.1 are clearly enactable. In respect of Article 14, there have been occasions when the democratic suppositions of the Article which particularly relate to Gypsies and travellers have worked both for and against those people it was designed to assist. The main benefits derived have been that it has at least shown that the court is willing to consider complaints on an individual basis and, furthermore, each case heard has included comment relating to the UK governments' failure to deliver an international commitment towards minority groups.

The cultural identity of the Gypsy Traveller communities

Although the Traveller lifestyle and culture sets them apart from the more sedentary population (Pavee Point 2002), Gypsy Travellers are not a homogenous sector of society, however, despite their diverse origins they do all have similarities in culture, many of which are defined by the nature of living a nomadic lifestyle. There are still a small number of Gypsies living in the UK who have Romany roots. These include: the Kale in Wales, the Romanicals in England, the Minceirs of Ireland, and the Nawkens of Scotland. In recent times these numbers have increased as Gypsies have migrated from Eastern Europe (Acton 2000). Okely (1983), among others, defines their culture as one based on economic need and its evolution. Traditionally, Gypsy Travellers were horse traders, musicians, sellers of homemade crafts and seasonal labourers who followed seasonal agricultural work around defined routes across the UK. More commonly these days, scrap metal dealing, tarmacking, roofing, domestic service trading, tree felling and landscape gardening have filled the gap left by the decline of seasonal picking and agricultural work. Travellers of Irish origin more commonly were tinsmiths, as were their Scottish counterparts, and were known as Tinkers or Tinklers. A small number of Gypsies follow a more settled life, which has included full time long-term education and a work life similar to others. Often these Travellers do not admit to their origins and roots for fear of prejudice. 'My daughter works in a good position in the bank, but she dare not ever own up to being a Gypsy. Some days she comes home to me and says, "They're at it again, calling us fit to burn"'. Scottish Traveller (as related to the author)

Gypsy travellers are adept at modernizing their traditional pursuits while retaining a self-employed independence (Okely 1983). Many Gypsy Travellers remain illiterate, dismissing formal schooling as irrelevant to their way of life. This, however, does not make them ignorant of the world or their local community. Attempts to assimilate Gypsy Travellers into the dominant society continue to fail and I list a number of reasons for this:

- Gypsy Travellers do not wish to live in a house all their lives. Those who do may continue to treat the house as though it were a caravan, spending a good deal of time out visiting kin on legal or transient sites
- Formal education has little to offer a traditional nomadic lifestyle
- All housing has internal bathrooms and toilets and for those Gypsy Travellers who continue to observe the notions of 'mochadi' or cleanliness it is not possible to have integral to living, cooking and sleeping areas.

It is impossible to do justice to an explanation of the cultural difference in this chapter. However, I will attempt to illustrate some cultural differences, which colour the way that many (but not all) groups of Gypsy Travellers view the world. Gypsy culture is largely governed by superstition. Some typical superstitions held by Gypsies are listed in Box 13.1.

Box 13.1 Some examples of Gypsy superstitions

- To speak of the Devil will make him appear
- If a daddy long legs walks over you, you will have new clothes
- A baby born at full moon will be lucky but if born at midnight before the Sabbath, it will be under a curse
- An itching of the right eye means sadness

(Jarman and Jarman 1991)

I asked a number of Irish Travellers if these sayings had any meaning for them and they agreed that, while not identical, some of these myths exist in similar forms in their culture as well as in the Welsh Romany. However, it is important to note that most Irish Travellers whether living in Ireland or Britain are Catholic (Kenrick 1998).

Cultural beliefs, whether they arise from superstition or religion, determine much of the Gypsy way of life. Marime or Makadi (Mochadi), for example, is the

Romany Gypsy hygiene code requiring that different wash bowls are used for clothes, dishes, the body, and for cleaning the home. The more common observance in the Irish Traveller community is two bowls, one for the dishes and one for cleaning. Even in a modern caravan with toilet facilities these remain unused and outside facilities are required. There is debate about the extent to which Mochadi is understood or practised by modern day British Gypsies and whether this continues to further extend to traditional beliefs about being unclean around menstruation and childbirth.

Additionally, beliefs about death and the ghost of the deceased have resulted in the burning of all belongings including the caravan of a Gypsy elder. While still clearly understood by the descendants, this seems to have varying degrees of observance. Some workers with Travellers report that following a death it is likely that Gypsy Travellers will move on, as they do not constantly wish to be reminded of the deceased (Derbyshire Gypsy Liaison Group 2004). This may be due to a fear of coming into contact with a spirit of a dead person. Traditionally two or three people kept vigil with the body of the deceased, for fear of a possible confrontation with the spirit (Jarman and Jarman 1991). This ritual may be further extended to include abstinence from a dead relative's favourite food or drink for many years as the belief was held that this might be perceived by the spirit as an invitation to join in.

Romany and Irish Travellers will travel across the width and breadth of the country to visit a sick relative or good friend. This is seen as a mark of respect, and a large number of visitors in the vicinity of a very ill person will be the measure of the esteem in which the person is held. This is carried through to the funeral, which is inevitably a huge affair with a large following and which lasts many days and nights.

Traditionally, Romany Gypsies and Irish and Scottish Travellers are bashful of sex education, sexuality, pregnancy and childbirth and the needs of young children are the concern of the women only. Indeed fathers do not usually stay with their wives during childbirth – it is more likely that the maternal grandmother will attend the birth or possibly an older sister who herself has had children (Derbyshire Gypsy Liaison Group 2003).

What remains apparent is that the majority of Gypsy Travellers' caravans gleam and sparkle and Gypsy Traveller women are taught to clean relentlessly from a very early age. These hygiene practices do not always translate into a clean external environment and again the extent of cleanliness varies from the caravan, its facilities and the defined pitch. Many sites have immaculate well hosed down pitches smelling strongly of bleach and disinfectant but the boundaries may be littered with rubbish. Many Gypsy Travellers believe in the concepts of purity and impurity and Vernon (1994) relates these to notions of good and bad fortune. This tends to impact upon health and illness behaviour, as can be seen by the following transcript from a conversation I had with a female Irish Traveller:

> Me: How is your grandson? I believe he had a serious accident in Ireland.

> Traveller: It is a miracle, he was run down by a lorry on the road by the site and they thought he was dead. He was spared and it's thanks be to God.

As Cleemput et al. (2007) point out in Gypsies and Travellers ill health is seen as normal and is stoically and fatalistically accepted.

A multi-agency approach to addressing the health needs and problems of access

Internationally, there is evidence to suggest that access to health of the Roma and Gypsy Traveller populations is problematic. A literature review of the health of the Roma people (Hajioff and McKee 2000) revealed poor access to health services and preventative care. A Scottish survey of Travellers' views (Lomax et al. 2000) also identified access to health care as a key concern raised in three of five key areas of concern raised by Travellers, as follows:

1   Access to housing and sites.
2   Access to education.
3   Legal advice and its charges.
4   Access on health care.
5   Advice on benefit and debts.

Poor access to health care is worrying as a recent study of Gypsies and Travellers in England (Parry et al. 2007) has revealed poorer health status than the settled population, as well as a higher incidence of long term illness and disabilities that limit daily or work activities. In an attempt to combat these problems, the Wrexham Multi-agency Forum has existed in Wrexham in North Wales for some years. Its membership has functioned and changed and for a period of time its existence was contentious resulting in it being temporarily disbanded. Since 1999, however, the Multi-agency Forum has gained in representation, membership, strength and purpose and currently meets at two monthly intervals with representation from:

● Community cohesion manager local authority
● Health services
● Midwifery services
● Domestic violence officer (police force)
● Commission for racial equality
● Police diversity officer
● Site management team
● Housing officer
● Voluntary services including home care services
● Traveller education service
● Youth offending team
● Youth work service
● Community housing association
● Catholic Traveller education forum
● Roman catholic church
● Traveller representatives

In the early stages of the development of this team the emphasis was on 'how best can we work together', developing terms of reference for the group, and identifying the skills, knowledge and expertise held within this diverse gathering of professionals and lay interested parties. As the group grew there was a recognition that individuals were working independently of each other, attempting to address many of the same themes that were identified by Scottish Travellers as important issues in their lives. The Wrexham Forum continued the attempt to address the needs of the local Traveller population through an inter-agency model with varying degrees of success until 2001.

It should be noted that a number of areas across the UK have operated inter-agency groups with the aim of targeting this socially excluded sector of society, most notably Pavee Point Northern Ireland. In addition, Streetly (1987) gives a good account of equal access for health care for Travellers, with services supported by representation from the Department of Education, Health and Social Services and other interested parties in Kent.

In 2001 the Welsh Assembly Government announced the availability of funding to redress inequalities in health in the Gypsy population. Some of this funding was targeted at reducing chronic disease and increasing access to healthcare. For some years, re-addressing these inequalities in health has been a priority for health policy development across Wales. A number of strategic and policy documents, including *Better Health Better Wales* (Welsh Assembly Government 1998) and *Better Wales/Plan for Wales* (Welsh Assembly Government 2001) have paved the way for the development of the Inequalities in Health Funded Projects. Particular attention was given in those documents to raising awareness of how cultural issues impact upon service delivery. In 2002 the chief medical officer for Wales noted in his report the disproportionate impact of inequality in health on marginalized groups including Travellers. Similarly, England, Scotland and Northern Ireland documents have highlighted the plight of Gypsies and Travellers in the UK. A successful bid to the Inequalities in Health Fund in Wales resulted in refocusing the ability to deliver an effective multi-agency service, in addition to providing an on-site health service to the Traveller community (Roberts et al. 2004).

The project: coronary heart disease and Gypsy/Travellers

The Wales Inequalities in Health Fund was designed in part to implement the National Assembly for Wales Service Framework, *Tackling Coronary Heart Disease in Wales: Implementing through Evidence* (DoH 2001a). One evidence-based standard from the plan states that: 'Health Authorities through their local groups and with local authorities in partnership through local health alliances should develop and monitor evidence based programmes to address tobacco use, diet and physical activity targeted at the most disadvantaged communities in Wales' (p. 23).

One of the requirements of the fund was that the responses made should be multi-agency in origin. A project steering group was formed from the existing Multi-agency Traveller Forum. Initial membership of the steering group has changed and now includes a project health worker, a full time researcher to evaluate the impact of the project, a professor of general practice in North Wales who is the research supervisor, myself as project lead and the chair of the Multi-agency Traveller Forum. This group steers the direction of the project ensuring that it will deliver upon its stated aims and objectives.

The major aims of the project are to describe the coronary health status and to redress the inequality of access to health care experienced by the Traveller population locally. At the present time the project is well underway and Figure 13.1 identifies the process as a continuous cycle. The research elements of the report are completed and as yet unpublished; further information is available from Dr Helen Lewis at: lewishj@cardiff.ac.uk.

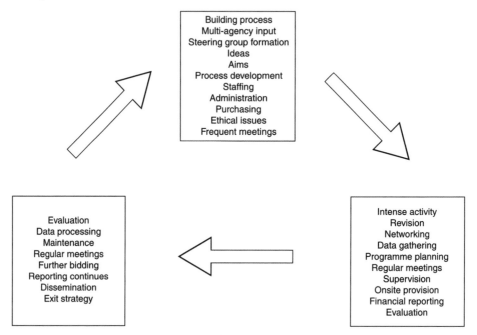

Figure 13.1 The continuous cycle of the project

As indicated in Figure 13.1, at all stages of development, the project has needed to take account of new challenges, changing needs, differing perspectives and overlapping areas of responsibility. The funding allowed for the purchase of a refitted motorized caravan, which enabled service delivery on site. Additionally, the Traveller community perceive the mobile caravan to be a private space, within which discussions concerning culturally difficult issues can be raised. These have included sexual health topics, pregnancy, informal counselling, domestic violence and mental health worries.

One finding from the project was that many Gypsies and Travellers suffer from severe and enduring mental health problems. The onset occurs when young and can last for decades. Mental ill health is perceived as a weakness and professional help is sought as a last resort. In an attempt to remedy this, the project appointed a mental health support worker to work proactively on site. The impact of this additional resource is currently being evaluated. A further development is that Gypsies and Travellers are now facilitated to attend mental health appointments. The local adult mental health service is also outreaching follow-on appointments on site. See Figure 13.2.

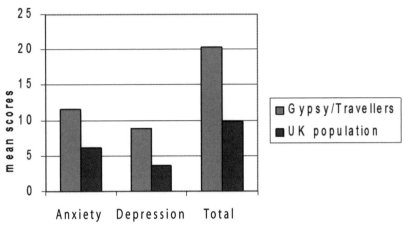

Figure 13.2 Mental health compared

The mobile unit has provided a focus for delivery of health and social welfare information and advice. The members of the Multi-agency Forum can deliver their own service, if required, from this vehicle by a collaboration partnership with the project health worker. Appropriate triage for medication advice, referral, liaison and treatment is available from the mobile unit, which visits the site three days a week. Settled Travellers can also access this facility or arrange home or clinic visits via this facility. The Multi-agency Forum is the inner core and building block of this project and this partnership way of working is illustrated in Figure 13.3.

The project views the Multi-agency Forum as an enabling, physically and emotionally supportive agency, which hosts a number of developments and approaches to the delivery of health and social care services. This form of interagency liaison is said to be vital and is highlighted in the work of Lawrie (1983), Rose (1993) and Mason and Brougton (2007). It enables service delivery and this project would echo those authors' conclusions. To date, the project's early findings have indicated value found in shared alliances between agencies, dissemination of good practice between organizations and provision of an outreach service, which provides for the cultural differences of Gypsy Travellers and respects their right to adopt a nomadic or semi-nomadic lifestyle while retaining the ability to access services. In common with Cemlyn (1995), we take the view that best practice is illustrated through service development, which includes mainstream development, encouraging 'flexible agendas; creative working areas across geographical, departmental, professional and agency boundaries' (p. 288).

Underpinning a good deal of the social exclusion that characterizes the life of Gypsy Travellers is the problem of discrimination and exclusion. Across Europe (Bancroft 2005) and the UK there is documented evidence that Gypsy Travellers are

Figure 13.3 Partnership way of working, with multi-agency forum at the central core

subjected to widespread prejudice and discrimination (Cleemput 2000). Anecdotal accounts are regularly reported in the *Traveller Times*, a magazine for Travellers edited by the Rural Media Company, and there are examples of widespread and vehement local opposition to the establishment of sites and stopping places (DoE 1982). Some authors take the view that conflict exists between Travellers and the settled society because of a lack of recognition of the nomadic way of life (Friends, Families and Travellers 2000). Ethnocentrism in the service delivery population is described by Smaje (1995) as resulting from an assumption formed on the basis of the majority example, which displays attitudes of prejudice and bias towards the minority needs of these groups. Further anecdotal evidence of discrimination is illustrated in the Scottish Survey of Travellers' Views (Lomax et al. 2000) and includes from a school child an account of bullying and children advising each other 'not to talk to the tink' (6.2). Further evidence from the report suggests that medical staff 'expected Travellers to be dirty and treated them differently' (6.9).

Attempts have been reported to development networks to build bridges between Gyspy/Traveller communities and service providers (Mason and Broughton 2007). A Multi-agency Forum creates opportunities for joint training aimed at dispelling stereotypes and encouraging cultural understanding. Good practice can be disseminated through the agencies' representatives to their fellow workers and the wider community. A Review of Service Provision for Gypsies and Travellers (National Assembly for Wales 2003) suggests that stereotypes around what is a 'real Gypsy' are misleading and used as an excuse to follow up with discriminatory comments. Multi-agency groups need to include representation from the Commission for Racial Equality to ensure that their membership challenges discrimination and prejudice at every level in the organization they represent. Groups should also include representation from the Gypsy Traveller community to offer guidance when developing service provision.

An English survey by Hussey (1989) demonstrated a lack of inter-service collaboration in health care, while Cemlyn (1995) comments upon the lack of specific policies and practices in social services departments reacting to Travellers at times when they become more vulnerable through eviction. Morris and Clements (2001) further conclude that the extent of unmet need for services provided by social services departments (children's or community care services) is unknown. Multi-agency partnerships, therefore, need to include representation from these services.

Service users are consulted at every stage of service development. The approach this project uses is informal as Gypsies and Travellers are difficult to engage formally. The project health worker canvasses the views and in this way we can assess what works and what is acceptable. Current developments include a peer education programme designed by the project health worker with a focus on understanding the body and good health.

It is essential that this service user group is approached for their views by a trusted person in order that they can be completely honest about their services preference. In the early days of the project we found that Gypsies and Travellers in this area would agree to many health promotion activities and lose interest very quickly.

Future developments

Having successfully piloted this outreach service and multi-agency partnership with local Gypsies and Travellers we see no reason why this health facility cannot be utilized with other hard to reach and vulnerable groups such as refugees, asylum seekers, migrant workers, homeless and roofless. The model ensures that all agencies engage quickly with new groups of service users. Useful and productive networks are facilitated and service users can be assisted to register with general practitioners and dentists and enabled to understand the complexities of primary and secondary NHS services.

Conclusion

In this chapter I have illustrated the background tensions, cultural differences, legal interpretations and nomadic lifestyle influences that impact upon the ability of

Gypsy Travellers to access health and social care services. Legislative changes are explained to demonstrate the interface issues which surround and compound the difficulties faced by this disadvantaged and hard to reach group. Cultural examples are also offered which have implications for the delivery of services, and the need to gain the trust of individual Gypsies and Travellers becomes apparent.

An example of a multi-agency approach is offered with an emphasis on the collective experience, expertise and partnership working capability. Shared experience, including that of service users themselves, is essential to prevent discriminatory practice. Anti-discriminatory training is crucial for service providers in these partnerships. I am aware of many other good models across the UK and would point the reader towards national associations, which seek to share good practice throughout their membership. The National Association for Health Workers for Travellers is a good starting point as is Pavee Point in Dublin.

Questions for further discussion

1   What problems might a worker face when advocating on behalf of Gypsy Travellers and how might these be addressed?
2   What considerations might your organization need to make before planning or carrying out care for Gypsy Travellers?
3   Prior to engaging in the care of a Gypsy or Traveller who is in need of your service, what should you learn about that individual and what skills will be required?

Useful websites:

• *Friends, Families and Travellers* (FFT): www.Gypsy-traveller.org/about/ An online registered charity working on behalf of all Gypsies and Travellers regardless of ethnicity, culture or background
• *The Equality and Human Rights Commission*: www.equalityhumanrights.com/ champions equality and human rights for all, working to eliminate discrimination, reduce inequality, protect human rights and to build good relations, ensuring that everyone has a fair chance to participate in society
• *Journey Folki*: http://journeyfolki.org.uk/aims to promote and perpetuate Gypsy and Traveller communities within Britain through information and education of their rights, beliefs and theologies

14   Effective partnerships to assist mentally disordered offenders

Virginia Minogue

This chapter will:

- Examine why a partnership response is seen as appropriate in the provision of services for mentally disordered offenders
- Explore the development of partnership and multi-agency responses to mentally disordered offenders, using case examples as illustrations
- Discuss the benefits, difficulties and dilemmas arising from partnership working
- Examine some of the issues of defining mentally disordered offenders and the impact this may have on their access to appropriate care and treatment

---

In the course of an evaluation of an inter-agency mentally disordered offender partnership group (Minogue 2000), agency managers were asked why partnership was the most appropriate approach to providing services to mentally disordered offenders. One respondent simply replied, 'because it is the only way to do it'. This response may have been based on experience of partnership working, a strongly held conviction, or could have been confirmation of their acceptance of local or national policy.

Concern about the effective treatment of mentally disordered offenders increased in the early 1990s.[1] There were two probable elements to this, the first being the report colloquially known as the *Reed Report* (DoH/Home Office 1992), which was the most far-reaching review of provision for mentally disordered offenders that had, hitherto, been undertaken. The second key factor was the re-evaluation of the care and treatment afforded to mentally disordered offenders brought about by the homicide committed by Christopher Clunis in 1992 (Reith 1998). However, although significant in marking a sea change in both professional and public interest, neither were remarkable in themselves as, some 16 years prior to the *Reed Report*, the Butler Committee (Home Office/DHSS 1975) had addressed very similar issues in relation to the care and treatment of 'offenders suffering from mental disorder or abnormality'. Furthermore, publications by the Zito Trust (Sheppard 1996) and Reith (1998) reflected a long-standing concern about care, instances of bad practice in the treatment of the mentally disordered, and the perceived risk posed by the mentally ill to others.

Early enquiries into the care of the mentally disordered tended to focus on the quality of institutional care and their criticisms may have, in part, contributed to the move towards community-based care in the 1990s (DoH 1990). However, the complex nature of providing care and treatment in the community requires, for any seriously mentally disordered person, a multi-dimensional package involving psychiatric and medical care, appropriate therapeutic intervention, control and management, and possibly, public protection. Adding offending behaviour to this equation multiplies the factors to be considered in assessing risk and in the control and management of a case. This underpins the unique nature of this minority group (mentally disordered offenders) and the characteristics of mental disorder and crime. Clearly, not all mentally disordered people offend and similarly, not all offenders are mentally disordered, but a subset of each group has both characteristics. Questions then arise, not only as to whether there is a relationship between the two conditions,[2] but also about the most appropriate method of care and treatment (i.e. from within health, social care or criminal justice systems). Mentally disordered offenders cross service boundaries and, as such, become the responsibility of a range of professionals, each working from a differing set of values, policies and organizational structures. It was clear that no single agency could provide a response and achieve the necessary outcomes for the effective treatment of the mentally disordered offender.

The study of mentally disordered offenders draws from a number of domains, criminology, sociology, mental health, psychiatry, to mention but a few. This, in turn, poses problems for multi-disciplinary work as no one philosophy or professional discourse can, on its own, provide a satisfactory explanation or a framework. The study and management of mentally disordered offenders illustrates how fine the dividing line can be between the perception and understanding of:

- Sanity and insanity
- Acceptable and unacceptable behaviour
- Madness and crime

It also illustrates how the boundaries between care and treatment can become similarly blurred and dependent on whether the offender/patient falls under the auspices of the criminal justice or health services. Robert Harris (1999) describes the mentally disordered offender as a sort of borderline figure who occupies the space somewhere between mental disorder and criminality, between criminality and social problem, and between petty nuisance and social casualty. This dichotomy presents the professional with several issues in determining the appropriate action:

- The general lack of any appropriate environment between hospital and prison
- The need or otherwise to attribute a causal relationship between the mental disorder and the crime

- The influence of subjective views on the clinical judgements of forensic practitioners

The criminal law, in the context of this debate, is a relatively straightforward process when dealing with offenders free from mental disorders. However, dealing with a mentally disordered offender is a far from straightforward process. The possibility of removing or 'diverting' the offender from the judicial process has existed since the introduction of the Mental Health Act 1983 (Home Office 1983) and can be utilized at several points in the system. Sections of the Act can also be invoked as part of the sentencing process,[3] further illustrating how treating mental disorder challenges the boundaries between mental health and the law. The common factor in each instance is the assessment of the mental disorder and judgement of the offender's culpability in relation to their crime. These assessments contribute to determining their disposal.

Defining mentally disordered offenders

Mentally disordered offenders are one of the most difficult groups to categorize. Not only does the terminology used to describe them differ but also the definition of a mentally disordered offender (DHSS 1974; DoH/Home Office 1992; Alberg et al. 1996; NACRO 2007). Although it may not be absolutely necessary to have a commonly agreed definition, lack of common understanding opens up the potential for ineffective or inappropriate responses to mentally disordered offenders, or even the possibility of them falling through the net of services (Peay 1999; Hagell 2002). Mentally disordered offenders are not a distinct group with clearly identifiable issues. Offending may range from comparatively minor offences such as petty theft or breaches of the peace, to serious offences of murder, while mental illness may range from a relatively mild depressive illness to paranoid schizophrenia. There may also be the additional impact of a substance misuse problem, behavioural disorder, personality disorder or sexual offending. The treatment needs of some patients categorized as mentally disordered offenders may fall outside the boundaries of general psychiatric treatment, for example, sexual offending and violent behaviour. Some may also require a number of services working in cooperation to address a range of problems. This may necessitate sharing of information which in turn can raise issues of confidentiality, particularly if it is third party information or intelligence about behavioural or offending patterns. Many inter-agency partnerships, such as panels meeting under the Multi-Agency Public Protection Arrangements (MAPPA),[4] have addressed this issue through the development of information sharing agreements.

The relationship between mental disorder and crime is a complex one. The mental disorder may be a disinhibiting factor but there may be other criminogenic or associative factors of equal relevance. Research has shown that offenders with mental health problems have a wide range of needs relating to age, employment status, homelessness, substance misuse and previous convictions (Cohen and Eastman 2000; Keene et al. 2003). Furthermore, attempts to define or establish categories become more complex if seen in the context of defining access to services. A serious incidence of offending is likely to increase the probability of intervention by the criminal justice system and lessen the possibility of accessing mental healthcare.

Even the most straightforward definitions can be problematic. The *Reed Report* (DoH 1992), for example, referred to mentally disordered offenders and others with similar needs as: 'a mentally disordered person who has broken the law'. This may intimate that a prosecution and contact with the courts is necessary, in order for an individual to be defined a mentally disordered offender. This then excludes those who have not been prosecuted or convicted, although their behaviour may have posed significant risk to others. Furthermore, the shift in policy predicated by Home Office Circular 66/1990 (Home Office 1990) and the Reed Report (DoH and Home Office 1992) saw the development of many diversion schemes. The majority of these worked on the principle of diverting the mentally disordered away from the criminal justice system at the earliest opportunity (i.e. pre-court). Many of these schemes, and other partnership arrangements, devised their own working definition of a mentally disordered offender in order to clarify the target group (see Box 14.1).

Box 14.1 Definitions of a mentally disordered offender

In 1996, in line with other definitions, the Leeds Mentally Disordered Offenders Partnership Group (LMDOPG 1996) provided a broad and inclusive definition of a mentally disordered offender as:

> People who offend and who, without access to health and/or social care, have difficulty in maintaining independent and offending free lifestyles. This means:
> - People with a mental disorder, as defined by the 1983 Mental Health Act;
> - People with mental health problems linked to alcohol and substance misuse;
> - People with significant behavioural and psychological problems associated with disordered personality development;
> - Those offenders who commit sexual offences where mental health problems are evident, or disordered personality development;
> - Offenders with problems of aggression associated with personality disorder who might benefit from complex psychological intervention and management.
>
> (LMDOPG 1996: 1)

In 2001, LMDOPG opted for a simplified and less explicit definition of mentally disordered offender: 'All those with mental health problems who come into contact with the criminal justice system as a result of activities that may be considered criminal'.

Part III of the Mental Health Act 1983 is specifically concerned with patients involved in criminal proceedings. Despite this, it has limitations and does not deal adequately with those who require specific interventions, for example, those offenders who require psychological rather than psychiatric intervention, and substance misusers. It also failed to clarify the nature and extent to which mental disorder should be seen as causing or impacting on offending behaviour and how this might affect any assessment of culpability or liability in prosecution procedures. As a result, the McNaughton Rules of 1843[5] remained the most significant determinant of a defendant's mental fitness in the legal arena. Evidence of the use of insanity as a defence for the commission of a crime stems from the sixteenth century, but it was the McNaughton trial in 1843 that led to the production of a set of rules on insanity. Critically, although this ruling placed the emphasis on the jury (comprising of lay people) making the decision about a defendant's sanity, it also introduced the concept of professional experts (i.e. psychiatrists) bringing medical evidence before the court.

By definition, mentally disordered offenders fall within, or between, the remit of a number of different service providers across the health/social care or criminal justice sectors. This poses several challenges for those trying to determine an appropriate response:

1   Should they see the mentally disordered offender as a person with a mental disorder who also offends, or as an offender who also has a mental disorder? (For a further examination of these issues see Columbo 1997; Laing 1999; Fennell and Yeates 2002).
2   Should treatment of the illness or punishment of the offence be the primary concern?
3   Where should the treatment or punishment be located – in the community, hospital or penal institution?
4   How can two potentially disparate forms of state intervention, the criminal justice system and healthcare, offer treatment, care, punishment, restriction or rehabilitation when operating from different ethical and philosophical standpoints?

Given the difficulties in categorizing mentally disordered offenders, it is of little surprise that the main published statistics relate to those patients subject to a restriction order admitted to, detained in and discharged from hospitals. The number of people detained in high secure and other hospitals has shown a steady increase over the last decade and in 2005, 3,395 were detained in hospital under restriction with 1350 having been admitted during that particular year (Home Office 2007b). 88% had a diagnosis of mental illness. The number of women within the hospital population remained at a similar level of between 11 and 13 percent. Examination of prison statistics demonstrates a somewhat different picture, with as many as 90 percent of adult prisoners and 95 percent of young offenders likely to have a mental illness (DoH and HMPS, 2001). A survey of psychiatric morbidity among prisoners in England (Singleton et al. 2000) found a prevalence of personality disorder in:

- 78 percent of male remand prisoners

- 64 percent male sentenced prisoners
- 50 percent female prisoners

Psychosis was prevalent in:

- 7 percent male sentenced prisoners
- 10 percent male remand
- 14 percent female prisoners

Further analysis revealed that nine out of ten detained young offenders showed evidence of mental disorder. Three-quarters of these had more than one disorder. Two-thirds of women prisoners in the survey were found to have a neurotic disorder, compared to women in the general population where only one-fifth were assessed as having similar problems. Approximately 40 percent female prisoners and 20 percent of male prisoners had help or treatment for a mental or emotional problem in the 12 months before going into prison. Moreover, in excess of half the budget for prison healthcare is being spent on mental health services.

However, a systematic review of the epidemiology of mentally disordered offenders (University of York 1999) demonstrated that their prevalence in the population is relatively low. Up to the age of 26–30, prevalence was between 2.1 and 2.8 percent for men and approximately half that number for women. All types of mental disorders were associated with all types of crime. Furthermore, it was apparent that the prevalence of mentally disordered offenders in the general psychiatric population was also small. Those who were diagnosed with schizophrenia were not more dangerous to others nor did they offend at any greater rate than the general population. Figures from the National Confidential Enquiry into Suicide and Homicide by People with Mental Illness (National Confidential Enquiry 2006) indicate there are 30 homicides per year committed by people with schizophrenia with 15 of those committing the offence being in contact with psychiatric services. Less than 1 percent of people detained in High Secure and other hospitals re-offended within two years of discharge (Home Office 2007b).

Developing inter-agency responses to mentally disordered offenders

The 1959 Mental Health Act reflected a shift from institutional care to community care for the mentally ill. This gained momentum in the 1960s and 1970s and was given further impetus in the 1980s and 1990s by the Conservative government and its hospital closure programme. However, by the 1990s care in the community was heavily criticized (Sheppard 1996; Howlett 1998; Reith 1998). This was in no small part due to the perceived failures in care indicated by the enquiries into serious incidents of harm involving mentally ill individuals (*National Confidential Inquiry into Suicide and Homicide by People with Mental Illness 2001*, Sheppard 1996). In response to the pressure for change, the government published its vision for the future of mental health services *Modernising Mental Health Services* (DoH 1998a), and subsequently the *Modern Standards and Service Models: Mental Health National Service Frameworks* (NHS 1999), and the White Paper, *Reforming the Mental Health Act* (DoH 2000d). The former introduced a raft of new or improved services such as outreach and crisis teams. However, both highlighted once again the tension between voluntary participation in healthcare and legally enforced compliance. The Mental Health Act 2007, reforms the 1983 Mental Health Act and:

- Extends the power to compel patients to undergo treatment both in hospital and the community
- Enhances the power of the Courts to order treatment in the community
- Allows the Court to make decisions regarding the compulsory treatment of mentally disordered offenders rather than a mental health review tribunal
- Introduces the use of compulsory treatment to those with personality disorders

Changes in relation to those with severe personality disorders arise out of concerns that those who present a high risk to the public fall through the net of existing services. Under the proposed changes these individuals could be detained and not released until they are judged to be a low risk to the public, the implication being that they could be subject to indeterminate detention.

There is no clear agreement about whether mentally disordered offenders should be cared for by general psychiatric or forensic psychiatric services. There are advantages and disadvantages to both but those advocating specialist services argue that specific skills are required, as well as specific treatments and provision (Tighe et al. 2002). Various interagency/partnership initiatives, testing this argument, have been developed over the last two decades including Court diversion schemes, panel assessment schemes, prison in-reach and out-reach schemes. Underpinning the drive towards the early development of inter-agency partnerships was Home Office Circular 66/1990 *Provision for Mentally Disordered Offenders*. This suggested that criminal justice agencies needed to increase their cooperation with health and social services (Home Office 1990) and was primarily aimed at the development of diversion schemes, the majority of which were based in police stations or courts. These schemes tended to involve a psychiatrist and/or community psychiatric nurse attending the police cells or court to undertake a psychiatric assessment of the defendant, as a result of a referral from the police, probation service, or other court-based service, and involved agencies cooperating by sharing information and discussing appropriate disposals. Other schemes were based on a 'panel assessment model', which involved a range of agencies forming a panel that met and formulated a management plan for each mentally disordered individual referred to them. Indications were that benefits were accrued in terms of provision of information, discontinuance of cases, increased understanding between agencies and, following initial pilots, other funding was made available to increase the number of diversion schemes nationally. However, an evaluation revealed that the panel assessment type schemes were not cost-effective and recommended discontinuing them (Home Office 1995a).

Court diversion schemes appeared to have more support and to be more effective in diverting people from custody and, by 2004, there were approximately

136 Court Diversion schemes in operation in England and Wales (NACRO 2005). However, not all partnership schemes were based on a simple diversion model. Some took on a wider remit and attempted to bring together a broad range of agencies in the provision of a package of care. Proponents of this approach (Staite et al. 1994; Haynes and Henfrey 1995), believed that to be successful in diverting the mentally disordered, the involvement of the prison service was crucial, offering the opportunity for more holistic provision across the social care and criminal justice systems, and also the possibility of involvement in the joint commissioning of some health care services.[6] Crucial to this change in thinking (and willingness to work in cooperation) on the part of health, social care and criminal justice agencies, was the availability of funding from government departments through the Mental Illness Specific Grant, which contributed to the development of court assessment schemes, inter-agency projects and services. Further investment by the Department of Health from 2001 (DoH and HMPS 2001) funded improvements in NHS services in 94 prisons across England and Wales.

A further Home Office circular in 1995 (Home Office 1995b) reiterated the importance of inter-agency working but also emphasized public safety considerations when making decisions regarding diversion. While still clearly supportive of diversion from the criminal justice system, this circular was a significant step away from wide-scale avoidance of prosecution for mentally disordered suspects. Enquiries such as Clunis (Ritchie et al. 1994) had called into question the validity of diverting those who were suspected of committing serious harm, and some of those who had committed lesser crimes, from the courts. This was felt to ignore the victim perspective and also the need to challenge an offender's offending behaviour. Home Office Circular 12/95 was accompanied by an advisory booklet, prepared by the Home Office and Department of Health, which outlined action the relevant services *might* take and described a number of existing examples of 'good practice'. Perhaps inevitably, given the absence of clear research-based evidence at this stage, service development lacked clarity of purpose in its intended outcomes.

As previously stated, caring for mentally disordered offenders held in the prison system is costly and rates of re-offending stand at 65 percent for those released from prison and 55 percent for all offenders (Home Office 2007e). Prison healthcare had not kept pace with developments in NHS mental healthcare and prisoners with mental health problems were not receiving services which met their needs or improved their health outcomes. Improving outcomes and the prospects for re-integration into the community could be beneficial in reducing the likelihood of re-offending and social exclusion. *Changing the Outlook* (DoH and HMPS 2001) proposed a review of mental healthcare in prisons and the creation of NHS in-reach teams. The aim was to improve NHS provision for prisoners through improved access, collaboration of NHS staff and skills sharing between NHS and prison staff. In turn this was intended to reduce the numbers of prisoners in prison healthcare centres and increase and improve wing-based support and care. An evaluation of the effectiveness of the increased investment has yet to report but indications are that there is no overall consensus about the role and function. This lack of consensus has undermined a number of attempts at partnership and inter-agency working and is discussed by Eastman (2006) who comments on the dissonance that exists between the interests of the Home Office and the clinician in relation to the mentally disordered offender. In his view there is no partnership because each party has different goals and does not share equal power.

Joint working arrangements

The emphasis on 'inter-agency' working was re-affirmed and reinforced by the document *Building Bridges* (DoH 1995a). This identified the agencies that should be involved in caring for mentally ill people, and outlined a number of key requirements for effective inter-agency working. For example, *Building Bridges* required a commitment to inter-agency working at all levels of the agency including senior management; a strategy which is jointly owned and agreed; agreed procedures; arrangements for exchanging information; consultation with, and commitment to, the involvement of service users and carers; joint commissioning in order to optimize resources; training within, and between, agencies which includes understanding of agency roles; review and evaluation.

Guidance was also published on the joint commissioning process advocated as an effective means of harnessing resources and coordinating services as well as overcoming some organizational boundaries. However, the green paper, *Developing Partnerships in Mental Health* (DoH 1997a), stated that while in some areas health and local authorities were engaged in successful partnerships, this was not a consistent pattern across England and Wales. Further evidence of persistent inequalities in service provision is indicated, by a subsequent secretary of state, in the publication of the *Mental Health National Service Frameworks* intended to ensure national standards apply to all aspects of provision (NHS 1999).

Department of Health guidance had tended to focus on the joint working arrangements of health and local authority departments such as social services, which had become even more critical since the full implementation in 1994 of the Care Programme Approach (introduced in 1991). Clearly, collaboration between health, social care and housing services was integral to any successful implementation and throughput of services to the mentally ill. However, practically all the aforementioned literature had referred to the need to work with other public sector organizations. Indeed, a number of the schemes already developed had involved the police and/or probation service and it was generally acknowledged that those services should share their skills in risk assessment, and in working with offenders and particular groups, such as sex offenders (Audit Commission 1994; DoH 1997a).

Although health and crime may not necessarily be linked in the perception of the general public, a document jointly produced by representatives of the Health and Probation Services was founded on the premise that crime had a definite impact on the nation's health (Home Office and DoH 1996). Apart from the impact of alcohol, drug, mental health problems and general health problems suffered by offenders, it was estimated that the effect on the health of victims of crime through their experience of being victimized was significant. Sex offenders, in particular, may have multiple victims. This advanced the view that benefits could be accrued by the two disciplines of health and criminal justice developing joint working and recommended collaboration to implement the various aims of the *Reed Review* (DoH and Home Office 1992), *Health of the Nation* (DoH 1992) and other documents. Principal among the reasons cited for collaborative working was improved risk assessment and management of mentally disordered offenders. Addressing the needs of substance misusers and sex offenders would also offer the opportunity to reduce future offending and overall these factors would produce benefits for victims. Much of the guidance document *Building Bridges* (DoH 1995a) focused on the development of joint policies and strategies, information sharing, offering joint training opportunities and maximizing access to effective services and offender programmes. Further suggestions included identifying liaison personnel in each agency, appointing managers from services to serve on boards or committees, and secondment of practitioner staff. An example of the development of joint working arrangements can be found in the following case study:

Box 14.1   Case study

In 1992, a multi-agency steering group was formed in the city of Leeds, West Yorkshire, to develop a diversion scheme at the Magistrates Court. In 1994, a partnership group was established to develop a strategic multi-agency approach to provide services for mentally disordered offenders. This arose from a recognition that people with mental health problems who offend were not always dealt with appropriately, and a belief that a partnership response was the most effective way of addressing the issues. The partnership group, which comprised a range of agencies who were providers and purchasers of services, had a core membership comprising the health authority, the community (mental) health trust, social services, the probation service, magistrates court and police. The Crown Prosecution Service and housing department also became members. Terms of reference for the group were produced in February 1995 and followed by an 'action plan' in December 1996. The key objectives in the plan came under the headings:

   1   Information awareness.
   2   Development of comprehensive services.
   3   Development of good practice.

The partnership group effectively separated out the purchaser/provider functions by setting up a 'provider group' in 1996. The group produced its first strategy in May 1999 and listed its key strategic objectives and an action plan under three headings:

   1   Policy.
   2   Practice.
   3   Information.

A more comprehensive strategy document was produced in July 2001 (LM-DOPG 2001). The action plan contained four objectives with separate tasks identified under each one that were to be taken forward by a series of sub-groups coordinated by a mentally disordered offenders development officer. An evaluation (Minogue 2000) found achievements could be categorized under the following headings:

1 *Relationship development and communication*:
   - Shared understanding
   - Agencies working together to achieve shared aims
   - Increased focus on mentally disordered offenders and their needs
   - Liaison with and training of sentencers

2 *Mutual advantage and resource exchange*:
   - Improved working relationships and inter-agency communication
   - Development of networks
   - Improved quality of work taking place in the courts through agencies allowing better access to their resources

3 *Specific outcomes*:
   - Development of a city-wide strategy
   - Development of a court-based diversion scheme
   - Good practice protocols
   - Mapped the numbers of mentally disordered offenders in the city
   - Production of a handbook for practitioners
   - Held inter-agency conferences and training
   - Development of care programme approach in a local prison
   - Undertook an audit of the use of acute beds by mentally disordered offenders
   - Took part in an independent review of the partnership and held internal review

Apart from recognition that it was important to acknowledge the benefits of including criminal justice agencies on a consultative and cooperative level in determining services to the mentally disordered offender, it is the relationship between the health and social services that is crucial in meeting the needs of the mentally ill. Community care legislation, and guidance on its provision, underlined this factor (NHS and Community Care Act 1990; DoH and Home Office 1992; DoH 1995a). The points at which mentally disordered offenders link the health and criminal justice systems have already been outlined, but the mentally disordered cross the boundaries of health and social care even more frequently. It is hard to visualize cases (other than long stay hospital patients where rehabilitation is not envisaged), where all needs are met by one service (see Figure 14.1).

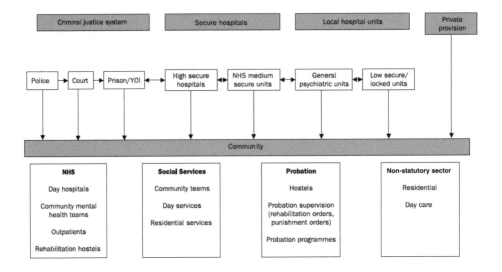

Figure 14.1   Service provision for mentally disordered offenders

Inpatient care may be predominantly the domain of healthcare workers but community care and rehabilitative services will be delivered by a range of practitioners from health and social services, for example, approved social workers, residential social workers, occupational therapists, community psychiatric nurses. Unlike 'physical' diseases, mental disorder rarely presents as a single episode and hence patients move from the care of one or more services to others over varying periods of time. Service models, therefore, have to ensure that they are built on systems that incorporate effective care management and public protection and that there are strong interfaces between health, criminal justice and other agencies, across the different levels of health care (see Figure 14.2).

Holistic partnership provision?

In order to provide interventions and treatments that are ultimately beneficial and lead to successful outcomes in terms of health gains and reduction in re-offending rates, health and other agencies have to understand what the needs of mentally disordered offenders are. After reviewing the literature Cohen and Eastman (2000) concluded that it was not possible to identify one model of 'what works' for mentally disordered offenders. The multi-dimensional nature of their problems and needs and the multi-professional aspects of their care, in addition to different theoretical perspectives make this a complex area in which to identify measurable outcomes. In order to do so, knowledge about the effectiveness of healthcare and other interventions is essential to know 'what works'.

For holistic partnership provision, encompassing community care, to become a reality (thus avoiding the critical conclusions of the enquiries mentioned several

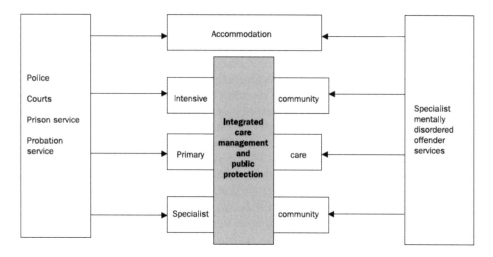

Figure 14.2 Effective care management and public protection service model

times previously), effective targeting and delivery of services is incumbent on health and social services. Implementation of effective packages of care, whether in the community or in a hospital setting, also increasingly depends on successful cooperation between health and social services and, to a certain extent, the voluntary and independent sector. The continued rise in the number of detained patients (Home Office 2007b) would appear to lend credence to this need to prevent further increases in the future. In response to the need to modernise and develop responsive services, a number of new interventions have been developed in recent years (e.g. Assertive Outreach, Crisis Resolution and Intensive Home Based Treatment Services, Early Intervention services). Although generally seen as positive developments they have not always been supported by evidence of their effectiveness. There is a sense that community care reforms implicitly assumed that the required improvements would result but perhaps did not pay sufficient regard to the fundamental differences in models of mental disorder employed by health and social services (i.e. bio-medical and social care models).

In the late 1990s commentators concluded that community care has failed the majority of mentally disordered patients (Reith 1998; Blom-Cooper 1999) although there were fewer homicides are committed by the mentally disordered than there were 30 to 40 years previously (Taylor and Gunn 1999). Undoubtedly, there were difficulties in operationalizing community care initiatives, particularly the care programme approach, which carried no additional funding to assist in implementation and administration. Consequently, differences in the scale of implementation, planning and procedures existed between health authorities. Government restrictions on public sector spending and increased pressure on NHS Trusts and other public sector organizations to reduce expenditure and debt have led to pressure on service delivery in some areas.

Involving the service user

Another critical factor in successful partnership working is the involvement of the service user and carer, not only in the care planning process but also in service planning and delivery. Service user involvement in health service delivery has been a policy directive in the NHS for over a decade (NHS 1999, 2000; DoH 2000c, 2001d, e, g, 2004b, 2005c) and is crucial to ensuring services reflect the needs of those they serve. There are many examples of service user involvement in mainstream mental health services and roles have been created to facilitate the increased inclusion of service users and carers (e.g. service user development workers, support time and recovery workers, public involvement departments, patient advice and liaison services). Issues relating to public protection and security, or the additional stigma of being a mentally disordered offender, have meant that service user involvement in forensic services has not been as strong as in other elements of mental healthcare. There are significant exceptions to this such as the Department of Health's National Programme on Forensic Mental Health Research and Development which involves service users in prioritizing and commissioning research. Nonetheless, involving service users in forensic mental health does pose a challenge as some individuals present a significant risk and are difficult to engage and treat. However, engaging with this challenge may ultimately provide us with a clearer idea of their needs and priorities. Box 14.2 identifies some of the opportunities and challenges involved in working in partnership with service users.

The active participation of the service user, and where relevant the carer, is an important factor in the management of risk. Some, but not all, mentally disordered offenders present a significant risk to others. In a naturally risk averse culture the management and minimisation of risk can dominate decisions made about care. Clinicians and professionals, making decisions either individually or as part of MAPPAs, may focus on the risk of violence or homicide rather than the mental illness and the individual service user. Fear of the 'blame culture' may predominate. The Royal College of Psychiatrists (Morgan 2007), suggests that the care programme approach, and partnerships with service users and carers could be used more effectively to reduce risk and improve risk management. However, this principle is not necessarily shared by other agencies, particularly criminal justice agencies, which do not have a history of service user involvement. The *National Probation Service Business Plan 2005–06* (Home Office 2005b), for example, has as one of its key priorities 'protecting the public from harm'. It aims to 'improve and consolidate' work with mentally disordered offenders and integrate health and offender services. Lay advisers are being recruited to assist in ensuring MAPPAs work but 'lay' does not necessarily bring the perspective of those with the most expertise and insight into their own experience of health and criminal justice systems. Expert patient programmes, survivor and advocacy groups have increasingly played a significant role in advising and informing the development of more appropriate and effective mental health services.

Box 14.2 Involving the service user

Service user involvement can take place at a number of different levels including: consultation, collaboration or partnership, training, user-led initiatives.

Why involve service users? There are a number of reasons why involvement can be a valuable addition to partnership working. They include:

- Ensuring policy, services, training, and research are relevant to the recipients of services (Staley and Minogue 2006)
- Allowing service improvement to be shaped by the experience of those who receive services
- Improving the quality of services
- Ensuring the right research questions are being asked
- Carrying out more meaningful research which is relevant to the needs of mentally disordered offenders
- Increasing the evidence base and knowledge of what works
- Providing opportunities for service users to share their experience, gain knowledge and skills, increase their self-esteem and confidence
- Reducing the stigma of forensic mental health services
- Increasing the understanding of mentally disordered offenders and improving the relationship between academics, mental health, social care, and criminal justice professionals and service users
- Reducing the social exclusion of mentally disordered offenders

There are various opportunities for involvement in mental health, social care, and criminal justice organizations including:

- Service planning
- Policy development
- Research
- Training of mental health, social care, and criminal justice professionals
- Committee membership e.g. patients forum, clinical governance councils, NHS Foundation Trust boards
- Staff recruitment panels
- Advocacy groups

However, there are many barriers that have prevented services users' involvement. They include:

- Security and risk issues: forensic environments, access to individuals and information.
- Confidentiality

- Attitudes of academics, mental health, social care and criminal justice professionals
- Reluctance of professionals to share control or power with service users
- Lack of opportunities for involvement
- Reluctance of those who use forensic services to engage
- Forensic service users' negative experiences or expectations of services making them reluctant to share their experience
- Forensic service users' perceptions of professionals and academics

The NHS and social care have developed significant expertise and good practice in involving service users, including marginalized groups, in service development, planning and delivery and overcoming some of the barriers outlined above. Service user involvement in research is particularly well developed and provides many examples of good practice.

(Lowes and Hulatt 2005, Involve 2007, SCIE 2007).

Conclusion

Mentally disordered offenders pose particular issues for the agencies providing care and treatment but the basic needs of the individuals receiving the care, and the basic principles of partnership working, are similar. Undoubtedly, there have been significant steps forward in inter-agency working in this area and strategic agreements exist between many of the main agencies. However, partnership cannot simply exist at a strategic level. Frontline staff need to understand the nature of partnership and be given adequate training in order for them to jointly manage care and public protection. Service users and carers are best placed to be able to identify their needs and to inform service development. Changes in general health and mental health services that have placed the patient much more centrally in the planning and delivery of services have gone some way to addressing the need to involve the service user. However, the mentally disordered offender is not always included, particularly where there are specific issues surrounding risk or public protection.

As Figures 14.1 and 14.2 illustrate, the provision of care for mentally disordered offenders is complex as it may cross different service tiers. The pattern of service delivery may be more complex still if the individual spends time in prison and is not identified through the in-reach or liaison systems linking the prison with community provision (in some establishments these may not yet be available). The most effective responses are those that are part of a coordinated partnership approach. However, setting up a partnership is only one element of what is needed. Operational policies and protocols are vital to a successful partnership but will require monitoring and evaluation to ensure they work in practice. Moreover, an agreement between agencies to work in partnership does not in itself ensure quality services or equal access to services. Unless different professional groups and organizations are prepared to remove some of the boundaries that prevent good communication, information sharing and cross-fertilization of skills, and work towards developing shared philosophies, it is unlikely that partnership working will be sustained in the longer term. A further fundamental aspect to a successful operational partnership is an effective communications network. Communication is fundamental on two levels: communication between strategic planners, managers and operational staff; information sharing between agencies to ensure effective care management and public protection. Partnership involves all stakeholders and this includes service users. Service user involvement in service planning and delivery, and in the monitoring and evaluation of services is the key to ensuring that provision is effective and relevant.

Finally, forward steps in any future attempts to develop and improve 'effective partnerships to assist mentally disordered offenders' should, I would propose, include two further radical developments. The service user view is often omitted from partnership working as is another stakeholder group, victims of crime. Victims, or the relatives of victims (where the offence is against the person), are rarely given prominence in discussions about partnership working and mentally disordered offenders. Is it time to include this stakeholder group as a key player in any partnership approach to planning, coordination and delivery? Second, Wolff (2002) had highlighted the policy implementation failures in the attempts to develop more integrated partnership services for mentally disordered offenders. Has the time not arrived for the traditional key players in this arena – health, social services and criminal justice agencies – to turn to management and business improvement theory, in order to iron out the process and communication failures which have frequently marked much of the partnership approaches to mentally disordered offenders? Approaches to quality improvement such as the European Excellence Model (Nabitz et al. 2000; Stahr et al. 2000) might very well assist all partnership players to break down the individualistic agency philosophies and processes which have hampered partnership working in the past by using such models as the building blocks of a truly *partnership* response to the needs of the mentally disordered offender. Managers may mistakenly believe strategy is simply about plans when in fact it is about taking action and committing resources to achieve clearly defined outcomes. Strategic management sets out to establish a clear strategy which is then implemented. Creativity and innovation ensure the strategy is responsive to change, of both a continuous and discontinuous nature, and, finally, strategic management manages change (Thompson and Martin 2005). Such an approach could turn partnership working on its head by beginning with the required outcome – care for the mentally disordered offender – rather than with the individual contribution of each agency.

The way forward

Agencies involved in the care of mentally disordered offenders need to build on the information sharing protocols that exist between them for dealing with risk management and public protection issues. Improved information sharing between agencies would address many of the criticisms relating to the failures in inter-agency communication that have led to serious incidents of harm. All stakeholders, including service users, carers and victims, should also be involved in the planning and delivery of services, if services are to be effective and relevant.

There are a high number of detained young offenders who show evidence of mental disorder, addressing their needs prior to them entering the criminal justice system should help to reduce the numbers of mentally disordered offenders in the prison system. The needs of those with a psychopathic disorder need to be similarly addressed, to avoid extended periods in secure conditions under proposed legislation.

A critical evaluation of the range of inter-agency partnerships that have been developed in response to mentally disordered offenders is needed. Although there have been evaluations of court diversion schemes and of local partnerships, there has been no meta-analysis to determine which models are most effective.

Questions for further discussion

1 To what extent are services for mentally disordered offenders best provided by (a) general psychiatric services, (b) forensic psychiatric services, or (c) specialist multi-disciplinary teams?
2 How can service users be involved in service planning and delivery, alongside other stakeholders, in a meaningful way?
3 To what extent do the Department of Health and the Home Office provide a clear lead on dealing with mentally disordered offenders?

Useful websites

- *Sainsbury Centre for Mental Health*: www.scmh.org.uk works to improve the quality of life for people with mental health problems by influencing policy and practice in mental health and related services
- *Revolving Doors Agency*: www.revolving-doors.org.uk is a UK charity dedicated to improving the lives of people who are caught up in a damaging cycle of crisis, crime and mental illness
- *Mental Health Primary Care in Prison*: www.prisonmentalhealth.org/ seeks to help individuals and organizations who work with adults and adolescents in prison who are struggling with mental ill health
- *National Association for the Resettlement of Offenders (NACRO)*: www.nacro.org.uk is a crime reduction charity that have over 200 projects running across England and Wales

---

Notes

1 Buchanan (Buchanan 2002) identifies 19 circulars containing guidance on mentally disordered offenders issued between 1990 and 1999.

2   Opinion on the relationship between crime and mental disorder differs. A great deal of the research has concentrated on the link between violence and mental health. For an overview of the research in this area see: the NHS Centre for Reviews and Dissemination (University of York 2000) *CRD Report 16: Scoping Review of Literature on the Health and Care of Mentally Disordered Offenders*.

3   Section 37 of the MHA 83 allows the Court to make a hospital order, or an interim hospital order can be made under Section 38, detaining a convicted patient in hospital for treatment. Section 41 adds a restriction to a hospital order requiring authority from the secretary of state for leave of absence or discharge from hospital. Section 37 also allows the making of a guardianship order placing a person under the guardianship of the local authority. Sections 35 and 36 allow the courts to remand a defendant to hospital for the preparation of reports or for treatment.

4   Multi-Agency Public Protection Arrangements (MAPPA) are arrangements set in place by agencies, including the police, probation and prison services, for assessing, managing and reviewing risk posed by serious and violent offenders. For further information see: www.probation.homeoffice.gov.uk

5   McNaughton committed an offence of murder (the victim was the prime minister's secretary) but was found not guilty by reason of insanity. This provoked a public outcry forcing the law lords to outline the criteria for the decision, thereby producing the rules of insanity known as the 'McNaughton Rules'.

6   At that point prison healthcare was outside the remit of the NHS and governors were required to devolve part of their budget to the purchase of healthcare services. Prison healthcare is now more clearly integrated with NHS services.

15 Partnership approaches to working with people with HIV

Ruth Wilson

This chapter will:

- Outline the extent of HIV/AIDS in the UK
- Explore the challenges presented by HIV/AIDS
- Present an overview of how and why multi-disciplinary and multi-agency working is essential in caring for people with the Human Immunodeficiency Virus (HIV)
- Explore the specific issues that confront staff in this dynamic and evolving area

---

The year 2006 marked the twenty-fifth anniversary of the first reported case of Acquired Immunodeficiency Syndrome (AIDS) and the beginning of HIV surveillance in the UK. In 2005 there were an estimated 63,500 people, aged between 15 and 59, living with HIV in the UK, of whom 20,100 (32%) had not been diagnosed. A total of 47,517 individuals (all ages) living with diagnosed HIV accessed HIV related care in the UK during 2005, a 13 percent increase since 2004. A total of 7,450 individuals were newly diagnosed with HIV in the UK in 2005.

The continued increase in HIV diagnoses is due to sustained levels of newly acquired infections in men who have sex with men; further diagnoses among heterosexual men and women who acquired their infection in Africa; much improved survival since the introduction of effective anti-retroviral therapy; and earlier and increased HIV testing. Each year since 1999, the number of new HIV diagnoses in heterosexuals has exceeded the number of new diagnoses in men who have sex with men, rising from 2031 in 2000 to 4,049 reported for 2005. Seventy-three percent of these were in people from Africa, or were associated with exposure there. However, the number of infections acquired as a result of sex between men also continues to rise due to increased testing and continued transmission. The 2,356 new diagnoses of HIV infection among men who have sex with men reported in 2005 was the highest ever. The Health Protection Agency estimates one in 20 gay men in the UK are living with HIV (UK Collaborative Group for HIV and STI (Sexually Transmitted Infections) Surveillance 2006).

The availability of anti-retroviral therapy has helped transform the course of HIV infection from a disease that inevitably progressed to death into a chronic condition requiring long term clinical management and monitoring (Carpenter *et al.* 1997; Brashers et al. 1999). The combined use of Viral Load and CD_4 monitoring and Antiretroviral Therapy (ART) have revolutionized HIV treatment, with consequent declines in morbidity and mortality (Carpenter et al. 1997; Gazzard 2002). People who were once given limited life expectancy are returning to work and leading full lives once again. The treatment consists of combinations of anti-retroviral drugs that require strict adherence in order to suppress viral replication and prevent resistance developing (Chesney et al. 1999; Carr and Cooper 2000; Paterson et al. 2000). The sustained decline in HIV associated deaths alongside a rise in the number of new diagnoses, has resulted in a steep increase in the number of people requiring long-term treatment. HIV has become a complex, chronic medical condition, and the model of care should be based on that of other such conditions. However, HIV remains an incurable condition with uncertain prognosis, and even the routine elements of HIV care are relatively complex and rapidly developing, involving specialized tests and combinations of drugs with significant potential for toxicity and interactions (BHIVA 2007). Recovery remains fragile, the future uncertain and the psychological ramifications unclear (Rabkin and Ferrando 1997; Sowell et al. 1998; Anderson and Weatherburn 1998; Brashers et al. 1999).

The multi-disciplinary team model of HIV care has evolved out of necessity due to the social impact of the disease, clinical needs and diverse characteristics of people with HIV (Pinching 1998; Sherer et al. 2002). The recommended standards for NHS HIV services set out by MedFASH (2002) clearly state services should be person centred, developed in partnership, equitable, integrated and outcome orientated, and stresses the importance of drawing on the knowledge and skills of health and social care professionals across a multi-disciplinary HIV healthcare team, including primary, social and specialist services. However, as Molyneux (2001) points out, there are challenges when working together in teams – disagreement, confusion, lack of cohesion, professional jealousy and poor communication. Inter-professional teams work well when there is good communication; respect for other professions; committed, professional staff; and when the opportunity is available to develop creative working methods. This relies on the professional maturity of staff who are sufficiently confident in their own role and professional identity to share ideas and expertise within the team and work effectively together in a user-focused way, allowing flexible boundaries to develop within the team. It is difficult to form collaborative ties when one is unsure of one's professional identity (Dombeck 1997), whereas an egalitarian working style allows trust and confidence to develop.

Working in a multi-disciplinary way with people with HIV therefore presents a number of challenges for professionals as indicated in Box 15.1.

Box 15.1 Challenges facing professionals working with people with HIV

- The challenge for the multi-disciplinary team of caring for people with HIV across the boundaries of primary, secondary and tertiary care.

- The challenge of conception, pregnancy and childbirth faced by the multi-disciplinary team.
- The challenge of treatment with Anti-retroviral Therapy (ART).
- The challenge of adherence to ART.
- The challenge of developing and maintaining partnerships between organizations involved in the monitoring, care and treatment of people with HIV.

This chapter will address each of the above challenges in turn.

The challenge of caring for people with HIV across the boundaries of primary, secondary and tertiary care

HIV is the only chronic and potentially fatal condition for which a patient is able to attend a hospital clinic directly, bypassing the general practitioner (GP). This may mean that the useful information the GP has about the home situation and other social and psychological issues is unavailable. Community nurse specialists/liaison nurses have the unique opportunity to cross the boundaries of primary and secondary care and into the patient's home. Gay men and drug users often have poor links with primary care services due to stigma and attitudes towards their lifestyle, as well as being a highly mobile population. Fears about medical reports for life insurances and mortgages may cause some patients to decline shared care. This means that issues of confidentiality need to be discussed and resolved within the primary care multi-disciplinary team to develop confidence in the patient to disclose.

A high proportion of people with HIV experience social exclusion problems related to housing issues, immigration status or financial hardship. These problems are likely to have a significant impact on mental health, treatment adherence, self-management and the ability to live well with HIV (BHIVA 2007). The management of HIV is also often complicated by complex clinical presentations including co infection with Tuberculosis (TB), Hepatitis B and/or C, with TB being one of the most common AIDS defining illnesses reported in the UK (UK Collaborative Group for HIV and STI Surveillance 2006).

The involvement of the wider multi-disciplinary team spanning a number of specialities is essential – see Box 15.2:

Box 15.2 The wider multi-disciplinary team

- Community/liaison nurses
- General practitioners
- Health advisors
- Dietitians
- Occupational therapists
- Physiotherapists

- Consultant physicians
- Sexual health clinic nurses
- Health visitors
- Midwives
- Pharmacists
- Welfare rights advisors

• Clinical psychologists	• Complementary therapists
• Mental health nurses	• Voluntary organizations
• Psychosexual counsellors	• Housing department
• Social workers	• TB specialist nurse
• Chaplains	• Hepatitis nurse specialist

Education, training and support from HIV specialist services will enable skill sharing and staff with any uncertainty should feel at ease in asking for help from specialists. Moreover, according to Theobald (2002), patients respect this and feel more confident if it is done. Although GPs may have few contacts with HIV-positive people, well-managed shared care with good communication can reduce hospital outpatient visits and the length of any inpatient stays (Theobald 2002). If primary care staff have had little or no involvement prior to the terminal stages of the illness, there is little opportunity for any relationships to develop, which creates difficulties for both staff and patients. Community nurses may be involved in the administration and supervision of medication, care of dressings and medium and long term intravenous access sites, parenteral feeding and personal care, when necessary.

As well as their involvement in primary care, the team is also involved at the hospital outpatient clinic during routine visits and with any inpatient admission. In addition, each team member possesses valuable information regarding dimensions of HIV care that are necessary in planning, implementing and evaluating a patient's individualized care. Sexual health advisors, for example, provide advice on safer sex and sexual health screening, as well as dealing with the sensitive issue of contact tracing. Clinical management of HIV can be further complicated by co-infection with other sexually transmitted infections, syphilis, lymphogranuloma venereum (LGV) and gonorrhoea as well as the increasing numbers of dual infections of HIV and Hepatitis C in men who have sex with men. Regular discussion regarding safer sex and sexual health screening should be an integral part of ongoing HIV treatment and care (UK Collaborative Group for HIV and STI Surveillance 2006).

Healthcare professionals also help patients come to terms with their diagnosis and reveal it appropriately to others, in particular their sexual partners. Trust is ultimately more powerful than any coercion and is essential in helping people work through the shame, guilt and fear associated with HIV infection and in dealing with any rejection and broken relationships that may result from disclosure. However, establishing trust may be difficult due to suspicion and fear, particularly with patients from different ethnic backgrounds.

Dietitians have an important role in assessing the patient's nutritional status and ensuring they have an adequate, nutritious and culturally appropriate diet. Dietitians regularly monitor weight, size and shape, using the Body Mass Index to give an accurate guide to any significant wasting. If nutritional support is needed they will advise on dietary supplements, appetite stimulants, anti-emetics and anti-diarrhoeals, as well as discussing food and water safety with patients who are susceptible to food poisoning because their immune system is compromised (i.e. if CD_4 is below 200). This would include advice on the safe purchase and storage of perishable foods, hand washing and kitchen hygiene generally, ensuring all fish, meat, poultry and eggs are thoroughly cooked and tap water is boiled for one minute before drinking or using to wash salads and so on, and to avoid water borne infections such as cryptosporidiosis. Dietitians also advise on dietary requirements of ART and give advice on metabolic abnormalities that may occur as side effects (Morlese 2002). Any lipoatrophy and lipodystrophy (body fat redistribution) detected may require changes to treatment and referral for specialist treatment. Discussion with the wider multi-disciplinary team may highlight financial difficulties which impact on the individual's ability to buy appropriate food, which can be addressed in the short term by applications to local and national HIV charities and by referral to welfare rights organizations such as the Citizens' Advice Bureau and also to social services, the Benefits Agency or asylum services, if appropriate. Local churches and other faith groups may also offer financial and practical assistance. For very sick and weak patients the dietitian may advise artificial feeding through an appropriate route. This could be via a nasogastric tube that goes through the nose and directly into the stomach, or a tube through the abdominal wall into the stomach (a gastrostomy) or other part of the gut. Patients whose gut is not functioning properly may be given total food replacement through a central venous catheter. This may be very traumatic for the patient and the involvement of a psychologist or counsellor may be required in accepting this treatment.

Another important member of the multi-disciplinary team is the occupational therapist, who will assess whether adaptations are necessary to the home and procure equipment (such as bath rails, level access showers, etc.) to facilitate activities of daily living. Any mobility difficulties will also be assessed by a physiotherapist. Such difficulties might result from side effects of medication, such as peripheral neuropathy, as a result of HIV brain impairment or following a period of artificial ventilation and immobilization.

Physical and psychological causes of loss of libido and erectile dysfunction also need to be investigated and treated. These may be side effects of medication or result from the psychological impact of HIV. The person may fear transmitting the virus and, therefore, a clinical psychologist or psychosexual counsellor would help them to explore and resolve these issues. The clinical psychologist can also offer psychological assessment of HIV related brain impairment and assessment of safety issues in HIV dementia and confusional states.

Recognizing the spiritual dimension to every person is essential but particularly for people who have been given a potentially life threatening diagnosis. Involving the appropriate chaplain in the ongoing care of patients is, therefore, important. Social services staff will also be involved in planning the discharge of patients from the inpatient setting. They will ensure appropriate home care services are in place and assess access requirements to accommodation, as well as the needs of any children in the family. Social worker involvement varies between centres, with some having a dedicated specialist social work team and others using generic social workers for the hospital or community. Encouraging patients to allow a referral to generic social services remains a challenge for health care staff due to patients' fears regarding confidentiality and where and how information about them may be stored. In cases where a specialist social worker attends the multi-disciplinary team meetings within the healthcare setting, patients regard them as part of the team and needs can be identified and met appropriately.

Confidentiality may present particular problems for the multi-disciplinary team when dealing with a gay man whose family have little or no knowledge of his lifestyle, living arrangements or his HIV diagnosis. For the inpatient this may be a particular problem regarding next of kin. In these circumstances a living will may be a useful tool in defining a person's wishes about who is consulted with regard to their care. If the man decides to disclose to his family, having appropriate people within the multi-disciplinary team, such as a psychologist or a specialist mental health worker, who are able to talk to them sensitively, listen to their fears and anxieties and answer their questions is essential.

The nursing care of someone with HIV is no different to the care of any other person with a chronic illness with periods of acute exacerbation. The differences arise because of the external factors such as stigma, fear and contagion, and attitudes towards sexual orientation associated with HIV. All nurses have the appropriate skills to care for the person with HIV. The HIV specialists need to support generic staff, enhancing their knowledge and skills rather than deskilling them. The wider multi-disciplinary team can have an important role in addressing the fears and concerns above and to enable assessment of how HIV is affecting the whole person.

Palliative care

Death is part of life and the process of dying is living the end of life. People need acceptance, love, the ability to give love, refuge or sanctuary, safety, comfort and belonging. The multi-disciplinary team needs to facilitate this process for the person who is dying with HIV/AIDS. There may be particular difficulties for the person rejected by their family because of HIV or those living alone in a foreign country, separated from friends and family and unable or unwilling to disclose their condition to them. The person will need support from different members of the multi-disciplinary team, such as the psychologist or counsellor as well as the nursing team. There may also be cultural aspects of death and dying that need to be identified and accommodated. It is important for the staff team to have adequate facilities to debrief, such as regular clinical supervision, when working with people who are dying. Multi-disciplinary meetings, with input from a clinical psychologist, counsellor or mental health nurse, can help facilitate discussion of feelings aroused by patient deaths or if there is a conflict between medical opinion and the patient's wishes, either in person or through a living will (also known as an advance directive). A living will that is completed when the person is competent, outlining their wishes for treatment and care if they become incompetent to make that decision, should be adhered to (Department of Health 2001d).

The challenge of conception, pregnancy and childbirth faced by the multi-disciplinary team

In the case of a couple where one partner is HIV positive and the other is HIV negative, consideration should be given to the options to prevent transmission of the virus when trying to conceive. The HIV-positive woman who has a negative partner can self-inseminate using sperm from her partner thus avoiding unprotected sexual contact. For the HIV-positive man with a negative partner there is the option of sperm washing and insemination at specialist centres. These challenges indicate how HIV intrudes into the intimate life of patients, making something that is usually private and special into something that has to be discussed openly.

In 2005, one in every 450 women giving birth in England and Scotland was HIV infected. The offer and recommendation of HIV testing to all pregnant women as a routine part of antenatal care has been established nationwide, and there is good evidence that most women are offered testing and accept it (RCPCH 2006). Around 95 percent of HIV infected pregnant women were diagnosed prior to delivery in 2005, compared with about 83 per cent in 2001, however, preventable HIV transmissions from mother to child are still occurring in women whose HIV infection is undetected (UK Collaborative Group for HIV and STI Surveillance 2006).

In order to facilitate antenatal testing, midwives have been trained in pre- and post-test counselling. Mothers who are found to be HIV positive are offered interventions that can reduce transmission of the virus to around 1 percent of babies. Guidelines giving up-to-date information on interventions to reduce the risk of mother to child transmission of the virus have been drawn up using best evidence (and expert opinion where limited evidence exists) by a multi-disciplinary group of clinicians and lay workers active in the management of pregnant women infected with HIV (Hawkins et al. 2005). These include taking anti-retroviral therapy in the latter weeks of pregnancy (dependant on Viral Load and CD_4 results); intravenous AZT during delivery by elective bloodless caesarean section; anti-retroviral therapy syrup for the baby for the first four to six weeks of life and not breastfeeding.

It is extremely traumatic for the woman diagnosed as HIV-positive in pregnancy. She not only has to deal with her own diagnosis and its implications for herself and her partner, but also decisions regarding treatment and delivery of her child. Liaison with obstetricians and paediatricians is essential with regard to antenatal care, delivery and postnatal care of mother and baby. Early discussions about treatment and delivery options enable the woman to make her own choices in consultation with the professionals. Regular perinatal meetings are necessary to facilitate this, and may include: HIV physicians, midwives, obstetricians, pharmacists, neonatal paediatricians, neonatal nurses, social workers, primary care teams, infectious disease paediatricians and HIV clinical nurse specialists.

Community midwives and health visitors have an important role in supporting mothers not to breastfeed, which may be extremely difficult for some mothers to contemplate or explain, particularly if their family is unaware of their diagnosis or if there is a strong cultural expectation to breastfeed. Every possible measure needs to be taken to reassure women that disclosure of their diagnosis to the primary care team will not compromise confidentiality in the local community. Failure to disclose the diagnosis to the GP and health visitor can result in conflicting advice being given by the primary care team and the hospital and midwifery teams with regard to issues such as breast feeding and infant immunization (RCPCH 2006).

Children who are found to be HIV-positive are referred to tertiary centres often some distance from the district general hospital. For this partnership to be successful it is vital that clear, effective lines of communication are established between the different centres in order to provide efficient and safe management of patients and accurate dissemination of information regarding treatments. The tertiary centre can share its knowledge and expertise, while local workers can identify the appropriate local services (White 2001). Any referral for shared care highlights concerns about confidentiality and disclosure for the family. The family's confidence needs to be gained by healthcare staff so they are open to referral to appropriate services and can gain benefit from shared care. The family affected by HIV may have experienced previous losses to HIV and more than one family member may be infected. Parents of a child with HIV have to cope with the knowledge of having transmitted HIV to their child and face the difficult decision of what, when and how to tell their child about their condition. They will therefore require skilled workers to explore the options open to them and their implications. HIV is a complex burden to carry for a young person who is developing his or her own sexual identity and requires sensitive handling by parents and specialist staff. More infected children are surviving into adolescence and adulthood, and this group have complex and specialized needs particularly as they make the transition between child and adult HIV services (BHIVA 2007).

The challenge of treatment with antiretroviral therapy (ART)

The introduction of ART has led to longer life expectancy and dramatic reduction in death rates for people with HIV. However, uncertainty remains about the long term effectiveness of treatment and patients' ability to continue treatment and tolerate side effects (Sowell et al. 1998; Brashers et al. 1999; Bogart et al. 2000; Rabkin et al. 2000). Given current knowledge, people will have to stay on antiretrovirals for the remainder of their lives, a daunting prospect (Bertholen et al. 1999). Concomitant infection with hepatitis or tuberculosis may mean additional treatment, with great potential for drug interactions (Pratt 2003) requiring input from other specialists. Excellent communication between services is, therefore, essential in monitoring treatment effectiveness and adherence.

The change of HIV from a fatal illness to a chronic disease as a result of ART demands dramatic psychological changes for individuals as they face the challenge of restructuring an unexpected future (Sowell et al. 1998; Brashers et al. 1999; Kylma et al. 2001). People who had been contemplating their own death may now be facing returning to work, rebuilding relationships and having to redefine their identity (Kalichman and Ramachandran 1999). Unexpected revival also has financial implications as for people who were aware of their limited life expectancy and had relied on state benefits, or cashed in their insurance policies and lived what they believed was the last part of their life to the full. They are now facing giving up the security of these entitlements and returning to work, despite having limited evidence of the long term effects of these medications (Rabkin and Ferrando 1997). This uncertainty, the magnitude and duration of improvement, the burden of an unremitting and onerous drug regime, anxiety about lapses in adherence and also the complex issues that an unanticipated future brings means the psychological burden of the illness remains (Anderson and Weatherburn 1998; Sowell et al. 1998; Trainor and Ezer 2000; Rabkin et al. 2000). A second life brings with it complex issues that seem largely irrelevant when there seems to be little time left and people are faced with balancing the idea of life being worth living against sinking into a narrowing existence due to the limitations of ART and its side effects.

Prior to ART, Kaposi's sarcoma, which causes purplish-black lesions on the skin, mucous membrane or internal organs, was for many a visible sign of HIV disease. This has largely disappeared due to the restoration of people's immune systems. However, as the length of time people have been taking ART increases, the emergence of longer term side effects of treatment, such as lipodystrophy, are causing similar problems for patients (Collins et al. 2000; Martinez et al. 2001). Lipodystrophy is a visible marker of HIV disease creating a similar look in many people to that of the HIV wasting, particularly in the face, common prior to treatment with ART. It can also lead to the development of a hump on the back of the neck, as well as increased chest and trunk fat with shrinkage of the buttocks, arms and legs. This easily identifies a person taking antiretrovirals to many of their peers and can have a negative effect on individuals' psychological and social lives, which can also impact their quality of life causing low self-esteem, isolation, depression and a narrowing of the patients' social world (Collins et al. 2000; Power et al. 2003).

Peripheral neuropathy is another disabling side effect of some HIV medication. It is important that the patient is aware of this and monitors for its development alongside the physician and specialist nurse so that a change in treatment can be instigated if necessary. Some patients may require the involvement of a neurologist, pharmacist and physiotherapist in its management and treatment.

People with HIV are seen regularly for follow-up, usually at three-monthly intervals when the Viral Load, CD_4 count and other routine tests are measured. For those on treatment there is the ongoing worry of treatment failure, raised lipids and abnormal liver function tests. Attendance at the outpatient clinic is a reminder of HIV and the ongoing need for monitoring of the disease process. The response to treatment failure is influenced by the patients' treatment history. A person who has had a number of regime changes as a result of failure becomes psychologically prepared (Kalichman and Ramachandran 1999), but they may need help to grieve, mourning the loss of hope and expressing anger, guilt and resentment.

GPs need ready access to HIV specialist advice when treating patients who are on ART and/or have advanced HIV disease, even for routine problems, because of the scope for serious interactions between some ART drugs and a wide range of other medications, and because of the risk of underestimating the seriousness of certain conditions in the immuno-compromised patient. Hence patients need to understand that care can only be safely delivered if the GP is kept informed about their HIV and is able to liaise with the HIV specialist. Unless a patient specifically objects, HIV services should routinely update the GP regarding the patient's state of health, test results and medication (BHIVA 2007).

The challenge of adherence to ART

Since the advent of ART we have seen dramatic improvements in CD_4 counts, Viral Loads and mortality among HIV-positive people, but these benefits are contingent on patients' adherence to treatment. Adherence in chronic diseases ranges from 15 to 93 per cent with average estimates of around 50 percent (Meichenbaum and Turk 1987; Singh et al. 1996; Dunbar-Jacob et al. 2000). Regimes of antiretrovirals are relatively inflexible and the need to maintain adequate levels of drug in the bloodstream means that patients must achieve near perfect adherence in order to give themselves the best possible chance of sustained viral suppression (Carr and Cooper 2000; Chesney 2000; Paterson et al. 2000). If adequate adherence is not maintained, the patient is likely to develop resistance to some or all classes of anti-retrovirals and not only face treatment failure but also may transmit resistant virus to any people he or she subsequently infects. As Rabkin and Chesney (1999) state, adherence is, therefore, not only a personal but also a public health issue. Combination therapy for HIV illness is perhaps the most rigorous, demanding and unforgiving of any oral outpatient treatment ever introduced, and may be prescribed for some patients without any current symptoms (Rabkin and Chesney 1999). To be effective ART has to maintain the balance between quality of life and quantity of life. People need to be able to live their life on therapy and live well.

Barriers to adherence

The literature indicates that adherence to treatment is difficult in the following circumstances:

- If the regime is complex
- If there are side effects
- If the demand is long-term
- If the regime interferes with daily living routines
- Where support and communications are nonoptimum

ART fulfils all these criteria (Sherr 2000). Adhering to medication is more difficult when the illness is chronic and the treatments are largely prophylactic (Loveday 2003). Patients who have never been ill as a result of HIV, but started treatment as a result of their CD_4 and Viral Load test results reaching the treatment range (Gazzard 2005, 2006) may not realize the significance of adherence to their treatment, or have the same commitment as someone who has been very ill as a result of HIV. It is difficult to gain a sense of the seriousness of their illness with only blood test results and the doctor's advice to rely on and when viral resistance seems unreal. Those who have 'returned from the dead' as a result of ART are more focused on their treatment. There is a need for excellent patient education and follow-up to facilitate the best adherence possible and to ensure patients are aware of the virological consequences of poor adherence (Anderson and Weatherburn 1998, 1999).

Patients with little or no social support are more likely to have difficulties with adherence (Anderson and Weatherburn 1999) and, therefore, may rely heavily on the team caring for them. For many, professionals involved in their care are the only people aware of their diagnosis and the burden of secrecy they are carrying. There are also many barriers to adherence evident within the literature, as indicated in Box 15.3:

Box 15.3   Potential barriers to adherence to ART

- Depression
- Current drug use
- Homelessness
- Alcohol use
- Concerns about confidentiality at home or work
- The constant reminder of HIV
- Dietary restrictions
- The nature and severity of side effects
- Medication being too large to carry conveniently
- Inconvenient dosing schedules
- Difficulty remembering
- Ethno-cultural factors such as a differing world view or lack of understanding of cultural influences
- Lack of knowledge or understanding about treatments
- Immigration difficulties
- Irregular working patterns
- Time and family pressures
- Financial insecurity
- Scepticism
- Difficulties with storage of medication (e.g. shared fridge)

(Chesney et al. 1995; Singh et al. 1996; Crespo-Fierro 1997; Rabkin and Chesney 1999; Catz et al. 2000; Mellins et al. 2003)

Multi-disciplinary teamwork can, however, improve adherence, and research has shown that patients who received help from social services, with transportation and mental health and chemical dependency issues addressed more likely to remain in contact with the HIV services (Sherer et al. 2002). Many African people receive an AIDS diagnosis alongside their HIV diagnosis as they often present late for testing (Del Amo et al. 1996) and need to start treatment quickly having had little time to build trusting relationships with healthcare staff. They may perceive their illness from a religious or spiritual standpoint in which it is a manifestation of evil or a sign from God and reject any HIV care, believing that God will cure them through prayer (King 1999). Plans to encourage and enhance adherence must incorporate person specific variables and be tailored to individualized needs (Crespo-Fierro 1997) – the multi-disciplinary team is well placed to do this.

Promoting adherence

The best combination for every patient is the combination they are willing and able to take (Catz et al. 2000), and efforts to maximize adherence must be started before the prescription is dispensed (Daar et al. 2003). Patients need to be *ready* to start treatment (Enriquez et al. 2004) and will be more likely to adhere if they have a clear understanding about HIV disease (Rabkin and Chesney 1999; Weiss et al. 2003). Reducing the pill burden increases the level of adherence (Altice and Friedland 1998; Anderson and Weatherburn 1999; Chesney 2000), and doctors will aim for the fewest tablets at the fewest dosing times. However, research has shown that it is the ease with which the regime is accommodated into the patient's daily routine that is crucial (Singh et al. 1996; Stone et al. 2001).

Multi-disciplinary discussion prior to treatment commencing enables potential barriers to adherence to be identified and appropriate referrals and action to be taken. An example of this in practice is shown in the case study in Box 15.4:

Box 15.4   Case study of adherence to treatment

Alice lives alone and none of her family, friends or colleagues is aware of her HIV diagnosis. She works two nights a week in a nursing home and also for a care agency on four or five other days each week, but doesn't have a regular shift pattern. Due to her declining test results the medical consultant planned to start Alice on ART, however, following discussion in the multi-disciplinary team meeting it became clear from other team members, combined with knowledge of Alice's work pattern and the potential side effects of Efavirenz, that the regime initially considered would be very difficult for Alice to adhere to.

An alternative regime was suggested taking into consideration Alice's blood test results and social requirements and the specialist nurse worked with Alice to identify the times that she could take it 12 hours apart and on an empty stomach as the regime required. Incorporating her work, eating and sleeping pattern and the need to take her medication in secret, Alice decided to take it at 6am and 6pm.

Despite having to set her alarm to wake her at 6 am when she is not working a night shift, Alice continues to adhere well to her regime, having been part of the decision making process and having committed herself to taking her medication at these times.

(N.B. Names have been changed to protect patient confidentiality).

The Department of Health has identified the need for patients to become 'experts' about their own health. Doctors, nurses and other health professionals who undertake long term follow-up and care of people with chronic diseases have recognized for many years that their patients understand their disease better than they do, and this knowledge and experience has been an untapped resource. Today's patients with chronic diseases need not be mere recipients of care – they can become key decision makers in the treatment process. By ensuring that knowledge of their condition is developed to a point where they are empowered to take some responsibility for its management and work in partnership with their health and social care providers, patients can be given greater control over their lives (Department of Health 2001f).

Multi-disciplinary working encourages collaborative treatment decision making and physician–patient partnerships lead to greater satisfaction and higher adherence for patients (Anderson and Zimmerman 1993; Chesney et al. 1999; Paterson 2001). Through talking with the patient about what they understand about HIV, its spread and treatment, multi-disciplinary team members can begin to understand and work with the patient to build on this knowledge, thus enhancing the patient's autonomy. Mutual respect and trust develops between the team and the patient, encouraging people to participate as equal partners in decisions about the health care they receive (Opie 1998). The goal of treatment plans is not to hand over the decision making to the patient, but rather to promote nonjudgemental dialogue and negotiation between patients and the team (Lerner et al. 1998).

Time spent with the doctor is usually limited and patients are often daunted, feeling more able to talk and confide in a nurse or social worker that they may meet for longer and perhaps in their own home. The nurse–patient relationship is a powerful tool that greatly affects adherence. In most settings it is the nurse who provides patient education surrounding treatment regimes and who is often privy to patients' reported challenges associated with adherence (Crespo-Fierro 1997; Halkitis and Kirton 1999). The community nurse specialist also has insight into the real home situation and can evaluate how this will impact on adherence. A genuine collaboration between patients and their healthcare providers regarding preferences and available options is essential. Identifying potential side effects of medication enables discussion with the individual about what they are prepared to tolerate. For example, one anti-retroviral –Efavirenz (Sustiva ©) – can cause vivid dreams and nightmares. For some people this is not a problem, others are unable to tolerate them. It is essential for the multi-disciplinary team to address the behavioural aspects of HIV therapies, taking account of optimal meal schedules, dietary considerations and dosing schedules, particularly with regard to holidays and travel (Kalichman and Ramachandran 1999) and to identify the difficulties patients face in their lives and to try to resolve them. This may involve referring them to a drug treatment programme, nutritionist, psychiatrist, pharmacist, case manager, welfare rights adviser, immigration solicitor or housing department (Gerbert et al. 2000). Partnership with HIV support centres is important as they can provide valuable information, advice, peer support, counselling and often therapies such as reflexology and aromatherapy massage, which are important in enabling patients to maintain adherence to medication.

There are many ways in which adherence can be enhanced, as indicated in Box 15.5, adapted from Rabkin and Chesney (1999) and Loveday (2003).

Box 15.5 Techniques to improve adherence

- Use of weekly or daily pill boxes
- Printed medication charts
- Alarms on watches or key fobs or mobile telephones
- Identification of lifestyle triggers and cues
- Designing a draft plan that integrates pill doses to established daily activities (e.g. keeping pills by the kettle or at the bedside)
- Using dummy pills or jelly sweets for trial runs
- Identification and resolution of dysfunctional attitudes
- Text reminders

In addition to the techniques in Box 15.5, referral to a psychologist for relaxation and guided imagery training and cognitive restructuring to focus on positive aspects of treatment is also useful. Culturally appropriate leaflets and information using CD-ROMs and videos about how pills are to be taken and possible side effects are useful tools provided by various HIV charities, pharmaceutical companies and information services and regular feedback of CD_4 and Viral Load test results by medical staff encourages continued adherence.

Confidentiality can be breached inadvertently, particularly when people live in close-knit communities (Gorna 1994), which leads to reluctance to fill in prescriptions in their home neighbourhood and hiding or relabelling medications to maintain secrecy within the home (Pediatrics 1998). Lack of disclosure of HIV creates specific problems, for example, having to store drugs in a refrigerator that may be available to others, or in a situation where a wider or extended family is living together. Finding appropriate, secret storage for medicines and disposal of packaging, continually hiding the process of taking medication at specific times and making plans and excuses for having medication are ongoing difficulties facing people on treatment for HIV, and has the potential to interfere with adherence to treatment. An example of how staff can help patients to deal with this is shown in Box 15.6:

Box 15.6 Case study of adherence to treatment

Grace is a 23-year-old Zimbabwean who came to England to study two years ago. She lives in a shared house with her two sisters and others from her home town. She shares a room with her older sister. Her parents and wider family remain in Zimbabwe. Grace was diagnosed HIV positive as part of a routine sexual health screen. She was very shocked at her diagnosis and decided not to tell anyone outside the clinic about her diagnosis, stating that her sisters would not be able to cope if she told them and they would in turn disclose to her family back in Zimbabwe.

Unfortunately Grace's results showed she needed to start on medication fairly soon after diagnosis. Because of the difficulties in maintaining confidentiality at home, she initially declined medication saying she was unable to hide anything from her sisters as they shared many possessions and had little or no privacy. She also often had to lie in order to attend the outpatient clinic. She began to develop symptoms of depression. The consultant discussed this within the multi-disciplinary team meeting and referral was made to the specialist community mental health nurse and they arranged to meet.

Grace was started on an anti-depressant and seen regularly for counselling and monitoring of her mood. She expressed great fear of disclosure but also recognized her need to start medication. Through discussing her fears and developing trust in the specialist nurse, she was able to identify a way she could use a dermatological problem as a reason to explain her need for medication to her sisters. Grace is now established on her anti-retroviral therapy, her confidentiality remains intact and her mental health has improved.

(N.B. Names have been changed to protect patient confidentiality.)

The challenge of developing and maintaining partnerships between organizations

Treatment for HIV is commenced when a person's blood test results and clinical picture reach limits set out in the BHIVA guidelines (Gazzard 2005, 2006). Now 13 years old, the British HIV Association is a well established and highly respected organization with national influence committed to providing excellence in the care of those living with and affected by HIV. Members are drawn from all disciplines and have also formed the Children's HIV Association of UK and Ireland (CHIVA), the Dietitians HIV Association (DHIVA), the National HIV Nurses Association (NHIVNA) and the HIV Pharmacists' Association (HIVPA), thus providing a breadth of experience and knowledge. Through critical examination of the research and through personal experience, the organization produces clear guidelines that are regularly updated and easily accessible on the internet for the treatment and care of people with HIV (see www.bhiva.org). This is essential in disseminating knowledge and sharing best practice to clinical staff, particularly those working outside large treatment centres, ensuring best possible treatment for patients. Due to the rapid changes and developments in treatments and care in HIV this partnership between clinicians and these associations is essential.

Stigma associated with HIV continues and fears, misconceptions and negative attitudes to people with HIV remain prevalent (Alonzo and Reynolds 1995; Katz 1996; Bunting 1996; Anderson and Weatherburn 1998; Brashers et al. 1999; Barroso and

Powell-Cope 2000; Taylor 2001). Fear of the disintegration of family relationships inhibits patients disclosing their status, even when it is necessary to access services (Anderson et al. 2000). HIV disease does not occur in a social vacuum, people who develop HIV infection often belong to a group that has experienced previous social rejection such as gay men, intravenous drug users and people from other ethnic groups (Catalan et al. 1995). Many are multiply disadvantaged, particularly those who are migrants to the UK having witnessed or experienced rape, torture or other severe trauma in their home country and have come as refugees with an uncertain future. As a result many are living in poor housing and become isolated due to cultural and language differences and fears about confidentiality. Refugees may take little interest in their health when their prime concern is for their relatives left behind or how they are going to negotiate the asylum system or pay their bills. Mental health problems are common (Himid et al. 1998). Counselling and support needs to be made available to help people to deal with the ongoing stigma of HIV and the effects of ART, as well as managing uncertainty and living with a chronic illness. Many have seen friends and family members with HIV dying and fear the same for themselves, reflecting the situation for many gay men who have seen many of their friends, living and dying with HIV, struggling with adherence to their medication, side effects and drug resistance. These multiple bereavements have a profound effect on the individual who then discovers they are HIV positive themselves. Fear of breach of confidentiality is the most common reason for Africans not accessing HIV services due to the continuing high level of stigmatization of HIV in African communities (McMunn et al. 1997). If their diagnosis is discovered, they fear abandonment by their family and social exclusion from previous sources of support such as friends, social networks and cultural groups. Many people do not disclose their diagnosis to anyone outside the healthcare provider setting and may become isolated as a result.

People with HIV draw their support from a variety of sources, both formal and informal, depending to a large extent on whom they trust, who is around and who makes a difference (Anderson et al. 2000). National support agencies such as Terence Higgins Trust, Positively Women, Body and Soul and others offer support groups, information and advice to HIV-positive people. These partners in supporting and caring for the individual with HIV can provide services in ways healthcare professionals are unable to. One important area is in peer support and self-help groups where patients can share personal stories and experiences and learn from each other. For many people, finding a safe place where they can be open about their diagnosis and discuss their fears, hopes, dreams and expectations with others who are facing the same situation is a lifeline. HIV support centres also fulfil an invaluable role in bringing together families affected by HIV to share experiences. Body and Soul, in particular, runs a youth club for teenagers with HIV, enabling them to relate to young people of their own age in a safe environment. There are also many local support centres and networks for people to access – ensuring that patients receive contact details and information about groups is important in maintaining this partnership. Self-referral to the group avoids any conflict over disclosure of confidential information, although an introduction to staff, volunteers or members of the group/centre can facilitate easier integration. The healthcare team will provide a letter confirming an HIV-positive diagnosis, if required, and may discuss patients' needs with staff with the patient's permission.

For those who have experienced revival as a result of ART, a crucial decision is whether to give up disability benefits, which, although limited, are secure and predictable, and return to work. Although feeling physically well enough to work, fear of employers' attitudes and trying to explain gaps in their CV due to periods of illness may make them reluctant to apply for jobs and training opportunities, again highlighting the impact of continuing stigma surrounding HIV. However, uncertainty about the durability of treatment response means people are attempting to reconcile the hope of regaining normal relationships, returning to work and having a future with the fear that their improved health may prove only transitory (Brashers et al. 1999). Advocacy programmes, advice on state benefits and 'back to work' and career counselling, are important facilities provided by many HIV support centres to help people cope with this uncertainty and take control of their life again.

Terence Higgins Trust, Avert and the National AIDS Manual provide excellent written information, covering a wide range of relevant topics, many of which are free to the HIV-positive person. These include a series written for gay men, young people and African men and women, recognizing that different groups require information written in culturally sensitive or age appropriate language. These organizations also provide excellent Internet websites that give accurate information on medical, treatment, and social and welfare issues, enabling people to access information in the privacy of their own home or through one of the local support groups. Magazines such as '+ve' provide excellent information and social contact details for patients. These are available at most treatment centres and HIV support centres and are free by post to individual patients.

Many patients welcome receipt of information via email or mobile phone text message, and this can be more confidential than a hospital envelope arriving on the doormat where it is visible to other household members. Patient choice in this area should not be restricted (BHIVA 2007).

Patient and public involvement

The challenge for the NHS, working in partnership with patient organizations and other government departments and agencies, is to bring about a fundamental shift in the way in which chronic diseases are managed – a shift which will encourage and enable patients to take an active role in their own care.

> Expert Patients Programmes', are not simply about educating or instructing patients about their condition and then measuring success on the basis of patient compliance. They are based on developing the confidence and motivation of patients to use their own skills and knowledge to take effective control over life with a chronic illness

> (Department of Health 2001f).

HIV services have matured within a true patient/clinician partnership where negotiation about care and respect for patient choice has dominated. This culture has largely been influenced by the sociological issues that have contributed to the uniqueness of the HIV speciality such as patient activism and advocacy in the early years of the epidemic, the young age of patients and the defined community of people affected compared to other illnesses (Nixon 2004). The standards for HIV clinical care (BHIVA 2007) state that 'Clinical care should be provided through partnership between clinicians, NHS organisations, patients and the wider public'. This reflects the government's approach to involve patients and the public in planning and helping to design services, the Kennedy Report (2002), recommended the representation of patient's interests 'on the inside' of the NHS at every level, following on from the development of the Expert Patient Programme. The white paper *'Our Health, Our Care, Our Say'* (DoH 2006b) outlines that a stronger voice for local people is needed. This means that NHS organizations, with their social care colleagues, need to have more effective and systematic ways of finding out what people want and need from their services. They need to reach out to those people whose needs are the greatest, to people who do not normally get involved and to people who find it hard to give their views. As a result, service users and their carers have more say over where, how and by whom their support is delivered, and have better access to information to help them make appropriate choices. Individuals and their communities are able to influence the shape and delivery of local services, and people using services are more satisfied with their overall experience of care.

Involving patients in the design of care services can provide new insights and leads to more patient focused and locally appropriate solutions. Everyone else on NHS teams is there to present a professional perspective (Squire et al. 2006). Patients should be viewed, not as raw material on which clinicians practise their skills, but as core team members who happen to have the clinical conditions at issue. Without the co-operation and collaboration of patients and their carers, no treatment plan can succeed, yet the expertise that patients possess is often ignored or disparaged by professionals (Kramer 2005). Clinical care should be provided through partnership between clinicians, NHS organizations, patients and the wider public. This entails patient and public involvement in planning and helping to design services, together with education and personalized information to support patients in taking part in shared decision making about their individual care (BHIVA 2007).

However, obtaining input from patients is not a trivial or ad hoc exercise; it demands careful thought and planning. Box 15.7 outlines this:

Box 15.7   Service user involvement – Issues to consider

- Confidentiality
- Clear aims and objectives
- Lines of communication
- Training and education
- Ensuring political will to be involved
- Adequate time and resources

- Adherence to timescales
- Empowering patients to be involved
- Accountability

Conclusion

HIV remains a complex and stigmatized disease that challenges professionals to work together to provide holistic, individualized care for patients. Significant advances in treatment mean that HIV, once considered uniformly fatal, is now regarded as a chronic disease. However, treatments are complex and require almost perfect adherence to achieve viral suppression. The rapid developments in treatment and psychosocial knowledge about HIV mean that healthcare staff need to constantly keep themselves updated in order to incorporate the latest evidence in their work. Being able to call on the knowledge and expertise of specialists and the guidelines produced through BHIVA, CHIVA, DHIVA and NHIVNA is essential in keeping on track with the latest developments. The role of the multi-disciplinary team in being able to assess and treat each person as a whole person and from different perspectives has been highlighted, as has the importance of developing a partnership with the patient to enhance adherence to treatment. The need for multi-agency working to enable people to cope with the psychosocial impact of HIV and of treatment with ART has been discussed and the valuable role support groups and information organizations play in the care of people with HIV has been identified. Many organizations have ceased during recent years due to withdrawal of funding. It is essential that those that remain continue to fulfil this function because of the stigma, prejudice and discrimination related to HIV.

Questions for further discussion

1 The treatment of HIV with ART has led to increasing complexities of medical treatment. How can members of the multi-disciplinary team ensure that they do not lose sight of the patient in the midst of the rapid developments?
2 HIV remains a stigmatized and largely secret disease and further changes of funding away from support and information agencies and towards treatment will leave people even more isolated and vulnerable. How can the multi-disciplinary team respond to this challenge?
3 HIV care has largely led the way on holistic, patient centred care. How are other areas of medicine and social care responding to the challenge?

Useful websites:

- *The British HIV Association*: www.bhiva.org has become the leading UK national advisory body for professionals involved in HIV care

- *National AIDS Manual Publications*: www.aidsmap.com is a UK charity that seeks to provide HIV information to HIV-positive people and to the professionals who treat, support and care for them
- *Positively Women*: www.positivelywomen.org.uk is a UK charity working to improve the quality of life of women and families affected by HIV
- *Terrence Higgins Trust*: www.tht.org.uk is one of the leading HIV and AIDS charity in the UK, and the largest in Europe

Part III:

Learning from partnerships

16　On the receiving end: reflections from a service user

Amir Minhas

This chapter will:

- Provide a very personal reflective account from an Asian man in his early 50s who is physically disabled and uses a wheelchair
- Share the journey, insights, and experiences of being dependent on outside help and support
- Provide a rich understanding that will be of interest and relevance to any service provider

---

I am an Asian male, born in Pakistan, who caught poliomyelitis in early childhood. The impact of 'polio' varies considerably from slight paralysis, in one or other limb, to almost total paralysis whereby the individual needs mechanical assistance to breathe and cannot independently move any part of the body apart from the head. In my case, the effect of poliomyelitis was to paralyse both legs resulting in impaired muscular and skeletal development of both legs. The impact of this impairment is that I am, for the most part, confined to a wheelchair. In a society like Pakistan people with disabilities have few life chances. There are no developed public sector welfare institutions able to address properly their needs. Had I stayed in the country and not moved to England, I would probably have been compelled either to beg for a living or to be entirely dependent upon one or other member of my family.

While recounting my early years in the UK I would like to mention that, in total, I attended three different boarding schools for 'handicapped' children: Staplefield Place School, Hatchford Park School and Lord Mayor Treloar College. The biography which follows is necessarily based upon personal recollections and personal experiences and so some of the details may not conform in terms of accuracy with regard to any specific location at a given time. The details in terms of the actual events are accurate.

Within this chapter I seek to portray and draw lessons from my life experience with a view to generating a discourse regarding some of the many issues pertaining to the 'human' services and explore the implications for multi-agency working. In particular, I intend the reader to identify and consider what the issues are, or what they may be. I raise issues for discussion and give personal opinions but am not attempting to provide answers.

Biography

I was born in 1956 in East Pakistan (now known as Bangladesh), the second youngest of six children. I caught poliomyelitis at 2 years of age and it left me with two paralysed legs. My father died when I was 3 years old, leaving my widowed mother with six children to raise within the context of an impoverished Muslim society, where women in the late 1950s and early 1960s did not have much opportunity for education, career or social independence. I am informed that, after a fruitless quest by both my parents in Pakistan to obtain treatment for poliomyelitis, my mother and father had planned to send me to England to receive treatment. However, my father's premature death had left the family destitute and, due to the difficult social conditions prevailing in Pakistan, my mother was not able to earn enough to look after my siblings adequately in terms of providing an education and meeting our material and emotional needs. Therefore, within this context and being influenced by other relatives, my mother decided it best to send me to England – telling me that I was going 'on holiday'.

At about 5 years of age, I was accompanied on an aeroplane by an old friend of my late father who was travelling to England (for I don't know what reason or for how long he had intended staying). On arrival in England I understand that my late father's friend took me straight to Tite Street Hospital, Chelsea, where he left me in the care of the hospital authorities for several months. I am told that the hospital conducted medical assessments and delivered appropriate treatment, but to no avail.

After all had been done that could be done, the hospital contacted the local London mosque, which then took charge of my welfare. It is important to note that the mosque is not only a building for prayers but is also a tightly knit community under the authority of the imam. The imam allocated my care to a young family who took me through religious duty rather than with any sense of welcoming acceptance. At some point the local education authority became involved and, in due course, I was sent to a 'boarding school for handicapped children', Staplefield Place School in Sussex. During the school holidays I returned to the mosque and to a different family. Some years later an 'uncle' of mine emigrated to England with a view to settling and bringing his own young family to the UK in due course. He had assured my mother that he would locate me and take personal responsibility for my care. The 'uncle' arrived in England and obtained work, which necessitated frequent trips around the country and living in 'digs' at various sites. However, he did locate me at boarding school, assumed my guardianship and arranged for me to be looked after by a kind old English lady (who had also suffered from poliomyelitis) and her blind and bedridden husband. This lady was only known to me as 'Sister Joan'.

The next year or so was spent at boarding school and with 'Sister Joan' during the school holidays until another friend of my father (Mr Khan) heard about my existence from the imam at the mosque. Out of his friendship for my deceased father, Mr Khan sought to take responsibility for my care. He contacted my 'uncle' and arranged for me to live with him and his English wife (Kathleen Khan) and their children during the school holidays. However, Kathleen did not really want to look after me (she had her own three preschool children to look after) but accepted me out of devotion to her husband. I do not recall for how long this arrangement lasted (probably about two years on and off), but it eventually broke down and I returned to live with 'Sister Joan' in the holidays. Staplefield Place School remained for me the only stable environment during my early childhood. School holidays had been spent in all sorts of places, including time at a residential children's home in Winchester and being fostered by an Asian family in Farnham, who kept me confined in one room of the house where I spent my days by myself and ate my meals alone.

However, when I was about 10 years old, Kathleen Khan contacted the school seeking to look after me during the holidays. It is my understanding that Kathleen's husband had died and that her resolve to look after me as a child was rooted in fulfilling a promise to her late husband. This arrangement lasted for about two years or so when, my 'uncle' and, by then legal, guardian had finally brought his own family over and settled in Liverpool and he was keen for me join his family. By this time I had, however, been socialized into Western society, culture and values and felt part of Kathleen's family. Although my 'uncle's' family were now settled in Liverpool, he had three preschool children who had just arrived in the UK from Pakistan and a wife who did not speak English and they were not integrated into Western society. I had forgotten how to speak in Urdu. From the age of 12, I regularly returned to my 'uncle's' family home in Liverpool during the school holidays and attempted to integrate – bearing in mind the cultural and communicational difficulties. By the time I was 15 I was free from statutory care and dependence and left 'home' in an attempt to lead an independent life, with albeit very limited, mobility.

Initially, I shared a flat with a friend for about two years and then I obtained my own independent accommodation. For the next 15 years or so I didn't 'live' life, and I didn't try to deal with the multi-faceted difficulties I faced in respect of disability, racism and cultural conflict. Tired of dependence and the stress and traumas it brought me, I wanted an independent life and simply 'existed'. I claimed all the benefits to which I was entitled; I escaped and occupied myself by regularly and excessively taking drugs; I watching TV all night, not starting my days until around 2pm and ending them in the early hours of the next morning. Not surprisingly, I sank into despair and depression. I drifted into a nihilistic view of life, with no purpose, no ambition, and no thoughts of ever having a loving relationship or meaningful career.

Towards the end of nearly 20 years of a purposeless existence, I chanced upon an old drugs misusing friend who had managed to extricate himself from a similar lifestyle. He persuaded me to attend an Access course (access to higher education for the unemployed). I undertook this course with no particular aim other than it would help fill my days. I successfully completed the course and went on to take a degree course, during which I established a committed relationship with a fellow student. She 'took charge' of my life. I needed help because by now I was dependent upon heroin. She moved in with me, cleaned up the flat and helped motivate me to seek employment. During this period I gained self-esteem and made some significant transitions. I embarked upon a methadone reduction course, achieved a good Bachelor of Arts degree at Christ and Notre Dame/St Kaths College and secured a position as a community service officer with Merseyside Probation Service.

After eighteen months I left my position as a community service officer, as I had been sponsored by the Home Office to attend Liverpool University to study a

Diploma in Social Work and Master of Arts (Social Work). Upon successful completion I was subsequently re-employed as a qualified probation officer with Merseyside Probation Service, where I have been employed for the past ten years.

Analysis and commentary

The reader will note that throughout this brief biography no mention has yet been made of social work and healthrelated interventions. During my childhood the role of the social worker was less formalized and more akin to that of a support worker cum guardian *ad litem* or *in loco parentis*, but without stringent, formalized structures of accountability. Consequently, as well as the potential for more meaningful, organic and 'natural' relationships between social workers and their clients, the lack of accountability opened the door to the potential for damaging abusive relationships. My knowledge and experience of the social worker–client relationship is based upon the memories of the accounts of childhood friends (all of whom seem to have had a social worker). As far as I am able to recall, no social worker was allocated to my case in the sense that I, as an individual, had any direct dealings with a social worker. However, social services must have been involved when I was placed in the children's home in Winchester and when fostered by the Asian family in Farnham. Essentially, decisions were made by I don't know whom about significant issues, without my involvement at any level, however elementary or basic. Again, this is possibly nothing out of the ordinary in terms of social work practice during the 1960s and early 1970s.

It is fair to assume that health, education and social services departments had been involved to varying degrees in making significant decisions about my physical, emotional and social welfare at different stages of my childhood development within the context of an inconsistent and variable 'home/family' setting. Such decisions were made without even the most basic consultation with me – it may be that as a child between the ages of 5 and 12 years it was the prevailing view among the agencies that consultation would not be appropriate or relevant. Most crucially, and this is really the main point, perhaps, clear explanations (reasons for the decisions) given in a sensitive and supportive way may have ameliorated some of the sense of absolute powerlessness I felt when, for example, I was told whether I was to stay with strangers in Farnham or with Kathleen in Fulham, or whether I was going to the children's home in Winchester during the summer holidays or to stay with my 'uncle's' family in Liverpool.

On reflection, the main issue for me as a child was not so much about not being involved in decision making or feeling I was not 'looked after', rather it was that I didn't have an enduring focal relationship with one individual who could be a source of support, information and explanation. In other words, an allocated social worker with whom a long term relationship could have developed. The psychological and emotional need for stability and continuity, from whatever source, was a paramount need, which appeared from my recollections to be neither recognized nor addressed. However, it is also true to say that the complex and difficult issues of emotional and psychological stability for a child in such circumstances is a problem which may never have been possible for a statutory agency to address satisfactorily (social workers come and go). In fairness, my material, educational and health needs were adequately met in terms of actual provision, although the quality of the provision was variable.

The issues of ongoing health care and the provision of aids (wheelchair, crutches, callipers, physiotherapy) were looked after by the residential school authorities directly, and so between the ages of 5 and 16 years, I had no direct knowledge of the necessary procedures and processes by which such services and aids could be accessed. The important point here is that at no time during my school years was I given information and help to independently access services and aids that I would need to access on a regular basis throughout the rest of my life. The presumption was that the parent(s)/guardian/care giver would either directly obtain such services and aids on my behalf or would inform me how to facilitate them. Unfortunately, my 'uncle' had no such knowledge or experience either, so he was not of much use to me in these respects.

On reaching adulthood and independent living all support from my 'uncle' ceased and I was left to my own devices in terms of self-care, obtaining employment, accessing services and aids, and expediting daily chores such as cooking, cleaning, shopping, laundry, which may be difficult for any 18-year-old, but are also physically much more challenging to a wheelchair user. My early experiences of living independently were fraught with great difficulties and yet I basked in the wonderful sense of freedom from residential care and a home life with my 'uncle', in which the culture, values and communication difficulties had stifled and constricted any sense of joy in being alive. However, that sense of freedom was an important but transitory feeling of elation as the harsh realities of unsupported living encroached upon my consciousness. Loneliness and despair soon became constant companions, and requests to my 'uncle' for practical support came to nothing: apparently, I had been a difficult child to look after and 'must now live the consequences of my circumstances'. His obligation to fulfil his promise to my mother had been discharged. So, how did I cope?

Well, I coped on an ad hoc basis. I ate as and when I was hungry; I slept as and when I felt like it; I laundered my clothes when the last clean shirt had become so dirty that even I felt the need for a change of clothes. Shopping occurred on a similar basis and cleaning my accommodation was last on the list of chores – except for obtaining employment, which was in all honesty not even on the list! My emotional and psychological circumstances were best characterized as being nihilistic and I very quickly resorted to taking drugs. The drug taking was not exclusively a response to personal despair but was, initially, also a response to my immature understanding of 'the evils of the world'. It was an expression of my rejection of Western capitalist values, which I held to be the fundamental cause of both global misery as well as my personal misery. It was also a lifestyle choice and recreational activity. As such I socialized with other drug users and constructed an identity that centred upon a community of outlaws and misfits – living off the 'dole', not giving a fig for 'the system' or the norms of society, while inexorably heading towards personal self-destruction without any regard for whether I lived or died.

Paradoxically, it was within this community of misfits and away from formal care, that I formed friendships which became sources of various types of informal support – predominantly emotional and psychological, but including practical support by negotiation and bartering. For example, in return for food and shelter, one friend would shop and clean the flat or would help to transport the washing to a public laundry. At other times I would provide a taxi service (in the car I got from Motobility) in return for help with the shopping. In other words, my daily needs were being met on the basis of exchange – sometimes direct cash payments for practical help, at other times help was given freely out of friendship. However, any semblance of truly autonomous living was not viable, given my disability without significant support.

With regard to the ongoing need for medical equipment/aids (crutches, wheel-chair), I would approach my GP and he/she would either make the appropriate referral or supply me with a relevant telephone number, and I would then pursue an application to its conclusion. My knowledge of sources of help was sparse in terms of the types of help available. However, I always knew enough to access a starting point. For example, if the need was medically related, then the starting point would be the GP. If it was a benefits issue, then I would approach the Citizens' Advice Bureau. If there was a social issue related to my impairment I would contact the local branch of the British Polio Fellowship or the Liverpool Association for the Disabled. The voluntary organizations were the primary sources of access to information and different forms of help, including welfare rights, housing and adult education. Any success I achieved rested upon my ability to communicate, engage and negotiate, with the impetus being generated by personal need and desire. If I did not have enough confidence and ability, then I would not have been able to access such services – and at times I did not do so. There was no 'one stop shop to which I could make an approach and from which the various types of support and help could be accessed. Nevertheless, I did manage to remain housed and fed, and eventually undertook relevant educational courses, which led to my becoming more integrated into mainstream society and, ultimately, achieving full time employment. The desire for integration and for employment could only have arisen and be sustained once I had been fortunate enough to have established a loving and committed relationship. It was the stability and nurturing aspects of this relationship that helped to heal the emotional and psychological damage sustained by a difficult childhood and a lifestyle that had subsequently become rooted in a total disregard for personal consequences.

I had always been wary of approaching social services and other statutory agencies since leaving 'home'. After all, I had never hitherto had any direct contact with social services and held the same prejudices and forebodings regarding the department's function and role as did all my contemporaries, believing it to be more an agency of control and surveillance than a source of help and support. I did once approach social services seeking nonspecific help (wishing to discuss my circum-stances with a view to changing my self-destructive lifestyle) but the initial assess-ment interview was such an appalling experience that I was relieved when no further contact was made by the department. The social worker appeared to be absolutely uninterested in my situation and made me feel that I should be grateful for not being even more deprived and oppressed than I actually was!

During my undergraduate days, while seeking to become less reliant upon personal relationships and friendships to meet my everyday needs, I applied to have a 'home help' (additional practical support at home). At this stage the Home Help Service was provided by the city council rather than by social services. I received three different home helps over a period of about four years. It was my impression that such people, while being pleasant enough as individuals, were underpaid and, in some cases, not properly trained. Household cleaning was often superficial; shopping would take an inordinately long time; a relationship would strike up in which much of the time was spent chatting and drinking cups of tea (not a bad thing except that it was at the expense of providing a service). Again, the relationship would become characterized in terms of dependency, and whether one received a half-way effective service or not, depended upon one's social and negotiating skills. It is my personal opinion that home help workers were 'disincentivized' by poor pay, unreasonable work schedules and poor training with little support from management. The priority of the employer would have been 'cost-effectiveness' (as usual). And the goal of cost-effectiveness within all public sector service provision too often boils down to doing the job as cheaply as you can get away with and having little or no regard for the consequences of the quality of service delivered or the long term impact on the client group. It appears to be an abiding governmental principle that is applied to all the public sector services (health, education, criminal justice, social services and police), while 'spin' uses spurious statistics to demonstrate 'successful outcomes'.

It is perhaps significant that my main experience of positive help was not as a client but as an employee during my initial spell of employment with Merseyside Probation Service, then during postgraduate studies at Liverpool University and finally again with Merseyside Probation Service. On first joining the probation service as a community service officer, I became aware of the concepts of anti-racism, anti-sexism, anti-oppressive practice and allied 'anti-isms'. In other words, I found myself employed by an organization that expressed anti-oppressive values and sought to promulgate a culture of inclusiveness and a commitment to a fair and just working environment for all its employees and in it's engagement with service users. I had very limited previous work experience and this was the first time that I had experienced positive support, understanding and help to facilitate and sustain employment in the context of the employer actively taking into account issues related to disability, with a view to overcoming any difficulties in conjunction and consultation with the disabled employee. For example, any problems or difficulties that did arise were open to discussion with management and with the personnel (human resources), and I was never made to feel that I was making unreasonable demands upon either a specific individual or the organization as a whole.

In my dealings with colleagues I felt listened to, consulted, taken seriously and involved in the process of finding solutions, without being held solely responsible for achieving solutions. In particular, the human resources department responded to issues positively and willingly, and continue to so do. A key factor here is that the assistant to the head of human resources (at the time) was available and responsive to me. She was an identified individual whom I could approach with any issues, regardless as to which area, section and/or function the issue pertained. A single identified individual with power in the organization developed a working relationship with me, which gave me the confidence to know that whatever difficulties I faced in employment with this organization, together we would seek to resolve issues without my having to take full responsibility for finding the solutions. This was a partnership on equal terms.

One such issue was the physical and emotional toll taken by me in attempting to fulfil my role as a probation officer on a full time basis. The help initiated by the human resources department was that arrangements were made to involve an organization called the Shaw Trust. In brief, this organization was able to fund one working day. This meant that in recognition of the additional challenges posed by my disability, positive action was taken that enabled me to be allocated 80 percent of the work of a full time probation officer, yet continue to receive a full salary and other entitlements of a full time employee. This was in recognition of the accumulative pressures of working in an environment that demands a high level of personal resources (physical and emotional energy) and, as a result, I would not be left feeling constantly exhausted at the end of every working week. Without this support I would not be able to sustain the role. Eventually, after becoming increasingly dissatisfied with the role of community service officer, I left the probation service and read for a diploma (social work) and Master of Arts (social work) at Liverpool University, although this environment posed additional challenges. I soon discovered that access to lecture rooms, seminar rooms, coffee bars, self-service cafeterias, notice boards, pigeon holes, etc. within the university was not straightforward as they were not wheelchair friendly. Like the probation service, the university staff were sympathetic and proactively helpful in achieving solutions. For example, they provided a dedicated parking space (shared) near the entrance to the relevant building, and they relocated the student pigeon hole to a lower height. Wheelchair access is a common issue in both the workplace and public buildings. At university the lecture rooms and tutors' offices were all on the second floor. Access to the only lift (which I think was predominantly designed and used for transporting laboratory equipment) involved time-consuming convoluted detours down long corridors, making it difficult to grab a coffee during short coffee breaks. However, at least a lift existed – which is not always the case!

While at university I returned to the probation service on my first assessed placement. At this purpose built probation office (known then as the South Knowsley Probation Centre) all the probation officers were located on the first floor. A lift had been especially installed for a previous wheelchair-bound employee. As a functional object, the lift, perhaps better described as a contraption, served its purpose. However, it actually resembled a forklift truck, with sides – a bit like a veal crate. It didn't look like it was designed for humans. As with so many aids for people with disabilities, the design (style, colour, materials, etc.) of such equipment focused on its functionality with little regard for the ergonomic and/or aesthetic impact upon the individual: if you have to use a noisy, slow and ugly looking goods lift frequently, and are separated from colleagues, you begin to feel like goods yourself.

I have often found that disabled access to places of work or other public buildings is achieved by a side or back entrance, where the entrance is usually locked, and the individual first has to locate a member of staff who holds the key and is invariably difficult to find. The design is invariably functional, crude and the cheapest available. The point here is not just about there being provision and availability of equipment, services and physical access, but that where such provision is available it usually unwittingly serves to separate, humiliate and alienate the individual even while achieving the functional objective (of, in this example, gaining access). Thereby, an accumulation of ad hoc solutions to various problems of disability helps to generate and reinforce an image of people with impairments reduced to the status of childlike dependency – at best, at worst the status of a burdensome problem that has to be reluctantly accommodated in order to demonstrate 'inclusiveness' and/or the expression of equal opportunities policies. The missing element is any sense of respect for the dignity or the value of people with impairments for who they are and what they have to offer. This is a general point about the expression of social attitudes to disability and the issue of empowering people with impairments to overcome a disabling society.

In my professional role I have become aware how the criminal justice system can so often devalue and oppress offenders by increasingly submitting them to processes and interventions without regard for their intrinsic value as human beings and their individual assessment and need. Of course the language of individual assessment and need is of top priority in policy and discourse within the system. However, the actual impact of current policy, dominated by exhaustive bureaucratic form filling and assessments, is to subvert professional judgements in order to fulfil targets, because targets are linked to budgets, and so are seen as evidence of successful outcomes (if they are achieved) – regardless of the counter-productive impact upon the individual. This obsession with targets pervades public services, but when applied to the human services (social work, probation, health and education) the systemic processes oppress those who are subject to them as well as those who are charged with implementing them.

The systems and processes that devalue people with impairments are not consciously formulated and written down as policy, as in the case of the public services analogy, but are rooted in historic attitudes (as is the case with racism and sexism) and reinforced by both physical and social structures. During my higher education I was exposed to a variety of sociological and psychological theories from which I have sought to analyse, interpret and elucidate models for understanding the dynamics and nature of the oppression of different vulnerable sectors of society, delivered, for example, by race, class, gender, age, sexual orientation, disability, nationality, culture or religion. These theories cover vast areas of psychosocial experiences and dynamics, cultural values and belief systems at the personal, familial, communal and societal levels. They seek to explain oppression and disadvantage with a view to informing government policies from which agency policies and procedures are derived, which, in turn, inform practice on a day to day level.

The agency policies and procedures are the framework within which the frontline worker is required to implement interventions. However, government priority is the delivery of services in a cost-effective and quantifiable manner and so practice guidance and policy frameworks are overlaid with bureaucratic procedures and productivity accountability systems, which seek to measure and demonstrate successful outcomes in order that politicians can evidence so called 'real improvements' in the delivery of public sector services. Inevitably these apparent improvements are measured in terms of achieving targets which are in turn linked to budgets. Consequently, the pressure on the public service sector to achieve targets then becomes the agency's top priority. The monumental task of achieving what appear to be arbitrary targets becomes the worker's priority because the achievement of targets is the measure of the worker's, team's, division's and agency's value. If quantitative targets are not achieved, financial penalties may be imposed which will further reduce resources and increase pressure on the worker. If these targets are achieved, then resources will be secured for the next financial year.

The point here is that the *quality* of service delivery is undermined and subverted by a mechanistic focus upon the quantifiable and measurable aspects of service delivery. In my own life experience I often received the services I needed (indeed this could have been measured and quantified), but it was often the way the services were qualitatively delivered that undermined the benefit of them to me, and at times this created additional difficulties. This is a subtle but crucial point. It isn't just *what* is done that matters, but it is also the *way* it's done.

It is fair to say that the lack of quality in the service I received during my childhood cannot be attributed to a social worker being driven by a 'target' agenda, because targets were not an accountability 'metric' during that period. However, part of the problem from my experience was that service I received was similarly too narrowly concerned with the visible practicalities such as provision for a wheelchair, crutches, a school, accommodation, etc., and insufficient attention was given to service delivery in terms of listening, empathizing, showing respect, caring, building up a rapport, responding individually and developing a relationship, etc. From my perspective the two need to go hand in hand if a service is going to be delivered successfully, but the latter aspect is getting marginalized in the human services in the twenty-first century.

Conclusion

To summarize I would make the following points. First, during my childhood and schoolboy years I did receive help and support from education, social services and the health departments. However, none of it, at any time and as best I can recall, actively involved me as an individual in any of the assessment or decision making processes. I received a number of different interventions, some of which should have involved my active participation at various stages. Statutory obligations were discharged by the relevant agencies, but I was often left feeling powerless, like a 'straw in the wind'. For example, the school holidays spent fostered with an Asian family in Farnham appears to have been arranged on the reductionist assumption that, because I was Asian, I would be best placed with an Asian family, as if somehow Asian people are a homogenous group. This was despite the fact that I was no longer able to speak Urdu and had never met the family before being placed with them. No account was taken of my Western socialization, developing identity or personal preferences.

Second, when I did leave the residential school and my 'uncle's' home in Liverpool, there arose a tension between two extremes: continuing to seek support from various agencies from which I was often left feeling powerless and patronized; and the freedom of living completely autonomously and independently. I opted for autonomous living with all its difficulties problems and dilemmas – most of which I did not foresee. For those I did foresee I did not have ready-made solutions, but attempted to resolve problems on an ad hoc basis. The solution depended upon the nature of the problem, the resources available at the time and my own inner resources. The point is that the lack of information, the lack of advice or guidance, the absence of any understanding or supportive relationship, compounded by previous difficult experiences from when I had received help, reinforced an aversion to availing myself of necessary support from the relevant statutory agencies.

Third, during my 'nonproductive' adult years obtaining appropriate help and support was often through trial and error. A myriad of organizations existed, both statutory and voluntary, yet I could only access assistance if I was capable and skilled enough to negotiate the bureaucracy and conduct myself in a manner that attracted a sympathetic understanding. There was no single, obvious access point (as in the more recent local authority initiative of 'one-stop-shops').

Fourth, significant support was made available when I obtained full time employment with Merseyside Probation Service. The support and social capital I gained here enabled me to sustain a demanding job and to develop both in my practice as a probation officer as well as in other personal areas, as a human being – notwithstanding managerial imperatives to fulfil targets set by Home Office officials. Of course, the rhetoric of impacting upon offending behaviour is prevalent through-out the criminal justice system and the intention in so doing is sincere and appropriate. However, it is the mechanistic application of the business model (in the interests of being cost-effective) to all the human services that I believe will ultimately prove to be counter-productive to the main purposes of any given agency. It is not the basic analyses and ideas in their entirety that are at fault; it is the inflexibility of target driven initiatives that damage both the client group and the workers who have to implement them.

Fifth, we live in an increasingly complicated and difficult world in which, as workers, we have to take into account various issues – many of which are only partly understood, sometimes contradictory, sometimes irreconcilable and which present dilemmas in practice, in order to practise our professions. With the increasing momentum towards multi-agency practice (involving different agency protocols, agendas and priorities) there arises the danger of compounding the complexities of delivering services and interventions. While we become preoccupied with negotiating the dynamics of multi-agency working, the prospect of losing sight of the purpose of all this work becomes a real possibility, and the client group risks becoming increasingly peripheral to the purposes of multi-agency partnerships and projects. Meetings will be held, emails exchanged, minutes circulated, documents sent out for consultation, faxes sent and received, working parties attended, and the telephone will never stop ringing – in the midst of all this you might find ten minutes to talk with the client!

Finally, I think what I am seeking to impart to the reader is that, from personal experience, as a recipient of services as well as a professional seeking to deliver services, you cannot underestimate the importance of engaging with whatever client group you work – in a spirit of truth, honesty, justice, care and respect. These attributes are harder to measure, they will probably not find their way into the mechanistic detail of targets, outcomes or deliverables. It is quite feasible for a partnership to demonstrate how successful it is 'on paper' and yet fail to deliver on these crucial values. From my experience, the single most important issue is not increasing the range of services we deliver, but rather improving the manner in which we deliver them: it's not so much what we do, but the way we do it that matters most to clients.

Questions for further discussion

1 How far does the account presented here reflect the experience of clients with whom you have had contact, or indeed your experience of receiving a service?

2 In your experience, has there been any improvement in user involvement in service delivery? If yes, what has been the nature of this improvement?

3 To what extent (if any) is the way in which a service is provided more important than the actual service itself?

4 Having read this personal account what would you say are the key lessons to be learnt for service delivery?

17 Evaluating partnerships

Ros Carnwell

This chapter will:

- Define evaluation in relation to partnership work.
- Identify what can be evaluated and who should be involved.
- Discuss the different models of evaluation.
- Consider the challenges of evaluation and how they can be overcome.

Partnership working is becoming increasingly prevalent as a means of addressing complex health and social care issues (Weiss et al. 2002), a fact which has become evident in earlier chapters of this book. However, according to Weiss et al. many partnerships have difficulty realizing the full potential of collaboration and need help in determining how well the collaborative process is working long before it is possible to measure the impact of the partnership's actions. Halliday et al. (2004) also point out the need for information about the 'health' of partnerships, including the identification of shortfalls and guidance about strategies for development. There is therefore a need for good evaluation of partnership work; however, as will be seen in this chapter, evaluating partnerships can be a complex task. The chapter will attempt to unravel this complexity, starting with an explanation of what evaluation is and how it applies to partnerships.

What is evaluation and who should be involved?

Evaluation can be defined as 'the systematic collection of information about the activities, characteristics, and outcomes of programs to make judgements about the program, improve program effectiveness, and/or inform decisions about future programming' (Patton 1997: 23). In relation to evaluating partnership, evaluation involves gathering information on how partnerships are working, in order to find out how effective they are, so that recommendations can then be made about any changes needed (Clarke 1999). Evaluation should be an ongoing process, during the creation and progress of the partnership right through to the point at which the partnership has achieved its objectives, rather than an event tagged on towards the end of the life of a partnership. The way in which the evaluation is conducted can be broadly divided into two overall approaches (formative or summative), although within these two approaches there are a number of different models, as will be discussed later in this chapter.

Formative evaluation, often referred to as *process evaluation*, is more concerned with the processes that are happening to deliver and run the partnership, rather than the outcomes the partnership produces. A process evaluation is concerned with the structures, the organization, the relationships, the interaction involvement and commitment with and between the different individuals and organizations that make up the partnership. Formative evaluators then:

- Work closely and interactively with everyone involved in the partnership
- Focus on processes not outcomes, such as activities that partners are engaged in, outputs and short term outcomes
- Share information with members of the partnership at all stages of the evaluation
- Enable corrections to be made as required throughout the development and progress of the partnership

(Scriven 1980; McCawley (undated); Kellogg Foundation 2004)

Summative evaluation, often referred to as *outcome evaluation*, focuses more on the end product than the processes involved in partnership work. A summative evaluation is concerned to look closely at what has been achieved by the partnership. Summative evaluators therefore:

- Focus on outputs, outcomes and resources employed
- Provide an assessment of the effects and efficiency of the partnership
- Help decision makers to decide whether to continue the partnership after the objectives have been achieved

(Scriven 1967)

What is being evaluated?

Most texts on evaluation refer to the evaluation of 'programmes' (e.g. Patton 1997). This chapter, however, is interested in the evaluation of partnerships, such as a case management partnership, or services that have been enhanced by different agencies working together in partnership, for example in respect of housing and homelessness (see Chapter 9). Some partnerships may be driven by policy directives which require partnerships to be established between organizations for example in respect of the provision of child protection (see Chapter 5).

Who should be involved in evaluation?

Most published evaluations are conducted by independent researchers who have been commissioned by organizations to conduct an independent evaluation. Being independent and separate from the partnership, such evaluations are free from the researcher bias that can occur if practitioners self-evaluate services that they are also responsible for delivering. Moreover, Shaw and Faulkner (2006) point out that involvement by social work practitioners in evaluation of their own services is rare, and that where it does exist, it has been criticized for a number of reasons, including its naive treatment of evidence, and its unquestioning insider standpoint. Despite these trends and criticisms, however, some argue that practitioners should be involved in evaluation by setting research priorities, so that research is perceived as relevant to practice (Attree 2006). Indeed, Shaw and Faulkner (2006) argue that practitioner involvement in small scale, local evaluation is 'an essential ingredient of good professional practice' (Shaw and Faulkner 2006: 45). A partnership can evaluate itself and this clearly has some merit but it also has some significant limitations compared to an independent evaluation.

Besides the lack of practitioners being involved in evaluation, there is also evidence of lack of service user involvement in designing evaluation (Simpson and House 2002, Shaw and Faulkner 2006). One explanation for this, according to Shaw and Faulkner's findings, centres upon the ethical issues of collecting research data from people that the researcher/practitioner worked with. It may also be possible that practitioners are reluctant to engage service users in research because of a concern that this might influence the findings. In a systematic review of literature concerning involvement of mental service users in the delivery and evaluation of services, for example, Simpson and House (2002) found that clients reported less satisfaction with services when interviewed by other users of the service in evaluation research. INVOLVE (2008), however, actively encourages user involvement in designing research and provides examples of good practice including:

- Helping researchers to identify and ask the right questions in the right way
- Ensuring that health and social care research is relevant to service users and the public
- Enabling service users to get involved in the research process itself, whether designing, managing, undertaking or disseminating research

Clearly then good independent evaluation needs to incorporate insights gained from service providers and from service users.

How to evaluate

Although models of evaluation vary in terms of the precise way in which evaluation is conducted, the process of evaluation generally involves four main stages (Owen and Rogers 1999). First, the evaluator will negotiate an evaluation plan with the *organization* commissioning the evaluation. Second, once the plan is agreed, evidence will be collected from across the different partner *organizations*. Third, the evidence will then be analysed in order to produce findings. Finally, the findings will be disseminated to the partner organizations to enable them to make decisions regarding the policy and/or practice implications. The main *focus* of the evaluation may differ, however, according to the requirements of the evaluation. Most writers agree that evaluation is concerned with 'processes', 'outputs', 'outcomes' (Tym and Partners 2006; McCawley (undated); Kellogg Foundation 2004) as well as 'inputs', 'activities' and 'impact' (McCawley (undated); Kellogg Foundation 2004). Each of these terms can be defined as follows:

- Input – resources invested into the partnership
- Activities – what is done by partners to achieve the desired outcomes
- Processes – events that take place during the implementation of the partnership arrangements, which determine *how* partnerships develop
- Outputs – what is achieved as a direct results of partnership (e.g. increased throughput, increase in patients seen)
- Outcomes – changes in socio-economic or physical conditions in the partnership (e.g. increased patient satisfaction, decrease in morbidity, which may be short of long term)
- Impact – changes achievable in the long term

(McCawley undated; Kellogg Foundation 2004; Tym and Partners 2006)

Depending on the method or model of evaluation adopted, the evaluator will focus to varying degrees on the activities listed above. An example of an evaluation focusing mainly on outcomes and impact is presented in Box 17.1:

Box 17.1 An evaluation of an intervention

In Sweden, a trial legislation was introduced in 1994 allowing the social insurance, social services and healthcare services to unite in co-financing under joint political steering. The aim was to improve the efficiency and effectiveness of the welfare systems for medical, social and work related rehabilitation (Hultberg et al. 2005).

Hultberg et al. describe how, in the city of Gothenburg, there was a trial area for 20 different projects under the name of DELTA, three of which concerned collaboration at primary health care centres. The co-financing project, enabled the DELTA health centres (intervention centres) to intensify rehabilitation work through teams including other professions, such as occupational therapists, physiotherapists, social workers and social insurance officers. The co-financing model involves joint financing, political steering and integration between services in primary health care, social services and social insurance.

Hultberg et al. (2005) conducted an evaluative study aimed to assess differences regarding change in physical, psychological and social status between patients with musculoskeletal diseases attending the health centres with the co-financed collaboration model, and patients attending a control health centre.

The study involved comparing patients attending three DELTA (intervention) centres with similar patients attending four (control) healthcentres not practising collaboration.

> The results found no evidence that the new inter-disciplinary team structure gave a better patient health outcome than conventional care. One explanation offered by the authors was that, although co-financing led to a new inter-disciplinary team structure, this did not change the actual rehabilitation that patients received.

Hultberg et al.'s (2005) evaluative study shows the limitations of focusing exclusively on outcomes and impact, rather than processes. Their study showed no difference in patient outcomes but did not consider that other important process factors, such as improved relationships between staff or improved staff morale may have been evident. If so, it could be possible that these important factors may ultimately result in improvements in patient outcome, if an evaluation were conducted at a later date.

Because of the limitations of focusing exclusively on outcomes and impacts, a number of authors have suggested different models of evaluation in order to successfully evaluate inputs, activities and processes as well as outcomes and impacts. In this chapter, four of these models will be discussed as they apply to evaluating partnerships. These are programme logic modelling, multi-method evaluation, evaluations based on theories of change and realistic evaluation. These models have been selected because of their applicability to partnership work.

Programme logic modelling

Programme logic modelling is a method of evaluation that maps the partnership to show the sequence of events connecting the need for the partnership with the desired results (Kellogg Foundation 2004). Programme logic modelling would therefore be based on the *planned work* and *intended results* of the partnership. As indicated in Table 17.1, the planned work includes resources or inputs (human, financial, organizational) needed to implement the partnership, and the partnership activities, such as processes, tools and events, as part of the implementation. The intended results include all of the partnership's desired results (outputs, outcomes and impact). Kellogg Foundation (2004: 2) defines outputs as 'types, levels and targets of services to be delivered by the programme'. By comparison, outcomes are 'specific changes in participants' behaviour, knowledge, skills, status and level of functioning', while the impact is defined as 'the intended or unintended change occurring in organisations, communities or systems as a result of partnership activities within 7 to 10 years' (Kellogg Foundation (2004: 2). Thus, according to this definition, impact often occurs after the conclusion of project funding. As indicated in Table 17.1, the programme logical model can be applied to evaluating partnerships. Resources, such as time and space, will need to be provided for partnerships to be established and activities, such as meetings will need to take place in order to agree working arrangements. In designing an evaluation it will be necessary to consider how such *planned work* will be measured in order to demonstrate its effectiveness as part of the *process evaluation*. Likewise, the *intended results*, expressed in terms of changes in knowledge about and commitment towards working arrangements, changes in local policy and ultimate changes in how services are provided, will also need to be measured as part of the *outcome evaluation.*

Table 17.1 Basic Logic Model format and potential problems with evaluating partnerships

Planned work			Intended results	
Resources/ Inputs *(Resources needed to achieve desired activities: what is invested)*	**Activities** *(Activities required to achieve outcomes: what is done)*	**Outputs** *(Outputs achievable as a consequence of activities: knowledge and attitudes).*	**Outcomes** *(Changes, behaviours, practices, policies) achievable in short term (1–3 years) and in the longer term (4–6 years)*	**Impact** *(Changes in environment or social conditions achievable in the long term – perhaps 7–10 years)*
Time for partners: to engage in strategic planning. Human resources to attend partnership meetings. Time for liaison between multi-disciplinary workers. Meeting place.	**Create schedule**: of partnership meetings. Agree terms of reference for partnerships. Formalize working arrangements.	**Stakeholders have**: improved knowledge of working arrangements of other partners. All stakeholders committed to partnership.	**Integrated local**: policies to involve all partners. Joint local strategies. Workers have ownership of process of partnership working.	**More effective**: communication between all stakeholders in partnership. Seamless provision of services to users. Less overlap of services. Increased service user satisfaction.

↓

Process evaluation

↓

Outcome evaluation

Potential problems in evaluating partnerships				
Duration of partnership planning may result in evaluator not being able to complete full evaluation within reasonable time scale. Funding may be spent on partnership development and not on evaluation.	Different partners may perceive 'success' differently. Staff may feel exposed to managerial scrutiny due to new arrangements and may not want to co-operate in evaluation. Partnership managers may want to 'appear' to be effective in order to maintain their funding.	Knowledge about other organizations and improved working relationships may have been achieved, but has this been achieved at the expense of professional morale and a stable workforce? What effect has closer collaboration between services had on the choice for users?	Workers may have been collaborating informally long before formal partnerships developed. Therefore, any benefits may result from a continuation of previous practices, rather than the effects of new arrangements. Records and data may not be available or may not be consistent across agencies.	Any differences in service user satisfaction could be due to other factors (e.g. training of staff) rather than partnership working. Evaluation may not be designed to distinguish between all the possible causes and effects.

Although there are a number of models to help with evaluating partnerships, partnership is a vague concept (see Chapter 1), capable of many interpretations, which makes evaluating partnership problematic (Glendinning 2002) (see Table 17.1). The problems of evaluating partnerships can be described in terms of: problems arising from funding and timescales, problems in attributing causes of success and problems in measuring success. Each of these is discussed below.

Problems arising from funding and timescales

Often initial funds are spent on the development of the partnership rather than setting aside funding for evaluation at the outset, with evaluation plans being added as an afterthought (Butterfoss and Francisco 2004). Partnership managers may also want to 'seen' to be effective in order to secure ongoing funding, so they seek an evaluation that might demonstrate 'hard' outcomes rather than one that is based on a solid logic model or theory. A narrowly focused outcome evaluation will struggle to distinguish between cause and effect, and it will be difficult to examine what proportion of the outcome could be attributed to which activity or what contribution each partner organization made (Butterfoss and Francisco 2004). As indicated by Glendinning (2002), for example, outcomes achieved may result from increased support and funding arising from the partnership. Therefore, once the funding is removed the outcomes may not be sustainable in the long term. The length of time required to make decisions and implement partnerships (often due to funding cycles) may also preclude the evaluation being possible within a reasonable timescale. This may limit evaluators to focusing only on the inputs, activities and processes involved in the partnership and possibly some outputs, as it may be too early for outcomes and impacts to be evident within the short timescale during which the evaluation has to take place.

Problems in attributing the causes of success

Glendinning (2002) argues three key points in relation to attributing the causes of success. First, successes may be unique to just one of the partners within the organisation and may not be typical of others. It cannot be assumed, for example, that because hospital admissions have been reduced in one partner organization following the partnership arrangements, the same will have occurred across other partners. The reduction in hospital admissions could have been due to many other factors, rather than the partnership, that are peculiar to the organization concerned.

Second, various stakeholders may perceive success and how it can be evaluated differently because of different professional perspectives. For example, 'success' in a drugs partnership might be viewed by the medical partners in relation to a reduction of infectious diseases such as Hepatitus and HIV, whereas criminal justice partners, might perceive 'success' in terms of a reduction in crime convictions.

Third, some successes may be achieved at the expense of other factors which in the longer term could have a detrimental impact upon future 'success'. There may, for example, be an increase in the number of clients being seen and referred onto to other services since the partnership arrangements were put in place, but there may also have been a reduction in staff morale, a higher staff turnover and unfilled vacancies due to difficulties in recruitment. While some outcomes may appear particularly positive, evaluators may argue that the partnership has been less success-ful overall, due to damage to the staff morale and stability of the workforce. Issues of quality may need to be considered as well as measurements of quantity.

In order to deal with these problems, Glendinning (2002) suggests that evaluators should identify the factors and circumstances that are likely to contribute to success. This would provide more information so that where possible the real causes of success could be identified and established.

Problems in measuring success

Due to the complexity of partnership arrangements, it is virtually impossible to ascertain whether an apparent outcome (such as increased satisfaction or easier access to services) is due to the partnership working or to some other factor, such as increased staffing or implementation of a training partnership in one of the partner organisations. Moreover, as Glendinning (2002) points out, costs are often easier to measure than benefits, such as those that are less tangible like increasing independence or quality of life. It is therefore easy enough for evaluators to obtain information about how much was invested into the partnership in terms of human and physical resources as these types of *inputs* can more easily be counted. However, if the desired outcome of health and social care partnerships is an increase in independence of older people in the community, it might be more complicated to establish criteria regarding what constitutes 'independence' in a way that any changes can consistently and accurately be measured.

Although evaluating partnerships does have its difficulties, if carefully planned, partnerships can be successfully evaluated. Careful planning first involves building an evaluation plan into the partnership structures and processes right at the beginning as this will ensure that information is available from which to construct baseline measurements, against which achievements can be evaluated (Tym and Partners 2006). Failure to do this, according to Tym and partners, would mean it was impossible to use findings of an evaluation to improve performance. Tym and partners (2006) also argue that a number of steps need to be followed for evaluation to be successful. These include:

- Establishing good quality baseline information at the outset. This means that if the intended outcome is to be an increase in client satisfaction, then client satisfaction surveys should be available at the start as a baseline against which future measurements can be compared
- Stating the objectives and outcomes of the partnership at the outset, so that measurements can be consistent with these
- Clearly stating who will benefit from the evaluation. There may, for example, be a number of beneficiaries, including senior managers, staff and service users
- Stating the intended achievements of different projects within the partnerships, together with details of costs and timescales. Some partnerships will comprise a number of different organizations, all of which might have different projects with different intended outcomes, although the accumulative effect of these may contribute to the overall effectiveness of the partnership
- Developing effective monitoring systems to ensure that outcomes of different projects are measured. As the projects within the different organizations are likely to be different, they will require different monitoring systems, although there may also be commonalities between them

It is evident then, that partnerships themselves are complicated and therefore that evaluating them will also be a complex task. A number of authors have addressed the problems of evaluating partnerships and have offered solutions. These include evaluating using *multiple methods* at different *levels* of the organization and using *theory-led* evaluations.

Multi-method evaluation

The complexity of partnerships, together with the problems of evaluating them have led some authors (e.g. Dickinson 2006; El Ansari and Weiss 2006) to argue that in order to understand the nature of partnership a pluralistic or multi-method approach is necessary. According to El Ansari and Weiss (2006), the traditional quantitative approach is inadequate and needs the additional rigour that a combination of qualitative and quantitative methods affords. To do this, they suggest that we need to make the quantitative and qualitative methodologies used in partnership research more robust by developing better tools in order to improve the evidence base for practitioners and policy makers. El Ansari and Weiss further argue that qualitative approaches provide insights into the data, identify relevant variables, develop appropriate outcome measures, and provide explanations from which hypotheses can be generated. The credibility of the emerging theory can then be tested through quantitative methods.

In addition to a multi-method approach, a multi-level evaluation is also recommended (Butterfoss and Fransisco 2004; El Ansari and Weiss 2006), which El Ansari and Weiss argue should embrace the perspectives of all stakeholders and the complexity of the phenomena under study. Moreover, Butterfoss and Francisco (2004) propose that partnerships should be evaluated at three levels (Table 17.2).

Table 17.2 What partners and evaluators do in multi-method and multi-level evaluation

	What partners do	What evaluators do	Type of data collected
Level 1: Infrastructure, function and processes	Develop mission statements. Conduct needs assessments. Produce action plans. Recruit and train leaders.	Document what was done and by whom. Document whether the partnerships were functioning as intended.	Qualitative and quantitative analysis of documents held by partners (e.g. annual reports, meeting minutes, activity logs, any surveys conducted by partners).
Level 2: Programmes and interventions	Engage in activities specified in action plans (e.g. delivery of services, interventions and training).	Look for evidence of achievement of partnership delivery of action plan.	Conduct quantitative surveys and qualitative interviews, focus groups, observations of interventions, records, home visits, logs and diaries.

	What partners do	What evaluators do	Type of data collected
Level 3: Health and community change outcomes	Continuance of delivery of activities to achieve outcomes.	Look for evidence of achievement of goals.	Qualitative analysis of user records to establish whether agreed changes in practice have been adopted. Analyse records to establish whether proposed policies were introduced. Interview key informants to assess whether local policies have changed as a result of partnership.

An example of using a multi-method, multi-level approach to evaluating a partnership can be seen in an evaluation of community mental health services, in which Freeman and Peck (2006) used multi-methods (through the various methods of data collection) and also a multi-level evaluation (Box 17.2). The multiple levels can be seen in the interviews of team managers (Level 1), questionnaires of staff (Level 2) and focus groups of users and carers (Level 3).

Box 17.2 Integrated community mental health services

Freeman and Peck (2006) evaluated a county-wide implementation of specialist integrated community mental health services in the UK.

As is typical of evaluation, the study began with a scoping exercise of the views of stakeholders, including users, carers, general practitioners, mental health leaders, senior managers and practitioners. Concerns identified from the scoping exercise were diverse and related to management (e.g. difficulties in bringing together personnel and procedures from health and social care); service users (e.g. benefits and difficulties) and staff (e.g. concerns over role clarity).

In order to capture the these diverse concerns, a multi-method evaluation was carried out which involved three sources of data:

- Focus groups with users and carers who had been in direct contact with both the new specialist team(s) and previous generalist provision
- Semi-structured interviews with each specialist and generalist team manager concerning the operation of the teams within their locality
- Quantitative self-completion questionnaires to each member of staff within the teams, in order to assess role clarity and job satisfaction within each of the new specialist teams and more traditional, generalist community mental health teams.

The results revealed general positive reactions towards the new provision although there were some concerns including issues of privacy and safety for service users. There were variations across partner organizations in relation to job satisfaction and role clarity.

Freeman and Peck's (2006) study shows the difficulties involved in evaluating the impact of complex service interventions on user, carer and staff perceptions of service quality, which were well illustrated by:

- The complexity of the proposed service interventions
- The diversity of *local* contexts, each with a wide range of prior experience of integrated working with potential to influence the extent to which participants were able to engage with the changes
- The dynamic *national* policy context requiring swift implementation of standard models of care
- Difficulties in comparing staff satisfaction levels at two different times due to high staff turnover during the interim period
- The introduction of different teams into the localities (as required by the intervention) – which meant there could be no direct pre–post-comparisons of team-based means. This illustrates the problems of not having base line measurements

(Tym and Partners 2006).

Freeman and Peck (2006) conclude that evaluating partnerships requires designs that are capable of taking account of the complex nature of the partnership interventions together with the heterogeneous contexts in which they occur. Moreover, as Judge and Bauld (2001) point out, many current policies involve complex interventions, which make contributions at different levels and which pose particular challenges for evaluation. One possible solution to this is to use *theory-based* designs (Judge and Bauld 2001, Freeman and Peck 2006).

Theory led evaluation

A method that encapsulates pluralistic approaches to evaluation, known as 'theory led' or 'theory-based' evaluation, has also become increasingly popular in partnership evaluation. This method, rather than being concerned only with causative links between the inputs to the partnership and the associated outcomes, is concerned to map out the entire process (Pawson and Tilley 1997), thus enabling evaluators to establish which parts of the partnership worked and why, and whether there were any unanticipated effects (Birckmayer and Weiss 2000).

Theory led approaches have arisen out of the inadequacy of previous approaches, which have been mainly concerned with the 'processes' of partnership work, such as *how* relationships between partners develop. While some approaches in the past have been relatively cheap, quick to use and applicable in a variety of contexts, these tools do not always enable the evaluator to accurately understand the connections between what was put into the partnership (input), what happened during the partnership (process); and what happened as a result of the partnership (outcome) (Dickinson 2006). Dickinson argues that it is these connections between input, process and outcome that quantitative and qualitative approaches are insufficiently able to deal with on their own. Theory led approaches are interested in unravelling the complex inter-connections in health and social care partnerships, and have understandably become more frequently used in partnership evaluations (Dickinson 2006). Theory-based evaluation therefore has the advantage of being capable of strengthening programme (and partnership) design and implementation, as well as promoting policy and practice learning about the most effective interventions for health improvement (Judge and Bauld 2001).

Two main theory led approaches have become influential (Wimbush and Watson 2000) and have been employed in the evaluation of health and social care partnerships (Dickinson 2006). These are 'theories of change' (Connell et al. 1995) and 'realistic evaluation' (Pawson and Tilley 1997).

The theories of change approach to evaluation

The 'theories of change' approach is relevant to the evaluation of partnerships because, according to Weiss (1995), all programmes (and thus partnerships) have explicit or implicit 'theories of change' about how and why they work. These theories influence decisions about the way in which partnerships develop, and when made explicit, can drive the development of an evaluation plan (Weiss 1995). Thus, the theories of change approach can capture the dynamics of relationships and performance at multiple levels with a diverse range of stakeholders, and it can articulate the processes and outcomes so that adjustments can be made to methods and goals along the way (Connell and Kubisch 1996, 1999). The theories of change approach, then, is mainly concerned with the *how* and *why* of change and offers the greatest promise for documenting the effectiveness of and improvements in community-based initiatives (McLeroy et al. 2003) with evaluators attempting to unravel in as much detail as possible about how and why a partnership works (Dickinson 2006). In doing so, evaluators make programme assumptions about relationships between activities and outcomes, as well as making the mediating factors more explicit. This would be done during the planning and at the commencement of the partnership, rather than after its completion, with different stakeholders exploring competing theories. The advantages of this approach are that it can overcome problems of ascribing causes and effects, it assists in planning and implementing initiatives, it engages in a deep analysis of internal processes and there is involvement of many stakeholders (Dickinson 2006).

An example of using a 'theories of change' approach to evaluating a partnership can be seen in Blamey *et al.*'s (2005) evaluation of 'Have a Heart Paisley (Box 17.3):

Box 17.3 An example of a 'theory of change' evaluation

Have a Heart Paisley (HaHP), established in October 2000, aimed to reduce the levels of inequality of Coronary Heart Disease in the town of Paisley, Scotland, through an integrated programme of secondary and primary prevention. The initiative involved 15 linked work strands designed to deliver interventions in partnership, engaging the community at all levels of the programme.

The evaluation consisted of four separate but linked approaches:

- Mapping the social context of the project area
- A quasi-experimental population survey and follow-up
- Integrated case studies of key settings (primary care, the community and the local authority) using qualitative and quantitative methods. The focus of this was largely on service development and impact of HaHP on professionals and/or agenda change, at both strategic and operational levels
- A theory-based/process evaluation to capture partnership plans and the extent of their delivery

According to Blamey et al. (2004, 2005) the *theory-based* approach involved a documentary review and initial interviews of managers in order to articulate the programme plans and theories. The plans and theories were represented as logic models, which were further developed with operational staff during in-depth interviews. Aspects of the evaluation focused on the extent to which HaHP successfully delivered its overall plans, in particular the cross-cutting mechanisms deemed crucial to success. The mechanisms related to the extent to which HaHP:

- Applied evidence-based and innovative practice
- Improved partnership working
- Fully engaged the community
- Achieved agenda change in the key agencies responsible for service delivery
- Saturated Paisley with opportunities to motivate behavioural and cultural change that reduced coronary heart disease
- Addressed health inequalities in relation to coronary heart disease

The 'theories of change' approach was used in Blamey et al.'s evaluation because of its focus on the inter-connections between the various partners. The deep analysis of internal processes involved in the theories of change approach enabled Blamey et al. to reveal the nature of some of the problems within the initiative, including the overambitious nature of some of the initial plans, which meant that timescales for delivery had to be lengthened and expectations with regard to outputs and outcomes reduced. The evaluators also discovered differences between the different partners in terms of developments of initiatives designed to prevent coronary heart disease.

In contrast to the theories of change approach, the *realistic evaluation* approach can also be usefully applied to evaluation of partnerships (Pawson and Tilley, 1997). This approach is also theory led, and while it may seem similar to the 'theories of change' approach, the two approaches fulfil different roles, and complement each other in a number of ways. As Dickinson (2006) points out, they have different functions for the evaluator. The 'theories of change' is prospective so that the evaluator is involved in a developmental process with the evaluation and with many stakeholders being involved in the evaluation process. By comparison, realistic evaluation is retrospective: the evaluator has a more traditional 'outside' role, with less involvement of various stakeholders in the evaluation.

The realistic evaluation approach

In the realistic evaluation approach, the combination of the *context* of the partnership and the *mechanisms* within it produce the *outcome* (i.e. context + mechanism = outcome) (Pawson and Tilley 1997). Because it is accepted that interventions cannot work for everyone and in every situation, realistic evaluation attempts to find out *which* mechanisms work for which *people* and within which *contexts*. In evaluating partnerships, evaluators would analyse relationships between all partners and activities within the partnerships in order to identify what it is about the partnerships and activities that might produce change, who might benefit and what social and cultural resources are necessary to sustain the changes (Wimbush and Watson 2000). Like the theory led evaluation, this approach also overcomes problems of ascribing cause and effect by uncovering theories at the micro level of the organization and also identifies which mechanisms work for which individuals, and in which contexts (Dickinson 2006). An example of an evaluation using the realistic approach is presented in Box 17.4:

Box 17.4   Realistic evaluation

Leone (2008) describes a realistic evaluation of an Italian sanctions-based two-year programme designed to dissuade drug users from consuming illicit drugs.

The aim of the evaluation was to provide regional decision makers and the local health units with useful indications to inform the redesign of the previous regional programme, and to implement the pilot programme. The project followed the logic of 'realistic evaluation', by not asking whether or not the programme worked, but instead exploring connections between:

- Context (i.e. organizational characteristics and institutional contexts and the subjects) (C)
- 'Mechanisms' developed in the field resulting from the interactions between the actions of the initiative and the reactions of the target group (M)
- Its theory about how programme resources will influence behaviour – outcomes (O)

Data collection involved a variety of methods as follows:

- Interviews with members of the services, social workers and the staff of operators
- Analysis of monitoring data provided by the organisation and by the local health units with reference to the two-year pilot programme
- A semi-structured telephone survey of 100 young people
- Three focus groups with the beneficiaries of the treatment provided by the different health units

The realistic evaluation approach seems to have been effective and Leone (2008) concluded that the use of the context, mechanism and outcome (CMO) configuration required by realistic evaluation proved useful to help them to find the right evaluation questions and to search for an explanation as to how the complexity of elements and dimensions were interacting. The concept of 'mechanism' enabled them to explain 'how' the subjects reacted to similar interventions developed in several contexts, and why different effects were observed.

Summary

By way of summarizing the key models discussed above, Table 17.3 outlines the key descriptions of each model.

Table 17.3 Key descriptions of the four evaluation models

	Characteristics	Advantages
Logic model	Describes logical linkages among resources, activities, outputs, audiences, and short, intermediate and long term outcomes related to a specific problem or situation. Once a programme has been described, critical measures of performance can be identified.	Identifies elements of partnership that are most likely to yield useful evaluation data. Identifies an appropriate sequence for collecting data and measuring progress.
Multi-method	Concerned to embrace the perspectives of all stakeholders and the complexity of the phenomena under study.	Qualitative approaches provide insights into the data, identify relevant variables, develop appropriate outcome measures and provide explanations from which hypotheses can be generated. The credibility of emerging theory can be tested through quantitative methods. (El Ansari and Weiss 2006).

	Characteristics	Advantages
Theories of change	Concerned with context of partnership, links between different activities, and outcomes. All involved in evaluation unravel in detail how and why partnership works. Takes place during planning and at commencement of partnership. Is prospective, with evaluator involved iteratively and with many stakeholders being involved in the evaluation process.	Overcomes problems of ascribing causes and effects. Assists in planning and implementing initiatives. Engages in deep analysis of internal processes. Involves many stakeholders (Dickinson 2006).
Realistic evaluation	Outcome arises from combination of context and mechanism. Attempts to find out *which* mechanisms work for which *people* and within which *contexts*. Is retrospective, with evaluator having a traditional 'outside' role and with less involvement of various stakeholders in the evaluation.	Overcomes problems of ascribing cause and effect by uncovering theories at the micro level of the organization. Identifies which mechanisms work for which individuals and in which contexts.

Conclusion

Partnerships between health and social care agencies are becoming increasingly common and often rely on funding to be sustainable in the long term. Funding of partnerships, however, is unlikely to be provided in the long term without the partnerships resulting in positive outcomes and impact on service users. Evidence of positive outcomes will therefore be needed, which can be provided by an independent evaluation. Initial funding for partnership work will normally include funding for evaluation, which will need to begin at the outset of the partnership. There is considerable debate about the extent to which practitioners and service users should be involved in this process. Involvement of practitioners in evaluating their own services is contentious, as they will have a vested interest in demonstrating positive outcomes as their employment might depend on future funding. Involving practitioners and service users in the design of the evaluation will be fruitful though as this will ensure that the evaluation is relevant to practice. Practitioners also need to be aware of the evaluation process so that they can contribute in an informed way to collection of data and can ensure that any information collected is as accurate and complete as possible. Involving service users in the collection of data also ensures that data collected does not only capture the views of service providers who may view the provision of their own service in a very positive light.

This chapter has highlighted the complex nature of partnership work and its evaluation. Evaluation strategies require careful consideration in order to discern the multiple and diverse factors involved in service delivery by different service providers and organizations working together in partnership. The limitations of focusing exclusively upon either a process or an outcome approach to evaluating partnerships, have been discussed. Instead, what is needed is an evaluation embedded from the outset of any partnership development and capable of embracing the complex dynamic of partnership work. The chapter has demonstrated how evaluation can be carried out using a variety of different models, most of which take into account the entire process of the development and implementation of partnership work, including, inputs, processes, outputs and outcomes.

Questions for further discussion

1 What scope is there for practitioners to become involved in evaluating partnerships and what issues does this raise?
2 What can be done to encourage service user involvement in the design of evaluations and what issues does this raise?
3 Of the four models discussed in this chapter, which do you think would be the most useful for evaluating health and social care partnerships?

---

18   Learning from partnerships: themes and issues

Ros Carnwell and Julian Buchanan

This chapter will:
- Reflect on the different meanings and interpretations given to the notion of partnership
- Discuss the political imperatives for working in partnership
- Explore the benefits and challenges of working in partnership

---

The meaning and interpretation of partnership

In Chapter 1 of this book the meanings of partnership and collaboration are highlighted together with the main attributes associated with these two concepts. In distinguishing between the two concepts, it is argued that collaboration (the verb) is *what* partners (the noun) *do* when they *work together*. However, although the two concepts are different, they do share some common features, such as:

- Trust and respect for partners or collaborators
- Respect for and sharing of expertise
- Joint working towards common goals
- Willingness to engage in teamwork

As pointed out in Chapter 6, partnership work is effective when partner agencies have a shared understanding of and respect for their different roles, when they share ownership of the partnerships aims and objectives, and have a shared commitment to address challenges ahead. Respect for others within partnerships also extends to service users. The notion of respect has in fact been enshrined in law; for example, Article 8 of the European Human Rights Act 1998, as it applies to Gypsy Travellers, refers to the right to respect for private and family life, home and correspondence (see Chapter 13). Moreover, as indicated in Chapter 3, recent recommendations from the review of UK discrimination laws in the UK, if successful, will ensure that public authorities show respect for the equal worth of different groups and foster good relations within and between groups (Department for Communities and Local Government 2007). It is not surprising, then, that the need for respect is also integrated into strategies, such as the *National Strategy for Carers* (DoH 1999d) which is based on respect and recognition of carers' expertise. This requires sharing of caring responsibilities between carers and service providers, in a way that the person they care for is respected (Chapter 15).

There is obviously a legal and political impetus then for professionals to work in a manner that is respectful to the people they serve and this same degree of respect needs to be afforded to other professions when working together. However, disagreement, confusion, lack of cohesion, professional jealousy and poor communication can all conspire to threaten effective teamwork (Molyneux 2001). Staff, therefore, need to have respect for others and to have the professional maturity and confidence in their own role and professional identity to share ideas and expertise and work effectively together (see Chapter 7). This will only be achieved though if professionals value each other's expertise. As illustrated in Chapter 6, failure to value the expertise of others can result in different teams using their specific knowledge to argue a particular position, which can create imbalance within and between teams so that tensions will arise. Interesting evidence is also provided in Chapter 10 of how drug dependency workers were much better prepared for dealing with drug users than other professional groups, and in fact considered that other professions tended to over react as a result of their lack of knowledge. Furthermore, professional groups either specialized in other areas, such as child protection, or provided a broader generic service. It is quite possible that these differences in expertise and professional orientation might affect the relationship between professional groups and hence their ability to work together. In such situations, shared training may be needed in order to enable different teams to develop mutual trust and respect for each other's judgement. Shared training will also help to break down professional boundaries that have evolved through perceived power and status associated with particular professional identities, such as those that professionals develop when working to safeguard children. As discussed in Chapter 5, professional roles can create barriers when working to safeguard children, as some professionals have a wide range of responsibilities and may argue that child protection is not their core business.

Another key attribute of partnership and collaboration is 'joint working'. Included within this term could be 'inter-agency' working, which has been reinforced in mental health policies since the 1990s. As discussed in Chapter 14, for example, *Building Bridges* (DoH 1995a), required a commitment to inter-agency working at all levels of the agency. This includes:

- A strategy which is jointly owned and agreed
- Agreed procedures
- Arrangements for exchanging information
- Consultation with, and commitment to, the involvement of service users and carers
- Joint commissioning in order to optimize resources
- Training within and between agencies, which includes understanding of agency roles
- Review and evaluation.

Only a year later, representatives of the Health and Probation Services jointly produced a document, which was founded on the premise that crime had a definite impact on the nation's health (Home Office and DoH 1996). Apart from the impact of alcohol, drug, mental health problems and general health problems suffered by offenders, it was estimated that the effect on the health of victims of crime through their experience of being victimized was significant. Thus, it was proposed that the two disciplines of health and criminal justice should develop joint working and collaboration to implement the various aims of the *Reed Review* (DoH and Home Office 1992), and *Health of the Nation* (DoH 1992; see Chapter 14).

Joint working is also enacted within the integration of children's services, in which there is a longstanding emphasis on 'joined-up' thinking and working. Joint working, however, seems to rely on the development of formal partnership arrangements, which may take the form of joined up services, such as children's trusts and joint commissioning of services which will bring together public, voluntary and private sector bodies as required by the children and young person's plans (see Chapter 5).

Joint working would have little value, however, if it did not have a positive impact on the experience of service users. Multi-disciplinary and partnership working builds mutual respect and trust between team members and service users, thus encouraging people to participate as equal partners in decisions about the care they receive (Opie 1998). In health care settings, collaborative treatment decision making and physician–patient partnerships lead to greater satisfaction and higher adherence for patients (Anderson and Zimmerman 1993; Chesney et al. 1999; Paterson 2001) and through sharing of knowledge between the multi-disciplinary team and the patients, patients' autonomy can be enhanced (see Chapter 7).

The final key characteristic of partnership is teamwork. Teamwork is the main focus of Chapter 6, in which it is argued that teamwork relies on a strategic approach and a highly skilled team leader for it to be successful. Methods of improving collaboration within teams are also discussed, such as whole systems working (e.g. shoring up team identity and control over work patterns); changing roles, so that staff extend their roles in directions previously undertaken by other professions; collaborative education; and clinical supervision, in which support, training and development is provided for team members.

Policy imperatives for partnership working

As we have seen from the above discussion, there are many examples of partnership work in health, social care and criminal justice. But what is the impetus for this type of activity? It is unlikely that so much attention would be given to this if it were not for the fact that working in partnership is at the heart of many government policies. These are wide ranging and include policies relating to children and older people, those related to cultural issues such as with travelling families, and policies relating to mental health, domestic violence and user involvement (see Table 18.1). Most of these policies focus on key concerns, such as integration of services, joint strategies, multi-agency working in assessment and delivery of care, and involvement of service users.

Table 18.1 Key policies and implications for partnership

Policy documents	Key emphasis	Implications for partnership
Every Child Matters (DfES 2004).	Safeguarding children.	Integrated children's services Common assessment framework.
The National Service Framework for Older People (Department of Health, 2001b); *Single Assessment Process Implementation Guidance* (DoH 2004c); *The Carers* (*Equal Opportunities*) *Act* (DoH 2004d); *Independence, Well-being and Choice: Our Vision for the Future of Social Care for Adults* (DoH 2005a); *Our Health, Our care, Our Say* (DoH 2006b).	Older people.	Improved, flexible, integrated and 'person centred' services for older people.
Building Bridges (DoH 1995a).	Raising awareness of how cultural issues impact upon service delivery.	Joint policies and strategies, information sharing, offering joint training opportunities and maximizing access to effective services and offender programmes.
Building Bridges (DoH 1995a).	Mental health.	Commitment to inter-agency working at all levels of the agency; a jointly owned and agreed strategy and procedures; and involvement of service users and carers.
Tackling Domestic Violence: Providing Support to Children Who Have Witnessed Domestic Violence (Home Office 2004b).	Domestic violence.	Multi-agency Risk Assessment Conferences (MARACs) screen for the level of risk in domestic violence cases, in order to identify those at greatest risk of serious harm.
The Health and Social Care Act 2001 (Home Office 2001).	Service user involvement.	Introduced a statutory duty to ensure public and patient involvement.

Within other chapters of this book, it becomes evident how government policy plays out in service developments. Some developments foster partnerships between different agencies, while others encourage partnerships between professionals and service users. In fact service user involvement has now resulted in a number of roles being created in mental health services, such as service user development workers, support time and recovery workers, public involvement departments, and patient advice and liaison services where the active participation of service users/carers is important in the management of risk (see Chapter 14).

Government policy also encourages partnership between practitioners and service users by creating opportunities for service users to become 'experts' about their own health, so that they can become key decision makers in the treatment process and hence gain more control over their lives (DoH 2001f). This trend in service user empowerment is simultaneous with increased use of the Internet by service users. Thus, patients are becoming more expert about their own health and are accessing the Internet to find out more about their ailments before visiting their general practitioner (see Chapter 2).

Benefits and challenges of working in partnership

Partnership working has a number of benefits and challenges. Its benefits are that it can create opportunities for joint training; it facilitates understanding and trust between partners, and it encourages involvement of service users in decisions. The Coventry domestic violence partnership, for example, discussed in Chapter 12, provided joint training across organizations as part of a three-year training project. This led to a more strategic approach to training, some of it generic, and some bespoke, utilizing the expertise of the Asian women's refuge or mental health professionals, or those working in drug and alcohol abuse. What is evident is that formal partnerships create opportunities for joint working. This in turn generates joint training, which provides the environment in which trust and understanding can flourish. As indicated in Chapter 9, it is easier to successfully negotiate with a person from a different agency if some basic trust and understanding has been built up through meeting individually or as a group. However, while individuals within different agencies may appreciate the importance of joint working and develop trust with other professionals it is helpful to have formal policy/practice support to validate and affirm this use of time and energy. It is the formal partnership arrangements that give this affirmation.

Most of the challenges of working in partnership arise as a result of moral and philosophical issues, structural issues and more practical concerns (see Box 18.1). In Chapter 4, a number of ethical and moral tensions are explored that might arise when working together. These include the need to recognize the limits to one's expertise and competence regardless of how long one may have been doing the job, while also highlighting that in inter-professional settings, it is uncomfortable to feel ill at ease or unskilled. There is a tendency to want to demonstrate competence and make a good representation on behalf of one's own agency in such settings. Moreover, the different types of expertise and working practices adopted by different agencies result in different types of intervention. As discussed in Chapters 8 and 14, for example, professionals from the healthcare system and the criminal justice system will offer treatment, care, punishment, restriction or rehabilitation, according to their philosophical standpoints. Related to these issues is the challenge of teamwork. As indicated in Chapter 15, teamwork can create disagreement, confusion and professional jealousy, which require a good deal of professional maturity and respect within team members in order to be overcome.

These challenges can often be overcome by adequate training to prepare professionals to work in partnership with different agencies and with service users. Time also needs to be devoted to enabling staff to work together effectively so that they begin to understand each others' roles.

Box 18.1   Challenges of partnership working

- Overcoming a desire to demonstrate competence to other agencies that might not be possessed
- Resolving differences in power, philosophy and working practices that exist between agencies
- Avoiding disagreement, confusion and professional jealousy
- Sharing professional expertise with service users
- Avoiding marginalization of service users and prospective clients

---

Another important challenge arises from partnership work with service users. As discussed above, service users are increasingly becoming empowered through their own means or through initiatives to improve their involvement. This means that professionals need to be prepared to share their knowledge and power in a way that they may have previously been unaccustomed to. General practitioners, for example, may have to allow more time to explain test results to a patient in order to dissuade them from believing that they have a condition that they have researched themselves on the Internet (see Chapter 3). On the other hand, some service users, such as older people and their carers may be less able to enter into a meaningful partnerships with service providers, as it may be difficult for carers to consider themselves to be equal partners while attempting to juggle many roles and maintaining some control over their whole life (see Chapter 7). Moreover, as Bates (2005) suggests, some service users may have historically been used to a fairly disempowering and patronizing relationship from particular agencies and will need to be empowered before they can fully participate and play a meaningful role in collaborative provision. As empowering users requires statutory bodies to relinquish some of their power, this is likely to remain contentious though some professionals may be more willing than others to devolve power to marginalized groups. This is exemplified in Chapter 16, in which the author recounts how he spent years attempting to access services individually, with no 'key worker' to ease this process. As he gained entry to educational systems he became more empowered and through that process was more able to access the services he needed.

Lack of attention to addressing challenges of working with service users is likely to result in marginalization of user groups and there is clear evidence of marginalization of service users and prospective clients. Chapter 15, for example, discusses the fact that barriers to working in partnership include fears, misconceptions and negative attitudes to certain groups of service users, such as those who are HIV positive. This same degree of marginalization is also often seen in work with Gypsy Travellers (Chapter 13) and other groups such as people with disabilities and chronic conditions, excluded older people, black and minority ethnic groups, homeless people, people living in poverty and some people living in rural areas (Chapter 3). Marginalization, then, remains a problem for those working within health and social care. This is not to say that partnership work is not addressing the issue of marginalization. What is important is that this is a major challenge for different agencies to overcome when they work together.

Conclusion

This chapter has explored the nature of partnership and collaboration as it is illustrated throughout this book. The attributes of partnership and collaboration have been discussed and policy drivers have been explained. What has emerged from the chapters of this book is that partnership working will by its very nature be fluid, but this can enable the agencies involved to respond better to the rapidly changing communities and needs that they serve. By comparison, agencies that work alone have a tendency to develop parochial interests and drift towards serving the needs of the employees and employers rather than responding to service user needs. Working in partnership is not easy, however, due to a number of reasons. Partnerships have to be sustained over a long period of time and this requires energy and commitment of all partners. This vulnerable lifespan is appropriate given that organizations can over time go stale and struggle to respond to changing demands. Expending time and effort sometimes means that partners may become involved in activities that arguably are not cost-effective. Furthermore, partnerships can sometimes rely too heavily upon the enthusiasm of a particular agency or individual and this may result in tensions between agencies. Their fluid nature can also make partnerships susceptible to being dominated by powerful individuals or agencies. Nevertheless, it is possible that long-term partnerships could erode the diverse identity of different agencies as they blend and converge.

Perhaps the future of partnerships lies primarily in a shared vision for service delivery. This shared vision should then be translated into three levels: strategic, operational and practice. Within the strategic level there should be a synergy between voluntary and statutory agencies and recognition of the need to understand and promote differences between agencies rather than to compete for resources. At the operational level, while policy directives will help drive resources, listening to service users and developing partnerships with voluntary groups will help keep services relevant and meaningful. At the practice level, greater understanding between personnel would be achieved by secondments between agencies, perhaps for six-month periods. The need to involve service users is also key to the development of partnerships, but this concept is underdeveloped both philosophically and practically. Service users would be more equally represented if service providers employed them, even if only on a consultancy or part time basis.

19 Developing best practice in partnership

Julian Buchanan and Ros Carnwell

This chapter will:

- Summarize what has been learnt about the development of partnership in the UK
- Identify key principles that appear to underpin best practice when developing partnerships

---

While statutory agencies such as the social services, education, health, housing and the police, and voluntary agencies such as Shelter, NSPCC, Prince's Trust and NACRO have distinctive roles and separate cultures and practices, they have a good track record for working together on discrete projects. However, over the past two decades statutory, voluntary and independent organizations have increasingly been required to work together on a day to day basis to deliver 'joined-up' services. Key factors that have made this shift towards partnership practice necessary include:

- An increasingly complex society resulting in multi-faceted needs that can no longer be met by a sole agency
- Changes in the structures, roles and function of statutory agencies, which made them more fluid, adaptable and able to work alongside other agencies
- The requirement for services that were once delivered exclusively by statutory bodies to be contracted out and delivered by outside voluntary or independent organizations
- The political drive from government policy to adopt a 'Third Way' approach to deliver services, which has resulted in a range of legislation and policy directives requiring agencies to work collaboratively in partnerships with voluntary and independent organizations to deliver seamless services

In the past, the focus was more often upon the service user seeking help from an individual agency. The response to service users' need tended to be a specific intervention strategy or therapy delivered sometimes exclusively from within the agency. While not mutually exclusive, the focus today draws upon enabling the individual to access a range of services and facilities available from different agencies

– statutory, voluntary and private. These agencies often work in collaboration with each other, sometimes informally, sometimes within formalized partnerships, to provide packages of care. A partnership may include various statutory, voluntary or independent/private organizations, and sometimes, though not often enough, service user involvement. This approach reflects the more diverse and fluid nature of society, the changing nature of the welfare state, the multi-faceted nature of individual needs, and the shift away from exclusive statutory provision to the expansion of 'contracted out' services provided by the voluntary and independent sector. This approach is at the heart of New Labour's 'Third Way'. The concept of partnership is now embedded within mainstream health, social care and criminal justice provision.

This shift of focus has significant implications for professionals in the health and social care sector (including criminal justice workers), many of whom have been used to working exclusively within their own organization and responding to need through their own in-house therapies, treatments or interventions. A particular challenge is ensuring staff possess the appropriate knowledge, skills and values to be able to work flexibly to develop, establish and maintain effective partnerships. Training and professional courses tend to lack inter-disciplinary opportunities for students from related disciples (such as nursing, social work, community work, youth work, medicine, probation work) to learn together, though there are now a growing number of modules appearing on courses that are concerned to equip students to understand inter-agency and partnership practice.

Relatively little has been written about partnerships, and what literature there is tends to concentrate upon the concept of partnership or the ideological basis of partnership. What is particularly lacking is literature concerned with the development of theory/practice knowledge in relation to partnership work that would inform and enable workers at the 'frontline' to be better equipped. There is a proliferation of partnerships, yet a relative dearth of knowledge, and a lack of training and education opportunities to inform practice wisdom to work effectively in partnership.

Key principles for effective practice when working in partnership

This final chapter will attempt to draw out some of the main messages from the text by identifying key principles for effective practice when working in partnership. We now offer 14 key principles of effective practice.

Devoting time to creating, nurturing and maintaining partnerships

Effective partnerships seem more successful when partners relate well and understand each other's roles. A good partnership cannot be rushed into existence. It is likely to require an initially heavy investment of time and even when established it will need ongoing attention. This is often best achieved by face-to-face contact that encourages informal, open dialogue between all partners exploring philosophy, vision, strategy and practice while at all times clarifying difference and sameness, strengths and weaknesses. This may be supplemented by new electronic forms of communication including email, dedicated mail databases, discussion boards, electronic communities, etc. Once partnerships are formed, agencies may find it useful to maintain dialogue and understanding through regular meetings, electronic communication and by involving staff from different agency partners in shared training events and role shadowing.

Developing a mutual understanding and respect between agency partners

A lot of misunderstanding occurs when agencies fail to appreciate the different roles and functions of the other agencies with whom they are seeking to work closely. Stereotypes and agency sub-cultures can hinder good working relationships with other agencies and fuel parochial attitudes and rivalry. Staff from all agencies need to be informed about each other's roles and to feel comfortable in embracing and respecting agency differences, even though at times they may be philosophically at odds with their own. This level of mature understanding, agreement and respect is not easily achieved and will often require considerable dialogue and investment of time to properly appreciate how other agencies 'see', and what they do.

Allowing time for partnerships to develop

In a climate of standardization and 'top-down' policy driven practice, an attempt may be made to force partnerships into existence by legislation. This can happen, but they will need time to develop as they are more fluid and organic by nature and are not easily created by bureaucratic mandates. This flexibility is, of course, a major strength of a partnership in that it is able to cater and respond to diverse local needs. This may sit uncomfortably with a centralist agenda, which promotes the creation of national standards, consistency and the rolling out of fixed models of partnership across the UK. Although easily created by statute or policy directives, regional and local differences will result in different partnership arrangements. Models of practice therefore, are best created at local levels to reflect the unique circumstances, such as rurality or cultural diversity. Partnership is a long term commitment that works best through good relationships and therefore need time invested to develop mutual trust, respect and understanding. A short term approach to partnership risks the creation of a false partnerships where agencies come together to fulfil a legal, political or policy requirement, to be 'seen' as a working in partnership, but in practice not be operating as one. This can benefit the agency in terms of finances and kudos in the short term, but doesn't benefit the service user.

Guarding against multi-agency inertia

Meeting together and discussing agendas, roles, philosophies as well as what the partnership could achieve is a relevant and important part of partnership development, but there is a risk that partnerships may become talk shops: places where good intentions and ideas are explored but never implemented. Personal agendas (sometimes hidden) and status arising from participating in partnerships can for some individuals be their sole reason for participating, these individuals can be quite destructive to the progress of any partnership.

Ensuring a shared interest in service delivery

As bidding for new tenders, contracts and monies becomes an integral part of the 'modernized' welfare state, it is easy for agencies to seek partnerships to attract funding, without giving proper consideration as to whether the partnership will, in practice, improve service delivery – thus chasing power and status and losing sight of the needs of service users. Agencies and partnerships can sometimes end up focusing upon the needs of their staff rather than the needs of service users. Effective partnership requires agencies to be focused on a shared commitment and interest in the needs of the service user, and a belief that much more can be achieved to the benefit of the service user by working together rather than working separately.

Developing strategic and operational commitment

Partnerships have a better chance of success when ownership and support exists both among grassroots staff, at the operational and practice level, and among staff at a managerial and strategic level. Support from legislative and policy directives can validate and sanction such moves. Without backing at this level, resources can be more difficult to acquire and the authority of the partnership can be undermined. Partnerships that are driven by enthusiastic individuals may be valid and effective, but if they lack strategic support, they can soon be left floundering once key personnel leave.

Being clear about the basis and boundaries of the partnership

This is a difficult issue to explore and may seem inappropriate, but the 'What if?' questions need exploring in order to be clear about the basis and boundaries of the partnership. The range of issues that may occur are wide ranging, but common issues may include:

- Can agencies withdraw from the partnership at any stage without notice?
- Are agencies able to compete independently to bid for contracts that the partnership may be also bidding for?
- Should agreements concerning service delivery be signed to form a legally binding contract?
- If legal or financial problems occur for the partnership, do all agencies share the burden equally?

Protecting your agency identity and difference

Agencies form partnerships to work closely together and gain benefit from what the other partner agencies can offer. There is a risk, however, that agencies that form a partnership could lose their focus and identity to a new corporate identity. A shared identity does help integration in that partners no longer see their separate identities as so significant. This does, however, present a constant tension within partnerships as the creation of a new single corporate agency could risk losing the benefits afforded by the many different agencies working together. This may be a particular issue for partnerships that unite together in shared premises, such as drug teams or youth offending teams. While partnerships should not be discouraged on account of this, the risk of agencies losing their identity needs to be acknowledged.

Promoting corporate identity

Agencies working collaboratively together in partnership may rigorously defend their own distinct identity, which arguably strengthens the partnership, but there needs to be a corporate identity, too, that is widely understood and promoted. If agencies are so busy promoting their own identity, who is promoting the partnership? One agency could take on this role, but that may lead to a power imbalance. All could share the role, but that would necessitate a considerable depth of understanding by all agency partners to avoid mixed messages. One solution to this problem is the appointment of an independent chair who has no allegiance to any single agency, can steer meetings and is able to act as a consultant promoting the partnership to outside bodies.

Looking beyond 'what is done' and concentrate on the 'way things are done'

In a climate of centralized bureaucracy and managerialism, which is preoccupied by objectives, targets, deliverables and outcomes, there is a danger of losing sight of the needs of the service user. Practice with service users driven by procedures can sometimes lead to 'empty' relationships, in which staff go through all the right motions, apparently deliver services, but fail to meet the service user's real need. The evidence in this book suggests service users do not want to receive a service that leaves them feeling like they have just been processed clinically along a conveyor belt in the health, social care and criminal justice factory. Service users are concerned about the way in which they are treated and not just about what services they receive. Service users want 'people friendly' services that are delivered by agency staff who have a genuine empathy and understanding of their situation and who are able to communicate clearly, honestly and respectfully.

Involving and listen to service users

There are few partnerships that fully involve service users in the running of them. It is easy for agencies to lose sight of the needs of service users while building the partnership. Service user involvement can help to address this problem and hold agencies to account by reminding them of why they exist. Service users can also provide valuable insights into their needs, which are not always fairly or comprehensively understood by agency representatives. It is easy for agencies to make erroneous assumptions about the needs of service users or to develop unfair stereotypes or prejudices. This is less likely to occur if service users are able to participate actively in the partnership. In order to enable service users to participate on an equal basis, partnerships may consider employing service users to work in the partnership, perhaps on a part time basis. This also addresses the problem of service users unfairly being expected to give up a lot of time on a voluntary basis.

Guarding against exploitation and power imbalance

Partnerships bring together a wide range of agencies: some may have considerable resources, a high percentage of qualified staff and excellent administrative support, while other partner agencies may be largely dependent upon unqualified staff and volunteer administrative support. It is easy in these circumstances for the larger agencies to dominate the partnership and to stifle the contribution of smaller agencies. Whenever possible, partners should be equal, when they are not, the basis and rationale for inequality needs to be openly established and agreed. Equality in partnership does, however, raise structural conflicts related to historical and largely fixed differences between partners concerning terms and conditions of service, and leading to wide variations in the partnership in relation to qualifications, salaries, pay, pensions and annual leave.

Clarifying the boundaries of confidentiality

This is a perennial issue that should not be avoided as it will eventually emerge when a serious issue arises. To what extent can agencies share information across the partnership, and precisely what information can be shared? Guidelines need to be established regarding sharing of information across boundaries and data protection. Signed consent from service users should also be obtained.

Evaluating the success of partnerships

It cannot be assumed that, because they have been formed, partnerships are working effectively. Factors such as different identities, different educational qualifications, different working conditions, as well as differences in vision, mission and cultures in organizations can all play a part in limiting effectiveness. Mechanisms are needed, therefore, at all levels of each organization within the partnership to ascertain effectiveness. Questions that could be asked within the evaluation include:

- Does each partner have equal commitment to the partnership and, if so, how is this demonstrated?
- Does the partnership promote ethical standards within its working practices?
- How is effective practice promoted and maintained throughout the partnership?
- How are professional conflicts between partners managed?
- Does the partnership have a corporate identity that is shared across agencies inside and outside the partnership?
- Does the partnership adequately take into account the need for comparable working conditions for comparable grades of staff?
- Is joint training in operation where needed?
- What are the service users' views and experiences of the partnership?
- What gaps in service delivery can be identified?
- What are the training needs of partner members?

Conclusion

This book seeks to help fill the current knowledge gap concerning the nature, context and form of partnerships. Part I explored the context within which partnerships operate. Part II looked at a partnership approach to tackling some of the most pressing and difficult health and social problems in the UK. We have been able to highlight many examples of partnership currently in existence responding to complex needs, such as homelessness, domestic violence, travellers and so on. The benefits and challenges involved in working in partnership have been carefully explored throughout. Our key concern is to develop 'effective practice' that actually makes a difference to the lives of vulnerable people in need. In many situations, this is best achieved by agencies working collaboratively together in partnership. We hope that the key principles we have presented in this final chapter offer a way forward for developing successful partnerships in practice.

References

Acheson, S. D. (1998) *Independent Inquiry into Inequalities and Health*. London: The Stationery office.

ACMD (Advisory Council on the Misuse of Drugs) (2002) *The Classification of Cannabis Under the Misuse of Drugs Act 1971*. London: Home Office.

ACMD (Advisory Council on the Misuse of Drugs) (2003) *Hidden Harm: Responding to the Needs of Problem Drug Users*. London: Home Office.

ACMD (Advisory Council on the Misuse of Drugs) (2007) *Hidden Harm: Three Years On: Realities, Challenges and Opportunities*. London: Home Office.

Acton, T. A. (2000) Patrin: the revival of Romani lobbying in Great Britain. *The Patrin Web Journal*. Available at: www.geocities.com/Paris/5121/lobbying-gb-htm

Adams, A., Attfield, S., and Blandford, A. (2004) Preprint. Paper presented at the ECDL workshop, Healthcare digital libraries: have digital resources taken a wrong turn on the health 'information journey'?

Adams, A., Blandford, A. and Attfield S. (2005) Implementing digital resources for clinicians' and patients' varying needs, *Proc. BCS Healthcare Computing*, 226–33.

Alberg, C., Hatfield, B. and Huxley, P. (eds) (1996) *Learning Materials on Mental Health: Risk Assessment*. University of Manchester, Manchester.

Allison, A. (1996) A framework for good practice: ethical issues in cognitive behaviour therapy, in S. Marshall, and J. Turnbull (eds), *Cognitive Behaviour Therapy: An Introduction to Theory and Practice*. London: Balliere Tindall.

Allison, A. and Ewens, A. (1998) Tensions in sharing client confidences while respecting autonomy: implications for interprofessional practice, *Nursing Ethics*, 5(5): 441–50.

Alonzo, A. A., and Reynolds, N. R. (1995) Stigma, HIV and AIDS: an exploration and elaboration of a stigma trajectory, *Social Science and Medicine*, 41(3): 303–15.

Altice, F. L. and Friedland, G. H. (1998) The era of adherence to HIV therapy, *Annals of Internal Medicine*, 129(6): 503–5.

Amnesty International (2007) Stop violence against women. Available at: www.amnesty.org.uk/content.asp?CategoryID=10459

Anaraki, S. Plugge, E. and Hill, A. (2003) Delivering primary care in prison: the need to improve health information, 11(4):191–4.

Anderson, G. (1987) *When Chemicals Come to School: The Student Assistance Programme Model*. London: Community Recovery Press

Anderson, W. and Weatherburn, P. (1998) *The Impact of Combination Therapy on the Lives of People with HIV*. London: Sigma Research.

Anderson, W. and Weatherburn, P. (1999) *Taking ART? The Impact of Combination Therapy on the Lives of People with HIV*. London: Sigma Research.

Anderson, L.A. and Zimmerman, M.A. (1993) Patient and physician perceptions of their relationship and patient satisfaction: a study of chronic disease management, *Patient Education and Counselling*, 20(1): 27–36.

Anderson, W., Weatherburn, P., Keogh, P. and Henderson, L. (2000) *Proceeding with Care: Phase 3 of an Ongoing Study of the Impact of Combination Therapies on the Needs of People with HIV*. London: Sigma Research.

Andolina, K. (1995) *Mental Health Critical Path/Care Map Tools and Case Management Systems*. South Natick: The Centre for Case Management.

Andrews, R., Cowell, R., Downe, J., Martin, S. and Turner, D. (2006) *Promoting Effective Citizenship and Community Empowerment – A Guide for Local Authorities on Enhancing Capacity for Public Participation*. London: Office of the Deputy Prime Minister.

Appleby, L., Shaw, J. and Amos, T. (1997) National confidential inquiry into suicide and homicide by people with mental illness, *British Journal of Psychiatry* 170: 101–2.

Arnstein, S. (1969) A ladder of participation, *Journal of the American Planning Association*, 35(4): 216–24

Ashwell, N. (2003) Perceptions of inter-agency collaboration: youth and health. Unpublished PhD thesis, University of Reading.

Askham, J. (1998) Supporting caregivers of older people: an overview of problems and priorities, *Australian Journal of Ageing*, 17(1): 5–7.

Attree, M. (2006) Evaluating healthcare education: issues and methods, *Nurse Education Today*, 26(8): 640–6.

Atwal, A. and Caldwell, K. (2006) Nurses' perceptions of multidisciplinary team work in acute health care, *International Journal of Nursing Practice*, 12(6): 359–65.

Audit Commission (1994) *Finding a Place: A Review of Mental Health Services for Adults*. London: HMSO.

Audit Commission (2000) *Listen Up! Effective Community Consultation*, London: Audit Commission.

Audit Commission (2004a) *Journey to Race Equality*. London: Audit Commission.

Audit Commission (2004b) *Older People: Independence and Well-being*. London: Audit Commission.

Aujoulat, I., d'Hoore, W. and Deccache, A. (2006) Patient empowerment in theory and practice: polysemy or cacophony? *Patient Education and Counselling*, 1–4, 1 Nov. Available at: www.sciencedirect.com (accessed 21 Nov. 2006).

Bancroft, A. (2005) *Roma and Gypsy Travellers in Europe: Modernity, Race, Space and Exclusion*. Aldershot: Ashgate.

Bancroft, A., Wilson, S, Cunningham-Burley, S., Backett-Milburn, K. and Masters, H. (2004) *Parental Drug and Alcohol Misuse: Resilience and Transition Among Young People*. York: Joseph Rowntree Foundation.

Banks, P. (1999) *Carer Support: Time for a Change of Direction*. London: King's Fund.

Barker, P. J. and Walker, L. (2000) Nurses' perceptions of multidisciplinary teamwork in acute psychiatric settings, *Journal of Psychiatric and Mental Health Nursing*, 7(6): 539–46.

Barnard, M. (2003) Between a rock and a hard place: the role of relatives in protecting children from the effects of parental drug problems, *Child and Family Social Work*, 8(4): 291–9.

Barnard, M., (2006) *Drug Addiction and Families*. London: Jessica Kingsley Publishers.

Barnes, D., Carpenter, J. and Dickinson, C. (2000) Interprofessional education for community mental health teams: attitudes to community care and professional stereotypes, *Social Work Education*, 19(6): 565–83.

Barnes, M., Newman, J. and Sullivan, H. (2007) *Power, Participation and Political Renewal: Case Studies in Public Participation*. Bristol: Policy Press.

Barr, O. (1997) Interdisciplinary teamwork: consideration of the challenges, *British Journal of Nursing*, 6(17): 1005–10.

Barr, H., Koppel, I. and Reeves, S. (2005) *Effective Interpersonal Education: Assumption, Argument and Evidence*. London: Blackwell.

Barroso, J. and Powell-Cope, G. M. (2000) Metasynthesis of qualitative research on living with HIV infection, *Qualitative Health Research*, 10(3): 340–53.

Bates, J. (2005) Embracing diversity in collaborative care, in R. Carnwell and J. Buchanan (eds), *Effective Practice in Health and Social Care: Working Together*. Maidenhead: Open University Press.

Bates, T., Buchanan, J., Corby, B. and Young, L. (1999) *Drug Use, Parenting and Child Protection: Towards an Effective Inter-agency Response*. Preston: University of Central Lancashire.

Bayles, M. D. (1989) *Professional ethics*, 2nd edn. Belmont, CA: Wadsworth Publishing Co.

Bayley, M. (1973) *Mental Handicap and Community Care*. London: Routledge and Kegan Paul.

BBC (2008) Bank's U-turn on student charges. Available at: http//news.bbc.co.uk/1/hi/education/6970570.stm

Beattie, A. (1995) War and peace amongst the health tribes, in K. Soothill, L. Mackay and C. Webb (eds), *Interprofessional Relations in Health Care*. London: Edward Arnold.

Begum, N. (2006), *Doing It For Themselves: Participation and black and minority ethnic service users*, Participation Report No. 14, London: Social Care Institute for Excellence in association with Race Equality Unit.

Benzeval, M., Judge, K. and Whitehead, M. (1995) *'Tackling Inequalities in Health': An Agenda for Action*. London: Kings Fund.

Beresford, P. (2004) Reframing the nurse's role through a social model approach: a rights-based approach to workers' development, *Journal of Psychiatric and Mental Health Nursing*, 11(3): 365–68.

Beresford, P. and Branfield, F. (2006) Developing inclusive partnerships: user-defined outcomes, networking and knowledge – a case study, *Health and Social Care in the Community*, 14(5): 436–44

Bernard, M. and Phillips, J. (1998) *The Social Policy of Old Age: Moving into the 21st Century*. London: Centre for Policy on Ageing.

Bertholon, D. R., Rossert, H. and Korsia, S. (1999) The patient's perspective on life with antiretroviral treatment: results of an 887-person survey, *The AIDS Reader*, Oct. pp. 462–9.

Bertram, G. and Stickley, T. (2005) Mental health nurses, promoters of inclusion or perpetuators of exclusion, *Journal of Psychiatric and Mental Health Nursing*, 12(4): 387–95.

Best, D., Homayoun, S. and Witton, J. (2008) Hidden harm: another postcode lottery? *Drink & Drug News*, 21 Apr.

Bewley, C. and Gibbs, A. (2002) Fact or fallacy? Domestic violence in pregnancy: an overview, *MIDIRS Midwifery Digest*, Sep., 12(2): S3–S5.

BHIVA (British HIV Association) (2007) *Standards for HIV Clinical Care*. Available at: www.bhiva.org

Bidmead, C. and Cowley, S. (2005) A concept analysis of partnership with clients, *Community Practitioner*, 78(6): 203–08.

Biggs, S. (2000) User voice, interprofessional and post modernity, in C. Davies, L. Finlay and A. Bullman (eds), *Changing Practice in Health and Social Care*. London: Open University Press and Sage.

Billingsley, R. D. and Lang, L. (2002) *The case for interprofessional learning in health and social care*, MCC: Building Knowledge for Integrated Care, 10(4):31–4

Birchall, E. and Hallet, C. (1995) *Working Together in Child Protection: Report of Phase Two. A Survey of the Experience and Perceptions of Six Key Professions*. Studies in child protection. London: The Stationery Office.

Birchwood, M., Smith, J., Cochrane, R., Wetton, S. and Copestake, S. (1990) The social functioning scale: the development and validation of a new scale of social adjustment for use in family intervention programmes with schizophrenic patients, *British Journal of Psychiatry*, 157: 853–9.

Birckmayer, J. D. and Weiss, C. H. (2000) Theory-based evaluation in practice: what do we learn? *Evaluation Review*, 24(4): 407–31.

Blamey, A., Ayana, M., Lawson, L. et al. (2004) *Final Report: The Independent Evaluation of Have a Heart Paisley*. Glasgow: University of Glasgow.

Blamey, A., Ayana, M., Lawson, L. et al. (2005) *Have A Heart Paisley: Executive Summary, Independent Evaluation*. Glasgow: University of Glasgow.

Blom-Cooper, L. (1999) Public inquiries in mental health, with particular reference to the Blackwood case at Broadmoor and the patient complaints of Ashworth Hospital, in D. Webb and R. Harris (eds), *Mentally Disordered Offenders: Managing People Nobody Owns*. London: Routledge.

BMA (British Medical Association) (1998) *Domestic Violence: A Health Care Issue?* British Medical Association: London.

Boardman, A. P., Hodgson, R. E. and Allen, K. (1997) Social indicators and the prediction of psychiatric admission in different diagnostic groups, *British Journal of Psychiatry*, 171: 457–62.

Bogart, L. M., Catz, S. L., Kelly, J. A., et al. (2000) Psychosocial issues in the era of new AIDS treatments from the perspective of persons living with HIV, *Journal of Health Psychology*, 5(4):500–16.

Boulanger, S., Deaville, J., Randall-Smith, and Wynn Jones, J. (1999) *Farm Suicide in Rural Wales: A Review of the Services in Powys and Ceredigion*. Newtown: Institute of Rural Health.

Bowles, N. and Dodds, P. (2002) Refocusing in acute psychiatry, *Nursing Times*, 98(22): 44–5.

Bowles, N. and Jones, A. (2005) Whole systems working and acute inpatient psychiatry: an exploratory study, *Journal of Psychiatric and Mental Health Nursing*, 12(3): 283–9.

Bowles, N., Dodds, P., Hackney, D., Sunderland, C. and Thomas, P. (2002) Formal observations and engagement: a discussion paper, *Journal of Psychiatric and Mental Health Nursing*, 9(3): 255–61.

Brashers, D. E., Neidig, J. L., Cardillo, L. K., Russell, J. A. and Haas, S. M. (1999) 'In an important way, I did die': Uncertainty and revival in persons living with HIV or AIDS, *AIDS CARE*, 11(2): 201–19.

Brechin, A., Walmsley, J., Katz, J. and Peace, S. (eds) (1998) *Care Matters: Concepts, Practice and Research in Health and Social Care*. London: Sage.

Bridge, The (Child Care Consultancy Service) (1991) *Sukina: An Evaluation of the Circumstances Leading to her Death.* London: The Bridge.

Bridge, The (Child Care Consultancy Service) (1995) *Paul: Death from Neglect.* London: The Bridge.

Brindlecombe, N. (2005) Asylum nursing in the UK at the end of the Victorian era: Hill End Asylum, *Journal of Psychiatric and Mental Health Nursing,* 12(1): 57–63.

Brooker, C. (2001) A decade of evidence-based training for work with people with serious mental health problems: progress in the development of psychosocial interventions, *Journal of Mental Health,* 10(1): 17–31.

Brooker, C., Saul, C., Robinson, J., King, J. and Dudley, M. (2003) Is training in psychosocial interventions worthwhile? Report of a psychosocial intervention trainee follow-up study, *International Journal of Nursing Studies,* 40(7): 731–47.

Brown, B., Crawford, P. and Darongkamas, J. (2000) Blurred roles and permeable boundaries: the experience of multidisciplinary working in community mental health, *Health and Social Care in the Community,* 8(6): 425–35.

Brown, J., Nolan, M. and Grant, G. (2001) Who's the expert? Redefining lay and professional relationships, in M. Nolan, S. Davies and G. Grant, (eds), *Working with Older People and their Families: Key Issues in Policy and Practice.* Buckingham: Open University Press.

Buchanan, A. (2002) Who does what? The relationships between generic and forensic psychiatric services, in A. Buchanan (ed.), *Care of the Mentally Disordered Offender.* Oxford: Oxford University Press.

Buchanan, J. (2004) Missing links: problem drug use and social exclusion, *Probation Journal Special Edition on Problem Drug Use,* 51(4): 387–97

Buchanan, J. (2006) Understanding problematic drug use: a medical matter or a social issue? *British Journal of Community Justice,* 4(2): 47–60.

Buchanan, J. and Young, L. (2000a) Examining the relationship between material conditions, long term problematic drug use and social exclusion: a new strategy for social inclusion, in J. Bradshaw and R. Sainsbury (eds), *Experiencing Poverty.* London: Ashgate Press, pp. 120–43.

Buchanan, J. and Young, L. (2000b) The war on drugs: a war on drug users, *Drugs: Education, Prevention Policy,* 7(4): 409–22.

Buchanan, J. and Young, L. (2001) Child protection and social work views, in Klee et al. (eds), *Issues in Motherhood and Substance Misuse.* London: Routledge.

Bunting, S. M. (1996) Sources of stigma associated with women with HIV, *Advances in Nursing Science,* 19(2): 64–73.

Burholt, V., Windle, G., Naylor, D. et al. (2007) *Looking to the Future: Ageing in Rural Communities.* Bangor: Centre for Social Policy Research and Development, University of Wales Bangor, and Age Concern Gwynedd.

Burke, L. (2001) Social policy. in: D. Sines, F, Appleby and E. Raymond (eds), *Community Health Care Nursing*, 2nd edn. Oxford: Blackwell Science.

Burke, B. and Harrison, P. (2002) Anti-oppressive practice, in R. Adams, L. Dominelli and M. Payne (eds), *Social Work: Themes, Issues and Critical Debates*, 2nd edn. Basinstoke: Palgrave.

Burkhardt, M. A. and Nathaniel, A. K. (2002) *Ethics and Issues in Contemporary Nursing*, 2nd edn. New York: Delmar.

Burns, T. and Lloyd, H. (2004) Is a team approach based on staff meetings cost effective in the delivery of mental health care? *Current Opinion in Psychiatry*, 17(4): 311–14.

Burr, J. (2002) Cultural stereotypes of women from South Asian communities: mental health care professionals' explanations for patterns of suicide and depression, *Social Science and Medicine*, 55(5): 835–45.

Butterfoss, F. D. and Francisco, V. T. (2004) Evaluating community partnerships and coalitions with practitioners in mind, *Health Promotion Practice*, 5(2): 108–14.

Cahill, J. (1996) Patient participation: a concept analysis, *Journal of Advanced Nursing*, 24(3): 561–71.

Calabretta, N. (2002) Consumer-driven, patient-centered health care in the age of electronic information, *Journal of the Medical Library Association*, 90(1): 32–7.

Carers UK (2005) Back me up. Available at: www.carersuk.org/policyandpractice

Carers UK (2006) In the know. Available at: www.carersuk.org/policyandpractice

Carers UK (2007) Real change not short change: time to deliver for carers. Available at: www.carersuk.org/policyandpractice

Carers UK and Sheffield Hallam University (2005a) Caring and older people. Available at: www.carersuk.org/policyandpractice

Carers UK and Sheffield Hallam University (2005b) Caring and pensioner poverty. Available at: www.carersuk.org/policyandpractice

Carlen, P. (1996) *Jigsaw: A Political Criminology of Youth Homelessness*. Buckingham: Open University Press.

Carnwell, R. and Baker, S. A. (2005a) An evalaution of Wrexham LEA. Unpublished report LEA Wrexham).

Carnwell, R. and Baker S. A. (2005b) A project to evaluate the student assistance programme for Wrexham LEA. Unpublished report, Wrexham LEA.

Carnwell, R. and Baker, S. A. (2007) A qualitative evaluation of a project to enhance pupils' emotional literacy through a student assistance programme, *Journal of Pastoral Care*.

Carpenter, C. C., Fischl, M. A., Hammer, S. M. et al. (1997) Antiretroviral therapy for HIV infection in 1997: updated recommendations of the International AIDS Society, *Journal of the American Medical Association*, 277(24): 1962–9.

Carr, S. (2004) *Has service user participation made a difference to social care services?* Social Care Institute for Excellence Position Paper No. 3. Mar. London: Social Care Institute for Excellence.

Carr, A. and Cooper, D. A. (2000) Adverse effects of antiretroviral therapy, *Lancet*, 356 (9239): 1423–30.

Catalan, J., Burgess, A. and Klimes, I. (1995) *Psychological Medicine of HIV Infection.* Oxford: Oxford University Press.

Catz, S. L., Kelly, J. A., Bogart, L. M., Benotsch, E. G. and McAuliffe, T. L. (2000) Patterns, correlates and barriers to medication adherence among persons prescribed new treatments for HIV disease, *Health Psychology*, 19(2): 124–33.

Cemlyn, S. (1995) Traveller children and the state: welfare or neglect? *Child Abuse Review* 4(4): 278–90

CCNAPP (Community Care Needs Assessment Project) (2001) *'Asking The Experts' – A Guide To Involving People In Shaping Health and Social Care Services.* Available from http://www.ccnap.org.uk

Chesney, M. A. (2000) Factors affecting adherence to antiretroviral therapy, *Clinical Infectious Diseases*, 30(2): S171–S176.

Chesney, M., Wall, T., Sorensen, J. L. et al. (1995) Adherence to zidovudine (AZT) among HIV infected methadone patients: a pilot study of supervised therapy and dispensing compared to usual care, *Drug and Alcohol Dependence*, 37: 261–9.

Chesney, M. A., Ickovics, J., Hecht, F. M., Sikipa, G. and Rabkin, J. (1999) Adherence: a necessity for successful HIV Combination Therapy, *AIDS 13*, Supplement A: S271–8.

CHI (Commission for Health Improvement) (2003a) *Nothing About Us Without Us: The Patient and the Public Strategy for CHI.* London: CHI.

CHI (Commission for Health Improvement) (2003b) *The Victoria Climbie Inquiry Report: Key Findings From the Self Audits of NHS Organizations, Social Services Departments and the Police.* London: CHI.

CHI (Commission for Health Improvement) (2004) *Involvement to Improvement.* London: CHI.

Chong, M. S., Wolff, K., Wise, K. et al. (2006) *Cannabis use in patients with multiple sclerosis* Multiple Sclerosis, 12(5): 646–51.

Clarke, A. (1999) *Evaluation Research: An Introduction to Principles, Method and Practice.* London: Sage.

Clarke, S. (2004) *Acute Inpatient Mental Health Care: Education, Training and Continuing Professional Education for all.* Leeds: NIMHE.

Cleaver, H., Unell, I. and Aldgate, J. (1999) *Children's Needs – Parenting Capacity: The Impact of Parental Mental Illness, Problem Alcohol and Drug Use and Domestic Violence on Children's Development*. London: The Stationery Office.

Cleemput, C. (2000) Health care needs of travellers, *Archives of Disease in Childhood*, 82(1): 32–7.

Cleemput, P., Parry, G., Thomas, K., Peters, J. and Cooper, C. (2007) Health-related beliefs and experiences of gypsies and travellers: a qualitative study, *Journal of Epidemiology and Community Health*, 61(3): 205–10.

Clifford, C. (2003) Working in parallel worlds. Key note presentation at the *Nurse Education Tomorrow Conference*, University of Durham, Durham.

Coaker, V. (2008) Tackling Drugs. Paper given at the Tackling Drugs – Reducing Crime European conference organized by the Nottinghamshire Police Authority, 7 Apr. Available at: http://press.homeoffice.gov.uk/Speeches/Speech-by-VC-Tackling-Crime

Coffey, M. and Jenkins, E. (2002) Power and control: forensic community mental health nurses' perceptions of team-working, legal sanction and compliance, *Journal of Psychiatric and Mental Health Nursing*, 9(5): 521–9.

Cohen, A. and Eastman, N. (2000). Needs assessment for mentally disordered offenders: measurement of 'ability to benefit' and outcome, *British Journal of Psychiatry*, 177: 493–98.

Coles, B., Britton, L. and Hicks, L. (2004) *Building Better Connections: Interagency Work and Connexions Service*. Bristol: Policy Press and Joseph Rowntree Foundation.

Collins, E., Wagner, C. and Walmsley, S. (2000) Psychosocial impact of the lipodystrophy syndrome in HIV infection, *The AIDS Reader*, 10(9): 546–51.

Columbo, A. (1997) *Understanding Mentally Disordered Offenders: A Multi-Agency Perspective*. London: Ashgate Publishing Ltd.

Commission for Healthcare Audit and Inspection (2007) No Ifs, *No Buts: Improving Services for Tobacco Control*. London: Health Commission.

Commission for Rural Communities (2008) Rural proofing. Available at: www.ruralcommunities.gov.uk//projects/ruralproofing

Communities and Local Government (2006) *Statutory Homelessness Statistical Release: 4th Quarter 2006, England*. London: Communities and Local Government.

Communities and Local Government (2007a) *Estimate of the Number of People Sleeping Rough in England: June 2007*. London: Communities and Local Government.

Communities and Local Government (2007b) *Statutory Homelessness Statistical Release: 1st Quarter 2007, England*. London: Communities and Local Government.

Communities and Local Government (2007c) *Statutory Homelessness Statistical Release: 2nd Quarter 2007, England*. London: Communities and Local Government.

Communities and Local Government (2007d) *Statutory Homelessness Statistical Release: 3rd Quarter 2007, England*. London: Communities and Local Government.

Condon, J. and Smith, N. (2003) *Prevalence of Drug Use: Key Findings from the 2002/2003 British Crime Survey*, Home Office Findings No. 229. London: Home Office.

Connell, J. P. and Kurbish, A. C. (1996) *Applying a Theories of Change Approach to the Evaluation of Comprehensive Community Initiatives*. Washington, DC: The Aspen Institute.

Connell, J. P. and Kubisch, A. C. (1999) Applying a theory of change approach to the evaluation of comprehensive community initiatives: progress, prospects, and problems, in K. Fullbright-Anderson, A. C. Kubisch and J. P. Connell (eds), *Theory, Measurement, and Analysis* Vol. 2. Washington DC: The Aspen Institute.

Connell, J. P., Kubisch, A. C., Schorr, L. B., and Weiss, C. H. (eds) (1995) *New Approaches to Evaluating Community Initiatives: Concepts, Methods and Contexts*. Washington, DC: The Aspen Institute.

Cooper, J. E. (1994) *ICD-10 Classification of Mental and Behavioural Disorders*. Edinburgh: Churchill Livingstone.

Cooper, H., Carlisle, C., Gibbs, T. and Watkins, C. (2001) Developing an evidence base for interdisciplinary learning: a systematic review, *Journal of Advanced Nursing*, 35(2): 228–37.

Corby, B. (2001) Interprofessional cooperation and inter-agency co-ordination and child protection, in K. Wilson and A. James (eds), *The Child Protection Handbook*, 2nd edn. London: Bailliere-Tindall, pp. 272–87.

Corby, B. (2003) Supporting families and protecting children: assisting child care professionals in initial decision-making and review of cases, *Journal of Social Work*, 3(2): 195–210.

Corby, B., Doig, A. and Roberts, V. (1998) Inquiries into child abuse, *Journal of Social Welfare and Family Law*, 20(4): 377–96.

Corby, B., Doig, A. and Roberts, V. (2001) *Public Inquiries into Abuse of Children in Residential Care*. London: Jessica Kingsley.

Corby, B., Millar, M. and Pope, A. (2002) Assessing children in need assessments – a parents' perspective, *Practice*, 14(4): 5–16.

Corston, J. (2007) *The Corston Report: A Review of Women with Particular Vulnerabilities in the Criminal Justice System*. London: Home Office.

Cott, C. (1998) Structure and meaning in multidisciplinary teamwork, *Sociology of Health and Illness*, 20(6): 848–73.

Courtney, R., Ballard, E., Fauver, S., Gariota, M. and Holland, L. (1996) The partnership model: working with individuals, families and communities towards a new vision of health, *Public Health Nursing*, 13(3): 177–86.

Coventry ACPC (Area Child Protection Committee) (2005) *Annual Report 2004–2005*. Coventry: Coventry ACPC.

Coventry Domestic Violence Focus Group (2000) *Coventry's Multi-Agency Strategy on Domestic Violence 2000–03*. Coventry: Coventry Domestic Violence Focus Group.

Craig, G. and Manthorpe, J. (2000) *Social Care in Rural Areas: Developing an Agenda for Research, Policy and Pactice*, Rowntree Research Findings No. 039. Available at: http://www.jrf.org.uk

Crane, M. and Warnes, A. (2001) *Single Homeless People in London*. Sheffield: Sheffield Institute for Studies on Ageing.

Crawford, M., Rutter, M. and Thelwall, S. (2003) *User Involvement in Change Manager: A Review of the Literature*, Report to the National Co-ordinating Centre for NHS Service Delivery and Organisation Research and Development (NSCCSDO). London: NSCCSDO.

CRE (Commission for Racial Equality) (2000) *Strengthening the Race Relations Act*. London: CRE.

Crespo-Fierro, M. (1997) Compliance/adherence and care management in HIV disease, *Journal of the Association of Nurses in AIDS Care*, 8(4): 43–54.

Crisis (2006) *Statistics about Homelessness October 2006*. London: Crisis.

CSCI (Commission for Social Care Inspection) (2006) Living well in later life, Available at: www.csci.org.uk

D'Amour, D., Ferrada-Videlai, M., San Martin Rodriguezi, L. and Beaulieu, M. D. (2005) The conceptual basis for interprofessional collaboration: core concepts and theoretical frameworks, *Journal of Interprofessional Care*, 1: 116–31.

Daar, E. S., Cohen, C., Remien, R., Sherer, R. and Smith, K. (2003) Improving adherence to antiretroviral therapy, *AIDS Reader*, 13(2): 81–90.

Dailey, G. (1993) Professional ideology or organisational tribalism? The health service-social work divide, in J. Walmersley, J. Reynolds, R. Shakespeare and R. Woolfe (eds), *Health, Welfare and Practice*. London: Sage.

Dale, P. Green, R. and Fellows, R. (2002) *What Really Happened? Child Protection Case Management of Infants with Serious Injuries and Discrepant Parental Explanations*. London: National Society for Prevention of Cruelty to Children.

Dalrymple, J. and Burke, B. (2006) *Anti-Oppressive Practice*. Maidenhead: Open University Press.

Danso, C., Greaves, H., Howell, S. et al. (2003) *The Involvement of Children and Young People in Promoting Change and Enhancing the Quality of Services: A Research Report for Social Care Institute for Excellence from the National Children's Bureau*, London: National Children's Bureau.

Dartington Social Research Unit (1995) *Child Protection: Messages from Research.* London: HMSO.

Davies, C. (2000) Getting health professionals to work together, *British Medical Journal.* 320(7241): 1021–2.

Davies, M. M. and Bath, P. A. (2001) The maternity information concerns of Somali women in the United Kingdom, *Journal of Advanced Nursing*, 36(2): 237–45.

Davis Smith J. (1998) *The 1997 National Survey of Volunteering.* London: National Centre for Volunteering.

Deaville, J. (2001) *The Nature of Rural General Practice in the UK: Preliminary Research. A Joint Report from the Institute of Rural Health and the General Practitioners Committee of the British Medical Association.* Powys: Institute of Rural Health.

Del Amo, J., Goh, B. T. and Forster, G. E. (1996) AIDS defining conditions in Africans resident in the United Kingdom, *International Journal of STDs and AIDS*, 7(11): 44–7.

Department for Children, School and Families (2007) Staying Safe: *A Consultation Document.* London: The Stationery Office.

Department for Communities and Local Government (2007) *Equality Impact Assessment: Discrimination Law Review. Consultation Proposals for a Single Equality Bill.* London: Department for Communities and Local Government.

DCFS (Department of Child and Family Services) (2007a) *The Children's Plan: Building Brighter Futures: Summary.* London: The Stationery Office. Available at: www.dfes.gov.uk/publications/childrensplan/downloads/ Childrens_Plan_Executive_Summary.pdf

DCFS (Department of Child and Family Services) (2007b) *Social and Emotional Aspects of Learning Secondary SEAL: A Quick Guide.* Available at: www.bandapilot.org.uk/ secondary/resources/welcome_page/sns_ssealguide0004307.pdf (accessed 27 Apr. 2008).

DETR (Department of the Environment, Transport and the Regions) (2000) *Our Countryside: The Future – A Fair Deal for Rural England.* London: The Stationery Office.

Derbyshire Gypsy Liaison Group (2003) *A Better Road.* Matlock: Derbyshire Gypsy Liaison Group, Ernest Bailey Community Centre.

DfES (Department for Education and Skills) (2004) *Every Child Matters: Change for Children.* Nottingham: HM Government.

DfES (Department for Education and Skills) (2006) *Working Together to Safeguard Children: A Guide to Interagency Working to Safeguard and Promote the Welfare of Children.* London: The Stationery Office.

DfES (Department for Education and Skills) (2007) *Local Safeguarding Children Boards: A Review of Progress.* London: HM Government.

DHSS (Department of Health and Social Security) (1974) *Report of the Committee of Inquiry into the Care and Supervision Provided in Relation to Maria Colwell.* London: HMSO.

DHSS (Department of Health and Social Security) (1979) *Patients First.* London: HMSO.

Dickinson, H. (2006) The evaluation of health and social care partnerships: an analysis of approaches and synthesis for the future, *Health and Social Care in the Community,* 14(5): 375–83.

DoE (Department of the Environment) (1982) *Management of Local Authority Gypsy sites.* Cardiff: DoE/Welsh Office.

DoH (Department of Health) (1990) *The NHS and Community Care Act.* London: HMSO.

DoH (Department of Health) (1991) *Child Abuse: A Study of Inquiry Reports 1980–1989.* London: HMSO.

DoH (Department of Health) (1992) *Health of the Nation.* London: HMSO.

DoH (Department of Health) (1995a) *Building Bridges: Arrangements for Inter-Agency Working for the Care and Protection of Severely Mentally Ill People.* London: HMSO.

DoH (Department of Health) (1995b) *The Carers (Recognition and Services) Act.* London: HMSO.

DoH (Department of Health) (1997a) *Developing Partnerships in Mental Health.* London: The Stationery Office.

DoH (Department of Health) (1997b) *The New NHS: Modern and Dependable.* London: The Stationery Office.

DoH (Department of Health) (1998a) *Modernising Mental Health Services: Safe, Sound, Supportive.* London: The Stationery Office.

DoH (Department of Health) (1998b) *Partnerships in Action: New Opportunities for Joint Working between Health and Social Services. A Discussion Document.* London: The Stationery Office.

DoH (Department of Health) (1999a) *Modernising Health and Social Services: Developing the Workforce.* London: The Stationary Office.

DoH (Department of Health) (1999b) *National Service Framework for Mental Health.* London: The Stationery Office.

DoH (Department of Health) (1999c) *Working Together to Safeguard Children: A Guide to Inter-agency Working to Safeguard and Promote the Welfare of Children.* London: The Stationery Office.

DoH (Department of Health) (1999d) *The National Strategy for Carers.* London: The Stationery Office.

DoH (Department of Health) (2000a) *Domestic Violence: A Resource Manual for Health Care Professionals*. London: The Stationery Office.

DoH (Department of Health) (2000b) *Framework for the Assessment of Children in Need and their Families*. London: The Stationery Office.

DoH (Department of Health) (2000c) *No Secrets: Guidance on Developing and Implementing Multiagency Policies and Procedures to Protect Vulnerable Adults from Abuse*. London: The Stationery Office.

DoH (Department of Health) (2000d) *Reforming the Mental Health Act*. London: The Stationery Office.

DoH (Department of Health) (2000e) *The Carers and Disabled Children Act*. London: The Stationery Office.

DoH (Department of Health) (2000f) *The NHS Plan*. London: The Stationery Office.

DoH (Department of Health) and DRES (Department for Education and Skills) (2004) *National Service Framework for Children, Young People and Maternity Services*. London: The Stationery Office.

DoH (Department of Health) and Home Office (1992) *Review of Health and Social Services for Mentally Disordered Offenders and Others Requiring Similar Services: Final Summary Report* (Reed report). Cm 2088. London: HMSO.

DoH (Department of Health) and Home Office (2006) *Domestic Abuse Training Manual for Health Professionals*. Available at: www.crimereduction.gov.uk/domesticviolence/domesticviolence58.htm

DoH (Department of Health) (2001a) *Coronary Heart Disease National Service Framework Implementation Plan for Wales: Tackling Coronary Heart Disease in Wales: Implementing through Evidence*. Wales: National Assembly.

DoH (Department of Health) (2001b) *National Service Framework for Older People*. London: The Stationery Office.

DoH (Department of Health) (2001c) *Health and Social Care Act 2001*. London: The Stationery Office.

DoH (Department of Health) (2001d) *Reference Guide to Consent for Examination or Treatment*. London: Department of Health (Crown Copyright).

DoH (Department of Health) (2001e) *Involving Patients and the Public in Health Care*. London: The Stationery Office.

DoH (Department of Health) (2001f) *The Expert Patient: A New Approach to Chronic Disease Management for the 21st Century*. London: Department of Health (Crown Copyright).

DoH (Department of Health) (2001g) *Research Governance Framework*. London: The Stationery Office.

DoH (Department of Health) (2002) *Adult Acute Inpatient Care Provision*. London: The Stationery Office.

DoH (Department of Health) (2003a): *Statistics on Smoking: Statistical Bulletin 2003/21*. London: The Stationery Office.

DoH (Department of Health) (2003b) *Building on the Best: Choice, Responsiveness and Equity*. London: The Stationery Office.

DoH (Department of Health) (2003c) *Safeguarding Children: What to Do if You're Worried a Child is Being Abused*. London: The Stationery Office.

DoH (Department of Health) (2004a) *National Service Framework for Children, Young People and Maternity Services: The Mental Health and Psychological Wellbeing of Children and Young People*. Available at: www.dh.gov.uk/en/Publicationsandstatistics/ Publications/PublicationsPolicyAndGuidance/DH_4089114 (accessed 21 Apr. 2008).

DoH (Department of Health) (2004b) *Choosing Health: Making Healthy Choices Easier*, CM 6374. London: The Stationery Office.

DoH (Department of Health) (2004c) *Single Assessment Process Implementation (SAP) Guidance*. London: The Stationery Office.

DoH (Department of Health) (2004d) *The Carers (Equal Opportunities) Act*. London: The Stationery Office.

DoH (Department of Health) (2004e) *The National Service Framework for Mental Health: 5 Years On*. London: The Stationery Office.

DoH (Department of Health) (2004f). *NHS Improvement Plan*. London: The Stationery office.

DoH (Department of Health) (2004g) *Mental Health Care Group Workforce Team*. London: The Stationery Office.

DoH (Department of Health) (2005a) *Independence, Well-being and Choice: Our Vision for the Future of Social Care for Adults*. London: The Stationery Office.

DoH (Department of Health) (2005b) *Responding to Domestic Abuse: A Handbook for Health Professionals*. London: The Stationery Office.

DoH (Department of Health) (2005c). *Creating a Patient Led NHS*. London: The Stationery Office.

DoH (Department of Health) (2006a) *Fourth Annual Report on Progress in Implementing the National Suicide Prevention Strategy for England*. London: The Stationery Office.

DoH (Department of Health) (2006b) *Our Health, Our Care, Our Say: A New Direction for Community Services*. London: Department of Health (Crown Copyright).

DoH (Department of Health) (2007a) New deal for carers. Available at: www.dh.gov.uk/en/Policyandguidance/Organisationpolicy/Healthreform/ NewDealforCarers/DH_075478

DoH (Department of Health) (2007b) *Creating an Interprofessional Workforce: An Education and Training Framework for Health and Social Care in England.* London: The Stationery Office.

DoH (Department of Health) and CSIP (2007a) *Guidance Statement on Fidelity and Best Practice for Crisis Services.* London: The Stationery Office.

DoH (Department of Health) (2007d) *Tackling Health Inequalities: 2004–2006 Data and Policy Update for the 2010 National Target.* London: The Stationery Office.

DoH (Department of Health) (2007e) *Creating Capable Teams Approach (CCTA): Best Practice Guidance to Support the Implementation of New Ways of Working and New Roles.* London: The Stationery Office.

DoH (Department of Health) (2007f) *New Ways of Working for Everyone: Best Practice Toolkit.* London: The Stationery Office.
DoH (Department of Health) (2008) New deal for carers. Available at: (www.dh.gov.uk/en/Policyandguidance/Organisationpolicy/Healthreform/NewDealforCarers/DH_075478

DoH (Department of Health) CSIP (2007b) *Onwards and Upwards: Sustaining Service Improvement in Acute Care.* London: The Stationery Office.

DoH (Department of Health) (2007c) *Safe. Sensible. Social. The Next Steps in the National Alcohol Strategy.* London: DH Publications.

DoH (Department of Health) and HMPS (Prison Service) (2001). *Changing the Outlook: A Strategy for Developing and Modernising Mental Health Services in Prisons.* London: The Stationery Office.

Dombeck, M. (1997) Professional personhood: training, territoriality and tolerance, *Journal of Interprofessional Care*, 11(1): 9–21.

Doran, T. (2001) Policy and practice: providing seamless community health and social services, *British Journal of Community Nursing*, 6(8): 387–90.

Dowling, B., Powell, M. and Glendinning, C. (2004) Conceptualising Successful Partnerships, *Health and Social Care in the Community*, 12(4): 309–17.

Downie, R. S. and Telfer, E. (1980) *Caring and Curing.* London: Methuen.

DTI (Department of Trade and Industry) (1999) *Employment Relations Act.* London: The Stationery Office.

DTI (Department of Trade and Industry) (2002) *Work–Life Balance Campaign.* Available at: www.dti.gov.uk

Dunbar-Jacob, J., Erlen, J. A., Schlenk, E. A. (2000) Adherence in chronic disease, *Annual Review of Nursing Research*, 18: 48–90.

DWP (Department for Work and Pensions) (2002) *Disabled for Life? Attitudes Towards and Experiences of Disability in Britain.* London: The Stationery Office.

DWP (Department for Work and Pensions) (2003) *Households Below Average Income.* London: The Stationery Office.

DWP (Department for Work and Pensions) (2004) *Opportunity for All: Sixth Annual Report 2004.* London: Stationery Office.

Eastman, N. (2006). *Can there be true partnership between clinicians and the Home Office? Advances in Psychiatric Treatment,* 12: 459–61.

ECM (Every Child Matters) (2008) *Delivering Services.* Available at: www.everychildmatters.gov.uk/deliveringservices/ (accessed 30 Jun. 2008).

Edwards, B., Goodwin, M., Pemberton, S. and Woods, M. (1999) Partnership working in rural regeneration, Rowntree Research Findings, No. 6039. Available at: www.jr-f.org.uk

El Ansari, W. and Phillips, C. (2001) Interprofessional collaboration: a stakeholder approach to evaluation of voluntary participation in community partnerships, *Journal of Interprofessional Care,* 15(4): 351–68.

El Ansari, W. and Weiss, E.S. (2006) Quality of research on community partnerships: developing the evidence base, *Health Education Research,* 21(2): 175–80.

Emmaus (2008) Emmaus communities. Available at: www.emmaus.org.uk

Enriquez, J., Lackey, N. R., O'Connor, M. and McKinsey, D. (2004) Successful adherence after multiple HIV treatment failures, *Journal of Advanced Nursing,* 45(4): 438–46.

Evans, J. and Lunt, I. (2002) Inclusive education: are there limits? *European Journal of Special Needs Education,* 17(1): 1–14.

Eysenbach, G. and Jadad, A. R. (2001) Evidence-based patient choice and consumer health informatics in the Internet age, *Journal of Medical Internet Research,* 3(2): 19–25 Available at: www.jmir.org/2001/2/e19/html (accessed Nov. 2006).

Facebook (2008) Dyslexia, it is a GIFT. Available at: www.facebook.com/group.php?gid=2227695776

Farhall J. and Cotton S. (2002) Implementing psychological treatments for psychosis in an area mental health service: the response of patients, therapists and managers, *Journal of Mental Health,* 11(5): 511–22.

Fennell, P. and Yeates, V. (2002). To serve which master? criminal justice policy, community care and the mentally disordered offender, in A. Buchanan (ed.), *Care of the Mentally Disordered Offender.* Oxford: Oxford University Press.

Fielding, J., Walterfang, M. and Dakis, J. (2002) The challenge of ongoing education in multidisciplinary mental health services, *Australasian Psychiatry,* 10(3): 224–8.

Finch, J. and Groves, D. (1983) *A Labour of Love: Women, Work and Caring.* London: Routledge and Kegan Paul.

Fish, D. and Coles, C. (1998) *Developing Professional Judgement in Health Care*. Oxford: Butterworth-Heinemann.

Fletcher, N. and Holt, T. (1995) *Ethics, Law and Nursing*. Manchester: Manchester University Press.

Ford, T. Vostanis, P. Meltzer, H. and Goodman, R. (2007) Psychiatric disorder among British children looked after by local authorities: comparison with children living in private households, *British Journal of Psychiatry*, 190: 319–25. Available at: http://bjp.rcpsych.org/cgi/content/full/190/4/319 (accessed 28 Apr. 2008).

Forrester, D. (2000) Parental substance misuse and child protection in a British sample: a survey of children on the Child Protection Register in an Inner London District Office, *Child Abuse Review*, 9: 235–46.

Fountain, J. and Howes, S. (2002) *Home and Dry? Homelessness and Substance Use*. London: Crisis.

Foyer (2008) *The Foyer Federation*. Available at: www.foyer.net/mpn/

Frankel, B. G. (1994) Patient–physician relationships: changing modes of interaction, in B. B. Singh and H. D. Dickinson (eds), *Health, Illness and Health Care in Canada*. London: Harcourt Brace, pp 183–98.

Freeman, M. (1999) Children are unbeatable, *Children & Society*, 13: 130–41.

Freeman, T. and Peck, E. (2006) Evaluating partnerships: a case study of integrated specialist mental health, *Services, Health and Social Care in the Community*, 14(5): 408–17.

Friends, Families and Travellers (2000) Unpublished information leaflet. Brighton: Community Base. Available at: www.gypsy-traveller.org/

Gallant, M. H., Beaulieu, M. C. and Carnevale, F. A. (2002) *Journal of Advanced Nursing*, 40(2), 149–57.

Gannon-Leary, P., Baines, S. and Wilson, R. (2006) Collaboration and partnership: a review and reflections on a national project to join up local services in England, *Journal of Interprofessional Care*, 20(6): 665–74.

Garcia, I. (2006) Leading the way in times of crisis, *Mental Health Practice*, 10(2): 22–3.

Gazzard, B. (on behalf of the British HIV Association (BHIVA) Writing Committee) (2005) British HIV Association (BHIVA) guidelines for the treatment of HIV-infected adults with antiretrovirals, *HIV Medicine*, 6(s2): 1–61.

Gazzard, B. (on behalf of the British HIV Association (BHIVA) Writing Committee) (2006) British HIV Association (BHIVA) guidelines for the treatment of HIV-infected adults with antiretrovirals, *HIV Medicine*, 7(8) 487–503.

Gazzard, B. G. (2002) Natural History of HIV infection, in B. G. Gazzard (ed.), *AIDS Care Handbook*. London: Mediscript.

Gelder, M., Mayou, R., and Cowen, P. (2002) *Shorter Oxford Textbook of Psychiatry: Part I.* Oxford: Oxford Medical Press.

Gelder, M., Mayou, R. and Cowen, P. (2004) *Shorter Oxford Textbook of Psychiatry: Part II.* Oxford: Oxford University Press.

Gerber, B. S. and Eiser, A. R. (2001) The patient–physician relationship in the Internet age: future prospects and the research agenda, *Journal of Medical Internet Research*, Apr.–Jun., 3(2): e15.

Gerbert, B., Bronstone, A., Clanon, K., Abercrombie, P. and Bangsberg, D. (2000) Combination antiretroviral therapy: health care providers confront emerging dilemmas, *AIDS Care*, 12(4): 409–21.

Gillon, R. (1986) *Philosophical Medical Ethics.* Chichester: John Wiley and Sons.

Glendinning, C. (2002) Partnerships between health and social services: developing a framework for evaluation, *Policy and Politics*, 30(1): 115–27.

Gorna, R. (1994) *Positive Practice*, 1st edn. London: Health Visitors' Association.

Grant, A. and Townend, M. (2007) Some emerging implications for clinical supervision in British mental health nursing, *Journal of Psychiatric and Mental Health Nursing* 14(6): 609–14.

Green, H., McGinnity, A., Meltzer, H., Ford, T. and Goodman, R. (2005) *Mental Health of Children and Young People in Great Britain, 2004*, Basingstoke: Palgrave Macmillan.

Greenall, P. (2006) The barriers to patient-driven treatment in mental health: why patients may choose to follow their own path, *Leadership in Health Services*, 19(1): xi–xxv.

Hagell, A. (2002) *The Mental Health of Young Offenders: Bright Futures. Working with Vulnerable Young People.* London: Mental Health Foundation.

Hague, G. (2000) *Reducing Domestic Violence: What Works. Multi-agency Fora.* London: Home Office.

Hague, G., Malos, E. and Dear, W. (1996) *Multi-agency Work and Domestic Violence: A National Study of Inter-agency Initiatives.* Bristol: The Policy Press.

Hajioff, S. and McKee, M. (2000) The health of the Roma people: a review of the published literature, *Journal of Epidemiology Community Health*, 54(11): 864–9.

Halkitis, P. N. and Kirton, C. (1999) Self-strategies as a means of enhancing adherence to HIV antiretroviral therapies: a Rogerian approach, *Journal of the New York State Nurses Association*, 30(2): 22–7.

Hallam, S. and Castle, F. (2000) Reducing exclusion from school: what really works. Paper presented at the European Conference on Educational Research, Edinburgh, 20–3 Sept. Available at: www.leeds.ac.uk/educol/documents/00001633.htm (accessed 29 Apr. 2008).

Halliday, J., Sheena Asthana, N. M. and Richardson, S. (2004) Evaluating partnership: the role of formal assessment tools, *Evaluation*, 10(3): 285–303.

Hamilton, B., Manias, E., Maude, P., Marjoribanks, T. and Cook, K. (2004) Perspectives of a nurse, a social worker and a psychiatrist regarding patient assessment in acute inpatient psychiatry settings: a case study approach, *Journal of Psychiatric and Mental Health Nursing*, 11(6): 683–9.

Hannigan, B. (1999) Joint working in community mental health: prospects and challenges, *Health and Social Care in the Community*, 7(1): 25–31.

Harbin, F. and Murphy, M. (eds) (2000) *Substance Misuse and Child Care: How to Understand, Assist and Intervene when Drugs Affect Parenting*. Lyme Regis: Russell House Publishing.

Harold, A. M. (1977) Psychiatrists and nurses in a Scottish hospital: a research note on conflict and its resolution in the ward situation, *Scottish Journal of Sociology*, 2: 87–96.

Harris, R. (1999) Mental disorder and social disorder: Underlying themes in crime management, in D. Webb and R. Harris (eds), *Mentally Disordered Offenders: Managing People Nobody Owns*. London: Routledge.

Hart, A., Henwood, F. and Wyatt, S. (2003) The role of the Internet in mediating relationships between patients and practitioners: hype and reality. Paper presented at the Making Sense of Health, Illness and Disease Conference, St Hilda's College, Oxford, 11–14 July.

Hawes, D. and Perez, B. (1996) *The Gypsy and the State: The Ethnic Cleansing of British Society*. Bristol: Policy Press.

Hawkins, D., Blott, M., Clayden, P. et al. on behalf of the British HIV Association (BHIVA) Guidelines Writing Committee (2005) Guidelines for the management of HIV infection in pregnant women and the prevention of mother-to-child transmission of HIV, *HIV Medicine*, 6(s2): 107–48.

Haynes, P. and Henfrey, D. (1995) *Progress in Partnership and Collaboration: An Evaluation of Multi-agency Working for Mentally Disordered Offenders in Surrey*. Brighton: Health and Social Policy Research Centre, University of Brighton.

Health Protection Agency (2003) *Renewing the Focus: HIV and other Sexually Transmitted Infections in the United Kingdom in 2002*. London: Health Protection Agency.

Health Protection Agency (2004) Health Protection Agency warns of impending HIV crisis. Press statement, Health Protection Agency, London.

Healthcare Commission (2007) *No Ifs, No Buts: Improving Services for Tobacco Control*. London: Commission for Healthcare Audit and Inspection.

Helft, P. R., Hlubocky, F. and Daugherty, C. K. (2003) American oncologists' views of Internet use by cancer patients: a mail survey of American Society of Clinical Oncology members, *Journal of Clinical Oncology*, 21(5): 942–7.

Henderson, J. (2001) He's not my carer – he's my husband: personal and policy constructions of care in mental health, *Journal of Social Work Practice*, 15(2): 149–59.

Hendessi, M. (1997) *Voices of Children Witnessing Domestic Violence: A Form of Child Abuse*. Coventry: Domestic Violence Focus Group.

Henneman, E. A., Lee, J. L. and Cohen, J. I. (1995) Collaboration: a concept analysis, *Journal of Advanced Nursing*, 21(1): 103–9.

Henwood, F. et al. (2003) Ignorance is bliss sometimes: constraints on the emergence of the 'informed patient' in the changing landscapes of health information, *Sociology of Health and Illness*, 25(6): 589–607.

Hester, M., Pearson, C. and Harwin, N. (1998) *Making an Impact: Children and Domestic Violence*. Bristol: Barnardos, NSPCC and University of Bristol.

Himid, K. A., Zwi, K., Welch, J. M. and Ball, C. S. (1998) The development of a community based family HIV service, *AIDS Care*, 10(2): 231–7.

HM Government (2007) *PSA Delivery Agreement 12: Improve the Health and Wellbeing of Children and Young People*. London: The Stationery Office. Available at: www.hm-treasury.gov.uk/media/C/F/pbr_csr07_psa12.pdf

HM Government (2008) *Drugs: Protecting Families and Communities. The 2008 Drug Strategy.* London: Prolog Home Office.

Homan, J. M. and J. J. McGowan (2002) The Medical Library Association: promoting new roles for health information professionals, *Journal of the Medical Library Association*, 90(1): 80–5.

Home Office (1983) *Mental Health Act 1983*. London: HMSO.

Home Office (1990) Probation circular 66/1990, *Provision for Mentally Disordered Offenders*. London: Home Office.

Home Office (1994) *Criminal Justice and Public Order Act 1994*. London: Home Office.

Home Office (1995a) Probation circular 21/1995: Home Office research study 138, *Public Interest Case Assessment Schemes*. London: Home Office.

Home Office (1995b) Probation circular 12/1995, *Mentally Disordered Offenders: Inter-agency Working*. London: Home Office.

Home Office (2000) *Multi-agency Guidance for Addressing Domestic Violence*. London: Home Office.

Home Office (2001) *Health and Social Care Act 2001*. London: The Stationery Office.

Home Office (2002) Updated drug strategy 2002, *Tackling Drugs*. London: Home Office Drugs Strategy Directorate.

Home Office (2004a) *Reducing Reoffending: National Action Plan*. London: Home Office.

Home Office (2004b) *Tackling Domestic Violence: Providing Support to Children Who Have Witnessed Domestic Violence*. London: Home Office.

Home Office (2005a) *National Report for Domestic Violence*. London: Home Office.

Home Office (2005b). Probation circular 24/2005 *National Probation Service Business Plan 2005 – 06*. London: Home Office.

Home Office (2006) *Crimes and Victims*. London: Home Office. Available at: www.homeoffice.gov.uk/crime-victims/reducing-crime/alcohol-related-crime/

Home Office (2007a) *Crime and Victims Factsheet*. Available at: www.homeoffice.gov.uk/crime-victims/reducing-crime/domestic-violence

Home Office (2007b) *Home Office Statistical Bulletin: Statistics of Mentally Disordered Offenders 2005*. London: Home Office Research Development and Statistics Directorate.

Home Office (2007c) *Domestic Violence Mini-site*. Available at: www.crimereduction.gov.uk/dv

Home Office (2007d) *Domestic Violence: Information Sharing Pathway*. Available at: www.crimereduction.gov.uk/isp01.htm

Home Office (2007e). *Home Office Statistical Bulletin: Re-offending of Adults. Results from the 2004 Cohort*. London: Home Office Research Development and Statistics Directorate.

Home Office (2008) Domestic violence. Available at: www.homeoffice.gov.uk/crime-victims/reducing-crime/domestic-violence/ (accessed Jun. 2008).

Home Office and DHSS (Department of Health and Social Security) (1975) *Report of the Committee on Mentally Abnormal Offenders*. The Butler Committee report, Cmnd 6244. London: Department of Health and Social Security.

Home Office and DoH (Department of Health) (1996) *A Guidance Document Aimed at Promoting Effective Working Between the Health and Probation Services*. London: HMSO.

Home Office and DoH (Department of Health) (1999) *Managing Dangerous People with Severe Personality Disorders*. London: The Stationery Office.

Homeless Link (2006) *Multiple Needs and Support: Homeless Link Membership Survey Summary Report September 2006*. London: Homeless Link.

Homeless Link (2007) *Effective and Strategic Partnership Working*. Available at: www.homeless.org.uk/developyourservice/partnership (accessed 28 Oct. 2007).

Hope, R. (2004) *The Ten Essential Shared Capabilities*. London: The Sainsbury Centre for Mental Health / NIMHE.

Horrigan, J. (2007) *A Typology of Information and Communication Technology Users*. Pew Internet and American Life Project. Washington, DC: Pew Internet. Available at: www.Pewinternet.Org/

House of Commons (2003a) *Every Child Matters*, CM5860. London: House of Commons.

House of Commons (2003b) *Keeping Children Safe: The Government's Response to the Victoria Climbie Inquiry Report and Joint Chief Inspectors' Report Safeguarding Children*, CM5861. London: House of Commons.

House of Commons Science and Technology Select Committee (2006) *Drug classification: making a hash of it?* Fifth report of session 2005–6, HC1031, 31 Jul. Available at: www.publications.parliament.uk/pa/cm200506/cmselect/cmsctech/1031/1031.pdf

Howlett, M. (1998) *Medication, Non-Compliance and Mentally Disordered Offenders: A Study of Independent Inquiry Reports*. London: The Zito Trust.

Hudson, B., Exworthy, M. and Peckham, S. (1998) *The Integration of Localised and Collaborative Purchasing: a Review of the Literature and Framework for Analysis*. Leeds and Southampton: Nuffield Institute for Health, University of Leeds and Institute for Health Policy Studies, University of Southampton.

Hughes, B. (1997) *Older People and Community Care*. Buckingham: Open University Press.

Hultberg, E., Nnroth, K. and Allebeck, P. (2005) Interdisciplinary collaboration between primary care, social insurance and social services in the rehabilitation of people with musculoskeletal disorder: effects on self-rated health and physical performance, *Journal of Interprofessional Care*, 19(2): 115–24.

Hummelvoll, J. K. and Severinsson, E. I. (2001) Imperative ideals and the strenuous reality: focusing on acute psychiatry, *Journal of Psychiatric and Mental Health Nursing*, 8(1): 17–24.

Hussey, R. (1989) Equal opportunities for gypsies, *Public Health*, 103(2): 79.

Husted, G. L. and Husted, J. H. (1991) *Ethical Decision Making in Nursing*. New York: Mosby.

Hutson, S. and Liddiard, M. (1994) *Youth Homelessness: The Construction of a Social Issue*. Basingstoke: Macmillan.

Iles, P. and Auluck, R. (1990) Team building, inter-agency team development and social work practice, *British Journal of Social Work*, 20(2): 151–64.

Institute of Medicine (1996) Fetal alcohol syndrome diagnosis, *Epidemiology, Prevention, and Treatment*. Washington, DC: National Academy Press.

Institute of Medicine, US (2001) *Crossing the Quality Chasm: A New Health System for the 21st Century*. Washington DC: National Academy of Sciences.

INVOLVE (2007) Promoting public involvement in NHS, public health and social care research. Available at: www.invo.org.uk. (Accessed 30 Jul. 2007).

INVOLVE (2008) Promoting public involvement in NHS, public health and social care research: good practice in active public involvement in research. Available at: www.invo.org.uk/pdfs/GoodPracticeD3.pdf (accessed Mar. 2008).

Irvine, R., Kerridge, I., McPhee, J. and Freeman, S. (2002) Interprofessionalism and ethics: consensus or clash of cultures? *Journal of Interprofessional Care*, 16(3): 200–10.

Jacobson, P. (2007) Empowering the physician–patient relationship: the effect of the Internet partnership, *Canadian Journal of Library and Information Practice and Research*, 2(1).

Jarman, B. (1983) Identification of underprivileged areas, *British Medical Journal*, 286(6365): 1705–9.

Jarman, A. O. H. and Jarman, E. (1991) *The Welsh Gypsies: Children of Abram Wood*. Cardiff: University of Wales Press.

Jefferies, H. and Chan, K. K. (2004) Multidisciplinary team working: is it both holistic and effective? *International Journal of Gynaecological Cancer*, 14(2): 210–11.

Jones, A. (2001) Role of care pathways in changing psychiatric practice: action research, *Journal of Integrated Care Pathways*, 5: 15–21.

Jones, A. (2006a) Multidisciplinary team working: collaboration and conflict, *International Journal of Mental Health Nursing*, 15(1): 19–28.

Jones, A. (2006b) Supplementary prescribing: relationships between nurses and psychiatrists on hospital psychiatric wards, *Journal of Psychiatric and Mental Health Nursing*, 13(1): 3–11.

Jones, A. (2008) Exploring independent nurse prescribing for mental health settings, *Journal of Psychiatric and Mental Health Nursing*, 15: 109–17.

Jones, A. and Bowles, N. (2005) Best practice from admission to discharge in acute inpatient care: considerations and standards from a whole system perspective, *Journal of Psychiatric and Mental Health Nursing*, 12(6): 642–7.

Jones, S., Drainey, S., Walker, L. and Rooney, J. (2004) *Collecting the Evidence: Clients' Views on Drug Services*. London: Addaction.

Joseph Rowntree Foundation (1999) *Evaluation of the National User Involvement Project*. York: Joseph Rowntree Foundation.

Joseph Rowntree Foundation (2006) *The Report of the Independent Working Group on Drug Consumption Rooms*. York: Joseph Rowntree Foundation.

Judge, K. and Bauld, L. (2001) Strong theory, flexible methods: evaluating complex community-based initiatives, *Critical Public Health*, 11(1): 19–38.

Kalichman, S. K. and Ramachandran, B. (1999) Mental health implication of new HIV treatments, in D. G. Ostrow and S. C. Kalichman (eds), *Psychosocial and Public Health Impacts of New HIV Therapies*. New York: Kluwer Academic/Plenum Publishers.

Katz, A. (1996) Gaining a new perspective on life as a consequence of uncertainty in HIV infection, *Journal of the Association of Nurses in AIDS Care*, 7(4): 51–60.

Keen, J. and Alison, L. H. (2001) Drug misusing parents: key points for health professionals, *Archives of Disease in Childhood*, 85: 296–9.

Keene, J., Janacek, J. and Howell, D. (2003) Mental health patients in criminal justice populations: needs, treatment and criminal behaviour, *Criminal Behaviour and Mental Health*, 13(3): 168–78.

Kellogg Foundation (2004) *Logic Model Development Guide: Using Logic Models to Bring Together Planning, Evaluation, and Action*. London: WK Kellog Foundation Ltd.

Kempe, C., Silverman, F., Steele, B., Droegemuller, W. and Silver, H. (1962) The battered child syndrome, *Journal of the American Medical Association*, 181: 17–24.

Kennedy, P. and Griffiths, H. (2001) General psychiatrists discovering new roles for a new era and removing work stress, *British Journal of Psychiatry*, 179: 283–5.

Kennedy Report, (2002) *Learning from Bristol*. London: The Stationery Office.

Kenrick, D. (1998) Timeline of Romani (gypsy) history, *Patrin Web Journal*. Available at: www.geocities.com/Paris/timeline.htm.

King, B. (1999) Caring for African clients with HIV, *Nursing Management (London)*, 6(6):14–17.

Kipping, C. and Hickey, G. (1998) Exploring mental health nurses' expectations and experiences of working in the community, *Journal of Clinical Nursing*, 7(6): 531–8.

Kirklees Ednet (2008) Kirklees SAFE Programme. Available at: www.kirklees-ednet.org.uk/subjects/eic/behaviour/SAFE.htm

Kitamura, H., Shioiri, T., Kimura, T., et al. (2006) Parietal white matter abnormalities in obsessive compulsive disorder: a magnetic resonance spectroscopy study at 3 Tesla, *Acta Psychiatrica Scandinavia*, 114(2): 101–8.

Kivits, J. (2006) Informed patients and the Internet: a mediated context for consultations with health professionals, *Journal of Health Psychology*, 11(2): 269–82.

Klee, H., Jackson, M. and Lewis, S. (eds) (2001) *Drug Misuse and Motherhood*. London: Routledge.

Klee, H., Wright, S. and Rothwell, J. (1998) *Drug Using Parents and Their Children: Risk and Protective Factors: Report to the Department of Health*. Manchester: Centre for Social Research on Health and Substance Use, Manchester Metropolitan University.

Kramer, I. (2005) Patients as experts, *Nursing Management*, 12(2): 14.

Kroll, B. (2004) Living with an elephant: growing up with parental substance misuse, *Child and Family Social Work*, 9(2): 129–40.

Kroll, B. and Taylor, A. (2003) *Parental Substance Misuse and Child Welfare*. London: Jessica Kingsley Publishers.

Kylma, J., Vehvilainen-Jlkunen, K. and Lahdevirta, J. (2001) Hope, despair and hopelessness in living with HIV/AIDS: a grounded theory study, *Journal of Advanced Nursing*, 33(6): 764–75.

Labonte, R. (1994) Health promotion and empowerment on professional practice, *Health Education Quarterly*, 21(2): 253–68.

Laing, J. (1999) *Mentally Disordered Offenders in the Criminal Justice System*. Oxford: Oxford University Press.

Laming, Lord (2003) *The Victoria Climbie Inquiry: Report of an Inquiry by Lord Laming*, CM5730. London: House of Commons.

Lanceley, A., Savage, J., Menon, U. and Jacobs, I. (2007) Influences on multidisciplinary team decision making, *International Journal of Gynaecological Cancer*, 18(2): 215–22.

Lawrie, B. (1983) Travelling families in East London: adapting health visiting methods to a minority group, *Health Visitor*, 56(1): 26–8.

Lazenbatt, A., Orr, J., Bradley, M. and McWhirter, E. (1999) The role of nursing partnership interventions in improving the health of disadvantaged women, *Journal of Advanced Nursing*, 30(6): 1280–8.

Leece, J. (2003) The development of domiciliary care: what does the future hold? *Practice*, 15(3): 17–30.

Leff, J., Trieman, N., Knapp, M. and Hallam, A. (2000) The TAPS Project: a report on 13 years of research, 1985–1998, *Psychiatric Bulletin*, 24: 165–8.

Leone, L. (2008) Realistic evaluation of an illicit drug deterrence programme: analysis of a case study, *Evaluation*, 14(1): 9–28.

Lerner, B., Gulick, R. M. and Dubler, N. N. (1998) Rethinking non adherence: historical perspectives on triple-drug therapy for HIV disease, *Annals of Internal Medicine*, 129(7): 573–8.

Lester, H., Wright, N., Heath, I. and RGCP Health Inequalities Standing Group (2002) Developments in the provision of primary care for homeless people, *British Journal of General Practice*, 52(475): 91–2

Lewis, G. (2002) Domestic violence: lessons from the 1997–99 confidential enquiry into maternal deaths, *MIDIRS Midwifery Digest*, Sep. 12(2): S6–S8.

Lewis, J. and Meredith, B. (1988) *Daughters who Care: Daughters Caring for Mothers at Home*. London: Routledge and Kegan Paul.

Liberman, R. P., Hilty, D. M., Drake, R. E. and Tsang, H. W. (2001) Requirements for multidisciplinary teamwork in psychiatric rehabilitation, *Psychiatric Services*, 52(10): 1331–42.

Lloyd, C., McKenna, C. and King, R. (2005) Sources of stress experienced by occupational therapists and social workers in mental health settings, *Occupational Therapy International*, 12(2): 81–94.

LMDOPG (Leeds Mentally Disordered Offender Partnership Group) (1996) *Action Plan 1996/7*. Leeds: Leeds Mentally Disordered Offender Partnership Group.

LMDOPG (Leeds Mentally Disordered Offender Partnership Group) (1999) *Mentally Disordered Offender Strategy 1999–2001: Breaking Down Barriers – Building Bridges*. Leeds: Leeds Mentally Disordered Offender Partnership Group.

LMDOPG (Leeds Mentally Disordered Offender Partnership Group) (2001) *Leeds Strategy for Mentally Disordered Offenders*. Leeds: Leeds Mentally Disordered Offender Partnership Group.

Lomax, D., Lancaster, S. and Gray, P. (2000) *Moving On: A Survey of Travellers' Views*. Edinburgh: The Scottish Executive Central Research Unit. Available at: http://www.scotland.gov.uk/cru/kd01/blue/moving-01.pdf

Loveday, H. (2003) Adherence to antiretroviral therapy, in R. Pratt (ed.), *HIV and AIDS: A Foundation for Nursing and Health Care Practice*. London: Arnold.

Lowes, L. and Hulatt, I. (eds) (2005) *Involving Service Users in Health and Social Care Research*. London: Routledge.

Lund, B. (2006) *Understanding Housing Policy*. Bristol: The Policy Press.

Lyotard, J. F. (1992) *The Postmodern Condition: A Report on Knowledge*. Manchester: Manchester University Press.

Lyttle, J. (1986) *Mental Disorder: Its Care and Treatment*. London: Baillière Tindall.

MacGregor, S. (2000), Editorial: the drugs-crime nexus, *Drugs: Education Prevention and Policy*, 7(4): 311–15.

Maguire, M. and Nolan, J. (2007) Accommodation and related services for ex-prisoners, in A. Hucklesby and L. Hagley-Dickinson (eds), *Prisoner Resettlement: Policy and Practice*. Cullompton: Willan Publishing.

Mairs, H. and Arkle, N. (2007) *Accredited Training in Psychosocial Interventions for Psychosis: A National Survey*. London: NIMHE.

Martinez, E., Garcia-Viejo, M. A., Blanch, L. and Gatell, J. M. (2001) Lipodystrophy syndrome in patients with HIV infection: quality of life issues, *Drug Safety*, 24(3): 157–66.

Mason, P. and Brougton, K. (2007) Gypsy/traveller children and families: the potential for working with networks, *Social Policy and Society*, 6(2): 243–53.

Mason, T., William, R. and Vivian-Byrne, S. (2002) Multidisciplinary working in a forensic mental health setting: ethical codes of reference, *Journal of Psychiatric and Mental Health Nursing*, 9(5): 563–72.

Masterson, A. (2002) Cross-boundary working: a macro-political analysis of the impact on professional roles, *Journal of Clinical Nursing*, 11(3): 331–9.

Matrix Knowledge Group (2008) *Dedicated Drug Court Pilots: A Process Report*. London: Ministry of Justice.

Mccallin, A. (2001) Interdisciplinary practice: a matter of teamwork. An integrated literature review, *Journal of Clinical Nursing*, 10(4): 419–28.

McCann, J., James, A., Wilson, S. and Dunn, G. (1996) Prevalence of psychiatric disorders in young people in the care system, *British Medical Journal*, 313: 1529–30.

McCawley, P. F. (undated) *The Logic Model for Programme Planning and Evaluation*. Idaho: University of Idaho Extension.

McLaughlin, H. (2004) Partnerships: panacea or pretence? *Journal of Interprofessional Care*, 18(2): 103–13.

McLeroy, K. R., Barbara, L., Norton, B. L. et al. (2003) Community-based interventions, *American Journal of Public Health*, 93(4): 529–33.

McMunn, A. M., Mwanje, R. and Pozniak, L. (1997) Issues facing Africans in London with HIV infection, *Genitourinary Medicine*, 73(3): 157–8.

McMurray, R. (2006) From partition to partnership: managing collaboration within a curative framework for NHS care, *International Journal of Public Sector Management*, 19(3): 238–49.

MedFASH (Medical Foundation for AIDS and Sexual Health) (2002) *Recommended Standards for NHS HIV Services*. London: MedFASH.

Meichenbaum, D. and Turk, D. C. (1987) Treatment and adherence: terminology, incidence and conceptualisation, *Facilitating Treatment Adherence*. New York: Plenum Press.

Mellins, C. A., Kang, E., Leu, C. S., Havens, J. F. and Chesney, M. A. (2003) Longitudinal study of mental health and psychosocial predictors of medical treatment adherence in mothers living with HIV disease, *AIDS Patient Care and STDs*, 17(8): 407–16.

Merrell, J., Mabbett, G. and Jones, M. (2005) *An evaluation of the volunteers' role in the 'bridging the Gap' project*. Unpublished report for Age Concern Swansea, School of Health Science, Swansea University, Swansea.

Miles, A. (1977) Staff relations in psychiatric hospitals, *British Journal of Psychiatry*, 130(1): 84–8.

Milewa, T., Dowswell, G. and Harrison, S. (2002) Partnerships, power and the 'new' politics of community participation in British health care, *Social Policy and Administration*, 36(7): 796–809.

Miller, W. R. and Rollnick, S. (2002) *Motivational Interviewing: Preparing People for Change*, 2nd edn. New York: The Guilford Press.

Minogue, V. (2000) Effective partnership working: developing a collaborative response to mentally disordered offenders. Unpublished PhD thesis.

Mirrlees-Black, C. (1998) *Domestic Violence: Findings from a New British Crime Survey Self-Completion Questionnaire*, Home Office Research Study 192. London: Home Office.

Molyneux, J. (2001) Interprofessional teamworking: what makes teams work well? *Journal of Interprofessional Care*, 15(1): 29–35.

Morgan, J. (2007) Giving up the culture of blame: risk assessment and risk management in psychiatric practice. Briefing document for the Royal College of Psychiatrists, February, Royal College of Psychiatrists, London.

Morlese, J. (2002) Abnormalities of lipid metabolism and body fat distribution, in B. G. Gazzard (ed.), *AIDS Care Handbook*. London: Mediscript.

Morris, R. (1996) *Factsheet: Travelling People in the United Kingdom*. Cardiff: Traveller Law Research Unit, Cardiff Law School.

Morris, R. and Clements, L. (2001) *Disability, Social Care, Health and Travelling People*. Cardiff: Traveller Law Research Unit, Cardiff Law School

Morrison, S. (2007) Working together: why bother with collaboration, *Work based Learning in Primary Care,* 5(2): 65–70.

Moxon, D. (1999) Criminal Justice Conference: violence against women. *Conference transcript.* Available at: www.homeOffice.gov.uk/domesticviolence

Mullender, A. (1996) *Rethinking Domestic Violence: The Social Work and Probation Response*. London: Routledge.

Munro, E. (2002) *Effective Child Protection*. London: Sage.

Murphy, J. M., Sobol, A. M., Olivier, D. C. et al. (1989) Prodromes of depression and anxiety: the Stirling County study, *British Journal of Psychiatry*, 155: 490–5.

Nabitz, U., Klazinga, N. and Walburg, J. (2000) The EFQM excellence model: European and Dutch experiences with the EFQM approach in health care, *International Journal of Health Care Quality Assurance*, 12(3): 191–201.

NatCen (National Centre for Social Research and the National Foundation for Educational Research for the Department of Health) (2004) *Drug Use, Smoking and Drinking Among Young People in England in 2003*. London: The Stationery Office.

NACRO (National Association for the Care and Resettlement of Offenders) (2005) *Findings of the 2004 Survey of Court Diversion/Criminal Justice Mental Health Liaison Schemes for Mentally Disordered Offenders in England and Wales*. London: NACRO.

NACRO (National Association for the Care and Resettlement of Offenders) (2007) NACRO mental health: frequently asked questions. Available at: www.nacro.org.uk/mhu/about/faqs.htm#q1. (accessed 29 May 2007).

National Assembly for Wales (2001) *Child and Adolescent Mental Health Services: Everybody's Business: Strategy Document,* Sept. Cardiff: National Assembly for Wales.

National Assembly for Wales (2003) *Review of Service Provision for Gypsy Travellers*. Cardiff: National Assembly for Wales.

National Confidential Enquiry (2001) National Confidential Enquiry into suicide and homicide by people with mental illness, *Safety First: Five year Report of the National Confidential Enquiry into Suicide and Homicide by People with Mental Illness*. London: National Confidential Enquiry.

National Confidential Enquiry (2006) National Confidential Enquiry into suicide and homicide by people with mental illness. *Avoidable Deaths: A Five Year Report of the National Confidential Enquiry into Suicide and Homicide by People with Mental Illness*. London: National Confidential Enquiry.

National Statistics (2008) Age-standardised alcohol-related death rates, United Kingdom, 1991 to 2006. Available at: www.statistics.gov.uk/statbase/Product.asp?vlnk=14496 (accessed 20 Mar. 2008).

Nazroo, J. (1997) *Health of Britain's Ethnic Minorities*. London: Policy Studies Institute.

Newburn, T. (1999) Drug prevention and youth justice: issues of philosophy, practice and policy, *British Journal of Criminology*, 39(4): 609–24.

NHS (National Health Service) (1999) *Modern Standards and Service Models: Mental Health National Service Frameworks*. London: Department of Health.

NHS (National Health Service) (2000) *The NHS Plan*. London: Department of Health.

NHS Executive (1998) *In the Public Interest: Developing a Strategy for Public Health Participation in the NHS*. Wetherby: Department of Health.

NHS (National Health Service) Health Advisory Service (1995) *Together We Stand*. London: NHS Health Advisory Service.

Niven, S. and Stewart, D. (2005) *Resettlement Outcomes on Release from Prison*, Findings 248. London: Home Office.

Nixon, E. (2004) The argument for patient and public involvement as an innovation, *HIV Nursing*, 4(4): 10–11.

Nolan, M., Grant, G. and Keady, J. (1996) *Understanding Family Care: A Multidimensional Model of Caring and Coping*. Buckingham: Open University Press.

Nolan, M., Davies, S. and Grant, G. (2001) *Working with Older People and their Families: Key Issues in Policy and Practice*. Buckingham: Open University Press.

Norman, R. (1983) *The Moral Philosophers: An Introduction to Ethics*. Oxford: Clarendon Press.

North Wales Police Community portal (2008) Chief Constable's blog. Available at: www.north-wales.police.uk/portal/blogs/cc/default.aspx

Nutt, D., King, L., Saulsbury, W. and Blakemore, C. (2007) Development of a rational scale to assess the harm of drugs of potential misuse, *Lancet*, 369(9566): 1047–53.

Nye, R. D. (1986) *Three Psychologies: Perspectives from Freud, Skinner and Rogers*. California: Brooks/Cole Publishing Company.

ODPM (Office of the Deputy Prime Minister) (2003) *More than a Roof: A Report into Tackling Homelessness, March 2003*. London: ODPM.

ODPM (Office of the Deputy Prime Minister) (2004a) *Action on Mental Health: A Guide to Promoting Social Inclusion*. London: ODPM.

ODPM (Office of the Deputy Prime Minister) (2004b) *Mental Health and Social Exclusion*. London: ODPM.

ODPM (Office of the Deputy Prime Minister) (2004c) *What is Supporting People?* London: ODPM.

ODPM (Office of the Deputy Prime Minister) (2005) *Sustainable Communities: Settled Homes, Changing Lives*, London: ODPM.

Office for National Statistics (2001a) *2001 Census of Population: First Results on Ethnic Groups and Identity*. Available at: www.wales.gov.uk/keypubstatisticsforwales/index.htm

Office of National Statistics (2001b) *Census 2001*: www.statistics.gov.uk, in M. Oliver and B. Sapey (1999) *Social Work with Disabled People*, 2nd edn. Basingstoke: Macmillan.

Office of National Statistics (2003) *General Household Survey 2003*. London: The Stationery Office.

Office of National Statistics (2006) *Life Expectancy Statistics*. Available at: www.statistics.gov.uk

Office of National Statistics (2008) Internet access. Available at: http://www.statistics.gov.uk/cci/nugget.asp?id=8

Okely, J. (1983) *The Traveller-Gypsies*. Cambridge: Cambridge University Press.

Oliver, M. and Sapey, B. (1999) *Social Work with Disabled People*, 2nd edn. Basingstoke: Macmillan.

Onyett, S. (2003) *Teamworking in Mental Health*. Basingstoke: Palgrave.

Opie, A. (1998) 'Nobody asked me for my view': Users' empowerment by multidisciplinary health teams, *Qualitative Health Research*, 8(2): 188–206.

O'Reilly, R. L. (1994) Viruses and schizophrenia, *Australian and New Zealand Psychiatry*, 28(2): 222.

Owen, J. M. and Rogers, P. J. (1999) *Progam Evaluation: Forms and Approaches*. London: Sage.

Parker, G. (1990) *With Due Care and Attention: A Review of the Research on Informal Care*, 2nd edn. London: Family Policy Studies Centre.

Parker, H., Aldridge, J. and Measham, F. (1998) *Illegal Leisure: The Normalisation of Adolescent Drug Use*. London: Routledge.

Parrott, L., Buchanan, J. and Williams, D. (2006) Volunteers, families and children in need: an evaluation of family, *Friends Child & Family Social Work*, 11: 147–55.

Parry, G., Cleemput, V., Peters, J. et al. (2007) Health status of gypsies and travellers in England, *Journal of Epidemiology and Community Health*, 61(3): 198–204.

Parsons, S. and Barker, P. (2000) The Phil Hearne course: an evaluation of a multidisciplinary mental health education programme for clinical practitioners, *Journal of Psychiatric and Mental Health Nursing* 7(2): 101–8.

Parsons, C. and Castle, F. (1998) Trends in exclusions from school – New Labour, new approaches? *Forum*, 40, (1): 11–14.

Paterson, B. (2001) Myth of empowerment in chronic illness, *Journal of Advanced Nursing*, 34(5): 574–81.

Paterson, D. L., Swindells, S., Mohr, J. et al. (2000) Adherence to protease inhibitor therapy and outcomes in patients with HIV infection, *Annals of Internal Medicine*, 133(1): 21–30.

Patton, M. Q. (1997) *Utilization-focused evaluation: A New Century Text.* London: Sage.

Pavee Point (2002) *Travellers Centre.* Dublin: Pavee Point. Available at: www.paveepoint.ie/

Pawson, R. and Tilley, N. (1997) *Realistic Evaluation.* Thousand Oaks, CA: Sage.

Peatfield, Z. (1998) Social exclusions, *Young Minds Magazine*, May/Jun, 34: 8.

Peay, J. (1999) Thinking horses, not zebras, in D. Webb and R. Harris (eds), *Mentally Disordered Offenders: Managing People Nobody Owns.* London: Routledge.

Peckham, S. and Exworthy, M. (2003) *Primary Care in the UK: Policy, Organisation and Management.* Basingstoke: Palgrave, Macmillan.

Pediatrics (1998) Antiretroviral therapy and medical management of pediatric HIV infection. (report by the Working Group on Antiretroviral Therapy and Medical Management of Infants, Children and Adolescents with HIV infection), *Pediatrics*, 102 (4 Suppl., Part 2): 1005–62.

Pence, G. (1993) Virtue theory, in P. Singer (ed.), *A Companion to Ethics.* Oxford: Blackwell.

Phillips, J. (1994) The employment consequences of caring for older people, *Health and Social Care in the Community*, 2(3): 143–52.

Phillips, J. (2000) Working carers: caring workers, in M. Bernard, J. Phillips, L. Machin and V. Harding-Davies, *Women Ageing: Changing Identities, Challenging Myths.* London: Routledge.

Phillips, J., Bernard, M. and Chittenden, M. (2002) *Juggling Work and Care: The Experiences of Working Carers of Older Adults.* Bristol: The Policy Press.

Pietroni, P. C. (1992) Towards reflective practice – the languages of health and social care, *Journal of Interprofessional Care*, 6(1): 7–16.

Pinching, A. (1998) In it together, *Nursing Standard*, 12(47): 18.

Potts, H. W. W. and Wyatt, J. C. (2002) Survey of doctors' experience of patients using the Internet, *Journal of Medical Internet Research,* 4(1): e5.

Power, R., Tate, H. L., McGill, S. M. and Taylor, C. (2003) A qualitative study of the psychosocial implications of Lipodystrophy Syndrome on HIV positive individuals, *Sexually Transmitted Infections*, 79(2): 137.

Pratt, R. (2003) *HIV and AIDS: A Foundation for Nursing and Health Care Practice.* London: Arnold.

Priestley, M. (1998) Discourse and resistance in care assessment: integrated living and Community Care, *British Journal of Social Work*, 28(5): 659–73.

Priestley, M. (1999) *Disability Politics and Community Care*. London: Jessica Kingsley.

Primary Review (2007) *Community Soundings: The Primary Review Regional Witness Sessions*. Cambridge: University of Cambridge Faculty of Education.

Prochaska, J. O., Norcross, J. C. and Di Clemente, C. C. (1994) *Changing for Good*. New York: William Morrow and Company, Inc.

Pugh, R. (2005) Working in partnership in rural areas, in R. Carnwell and J. Buchanan (eds), *Effective Practice in Health and Social Care A Partnership Approach*. Maidenhead: Open University Press.

Rabkin, J. G. and Chesney, M. (1999) Treatment adherence to new HIV therapies: the Achilles heel of the new therapeutics, in D. G. Ostrow and S. C. Kalichman (eds), *Psychosocial and Public Health Impacts of new HIV Therapies*. New York: Kluwer Academic/Plenum Publishers.

Rabkin, J. G. and Ferrando, S. (1997) A second life agenda: psychiatric research issues raised by protease inhibitor treatments for people with the Human Immunodeficiency Virus or the Acquired Immunodeficiency Syndrome, *Archives of General Psychiatry*, 54(11): 1049–53.

Rabkin, J. G., Ferrando, S. J., Lin, S., Sewell, M. and McElhiney, M. (2000) Psychological effects of ART: a 2-year study, *Psychosomatic Medicine*, 62(3): 413–22.

Race Equality West Midlands (2005) *Gypsies and Travellers: Disadvantages and Discrimination. How Race Equality Councils and Other Voluntary Bodies Can Help*. Birmingham: Race Equality West Midlands.

Ray, M. and Chambers, P. (2007) 'Social work and social gerontology: distant relations or natural allies?' *Generations Review*. Available at: www.britishgerontology.org.uk

RCPCH (Royal College of Paediatrics and Child Health) (2006) *Reducing Mother to Child Transmission of HIV: Update Report of an Intercollegiate Working Party*. Report by the Royal College of Paediatrics and Child Health, Royal College of Midwives, Royal

College of General Practitioners, Royal College of Nursing, Faculty of Public Health, Royal College of Pathologists, Royal College of Obstetricians and Gynaecologists, Royal College of Physicians, Health Protection Agency. London: RCPCH.

Reder, P. and Duncan, S. (2003) Making the most of the Victoria Climbié Inquiry, *Child Abuse Review*, 13(2): 95–11.

Reder, P., Duncan, J. and Grey, M. (1993) *Beyond Blame: Child Abuse Tragedies Revisited*. London: Routledge.

Rees, D. and Smith, S. (1991) Work stress in occupational therapists assessed by the occupational stress indicator, *British Journal of Occupational Therapy*, 54(8): 289–94.

Reeves, S. and Freeth, D. (2006) Re-examining the evaluation of interprofessional education for community mental health teams with a different lens: understanding presage, process and product factors, *Journal of Psychiatric and Mental Health Nursing*, 13(6): 765–70.

Rehm, J., Room, R., Monteiro, M. et al. (2004) 'Alcohol,' in World Health Organization (WHO) (ed.), *Comparative Quantification of Health Risks: Global and Regional Burden of Disease Due to Selected Major Risk Factors*. Geneva: WHO.

Reith, M. (1998) *Community Care Tragedies: A Practice Guide to Mental Health Inquiries*. Birmingham: Venture Press.

Reuter, P. and Stevens, A. (2007) *An Analysis of UK Drug Policy*, London: UK Drug Policy Commission.

Reynolds, G. P. (1989) Beyond the hypothesis: the neurochemical pathology of schizophrenia, 155: 305–16.

Rhodes, D. (2003) *Better Informed? Inspection of the Management and Use of Information in Social Care*. London: Department of Health.

Ritchie, J. H., Dick, D. and Lingham, R. (1994) *Report of the Inquiry into the Care and Treatment of Christopher Clunis*. London: HMSO.

Roberts, K. (2002) Exploring participation: older people on discharge from hospital, *Journal of Advanced Nursing*, 40(4): 413–20.

Roberts, K. J. (1999) Patient empowerment in the United States: a critical commentary, *Health Expectations: An International Journal of Public Participation in Health Care and Health Policy*, 2(2): 82–92.

Roberts, A., Lewis, H., Degale, J. and Wilkinon, C. (2004) *Coronary Heart Disease and Gypsy/Travellers: Redressing the balance: Annual Report 2003–2004 Welsh Assembly Government IIH Fund*. Cardiff: Welsh Assembly.

Robinson, M. and Cottrel, D. (2005) Health professionals in multi-disciplinary and multi-agency teams: changing professional practice, *Journal of Interprofessional Care*, 19(6): 547–60.

Roche, M. (2004) Complicated problems, complicated solutions? Homelessness and joined-up policy responses, *Social Policy and Administration*, 38(7): 758–74.

Rodgers, B. L. (2000) Concept analysis: an evolutionary view, in B. L. Rodgers and K. A. Knafl (eds), *Concept Development in Nursing: Foundations, Techniques and Applications*, 2nd edn. Philadelphia: Saunders, pp 77–102.

Roe, S. and Man, L. (2006). Drug misuse declared: findings from the 2005/06 British Crime Survey, *Home Office Statistical Bulletin 15/06*. London: Home Office.

Rolls, L., Davis, E. and Coupland, K. (2002) Improving serious mental illness through interprofessional education, *Journal of Psychiatric and Mental Health Nursing*, 9(3): 317–24.

Rose, V. (1993) On the road, *Health Visitor*, 89(33): 30–1.

Rough Sleepers Unit (1999) *Coming in from the Cold: The Government's Strategy on Rough Sleeping*. London: Department of the Environment, Transport and the Regions.

Rough Sleepers Unit (2000) *Coming in from the Cold: Progress Report on the Government's Strategy on Rough Sleeping*, London: Department of the Environment, Transport and the Regions.

Rural Media (2004) *The Travellers Times*, Summer, 20. Hereford: The Rural Media Company.

Saltus, R., Hawthorn, K., Karani, G. et al. (2005) *Scoping Study to Explore the Feasibility of a Health and Social Care Research and Development Network Covering Black and Minority Ethnic Groups in Wales: Report for Wales Office of Research and Development*. Available at: www.wedhs.org.uk

SANE, (2008) SANEmail 'tap into help online'. Available at: www.sane.org.uk/app/webroot/DiscussionBoard/

Scottish Executive (2002) *'It's Everyone's Job to Make Sure I'm Alright': Report of the Child Protection Audit and Review*. Edinburgh: Scottish Government.

Scottish Executive (2006) *Good Practice Guidance for working with Children and Families affected by Substance Misuse: Getting Our Priorities Right*. Edinburgh: Scottish Executive.

Scriven, M. (1967) *The Methodology of Evaluation: Perspectives on Curriculum Evaluation*, AERA Monograph Series on Curriculum Evaluation, No. 1. Chicago, IL: Rand McNally.

Scriven, M. (1980) *The Logic of Evaluation*. California: Edgepress.

Secker, J. and Hill, K. (2001) Broadening the partnerships: experiences of working across community agencies, *Journal of Interprofessional Care*, 15(4): 341–50.

Senior, P., Buchanan, J., Baker, S. and Evans, M. (2007) *Process and Outcome Evaluation of Dawn Project*. Sheffield: Hallam Centre for Community Justice.

SEU (Social Exclusion Unit) (1998) *Rough Sleeping*. London: Cabinet Office.

SEU (Social Exclusion Unit) (2001) *A New Commitment to Neighbourhood Renewal*. London: Office of the Deputy Prime Minister.

SEU (Social Exclusion Unit) (2002) *Reducing Re-offending by Ex-prisoners*. London: Available at: www.socialexclusionunit.gov.uk/reduce_reoff/rr_main.pdf

SEU (Social Exclusion Unit) (2004) *Breaking the Cycle – Taking Stock of Progress and Priorities for the Future*. London: Office of the Deputy Prime Minister.

SEU (Social Exclusion Unit) (2005) *Improving Services, Improving Lives: Evidence and Key Themes. A Social Exclusion Unit Interim Report*. London: Office of the Deputy Prime Minister.

Sharkey, S. B. and Sharples, A. (2003) The impact on work related stress of mental health teams following team based learning on clinical risk management, *Journal of Psychiatric and Mental Health Nursing*, 10(1): 73–81.

Shaw, I. and Faulkner, A. (2006) Practitioner evaluation at work, *American Journal of Evaluation*, 27(1): 44–63.

Shelter (2007) *Homelessness Strategies*. Available at: http://england.shelter.org.uk/policy/policy-6691.cfm (accessed 28 Oct. 2007).

Sheppard, D. (1996) *Learning the Lessons: Mental Health Inquiry Reports Published in England and Wales between 1969 and 1996 and their Recommendations for Improving Practice*, 2nd edn. London: Zito Trust.

Sherer, R., Stieglitz, K., Narra, J. et al. (2002) HIV multidisciplinary teams work: support services improve access to and retention in HIV primary care, *AIDS Care*, 14 (1): S31–44.

Sherr, L. (2000) Adherence – sticking to the evidence, *AIDS Care*, 12(4): 373–6.

Simpson, E. L. and House, A. O. (2002) Involving users in the delivery and evaluation of mental health services: systematic review, *British Medical Journal*, 325, 1265–70.

Singh, N., Squier, C., Sivek, C. et al. (1996) Determinants of compliance with antiretroviral therapy in patients with HIV: prospective assessment with implications for enhancing compliance, *AIDS Care*, 8(3): 261–9.

Singleton, N., Meltzer, H. and Gatward, R. (2000) *Psychiatric Morbidity Among Prisoners*. London: Office for National Statistics.

Smaje, C. (1995) *Health, Race and Ethnicity*. London: King's Fund Institute.

SCIE (Social Care Institute for Excellence) (2007). *Participation: Finding Out What Difference it Makes*. London: SCIE.

Social Trends (2007) *Social Trends*. London: The Stationery Office.

Soothill, K., Mackay, L. and Webb, C. (1995) Troubled times: the context for interprofessional collaboration? in K. Soothill, L. Mackay and C. Webb (eds), *Interprofessional Relations in Health Care*. London: Edward Arnold.

Sowell, R. L., Phillips, K. D. and Grier, J. (1998) Restructuring life to face the future: the perspective of men after a positive response to protease inhibitor therapy, *AIDS Patient Care and STDs,* 12(1): 33–42.

Spratt, T. (2001) The Influence of Child Protection Orientation on Child Welfare Practice, *British Journal of Social Work,* 31(6): 933–54.

Squire, S., Greco, M., O'Hagan, B., Dickinson, K., and Wall, D. (2006) Being patient-centered: creating health care for our grandchildren, *Clinical Governance,* 11(1): 8–9.

SSI (Social Services Inspectorate) (1996) *A Matter of Chance for Carers.* London: HMSO.

Stahr, H., Bulman, B. and Stead, M. (2000) *The Excellence Model in the Health Service: Sharing Good Practice.* Chichester: Kingsham.

Staite, C., Martin, N., Bingham, M. and Daly, R. (1994) *Diversion from Custody for Mentally Disordered Offenders.* Harlow: Longman.

Staley, K. and Minogue, V. (2006) User involvement leads to more ethically sound research, *Clinical Ethics,* 1.

Stanko, E. (2000) *The Day to Count.* Available at: www.domesticviolencedata.org

Stark, S., Stronach, I. and Warne, T. (2002) Teamwork in mental health: rhetoric and reality, *Journal of Psychiatric and Mental Health Nursing* 9(4): 411–18.

Steel, R. (2004) *Involving Marginalised and Vulnerable People in Research: A Consultation Document.* Available at: www.involve.org.uk

Steen, R. G., Mull, C., McClure, R., Hamer, R. M. and Lieberman, J. A. (2006) Brain volume in first episode schizophrenia, *British Journal of Psychiatry,* 188: 510–18.

Stevens, A. (2007) When two dark figures collide: evidence and discourse on drug-related crime, *Critical Social Policy,* 27(1) 77–99.

Stewart, M. J. and Reutter, L. (2001) Fostering partnerships between peers and professionals, *Canadian Journal of Nursing Research,* 33(1): 97–116

Stone, V. E., Hogan, J. W., Shuman, P. et al. (2001) Antiretroviral regimen complexity, self-reported adherence and HIV patients' understanding of their regimens: survey of women in HER study, *Journal of Acquired Immune Deficiency Syndromes,* 28(2): 124–31.

Straussner, S. L. A. and Fewell, C. H. (2006) *Impact of Substance Abuse on Children and Families: Research and Practice Implications.* Philadelphia: Haworth Press Inc.

Streetly, A. (1987) Health care for travellers: one year's experience, *British Medical Journal,* 294: 492–4.

Swindlehurst, H. (2003) Rural Proofing for Health: Analysis of the Consultation with Primary Care Trusts. London: Institute of Rural Health. Available at: www.ruralhealth-goodpractice.org.uk

Tarrier, N., Barrowclough, C. and McGovern, J. (1999) The dissemination of innovative cognitive behavioural psychosocial treatments for schizophrenia, *Journal of Mental Health*, 8(6): 569–82.

Taylor, B. (2001) HIV, stigma and health: integration of theoretical concepts and the lived experience of individuals, *Journal of Advanced Nursing*, 35(5): 792–8.

Taylor, P. J. and Gunn, J. (1999) Homicides by people with mental illness: myth and reality, *The British Journal of Psychiatry*, 174: 1–14.

Taylor, I. and Le Riche, P. (2006) What do we know about partnership with service users and carers in social work education and how robust is the evidence base? *Health and Social Care in the Community*, 14(5): 418–25.

Tempest, S. and Mcintyre, A. (2006) Using the ICF to clarify team roles and demonstrate clinical reasoning in stroke rehabilitation, *Disability and Rehabilitation*, 28(10): 663–7.

Templeton, L., Zohhadi, S., Galvani, S. and Velleman, R., (2006) '*Looking Beyond Risk: Parental Substance Misuse. Scoping Study.* Edinburgh: Scottish Executive.

Texas SAP (2008) Texas Student Assistance Program Initiative. Available at: www.studentassistance.org/frameabout.html (accessed 21 Apr. 2008).

Theobald, N. (2002) Caring in the community, in B.G. Gazzard (ed.), *AIDS Care Handbook*. London: Mediscript.

Thompson, J. and Martin, F. (2005). *Strategic Management. Awareness and Change.* 5th Edn. London: Thomson.

Thornicroft, G. (1991) Social deprivation and rates of treated mental disorder: developing statistical models to predict psychiatric service utilisation, *British Journal of Psychiatry*, 158: 475–84.

Tighe, J., Henderson, C. and Thornicroft, G. (2002) Mentally disordered offenders and models of community care, in A. Buchanan (ed.), *Care of the Mentally Disordered Offender*. Oxford: Oxford University Press.

Townend, M. (2005) Interprofessional supervision from the perspectives of both mental health nurses and other professionals in the field of cognitive behavioural psychotherapy, *Journal of Psychiatric and Mental Health Nursing*, 12(5): 582–8.

Townsend, P., Davidson, N. and Whitehead, M. (1988) *Inequalities in Health: The Black Report and The Health Divide*. Harmondsworth: Penguin.

Townsend, P., Phillimore, P. and Beattie, A. (1988) *Health and Deprivation: Inequality and the North*. London: Routledge.

Treasury The (2005) *Supporting Parents: The Best Start for Children*. London: The Stationery Office.

Trainor, A. and Ezer, H. (2000) Rebuilding life: the experience of living with AIDS after facing imminent death, *Qualitative Health Research*, 10(5): 646–60.

Tunnard, J. (2002) Parental drug misuse: a review of impact and intervention studies, *Research in Practice*. Available at: www.rip.org.uk

Turner, B. S. (1987) *Medical Power and Social Knowledge*. London: Sage.

Twigg, J. (ed.) (1992) *Carers: Research and Practice*. London: HMSO.

Twigg, J. and Aitken, K. (1994) *Carers Perceived: Policy and Practice in Informal Care*. Buckingham: Open University Press.

Tym, R. and Partners (2006) *Local Evaluation for Regeneration Partnerships: Good Practice Guide*. London: Department of the Environment, Transport and Regions.

Tyrer, P. and Steinberg, D. (2005) *Models for Mental Disorder*. Brighton: John Wiley and Sons.

UK Collaborative Group for HIV and STI (Sexually Transmitted Infections) Surveillance (2006). A Complex Picture: HIV and other sexually transmitted infections in the United Kingdom. London: Centre for Infections, Health Protection Agency. Centre for Infections. Available at: www.hpa.org.uk/publications/2006/hiv_sti_2006/contents.htm (accessed Nov. 2006).

UKDPC (UK Drug Policy Commission) (2008). *Reducing Drug Use: Reducing Reoffending*. London: UKDPC.

Ungerson, C. (1987) *Policy is Personal: Sex, Gender and Informal Care*. London: Tavistock.

United Nations (1948) *Universal Declaration of Human Rights*. Available at: www.unhchr.ch/udhr (accessed 10 May 2001).

University of York, (1999) *CRD Report 15: Systematic Review of the International Literature on the Epidemiology of Mentally Disordered Offenders*. York: NHS Centre for Reviews and Dissemination, University of York.

University of York (2000) *CRD Report 16: Scoping Review of Literature on the Health and Care of Mentally Disordered Offenders*. York: NHS Centre for Reviews and Dissemination (CRD), University of York.

UNODC United Nations Office for Drugs and Crime) (2007) World Drugs Report 2007. Available at: www.unodc.org/pdf/research/wdr07/WDR_2007.pdf

Vernon, D. (1994) The health of traveller-gypsies, *British Journal of Nursing*, 3(18): 969–72.

WAFE (Women's Aid Federation of England) (2006) *2005 Survey of Domestic Violence Services Findings*. Available at: www.womenaid.org.uk.

WAG (2006) *National Service Framework for Children, Young People and Maternity Services in Wales*, Feb. CMK-22–12–051.

Wagner, E. F., Tubman, J. G. and Gil, A. G. (2004) Implementing school-based substance abuse interventions: methodological dilemmas and recommended solutions, *Addiction*, 99(Suppl. 2): 106–19.

Walby, S. (2004) *The Cost of Domestic Violence*. London: Women and Equality Unit.

Walker, L. O. and Avant, K. C. (1995) *Strategies of Theory Construction in Nursing*, 3rd edn. London: Norwalk SCT Appleton and Lange.

Warner, L. and Hoadley, A. (2004) Blocked pathways, *Health Service Journal* 114: 36.

Watkins, C. (1994) Student support groups: help and healing through the education system, *International Schools Journal*, 27: 7–14.

Watkins, C. (1999) *Student Assistance Program Training*. Phoenix, AZ: Student Assistance Training International.

Watkins, C. (2008) International Student Assistance Programme Training. Available at: www.cwsap.com/ (accessed 30 Apr. 2008).

Watson, J., Global Partners and Associates (2006) Whose Rights Are They Anyway? Carers and the Human Rights Act. Available at: www.carersuk.org/policyandpractice

Watson, S. and Austerberry, H. (1986) *Housing and Homelessness: A Feminist Perspective*. London: Routledge and Kegan Paul.

Weare, K. (2000) *Promoting Mental, Emotional and Social Health: A Whole School Approach*. London: Routledge.

Webb, A. (1991) Co-ordination: a problem in public sector management, *Policy and Politics*, 19(4): 229–42.

Weiss, C. H. (1995) Nothing as practical as a good theory: exploring theory-based evaluation, in J. P. Connell, A. C. Kubisch, L. B. Schorr and C. H. Weiss (eds), *New Approaches to Evaluating Community Initiatives: Concepts, Methods and Contexts*. Washington, DC: The Aspen Institute.

Weiss, E. S., Miller Anderson, R. and Lasker, R. D. (2002) Partnership functioning: making the most of collaboration: exploring the relationship between partnership synergy and implications for research and practice, *Health Education Behaviour*, 29(6): 683–98.

Weiss, L., French, T., Finkelstein, R., Mukherjee, R. and Agins, B. (2003) HIV-related knowledge and Adherence to ART, *AIDS Care*, 15(5): 673–9.

Welsh Assembly Government (1998) *Better Health: Better Wales*. Cardiff: Welsh Assembly Government.

Welsh Assembly Government (2001) *Better Wales: Plan for Wales*. Cardiff: Welsh Assembly Government.

Welsh Assembly Government (2002) *National Service Framework for Mental Health*. Welsh Assembly Government, Cardiff

Welsh Assembly Government (2005) *National Service Framework for Children, Young People and Maternity Services*. Cardiff: Welsh Assembly Government.

Welsh Assembly Government (2006) *National Service Framework for Older People*. Cardiff: Welsh Assembly Government.

Welsh Assembly Government (2007) Fulfilled Lives, Supportive Communities. Available at: http://new.wales.gov.uk/topics/health/publications/health_social_care_strategies/fulfilledlives/?lang=en

Welsh Assembly Government (2008) Working Together to Reduce Harm: The Substance Misuse Strategy for Wales 2008–2018. Available at: http://tiny.cc/6frOg

White, J. (2001) Sharing the care of children with HIV infection, *Nursing Standard*, 15(20): 42–6.

WHO/UNICEF (1978) *Primary Health Care: Report of the International Conference on Primary Care*, Alma Ata USSR, 6–12 Sept. Geneva: WHO/UNICEF.

Wibberley, G. (1986) *A Report on the Analysis of Response to Consultation on the Operation of The Caravan Sites Act 1968*. London: Department of Education. Available at: www scotland.gov.uk/kd01/blue/moving-10.htm-30k

Williams, B. (2002) Using collage art work as a common medium for communication in interprofessional workshops, *Journal of Interprofessional Care*, 16(1): 53–8.

Williams, A., Merrell, J., Jones, M. et al. (2002) Evaluation of Caerphilly Sure Start and children and youth programmes. Unpublished report for Caerphilly County Borough Council, School of Health Science, Swansea University.

Wilson, R. and Lewis, H (2006) *A Part of Society Refugees and Asylum Seekers Volunteering in the UK*. Leeds: Tandem.

Wimbush, E. and Watson, J. (2000) An evaluation framework for health promotion: theory, quality and effectiveness, *Evaluation*, 6(3): 301–21.

Wincup, E. and Norvell, S. (2004) *Accommodating the Needs of Female Offenders: Report to the East of England Region of the National Probation Service*. Cambridge: East of England Region of the National Probation Service.

Wincup, E., Buckland, G. and Bayliss, R. (2003) *Youth Homelessness and Substance Use: A Report to the Drugs and Alcohol Research Unit*. Home Office Research Study No. 258. London: Home Office.

Wolff, N. (2002) (New) public management of mentally disordered offenders Part II: A vision with promise, *International Journal of Law and Psychiatry*, 25: 427–44.

Women's Unit (1999) *Tackling Violence Against Women*. London: Cabinet Office.

Woolf, S. H., Chan, E. C., Harris, R. et al. (2005) Promoting informed choice: transforming health care to dispense knowledge for decision making, *Annals of Internal Medicine*, 143(4): 293–300.

WHO World Health Organization (1995) *Global School Health Initiative*. Available at: www.who.int/school_youth_health/gshi/en/ (accessed 9 Nov. 2007).

Wright, N., Tompkins, C. and Oldham, N. (2004) Homelessness and health: what can be done in general practice? *Journal of the Royal Society of Medicine*, 97(4): 170–3.

Wyner, R. (2005) Working together with people who are homeless, in R. Carnwell and J. Buchanan (eds) *Effective Practice in Health and Social Care: A Partnership Approach*, 1st edn. Maidenhead: Open University Press.

Zubin, J. and Spring, B. (1977) Vulnerability: a new view of schizophrenia, *Journal of Abnormal Psychology*, 86(2): 103–24.

Zwarenstein, M. and Reeves, S. (2006) Knowledge translation and interprofessional collaboration: where the rubber of evidence based care hits the road of teamwork, *Journal of Continuing Education in the Health Professions*, 26(1): 46–54.

Index

The index entries appear in word-by-word alphabetical order.

AIDS, *see* HIV/AIDS
Anxiety, institutional 94
Arnstein's ladder of citizen participation
    13–14, 35–6
Behavioural problems, classroom, *see*
    Classroom behavioural problems
Best practice development 289–94
Black and minority ethnic (BME) groups:
    and domestic violence 182–3
    equality legislation 33–4
    personal account of service use 251–62
    population statistics 32
    rural service provision 45–6
    staff training issues 39
    see also Disadvantaged groups
Boundaries, partnership 291
Building Bridges 217, 218, 282, 284
Candour 58
Care pathways 86
Carer partnerships 97–9, 101–9
    carer expertise 106
    carer models 104–6
    diversity of 99–101
    employment 100, 103, 104, 108–9
    evaluation of 107
    good practice development 107–9
    national statistics 99
    power balance 103–5, 107
Carers and Disabled Children Act (2000)
    97, 102–3
Carer's assessments 97, 98, 102–3, 107
Carers (Recognitions and Services) Act
    (1995) 97
Caring:
    costs and benefits of 100–1
    social and legal context of 97–103,
        282, 284
    temporality of 106, 107
Child protection 65–79
    case range 68, 74
child poverty 68
Children and Young Person's Plans
    (CYPP) 72, 77
Common Assessment Framework (CAF)
    72–3, 77
domestic violence 180–1
families in need perspective 69, 146

Integrated Children's System (ICS) 73
inter-professional barriers 68, 74
inter-professional communication 65–7,
    73–8
    Laming Inquiry 65, 66–7, 75, 78, 146
local safeguarding children boards
    (LSCBs) 71, 73, 76, 77
    partnership working improvement
        strategies 77–8
    post-Laming Inquiry policy
        development 68–71, 77, 284
    professional defensiveness 146, 156
resources 67, 68, 69, 74
service integration 71–2
    service user participation 74–5
system complexity 67–8, 74–5
training 67, 68, 75–6, 77–8
see also Child protection and problem
    drug use; Children's services
Child protection and problem drug use
    143–59
    attitudes and values 150–1, 157
    case study 154–5
    confidentiality 152
    focus of intervention 148, 157
    inter-professional issues 148–50, 157
    inter-professional training 153–5, 157
    parental engagement 156–7
    parents' perspectives 155–6, 157–8
    practice guidelines 147–8
    professional knowledge 151–2, 157
    professional perspectives 145–6, 150–5
    roles and boundaries 152
    social exclusion 143–5
    statistics 147
    see also Child protection; Children's
        services; Problem drug use
Children Act (2004) 68, 69, 70–1, 162
Children and Young Person's Plans
    (CYPP) 72, 77
Children's Plan, The 162
Children's services:
    Common Assessment Framework
        (CAF) 72–3, 77
    and emotional health 161–2
    Integrated Children's System (ICS) 73
    integration of 71–2, 74, 283, 284

inter-professional communication
   issues 65–7, 73–8
inter-professional training 67, 68,
   75–6, 77–8, 153–5, 157
   policy developments in 67, 68–71, 77,
     161–2, 284
   whole school initiatives 162–3
   see also Child protection; Child
     protection and problem drug use;
     Student Assistance Programmes
Citizen participation:
   Arnstein's ladder of 13–14, 35–6
   see also Service user involvement
Classroom behavioural problems:
   causes of 160–1
   whole school intiatives 162–3
   see also Student Assistance
     Programmes
Climbie, Victoria, *see* Laming Inquiry
Clinical supervision 93–4
Collaboration:
   context of 10
   definitions of 8–9, 10
   and partnership similarities 281–3
   terminology 3–4
Collaboration concept analysis:
   antecedents 9, 18
   attributes 8–9, 14–15
   consequences 9, 20
   empirical referents 20
   model, related and contrary cases
     16–18
Colwell, Maria 65
Commitment 7, 291
Common Assessment Framework (CAF)
   72–3, 77
Communication:
   in child protection 65–7, 73–8
   and disease classification 85
   electronic forms of 29–30, 290
   partnership development 289–90
Community Care Needs Assessment
   Project (CCNAP) 40
Competence 58–9, 285–6
see also expertise
Confidence, professional 86–7, 229
Confidentiality 19, 44, 58, 60, 152, 293
   HIV/AIDS care issues 230, 233, 241,
     243
Coventry Domestic Violence Partnership
   13, 185–90, 191, 192, 285
Creating Capable Teams (CCT) 93
Crime and Disorder Act 1998 178

Criminal Justice and Public Order
   Act 1994 198
Defensiveness, professional 87, 146, 156
Deontology 50–1
Diligence 59
Disability:
   equality legislation 33–4
   personal account of service use 251–62
   population statistics 32
   see also Disadvantaged groups
Disadvantaged groups:
   definition of 32
   equality/discrimination legislation
     33–4, 198–9, 281
   involvement promotion 39–40, 286–7
   personal capacity building 41–3
   rural service provision 45–6
   staff training role 39
Discretion 60
Discrimination laws 33–4, 198–9, 281
Domestic violence 177–94
   case study 187–8
   and child abuse 180–1
   coordinator role 185–6
   Coventry Domestic Violence
     Partnership 13, 185–90, 191, 192,
     285
   cultural context 182–3
   extent of 179–80
   forms of 180
   and pregnancy 181
   productive partnership 184–5, 190–3
   social and political context 177–9,
     193, 284
   staff training 181–2
   summary of 183–4
   and vulnerable adult abuse 183
Drug use, *see* Child protection and
   problem drug use; Problem drug use;
   Recreational drug use
Drugs Act (2005) 112
Employer–employee partnership 58,
   257–8
Equality legislation 33–4
see also Discrimination laws
Ethical issues 47–62, 285
   case study 49–50, 57
   ethics/morals distinction 48
   fiduciary relationship 55–6
   in inter-professional practice 47–8,
     53–5, 56–61, 285
   professional virtues 56, 58–61
   and schools of philosophical thought
     50–1

Ethical partnerships 13
Evaluation 107, 263–80, 293–4
   causes of success attribution problems
      269, 270
   example of 273–4
   formative/process 264, 267
   funding and timescale problems
      269–70
   independent 264–5
   multi-method, multi-level approach
      271–4, 278
   planning for 271
   practitioner involvement in 265, 279
   process of 265–6
   programme logic modelling 267–9,
      278
   realistic evaluation approach 274–5,
      277–8, 279
   research deficit 35
   service user involvement in 35, 38–9,
      46, 265, 279
   success measurement problems 269,
      270–1
   summative/outcome 264, 266–7
   terminology definitions 263–4, 266
   theories of change approach 274–7,
      279
Every Child Matters 68, 70, 162, 284
Expertise:
   carer 106
   limit recognition 53, 59, 301
   patient 245, 244, 240
   rural services 45–6
Fairness 60
Family work 89, 94
Fiduciary relationship 55–6
Financial issues:
   mentally disordered offenders' care
      216, 221, 227
   partnership evaluation 269–70, 279
   rural services 44, 45
Gypsy travellers 195–208
   a coronary heart disease project 203–7
   cultural identity of 199–201
   health care access issues 202–3
   historical legislation 196, 197, 281
   mental health issues 204, 205
   Multi-agency traveller Forums 202–7,
      208
   origins of 195–6
   population statistics 196
   recent legislation and effects 198–9
   Romany (Gypsy) history 197
   staff training 206–7, 208

   see also Disadvantaged groups
Health and Social Care Act (2001) 38, 284
HIV/AIDS care
   Antiretroviral therapy (ART) 229,
      235–42, 244
   conception, pregnancy and childbirth
      234–5
   confidentiality issues 230, 233, 241,
      243
   crossing care boundaries 230–3
   diagnostic non-disclosure 238, 239,
      241–2
   disease prevalence 228
   need diversity 229
   organization partnerships 242–4
   service user involvement 244–6
   social exclusion problems 230
   specialist training/support 231, 236–7,
      242–4
   stigmatization issues 230, 242–3, 244
   team members and roles 230–3, 240–1
Homelessness 129–42
   housing access barriers 133–5
   meaning of 129–30
   and multiple need 132–3, 136–8
   offender resettlement 139–41
   partnership typology 138–9
   partnership working 138–41
   policy developments 131–2
   prevalence of 130–1
   rough sleepers 130, 131, 133, 135
   service provision forms 135, 136–8
   service user engagement 138
   statutory 130, 133–4
   voluntary–statutory sector
      relationship 134, 137–8
   see also Disadvantaged groups
Homelessness Act (2002) 131, 134, 139
Honesty 58
Human Rights Act (1998) 103, 198–9
Identity:
in partnership 11–12, 292
see also Professional identity
Ideological partnerships 12–13
Independence, Well-being and Choice 102
Information technology and the Internet
   22–30
   active/passive usage 23
   communication tools 28–30
   health information journey 22–3, 24
   information quality and interpretation
      23–5, 28, 30
   Internet access issues 25–6

in partnership working 28, 29, 30, 285, 286
and patient–practitioner relationships 26–7, 285, 286–7
technical competence 26
usage statistics 22–3
virtual communities 28–30
Integrated Children's System (ICS) 73
Internet, the *see* Information technology and the Internet
Joint working 282–3, 285
in children's services 71–2, 74, 283, 284
in health and criminal justice 217–20, 221, 224–5, 283
in partnership and collaboration concepts 8, 9, 14, 15
in rural areas 44
see also Partnership working
Laming Inquiry 65, 66–7, 75, 78, 146
subsequent legislation and guidance 68–71, 77, 274
Local safeguarding children boards (LSCBs) 71, 73, 76, 77
Local strategic partnerships 44–5
Loyalty 59
McNaughton Rules 213, 227
Mental Health Act (1983) 86, 211, 213, 227
reform of 215
Mental health services 80–95
assertive community treatment approach 84, 90
care pathways 86
clinical supervision 93–4
effective teamwork examples 83
and Gypsy travellers 204, 205
inter-professional education 93
Mental Health Act (1983) 86, 211, 213, 215, 227
multi-disciplinary team (MDT) models 87–91
National Service Framework for Mental Health 92, 97, 215, 217
partnership evaluation example 94, 273–4
role changes 92–3, 284–5
strategic and political context 80–1, 284
successful team attributes 85–6, 94
team conflict 83–7, 90
team leadership 81–2
whole systems working 91–2

see also Mentally disordered offenders' care
Mentally disordered offenders' care 209–27
Building Bridges 217, 218, 282, 284
court diversion schemes 215–16
crime and mental disorder relationship 210, 211–12, 227
criminal justice/health services boundary 210–11
future partnership development 225–6
holistic partnership provision 220–2
inter-agency response development 214–17
joint working arrangements 217–20, 220, 221, 224–5, 283
McNaughton Rules 213, 227
Multi-agency Public Protection Arrangements (MAPPA) 211, 222, 227
panel assessment schemes 215
Reed Report 209, 212, 218, 283
related statistics 213–14
risk management 222
service user involvement 222–4, 225–6
terminology 211–14
victim involvement 225
Misuse of Drugs Act (MDA) 1971 111–12
Models:
carer 104–6
multi-disciplinary team 87–91
partnership working 35–7
Morals, and ethics distinction 48
Multi-agency inertia 290–1
Multi-agency Public Protection Arrangements (MAPPA) 211, 222, 227
National Service Frameworks 34
for Children, Young People and Maternity Services 162
for Mental Health 92, 97, 215, 217
for Older People 96, 97, 284
National Strategy for Carers 97, 99, 101–2, 106, 282
Negotiation 14
New ways of working programme 93
NHS and Community Care Act (1990) 97, 105
Offenders:
resettlement of 139–41
see also Mentally disordered offenders' care
Older people:
informal/formal care interface 96–110
involvement of 96

key policies and implications 284
National Service Framework for 96, 97, 284
population statistics 32
rural care needs study 42–3
see also Carer Partnerships; Caring; Disadvantaged groups
Partnership:
    collaboration similarities 281–3
    context of 6–7
    definitions of 6–7, 8–9
    process of 13, 14
    terminology of 3–4
    types of 12–14
Partnership concept analysis:
    antecedents 9, 18
    attributes 8–9, 11–14
    consequences 9, 18–19
    definitions 6–7, 8–9
    empirical referents 20
    model, related and contrary cases 16–17
Partnership working:
    benefits and challenges summary 285–7
    fluid nature of 287
    inter-professional practice context 51–4
    necessity of 288
    policy context of 34–5
    promotion of 31–46
    see also Joint working
Patient participation, *see* Service user involvement
Personal capacity building 41–3
Philosophy, and partnerships 4–5
Philosophical thought, schools of 50–1
Policy:
    in children's services 67, 68–71, 77, 161–2, 284
    and collaboration 10
    drug use 111–13
    homelessness 131–2
    key policies and implications 284
    in mental health services 80–1, 284
    partnership working emphasis 4–5, 6–7, 34–5, 37–8, 52, 283–5
Poverty:
    child 68
    and health 32
    see also Disadvantaged groups
Power imbalance 103–4, 107, 293
Power sharing 14, 36, 293

Prisoners, *see* Mentally disordered offenders' care; Offenders
Problem drug use 111–16, 118–28
case study 124–5
components of 121–4
    and crime relationship 118–19
    daily cycle of 12
and inter-professional partnerships 121, 126–8
legal/illegal divide 113–14, 144
    legal policy context 111–13
personal account of 253, 255–6
    prevalence 144
    risks 114–17, 144
    social exclusion 119–21, 143–5
treatment approaches 125–6
see also Child protection and problem drug use
Problem oriented partnerships 12
Problem-specific professions 5
Professional identity:
    confidence in 86–7, 229
    erosion of 11–12, 19
    and inter-professional respect 282
    and language use 17–18, 19, 84–5
    and status 75
Professional practice:
    challenges to 47–8
    culture change in 38–41, 52
    stereotyping of 16
Project partnership 12
Race Relations Amendment Act (2000) 198
Recreational drug use:
    legal/illegal divide 113–14
    perceived problems 116–18
    prevalence of 117
    risks of 114–16, 117
    see also Problem drug use
Reed Review 209, 212, 218, 283
Refocusing projects 91
Respect 281–2, 290
Responsibility, distributed 93
Role boundary conflicts 19
Role changes 92–3
Role convergence 11–12, 19
Rural proofing 46
Rural services 31–2, 43–6
    financial issues 44, 45
    older people care needs study 42–3
    partnership working extent 44–5
    staff expertise 45–6

Safeguarding children, *see* Child
    protection; Child protection and
    problem drug use; Children's services
Scepticism, to partnership approach 19
Service access 288–9
    personal account of 255, 256–7, 261
Service delivery:
    key policies and implications 284
    manner of 262, 292
    shared interest in 291
    three levels of 287
Service design, problem oriented 4–5
Service Level Agreements (SLAs) 10
Service provision 18–19
    and quantitative targets 259–60, 261
Service user involvement 13–14, 285,
    286, 287, 293
    Arnstein's ladder of citizen
        participation 13–14, 35–6
    in child protection 74–5, 156–7
    continuum of involvement 17
    and culture change 38–41
    effectiveness evaluation 35, 38–9, 46,
        265, 279
    guidance resources 40
    institutional types 36–7
    patient participation concept analysis
        17
    personal account of 251–62
    rules of engagement 40
    statutory duty of 37–8, 284
training 41
Service users:
    empowerment of 4–5, 26–7, 39, 52–3,
        285, 286
    expertise of 106, 240, 244, 245, 285
    reflective account of 251–62
Social exclusion 32–4
    and children's emotional health 161
    definition of 32–3
    HIV/AIDS 230
    homelessness 131, 132
    problem drug use 119–21
    see also Disadvantaged groups
Staff training, *see* Training
Student Assistance Programmes (SAPs)
    163–76
    advisory group formation 164
    boundary transitions 172–3
    Caerphilly case study 168, 174–5
    community networking 167
    curriculum infusion 167, 171
    evaluation of 167, 172
    Kirklees case study 168, 173–4

leadership and administration 167
parental and community involvement
    166–7, 173
participant identification and referral
    165
policy targets 175
prevention activities 166, 171
relationship building skills 172
staff training 165, 170
staff wellness 168, 171
support groups 165–6, 169–70, 173,
    174
Wrexham case study 168–73
Support groups 25, 29–30
    in Student Assistance Programmes
        165–6, 169–70, 173, 174
Supporting People programme 132
Targets, quantitative 259–60, 261
Teamwork 283, 285–6
    collaborative education 93
    conflict 83–7
    success factors 85–6, 94–5
    leadership 81–2
    in mental health services 80–95
    role changes in 92–3
    whole systems working 81, 91–2
Third parties, professional obligation to
    54–5, 59
Tokenism 10, 36, 40
Training 285, 286
    anti-discriminatory 206–7, 208
    in children's services 67, 68, 75–6,
        77–8, 153–5, 157
    collaborative 93
    by disadvantaged groups 39
    domestic violence 181–2
    HIV/AIDS care 231, 236–7, 242–4
    problem drug use 153–5, 157
    service user 41
Tribalism 56
Utilitarianism 50, 51
Virtue ethics 51, 56
Virtues, professional 56, 58–61
Volunteering 42
Vulnerable adult abuse 183
Whole systems working 81, 91–2

THE HANDBOOK FOR ADVANCED PRIMARY CARE NURSES

Rebecca Neno and Debby Price (eds)

'I believe that The Handbook for Advanced Primary Care Nurses *should be extensively read and that it will prove to be an essential resource for nurses striving to improve public health and patient care in the communities of today and tomorrow. It may, with political will and a skilled and determined workforce help Florence Nightingale's vision come true.'*

Lynn Young, Primary Health Care Adviser, Royal College of Nursing, UK

This important new handbook for Primary Care Nurses is designed to assist senior nurses in developing the understanding and skills required to be effective at both strategic and operational levels. As well as exploring the context of advanced primary care practice, the book provides the tools needed for enhancing care delivery within both primary care and community settings.

The Handbook for Advanced Primary Care Nurses is an accessible guide to working strategically in primary care. It offers practical support across a range of core areas, including:

- Case finding and case management
- Mentorship
- Leadership and management
- Needs assessment
- Interprofessional working
- Prescribing

Neno and Price encourage readers to think analytically about their practice and include activities and reflection points throughout the book to help with this.

This book is the ideal companion both for nurse practitioners undertaking courses at advanced practice level and for professionals working at all levels in primary care.

Contents: *Foreword – Contributors – Introduction – Part 1: Context – Emergence of the advanced primary care nurse – Part 2: Enhancing care delivery – Legal and ethical issues in advanced practice – Case finding – Case management – First contact and complex needs assessment – Non-medical prescribing – Part 3: Enhancing strategic skills – Developing whole systems thinking – Transformational leadership – Developing and sustaining the advanced practitioner role – Developing and sustaining professional partnerships – From involvement to partnerships and beyond Part 4: Developing skills for the future – Commissioning in health and social care – Social enterprise and business skills – Influencing and getting your message across – Part 5: Future directions – The future for advanced primary care nurses – Index.*

2008   224pp
978-0-335-22353-4 (Paperback) 978-0-335-22354-1 (Hardback)

PREFACE

E-commerce. Business. Technology. Society. Global Edition 11e provides you with an in-depth introduction to the field of global e-commerce. We focus on concepts that will help you understand and take advantage of the evolving world of opportunity offered by e-commerce, which is dramatically altering the way business is conducted and driving major shifts in the global economy. E-commerce is a global phenomenon affecting economic and social life throughout the world. The Global Edition is aimed at students and professionals in the European Union, the Middle East, Asia Pacific, Australia, and South Africa. Case studies reflect e-commerce firms in these regions, and figures and tables relate to these regional sources wherever possible.

Just as important as our global orientation, we have tried to create a book that is thought-provoking and current. We use the most recent data available, and focus on companies that you are likely to encounter on a daily basis in your everyday life, such as Facebook, Google, Twitter, Amazon, YouTube, Pinterest, eBay, Uber, WhatsApp, Snapchat, and many more that you will recognize, as well as some exciting startups that may be new to you. Global Edition cases include PUMA, Financial Times, Beatgroup, InMobi, Just Falafel, Spotify, Deezer, Viadeo, Souk, Alibaba, and RocketInternet, among others. We also have up-to-date coverage of the key topics in e-commerce today, from privacy and piracy, to government surveillance, cyberwar, social, local, and mobile marketing, Internet sales taxes, intellectual property, and more. You will find here the most up-to-date and comprehensive overview of e-commerce today.

The e-commerce concepts you learn in this book will make you valuable to potential employers. The e-commerce job market is expanding rapidly. Many employers expect new employees to understand the basics of e-commerce, social and mobile marketing, and how to develop an e-commerce presence. Every industry today is touched in at least some way by e-commerce. The information and knowledge you find in this book will be valuable throughout your career, and after reading this book, we expect that you will be able to participate in, and even lead, management discussions of e-commerce for your firm.

WHAT'S NEW IN THE 11TH GLOBAL EDITION

Currency

The 11th edition features new or updated opening, closing, and "Insight on" cases. The text, as well as all of the data, figures, and tables in the book, have been updated through October 2014 with the latest marketing and business intelligence available from eMarketer, Pew Research Center, Forrester Research, comScore, Gartner Research, and other industry sources.

In addition, we have added new material throughout the text on a number of e-commerce topics that have appeared in the headlines during 2014, including the following:

- Sharing economy companies such as Uber and Airbnb (Chapters 1, 5, and 11)

- Public, private, and hybrid clouds; Amazon Web Services; proposed changes in Internet governance; Internet access drones; the Internet of Things, wearable computing (Apple Watch), smart houses, and connected cars (Chapter 2)
- PHP, Ruby on Rails, Django, PHP, LAMP, Python; mobile first design, responsive Web design, and adaptive Web design; cross-platform mobile app development tools (Chapter 3)
- Heartbleed bug; Cryptolocker and other forms of ransomware; carder forums; the Target and JPMorgan Chase data breaches; DDoS smokescreening; OpenSSL flaws; code signing for mobile devices; next generation firewalls; Bitcoin and mobile payment systems such as Apple Pay (Chapter 4)
- Information technology and business model disruption (Chapter 5)
- Native advertising; Google search algorithm changes; programmatic advertising; ad fraud and viewability issues; marketing automation systems (Chapter 6)
- Dark social; changes to Facebook's marketing tools; Twitter's new marketing tools and MoPub advertising network; Pinterest's Promoted Pins; proximity marketing; BLE; and Apple iBeacons (Chapter 7)
- The Right to be Forgotten; data brokers; facial recognition technology; NSA surveillance; the privacy implications of Big Data; Apple iPhone and Google Android encryption algorithms; Facebook and OKCupid social experiment furor; and continuing issues about net neutrality (Chapter 8)
- Amazon, Yahoo, and YouTube enter the entertainment business; new "digital-first" newspaper business models and the emergence of all-digital news sites such as Vox and Vice; e-book business model turmoil; Apple e-book price-fixing case; social TV (Chapter 9)
- Apps and social networks; mobile messaging apps such as WhatsApp, Snapchat, Slingshot, and Bolt; social network monetization; Yahoo portal struggles (Chapter 10)
- Social commerce Buy buttons; subscription-based retail business models; omnichannel retailing; the use of Big Data in retail marketing; sharing economy companies (Chapter 11)
- Impact of B2C e-commerce on B2B e-commerce; supply chain visibility; cloud-based B2B; mobile B2B; Collaboration 2.0 (Chapter 12)

Themes

E-commerce today is greatly different from e-commerce only seven years ago. The iPhone was introduced in 2007. The iPad tablet was first introduced in 2010 and has already gone through several generations! The smartphone and tablet devices have changed e-commerce into a social, local, and mobile experience. The 11th edition spotlights the following themes and content:

Headlines

- Social, Mobile, Local: We have included an entire chapter describing social, mobile, and local marketing. Content about social networks, the mobile platform, and local e-commerce appears throughout the book.

- » Social networks such as Facebook, Twitter, Pinterest, and LinkedIn continue their rapid growth, laying the groundwork for a social network marketing platform
- » The mobile platform composed of smartphones and tablet computers takes off and becomes a major factor in search, marketing, payment, retailing and services, and online content. Mobile device use poses new security and privacy issues as well.
- » Location-based services lead to explosive growth in local advertising and marketing.
- Online privacy continues to deteriorate, driven by a culture of self-revelation and powerful technologies for collecting personal information online without the knowledge or consent of users.
- Internet security risks increase; cyberwarfare becomes a new way of conducting warfare among nation-states and a national security issue.

Business

- Global e-commerce revenues surge after the recession.
- Internet advertising growth resumes, at a faster rate than traditional advertising.
- Social marketing grows faster than traditional online marketing like search and display advertising.
- E-books take off and expand the market for text, supported by the iPad, Kindle, Nook, and iPhone.
- Newspapers struggle to define a digital first news service
- Streaming of popular TV shows and movies (Netflix, Amazon, and Hulu.com) becomes a reality, as Internet distributors and Hollywood and TV producers strike deals for Web distribution that also protects intellectual property.
- "Free" and "freemium" business models compete to support digital content.
- New mobile payment platforms emerge to challenge PayPal.
- B2B e-commerce exceeds pre-recession levels as firms become more comfortable with digital supply chains.

Technology

- Smartphones, tablets, and e-book readers, along with associated software applications, and coupled with 4G cellular network expansion, fuel rapid growth of the mobile platform.
- Investment in cloud computing increases, providing the computing infrastructure for a massive increase in online digital information and e-commerce.
- Cloud-based streaming services for music and video challenge sales of downloads and physical product.
- Software apps fuel growth in app sales, marketing, and advertising; transforming software production and distribution.
- Touch interface operating systems dominate mobile devices. Windows 8 introduced with a touch screen interface, mimicking Apple's iOS and Google Android smartphones.

- The cost of developing sophisticated Web sites continues to drop due to declining software and hardware prices and open source software tools.
- Internet and cellular network capacity is challenged by the rapid expansion in digital traffic generated by mobile devices; the use of bandwidth caps tier-pricing expands.
- Internet telecommunications carriers support differential pricing to maintain a stable Internet; opposed by Net neutrality groups pushing non-discriminatory pricing.

Society

- The mobile, "always on" culture in business and family life continues to grow.
- European countries adopt "right to be forgotten" laws.
- U.S. state governments heat up the pursuit of taxes on Internet sales by Amazon and others.
- Intellectual property issues remain a source of conflict with significant movement toward resolution in some areas, such as Google's deals with Hollywood and the publishing industry, and Apple's and Amazon's deals with e-book and magazine publishers.
- P2P piracy traffic declines as paid streaming music and video gains ground, although digital piracy of online content remains a significant threat to Hollywood and the music industry.
- Governments around the world increase surveillance of Internet users and Web sites in response to national security threats; Google continues to tussle with China and other countries over censorship and security issues.
- Venture capital investing in e-commerce explodes for social, mobile, and local software applications. Crowdfunding becomes a new source of funding for e-commerce start-ups.

WELCOME TO E-COMMERCE 2015

Since it began in 1995, global e-commerce has grown from a standing start to a €1.2 trillion retail, travel, and media business and a €12.4 trillion business-to-business juggernaut, bringing about enormous change in business firms, markets, and consumer behavior. Economies and business firms around the globe are being similarly affected. During this relatively short time, e-commerce has itself been transformed from its origin as a mechanism for online retail sales into something much broader. Today, e-commerce has become the platform for media and new, unique services and capabilities that aren't found in the physical world. There is no physical world counterpart to Facebook, Twittter, Google search, or a host of other recent online innovations from Pinterest and iTunes to Tumblr. Welcome to the new e-commerce!

E-commerce is projected to continue growing at double-digit rates over the next five years, remaining the fastest growing form of commerce. Just as automobiles, airplanes, and electronics defined the twentieth century, so will e-commerce of all kinds define business and society in the twenty-first century. The rapid movement toward an e-commerce economy and society is being led by both established business firms such as Tesco, Ford, IBM, Carrefours, and General Electric, and pure online firms such as Google, Amazon, Apple, Facebook, Yahoo, Twitter, and YouTube. Students of business and information technology need a thorough grounding in e-commerce in order to be effective and successful managers in the next decade.

While firms such as Facebook, Tumblr, YouTube, Twitter, Pinterest, and Uber have grown explosively in the last two years and grab our attention, the traditional forms of retail e-commerce and services also remain vital and have proven to be more resilient than traditional retail channels in facing the economic recession. The experience of these firms from 1995 to the present is also a focus of this book. The defining characteristic of these firms is that they are profitable, sustainable, efficient, and innovative, with powerful brand names. Many of these now-experienced retail and service firms, such as eBay, Amazon, Priceline, and Expedia, are survivors of the first era of e-commerce, from 1995 to spring 2000. These surviving firms have evolved their business models, integrated their online and offline operations, and changed their revenue models to become profitable. Understanding how these online businesses succeeded will help students to manage their own firms in the current omni-channel business environment.

It would be foolish to ignore the lessons learned in the early period of e-commerce. Like so many technology revolutions in the past—automobiles, electricity, telephones, television, and biotechnology—there was an explosion of entrepreneurial efforts, followed by consolidation. By 2005, the survivors of the early period were moving to establish profitable businesses while maintaining rapid growth in revenues. In 2014, e-commerce is in the midst of a new period of explosive entrepreneurial activity focusing on social networks and the mobile platform created by smartphones and tablet computers. These technologies and social behaviors are bringing about extraordinary changes to our personal lives, markets, industries, individual businesses, and society as a whole. In 2013–2014, the stock values of Apple, Google, and Amazon hit new highs, along with many start-ups. E-commerce is generating thousands of new jobs in all fields from marketing to management, entrepreneurial studies, and information systems. Today, e-commerce has moved into the mainstream life of established businesses that have the market brands and financial muscle required for the long-term deployment of e-commerce technologies and methods. If you are working in an established business, chances are the firm's e-commerce capabilities and Web presence are important factors for its success. If you want to start a new business, chances are very good that the knowledge you learn in this book will be very helpful.

BUSINESS. TECHNOLOGY. SOCIETY.

We believe that in order for business and technology students to really understand e-commerce, they must understand the relationships among e-commerce business concerns, Internet technology, and the social and legal context of e-commerce. These three themes permeate all aspects of e-commerce, and therefore, in each chapter, we present material that explores the business, technological, and social aspects of that chapter's main topic.

Given the continued growth and diffusion of e-commerce, all students—regardless of their major discipline—must also understand the basic economic and business forces driving e-commerce. E-commerce has created new digital markets where prices are more transparent, markets are global, and trading is highly efficient, though not perfect. E-commerce has a direct impact on a firm's relationship with suppliers, customers, competitors, and partners, as well as how firms market products, advertise, and use brands. Whether you are interested in marketing and sales, design, production, finance, information systems, or logistics, you will need to know how e-commerce technologies can be used to reduce supply chain costs, increase production efficiency, and tighten the relationship with customers. This text is written to help you understand the fundamental business issues in e-commerce.

We spend a considerable amount of effort analyzing the business models and strategies of "pure-play" online companies and established businesses now employing "bricks-and-clicks" business models. We explore why e-commerce firms fail and the strategic, financial, marketing, and organizational challenges they face. We also discuss how e-commerce firms learned from the mistakes of early firms, and how established firms are using e-commerce to succeed. Above all, we attempt to bring a strong sense of business realism and sensitivity to the often exaggerated descriptions of e-commerce. As founders of a dot.com company and participants in the e-commerce revolution, we have learned that the "e" in e-commerce does not stand for "easy."

The Web and mobile platform have caused a major revolution in marketing and advertising in the United States. We spend two chapters discussing online marketing and advertising. Chapter 6 discusses "traditional" online marketing formats like search engine marketing, display advertising, and e-mail, as well as various Internet marketing technologies underlying those efforts, and metrics for measuring marketing success. Chapter 7 provides an in-depth examination of social, mobile, and local marketing, which relies on mobile devices and social networks.

E-commerce is driven by Internet technology. Internet technology, and information technology in general, is perhaps the star of the show. Without the Internet, e-commerce would be virtually nonexistent. Accordingly, we provide three chapters specifically on the Internet and e-commerce technology, and in every chapter we provide continuing coverage by illustrating how the topic of the chapter is being shaped by new information technologies. For instance, Internet technology drives developments in security and payment systems, marketing strategies and advertising, financial applications, media distribution, business-to-business trade, and retail e-commerce. We discuss the rapid growth of the mobile platform, the emergence of cloud computing, new open source software tools and applications that enable Web 2.0, and new types of Internet-based information systems that support digital business-to-business markets.

E-commerce is not only about business and technology, however. The third part of the equation for understanding e-commerce is society. E-commerce and Internet technologies have important social consequences that business leaders can ignore only at their peril. E-commerce has challenged our concepts of privacy, intellectual property, and even our ideas about national sovereignty and governance. Google, Facebook, Apple, Amazon, and assorted advertising networks maintain profiles on millions of shoppers and consumers worldwide. The proliferation of illegally copied music and videos on the Internet, and the growth of social network sites often based on displaying copyrighted materials without permission, are challenging the intellectual property rights of record labels, Hollywood studios, and artists. And many countries—including the United States—are demanding to control the content of Web sites displayed within their borders for political and social reasons. Tax authorities in the United States and Europe are demanding that e-commerce sites pay sales taxes just like ordinary brick and mortar stores on Main Street. As a result of these challenges to existing institutions, e-commerce and the Internet are the subject of increasing investigation, litigation, and legislation. Business leaders need to understand these societal developments, and they cannot afford to assume any longer that the Internet is borderless, beyond social control and regulation, or a place where market efficiency is the only consideration. In addition to an entire chapter devoted to the social and legal implications of e-commerce, each chapter contains material highlighting the social implications of e-commerce.

FEATURES AND COVERAGE

Strong Conceptual Foundation The book emphasizes the three major driving forces behind e-commerce: business development and strategy, technological innovations, and social controversies and impacts. Each of these driving forces is represented in every chapter, and together they provide a strong and coherent conceptual framework for understanding e-commerce. We analyze e-commerce, digital markets, and e-business firms just as we would ordinary businesses and markets using concepts from economics, marketing, finance, sociology, philosophy, and information systems. We strive to maintain a critical perspective on e-commerce and avoid industry hyperbole.

Some of the important concepts from economics and marketing that we use to explore e-commerce are transaction cost, network externalities, information asymmetry, social networks, perfect digital markets, segmentation, price dispersion, targeting, and positioning. Important concepts from the study of information systems and technologies play an important role in the book, including Internet standards and protocols, client/server computing, multi-tier server systems, cloud computing, mobile platform and wireless technologies, and public key encryption, among many others. From the literature on ethics and society, we use important concepts such as intellectual property, privacy, information rights and rights management, governance, public health, and welfare.

From the literature on business, we use concepts such as business process design, return on investment, strategic advantage, industry competitive environment, oligopoly, and monopoly. We also provide a basic understanding of finance and accounting issues, and extend this through an "E-commerce in Action" case that critically examines the financial statements of Amazon. One of the witticisms that emerged from the early years of e-commerce and that still seems apt is the notion that e-commerce changes everything except the rules of business. Businesses still need to make a profit in order to survive in the long term.

Currency Important new developments happen almost every day in e-commerce and the Internet. We try to capture as many of these important new developments as possible in each annual edition. You will not find a more current book for a course offered for the 2015 academic year. Many other texts are already six months to a year out of date before they even reach the printer. This text, in contrast, reflects extensive research through October 2014, just weeks before the book hits the press.

Real-World Global Business Firm Focus and Cases From Akamai Technologies to Google, Microsoft, Apple, and Amazon, to Facebook, Twitter, and Tumblr, to Netflix, Pandora, and Elemica, this book contains hundreds of real-company examples and over 60 more extensive cases that place coverage in the context of actual e-commerce businesses. You'll find these examples in each chapter, as well as in special features such as chapter-opening, chapter-closing, and "Insight on" cases. The book takes a realistic look at the world of e-commerce, describing what's working and what isn't, rather than presenting a rose-colored or purely "academic" viewpoint.

In-depth Coverage of Marketing and Advertising The text includes two chapters on marketing and advertising, both traditional online marketing and social, mobile, and local marketing. Marketing concepts, including market segmentation, personalization, click-stream analysis, bundling of digital goods, long-tail marketing, and dynamic pricing, are used throughout the text.

In-depth Coverage of B2B E-commerce We devote an entire chapter to an examination of B2B e-commerce. In writing this chapter, we developed a unique and easily understood classification schema to help students understand this complex arena of e-commerce. This chapter covers four types of Net marketplaces (e-distributors, e-procurement companies, exchanges, and industry consortia) as well as the development of private industrial networks and collaborative commerce.

Current and Future Technology Coverage Internet and related information technologies continue to change rapidly. The most important changes for e-commerce include dramatic price reductions in e-commerce infrastructure (making it much less expensive to develop a sophisticated e-commerce presence), the explosive growth in the mobile platform such as iPhones, iPads, tablet computers, and expansion in the development of social technologies, which are the foundation of online social networks. What was once a shortage of telecommunications capacity has now turned into a surplus, PC prices have continued to fall, smartphone and tablet sales have soared, Internet high-speed broadband connections are now typical and are continuing to show double-digit growth, and wireless technologies such as Wi-Fi and cellular broadband are transforming how, when, and where people access the Internet. While we thoroughly discuss the current Internet environment, we devote considerable attention to describing Web 2.0 and emerging technologies and applications such as the Internet of Things, advanced network infrastructure, fiber optics, wireless Web and 4G technologies, Wi-Fi, IP multicasting, and future guaranteed service levels.

Up-to-Date Coverage of the Research Literature This text is well grounded in the e-commerce research literature. We have sought to include, where appropriate, references and analysis of the latest e-commerce research findings, as well as many classic articles, in all of our chapters. We have drawn especially on the disciplines of economics, marketing, and information systems and technologies, as well as law journals and broader social science research journals including sociology and psychology.

We do not use references to Wikipedia in this text, for a variety of reasons. Most colleges do not consider Wikipedia a legitimate or acceptable source for academic research and instruct their students not to cite it. Material found on Wikipedia may be out of date, lack coverage, lack critical perspective, and cannot necessarily be trusted. Our references are to respected academic journals; industry sources such as eMarketer, comScore, Hitwise, Nielsen, and Gartner; newspapers such as the *New York Times* and *Wall Street Journal*; and industry publications such as *Computerworld* and *Information-Week*, among others. Figures and tables sourced to "authors' estimates" reflect analysis of data from the U.S. Department of Commerce, estimates from various research firms, historical trends, revenues of major online retailers, consumer online buying trends, and economic conditions.

Special Attention to the Social and Legal Aspects of E-commerce We have paid special attention throughout the book to the social and legal context of e-commerce. Chapter 8 is devoted to a thorough exploration of four ethical dimensions of e-commerce: information privacy, intellectual property, governance, and protecting public welfare on the Internet. We have included an analysis of the latest Federal Trade Commission and other regulatory and nonprofit research reports, and their likely impact on the e-commerce environment.

A major theme throughout this chapter, and the remainder of the book, is the impact of social, mobile, and local commerce on how consumers use the Internet.

Writing That's Fun to Read Unlike some textbooks, we've been told by many students that this book is actually fun to read and easy to understand. This is not a book written by committee—you won't find a dozen different people listed as authors, co-authors, and contributors on the title page. We have a consistent voice and perspective that carries through the entire text and we believe the book is the better for it.

OVERVIEW OF THE BOOK

The book begins with an introductory chapter that provides an introduction to the major themes of the book. Chapter 1 defines e-commerce, distinguishes between e-commerce and e-business, and defines the different types of e-commerce. Chapter 2 traces the historical development of the Internet and thoroughly describes how today's Internet works. A major focus of this chapter is mobile technology, Web 2.0 applications, and the near-term future Internet that is now under development and will shape the future of e-commerce. Chapter 3 builds on the Internet chapter by focusing on the steps managers need to follow in order to build an e-commerce presence. This e-commerce infrastructure chapter covers the process that should be followed in building an e-commerce presence; the major decisions regarding outsourcing site development and/or hosting; how to choose software, hardware, and other tools that can improve Web site performance, and issues involved in developing a mobile Web site and mobile applications. Chapter 4 focuses on e-commerce security and payments, building on the e-commerce infrastructure discussion of the previous chapter by describing the ways security can be provided over the Internet. This chapter defines digital information security, describes the major threats to security, and then discusses both the technology and policy solutions available to business managers seeking to secure their firm's sites. This chapter concludes with a section on e-commerce payment systems. We identify the various types of online payment systems (credit cards, stored value payment systems such as PayPal, digital wallets such as Google Wallet, and others), and the development of mobile payment systems such as Apple Pay.

The next four chapters focus directly on the business concepts and social-legal issues that surround the development of e-commerce. Chapter 5 introduces and defines the concepts of business model and revenue model, describes the major e-commerce business and revenue models for both B2C and B2B firms, and introduces the basic business concepts required throughout the text for understanding e-commerce firms including industry structure, value chains, and firm strategy. Chapter 6 focuses on e-commerce consumer behavior, the Internet audience, and introduces the student to the basics of online marketing and branding, including traditional online marketing technologies and marketing strategies. Topics include the Web site as a marketing platform, search engine marketing and advertising, display ad marketing, e-mail campaigns, affiliate and lead generation marketing programs, multichannel marketing, and various customer retention strategies such as personalization (including interest-based advertising, also known as behavioral targeting) and customer service tools. The chapter also covers other marketing strategies such as pricing and long-tail marketing. Internet marketing technologies (Web transaction logs, tracking files, data mining, and Big Data) and marketing automation and CRM systems are also explored. The chapter concludes with a section on understanding the costs and benefits of various types of online marketing, including a new section on Web analytics software. Chapter 7 is devoted to an in-depth analysis of social, mobile, and local marketing. Topics include Facebook, Twitter, and Pinterest marketing platforms, the evolution of mobile marketing and the growing use of geo-aware technologies to support proximity marketing. Chapter 8 provides a thorough introduction to the social and legal environment of e-commerce. Here, you will find a description of the ethical and legal dimensions of e-commerce, including a thorough discussion of the latest developments in personal information privacy, intellectual property, Internet governance, jurisdiction, and public health and welfare issues such as pornography, gambling, and health information.

The final four chapters focus on real-world e-commerce experiences in retail and services, online media, auctions, portals, and social networks, and business-to-business e-commerce. These chapters take a sector approach rather than the conceptual approach used in the earlier chapters. E-commerce is different in each of these sectors. Chapter 9 explores the world of online content and digital media and examines the enormous changes in online publishing and entertainment industries that have occurred over the last two years, including streaming movies, e-books, and online newspapers and magazines. Chapter 10 explores the online world of social networks, auctions, and portals. Chapter 11 takes a close look at the experience of firms in the retail marketplace for both goods and services, as well as new shared economy companies such as Uber and Airbnb. Chapter 11 also includes an "E-commerce in Action" case that provides a detailed analysis of the business strategies and financial operating results of Amazon, which can be used as a model to analyze other e-commerce firms. Chapter 12 concentrates on the world of B2B e-commerce, describing both Net marketplaces and the less-heralded, but very large arena of private industrial networks and the movement toward collaborative commerce.

PEDAGOGY AND CHAPTER OUTLINE

The book's pedagogy emphasizes student cognitive awareness and the ability to analyze, synthesize, and evaluate e-commerce businesses. While there is a strong data and conceptual foundation to the book, we seek to engage student interest with lively writing about e-commerce businesses and the transformation of business models at traditional firms.

Each chapter contains a number of elements designed to make learning easy as well as interesting.

Learning Objectives A list of learning objectives that highlights the key concepts in the chapter guides student study.

Chapter-Opening Cases Each chapter opens with a story about a leading e-commerce company that relates the key objectives of the chapter to a real-life e-commerce business venture. The cases focus specifically on global aspects of e-commerce and companies with a presence in Europe, the Middle East, Africa, Asia and/or Australia.

Just Falafel
Soars with Social Media

When Reema Shetty and her longtime friend from high school, Alia Al Mazrouei, were kicking around ideas for a healthy fast food outlet in the United Arab Emirates, their mutual friend, Mohammad Bitar, suggested promoting Middle Eastern and Lebanese delicacies. By the time the trio was ready to open their first restaurant in Abu Dhabi in 2007, they were already dreaming big. They believed they could take a 1000 year-old vegetarian staple, whose main marketplace incarnation had been as street vender food, to mall food courts and compete head to head with the likes of McDonald's, Subway, and Sbarro.

Falafel, they thought, had a number of propitious characteristics. Made from either ground chick peas or fava beans, it could be marketed as a wholesome alternative to typical preservative and fat-laden food court fare. It had never been adapted for food court distribution, so they would have first mover advantage. By using the best ingredients, they would create a superior, more delicious product than the competition, and by diversifying condiments and breads, they could internationalize the fried patties, appealing to a wide range of palates. A falafel aficionado, Bitar believed that with the proper attention, this poor man's food could be elevated to equal standing with its competitors.

To start, Just Falafel offered the Original, served with tahini and pickles in pita bread, a Greek version with Tzatziki dressing and olives on tortilla bread, and an Indian version with spicy Indian dressing and cucumber pickles, also on tortilla bread. By 2010, it had five locations and had gained acclaim as the caterer for some of the UAE's biggest sporting events. Bitar and Shetty, now married, believed that Just Falafel's business proposition—from a menu standpoint—was nearing completion. Mexican, Italian, Lebanese, American, and Japanese flavors were offered, and Just Falafel began soliciting on its six-month-old Facebook page for suggestions for an Emirati version. A YouTube channel was launched in November. Though not quite sure yet how to leverage their social media channels, the founders had a new dream: global expansion.

As 2011 began, they set a goal to have 75 stores in the UAE within the next five years. Franchising was the only way to achieve this. Just Falafel would need partners on the retail front-end so that it could reinvest on the back-end. Fadi Malas was brought

© maigi/Fotolia.com

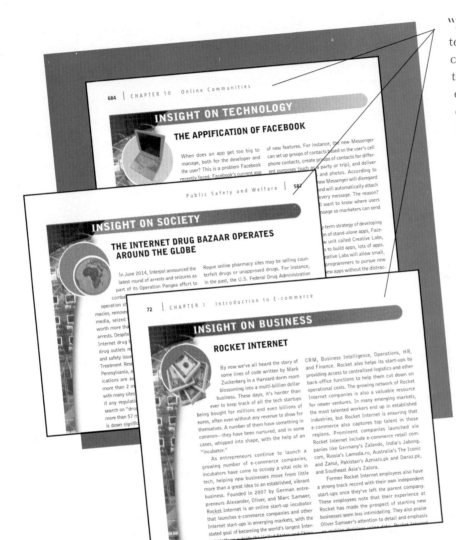

"Insight on" Cases Each chapter contains three real-world cases illustrating the themes of technology, business, and society. These cases take an in-depth look at relevant topics to help describe and analyze the full breadth of the field of e-commerce. The cases probe such issues as the ability of governments to regulate Internet content, how to design Web sites for accessibility, the challenges faced by luxury marketers in online marketing, and smartphone security.

Margin Glossary Throughout the text, key terms and their definitions appear in the text margin where they are first introduced.

Real-Company Examples Drawn from actual e-commerce ventures, well over 100 pertinent examples are used throughout the text to illustrate concepts.

Chapter-Closing Case Studies Each chapter concludes with a robust case study based on a real-world organization. These cases help students synthesize chapter concepts and apply this knowledge to concrete problems and scenarios such as evaluating Pandora's freemium business model, ExchangeHunterJumper's efforts to build a brand, and the fairness of the Google Books settlement.

Chapter-Ending Pedagogy Each chapter contains extensive end-of-chapter materials designed to reinforce the learning objectives of the chapter.

Key Concepts Keyed to the learning objectives, Key Concepts present the key points of the chapter to aid student study.

Review Questions Thought-provoking questions prompt students to demonstrate their comprehension and apply chapter concepts to management problem solving.

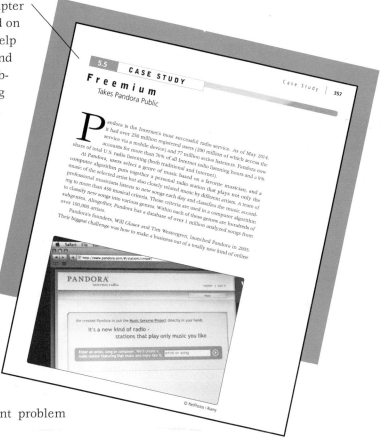

Projects At the end of each chapter are a number of projects that encourage students to apply chapter concepts and to use higher-level evaluation skills. Many make use of the Internet and require students to present their findings in an oral or electronic presentation or written report. For instance, students are asked to evaluate publicly available information about a company's financials at the SEC Web site, assess payment system options for companies across international boundaries, or search for the top 10 cookies on their own computer and the sites they are from.

Web Resources Web resources that can extend students' knowledge of each chapter with projects, exercises, and additional content are available at www.azimuth-interactive.com/ecommerce11e. The Web site contains the following content provided by the authors:

- Additional projects, exercises, and tutorials
- Information on how to build a business plan and revenue models
- Essays on careers in e-commerce

INSTRUCTOR RESOURCES

At the Instructor Resource Center, accessible through www.pearsonglobaleditions. com/Laudon, instructors can easily register to gain access to a variety of instructor resources available with this text in downloadable format. If assistance is needed, our dedicated technical support team is ready to help with the media supplements that accompany this text. Visit http://247.pearsoned.com for answers to frequently asked questions and toll-free user support phone numbers.

The following supplements are available with this text:

- **Instructor's Resource Manual**
- **Test Bank**
- **TestGen® Computerized Test Bank**
- **PowerPoint Presentation**
- **Learning Tracks** These additional essays, created by the authors, provide instructors and students with more in-depth content on selected topics in e-commerce.

  Chapter 1
  1.1 Global E-commerce Europe
  1.2 Global E-commerce Latin America
  1.3 Global E-commerce China

  Chapter 6
  6.1 Basic Marketing Concepts
  6.2 Consumer Behavior: Cultural, Social, and Psychological Background Factors
  6.3 Social Media Marketing—Blogging

  Chapter 7
  Social Media Marketing: Facebook
  Social Media Marketing: Twitter

- **Video Cases** The authors have created a collection of video case studies that integrate short videos, supporting case study material, and case study questions. Video cases can be used in class to promote discussion or as written assignments.

  Chapter 1
  1.1 The Future of E-commerce

  Chapter 2
  2.1 Google Data Center Efficiency Best Practices
  2.2 NBA: Competing on Global Delivery

  Chapter 3
  3.1 ESPN Goes to eXtreme Scale
  3.2 Data Warehousing at REI: Understanding the Customer

  Chapter 4
  4.1 Cyberespionage: The Chinese Threat
  4.2 Stuxnet and Cyberwarfare

4.3 IBM Zone Trusted Information Channel (ZTIC)
4.4 Open ID and Web Security

Chapter 5
5.1 Deals Galore at Groupon
5.2 Angel Investing

Chapter 6
6.1 Nielsen Online Campaign Ratings

Chapter 7
7.1 The Power of Like
Chapter 8
8.1 Facebook Privacy
8.2 What Net Neutrality Means for You
8.3 Lawrence Lessig on Net Neutrality

Chapter 9
9.1 YouTube's 7th Birthday

Chapter 10
10.1 Mint Returns for Goodwill's eBay Auctions of Thrift-Store Finds

Chapter 11
11.1 Etsy: A Marketplace and a Community

Chapter 12
12.1 Ford AutoXchange B2B Marketplace
12.2 Flextronics Uses Elementum's Cloud-based Mobile Supply Chain Apps

ACKNOWLEDGMENTS

Pearson Education sought the advice of many excellent reviewers, all of whom strongly influenced the organization and substance of this book. The following individuals provided extremely useful evaluations of this and previous editions of the text:

Deniz Aksen, Koç University (Istanbul)

Carrie Andersen, Madison Area Technical College

Christine Barnes, Lakeland Community College

Dr. Shirley A. Becker, Northern Arizona University

Prasad Bingi, Indiana-Purdue University, Fort Wayne

Joanna Broder, Pima Community College

James Buchan, College of the Ozarks

Ashley Bush, Florida State University

Cliff Butler, North Seattle Community College

Adnan Chawdhry, California University of Pennsylvania

Mark Choman, Luzerne City Community College

Andrew Ciganek, Jacksonville State University

Daniel Connolly, University of Denver

Tom Critzer, Miami University

Dursan Delen, Oklahoma State University

Abhijit Deshmukh, University of Massachusetts

Brian L. Dos Santos, University of Louisville

Robert Drevs, University of Notre Dame

Akram El-Tannir, Hariri Canadian University, Lebanon

Kimberly Furumo, University of Hawaii at Hilo

John H. Gerdes, University of California, Riverside

Philip Gordon, University of California at Berkeley

Allan Greenberg, Brooklyn College

Bin Gu, University of Texas at Austin

Norman Hahn, Thomas Nelson Community College

Peter Haried, University of Wisconsin- La Crosse

Sherri Harms, University of Nebraska at Kearney

Sharon Heckel, St. Charles Community College

David Hite, Virginia Intermont College

Gus Jabbour, George Mason University

Kevin Jetton, Texas State University, San Marcos

Ellen Kraft, Georgian Court University

Gilliean Lee, Lander University

Zoonky Lee, University of Nebraska, Lincoln

Andre Lemaylleux, Boston University, Brussels

Haim Levkowitz, University of Massachusetts, Lowell

Yair Levy, Nova Southeastern University

Richard Lucic, Duke University

John Mendonca, Purdue University

Dr. Abdulrahman Mirza, DePaul University

Barbara Ozog, Benedictine University

Kent Palmer, MacMurray College

Karen Palumbo, University of St. Francis

James Pauer, Lorain County Community College

Wayne Pauli, Dakota State University

Sam Perez, Mesa Community College

Jamie Pinchot, Thiel College

Kai Pommerenke, University of California at Santa Cruz

Barry Quinn, University of Ulster, Northern Ireland

Michelle Ramim, Nova Southeastern University

Jay Rhee, San Jose State University

Jorge Romero, Towson University

John Sagi, Anne Arundel Community College

Patricia Sendall, Merrimack College

Dr. Carlos Serrao, ISCTE/DCTI, Portugal

Neerja Sethi, Nanyang Business School, Singapore

Amber Settle, DePaul CTI

Vivek Shah, Texas State University-San Marcos

Wei Shi, Santa Clara University

Seung Jae Shin, Mississippi State University

Sumit Sircar, University of Texas at Arlington

Hongjun Song, University of Memphis

Pamela Specht, University of Nebraska at Omaha

Esther Swilley, Kansas State University

Tony Townsend, Iowa State University

Bill Troy, University of New Hampshire

Susan VandeVen, Southern Polytechnic State University

Hiep Van Dong, Madison Area Technical College

And Michael Van Hilst, Nova Southeastern University

Mary Vitrano, Palm Beach Community College

Andrea Wachter, Point Park University

Catherine Wallace, Massey University, New Zealand

Biao Wang, Boston University

Haibo Wang, Texas A&M International University

Harry Washington, Lincoln University

Rolf Wigand, University of Arkansas at Little Rock

Erin Wilkinson, Johnson & Wales University

Alice Wilson, Cedar Crest College

Dezhi Wu, Southern Utah University

Gene Yelle, SUNY Institute of Technology

David Zolzer, Northwestern State University

We would like to thank eMarketer, Inc. and David Iankelevich for their permission to include data and figures from their research reports in our text. eMarketer is one of the leading independent sources for statistics, trend data, and original analysis covering many topics related to the Internet, e-business, and emerging technologies. eMarketer aggregates e-business data from multiple sources worldwide.

In addition, we would like to thank all those at Pearson who have worked so hard to make sure this book is the very best it can be. We want to thank Nicole Sam, Acquisitions Editor of the Pearson MIS list, and Karalyn Holland, Project Manager, for their support; Judy Leale for overseeing production of this project; and DePinho Design for the outstanding cover design. Very special thanks to Megan Miller, Will Anderson, and Robin Pickering at Azimuth Interactive, Inc., for all their hard work on the production of, and supplements for, this book.

A special thanks also to Susan Hartman, Executive Editor for the first and second editions and to Frank Ruggirello, Publisher at Addison-Wesley when we began this project, and now Vice President and Editorial Director at Benjamin-Cummings.

Finally, last but not least, we would like to thank our family and friends, without whose support this book would not have been possible.

Kenneth C. Laudon
Carol Guercio Traver

Brief Contents

1	INTRODUCTION TO E-COMMERCE	42
2	E-COMMERCE INFRASTRUCTURE	94
3	BUILDING AN E-COMMERCE PRESENCE	170
4	E-COMMERCE SECURITY AND PAYMENT SYSTEMS	234
5	E-COMMERCE BUSINESS STRATEGIES	312
6	E-COMMERCE MARKETING AND ADVERTISING	366
7	SOCIAL, MOBILE, AND LOCAL MARKETING	456
8	ETHICS, LAW, AND E-COMMERCE	524
9	ONLINE MEDIA	602
10	ONLINE COMMUNITIES	676
11	E-COMMERCE RETAILING AND SERVICES	718
12	B2B E-COMMERCE	784

Contents

1 **INTRODUCTION TO E-COMMERCE** **42**

Learning Objectives 42

Puma Goes Omni *43*

1.1 E-commerce: The Revolution Is Just Beginning 46
The First 30 Seconds 48
What Is E-commerce? 49
The Difference Between E-commerce and E-business 49
Why Study E-commerce? 50
Eight Unique Features of E-commerce Technology 51
Ubiquity 52
Global Reach 52
Universal Standards 53
Richness 53
Interactivity 53
Information Density 54
Personalization/Customization 54
Social Technology: User Content Generation and Social Networking 54
Web 2.0: Play My Version 56
Types of E-commerce 57
Business-to-Consumer (B2C) E-commerce 57
Business-to-Business (B2B) E-commerce 58
Consumer-to-Consumer (C2C) E-commerce 58
Mobile E-commerce (M-commerce) 59
Social E-commerce 59
Local E-commerce 60
Growth of the Internet, Web, and Mobile Platform 61
Insight on Technology: Will Apps Make the Web Irrelevant? *64*
Origins and Growth of E-commerce 66

1.2 E-commerce: A Brief History 66
E-commerce 1995–2000: Invention 67
E-commerce 2001–2006: Consolidation 70

E-commerce 2007–Present: Reinvention   71

Assessing E-commerce: Successes, Surprises, and Failures   71

Insight on Business: Rocket Internet   *72*

Predictions for the Future: More Surprises   76

1.3   *Understanding E-commerce: Organizing Themes*   *79*

Technology: Infrastructure   79

Business: Basic Concepts   80

Society: Taming the Juggernaut   80

Insight on Society: Facebook and the Age of Privacy   *82*

Academic Disciplines Concerned with E-commerce   84

Technical Approaches   84

Behavioral Approaches   84

1.4   *Case Study: The Pirate Bay: Searching for a Safe Haven*   *86*

1.5   *Review*   *89*

Key Concepts   89

Questions   91

Projects   92

References   92

| 2 | **E-COMMERCE INFRASTRUCTURE** | **94** |

Learning Objectives   94

Wikitude, Layar, and Blippar: Augment My Reality   *95*

2.1   *The Internet: Technology Background*   *98*

The Evolution of the Internet: 1961—The Present   100

The Internet: Key Technology Concepts   101

Packet Switching   101

Transmission Control Protocol/Internet Protocol (TCP/IP)   106

IP Addresses   106

Domain Names, DNS, and URLs   108

Client/Server Computing   108

The New Client: The Mobile Platform   111

The Internet "Cloud Computing" Model: Hardware and Software as a
Service   111

Other Internet Protocols and Utility Programs   113

2.2   *The Internet Today*   *115*

The Internet Backbone   117

Internet Exchange Points   118

Campus Area Networks   118

Internet Service Providers   118

Intranets   121

Who Governs the Internet?   122

2.3   *The Future Internet Infrastructure*   *124*

Limitations of the Current Internet   124

Insight on Society: Government Regulation and Surveillance of the Internet   125

The Internet2® Project   128

The First Mile and the Last Mile   129

Fiber Optics and the Bandwidth Explosion in the First Mile   130

The Last Mile: Mobile Internet Access   130

Internet Access Drones   134

The Future Internet   135

Latency Solutions   135

Guaranteed Service Levels and Lower Error Rates   135

Declining Costs   135

The Internet of Things   136

2.4   *The Web*   *137*

Hypertext   139

Markup Languages   141

HyperText Markup Language (HTML)   141

eXtensible Markup Language (XML)   142

Insight on Technology: Is HTML5 Ready for Prime Time?   143

Web Servers and Clients   145

Web Browsers   147

2.5   *The Internet and the Web: Features and Services*   *147*

E-mail   147

Instant Messaging   148

Search Engines   148

Online Forums   151

Streaming Media   151

Cookies   152

Web 2.0 Features and Services   152

Online Social Networks   152

Blogs   152

Really Simple Syndication (RSS)   153

Podcasting   153

Wikis   154

Music and Video Services   154

Internet Telephony   155

Video Conferencing, Video Chatting, and Telepresence   156

Online Software and Web Services: Web Apps, Widgets, and Gadgets   156

Intelligent Personal Assistants   156

2.6   *Mobile Apps: The Next Big Thing Is Here*   157

Platforms for Mobile Application Development   158

App Marketplaces   158

Insight on Business: Apps for Everything: The App Ecosystem   159

2.7   *Case Study: Akamai Technologies: Attempting to Keep Supply Ahead of Demand*   161

2.8   *Review*   165

Key Concepts   165

Questions   166

Projects   167

References   167

---

3   BUILDING AN E-COMMERCE PRESENCE   170

Learning Objectives   170

The Financial Times: A Remodel for 21st Century Publishing Profitability   171

3.1   *Imagine Your E-commerce Presence*   174

What's the Idea? (The Visioning Process)   174

Where's the Money: Business and Revenue Model   174

Who and Where Is the Target Audience   175

What Is the Ballpark? Characterize the Marketplace   175

Where's the Content Coming From?   176

Know Yourself: Conduct a SWOT Analysis   177

Develop an E-commerce Presence Map   178

Develop a Timeline: Milestones   179

How Much Will This Cost?   179

3.2   *Building an E-commerce Presence: A Systematic Approach*   180

Planning: The Systems Development Life Cycle   182

Systems Analysis/Planning: Identify Business Objectives, System Functionality, and Information Requirements   182

System Design: Hardware and Software Platforms   184

Building the System: In-house Versus Outsourcing   184

Build Your Own versus Outsourcing   184

Host Your Own versus Outsourcing   188

Insight on Business: Weebly Makes Creating Web Sites Easy   189

Testing the System   191

Implementation and Maintenance   191
Factors in Optimizing Web Site Performance   192

3.3   Choosing Software   193
Simple Versus Multi-Tiered Web Site Architecture   193
Web Server Software   194
    Site Management Tools   196
    Dynamic Page Generation Tools   198
Application Servers   199
E-commerce Merchant Server Software Functionality   200
    Online Catalog   200
    Shopping Cart   201
    Credit Card Processing   201
Merchant Server Software Packages (E-commerce Software Platforms)   201
    Choosing an E-commerce Software Platform   203

3.4   Choosing Hardware   204
Right-sizing Your Hardware Platform: The Demand Side   204
Right-sizing Your Hardware Platform: The Supply Side   207

3.5   Other E-commerce Site Tools   209
Web Site Design: Basic Business Considerations   209
Tools for Web Site Optimization   210
Tools for Interactivity and Active Content   211
    Common Gateway Interface (CGI)   211
    Active Server Pages (ASP and ASP.NET)   212
    Java, Java Server Pages (JSP), and JavaScript   212
    ActiveX and VBScript   213
    ColdFusion   213
    PHP, Ruby on Rails (RoR), and Django   213
    Web 2.0 Design Elements   214
Personalization Tools   215
The Information Policy Set   215
    Insight On Society: Designing for Accessibility   216

3.6   Developing a Mobile Web Site and Building Mobile Applications   218
Planning and Building a Mobile Presence   219
Mobile Presence: Design Considerations   220
Cross-platform Mobile App Development Tools   222
Mobile Presence: Performance and Cost Considerations   222
    Insight on Technology: Building a Mobile Presence   223

3.7   Case Study: Orbitz Worldwide Charts Its Mobile Trajectory   226

3.8   Review   230

Key Concepts   230
Questions   232
Projects   232
References   233

| 4 | E-COMMERCE SECURITY AND PAYMENT SYSTEMS | 234 |

Learning Objectives   234

Europol Takes on Cybercrime with EC3   **235**

4.1   *The E-commerce Security Environment*   238
The Scope of the Problem   239
The Underground Economy Marketplace: The Value of Stolen
Information   240
What Is Good E-commerce Security?   242
Dimensions of E-commerce Security   243
The Tension Between Security and Other Values   244
Ease of Use   244
Public Safety and the Criminal Uses of the Internet   245

4.2   *Security Threats in the E-commerce Environment*   246
Malicious Code   247
Potentially Unwanted Programs (PUPs)   250
Phishing   252
Hacking, Cybervandalism, and Hacktivism   253
Data Breaches   254
    Insight on Business: Hackers Infiltrate Target   255
Credit Card Fraud/Theft   257
Identity Fraud   258
Spoofing, Pharming, and Spam (Junk) Web Sites   258
Denial of Service (DOS) and Distributed Denial of Service (DDOS) Attacks   259
Sniffing   260
Insider Attacks   260
Poorly Designed Software   261
Social Network Security Issues   262
Mobile Platform Security Issues   262
    Insight on Technology: Think Your Smartphone Is Secure?   264
Cloud Security Issues   266

4.3   *Technology Solutions*   266
Protecting Internet Communications   266
Encryption   267

Symmetric Key Cryptography   268

Public Key Cryptography   269

Public Key Cryptography Using Digital Signatures and Hash Digests   270

Digital Envelopes   273

Digital Certificates and Public Key Infrastructure (PKI)   274

Limitations to Encryption Solutions   275

Securing Channels of Communication   276

Secure Sockets Layer (SSL) and Transport Layer Security (TLS)   276

Virtual Private Networks (VPNs)   278

Wireless (Wi-Fi) Networks   278

Protecting Networks   278

Firewalls   279

Proxy Servers   279

Intrusion Detection and Prevention Systems   281

Protecting Servers and Clients   281

Operating System Security Enhancements   281

Anti-Virus Software   281

4.4 *Management Policies, Business Procedures, and Public Laws*   **282**

A Security Plan: Management Policies   282

The Role of Laws and Public Policy   284

Private and Private-Public Cooperation Efforts   285

Government Policies and Controls on Encryption Software   287

4.5 *E-commerce Payment Systems*   **287**

Online Credit Card Transactions   289

Credit Card E-commerce Enablers   291

Limitations of Online Credit Card Payment Systems   291

Alternative Online Payment Systems   291

Mobile Payment Systems: Your Smartphone Wallet   293

Digital Cash and Virtual Currencies   294

4.6 *Electronic Billing Presentment and Payment*   **294**

Insight on Society: Bitcoin   **295**

Market Size and Growth   297

EBPP Business Models   297

4.7 *Case Study: The Mobile Payment Marketplace: Goat Rodeo*   **299**

4.8 *Review*   **305**

Key Concepts   305

Questions   307

Projects   308

References   308

| 5 | E-COMMERCE BUSINESS STRATEGIES | 312 |

Learning Objectives   312

Beatguide: Turning a Passion into a Business   *313*

5.1   *E-commerce Business Models*   *316*
Introduction   316
Eight Key Elements of a Business Model   316
    Value Proposition   317
    Revenue Model   318
    Insight on Society: Foursquare: Check Your Privacy at the Door   *320*
    Market Opportunity   322
    Competitive Environment   322
    Competitive Advantage   323
    Market Strategy   325
    Organizational Development   325
    Management Team   326
Raising Capital   326
    Insight on Business: Crowdfunding Takes Off   *328*
Categorizing E-commerce Business Models: Some Difficulties   330

5.2   *Major Business-to-Consumer (B2C) Business Models*   *332*
E-tailer   332
Community Provider   332
Content Provider   334
Portal   335
    Insight on Technology: Battle of the Titans: Music in the Cloud   *336*
Transaction Broker   338
Market Creator   339
Service Provider   340

5.3   *Major Business-to-Business (B2B) Business Models*   *341*
E-distributor   342
E-procurement   342
Exchanges   342
Industry Consortia   343
Private Industrial Networks   343

**5.4   *How E-commerce Changes Business: Strategy, Structure, and
    Process*   *344***
Industry Structure   344
Industry Value Chains   348
Firm Value Chains   349

Firm Value Webs   349

Business Strategy   350

E-commerce Technology and Business Model Disruption   354

5.5   *Case Study: Freemium Takes Pandora Public*   357

5.6   *Review*   361

Key Concepts   361

Questions   362

Projects   363

References   363

| 6 | **E-COMMERCE MARKETING AND ADVERTISING** | **366** |

Learning Objectives   366

InMobi's Global Mobile Ad Network   367

6.1   *Consumers Online: The Internet Audience and Consumer Behavior*   370

Internet Traffic Patterns: The Online Consumer Profile   370

Intensity and Scope of Usage   371

Demographics and Access   372

Type of Internet Connection: Broadband and Mobile Impacts   373

Community Effects: Social Contagion in Social Networks   373

Consumer Behavior Models   374

Profiles of Online Consumers   374

The Online Purchasing Decision   375

Shoppers: Browsers and Buyers   378

What Consumers Shop for and Buy Online   379

Intentional Acts: How Shoppers Find Vendors Online   379

Why More People Don't Shop Online   380

Trust, Utility, and Opportunism in Online Markets   380

6.2   *Digital Commerce Marketing and Advertising Strategies and Tools*   381

Strategic Issues and Questions   381

The Web Site as a Marketing Platform: Establishing the Customer Relationship   383

Traditional Online Marketing and Advertising Tools   384

Search Engine Marketing and Advertising   386

Display Ad Marketing   390

E-mail Marketing   397

Affiliate Marketing   399

Viral Marketing   400

Lead Generation Marketing   400

Social, Mobile, and Local Marketing and Advertising   401

Social Marketing and Advertising   401

Mobile Marketing and Advertising   402

Local Marketing: The Social-Mobile-Local Nexus   403

Multi-channel Marketing: Integrating Online and Offline Marketing   404

Other Online Marketing Strategies   405

Customer Retention Strategies   405

Insight on Business: Are the Very Rich Different from You and Me?   *406*

Pricing Strategies   413

Long Tail Marketing   419

Insight on Technology: The Long Tail: Big Hits and Big Misses   *420*

6.3   *Internet Marketing Technologies*   *422*

The Revolution in Internet Marketing Technologies   422

Web Transaction Logs   422

Supplementing the Logs: Tracking Files   424

Databases, Data Warehouses, Data Mining, and Big Data   425

Insight on Society: Every Move You Take, Every Click You Make, We'll Be Tracking You   *426*

Databases   428

Data Warehouses and Data Mining   428

Hadoop and the Challenge of Big Data   430

Marketing Automation and Customer Relationship Management (CRM) Systems   431

6.4   *Understanding the Costs and Benefits of Online Marketing Communications*   *433*

Online Marketing Metrics: Lexicon   433

How Well Does Online Advertising Work?   437

The Costs of Online Advertising   439

Web Analytics: Software for Measuring Online Marketing Results   441

6.5   *Case Study: Programmatic Advertising: Real-Time Marketing*   *444*

6.6   *Review*   *448*

Key Concepts   448

Questions   450

Projects   450

References   451

| 7 | SOCIAL, MOBILE, AND LOCAL MARKETING | 456 |

Learning Objectives   456

Just Falafel: Soars with Social Media   457

7.1   *Introduction to Social, Mobile, and Local Marketing   460*
From Eyeballs to Conversations   460
From the Desktop to the Smartphone and Tablet   460
The Social, Mobile, Local Nexus   462

7.2   *Social Marketing   463*
Social Marketing Players   463
The Social Marketing Process   464
Facebook Marketing   466
    Basic Facebook Features   466
    Facebook Marketing Tools   466
    Starting a Facebook Marketing Campaign   470
    Measuring Facebook Marketing Results   472
Twitter Marketing   474
    Basic Twitter Features   474
    Insight on Technology: Fairmont Hotels: Using Google Analytics to Optimize Social and Mobile Marketing   475
    Twitter Marketing Tools   477
    Starting a Twitter Marketing Campaign   479
    Measuring Twitter Marketing Results   480
Pinterest Marketing   481
    Basic Pinterest Features   482
    Pinterest Marketing Tools   482
    Starting a Pinterest Marketing Campaign   485
    Measuring Pinterest Marketing Results   487
The Downside of Social Marketing   488

7.3   *Mobile Marketing   488*
Overview: M-commerce Today   488
    Insight on Society: Marketing to Children of the Web in the Age of Social Networks   489
    How People Actually Use Mobile Devices   492
    In-App Experiences and In-App Ads   493
    How the Multi-Screen Environment Changes the Marketing Funnel   495
Basic Mobile Marketing Features   495
    The Technology: Basic Mobile Device Features   496

Mobile Marketing Tools: Ad Formats   498

Starting a Mobile Marketing Campaign   499

Insight on Business: Mobile Marketing: Land Rover Seeks Engagement on the Small Screen   500

Measuring Mobile Marketing Results   503

7.4 *Local and Location-Based Mobile Marketing*   *504*

The Growth of Local Marketing   504

The Growth of Location-Based (Local) Mobile Marketing   505

Location-Based Marketing Platforms   506

Location-Based Mobile Marketing: The Technologies   507

Why Is Local Mobile Attractive to Marketers?   509

Location-Based Marketing Tools   509

A New Lexicon: Location-Based Digital Marketing Features   509

Proximity Marketing with Beacons   510

Starting a Location-Based Marketing Campaign   511

Measuring Location-Based Marketing Results   512

7.5 *Case Study: ExchangeHunterJumper.com: Building a Brand with Social Marketing   513*

7.6 *Review   519*

Key Concepts   519

Questions   521

Projects   522

References   522

| 8 | **ETHICS, LAW, AND E-COMMERCE** | **524** |

Learning Objectives   524

The EU Objects to Google's New Privacy Policy   525

8.1 *Understanding Ethical, Social, and Political Issues in E-commerce   528*

A Model for Organizing the Issues   529

Basic Ethical Concepts: Responsibility, Accountability, and Liability   531

Analyzing Ethical Dilemmas   533

Candidate Ethical Principles   534

8.2 *Privacy and Information Rights   535*

Information Collected at E-commerce Sites   536

Social Networks and Privacy   538

Mobile and Location-Based Privacy Issues   539

Profiling and Behavioral Targeting   540

The Internet and Government Invasions of Privacy: E-commerce
        Surveillance   542
Legal Protections   545
    Informed Consent and Notice   546
        The Federal Trade Commission's Fair Information Practices Principles   549
        The European Data Protection Directive   553
Private Industry Self-Regulation   554
Privacy Advocacy Groups   556
The Emerging Privacy Protection Business   556
Technological Solutions   557

8.3   *Intellectual Property Rights*   *558*
Types of Intellectual Property Protection   559
Copyright: the Problem of Perfect Copies and Encryption   559
    Look and Feel   560
    Fair Use Doctrine   560
    The Digital Millennium Copyright Act of 1998   561
Patents: Business Methods and Processes   564
    E-commerce Patents   565
    *Insight on Technology: Apple and Samsung Fight a Patent Battle Around the
    Globe   566*
Trademarks: Online Infringement and Dilution   571
    Trademarks and the Internet   571
    Cybersquatting and Brandjacking   572
    Cyberpiracy   573
    Metatagging   574
    Keywording   575
    Linking   575
    Framing   576
Challenge: Balancing the Protection of Property with Other Values   576

8.4   *Governance*   *577*
Can the Internet Be Controlled?   577
Taxation   578
    Insight on Business: New Rules Extend EU Taxation of E-commerce   580
Net Neutrality   582

8.5   *Public Safety and Welfare*   *584*
Protecting Children   585
Cigarettes, Gambling, and Drugs: Is the Web Really Borderless?   586
    Insight on Society: The Internet Drug Bazaar Operates Around the Globe   587

8.6   *Case Study: The Google Books Settlement: Is It Fair?*   *590*

8.7   *Review*   *595*
      Key Concepts   595
      Questions   597
      Projects   598
      References   598

9   **ONLINE CONTENT**   **602**

      Learning Objectives   602

      Spotify and Deezer: European Streaming Music Services Spread Around the Globe   *603*

9.1   *Online Content*   *607*
      Content Audience and Market: Where Are the Eyeballs and the Money?   609
         Media Utilization: A Converging Digital Stream   609
         Internet and Traditional Media: Cannibalization versus
            Complementarity   610
         Media Revenues   610
         Three Revenue Models for Digital Content Delivery: Subscription, A La Carte,
            and Advertising-Supported (Free and Freemium)   611
         Online Content Consumption   612
         Free or Fee: Attitudes About Paying for Content and the Tolerance for
            Advertising   613
      Digital Rights Management (DRM) and Walled Gardens   615
      Media Industry Structure   616
      Media Convergence: Technology, Content, and Industry Structure   617
         Technological Convergence   617
         Content Convergence   617
         Industry Structure Convergence   618
      Making a Profit with Online Content: From Free to Fee   620

9.2   *The Online Publishing Industry*   *621*
      Online Newspapers   621
         Newspapers: Searching for a Digital Business Model   621
         From Print-centric to Digital First: The Evolution of Newspaper Online
            Business Models, 1995–2014   623
         Assets: Newspaper Audience Size and Growth   626
         Challenge: Digital Ad Revenue   627
         Strength: Content Is King   627
         Challenge: Finding a Revenue Model   629
         Challenge: Growth of Pure Digital Competitors   630
         Can Newspapers Survive Digital Disruption?   632
      Magazines Rebound on the Tablet Platform   633

Insight on Society: Vox: The All-Digital News Site   *634*

E-Books and Online Book Publishing   638

Insight on Business: Digital Newsstands Grow   *639*

Amazon and Apple: The New Digital Media Ecosystems   642

E-Book Business Models   644

The Challenges of the Digital E-Book Platform   646

Interactive Books: Converging Technologies   647

9.3   *The Online Entertainment Industry*   *648*

Online Entertainment Audience Size and Growth   650

Television and Premium Video   651

Movies   653

Music   657

Insight on Technology: Hollywood and the Internet: Let's Cut a Deal   *658*

Games   664

9.4   *Case Study: Netflix: How Does This Movie End?*   *667*

9.5   *Review*   *671*

Key Concepts   671

Questions   673

Projects   673

References   674

| 10 | **ONLINE COMMUNITIES** | **676** |

Learning Objectives   676

Viadeo Challenges LinkedIn with a Multi-Local Approach   *677*

10.1   *Social Networks and Online Communities*   *679*

What Is an Online Social Network?   681

The Growth of Social Networks and Online Communities   681

Insight on Technology: The Appification of Facebook   *684*

Turning Social Networks into Businesses   686

Types of Social Networks and Their Business Models   688

Insight on Society: The Dark Side of Social Networks   *689*

Social Network Features and Technologies   692

The Future of Social Networks   693

10.2   *Online Auctions*   *694*

Benefits and Costs of Auctions   695

Benefits of Auctions   695

Risks and Costs of Auctions   696

Auctions as an E-commerce Business Model   697
Types and Examples of Auctions   697
When to Use Auctions (and for What) in Business   698
Auction Prices: Are They the Lowest?   700
Consumer Trust in Auctions   701
When Auction Markets Fail: Fraud and Abuse in Auctions   701

10.3   *E-commerce Portals*   *702*
The Growth and Evolution of Portals   703
Types of Portals: General-Purpose and Vertical Market   704
Insight on Business: The Transformation of AOL   *705*
Portal Business Models   708

10.4   *Case Study: eBay Evolves*

10.5   *Review*   *714*
Key Concepts   714
Questions   716
Projects   716
References   716

| 11 | **E-COMMERCE RETAILING AND SERVICES** | **718** |

Learning Objectives   718

Souq.com: The Amazon of the Middle East   *719*

11.1   *The Online Retail Sector*   *723*
The Retail Industry   724
Online Retailing   725
E-commerce Retail: The Vision   725
The Online Retail Sector Today   726

11.2   *Analyzing the Viability of Online Firms*   *730*
Strategic Analysis   730
Financial Analysis   731

11.3   *E-commerce in Action: E-tailing Business Models*   *733*
Virtual Merchants   733
Amazon   734
The Vision   734
Business Model   735
Financial Analysis   738

Strategic Analysis—Business Strategy   740

Strategic Analysis—Competition   741

Strategic Analysis—Technology   742

Strategic Analysis—Social and Legal Challenges   742

Future Prospects   742

Omni-Channel Merchants: Bricks-and-Clicks   743

Catalog Merchants   744

Manufacturer-Direct   745

Common Themes in Online Retailing   747

11.4   *The Service Sector: Offline and Online*   749

Insight on Technology: Big Data and Predictive Marketing   750

11.5   *Online Financial Services*   752

Online Financial Consumer Behavior   752

Online Banking and Brokerage   753

Multi-Channel vs. Pure Online Financial Services Firms   754

Financial Portals and Account Aggregators   755

Online Mortgage and Lending Services   755

Online Insurance Services   756

Online Real Estate Services   757

11.6   *Online Travel Services*   759

Why Are Online Travel Services So Popular?   760

The Online Travel Market   760

Online Travel Industry Dynamics   761

Insight on Society

Phony Reviews   763

11.7   *Online Career Services*   765

It's Just Information: The Ideal Web Business?   765

Online Recruitment Industry Trends   767

11.8   *Sharing Economy Companies*   769

Insight on Business: Airbnb Takes Off   771

11.9   *Case Study: OpenTable: Your Reservation Is Waiting*   774

11.10 *Review*   779

Key Concepts   779

Questions   781

Projects   782

References   782

| **12** | **B2B E-COMMERCE** | **784** |

Learning Objectives   784

Alibaba: China's E-commerce King   *785*

12.1 *An Overview of B2B E-commerce*   *789*
Some Basic Definitions   790
The Evolution of B2B E-commerce   790
The Growth of B2B E-commerce   793
Potential Benefits and Challenges of B2B E-commerce   794

12.2 *The Procurement Process and Supply Chains*   *795*
Steps in the Procurement Process   795
  Insight on Society: Where's My iPad? Global Supply Chain Risk and Vulnerability   796
Types of Procurement   798
Multi-Tier Supply Chains   799
Visibility and Other Concepts in Supply Chain Management   800
The Role of Existing Legacy Computer Systems and Enterprise Systems in Supply Chains   800

12.3 *Trends in Supply Chain Management and Collaborative Commerce*   *801*
Just-in-Time and Lean Production   802
Supply Chain Simplification   802
Supply Chain Black Swans: Adaptive Supply Chains   802
Accountable Supply Chains: Labor Standards   804
Sustainable Supply Chains: Lean, Mean, and Green   805
Electronic Data Interchange (EDI)   806
Mobile B2B   808
B2B in the Cloud   809
  Insight on Technology: Your Shoes Are in the Cloud   811
Supply Chain Management Systems   812
Collaborative Commerce   814
  Collaboration 2.0: Cloud, Web, Social, and Mobile   815
Social Networks and B2B: The Extended Social Enterprise   816

12.4 *Net Marketplaces*   *817*
Characteristics of Net Marketplaces   817
Types of Net Marketplaces   818
  E-distributors   819
  E-procurement   820

Exchanges   822

Industry Consortia   824

12.5 Private Industrial Networks   826

Objectives of Private Industrial Networks   827

Private Industrial Networks and Collaborative Commerce   828

Insight on Business: Walmart Develops a Private Industrial Network   829

Implementation Barriers   832

**12.6 Case Study: Elemica: Cooperation, Collaboration, and
Community   833**

12.7 Review   839

Key Concepts   839

Questions   841

Projects   842

References   842

Index   845

Credits   905

CHAPTER 1

Introduction to E-commerce

Puma

Goes Omni

When Puma, one of the world's top sports footwear, apparel, and accessories brands conceived its Love=Football campaign in 2010, the goal was to create a memorable tagline in a language that would be understood the world over—pictures. In the process, the company stumbled upon the power of social marketing. Puma's ad agency, Droga5, filmed a light-hearted commercial featuring scruffy everyday men in a Tottenham pub singing love songs to their Valentines. The video went viral, garnering more than 130 million impressions and spawning hundreds of homemade response videos. Featured in stories in every U.K. newspaper, the video was nominated in the Best Use of Social Media Marketing category at the Cannes Lions International Festival of Creativity.

© ngaga35/Fotolia.com

Its eyes opened by the success of the video, it was not long before Puma established a reputation as a social marketing pioneer. It developed an extensive presence on Facebook, Twitter, Instagram, Pinterest, Google+, and YouTube, closely integrating its social strategy with its other marketing channels with an eye towards driving the conversation and deepening its engagement with consumers. Its partnership with Droga5 produced several more award-winning videos and its Instagram social branding work earned marketing media praise.

But with a product distribution reach into more than 120 countries, Puma had to understand its different regional and sub-brand audiences. Not all content is suitable for every one of its 13.5 million global Facebook fans. Dedicated sport, country, region, and product category pages were created for each social network. For several years, Puma took a trial-and-error approach, focusing on building its follower base. Today, Puma uses a data-driven approach, geo-targeting posts at the appropriate times of day to maximize fan engagement and generate the right mix of online content to best drive sales. A tab for its iPhone app sends followers directly to Apple's App Store, substantially boosting sales. This integration of channels into a cohesive customer acquisition strategy is in a fact a key element of the emerging world of omni-channel retailing.

The advent of the term omni-channel signals the evolution of multi-channel or cross-channel retailing to encompass all digital and social technologies. The idea is that customers can examine, access, purchase, and return goods from any channel, and even change channels during the process, and at each step along the way and in each channel, receive timely and relevant product information. The rise of social networks and the personalized retail it engenders is a primary driver of omni-channel—the complete integration of the shopping and brand experience. Marketing efforts must be unified undertakings combining offline events and sales and online promotions and brand building that not only employ all available channels but provide multiple opportunities for customer involvement. For a company with e-commerce sites in the United States, Russia, Canada, China, India, Switzerland, Germany, France, the U.K., and a European site that serves multiple countries in multiple languages, this presents quite a challenge.

Puma's Global Head of E-Commerce, Tom Davis, has overseen a major restructuring of its e-commerce business. Puma was not fully prepared to compete in a global market that was rapidly shifting away from mature Western markets and desktop commerce. To coordinate market rollouts and ensure a unified brand image, Puma's regional e-commerce teams needed oversight. A command center took over brand strategy and investment decisions, leaving daily operational and locality-based decision-making to the regional teams. Unified content and product strategies were developed as well as a centralized product database. One central Web site replaced multiple e-commerce sites on different platforms. Demandware, Puma's main e-commerce platform, was used to simplify managing global e-commerce operations from a central digital platform, though several other e-commerce platforms are still used. The goal was to achieve a consistent and cohesive brand building strategy so that the teams would all be on the same page and decisions could be more quickly reached. Yet local customization of the message and ensuring that globally produced goods meet local requirements would still be most efficiently handled.

Web site overhaul was assigned to Viget, a Web design firm. It created templates to unite several Puma sites into one and unify the look across numerous categories and content types. A dozen category sites now complement Puma.com, with a custom-built content management system (CMS) ensuring that consistent Puma branding and navigation are maintained across all sub-sites and pages. Category managers can customize home pages outside of the template layout. The flexibility to roll out local, regional, or global campaigns is thus built into the Web site design. What's more, the CMS integrates with Puma's product inventory manager, Storefinder, and language translation tool. The design changes have improved site visualization and navigation, prompting customers to spend twice as much time on the site and raising the order rate by 7.1%.

The Viget team then turned to the mobile site, first incorporating Storefinder into the interface. Using the GPS capability of the mobile device, Puma stores nearest to the user can be located, along with address and contact information. Users experience the same content and appearance as Puma.com and each of the category sites, managed by the same CMS. With future modifications still on the horizon, Puma incorporated mobile into its omni-channel marketing strategy. The Puma Joy Pad—32 synchronized iPads mounted on a wall—allows shoppers at its flagship Paris store and other select locations to play games and experiment with Web apps. In the near future, shoppers will be able to generate content that they can share with their social networks, and walls will be connected so that customers in stores around the globe will be able to share their shopping experiences.

In October 2013, Puma released PUMATRAC, an iPhone app that automatically analyzes environmental conditions to give runners feedback on how these variables impact their performance. Once runners understand their own personal set of optimum conditions, they can modify adjustable variables to maximize performance. Scores and personal insights can be shared with runners in the region as can running routes. Stats can also be shared on social media sites, even as they are occurring. When traveling, GPS functionality enables sharing top running routes in the area, and, of course, the app is integrated with the E-store so that users will never be more than a few clicks away from the newest gear and nearest store.

In 2014, Puma's focus is to unify its branding and e-commerce Web sites into one site that delivers both experiences, as many other major apparel brands have done. The company has also solidified its worldwide e-commerce teams. In the past, Puma maintained nine independent e-commerce teams on five continents. Currently, it is working towards teams divided into the three major segments that comprise the majority of its sales—North America, Europe, Asia Pacific—as well as a global unit that operates at a level above these regional segments. The goal is to centralize Puma's e-commerce business both at one e-commerce site as well as internally within the company. At the same time, the company hopes to pursue a strategy that is flexible and that is focused more on the precise local needs in individual markets. These changes have already reaped rewards, improving conversion rates from 10% to 20% and boosting average order value by 12%. Centralizing its e-commerce operations under a single site also helps Puma better collect customer data to personalize marketing and develop more appealing products.

Although over the past three years Puma has gained invaluable omni-channel experience, racked up social marketing accomplishments, and laid the groundwork for resurgent e-commerce success, implementing a successful omni-channel strategy is a monumental task. Although Puma's sales increased by 3.7% in the third quarter of 2014, Puma's profits fell significantly from its 2013 levels, and the company cited marketing expenses as one of the primary causes. Puma cannot compete on price with mass merchandisers such as Amazon and Zappos, and it cannot control Puma product presentation in those venues. External loss of brand control necessitates superior product content, product information management, and shopping experience internally, precisely the skills it has been nurturing. Puma's ability to adapt its strategy to individual areas is also likely to help the company advance into China, a growing market where Puma has traditionally had minimal presence. This flexibility allowed Puma to adapt to Chinese e-commerce giant Alibaba's Tmall platform, where it holds a strong brand score.

SOURCES: "Puma Profits Drop in Q3 on Marketing, Forex Costs," Afp.com, November 7, 2014; "The Case of Puma: Can Tmall and In-House E-Store Co-Exist in China?" by Gelati Ting, Fashionbi.com, June 26, 2014; "Puma Understands the Importance of Local Needs in a Global E-commerce Rollout," by Derek Du Preez, Diginomica.com, June 24, 2014; "Puma and Newegg Discuss Their Entry Into the China E-commerce Market," Cdnetworks.com, June 3, 2014; "How Puma is Improving Sales Operations Through E-commerce," by Paul Demery, Internetretailer.com, May 20, 2014; "Clients: Puma," Demandware.com, accessed October 20, 2013; "Droga5 Case Studies: The HardChorus," Droga5.com, accessed October 20, 2013; "Puma Launches Innovative New Running App," News.puma.com, October 2, 2013; "Puma's Unified Approach to Global E-commerce," Ecommercefacts.com, August 5, 2013; "Puma's Head of E-Commerce: Changes and Challenges of Customization in the Apparel Industry," Masscustomization.de, July 16, 2013; "Puma Tries Out Mobile Photo-sharing with Rewards-based Campaign," by Lauren Johnson, Mobilemarketer.com, June 21, 2013; "PUMA: Challenges in an Omni-channel World," Embodee.com, May 3, 2013; "Puma Goes Mobile to Create Urban Playgrounds in Asia," by Adaline Lau, Clickz.com, November 23, 2012; "Puma Embraces Mobile, Fun Tech to Attract Buyers," by Mark Walsh, Mediapost.com, November 14, 2012; "The 10 Best-Branded Companies on Instagram," by Allyson Galle, Blog.hubspot.com, May 18, 2012; "3 Shoe Brands Kicking Butt with Social Media," by Lauren Indvik, Mashable.com, February 6, 2012; "Why Brands Like Puma and GE Are Flocking to Instagram," by Cotton Delo, Adage.com, January 17, 2012.

In 1994, e-commerce as we now know it did not exist. In 2014, just 20 years later, around 1.2 billion consumers worldwide are expected to spend about €1.18 trillion, and businesses more than €12.4 trillion, purchasing goods and services online or via a mobile device. And in this short period of time, e-commerce has been reinvented not just once, but twice.

The early years of e-commerce, during the late 1990s, were a period of business vision, inspiration, and experimentation. It soon became apparent, however, that establishing a successful business model based on those visions would not be easy. There followed a period of retrenchment and reevaluation, which led to the stock market crash of 2000–2001, with the value of e-commerce, telecommunications, and other technology stocks plummeting. After the bubble burst, many people were quick to write off e-commerce. But they were wrong. The surviving firms refined and honed their business models, and the technology became more powerful and less expensive, ultimately leading to business firms that actually produced profits. Between 2002–2008, retail e-commerce grew at more than 25% per year.

Today, we are in the middle of yet another transition. Social networks such as Facebook, Twitter, YouTube, Pinterest, and Tumblr, which enable users to distribute their own content (such as videos, music, photos, personal information, commentary, blogs, and more), have rocketed to prominence. Never before in the history of media have such large audiences been aggregated and made so accessible. Businesses are grappling with how best to approach this audience from a marketing, advertising, and sales perspective. At the same time, the traditional desktop platform and Web browser that most consumers have used to access the Internet in the past is being supplanted by mobile devices such as smartphones and tablet computers, and mobile apps. Facilitated by technologies such as cloud computing, mobile devices have become shopping, reading, and media viewing machines, and in the process, consumer behavior is being transformed yet again. Mobile, social, and local have become driving forces in e-commerce. It's probably safe to predict that this will not be the last transition for e-commerce, either. For instance, companies like Uber and Airbnb are part of a new wave of companies based on a disruptive "sharing economy" business model that may be the beginnings of yet another big shift in e-commerce.

1.1 E-COMMERCE: THE REVOLUTION IS JUST BEGINNING

Table 1.1 describes the major trends in e-commerce in 2014–2015. The mobile platform based on smartphones and tablet computers has finally arrived with a bang, making true mobile e-commerce a reality. Social networks are enabling social e-commerce by providing search, advertising, and payment services to vendors and customers. More and more people and businesses are using the Internet to conduct commerce; smaller, local firms are learning how to take advantage of the Internet as Web services and Web site tools become very inexpensive. New e-commerce brands have emerged while traditional retail brands such as Tesco and Carrefour are further extending their multi-channel, bricks-and-clicks strategies and retaining their dominant retail positions by strengthening their Internet operations. At the societal level, other trends are apparent. The Internet has created a platform for millions of people to create and share content,

TABLE 1.1	MAJOR TRENDS IN E-COMMERCE 2014–2015

BUSINESS

- B2C e-commerce continues to grow worldwide, with a global growth rate of almost 20%, and even higher in emerging markets such as China, India, and Brazil.
- Mobile e-commerce explodes growing from about €10.5 billion in 2013 to estimated €17.7 billion in 2014 in the United Kingdom.
- A new mobile app-based online economy grows alongside traditional Internet e-commerce, generating an estimated €25.8 billion in revenue from sales of apps and in-app purchases worldwide in 2014.
- Social e-commerce, based on social networks and supported by advertising, emerges and grows by over 60% from 2012 to 2013, generating over $2.7 billion in revenue for the top 500 social media retailers in the United States.
- Local e-commerce, the third dimension of the mobile, social, local e-commerce wave, also is growing in the United States, to an estimated $4.8 billion in 2014.
- Companies such as Airbnb and Uber, sometimes referred to as sharing economy companies, garner multi-billion dollar valuations.
- Mobile and social advertising platforms show strong growth and begin to challenge search engine marketing.
- Small businesses and entrepreneurs continue to flood into the e-commerce marketplace, often riding on the infrastructures created by industry giants such as Apple, Facebook, Amazon, Google, and eBay.
- B2B e-commerce worldwide continues to strengthen and grow beyond the €12.4 trillion mark.

TECHNOLOGY

- A mobile computing and communications platform based on smartphones and tablet computers and mobile apps becomes a reality and begins to rival the PC platform, creating a new platform for online transactions, marketing, advertising, and media viewing.
- Cloud computing completes the transformation of the mobile platform by storing consumer content and software on Internet servers and making it available to any consumer-connected device from the desktop to a smartphone.
- Computing and networking component prices continue to fall dramatically.
- As firms track the trillions of online interactions that occur each day, a flood of data, typically referred to as Big Data, is being produced.
- In order to make sense out of Big Data, firms turn to sophisticated software called business analytics (or Web analytics) that can identify purchase patterns as well as consumer interests and intentions in milliseconds.

SOCIETY

- Consumer- and user-generated content, and syndication in the form of social networks, tweets, blogs, and wikis, continue to grow and provide an entirely new self-publishing forum that engages millions of consumers.
- Social networks encourage self-revelation, while threatening privacy.
- Participation by adults in social networks on the Internet increases; Facebook becomes ever more popular in all demographic categories.
- Conflicts over copyright management and control continue, but there is substantial agreement among Internet distributors and copyright owners that they need one another.
- Taxation of Internet sales poses challenges for governments.
- Surveillance of Internet communications by both repressive regimes and Western democracies grows.
- Concerns over commercial and governmental privacy invasion increase.
- Internet security continues to decline as major sites are hacked and lose control over customer information.
- Spam remains a significant problem.

establish new social bonds, and strengthen existing ones through social networks, blogging, and photo- and video-posting sites. These same social networks have created significant privacy issues. The major digital copyright owners have increased their pursuit of online file-swapping services with mixed success, while reaching broad agreements with the big technology players like Apple, Amazon, and Google to protect intellectual property rights. Taxation of Internet sales continues to pose challenges for governments. Sovereign nations have expanded their surveillance of, and control over, Internet communications and content as a part of their anti-terrorist activities and their traditional interest in snooping on citizens. Privacy seems to have lost some of its meaning in an age when millions create public online personal profiles.

THE FIRST 30 SECONDS

It is important to realize that the rapid growth and change that has occurred in the first 20 years of e-commerce represents just the beginning—what could be called the first 30 seconds of the e-commerce revolution. Technology continues to evolve at exponential rates. This underlying ferment presents entrepreneurs with new opportunities to both create new businesses and new business models in traditional industries, and also to destroy old businesses. Business change becomes disruptive, rapid, and even destructive, while offering entrepreneurs new opportunities and resources for investment.

Improvements in underlying information technologies and continuing entrepreneurial innovation in business and marketing promise as much change in the next decade as was seen in the last decade. The twenty-first century will be the age of a digitally enabled social and commercial life, the outlines of which we can barely perceive at this time. Analysts estimate that by 2018, U.S. consumers will be spending almost $700 billion and businesses almost $8 trillion in online transactions. By 2020, some industry analysts believe e-commerce may account for 20% of all retail sales in the United States and Europe (eMarketer, Inc., 2013a). It appears likely that e-commerce will eventually impact nearly all commerce, and that most commerce will be e-commerce by the year 2050.

Can e-commerce continue to grow indefinitely? It's possible that at some point, e-commerce growth may slow simply as a result of overload: people may just not have the time to watch yet another online video, open another e-mail, or read another blog, tweet, or Facebook update. However, currently, there is no foreseeable limit to the continued rapid development of Internet and e-commerce technology, or limits on the inventiveness of entrepreneurs to develop new uses for the technology. Therefore, for now at least, it is likely that the disruptive process will continue.

Business fortunes are made—and lost—in periods of extraordinary change such as this. The next five years hold out extraordinary opportunities—as well as risks—for new and traditional businesses to exploit digital technology for market advantage. For society as a whole, the next few decades offer the possibility of extraordinary gains in social wealth as the digital revolution works its way through larger and larger segments of the world's economy, offering the possibility of high rates of productivity and income growth in an inflation-free environment.

As a business or technology student, this book will help you perceive and understand the opportunities and risks that lie ahead. By the time you finish, you will be able to identify the technological, business, and social forces that have shaped the growth of e-commerce and extend that understanding into the years ahead.

WHAT IS E-COMMERCE?

Our focus in this book is **e-commerce**—the use of the Internet, the World Wide Web (Web), and mobile apps to transact business. Although the terms Internet and Web are often used interchangeably, they are actually two very different things. The *Internet* is a worldwide network of computer networks, and the *Web* is one of the Internet's most popular services, providing access to billions of Web pages. An *app* (short-hand for application) is a software application. The term is typically used when referring to mobile applications, although it is also sometimes used to refer to desktop computer applications as well. (We describe the Internet, Web, and apps more fully later in this chapter and in Chapters 3 and 4.) More formally, we focus on digitally enabled commercial transactions between and among organizations and individuals. Each of these components of our working definition of e-commerce is important. *Digitally enabled transactions* include all transactions mediated by digital technology. For the most part, this means transactions that occur over the Internet, the Web, and/or via mobile apps. *Commercial transactions* involve the exchange of value (e.g., money) across organizational or individual boundaries in return for products and services. Exchange of value is important for understanding the limits of e-commerce. Without an exchange of value, no commerce occurs.

The professional literature sometimes refers to e-commerce as digital commerce in part to reflect the fact that in 2014, apps account for a growing amount of e-commerce revenues. For our purposes, we consider e-commerce and digital commerce to be synonymous.

THE DIFFERENCE BETWEEN E-COMMERCE AND E-BUSINESS

There is a debate about the meaning and limitations of both e-commerce and e-business. Some argue that e-commerce encompasses the entire world of electronically based organizational activities that support a firm's market exchanges—including a firm's entire information system's infrastructure (Rayport and Jaworski, 2003). Others argue, on the other hand, that e-business encompasses the entire world of internal and external electronically based activities, including e-commerce (Kalakota and Robinson, 2003).

We think it is important to make a working distinction between e-commerce and e-business because we believe they refer to different phenomena. E-commerce is not "anything digital" that a firm does. For purposes of this text, we will use the term **e-business** to refer primarily to the digital enabling of transactions and processes *within* a firm, involving information systems under the control of the firm. For the most part, in our view, e-business does not include commercial transactions involving an exchange of value across organizational boundaries. For example, a company's online inventory control mechanisms are a component of e-business, but such internal processes do not directly generate revenue for the firm from outside businesses or consumers, as e-commerce, by definition, does. It is true, however, that a firm's e-business infrastructure provides support for online e-commerce exchanges; the same infrastructure and skill sets are involved in both e-business and e-commerce. E-commerce and e-business systems blur together at the business firm boundary, at the point

e-commerce
the use of the Internet, the Web, and apps to transact business. More formally, digitally enabled commercial transactions between and among organizations and individuals

e-business
the digital enabling of transactions and processes within a firm, involving information systems under the control of the firm

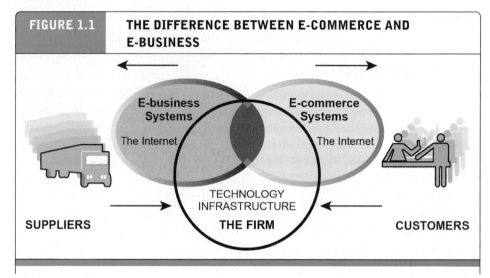

| FIGURE 1.1 | THE DIFFERENCE BETWEEN E-COMMERCE AND E-BUSINESS |

E-commerce primarily involves transactions that cross firm boundaries. E-business primarily involves the application of digital technologies to business processes within the firm.

where internal business systems link up with suppliers or customers (see **Figure 1.1**). E-business applications turn into e-commerce precisely when an exchange of value occurs (see Mesenbourg, U.S. Department of Commerce, 2001, for a similar view). We will examine this intersection further in Chapter 12.

WHY STUDY E-COMMERCE?

Why are there college courses and textbooks on e-commerce when there are no courses or textbooks on "TV Commerce," "Radio Commerce," "Railroad Commerce," or "Highway Commerce," even though these technologies had profound impacts on commerce in the twentieth century and account for far more commerce than e-commerce?

The reason for the interest specifically in e-commerce is that e-commerce technology (discussed in detail in Chapters 3 and 4) is different and more powerful than any of the other technologies we have seen in the past century. E-commerce technologies—and the digital markets that result—have brought about some fundamental, unprecedented shifts in commerce. While these other technologies transformed economic life in the twentieth century, the evolving Internet and other information technologies are shaping the twenty-first century.

Prior to the development of e-commerce, the marketing and sale of goods was a mass-marketing and sales force–driven process. Marketers viewed consumers as passive targets of advertising campaigns and branding "blitzes" intended to influence their long-term product perceptions and immediate purchasing behavior. Companies sold their products via well-insulated channels. Consumers were trapped by geographical and social boundaries, unable to search widely for the best price and quality. Information about prices, costs, and fees could be hidden from the consumer, creating profitable information asymmetries for the selling firm. **Information asymmetry** refers to any disparity in relevant market information among parties in a transaction. It was so expensive to change

information asymmetry

any disparity in relevant market information among parties in a transaction

national or regional prices in traditional retailing (what are called *menu costs*) that one national price was the norm, and dynamic pricing to the marketplace let alone to individuals in the marketplace—changing prices in real time—was unheard of. In this environment, manufacturers prospered by relying on huge production runs of products that could not be customized or personalized. One of the shifts that e-commerce is bringing about is a reduction in information asymmetry among market participants (consumers and merchants). Preventing consumers from learning about costs, price discrimination strategies, and profits from sales becomes more difficult with e-commerce, and the entire marketplace potentially becomes highly price competitive. At the same time, online merchants gain considerable market power over consumers by using consumer personal information in ways inconceivable 10 years ago to maximize their revenues.

EIGHT UNIQUE FEATURES OF E-COMMERCE TECHNOLOGY

Figure 1.2 illustrates eight unique features of e-commerce technology that both challenge traditional business thinking and explain why we have so much interest in e-commerce. These unique dimensions of e-commerce technologies suggest many new possibilities for marketing and selling—a powerful set of interactive, personalized, and rich messages are available for delivery to segmented, targeted audiences. E-commerce technologies make it possible for merchants to know much more about consumers and to be able to use this information more effectively than was ever true

FIGURE 1.2	EIGHT UNIQUE FEATURES OF E-COMMERCE TECHNOLOGY

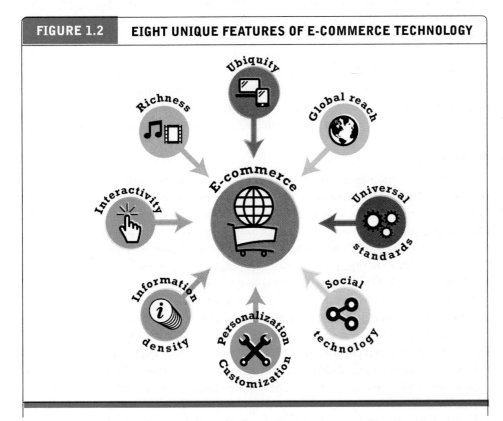

E-commerce technologies provide a number of unique features that have impacted the conduct of business.

in the past. Online merchants can use this new information to develop new information asymmetries, enhance their ability to brand products, charge premium prices for high-quality service, and segment the market into an endless number of subgroups, each receiving a different price. To complicate matters further, these same technologies make it possible for merchants to know more about other merchants than was ever true in the past. This presents the possibility that merchants might collude on prices rather than compete and drive overall average prices up. This strategy works especially well when there are just a few suppliers (Varian, 2000a). We examine these different visions of e-commerce further in Section 1.2 and throughout the book.

Each of the dimensions of e-commerce technology illustrated in Figure 1.2 deserves a brief exploration, as well as a comparison to both traditional commerce and other forms of technology-enabled commerce.

Ubiquity

marketplace

physical space you visit in order to transact

ubiquity

available just about everywhere, at all times

marketspace

marketplace extended beyond traditional boundaries and removed from a temporal and geographic location

In traditional commerce, a **marketplace** is a physical place you visit in order to transact. For example, television and radio typically motivate the consumer to go someplace to make a purchase. E-commerce, in contrast, is characterized by its **ubiquity**: it is available just about everywhere, at all times. It liberates the market from being restricted to a physical space and makes it possible to shop from your desktop, at home, at work, or even from your car, using mobile e-commerce. The result is called a **marketspace**—a marketplace extended beyond traditional boundaries and removed from a temporal and geographic location. From a consumer point of view, ubiquity reduces *transaction costs*—the costs of participating in a market. To transact, it is no longer necessary that you spend time and money traveling to a market. At a broader level, the ubiquity of e-commerce lowers the cognitive energy required to transact in a marketspace. *Cognitive energy* refers to the mental effort required to complete a task. Humans generally seek to reduce cognitive energy outlays. When given a choice, humans will choose the path requiring the least effort—the most convenient path (Shapiro and Varian, 1999; Tversky and Kahneman, 1981).

Global Reach

E-commerce technology permits commercial transactions to cross cultural, regional, and national boundaries far more conveniently and cost-effectively than is true in traditional commerce. As a result, the potential market size for e-commerce merchants is roughly equal to the size of the world's online population (an estimated 2.8 billion in 2014) (eMarketer, Inc., 2014a). More realistically, the Internet makes it much easier for start-up online merchants within a single country to achieve a national audience than was ever possible in the past. The total number of users or customers an e-commerce business can obtain is a measure of its **reach** (Evans and Wurster, 1997).

reach

the total number of users or customers an e-commerce business can obtain

In contrast, most traditional commerce is local or regional—it involves local merchants or national merchants with local outlets. Television and radio stations, and newspapers, for instance, are primarily local and regional institutions with limited but powerful national networks that can attract a national audience. In contrast to e-commerce technology, these older commerce technologies do not easily cross national boundaries to a global audience.

Universal Standards

One strikingly unusual feature of e-commerce technologies is that the technical standards of the Internet, and therefore the technical standards for conducting e-commerce, are **universal standards**—they are shared by all nations around the world. In contrast, most traditional commerce technologies differ from one nation to the next. For instance, television and radio standards differ around the world, as does cell phone technology. The universal technical standards of the Internet and e-commerce greatly lower *market entry costs*—the cost merchants must pay just to bring their goods to market. At the same time, for consumers, universal standards reduce *search costs*—the effort required to find suitable products. And by creating a single, one-world marketspace, where prices and product descriptions can be inexpensively displayed for all to see, *price discovery* becomes simpler, faster, and more accurate (Banerjee et al., 2005; Bakos, 1997; Kambil, 1997). Users of the Internet, both businesses and individuals, also experience *network externalities*—benefits that arise because everyone uses the same technology. With e-commerce technologies, it is possible for the first time in history to easily find many of the suppliers, prices, and delivery terms of a specific product anywhere in the world, and to view them in a coherent, comparative environment. Although this is not necessarily realistic today for all or even most products, it is a potential that will be exploited in the future.

universal standards
standards that are shared by all nations around the world

Richness

Information **richness** refers to the complexity and content of a message (Evans and Wurster, 1999). Traditional markets, national sales forces, and small retail stores have great richness: they are able to provide personal, face-to-face service using aural and visual cues when making a sale. The richness of traditional markets makes them a powerful selling or commercial environment. Prior to the development of the Web, there was a trade-off between richness and reach: the larger the audience reached, the less rich the message. The Internet has the potential for offering considerably more information richness than traditional media such as printing presses, radio, and television because it is interactive and can adjust the message to individual users. Chatting with an online sales person, for instance, comes very close to the customer experience in a small retail shop. The richness enabled by the Internet allows retail and service merchants to market and sell "complex" goods and services that heretofore required a face-to-face presentation by a sales force to a much larger audience.

richness
the complexity and content of a message

Interactivity

Unlike any of the commercial technologies of the twentieth century, with the possible exception of the telephone, e-commerce technologies allow for **interactivity**, meaning they enable two-way communication between merchant and consumer and among consumers. Traditional television, for instance, cannot ask viewers questions or enter into conversations with them, or request that customer information be entered into a form. In contrast, all of these activities are possible on an e-commerce site and are now commonplace with smartphones, social networks, and Twitter. Interactivity allows an online merchant to engage a consumer in ways similar to a face-to-face experience.

interactivity
technology that allows for two-way communication between merchant and consumer

Information Density

information density
the total amount and quality of information available to all market participants

E-commerce technologies vastly increase **information density**—the total amount and quality of information available to all market participants, consumers, and merchants alike. E-commerce technologies reduce information collection, storage, processing, and communication costs. At the same time, these technologies greatly increase the currency, accuracy, and timeliness of information—making information more useful and important than ever. As a result, information becomes more plentiful, less expensive, and of higher quality.

A number of business consequences result from the growth in information density. In e-commerce markets, prices and costs become more transparent. *Price transparency* refers to the ease with which consumers can find out the variety of prices in a market; *cost transparency* refers to the ability of consumers to discover the actual costs merchants pay for products (Sinha, 2000). But there are advantages for merchants as well. Online merchants can discover much more about consumers; this allows merchants to segment the market into groups willing to pay different prices and permits them to engage in *price discrimination*—selling the same goods, or nearly the same goods, to different targeted groups at different prices. For instance, an online merchant can discover a consumer's avid interest in expensive exotic vacations, and then pitch expensive exotic vacation plans to that consumer at a premium price, knowing this person is willing to pay extra for such a vacation. At the same time, the online merchant can pitch the same vacation plan at a lower price to more price-sensitive consumers. Merchants also have enhanced abilities to differentiate their products in terms of cost, brand, and quality.

Personalization/Customization

personalization
the targeting of marketing messages to specific individuals by adjusting the message to a person's name, interests, and past purchases

customization
changing the delivered product or service based on a user's preferences or prior behavior

E-commerce technologies permit **personalization**: merchants can target their marketing messages to specific individuals by adjusting the message to a person's name, interests, and past purchases. Today this is achieved in a few milliseconds and followed by an advertisement based on the consumer's profile. The technology also permits **customization**—changing the delivered product or service based on a user's preferences or prior behavior. Given the interactive nature of e-commerce technology, much information about the consumer can be gathered in the marketplace at the moment of purchase. With the increase in information density, a great deal of information about the consumer's past purchases and behavior can be stored and used by online merchants. The result is a level of personalization and customization unthinkable with traditional commerce technologies. For instance, you may be able to shape what you see on television by selecting a channel, but you cannot change the contents of the channel you have chosen. In contrast, the online version of *The Financial Times* allows you to select the type of news stories you want to see first, and gives you the opportunity to be alerted when certain events happen. Personalization and customization allow firms to precisely identify market segments and adjust their messages accordingly.

Social Technology: User Content Generation and Social Networking

In a way quite different from all previous technologies, e-commerce technologies have evolved to be much more social by allowing users to create and share content with a worldwide community. Using these forms of communication, users are able to create new social networks and strengthen existing ones. All previous mass media in modern history, including the printing press, used a broadcast model (one-to-many) where content is created in a central location by experts (professional writers, editors, directors, actors, and producers) and audiences are concentrated in huge aggregates to consume a standardized product. The telephone would appear to be an exception but it is not a mass communication technology. Instead the telephone is a one-to-one technology. The Internet and e-commerce technologies have the potential to invert this standard media model by giving users the power to create and distribute content on a large scale, and permit users to program their own content consumption. The Internet provides a unique, many-to-many model of mass communication.

Table 1.2 provides a summary of each of the unique features of e-commerce technology and their business significance.

TABLE 1.2	BUSINESS SIGNIFICANCE OF THE EIGHT UNIQUE FEATURES OF E-COMMERCE TECHNOLOGY
E-COMMERCE TECHNOLOGY DIMENSION	**BUSINESS SIGNIFICANCE**
Ubiquity—Internet/Web technology is available everywhere: at work, at home, and elsewhere via mobile devices, anytime.	The marketplace is extended beyond traditional boundaries and is removed from a temporal and geographic location. "Marketspace" is created; shopping can take place anywhere. Customer convenience is enhanced, and shopping costs are reduced.
Global reach—The technology reaches across national boundaries, around the earth.	Commerce is enabled across cultural and national boundaries seamlessly and without modification. "Marketspace" includes potentially billions of consumers and millions of businesses worldwide.
Universal standards—There is one set of technology standards, namely Internet standards.	There is a common, inexpensive, global technology foundation for businesses to use.
Richness—Video, audio, and text messages are possible.	Video, audio, and text marketing messages are integrated into a single marketing message and consuming experience.
Interactivity—The technology works through interaction with the user.	Consumers are engaged in a dialog that dynamically adjusts the experience to the individual, and makes the consumer a co-participant in the process of delivering goods to the market.
Information density—The technology reduces information costs and raises quality.	Information processing, storage, and communication costs drop dramatically, while currency, accuracy, and timeliness improve greatly. Information becomes plentiful, cheap, and accurate.
Personalization/Customization—The technology allows personalized messages to be delivered to individuals as well as groups.	Personalization of marketing messages and customization of products and services are based on individual characteristics.
Social technology—User content generation and social networks.	New Internet social and business models enable user content creation and distribution, and support social networks.

WEB 2.0: PLAY MY VERSION

Web 2.0

a set of applications and technologies that allows users to create, edit, and distribute content; share preferences, bookmarks, and online personas; participate in virtual lives; and build online communities

Many of the unique features of e-commerce technology and the Internet come together in a set of applications and social media technologies referred to as **Web 2.0**. The Internet started out as a simple network to support e-mail and file transfers among remote computers. The Web started out as a way to use the Internet to display simple pages and allow the user to navigate among the pages by linking them together electronically. You can think of this as Web 1.0. By 2007 something else was happening. The Internet and the Web had evolved to the point where users could create, edit, and distribute content to others; share with one another their preferences, bookmarks, and online personas; participate in virtual lives; and build online communities. This "new" Web is called by many Web 2.0, and while it draws heavily on the "old" Web 1.0, it is nevertheless a clear evolution from the past.

Let's take a quick look at some examples of Web 2.0 applications and sites:

- Twitter is a social network/micro-blogging service that encourages users to enter 140-character messages ("tweets") in answer to the question "What are you doing?" Twitter has more than 270 million active users worldwide, sending around 500 million tweets per day and more than 16 billion tweets a month. Twitter has begun to monetize its subscribers by developing an ad platform and providing marketing services to firms that want to stay in instant contact with their customers.

- YouTube, owned by Google, is the world's largest online consumer-generated video-posting site. YouTube is now morphing into a premium video content distributor and video producer, offering feature-length movies, television series, and its own original content. In April 2014, YouTube had more than 1 billion unique viewers a month worldwide. According to YouTube, 100 hours of video are posted to the site every minute, and over 6 billion hours of video are watched each month, with almost 40% of that time on mobile devices (YouTube, 2014; comScore, 2014a).

- Instagram is a mobile photo-sharing application that allows users to easily apply a variety of different photo filters and borders, and then post the photos to social networks such as Facebook, Twitter, Foursquare, Tumblr, and Flickr. Launched in November 2010, Instagram quickly attracted more than 50 million users and in April 2012 was purchased by Facebook for $1 billion. It has over 200 million active users as of May 2014 (Buck, 2012; Instagram.com, 2014).

- Wikipedia allows contributors around the world to share their knowledge and in the process has become the most successful online encyclopedia, far surpassing "professional" encyclopedias such as Encarta and Britannica. Wikipedia is one of the largest collaboratively edited reference projects in the world, with more than 4.5 million articles available in English and more than 30 million in total, in 287 languages. Wikipedia relies on volunteers, makes no money, and accepts no advertising. Wikipedia is consistently ranked as one of the top 10 most visited sites on the Web (Wikipedia.org, 2014; Wikimedia Foundation, 2011; comScore, 2014b).

- Tumblr, now owned by Yahoo, is a combination of blog platform and social network. It allows users to easily post text, photos, links, music, videos, and more. As of June

2014, Tumblr hosts over 190 million blogs, containing over 83 billion posts. On a typical day, users make almost 95 million posts (Tumblr.com, 2014).

- Uber is a company that has created a social and economic platform that allows providers who have an available car to connect with consumers that do not have a car but need transportation. Uber's so-called "mesh" or "sharing economy" business model is based on smartphone apps and cloud servers. Uber had over $200 million in revenue in 2013 based on more than $1 billion in bookings, and in June 2014, was valued at a shocking $18 billion.

What do these Web 2.0 applications and sites have in common? First, they rely on user- and consumer-generated content. "Regular" people (not just experts or professionals) are creating, sharing, modifying, and broadcasting content to huge audiences. Second, easy search capability is a key to their success. Third, they are inherently highly interactive, creating new opportunities for people to socially connect to others. They are social sites because they support interactions among users. Fourth, they rely on broadband connectivity. Fifth, many of them are currently only marginally profitable, and their business models are unproven despite considerable investment. Nevertheless, the potential monetary rewards for social sites with huge audiences is quite large. Sixth, they attract extremely large audiences when compared to traditional Web 1.0 applications, exceeding in many cases the audience size of national broadcast and cable television programs. These audience relationships are intensive and long-lasting interactions with millions of people. In short, they attract eyeballs in very large numbers. Hence, they present marketers with extraordinary opportunities for targeted marketing and advertising. They also present consumers with the opportunity to rate and review products, and entrepreneurs with ideas for future business ventures. Last, these sites act as application development platforms where users can contribute and use software applications for free. Briefly, it's a whole new world from what has gone before.

TYPES OF E-COMMERCE

There are several different types of e-commerce and many different ways to characterize them. **Table 1.3** lists the major types of e-commerce discussed in this book.[1] For the most part, we distinguish different types of e-commerce by the nature of the market relationship—who is selling to whom. Mobile, social, and local e-commerce can be looked at as subsets of these types of e-commerce.

Business-to-Consumer (B2C) E-commerce

The most commonly discussed type of e-commerce is **business-to-consumer (B2C) e-commerce**, in which online businesses attempt to reach individual consumers. B2C commerce includes purchases of retail goods, travel services, and online content. B2C e-commerce has grown exponentially since 1995, and is the type of e-commerce that

business-to-consumer (B2C) e-commerce
online businesses selling to individual consumers

---

[1] For the purposes of this text, we subsume business-to-government (B2G) e-commerce within B2B e-commerce, viewing the government as simply a form of business when it acts as a procurer of goods and/or services.

TABLE 1.3	MAJOR TYPES OF E-COMMERCE
TYPE OF E-COMMERCE	EXAMPLE
B2C—business-to-consumer	Amazon is a general merchandiser that sells consumer products to retail consumers.
B2B—business-to-business	Go2Paper is an independent third-party marketplace that serves the paper industry.
C2C—consumer-to-consumer	Auction sites such as eBay, and listing sites such as Craigslist, enable consumers to auction or sell goods directly to other consumers. Airbnb and Uber provide similar platforms for services such as room rental and transportation.
M-commerce—mobile e-commerce	Mobile devices such as tablet computers and smartphones can be used to conduct commercial transactions.
Social e-commerce	Facebook is both the leading social network and social e-commerce site.
Local e-commerce	Groupon offers subscribers daily deals from local businesses in the form of Groupons, discount coupons that take effect once enough subscribers have agreed to purchase.

most consumers are likely to encounter (see **Figure 1.3**). In 2014, global B2C sales are estimated to be about €1.18 trillion, growing to over €2.35 trillion by 2018. North America is still the region with the highest e-commerce sales in 2014, but by 2015, the Asia-Pacific region is expected to surpass North America and will grow faster through 2018. Within the B2C category, there are many different types of business models. Chapter 2 has a detailed discussion of seven different B2C business models: portals, online retailers, content providers, transaction brokers, market creators, service providers, and community providers.

Business-to-Business (B2B) E-commerce

business-to-business (B2B) e-commerce

online businesses selling to other businesses

Business-to-business (B2B) e-commerce, in which businesses focus on selling to other businesses, is the largest form of e-commerce, with over $5.7 trillion in transactions in the United States (see **Figure 1.4** on page 60) and about €12.4 trillion worldwide in 2014. This is a small portion of total B2B commerce (which remains largely non-automated), suggesting that B2B e-commerce has significant growth potential. The ultimate size of B2B e-commerce is potentially huge. There are two primary business models used within the B2B arena: Net marketplaces, which include e-distributors, e-procurement companies, exchanges and industry consortia, and private industrial networks.

Consumer-to-Consumer (C2C) E-commerce

consumer-to-consumer (C2C) e-commerce

consumers selling to other consumers

Consumer-to-consumer (C2C) e-commerce provides a way for consumers to sell to each other, with the help of an online market maker (also called a platform provider) such as eBay or Etsy, the classifieds site Craigslist, or newer sharing companies such as Airbnb and Uber. Given that in 2014, eBay is likely to generate over €64 billion in gross merchandise volume around the world, it is probably safe to estimate that the size of the global C2C market in 2014 is more than €80 billion (eBay, 2014). In C2C e-commerce, the consumer prepares the product for market, places the product for auction or sale, and relies on the market maker to provide catalog, search engine, and transaction-clearing capabilities so that products can be easily displayed, discovered, and paid for.

Mobile E-commerce (M-commerce)

Mobile e-commerce, or m-commerce, refers to the use of mobile devices to enable online transactions. Described more fully in Chapter 2, m-commerce involves the use of cellular and wireless networks to connect laptops, smartphones such as the iPhone, Android, and BlackBerry, and tablet computers such as the iPad to the Internet. Once connected, mobile consumers can conduct transactions, including stock trades, in-store price comparisons, banking, travel reservations, and more. Mobile retail purchases are expected to reach over €17.7 billion in 2014 in the United Kingdom, for instance, and to continue to grow rapidly over the next five years.

mobile e-commerce (m-commerce)
use of mobile devices to enable online transactions

Social E-commerce

Social e-commerce is e-commerce that is enabled by social networks and online social relationships. It is sometimes also referred to as Facebook commerce, but in

social e-commerce
e-commerce enabled by social networks and online social relationships

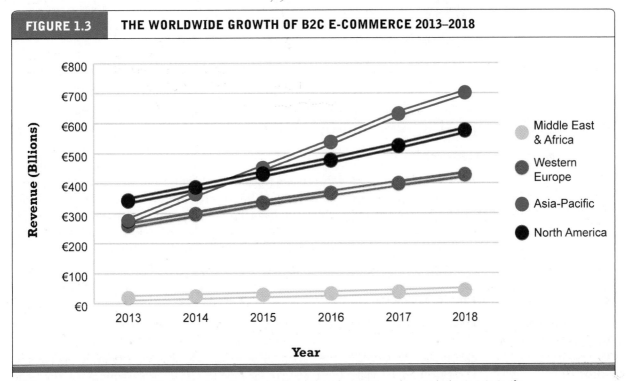

| **FIGURE 1.3** | **THE WORLDWIDE GROWTH OF B2C E-COMMERCE 2013–2018** |

B2C e-commerce is growing rapidly in all regions. Overall global growth is about 20%, and is even higher in Asia-Pacific.
SOURCES: Based on data from eMarketer, Inc., 2014b; authors' estimates.

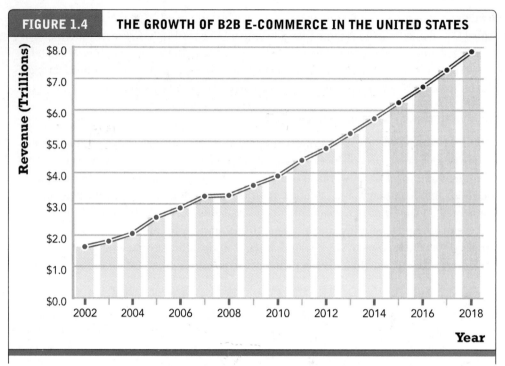

FIGURE 1.4   THE GROWTH OF B2B E-COMMERCE IN THE UNITED STATES

B2B e-commerce in the United States is about 10 times the size of B2C e-commerce. In 2018, B2B e-commerce is projected to be almost $8 trillion. (Note: Does not include EDI transactions.)

SOURCES: Based on data from U.S. Census Bureau, 2014; authors' estimates.

actuality is a much larger phenomenon that extends beyond just Facebook. The growth of social e-commerce is being driven by a number of factors, including the increasing popularity of social sign-on (signing onto Web sites using your Facebook or other social network ID), network notification (the sharing of approval or disapproval of products, services, and content via Facebook's Like button or Twitter tweets), online collaborative shopping tools, and social search (recommendations from online trusted friends). Social e-commerce is still in its infancy, but in 2013, the top 500 retailers in Internet Retailer's Social Media 500 earned about $2.7 billion from social commerce, a 60% increase over 2012, and shoppers clicking from social networks to retailers' Web sites accounted for 7.7% of all traffic to those Web sites in November 2013, up from 6.6% in the previous year (Internet Retailer, 2014a; Stambor, 2014).

Local E-commerce

local e-commerce
e-commerce that is focused on engaging the consumer based on his or her current geographic location

Local e-commerce, as its name suggests, is a form of e-commerce that is focused on engaging the consumer based on his or her current geographic location. Local merchants use a variety of online marketing techniques to drive consumers to their stores. Local e-commerce is the third prong of the mobile, social, local e-commerce wave, and is expected to grow in the United States to an estimated $4.8 billion in 2014 (eMarketer, Inc., 2012).

Figure 1.5 illustrates the relative size of all of the various types of e-commerce.

GROWTH OF THE INTERNET, WEB, AND MOBILE PLATFORM

The technology juggernauts behind e-commerce are the Internet, the Web, and increasingly, the mobile platform. We describe the Internet, Web, and mobile platform in some detail in Chapter 3. The **Internet** is a worldwide network of computer networks built on common standards. Created in the late 1960s to connect a small number of mainframe computers and their users, the Internet has since grown into the world's largest network. It is impossible to say with certainty exactly how many computers and other wireless access devices such as smartphones are connected to the Internet worldwide at any one time, but the number is clearly more than 1 billion. The Internet links businesses, educational institutions, government agencies, and individuals together, and provides users with services such as e-mail, document transfer, shopping, research, instant messaging, music, videos, and news.

One way to measure the growth of the Internet is by looking at the number of Internet hosts with domain names. (An *Internet host* is defined by the Internet Systems Consortium as any IP address that returns a domain name in the in-addr.arpa domain,

Internet
worldwide network of computer networks built on common standards

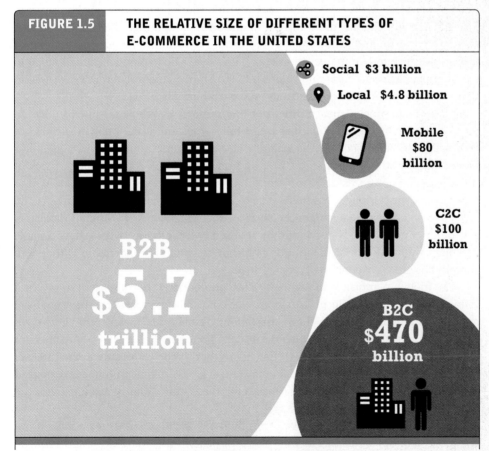

| FIGURE 1.5 | THE RELATIVE SIZE OF DIFFERENT TYPES OF E-COMMERCE IN THE UNITED STATES |

Social $3 billion

Local $4.8 billion

Mobile $80 billion

C2C $100 billion

B2B $5.7 trillion

B2C $470 billion

B2B e-commerce dwarfs all other forms of e-commerce; mobile, social, and local e-commerce, although growing rapidly, are still relatively small in comparison to "traditional" e-commerce.

which is a special part of the DNS namespace that resolves IP addresses into domain names.) In January 2014, there were more than 1 billion Internet hosts in over 245 countries, up from just 70 million in 2000 (Internet Systems Consortium, 2014).

The Internet has shown extraordinary growth patterns when compared to other electronic technologies of the past. It took radio 38 years to achieve a 30% share of U.S. households. It took television 17 years to achieve a 30% share. It took only 10 years for the Internet/Web to achieve a 53% share of U.S. households once a graphical user interface was invented for the Web in 1993.

World Wide Web (the Web)
provides access to billions of Web pages

The **World Wide Web (the Web)** is one of the most popular services that runs on the Internet infrastructure. The Web was the original "killer app" that made the Internet commercially interesting and extraordinarily popular. The Web was developed in the early 1990s and hence is of much more recent vintage than the Internet. We describe the Web in some detail in Chapter 3. The Web provides access to billions of Web pages indexed by Google and other search engines. These pages are created in a language called *HTML (HyperText Markup Language)*. HTML pages can contain text, graphics, animations, and other objects. You can find an exceptionally wide range of information on Web pages, ranging from the entire collection of public records from the Securities and Exchange Commission, to the card catalog of your local library, to millions of music tracks and videos. The Internet prior to the Web was primarily used for text communications, file transfers, and remote computing. The Web introduced far more powerful and commercially interesting, colorful multimedia capabilities of direct relevance to commerce. In essence, the Web added color, voice, and video to the Internet, creating a communications infrastructure and information storage system that rivals television, radio, magazines, and even libraries.

There is no precise measurement of the number of Web pages in existence, in part because today's search engines index only a portion of the known universe of Web pages, and also because the size of the Web universe is unknown. Google has identified over 60 trillion unique URLs, up from 1 trillion in 2008, although many of these pages do not necessarily contain unique content (Google, 2014). In addition to this "surface" or "visible" Web, there is also the so-called deep Web that is reportedly 1,000 to 5,000 times greater than the surface Web. The deep Web contains databases and other content that is not routinely indexed by search engines such as Google. Although the total size of the Web is not known, what is indisputable is that Web content has grown exponentially since 1993.

mobile platform
provides the ability to access the Internet from a variety of highly mobile devices such as smartphones, tablets, and other ultra-lightweight laptop computers

The mobile platform is the newest "latest and greatest" development in Internet infrastructure. The **mobile platform** provides the ability to access the Internet from a variety of mobile devices such as smartphones, tablets, and other ultra-lightweight laptop computers via wireless networks or cell phone service. In 2014, there are over 365 million mobile devices in the United States that can be connected to the Internet (more than 1 device for each person in the United States), and that number is expected to grow to over 385 million by 2018 (eMarketer, Inc., 2014c). **Figure 1.6** illustrates the rapid growth of mobile Internet access.

Read *Insight on Technology: Will Apps Make the Web Irrelevant?* for a look at the challenge that apps and the mobile platform pose to the Web's dominance of the Internet ecosphere.

FIGURE 1.6 — MOBILE INTERNET ACCESS IN THE UNITED STATES

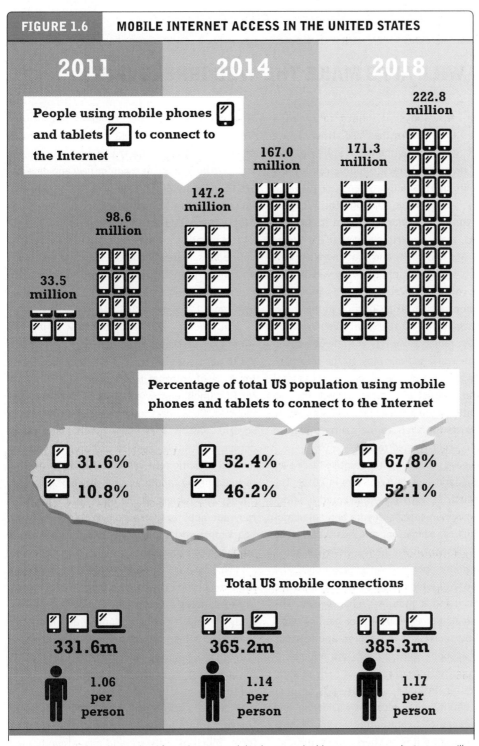

Continued growth in the number of people using mobile phones and tablets to connect to the Internet will provide a significant stimulus to mobile e-commerce.

SOURCES: Based on data from eMarketer, Inc., 2013b, 2013c, 2013d, 2014c, 2014d.

INSIGHT ON TECHNOLOGY

WILL APPS MAKE THE WEB IRRELEVANT?

Nowadays, it's hard to recall a time before the Web. How did we get along without the ability to pull up a Web browser and search for any item, learn about any topic, or play just about any type of game? Though the Web has come a remarkably long way from its humble beginnings, many experts claim that the Web's best days are behind it, and that there's a new sheriff in town: apps. Opinions vary widely over the future role of the Web in a world where apps have become an ever larger portion of the Internet marketspace. In 10 years, will Web browsers be forgotten relics, as we rely entirely on apps to do both our work and our play on the Internet? Will the Web and apps coexist peacefully as vital cogs in the Internet ecosystem? Or will the app craze eventually die down as tech users gravitate back towards the Web as the primary way to perform Internet-related tasks?

Apps have grown into a disruptive force ever since Apple launched its App Store in 2008. The list of industries apps have disrupted is wide-ranging: communications, media and entertainment, logistics, education, and healthcare. The average U.S. consumer spends almost 2 hours and 45 minutes per day on smartphones and tablets, 86% of which is spent within apps and only 14% using a mobile Web browser. The primary amount of time spent is on gaming apps, followed by social and messaging applications such as Facebook and Twitter, and entertainment sites as YouTube. Despite not even existing prior to 2008, in 2014, sales of apps account for about €20 billion in revenues worldwide, and the app economy is continuing to show robust growth, suggesting it is nowhere near saturated.

Not only that, but the growth is not coming from more users trying the same small number of apps. Consumers are trying new apps all the time, leaving plenty of room for new app developers to innovate and create best-selling apps. In fact, according to mobile advertising company Flurry, over 175 million people in the United States qualify as mobile addicts, which they define as someone who launches a smartphone app more than 60 times a day. According to Flurry, the number of such addicts has increased by almost 125% from 2013 to 2014.

In January 2014, for the first time ever, Americans used apps more than desktop computers to access the Internet, with apps accounting for 47% of Internet traffic, compared to 45% for PCs (mobile browsers comprised the remaining 8%). Consumers have gravitated to apps for several reasons. First, smartphones and tablet computers enable users to use apps anywhere, instead of being tethered to a desktop or having to lug a heavy laptop around. Of course, smartphones and tablets enable users to use the Web too, but apps are often more convenient and boast more streamlined, elegant interfaces than mobile Web browsers.

Not only are apps more appealing in certain ways to consumers, they are much more appealing to content creators and media companies. Apps are much easier to control and monetize than Web sites, not to mention they can't be crawled by Google or other services. On the Web, the average price of ads per thousand impressions is falling, and after twenty years, many content providers are still mostly struggling to turn the Internet into a profitable content delivery platform. Much of software and media companies' focus has shifted to developing mobile apps for this reason.

These trends are why some pundits boldly proclaim that the Web is dead, and that the shift from the Web to apps has only just started. These analysts believe that the Internet will be used to transport data, but individual app interfaces will replace the Web browser as the most common way to access and display content. Even the creator of the Web, Tim Berners-Lee, feels that the Web as we know it is being threatened. That's not a good sign.

But there is no predictive consensus about the role of the Web in our lives in the next decade and beyond. Many analysts believe the demise of the Web has been greatly exaggerated, and that the Web boasts many advantages over today's apps that users will be unwilling to relinquish. Although apps may be more convenient than the Web in many respects, the depth of the Web browsing experience trumps that of apps. The Web is a vibrant, diverse array of sites, and browsers have an openness and flexibility that apps lack. The connections between Web sites enhance their usefulness and value to users, and apps that instead seek to lock users in cannot offer the same experience.

Other analysts who are more optimistic about the Web's chances to remain relevant in an increasingly app-driven online marketplace feel this way because of the emergence of HTML5. HTML5 is a new markup language that will enable more dynamic Web content and allow for browser-accessible Web apps that are as appealing as device-specific apps. In fact, there is another group of analysts who believe that apps and the Web are going to come together, with HTML5 bringing the best of the app experience to the Web, and with apps developing new Web-like capabilities. Already, work is underway to create more "smart" apps that handle a wider array of tasks than today's apps can handle, such as Google Glasses or apps with Siri integration.

A shift towards apps and away from the Web would have a ripple effect on e-commerce firms. As the pioneer of apps and the market leader in apps, smartphones, and tablet computers, Apple stands to gain from a shift towards apps, and although they will also face increasing opposition from other companies, including Google, the established success of the App Store will make it next to impossible to dethrone them. Google's search business is likely to suffer from all of the "walled garden" apps that it cannot access, but it also has a major stake in the world of smartphones, tablets, and apps itself with its fleet of Android-equipped devices. Facebook has already seen its members make the transition from using its site on the Web to using its mobile app and has made, and continues to make, significant investments in standalone apps, such as Instagram and WhatsApp. Web-based companies that fail to find an answer to this problem may eventually fall by the wayside. The one sure bet is that nobody knows for sure exactly what the future holds for apps, the Web, and the Internet.

■■ **SOURCES:** "More People Are Opening More Mobile Apps Every Day," by Ewan Spence, Forbes.com, April 24, 2014; "The Rise of the Mobile Addict," by Simon Khalaf, Flurry.com, April 22, 2014; "How Apps Won the Mobile Web," by Thomas Claburn, Informationweek.com, April 3, 2014; "Apps Solidify Leadership Six Years into the Mobile Revolution," by Simon Khalaf, Flurry.com, April 1, 2014; "Mobile Apps Overtake PC Internet Usage in U.S.," by James O'Toole, Money.cnn.com, February 28, 2014; "Convergence of User Experiences," Savas.me, April 4, 2013; "Flurry Five-Year Report: It's an App World. The Web Just Lives in It," by Simon Khalaf, Flurry.com, April 3, 2013; "Here's Why Google and Facebook Might Completely Disappear in the Next 5 Years," by Eric Jackson, Forbes.com, April 30, 2012; "Is The Web Dead In the Face of Native Apps? Not Likely, But Some Think So," by Gabe Knuth, Brianmadden.com, March 28, 2012; "Imagining the Internet," by Janna Quitney Anderson and Lee Rainie, Pew Internet and American Life Project, March 23, 2012; "The Web is Dead. Long Live the Internet," by Chris Anderson and Michael Wolff, Wired.com, August 17, 2010; "The Web is Dead? A Debate," by Chris Anderson, Wired.com, August 17, 2010.

ORIGINS AND GROWTH OF E-COMMERCE

It is difficult to pinpoint just when e-commerce began. There were several precursors to e-commerce. In the late 1970s, a pharmaceutical firm named Baxter Healthcare initiated a primitive form of B2B e-commerce by using a telephone-based modem that permitted hospitals to reorder supplies from Baxter. This system was later expanded during the 1980s into a PC-based remote order entry system and was widely copied throughout the United States long before the Internet became a commercial environment. The 1980s saw the development of Electronic Data Interchange (EDI) standards that permitted firms to exchange commercial documents and conduct digital commercial transactions across private networks.

In the B2C arena, the first truly large-scale digitally enabled transaction system was deployed in France in 1981. The Minitel was a French videotext system that combined a telephone with an 8-inch screen. By the mid-1980s, more than 3 million Minitels were deployed, and more than 13,000 different services were available, including ticket agencies, travel services, retail products, and online banking. The Minitel service continued in existence until December 31, 2006, when it was finally discontinued by its owner, France Telecom.

However, none of these precursor systems had the functionality of the Internet. Generally, when we think of e-commerce today, it is inextricably linked to the Internet. For our purposes, we will say e-commerce begins in 1995, following the appearance of the first banner advertisements placed by AT&T, Volvo, Sprint, and others on Hotwired in late October 1994, and the first sales of banner ad space by Netscape and Infoseek in early 1995. Since then, e-commerce has been the fastest growing form of commerce in the United States.

The data suggests that, over the next five years, B2C e-commerce in the United States will grow by about 13% annually, much faster than traditional retail sales (which are growing at only about 4% a year). There is tremendous upside potential. Today, for instance, B2C retail e-commerce is still a very small part (around 6–7%) of the overall $4.7 trillion retail market in the United States, and under current projections, will only be slightly higher than Walmart's fiscal 2014 revenue ($473 billion) in 2018. There is obviously much room to grow (see **Figure 1.7**). However, it's not likely that B2C e-commerce revenues will continue to expand forever at double-digit rates. As online sales become a larger percentage of all sales, online sales growth will likely eventually decline to that growth level. This point still appears to be a long way off. Online content sales, everything from music, to video, medical information, games, and entertainment, have an even longer period to grow before they hit any ceiling effects.

1.2   E-COMMERCE: A BRIEF HISTORY

Although e-commerce is not very old, it already has a tumultuous history. The history of e-commerce can be usefully divided into three periods: 1995–2000, the period of invention; 2001–2006, the period of consolidation; and 2007–present, a period of

FIGURE 1.7	**ROOM TO GROW**

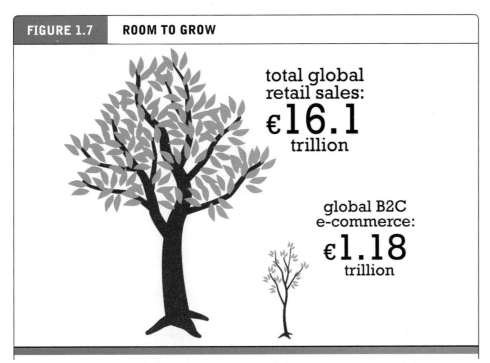

total global
retail sales:
€16.1
trillion

global B2C
e-commerce:
€1.18
trillion

The B2C e-commerce market is still just a small part of the overall global retail market, but with much room to grow in the future.

SOURCES: Based on data from IORMA, 2014.

reinvention with social, mobile, and local expansion. The following examines each of these periods briefly, while **Figure 1.8** places them in context along a timeline.

E-COMMERCE 1995–2000: INVENTION

The early years of e-commerce were a period of explosive growth and extraordinary innovation, beginning in 1995 with the first widespread use of the Web to advertise products. During this Invention period, e-commerce meant selling retail goods, usually quite simple goods, on the Internet. There simply was not enough bandwidth for more complex products. Marketing was limited to unsophisticated static display ads and not very powerful search engines. The Web policy of most large firms, if they had one at all, was to have a basic static Web site depicting their brands. The rapid growth in e-commerce was fueled by over $125 billion in U.S. venture capital. This period of e-commerce came to a close in 2000 when stock market valuations plunged, with thousands of companies disappearing (the "dot-com crash").

The early years of e-commerce were also one of the most euphoric of times in commercial history. It was also a time when key e-commerce concepts were developed. For computer scientists and information technologists, the early success of e-commerce was a powerful vindication of a set of information technologies that had developed over a period of 40 years—extending from the development of the early Internet, to the PC, to local area networks. The vision was of a universal

FIGURE 1.8	PERIODS IN THE DEVELOPMENT OF E-COMMERCE

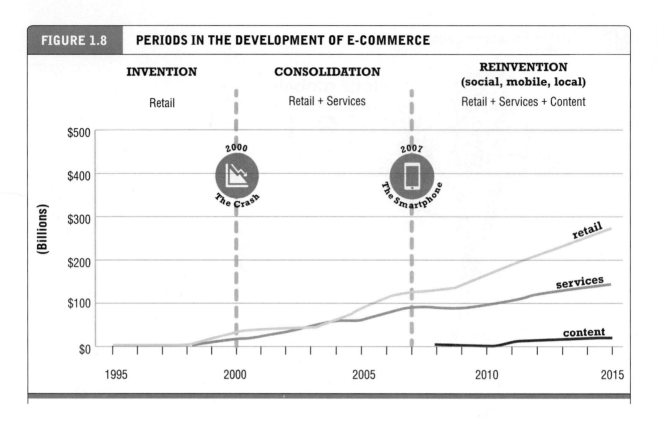

communications and computing environment that everyone on Earth could access with cheap, inexpensive computers—a worldwide universe of knowledge stored on HTML pages created by hundreds of millions of individuals and thousands of libraries, governments, and scientific institutes. Technologists celebrated the fact that the Internet was not controlled by anyone or any nation, but was free to all. They believed the Internet—and the e-commerce that rose on this infrastructure—should remain a self-governed, self-regulated environment.

For economists, the early years of e-commerce raised the realistic prospect of a nearly perfect competitive market: where price, cost, and quality information are equally distributed, a nearly infinite set of suppliers compete against one another, and customers have access to all relevant market information worldwide. The Internet would spawn digital markets where information would be nearly perfect—something that is rarely true in other real-world markets. Merchants in turn would have equal direct access to hundreds of millions of customers. In this near-perfect information marketspace, transaction costs would plummet because search costs—the cost of searching for prices, product descriptions, payment settlement, and order fulfillment—would all fall drastically (Bakos, 1997). For merchants, the cost of searching for customers would also fall, reducing the need for wasteful advertising. At the same time, advertisements could be personalized to the needs of every customer. Prices and even costs would be increasingly transparent to the consumer, who could now know exactly and instantly the worldwide best price, quality, and availability of most products. Information asymmetry would be greatly reduced. Given the instant nature of Internet communications, the availability of powerful sales information systems, and the low cost involved in changing prices on a Web site (low menu costs), producers could dynamically price their products to reflect actual demand, ending the idea of one national price, or one suggested manufacturer's list price. In turn, market middlemen—the distributors and wholesalers who are intermediaries between producers and consumers, each demanding a payment and raising costs while adding little value—would disappear (**disintermediation**). Manufacturers and content originators would develop direct market relationships with their customers. The resulting intense competition, the decline of intermediaries, and the lower transaction costs would eliminate product brands, and along with these, the possibility of *monopoly profits* based on brands, geography, or special access to factors of production. Prices for products and services would fall to the point where prices covered costs of production plus a fair, "market rate" of return on capital, plus additional small payments for entrepreneurial effort (that would not last long). Unfair competitive advantages (which occur when one competitor has an advantage others cannot purchase) would be eliminated, as would extraordinary returns on invested capital. This vision was called **friction-free commerce** (Smith et al., 2000).

For real-world entrepreneurs, their financial backers, and marketing professionals, e-commerce represented an extraordinary opportunity to earn far above normal returns on investment. The e-commerce marketspace represented access to millions of consumers worldwide who used the Internet and a set of marketing communications technologies (e-mail and Web pages) that was universal, inexpensive, and powerful. These new technologies would permit marketers to practice what they always had done—segmenting the market into groups with different needs and price sensitivity, targeting the segments with branding and promotional messages, and positioning the product and pricing for each group—but with even more precision. In this new marketspace, extraordinary profits would go to **first movers**—those firms who were first to market in a particular area and who moved quickly to gather market share. In a "winner take all" market, first movers could establish a large customer base quickly, build brand name recognition early, create an entirely new distribution channel, and then inhibit competitors (new entrants) by building in *switching costs* for their customers through proprietary interface designs and features available only at one site. The idea for entrepreneurs was to create near monopolies online based on size, convenience, selection, and brand. Online businesses using the new technology could create informative, community-like features unavailable to traditional merchants. These "communities of consumption" also would add value and be difficult for traditional merchants to imitate. The thinking was that once customers became accustomed to using a company's unique Web interface and feature set, they could not easily be switched to competitors. In the best case, the entrepreneurial firm would invent proprietary technologies and techniques that almost everyone adopted, creating a network effect. A **network effect** occurs where all participants receive value from the fact that everyone else uses the same tool or product (for example, a common operating system, telephone system, or software application such as a proprietary instant messaging standard or an operating system such as Windows), all of which increase in value as more people adopt them.[2]

---

[2] The network effect is quantified by Metcalfe's Law, which argues that the value of a network grows by the square of the number of participants.

disintermediation
displacement of market middlemen who traditionally are intermediaries between producers and consumers by a new direct relationship between producers and consumers

friction-free commerce
a vision of commerce in which information is equally distributed, transaction costs are low, prices can be dynamically adjusted to reflect actual demand, intermediaries decline, and unfair competitive advantages are eliminated

first mover
a firm that is first to market in a particular area and that moves quickly to gather market share

network effect
occurs where users receive value from the fact that everyone else uses the same tool or product

To initiate this process, entrepreneurs argued that prices would have to be very low to attract customers and fend off potential competitors. E-commerce was, after all, a totally new way of shopping that would have to offer some immediate cost benefits to consumers. However, because doing business on the Web was supposedly so much more efficient when compared to traditional "bricks-and-mortar" businesses (even when compared to the direct mail catalog business) and because the costs of customer acquisition and retention would supposedly be so much lower, profits would inevitably materialize out of these efficiencies. Given these dynamics, market share, the number of visitors to a site ("eyeballs"), and gross revenue became far more important in the earlier stages of an online firm than earnings or profits. Entrepreneurs and their financial backers in the early years of e-commerce expected that extraordinary profitability would come, but only after several years of losses.

Thus, the early years of e-commerce were driven largely by visions of profiting from new technology, with the emphasis on quickly achieving very high market visibility. The source of financing was venture capital funds. The ideology of the period emphasized the ungoverned "Wild West" character of the Web and the feeling that governments and courts could not possibly limit or regulate the Internet; there was a general belief that traditional corporations were too slow and bureaucratic, too stuck in the old ways of doing business, to "get it"—to be competitive in e-commerce. Young entrepreneurs were therefore the driving force behind e-commerce, backed by huge amounts of money invested by venture capitalists. The emphasis was on *deconstructing* (destroying) traditional distribution channels and disintermediating existing channels, using new pure online companies who aimed to achieve impregnable first-mover advantages. Overall, this period of e-commerce was characterized by experimentation, capitalization, and hypercompetition (Varian, 2000b).

E-COMMERCE 2001–2006: CONSOLIDATION

In the second period of e-commerce, from 2000 to 2006, a sobering period of reassessment of e-commerce occurred, with many critics doubting its long-term prospects. Emphasis shifted to a more "business-driven" approach rather than being technology driven; large traditional firms learned how to use the Web to strengthen their market positions; brand extension and strengthening became more important than creating new brands; financing shrunk as capital markets shunned start-up firms; and traditional bank financing based on profitability returned.

During this period of consolidation, e-commerce changed to include not just retail products but also more complex services such as travel and financial services. This period was enabled by widespread adoption of broadband networks in American homes and businesses, coupled with the growing power and lower prices of personal computers that were the primary means of accessing the Internet, usually from work or home. Marketing on the Internet increasingly meant using search engine advertising targeted to user queries, rich media and video ads, and behavioral targeting of marketing messages based on ad networks and auction markets. The Web policy of both large and small firms expanded to include a broader "Web presence" that included not just Web sites, but also e-mail, display, and search engine campaigns; multiple Web sites for each product; and the building of some limited community feedback facilities. E-commerce in this period was growing again by more than 10% a year.

E-COMMERCE 2007–PRESENT: REINVENTION

Beginning in 2007 with the introduction of the iPhone, to the present day, e-commerce has been transformed yet again by the rapid growth of online social networks, widespread adoption of consumer mobile devices such as smartphones and tablet computers, and the expansion of e-commerce to include local goods and services. The defining characteristics of this period are often characterized as the "social, mobile, local" online world. In this period, entertainment content begins to develop as a major source of e-commerce revenues and mobile devices become entertainment centers, as well as on-the-go shopping devices for retail goods and services. Marketing is transformed by the increasing use of social networks, word-of-mouth, viral marketing, and much more powerful data repositories and analytic tools for truly personal marketing. Firms' online policies expand in the attempt to build a digital presence that surrounds the online consumer with coordinated marketing messages based on their social network memberships, use of search engines and Web browsers, and even their personal e-mail messages. This period is both a sociological phenomenon as well as a technological and business phenomenon. The *Insight on Business* case, *Rocket Internet,* takes a look at Rocket Internet, which has mentored a number of these new social, mobile, and local e-commerce ventures.

Table 1.4 on page 74 summarizes e-commerce in each of these three periods.

ASSESSING E-COMMERCE: SUCCESSES, SURPRISES, AND FAILURES

Looking back at the early years of e-commerce, it is apparent that e-commerce has been, for the most part, a stunning technological success as the Internet and the Web ramped up from a few thousand to billions of e-commerce transactions per year, and this year will generate an estimated €1.12 trillion in total B2C global revenues and around €12.4 trillion in B2B revenues, with around 1.2 billion online buyers worldwide. With enhancements and strengthening, described in later chapters, it is clear that e-commerce's digital infrastructure is solid enough to sustain significant growth in e-commerce during the next decade. The Internet scales well. The "e" in e-commerce has been an overwhelming success.

From a business perspective, though, the early years of e-commerce were a mixed success, and offered many surprises. Only about 10% of dot-coms formed since 1995 have survived as independent companies in 2014. Only a very tiny percentage of these survivors are profitable. Yet online B2C sales of goods and services are still growing very rapidly. Contrary to economists' hopes, increasingly online sales are concentrated in the top ten retailers who account for over 50% of all online retail sales. So thousands of firms fail, and those few that survive dominate the market. The idea of thousands of suppliers competing on price has been replaced by a market dominated by giant firms. Consumers have learned to use the Web as a powerful source of information about products they actually purchase through other channels, such as at a traditional bricks-and-mortar store. For instance, a November 2013 study by consulting firm Accenture found that over 75% of those surveyed "webroomed" (researched a product online before purchasing at a physical store) (eMarketer, Inc., 2014a). This is

INSIGHT ON BUSINESS

ROCKET INTERNET

By now we've all heard the story of some lines of code written by Mark Zuckerberg in a Harvard dorm room blossoming into a multi-billion dollar business. These days, it's harder than ever to keep track of all the tech startups being bought for millions and even billions of euros, often even without any revenue to show for themselves. A number of them have something in common—they have been nurtured, and in some cases, whipped into shape, with the help of an "incubator."

As entrepreneurs continue to launch a growing number of e-commerce companies, incubators have come to occupy a vital role in tech, helping new businesses move from little more than a great idea to an established, vibrant business. Founded in 2007 by German entrepreneurs Alexander, Oliver, and Marc Samwer, Rocket Internet is an online start-up incubator that launches e-commerce companies and other Internet start-ups in emerging markets, with the stated goal of becoming the world's largest Internet platform outside the United States and China. Headquartered in Berlin and with 25 additional international offices, Rocket Internet has over 75 independent companies active in 100 countries in its portfolio of start-ups. In 2014, Rocket launched a much-anticipated IPO on the Frankfurt Stock Exchange, representing the largest German technology IPO in the past decade. The initial pricing valued the company at around €6.5 billion. In the previous two years, the company had raised nearly €3.2 billion from investors.

Rocket bills itself as more than a venture capital firm or typical incubator. Rocket has a variety of teams that work closely with each of its ventures, including teams focused on Engineering and Product Development, Online Marketing, CRM, Business Intelligence, Operations, HR, and Finance. Rocket also helps its start-ups by providing access to centralized logistics and other back-office functions to help them cut down on operational costs. The growing network of Rocket Internet companies is also a valuable resource for newer ventures. In many emerging markets, the most talented workers end up in established industries, but Rocket Internet is ensuring that e-commerce also captures top talent in those regions. Prominent companies launched via Rocket Internet include e-commerce retail companies like Germany's Zalando, India's Jabong. com, Russia's Lamoda.ru, Australia's The Iconic and Zanui, Pakistan's Azmalo.pk and Daraz.pk, and Southeast Asia's Zalora.

Former Rocket Internet employees also have a strong track record with their own independent start-ups once they've left the parent company. These employees note that their experience at Rocket has made the prospect of starting new businesses seem less intimidating. They also praise Oliver Samwer's attention to detail and emphasis on making decisions using data. Rocket Internet start-ups invariably collect and analyze as much data as possible to learn about customer behavior and the markets in which they operate. They also report that their association with Rocket Internet gives them more credibility with major investors.

Rocket Internet has yet to launch many new businesses in the United States, where the competitive environment for tech ventures is much more difficult than in emerging markets and even Europe. Many of Rocket's ventures focus on emerging markets because the profit margins are higher, although the markets are smaller. This is in contrast to Amazon, for example, which has razor-thin margins but enormous scope and market reach. Critics of Rocket Internet claim that the company is less concerned with innovation than it is with launching clones of successful United States-based businesses in other markets. For instance, in 2014, Rocket launched Zipjet, an on-demand laundry service modeled after U.S. counterpart Washio, and ShopWings, an online supermarket resembling Instacart, a similar service launched in major U.S. cities. Oliver Samwer counters talk of site clones by noting that for the majority of these types of businesses, truly disruptive innovation is rare, and the business succeeds or does not succeed based on the efficiency of its business processes. Marc Samwer adds that Rocket Internet takes the best ideas and improves on them by localizing them to better fit specific areas. Investors are also concerned about the profitability of Rocket's portfolio. Many of Rocket's companies have market leader status in their respective areas, but nearly all of them are not currently profitable, including Zalora and Jabong. Rocket contends that by focusing on growth in emerging markets first, profits will come in time.

Rocket has done well by launching companies modeled after established businesses in emerging markets, and then selling these ventures to those established businesses when they're looking to expand into those markets. eBay's acquisition of Germany's leading auction site, Alando, is an example. Amazon is rumored to be interested in Jabong, and Africa-based Jumia and Southeast Asia-based Lazada, also modeled after Amazon, could conceivably be additional targets for Amazon. Payleven is a European mobile payment company modeled after Square and Paypal. Increasingly, however, Rocket is looking to create sustainable companies who are focused less on their eventual sale to bigger companies and more on their own growth. Oliver Samwer believes that in the past, it may have sold some businesses, such as Alando, too early, but that it was necessary in order for Rocket to build a track record. Now that it has, it can afford to take a longer-term view.

Startupbootcamp is another start-up accelerator based in Europe that selects 10 start-ups from a pool of hundreds of applicants and provides cutting edge training and a network of professionals to help them go from an idea to a thriving business. Via its flagship locations in Amsterdam, applicants receive coaching from a network of 750 volunteer mentors from successful tech companies as well as significant stipends for living expenses and partner deals. After 3 months, start-ups pitch their businesses to venture capitalists and investors. Established companies also have made deals with Startupbootcamp to mentor specific types of businesses, such as AVG Technologies' 2013 agreement to invest in Startupbootcamp's NFC and Contactless division. Though Internet start-ups have boomed, busted, and are now booming again, as the global economy continues to rely more on the Internet and Internet-based services, incubators and accelerators like Rocket Internet and Startupbootcamp are here to stay.

SOURCES: "Fear And Laundry In London As Rocket Internet's ZipJet Launches In The U.K. Capital City," by Steve O'Hear, Techcrunch.com, November 3, 2014; "With ShopWings, Instacart Gets a Wink and a Clone From Rocket Internet," by Ingrid Lunden, Techcrunch.com, October 13, 2014; "Rocket Internet – First Mover in Asia?" by Susan Cunningham, *Forbes*, October 5, 2014; "Rocket Internet Shares End Lower," by Friedrich Geiger, *Wall Street Journal*, October 3, 2014; "Rocket Internet Drops 13% in Debut," by Chase Gummer, *Wall Street Journal*, October 2, 2014; "Rocket Internet's Linio Picks Up $50M to Further Build Out Its Latin American Amazon-style Marketplace," by Ingrid Lunden, Techcrunch.com, November 5, 2013; "Rocket Internet Is Getting Ready to Launch Peer-to-Peer Lending Platform Lendico," Venturevillage.eu, October 30, 2013; "Rocket Internet's Marc Samwar on Cloning: We Make Business Models Better Because We Localize," by Leena Rao, Techcrunch.com, October 28, 2013; "5 Reasons Why Rocket Internet Graduates Become Good Entrepreneurs," Vntureburn.com, October 17, 2013; "About Startupbootcamp," startupbootcamp.com, accessed October 2013; "AVG Invests in Startupbootcamp NFC & Contactless Program in Amsterdam," Wall Street Journal, September 26, 2013; "Rocket Internet Raises $500M from Kinnevik and Access, Plans More E-Commerce in Emerging Markets," by Ingrid Lunden, TechCrunch, July 16, 2013; "Rocket Internet Raises $500M To Be the Biggest e-Commerce Incubator on Earth," by Sean Ludwig, VentureBeat.com, July 16, 2013; "eBay Acquires Germany's Leading Onine Person-to-Person Trading Site – Alando.de AG," Prnewswire, June 22, 2013; "Payleven, The Samwer's Square/PayPal Rival, Ramps Up Security with FSA Authorization, MasterCard mPOS Scheme," by Ingrid Lunden, TechCrunch.com, March 27, 2013; "Rocket Internet's New Site Reveals a Huge Global Cloning Operation in Full Flow," by Mike Butcher, TechCrunch.com, July 20, 2012.

TABLE 1.4	EVOLUTION OF E-COMMERCE	
1995–2000 INVENTION	2001–2006 CONSOLIDATION	2007–PRESENT REINVENTION
Technology driven	Business driven	Mobile technology enables social, local, and mobile commerce
Revenue growth emphasis	Earnings and profits emphasis	Audience and social network connections emphasis
Venture capital financing	Traditional financing	Smaller VC investments; early small-firm buyouts by large online players
Ungoverned	Stronger regulation and governance	Extensive government surveillance
Entrepreneurial	Large traditional firms	Entrepreneurial social and local firms
Disintermediation	Strengthening intermediaries	Proliferation of small online intermediaries renting business processes of larger firms
Perfect markets	Imperfect markets, brands, and network effects	Continuation of online market imperfections; commodity competition in select markets
Pure online strategies	Mixed "bricks-and-clicks" strategies	Return of pure online strategies in new markets; extension of bricks-and-clicks in traditional retail markets
First-mover advantages	Strategic-follower strength; complementary assets	First-mover advantages return in new markets as traditional Web players catch up
Low-complexity retail products	High-complexity retail products and services	Retail, services, and content

especially true of expensive consumer durables such as appliances, automobiles, and electronics. This offline "Internet-influenced" commerce is very difficult to estimate, but is believed to be somewhere around $1.4 trillion in the United States in 2014 (Barberi, 2014). Altogether then, B2C retail e-commerce (both actual purchases and purchases influenced by online shopping but actually buying in a store) is expected to amount to over $1.7 trillion in 2014, or over a third of total retail sales in the United States. The "commerce" in e-commerce is basically very sound, at least in the sense of attracting a growing number of customers and generating revenues.

Although e-commerce has grown at an extremely rapid pace in customers and revenues, it is clear that many of the visions, predictions, and assertions about e-commerce developed in the early years have not have been fulfilled. For instance, economists' visions of "friction-free" commerce have not been entirely realized. Prices are sometimes lower online, but the low prices are sometimes a function of entrepreneurs selling products below their costs. Consumers are less price sensitive than expected; surprisingly, the Web sites with the highest revenue often have the highest prices. There remains considerable persistent and even increasing price dispersion: online competition has lowered prices, but price dispersion remains pervasive in many markets despite lower search costs (Levin, 2011; Ghose and Yao, 2010). The concept of one world, one market, one price has not occurred in reality as entrepreneurs discover new ways to differentiate their products and services. While for the most part Internet prices save consumers about 20% on average when compared to in-store prices, sometimes online prices are higher than for similar products purchased offline, especially if shipping costs are considered. For instance, prices on books and CDs vary by as much as 50%, and prices for airline tickets as much as 20% (Alessandria, 2009; Aguiar and Hurst, 2008; Baye, 2004; Baye et al., 2004; Brynjolfsson and Smith, 2000; Bailey, 1998a, b). Merchants have adjusted to the competitive Internet environment by engaging in "hit-and-run pricing" or changing prices every day or hour (using "flash pricing" or "flash sales") so competitors never know what they are charging (neither do customers); by making their prices hard to discover and sowing confusion among consumers by "baiting and switching" customers from low-margin products to high-margin products with supposedly "higher quality." Finally, brands remain very important in e-commerce—consumers trust some firms more than others to deliver a high-quality product on time (Rosso and Jansen, 2010).

The "perfect competition" model of extreme market efficiency has not come to pass. Merchants and marketers are continually introducing information asymmetries. Search costs have fallen overall, but the overall transaction cost of actually completing a purchase in e-commerce remains high because users have a bewildering number of new questions to consider: Will the merchant actually deliver? What is the time frame of delivery? Does the merchant really stock this item? How do I fill out this form? Many potential e-commerce purchases are terminated in the shopping cart stage because of these consumer uncertainties. Some people still find it easier to call a trusted catalog merchant on the telephone than to order on a Web site. Finally, intermediaries have not disappeared as predicted. Most manufacturers, for instance, have not adopted the Dell model of online sales (direct sales by the manufacturer to the consumer), and Dell itself has moved towards a mixed model heavily reliant on in-store sales where customers can "kick the tires" by trying the keyboard and viewing the screen. Apple stores are among the most successful stores in the world, with sales of about $5,600 per square foot, about 20 times the average for retail stores. People still like to shop in a physical store.

If anything, e-commerce has created many opportunities for middlemen to aggregate content, products, and services into portals and search engines and thereby introduce themselves as the "new" intermediaries. Yahoo, MSN, and Amazon, along with third-party travel sites such as Travelocity, Orbitz, and Expedia, are all examples of this kind of intermediary. As illustrated in **Figure 1.9**, e-commerce has not driven existing retail chains and catalog merchants out of business, although it has created opportunities for entrepreneurial Web-only firms to succeed.

The visions of many entrepreneurs and venture capitalists for e-commerce have not materialized exactly as predicted either. First-mover advantage appears to have succeeded only for a very small group of sites. Historically, first movers have been long-term

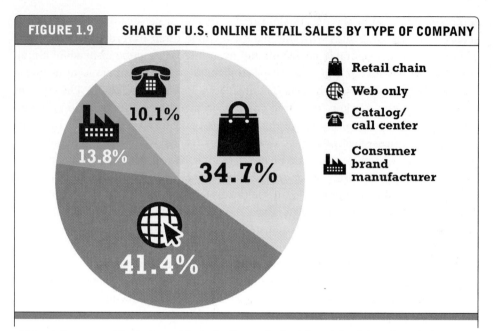

| FIGURE 1.9 | SHARE OF U.S. ONLINE RETAIL SALES BY TYPE OF COMPANY |

Web-only firms account for the largest share of online retail sales, followed closely by online sales by traditional retail chain stores.

SOURCE: Based on data from Internet Retailer, 2014b.

losers, with the early-to-market innovators usually being displaced by established "fast-follower" firms with the right complement of financial, marketing, legal, and production assets needed to develop mature markets, and this has proved true for e-commerce as well. Many e-commerce first movers, such as eToys, FogDog (sporting goods), Webvan (groceries), and Eve.com (beauty products), are out of business. Customer acquisition and retention costs during the early years of e-commerce were extraordinarily high, with some firms, such as E*Trade and other financial service firms, paying up to $400 to acquire a new customer. The overall costs of doing business online—including the costs of technology, site design and maintenance, and warehouses for fulfillment—are often no lower than the costs faced by the most efficient bricks-and-mortar stores. A large warehouse costs tens of millions of dollars regardless of a firm's online presence. The knowledge of how to run the warehouse is priceless, and not easily moved. The start-up costs can be staggering. Attempting to achieve or enhance profitability by raising prices has often led to large customer defections. From the e-commerce merchant's perspective, the "e" in e-commerce does not stand for "easy."

PREDICTIONS FOR THE FUTURE: MORE SURPRISES

Given that e-commerce has changed greatly in the last several years, its future cannot be predicted except to say "Watch for more surprises." There are several factors that will help define the future of e-commerce. First, there is little doubt that the technology of e-commerce—the Internet, the Web, and the growing number of mobile devices, including smartphones and tablet computers—will continue to propagate through all commercial activity. The overall global revenues from B2C e-commerce are expected to continue to rise, most likely at an annualized rate of about 14% per year through 2018. The number of products and services sold online and the size of the average purchase order both will continue to grow at near double-digit rates. The number of online shoppers will also continue to grow, although at a much more modest rate of about 1% per year. There has also been a significant broadening of the online product mix compared to the early years when books, computer software, and hardware dominated e-commerce. Today, although computers and electronics and books, music, and video together still account for almost a third of all e-commerce revenues, product categories such as apparel and accessories, autos and auto parts, and furniture and home furnishings, which were not often sold online during the early years of e-commerce, now comprise a significant percentage of e-commerce revenues (see **Figure 1.10**). This trend will continue. (See Chapter 9 for changes in retail products and services.)

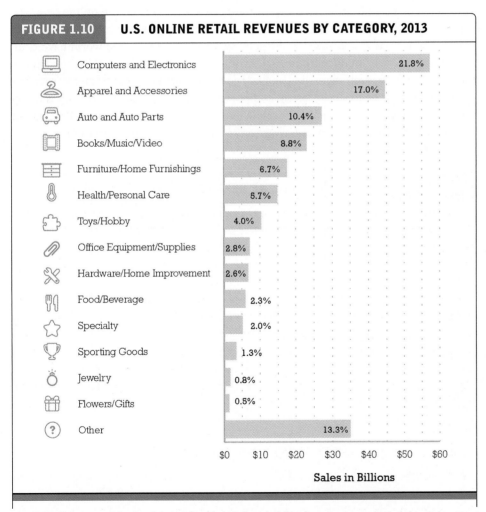

| FIGURE 1.10 | **U.S. ONLINE RETAIL REVENUES BY CATEGORY, 2013** |

- Computers and Electronics — 21.8%
- Apparel and Accessories — 17.0%
- Auto and Auto Parts — 10.4%
- Books/Music/Video — 8.8%
- Furniture/Home Furnishings — 6.7%
- Health/Personal Care — 5.7%
- Toys/Hobby — 4.0%
- Office Equipment/Supplies — 2.8%
- Hardware/Home Improvement — 2.6%
- Food/Beverage — 2.3%
- Specialty — 2.0%
- Sporting Goods — 1.3%
- Jewelry — 0.8%
- Flowers/Gifts — 0.5%
- Other — 13.3%

Sales in Billions ($0, $10, $20, $30, $40, $50, $60)

The mix of products sold online has significantly broadened, although computers and other electronics remain the leading category, with $57.4 billion in sales (accounting for over 20% of all online retail revenues).

SOURCES: Based on data from eMarketer, Inc., 2014b; Internet Retailer, 2014b; authors' estimates.

Second, traditional, well-endowed, experienced U.S. Fortune 500 companies will continue to play a dominant role in e-commerce, while new start-up ventures will quickly gain large online audiences for new products and services not dominated by the large players. There will also be a continuation of audience consolidation on the Internet in general, with the top 100 sites garnering almost 85% of all online sales (Internet Retailer, 2014b). **Table 1.5** lists the top 15 U.S. online retailers, as ranked by 2013 online sales. The table shows an unmistakable trend toward well-known, traditional brands from strong traditional retail chains, with Staples, Walmart, Sears, Macy's, Office Depot, OfficeMax, Costco, and Best Buy all in the top 15.

Third, the number of successful purely online companies will remain smaller than integrated online/offline stores that combine traditional sales channels such as physical stores and printed catalogs with online efforts. For instance, traditional catalog sales firms such as L.L.Bean have transformed themselves into integrated online and direct mail firms with more than half of their sales coming from the online channel.

The future of e-commerce will include the continued growth of regulatory activity both in the United States and worldwide. Governments around the world have challenged the early vision of computer scientists and information technologists that the Internet should be a self-regulating and self-governing phenomenon. The Internet and e-commerce have been so successful and powerful, so all-pervasive, that they directly involve the social, cultural, and political life of entire nations and cultures. Throughout history, whenever technologies have risen to this level of social importance, power,

TABLE 1.5	**TOP 15 U.S. ONLINE RETAILERS RANKED BY ONLINE SALES**
ONLINE RETAILER	ONLINE SALES (2013) (IN BILLIONS)
Amazon	$67.9
Apple	$18.3
Staples	$10.4
Walmart	$10.0
Sears	$4.9
Liberty Interactive (QVC, etc.)	$4.8
Netflix	$4.4
Macy's	$4.2
Office Depot	$4.1
Dell	$3.6
CDW	$3.4
OfficeMax	$3.2
W.W. Grainger	$3.1
Costco	$3.1
Best Buy	$3.0

SOURCES: Based on data from Internet Retailer, 2014b; company reports on Form 10-K filed with the Securities and Exchange Commission.

and visibility, they become the target of efforts to regulate and control the technology to ensure that positive social benefits result from their use and to guarantee the public's health and welfare. Radio, television, automobiles, electricity, and railroads are all the subject of regulation and legislation. Likewise, with e-commerce. In both the European Union and the U.S. Congress, there have already been a number of bills passed (as well as hundreds proposed) to control various facets of the Internet and e-commerce, from consumer privacy to pornography, gambling, and encryption. We can expect these efforts at regulation in the United States and around the world to increase as e-commerce extends its reach and importance.

A relatively new factor that will influence the growth of e-commerce is the cost of energy, in particular gasoline and diesel. As fuel costs rise, traveling to shop at physical locations can be very expensive. Buying online can save customers time and energy costs. There is growing evidence that shoppers are changing their shopping habits and locales because of fuel costs, and pushing the sales of online retailers to higher levels.

In summary, the future of e-commerce will be a fascinating mixture of traditional retail, service, and media firms extending their brands to online markets; early-period e-commerce firms such as Amazon and eBay strengthening their financial results and dominant positions; and a bevy of entirely new entrepreneurial firms with the potential to rocket into prominence by developing huge new audiences in months. Firms that fit this pattern include Facebook, Twitter, Pinterest, and Uber.

1.3 UNDERSTANDING E-COMMERCE: ORGANIZING THEMES

Understanding e-commerce in its totality is a difficult task for students and instructors because there are so many facets to the phenomenon. No single academic discipline is prepared to encompass all of e-commerce. After teaching the e-commerce course for several years and writing this book, we have come to realize just how difficult it is to "understand" e-commerce. We have found it useful to think about e-commerce as involving three broad interrelated themes: technology, business, and society. We do not mean to imply any ordering of importance here because this book and our thinking freely range over these themes as appropriate to the problem we are trying to understand and describe. Nevertheless, as in previous technologically driven commercial revolutions, there is a historic progression. Technologies develop first, and then those developments are exploited commercially. Once commercial exploitation of the technology becomes widespread, a host of social, cultural, and political issues arise.

TECHNOLOGY: INFRASTRUCTURE

The development and mastery of digital computing and communications technology is at the heart of the newly emerging global digital economy we call e-commerce. To understand the likely future of e-commerce, you need a basic understanding of the information technologies upon which it is built. E-commerce is above all else a technologically driven phenomenon that relies on a host of information technologies as well as fundamental concepts from computer science developed over a 50-year period. At the core of e-commerce are the Internet and the Web, which we describe in detail in Chapter 3. Underlying these technologies are a host of complementary technologies: cloud computing, personal computers, smartphones, tablet computers, local area networks, relational and non-relational databases, client/server computing, data mining, and fiber-optic switches, to name just a few. These technologies lie at the heart of sophisticated business computing applications such as enterprise-wide computing systems, supply chain management systems, manufacturing resource planning systems, and customer relationship management systems. E-commerce relies on all these basic technologies—not just the Internet. The Internet, while representing a sharp break from prior corporate computing and communications technologies, is nevertheless just the latest development in the evolution of corporate computing and part of the continuing chain of computer-based innovations in business. **Figure 1.11** illustrates the major stages in the development of corporate computing and indicates how the Internet and the Web fit into this development trajectory.

To truly understand e-commerce, you will need to know something about packet-switched communications, protocols such as TCP/IP, client/server and cloud computing, mobile digital platforms, Web servers, HTML5, CSS, and software programming tools such as Flash and JavaScript on the client side, and Java, PHP, Ruby on Rails, and ColdFusion on the server side. All of these topics are described fully in Part 2 of the book (Chapters 3–5).

BUSINESS: BASIC CONCEPTS

While technology provides the infrastructure, it is the business applications—the potential for extraordinary returns on investment—that create the interest and excitement in e-commerce. New technologies present businesses and entrepreneurs with new ways of organizing production and transacting business. New technologies change the strategies and plans of existing firms: old strategies are made obsolete and new ones need to be invented. New technologies are the birthing grounds where thousands of new companies spring up with new products and services. New technologies are the graveyard of many traditional businesses, such as record stores. To truly understand e-commerce, you will need to be familiar with some key business concepts, such as the nature of digital markets, digital goods, business models, firm and industry value chains, value webs, industry structure, digital disruption, and consumer behavior in digital markets, as well as basic concepts of financial analysis. We'll examine these concepts further in Chapters 5, 6, 7, and 9 through 12.

SOCIETY: TAMING THE JUGGERNAUT

With more than 2.8 billion people now using the Internet, many for e-commerce purposes, the impact of the Internet and e-commerce on society is significant and global. Increasingly, e-commerce is subject to the laws of nations and global entities. You will need to understand the pressures that global e-commerce places on contemporary society in order to conduct a successful e-commerce business or understand the e-commerce phenomenon. The primary societal issues we discuss in this book are individual privacy, intellectual property, and public welfare policy.

Because the Internet and the Web are exceptionally adept at tracking the identity and behavior of individuals online, e-commerce raises difficulties for preserving

FIGURE 1.11	THE INTERNET AND THE EVOLUTION OF CORPORATE COMPUTING

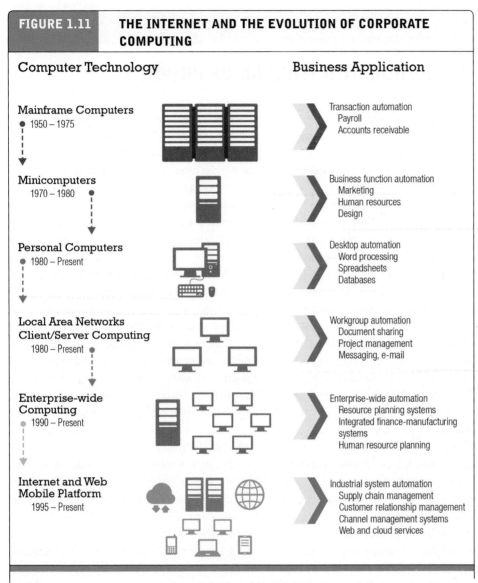

Computer Technology

Mainframe Computers
● 1950 – 1975

Minicomputers
1970 – 1980 ●

Personal Computers
● 1980 – Present

Local Area Networks Client/Server Computing
1980 – Present ●

Enterprise-wide Computing
● 1990 – Present

Internet and Web Mobile Platform
1995 – Present

Business Application

Transaction automation
Payroll
Accounts receivable

Business function automation
Marketing
Human resources
Design

Desktop automation
Word processing
Spreadsheets
Databases

Workgroup automation
Document sharing
Project management
Messaging, e-mail

Enterprise-wide automation
Resource planning systems
Integrated finance-manufacturing systems
Human resource planning

Industrial system automation
Supply chain management
Customer relationship management
Channel management systems
Web and cloud services

The Internet and Web, and the emergence of a mobile platform held together by the Internet cloud, are the latest in a chain of evolving technologies and related business applications, each of which builds on its predecessors.

privacy—the ability of individuals to place limits on the type and amount of information collected about them, and to control the uses of their personal information. Read the *Insight on Society* case, *Facebook and the Age of Privacy,* to get a view of some of the ways e-commerce sites use personal information.

Because the cost of distributing digital copies of copyrighted intellectual property—tangible works of the mind such as music, books, and videos—is nearly zero on the Internet, e-commerce poses special challenges to the various methods societies have used in the past to protect intellectual property rights.

INSIGHT ON SOCIETY

FACEBOOK AND THE AGE OF PRIVACY

In a January 2010 interview, Mark Zuckerberg, the founder of Facebook, proclaimed that the age of privacy had to come to an end. According to Zuckerberg, people were no longer worried about sharing their personal information with friends, friends of friends, or even the entire Web. This view is in accordance with Facebook's broader goal, which is to make the world a more open and connected place. Supporters of Zuckerberg's viewpoint believe the twenty-first century is a new era of openness and transparency.

However, not everyone is a true believer. Privacy—limitations on what personal information government and private institutions can collect and use—is a founding principle of democracies. A decade's worth of privacy surveys in the United States show that well over 80% of the American public fear the Internet is a threat to their privacy.

With more than 1.3 billion users worldwide, and about 240 million in North America, Facebook's privacy policies are going to shape privacy standards on the Internet for years to come. The economic stakes in the privacy debate are quite high, involving billions in advertising and transaction dollars. Social network sites such as Facebook use a model based on building a database of hundreds of millions of users who post personal information, preferences, and behaviors, and who are encouraged, or even perhaps deceived, into relinquishing control over their information, which is then sold to advertisers and outside third parties. The less privacy Facebook's users want or have, the more Facebook profits.

Facebook's current privacy policies are quite a flip-flop from its original policy in 2004, which promised users near complete control over who could see their personal profile. However, every year since 2004, Facebook has attempted to extend its control over user information and content, usually without notice.

For instance, in 2007, Facebook introduced the Beacon program, which was designed to broadcast users' activities on participating Web sites to their friends. After a public outcry, Facebook terminated the Beacon program in 2009, and paid $9.5 million to settle a host of class action lawsuits.

In 2009, undeterred by the Beacon fiasco, Facebook unilaterally decided that it would publish users' basic personal information on the public Internet, and announced that whatever content users had contributed belonged to Facebook, and that its ownership of that information never terminated. However, as with the Beacon program, Facebook's efforts to take permanent control of user information resulted in users joining online resistance groups and it was ultimately forced to withdraw this policy as well.

In 2009, Facebook also introduced the Like button, and in 2010 extended it to third-party Web sites to alert Facebook users to their friends' browsing and purchases. In 2011, it began publicizing users' "likes" of various advertisers in Sponsored Stories (i.e., advertisements) that included the users' names and profile pictures without their explicit consent, without paying them, and without giving them a way to opt out. This resulted in yet another class action lawsuit, which Facebook settled for $20 million in June 2012. As part of the settlement, Facebook agreed to make it clear to users that information like their names and profile pictures might be used in Sponsored Stories. (Facebook dropped Sponsored Stories in April 2014.) In 2011, Facebook enrolled all Facebook subscribers into its facial recognition program without notice. This too raised the privacy alarm, forcing Facebook to make it easier for users to opt out. In 2012, Facebook, under pressure from European regulators, promised that it would not use the Tag Suggestion feature, which allows photos to be automatically matched with particular users.

In May 2012, Facebook went public, creating even more pressure to increase revenues and profits to justify its stock market value. Shortly thereafter, Facebook announced that it was launching a mobile advertising product that pushes ads to the mobile news feeds of users based on the apps they use through the Facebook Connect feature, without explicit permission from the user to do so. It also announced Facebook Exchange, a program that allows advertisers to serve ads to Facebook users based on their browsing activity while not on Facebook. Privacy advocates raised the alarm yet again and more lawsuits were filed by users who claimed that Facebook invaded their privacy by tracking their Internet use even after they had logged off from Facebook. In February 2013, Facebook agreed to partner with Acxiom, Epsilon, and Datalogix—all data marketing companies that deliver targeted ads based on offline data. The firms provide customer data to Facebook, which then allows Facebook advertisers to target their ads to those users based on that data. In June 2013, Facebook introduced searchable hashtags, whose use has been popularized by Twitter, Tumblr, and other social media sites. This is just one further step moving Facebook away from its initial origins as a place for friends to connect and toward a public platform where what one posts becomes part of a public conversation.

In December 2013, another class action lawsuit was filed against Facebook by users alleging that it violated their privacy by scanning users' private Facebook messages and mining them for data such as references to URLs that Facebook could then sell to advertisers. In May 2014, an enhancement to Facebook's mobile app that allows the app to recognize the music, television show, or movie playing in the background when a user makes a status update raised a new privacy alarm.

It appears that Zuckerberg's proclamation that the age of privacy is over was premature. Instead, privacy issues may turn out to be an enduring headache and perhaps ultimately Facebook's Achilles heel. As Facebook itself noted in its S-1 filing with the Securities and Exchange Commission, if it adopts "policies or procedures related to areas such as sharing or user data that are perceived negatively by our users or the general public," its revenue, financial results, and business could be significantly harmed. And this, more than anything else, may be the savior for privacy at Facebook.

In fact, in June 2014, Facebook, in apparent recognition of the fact that its future growth might depend on users' feeling more confident that they are sharing information only with those they want, announced that it was switching its default privacy setting for new users from Public to Friends and providing a Privacy Checkup tool for all users. In addition, Facebook announced that it was going to give its users the ability to see the data it keeps on their likes and interests and enable users to change, delete, or add to that data, giving users more control over ads they are shown. Is this an indication that Facebook is turning over a new leaf when it comes to privacy? Only time will tell.

SOURCES: "Faceboook to Let Users Alter Their Ad Profiles," by Vindu Goel, *New York Times*, June 12, 2014; "Facebook Stops Irresponsibly Defaulting Privacy of New Users' Posts to 'Public,' Changes to 'Friends,'" by Josh Constine, Techcrunch.com, May 22, 2014; "Facebook Users Revolt Over Privacy Feature—Enables Microphone in Apps," by Jan Willem Aldershoff, Myce.com, June 9, 2014; "Facebook Eliminates Sponsored Stories—Will It Matter to Advertisers?," by Amy Durbin, Mediapost.com, February 25, 2014; "Facebook Sued for Allegedly Intercepting Private Messages," by Jennifer Van Grove, Cnet.com, January 2, 2014; "Facebook Introduces Hashtags, Moving Away From Friends," by Bianca Bosker, Huffingtonpost.com, June 16, 2013; "Facebook To Partner With Data Brokers," by Bob Sullivan, Redtape.nbcnews.com, February 26, 2013; "Facebook Exchange Ads Raise Privacy Concerns," by Mikal E. Belicove, Cnbc.com, June 21, 2012; "Facebook Suit Over Subscriber Tracking Seeks $15 Billion," by Kit Chellel and Jeremy Hodges, Bloomberg.com, May 19, 2012; Facebook Inc. Form S-1/A filed with the Securities and Exchange Commission, May 16, 2012; "German State to Sue Facebook over Facial Recognition Feature," by Emil Protalinski, Zdnet.com, November 10, 2011; "Facebook Aims to Simplify Privacy Settings," by Somini Sengupta, *New York Times*, August 23, 2011; "Facebook Redesigns Privacy Controls," by Ben Worthen, *Wall Street Journal*, May 27, 2010; "How Facebook Pulled a Privacy Bait and Switch," by Dan Tynan, *PC World*, May 2010.

The global nature of e-commerce also poses public policy issues of equity, equal access, content regulation, and taxation. For instance, in the United States, public telephone utilities are required under public utility and public accommodation laws to make basic service available at affordable rates so everyone can have telephone service. Should these laws be extended to the Internet and the Web? If goods are purchased by a New York State resident from a Web site in California, shipped from a center in Illinois, and delivered to New York, what state has the right to collect a sales tax? Should some heavy Internet users who consume extraordinary amounts of bandwidth by streaming endless movies be charged extra for service, or should the Internet be neutral with respect to usage? What rights do nation-states and their citizens have with respect to the Internet, the Web, and e-commerce? We address issues such as these in Chapter 8, and also throughout the text.

ACADEMIC DISCIPLINES CONCERNED WITH E-COMMERCE

The phenomenon of e-commerce is so broad that a multidisciplinary perspective is required. There are two primary approaches to e-commerce: technical and behavioral.

Technical Approaches

Computer scientists are interested in e-commerce as an exemplary application of Internet technology. They are concerned with the development of computer hardware, software, and telecommunications systems, as well as standards, encryption, and database design and operation. Operations management scientists are primarily interested in building mathematical models of business processes and optimizing these processes. They are interested in e-commerce as an opportunity to study how business firms can exploit the Internet to achieve more efficient business operations. The information systems discipline spans the technical and behavioral approaches. Technical groups within the information systems specialty focus on data mining, search engine design, and artificial intelligence.

Behavioral Approaches

From a behavioral perspective, information systems researchers are primarily interested in e-commerce because of its implications for firm and industry value chains, industry structure, and corporate strategy. Economists have focused on online consumer behavior, pricing of digital goods, and on the unique features of digital electronic markets. The marketing profession is interested in marketing, brand development and extension, online consumer behavior, and the ability of e-commerce technologies to segment and target consumer groups, and differentiate products. Economists share an interest with marketing scholars who have focused on e-commerce consumer response to marketing and advertising campaigns, and the ability of firms to brand, segment markets, target audiences, and position products to achieve above-normal returns on investment.

Management scholars have focused on entrepreneurial behavior and the challenges faced by young firms who are required to develop organizational structures in short time spans. Finance and accounting scholars have focused on e-commerce firm valuation and accounting practices. Sociologists—and to a lesser extent, psychologists—have focused on general population studies of Internet usage, the role of social inequality in skewing Internet benefits, and the use of the Web as a social network and group communications tool. Legal scholars are interested in issues such as preserving intellectual property, privacy, and content regulation.

No one perspective dominates research about e-commerce. The challenge is to learn enough about a variety of academic disciplines so that you can grasp the significance of e-commerce in its entirety.

The Pirate Bay:

Searching for a Safe Haven

The Pirate Bay (TPB) is one of the world's most popular pirated music and content sites, offering free access to millions of copyrighted songs and thousands of copyrighted Hollywood movies, television shows, and video games. It claims it is the world's largest BitTorrent tracker. In April 2014, TPB reported that it had processed its 10 millionth torrent upload. As of June 2014, it claimed to have over 6 million registered users, and according to Alexa.com, a site that tracks Web usage, was one of the top 100 Web sites in the world in terms of global traffic, with about 20% of the visitors coming from the United States. It even has a Facebook page and Twitter feed. This despite the fact that TPB has been subjected to repeated legal efforts to shut it down. In fact, the authorities pursuing TPB must feel as if they are engaged in a never-ending game of Whack-a-mole, as each time they "whack" TPB, it somehow manages to reappear. But the battle is far from over. The Internet is becoming a tough place for music and video pirates to make a living in part because of enforcement actions, but more importantly because of new mobile

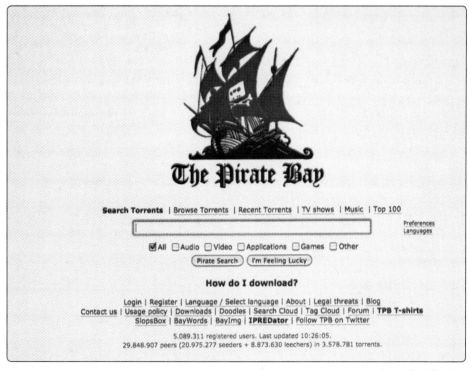

© Tommy (Louth) / Alamy

and wireless technologies that enable high-quality content to be streamed for just a small fee.

TPB is part of a European social and political movement that opposes copyrighted content and demands that music, videos, TV shows, and other digital content be free and unrestricted. TPB does not operate a database of copyrighted content. Neither does it operate a network of computers owned by "members" who store the content, nor does it create, own, or distribute software (like BitTorrent and most other so-called P2P networks) that permit such networks to exist in the first place. Instead, TPB simply provides a search engine that responds to user queries for music tracks, or specific movie titles, and generates a list of search results that include P2P networks around the world where the titles can be found. By clicking on a selected link, users gain access to the copyrighted content, but only after downloading software and other files from that P2P network.

TPB claims it is merely a search engine providing pointers to existing P2P networks that it does not itself control. It says that it cannot control what content users ultimately find on those P2P networks, and that it is no different from any other search engine, such as Google or Bing, which are not held responsible for the content found on sites listed in search results. From a broader standpoint, TPB's founders also claim that copyright laws in general unjustly interfere with the free flow of information on the Internet, and that in any event, they were not violating Swedish copyright law, which they felt should be the only law that applied. And they further claimed they did not encourage, incite, or enable illegal downloading. Nevertheless, the defendants have never denied that theirs was a commercial enterprise. Despite all the talk calling for the free, unfettered spread of culture, TPB was a money-making operation from the beginning, designed to produce profits for its founders, with advertising as the primary source of revenue.

However, the First Swedish Court in Stockholm declared TPB's four founders guilty of violating Swedish copyright law, and sentenced each to one year in prison and payment of €2.8 million in restitution to the plaintiffs, all Swedish divisions of the major record firms (Warner Music, Sony, and EMI Group among them). The court found that the defendants had incited copyright infringement by providing a Web site with search functions, easy uploading and storage possibilities, and a tracker. The court also said that the four defendants had been aware of the fact that copyrighted material was shared with the help of their site and that the defendants were engaged in a commercial enterprise, the basis of which was encouraging visitors to violate the copyrights of owners. In fact, the primary purpose of TPB was to violate copyrights in order to make money for the owners (commercial intent).

Meanwhile, the U.S. government pressured the Swedish government to strengthen its copyright laws to discourage rampant downloading. In Sweden, downloading music and videos from illegal sites was very popular, engaged in by 43% of the Swedish Internet population. To strengthen its laws, Sweden adopted the European Union convention on copyrights, which allows content owners to receive from Internet providers the names and addresses of people suspected of sharing pirated files. In France, participating in these pirate sites will result in banishment from the Internet

SOURCES: Thepiratebay.se, accessed July 30, 2014; "The Piratebay.se," Alexa.com, accessed July 30, 2014; "Pirate Bay Launches Mobile Site, Teases More Expansion," by Ernesto, Torrentfreak.com, July 24, 2014; "Pirate Bay Co-Founder Peter Sunde Arrested Years After Conviction," by Natasha Lomas, Techcrunch.com, June 1, 2014; "The Pirate Bay and the Business of Piracy;" by Leo Sun, Fool.com, May 21, 2014; "Pirate Bay's Anti-censorship Browser Clocks 5,000.000 Downloads," by Ernesto, Torrentfreak.com, May 16, 2014; "The Pirate Bay Celebrates Its 10 Millionth Torrent Upload," by Dennis Lynch, Ibtimes.com, April 24, 2014; "Google Asked to Censor Two Million Pirate Bay URLs," by Ernesto, Torrentfreak.com, April 20, 2014; "Singapore Proposes Law to Block Sites such as Pirate Bay," by Aloysius Low, Cnet.com, April 7, 2014; "Pirate Bay Docks in Peru: New System Will Make Domains 'Irrelevant,'" by Andy, Torrentfreak.com, December 12, 2013; "MPAA Still Hunting For Cash as Pirate Bay Financier Set to Go Bankrupt," by Andy, Torrentfreak.com, June 10, 2013; "Pirate Bay Founder Submits Emotional Plea for Pardon," by Ernesto, Torrentfreak.com, July 7, 2012; "The Pirate Bay Evades ISP Blockade with IPv6, Can Do It 18 Quintillion More Times," by Sebastian Anthony, Extremetech.com, June 8, 2012; "World's Biggest Ad Agency Keelhauls 2,000 Pirate Sites," by Natalie Apostolu, *The Register*, June 14, 2011; "Internet Piracy and How to Stop It," *New York Times*, June 8, 2011; "The Pirate Bay: Five Years After the Raid," by Ernesto, Torrentfreak.com, May 31, 2011; "The Protect IP Act: COICA Redux," by Abigail Phillips, Electronic Frontier Foundation, May 12, 2011; "Pirate Bay Keeps Sinking: Another Law Suit Coming," by Stan Schroeder, Mashable.com, June 22, 2010; "Pirate Bay Sunk by Hollywood Injunction For Now," by Charles Arthur, *The Guardian*, May 17, 2010; "British Put Teeth in Anti-Piracy Proposal," by Eric Pfanner, *New York Times,* March 14, 2010.

for up to three years. As a result, Internet traffic in Sweden declined by 40%, and has stayed there.

TPB has appealed the court judgment and has not paid any fines. That doesn't mean that TPB has not been affected by the lawsuits, however. In 2011, the firm moved its servers into caves in Sweden, and dispersed multiple copies of its program to other countries. In response to the lawsuits, police raids, and confiscation of servers, TPB has had stints in France, Finland, Italy, Germany, Denmark, Ireland, the U.K., and Greece within the last few years. These countries have in some cases refused to allow Internet service providers in their countries to host TPB, or link to TPB, no matter where in the world its servers are located. In 2013, authorities shut down TPB's top-level domains in Sweden, Greenland, and Iceland, but TPB has continued to try to operate by hopping from country to country, moving to Saint Maarten, to tiny Ascension Island, to Peru, and back again to Sweden.

In 2014, TPB has proven as elusive as ever for law enforcement, although co-founder Gottfrid Svartholm Warg is now in prison in Denmark, co-founder Peter Sunde was arrested after years on the run, and is expected to begin serving an eight-month prison term for copyright violation, and the company's financial resources have begun to run dry. As interest has continued to accrue on financial penalties previously levied on TPB, Carl Lundstrom, the site's primary financial backer, has declared bankruptcy. Consistently relocating operations from country to country costs money.

However, TPB has developed a Firefox-based browser it calls PirateBrowser that uses the Tor network and allows users to bypass ISP filtering and access blocked Web sites. As of May 2014, it has been downloaded by more than 5 million users. In addition TPB is developing a P2P BitTorrent browser application that will let its users distribute and store the site and others on their own computers without having to access a central host. Once it releases this application, TPB will no longer have a central location for attack, and piracy enforcement efforts may become even more difficult. In July 2014, it launched a mobile version that it calls The Mobile Bay. It also plans to develop separate television, music, and movie sites, all in an effort to make it even more resilient than it has been.

TPB has caused England, France, Malaysia, Finland, and the United States to consider strong intellectual property protection laws that will prevent domestic search engines and ISPs from linking to infringing sites, or resolving their domain names. In addition, the world's largest advertising agency, GroupM, has put TPB and 2,000 other sites on its blacklist of copyright infringing sites where it will not buy advertising space.

The record industry's struggle against TPB is just part of the battle that it has been waging for some time. In 2005, the Supreme Court ruled in the ground-breaking *Metro-Goldwyn Mayer v. Grokster, et al.* case that the original peer-to-peer file sharing services, such as Grokster, Kazaa, and StreamCast, could be held liable for copyright infringement, because they had intentionally sought to encourage users to share copyrighted material. All of these services have since gone out of business. But these legal victories, and stronger government enforcement of copyright laws, have not proven to be the magic bullet that miraculously solves all the problems facing the music industry. The music industry has had to drastically change its business model and decisively move towards digital distribution platforms. They have made striking progress, and, for the first time, in 2011 sales of music in a purely digital format accounted for more revenue than sales of music in a physical format. To do so, the music industry employed a number of different business models and online delivery platforms, including Apple's iTunes pay-per-download model, subscription models, streaming models, and now music in the cloud.

In each of these new media delivery platforms, the copyright owners—record companies, artists, and Hollywood studios—have struck licensing deals with the technology platform owners and distributors (Apple, Amazon, and Google). These new platforms offer a win-win solution. Consumers are benefitted by having near instant access to high-quality music tracks and videos without the hassle of P2P software downloads. Content owners get a growing revenue stream and protection for their copyrighted content. And the pirates? TPB and other pirate sites may not be able to compete with new and better ways to listen to music and view videos. Like the real pirates of the Caribbean, who are now just a footnote in history books, technology and consumer preference for ease of use may leave them behind.

Case Study Questions

1. Why did TPB believe it was not violating copyright laws? What did the Swedish court rule?

2. How has TPB managed to continue operating despite being found in violation of copyright laws?

3. How has the music industry reacted to the problems created by pirates like TPB?

1.5 REVIEW

KEY CONCEPTS

■ Define e-commerce and describe how it differs from e-business.

- E-commerce involves digitally enabled commercial transactions between and among organizations and individuals. Digitally enabled transactions include all those mediated by digital technology, meaning, for the most part, transactions that occur over the Internet, the Web, and/or via mobile apps. Commercial transactions involve the exchange of value (e.g., money) across organizational or individual boundaries in return for products or services.
- E-business refers primarily to the digital enabling of transactions and processes within a firm, involving information systems under the control of the firm. For the most part, e-business does not involve commercial transactions across organizational boundaries where value is exchanged.

■ Identify and describe the unique features of e-commerce technology and discuss their business significance.

There are eight features of e-commerce technology that are unique to this medium:

- *Ubiquity*—available just about everywhere, at all times, making it possible to shop from your desktop, at home, at work, or even from your car.
- *Global reach*—permits commercial transactions to cross cultural and national boundaries far more conveniently and cost-effectively than is true in traditional commerce.
- *Universal standards*—shared by all nations around the world, in contrast to most traditional commerce technologies, which differ from one nation to the next.
- *Richness*—enables an online merchant to deliver marketing messages in a way not possible with traditional commerce technologies.
- *Interactivity*—allows for two-way communication between merchant and consumer and enables the merchant to engage a consumer in ways similar to a face-to-face experience, but on a much more massive, global scale.
- *Information density*—is the total amount and quality of information available to all market participants. The Internet reduces information collection, storage, processing, and communication costs while increasing the currency, accuracy, and timeliness of information.
- *Personalization* and *customization*—the increase in information density allows merchants to target their marketing messages to specific individuals and results in a level of personalization and customization unthinkable with previously existing commerce technologies.
- *Social technology*—provides a many-to-many model of mass communications. Millions of users are able to generate content consumed by millions of other users. The result is the formation of social networks on a wide scale and the aggregation of large audiences on social network platforms.

■ Recognize and describe Web 2.0 applications.

- Web 2.0 applications attract huge audiences and represent significant opportunities for e-commerce revenues. Web 2.0 applications such as social networks, photo- and video-sharing sites, and blog platforms support very high levels of interactivity compared to other traditional media.

■ Describe the major types of e-commerce.

There are five major types of e-commerce:
- *B2C e-commerce* involves businesses selling to consumers and is the type of e-commerce that most consumers are likely to encounter.
- *B2B e-commerce* involves businesses selling to other businesses and is the largest form of e-commerce.
- *C2C e-commerce* is a means for consumers to sell to each other. In C2C e-commerce, the consumer prepares the product for market, places the product for auction or sale, and relies on the market maker to provide catalog, search engine, and transaction clearing capabilities so that products can be easily displayed, discovered, and paid for.
- *Social e-commerce* is e-commerce that is enabled by social networks and online social relationships.
- *M-commerce* involves the use of wireless digital devices to enable online transactions.
- *Local e-commerce* is a form of e-commerce that is focused on engaging the consumer based on his or her current geographic location.

■ Understand the evolution of e-commerce from its early years to today.

E-commerce has gone through three stages: innovation, consolidation, and reinvention.
- The early years of e-commerce were a technological success, with the digital infrastructure created during the period solid enough to sustain significant growth in e-commerce during the next decade, and a mixed business success, with significant revenue growth and customer usage, but low profit margins.
- E-commerce entered a period of consolidation beginning in 2001 and extending into 2006.
- E-commerce entered a period of reinvention in 2007 with the emergence of the mobile digital platform, social networks, and Web 2.0 applications that attracted huge audiences in a very short time span.

■ **Identify the factors that will define the future of e-commerce.**

Factors that will define the future of e-commerce include the following:
*   E-commerce technology (the Internet, the Web, and the mobile platform) will continue to propagate through all commercial activity, with overall revenues from e-commerce and the number of products and services sold all rising.
*   Traditional well-endowed and experienced Fortune 500 companies will continue to play a dominant role.
*   The number of successful purely online companies will continue to decline, and most successful e-commerce firms will adopt an integrated, multi-channel bricks-and-clicks strategy.
*   Regulation of the Internet and e-commerce by government will grow both in the United States and worldwide.

■ **Describe the major themes underlying the study of e-commerce.**

E-commerce involves three broad interrelated themes:
*   *Technology*—To understand e-commerce, you need a basic understanding of the information technologies upon which it is built, including the Internet, the Web, and mobile platform, and a host of complementary technologies—cloud computing, personal computers, smartphones, tablet computers, local area networks, client/server computing, packet-switched communications, protocols such as TCP/IP, Web servers, HTML, and relational and non-relational databases, among others.
*   *Business*—While technology provides the infrastructure, it is the business applications—the potential for extraordinary returns on investment—that create the interest and excitement in e-commerce. Therefore, you also need to understand some key business concepts such as electronic markets, information goods, business models, firm and industry value chains, industry structure, and consumer behavior in digital markets.
*   *Society*—Understanding the pressures that global e-commerce places on contemporary society is critical to being successful in the e-commerce marketplace. The primary societal issues are intellectual property, individual privacy, and public policy.

■ **Identify the major academic disciplines contributing to e-commerce.**

There are two primary approaches to e-commerce: technical and behavioral. Each of these approaches is represented by several academic disciplines. On the technical side, this includes computer science, operations management, and information systems. On the behavioral side, it includes information systems as well as sociology, economics, finance and accounting, management, and marketing.

QUESTIONS

1. What does omni-channel mean in terms of e-commerce presence?
2. What is information asymmetry?
3. What are some of the unique features of e-commerce technology?
4. Why has Rocket Internet been criticized, and how do the Samwer brothers respond to that criticism?
5. What are three benefits of universal standards?
6. What are some of the factors driving the growth of social e-commerce?
7. Name three of the business consequences that can result from growth in information density.
8. What is Web 2.0? Give examples of Web 2.0 sites and explain why you included them in your list.
9. Give examples of B2C, B2B, C2C, and social, mobile, and local e-commerce besides those listed in the chapter materials.
10. How are e-commerce technologies similar to or different from other technologies that have changed commerce in the past?
11. Describe the three different stages in the evolution of e-commerce.

12. Define disintermediation and explain the benefits to Internet users of such a phenomenon. How does disintermediation impact friction-free commerce?
13. What are some of the major advantages and disadvantages of being a first mover?
14. What is a network effect, and why is it valuable?
15. Discuss the ways in which the early years of e-commerce can be considered both a success and a failure.
16. What are five of the major differences between the early years of e-commerce and today's e-commerce?
17. What factors will help define the future of e-commerce over the next five years?
18. Why is a multidisciplinary approach necessary if one hopes to understand e-commerce?
19. What are some of the privacy issues that Facebook has created?
20. What are those who take a behavioral approach to studying e-commerce interested in?

PROJECTS

1. Choose an e-commerce company and assess it in terms of the eight unique features of e-commerce technology described in Table 1.2. Which of the features does the company implement well, and which features poorly, in your opinion? Prepare a short memo to the president of the company you have chosen detailing your findings and any suggestions for improvement you may have.

2. Search the Web for an example of each of the major types of e-commerce described in Section 1.1 and listed in Table 1.3. Create a presentation or written report describing each company (take a screenshot of each, if possible), and explain why it fits into the category of e-commerce to which you have assigned it.

3. Given the development and history of e-commerce in the years from 1995–2014, what do you predict we will see during the next five years of e-commerce? Describe some of the technological, business, and societal shifts that may occur as the Internet continues to grow and expand. Prepare a brief presentation or written report to explain your vision of what e-commerce will look like in 2018.

4. Prepare a brief report or presentation on how companies are using Instagram or another company of your choosing as a social e-commerce platform.

5. Follow up on events at Puma since November 2014 (when the opening case was prepared). Prepare a short report on your findings.

REFERENCES

Aguiar, Mark and Erik Hurst. "Life-Cycle Prices and Production." *American Economic Review* 97:5, 1533-1559. (January 1, 2008).

Alessandria, George. "Consumer Search, Price Dispersion, and International Relative Price Fluctuations." *International Economic Review* 50:3, 803-829 (September 1, 2009).

Bailey, Joseph P. *Intermediation and Electronic Markets: Aggregation and Pricing in Internet Commerce.* Ph. D., Technology, Management and Policy, Massachusetts Institute of Technology (1998a).

Bakos, Yannis. "Reducing Buyer Search Costs: Implications for Electronic Marketplaces." *Management Science* (December 1997).

Banerjee, Suman and Chakravarty, Amiya. "Price Setting and Price Discovery Strategies with a Mix of Frequent and Infrequent Internet Users." (April 15, 2005). SSRN: http://ssrn.com/abstract = 650706.

Barberi, Mauricio. "How Will Forrester's Predicted $1.4 Trillion in Web-Influenced Sales Affect Competitive Retail in 2014." Upstreamcommerce.com (January 21, 2014).

Baye, Michael R. "Price Dispersion in the Lab and on the Internet: Theory and Evidence." *Rand Journal of Economics* (2004).

Baye, Michael R., John Morgan, and Patrick Scholten. "Temporal Price Dispersion: Evidence from an Online Consumer Electronics Market." *Journal of Interactive Marketing* (January 2004).

Brynjolfsson, Erik, and Michael Smith. "Frictionless Commerce? A Comparison of Internet and Conventional Retailers." *Management Science* (April 2000).

Buck, Stephanie. "The Beginner's Guide to Instagram." Mashable.com (May 29, 2012).

comScore. "comScore Releases April 2014 U.S. Online Video Rankings." (May 21, 2014a).

comScore. "comScore Media Metrix Ranks Top 50 U.S. Web Properties for April 2014." (May 23, 2014b).

eBay, Inc. "eBay Inc. Reports Second Quarter Results." (July 16, 2014.)

eMarketer, Inc. "Comparative Estimates, Internet Users Worldwide." (accessed April 30, 2014a).

eMarketer, Inc. (Alison McCarthy) "Worldwide B2C Ecommerce: Q3 2014 Complete Forecast. " (August 2014b).

eMarketer, Inc. (Alison McCarthy). "US Mobile Users: 2014 Complete Forecast." (April 2014c).

eMarketer, Inc. (Alison McCarthy). "US Tablet Users: Q1 2014 Forecast and Comparative Estimates." (May 2014d).

eMarketer, Inc. (Jeffrey Grau). "US Retail Ecommerce: 2013 Forecast and Comparative Estimates." (April 2013a).

eMarketer, Inc. , "US Mobile Connections, 2011–2017." (March 2013b)

eMarketer, Inc. "US Mobile Phone Internet Users and Penetration, 2011–2017." (March 2013c).

eMarketer, Inc. "US Tablet Users and Penetration, 2011–2017." (March 2013d).

eMarketer, Inc. "US Daily Deal Site Revenues, 2011–2016 (billions)." (September 17, 2012).

Evans, Philip, and Thomas S. Wurster. "Getting Real About Virtual Commerce." *Harvard Business Review* (November-December 1999).

Evans, Philip, and Thomas S. Wurster. "Strategy and the New Economics of Information." *Harvard Business Review* (September-October 1997).

Ghose, Anindya, and Yuliang Yao. "Using Transaction Prices to Re-Examine Price Dispersion in Electronic Markets." Information Systems Research, Vol. 22 No. 2. (June 2011).

Google. "How Search Works: From Algorithms to Answers." (accessed June 17, 2014).

Instagram.com "Press News." (accessed June 17, 2014).

Internet Retailer. "There's a Lot to 'Like' in the Social Media 500." Internetretailer.com (January 2014a).

Internet Retailer. "Top 500 Guide 2014 Edition." (2014b).

Internet Systems Consortium, Inc. "ISC Internet Domain Survey." (April 2014).

IORMA. "Global Retail Trends...in an Omni World." (2014).

Kalakota, Ravi, and Marcia Robinson. *e-Business 2.0: Roadmap for Success, 2nd edition*. Reading, MA: Addison Wesley (2003).

Kambil, Ajit. "Doing Business in the Wired World." *IEEE Computer* (May 1997).

Levin, Jonathon. "The Economics of Internet Markets." Stanford University, Draft, February 18, 2011.

Mesenbourg, Thomas L. "Measuring Electronic Business: Definitions, Underlying Concepts, and Measurement Plans." U. S. Department of Commerce Bureau of the Census (August 2001).

Rayport, Jeffrey F., and Bernard J. Jaworski. *Introduction to E-commerce, 2nd edition*. New York: McGraw-Hill (2003).

Rosso, Mark and Bernard Janse. "Smart Marketing or Bait & Switch: Competitors' Brands as Keywords in Online Advertising." Proceedings of the 4th Workshop on Information Credibility. ACM (2010).

Shapiro, Carl, and Hal R. Varian. *Information Rules. A Strategic Guide to the Network Economy*. Cambridge, MA: Harvard Business School Press (1999).

Sinha, Indajit. "Cost Transparency: The Net's Threat to Prices and Brands." *Harvard Business Review* (March-April 2000).

Smith, Michael; Joseph Bailey; and Erik Brynjolfsson. "Understanding Digital Markets: Review and Assessment." In Erik Brynjolfsson and Brian Kahin (eds.) *Understanding the Digital Economy*. Cambridge MA: MIT Press (2000).

Stambor, Zak. "Social Networks Drive 7.7% of Visits to Retail Web Sites." Internetretailer.com (March 28, 2014).

Tumblr.com. "Press Information." (accessed June 17, 2014).

Tversky, A., and D. Kahneman. "The Framing of Decisions and the Psychology of Choice." *Science* (January 1981).

U.S. Census Bureau. "E-Stats." (May 22, 2014).

Varian, Hal R. "When Commerce Moves On, Competition Can Work in Strange Ways." *New York Times* (August 24, 2000a).

Varian, Hal R. "5 Habits of Highly Effective Revolution." *Forbes ASAP* (February 21, 2000b).

Wikipedia.org. "Wikipedia: About." (accessed June 17, 2014).

Wikimedia Foundation. "Wikipedia Celebrates 10 Years of Free Knowledge." (January 12, 2011).

YouTube.com. "Statistics." (accessed June 17, 2014).

CHAPTER 2

E-commerce Infrastructure

After reading this chapter, you will be able to:

- Discuss the origins of, and the key technology concepts behind, the Internet.
- Explain the current structure of the Internet.
- Understand the limitations of today's Internet and the potential capabilities of the Internet of the future.
- Understand how the Web works.
- Describe how Internet and Web features and services support e-commerce.
- Understand the impact of m-commerce applications.

Wikitude, Layar, and Blippar:

Augment My Reality

Walk down the street in any city and count the number of people pecking away at their smartphones. Ride the train, and observe how many fellow travelers are using a tablet. Today, the primary means of accessing the Internet is via a mobile device. Traditional PCs still play a role, but in 2014, almost 80% of the Internet population uses a mobile device to access the Internet, and over 30% of total Internet traffic comes from mobile devices. That percentage is only going to grow. The mobile platform provides the foundation for a number of unique new services, including augmented reality, which involves content (text, video, and sound) that is superimposed over live images in order to enrich the user's experience.

Augmented reality combines the geolocating

© fairoesh/Fotolia.com

functionality built into smartphones to bring together location, and context, helping the user understand his or her environment better. There are many start-up companies working on augmented reality apps in this emerging marketspace. Wikitude is one of the most prominent examples of an online augmented reality mobile platform. It is a "points of interest" location-based service that uses the same kind of wiki tools that power Wikipedia, the online encyclopedia. The Wikitude 8 app is available for all major mobile operating systems, and the company released the latest edition of its developer kit, SDK 4.0, in July 2014. The app displays information about whatever the user's phone camera is pointed at. Using the smartphone's GPS, accelerometer, and compass, the app knows where it is located, and what direction it is pointing. The app then accesses the Wikitude database to provide text information on the object being looked at by the user, including identifying the object or scene, history, and related points of interest. The app currently provides support for 12 languages, and Wikitude's database contains information on over 100 million points of interest. It obtains this information from Wikipedia, the online encyclopedia, as well as third-party services such as TripAdvisor, Foursquare, and Yelp. You can snap a picture of an object and let Wikitude describe its historical significance, or you can use the app to find, say, a Thai restaurant nearby. You can think of Wikitude as a very sophisticated travel guide, which is precisely its most common use. In addition, merchants can advertise their local offerings and discount coupons based on where the user is located. Wikitude is therefore an advertising platform as well as a travel guide.

Organizations throughout Europe and the rest of world are using Wikitude to create custom apps for a variety of purposes. The Trentino 2013 Fiemme Nordic Ski Championships used an app powered by Wikitude to guide visitors and provide locations of event facilities and nearby attractions. Fashion retailer Zalando and concept car manufacturer Rinspeed collaborated with Wikitude to produce an augmented reality display inside Rinspeed's latest vehicle. Wikitude and eoVision, which offers services and products related to Earth's observation and geoinformation, collaborated on a book entitled "one earth," which has 119 pages of satellite images that analyze the environment and display maps, descriptions, 3D modeling, and advanced augmented reality technology to deliver an entirely new media experience. Wikitude technology also features prominently in the companion app to "Who We Are: One Direction," an autobiography of the popular band One Direction, released in September 2014. App users can place their mobile device over photographs and other areas of the book, allowing them to view exclusive videos, interviews, and other interactive material. The app was downloaded more than 60,000 times in the two weeks after its launch.

In February 2014, Wikitude announced that it was bringing its app and developer's kit to Google Glass. The kit will allow developers to create apps with Wikitude's Image Recognition engine and location-based augmented reality services. One problem with Google Glass is that the screen sits above and to the right of the user's line of sight. For Wikitude to work best, it should ideally be overlaid directly in the user's eye line. Still, Wikitude's array of apps are exactly what many prospective users of Google Glass are expecting from the device.

Layar, a Wikitude competitor that also offers an augmented reality browser, has traditionally been friendly to iOS developers in an attempt to commercialize augmented reality services. Services like Layar Vision allow users to hold up a smartphone to a real life object and receive an overlay of data about it, including advertising offers. Layar believes that augmented reality will ultimately become essential to consumers' mobile experiences. As Layar strategist Gene Becker noted, the challenge now is to really get into the business of creating a medium that people can use to express, connect, and communicate. In 2013, Layar collaborated with the Toronto Star and a number of other major newspapers to release an augmented reality version of individual newspapers.

In 2014, Layar followed in Wikitude's footsteps, announcing that a beta version of its own app was available for download for Google Glass. Simply saying "OK Glass, scan this" allows users to see extra information from magazines, local real estate, or movie trailers. It also allows users to scan QR codes to get extra information about a variety of items.

Later in 2014, Layar was acquired by fellow augmented reality start-up Blippar, an image recognition platform used in digital advertising. Blippar creates "blipps" in which users snap pictures of products to view content-rich, interactive experiences via mobile devices. Because both companies are focused primarily on advertising via graphical overlays, the two companies were a natural fit. The move gives the combined entity the ability to compete with a wider array of AR and VR companies. As of yet, gaming headset developer Oculus VR is the only company in this space to generate major consumer buzz, but that company was purchased by Facebook for $2 billion, indicating there is an

SOURCES: "One Direction '1D Official Book' Companion App", Wikitude.com, accessed November 25, 2014; "castAR Bets Big on its Augmented Reality Hardware with

opportunity for the Blippar-Layar combination, as well as Wikitude and other competing firms like Metaio and Vuforia.

More and more commercial applications of augmented reality technology are being introduced every day. Yellow Pages has tested the use of augmented reality to overlay advertisements, paid for by business, to street views where its app is used. Another variation is a real estate app tested by RightMove.com that allows users to point their phone up and down a street and find out what is for sale or for rent, and how much it costs. It also provides contact information for each of the properties. Yelp, TripAdvisor, and Lonely Planet are just a few of the travel companies that have introduced some aspects of augmented reality to their apps.

Yet another current use of augmented reality is to allow users to simulate "trying on" the product. For instance, eBay's Fashion iPhone app lets users virtually try on sunglasses using the phone's front-facing camera to take a picture of themselves and then virtually "fit" the sunglasses to their face. Watchmaker Neuvo offers a similar app that lets users virtually try on watches, while a Converse app lets you do the same with Converse shoes. Software from Zugara allows you try on clothing from online shops.

Gaming is another area where augmented reality is expected to make a big splash. The aforementioned Oculus VR is gaining traction despite the fact that its Oculus Rift headset is several months away from a consumer release, currently expected in late 2014. Although the headset was originally conceived as a gaming platform, Oculus Rift has potential applications for virtual reality training programs, performing advanced medical procedures, and any number of other more practical uses. And the VR gaming landscape is getting more crowded. Two former employees from gaming company Valve received over $400,000 in Kickstarter funding in under two days for its castAR augmented reality gaming project, which uses glasses, an RFID tracking grid, and a controller to enable augmented reality gaming. The company has raised over $1 million in funding via Kickstarter to date and moved to Silicon Valley in 2014 to hire more talented hardware engineers and meet increased production demands. Google is also developing an augmented reality game called Ingress that will function seamlessly with Google Glass. Players will explore real world environments and will team up with other players to achieve in-game goals. Many other gaming companies are considering the possibilities for augmented reality in future projects.

Rumor also has it that Apple may be planning its own augmented reality foray, which may be the final push needed to put augmented reality squarely into the mainstream. Apple applied for and won patents for an augmented reality system for mobile devices in 2013, though as of yet nothing concrete has been announced. In 2014, Apple submitted more patents for iOS for augmented reality systems. Apple appears to be developing a system that can provide virtual overlays of their surroundings akin to Layar, but which also will include "x-ray vision" that allows users to look behind walls of select structures. A combination of a live feed from the iPhone's camera and local sensor information would pinpoint a user's position and generate an interactive wireframe model of their immediate surroundings. Users will be able to manipulate the frame so that it matches their view. Applications for the service could be as an advanced version of Apple's Maps service, complete with capability for local businesses to advertise and generate special offers based on Apple's granular user data.

Move to Silicon Valley," by Nicole Lee, Engadget.com, October 17, 2014; "Apple's iPhone-based Augmented Reality Navigation Concept has 'X-Ray Vision' Features," by Mikey Campbell, Appleinsider.com, September 4, 2014; "UK Startup Blippar Confirms It Has Acquired AR Pioneer Layar," by Mike Butcher, Techcrunch.com, June 18, 2014; "Augmented Reality Augmentation: Blippar Has Bought Layar," by Ingrid Lunden, Techcrunch.com, June 10, 2014; "Layar Now Wants to Augment Your Reality with its Google Glass App," by Ben Woods, Thenextweb.com, March 19, 2014; "Wikitude Opens its Augmented Reality SDK to Glass Developers," Matt McGee, Glassalmanac.com, February 21, 2014; "Trentino 2013 Fiemme Nordic Ski Championships," Wikitude.com, accessed October 2013; "Augmented Reality Tech Hits Funding Goal," by Eddie Makuch, Gamespot.com, October 16, 2013; "Google Niantic's Ingress Augmented-Reality Game Grows With Real-Time Events," by Dean Takahashi, VentureBeat, October 15, 2013; "Wikitude and eoVision Bring Augmented Reality to the Frankfurt Book Fair," Wikitude.com, October 10, 2013; "Meet the Toronto STar's Layar Edition," Thestar.com, September 18, 2013; "Zalando Scans Fashion with Wikitude Augmented Reality at 83rd Annual Geneva Motor Show," Wikitude.com, March 5, 2013; "Apple Patent Hints at Augmented Reality Camera App," by Josh Lowensohn, News.cnet.com; August 18, 2011; "Augmented Reality Kills the QR Code Star," by Kit Eaton, Fastcompany.com, August 4, 2011; "Qualcomm's Awesome Augmented Reality SDK Now Available for iOS," Telecrunch.com, July 27, 2011; "Real Life or Just Fantasy," by Nick Clayton, *Wall Street Journal*, June 29, 2011; "Augmented Reality Comes Closer to Reality," by John Markoff, *New York Times*, April 7, 2011; "Augmented Reality's Industry Prospects May Get Very Real, Very Fast," by Danny King, Dailyfinance.com; "Even Better Than the Real Thing," by Paul Skelton, *Wall Street Journal*, February 15, 2011; "Wikitude Goes Wimbledon 2010," press release, Wikitude.com, June 20, 2010.

his chapter examines the Internet, Web, and mobile platform of today and tomorrow, how it evolved, how it works, and how its present and future infrastructure enables new business opportunities.

The opening case illustrates how important it is for business people to understand how the Internet and related technologies work, and to be aware of what's new. Operating a successful e-commerce business and implementing key e-commerce business strategies such as personalization, customization, market segmentation, and price discrimination require that business people understand Internet technology and keep track of Web and mobile platform developments.

The Internet and its underlying technology is not a static phenomenon in history, but instead continues to change over time. Computers have merged with cell phone services; broadband access in the home and broadband wireless access to the Internet via smartphones, tablet computers, and laptops are expanding rapidly; self-publishing on the Web via blogging, social networking, and podcasting now engages millions of Internet users; and software technologies such as Web services, cloud computing, and smartphone apps are revolutionizing the way businesses are using the Internet. Looking forward a few years, the business strategies of the future will require a firm understanding of these technologies and new ones, such as the Internet of Things, wearable technology, and the "smart/connected" movement (smart homes, smart TVs, and connected cars) to deliver products and services to consumers. **Table 2.1** summarizes some of the most important developments in e-commerce infrastructure for 2014–2015.

2.1   THE INTERNET: TECHNOLOGY BACKGROUND

What is the Internet? Where did it come from, and how did it support the growth of the Web? What are the Internet's most important operating principles? How much do you really need to know about the technology of the Internet?

Let's take the last question first. The answer is: it depends on your career interests. If you are on a marketing career path, or general managerial business path, then you need to know the basics about Internet technology, which you'll learn in this and the following chapter. If you are on a technical career path and hope to become a Web designer, or pursue a technical career in Web infrastructure for businesses, you'll need to start with these basics and then build from there. You'll also need to know about the business side of e-commerce, which you will learn about throughout this book.

As noted in Chapter 1, the **Internet** is an interconnected network of thousands of networks and millions of computers (sometimes called *host computers* or just *hosts*) linking businesses, educational institutions, government agencies, and individuals. The Internet provides approximately 2.8 billion people around the world with services such as e-mail, apps, newsgroups, shopping, research, instant messaging, music, videos, and news (eMarketer, Inc., 2014a, 2014b). No single organization controls the Internet or how it functions, nor is it owned by anybody, yet it has provided the

Internet

an interconnected network of thousands of networks and millions of computers linking businesses, educational institutions, government agencies, and individuals

TABLE 2.1	**TRENDS IN E-COMMERCE INFRASTRUCTURE 2014–2015**

BUSINESS

- Mobile devices become the primary access point to social network services and a rapidly expanding social marketing and advertising platform, and create a foundation for location-based Web services and business models.
- Explosion of Internet content services and mobile access devices strains the business models of Internet backbone providers (the large telecommunication carriers).
- The growth in cloud computing and bandwidth capacity enables new business models for distributing music, movies, and television.
- Search becomes more social and local, enabling social and local commerce business models.
- Internet backbone carriers initiate differential pricing models so that users pay for bandwidth usage.
- "Big Data" produced by the Internet creates new business opportunities for firms with the analytic capability to understand it.

TECHNOLOGY

- Mobile devices such as smartphones and tablet computers have become the dominant mode of access to the Internet. The new client is mobile.
- The explosion of mobile apps threatens the dominance of the Web as the main source of online software applications and leads some to claim the Web is dead.
- HTML5 grows in popularity among publishers and developers and makes possible Web applications that are just as visually rich and lively as native mobile apps.
- Cloud computing reshapes computing and storage, and becomes an important force in the delivery of software applications and online content.
- The Internet runs out of IPv4 addresses; transition to IPv6 begins.
- The shipment of tablet computers exceeds the shipment of PCs.
- The decreased cost of storage and advances in database software lead to explosion in online data collection known as Big Data and creates new business opportunities for firms with the analytic capability to understand it.
- The Internet of Things, with millions of sensor-equipped devices connecting to the Internet, starts to become a reality, and is powering the development of smart connected "things" such as televisions, houses, cars, and wearable technology.

SOCIETY

- Governance of the Internet becomes more involved with conflicts between nations; the United States plans to give up control over IANA, which administers the Internet's IP addressing system.
- Government control over, and surveillance of, the Internet is expanded in most advanced nations, and in many nations the Internet is nearly completely controlled by government agencies.
- The growing Web-based infrastructure for tracking online and mobile consumer behavior conflicts with individual claims to privacy and control over personal information.

infrastructure for a transformation in commerce, scientific research, and culture. The word *Internet* is derived from the word *internetwork*, or the connecting together of two or more computer networks. The **Web** is one of the Internet's most popular services, providing access to billions, perhaps trillions, of Web pages, which are documents created in a programming language called HTML that can contain text, graphics, audio, video, and other objects, as well as "hyperlinks" that permit users to jump easily from one page to another. Web pages are navigated using browser software.

the Web
one of the Internet's most popular services, providing access to billions, and perhaps trillions, of Web pages

THE EVOLUTION OF THE INTERNET: 1961—THE PRESENT

Today's Internet has evolved over the last 50 or so years. In this sense, the Internet is not "new;" it did not happen yesterday. Although journalists talk glibly about "Internet" time—suggesting a fast-paced, nearly instant, worldwide global change mechanism—in fact, it has taken about 50 years of hard work to arrive at today's Internet.

The history of the Internet can be segmented into three phases (see **Figure 2.1**). In the first phase, the *Innovation Phase,* from 1961 to 1974, the fundamental building blocks of the Internet were conceptualized and then realized in actual hardware and software. The basic building blocks are packet-switching hardware, a communications protocol called TCP/IP, and client/server computing (all described more fully later in this section). The original purpose of the Internet, when it was conceived in the 1960s, was to link large mainframe computers on different college campuses. This kind of one-to-one communication between campuses was previously only possible through the telephone system or private networks owned by the large computer manufacturers.

In the second phase, the *Institutionalization Phase*, from 1975 to 1995, large institutions such as the U.S. Department of Defense (DoD) and the National Science Foundation (NSF) provided funding and legitimization for the fledging invention called the Internet. Once the concepts behind the Internet had been proven in several government-supported demonstration projects, the DoD contributed $1 million to further develop them into a robust military communications system that could withstand nuclear war. This effort created what was then called ARPANET (Advanced Research Projects Agency Network). In 1986, the NSF assumed responsibility for the development of a civilian Internet (then called NSFNET) and began a 10-year-long $200 million expansion program.

FIGURE 2.1	STAGES IN THE DEVELOPMENT OF THE INTERNET

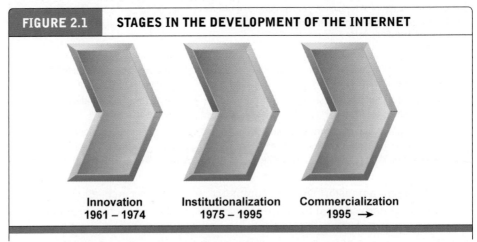

Innovation
1961 – 1974

Institutionalization
1975 – 1995

Commercialization
1995 →

The Internet has developed in three stages over approximately a 50-year period from 1961 to the present. In the Innovation stage, basic ideas and technologies were developed; in the Institutionalization stage, these ideas were brought to life; in the Commercialization stage, once the ideas and technologies had been proven, private companies brought the Internet to millions of people worldwide.

In the third phase, the *Commercialization Phase*, from 1995 to the present, government agencies encouraged private corporations to take over and expand both the Internet backbone and local service to ordinary citizens—families and individuals across the world who were not students on campuses. By 2000, the Internet's use had expanded well beyond military installations and research universities. See **Table 2.2** on pages 102–104 for a closer look at the development of the Internet from 1961 on.

THE INTERNET: KEY TECHNOLOGY CONCEPTS

In 1995, the Federal Networking Council (FNC) passed a resolution formally defining the term *Internet* as a network that uses the IP addressing scheme, supports the Transmission Control Protocol (TCP), and makes services available to users much like a telephone system makes voice and data services available to the public (see **Figure 2.2**).

Behind this formal definition are three extremely important concepts that are the basis for understanding the Internet: packet switching, the TCP/IP communications protocol, and client/server computing. Although the Internet has evolved and changed dramatically in the last 30 years, these three concepts are at the core of the way the Internet functions today and are the foundation for the Internet of the future.

Packet Switching

Packet switching is a method of slicing digital messages into discrete units called **packets**, sending the packets along different communication paths as they become available, and then reassembling the packets once they arrive at their destination (see

packet switching
a method of slicing digital messages into packets, sending the packets along different communication paths as they become available, and then reassembling the packets once they arrive at their destination

packets
the discrete units into which digital messages are sliced for transmission over the Internet

---

FIGURE 2.2   **RESOLUTION OF THE U.S. FEDERAL NETWORKING COUNCIL**

"The Federal Networking Council (FNC) agrees that the following language reflects our definition of the term 'Internet.'

'Internet' refers to the global information system that—

(i) is logically linked together by a globally unique address space based on the Internet Protocol (IP) or its subsequent extensions/follow-ons;

(ii) is able to support communications using the Transmission Control Protocol/Internet Protocol (TCP/IP) suite or its subsequent extensions/ follow-ons, and/or other IP-compatible protocols; and

(iii) provides, uses or makes accessible, either publicly or privately, high level services layered on the communications and related infrastructure described herein."

Last modified on October 30, 1995.

SOURCE: Federal Networking Council, 1995

TABLE 2.2	DEVELOPMENT OF THE INTERNET TIMELINE

YEAR	EVENT	SIGNIFICANCE
INNOVATION PHASE 1961–1974		
1961	Leonard Kleinrock (MIT) publishes a paper on "packet switching" networks.	The concept of packet switching is born.
1962	J.C.R. Licklider (MIT) writes memo calling for an "Intergalatic Computer Network."	The vision of a global computer network is born.
1969	BBN Technologies awarded ARPA contract to build ARPANET.	The concept of a packet-switched network moves closer toward physical reality.
1969	The first packet-switched message is sent on ARPANET from UCLA to Stanford.	The communications hardware underlying the Internet is implemented for the first time. The initial ARPANET consisted of four routers (then called Interface Message Processors (IMPs)) at UCLA, Stanford, UCSB, and the University of Utah.
1972	E-mail is invented by Ray Tomlinson of BBN. Larry Roberts writes the first e-mail utility program permitting listing, forwarding, and responding to e-mails.	The first "killer app" of the Internet is born.
1973	Bob Metcalfe (XeroxParc Labs) invents Ethernet and local area networks.	**Client/server computing is invented.** Ethernet permitted the development of local area networks and client/server computing in which thousands of fully functional desktop computers could be connected into a short-distance (<1,000 meters) network to share files, run applications, and send messages.
1974	"Open architecture" networking and TCP/IP concepts are presented in a paper by Vint Cerf (Stanford) and Bob Kahn (BBN).	**TCP/IP invented.** The conceptual foundation for a single common communications protocol that could potentially connect any of thousands of disparate local area networks and computers, and a common addressing scheme for all computers connected to the network, are born. Prior to this, computers could communicate only if they shared a common proprietary network architecture. With TCP/IP, computers and networks could work together regardless of their local operating systems or network protocols.
INSTITUTIONALIZATION PHASE 1975–1995		
1977	Lawrence Landweber envisions CSNET (Computer Science Network)	CSNET is a pioneering network for U.S. universities and industrial computer research groups that could not directly connect to ARPANET, and was a major milestone on the path to the development of the global Internet.
1980	TCP/IP is officially adopted as the DoD standard communications protocol.	The single largest computing organization in the world adopts TCP/IP and packet-switched network technology.
1980	Personal computers are invented.	Altair, Apple, and IBM personal desktop computers are invented. These computers become the foundation for today's Internet, affording millions of people access to the Internet and the Web.

TABLE 2.2	DEVELOPMENT OF THE INTERNET TIMELINE (CONTINUED)

YEAR	EVENT	SIGNIFICANCE
1984	Apple Computer releases the HyperCard program as part of its graphical user interface operating system called Macintosh.	The concept of "hyperlinked" documents and records that permit the user to jump from one page or record to another is commercially introduced.
1984	Domain Name System (DNS) introduced.	DNS provides a user-friendly system for translating IP addresses into words that people can easily understand.
1989	Tim Berners-Lee of CERN in Switzerland proposes a worldwide network of hyperlinked documents based on a common markup language called HTML—HyperText Markup Language.	**The concept of an Internet-supported service called the World Wide Web based on HTML pages is born**. The Web would be constructed from "pages" created in a common markup language, with "hyperlinks" that permitted easy access among the pages.
1990	NSF plans and assumes responsibility for a civilian Internet backbone and creates NSFNET.[1] ARPANET is decommissioned.	The concept of a "civilian" Internet open to all is realized through nonmilitary funding by NSF.
1993	The first graphical Web browser called Mosaic is invented by Marc Andreessen and others at the National Center for Supercomputing Applications at the University of Illinois.	Mosaic makes it very easy for ordinary users to connect to HTML documents anywhere on the Web. The browser-enabled Web takes off.
1994	Andreessen and Jim Clark form Netscape Corporation.	The first commercial Web browser—Netscape—becomes available.
1994	The first banner advertisements appear on Hotwired.com in October 1994.	**The beginning of e-commerce**.

COMMERCIALIZATION PHASE 1995–PRESENT

1995	NSF privatizes the backbone, and commercial carriers take over backbone operation.	**The fully commercial civilian Internet is born**. Major long-haul networks such as AT&T, Sprint, GTE, UUNet, and MCI take over operation of the backbone. Network Solutions (a private firm) is given a monopoly to assign Internet addresses.
1995	Jeff Bezos founds Amazon; Pierre Omidyar forms AuctionWeb (eBay).	E-commerce begins in earnest with pure online retail stores and auctions.
1998	The U.S. federal government encourages the founding of the Internet Corporation for Assigned Names and Numbers (ICANN).	Governance over domain names and addresses passes to a private nonprofit international organization.
1999	The first full-service Internet-only bank, First Internet Bank of Indiana, opens for business.	Business on the Web extends into traditional services.
2003	The Internet2 Abilene high-speed network is upgraded to 10 Gbps.	A major milestone toward the development of ultra-high-speed transcontinental networks several times faster than the existing backbone is achieved.

[1] "Backbone" refers to the U.S. domestic trunk lines that carry the heavy traffic across the nation, from one metropolitan area to another. Universities are given responsibility for developing their own campus networks that must be connected to the national backbone.

(continued)

TABLE 2.2	DEVELOPMENT OF THE INTERNET TIMELINE (CONTINUED)

YEAR	EVENT	SIGNIFICANCE
2005	NSF proposes the Global Environment for Network Innovations (GENI) initiative to develop new core functionality for the Internet.	Recognition that future Internet security and functionality needs may require the thorough rethinking of existing Internet technology.
2006	The U.S. Senate Committee on Commerce, Science, and Transportation holds hearings on "Network Neutrality."	The debate grows over differential pricing based on utilization that pits backbone utility owners against online content and service providers and device makers.
2007	The Apple iPhone is introduced.	The introduction of the iPhone represents the beginning of the development of a viable mobile platform that will ultimately transform the way people interact with the Internet.
2008	The Internet Society (ISOC) identifies Trust and Identity as a primary design element for every layer of the Internet, and launches an initiative to address these issues.	The leading Internet policy group recognizes the current Internet is threatened by breaches of security and trust that are built into the existing network.
2008	Internet "cloud computing" becomes a billion-dollar industry.	Internet capacity is sufficient to support on-demand computing resources (processing and storage), as well as software applications, for large corporations and individuals.
2009	Internet-enabled smartphones become a major new Web access platform.	Smartphones extend the reach and range of the Internet to more closely realize the promise of the Internet anywhere, anytime, anyplace.
2009	Broadband stimulus package and Broadband Data Improvement Act enacted.	President Obama signs stimulus package containing $7.2 billion for the expansion of broadband access in the United States.
2011	ICANN expands domain name system.	ICANN agrees to permit the expansion of generic top-level domain names from about 300 to potentially thousands using any word in any language.
2012	World IPv6 Launch day.	Major ISPs, home networking equipment manufacturers, and Web companies begin to permanently enable IPv6 for their products and services as of June 6, 2012.
2013	The Internet of Things (IoT) starts to become a reality.	Internet technology spreads beyond the computer and mobile device to anything that can be equipped with sensors, leading to predictions that up to 100–200 billion uniquely identifiable objects will be connected to the Internet by 2020.
2014	Apple introduces Apple Pay and Apple Watch	Apple Pay is likely to become the first widely adopted mobile payment system; Apple Watch may usher in a new era of wearable Internet-connected technology and is a further harbinger of the Internet of Things.

SOURCES: Based on Leiner et al., 2000; Zakon, 2005; Gross, 2005; Geni.net, 2007; ISOC.org, 2010; Arstechnica.com, 2010; ICANN, 2011a; Internet Society, 2012; IEEE Computer Society, 2013.

Figure 2.3). Prior to the development of packet switching, early computer networks used leased, dedicated telephone circuits to communicate with terminals and other computers. In circuit-switched networks such as the telephone system, a complete point-to-point circuit is put together, and then communication can proceed. However, these "dedicated" circuit-switching techniques were expensive and wasted available communications capacity—the circuit would be maintained regardless of whether any

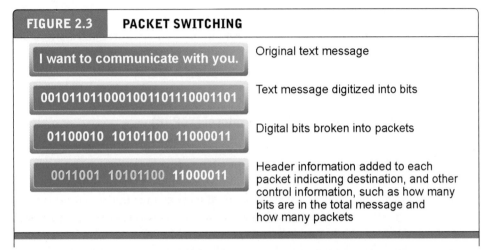

FIGURE 2.3	**PACKET SWITCHING**
I want to communicate with you.	Original text message
00101101100010011011110001101	Text message digitized into bits
01100010 10101100 11000011	Digital bits broken into packets
0011001 10101100 **11000011**	Header information added to each packet indicating destination, and other control information, such as how many bits are in the total message and how many packets

In packet switching, digital messages are divided into fixed-length packets of bits (generally about 1,500 bytes). Header information indicates both the origin and the ultimate destination address of the packet, the size of the message, and the number of packets the receiving node should expect. Because the receipt of each packet is acknowledged by the receiving computer, for a considerable amount of time, the network is not passing information, only acknowledgments, producing a delay called latency.

data was being sent. For nearly 70% of the time, a dedicated voice circuit is not being fully used because of pauses between words and delays in assembling the circuit segments, both of which increase the length of time required to find and connect circuits. A better technology was needed.

The first book on packet switching was written by Leonard Kleinrock in 1964 (Kleinrock, 1964), and the technique was further developed by others in the defense research labs of both the United States and England. With packet switching, the communications capacity of a network can be increased by a factor of 100 or more. (The communications capacity of a digital network is measured in terms of bits per second.[2]) Imagine if the gas mileage of your car went from 15 miles per gallon to 1,500 miles per gallon—all without changing too much of the car!

In packet-switched networks, messages are first broken down into packets. Appended to each packet are digital codes that indicate a source address (the origination point) and a destination address, as well as sequencing information and error-control information for the packet. Rather than being sent directly to the destination address, in a packet network, the packets travel from computer to computer until they reach their destination. These computers are called routers. A **router** is a special-purpose computer that interconnects the different computer networks that make up the Internet and routes packets along to their ultimate destination as they travel. To ensure that packets take the best available path toward their destination, routers use a computer program called a **routing algorithm**.

router
special-purpose computer that interconnects the computer networks that make up the Internet and routes packets to their ultimate destination as they travel the Internet

routing algorithm
computer program that ensures that packets take the best available path toward their destination

[2] A bit is a binary digit, 0 or 1. A string of eight bits constitutes a byte. A home telephone dial-up modem connects to the Internet usually at 56 Kbps (56,000 bits per second). Mbps refers to millions of bits per second, whereas Gbps refers to billions of bits per second.

Packet switching does not require a dedicated circuit, but can make use of any spare capacity that is available on any of several hundred circuits. Packet switching makes nearly full use of almost all available communication lines and capacity. Moreover, if some lines are disabled or too busy, the packets can be sent on any available line that eventually leads to the destination point.

Transmission Control Protocol/Internet Protocol (TCP/IP)

While packet switching was an enormous advance in communications capacity, there was no universally agreed-upon method for breaking up digital messages into packets, routing them to the proper address, and then reassembling them into a coherent message. This was like having a system for producing stamps but no postal system (a series of post offices and a set of addresses). The answer was to develop a **protocol** (a set of rules and standards for data transfer) to govern the formatting, ordering, compressing, and error-checking of messages, as well as specify the speed of transmission and means by which devices on the network will indicate they have stopped sending and/or receiving messages.

Transmission Control Protocol/Internet Protocol (TCP/IP) has become the core communications protocol for the Internet (Cerf and Kahn, 1974). **TCP** establishes the connections among sending and receiving Web computers, and makes sure that packets sent by one computer are received in the same sequence by the other, without any packets missing. **IP** provides the Internet's addressing scheme and is responsible for the actual delivery of the packets.

TCP/IP is divided into four separate layers, with each layer handling a different aspect of the communication problem (see **Figure 2.4**). The **Network Interface Layer** is responsible for placing packets on and receiving them from the network medium, which could be a LAN (Ethernet) or Token Ring network, or other network technology. TCP/IP is independent from any local network technology and can adapt to changes at the local level. The **Internet Layer** is responsible for addressing, packaging, and routing messages on the Internet. The **Transport Layer** is responsible for providing communication with the application by acknowledging and sequencing the packets to and from the application. The **Application Layer** provides a wide variety of applications with the ability to access the services of the lower layers. Some of the best-known applications are HyperText Transfer Protocol (HTTP), File Transfer Protocol (FTP), and Simple Mail Transfer Protocol (SMTP), all of which we will discuss later in this chapter.

IP Addresses

The IP addressing scheme answers the question "How can billions of computers attached to the Internet communicate with one another?" The answer is that every computer connected to the Internet must be assigned an address—otherwise it cannot send or receive TCP packets. For instance, when you sign onto the Internet using a dial-up, DSL, or cable modem, your computer is assigned a temporary address by your Internet Service Provider. Most corporate and university computers attached to a local area network have a permanent IP address.

---

protocol
a set of rules and standards for data transfer

Transmission Control Protocol/Internet Protocol (TCP/IP)
the core communications protocol for the Internet

TCP
protocol that establishes the connections among sending and receiving Web computers and handles the assembly of packets at the point of transmission, and their reassembly at the receiving end

IP
protocol that provides the Internet's addressing scheme and is responsible for the actual delivery of the packets

Network Interface Layer
responsible for placing packets on and receiving them from the network medium

Internet Layer
responsible for addressing, packaging, and routing messages on the Internet

Transport Layer
responsible for providing communication with the application by acknowledging and sequencing the packets to and from the application

Application Layer
provides a wide variety of applications with the ability to access the services of the lower layers

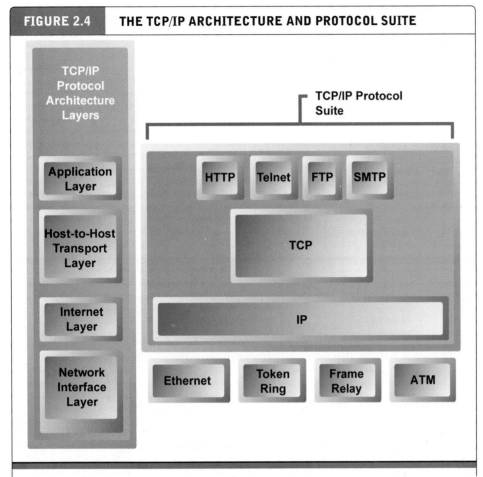

FIGURE 2.4   **THE TCP/IP ARCHITECTURE AND PROTOCOL SUITE**

TCP/IP is an industry-standard suite of protocols for large internetworks. The purpose of TCP/IP is to provide high-speed communication network links.

There are two versions of IP currently in use: IPv4 and IPv6. An **IPv4 Internet address** is a 32-bit number that appears as a series of four separate numbers marked off by periods, such as 64.49.254.91. Each of the four numbers can range from 0–255. This "dotted quad" addressing scheme supports up to about 4 billion addresses (2 to the 32nd power). In a typical Class C network, the first three sets of numbers identify the network (in the preceding example, 64.49.254 is the local area network identification) and the last number (91) identifies a specific computer.

Because many large corporate and government domains have been given millions of IP addresses each (to accommodate their current and future work forces), and with all the new networks and new Internet-enabled devices requiring unique IP addresses being attached to the Internet, by 2011, there were only an estimated 76 million IPv4 addresses left, declining at the rate of 1 million per week. IPv6 was created to address this problem. An **IPv6 Internet address** is 128 bits, so it can support up to 2^{128} (3.4×10^{38}) addresses, many more than IPv4.

IPv4 Internet address

Internet address expressed as a 32-bit number that appears as a series of four separate numbers marked off by periods, such as 64.49.254.91

IPv6 Internet address

Internet address expressed as a 128-bit number

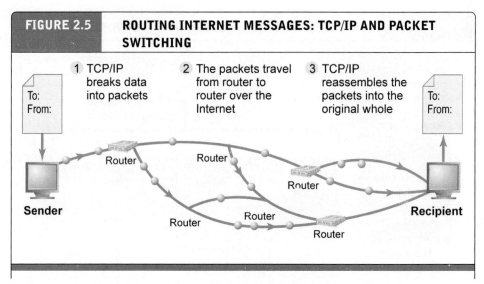

FIGURE 2.5 | **ROUTING INTERNET MESSAGES: TCP/IP AND PACKET SWITCHING**

1 TCP/IP breaks data into packets

2 The packets travel from router to router over the Internet

3 TCP/IP reassembles the packets into the original whole

Sender

Router

Router

Router

Router

Router

Router

Recipient

The Internet uses packet-switched networks and the TCP/IP communications protocol to send, route, and assemble messages. Messages are broken into packets, and packets from the same message can travel along different routes.

Figure 2.5 illustrates how TCP/IP and packet switching work together to send data over the Internet.

Domain Names, DNS, and URLs

domain name
IP address expressed in natural language

Domain Name System (DNS)
system for expressing numeric IP addresses in natural language

Uniform Resource Locator (URL)
the address used by a Web browser to identify the location of content on the Web

Most people cannot remember 32-bit numbers. An IP address can be represented by a natural language convention called a **domain name**. The **Domain Name System (DNS)** allows expressions such as Cnet.com to stand for a numeric IP address (cnet.com's numeric IP is 216.239.113.101).[3] A **Uniform Resource Locator (URL)**, which is the address used by a Web browser to identify the location of content on the Web, also uses a domain name as part of the URL. A typical URL contains the protocol to be used when accessing the address, followed by its location. For instance, the URL http://www.azimuth-interactive.com/flash_test refers to the IP address 208.148.84.1 with the domain name "azimuth-interactive.com" and the protocol being used to access the address, HTTP. A resource called "flash_test" is located on the server directory path /flash_test. A URL can have from two to four parts; for example, name1.name2.name3.org. We discuss domain names and URLs further in Section 2.4. **Figure 2.6** illustrates the Domain Name System and **Table 2.3** summarizes the important components of the Internet addressing scheme.

Client/Server Computing

While packet switching exploded the available communications capacity and TCP/IP provided the communications rules and regulations, it took a revolution in computing

[3] You can check the IP address of any domain name on the Internet. In Windows 7 or Vista, use Start/cmd to open the DOS prompt. Type ping < Domain Name >. You will receive the IP address in return.

| FIGURE 2.6 | THE HIERARCHICAL DOMAIN NAME SYSTEM |

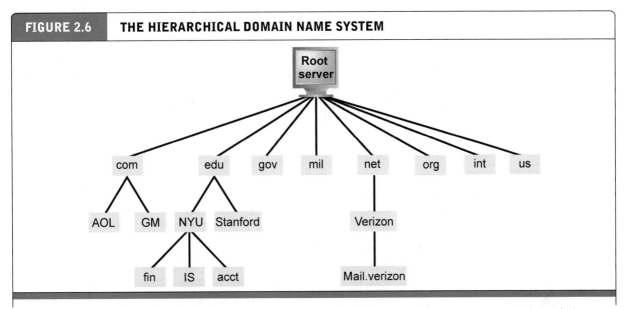

The Domain Name System is a hierarchical namespace with a root server at the top. Top-level domains appear next and identify the organization type (such as .com, .gov, .org, etc.) or geographic location (such as .uk [Great Britain] or .ca [Canada]). Second-level servers for each top-level domain assign and register second-level domain names for organizations and individuals such as IBM.com, Microsoft. com, and Stanford.edu. Finally, third-level domains identify a particular computer or group of computers within an organization, e.g., www.finance.nyu.edu.

to bring about today's Internet and the Web. That revolution is called client/server computing and without it, the Web—in all its richness—would not exist. **Client/server computing** is a model of computing in which powerful personal computers and other Internet devices called **clients** are connected in a network to one or more server computers. These clients are sufficiently powerful to accomplish complex tasks such as displaying rich graphics, storing large files, and processing graphics and sound files,

client/server computing

a model of computing in which powerful personal computers are connected in a network together with one or more servers

client

a powerful personal computer that is part of a network

TABLE 2.3	PIECES OF THE INTERNET PUZZLE: NAMES AND ADDRESSES
IP addresses	Every device connected to the Internet must have a unique address number called an Internet Protocol (IP) address.
Domain names	The Domain Name System allows expressions such as Pearsoned.com (Pearson Education's Web site) to stand for numeric IP locations.
DNS servers	DNS servers are databases that keep track of IP addresses and domain names on the Internet.
Root servers	Root servers are central directories that list all domain names currently in use for specific domains; for example, the .com root server. DNS servers consult root servers to look up unfamiliar domain names when routing traffic.

server

networked computer dedicated to common functions that the client computers on the network need

all on a local desktop or handheld device. **Servers** are networked computers dedicated to common functions that the client computers on the network need, such as file storage, software applications, utility programs that provide Web connections, and printers (see **Figure 2.7**). The Internet is a giant example of client/server computing in which millions of Web servers located around the world can be easily accessed by millions of client computers, also located throughout the world.

To appreciate what client/server computing makes possible, you must understand what preceded it. In the mainframe computing environment of the 1960s and 1970s, computing power was very expensive and limited. For instance, the largest commercial mainframes of the late 1960s had 128k of RAM and 10-megabyte disk drives, and occupied hundreds of square feet. There was insufficient computing capacity to support graphics or color in text documents, let alone sound files, video, or hyperlinked documents.

With the development of personal computers and local area networks during the late 1970s and early 1980s, client/server computing became possible. Client/server computing has many advantages over centralized mainframe computing. For instance, it is easy to expand capacity by adding servers and clients. Also, client/server networks are less vulnerable than centralized computing architectures. If one server goes down, backup or mirror servers can pick up the slack; if a client computer is inoperable, the rest of the network continues operating. Moreover, processing load is balanced over many powerful smaller computers rather than being concentrated in a single huge computer that performs processing for everyone. Both software and hardware in client/server environments can be built more simply and economically.

Estimates of the number of personal computers in use around the world in 2014 range from 1.6 billion to 1.74 billion (Keizer, 2014). Personal computing capabilities have also moved to smartphones and tablet computers (all much "thinner" clients with a bit less computing horsepower, and limited memory, but which rely on Internet servers to accomplish their tasks). In the process, more computer processing will be performed by central servers.

FIGURE 2.7	THE CLIENT/SERVER COMPUTING MODEL

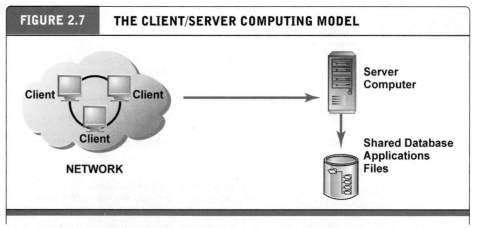

In the client/server model of computing, client computers are connected in a network together with one or more servers.

THE NEW CLIENT: THE MOBILE PLATFORM

There's a new client in town. The primary means of accessing the Internet worldwide is now through highly portable smartphones and tablet computers, and not traditional desktop or laptop PCs. This means that the primary platform for e-commerce products and services is also changing to a mobile platform.

The change in hardware has reached a tipping point. The form factor of PCs has changed from desktops to laptops and tablet computers such as the iPad (and more than 100 other competitors). Tablets are lighter, do not require a complex operating system, and rely on the Internet cloud to provide processing and storage. And, while there are an estimated 1.6 to 1.74 billion PCs in the world, the number of cell phones long ago exceeded the population of PCs. In 2014, there are an estimated 4.65 billion worldwide mobile phone users, with 252 million in the United States, around 1.1 billion in China, and 581 million in India. The population of mobile phone users is almost three times that of PC owners. Around 38%, or 1.76 billion, of the world's mobile phone users are smartphone users. Around 2.25 billion people around the world access the Internet using mobile devices, mostly smartphones and tablets (eMarketer, Inc., 2014c, 2014d, 2014e). Briefly, the Internet world is turning into a lighter, mobile platform. The tablet is not replacing PCs so much as supplementing PCs for use in mobile situations.

Smartphones are a disruptive technology that radically alters the personal computing and e-commerce landscape. Smartphones involve a major shift in computer processors and software that is disrupting the 40-year dual monopolies established by Intel and Microsoft, whose chips, operating systems, and software applications have dominated the PC market since 1982. Few smartphones use Intel chips, which power 90% of the world's PCs; only a small percentage of smartphones use Microsoft's operating system (Windows Mobile). Instead, smartphone manufacturers either purchase operating systems such as Symbian, the world leader, or build their own, such as Apple's iPhone iOS and BlackBerry's OS, typically based on Linux and Java platforms. Smartphones do not use power-hungry hard drives but instead use flash memory chips with storage up to 64 gigabytes that also require much less power.

The mobile platform has profound implications for e-commerce because it influences how, where, and when consumers shop and buy.

THE INTERNET "CLOUD COMPUTING" MODEL: HARDWARE AND SOFTWARE AS A SERVICE

The growing bandwidth power of the Internet has pushed the client/server model one step further, towards what is called the "cloud computing model" (**Figure 2.8**). **Cloud computing** refers to a model of computing in which firms and individuals obtain computing power and software applications over the Internet, rather than purchasing the hardware and software and installing it on their own computers.

A number of different types of cloud computing models have developed. The most well-known type is referred to as a public cloud. A **public cloud** is offered by a third-party service provider, such as Amazon Web Services, IBM, HP, and Dell, who own and manage very large, scalable cloud computing centers that provide computing power, data storage, and high-speed Internet connections to multiple customers who

cloud computing
model of computing in which firms and individuals obtain computing power and software over the Internet

public cloud
third-party service providers that own and manage large, scalable data centers that offer computing, data storage, and high speed Internet to multiple customers who pay for only the resources they use

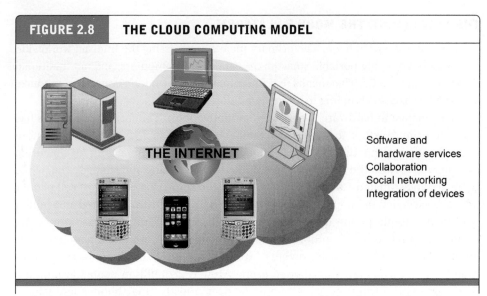

FIGURE 2.8 | **THE CLOUD COMPUTING MODEL**

THE INTERNET

Software and
hardware services
Collaboration
Social networking
Integration of devices

In the cloud computing model, hardware and software services are provided on the Internet by vendors operating very large server farms and data centers.

are able to choose from a variety of options, such as servers, operating systems, storage, and bandwidth, and pay only for the resources they use. Gartner estimates that spending on public cloud services worldwide will grow almost 20% in 2014, to about €126 billion (Gartner, Inc., 2014a). A **private cloud** provides similar options but has only a single tenant (either on the customer's premises or off the premises), and is most often used for customers who require enhanced security or compliance for their applications, such as the financial services or medical service providers. A **hybrid cloud** is one that offers customers both options—both a public cloud and a private cloud.

Software firms such as Google, Microsoft, SAP, Oracle, and Salesforce.com sell software applications that are Internet-based. Instead of software as a product, in the cloud computing model, software is a service provided over the Internet (referred to as SaaS—software as a service). For instance, Google claims there are around 50 million active users and 5 million businesses that use Google Apps, its suite of office software applications such as word processing, spreadsheets, and calendars, that users access over the Internet. More than 100,000 firms and organizations use Salesforce.com's customer relationship management software.

Microsoft, which in the past has depended on selling boxed software to firms and individuals, is adapting to this new marketplace with its own "software plus service" (buy the boxed version and get "free" online services), Windows Live, and online technology initiatives.

Cloud computing has many significant implications for e-commerce. For e-commerce firms, cloud computing radically reduces the cost of building and operating Web sites because the necessary hardware infrastructure and software can be licensed as a service from Internet providers at a fraction of the cost of purchasing these services as products. This means firms can adopt "pay-as-you-go" and "pay-as-you-grow" strategies

private cloud
provides similar options as public cloud but only to a single tenant

hybrid cloud
offers customers both a public cloud and a private cloud

when building out their Web sites. For instance, according to Amazon, hundreds of thousands of customers use Amazon's Web Services arm, which provides storage services, computing services, database services, messaging services, and payment services. For individuals, cloud computing means you no longer need a powerful laptop or desktop computer to engage in e-commerce or other activities. Instead, you can use much less-expensive tablet computers or smartphones that cost a few hundred dollars. For corporations, cloud computing means that a significant part of hardware and software costs (infrastructure costs) can be reduced because firms can obtain these services online for a fraction of the cost of owning, and they do not have to hire an IT staff to support the infrastructure. These benefits come with some risks: firms become totally dependent on their cloud service providers.

OTHER INTERNET PROTOCOLS AND UTILITY PROGRAMS

There are many other Internet protocols and utility programs that provide services to users in the form of Internet applications that run on Internet clients and servers. These Internet services are based on universally accepted protocols—or standards— that are available to everyone who uses the Internet. They are not owned by any organization, but they are services that have been developed over many years and made available to all Internet users.

HyperText Transfer Protocol (HTTP) is the Internet protocol used to transfer Web pages (described in the following section). HTTP was developed by the World Wide Web Consortium (W3C) and the Internet Engineering Task Force (IETF). HTTP runs in the Application Layer of the TCP/IP model shown in Figure 2.4 on page 107. An HTTP session begins when a client's browser requests a resource, such as a Web page, from a remote Internet server. When the server responds by sending the page requested, the HTTP session for that object ends. Because Web pages may have many objects on them—graphics, sound or video files, frames, and so forth—each object must be requested by a separate HTTP message. For more information about HTTP, you can consult RFC 2616, which details the standards for HTTP/1.1, the version of HTTP most commonly used today (Internet Society, 1999). (An RFC is a document published by the Internet Society [ISOC] or one of the other organizations involved in Internet governance that sets forth the standards for various Internet-related technologies. You will learn more about the organizations involved in setting standards for the Internet later in the chapter.)

E-mail is one of the oldest, most important, and frequently used Internet services. Like HTTP, the various Internet protocols used to handle e-mail all run in the Application Layer of TCP/IP. **Simple Mail Transfer Protocol (SMTP)** is the Internet protocol used to send e-mail to a server. SMTP is a relatively simple, text-based protocol that was developed in the early 1980s. SMTP handles only the sending of e-mail. To retrieve e-mail from a server, the client computer uses either **Post Office Protocol 3 (POP3)** or **Internet Message Access Protocol (IMAP)**. You can set POP3 to retrieve e-mail messages from the server and then delete the messages on the server, or retain them on the server. IMAP is a more current e-mail protocol supported by all browsers and most servers and ISPs. IMAP allows users to search, organize, and filter their mail prior to downloading it from the server.

HyperText Transfer Protocol (HTTP)
the Internet protocol used for transferring Web pages

Simple Mail Transfer Protocol (SMTP)
the Internet protocol used to send mail to a server

Post Office Protocol 3 (POP3)
a protocol used by the client to retrieve mail from an Internet server

Internet Message Access Protocol (IMAP)
a more current e-mail protocol that allows users to search, organize, and filter their mail prior to downloading it from the server

File Transfer Protocol (FTP)

one of the original Internet services. Part of the TCP/IP protocol that permits users to transfer files from the server to their client computer, and vice versa

Telnet

a terminal emulation program that runs in TCP/IP

Secure Sockets Layer (SSL) /Transport Layer Security (TLS)

protocols that secure communications between the client and the server

Ping

a program that allows you to check the connection between your client and the server

Tracert

one of several route-tracing utilities that allow you to follow the path of a message you send from your client to a remote computer on the Internet

File Transfer Protocol (FTP) is one of the original Internet services. FTP runs in TCP/IP's Application Layer and permits users to transfer files from a server to their client computer, and vice versa. The files can be documents, programs, or large database files. FTP is the fastest and most convenient way to transfer files larger than 1 megabyte, which some e-mail servers will not accept. More information about FTP is available in RFC 959 (Internet Society, 1985).

Telnet is a network protocol that also runs in TCP/IP's Application Layer and is used to allow remote login on another computer. The term Telnet also refers to the Telnet program, which provides the client part of the protocol and enables the client to emulate a mainframe computer terminal. (The industry-standard terminals defined in the days of mainframe computing are VT-52, VT-100, and IBM 3250.) You can then attach yourself to a computer on the Internet that supports Telnet and run programs or download files from that computer. Telnet was the first "remote work" program that permitted users to work on a computer from a remote location.

Secure Sockets Layer (SSL)/Transport Layer Security (TLS) are protocols that operate between the Transport and Application Layers of TCP/IP and secure communications between the client and the server. SSL/TLS helps secure e-commerce communications and payments through a variety of techniques, such as message encryption and digital signatures, that we will discuss further in Chapter 4.

Packet InterNet Groper (Ping) is a utility program that allows you to check the connection between a client computer and a TCP/IP network (see **Figure 2.9**). Ping will also tell you the time it takes for the server to respond, giving you some idea about the speed of the server and the Internet at that moment. You can run Ping from the DOS prompt on a personal computer with a Windows operating system by typing: ping < domain name >. We will discuss Ping further in Chapter 4, because one way to slow down or even crash a domain server is to send it millions of ping requests.

Tracert is one of several route-tracing utilities that allow you to follow the path of a message you send from your client to a remote computer on the Internet. **Figure 2.10** shows the result of a message sent to a remote host using a visual route-tracing program called VisualRoute (available from Visualware).

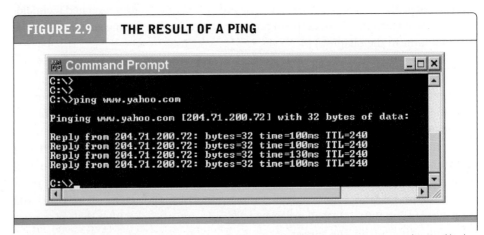

| FIGURE 2.9 | THE RESULT OF A PING |

A ping is used to verify an address and test the speed of the round trip from a client computer to a host and back.

| FIGURE 2.10 | **TRACING THE ROUTE A MESSAGE TAKES ON THE INTERNET** |

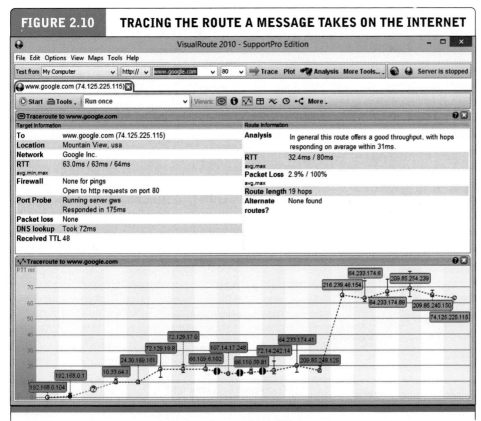

VisualRoute and other tracing programs provide some insight into how the Internet uses packet switching. This particular message traveled to a Google server in Mountain View, California.

SOURCE: Visualware, Inc., 2014.

THE INTERNET TODAY

In 2014, there are an estimated 2.8 billion Internet users worldwide, up from 100 million users at year-end 1997. While this is a huge number, it represents only about 40% of the world's population (eMarketer, Inc., 2014a). Although Internet user growth has slowed in the United States to about 1%–2% annually, in the Asia-Pacific region, Internet growth is about 10% annually, while in India it is over 25%, and by 2018, it is expected that there will be about 3.45 billion Internet users worldwide. One would think the Internet would be overloaded with such incredible growth; however, this has not been true for several reasons. First, client/server computing is highly extensible. By simply adding servers and clients, the population of Internet users can grow indefinitely. Second, the Internet architecture is built in layers so that each layer can change without disturbing developments in other layers. For instance, the technology used to move messages through the Internet can go through radical changes to make service faster without being disruptive to your desktop applications running on the Internet.

Network Technology Substrate layer

layer of Internet technology that is composed of telecommunications networks and protocols

Transport Services and Representation Standards layer

layer of Internet architecture that houses the TCP/IP protocol

Applications layer

layer of Internet architecture that contains client applications

Middleware Services layer

the "glue" that ties the applications to the communications networks and includes such services as security, authentication, addresses, and storage repositories

Figure 2.11 illustrates the "hourglass" and layered architecture of the Internet. The Internet can be viewed conceptually as having four layers: Network Technology Substrates, Transport Services and Representation Standards, Middleware Services, and Applications.[4] The **Network Technology Substrate layer** is composed of telecommunications networks and protocols. The **Transport Services and Representation Standards layer** houses the TCP/IP protocol. The **Applications layer** contains client applications such as the World Wide Web, e-mail, and audio or video playback. The **Middleware Services layer** is the glue that ties the applications to the communications networks and includes such services as security, authentication, addresses, and

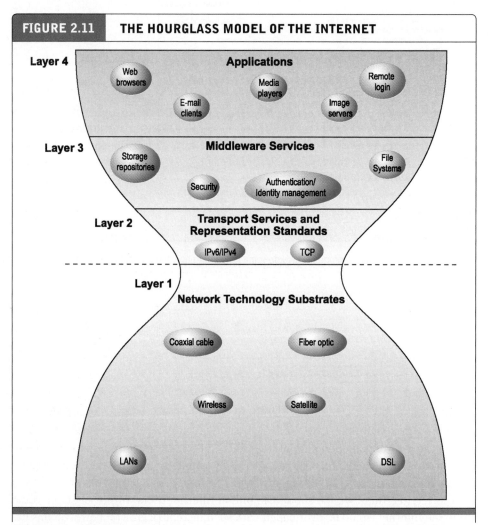

FIGURE 2.11 | **THE HOURGLASS MODEL OF THE INTERNET**

The Internet can be characterized as an hourglass modular structure with a lower layer containing the bit-carrying infrastructure (including cables and switches) and an upper layer containing user applications such as e-mail and the Web. In the narrow waist are transportation protocols such as TCP/IP.

[4] Recall that the TCP/IP communications protocol also has layers, not to be confused with the Internet architecture layers.

storage repositories. Users work with applications (such as e-mail) and rarely become aware of middleware that operates in the background. Because all layers use TCP/IP and other common standards linking all four layers, it is possible for there to be significant changes in the Network layer without forcing changes in the Applications layer.

THE INTERNET BACKBONE

Figure 2.12 illustrates some of the main physical elements of today's Internet. Originally, the Internet had a single backbone, but today's Internet has several backbones that are physically connected with each other and that transfer information from one private network to another. These private networks are referred to as **Network Service Providers (NSPs)**, which own and control the major backbone networks (see **Table 2.4**). For the sake of clarity we will refer to these networks of backbones as a single "backbone." The **backbone** has been likened to a giant pipeline that transports data around the world in milliseconds. The backbone is typically composed of fiber-optic cable with bandwidths ranging from 155 Mbps to 2.5 Gbps. **Bandwidth** measures how much data can be transferred over a communications medium within a fixed period of time and is usually expressed in bits per second (bps), kilobits (thousands of bits) per second (Kbps), megabits (millions of bits) per second (Mbps), or gigabits (billions of bits) per second (Gbps).

Network Service Provider (NSP)
owns and controls one of the major networks comprising the Internet's backbone

backbone
high-bandwidth fiber-optic cable that transports data across the Internet

bandwidth
measures how much data can be transferred over a communications medium within a fixed period of time; is usually expressed in bits per second (bps), kilobits per second (Kbps), megabits per second (Mbps), or gigabits per second (Gbps)

FIGURE 2.12	INTERNET NETWORK ARCHITECTURE

Today's Internet has a multi-tiered open network architecture featuring multiple national backbones, regional hubs, campus area networks, and local client computers.

Connections to other continents are made via a combination of undersea fiber-optic cable and satellite links. The backbones in foreign countries typically are operated by a mixture of private and public owners. The backbone has built-in redundancy so that if one part breaks down, data can be rerouted to another part of the backbone. **Redundancy** refers to multiple duplicate devices and paths in a network.

INTERNET EXCHANGE POINTS

Hubs where the backbone intersects with regional and local networks, and where the backbone owners connect with one another, were originally called Network Access Points (NAPs) or Metropolitan Area Exchanges (MAEs), but now are more commonly referred to as **Internet Exchange Points (IXPs)** (see **Figure 2.13**). IXPs use high-speed switching computers to connect the backbone to regional and local networks, and exchange messages with one another. The regional and local networks are owned by private telecommunications firms; they generally are fiber-optic networks operating at more than 100 Mbps. The regional networks lease access to ISPs, private companies, and government institutions.

CAMPUS AREA NETWORKS

Campus area networks (CANs) are generally local area networks operating within a single organization—such as New York University or Microsoft Corporation. In fact, most large organizations have hundreds of such local area networks. These organizations are sufficiently large that they lease access to the Web directly from regional and national carriers. These local area networks generally are running Ethernet (a local area network protocol) and have network operating systems such as Windows Server or Linux that permit desktop clients to connect to the Internet through a local Internet server attached to their campus networks. Connection speeds in campus area networks are in the range of 10–100 Mbps to the desktop.

INTERNET SERVICE PROVIDERS

The firms that provide the lowest level of service in the multi-tiered Internet architecture by leasing Internet access to home owners, small businesses, and some large institutions are called **Internet Service Providers (ISPs)**. ISPs are retail providers. They deal

redundancy
multiple duplicate devices and paths in a network

Internet Exchange Point (IXP)
hub where the backbone intersects with local and regional networks and where backbone owners connect with one another

campus area network (CAN)
generally, a local area network operating within a single organization that leases access to the Web directly from regional and national carriers

Internet Service Provider (ISP)
firm that provides the lowest level of service in the multi-tiered Internet architecture by leasing Internet access to home owners, small businesses, and some large institutions

TABLE 2.4	MAJOR INTERNET BACKBONE OWNERS
AT&T	Tata Communications
Cogent	Verio (NTT Communications)
Level 3 Communications	Verizon
Sprint	Vodafone

FIGURE 2.13	SOME MAJOR U.S. INTERNET EXCHANGE POINTS (IXPs)

Region	Name	Location	Operator
EAST	Boston Internet Exchange (BOSIX)	Boston	Markley
	New York International Internet Exchange (NYIIX)	New York	Telehouse
	Peering and Internet Exchange (PAIX)	New York, Virginia, Atlanta	Equinix
	NAP of the Americas	Miami	Verizon Terremark
CENTRAL	Any2 Exchange	Chicago	CoreSite
	Peering and Internet Exchange (PAIX)	Dallas	Equinix
	Midwest Internet Cooperative Exchange	Minneapolis	Members
WEST	Peering and Internet Exchange (PAIX)	Seattle, Palo Alto	Equinix
	Los Angeles International Internet Exchange (LAIIX)	Los Angeles	Telehouse
	Any2 Exchange	San Jose, Los Angeles	CoreSite
	Seattle Internet Exchange (SIX)	Seattle	Members

with "the last mile of service" to the curb—homes and business offices. ISPs typically connect to IXPs with high-speed telephone or cable lines (45 Mbps and higher).

There are a number of major ISPs throughout Europe, such as BT (Plus Net), Sky Broadband, Virgin Media, and TalkTalk in the U.K; Orange, Free, and Alice in France; and Tiscali, BT Italia, and Fastweb in Italy. If you have home or small business Internet access, an ISP likely provides the service to you.

Table 2.5 summarizes the variety of services, speeds, and costs of ISP Internet connections. There are two types of ISP service: narrowband and broadband. **Narrowband** service is the traditional telephone modem connection now operating at 56.6 Kbps (although the actual throughput hovers around 30 Kbps due to line noise that causes extensive resending of packets). This used to be the most common form of connection worldwide but it has been largely replaced by broadband connections in the United States, Europe, and Asia. Broadband service is based on DSL (including high speed fiber-optic service), cable, telephone (T1 and T3 lines), and satellite technologies. **Broadband**, in the context of Internet service, refers to any communication technology that permits clients to play streaming audio and video files at acceptable speeds—generally anything above .5 Mbps.In 2014, there are an estimated 640 million broadband households worldwide (about 30% of all households) (eMarketer, Inc., 2014f). According to Akamai, the leader in average connection speed is South Korea, with an average rate of 23.6 Mbps (Akamai, 2014).

The actual throughput of data will depend on a variety of factors including noise in the line and the number of subscribers requesting service. Service-level speeds quoted are typically only for downloads of Internet content; upload speeds tend to be slower, although recently a number of broadband ISPs have announced plans that offer the same upload as download speed. T1 and T3 lines are publicly regulated utility lines

narrowband
the traditional telephone modem connection, now operating at 56.6 Kbps

broadband
refers to any communication technology that permits clients to play streaming audio and video files at acceptable speeds—generally anything above 100 Kbps

TABLE 2.5	U.S. ISP SERVICE LEVELS AND BANDWIDTH CHOICES	
SERVICE	COST/MONTH	SPEED TO DESKTOP (DOWNLOAD)
Telephone modem	$10–$25	30–56 Kbps
DSL	$20–$30	1–15 Mbps
FiOS	$50–$300	25 Mbps–500 Mbps
Cable Internet	$35–$199	1 Mbps–500 Mbps
Satellite	$39–$129	5–15 Mbps
T1	$200–$300	1.54 Mbps
T3	$2,500–$10,000	45 Mbps

that offer a guaranteed level of service, but the actual throughput of the other forms of Internet service is not guaranteed.

Digital Subscriber Line (DSL) service is a telephone technology that provides high-speed access to the Internet through ordinary telephone lines found in a home or business. Service levels range from about .5 to 15 Mbps. DSL service requires that customers live within two miles (about 4,000 meters) of a neighborhood telephone switching center. In order to compete with cable companies, telephone companies now also offer an advanced form of DSL called **FiOS (fiber-optic service)** that provides up to 500 Mbps to homes and businesses.

Cable Internet refers to a cable television technology that piggybacks digital access to the Internet using the same analog or digital video cable providing television signals to a home. Cable Internet is a major broadband alternative to DSL service, generally providing faster speeds and a "triple play" subscription: telephone, television, and Internet for a single monthly payment. Cable Internet services range from 1 Mbps up to 500 Mbps. Deutsche Telekom, Vodafone, Telefonica, and Liberty Global are some of the major cable Internet providers in Europe.

T1 and T3 are international telephone standards for digital communication. **T1** lines offer guaranteed delivery at 1.54 Mbps, while **T3** lines offer 45 Mbps. In the U.S., T1 lines cost about $200–$300 per month, and T3 lines around $2500–$6000 per month. These are leased, dedicated, guaranteed lines suitable for corporations, government agencies, and businesses such as ISPs requiring high-speed guaranteed service levels.

Satellite Internet is offered by satellite companies that provide high-speed broadband Internet access primarily to homes and offices located in rural areas where DSL or cable Internet access is not available. Access speeds and monthly costs are comparable to DSL and cable, but typically require a higher initial payment for installation of a small (18-inch) satellite dish. Upload speeds tend to be slower, typically 1–3 Mbps. Satellite providers typically have policies that limit the total megabytes of data that a single account can download within a set period, usually monthly. Major satellite providers in Europe include Hughes, Telefonica, Europasat, and Bentley-Walker, among others.

Nearly all large business firms and government agencies have broadband connections to the Internet. Demand for broadband service has grown so rapidly because it greatly speeds up the process of downloading Web pages and increasingly, large video and audio files located on Web pages (see **Table 2.6**). As the quality of Internet service offerings expands to include Hollywood movies, music, games, and other rich media-streaming content, the demand for broadband access will continue to swell. In order to compete with cable companies, telephone companies provide an advanced form of DSL called FiOS (fiber-optic service) that provides up to 50 Mbps speeds for households, which is much faster than cable systems.

INTRANETS

The very same Internet technologies that make it possible to operate a worldwide public network can also be used by private and government organizations as internal networks. An **intranet** is a TCP/IP network located within a single organization for

Digital Subscriber Line (DSL)
delivers high-speed access through ordinary telephone lines found in homes or businesses

FiOS (fiber-optic service)
a form of DSL that provides speeds of up to 500 Mbps

cable Internet
piggybacks digital access to the Internet on top of the analog video cable providing television signals to a home

T1
an international telephone standard for digital communication that offers guaranteed delivery at 1.54 Mbps

T3
an international telephone standard for digital communication that offers guaranteed delivery at 45 Mbps

satellite Internet
high-speed broadband Internet access provided via satellite

intranet
a TCP/IP network located within a single organization for purposes of communications and information processing

TABLE 2.6	TIME TO DOWNLOAD A 10-MEGABYTE FILE BY TYPE OF INTERNET SERVICE	
TYPE OF INTERNET SERVICE		TIME TO DOWNLOAD
NARROWBAND SERVICES		
Telephone modem		25 minutes
BROADBAND SERVICES		
DSL @ 1 Mbps		1.33 minutes
Cable Internet @ 10 Mbps		8 seconds
T1		52 seconds
T3		2 seconds

purposes of communications and information processing. Internet technologies are generally far less expensive than proprietary networks, and there is a global source of new applications that can run on intranets. In fact, all the applications available on the public Internet can be used in private intranets. The largest provider of local area network software is Microsoft, followed by open source Linux, both of which use TCP/IP networking protocols.

WHO GOVERNS THE INTERNET?

Aficionados and journalists often claim that the Internet is governed by no one, and indeed cannot be governed, and that it is inherently above and beyond the law. What these people forget is that the Internet runs over private and public telecommunications facilities that are themselves governed by laws, and subject to the same pressures as all telecommunications carriers. In fact, the Internet is tied into a complex web of governing bodies, national governments, and international professional societies. There is no one single governing organization that controls activity on the Internet. Instead, there are a number of organizations that influence the system and monitor its operations. Among the governing bodies of the Internet are:

- The *Internet Corporation for Assigned Names and Numbers (ICANN)*, which coordinates the Internet's systems of unique identifiers: IP addresses, protocol parameter registries, and the top-level domain systems. ICANN was created in 1998 as a nonprofit organization and currently manages the Internet Assigned Numbers Authority (IANA), which is in charge of assigning IP addresses, under a contract from the U.S. National Telecommunications and Information Administration (NTIA), an agency of the U.S. Department of Commerce.

- The *Internet Engineering Task Force (IETF)*, which is an open international community of network operators, vendors, and researchers concerned with the evolution of the Internet architecture and operation of the Internet. The IETF has a number of working groups, organized into several different areas, that develop and promote Internet standards, which influence the way people use and manage the Internet.

- The *Internet Research Task Force (IRTF)*, which focuses on the evolution of the Internet. The IRTF has a number of long-term research groups working on various topics such as Internet protocols, applications, applications, and technology.

- The *Internet Engineering Steering Group (IESG)*, which is responsible for technical management of IETF activities and the Internet standards process.

- The *Internet Architecture Board (IAB)*, which helps define the overall architecture of the Internet and oversees the IETF and IRTF.

- The *Internet Society (ISOC)*, which is a consortium of corporations, government agencies, and nonprofit organizations that monitors Internet policies and practices.

- The *Internet Governance Forum (IGF)*, which is a multi-stakeholder open forum for debate on issues related to Internet governance.

- The *World Wide Web Consortium (W3C)*, which is a largely academic group that sets HTML and other programming standards for the Web.

- The *Internet Network Operators Groups (NOGs),* which are informal groups that are made up of ISPs, IXPs, and others that discuss and attempt to influence matters related to Internet operations and regulation.

While none of these organizations has actual control over the Internet and how it functions, they can and do influence government agencies, major network owners, ISPs, corporations, and software developers with the goal of keeping the Internet operating as efficiently as possible. ICANN comes closest to being a manager of the Internet and reflects the powerful role that the U.S. Department of Commerce has played historically in Internet governance. The United States has been responsible for the IANA function since the beginning of the Internet. After the creation of ICANN, however, the expectation was the function would eventually be transferred out of the U.S. government's control. In 2006, however, the U.S. Department of Commerce announced that the U.S. government would retain oversight over the root servers, contrary to initial expectations. There were several reasons for this move, including the use of the Internet for basic communications services by terrorist groups and the uncertainty that might be caused should an international body take over. In 2008, the Department of Commerce reaffirmed this stance, stating that it "has no plans to transition management of the authoritative root zone file to ICANN" (U.S. Department of Commerce, 2008). At the same time, growing Internet powers China and Russia were lobbying for more functions of the Internet to be brought under the control of the United Nations, raising fears that governance of the Internet could become even more politicized (Pfanner, 2012). In 2014, the United States, under continued pressure from other countries, finally announced its willingness to transition control of IANA, provided that certain stipulations are met, including that the organization managing the IANA functions not be specifically controlled by any other government or intergovernmental organization (such as the United Nations). The transition is intended to take place by September 2015, although it could be extended to as late as September 2019.

In addition to these professional bodies, the Internet must also conform to the laws of the sovereign nation-states in which it operates, as well as the technical infrastructures that exist within each nation-state. Although in the early years of the Internet there was very little legislative or executive interference, this situation is changing as the Internet plays a growing role in the distribution of information and knowledge, including content that some find objectionable.

Read *Insight on Society: Government Regulation and Surveillance of the Internet* for a further look at the issue of censorship of Internet content and substance.

2.3   THE FUTURE INTERNET INFRASTRUCTURE

The Internet is changing as new technologies appear and new applications are developed. The next era of the Internet is being built today by private corporations, universities, and government agencies. To appreciate the potential benefits of the Internet of the future, you must first understand the limitations of the Internet's current infrastructure.

LIMITATIONS OF THE CURRENT INTERNET

Much of the Internet's current infrastructure is several decades old (equivalent to a century in Internet time). It suffers from a number of limitations, including:

- *Bandwidth limitations.* There is insufficient capacity throughout the backbone, the metropolitan switching centers, and most importantly, the "last mile" to the house and small businesses. The result is slow peak-hour service (congestion) and a limited ability to handle high volumes of video and voice traffic.

- *Quality of service limitations.* Today's information packets take a circuitous route to get to their final destinations. This creates the phenomenon of **latency**—delays in messages caused by the uneven flow of information packets through the network. In the case of e-mail, latency is not noticeable. However, with streaming video and synchronous communication, such as a telephone call, latency is noticeable to the user and perceived as "jerkiness" in movies or delays in voice communication. Today's Internet uses "best-effort" quality of service (QOS), which makes no guarantees about when or whether data will be delivered, and provides each packet with the same level of service, no matter who the user is or what type of data is contained in the packet. A higher level of service quality is required if the Internet is to keep expanding into new services, such as video on demand and telephony.

- *Network architecture limitations.* Today, a thousand requests for a single music track from a central server will result in a thousand efforts by the server to download the music to each requesting client. This slows down network performance, as the same music track is sent out a thousand times to clients that might be located in the same metropolitan area. This is very different from television, where the program is broadcast once to millions of homes.

- *Wired Internet.* The Internet is still largely based on cables—fiber-optic and coaxial copper cables. Copper cables use a centuries-old technology, and fiber-optic cable is

latency

delays in messages caused by the uneven flow of information packets through the network

INSIGHT ON SOCIETY

GOVERNMENT REGULATION AND SURVEILLANCE OF THE INTERNET

Hardly a week goes by without reports that a massive protest has occurred in the streets of a big city somewhere in the world. Invariably, the Internet, social media, and mobile phones are either blamed or praised for enabling these popular expressions of discontent with political regimes, corrupt officials, unemployment, or wealth inequality. Events such as the Jasmine Revolution in Tunisia and the Arab Spring in Egypt in 2010, and more recently, the 2014 protests in Madrid, Caracas, Moscow, Pakistan, and even heretofore quiet U.S. Midwestern towns like Ferguson, Missouri, encourage us all to think of the Internet and the Web as an extraordinary technology unleashing torrents of human creativity, innovation, expression, and sometimes, popular rebellion, and even democracy. In the United States, in 2011, a short-lived political action group called Occupy Wall Street spread its protest message against income inequality, greed, and corruption to over 2,600 cities worldwide in a few weeks, and changed the talking points of presidential candidates. The rapid spread of this group's message was attributed to social media.

How ironic then that the same Internet has spawned an explosion in government control and surveillance of individuals on the Internet. Totalitarian dictators of the mid-twentieth century would have given their eyeteeth for a technology such as this, that can track what millions of people do, say, think, and search for in billions of e-mails, searches, blogs, and Facebook posts every day.

In the early years of the Internet and the Web, many people assumed that because the Internet is so widely dispersed, it must be difficult to control or monitor. Legions of music and video pirates still believe they are anonymous on the Internet and cannot possibly be held accountable for what they do. But the reality is quite different. We now know that just about all governments assert some kind of control and surveillance over Internet content and messages, and in many nations this control over the Internet and the people who use it is very extensive.

While the Internet is a decentralized network, Internet traffic in all countries runs through large fiber-optic trunk lines that are controlled by national authorities or private firms. In China, there are three such lines, and China requires the companies that own these lines to configure their routers for both internal and external service requests. When a request originates in China for a Web page in Chicago, Chinese routers examine the request to see if the site is on a blacklist, and then examine words in the requested Web page to see if it contains blacklisted terms. Blacklisted terms include "falun" (a suppressed religious group in China) and "Tiananmen Square massacre" (or any symbols that might lead to such results such as "198964," which signifies June 4, 1989, the date of the massacre), among many others. The system is often referred to as "The Great Firewall of China" and is implemented with the assistance of Cisco Systems (the U.S. firm that is the largest manufacturer of routers in the world). Other U.S. Internet firms are also involved in China's censorship and surveillance efforts, including Yahoo, Microsoft, and Juniper Networks, among many others.

In 2014, China strengthened and extended its regulation of the Internet. A new law allows Web users to be jailed for up to three years if

(continued)

they post defamatory rumors that are read by more than 5,000 people. China also issued new rules to restrict the dissemination of political news and opinions on instant messaging applications such as WeChat, a text messaging app similar to Twitter and WhatsApp. Users are required to post political opinions and news only to state-authorized media outlets and are required to use their own names when establishing accounts. Authorities explain that the new restrictive laws are needed for social stability, and that every country seeks to regulate the Internet. In March 2014 Google began to encrypt searches originating in China in order to prevent surveillance by state agencies. In June 2014 the Chinese authorities severely disrupted Google search access, as well as popular services like Google Maps and Gmail. The disruption occurred on the 25th anniversary of the government's crackdown on the pro-democracy demonstrations in Tiananmen Square. Facebook, Twitter, Flickr, and YouTube have been blocked in China for years. In July, access to Google was restored.

While China is often criticized for its extensive Internet controls, other countries are not far behind. Iran's Internet surveillance of its citizens is considered by security experts to be one of the world's most sophisticated mechanisms for controlling and censoring the Internet, allowing it to examine the content of individual online communications on a massive scale, far more sophisticated than even China's Internet surveillance activities. The Iranian system goes far beyond preventing access to specific sites such as BBC World News, Google, and Facebook. One technique is deep packet inspection of every e-mail, text, or tweet. Deep packet inspection allows governments to read messages, alter their contents for disinformation purposes, and identify senders and recipients. It is accomplished by installing computers in the line between users and ISPs, opening up every digitized packet, inspecting for keywords and images, reconstructing the message, and sending it on. This is done for all Internet traffic including Skype, Facebook, e-mail, tweets, and messages sent to proxy servers.

In Russia, a new law took effect in February 2014 that allows the government to close Web sites without a court decision if they contain undesirable content. Sites can be closed if the General Prosecutor's office declares the material on a site to be "extremist." In August 2014, Russia expanded Internet regulations to the blogosphere, requiring bloggers with more than 3,000 daily readers to register their real names and contact information with Russia's communications regulator.

In January 2014, the Turkish government shut down the file-sharing site SoundCloud after recordings of Prime Minister Recep Tayyip Erdogan arranging to obtain two villas for his family in return for a zoning change to construction tycoon surfaced. When the recordings moved to YouTube, Turkey shut down YouTube. Turkey already has extensive regulations of the Internet prohibiting pornography, gambling, and criticism of the founder of modern Turkey, Mustafa Kemal Attaturk. In April 2014 the Turkish Constitutional Court ordered the government to restore access to YouTube, Twitter, SoundCloud, and other sites because the shutdowns were a violation of freedom of expression.

Not to be outdone, both Europe and the United States have at various times taken steps to control access to Internet sites, censor Web content, and engage in extensive surveillance of communications, although not to the extent of Iran, China, and many other nations. For instance, Britain has a list of blocked sites, as do Germany and France. The Australian Communications and Media Authority has developed a list of several hundred Web sites that have been refused registration in Australia, mostly violent video game and online pornography sites. The United States and European countries generally ban the sale, distribution, and/or possession of online child pornography. Both France and Germany bar online Nazi memorabilia. Even in South Korea, one of the world's most wired countries, there are restrictions on pornographic sites, games sites, and limits on Google Maps.

In response to terrorism threats and other crimes, European governments and the U.S. government have also initiated deep packet inspection of e-mail and text communications. This surveillance is not limited to cross-border international data flows and includes large-scale domestic surveillance and analysis of routine e-mail, tweets, and other messages. For instance, the FBI has recently created a secret Internet surveillance unit, the National Domestic Communications Assistance Center, in a collaborative effort with the U.S. Marshals Service and the Drug Enforcement Agency. The NDCAC's mission is to assist in the development of new surveillance technologies that will allow authorities to increase the interception of Internet, wireless, and VoIP communications. Although it may seem preposterous that any U.S. government agency could read an estimated 150 billion daily e-mails, this task is, in reality, far less complicated than Google's handling of 10 to 12 billion search queries per month.

For instance, in 2013, NSA contractor Edward Snowden made headlines by leaking classified NSA documents shedding light on the NSA's PRISM program, which grants the agency unauthorized access to the servers of major Internet companies such as Facebook, Google, Apple, Microsoft, and many others. Additionally, the documents revealed the existence of the NSA's XKeyscore program, which allows analysts to search databases of e-mails, chats, and browsing histories of individual citizens without any authorization. Warrants, court clearance, or other forms of legal documentation are not required for analysts to use the technology. Snowden's documents also showed spy agencies were tapping data from smartphone apps like Candy Crush, and most others, and that the NSA was tapping the flow of personal user information among Google and Yahoo. The NSA claims that the program was only used to monitor foreign intelligence targets and that the information it collects has assisted in apprehending terrorists.

Efforts are underway in the United States to curb domestic and international counter-terrorist agencies like the NSA from conducting dragnet surveillance of the entire American population, strengthen court oversight of surveillance, limit surveillance to specific individuals, and ease disclosure rules for Internet firms who receive requests from government agencies. It is unclear at this time if any of these proposed measures will become law.

SOURCES: "China Tightens Message App Rules for Public Information," by Bloomberg.com, September 1, 2014; "Russia Forces Its Popular Bloggers to Register—Or Else," by Ilya Khrennikov, Bloomberg.com, August 19, 2014; "A Stronger Bill to Limit Surveillance," *New York Times*, July 27, 2014; "Access to Google Services Within China Returns," by Paul Carsten, Reuters.com, July 10, 2014; "Turkey Lifts Twitter Ban After Court Ruling," by Daren Butler, Reuters.com, April 3, 2014; "NSA Top Lawyer Says Tech Giants Knew About Data Collection," Cnet.com, March 19, 2014; "Documents Say NSA Pretends to Be Facebook in Surveillance," by Reed Albergotti, *Wall Street Journal*, March 12, 2014; Amid Flow of Leaks, Turkey Moves to Crimp Internet," by Tim Arango and Ceylan Yeginsu, *New York Times*, February 6, 2014; "U.S. Eases Disclosure Rules for Net Firms," by Devlin Barrett and Danny Yadron, *Wall Street Journal*, January 28, 2014; "Spy Agencies Tap Data Streaming From Phone Apps," by James Glanz, Jeff Larson, and Andrew Lehren, *New York Times*, January 27, 2014; "Big Web Crash in China: Experts Suspect Great Firewall," by Nicole Perlroth, *New York Times*, January 22, 2014; "NSA Surveillance Covers 75 Percent of U.S. Internet Traffic: WSJ," by Reuters, News.Yahoo.com, August 20, 2013; "New Snowden Leak: NSA Program Taps All You Do Online," by Amanda Wills, Mashable.com, August 1, 2013; "Report: Snowden Says NSA Can Tap E-mail, Facebook Chats," by Doug Stanglin, USAToday.com, July 31, 2013; "Snowden: NSA Collects 'Everything,' Including Content of Emails," by Eyder Peralta, NPR.org, June 17, 2013; "FBI Quietly Forms Secret Net-Surveillance Unit," by Declan McCullagh, News.cnet.com, May 22, 2012; "Catching Scent of Revolution, China Moves to Snip Jasmine," by Andrew Jacobs and Jonathon Ansfield, *New York Times*, May 10, 2011; "Google Accuses Chinese of Blocking Gmail Service," by David Barboza and Claire Cain Miller, *New York Times*, March 20, 2011; "Bullets Stall Youthful Push for Arab Spring," by Michael Slackman, *New York Times*, March 17, 2011.

expensive to place underground. The wired nature of the Internet restricts mobility of users although it is changing rapidly as Wi-Fi hotspots proliferate, and cellular phone technology advances. However, cellular systems are often overloaded due to the growth in the number of smartphones.

Now imagine an Internet at least 1,000 times as powerful as today's Internet, one that is not subjected to the limitations of bandwidth, protocols, architecture, physical connections, and language detailed previously. Welcome to the world of the future Internet, and the next generation of e-commerce services and products!

THE INTERNET2® PROJECT

Internet2®

advanced networking consortium of more than 350 member institutions working in partnership to facilitate the development, deployment, and use of revolutionary Internet technologies

Internet2® is an advanced networking consortium of more than 440 member institutions including universities, corporations, government research agencies, and not-for-profit networking organizations, all working in partnership to facilitate the development, deployment, and use of revolutionary Internet technologies. The broader Internet2 community includes more than 93,000 institutions across the United States and international networking partners in more than 100 countries. Internet2's work is a continuation of the kind of cooperation among government, private, and educational organizations that created the original Internet.

The advanced networks created and in use by Internet2 members provide an environment in which new technologies can be tested and enhanced. For instance, Internet2 provides a next-generation, nationwide 100 gigabit-per-second network that not only makes available a reliable production services platform for current high-performance needs but also creates a powerful experimental platform for the development of new network capabilities. See **Table 2.7** to get some sense of just how fast a 100-Gbps network is in terms of data transmission times. The fourth generation of this network, built through a federal stimulus grant from the National Telecommunications and Information Administration's Broadband Technology Opportunities Program, has now been deployed. The hybrid optical and packet network provides 8.8 terabits of capacity with the ability to seamlessly scale as requirements grow, includes over 15,000 miles of owned fiber optic cable, and reaches into underserved areas of the country, supporting connectivity for approximately 200,000 U.S. community anchor institutions (schools, local libraries, and museums), and enabling them to provide citizens across the country with telemedicine, distance learning, and other advanced applications not possible with consumer-grade Internet services. The infrastructure supports a wide range of IP and optical services already available today and also will stimulate a new generation of innovative services. The goal is to create an intelligent global ecosystem

TABLE 2.7	HOW FAST IS A 100-GBPS NETWORK?
DATA	TIME TO TRANSMIT
8.5 million electronic records	1 minute
300,000 X-rays	1 minute
1.8 million e-books simultaneously downloaded	2 minute

TABLE 2.8	PROJECTS BEING ENABLED BY INTERNET2'S 100-GBPS NETWORK
PROJECT	DESCRIPTION
XSEDE (Extreme Science and Engineering Discovery Environment).	In 2013, XSEDE upgraded from a 10-Gbps network to Internet2's 100-Gbps network. XSEDE supports over 8,000 members of the global scientific community and 17 supercomputers, and is being used for: • Galaxy, a data-intensive cancer research program, with more than 10,000 users who run 4,000-5,000 DNA sequence analyses daily. • Advanced chemistry research, which has discovered new materials such as two-dimensional metals. • Simulations of the impact of orbital debris on spacecraft and fragment impacts on body armor. • Research into healthcare contract economics.
CloudLab	Cloud computing test beds based at the University of Utah, Clemson, and the University of Wisconsin-Madison, connected by Internet2's 100-Gbps network. Focusing on the development of novel cloud architectures and new cloud computing applications. Will enable researchers to build their own clouds and experiment with applications such as real-time disaster response and medical record security.
University of Florida	Support for Compact Muon Solenoid (CMS) experiments at CERN's Hadron collider (contributed to discovery of the Higgs Particle, which earned 2013 Nobel Prize).

that will enable researchers, scientists, and others to "turn on" high-capacity network connections whenever and wherever they are needed. **Table 2.8** describes some of the projects that Internet2's 100-Gbps network is enabling. Other initiatives involve science and engineering (advanced network applications in support of distributed lab environments, remote access to rare scientific instruments, and distributed large-scale computation and data access), health sciences and health networks (telemedicine, medical and biological research, and health education and awareness), and arts and humanities (collaborative live performances, master classes, remote auditions, and interactive performing arts education and media events).

THE FIRST MILE AND THE LAST MILE

The Internet2 project is just the tip of the iceberg when it comes to future enhancements to the Internet. In 2007, the NSF began work on the Global Environment for Network Innovations (GENI) initiative. GENI is a unique virtual laboratory for exploring future internets at scale. GENI aims to promote innovations in network science, security technologies, services, and applications. GENI is a partnership of leading academic centers and private corporations such as Cisco, IBM, and HP, among many others. To date, awards have been made to 83 academic/industry teams for various projects to build, integrate, and operate early prototypes of the GENI virtual laboratory (Geni.net, 2014). In 2012, the NSF announced that it would be building on the GENI project as part of US Ignite, a White House initiative aimed at realizing the potential of fast, open, next-generation networks. GENI will underlie US Ignite and provide a virtual laboratory for experiments that the NSF hopes will transform cybersecurity, network performance, and cloud computing research (National Research Foundation, 2012).

The most significant privately initiated (but often government-influenced) changes are coming in two areas: fiber-optic trunk line bandwidth and wireless Internet services. Fiber optics is concerned with the first mile or backbone Internet services that carry bulk traffic long distances. Wireless Internet is concerned with the last mile—from the larger Internet to the user's smartphone, tablet computer, or laptop.

Fiber Optics and the Bandwidth Explosion in the First Mile

fiber-optic cable

consists of up to hundreds of strands of glass or plastic that use light to transmit data

Fiber-optic cable consists of up to hundreds of strands of glass that use light to transmit data. It often replaces existing coaxial and twisted pair cabling because it can transmit much more data at faster speeds, with less interference and better data security. Fiber-optic cable is also thinner and lighter, taking up less space during installation. The hope is to use fiber optics to expand network bandwidth capacity in order to prepare for the expected increases in Web traffic once next-generation Internet services are widely adopted.

Telecommunication firms have made substantial investments in fiber optic cross-country and regional cable systems in the last decade. This installed base of fiber optic cable represents a vast digital highway that is currently being exploited by YouTube (Google), Facebook, and other high-bandwidth applications. Telecommunications companies are recapitalizing and building new business models based on market prices for digital traffic. The net result is that society ultimately benefited from extraordinarily low-cost, long-haul, very high-bandwidth communication facilities that are already paid for.

Demand for fiber-optic cable has begun to strengthen as consumers demand integrated telephone, broadband access, and video from a single source. In 2011, around 19 million miles of optical fiber were installed in the United States, the most since 2000. Verizon has spent over $23 billion since 2004 building and expanding its FiOS fiber-optic Internet service. In 2014, there are about 5.6 million Verizon FiOS broadband customers. FiOS provides download and upload speeds of up to 500 Mbps. In 2011, Google joined the fray with Google Fiber, a 1 Gbps fiber optic network. Currently, Google Fiber is available in Kansas City, Kansas and Missouri, with plans to expand to 34 more cities. But despite the interest in fiber, only about 7.7% of U.S. homes have fiber connections as of 2014, a much lower percentage than a number of other countries around the world (Murphy, 2014). **Table 2.9** illustrates several optical bandwidth standards and compares them to traditional T lines.

The Last Mile: Mobile Internet Access

Fiber-optic networks carry the long-haul bulk traffic of the Internet—and in the future will play an important role in bringing high-speed broadband to the household and small business. The goal of the Internet2 and GENI projects is to bring gigabit and ultimately terabit bandwidth to the household over the next 20 years. But along with fiber optics, arguably the most significant development for the Internet and Web in the last five years has been the emergence of mobile Internet access.

Wireless Internet is concerned with the last mile of Internet access to the user's home, office, car, smartphone, or tablet computer, anywhere they are located. Up until

TABLE 2.9	HIGH-SPEED OPTICAL BANDWIDTH STANDARDS
STANDARD	**SPEED**
T1	1.544 Mbps
T3	43.232 Mbps
OC-3	155 Mbps
OC-12	622 Mbps
OC-48	2.5 Gbps
OC-192	9.6 Gbps

Note: "OC" stands for Optical Carrier and is used to specify the speed of fiber-optic networks conforming to the SONET standard. SONET (Synchronous Optical Networks) includes a set of signal rate multiples for transmitting digital signals on optical fiber. The base rate (OC-1) is 51.84 Mbps.

2000, the last-mile access to the Internet—with the exception of a small satellite Internet connect population—was bound up in land lines of some sort: copper coaxial TV cables or telephone lines or, in some cases, fiber-optic lines to the office. Today, in comparison, high-speed cell phone networks and Wi-Fi network hotspots provide a major alternative.

Today, sales of desktop computers have been eclipsed by sales of tablet and ultra-mobile laptop computers with built-in wireless networking functionality. Sales of smartphones are expected to reach 1.2–1.3 billion units in 2014 (Gartner, Inc. 2014b). Clearly, a large part of the Internet is now mobile, access-anywhere broadband service for the delivery of video, music, and Web search. According to eMarketer, there are more than 2.25 billion mobile Internet users worldwide (eMarketer, Inc., 2014e; 2014g).

Telephone-based versus Computer Network-based Wireless Internet Access There are two different basic types of wireless Internet connectivity: telephone-based and computer network-based systems.

Telephone-based wireless Internet access connects the user to a global telephone system (land, satellite, and microwave) that has a long history of dealing with thousands of users simultaneously and already has in place a large-scale transaction billing system and related infrastructure. Cellular telephones and the telephone industry are currently the largest providers of wireless access to the Internet today. In 2013, there were more than 1.8 billion mobile phones sold worldwide, with a similar amount expected to be sold in 2014. The percentage of smartphones sold exceeded regular mobile phones for the first time during the second quarter of 2013, accounting for over 51% of all mobile phone sales (Gartner, Inc., 2013). **Table 2.10** summarizes the various telephone technologies used for wireless Internet access.

Smartphones, such as an iPhone, Android, or BlackBerry, combine the functionality of a cell phone with that of a laptop computer with Wi-Fi capability. This makes it possible to combine in one device music, video, Web access, and telephone service.

Wireless local area network (WLAN)-based Internet access derives from a completely different background from telephone-based wireless Internet access. Popularly known as **Wi-Fi**, WLANs are based on computer local area networks where the task is to

Wi-Fi

Wireless standard for Ethernet networks with greater speed and range than Bluetooth

TABLE 2.10	WIRELESS INTERNET ACCESS TELEPHONE TECHNOLOGIES		
TECHNOLOGY	SPEED	DESCRIPTION	PLAYERS
3G (THIRD GENERATION)			
CDMA2000 EV-DO HSPA (W-CDMA)	144 Kbps–2 Mbps	High-speed, mobile, always on for e-mail, browsing, instant messaging. Implementing technologies include versions of CDMA2000 EV-DO (used by CDMA providers) and HSPDA (used by GSM providers). Nearly as fast as Wi-Fi.	Verizon, Sprint, AT&T, T-Mobile, Vodafone
3.5G (3G+)			
CDMA2000 EV-DO, Rev.B	Up to 14.4 Mbps	Enhanced version of CDMA 2000 EV-DO.	Verizon, Sprint
HSPA+	Up to 11 Mbps	Enhanced version of HSPA.	AT&T, T-Mobile
4G (FOURTH GENERATION)			
Long-Term Evolution (LTE)	Up to 100 Mbps	True broadband on cell phone.	AT&T, Verizon, Sprint, T-Mobile (in 2013)

connect client computers (generally stationary) to server computers within local areas of, say, a few hundred meters. WLANs function by sending radio signals that are broadcast over the airwaves using certain radio frequency ranges (2.4 GHz to 5.875 GHz, depending on the type of standard involved). The major technologies here are the various versions of the Wi-Fi standard, WiMax, and Bluetooth (see **Table 2.11**).

In a Wi-Fi network, a *wireless access point* (also known as a "hot spot") connects to the Internet directly via a broadband connection (cable, DSL telephone, or T1 line) and then transmits a radio signal to a transmitter/receiver installed in a laptop computer or PDA, either as a PC card or built-in at manufacture (such as Intel's Centrino processor, which provides built-in support for Wi-Fi in portable devices). **Figure 2.14** illustrates how a Wi-Fi network works.

Wi-Fi provided under the 802.11 a/b/g/n specifications offers high-bandwidth capacity from 11 Mbps to 70 Mbps—far greater than any 3G or 4G service currently in existence—but has a limited range of 300 meters, with the exception of WiMax discussed below. Wi-Fi is also exceptionally inexpensive. The cost of creating a corporate Wi-Fi network in a single 14-story building with an access point for each floor is less than $100 an access point. It would cost well over $500,000 to wire the same building with Ethernet cable. IEEE 802.11ac is a new version of the 802.11 specification approved in 2014 that will be able to provide throughputs of between 500 Mbps to over 1 Gbps. Sales of 802.11ac devices are expected to exceed 1 billion by 2015.

While initially a grass roots, "hippies and hackers" public access technology, billions of dollars have subsequently been poured into private ventures seeking to create for-profit Wi-Fi networks. One of the most prominent networks has been created by Boingo Wireless with more than 1 million hot spots around the globe. Optimum WiFi (available to Optimum Online customers for free) also offers over 1 million hotspots around the world. AT&T Wi-Fi Services (formerly Wayport) created another

TABLE 2.11	WIRELESS INTERNET ACCESS NETWORK TECHNOLOGIES		
TECHNOLOGY	RANGE/ SPEED	DESCRIPTION	PLAYERS
Wi-Fi (IEEE 802.11 a/b/g/n)	300 feet/ 11–70 Mbps	Evolving high-speed, fixed broadband wireless local area network for commercial and residential use	Linksys, Cisco, and other Wi-Fi router manufacturers; entrepreneurial network developers
802.11ac	500 Mbps-1 Gbps		
WiMax (IEEE 802.16)	30 miles/ 50–70 Mbps	High-speed, medium-range, broadband wireless metropolitan area network	Clearwire, Sprint, Fujitsu, Intel, Alcatel, Proxim
Bluetooth (wireless personal area network)	1–30 meters/ 1–3 Mbps	Modest-speed, low-power, short-range connection of digital devices	Sony Ericsson, Nokia, Apple, HP, and other device makers

large network that provides Wi-Fi service at hotels, airports, McDonald's, and IHOP restaurants, and Hertz airport rental offices, with more than 30,000 hot spots in the United States and access to Boingo's wireless network internationally. T-Mobile and Sprint have also established Wi-Fi services at 2,000 Starbucks coffee shops and thousands of other public locations in the United States. Apple, in turn, has made Wi-Fi

FIGURE 2.14 | **WI-FI NETWORKS**

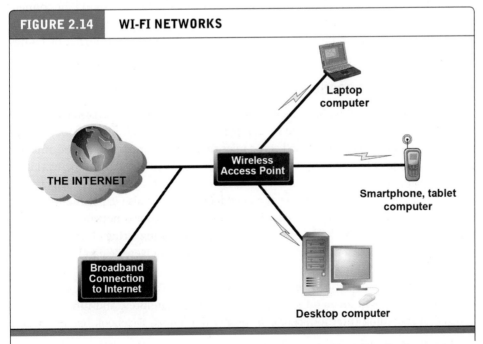

In a Wi-Fi network, wireless access points connect to the Internet using a land-based broadband connection. Clients, which could be laptops, desktops, or tablet computers, connect to the access point using radio signals.

automatically available to iPhone and iPad devices as an alternative to the more expensive and much slower 3G and 4G cellular systems.

Will WLAN compete directly against far more expensive telephone 4G services? The answer is "eventually, but not right now." Wi-Fi was originally a local area network technology of limited range, for stationary client computers, but with high capacity suitable for most Web surfing and some corporate uses with modest bandwidth demands. Cellular phone systems are wide area networks of nearly unlimited range, for mobile client computers and handhelds, and with modest but rapidly increasing capacity suitable for e-mail, photos, and Web browsing (on very small screens). However, the rock-bottom price of Wi-Fi coupled with ambitious plans for a 30-mile-range WiMax (802.16) service suggests that Wi-Fi could drain significant business from far more capital-intensive cellular systems.

A second WLAN technology for connecting to the Internet, and for connecting Internet devices to one another, is called Bluetooth. **Bluetooth** is a personal connectivity technology that enables links between mobile devices and connectivity to the Internet (Bluetooth.com, 2014). Bluetooth is the universal cable cutter, promising to get rid of the tangled mess of wires, cradles, and special attachments that plague the current world of personal computing. With Bluetooth, users can wear a wireless earbud, share files in a hallway or conference room, synchronize their smartphone with their laptop without a cable, send a document to a printer, and even pay a restaurant bill from the table to a Bluetooth-equipped cash register. Bluetooth is also an unregulated media operating in the 2.4 GHz spectrum but with a very limited range of 30 feet or less. It uses a frequency hopping signal with up to 1,600 hops per second over 79 frequencies, giving it good protection from interference and interception. Bluetooth-equipped devices constantly scan their environments looking for connections to compatible devices. Today, almost all mobile devices are Bluetooth-enabled. Bluetooth may also play a role in the future as a platform for the Internet of Things (see page 136).

Bluetooth

technology standard for short-range wireless communication under 30 feet

INTERNET ACCESS DRONES

A new method of providing Internet access to areas that are not well served by wired or cellular networks is being explored by companies such as Google and Facebook. Both companies have recently purchased companies that make drones (unmanned aircraft/satellites) that may be used to provide Internet access to remote parts of the world.

In April 2014, Google purchased Titan Aerospace, which makes solar-powered drones that can fly for several years at 65,000 feet. Google is also experimenting with high-altitude balloons with its Project Loon. Google envisions a network of balloons circling high above the earth in the stratosphere, establishing a ring of uninterrupted connectivity. A pilot test of the concept was conducted over New Zealand in 2013, and will be expanded through 2014.

In a similar effort, Facebook has put together the Facebook Connectivity Lab, where engineers will focus on solar-powered drones, satellites, and infrared lasers capable of providing Internet access. To propel that effort, Facebook has purchased the British company Ascenta, whose founders helped create the world's longest flying solar-powered drone.

THE FUTURE INTERNET

The increased bandwidth and expanded wireless network connectivity of the Internet of the future will result in benefits beyond faster access and richer communications. First-mile enhancements created by fiber-optic networks will enhance reliability and quality of Internet transmissions and create new business models and opportunities. Some of the major benefits of these technological advancements include latency solutions, guaranteed service levels, lower error rates, and declining costs. Widespread wireless access to the Internet will also essentially double or even triple the size of the online shopping marketspace because consumers will be able to shop and make purchases just about anywhere. We describe some of these benefits in more detail in the following sections.

Latency Solutions

One of the challenges of packet switching, where data is divided into chunks and then sent separately to meet again at the destination, is that the Internet does not differentiate between high-priority packets, such as video clips, and those of lower priority, such as self-contained e-mail messages. Because the packets cannot yet be simultaneously reassembled, the result can be distorted audio and video streams.

Differentiated quality of service (**diffserv**) is a technology that assigns levels of priority to packets based on the type of data being transmitted. Video conference packets, for example, which need to reach their destination almost instantaneously, receive much higher priority than e-mail messages. In the end, the quality of video and audio will skyrocket without undue stress on the network. Differential service is very controversial because it means some users may get more bandwidth than others, and potentially they may have to pay a higher price for more bandwidth.

differentiated quality of service (diffserv)
a new technology that assigns levels of priority to packets based on the type of data being transmitted

Guaranteed Service Levels and Lower Error Rates

In today's Internet, there is no service-level guarantee and no way to purchase the right to move data through the Internet at a fixed pace. Today's Internet promises only "best effort." The Internet is democratic—it speeds or slows everyone's traffic alike. In the future, it will be possible to purchase the right to move data through the network at a guaranteed speed in return for higher fees.

Declining Costs

As the Internet pipeline is upgraded, the availability of broadband service will expand beyond major metropolitan areas, significantly reducing the cost of access. More users means lower cost, as products and technology catch on in the mass market. Higher volume usage enables providers to lower the cost of both access devices, or clients, and the service required to use such products. Both broadband and wireless service fees are expected to decline as geographic service areas increase, in part due to competition for that business.

The Internet of Things

Internet of Things (IoT)

Use of the Internet to connect a wide variety of devices, machines, and sensors

No discussion of the future Internet would be complete without mentioning the **Internet of Things (IoT)**, also sometimes referred to as the Industrial Internet. Internet technology is spreading beyond the desktop, laptop, and tablet computer, and beyond the smartphone, to consumer electronics, electrical appliances, cars, medical devices, utility systems, machines of all types, even clothing—just about anything that can be equipped with sensors that can collect data and connect to the Internet, enabling the data to be analyzed with data analytics software.

IoT builds on a foundation of existing technologies, such as RFID, and is being enabled by the availability of low-cost sensors, the drop in price of data storage, the development of "Big Data" analytics software that can work with trillions of pieces of data, as well as implementation of IPV6, which will allow Internet addresses to be assigned to all of these new devices. Although IoT devices don't necessarily have to be wireless, most use wireless communications technology previously discussed, such as cellular networks, Wi-Fi, Bluetooth, or other wireless protocols such as Zigbee or Z-Wave, to connect either directly or via a mobile app to the Internet (often a cloud service).

IoT technology is powering the development of "smart" connected "things"— televisions, houses, and cars, as well as wearable technology—clothing and devices like Google Glass, profiled in the opening case. Smart televisions that integrate the Internet directly into the set and can run apps are starting to become popular. In 2013, 22% of televisions sold in the United States were smart, Internet-connected TVs, double the number sold the previous year (Chen and Wingfield, 2014). Smart houses have attracted even more interest, fueled by Google's purchase of Nest Labs for $3.2 billion in January 2014. Nest Labs makes smart thermostats and smoke and carbon monoxide alarms. Nest purchased Dropcam (maker of Wi-Fi-enabled security cameras) for $555 million in June 2014. Apple announced a smart home platform that it calls Homekit in June 2014. Homekit is a framework and network protocol for controlling devices in the home. Many cable companies such as Time Warner Cable, Comcast, and AT&T already offer connected home systems that include appliances and lights. All in all, the global market for smart house products is expected to be as much as €32 billion in next 5 to 7 years.

In September 2014, Apple introduced the Apple Watch, a smartwatch designed to be used in conjunction with an iPhone 5 or 6, that will be first available in early 2015. The Apple Watch features a fitness/activity tracker similar to that offered by the already popular Fitbit, Nike + , FuelBand, and Jawbone Up, will be able to access a wide variety of apps, and also will work with Apple Pay, Apple's new mobile payment service. A number of other manufacturers, such as Samsung, LG, Motorola, and Swatch have also introduced smartwatches in 2014. Gartner estimates that wearable devices will be a €8 billion market by 2016.

Connected cars that have built-in Internet access are also on the horizon. Here too, Google and Apple are major players. In January 2014, Google announced the Open Automotive Alliance, a group of leading automakers and technology companies focused on bringing the Android platform to cars. In March 2014, Apple announced CarPlay, a software platform that synchronizes iPhones to the car's infotainment system. CarPlay-enabled vehicles are expected to be available in 2015. Connected cars are likely to be integrated with smart home initiatives in the future. Already, iControl, which provides the software underlying automated home systems from Comcast, TimeWarner, ADT, and others, has entered into a partnership with Zubie, a provider of connected car services.

Despite all of the IoT activity, however, interoperability remains a major concern. As with many technologies in the early stages of development, many organizations are fighting to create the standards that participants in the market will follow. The AllSeen Alliance, formed by Qualcomm in December 2013 with 50 other companies, including Microsoft and Cisco, is one group that hopes to create an open source standard. Another group, the Open Interconnect Consortium, formed by Intel, Broadcom, Dell, and others apparently not happy with the AllSeen effort, formed in July 2014. A different group, the Industrial Internet Consortium, has been formed by AT&T, Cisco, GE, IBM, and Intel to focus on engineering standards for industrial assets. The Wolfram Connected Devices Project is aimed at developing a database of IoT devices, and currently includes more than 2,000. And as with many other types of Internet-related technology, Google with its Android operating system and Apple with AirPlay may be trying to create their own standards.

Other concerns include security and privacy. Security experts believe that IoT devices could potentially be a security disaster, with the potential for malware being spread through a connected network, and difficulty in issuing patches to devices, leaving them vulnerable (SANS, 2014). Data from stand-alone smart devices can reveal much personal detail about a consumer's life, and if those devices are all ultimately interconnected, there will be little that is truly private.

Although challenges remain before the Internet of Things is fully realized, it is coming closer and closer to fruition, and predictions indicate that there could be up to 100 to 200 billion "things" connected to the Internet by 2020, with 25–30 billion of those connected autonomous devices (IEEE Computer Society, 2013; IDC, 2013; Gartner, 2013).

2.4 THE WEB

Without the Web, there would be no e-commerce. The invention of the Web brought an extraordinary expansion of digital services to millions of amateur computer users, including color text and pages, formatted text, pictures, animations, video, and sound. In short, the Web makes nearly all the rich elements of human expression needed to establish a commercial marketplace available to nontechnical computer users worldwide.

While the Internet was born in the 1960s, the Web was not invented until 1989–1991 by Dr. Tim Berners-Lee of the European Particle Physics Laboratory, better known as CERN (Berners-Lee et al., 1994). Several earlier authors—such as Vannevar

Bush (in 1945) and Ted Nelson (in the 1960s)—had suggested the possibility of organizing knowledge as a set of interconnected pages that users could freely browse (Bush, 1945; Ziff Davis Publishing, 1998). Berners-Lee and his associates at CERN built on these ideas and developed the initial versions of HTML, HTTP, a Web server, and a browser, the four essential components of the Web.

First, Berners-Lee wrote a computer program that allowed formatted pages within his own computer to be linked using keywords (hyperlinks). Clicking on a keyword in a document would immediately move him to another document. Berners-Lee created the pages using a modified version of a powerful text markup language called Standard Generalized Markup Language (SGML).

Berners-Lee called this language HyperText Markup Language, or HTML. He then came up with the idea of storing his HTML pages on the Internet. Remote client computers could access these pages by using HTTP (introduced earlier in Section 2.1 and described more fully in the next section). But these early Web pages still appeared as black and white text pages with hyperlinks expressed inside brackets. The early Web was based on text only; the original Web browser only provided a line interface.

Information being shared on the Web remained text-based until 1993, when Marc Andreessen and others at the National Center for Supercomputing Applications (NCSA) at the University of Illinois created a Web browser with a graphical user interface (GUI) called **Mosaic** that made it possible to view documents on the Web graphically—using colored backgrounds, images, and even primitive animations. Mosaic was a software program that could run on any graphically based interface such as Macintosh, Windows, or Unix. The Mosaic browser software read the HTML text on a Web page and displayed it as a graphical interface document within a GUI operating system such as Windows or Macintosh. Liberated from simple black and white text pages, HTML pages could now be viewed by anyone in the world who could operate a mouse and use a Macintosh or PC.

Aside from making the content of Web pages colorful and available to the world's population, the graphical Web browser created the possibility of **universal computing**, the sharing of files, information, graphics, sound, video, and other objects across all computer platforms in the world, regardless of operating system. A browser could be made for each of the major operating systems, and the Web pages created for one system, say, Windows, would also be displayed exactly the same, or nearly the same, on computers running the Macintosh or Unix operating systems. As long as each operating system had a Mosaic browser, the same Web pages could be used on all the different types of computers and operating systems. This meant that no matter what kind of computer you used, anywhere in the world, you would see the same Web pages. The browser and the Web have introduced us to a whole new world of computing and information management that was unthinkable prior to 1993.

In 1994, Andreessen and Jim Clark founded Netscape, which created the first commercial browser, **Netscape Navigator**. Although Mosaic had been distributed free of charge, Netscape initially charged for its software. In August 1995, Microsoft Corporation released its own free version of a browser, called **Internet Explorer**. In the ensuing years, Netscape fell from a 100% market share to less than .5% in 2009. The

Mosaic
Web browser with a graphical user interface (GUI) that made it possible to view documents on the Web graphically

universal computing
the sharing of files, information, graphics, sound, video, and other objects across all computer platforms in the world, regardless of operating system

Netscape Navigator
the first commercial Web browser

Internet Explorer
Microsoft's Web browser

fate of Netscape illustrates an important e-commerce business lesson. Innovators usually are not long-term winners, whereas smart followers often have the assets needed for long-term survival. Much of the Netscape browser code survives today in the Firefox browser produced by Mozilla, a nonprofit heavily funded by Google.

HYPERTEXT

Web pages can be accessed through the Internet because the Web browser software on your PC can request Web pages stored on an Internet host server using the HTTP protocol. **Hypertext** is a way of formatting pages with embedded links that connect documents to one another and that also link pages to other objects such as sound, video, or animation files. When you click on a graphic and a video clip plays, you have clicked on a hyperlink. For example, when you type a Web address in your browser such as http://www.sec.gov, your browser sends an HTTP request to the sec.gov server requesting the home page of sec.gov.

hypertext
a way of formatting pages with embedded links that connect documents to one another, and that also link pages to other objects such as sound, video, or animation files

HTTP is the first set of letters at the start of every Web address, followed by the domain name. The domain name specifies the organization's server computer that is housing the document. Most companies have a domain name that is the same as or closely related to their official corporate name. The directory path and document name are two more pieces of information within the Web address that help the browser track down the requested page. Together, the address is called a Uniform Resource Locator, or URL. When typed into a browser, a URL tells it exactly where to look for the information. For example, in the following URL:

http://www.megacorp.com/content/features/082602.html

http = the protocol used to display Web pages

www.megacorp.com = domain name

content/features = the directory path that identifies where on the domain Web server the page is stored

082602.html = the document name and its format (an HTML page)

The most common domain extensions (known as general top-level domains, or gTLDs) currently available and officially sanctioned by ICANN are shown in **Table 2.12**. Countries also have domain names, such as .uk, .au, and .fr (United Kingdom, Australia, and France, respectively). These are sometimes referred to as country-code top-level domains, or ccTLDs. In 2008, ICANN approved a significant expansion of gTLDs, with potential new domains representing cities (such as .berlin), regions (.africa), ethnicity (.eus), industry/activities (such as .health), and even brands (such as .deloitte). In 2009, ICANN began the process of implementing these guidelines. In 2011, ICANN removed nearly all restrictions on domain names, thereby greatly expanding the number of different domain names available. As of August 2014, around 1400 new gTLDs have been applied for and acquired, and they began to be launched as of late 2013. The new gTLDs are in multiple languages and scripts/characters (including

TABLE 2.12	**TOP-LEVEL DOMAINS**		
GENERAL TOP-LEVEL DOMAIN (GTLD)	YEAR(S) INTRODUCED	PURPOSE	SPONSOR/ OPERATOR
.com	1980s	Unrestricted (but intended for commercial registrants)	VeriSign
.edu	1980s	U.S. educational institutions	Educause
.gov	1980s	U.S. government	U.S. General Services Administration
.mil	1980s	U.S. military	U.S. Department of Defense Network Information Center
.net	1980s	Unrestricted (but originally intended for network providers, etc.)	VeriSign
.org	1980s	Unrestricted (but intended for organizations that do not fit elsewhere)	Public Interest Registry (was operated by VeriSign until December 31, 2002)
.int	1998	Organizations established by international treaties between governments	Internet Assigned Numbers Authority (IANA)
.aero	2001	Air-transport industry	Societé Internationale de Telecommunications Aeronautiques SC (SITA)
.biz	2001	Businesses	NeuLevel
.coop	2001	Cooperatives	DotCooperation LLC
.info	2001	Unrestricted use	Afilias LLC
.museum	2001	Museums	Museum Domain Name Association (MuseDoma)
.name	2001	For registration by individuals	Global Name Registry Ltd.
.pro	2002	Accountants, lawyers, physicians, and other professionals	RegistryPro Ltd
.jobs	2005	Job search	Employ Media LLC
.travel	2005	Travel search	Tralliance Corporation
.mobi	2005	Web sites specifically designed for mobile phones	mTLD Top Level Domain, Ltd.
.cat	2005	Individuals, organizations, and companies that promote the Catalan language and culture	Fundació puntCAT
.asia	2006	Regional domain for companies, organizations, and individuals based in Asia	DotAsia Organization
.tel	2006	Telephone numbers and other contact information	ICM Registry
.xxx	2010	New top-level domain for pornographic content	None yet approved

SOURCE: Based on data from ICANN, 2011b.

FIGURE 2.15   **EXAMPLE HTML CODE (A) AND WEB PAGE (B)**

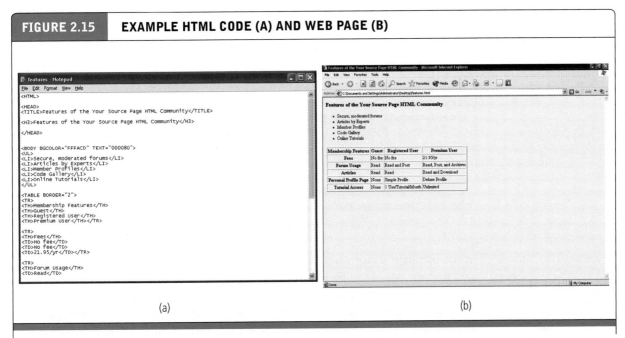

(a)   (b)

HTML is a text markup language used to create Web pages. It has a fixed set of "tags" that are used to tell the browser software how to present the content on screen. The HTML shown in Figure 2.15 (a) creates the Web page seen in Figure 2.15 (b).

Arabic, Chinese, Japanese, and Russian) and include geographic place names such as .nyc, .london, and .berlin, business identifiers such as .restaurant, .realtor, .technology, .lawyer, brand names such as .bmw and .suzuki; and a whole host of other descriptive names.

MARKUP LANGUAGES

Although the most common Web page formatting language is HTML, the concept behind document formatting actually had its roots in the 1960s with the development of Generalized Markup Language (GML).

HyperText Markup Language (HTML)

HyperText Markup Language (HTML) is a GML that is relatively easy to use. HTML provides Web page designers with a fixed set of markup "tags" that are used to format a Web page (see **Figure 2.15**). When these tags are inserted into a Web page, they are read by the browser and interpreted into a page display. You can see the source HTML code for any Web page by simply clicking on the "Page Source" command found in all browsers. In Figure 2.16, the HTML code in the first screen produces the display in the second screen.

HTML defines the structure and style of a document, including the headings, graphic positioning, tables, and text formatting. Since its introduction, the major browsers have continuously added features to HTML to enable programmers to further refine their page layouts. Unfortunately, some browser enhancements may work only

HyperText Markup Language (HTML)
GML that is relatively easy to use in Web page design. HTML provides Web page designers with a fixed set of markup "tags" that are used to format a Web page

FIGURE 2.16	A SIMPLE XML DOCUMENT

```
<?xml version="1.0"?>
<note>
<to>George</to>
<from>Carol</from>
<heading>Just a Reminder</heading>
<body>Don't forget to order the groceries from FreshDirect!</body>
</note>
```

The tags in this simple XML document, such as <note>, <to>, and <from>, are used to describe data and information, rather than the look and feel of the document.

in one company's browser. Whenever you build an e-commerce site, you should take care that the pages can be viewed by the major browsers, even outdated versions of browsers. HTML Web pages can be created with any text editor, such as Notepad or WordPad, using Microsoft Word (simply save the Word document as a Web page), or any one of several Web page development tools such as Microsoft Expression Web or Adobe Dreamweaver CC.[5]

The most recent version of HTML is HTML5. HTML5 introduces features like video playback and drag-and-drop that in the past were provided by plug-ins like Adobe Flash. HTML5 is also used in the development of mobile Web sites and mobile apps, and is an important tool in both responsive Web design and adaptive Web delivery, all of which are discussed more fully in Chapter 3. The *Insight on Technology* case, *Is HTML5 Ready for Prime Time?* examines some of the issues associated with use of HTML5.

eXtensible Markup Language (XML)

eXtensible Markup Language (XML)
a markup language specification developed by the World Wide Web Consortium (W3C) that is designed to describe data and information

eXtensible Markup Language (XML) takes Web document formatting a giant leap forward. XML is a markup language specification developed by the W3C that is similar to HTML, but has a very different purpose. Whereas the purpose of HTML is to control the "look and feel" and display of data on the Web page, XML is designed to describe data and information. For example, consider the sample XML document in **Figure 2.16**. The first line in the sample document is the XML declaration, which is always included; it defines the XML version of the document. In this case, the document conforms to the 1.0 specification of XML. The next line defines the first element of the document (the root element): < note >. The next four lines define four child elements of the root (to, from, heading, and body). The last line defines the end of the root element. Notice that XML says nothing about how to display the data, or how the text should look on the screen. HTML is used for information display in combination with XML, which is used for data description.

---

[5] A detailed discussion of how to use HTML is beyond the scope of this text.

INSIGHT ON TECHNOLOGY

IS HTML5 READY FOR PRIME TIME?

Can HTML5 save businesses billions of dollars in development costs and bring about the demise of the native app? Possibly! The newest standard for how Web pages should be rendered by a browser has been welcomed by developers far in advance of ratification by the W3C, currently scheduled for the end of 2014. Advocated by Apple founder Steve Jobs as the preferred method for displaying video on the Web, HTML5's video element replaces plug-ins such as Flash, QuickTime, and RealPlayer, and represents a dramatic breakthrough in Web page design. As a result, HTML5 has become the de facto standard for display of video on mobile devices.

HTML5 has become a catch-all term that encompasses not only the video element but also the use of the newest versions of Cascading Style Sheets (CSS3) and JavaScript, and another new tool, HTML5 Canvas. Also intended to replace plug-ins, it is used with a set of JavaScript functions to render simple animations, which reduces page load time. Multi-platform Web developers began using HTML5 because these new elements provided device independence, but soon discovered that they could do even more. The built-in functionality of mobile devices, including GPS and swiping, can be accessed, enabling m-commerce sites to build Web-based mobile apps that can replicate the native app experience. Web-based mobile apps (HTML5 apps) work just like Web pages. When a user navigates to the page containing the mobile app, the page content, including graphics, images, and video, are loaded into the browser from the Web server, rather than residing in the mobile device hardware like a native app. This concept has been embraced by mobile developers who naturally dream of being able to reach all platforms with a single product.

For businesses, the cost savings of HTML5 are obvious. A single HTML5 app requires far less effort to build than multiple native apps for the iOS, Android, Windows Phone, and other platforms. HTML5 apps can more easily be linked to and shared on social networks, encouraging viral distribution. Some HTML5 apps can even be designed so that they can be run on mobile devices when they are offline. Differences in how apps run across different platforms and workarounds are eliminated.

In April 2014, the Interactive Advertising Bureau (IAB), together with a number of the largest publishers and advertising firms, urged advertisers to implement HTML5 as the standard for mobile ads in order to guarantee that ads will run and look good on different platforms. The shift toward HTML5 is expected to be one of the most important changes in digital advertising in 2014.

In 2014, almost 50% of Internet Retailer's top 500 mobile retailers use HTML5 for their smartphone or tablet mobile sites. One example is eBags, a niche e-tailer of handbags, which used HTML5 to help create a responsive design/adaptive delivery (see Chapter 3 for a further discussion of responsive design and adaptive deliver) mobile Web site. HTML5 was used to create a pop-up keyboard to enable easy data input for fields such as phone numbers and ZIP codes. eBags also used HTML's local storage, which allows it to store Web page content within the cache of a mobile Web browser, to improve page load times . Performance was also enhanced by HTML5's asynchronous download capabilities, which enables the simultaneous download of JavaScript files and Web page content files. Since implementing the new mobile site, eBags has significantly improved its conversion rate on all devices.

(continued)

Rakuten is another etailer using HTML5 with success. Rakuten Shopping is an online retailer that offers a wide variety of goods online, and is currently ranked as one of Internet Retailer's top 30 mobile retailers in 2014. Using HTML5 has enabled Rakuten to shift away from using cookies to store customer attributes and has lightened the load on its servers, which are receiving fewer calls from mobile devices because once content is downloaded, it is then stored locally in the device's browser. HTML5's video tag has also enabled Rakuten to embed video within HTML pages on a mobile device.

The *Financial Times*'s HTML5 app has proven to be an important driver for FT's business. FT first switched from a native app to HTML5 in 2011, in part to make maintaining the app across multiple platforms and devices easier. In 2013, FT rolled out a redesign of the app, featuring even more videos and personalization features. FT's managing director, Robert Grimshaw, believes that those who have chosen to develop native apps in parallel will struggle with the overhead of maintaining and developing them.

One of the biggest challenges of HTML5 apps is to meet and then attempt to surpass the user experience and performance level of native apps. Although HTML5 sites load faster than first-generation mobile commerce sites, native apps generally still trump HTML5 apps on speed because a great deal of the interface already resides on the mobile device. Only newly requested data must be loaded. The mobile device platform also provides a standard user interface that native app developers can exploit to provide ease of execution for the user. HTML5 also faces challenges due to the fact that it depends on a mishmash of and lacks a robust toolset and developers with HTML5 experience.

In fact, according to Indeed, which searches millions of jobs from thousands of different job sites, in 2014, "HTML5" is the fastest growing keyword found in online job postings, ahead of iOS and Android. As a result, HTML5 projects typically take longer to develop than planned, according to a Forrester survey.

According to Tim Berners-Lee, founder and chief of the W3C and an ardent opponent of native apps because they remove functionality from the Web, HTML5 security and access control issues are currently being addressed. For instance, HTML5 does not support digital rights management (DRM). In the past, media companies developed their own copy protection standards based on geographical region and/or whether payment had been proffered. These were enforced through their own media players. Because HTML5 does not require plug-ins to play video (or audio), and further, because HTML5 is an official W3C standard charged with remaining vendor neutral, this presents a challenge to the HTML5 working group.

Although HTML5 is being widely adopted on e-commerce and m-commerce sites, native apps aren't going anywhere. Instead, developers are incorporating HTML5 code into native apps, creating a kind of hybrid or mixed mode app. Gartner expects that more than 50% of mobile applications will be hybrid by 2016. While the lure of reaching all platforms with a single product is potent, if developers cannot produce a product that equals the performance of native apps, they will stick with the side their bread is buttered on and continue to develop native apps for the top sellers. For example, Facebook and LinkedIn have decided to focus on developing native apps in order to provide more performance with rich functionality.

SOURCES: "Mobile HTML5 Remains Relevant, But Faces Challenges," by George Lawton, Techtarget.com, August 28, 2014; "RIP Flash: Why HTML5 Will Finally Take Over Video and the Web This Year," by Erika Trautman, Thenextweb.com, April 19, 2014; "Forrester: HTML5 Apps Still Not As Good As Native Apps," by Serdar Yegulalp, Infoworld.com, February 3, 2014; "Top Mobile Retailers Reap Rewards Using the Magical HTML5," by Bill Siwicki, Internetretailer.com, December 13, 2013; "Financial Times: 'There is No Drawback to Working in HTML5'," by Stuart Dredge, TheGuardian.com, April 29, 2013; "The HTML5 Promise: Responsive Web Design for Any Screen," by Tom Foremski, Siliconvalleywatcher.com, April 16, 2013; "HTML5 Mobile Sites Give Apps a Run for their Money," by Bill Siwicki, Internet Retailer, February 3, 2012; "HTML5 Is Popular, Still Unfinished," by Don Clark, *Wall Street Journal*, November 11, 2011; "Adobe's Flash Surrender Proves Steve Jobs And Apple Were Right All Along With HTML5," by Nigam Arora, *Forbes*, November, 9, 2011.

FIGURE 2.17	**SAMPLE XML CODE FOR A COMPANY DIRECTORY**

```
<?xml version="1.0"?>
<Companies>
    <Company>
          <Name>Azimuth Interactive Inc.</Name>
       <Specialties>
                 <Specialty>HTML development</Specialty>
                  <Specialty>technical documentation</Specialty>
               <Specialty>ROBO Help</Specialty>
               <Country>United States</Country>
        </Specialties>
        <Location>
                 <Country>United States</Country>
             <State />
              <City>Chicago</City>
        </Location>
             <Telephone>301-555-1212</Telephone>
    </Company>
    <Company>
       ...
    </Company>
   ...
</Companies>
```

This XML document uses tags to define a database of company names.

Figure 2.17 shows how XML can be used to define a database of company names in a company directory. Tags such as < Company >, < Name >, and < Specialty > can be defined for a single firm, or an entire industry. On an elementary level, XML is extraordinarily easy to learn and is very similar to HTML except that you can make up your own tags. At a deeper level, XML has a rich syntax and an enormous set of software tools, which make XML ideal for storing and communicating many types of data on the Web.

XML is "extensible," which means the tags used to describe and display data are defined by the user, whereas in HTML the tags are limited and predefined. XML can also transform information into new formats, such as by importing information from a database and displaying it as a table. With XML, information can be analyzed and displayed selectively, making it a more powerful alternative to HTML. This means that business firms, or entire industries, can describe all of their invoices, accounts payable, payroll records, and financial information using a Web-compatible markup language. Once described, these business documents can be stored on intranet Web servers and shared throughout the corporation.

WEB SERVERS AND CLIENTS

We have already described client/server computing and the revolution in computing architecture brought about by client/server computing. You already know that a server is a computer attached to a network that stores files, controls peripheral devices, interfaces with the outside world—including the Internet—and does some processing for other computers on the network.

Web server software
software that enables a computer to deliver Web pages written in HTML to client computers on a network that request this service by sending an HTTP request

But what is a Web server? **Web server software** refers to the software that enables a computer to deliver Web pages written in HTML to client computers on a network that request this service by sending an HTTP request. The two leading brands of Web server software are Apache, which is free Web server shareware that accounts for about 51% of the market, and Microsoft's Internet Information Services (IIS), which accounts for about 12% of the market (Netcraft, 2014).

Aside from responding to requests for Web pages, all Web servers provide some additional basic capabilities such as the following:

- *Security services*—These consist mainly of authentication services that verify that the person trying to access the site is authorized to do so. For Web sites that process payment transactions, the Web server also supports SSL and TLS, the protocols for transmitting and receiving information securely over the Internet. When private information such as names, phone numbers, addresses, and credit card data needs to be provided to a Web site, the Web server uses SSL to ensure that the data passing back and forth from the browser to the server is not compromised.

- *FTP*—This protocol allows users to transfer files to and from the server. Some sites limit file uploads to the Web server, while others restrict downloads, depending on the user's identity.

- *Search engine*—Just as search engine sites enable users to search the entire Web for particular documents, search engine modules within the basic Web server software package enable indexing of the site's Web pages and content and permit easy keyword searching of the site's content. When conducting a search, a search engine makes use of an index, which is a list of all the documents on the server. The search term is compared to the index to identify likely matches.

- *Data capture*—Web servers are also helpful at monitoring site traffic, capturing information on who has visited a site, how long the user stayed there, the date and time of each visit, and which specific pages on the server were accessed. This information is compiled and saved in a log file, which can then be analyzed. By analyzing a log file, a site manager can find out the total number of visitors, the average length of each visit, and the most popular destinations, or Web pages.

The term *Web server* is also used to refer to the physical computer that runs Web server software. Leading manufacturers of Web server computers include IBM, Dell, and Hewlett-Packard. Although any personal computer can run Web server software, it is best to use a computer that has been optimized for this purpose. To be a Web server, a computer must have the Web server software installed and be connected to the Internet. Every public Web server computer has an IP address. For example, if you type http://www.pearsonhighered.com/laudon in your browser, the browser software sends a request for HTTP service to the Web server whose domain name is pearsonhighered.com. The server then locates the page named "laudon" on its hard drive, sends the page back to your browser, and displays it on your screen. Of course, firms also can use Web servers for strictly internal local area networking in intranets.

Aside from the generic Web server software packages, there are actually many types of specialized servers on the Web, from **database servers** that access specific information within a database, to **ad servers** that deliver targeted banner ads, to **mail servers** that provide e-mail messages, and **video servers** that provide video clips. At a small e-commerce site, all of these software packages might be running on a single computer, with a single processor. At a large corporate site, there may be hundreds or thousands of discrete server computers, many with multiple processors, running specialized Web server functions. We discuss the architecture of e-commerce sites in greater detail in Chapter 3.

A **Web client**, on the other hand, is any computing device attached to the Internet that is capable of making HTTP requests and displaying HTML pages. The most common client is a Windows or Macintosh computer, with various flavors of Unix/Linux computers a distant third. However, the fastest growing category of Web clients are not computers at all, but smartphones, tablets, and netbooks outfitted with wireless Web access software. In general, Web clients can be any device—including a printer, refrigerator, stove, home lighting system, or automobile instrument panel—capable of sending and receiving information from Web servers.

WEB BROWSERS

A **Web browser** is a software program whose primary purpose is to display Web pages. Browsers also have added features, such as e-mail and newsgroups (an online discussion group or forum). The leading Web browser is Microsoft Internet Explorer, with about 58% of the market as of August 2014. The second most popular browser, with about a 20% market share, is Google's Chrome, a small, yet technologically advanced open source browser. Mozilla Firefox has dropped to third place, with only about 15% of the U.S. Web browser market. First released in 2004, Firefox is a free, open source Web browser for the Windows, Linux, and Macintosh operating systems, based on Mozilla open source code (which originally provided the code for Netscape). It is small and fast and offers many features such as pop-up blocking and tabbed browsing. Apple's Safari browser is fourth, with about 5% of the market (Marketshare.hitslink.com, 2014).

database server
server designed to access specific information within a database

ad server
server designed to deliver targeted banner ads

mail server
server that provides e-mail messages

video server
server that serves video clips

Web client
any computing device attached to the Internet that is capable of making HTTP requests and displaying HTML pages, most commonly a Windows PC or Macintosh

Web browser
software program whose primary purpose is to display Web pages

2.5	**THE INTERNET AND THE WEB: FEATURES AND SERVICES**

The Internet and the Web have spawned a number of powerful software applications upon which the foundations of e-commerce are built. You can think of all these as Web services, and it is interesting as you read along to compare these services to other traditional media such as television or print media. If you do, you will quickly realize the richness of the Internet environment.

E-MAIL

Since its earliest days, **electronic mail**, or **e-mail**, has been the most-used application of the Internet. Worldwide, there are an estimated 4.1 billion e-mail accounts, sending

electronic mail (e-mail)
the most-used application of the Internet. Uses a series of protocols to enable messages containing text, images, sound, and video clips to be transferred from one Internet user to another

an estimated 196 billion e-mails a day. There are an estimated 1.1 billion mobile e-mail users worldwide, and their number is expected to double, to 2.2 billion, by 2016 (Radicati Group, 2014). Estimates vary on the amount of spam, ranging from 40% to 90%. E-mail marketing and spam are examined in more depth in Chapter 6.

E-mail uses a series of protocols to enable messages containing text, images, sound, and video clips to be transferred from one Internet user to another. Because of its flexibility and speed, it is now the most popular form of business communication—more popular than the phone, fax, or snail mail (the Postal Service). In addition to text typed within the message, e-mail also allows **attachments**, which are files inserted within the e-mail message. The files can be documents, images, sounds, or video clips.

attachment
a file inserted within an e-mail message

INSTANT MESSAGING

instant messaging (IM)
displays words typed on a computer almost instantaneously. Recipients can then respond immediately to the sender the same way, making the communication more like a live conversation than is possible through e-mail

Instant messaging (IM) allows you to send messages in real time, one line at a time, unlike e-mail. E-mail messages have a time lag of several seconds to minutes between when messages are sent and received. IM displays lines of text entered on a computer almost instantaneously. Recipients can then respond immediately to the sender the same way, making the communication more like a live conversation than is possible through e-mail. To use IM, users create a buddy list they want to communicate with, and then enter short text messages that their buddies will receive instantly (if they are online at the time). And although text remains the primary communication mechanism in IM, more advanced systems also provide voice and video chat functionality. Instant messaging over the Internet competes with wireless phone Short Message Service (SMS) texting, which is far more expensive than IM.

The major IM systems are Skype, Yahoo Messenger, Google Talk, and AIM (AOL Instant Messenger). Facebook also offers instant messaging services via Facebook Chat. IM systems were initially developed as proprietary systems, with competing firms offering versions that did not work with one another. Today, there still is no built-in interoperability among the major IM systems. Mobile messaging apps, such as Facebook Messenger, WhatsApp (purchased by Facebook for $16 billion in 2014), Snapchat (which allows users to send pictures, videos, and texts that will disappear after a short period of time), Viber, MessageMe, and others are also becoming very popular, providing competition for both traditional desktop IM systems and SMS text messaging.

SEARCH ENGINES

search engine
identifies Web pages that appear to match keywords, also called queries, entered by the user and then provides a list of the best matches

Search engines identify Web pages that appear to match keywords, also called queries, entered by a user and then provide a list of the best matches (search results). Worldwide, over 50% of Internet users actively use search engines when looking for information about brands, products, or services (eMarketer, Inc., 2014h). There are hundreds of different search engines, but in the United States, the vast majority of the search results are supplied by the top five providers (see **Figure 2.18**). Google, Bing, Ask and Yahoo are also major search providers in Europe. Other popular European search providers include T-Online (in Germany), and Delta-Search (in Spain and France). In China, Baidu, Qihoo 360, Sohu Sogou and Tencent Soso are major search engine providers.

Web search engines started out in the early 1990s shortly after Netscape released the first commercial Web browser. Early search engines were relatively simple software programs that roamed the nascent Web, visiting pages and gathering information about the content of each Web page. These early programs were called variously crawlers, spiders, and wanderers; the first full-text crawler that indexed the contents of an entire Web page was called WebCrawler, released in 1994. AltaVista (1995), one of the first widely used search engines, was the first to allow "natural language" queries such as "history of Web search engines" rather than "history + Web + search engine."

The first search engines employed simple keyword indexes of all the Web pages visited. They would count the number of times a word appeared on the Web page, and store this information in an index. These search engines could be easily fooled by Web designers who simply repeated words on their home pages. The real innovations in search engine development occurred through a program funded by the Department of Defense called the Digital Library Initiative, designed to help the Pentagon find research papers in large databases. Stanford, Berkeley, and three other universities became hotbeds of Web search innovations in the mid-1990s. At Stanford in 1994, two computer science students, David Filo and Jerry Yang, created a hand-selected list of their favorite Web pages and called it "Yet Another Hierarchical Officious Oracle," or Yahoo!. Yahoo initially was not a real search engine, but rather an edited selection of Web sites organized by categories the editors found useful. Yahoo later developed "true" search engine capabilities.

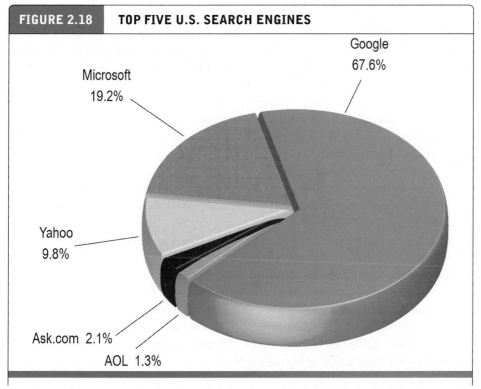

FIGURE 2.18 | **TOP FIVE U.S. SEARCH ENGINES**

Google 67.6%

Microsoft 19.2%

Yahoo 9.8%

Ask.com 2.1%

AOL 1.3%

Google is, by far, the leading search engine based on its percentage share of the number of searches.
SOURCE: Based on data from comScore, 2014a.

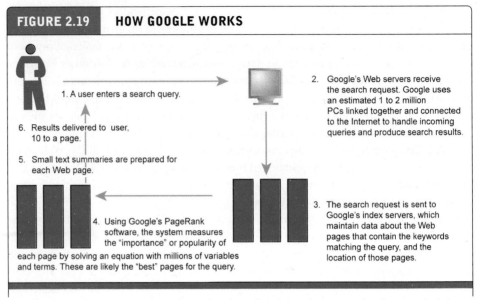

FIGURE 2.19   **HOW GOOGLE WORKS**

1. A user enters a search query.

6. Results delivered to user, 10 to a page.

5. Small text summaries are prepared for each Web page.

4. Using Google's PageRank software, the system measures the "importance" or popularity of each page by solving an equation with millions of variables and terms. These are likely the "best" pages for the query.

2. Google's Web servers receive the search request. Google uses an estimated 1 to 2 million PCs linked together and connected to the Internet to handle incoming queries and produce search results.

3. The search request is sent to Google's index servers, which maintain data about the Web pages that contain the keywords matching the query, and the location of those pages.

The Google search engine is continuously crawling the Web, indexing the content of each page, calculating its popularity, and caching the pages so that it can respond quickly to your request to see a page. The entire process takes about one-half of a second.

In 1998, Larry Page and Sergey Brin, two Stanford computer science students, released their first version of the Google search engine. This search engine was different: not only did it index each Web page's words, but Page had discovered that the AltaVista search engine not only collected keywords from sites but also calculated what other sites linked to each page. By looking at the URLs on each Web page, they could calculate an index of popularity. AltaVista did nothing with this information. Page took this idea and made it a central factor in ranking a Web page's appropriateness to a search query. He patented the idea of a Web page ranking system (PageRank System), which essentially measures the popularity of the Web page. Brin contributed a unique Web crawler program that indexed not just keywords on a Web page, but combinations of words (such as authors and their article titles). These two ideas became the foundation for the Google search engine (Brandt, 2004). **Figure 2.19** illustrates how Google works.

Initially, few understood how to make money from search engines. That changed in 2000 when Goto.com (later Overture) allowed advertisers to bid for placement on their search engine results, and Google followed suit in 2003 with its AdWords program, which allowed advertisers to bid for placement of short text ads on Google search results. The spectacular increase in Internet advertising revenues (which have been growing at around 20%–25% annually over the last few years) has helped search engines transform themselves into major shopping tools and created an entire new industry called "search engine marketing."

When users enter a search term at Google, Bing, Yahoo, or any of the other Web sites serviced by these search engines, they receive two types of listings: sponsored links, for which advertisers have paid to be listed (usually at the top of the search results page), and unsponsored "organic" search results. In addition, advertisers can purchase small text ads on the right side of the search results page. Although the major search engines are used for locating general information of interest to users, search engines have also become a crucial tool within e-commerce sites. Customers can more easily search for the product information they want with the help of an internal search program; the difference is that within Web sites, the search engine is limited to finding matches from that one site. In addition, search engines have extended their services to include news, maps, satellite images, computer images, e-mail, group calendars, group meeting tools, and indexes of scholarly papers. In 2012, Google and Bing added social search terms to their search results. Whatever these search engines can glean from your e-mails and social network posts they can use in response to your searches to make the results more "personal" and social.

ONLINE FORUMS

An **online forum** (also referred to as a message board, bulletin board, discussion board, discussion group, or simply a board or forum) is a Web application that enables Internet users to communicate with each other, although not in real time. A forum provides a container for various discussions (or "threads") started (or "posted") by members of the forum, and depending on the permissions granted to forum members by the forum's administrator, enables a person to start a thread and reply to other people's threads. Most forum software allows more than one forum to be created. The forum administrator typically can edit, delete, move, or otherwise modify any thread on the forum. Unlike an electronic mailing list (such as a listserv), which automatically sends new messages to a subscriber, an online forum typically requires that the member visit the forum to check for new posts. Some forums offer an "e-mail notification" feature that notifies users that a new post of interest to them has been made.

online forum
a Web application that allows Internet users to communicate with each other, although not in real time

STREAMING MEDIA

Streaming media enables live Web video, music, video, and other large-bandwidth files to be sent to users in a variety of ways that enable the user to play back the files. In some situations, such as live Web video, the files are broken into chunks and served by specialized video servers to users in chunks. Client software puts the chunks together and plays the video. In other situations, such as YouTube, a single large file is downloaded from a standard Web server to users who can begin playing the video before the entire file is downloaded. Streamed files must be viewed "live"; they cannot be stored on client hard drives without special software. Streamed files are "played" by a software program such as Windows Media Player, Apple QuickTime, Flash, and RealMedia Player. There are a number of tools used to create streaming files, but one of the most common is Adobe's Flash program. The Flash player has the advantage of being built into most client browsers; no plug-in is required to play Flash files.

streaming media
enables music, video, and other large files to be sent to users in chunks so that when received and played, the file comes through uninterrupted

Sites such as YouTube, Metacafe, and Facebook have popularized user-generated video streaming. Web advertisers increasingly use video to attract viewers. Streaming audio and video segments used in Web ads and news stories are perhaps the most frequently used streaming services. As the capacity of the Internet grows, streaming media will play an even larger role in e-commerce.

COOKIES

cookie

a tool used by Web sites to store information about a user. When a visitor enters a Web site, the site sends a small text file (the cookie) to the user's computer so that information from the site can be loaded more quickly on future visits. The cookie can contain any information desired by the site designers

A **cookie** is a tool used by a Web site to store information about a user. When a visitor enters a Web site, the site sends a small text file (the cookie) to the user's computer so that information from the site can be loaded more quickly on future visits. The cookie can contain any information desired by the Web site designers, including customer number, pages visited, products examined, and other detailed information about the behavior of the consumer at the site. Cookies are useful to consumers because the Web site will recognize returning patrons and not ask them to register again. Cookies are also used by advertisers to ensure visitors do not receive the same advertisements repeatedly. Cookies can also help personalize a Web site by allowing the site to recognize returning customers and make special offers to them based on their past behavior at the site. Cookies allow Web marketers to customize products and segment markets—the ability to change the product or the price based on prior consumer information (described more fully in later chapters). As we will discuss throughout the book, cookies also can pose a threat to consumer privacy, and at times they are bothersome. Many people clear their cookies at the end of every day. Some disable them entirely using tools built into most browsers.

WEB 2.0 FEATURES AND SERVICES

Today's broadband Internet infrastructure has greatly expanded the services available to users. These new capabilities have formed the basis for new business models. Digital content and digital communications are the two areas where innovation is most rapid. Web 2.0 applications and services are "social" in nature because they support communication among individuals within groups or social networks.

Online Social Networks

Online social networks are services that support communication within networks of friends, colleagues, and entire professions. Online social networks have developed very large worldwide audiences and form the basis for new advertising platforms and for social e-commerce (see Chapters 6, 7, and 11). The largest social networks are Facebook (1.3 billion members worldwide), Google+ (540 million members worldwide), LinkedIn (more than 310 million members worldwide), Twitter (more than 270 million active users worldwide), and Pinterest (around 70 million active users). These networks rely on user-generated content (messages, photos, and videos) and emphasize sharing of content. All of these features require significant broadband Internet connectivity and equally large cloud computing facilities to store content.

Blogs

blog

personal Web page that is created by an individual or corporation to communicate with readers

A **blog** (originally called a **weblog**) is a personal Web page that typically contains a series of chronological entries (newest to oldest) by its author, and links to related Web pages. The blog may include a blogroll (a collection of links to other blogs) and trackbacks (a list of entries in other blogs that refer to a post on the first blog). Most blogs allow readers to post comments on the blog entries as well. The act of creating a blog is often referred to as "blogging." Blogs are either hosted by a third-party site such as Blogger, LiveJournal, TypePad, Xanga, WordPress, and Tumblr, or prospective bloggers can download software such as Movable Type to create a blog that is hosted by the user's ISP. Blog pages are usually variations on templates provided by the blogging service or software and hence require no knowledge of HTML. Therefore, millions of people without HTML skills of any kind can post their own Web pages, and share content with friends and relatives. The totality of blog-related Web sites is often referred to as the "blogosphere."

Blogs have become hugely popular. Tumblr, WordPress, and LiveJournal together hosted over 325 million blogs as of August 2014, so it is likely that the total number is significantly higher. According to eMarketer, there are an estimated 27 million active U.S. bloggers, and 76 million U.S. blog readers (eMarketer, Inc., 2014i, 2014j). No one knows how many of these blogs are kept up to date or are just yesterday's news. And no one knows how many of these blogs have a readership greater than one (the blog author). In fact, there are so many blogs you need a blog search engine just to find them (such as Google's or Technorati's search engine), or you can just go to a list of the most popular 100 blogs and dig in. We discuss blogs further in Chapters 6 and 7 as a marketing and advertising mechanism, and in Chapter 9 as a part of the significant growth in user-generated content.

Really Simple Syndication (RSS)

The rise of blogs is correlated with a distribution mechanism for news and information from Web sites that regularly update their content. **Really Simple Syndication (RSS)** is an XML format that allows users to have digital content, including text, articles, blogs, and podcast audio files, automatically sent to their computers over the Internet. An RSS aggregator software application that you install on your computer gathers material from the Web sites and blogs that you tell it to scan and brings new information from those sites to you. Sometimes this is referred to as "syndicated" content because it is distributed by news organizations and other syndicators (or distributors). Users download an RSS aggregator and then "subscribe" to the RSS "feeds." When you go to your RSS aggregator's page, it will display the most recent updates for each channel to which you have subscribed. RSS has rocketed from a "techie" pastime to a broad-based movement. Although Google has closed down Google Reader, a popular RSS product, a number of other RSS reader options remain, including Feedly, Reeder, and NewsBlur.

Really Simple Syndication (RSS)
program that allows users to have digital content, including text, articles, blogs, and podcast audio files, automatically sent to their computers over the Internet

Podcasting

A **podcast** is an audio presentation—such as a radio show, audio from a movie, or simply a personal audio presentation—stored as an audio file and posted to the Web. Listeners download the files from the Web and play them on their players or computers. While commonly associated with Apple's iPod portable music player, you can listen to MP3 podcast files with any MP3 player. Podcasting has transitioned from an amateur independent producer media in the "pirate radio" tradition to a professional news and talk content distribution channel.

podcast
an audio presentation—such as a radio show, audio from a movie, or simply a personal audio presentation—stored as an audio file and posted to the Web

Wikis

wiki

Web application that allows
a user to easily add and edit
content on a Web page

A **wiki** is a Web application that allows a user to easily add and edit content on a Web page. (The term wiki derives from the "wiki wiki" (quick or fast) shuttle buses at Honolulu Airport.) Wiki software enables documents to be written collectively and collaboratively. Most wiki systems are open source, server-side systems that store content in a relational database. The software typically provides a template that defines layout and elements common to all pages, displays user-editable source code (usually plain text), and then renders the content into an HTML-based page for display in a Web browser. Some wiki software allows only basic text formatting, whereas others allow the use of tables, images, or even interactive elements, such as polls and games. Because wikis by their very nature are very open in allowing anyone to make changes to a page, most wikis provide a means to verify the validity of changes via a "Recent Changes" page, which enables members of the wiki community to monitor and review the work of other users, correct mistakes, and hopefully deter "vandalism."

The most well-known wiki is Wikipedia, an online encyclopedia that contains more than 4.5 million English-language articles on a variety of topics, appears in 287 languages, and has around 500 million unique visitors each month worldwide. The Wikimedia Foundation, which operates Wikipedia, also operates a variety of related projects, including Wikibooks, a collection of collaboratively written free textbooks and manuals; Wikinews, a free content news source; and Wiktionary, a collaborative project to produce a free multilingual dictionary in every language, with definitions, etymologies, pronunciations, quotations, and synonyms.

Music and Video Services

With the low-bandwidth connections of the early Internet, audio and video files were difficult to download and share, but with the huge growth in broadband connections, these files are not only commonplace but today constitute the majority of Web traffic. Spurred on by the worldwide sales of more than 800 million iOS devices (iPhones, iPads, and iPod Touches) through June 2014, as well as millions of other smartphones, the Internet has become a virtual digital river of music and video files (Ingraham, 2014).

The Apple iTunes store is probably the most well-known repository of digital music tracks online, with a catalog of more than 37 million songs in its catalog as of August 2014. Google Play offers over 25 million, Amazon MP3 more than 20 million, and there are hundreds of other sites offering music downloads as well. In addition, streaming music services (see the *Insight on Technology* case study, *Battle of the Titans: Music in the Cloud* in Chapter 5) and Internet radio add to the bandwidth devoted to the delivery of online music.

Online video viewing has also exploded in popularity. In 2014, for instance, around 1.48 billion people around the world watch online video on a monthly basis, averaging 15 hours per viewer (comScore, 2014b). By far, the most common type of Internet video is provided by YouTube, with more than 1 billion unique visitors worldwide each month who watch more than 6 billion hours of video, most of it short clips taken from television shows, or user-generated content. The largest sources of legal, paid television content are the iTunes Store, where you can purchase specific episodes or entire seasons of TV shows, and Hulu, which is owned by major television producers NBCUniversal, News Corp., The Walt Disney Company, and Providence Equity Partners.

Internet advertising makes extensive use of streaming video ads: in March 2014, Americans watched around 29 billion video ads, almost 50% more than the previous year. Companies that want to demonstrate use of their products have found video clips to be extremely effective. And audio reports and discussions also have become commonplace, either as marketing materials or customer reports.

Future digital video networks will be able to deliver better-than-broadcast-quality video over the Internet to computers and other devices in homes and on the road. High-quality interactive video and audio makes sales presentations and demonstrations more effective and lifelike and enables companies to develop new forms of customer support. The Internet has become a major distribution channel for movies, television shows, and sporting events (see Chapter 9).

Internet Telephony

If the telephone system were to be built from scratch today, it would be an Internet-based, packet-switched network using TCP/IP because it would be less expensive and more efficient than the alternative existing system, which involves a mix of circuit-switched legs with a digital backbone. Likewise, if cable television systems were built from scratch today, they most likely would use Internet technologies for the same reasons.

IP telephony is a general term for the technologies that use **Voice over Internet Protocol (VoIP)** and the Internet's packet-switched network to transmit voice, fax, and other forms of audio communication over the Internet. VoIP can be used over a traditional handset as well as over a mobile device. VoIP avoids the long distance charges imposed by traditional phone companies.

There were about 212 million residential VoIP subscribers worldwide in 2013, and in the United States, almost half (47%) of residential customers are now using VoIP, and this number is expanding rapidly as cable systems provide telephone service as part of their "triple play": voice, Internet, and TV as a single package. This number is dwarfed, however, by the number of mobile VoIP subscribers, which has grown explosively over the last several years and was estimated to be around 1 billion in 2013 (Infonetics Research, 2014; Hamilton, 2014).

VoIP is a disruptive technology. In the past, voice and fax were the exclusive provenance of the regulated telephone networks. With the convergence of the Internet and telephony, however, this dominance is already starting to change, with local and long distance telephone providers and cable companies becoming ISPs, and ISPs getting into the phone market. Key players in the VoIP market include independent service providers such as VoIP pioneers Vonage and Skype (now owned by Microsoft), as well as traditional players such as telephone and cable companies that have moved aggressively into the market. Skype currently dominates the international market, and in 2013 carried an estimated 214 billion minutes of international calls from one Skype app to another, constituting almost 40% of the entire conventional international telecommunications market (Gara, 2014).

IP telephony
a general term for the technologies that use VoIP and the Internet's packet-switched network to transmit voice and other forms of audio communication over the Internet

Voice over Internet Protocol (VoIP)
protocol that allows for transmission of voice and other forms of audio communication over the Internet

Video Conferencing, Video Chatting, and Telepresence

Internet video conferencing is accessible to anyone with a broadband Internet connection and a Web camera (webcam). The most widely used Web conferencing suite of tools is WebEx (now owned by Cisco). VoIP companies such as Skype and ooVoo also provide more limited Web conferencing capabilities, commonly referred to as video chatting. Apple's FaceTime is another video chatting technology available for iOS mobile devices with a forward-facing camera and Macintosh computers equipped with Apple's version of a webcam, called a FaceTime camera.

Telepresence takes video conferencing up several notches. Rather than single persons "meeting" by using webcams, telepresence creates an environment in a room using multiple cameras and screens, which surround the users. The experience is uncanny and strange at first because as you look at the people in the screens, they are looking directly at you. Broadcast quality and higher screen resolutions help create the effect. Users have the sensation of "being in the presence of their colleagues" in a way that is not true for traditional webcam meetings. Providers of telepresence software and hardware include Cisco, HP, and Teliris.

Online Software and Web Services: Web Apps, Widgets, and Gadgets

We are all used to installing software on our PCs. But as the Web and e-commerce move towards a service model, applications increasingly will be running off Web servers. Instead of buying a "product" in a box, you will be paying for a Web service instead. There are many kinds of Web services now available, many free, all the way from full-function applications, such as Microsoft Office 365, to much smaller chunks of code called "widgets" and "gadgets."

Widgets pull content and functionality from one place on the Web to a place where you want it, such as on your Web page, blog, or Facebook page. You can see Web widget services most clearly in photo sites such as Picnik.com, which offers a free photo-editing application that is powerful and simple to use. Facebook's Like button is a widget that is embedded in more than 7.5 million Web sites. Walmart, eBay, and Amazon, along with many other retailers, are creating shopping widgets that users can drag to their blogs or profile pages on various social networks so visitors can shop at a full-function online store without having to leave the page. Yahoo, Google, MSN, and Apple all have collections of hundreds of widgets available on their Web sites.

Gadgets are closely related to widgets. They are small chunks of code that usually supply a single limited function such as a clock, calendar, or diary. You can see a collection of gadgets at http://www.google.com/ig/directory?synd=open.

Intelligent Personal Assistants

The idea of having a conversation with a computer, having it understand you and be able to carry out tasks according to your direction, has long been a part of science fiction, from the 1968 Hollywood movie *2001: A Space Odyssey*, to an old Apple promotional video depicting a professor using his personal digital assistant to organize his life, gather data, and place orders at restaurants. That was all fantasy. But Apple's Siri, billed as an intelligent personal assistant and knowledge navigator and released in October 2011 for the iPhone 4S, has many of the capabilities of the computer assistants found in fiction. Siri has a natural language, conversational interface, situational awareness, and is capable of carrying out many tasks based on verbal commands by delegating requests to a variety of different Web services. For instance, you can ask Siri to find a restaurant nearby that serves Italian food. Siri may show you an ad for a local restaurant in the process. Once you have identified a restaurant you would like to eat at, you can ask Siri to make a reservation using OpenTable. You can also ask Siri to place an appointment on your calendar, search Google (or Bing) for airline flights, and figure out what's the fastest route between your current location and a destination using public transit. The answers are not always completely accurate, but critics have been impressed with its uncanny abilities. Siri is currently available on the iPhone 4S, the iPhone 5, the third and fourth generation iPad, iPad Mini, and the fifth generation iPod Touch.

In 2012, Google released its version of an intelligent assistant for Android-based smartphones, which it calls Google Now. Google Now is part of the Google Search mobile application. While Google Now has many of the capabilities of Apple's Siri, it attempts to go further by predicting what users may need based on situational awareness, including physical location, time of day, previous location history, calendar, and expressed interests based on previous activity, as described in its patent application (United States Patent Office, 2012). For instance, if you often search for a particular musician or style of music, Google Now might provide recommendations for similar music. If it knows that you go to a health club every other day, Google Now will remind you not to schedule events during these periods. If it knows that you typically read articles about health issues, the system might monitor Google News for similar articles and make recommendations. Other intelligent personal assistants include Samsung's S Voice, LG's Voice Now, and Microsoft's Cortana.

2.6 MOBILE APPS: THE NEXT BIG THING IS HERE

The use of mobile devices such as smartphones and tablet computers in e-commerce has truly exploded, as has the use of mobile apps. Worldwide, according to 451 Research, there are over 1.8 billion active mobile app users worldwide, and this number is expected to increase to over 3 billion by 2018. Although the United States accounts for the most mobile app downloads on an absolute basis, countries in Asia, such as Malaysia, Indonesia, the Philippines, South Korea, and Taiwan, have much higher app download rates on a per-user basis, based on activity on InMobi's mobile ad network (see the opening case in Chapter 6, *InMobi's Global Mobile Ad Network* for further information on InMobi).

Although using mobile browsers to access mobile Web sites remains popular, increasingly more and more time is being spent with mobile apps. For instance, the average U.S. consumer spends almost 2 hours and 45 minutes per day on smartphones and tablets, 86% of which is spent within apps and only 14% using a mobile Web browser (Khalaf, 2014). In United Kingdom, a much higher percentage of users access

Twitter, Facebook, and LinkedIn via a mobile app versus a mobile browser. However, mobile phone users in the United Kingdom are still more likely to use a mobile Web browser for shopping than an app.

In Finland, 80% of smartphone owners in 2014 used mobile apps on their devices, a 150% increase from 2012. Activities that are popular on apps include accessing social networks such as Facebook and Instagram, using Google Maps, using messaging apps such as WhatsApp, listening to music on Spotify, watching online video on YouTube, and playing games. Social networks are the dominant mobile app activity in Australia, with almost two-thirds of mobile Internet users using such apps monthly. As with Finland, games, maps, and entertainment apps are also popular. In France, the top mobile app ranked by unique visitors is YouTube. We examine development of mobile apps and mobile Web sites in further detail in Chapter 3. *Insight on Business: Apps For Everything: The App Ecosystem* also gives you some further background on mobile apps.

PLATFORMS FOR MOBILE APPLICATION DEVELOPMENT

Unlike mobile Web sites, which can be accessed by any Web-enabled mobile device, native apps, which are designed specifically to operate using the mobile device's hardware and operating system, are platform-specific. Applications for the iPhone, iPad, and other iOS devices are written in the Objective-C programming language using the iOS SDK (software developer kit). Applications for Android operating system–based phones typically are written using Java, although portions of the code may be in the C or C++ programming language. BlackBerry apps also are written in Java. Applications for Windows mobile devices are written in C or C++. In addition to creating native apps using a programming language such as Objective-C or Java, there are also hundreds of low-cost or open source app development toolkits that make creating cross-platform mobile apps relatively easy and inexpensive without having to use a device-specific programming language. See Section 3.6 in Chapter 3 for more information.

APP MARKETPLACES

Once written, applications are distributed through various marketplaces. Android apps for Android-based phones are distributed through Google Play, which is controlled by Google. iPhone applications are distributed through Apple's App Store. BlackBerry applications can be found in RIM's App World, while Microsoft operates the Windows Phone Marketplace for Windows mobile devices. Apps can also be purchased from third-party vendors such as Amazon's Appstore. It is important to distinguish "native" mobile apps, which run directly on a mobile device and rely on the device's internal operating system, from Web apps referred to in Section 2.5, which install into your browser, although these can operate in a mobile environment as well.

INSIGHT ON BUSINESS

APPS FOR EVERYTHING: THE APP ECOSYSTEM

When Steve Jobs introduced the iPhone in January 2007, no one—including himself—envisioned that the device would launch a revolution in consumer and business software, or become a major e-commerce platform, let alone a game platform, advertising platform, and general media platform for television shows, movies, videos, and e-books. In short, it's become the personal computer all over again, just in a much smaller form factor.

The iPhone's original primary functions, beyond being a cell phone, were to be a camera, text messaging device, and Web browser. What Apple initially lacked for the iPhone were software applications that would take full advantage of its computing capabilities. The solution was software developed by outside developers—tens of thousands of outside developers—who were attracted to the mission by potential profits and fame from the sale or free distribution of their software applications on a platform approved by the leading innovator in handheld computing and cellular devices. More than two-thirds of apps are free. Every month, Apple receives thousands of new apps from over 9 million registered developers who may be teenagers in a garage, major video game developers, or major publishers, as well as Fortune 500 consumer products firms using apps for marketing and promotion.

In July 2008, Apple introduced the App Store, which provides a platform for the distribution and sale of apps by Apple as well as by independent developers. Following in the footsteps of the iTunes music store, Apple hoped that the software apps—most free—would drive sales of the iPhone device. It was not expecting the App Store itself to become a major source of revenue. Fast forward to 2014: there are now an estimated 1.2 million approved apps available for download from the App Store. Other smartphone developers

also followed suit: there are also thousands of apps available for Android phones, BlackBerrys, and Windows phones. As of June 2014, more than 75 billion apps had been downloaded from the App Store, and somewhere between 2 and 3 billion apps are downloaded each month. Apple has reported that customers spent over $10 billion in the App Store in 2013, generating an estimated profit for Apple of about $3 billion. Even so, Apple's primary goal in offering apps is not to make money from them, but instead to drive sales of devices—the iPhones, iPads, and iPods that need software to become useful. It's the reverse of printer companies who make cheap printers in order to sell expensive ink. At the same time, apps tie the customer to a hardware platform: as you add more and more apps to your phone, the cost of switching to, say, an Android, rises with each new app installed.

The app phenomenon, equally virulent on Android and BlackBerry operating system platforms, has spawned a new digital ecosystem: tens of thousands of developers, a wildly popular hardware platform, and millions of consumers looking for a computer in their pocket that can replace their now clunky desktop-laptop Microsoft Windows computers, do a pretty good job as a digital media center while on the road, and, by the way, serve as a cell phone.

The range of applications among the 1.2 million or so apps on the Apple platform is staggering and defies brief description. Currently, there are 24 different categories. You can use the Genius feature to recommend new apps based on ones you already have. There are so many apps that searching for a particular app can be a problem unless you know the name of the app or the developer. Google is probably the best search engine for apps. Enter a search term like "Kraft app" and you'll find that Kraft has an app called iFood Assistant that provides recipes

(continued)

using Kraft products. The most popular app categories are games, education, business, lifestyle, and entertainment.

The implications of the app ecosystem for e-commerce are significant. The smartphone in your pocket becomes not only a general-purpose computer, but also an always-present shopping tool for consumers, as well as an entirely new marketing and advertising platform for vendors. Early e-commerce applications using desktops and laptops were celebrated as allowing people to shop in their pajamas. Smartphones extend this range from pajamas to office desktops to trains, planes, and cars, all fully clothed. You can shop anywhere, shop everywhere, and shop all the time, in between talking, texting, watching video, and listening to music.

Almost all of the top 100 brands have a presence in at least one of the major app stores, and more than 90% have an app in the Apple App Store. Here are a few examples of how some different firms are using apps to advance and support their brands:

- Converse's Sampler: Allows users to take a picture and "try on" a pair of shoes to see how they look in the clothes they're wearing, as well as to immediately purchase the shoes
- Benjamin Moore's Color Capture: Enables users to match colors and paints
- Colgate-Palmolive's Max White Photo Recharger: Enables users to whiten their teeth in photos
- Tiffany's Engagement Ring Finder: Lets users view diamonds by size, shape, setting, metal, and design
- Charmin's SitOrSquat: Restroom Finder: Provides users with locations of nearest public

bathrooms, including cleanliness reviews, availability of changing tables, and handicapped access.

There are, of course, dangers in any ecosystem dominated by a single company. The Apple iOS platform is closed and proprietary, a walled garden, a limiting sandbox. The apps you buy there can play nowhere else. Many apps are incredibly single-purposed and limited in applicability. The apps don't come with any warranty. Because Apple controls who can play in the sandbox, there is the possibility, even the likelihood, that Apple acts as a censor of content, or as a monopolist that prevents certain applications from entering the marketplace, or more likely, as an arbitrary, inscrutable bureaucratic machine that decides which apps will play and which will not. For instance, Apple has removed applications because of sexually themed content. Such programs often appear on the store's list of most-downloaded apps. Clearly Apple is concerned the App Store might become an adult digital theme park that would turn off parents and families who are the target audience for iPhone and iPad sales. In 2012, for the first time, Apple was forced to remove malware from its App Store. A Russian app entitled "Find and Call" purported to simplify users' contacts lists, but instead stole those contacts and uploaded the address book to a remote server, spamming those addresses. In 2013, researchers at Georgia Tech created an app that was able to elude all of Apple iOS's most current security tools, including sandboxing, code signing, and various anti-exploit technologies. Thus far, most Apple app malware has been targeted toward jailbroken iPhones. However, clearly, the app ecosystem is not immune to many of the same issues that apply to the Internet and e-commerce at large.

SOURCES: "App Store Metrics," Pocketgamer.biz, accessed September 3, 2014; "iTunes App Store Now Has 1.2 Million Apps, Has Seen 75 Billion Downloads to Date," by Sara Perez, Techcrunch.com, June 2, 2014; "Apple's 2013 App Sales Top $10 Billion," by Daisuke Wakabayahsi, *Wall Street Journal*, January 7, 2014; "Global Brands in the Mobile Landscape," by Anne Hezemans, *Distimo*, October 2013; "Researchers Outwit Apple, Plant Malware in App Store," by Gregg Keizer, *Computerworld*, August 20, 2013; "Apple: App Store Now Makes Over $1 Billion in Profits Per Year," SeekingAlpha.com, May 30, 2013; "First Instance of iOS App Store Malware Detected, Removed," by Christina Bonnington, Wired.com, July 5, 2012; "The Apps Strategies of the Top 100 Brands," by Haydn Shaughnessy, Forbes.com, October 27, 2011; "The State of Mobile Apps," by The Nielsen Company, June 1, 2010; "Mobile Apps and Consumer Product Brands," by Tobi Elkin, eMarketer, March 2010; "Apple Bans Some Apps for Sex-Tinged Content," by Jenna Wortham, *New York Times*, February 22, 2010; "Inside the App Economy," by Douglas MacMillan, *BusinessWeek*, October 22, 2009.

CASE STUDY

Akamai Technologies:
Attempting to Keep Supply Ahead of Demand

I n 2014, the amount of Internet traffic generated by YouTube alone is greater than the amount of traffic on the entire Internet in 2000. Because of video streaming and the explosion in mobile devices demanding high-bandwidth applications, Internet traffic has increased over 500% since 2009 and is predicted to triple over the next 5 years (see **Figure 2.20**). Internet video is now a majority of Internet traffic and will reach almost 80% by 2018, according to Cisco. Experts call services like YouTube, Netflix, and high definition streaming video "net bombs" because they threaten the effective operation of the Internet. Mobile platform

| FIGURE 2.20 | THE GROWTH OF INTERNET TRAFFIC |

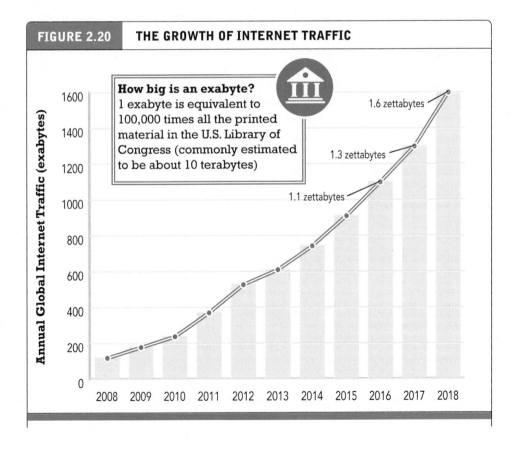

How big is an exabyte?
1 exabyte is equivalent to 100,000 times all the printed material in the U.S. Library of Congress (commonly estimated to be about 10 terabytes)

traffic is growing at over 60% and will soon push cellular networks and the Internet to their capacities. Cisco estimates that annual global Internet traffic will be around 1.6 zettabytes in 2018: that's 1,600 exabytes, or, in other words, 16 with 19 zeroes behind it!

Analysts differ on how fast Internet capacity is growing. Large telecommunication companies argue that demand will soon overwhelm capacity, while other experts argue that Internet bandwidth can double every year for a very long time and easily keep up with demand. Perhaps they're both right: Internet capacity can expand to keep up with demand if sufficient capital is invested in backbone and local networks. That's a big "if." As a result, and in order to raise revenue, nearly all the large ISPs have bandwidth caps that require heavy users of video to pay more for their Internet service. More charges based on usage are in the pipeline.

In today's broadband environment, the threshold of patience is very low. Increased video and audio customer expectations are bad news for anyone seeking to use the Web for delivery of high-quality multimedia content and high definition video. Akamai is one of the Web's major helpers, and an overwhelming majority of the Web's top companies use Akamai's services to speed the delivery of content. Akamai serves more than 15 terabits of Web traffic per second.

Slow-loading Web pages and Web content sometimes result from poor design, but more often than not, the problem stems from the underlying infrastructure of the Internet. The Internet is a collection of networks that has to pass information from one network to another. Sometimes the handoff is not smooth. Every 1,500-byte packet of information sent over the Internet must be verified by the receiving server and an acknowledgment sent to the sender. This slows down not only the distribution of content such as music, but also slows down interactive requests, such as purchases, that require the client computer to interact with an online shopping cart. Moreover, each packet may go through many different servers on its way to its final destination, multiplying by several orders of magnitude the number of acknowledgments required to move a packet from New York to San Francisco. The Internet today spends much of its time and capacity verifying packets, contributing to a problem called "latency" or delay. For this reason, a single e-mail with a 1-megabyte attached PDF file can create more than 50 megabytes of Internet traffic and data storage on servers, client hard drives, and network backup drives.

Akamai Technologies was founded by Tom Leighton, an MIT professor of applied mathematics, and Daniel Lewin, an MIT grad student, with the idea of expediting Internet traffic to overcome these limitations. Lewin's master's thesis was the theoretical starting point for the company. It described storing copies of Web content such as pictures or video clips at many different locations around the Internet so that one could always retrieve a nearby copy, making Web pages load faster.

Officially launched in August 1998, Akamai's current products are based on the Akamai Intelligent Platform, a cloud platform made up of over 150,000 servers in 92 countries within over 1,200 networks around the world, and all within a single network hop of 85% of all Internet users. Akamai software on these servers allows the platform to identify and block security threats and provide comprehensive knowledge of network conditions, as well as instant device-level detection and optimization.

Akamai's site performance products allow customers to move their Web content closer to end users so a user in New York City, for instance, will be served L.L.Bean pages from the New York Metro area Akamai servers, while users of the L.L.Bean site in San Francisco will be served pages from Akamai servers in San Francisco. Akamai has a wide range of large corporate and government clients: 1 out of every 3 global Fortune 500 companies, the top 30 media and entertainment companies, 97 of the top 100 online U.S. retailers, all branches of the U.S. military, all the top Internet portals, all the major U.S. sports leagues, and so on. In 2014, Akamai delivers between 15% and 30% of all Web traffic, and over 2 trillion daily Internet interactions. Other competitors in the content delivery network (CDN) industry include Limelight Networks, Level 3 Communications, and Mirror Image Internet.

Accomplishing this seemingly simple task requires that Akamai monitor the entire Internet, locating potential sluggish areas and devising faster routes for information to travel. Frequently used portions of a client's Web site, or large video or audio files that would be difficult to send to users quickly, are stored on Akamai's servers. When a user requests a song or a video file, his or her request is redirected to an Akamai server nearby and the content served from this local server. Akamai's servers are placed in Tier 1 backbone supplier networks, large ISPs, universities, and other networks. Akamai's software determines which server is optimum for the user and then transmits the "Akamaized" content locally. Web sites that are "Akamaized" can be delivered anywhere from 4 to 10 times as fast as non-Akamaized content. Akamai has developed a number of other business services based on its Internet savvy, including targeted advertising based on user location and zip code, content security, business intelligence, disaster recovery, on-demand bandwidth and computing capacity during spikes in Internet traffic, storage, global traffic management, and streaming services. Akamai also offers a product called Advertising Decision Solutions, which provides companies with intelligence generated by the Internet's most accurate and comprehensive knowledge base of Internet network activity. Akamai's massive server deployment and relationships with networks throughout the world enable optimal collection of geography and bandwidth-sensing information. As a result, Akamai provides a highly accurate knowledge base with worldwide coverage. Customers integrate a simple program into their Web server or application server. This program communicates with the Akamai database to retrieve the very latest information. The Akamai network of servers is constantly mapping the Internet, and at the same time, each company's software is in continual communication with the Akamai network. The result: data is always current. Advertisers can deliver ads based on country, region, city, market area, area code, county, zip code, connection type, and speed. You can see several interesting visualizations of the Internet that log basic real-time Web activity by visiting the Akamai Web site.

The shift towards cloud computing and the mobile platform as well as the growing popularity of streaming video have provided Akamai with new growth opportunities. As more businesses and business models are moving to the Web, Akamai has seen its client base continue to grow beyond the most powerful Internet retailers and online content providers. In 2014, Akamai made a push to encourage Hollywood studios to

SOURCES: "Facts & Figures," Akamai.com, accessed September 3, 2014; "Akamai in 60 Seconds," Akamai.com, accessed September 3, 2014; "The State of the Internet, 1st Quarter 2014 Report," by Akamai Technologies, Inc., June 28, 2014; "Cisco Visual Networking Index, 2013–2018," by Cisco Systems, Inc., June 10, 2014; "Akamai Appeals to Hollywood Studios at NAB 2014," by Troy Dreier, Streamingmedia.com, April 7, 2014; "Akamai Completes Acquisition of Prolexic," Akamai.com, February 18, 2014; "You Think the Internet is Big Now? Akamai Needs to Grow 100-Fold," by Mathew Ingram, GigaOM.com, June 20, 2012; "Akamai Eyes Acceleration Boost for Mobile Content," by Stephen Lawson, *Computerworld*, March 20, 2012; "To Cash In on Wave of Web Attacks, Akamai Launches Standalone Security Business," by Andy Greenberg, Forbes.com, February 21, 2012.

use the cloud for feature films. Akamai announced that it was partnering with Aspera, a high-speed file transfer company, to develop the capability to upload and download large video files fast enough for business use, including feature films. Akamai had already developed partnerships with companies that allow movie studios to convert movie files from one format to another as well as to apply DRM protections all in one step. Establishing partnerships with movie studios represents big business for Akamai, with an increasing amount of media consumption taking place on mobile devices through the cloud.

Akamai is also acutely aware of the increase in cybercrime as more traffic migrates to the Internet. Growth in Internet traffic is good news for Akamai, but the company must also now deal with politically motivated cyberattacks, organized crime online, and state-sponsored cyberwarfare. In 2014, Akamai improved its Kona Site Defender tool, which offers a variety of security measures for Akamai clients. The tool protects against Distributed Denial of Service (DDoS) attacks and includes a firewall for Web applications. Akamai also upgraded Site Defender's Web Application Firewall feature and developed modifications to the tool that make it easier for its users to use. Akamai has continued to acquire security companies in 2014, purchasing Prolexic Technologies, a cloud-based security provider specializing in protecting data centers from DDoS attacks. With so many businesses now dependent on the uninterrupted flow of content over the Internet, Akamai is in a very strong position to sell security services to its customers. However, as impressive as Akamai's operation has become, it may not be nearly enough to cope with the next 5 to 10 years of Internet growth.

Case Study Questions

1. Why does Akamai need to geographically disperse its servers to deliver its customers' Web content?

2. If you wanted to deliver software content over the Internet, would you sign up for Akamai's service? Why or why not?

3. What advantages does an advertiser derive from using Akamai's service? What kinds of products might benefit from this kind of service?

4. Do you think Internet users should be charged based on the amount of bandwidth they consume, or on a tiered plan where users would pay in rough proportion to their usage?

| 2.8 | **REVIEW** |

KEY CONCEPTS

- ■ Discuss the origins of, and the key technology concepts behind, the Internet.

- The Internet has evolved from a collection of mainframe computers located on a few U.S. college campuses to an interconnected network of thousands of networks and millions of computers worldwide.
- The history of the Internet can be divided into three phases: the Innovation Phase (1961-1974), the Institutionalization Phase (1975-1995), and the Commercialization Phase (1995 to the present).
- Packet switching, TCP/IP, and client/server technology are key technology concepts behind the Internet.
- The mobile platform has become the primary means for accessing the Internet.
- Cloud computing refers to a model of computing in which firms and individuals obtain computing power and software applications over the Internet, rather than purchasing the hardware and software and installing it on their own computers.
- Internet protocols and utility programs such as HTTP, SMTP and POP, SSL and TLS, FTP, Telnet, Ping, and Tracert provide a number of Internet services.

- ■ Explain the current structure of the Internet.

- The main structural elements of the Internet are: the backbone (composed primarily high-bandwidth fiber optic cable), IXPs (hubs that use high-speed switching computers to connect to the backbone), CANs (campus areas networks) and ISPs (which deal with the "last mile" of service to homes and offices).
- *Governing bodies*, such as IAB, ICANN, IESG, IETF, ISOC, and W3C. Although they do not control the Internet, they have influence over it and monitor its operations.

- ■ Understand the limitations of today's Internet and the potential capabilities of the Internet of the future.

- To envision what the Internet of tomorrow will look like, we must first look at the limitations of today's Internet, which include bandwidth limitations, quality of service limitations, network architecture limitations, language limitations, and limitations arising from the wired nature of the Internet.
- Internet2 is a consortium working together to develop and test new technologies for potential use on the Internet. Other groups are working to expand Internet bandwidth via improvements to fiber optics. Wireless LAN and 4G technologies are providing users of smartphones and tablet computers with increased access to the Internet and its various services. The increased bandwidth and expanded connections will result in a number of benefits, including latency solutions; guaranteed service levels; lower error rates; and declining costs. The Internet of Things will be a big part of the Internet of the future, with more and more sensor-equipped machines and devices connected to the Internet.

- ■ Understand how the Web works.

- The Web was developed during 1989–1991 by Dr. Tim Berners-Lee, who created a computer program that allowed formatted pages stored on the Internet to be linked using keywords (hyperlinks). In 1993, Marc Andreessen created the first graphical Web browser, which made it possible to view documents on the Web graphically and created the possibility of universal computing.
- The key concepts you need to be familiar with in order to understand how the Web works are hypertext, HTTP, URLS, HTML, XML, Web server software, Web clients, and Web browsers.

■ **Describe how Internet and Web features and services support e-commerce.**

• Together, the Internet and the Web make e-commerce possible by allowing computer users to access product and service information and to complete purchases online.

• Some of the specific features that support e-commerce include e-mail, instant messaging, search engines, online forums (message boards), streaming media, and cookies.

• Web 2.0 features and services include social networks, blogs, RSS, podcasts, wikis, music and video services, Internet telephony, and online software and services.

■ **Understand the impact of m-commerce applications.**

• The use of mobile devices such as smartphones and tablet computers in e-commerce has truly exploded, as has the use of mobile apps.

• Smartphone and tablet users spent the majority of their time using mobile apps rather than the mobile Web.

• There are a variety of different platforms for mobile application development including Objective-C (for iOS devices), Java (BlackBerrys and Android smartphones), and C and C++ (Windows mobile devices and some BlackBerry coding).

• Mobile apps for the iPhone are distributed through Apple's App Store, for BlackBerrys through RIM's App World, for Android devices through Google Play, and for Windows mobile devices through Microsoft's Windows Phone Marketplace. There are also third-party vendors such as Amazon's Appstore.

QUESTIONS

1. What advantages does client/server computing have over mainframe computing?
2. What are three different types of cloud computing models that have been developed?
3. Why is packet switching so essential to the Internet?
4. What are four Internet protocols besides HTTP (the Web) and sending e-mail (SMTP)?
5. What are the three main phases in the evolution of the Internet? Briefly describe each.
6. What is the difference between video conferencing and telepresence?
7. Why are smartphones a disruptive technology?
8. What types of companies form the Internet backbone today?
9. Identify the various types of narrowband and broadband ISP Internet connections. Of all, which is the fastest and which is the slowest?
10. What is the Internet of Things and how is it being created and enabled?
11. Explain what domain names, URLs, and IP addresses are and provide an example of each. How are they used when a user is browsing the Web?
12. What are the main mobile platforms used by mobile devices?
13. What technologies and tools do governments use to monitor, censor, and limit their citizens' activities on the Internet?
14. Identify the layers used in Internet technology. What is their importance to Internet communications?
15. Describe at least two differences between a public Web server connected to the Internet and an end-user's computer connected to the Internet.
16. Define and contrast the "First Mile" and "Last Mile." What is the importance of making these distinctions in Internet telecommunications?
17. What are three concerns about the Internet of Things?
18. What is the difference between HTML and XML?
19. Identify and describe four Internet services besides e-mail that enable individual users to communicate with each other through text.
20. Explain how apps are distributed once they have been created.

PROJECTS

1. Review the opening case on augmented reality. What developments have occurred since this case was written in November 2014?

2. Locate where cookies are stored on your computer. (They are probably in a folder entitled "Cookies" within your browser program.) List the top 10 cookies you find and write a brief report describing the kinds of sites that placed the cookies. What purpose do you think the cookies serve? Also, what do you believe are the major advantages and disadvantages of cookies? In your opinion, do the advantages outweigh the disadvantages, or vice versa?

3. Call or visit the Web sites of a cable provider, DSL provider, and satellite provider to obtain information on their Internet services. Prepare a brief report summarizing the features, benefits, and costs of each. Which is the fastest? What, if any, are the downsides of selecting any of the three for Internet service (such as additional equipment purchases)?

4. Select two countries (excluding the United States) and prepare a short report describing their basic Internet infrastructure. Are they public or commercial? How and where do they connect to backbones within the United States?

5. Investigate the Internet of Things. Select one example and describe what it is and how it works.

REFERENCES

Arstechnica.com. "Capitol Hill, The Internet, and Broadband: An Ars Technica Quarterly Report." (September 2010).

Akamai Inc. "Akamai's State of the Internet Q1 2014 Report." (August 2014).

Berners-Lee, Tim; Robert Cailliau; Ari Luotonen; Henrik Frystyk Nielsen; and Arthur Secret. "The World Wide Web." *Communications of the ACM* (August 1994).

Bluetooth.com. "What Is Bluetooth Technology." (2014).

Brandt, Richard. "Net Assets: How Stanford's Computer Science Department Changed the Way We Get Information." *Stanford Magazine* (November/December 2004).

Bush, Vannevar. "As We May Think." *Atlantic Monthly* (July 1945).

Cerf, V., and R. Kahn, "A Protocol for Packet Network Intercommunication." *IEEE Transactions on Communications*, Vol. COM-22, No. 5, pp 637-648 (May 1974).

Chen, Brian X., and Nick Wingfield. "Smart TVs are Next Bet for Makers as Sales Languish." *New York Times* (January 6. 2014).

comScore. "comScore Releases July 2014 U.S. Search Engine Rankings." (August 14, 2014a).

comScore. "Video in Canada." (September 22, 2014b).

eMarketer, Inc. "Internet Users and Penetration Worldwide, 2012–2018." (May 2014a).

eMarketer, Inc. "US Internet Users and Population, 2012–2018." (February 2014b).

eMarketer, Inc. "Mobile Phone Users Worldwide, 2012–2018." (June 2014c).

eMarketer, Inc. "Smartphone Users and Penetration Worldwide, 2012–2018." (June 2014d).

eMarketer, Inc. "US Mobile Phone Internet Users and Penetration, 2012–2018." (April 2014e).

eMarketer, Inc. "Fixed Broadband Households and Penetration Worldwide, by Region, 2013–2018." (November 13, 2014f).

eMarketer, Inc. "Mobile Phone Internet Users and Penetration Worldwide, 2012–2018." (June 2014g).

eMarketer, Inc. "Search Engine Users Worldwide, by Age and Region, Q4 2013." (March 4, 2014h).

eMarketer, Inc., "US Bloggers, 2012–2018." (March 2014i).

eMarketer, Inc. "US Blog Readers, 2012–2018." (February 2014j).

Federal Networking Council. "FNC Resolution: Definition of 'Internet.'" (October 24, 1995).

Gara, Tom. "Skype's Incredible Rise, in One Image." Blogs.wsj.com (January 15, 2014).

Gartner, Inc. "Forecast: Public Cloud Services, Worldwide, 2012–2018, 1Q14 Update." (March 31, 2014a).

Gartner, Inc. "Gartner Says Annual Smartphone Sales Surpassed Sales of Feature Phones for the First Time in 2013." (February 13, 2014b).

Gartner, Inc. "Gartner Says Smartphone Sales Grew 46.5 Percent in Second Quarter of 2013 and Exceeded Feature Phone Sales for First Time." (August 14, 2013).

Gartner, Inc. "Gartner Says the Internet of Things Installed Base Will Grow to 26 Billion Units by 2020." (December 12, 2013).

Geni.net. "Global Environment for Network Innovations." (accessed September 2014).

Gross, Grant. "NSF Seeks Ambitious Next-Generation Internet Project." *Computerworld* (August 29, 2005).

Hamilton, David. "US Phone Customers Move from Incumbent Carriers to VoIP: Fcc Report." Thewhir.com (July 21, 2014).

IDC. "The Internet of Things is Poised to Change Everything, Says IDC." (October 3, 2013).

IEEE Computer Society. "Top Trends for 2013." (2013).

Infonetics Research. "2014 VoIP and UC Services and Subscribers." (April 2014).

Ingraham, Nathan. "Apple Has Sold More Than 800 Million iOS Devices, 130 Million New iOS Users in the Last Year." Theverge.com (June 2, 2014).

Internet2. "Internet2 Planned 100 Gigabit Infrastructure Topology; Internet2 Network." Internet2.edu (September 2011).

Internet Corporation for Assigned Names and Numbers (ICANN). "ICANN Approves Historic Change to Internet 's Domain System." (June 20, 2011a).

Internet Corporation for Assigned Names and Numbers (ICANN). "Top-Level Domains (gTLDs)." (2011b).

ISOC.org. "ISOC's Standards Actitivies." *Internet Society* (September 2010).

Internet Society. " World IPv6 Launch on June 6, 2012, To Bring Permanent IPv6 Deployment." (January 2012).

Internet Society. "RFC 2616: Hypertext Transfer Protocol-HTTP/1.1." (June 1999).

Internet Society. "RFC 0959: File Transfer Protocol." (October, 1985).

Keizer, Gregg. "Windows 8 May Be Selling, But Different Figures Define Its Use." Pcworld.com (February 23, 2014).

Khalef, Simon. "Apps Solidify Leadership Six Years into the Mobile Revolution." Flurry.com (April 1, 2014).

Kleinrock, Leonard. *1964 Communication Nets: Stochastic Message Flow and Delay.* New York: McGraw-Hill (1964).

Leiner, Barry M.; Vinton G. Cerf; David D. Clark; Robert E. Kahn; Leonard Kleinrock; Daniel C. Lynch; Jon Postel; Larry G. Roberts; and Stephen Wolff. "All About the Internet: A Brief History of the Internet." *Internet Society* (ISOC) (August 2000).

Marketshare.hitslink.com. "Top Browser Share Trend." (August 2014).

Murphy, Kate. "For the Tech-Savy With a Need for Speed, a Limited Choice of Towns With Fiber." *New York Times* (April 2, 2014).

National Research Foundation. "NSP Leadership in Discovery and Initiative Sparks White House US Ignite Initiative." (June 13, 2012).

Netcraft. "August 2014 Web Server Survey." (August 2014).

Nielsen. "A Look Across Screens: The Cross-Platform Report." (June 2013).

Nielsen. "Mobile Apps Beat the Mobile Web Among US Android Smartphone Users." (August 18, 2011).

Pfanner, Eric. "Ethics Fight Over Domain Names Intensifies." *New York Times* (March 18, 2012).

Radicati Group. "Email Statistics Report, 2014–2018." (April 2014).

SANS Institute (John Pescatore). "Security the 'Internet of Things' Survey." (January 2014).

Troianovski, Anton. "Optical Delusion? Fiber Booms Again, Despite Bust." *Wall Street Journal* (April 2, 2012).

U.S. Department of Commerce. "Letter to ICANN Chairman." http://www.ntia.doc.gov/comments/2008/ICANN_080730.html (July 30, 2008).

Visualware, Inc., "VisualRoute Traceroute Server." (2014).

Zakon, Robert H. "Hobbes' Internet Timeline v8.1." Zakon.org (2005).

Ziff-Davis Publishing. "Ted Nelson: Hypertext Pioneer." Techtv.com (1998).

CHAPTER 3

Building an E-commerce Presence

After reading this chapter, you will be able to:

- Understand the questions you must ask and answer, and the steps you should take, in developing an e-commerce presence.
- Explain the process that should be followed in building an e-commerce presence.
- Identify and understand the major considerations involved in choosing Web server and e-commerce merchant server software.
- Understand the issues involved in choosing the most appropriate hardware for an e-commerce site.
- Identify additional tools that can improve Web site performance.
- Understand the important considerations involved in developing a mobile Web site and building mobile applications.

The Financial Times

A Remodel for 21st Century Publishing Profitability

When the 125-year-old London-based Financial Times (FT) updated its apps with a new browser-based HTML5 Web app in 2011, it became the first major news outlet to employ responsive design tools to create a single app for multiple platforms. FT believed that the HMTL5 app would yield significant cost savings in comparison to building multiple native apps for different platforms, and would also liberate it from app stores and their attendant commission fees. The decision was also triggered by Apple's pronouncement that it would no longer share subscriber data from subscriptions purchased through its App Store.

So when FT began considering its next

© Azimuth Interactive, Inc.

upgrade, it had a firm technological base on which to build. Its next major goal was to satisfy the yearning of a significant portion of its readership who still wanted to be able to read the paper as they always did, from cover to cover. Released in 2013, FT's new Web app has two modes: Live and Morning. The Live version provides frequently updated stories and shifting article arrangement. The Morning version, on the other hand, reproduces the experience of yesteryear, presenting a snapshot of the previous day's news just like the print edition. Because the majority of FT Web app users access the site from their iPads, the upgrade applied only to that channel. A navigation bar allows readers to easily toggle between the two versions and also presents thumbnails for easy navigation to newspaper sections, a search bar, and a refresh button. A new section, My FT, provides article recommendations based on reading history and a place to store personal portfolios and clippings. Clippings are saved articles and links that readers can share with other FT.com users. Articles can be clipped from the Web site on a desktop and saved for later reading within the Web app. Portfolios can include any personal investments the user wants to track. Personal notes can be added to any holding, and articles pertaining to any company or investment can be automatically added to the News tab. Subscribers can also create personalized charts to monitor investment performance vs. performance benchmarks and organize how they view their portfolio. While some of these tools had been available in the original Web app, My FT consolidated them in a handy single-page hub.

But while FT.com subscribers have access to the latest tools and technologies for managing, monitoring, and viewing their investments and sharing articles with fellow readers, they now also experience a digital design that simulates the reading of a newspaper. A fixed-height page and two-column layout limits the amount of up and down scrolling needed to read an article, and a left-to-right swipe navigates to the next article. This format has been found to keep readers engaged longer as they dig deeper into the site. Full-page ads, often including multimedia content, are interspersed between articles and display at each section change. Simulating a television commercial break or an advertisement encountered while turning the pages of a magazine, these ads command a premium. FT's digital subscriptions have long since surpassed print circulation, and the new app design provides additional opportunities for digital advertising growth, including space on article pages in addition to the interstitials. In 2014, a full half of FT's total traffic comes via mobile devices.

Other changes aimed at enhancing the reader experience included new sections for the weekly publications FT Money and FTfm, an analysis of the fund management industry, a new index hub for FT blogs, and beefed-up multimedia story accompaniments such as slideshows and videos. Another new attraction is fastFT, a market-focused, Monday through Friday, live commentary and reporting service offering up short summaries of significant market events that can be expanded to the full story length if desired. In 2014, FT launched its fastFT service for the Samsung Gear S smartwatch, representing its first foray into wearable electronics. The service will stream fastFT headlines to smartwatch users at customizable speeds. FT also made upgrades to its Android app in 2014. The Android version now allows video content, high resolution images optimized for mobile screens, clearer design, and embedded slideshows.

The overarching goal of the revamp was to balance the desires of FT's older, but technologically proficient, audience with the expectations of its newer younger audience. FT wanted to provide its older subscribers a soothingly familiar experience while introducing them to the convenience and efficiencies of modern tools. At the same time, it hoped to keep its younger audience on the site longer, giving FT advertisers more marketing opportunities. Thus far, the results of FT's efforts have been a resounding success. In 2014, FT announced that its circulation had reached an all-time high at 677,000 subscribers, a 13% increase over the previous year. About two-thirds of that total are digital subscribers, and that segment of FT's subscriber base grew 33% over the previous year.

The FT app experience, like that of several other prominent publishers, is essentially marrying the print experience and the digital experience, mixing static daily print content and a more print-like reading experience with dynamic Web-only content and content management tools. But the FT.com—Web app union is equally important. FT wanted to further encourage an emerging trend it had observed among its million readers: channel hopping.

FT invested significant time and resources into adapting storage tools and methods including cookies, the application cache (AppCache), IndexDB, and the bootstrap process so that subscribers could have access even when they had no network connection. The majority of each Web page is JavaScript, Cascading Style Sheets (CSS), templates, advertising, and UI images that do not change from page to page. Most goes into local storage. The Web app automatically caches the content on load, and the page is assembled in the browser using JavaScript. When an online reader goes to an article page, the server only has to send the article content. Everything else is added to the page in the browser. For FT's audience, many of whom switch back and forth between workplace computers and mobile devices, and which also includes a sizable business traveler audience, this means that cached articles, clipped articles, My FT, and even video content is available offline and can even be streamed to in-flight entertainment screens without a network connection.

What's more, FT has discovered that tablet use is more conducive to the consumption of longer, more in-depth pieces. While the smartphone is clearly a device designed for the consumption of short bursts of pertinent information, on first glance, the largest screen would seem to be the most conducive to online reading. But reading in a computer chair at a desk is uncomfortable, and in fact, least reproduces how people used to read books, magazines, and newspapers. With a tablet, readers can relax on the couch or in a cozy chair with a drink and a snack nearby and peacefully scroll through a long article. Both of these observations about its readership informed the decision to offer the static edition. Tablet users, either offline or on, have only limited time to catch up on financial news. If they are inclined to read more and longer, this is not only a positive development for in-depth journalism in general but for FT in particular.

In 2014, Tom Betts, VP of Customer Analytics at FT, and his team also observed that during normal business hours, the desktop site gets the most traffic, but during weekends, a whopping 75% of traffic comes from mobile devices. This informed FT's decision to split its Weekend section into a separate app, FT Weekend. FT Weekend is a graphically rich, premium print product focusing on lifestyle, and the app focuses more on these qualities than the flagship site. FT launched the app in 2014 across all major platforms along with a digital marketing campaign to raise awareness of the new offering. Although there's some chance that FT Weekend will cannibalize some of their main subscriber base going forward, FT is confident that new subscribers who wouldn't otherwise pay for digital editions will do so for premium content from FT Weekend, and that many readers will want access to both. FT will also be able to upsell FT Weekend subscribers, offering them deals on the full version.

FT's revenue mix, like most other former print-only publications, has rapidly morphed from being primarily advertising-based to being primarily subscription-based, with profits declining commensurately. So while the Web app upgrade focused heavily on the goal of increasing subscriptions, it was also designed to bolster stalling digital and mobile advertising revenue, which so far have not been able to replace lost print advertising dollars. Rich media ads, which FT is betting are the future of Web advertising, can be cached on devices and served to the Web app offline. No click is required to reach multimedia content; instead it is part of the content stream as readers move between articles and sections. FT prefers this quality over quantity approach, aiming to persuade advertisers that high-quality rich media ads that directly engage the viewer are worth the premium. Awareness of the browsing and reading habits of its audience is a springboard for further differentiation to come in how content—and advertising—is displayed in each channel. FT's stance on spin-off efforts like FT Weekend is that they're willing to do so, but only if they see both a need and an opportunity.

SOURCES: "The FT Web App," labs.ft.com/articles, accessed November 24, 2014; "Financial Times Moves Into Wearables With Launch of fastFT App on Samsung Gear S," by Angela Haggerty, Thedrum.com, August 29, 2014; "The Financial Times' Mobile-Led Weekend Evolution", World News Publishing Focus, July 26, 2014; "Financial Times Circulation Reaches All-time High at 677,000 Total," by Roy Greenslade, Theguardian.com, July 25, 2014; "More Products, Better Treatment: How and Why the Financial Times Built a Digital FT Weekend," by Jasper Jackson, Themediabriefing. com, July 22, 2014; "Financial Times Debuts FT Weekend App For Growing Lifestyle Audience," FT. com, July 3, 2014; "Financial Times Weighs In on Web vs. Native App Debate, How Technology Has Shaped Its Own Digital Strategy," by Graham Hinchly, Inma.org, January 20, 2014; "The FT Launches FastFT for Live Commentary on 'Market-moving news.' It's Like Twitter with Context," by Paul Sawers, Thenextweb.com, May 29, 2013; "Building The New Financial Times Web App (A Case Study)," by Wilson Page, Smashing Magazine, May 23rd, 2013; "FT App Blends Features of Print, Web," by Charlotte Woolard, BtoB Media Business, May 7, 2013; "Financial Times: 'There is No Drawback to Working in HTML5'," by Stuart Dredge, Apps Blog, Theguardian. com. April 29, 2013; "'Financial Times' Relaunches Web App With 'Live' and 'Morning' Editions," by Lauren Indvik, Mashable.com, April 3, 2013 "FT Relaunches Web App: New App Facilitates Tighter Integration with FT.com," by Bill Mickey, Foliomag.com, April 3, 2013; "The 'Financial Times' Has a Secret Weapon: Data," by Lauren Indvik, Mashable.com, April, 2, 2013.

I n Chapter 2, you learned about e-commerce's technological foundation: the Internet, Web, and the mobile platform. In this chapter, you will examine the important factors that a manager needs to consider when building an e-commerce presence. The focus will be on the managerial and business decisions you must make before you begin, and that you will continually need to make. Although building a sophisticated e-commerce presence isn't easy, today's tools are much less expensive and far more powerful than they were during the early days of e-commerce. You do not have to be Amazon or eBay to create a successful Web e-commerce presence. In this chapter, we focus on both small and medium-sized businesses as well as much larger corporate entities that serve thousands of customers a day, or even an hour. As you will see, although the scale may be very different, the principles and considerations are basically the same.

3.1 IMAGINE YOUR E-COMMERCE PRESENCE

Before you begin to build a Web site or app of your own, there are some important questions you will need to think about and answer. The answers to these questions will drive the development and implementation of your e-commerce presence.

WHAT'S THE IDEA? (THE VISIONING PROCESS)

Before you can plan and actually build an e-commerce presence, you need to have a vision of what you hope to accomplish and how you hope to accomplish it. The vision includes not just a statement of mission, but also identification of the target audience, characterization of the market space, a strategic analysis, a marketing matrix, and a development timeline. It starts with a dream of what's possible, and concludes with a timeline and preliminary budget for development.

If you examine any successful Web site, you can usually tell from the home page what the vision that inspires the site is. If the company is a U.S. public company, you can often find a succinct statement of its vision or mission in the reports it files with the U.S. Securities and Exchange Commission. For Amazon, it's to become the largest marketplace on earth. For Facebook, it's to make the world more open and connected. For Google, it's to organize the world's information and make it universally accessible and useful. The e-commerce presence you want to build may not have such all-encompassing ambitions, but a succinct statement of mission, purpose, and direction is the key factor in driving the development of your project. For instance, the mission of Theknot is to be the Internet's comprehensive, one-stop wedding planning solution.

WHERE'S THE MONEY: BUSINESS AND REVENUE MODEL

Once you have defined a mission statement, a vision, you need to start thinking about where the money will be coming from. You will need to develop a preliminary idea of your business and revenue models. You don't need detailed revenue and cost projections at this point. Instead, you need a general idea of how your business will generate revenues. The basic choices are described in Chapter 5. Basic business models are portal, e-tailer, content provider, transaction broker, market creator, service provider, and community provider (social network).

The basic revenue model alternatives are advertising, subscriptions, transaction fees, sales, and affiliate revenue. There's no reason to adopt a single business or revenue model, and in fact, many firms have multiple models. For instance, *The Financial Times* digital business model is to both sell subscriptions and sell ad space. In addition, they sell unique photographs and gifts. At Theknot, a vertical portal for the wedding industry, you will find ads, affiliate relationships, and sponsorships from major creators of wedding products and services, including a directory to local wedding planners, all of which produce revenue for Theknot.com. Petsmart, the most popular pet Web site in the United States, has a more focused sales revenue model, and presents itself almost entirely as an e-tailer of pet supplies.

WHO AND WHERE IS THE TARGET AUDIENCE

Without a clear understanding of your target audience, you will not have a successful e-commerce presence. There are two questions here: who is your target audience and where can you best reach them? Your target audience can be described in a number of ways: demographics, behavior patterns (lifestyle), current consumption patterns (online vs. offline purchasing), digital usage patterns, content creation preferences (blogs, social networks, sites like Pinterest), and buyer personas (profiles of your typical customer). Understanding the demographics of your target audience is usually the first step. Demographic information includes age, income, gender, and location. In some cases, this may be obvious and in others, much less so. For instance, Harley-Davidson sells motorcycles to a very broad demographic range of varying ages, incomes, and locations, from 34-year-olds to 65-year-olds. Although most of the purchasers are middle-aged men, with middle incomes, many of the men ride with women, and the Harley-Davidson Web site has a collection of women's clothing and several Web pages devoted to women riders. While the majority of men who purchase Harley-Davidsons have modest incomes, a significant group of purchasers are professionals with above-average incomes. Hence, the age and income demographic target is quite broad. What ties Harley-Davidson riders together is not their shared demographics, but their love of the motorcycles and the brand, and the lifestyle associated with touring the highways of America on a powerful motorcycle that sounds like a potato popper. In contrast, a company like Theknot is aimed at women in the 18–34-year-old range who are in varying stages of getting married, with lifestyles that include shopping online, using smartphones and tablets, downloading apps, and using Facebook. This audience is technologically hip. These women read and contribute to blogs, comment on forums, and use Pinterest to find ideas for fashion. A "typical" visitor to Theknot would be a 28-year-old woman who has an engagement ring, is just starting the wedding planning process, has an income of $45,000, lives in the Northeast, and is interested in a beach wedding. There are, of course, other "typical" profiles. For each profile for your Web site you will need to develop a detailed description.

WHAT IS THE BALLPARK? CHARACTERIZE THE MARKETPLACE

The chances of your success will depend greatly on the characteristics of the market you are about to enter, and not just on your entrepreneurial brilliance. Enter into a declining market filled with strong competitors, and you will multiply your chances of failure. Enter into a market that is emerging, growing, and has few competitors, and you stand a better chance. Enter a market where there are no players, and you will either be rewarded handsomely with a profitable monopoly on a successful product no one else thought of (Apple) or you will be quickly forgotten because there isn't a market for your product at this point in time (the Franklin e-book reader circa 1999).

Features of the marketplace to focus on include the demographics of the market and how an e-commerce presence fits into the market. In addition, you will want to know about the structure of the market: competitors and substitute products.

What are the features of the marketplace you are about to enter? Is the market growing, or receding in size? If it's growing, among which age and income groups? Is the marketplace shifting from offline to online delivery? If so, is the market moving towards traditional Web sites, mobile, and/or tablets? Is there a special role for a mobile presence in this market? What percentage of your target audience uses a Web site, smartphone, or tablet? What about social networks? What's the buzz on products like yours? Are your potential customers talking about the products and services you want to offer on Facebook, Twitter, or blogs? How many blogs focus on products like yours? How many Twitter posts mention similar offerings? How many Facebook Likes (signs of customer engagement) are attached to products you want to offer?

The structure of the market is described in terms of your direct competitors, suppliers, and substitute products. You will want to make a list of the top five or ten competitors and try to describe their market share, and distinguishing characteristics. Some of your competitors may offer traditional versions of your products, while others will offer new renditions or versions of products that have new features. You need to find out everything you can about your competitors. What's the market buzz on your competitors? How many unique monthly visitors (UMVs) do they have? How many Facebook Likes, Twitter followers, and/or Pinterest followers? How are your competitors using social sites and mobile devices as a part of their online presence. Is there something special you could do with social networks that your competitors do not? Do a search on customer reviews of their products. You can find online services (some of them free) that will measure the number of online conversations about your competitors, and the total share of Internet voice each of your competitors receives. Do your competitors have a special relationship with their suppliers that you may not have access to? Exclusive marketing arrangements would be one example of a special supplier relationship. Finally, are there substitutes for your products and services? For instance, your site may offer advice to the community of pet owners, but local pet stores or local groups may be a more trusted source of advice on pets.

WHERE'S THE CONTENT COMING FROM?

Web sites are like books: they're composed of a lot of pages that have content ranging from text, to graphics, photos, and videos. This content is what search engines catalog as they crawl through all the new and changed Web pages on the Internet. The content is why your customers visit your site and either purchase things or look at ads that generate revenue for you. Therefore, the content is the single most important foundation for your revenue and ultimate success.

There are generally two kinds of content: static and dynamic. Static content is text and images that do not frequently change, such as product descriptions, photos, or text that you create to share with your visitors. Dynamic content is content that changes regularly, say, daily or hourly. Dynamic content can be created by you, or increasingly, by bloggers and fans of your Web site and products. User-generated content has a number of advantages: it's free, it engages your customer fan base, and search engines are more likely to catalog your site if the content is changing. Other sources of content, especially photos, are external Web sites that aggregate content such as Pinterest, discussed in the opening case in Chapter 1.

KNOW YOURSELF: CONDUCT A SWOT ANALYSIS

A **SWOT analysis** is a simple but powerful method for strategizing about your business and understanding where you should focus your efforts. In a SWOT analysis you describe your strengths, weaknesses, threats, and opportunities. In the example SWOT analysis in **Figure 3.1**, you will see a profile of a typical start-up venture that includes a unique approach to an existing market, a promise of addressing unmet needs in this market, and the use of newer technologies (social and mobile platforms) that older competitors may have overlooked. There are many opportunities to address a large market with unmet needs, as well as the potential to use the initial Web site as a home base and spin-off related or nearby sites, leveraging the investment in design and technology. But there are also weaknesses and threats. Lack of financial and human resources are typically the biggest weakness of start-up sites. Threats include competitors that could develop the same capabilities as you, and low market entry costs, which might encourage many more start-ups to enter the marketplace.

Once you have conducted a SWOT analysis, you can consider ways to overcome your weaknesses and build on your strengths. For instance, you could consider hiring

SWOT analysis
describes a firm's strengths, weaknesses, opportunities, and threats

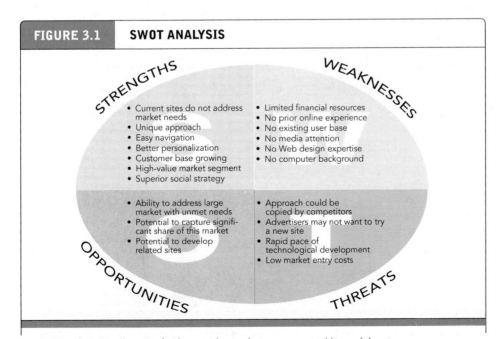

| FIGURE 3.1 | SWOT ANALYSIS |

STRENGTHS
- Current sites do not address market needs
- Unique approach
- Easy navigation
- Better personalization
- Customer base growing
- High-value market segment
- Superior social strategy

WEAKNESSES
- Limited financial resources
- No prior online experience
- No existing user base
- No media attention
- No Web design expertise
- No computer background

OPPORTUNITIES
- Ability to address large market with unmet needs
- Potential to capture significant share of this market
- Potential to develop related sites

THREATS
- Approach could be copied by competitors
- Advertisers may not want to try a new site
- Rapid pace of technological development
- Low market entry costs

A SWOT analysis describes your firm's strengths, weaknesses, opportunities, and threats.

or partnering to obtain technical and managerial expertise, and looking for financing opportunities (including friends and relatives).

DEVELOP AN E-COMMERCE PRESENCE MAP

E-commerce has moved from being a PC-centric activity on the Web to a mobile and tablet-based activity as well. While 80% or more of e-commerce today is conducted using PCs, increasingly smartphones and tablets will be used for purchasing. Currently, smartphones and tablets are used by a majority of Internet users in the United States to shop for goods and services, explore purchase options, look up prices, and access social sites. Your potential customers use these various devices at different times during the day, and involve themselves in different conversations depending on what they are doing—touching base with friends, tweeting, or reading a blog. Each of these are "touch points" where you can meet the customer, and you have to think about how you develop a presence in these different virtual places. **Figure 3.2** provides a roadmap to the platforms and related activities you will need to think about when developing your e-commerce presence.

Figure 3.2 illustrates four different kinds of e-commerce presence: Web site/App, e-mail, social media, and offline media. For each of these types there are different platforms that you will need to address. For instance, in the case of Web sites and/or apps, there are three different platforms: traditional desktop, tablets, and smartphones, each with different capabilities. And for each type of e-commerce presence there are related activities you will need to consider. For instance, in the case of Web sites and apps, you will want to engage in search engine marketing, display ads, affiliate programs, and sponsorships. Offline media, the fourth type of e-commerce presence,

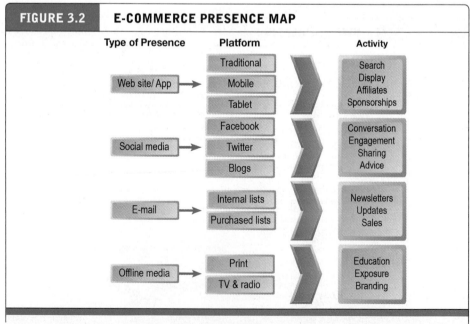

An e-commerce presence requires firms to consider the four different kinds of presence, and the platforms and activities associated with each type of presence.

is included here because many firms use multiplatform or integrated marketing where print ads refer customers to Web sites and apps. The marketing activities in Figure 3.2 are described in much greater detail in Chapters 6 and 7.

DEVELOP A TIMELINE: MILESTONES

Where would you like to be a year from now? It's a good idea for you to have a rough idea of the time frame for developing your e-commerce presence when you begin. You should break your project down into a small number of phases that could be completed within a specified time. Six phases are usually enough detail at this point. **Table 3.1** illustrates a one-year timeline for the development of a start-up Web site.

Note that this example timeline defers the development of a mobile plan until after a Web site and social media plan have been developed and implemented. There is a growing trend, however, to flip this timeline around, and begin with a mobile plan instead (sometimes referred to as mobile first design). Mobile first design has both advantages and disadvantages that will be examined more fully in Section 3.6.

HOW MUCH WILL THIS COST?

It's too early in the process to develop a detailed budget for your e-commerce presence, but it is a good time to develop a preliminary idea of the costs involved. How much you spend on a Web site, for instance, depends on what you want it to do. Simple Web sites can be built and hosted with a first-year cost of €4,000 or less if all the work is done in-house by yourself and others willing to work without pay. A more reasonable budget for a small Web start-up might be €20,000 to €40,000. Here the firm owner would develop all the content at no cost, and a Web designer and programmer would be hired to implement the initial Web site. As discussed later, the Web site would be hosted on a cloud-based server. The Web sites of large firms that offer high levels of

TABLE 3.1	E-COMMERCE PRESENCE TIMELINE	
PHASE	ACTIVITY	MILESTONE
Phase 1: Planning	Envision e-commerce presence; determine personnel	Mission statement
Phase 2: Web site development	Acquire content; develop a site design; arrange for hosting the site	Web site plan
Phase 3: Web Implementation	Develop keywords and metatags; focus on search engine optimization; identify potential sponsors	A functional Web site
Phase 4: Social media plan	Identify appropriate social platforms and content for your products and services	A social media plan
Phase 5: Social media implementation	Develop Facebook, Twitter, and Pinterest presence	Functioning social media presence
Phase 6: Mobile plan	Develop a mobile plan; consider options for porting your Web site to smartphones	A mobile media plan

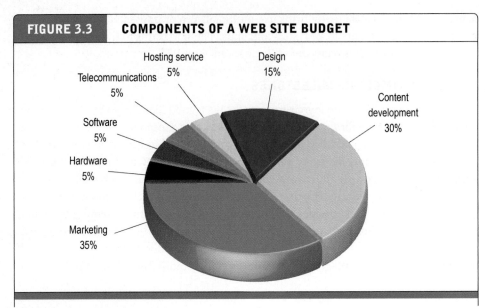

FIGURE 3.3 | **COMPONENTS OF A WEB SITE BUDGET**

While hardware and software costs have fallen dramatically, Web sites face significant design, content development, and marketing costs.

interactivity and linkage to corporate systems can cost several hundred thousand to millions of dollars a year to create and operate.

While how much you spend to build a Web site depends on how much you can afford, and, of course, the size of the opportunity, **Figure 3.3** provides some idea of the relative size of various Web site costs. In general, the cost of hardware, software, and telecommunications for building and operating a Web site has fallen dramatically (by over 50%) in the last decade, making it possible for very small entrepreneurs to build fairly sophisticated sites. At the same time, while technology has lowered the costs of system development, the costs of marketing, content development, and design have risen to make up more than half of typical Web site budgets. The longer-term costs would also have to include site and system maintenance, which are not included here. The costs of developing a mobile site and apps are discussed in Section 3.6.

3.2 | BUILDING AN E-COMMERCE PRESENCE: A SYSTEMATIC APPROACH

Once you have developed a vision of the e-commerce presence you want to build, it's time to start thinking about how to build and implement that presence. Building a successful e-commerce presence requires a keen understanding of business, technology, and social issues, as well as a systematic approach. E-commerce is just too important to be left totally to technologists and programmers.

The two most important management challenges are (1) developing a clear understanding of your business objectives and (2) knowing how to choose the right technology to achieve those objectives. The first challenge requires you to build a plan for developing your firm's presence. The second challenge requires you to understand some of the basic elements of e-commerce infrastructure. Let the business drive the technology.

Even if you decide to outsource the development effort and operation to a service provider, you will still need to have a development plan and some understanding of the basic e-commerce infrastructure issues such as cost, capability, and constraints. Without a plan and a knowledge base, you will not be able to make sound management decisions about e-commerce within your firm.

Let's assume you are a manager for a medium-sized industrial parts firm in Munich, Germany. You have been given a budget of €80,000 to develop an e-commerce presence for the firm. The purpose will be to sell and service the firm's customers, who are mostly small machine and metal fabricating shops, and to engage your customers through a blog and user forum. Where do you start? In the following sections, we will examine developing an e-commerce Web site, and then, at the end of the chapter, discuss some of the more specific considerations involved in developing a mobile site and building mobile applications.

First, you must be aware of the main areas where you will need to make decisions (see **Figure 3.4**). On the organizational and human resources fronts, you will have to bring together a team of individuals who possess the skill sets needed to build and manage a successful e-commerce presence. This team will make the key decisions about business objectives and strategy, technology, design, and social and information policies. The entire development effort must be closely managed if you hope to avoid the disasters that have occurred at some firms.

You will also need to make decisions about hardware, software, and telecommunications infrastructure. The demands of your customers should drive your choices of technology. Your customers will want technology that enables them to find what they want easily, view the product, purchase the product, and then receive the product from

FIGURE 3.4	**FACTORS TO CONSIDER IN DEVELOPING AN E-COMMERCE PRESENCE**

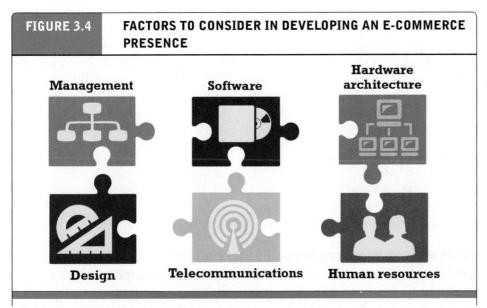

Building an e-commerce presence requires that you systematically consider the many factors that go into the process.

FIGURE 3.5	WEB SITE SYSTEMS DEVELOPMENT LIFE CYCLE

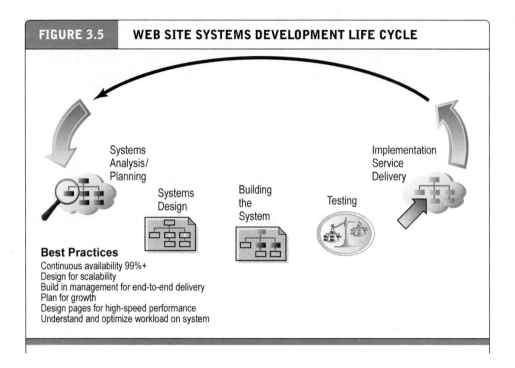

your warehouses quickly. You will also have to carefully consider design. Once you have identified the key decision areas, you will need to think about a plan for the project.

PLANNING: THE SYSTEMS DEVELOPMENT LIFE CYCLE

systems development life cycle (SDLC)
a methodology for understanding the business objectives of any system and designing an appropriate solution

Your second step in building an e-commerce Web site will be creating a plan document. In order to tackle a complex problem such as building an e-commerce site, you will have to proceed systematically through a series of steps. One methodology is the systems development life cycle. The **systems development life cycle (SDLC)** is a methodology for understanding the business objectives of any system and designing an appropriate solution. Adopting a life cycle methodology does not guarantee success, but it is far better than having no plan at all. The SDLC method also helps in creating documents that communicate objectives, important milestones, and the uses of resources to management. **Figure 3.5** illustrates the five major steps involved in the systems development life cycle for an e-commerce site:

- Systems analysis/planning
- Systems design
- Building the system
- Testing
- Implementation

SYSTEMS ANALYSIS/PLANNING: IDENTIFY BUSINESS OBJECTIVES, SYSTEM FUNCTIONALITY, AND INFORMATION REQUIREMENTS

In the systems analysis/planning step of the SDLC, you try to answer the question, "What do we want this e-commerce site to do for our business?" The key point is to let the business decisions drive the technology, not the reverse. This will ensure that your technology platform is aligned with your business. We will assume here that you have identified a business strategy and chosen a business model to achieve your strategic objectives (see Chapter 5). But how do you translate your strategies, business models, and ideas into a working e-commerce Web site?

One way to start is to identify the specific business objectives for your site, and then develop a list of system functionalities and information requirements. **Business objectives** are simply capabilities you want your site to have.

System functionalities are types of information systems capabilities you will need to achieve your business objectives. The **information requirements** for a system are the information elements that the system must produce in order to achieve the business objectives. You will need to provide these lists to system developers and programmers so they know what you as the manager expect them to do.

Table 3.2 describes some basic business objectives, system functionalities, and information requirements for a typical e-commerce site. As shown in the table, there are nine basic business objectives that an e-commerce site must deliver. These objectives must be translated into a description of system functionalities and ultimately into a set of precise information requirements. The specific information requirements for a system

business objectives
capabilities you want your site to have

system functionalities
types of information systems capabilities you will need to achieve your business objectives

information requirements
the information elements that the system must produce in order to achieve the business objectives

TABLE 3.2	SYSTEM ANALYSIS: BUSINESS OBJECTIVES, SYSTEM FUNCTIONALITIES, AND INFORMATION REQUIREMENTS FOR A TYPICAL E-COMMERCE SITE	
BUSINESS OBJECTIVE	**SYSTEM FUNCTIONALITY**	**INFORMATION REQUIREMENTS**
Display goods	Digital catalog	Dynamic text and graphics catalog
Provide product information (content)	Product database	Product description, stocking numbers, inventory levels
Personalize/customize product	Customer on-site tracking	Site log for every customer visit; data mining capability to identify common customer paths and appropriate responses
Engage customers in conversations	On-site blog	Software with blogging and community response functionality
Execute a transaction	Shopping cart/payment system	Secure credit card clearing; multiple payment options
Accumulate customer information	Customer database	Name, address, phone, and e-mail for all customers; online customer registration
Provide after-sale customer support	Sales database	Customer ID, product, date, payment, shipment date
Coordinate marketing/advertising	Ad server, e-mail server, e-mail, campaign manager, ad banner manager	Site behavior log of prospects and customers linked to e-mail and banner ad campaigns
Understand marketing effectiveness	Site tracking and reporting system	Number of unique visitors, pages visited, products purchased, identified by marketing campaign
Provide production and supplier links	Inventory management system	Product and inventory levels, supplier ID and contact, order quantity data by product

typically are defined in much greater detail than Table 3.2 indicates. To a large extent, the business objectives of an e-commerce site are not that different from those of an ordinary retail store. The real difference lies in the system functionalities and information requirements. In an e-commerce site, the business objectives must be provided entirely in digital form without buildings or salespeople, 24 hours a day, 7 days a week.

SYSTEM DESIGN: HARDWARE AND SOFTWARE PLATFORMS

Once you have identified the business objectives and system functionalities, and have developed a list of precise information requirements, you can begin to consider just how all this functionality will be delivered. You must come up with a **system design specification**—a description of the main components in the system and their relationship to one another. The system design itself can be broken down into two components: a logical design and a physical design. A **logical design** includes a data flow diagram that describes the flow of information at your e-commerce site, the processing functions that must be performed, and the databases that will be used. The logical design also includes a description of the security and emergency backup procedures that will be instituted, and the controls that will be used in the system.

A **physical design** translates the logical design into physical components. For instance, the physical design details the specific model of server to be purchased, the software to be used, the size of the telecommunications link that will be required, the way the system will be backed up and protected from outsiders, and so on.

Figure 3.6(a) presents a data flow diagram for a simple high-level logical design for a very basic Web site that delivers catalog pages in HTML in response to HTTP requests from the client's browser, while **Figure 3.6(b)** shows the corresponding physical design. Each of the main processes can be broken down into lower-level designs that are much more precise in identifying exactly how the information flows and what equipment is involved.

BUILDING THE SYSTEM: IN-HOUSE VERSUS OUTSOURCING

Now that you have a clear idea of both the logical and physical designs for your site, you can begin considering how to actually build the site. You have many choices, and much depends on the amount of money you are willing to spend. Choices range from outsourcing everything (including the actual systems analysis and design) to building everything yourself (in-house). **Outsourcing** means that you will hire an outside vendor to provide the services involved in building the site rather than using in-house personnel. You also have a second decision to make: will you host (operate) the site on your firm's own servers or will you outsource the hosting to a Web host provider? These decisions are independent of each other, but they are usually considered at the same time. There are some vendors who will design, build, and host your site, while others will either build or host (but not both). **Figure 3.7** on page 186 illustrates the alternatives.

Build Your Own versus Outsourcing

Let's take the building decision first. If you elect to build your own site, there are a range of options. Unless you are fairly skilled, you should use a pre-built template to create the Web site. For example, Yahoo Stores, Amazon Stores, and eBay all provide

---

system design specification

description of the main components in a system and their relationship to one another

logical design

describes the flow of information at your e-commerce site, the processing functions that must be performed, the databases that will be used, the security and emergency backup procedures that will be instituted, and the controls that will be used in the system

physical design

translates the logical design into physical components

outsourcing

hiring an outside vendor to provide the services you cannot perform with in-house personnel

FIGURE 3.6	A LOGICAL AND A PHYSICAL DESIGN FOR A SIMPLE WEB SITE

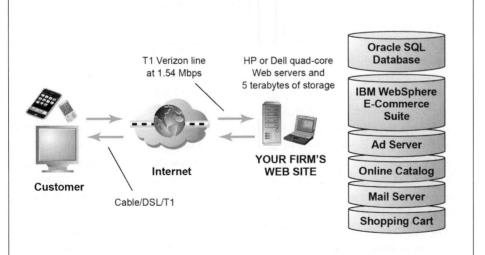

(a) Simple Data Flow Diagram.
This data flow diagram describes the flow of information requests and responses for a simple Web site.

(b) Simple Physical Design.
A physical design describes the hardware and software needed to realize the logical design.

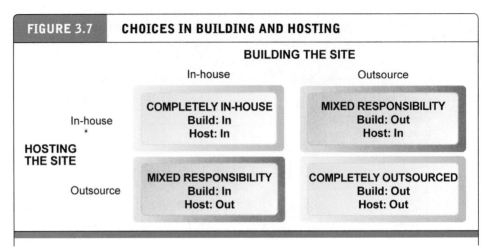

| FIGURE 3.7 | CHOICES IN BUILDING AND HOSTING |

You have a number of alternatives to consider when building and hosting an e-commerce site.

templates that merely require you to input text, graphics, and other data, as well as the infrastructure to run a sales-oriented Web site once it has been created.

If your Web site is not a sales-oriented site requiring a shopping cart, one of the least expensive and most widely used site building tools is WordPress. **WordPress** is a Web site development tool with a sophisticated content management system. A **content management system (CMS)** is a database software program specifically designed to manage structured and unstructured data and objects in a Web site environment. A CMS provides Web managers and designers with a centralized control structure to manage Web site content. WordPress also has thousands of user-built plug-ins and widgets that you can use to extend the functionality of a Web site. Web sites built in WordPress are treated by search engines like any other Web site: their content is indexed and made available to the entire Web community. Revenue-generating ads, affiliates, and sponsors are the main sources of revenue for WordPress sites. Other similar Web site building tools are provided by Google Sites, Wix, Squarespace, and Weebly. While these are the least costly ways to create a Web site, you will be limited to the "look and feel" and functionality provided by the templates and infrastructure supplied by these vendors.

If you have some programming experience, you might decide to build the site yourself "from scratch." There are a broad variety of tools, ranging from those that help you build everything truly "from scratch," such as Adobe Dreamweaver CC and Microsoft Visual Studio, to top-of-the-line prepackaged site-building tools that can create sophisticated sites customized to your needs. **Figure 3.8** illustrates the spectrum of tools available. We will look more closely at the variety of e-commerce software available in Section 3.3.

The decision to build a Web site on your own has a number of risks. Given the complexity of features such as shopping carts, credit card authentication and processing, inventory management, and order processing, the costs involved are high, as are the risks of doing a poor job. You will be reinventing what other specialized firms have already built, and your staff may face a long, difficult learning curve, delaying your entry to market. Your efforts could fail. On the positive side, you may be better able to build a site that does exactly what you want, and, more importantly, develop

WordPress
open source content management and Web site design tool

content management system (CMS)
organizes, stores, and processes Web site content

FIGURE 3.8 THE SPECTRUM OF TOOLS FOR BUILDING YOUR OWN E-COMMERCE SITE

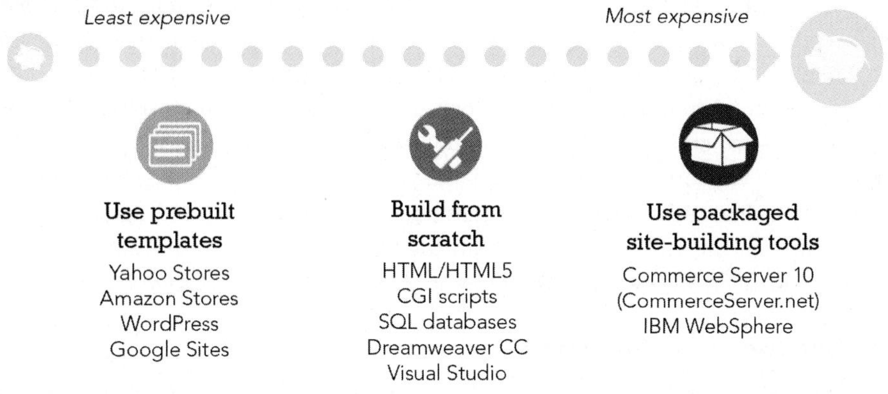

Least expensive
Most expensive
Use prebuilt templates
Yahoo Stores
Amazon Stores
WordPress
Google Sites
Build from scratch
HTML/HTML5
CGI scripts
SQL databases
Dreamweaver CC
Visual Studio
Use packaged site-building tools
Commerce Server 10
(CommerceServer.net)
IBM WebSphere

the in-house knowledge to allow you to change the site rapidly if necessary due to a changing business environment.

If you choose more expensive site-building packages, you will be purchasing state-of-the art software that is well tested. You could get to market sooner. However, to make a sound decision, you will have to evaluate many different packages, and this can take a long time. You may have to modify the package to fit your business needs and perhaps hire additional outside vendors to do the modifications. Costs rise rapidly as modifications mount. A €3,200 package can easily become a €32,000 to €48,000 development project (see **Figure 3.9**).

FIGURE 3.9 COSTS OF CUSTOMIZING E-COMMERCE SOFTWARE PACKAGES

Implementation Costs Factor
12
10
8
6
4
2
0
0
2
4
6
8
10
12
Percent Lines of Code Changed

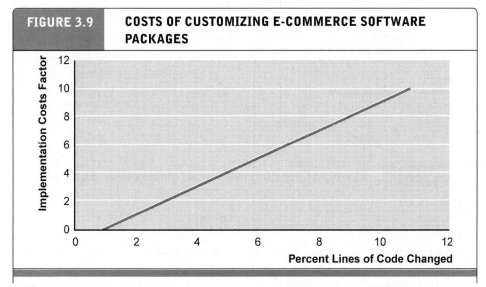

While sophisticated site development software packages appear to reduce costs and increase speed to market, as the modifications required to fit the package to your business needs rise, costs rise rapidly.

In the past, bricks-and-mortar retailers in need of an e-commerce site typically designed the site themselves (because they already had the skilled staff in place and had extensive investments in information technology capital such as databases and telecommunications). However, as Web applications have become more sophisticated, larger retailers today rely heavily on vendors to provide sophisticated Web site capabilities, while also maintaining a substantial internal staff. Small start-ups may build their own sites from scratch using in-house technical personnel in an effort to keep costs low. Medium-size start-ups will often purchase a Web site design and programming expertise from vendors. Very small mom-and-pop firms seeking simple storefronts will use templates like WordPress. For e-commerce sites, the cost of building has dropped dramatically in the last five years, resulting in lower capital requirements for all players (see *Insight on Business: Weebly Makes Building Web Sites Easy and Inexpensive.*)

Host Your Own versus Outsourcing

Now let's look at the hosting decision. Most businesses choose to outsource hosting and pay a company to host their Web site, which means that the hosting company is responsible for ensuring the site is "live," or accessible, 24 hours a day. By agreeing to a monthly fee, the business need not concern itself with many of the technical aspects of setting up a Web server and maintaining it, telecommunications links, nor with staffing needs.

co-location

when a firm purchases or leases a Web server (and has total control over its operation) but locates the server in a vendor's physical facility. The vendor maintains the facility, communications lines, and the machinery

You can also choose to *co-locate*. With a **co-location** agreement, your firm purchases or leases a Web server (and has total control over its operation) but locates the server in a vendor's physical facility. The vendor maintains the facility, communications lines, and the machinery. Co-location has expanded with the spread of virtualization where one server has multiple processors (4 to 16) and can operate multiple Web sites at once with multiple operating systems. In this case, you do not buy the server but rent its capabilities on a monthly basis, usually at one-quarter of the cost of owning the server itself. See **Table 3.3** for a list of some of the major hosting/co-location providers. There is an extraordinary range of prices for co-location, ranging from a few euros a month, to several hundred thousands of euros per month depending on the size of the Web site, bandwidth, storage, and support requirements.

While co-location involves renting physical space for your hardware, you can think of using a cloud service provider as renting virtual space in your provider's infrastructure. Cloud services are rapidly replacing co-location because they are less expensive, and arguably more reliable. Unlike with co-location, your firm does not own

TABLE 3.3	KEY PLAYERS: HOSTING/CO-LOCATION/CLOUD SERVICES
Amazon Web Services (AWS) EC2	Microsoft
CenturyLink	Rackspace
Digital Realty Trust	SoftLayer (IBM)
Fujitsu	Verizon/Terremark
Joyent	Virtualstream
IBM Global Services	

INSIGHT ON BUSINESS

WEEBLY MAKES CREATING WEB SITES EASY

With so many big companies dominating the e-commerce scene, you may wonder if there's a chance for the little guy anymore. The answer is yes: there are still billions left in potential online retail sales, with additional money to be made from advertising revenues. In fact, there's an e-commerce frenzy going on that nearly rivals the dot-com era with one exception: the start-ups have much leaner development models made possible in part by much cheaper technology and social media that can provide inexpensive marketing and sales.

Weebly, a company that was once a "little guy" itself, makes its living by providing valuable Web site solutions to other small businesses. Founded in 2007 by Penn State graduates David Rusenko, Chris Fanini, and Dan Veltri, Weebly provides Web site templates that allow small businesses to create their own Web sites with a full suite of features, including blogs, online stores, and mobile compatibility. Weebly hosts over 20 million sites created with its Web site tools that have over 140 million monthly unique visitors. Users create sites using a drag-and-drop, widget-based tool that works within a Web browser. Weebly's primary customers are the "little guys" hoping to harness the site tools traditionally available only to bigger Web sites and retailers.

Weebly is just one option in an increasingly crowded marketplace for website creation services. Today's offerings are a far cry from early services like GeoCities and AngelFire, which look crude by today's standards. Weebly and its competitors, including Squarespace, Wix, and WordPress, offer much more polished products than their predecessors. The company has a free option with basic features as well as premium plans starting at $4 per month and increasing to only $29 per month for its high-end Business Plan. Over the course of its growth, Weebly has added Google AdSense monetization features, CSS/HTML editing support, and the ability to generate a mobile version of each Web site automatically.

Weebly has increasingly focused on improving its e-commerce services, such as a mobile store and checkout capability, integrated shopping cart, and filtered product search. It also offers basic support for PayPal and Google Checkout. By revamping its e-commerce tools, Weebly hopes to better compete with Amazon, as well as similar user-friendly marketplaces such as Etsy and Shopify. Sixty percent of Weebly users identify themselves as entrepreneurs hoping to create an online presence for their business. One example is Kim Beers. Beers had recently graduated from the University of New Hampshire with a degree in environmental chemistry and had large student loans to pay back. Strapped for cash and looking to come up with thoughtful Christmas gifts for friends, Beers began to make pet toys. They were so well received that she decided to start selling them under the name Woof Purr Studio. Working from her apartment in Concord, New Hampshire, she fashions about 20 different types of non-toxic, environmentally-friendly pet toys from recycled items such as tennis balls, milk inflaters, fleece purchased on clearance, and squeakers. Beers first tried selling on Etsy and eBay, which enabled her to build an initial following. However, she was dissatisfied with the inability to control how her products were displayed and the fees that Etsy and

(continued)

eBay charged. She felt it was important to start selling directly from her own Web site to increase her margins and grow her business. So, she decided to create her own Web site with Weebly, starting with Weebly's Basic version for her first Web site, and then in, 2013, upgrading to its Business version, which allows for an unlimited number of products to be displayed for a flat monthly and no transaction fees. Beers reports a much better user experience, with the ability to display larger images and videos, offer coupon codes and ship items internationally more easily. Even better, she has experienced an increase in sales after switching, an increase she attributes to her ability to be able to explain in a video on the site why her toys are better although they cost more than toys made in China from potentially chemical-laced materials.

Although Weebly doesn't disclose its revenue, the company is profitable and has been since 2009. This is an attractive quality for a start-up company, many of which have historically sought growth first and profitability later. In 2014, Weebly received $35 million in venture capital funding that valued the company at $455 million. Weebly is one of the more valuable companies to graduate the technology incubator Y Combinator, which its founders attended in 2007. In anticipation of its future growth, Weebly has continued to expand its physical presence and workforce beyond the 80 employees it had in 2013 in its San Francisco and New York offices, building new headquarters in San Francisco in 2013 and a new office in Scottsdale, Arizona, in 2014. Weebly plans to hire 150 employees in Scottsdale by next year and approximately 500 new employees overall over the long term, most of whom will be engineers and designers.

Because so many businesses still don't have an online presence, Weebly's prospects for growth are bright. Less than 40% of restaurants have online menus, for example. Although its competitors, such as Wix, are also growing fast, there appears to be enough room in this market for several companies. In 2013, Wix launched an initial public offering, but the response was lukewarm, with investors expressing concern over its lack of profitability. So far, that's an advantage for Weebly, but with its recent aggressive push for growth, Weebly may suffer in this regard in the near-term future.

Weebly is just one example of a larger trend toward leaner business models that rely on outside help for many of their business functions. Although hardware has become less expensive over time, many startup firms have found that cloud computing and social marketing greatly reduce the costs of starting a company. Market intelligence, public relations, and even design services can be found online for a fraction of the cost of traditional service firms. It's never been cheaper to start an e-commerce company. In fact, a slow economy may be an entrepreneur's best friend. Failures are not so noticeable, which creates a better environment for risk-taking, which encourages innovation.

SOURCES: "About Weebly," Weebly.com, accessed August 20, 2014; "Weebly Expanding Into Scottsdale, Plans to Hire 250," by Hayley Ringle, *Phoenix Business Journal*, June 3, 2014; "Weebly Valued at $455 Million Amid Website-Building Boom," by Douglas Macmillan, *Wall Street Journal*, April 22, 2014; "Woof Purr Has Everything You Need for That Special Pet in Your Life," by Tim Goodwin, Theconcordinsider.com, December 31, 2013; "Weebly Website Creator Attracts Online Sellers with Store Features," by Greg Holden, Ecommercebytes.com, December 8, 2013; "A Tiny Web Merchant, But a Global Reach," by Paul Demery, Internetretailer.com, November 19, 2013; "With 30K Active Online Stores, Weebly Launches DIY eCommerce Platform to Take On Amazon and Shopify," by Rip Empson, Techcrunch.com, November 6, 2013; "Weeby Arms Entrepreneurs with Superior eCommerce to Boost Shopper Experience and Sell More Both Online and on Mobile," Reuters.com, November 6, 2013; "As Wix Heads Toward IPO, Weebly Looks to Expand with Big New SF Headquarters, Plans to Add 500+ Employees," by Rip Empson, TechCrunch, August 24, 2013.

the hardware. Cloud service providers offer a standardized infrastructure, virtualization technology, and usually employ a pay-as-you-go billing system.

Hosting, co-location, and cloud services have become a commodity and a utility: costs are driven by very large providers (such as IBM) who can achieve large economies of scale by establishing huge "server farms" located strategically around the country and the globe. This means the cost of pure hosting has fallen as fast as the fall in server prices, dropping about 50% every year! Telecommunications costs have also fallen. As a result, most hosting services seek to differentiate themselves from the commodity hosting business by offering extensive site design, marketing, optimization, and other services. Small, local ISPs also can be used as hosts, but service reliability is an issue. Will the small ISPs be able to provide uninterrupted service, 24 hours a day, 7 days a week, 365 days a year? Will they have service staff available when you need it?

There are several disadvantages to outsourcing hosting. If you choose a vendor, make sure the vendor has the capability to grow with you. You need to know what kinds of security provisions are in place for backup copies of your site, internal monitoring of activity, and security track record. Is there a public record of a security breach at the vendor? Most Fortune 500 firms have their own private cloud data centers so they can control the Web environment. On the other hand, there are risks to hosting your own site if you are a small business. Your costs will be higher than if you had used a large outsourcing firm because you don't have the market power to obtain low-cost hardware and telecommunications. You will have to purchase hardware and software, have a physical facility, lease communications lines, hire a staff, and build security and backup capabilities yourself.

TESTING THE SYSTEM

Once the system has been built and programmed, you will have to engage in a testing process. Depending on the size of the system, this could be fairly difficult and lengthy. Testing is required whether the system is outsourced or built in-house. A complex e-commerce site can have thousands of pathways through the site, each of which must be documented and then tested. **Unit testing** involves testing the site's program modules one at a time. **System testing** involves testing the site as a whole, in the same way a typical user would when using the site. Because there is no truly "typical" user, system testing requires that every conceivable path be tested. Final **acceptance testing** requires that the firm's key personnel and managers in marketing, production, sales, and general management actually use the system as installed on a test Internet or intranet server. This acceptance test verifies that the business objectives of the system as originally conceived are in fact working. It is important to note that testing is generally underbudgeted. As much as 50% of the software effort can be consumed by testing and rebuilding (usually depending on the quality of the initial design).

unit testing
involves testing the site's program modules one at a time

system testing
involves testing the site as a whole, in a way the typical user will use the site

acceptance testing
verifies that the business objectives of the system as originally conceived are in fact working

IMPLEMENTATION AND MAINTENANCE

Most people unfamiliar with systems erroneously think that once an information system is installed, the process is over. In fact, while the beginning of the process is over, the operational life of a system is just beginning. Systems break down for a variety of reasons—most of them unpredictable. Therefore, they need continual checking, testing, and repair. Systems maintenance is vital, but sometimes not budgeted for. In general, the annual system maintenance cost will roughly parallel the development cost. An e-commerce site that cost €32,000 to develop is likely to require a €32,000 annual expenditure to maintain. Very large e-commerce sites experience some economies of scale, so that, for example, a site that cost €1 million to develop is likely to require an annual maintenance budget of perhaps half to three-quarters of that cost.

Why does it cost so much to maintain an e-commerce site? Unlike payroll systems, for example, e-commerce sites are always in a process of change, improvement, and correction. Studies of traditional systems maintenance have found 20% of the time is devoted to debugging code and responding to emergency situations (for example, a new server was installed by your ISP, and all your hypertext links were lost and CGI scripts disabled—the site is down!) (Lientz and Swanson, 1980; Banker and Kemerer, 1989). Another 20% of the time is concerned with changes in reports, data files, and links to backend databases. The remaining 60% of maintenance time is devoted to general administration (making product and price changes in the catalog) and making changes and enhancements to the system. E-commerce sites are never finished: they are always in the process of being built and rebuilt. They are dynamic—much more so than payroll systems.

The long-term success of an e-commerce site will depend on a dedicated team of employees (the Web team) whose sole job is to monitor and adapt the site to changing market conditions. The Web team must be multi-skilled; it will typically include programmers, designers, and business managers drawn from marketing, production, and sales support. One of the first tasks of the Web team is to listen to customers' feedback on the site and respond to that feedback as necessary. A second task is to develop a systematic monitoring and testing plan to be followed weekly to ensure all the links are operating, prices are correct, and pages are updated. A large business may have thousands of Web pages, many of them linked, that require systematic monitoring. Other important tasks of the Web team include **benchmarking** (a process in which the site is compared with those of competitors in terms of response speed, quality of layout, and design) and keeping the site current on pricing and promotions. The Web is a competitive environment where you can very rapidly frustrate and lose customers with a dysfunctional site.

benchmarking
a process in which the site is compared with those of competitors in terms of response speed, quality of layout, and design

FACTORS IN OPTIMIZING WEB SITE PERFORMANCE

The purpose of a Web site is to deliver content to customers and to complete transactions. The faster and more reliably these two objectives are met, the more effective the Web site is from a commerce perspective. If you are a manager or marketing executive, you will want the Web site operating in a way that fulfills customers' expectations. You'll have to make sure the Web site is optimized to achieve this business objective. The optimization of Web site performance is more complicated than it seems and involves at least three factors: page content, page generation, and page delivery (see **Figure 3.10**). In this chapter, we describe the software and hardware choices you will need to make in building an e-commerce site; these are also important factors in Web site optimization.

Using efficient styles and techniques for *page design* and *content* can reduce response times by two to five seconds. Simple steps include reducing unnecessary

FIGURE 3.10	**FACTORS IN WEB SITE OPTIMIZATION**

Page Delivery

Content delivery networks
Edge caching
Bandwidth

Page Generation

Server response time
Device-based accelerators
Efficient resource allocation
Resource utilization thresholds
Monitoring site performance

Page Content

Optimize HTML
Optimize images
Site architecture
Efficient page style

Web site optimization requires that you consider three factors: page content, page generation, and page delivery.

HTML comments and white space, using more efficient graphics, and avoiding unnecessary links to other pages in the site. *Page generation* speed can be enhanced by segregating computer servers to perform dedicated functions (such as static page generation, application logic, media servers, and database servers), and using various devices from vendors to speed up these servers. Using a single server or multiple servers to perform multiple tasks reduces throughput by more than 50%. *Page delivery* can be speeded up by using edge-caching services such as Akamai, or specialized content delivery networks such as RealNetworks, or by increasing local bandwidth. We will discuss some of these factors throughout the chapter, but a full discussion of Web site optimization is beyond the scope of this text.

3.3 CHOOSING SOFTWARE

Along with telecommunications, software and hardware constitute the infrastructure of an e-commerce presence. As a business manager in charge of creating an e-commerce presence, you will need to know some basic information about both.

SIMPLE VERSUS MULTI-TIERED WEB SITE ARCHITECTURE

Prior to the development of e-commerce, Web sites simply delivered Web pages to users who were making requests through their browsers for HTML pages with content of various sorts. Web site software was appropriately quite simple—it consisted of a server computer running basic Web server software. We might call this arrangement

system architecture
the arrangement of software, machinery, and tasks in an information system needed to achieve a specific functionality

a single-tier system architecture. **System architecture** refers to the arrangement of software, machinery, and tasks in an information system needed to achieve a specific functionality (much like a home's architecture refers to the arrangement of building materials to achieve a particular functionality). The NaturallyCurly Web site started this way—there were no monetary transactions. Tens of thousands of dot-com sites still perform this way. Orders can always be called in by telephone and not taken online.

However, the development of e-commerce required a great deal more interactive functionality, such as the ability to respond to user input (name and address forms), take customer orders for goods and services, clear credit card transactions on the fly, consult price and product databases, and even adjust advertising on the screen based on user characteristics. This kind of extended functionality required the development of Web application servers and a multi-tiered system architecture to handle the processing loads. *Web application servers*, described more fully later in this section, are specialized software programs that perform a wide variety of transaction processing required by e-commerce.

In addition to having specialized application servers, e-commerce sites must be able to pull information from and add information to pre-existing corporate databases. These older databases that predate the e-commerce era are called *backend* or *legacy* databases. Corporations have made massive investments in these systems to store their information on customers, products, employees, and vendors. These backend systems constitute an additional layer in a multi-tiered site.

Figure 3.11 illustrates a simple two-tier and a more complex multi-tier e-commerce system architecture. In **two-tier architecture**, a Web server responds to requests for Web pages and a database server provides backend data storage. In a **multi-tier architecture**, in contrast, the Web server is linked to a middle-tier layer that typically includes a series of application servers that perform specific tasks, as well as to a backend layer of existing corporate systems containing product, customer, and pricing information. A multi-tiered site typically employs several physical computers, each running some of the software applications and sharing the workload across many physical computers.

The remainder of this section describes basic Web server software functionality and the various types of Web application servers.

two-tier architecture
e-commerce system architecture in which a Web server responds to requests for Web pages and a database server provides backend data storage

multi-tier architecture
e-commerce system architecture in which the Web server is linked to a middle-tier layer that typically includes a series of application servers that perform specific tasks as well as a backend layer of existing corporate systems

WEB SERVER SOFTWARE

All e-commerce sites require basic Web server software to answer requests from customers for HTML and XML pages.

When you choose Web server software, you will also be choosing an operating system for your site's computers. Apache, which works with Linux and Unix operating systems, is the leading Web server software, and is currently being used by about 51% of 155 million active sites included in Netcraft's July 2014 Web Server Survey (Netcraft, 2014). Unix is the original programming language of the Internet and Web, and Linux is a derivative of Unix designed for the personal computer. Apache was developed by a worldwide community of Internet innovators. Apache is free and can be downloaded from many sites on the Web; it also comes installed on most IBM Web servers. Literally

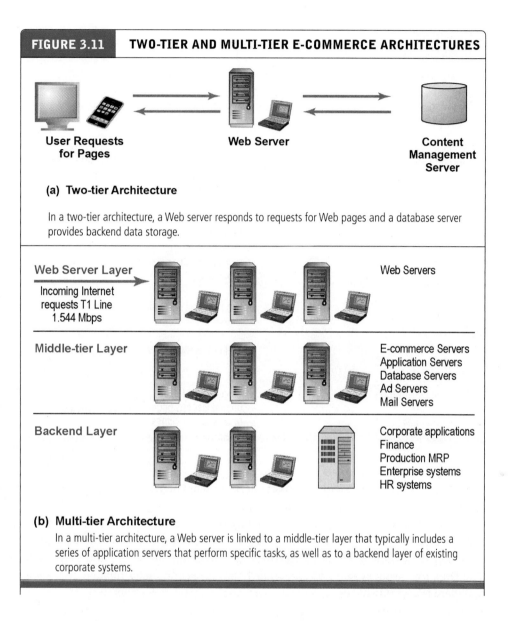

FIGURE 3.11   **TWO-TIER AND MULTI-TIER E-COMMERCE ARCHITECTURES**

User Requests for Pages

Web Server

Content Management Server

(a) Two-tier Architecture

In a two-tier architecture, a Web server responds to requests for Web pages and a database server provides backend data storage.

Web Server Layer

Incoming Internet requests T1 Line 1.544 Mbps

Web Servers

Middle-tier Layer

E-commerce Servers
Application Servers
Database Servers
Ad Servers
Mail Servers

Backend Layer

Corporate applications
Finance
Production MRP
Enterprise systems
HR systems

(b) Multi-tier Architecture

In a multi-tier architecture, a Web server is linked to a middle-tier layer that typically includes a series of application servers that perform specific tasks, as well as to a backend layer of existing corporate systems.

thousands of programmers have worked on Apache over the years; thus, it is extremely stable. There are thousands of utility software programs written for Apache that can provide all the functionality required for a contemporary e-commerce site. In order to use Apache, you will need staff that is knowledgeable in Unix or Linux.

Microsoft Internet Information Services (IIS) is the second major Web server software available, and is being used by about 12% of active sites in the Netcraft July 2014 survey. IIS is based on the Windows operating system and is compatible with a wide selection of Microsoft utility and support programs. These numbers are different among the Fortune 1000 firms, and different again if you include blogs, which are served up by Microsoft and Google at their own proprietary sites.

TABLE 3.4	BASIC FUNCTIONALITY PROVIDED BY WEB SERVERS
FUNCTIONALITY	DESCRIPTION
Processing of HTTP requests	Receive and respond to client requests for HTML pages
Security services (Secure Sockets Layer)/ Transport Layer Security	Verify username and password; process certificates and private/public key information required for credit card processing and other secure information
File Transfer Protocol	Permits transfer of very large files from server to server
Search engine	Indexing of site content; keyword search capability
Data capture	Log file of all visits, time, duration, and referral source
E-mail	Ability to send, receive, and store e-mail messages
Site management tools	Calculate and display key site statistics, such as unique visitors, page requests, and origin of requests; check links on pages

There are also at least 100 other smaller providers of Web server software, most of them based on the Unix or Sun Solaris operating systems. Note that the choice of Web server has little effect on users of your system. The pages they see will look the same regardless of the development environment. There are many advantages to the Microsoft suite of development tools—they are integrated, powerful, and easy to use. The Unix operating system, on the other hand, is exceptionally reliable and stable, and there is a worldwide open software community that develops and tests Unix-based Web server software.

Table 3.4 shows the basic functionality provided by all Web servers.

Site Management Tools

site management tools
verify that links on pages are still valid and also identify orphan files

In Chapter 2, we described most of the basic functionality of the Web servers listed in Table 3.4. Another functionality not described previously is site management tools. **Site management tools** are essential if you want to keep your site working, and if you want to understand how well it is working. Site management tools verify that links on pages are still valid and also identify orphan files, or files on the site that are not linked to any pages. By surveying the links on a Web site, a site management tool can quickly report on potential problems and errors that users may encounter. Your customers will not be impressed if they encounter a "404 Error: Page Does Not Exist" message on your Web site. Links to URLs that have moved or been deleted are called dead links; these can cause error messages for users trying to access that link. Regularly checking that all links on a site are operational helps prevent irritation and frustration in users who may decide to take their business elsewhere to a better functioning site.

Even more importantly, site management tools can help you understand consumer behavior on your Web site. Site management software and services, such as those provided by Webtrends, can be purchased in order to more effectively monitor customer purchases and marketing campaign effectiveness, as well as keep track of standard hit counts and page visit information. **Figure 3.12** shows a screenshot that illustrates Webtrends Analytics 10.

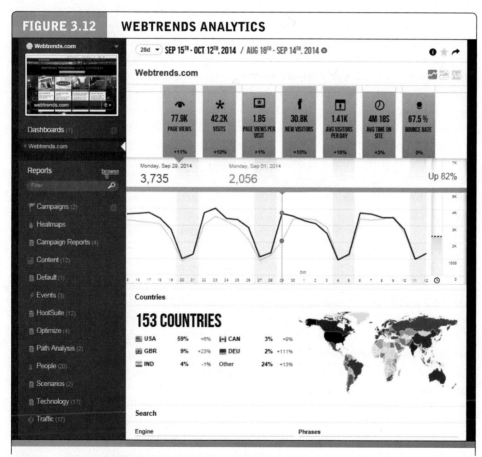

FIGURE 3.12   **WEBTRENDS ANALYTICS**

Using a sophisticated Web analytics solution such as Webtrends Analytics, managers can quickly understand the return on investment of their online marketing efforts and determine how to improve conversion by drilling down into abandonment paths, product preferences, and successful campaign elements for different types of customers.

SOURCE: Webtrends, Inc., 2014.

Dynamic Page Generation Tools

One of the most important innovations in Web site operation has been the development of dynamic page generation tools. Prior to the development of e-commerce, Web sites primarily delivered unchanging static content in the form of HTML pages. While this capability might be sufficient to display pictures of products, consider all the elements of a typical e-commerce site today by reviewing Table 3.2 (on page 183), or visit what you believe is an excellent e-commerce site. The content of successful e-commerce sites is always changing, often day by day. There are new products and promotions, changing prices, news events, and stories of successful users. E-commerce sites must intensively interact with users who not only request pages but also request product, price, availability, and inventory information. One of the most dynamic sites is eBay—the auction site. There, the content is changing minute by minute. E-commerce sites are just like real markets—they are dynamic. News sites, where stories change constantly, also are dynamic.

dynamic page generation

the contents of a Web page are stored as objects in a database, rather than being hard-coded in HTML. When the user requests a Web page, the contents for that page are then fetched from the database

The dynamic and complex nature of e-commerce sites requires a number of specialized software applications in addition to static HTML pages. Perhaps one of the most important is dynamic page generation software. With **dynamic page generation**, the contents of a Web page are stored as objects in a database, rather than being hard-coded in HTML. When the user requests a Web page, the contents for that page are then fetched from the database. The objects are retrieved from the database using Common Gateway Interface (CGI), Active Server Pages (ASP), Java Server Pages (JSP), or other server-side programs. CGI, ASP, and JSP are described in the last section of this chapter. This technique is much more efficient than working directly in HTML code. It is much easier to change the contents of a database than it is to change the coding of an HTML page. A standard data access method called *Open Database Connectivity (ODBC)* makes it possible for applications written in the C programmming language to access data from any database regardless of the database and operating system software being used via an ODBC driver that serves as a translator between the application and the database. ODBC drivers are available for most of the major database management systems offered by companies such as Oracle, SAP, Sybase, and IBM. Java Database Connectivity (JDBC) is a version of ODBC that provides connectivity between applications written in the Java programming language and a wide range of databases. However, while ODBC remains the de facto standard for cross-platform data access, today many web development platforms provide functionality that allows a programmer to directly link to a target database, making ODBC/JDBC drivers unnecessary.

Dynamic page generation gives e-commerce several significant capabilities that generate cost and profitability advantages over traditional commerce. Dynamic page generation lowers *menu costs* (the costs incurred by merchants for changing product descriptions and prices). Dynamic page generation also permits easy online *market segmentation*—the ability to sell the same product to different markets. For instance, you might want variations on the same banner ad depending on how many times the customer has seen the ad. In the first exposure to a car ad, you might want to emphasize brand identification and unique features. On the second viewing you might want to emphasize superlatives like "most family friendly" to encourage comparison to other brands. The same capability makes possible nearly cost-free *price discrimination*—the ability to sell the same product to different customers at different prices. For instance, you might want to sell the same product to corporations and government agencies but use different marketing themes. Based on a cookie you place on client computers, or in response to a question on your site that asks visitors if they are from a government agency or a corporation, you would be able to use different marketing and promotional materials for corporate clients and government clients. You might want to reward loyal customers with lower prices, say on DVDs or musical tracks, and charge full price to first-time buyers. Dynamic page generation allows you to approach different customers with different messages and prices.

Dynamic page generation also enables the use of a content management system (CMS). As previously described, a CMS is used to create and manage Web content. A CMS separates the design and presentation of content (such as HTML documents, images, video, audio) from the content creation process. The content is maintained in a database and dynamically linked to the Web site. A CMS usually includes templates that can be automatically applied to new and existing content, WYSIWYG editing tools that make it easy to edit and describe (tag) content, and collaboration, workflow, and document management tools. Typically, an experienced programmer is needed to install the system, but thereafter, content can be created and managed by non-technical staff. There are a wide range of commercial CMSs available, from top-end enterprise systems offered by HP Autonomy, EMC Documentum, OpenText, IBM, and Oracle, to mid-market systems by Ixiasoft, PaperThin, and Ektron, as well as hosted software as a service (SaaS) versions by Clickability, CrownPeak Technology, and OmniUpdate. There are also several open source content management systems available, such as WordPress, Joomla, Drupal, OpenCms, and others.

APPLICATION SERVERS

Web application servers are software programs that provide the specific business functionality required of a Web site. The basic idea of application servers is to isolate the business applications from the details of displaying Web pages to users on the front end and the details of connecting to databases on the back end. Application servers are a kind of middleware software that provides the glue connecting traditional corporate systems to the customer as well as all the functionality needed to conduct e-commerce. In the early years, a number of software firms developed specific separate programs for each function, but increasingly, these specific programs are being replaced by integrated software tools that combine all the needed functionality for an e-commerce site into a single development environment, a packaged software approach.

Table 3.5 on page 200 illustrates the wide variety of application servers available in the marketplace. The table focuses on "sell-side" servers that are designed to enable selling products on the Web. So-called "buy-side" and "link" servers focus on the needs of businesses to connect with partners in their supply chains or find suppliers for specific

Web application server
software programs that provide specific business functionality required of a Web site

TABLE 3.5	APPLICATION SERVERS AND THEIR FUNCTION
APPLICATION SERVER	FUNCTIONALITY
Catalog display	Provides a database for product descriptions and prices
Transaction processing (shopping cart)	Accepts orders and clears payments
List server	Creates and serves mailing lists and manages e-mail marketing campaigns
Proxy server	Monitors and controls access to main Web server; implements firewall protection
Mail server	Manages Internet e-mail
Audio/video server	Stores and delivers streaming media content
Chat server	Creates an environment for online real-time text and audio interactions with customers
News server	Provides connectivity and displays Internet news feeds
Fax server	Provides fax reception and sending using a Web server
Groupware server	Creates workgroup environments for online collaboration
Database server	Stores customer, product, and price information
Ad server	Maintains Web-enabled database of advertising banners that permits customized and personalized display of advertisements based on consumer behavior and characteristics
Auction server	Provides a transaction environment for conducting online auctions
B2B server	Implements buy, sell, and link marketplaces for commercial transactions

parts and assemblies. These buy-side and link servers are described more fully in Chapter 12. There are several thousand software vendors that provide application server software. For Linux and Unix environments, many of these capabilities are available free on the Internet from various sites. Most businesses—faced with this bewildering array of choices—choose to use integrated software tools called merchant server software.

E-COMMERCE MERCHANT SERVER SOFTWARE FUNCTIONALITY

e-commerce merchant server software
software that provides the basic functionality needed for online sales, including an online catalog, order taking via an online shopping cart, and online credit card processing

E-commerce merchant server software provides the basic functionality needed for online sales, including an online catalog, order taking via an online shopping cart, and online credit card processing.

Online Catalog

online catalog
list of products available on a Web site

A company that wants to sell products on the Web must have a list, or **online catalog**, of its products, available on its Web site. Merchant server software typically includes a database capability that will allow for construction of a customized online catalog.

The complexity and sophistication of the catalog will vary depending on the size of the company and its product lines. Small companies, or companies with small product lines, may post a simple list with text descriptions and perhaps color photos. A larger site might decide to add sound, animations, or videos (useful for product demonstrations) to the catalog, or interactivity, such as customer service representatives available via instant messaging to answer questions. Today, larger firms make extensive use of streaming video.

Shopping Cart

Online **shopping carts** are much like their real-world equivalent; both allow shoppers to set aside desired purchases in preparation for checkout. The difference is that the online variety is part of a merchant server software program residing on the Web server, and allows consumers to select merchandise, review what they have selected, edit their selections as necessary, and then actually make the purchase by clicking a button. The merchant server software automatically stores shopping cart data.

Credit Card Processing

A site's shopping cart typically works in conjunction with credit card processing software, which verifies the shopper's credit card and then puts through the debit to the card and the credit to the company's account at checkout. Integrated e-commerce software suites typically supply the software for this function. Otherwise, you will have to make arrangements with a variety of credit card processing banks and intermediaries.

MERCHANT SERVER SOFTWARE PACKAGES (E-COMMERCE SOFTWARE PLATFORMS)

Rather than build your site from a collection of disparate software applications, it is easier, faster, and generally more cost-effective to purchase a **merchant server software package** (also called an **e-commerce software platform**). Merchant server software offers an integrated environment that promises to provide most or all of the functionality and capabilities you will need to develop a sophisticated, customer-centric site. An important element of merchant sofware packages is a built-in shopping cart that can display merchandise, manage orders, and clear credit card transactions. E-commerce software platforms come in three general ranges of price and functionality.

While existing firms often have the financial capital to invest in commercial merchant server software, many small firms and start-up firms do not. There are really two options here, the key factor being how much programming experience and time you have. One option is to utilize the e-commerce merchant services provided by sites such as Yahoo Stores. For instance, for $26 a month and a 1.5% transaction fee for each transaction processed through the store, Yahoo Stores Professional makes it easy to create an e-commerce Web site with customizable templates. An e-commerce template is a predesigned Web site that allows users to customize the look and feel of the site to fit their business needs and provides a standard set of functionalities. Most templates today contain ready-to-go site designs with built-in e-commerce functionality like shopping carts, payment clearance, and site management tools. Yahoo Stores also

shopping cart
allows shoppers to set aside desired purchases in preparation for checkout, review what they have selected, edit their selections as necessary, and then actually make the purchase by clicking a button

merchant server software package (e-commerce software platform)
offers an integrated environment that provides most or all of the functionality and capabilities needed to develop a sophisticated, customer-centric site

TABLE 3.6	OPEN SOURCE SOFTWARE OPTIONS
FUNCTIONALITY	OPEN SOURCE SOFTWARE
Web server	Apache (the leading Web server for small and medium businesses)
Shopping cart, online catalog	Many providers: osCommerce, Zen Cart, AgoraCart, X-cart, AspDotNetStorefront
Credit card processing	Credit card acceptance is typically provided in shopping cart software but you may need a merchant account from a bank as well.
Database	MySQL (the leading open source SQL database for businesses)
Programming/scripting language	PHP is a scripting language embedded in HTML documents but executed by the server, providing server-side execution with the simplicity of HTML editing. Perl is an alternative language. JavaScript programs are client-side programs that provide user interface components. Ruby on Rails (RoR, Rails) and Django are other popular open source Web application frameworks.
Analytics	Analytics keep track of your site's customer activities and the success of your Web advertising campaign. You can also use Google Analytics if you advertise on Google, which provides good tracking tools; most hosting services will provide these services as well. Other open source analytic tools include Piwik, CrawlTrack, and Open Web Analytics.

includes a mobile storefront, search engine optimization tools, social media support, and a variety of other marketing tools. Amazon Stores, eBay, and many others, such as Bigcommerce, Homestead, Vendio, Shopify offer similar services.

open source software
software that is developed by a community of programmers and designers, and is free to use and modify

If you have considerable, or at least some, programming background, you can consider open source merchant server software. **Open source software** is software developed by a community of programmers and designers, and is free to use and modify. **Table 3.6** provides a description of some open source options. The advantage of using open source Web building tools is that you get exactly what you want, a truly customized unique Web site. The disadvantage is that it will take several months for a single programmer to develop the site and get all the tools to work together seamlessly. How many months do you want to wait before you get to market with your ideas?

Midrange e-commerce software platforms include IBM WebSphere Commerce Express Edition and Commerce Server (formerly Microsoft Commerce Server). High-end enterprise solutions for large global firms are provided by IBM WebSphere's Commerce on Cloud, Professional, and Enterprise Editions, Oracle ATG Web Commerce, eBay Enterprises (formerly GSI Commerce), Demandware, Magento, NetSuite, and others. Many of these e-commerce software platforms are now available on a Software as a Service (SaaS) basis, a model in which the software is hosted in the cloud and run by the client via a Web browser. This model enables a firm to launch an e-commerce site very quickly. For instance, Williams-Sonoma, a housewares retail chain in the United States, used Web-hosted e-commerce software from NetSuite to launch an e-commerce site in Australia in only 3 months time (Dusto, 2014). There are several hundred software firms that provide e-commerce software, which raises the costs of making sensible decisions on this matter.

Choosing an E-commerce Software Platform

With all of these vendors, how do you choose the right one? Evaluating these tools and making a choice is one of the most important and uncertain decisions you will make in building an e-commerce site. The real costs are hidden—they involve training your staff to use the tools and integrating the tools into your business processes and organizational culture. The following are some of the key factors to consider:

- Functionality, including availability on an SaaS basis
- Support for different business models, including mobile commerce
- Business process modeling tools
- Visual site management tools and reporting
- Performance and scalability
- Connectivity to existing business systems
- Compliance with standards
- Global and multicultural capability
- Local sales tax and shipping rules

For instance, although e-commerce software platforms promise to do everything, your business may require special functionality—such as streaming audio and video. You will need a list of business functionality requirements. Your business may involve several different business models—such as a retail side and a business-to-business side; you may run auctions for stock excess as well as fixed-price selling. Be sure the package can support all of your business models. You may wish to change your business processes, such as order taking and order fulfillment. Does the platform contain tools for modeling business process and work flows? Understanding how your site works will require visual reporting tools that make its operation transparent to many different people in your business. A poorly designed software package will drop off significantly in performance as visitors and transactions expand into the thousands per hour, or minute. Check for performance and scalability by stress-testing a pilot edition or obtaining data from the vendor about performance under load. You will have to connect the e-commerce platform to your traditional business systems. How will this connection to existing systems be made, and is your staff skilled in making the connection? Because of the changing technical environment—in particular, changes in mobile commerce platforms—it is important to document exactly what standards the platform supports now, and what the migration path will be toward the future. Finally, your e-commerce site may have to work both globally and locally. You may need a foreign language edition using foreign currency denominations. And you will have to collect sales taxes across many local, regional, and national tax systems. Does the e-commerce platform support this level of globalization and localization?

3.4 CHOOSING HARDWARE

hardware platform
refers to all the underlying computing equipment that the system uses to achieve its e-commerce functionality

Whether you host your own site or outsource the hosting and operation of your site, you will need to understand certain aspects of the computing hardware platform. The **hardware platform** refers to all the underlying computing equipment that the system uses to achieve its e-commerce functionality. Your objective is to have enough platform capacity to meet peak demand (avoiding an overload condition), but not so much platform that you are wasting money. Failing to meet peak demand can mean your site is slow, or actually crashes. How much computing and telecommunications capacity is enough to meet peak demand? How many hits per day can your site sustain?

To answer these questions, you will need to understand the various factors that affect the speed, capacity, and scalability of an e-commerce site.

RIGHT-SIZING YOUR HARDWARE PLATFORM: THE DEMAND SIDE

The most important factor affecting the speed of your site is the demand that customers put on the site. **Table 3.7** lists the most important factors to consider when estimating the demand on a site.

Demand on a Web site is fairly complex and depends primarily on the type of site you are operating. The number of simultaneous users in peak periods, the nature of customer requests, the type of content, the required security, the number of items in inventory, the number of page requests, and the speed of legacy applications that may be needed to supply data to the Web pages are all important factors in overall demand on a Web site system.

stateless
refers to the fact that the server does not have to maintain an ongoing, dedicated interaction with the client

Certainly, one important factor to consider is the number of simultaneous users who will likely visit your site. In general, the load created by an individual customer on a server is typically quite limited and short-lived. A Web session initiated by the typical user is **stateless**, meaning that the server does not have to maintain an ongoing, dedicated interaction with the client. A Web session typically begins with a page request, then a server replies, and the session is ended. The sessions may last from tenths of a second to a minute per user. Nevertheless, system performance does degrade as more and more simultaneous users request service. Fortunately, degradation (measured as "transactions per second" and "latency" or delay in response) is fairly graceful over a wide range, up until a peak load is reached and service quality becomes unacceptable (see **Figure 3.13** on page 206).

TABLE 3.7	FACTORS IN RIGHT-SIZING AN E-COMMERCE PLATFORM				
SITE TYPE	PUBLISH/ SUBSCRIBE	SHOPPING	CUSTOMER SELF-SERVICE	TRADING	WEB SERVICES/ B2B
Examples	WSJ.com	Amazon	Travelocity	E*Trade	Ariba e-procurement exchanges
Content	Dynamic Multiple authors High volume Not user-specific	Catalog Dynamic items User profiles with data mining	Data in legacy applications Multiple data sources	Time sensitive High volatility Multiple suppliers and consumers Complex transactions	Data in legacy applications Multiple data sources Complex transactions
Security	Low	Privacy Nonrepudiation Integrity Authentication Regulations	Privacy Nonrepudiation Integrity Authentication Regulations	Privacy Nonrepudiation Integrity Authentication Regulations	Privacy Nonrepudiation Integrity Authentication Regulations
Percent secure pages	Low	Medium	Medium	High	Medium
Cross session information	No	High	High	High	High
Searches	Dynamic Low volume	Dynamic High volume	Nondynamic Low volume	Nondynamic Low volume	Nondynamic Moderate volume
Unique items (SKUs)	High	Medium to high	Medium	High	Medium to high
Transaction volume	Moderate	Moderate to high	Moderate	High to extremely high	Moderate
Legacy integration complexity	Low	Medium	High	High	High
Page views (hits)	High to very high	Moderate to high	Moderate to low	Moderate to high	Moderate

Serving up static Web pages is **I/O intensive**, which means it requires input/ output (I/O) operations rather than heavy-duty processing power. As a result, Web site performance is constrained primarily by the server's I/O limitations and the telecommunications connection, rather than the speed of the processor.

Other factors to consider when estimating the demand on a Web site are the user profile and the nature of the content. If users request searches, registration forms, and order taking via shopping carts, then demands on processors will increase markedly.

I/O intensive

requires input/output operations rather than heavy-duty processing power

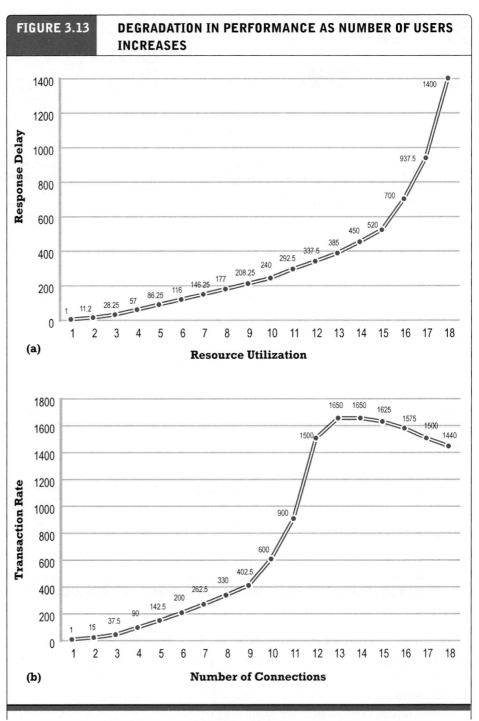

FIGURE 3.13 **DEGRADATION IN PERFORMANCE AS NUMBER OF USERS INCREASES**

Degradation in Web server performance occurs as the number of users (connections) increases, and as the system's resources (processors, disk drives) become more utilized. In (a), as resource utilization grows, response delay increases, and eventually rises exponentially to an unacceptable level. In (b), as the number of connections (users) increases, the transaction rises gracefully until, at a certain inflection point, the transaction rate declines and the system slows down or crashes.

RIGHT-SIZING YOUR HARDWARE PLATFORM: THE SUPPLY SIDE

Once you estimate the likely demand on your site, you will need to consider how to scale up your site to meet demand. We have already discussed one solution that requires very little thought: outsource the hosting of your Web site to a cloud-based service. See Chapter 2 for a discussion of cloud-based computing services. However, if you decide to host your own Web site, scalability is an important consideration. **Scalability** refers to the ability of a site to increase in size as demand warrants. There are three steps you can take to meet the demands for service at your site: scale hardware vertically, scale hardware horizontally, and/or improve the processing architecture of the site (see **Table 3.8**). **Vertical scaling** refers to increasing the processing power of individual components. **Horizontal scaling** refers to employing multiple computers to share the workload and increase the "footprint" of the installation (IBM, 2002).

You can scale your site vertically by upgrading the servers from a single processor to multiple processors. You can keep adding processors to a computer depending on the operating system and upgrade to faster chip speeds as well.

There are two drawbacks to vertical scaling. First, it can become expensive to purchase additional processors with every growth cycle, and second, your entire site becomes dependent on a small number of very powerful computers. If you have two such computers and one goes down, half of your site, or perhaps your entire site, may become unavailable.

scalability
the ability of a site to increase in size as demand warrants

vertical scaling
increasing the processing power of individual components

horizontal scaling
employing multiple computers to share the workload

TABLE 3.8	VERTICAL AND HORIZONTAL SCALING TECHNIQUES
TECHNIQUE	APPLICATION
Use a faster computer	Deploy edge servers, presentation servers, data servers, etc.
Create a cluster of computers	Use computers in parallel to balance loads.
Use appliance servers	Use special-purpose computers optimized for their task.
Segment workload	Segment incoming work to specialized computers.
Batch requests	Combine related requests for data into groups, process as group.
Manage connections	Reduce connections between processes and computers to a minimum.
Aggregate user data	Aggregate user data from legacy applications in single data pools.
Cache	Store frequently used data in cache rather than on the disk.

TABLE 3.9	IMPROVING THE PROCESSING ARCHITECTURE OF YOUR SITE
ARCHITECTURE IMPROVEMENT	DESCRIPTION
Separate static content from dynamic content	Use specialized servers for each type of workload.
Cache static content	Increase RAM to the gigabyte range and store static content in RAM.
Cache database lookup tables	Use cache tables used to look up database records.
Consolidate business logic on dedicated servers	Put shopping cart, credit card processing, and other CPU-intensive activity on dedicated servers.
Optimize ASP code	Examine your code to ensure it is operating efficiently.
Optimize the database schema	Examine your database search times and take steps to reduce access times.

Horizontal scaling involves adding multiple single-processor servers to your site and balancing the load among the servers. You can then partition the load so some servers handle only requests for HTML or ASP pages, while others are dedicated to handling database applications. You will need special load-balancing software (provided by a variety of vendors such as Cisco, Microsoft, and IBM) to direct incoming requests to various servers.

There are many advantages to horizontal scaling. It is inexpensive and often can be accomplished using older PCs that otherwise would be disposed of. Horizontal scaling also introduces redundancy—if one computer fails, chances are that another computer can pick up the load dynamically. However, when your site grows from a single computer to perhaps 10 to 20 computers, the size of the physical facility required (the "footprint") increases and there is added management complexity.

A third alternative—improving the processing architecture—is a combination of vertical and horizontal scaling, combined with artful design decisions. **Table 3.9** lists some of the more common steps you can take to greatly improve performance of your site. Most of these steps involve splitting the workload into I/O-intensive activities (such as serving Web pages) and CPU-intensive activities (such as taking orders). Once you have this work separated, you can fine-tune the servers for each type of load. One of the least expensive fine-tuning steps is to simply add RAM to a few servers and store all your HTML pages in RAM. This reduces load on your hard drives and increases speed dramatically. RAM is thousands of times faster than hard disks, and RAM is inexpensive. The next most important step is to move your CPU-intensive activities, such as order taking, onto a high-end, multiple-processor server that is dedicated to handling orders and accessing the necessary databases. Taking these steps can permit you to reduce the number of servers required to service 10,000 concurrent users from 100 down to 20, according to one estimate.

3.5	**OTHER E-COMMERCE SITE TOOLS**

Now that you understand the key factors affecting the speed, capacity, and scalability of your Web site, we can consider some other important requirements. You will need a coherent Web site design that makes business sense—not necessarily a site to wow visitors or excite them, but to sell them something. You will also need to know how to build active content and interactivity into your site—not just display static HTML pages. You must be able to track customers who come, leave, and return to your site in order to be able to greet return visitors ("Hi Sarah, welcome back!"). You will also want to track customers throughout your site so you can personalize and customize their experience. You will definitely want the ability for customers to generate content and feedback on your site to increase their engagement with your brand. Finally, you will need to establish a set of information policies for your site—privacy, accessibility, and access to information policies.

In order to achieve these business capabilities, you will need to be aware of some design guidelines and additional software tools that can cost-effectively achieve the required business functionality.

WEB SITE DESIGN: BASIC BUSINESS CONSIDERATIONS

This is not a text about how to design Web sites. (In Chapter 6, we discuss Web site design issues from a marketing perspective.) Nevertheless, from a business manager's perspective, there are certain design objectives you must communicate to your Web site designers to let them know how you will evaluate their work. At a minimum, your customers will need to find what they need at your site, make a purchase, and leave. A Web site that annoys customers runs the risk of losing the customer forever. See **Table 3.10** for a list of the most common consumer complaints about Web sites.

TABLE 3.10	**E-COMMERCE WEB SITE FEATURES THAT ANNOY CUSTOMERS**
• Requiring user to view ad or Flash introduction before going to Web site content	• Inability to use browser's Back button
• Pop-up and pop-under ads and windows	• No contact information available (Web form only)
• Too many clicks to get to the content	• Unnecessary splash/flash screens, animation, etc.
• Links that don't work	• Music or other audio that plays automatically
• Confusing navigation; no search function	• Unprofessional design elements
• Requirement to register and log in before viewing content or ordering	• Text not easily legible due to size, color, format
• Slow loading pages	• Typographical errors
• Content that is out of date	• No or unclear returns policy

TABLE 3.11	THE EIGHT MOST IMPORTANT FACTORS IN SUCCESSFUL E-COMMERCE SITE DESIGN
FACTOR	DESCRIPTION
Functionality	Pages that work, load quickly, and point the customer toward your product offerings
Informational	Links that customers can easily find to discover more about you and your products
Ease of use	Simple foolproof navigation
Redundant navigation	Alternative navigation to the same content
Ease of purchase	One or two clicks to purchase
Multi-browser functionality	Site works with the most popular browsers
Simple graphics	Avoids distracting, obnoxious graphics and sounds that the user cannot control
Legible text	Avoids backgrounds that distort text or make it illegible

Some critics believe poor design is more common than good design. It appears easier to describe what irritates people about Web sites than to describe how to design a good Web site. The worst e-commerce sites make it difficult to find information about their products and make it complicated to purchase goods; they have missing pages and broken links, a confusing navigation structure, and annoying graphics or sounds that you cannot turn off. **Table 3.11** restates these negative experiences as positive goals for Web site design.

TOOLS FOR WEB SITE OPTIMIZATION

A Web site is only as valuable from a business perspective as the number of people who visit. Web site optimization (as we use it here) means how to attract lots of people to your site. One solution is through search engines such as Google, Bing, Ask, and several hundred others. The first stop for most customers looking for a product or service is to start with a search engine, and follow the listings on the page, usually starting with the top three to five listings, then glancing to the sponsored ads to the right. The higher you are on the search engine pages, the more traffic you will receive. Page 1 is much better than Page 2. So how do you get to Page 1 in the natural (unpaid) search listings? While every search engine is different, and none of them publish their algorithms for ranking pages, there are some basic ideas that work well:

- **Metatags, titles, page contents:** Search engines "crawl" your site and identify keywords as well as title pages and then index them for use in search arguments. Pepper your pages with keywords that accurately describe what you say you do in your metatag site "description" and "keywords" sections of your source code. Experiment: use different keywords to see which work. "Vintage cars" may attract more visitors than "antique cars" or "restored cars."

- **Identify market niches:** Instead of marketing "jewelry," be more specific, such as "Victorian jewelry," or "1950s jewelry" to attract small, specific groups who are intensely interested in period jewelry and closer to purchasing.

- **Offer expertise:** White papers, industry analyses, FAQ pages, guides, and histories are excellent ways to build confidence on the part of users and to encourage them to see your Web site as the place to go for help and guidance.

- **Get linked up:** Encourage other sites to link to your site; build a blog that attracts people and who will share your URL with others and post links in the process. List your site with Yahoo Directory. Build a Facebook page for your company, and think about using Twitter to develop a following or fan base for your products.

- **Buy ads:** Complement your natural search optimization efforts with paid search engine keywords and ads. Choose your keywords and purchase direct exposure on Web pages. You can set your budget and put a ceiling on it to prevent large losses. See what works, and observe the number of visits to your site produced by each keyword string.

- **Local e-commerce:** Developing a national market can take a long time. If your Web site is particularly attractive to local people, or involves products sold locally, use keywords that connote your location so people can find you nearby. Town, city, and region names in your keywords can be helpful, such as "Vermont cheese" or "San Francisco blues music."

TOOLS FOR INTERACTIVITY AND ACTIVE CONTENT

The more interactive a Web site is, the more effective it will be in generating sales and encouraging return visitors. Although functionality and ease of use are the supreme objectives in site design, you will also want to interact with users and present them with a lively, "active" experience. You will want to personalize the experience for customers by addressing their individual needs, and customize the content of your offerings based on their behavior or expressed desires. In order to achieve these business objectives, you will need to consider carefully the tools necessary to build these capabilities. Simple interactions such as a customer submitting a name, along with more complex interactions involving credit cards, user preferences, and user responses to prompts, all require special programs. The following sections provide a brief description of some commonly used software tools for achieving high levels of site interactivity.

Common Gateway Interface (CGI)

Common Gateway Interface (CGI) is a set of standards for communication between a browser and a program running on a server that allows for interaction between the user and the server. CGI permits an executable program to access all the information within incoming requests from clients. The program can then generate all the output required to make up the return page (the HTML, script code, text, etc.), and send it back to the client via the Web server. For instance, if a user clicks the My Shopping Cart button, the server receives this request and executes a CGI program. The CGI program

Common Gateway Interface (CGI)
a set of standards for communication between a browser and a program running on a server that allows for interaction between the user and the server

retrieves the contents of the shopping cart from the database and returns it to the server. The server sends an HTML page that displays the contents of the shopping cart on the user's screen. Notice that all the computing takes place on the server side (this is why CGI programs and others like it are referred to as "server-side" programs).

CGI programs can be written in nearly any programming language as long as they conform to CGI standards. Currently, Perl is one of the most popular languages for CGI scripting. Generally, CGI programs are used with Unix servers. CGI's primary disadvantage is that it is not highly scalable because a new process must be created for each request, thereby limiting the number of concurrent requests that can be handled. CGI scripts are best used for small to medium-sized applications that do not involve a high volume of user traffic. There are also Web server extensions available, such as FastCGI, that improve CGI's scalability and SCGI, which is a simpler version of FastCGI (Doyle and Lopes, 2005).

Active Server Pages (ASP and ASP.NET)

Active Server Pages (ASP)

a proprietary software development tool that enables programmers using Microsoft's IIS package to build dynamic pages

Active Server Pages (ASP) is Microsoft's original version of server-side programming for Windows. Invented by Microsoft in late 1996, ASP grew rapidly to become the major technique for server-side Web programming in the Windows environment. ASP enables developers to easily create and open records from a database and execute programs within an HTML page, as well as handle all the various forms of interactivity found on e-commerce sites. Like CGI, ASP permits an interaction to take place between the browser and the server. ASP uses the same standards as CGI for communication with the browser. ASP programs are restricted to use on Windows servers running Microsoft's IIS Web server software. ASP.NET, first released in January 2002, and part of Microsoft's .NET framework, is the successor to ASP.

Java, Java Server Pages (JSP), and JavaScript

Java

a programming language that allows programmers to create interactivity and active content on the client computer, thereby saving considerable load on the server

Java is a programming language that allows programmers to create interactivity and active content on the client computer, thereby saving considerable load on the server. Java was invented by Sun Microsystems in 1990 as a platform-independent programming language for consumer electronics. The idea was to create a language whose programs (so-called Write Once Run Anywhere [WORA] programs) could operate on any computer regardless of operating system. This would be possible if every operating system at the time (Macintosh, Windows, Unix, DOS, and mainframe MVS systems) had a Java Virtual Machine (VM) installed that would interpret the Java programs for that environment.

By 1995, it had become clear, however, that Java was more applicable to the Web than to consumer electronics. Java programs (known as Java applets) could be downloaded to the client over the Web and executed entirely on the client's computer. Applet tags could be included in an HTML page. To enable this, each browser would have to include a Java VM. Today, the leading browsers do include a VM to run Java programs. When the browser accesses a page with an applet, a request is sent to the server to download and execute the program and allocate page space to display the results of the program. Java can be used to display interesting graphics, create interactive environments (such as a mortgage calculator), and directly access the Web server.

Java Server Pages (JSP), like CGI and ASP, is a Web page coding standard that allows developers to use a combination of HTML, JSP scripts, and Java to dynamically generate Web pages in response to user requests. JSP uses Java "servlets," small Java programs that are specified in the Web page and run on the Web server to modify the Web page before it is sent to the user who requested it. JSP is supported by most of the popular application servers on the market today.

JavaScript is a programming language invented by Netscape that is used to control the objects on an HTML page and handle interactions with the browser. It is most commonly used on the client side to handle verification and validation of user input, as well as to implement business logic. For instance, JavaScript can be used on customer registration forms to confirm that a valid phone number, zip code, or even e-mail address has been given. Before a user finishes completing a form, the e-mail address given can be tested for validity. JavaScript appears to be much more acceptable to corporations and other environments in large part because it is more stable and also it is restricted to the operation of requested HTML pages. JavaScript is also used as part of Node.js, a cross-platform environment for server-side applications (including mobile), which has been used by companies such as Walmart, LinkedIn, and Groupon. *Ajax (asynchronous JavaScript and XML)* uses a variety of different tools, including JavaScript, to allow Web pages to be updated asynchronously (i.e., updating only parts of the page rather than having to reload the entire page to change just part of the content).

ActiveX and VBScript

Microsoft invented the **ActiveX** programming language to compete with Java and **VBScript** to compete with JavaScript. When a browser receives an HTML page with an ActiveX control (comparable to a Java applet), the browser simply executes the program. Unlike Java, however, ActiveX has full access to all the client's resources— printers, networks, and hard drives. VBScript performs in the same way as JavaScript. ActiveX and VBScript work only if you are using Internet Explorer. Otherwise, that part of the screen is blank.

ColdFusion

ColdFusion is an integrated server-side environment for developing interactive Web and mobile applications. Originally developed by Macromedia and now offered by Adobe, ColdFusion combines an intuitive tag-based scripting language and a tag-based server scripting language (CFML) that lowers the cost of creating interactive features. ColdFusion offers a powerful set of visual design, programming, debugging, and deployment tools.

PHP, Ruby on Rails (RoR), and Django

PHP is an open source, general purpose scripting language that is most frequently used in server-side Web applications to generate dynamic Web page content, although it can also be used for client-side graphical user interface applications. PHP is also a part of many Web application development frameworks, such as CakePHP, CodeIgniter, and others, and is also part of the LAMP (Linux, Apache, MySQL, PHP) open source Web development model for building dynamic Web sites and web applications (Perl

---

Java Server Pages (JSP)
like CGI and ASP, a Web page coding standard that allows developers to dynamically generate Web pages in response to user requests

JavaScript
a programming language invented by Netscape that is used to control the objects on an HTML page and handle interactions with the browser

ActiveX
a programming language created by Microsoft to compete with Java

VBScript
a programming language invented by Microsoft to compete with JavaScript

ColdFusion
an integrated server-side environment for developing interactive Web applications

and Python are sometimes substituted for PHP in some LAMP projects). According to W3Techs, PHP is, by far and away, the most commonly used server-side scripting language (used by over 80% of the Web sites whose server-side programming language it was able to identify), with ASP.NET a distant second, used by less than 20%, followed by Java, with 2.7%. ColdFusion, Perl, Ruby on Rails, Python, and JavaScript were all less than 1% (W3techs.com, 2014). Netcraft's Web Server Survey has found PHP on over 240 million sites (Netcraft, 2014).

Ruby on Rails (RoR or Rails) is an open source Web application framework based on the Ruby programming language. RoR is based on a philosophy known as convention over configuration, or coding by convention (CoC), which means that the framework provides a structured layout that minimizes the number of decisions that the programmer needs to make, thereby simplifying and speeding development. JavaScript and Ajax are highly integrated into RoR, which makes it easy to handle Ajax requests for page updates. Some well-known Web sites based on RoR include Shopify, Groupon, Indiegogo, and Airbnb (Codefactory, 2014).

Django is also an open source Web application framework. It is based on the Python programming language. Django is optimized for the creation of complex, database-driven Web sites. It allows for fast development, focuses on automating as much as possible, emphasizes the reusability of various components, and follows the DRY (Don't Repeat Yourself) programming principle. Some well-known Web sites based on Django include Instagram, Pinterest, and the satirical news site, The Onion (Codecondo, 2013).

Web 2.0 Design Elements

widget
a small, prebuilt chunk of code that executes automatically in your HTML Web page; capable of performing a wide variety of tasks

One easy way to pump up the energy on your Web site is to include some appropriate widgets (sometimes called gadgets, plug-ins, or snippets). **Widgets** are small chunks of code that execute automatically in your HTML Web page. They are prebuilt and many are free. Social networks and blogs use widgets to present users with content drawn from around the Web (news headlines from specific news sources, announcements, press releases, and other routine content), calendars, clocks, weather, live TV, games, and other functionality. You can copy the code to an HTML Web page. You can find widgets at Apple's Dashboard Widgets, Wolfram|Alpha Widgets, and SIMILE Widgets. There are also widgets for specific platforms such as WordPress, Amazon Widgets, and Pinterest's Widget Builder.

Mashups are a little more complicated and involve pulling functionality and data from one program and including it in another. The most common mashup involves using Google Maps data and software and combining it with other data. For instance, if you have a local real estate Web site, you can download Google Maps and satellite image applications to your site so visitors can get a sense of the neighborhood. There are thousands of Google Map mashups, from maps of Myanmar political protests, to maps of the Fortune 500 companies, all with associated news stories and other content. Other mashups involve sports, photos, video, shopping, and news.

The point of these Web 2.0 applications is to enhance user interest and engagement with your Web site and brand.

PERSONALIZATION TOOLS

You will definitely want to know how to treat each customer on an individual basis and emulate a traditional face-to-face marketplace. *Personalization* (the ability to treat people based on their personal qualities and prior history with your site) and *customization* (the ability to change the product to better fit the needs of the customer) are two key elements of e-commerce that potentially can make it nearly as powerful as a traditional marketplace, and perhaps even more powerful than direct mail or shopping at an anonymous suburban shopping mall. Speaking directly to the customer on a one-to-one basis, and even adjusting the product to the customer is quite difficult in the usual type of mass marketing, one-size-fits-all commercial transaction that characterizes much of contemporary commerce.

There are a number of methods for achieving personalization and customization. For instance, you could personalize Web content if you knew the personal background of the visitor. You could also analyze the pattern of clicks and sites visited for every customer who enters your site. We discuss these methods in later chapters on marketing. The primary method for achieving personalization and customization is through the placement of cookie files on the user's client computer. As we discussed in Chapter 2, a cookie is a small text file placed on the user's client computer that can contain any kind of information about the customer, such as customer ID, campaign ID, or purchases at the site. And then, when the user returns to the site, or indeed goes further into your site, the customer's prior history can be accessed from a database. Information gathered on prior visits can then be used to personalize the visit and customize the product.

For instance, when a user returns to a site, you can read the cookie to find a customer ID, look the ID up in a database of names, and greet the customer ("Hello Mary! Glad to have you return!"). You could also have stored a record of prior purchases, and then recommend a related product ("How about the wrench tool box now that you have purchased the wrenches?"). And you could think about customizing the product ("You've shown an interest in the elementary training programs for Word. We have a special 'How to Study' program for beginners in Office software. Would you like to see a sample copy online?").

We further describe the use of cookies in Chapter 6.

THE INFORMATION POLICY SET

In developing an e-commerce site, you will also need to focus on the set of information policies that will govern the site. You will need to develop a **privacy policy**—a set of public statements declaring to your customers how you treat their personal information that you gather on the site. You also will need to establish **accessibility rules**—a set of design objectives that ensure disabled users can effectively access your site. There are more than 650 million people worldwide who are disabled and many of whom may require special help in order to be able to access computer systems (see *Insight on Society: Designing for Accessibility*). E-commerce information policies are described in greater depth in Chapter 8.

privacy policy
a set of public statements declaring to your customers how you treat their personal information that you gather on the site

accessibility rules
a set of design objectives that ensure disabled users can effectively access your site

INSIGHT ON SOCIETY

DESIGNING FOR ACCESSIBILITY

About 10% of the population worldwide has a disability that affects their ability to use the Internet. There are approximately 360 million people worldwide with hearing loss and 285 million with significant vision loss. These and other disabilities, such as motor and mobility impairments, often can be addressed with intelligent software and hardware design. But, for the most part, this has not yet occurred. As a result, the Internet and mobile devices are unfriendly places for many disabled.

So how should designers build in accessibility for the blind? One tool is screen-reader software that translates text information on the screen into synthesized speech or Braille. A blind person navigates a Web page by checking the hypertext links on the page, usually by jumping from link to link with the Tab key; the screen-reader software automatically reads the highlighted text as the focus moves from link to link. The screen-reader software is looking for ASCII text, which it can convert to speech or Braille. Once the desired hypertext link has been located, the blind person presses the Enter key (clicks on the link) to go where the link points. Examples of such software include Freedom Scientific's Job Access with Speech (JAWS) and Macfortheblind's VoiceOver.

There are also several simple strategies Web designers can use to improve accessibility. Embedding text descriptions behind images is one example that allows screen readers to announce those descriptions. So instead of hearing "Image," when a screen reader passes over an image, the visually impaired user can hear "Photo of a cruise ship sitting in a harbor." Allowing users to set the color and font schemes also can make a difference for the visually impaired. Adding screen magnification tools and sound labels where hyperlinks appear are two additional ways to increase accessibility. For those who are hearing impaired, access to close-captioned video with subtitles , as mandated by the United States' 21st Century Communications and Video Accessibility Act, can also be helpful.

These are examples of "equivalent alternatives" that disability advocates suggest should be required, both for visual and auditory content, to ensure individuals with disabilities have equal access to information that appears on-screen. Guidelines for creating accessible Web pages include ensuring that text and graphics are understandable when viewed without color, using features that enable activation of page elements via a variety of input devices (such as keyboard, head wand, or Braille reader), and providing clear navigation mechanisms (such as navigation bars or a site map) to aid users.

The World Wide Web Consortium (W3C) issued Web Content Accessibility Guidelines (WCAG) 2.0 in June 2010 (final draft form) that provide all organizations with strategies in Web design for accommodating people with many different kinds of disabilities.

Ensuring accessibility of mobile devices has its own set of issues, in many instances ones that are even more challenging than those associated with the Web. There is only a limited selection of mobile devices with built-in accessibility features. The small size of the device, screen, and keypad presents its own problems. Third-party applications, such as text-to-speech/screen readers and screen magnifiers, are starting to become available, but much work still needs to be done. For instance, many mobile devices come equipped with voice control capabilities and audio alerts, which could be helpful to those with vision or motor difficulties, but in most cases, these are still limited to simple tasks, and do not provide access to the full functionality of the device. In addition, the deaf community cannot rely on audio content or alerts, so developers need to provide text or other alternatives for auditory information. Those with impaired motor functionality also face great challenges in dealing with input to mobile devices. To deal with these challenges, the WC3 recommends that mobile content developers follow WCAG 2.0 and its guidelines on mobile Web best practices.

Web accessibility is not just a concern for Web developers or a question of technical Web standards. It is also a matter of government policy. Article 9 of the United Nations' *Convention on the Rights of Persons with Disabilities* requires that as a matter of basic human rights, appropriate measures must be taken to ensure access to information and communications technologies for persons with disabilities on an equal basis with others. Despite this, actual accessibility of both government and private Web sites remains quite low. For instance, the most recent European Commission report on monitoring accessibility found that only one-third of the content generated by public authorities was accessible. In December 2012, the European Commission adopted a proposal for a directive on the accessibility of public sector bodies' Web sites, as a forerunner of a planned European Accessibility Act that the Commission is considering. In March 2014, members of the European Parliament voted to strengthen the proposed directive, requiring EU member states to ensure that not only all public Web and mobile sites are fully accessible, but also Web and mobile sites run by entities performing public tasks such as utility, health care, and transporation companies.

Various countries have also implemented accessibility legislation. In many cases, standards apply only to government agency Web sites and not private Web sites. For example French law requires all French public Web sites to comply with its standard, RGAA 2.2.1, which is based on WCAG2. In Germany, all government Web sites must comply with BITV 2 (also based on WCAG 2). One

exception is Australia, which requires non-government, as well as government Web sites to comply with WCAG 2. In the U.K., service providers must make reasonable adjustments to ensure their Web sites are accessible to all users. In determining what is reasonable, the Statutory Code of Practice indicates that factors to be taken into account include the service provider's financial and other resources, the amount of resources already spent on making adjustments, and the extent of any disruption that it would cause the service provider. Large companies will clearly have a more difficult time justifying any failure to make their Web sites accessible. In the United States, several statutes, including the Rehabilitation Act (Section 508), the Americans with Disabilities Act (the ADA), and the 21st Century Communications and Video Accessibility Act, impose various obligations with respect to accessibility.

Disability advocates are also using lawsuits as a way to move the ball forward. In January 2012, the Royal National Institute of the Blind (RNIB) brought a court case in the U.K. against BMI Baby, a British travel agency. In April 2012, BMI Baby agreed to make changes to its Web site to enable the blind to book flights. In the United States, the National Association of the Deaf sued Netflix, charging that its "Watch Instantly" feature does not provide equal access, which it must do as a "place of exhibition or entertainment" under the ADA. In 2012, a U.S. federal district court ruled that Web sites can be considered "public accommodation," and as such do fall under the jurisdiction of the ADA. In October 2012, Netflix settled the case, agreeing to caption all of its streaming videos by 2014. Despite these successes, however, much remains to be done to make Web sites, mobile sites, and apps fully accessible to the disabled.

SOURCES: "Digital Agenda for Europe: A Europe 2020 Initiative/Web Accessibility," European Commission, accessed December 1, 2014; "Tough new EU Public Sector Web Accessibility Rules Take Shape," by Dan Jellinek, UKAuthority.com, March 4, 2014; "Disabled Consumers' Ownership of Communications Services," Ofcom, September 25, 2013; "Digital Britain 2: Putting Users at the Heart of Government's Digital Services," National Audit Office, March 28, 2013; "Government Accessiblity Standards and WCAG 2.0," by Mark Rodgers, Blog.powermapper.com, November 13, 2012; "Mobile Web Accessibility," by Tim Shelton, Accessibletech.com, July 2011; "For the Disabled, Just Getting Online is a Struggle," by Wilson Rotham, Technolog.msnbc.msn.com, January 21, 2011; "W3C Web Accessibility Initiative [Final Draft]," WC3.org, June 2010; "Web Accessibility: Making Your Site Accessible to the Blind," by Curtis Chong, National Federation of the Blind, accessed August 14, 2009.

3.6   DEVELOPING A MOBILE WEB SITE AND BUILDING MOBILE APPLICATIONS

Today, building a Web site is just one part of developing an e-commerce presence. Given that around 2.25 billion Internet users worldwide (about 80% of all Internet users) access the Web at least part of the time from mobile devices, businesses today need to develop mobile Web sites, and mobile Web apps, native apps, or hybrid apps, in order to interact with customers, suppliers, and employees. Deciding which of these extended Web presence tools to use is a first step.

mobile Web site

version of a regular desktop Web site that is scaled down in content and navigation

There are kinds of mobile e-commerce platform offerings to consider, each with unique advantages and costs. A **mobile Web site** is a version of a regular Web site that is scaled down in content and navigation so that users can find what they want and move quickly to a decision or purchase. You can see the difference between a regular Web site and a mobile site by visiting the Amazon Web site from your desktop computer and then a smartphone or tablet computer. Amazon's mobile site is a cleaner, more interactive site suitable for finger navigation, and efficient consumer decision making. Like traditional Web sites, mobile Web sites run on a firm's servers, and are built using standard Web tools such as server-side HTML, Linux, PHP, and SQL. Like all Web sites, the user must be connected to the Web and performance will depend on bandwidth. Generally, mobile Web sites operate more slowly than traditional Web sites viewed on a desktop computer connected to a broadband office network. Most large firms today have mobile Web sites.

mobile Web app

application built to run on the mobile Web browser built into a smartphone or tablet computer

A **mobile Web app** is an application built to run on the mobile Web browser built into a smartphone or tablet computer. In the case of Apple, the native browser is Safari. Generally it is built to mimic the qualities of a native app using HTML5 and Java. Mobile Web apps are specifically designed for the mobile platform in terms of screen size, finger navigation, and graphical simplicity. Mobile Web apps can support complex interactions used in games and rich media, perform real-time, on-the-fly calculations, and can be geo-sensitive using the smartphone's built-in global positioning system (GPS) function. Mobile Web apps typically operate faster than mobile Web sites but not as fast as native apps.

native app

application designed specifically to operate using the mobile device's hardware and operating system

A **native app** is an application designed specifically to operate using the mobile device's hardware and operating system. These stand-alone programs can connect to the Internet to download and upload data, and can operate on this data even when not connected to the Internet. Download a book to an app reader, disconnect from the Internet, and read your book. Because the various types of smartphones have different hardware and operating systems, apps are not "one size fits all" and therefore need to be developed for different mobile platforms. An Apple app that runs on an iPhone cannot operate on Android phones. As you learned in Chapter 2, native apps are built using different programming languages depending on the device for which they are intended, which is then compiled into binary code, and which executes extremely fast on mobile devices, much faster than HTML or Java-based mobile Web apps. For this reason, native apps are ideal for games, complex interactions, on-the-fly calculations, graphic manipulations, and rich media advertising.

Increasingly, developers are combining elements of native apps and mobile Web apps into hybrid apps. A **hybrid app** has many of the features of both a native app and a mobile Web app. Like a native app, it runs inside a native container on the mobile device and has access to the device's APIs, enabling it to take advantage of many of the device's features, such as a gyroscope, that are normally not acessible by a mobile Web app. It can also be packaged as an app for distribution from an App store. Like a mobile Web app, it is based on HTML5, CSS3, and JavaScript, but uses the device's browser engine to render the HTML5 and process the JavaScript locally.

hybrid app
has many of the features of both a native app and a mobile Web app

PLANNING AND BUILDING A MOBILE PRESENCE

What is the "right" mobile presence for your firm? The answer depends on identifying the business objectives, and from these, deriving the information requirements of your mobile presence. The same kind of systems analysis and design (SAD) reasoning described earlier in the chapter is needed for planning and building a mobile presence, although there are important differences.

The first step is to identify the business objectives you are trying to achieve. **Table 3.12** illustrates the thought process for the analysis stage of building a mobile presence. Why are you developing a mobile presence? Is it to drive sales by creating an easily browsed catalog where users can shop and purchase? Strengthen your brand by creating an engaging, interactive experience? Enable customers to interact with your customer community? How are your competitors using their mobile presence? Once you have a clear sense of business objectives, you will be able to describe the kind of system functionality that is needed and specify the information requirements for your mobile presence.

After you have identified the business objectives, system functionality, and information requirements, you can think about how to design and build the system. Now

TABLE 3.12	SYSTEMS ANALYSIS FOR BUILDING A MOBILE PRESENCE	
BUSINESS OBJECTIVE	**SYSTEM FUNCTIONALITY**	**INFORMATION REQUIREMENTS**
Drive sales	Digital catalog; product database	Product descriptions, photos, SKUs, inventory
Branding	Showing how customers use your products	Videos and rich media; product and customer demonstrations
Building customer community	Interactive experiences, games with multiple players	Games, contests, forums, social sign-up to Facebook
Advertising and promotion	Coupons and flash sales for slow-selling items	Product descriptions, coupon management, and inventory management
Gathering customer feedback	Ability to retrieve and store user inputs including text, photos, and video	Customer sign-in and identification; customer database

is the time to consider which to develop: a mobile Web site, a mobile Web app, or a native app. For instance, if your objective is branding or building community, a native app might be the best choice because it enables you to deliver a rich, interactive, and immersive experience that can strengthen the emotional connection with the brand. Because native apps are stored locally on the device, they can be accessed even when the user is offline, enabling the user to more deeply engage. In addition, native apps can take advantage of the mobile device's unique characteristics, such as using the gyroscope to deliver a 360-degree view. If your objective, on the other hand, is to create broad awareness, provide specific information on particular products, or drive sales, then a mobile Web site or mobile Web app makes more sense, because it is relatively easy and inexpensive to simply publish information to the mobile Web and consumers are still most comfortable completing transactions on the Web (although this is changing as more and more retailers add e-commerce functionality directly into apps). Increasingly, however, the choice will not be an either/or decision. Mobile apps and mobile Web sites each offer distinct benefits, and in most cases, the best strategy will be to plan to deliver compelling content across all devices.

MOBILE PRESENCE: DESIGN CONSIDERATIONS

Designing a mobile presence is somewhat different from traditional desktop Web site design because of different hardware, software, and consumer expectations. **Table 3.13** describes some of the major differences.

Designers need to take mobile platform constraints into account when designing for the mobile platform. File sizes should be kept smaller and the number of files sent to the user reduced. Focus on a few, powerful graphics, and minimize the number of images sent to the user. Simplify choice boxes and lists so the user can easily scroll and touch-select the options.

TABLE 3.13	UNIQUE FEATURES THAT MUST BE TAKEN INTO ACCOUNT WHEN DESIGNING A MOBILE PRESENCE
FEATURE	IMPLICATIONS FOR MOBILE PLATFORM
Hardware	Mobile hardware is smaller, and there are more resource constraints in data storage and processing power.
Connectivity	The mobile platform is constrained by slower connection speeds than desktop Web sites.
Displays	Mobile displays are much smaller and require simplification. Some screens are not good in sunlight.
Interface	Touch-screen technology introduces new interaction routines different from the traditional mouse and keyboard. The mobile platform is not a good data entry tool but can be a good navigational tool.

Mobile presence has become so important that it is fueling a growing trend to flip the traditional e-commerce development process and begin instead with development of a mobile presence rather than a desktop Web site (known as **mobile first design**). Mobile first design has several advantages. Instead of creating a full-featured design for a desktop Web site that then needs to be scaled back, mobile first design focuses on creating the best possible experience given mobile platform constraints and then adding back elements for the desktop platform, progressively enhancing the the functionality of the site. Proponents of mobile first design argue that it forces designers to focus on what is most important, and this helps create a lean and efficient mobile design that functions much better than a design that begins with a traditional platform that must be stripped down to work on mobile. Mobile first design is not without its challenges, however. It can be more difficult for designers who are more comfortable with the more traditional process (Byers, 2013).

Other important trends in the development of mobile Web sites include responsive Web design and adaptive Web design.

Responsive Web design (RWD) tools and design techniques make it possible to design a Web site that automatically adjusts its layout and display according to the screen resolution of the device on which it is being viewed, whether a desktop, tablet, or smartphone. RWD tools include HTML5 and CSS3 and its three key design principles involve using flexible grid-based layouts, flexible images and media, and media queries. RDW uses the same HTML code and design for each device, but uses CSS (which determines the layout of the Web page) to adjust the layout and display to the screen's form factor. RWD sites typically work well for sites with relatively simple functionality (i.e., sites that primarily deliver content) and that users engage with in a similar manner no matter the device being used. However, using RWD can be costly, often requiring a complete redesign of the Web site's interface. Another problem with RDW, particularly if not coupled with mobile first design, is that the responsive Web site still has the size and complexity of a traditional desktop site, sometimes making it slow to load and perform on a mobile device. Another technique, known as adaptive Web design, has been developed to deal with this issue.

With **adaptive Web design (AWD)** (sometimes also referred to as *adaptive delivery or responsive Web design with server-side components (RESS)*), the server hosting the Web site detects the attributes of the device making the request and, using predefined templates based on device screen size along with CSS and JavaScript, loads a version of the site that is optimized for the device. AWD has a number of advantages, including faster load times, the ability to enhance or remove functionality on the fly, and typically a better user experience, particularly for businesses where user intent differs depending on the platform being used. For example, creating its mobile Web site with AWD enabled Lufthansa to focus on actions its mobile users are most likely to take, such as checking in, getting flight status information, and looking up travel itineraries, and to provide a differentiated experience from its traditional desktop site (Pratap, 2013). A variation on AWD uses a cloud-based platform to provide similar functionality (Moovweb, 2013).

mobile first design
beginning the e-commerce development process with a mobile presence rather than a desktop Web site

responsive Web design (RWD)
tools and design principles that automatically adjust the layout of a Web site depending on the screen resolution of the device on which it is being viewed

adaptive Web design (AWD)
server-side technique that detects the attributes of the device making the request and, using predefined templates based on device screen size along with CSS and JavaScript, loads a version of the site that is optimized for the device

CROSS-PLATFORM MOBILE APP DEVELOPMENT TOOLS

In addition to creating native apps from scratch using a programming language such as Objective C or Java (as described in Chapter 2), there are hundreds of low-cost or open source app development toolkits that make creating cross-platform mobile apps relatively easy and inexpensive without having to use a device-specific programming language.

Tools include Appery.io, a cloud-based platform that enables you to a drag-and-drop visual builder tool to create HTML5 apps using jQuery Mobile. Appery.io supports Android, iOS, and Windows Phone applications. Codiqua is a similar tool that is even easier to use. It also provides a drag-and-drop interface and builds an app with 100% HTML5 components, without the need to do any coding. For those who are even less technical, Conduit is a free mobile app builder that allows you to include a variety of functionality, including e-commerce, notifications, and a social feed.

On the more technical side, PhoneGap is a mobile development framework that uses software called Apache Cordova to enable building hybrid mobile applications using HTML, CSS, and JavaScript. MoSynch is another advanced tool for developing cross-platform apps for iOS, Android, Linux Mobile, Windows Mobile, and Symbian operating systems. Appcelerator is a similar, less technical tool for creating and managing hybrid mobile apps.

MOBILE PRESENCE: PERFORMANCE AND COST CONSIDERATIONS

If you don't have an existing Web site, the most efficient process may be to use a mobile first design philosophy and design a mobile site first. Alternatively, you may choose to build a traditional Web site using RWD or AWD techniques. If you already have a Web site that you don't want to totally redevelop, the least expensive path is to resize it to create a smartphone-friendly mobile site. Doing so typically will not require a complete redesign effort. You will need to reduce the graphics and text, simplify the navigation, and focus on improving the customer experience so you do not confuse people. Because your customers might still need to use a relatively slow cell connection at times, you will need to lighten up the amount of data you send. Also, given the difficulty of customer data entry on a mobile device, you cannot expect customers to happily enter long strings of numbers or text characters. For marketing clarity, make sure the brand images used on the mobile Web site match those on the traditional Web site. The cost of developing a mobile Web site can range widely, from upwards of €1 million for a custom-designed site for a large global enterprise to well under €1,000 for a small business who chooses a company such as Wix or Mofuse that offers a template or mobile Web site creator, as described in the *Insight on Technology* case, *Building a Mobile Presence*.

Building a mobile Web app that uses the mobile device's browser requires more effort and cost than developing a mobile Web site, suffers from the same limitations as any browser-based application, but does offer some advantages such as better graphics, more interactivity, and faster local calculations as, for instance, in mobile geo-location applications like Foursquare that require local calculations of position and then communication with the site's Web server.

INSIGHT ON TECHNOLOGY

BUILDING A MOBILE PRESENCE

Today, almost every company with a Web presence is thinking about or developing mobile applications and a mobile Web site. Customers expect, and even demand, to be able to use a mobile device of their choice to obtain information or perform a transaction anywhere and at any time. So, if a company wants to stay connected to its customers, it needs a mobile presence.

Developing mobile apps or a mobile Web site has some special challenges. The user experience on a mobile device is fundamentally different from that on a desktop computer. There are special features on mobile devices such as location-based services that give a company the potential to interact with customers in new ways. Businesses need to be able to take advantage of those features while delivering an experience that is appropriate to a small screen. You can't just port a Web site or desktop application to a smartphone or tablet. There are multiple mobile platforms to work with—iPhone, Android, Black-Berry, and Windows—and a company may need a different version of an application to run on each of these. Increasingly, mobile-optimized Web sites are "responsive," which means they adapt their displays based on the screen resolution of the mobile device used to view the site. Some mobile sites have tweaks to their layout that factor in the smartphone browsing experience, such as placing company contact information at the top of the screen on every page instead of at the bottom of only certain pages.

It's important to understand how, why, and where customers use mobile devices and how these mobile experiences change business interactions and behavior. For example, do customers who use an app conduct a greater number of transactions (like purchasing) on apps when compared to a mobile browser? When compared to a tablet computer, do customers spend more or less time researching products and shopping from a smartphone?

Local businesses may stand to significantly gain from the shift to mobile. Approximately half of all mobile searches are done in search of a nearby business. The total number of local business searches performed on mobile phones has been growing explosively, along with nearly every other statistic related to mobile devices or mobile apps. Over 50% of the U.S. population has a smartphone and almost as many (46%) own a tablet.

The number of small businesses with Web sites optimized for mobile navigation is trailing behind those numbers. Only about 15% of small businesses have mobile Web sites with responsive design, and approximately half of all businesses lack a mobile site or app entirely. These numbers are expected to rise over time as the businesses that optimize their sites first reap the benefits, such as increased traffic and better standing in Google searches and other search engines. A 2013 report by Adobe showed that companies investing in mobile-optimized sites are three times more likely to achieve mobile conversion rates of 5% or higher than companies relying exclusively on traditional desktop Web sites. During the original dot-com boom, companies that were quick to adjust to the new online business environment gained an edge on their competitors. The same thing is happening with the mobile platform today.

Before entering the mobile sphere, companies should develop a clear strategy and goals they hope to accomplish. A mobile strategy involves

(continued)

more than selecting mobile devices, operating systems, and applications. It also involves changes to the way a business interacts with its customers. Mobile technology can streamline processes, make them more portable, and enhance them with capabilities such as touch interfaces, location and mapping features, alerts, texting, cameras, and video functionality. The technology can also create less efficient processes or fail to deliver benefits if the mobile application is not properly designed.

Many small businesses have struggled to adapt to the changes of designing for mobile. Often, businesses design their Web sites with artistic considerations in mind, but mobile users are less interested in presentation and more interested in functionality. Sites with Flash elements are incompatible with the iPhone, which makes the mobile browsing experience incomplete or frustrating for the user. Many times with mobile, less is more when it comes to design. Common features of today's mobile Web sites are a navigation bar at the top of each page that persists throughout browsing, collapsible sets of data that cut down on screen space unless users specifically request to see the complete set of information, such as a restaurant menu or full mailing address, and simple, easy-to-read icons and buttons such as a Facebook "like" button.

Many businesses are still getting used to the costs of maintaining a Web site and aren't willing to redo that work and spend more time and resources to incorporate responsive design. In one survey of small businesses, businesses not using any mobile solutions said that the two biggest reasons for staying away from mobile were lack of customer demand and lack of ability to deploy and use them. But the total number of businesses that say they have no intention of entering the mobile arena is going down precipitously. In the same survey, only 8% of businesses reported no plans to have a mobile-optimized Web site. That number was down from 28% of businesses in 2013.

There are a number of Web site design companies that offer templates that can automatically convert Web sites into mobile-only versions of the same site. For example, you can create a desktop Web site using a template provided by Wix, and it will automatically create a mobile version of the site. A Mobile Editor enables you to change the design of the mobile site without affecting the desktop version of the site, giving businesses more creative freedom. Mofuse is another company that offers an easy-to-use mobile Web site creator. For those who are challenged by even that prospect, Mofuse will create the site for you. Developing mobile apps is probably a bit more daunting for the average small business, but there are number of platforms that can help you build a mobile app on a budget without any programming knowledge. For example BiznessApps enables you to use a drag-and-drop template to quickly and easily build iPhone, iPad, Android, and HMTL5 apps that include functionality such as dynamic content, one-touch calling, push notifications, built-in sharing capabilities, a shopping cart, loyalty program, in-app purchases, and much more. It also offers templates optimized for various industries, such as restaurants, bars and clubs, realtors, lawyers, gyms and fitness centers, and spas and salons. A content management system allows the apps to be easily customized and updated. More than 100,000 small businesses around the world have used BiznessApps.

SOURCES: "Overview," Biznessapps.com, August 22, 2014; "Mobile Madness: Small Business Mobile Adoption on the Rise," by Jason Fidler, Business2community.com, July 30, 2014; "Making Sure Your Website is Ready for Smartphones," by Eilene Zimmerman, *New York Times*, January 8, 2014; "10 Excellent Platforms for Building Mobile Apps," by Grace Smith, Mashable.com, December 3, 2013; "New Mobile Solution from Wix — Better, Faster and 100% Free Mobile Websites," Wix.com, October 2, 2013; "4 Examples of Stellar Small Business Mobile Websites," by Sebastian Agosta, Experiencedmg.com, April 11, 2013; "45% of Businesses Still Don't Have a Mobile Site or App," by David Moth, Econsultancy.com, May 2, 2013; "Mobility Transforms the Customer Relationship," by Samuel Greengard, Baseline, February 2012; "Going Mobile: A Portable Approach to Process Improvement," *Business Agility Insights*, June 2012.

The most expensive path to a mobile presence is to build a native app. Native apps can require more extensive programming expertise. In addition, virtually none of the elements used in your existing Web site can be reused, and you will need to redesign the entire logic of the interface and carefully think out the customer experience. For instance, there is a fairly stable HTML traditional Web site interface with buttons, graphics, videos, and ads that has developed over the last decade. This is not true for apps. There is no set of standards or expectations even on the part of users—every app looks different from every other app. This means the user confronts large variations in app design, so your interface must be quite simple and obvious. Many of the bells and whistles found on the large desktop Web site screen cannot be used in mobile apps. You'll need even greater simplification and focus. These weaknesses are also native apps' greatest strength: you have the opportunity to create a really stunning, unique customer experience where users can interact with your brand. If you want an intense branding experience with your customers, where interaction between your brand and customers is effortless and efficient, then native apps are the best choice.

Orbitz Worldwide Charts
Its Mobile Trajectory

When it comes to mobile apps and gauging their impact on consumers and business, there's no better industry to look at than the online travel industry and its airline and hotel reservation systems. And there's no better company in this industry in developing mobile apps than Orbitz Worldwide Inc., the leading online travel site. Orbitz connects consumers to hundreds of airlines, over 80,000 hotels, 15 rental car agencies, as well as cruises and vacation packages. Orbitz typically has over 8 million unique visitors to its Web site each month.

As early as 1999, fledgling Internet travel companies such as Priceline, Expedia, and Travelocity were already transforming the travel industry. Recognizing the threat, and the opportunity, five major airlines—United, Delta, Continental, Northwest, and American—banded together to form a new venture that would become Orbitz. By the

© NetPhotos/Alamy

time the site launched in 2001, six other airlines had invested and anti-trust objections from consumer groups and competitors had been rejected by the U.S. Department of Transportation. Even at that early date, the Orbitz management team was forward-thinking, providing the capability for consumers to access flight updates and cancellations via pagers and mobile phones. By the time the Department of Justice had completely cleared Orbitz for takeoff and it had completed its IPO in November 2003, Orbitz had recruited more than 100 independent hotels in addition to its initial TravelWeb syndicate, which included the big players such as Marriott, Hilton, and Hyatt.

In 2006, Orbitz became the first Internet travel company to offer a WML-only (Wireless Markup Language) mobile Web site in the United States. (Expedia had a mobile site for its UK customers.) Users could check flight statuses for 27 airlines, some of which did not yet have a mobile site, and search for hotels in the 19 largest destination markets in the United States and in Cancun, Mexico. They also had access to a personal page dedicated to itineraries for Orbitz-booked trips and links to autodial Orbitz customer service. Additional services added in 2007 included enabling mobile users to view average wait times to get through security and available Wi-Fi services for a particular airport. A data feedback system was instituted to compute check-in delays and taxi line wait-times based on customer-inputted experiences. In 2008, Orbitz added an iPhone/iPod–specific app with the same capabilities for itinerary, flight status, WiFi availability, and wait-time checking as well as the ability to view weather and traffic conditions, reports from other travelers, and information about where to park and ground transportation. Customers could also now use technology specifically designed for touch-based Safari browsers to book a hotel room during inclement weather.

By 2010, market research had pushed Orbitz to increase its investment in mobile technology. It launched a redesigned mobile Web site in July, and a smartphone app for Google Inc.'s Android operating system in November, along with an updated iPhone app. Users of any Web-enabled device could now access a tool set comparable to the one available on its regular Web site to purchase flights, book car rentals, and secure hotel accommodations, including same-day reservations, as well as Orbitz's Price Assurance service, which guarantees consumers an automatic refund if another Orbitz customer books the same service for less. The native apps and redesigned mobile site were developed in-house with input from an unnamed outside vendor.

In 2011, Orbitz was the first to launch an m-commerce site designed for business users. The site was accessible from any Web-enabled device, which avoided the pitfalls of developing native apps for the wide variety of different devices its customers used. Users could enter and modify their trips via the app and give preference to a preferred vendor, which helped to adhere to company-specific travel policies. They also launched a hotel-booking app for iPad users. The app used the GPS function to display a detailed map of the user's location, with pins denoting nearby hotels and providing hotel details like address, phone number, and cost per night. Barney Harford, CEO of Orbitz Worldwide, touted the ability to book a hotel room in just three taps.

The rollout of the m-commerce site and iPad app prepared Orbitz to create second-generation applications that could meet evolving consumer expectations and adjust to the rapidly expanding and changing mobile environment. Three main improvements were made to the second-generation m-commerce site. First, it was optimized

SOURCES: "Orbitz Lets Users Resume Searches Across Devices," by Mark Walsh, Mediapost.com, August 19, 2014; "Orbitz for Business See Strong Growth in Best-in-Class Mobile Booking Tool," Orbitz.com, July 29, 2014; "The Orbitz App is on Fire," Orbitz. com, July 25, 2014; "Orbitz Flights, Hotels, Cars App Wins Appy Award for Best Travel App," Marketwatch. com, May 22, 2014; "Orbitz Reports Strong Q1 Growth Backed By Enhanced Mobile and Rewards," Pymnts.com, May 14, 2014; "Orbitz.com Rated #1 Online Travel Provider in ACSI Customer Satisfaction Survey," *Wall Street Journal*, April 23, 2014; "Orbitz.com Rated #1 Online Travel Provider in ACSI Customer Satisfaction Survey," *Wall Street Journal*, April 23, 2014; "Orbitz for Business Rolls Out Major Update to Best-in-Class Mobile Booking Tool," GlobeNewswire.com, March 26, 2014; "Expedia, Orbitz, Harness Big Data for Next-Generation Mobile Booking," by Chantal Tode, Mobilecommercedaily.com, January 30, 2014; "Orbitz.com Rolls Out Major Update to Orbitz Flights, Hotels, Cars App for Android," marketwatch.com, Orbitz.com, August 21, 2013; "Orbitz Releases the First Native App for iPad that Allows Consumers to Book Flights, Hotels, and Rental Cars," Orbitz.com, February 25, 2013; "How to Embark upon an M-commerce Redesign," by Kevin Woodward, *Internet Retailer*, August 10, 2012; "Orbitz Revamps iPhone App with Focus on Streamlined Booking, Deals," by Lauren Johnson, *Mobile Commerce Daily*, June 22, 2012; "Orbitz Rolls Out Major Update to App for iPhone and iPod Touch," Orbitz, June 21, 2012; "Orbitz Releases New Travel App," by Emily Brennan, *New York Times*, June 21, 2012; "Orbitz Launches New iPhone App, Bets on Mobile Growth," by Erica Ogg, Gigaom.com, June 21, 2012; "Orbitz: Mobile Searches May Yield Better Hotel Deals," by Barbara De Lollis, *USA Today*, May 10, 2012; "Orbitz Launches Revamped Mobile Site, Daily Deals to Capitalize on Last-Minute Travel,"

to accommodate the small screen size of any Web-enabled mobile device. Second, it was updated to accommodate swiping gestures, and third, it was revamped to expedite touch screen transactions. HTML5 enabled Orbitz to incorporate features traditionally associated with apps, such as swiping and faster browsing. Features were also added, including the ability to book vacation packages, view savings made by booking flight and hotel rooms at once, improved search and filtering capabilities, and linking an online profile to credit cards to hasten the checkout process.

Looking to capitalize on the market research findings that highlighted the burgeoning role of Web-enabled mobile devices in securing same-day accommodations, Orbitz also instituted mobile-exclusive same-day deals. These specials, called Mobile Steals, are available both on the m-commerce site and through the Hotels by Orbitz app, which was also released for the Android and iPhone. Last-minute perishable goods are available in more than 50 markets worldwide, benefitting both lodging proprietors and consumers. Proprietors are able to fill rooms that might otherwise remain vacant, and consumers enjoy savings of up to 50% off the standard rate.

With mobile transaction customers doubling in one year's time, Orbitz decided that an overhaul of its native iPhone app was also in order. When relaunched in June 2012, the iOS app included an improved filtering tool that enabled users to search and compare offerings by cost, distance from destination, and star ratings. Securing flight, lodging, and car rental reservations was simplified, eliminating browser screens and data entry repetition, and allowing users to perform all three operations in a continuous in-app stream unassociated with a mobile Web site. This was the heart of the redesign: to eliminate the mobile Web site and consolidate the entire search and reservation process within the native app so that users would no longer experience disruptive and time-consuming redirects either to Orbitz's mobile site or to an airline, hotel, or car rental agency site to complete the booking. The goal was to trump its competitors on speed and ease of use.

In order to verify that its goals for the app had been achieved, Orbitz commissioned a speed comparison study with Atmosphere Research Group and C + R Research. The travel apps, m-commerce sites, and e-commerce sites of its major competitors, including Kayak, Expedia, Priceline, and Travelocity, were pitted against the Orbitz iPhone app. The study found that Orbitz iPhone app users were able to book a round-trip flight to Hilton Head, South Carolina, a hotel reservation, and a car rental in slightly more than seven minutes, twice as fast as people using its iPhone app competitors. Only 60% of study participants using a competitor's product (aggregated) were able to complete the task as quickly. The Orbitz iPhone app transaction speed also surpassed comparable iPad and Android apps as well as desktop e-commerce site experiences. Study participants overwhelmingly awarded positive marks to the completely in-house–built Orbitz iPhone app in comparison to its competitors, 92% and 30%, respectively.

To speed the identification and fulfillment of future needs, customers' search history, personal information, frequent flyer program data, and travel preferences are saved within the app, enabling one-tap access to recent searches and automatic search suggestions. Itineraries can be accessed even while offline, and flight status and gate change data can be accessed with a single tap. Trips can also be easily added to the Apple Calendar app, formerly called iCal, used by many iPhone and iPod touch users.

Since then, Orbitz has continued to expand its array of apps across different operating systems and platforms. In 2013, it launched a full version of its *Flights, Hotels, Cars* app as a native app optimized for iPad, the first of its kind among travel service providers. Orbitz also fully overhauled the same app for Android, marking the third generation of its Android native app. Orbitz plans to continue its mobile development across all platforms. In October 2013, Orbitz launched Orbitz Rewards, a rewards program that has led to a marked increase in mobile purchases. The program already has over 2 million members, many of which are entirely new customers to Orbitz. In January 2014, Orbitz introduced Orbitz Labs, as part of an effort to use the increasing amount of data its users generate to provide better services and drive more bookings. Orbitz is using Orbitz Labs to test out new features and keep track of which ones are most popular with users, with the intent of incorporating those popular features into the Orbitz mobile app. In March 2014, Orbitz released a new version of its Orbitz for Business mobile site, with a new design that increases ease of use and provides improved speed and touch responsiveness. In July 2014, it released an app for the Amazon Fire phone that is customized to take advantage of the unique technology that the Fire phone employs, such as its Dynamic Perspective technology that allows users to view in multiple dimensions and provides an immersive experience. In addition, it is rolling out a responsive design approach across devices, and has started syncing user searches across devices so that users can pick up where they left off, no matter what device they are using. Orbitz has earned rave reviews for its efforts, winning the APPY Award for best travel app and receiving the top rating in customer satisfaction among all online travel Web sites. The efforts are paying off. Orbitz reports that more than 30% of its hotel bookings now come via a mobile channel, compared to only 3% in 2010, and up from 24% in 2013.

by Lauren Johnson, *Mobile Commerce Daily*, December 13, 2011; "Orbitz Travels the M-commerce Site Redesign Route," by Bill Siwicki, *Internet Retailer*, December 13, 2011; "Orbitz Unveils Powerful New Mobile Website and Introduces New 'Mobile Steals' Program Offering Discounted Mobile-only Rates on Hotels," Orbitz, December 12, 2011; "Orbitz Launches New 'Orbitz Hotels' App for iPad®," Orbitz, July 6, 2011; "Orbitz for Business Debuts Mobile Booking Site Targeting Corporate Travelers," by Dan Butcher, *Mobile Commerce Daily*, April 15, 2011; "Two Travel Providers Make Mobile Moves," by Katie Deatsch, *Internet Retailer*, November 16, 2010; "Orbitz Launches Native iPhone® and Android™ Applications That Allow Consumers to Shop and Book Flight, Hotel and Car Rental Options," Orbitz, November 15, 2010; "Orbitz for iPhone Review," by Joe Seifi, AppSafari.com, November 13th, 2008; "Orbitz Goes Mobile," by Russell Buckley, MobHappy.com, September 6, 2007; "Orbitz Mobile," by Dennis Bournique, WAPReview.com, August 15, 2006.

Case Study Questions

1. When compared to traditional desktop customers, why are mobile phone users much more likely to book a room or airline reservation for the same day?

2. In the mobile design project of 2011, why did Orbitz management decide to construct a mobile Web site for corporate users rather than a native app?

3. Why has Orbitz decided to go with native apps for each mobile platform (iOS, Android, and Kindle Fire) instead of a single mobile Web site as it did with the Orbitz for Business mobile site?

4. What issues does syncing recent user searches across devices pose?

3.8   REVIEW

KEY CONCEPTS

- ■ **Understand the questions you must ask and answer, and the steps you should take, in developing an e-commerce presence.**

- Questions you must ask and answer when developing an e-commerce presence include:
  - What is your vision and how do you hope to accomplish it?
  - What is your business and revenue model?
  - Who and where is the target audience?
  - What are the characteristics of the marketplace?
  - Where is the content coming from?
  - Conduct a SWOT analysis.
  - Develop an e-commerce presence map.
  - Develop a timeline.
  - Develop a detailed budget.

- ■ **Explain the process that should be followed in building an e-commerce presence.**

- Factors you must consider when building an e-commerce site include hardware, software, telecommunications capacity, Web site and mobile platform design, human resources, and organizational capabilities.
- The systems development life cycle (a methodology for understanding the business objectives of a system and designing an appropriate solution) for building an e-commerce Web site involves five major steps:
- Identify the specific business objectives for the site, and then develop a list of system functionalities and information requirements.
- Develop a system design specification (both logical design and physical design).
- Build the site, either by in-house personnel or by outsourcing all or part of the responsibility to outside contractors.
- Test the system (unit testing, system testing, and acceptance testing).
- Implement and maintain the site.
- The basic business and system functionalities an e-commerce site should contain include a digital catalog, a product database, customer tracking, shopping cart/payment system, an on-site blog, a customer database, an ad server, a site tracking and reporting system, and an inventory management system.
- Advantages of building a site in-house include the ability to change and adapt the site quickly as the market demands and the ability to build a site that does exactly what the company needs.
- Disadvantages of building a site in-house include higher costs, greater risks of failure, a more time-consuming process, and a longer staff learning curve that delays time to market.
- Using design templates cuts development time, but preset templates can also limit functionality.
- A similar decision is also necessary regarding outsourcing the hosting of the site versus keeping it in-house. Relying on an outside vendor places the burden of reliability on someone else in return for a monthly hosting fee. The downside is that if the site requires fast upgrades due to heavy traffic, the chosen hosting company may or may not be capable of keeping up. Reliability versus scalability is the issue in this instance.

- ■ **Identify and understand the major considerations involved in choosing Web server and e-commerce merchant server software.**

- Early Web sites used single-tier system architecture and consisted of a single-server computer that delivered static Web pages to users making requests through their browsers. The extended functionality of today's Web sites requires the development of a multi-tiered systems architecture, which utilizes a variety of specialized Web servers, as well as links to pre-existing backend or legacy corporate databases.

- All e-commerce sites require basic Web server software to answer requests from customers for HTML and XML pages. When choosing Web server software, companies are also choosing what operating system the site will run on. Apache, which runs on the Unix system, is the market leader.
- Web servers provide a host of services, including processing user HTML requests, security services, file transfer, a search engine, data capture, e-mail, and site management tools.
- Dynamic server software allows sites to deliver dynamic content, rather than static, unchanging information. Web application server programs enable a wide range of e-commerce functionality, including creating a customer database, creating an e-mail promotional program, and accepting and processing orders, as well as many other services.
- E-commerce merchant server software is another important software package that provides catalog displays, information storage and customer tracking, order taking (shopping cart), and credit card purchase processing. E-commerce software platforms can save time and money, but customization can significantly drive up costs. Factors to consider when choosing an e-commerce software platform include its functionality, support for different business models, visual site management tools and reporting systems, performance and scalability, connectivity to existing business systems, compliance with standards, and global and multicultural capability.

■ **Understand the issues involved in choosing the most appropriate hardware for an e-commerce site.**

- Speed, capacity, and scalability are three of the most important considerations when selecting an operating system, and therefore the hardware that it runs on.
- To evaluate how fast the site needs to be, companies need to assess the number of simultaneous users the site expects to see, the nature of their requests, the type of information requested, and the bandwidth available to the site. The answers to these questions will provide guidance regarding the processors necessary to meet customer demand. In some cases, additional processing power can increase capacity, thereby improving system speed.
- Scalability is also an important issue. Increasing processing supply by scaling up to meet demand can be done through vertical or horizontal scaling or by improving processing architecture.

■ **Identify additional tools that can improve Web site performance.**

- In addition to providing a speedy Web site, companies must also strive to have a well-designed site that encourages visitors to buy. Building in interactivity improves site effectiveness, as do personalization techniques.
- Commonly used software tools for achieving high levels of Web site interactivity and customer personalization include Common Gateway Interface (CGI) scripts, Active Server Pages (ASP), Java applets, JavaScript, ActiveX and VBScript, Ajax, PHP, Ruby on Rails (RoR or Rails), and Django.

■ **Understand the important considerations involved in developing a mobile Web site and building mobile applications.**

- When developing a mobile presence, it is important to understand the difference between a mobile Web site, mobile Web apps, native apps, and hybrid apps.
- The first step is to identify business objectives, because they help determine which type of mobile presence is best.
- Design should take into account mobile platform constraints. Recent trends include mobile first design, responsive Web design, and adaptive Web delivery.
- Developing a mobile Web site is likely to be the least expensive option; mobile Web apps require more effort and cost; native apps are likely to be the most expensive to develop.

QUESTIONS

1. What elements do you need to address when developing a vision for an e-commerce presence?
2. Name the four main kinds of e-commerce presence and the different platforms for each type.
3. Identify the different phases used in a one-year timeline for the development of an e-commerce presence, and the related milestones for each phase.
4. Define the systems development life cycle and discuss the various steps involved in creating an e-commerce site.
5. Discuss the differences between a simple logical and a simple physical Web site design.
6. Why is a Web site so costly to maintain? Discuss the main factors that impact cost.
7. What are the main differences between single-tier and multi-tier site architecture?
8. What is a content management system and what function does it serve?
9. What is open source software and how can it be used in creating an e-commerce presence?
10. What are the main factors to consider when choosing an e-commerce suite?
11. What are some methods for achieving personalization and customization?
12. What are the eight most important factors impacting Web site design, and how do they affect a site's operation?
13. What is CGI and how does it enable interactivity?
14. What are some of the unique features that must be taken into account when designing a mobile Web presence?
15. What are Java and JavaScript? What role do they play in Web site design?
16. What are the advantages and disadvantages of mobile first design?
17. What is the difference between a mobile Web app and a native app?
18. In what ways does a hybrid mobile app combine the functionality of a mobile Web app and a native app?
19. What is PHP and how is it used in Web development?
20. How does responsive Web design differ from adaptive Web delivery?

PROJECTS

1. Go to the Web site of Wix, Weebly, or another provider of your choosing that allows you to create a simple e-tailer Web site for a free trial period. Create a Web site. The site should feature at least four pages, including a home page, product page, shopping cart, and contact page. Extra credit will be given for additional complexity and creativity. Come to class prepared to present your e-tailer concept and Web site.

2. Visit several e-commerce sites, not including those mentioned in this chapter, and evaluate the effectiveness of the sites according to the eight basic criteria/functionalities listed in Table 3.11. Choose one site you feel does an excellent job on all the aspects of an effective site and create an electronic presentation, including screen shots, to support your choice.

3. Imagine that you are in charge of developing a fast-growing start-up's e-commerce presence. Consider your options for building the company's e-commerce presence in-house with existing staff, or outsourcing the entire operation. Decide which strategy you believe is in your company's best interest and create a brief presentation outlining your position. Why choose that approach? And what are the estimated associated costs, compared with the alternative? (You'll need to make some educated guesses here—don't worry about being exact.)

4. Choose two e-commerce software packages and prepare an evaluation chart that rates the packages on the key factors discussed in the section "Choosing an E-commerce Software Platform." Which package would you choose if you were developing a Web site of the type described in this chapter, and why?

5. Choose one of the open source Web content management systems such as WordPress, Joomla, or Drupal or another of your own choosing and prepare an evaluation chart similar to that required by Project 4. Which system would you choose and why?

REFERENCES

Banker, Rajiv D., and Chris F. Kemerer. "Scale Economies in New Software Development." *IEEE Transactions on Software Engineering*, Vol. 15, No. 10 (1989).

Byers, Josh. "Three Reasons a "Mobile First" Philosophy is Critical to Achieving Your Business Goals." Copyblogger.com (May 11, 2013).

Codecondo. "10 Popular Sites Powered by Django Web Framework." (December 21, 2013).

Coderfactory. "Top 15 Sites Built with Ruby on Rails." (February 26, 2014).

Doyle, Barry, and Cristina Videria Lopes. "Survey of Technologies for Web Application Development." *ACM*, Vol. 2., No. 3. (June 2005).

Dusto, Amy. "The Top E-commerce Platform Vendors for Midmarket Retailers." Internetretailer.com (January 10, 2014).

IBM (High Volume Web Sites Team). "Best Practices for High-Volume Web Sites." *IBM Redbooks* (December 2002).

Lientz, Bennet P., and E. Burton Swanson. *Software Maintenance Management*. Reading MA: Addison-Wesley (1980).

Moovweb. "Responsive Delivery." (accessed August 27, 2014).

Netcraft. "PHP Just Grows and Grows." (accessed August 19, 2014).

Pratap, Ravi. "Responsive Design vs. Adaptive Delivery: Which One's Right for You?" Venturebeat.com (November 19, 2013).

W3Techs. "Server-side Languages." (accessed August 19, 2014).

Webtrends, Inc. "Webtrends Analytics 10." (2014).

CHAPTER 4

E-commerce Security and Payment Systems

After reading this chapter, you will be able to:

- Understand the scope of e-commerce crime and security problems, the key dimensions of e-commerce security, and the tension between security and other values.
- Identify the key security threats in the e-commerce environment.
- Describe how technology helps secure Internet communications channels and protect networks, servers, and clients.
- Appreciate the importance of policies, procedures, and laws in creating security.
- Identify the major e-commerce payment systems in use today.
- Describe the features and functionality of electronic billing presentment and payment systems.

Europol

Takes on Cybercrime with EC3

From the earliest of days, humans have warred against and stolen from each other, with the tools evolving over time from sticks and stones, to arrows and spears, to guns and bombs. Physical weaponry is familiar and readily recognizable. But today, algorithms and computer code have moved to the forefront. Cyberspace has become a new battlefield, one that often involves targets such as financial systems and communications networks.

© Rafal Olechowski / Fotolia

In 2013, the European Cybercrime Center (EC3) was created at Europol, the European law enforcement agency in The Hague, to combat the rise of cybercrime and cyberattacks throughout Europe and the rest of the world. More than half of the EU's population is now online, meaning that an organization like the EC3 is needed in Europe now more than ever before.

A major challenge in fighting cybercrime is to even concretely define it and measure the amount of cybercrime taking place. Estimates of how much cybercrime costs companies and individuals vary widely. For example, some experts indicate that cybercrime has cost €2 billion in the United Kingdom, but other estimates put the total global effect of cybercrime at hundreds of billions of euros. Not only that, but cybercrime is also a global problem, and countries have attempted many different strategies to fight it with a standard approach. The EC3 will help to standardize approaches to better counteract European cybercrime, and will help set guidelines regarding what incidents constitute cybercrime.

EC3 began operations out of The Hague on January 1, 2013, with a focus on three areas of cybercrime: crime committed by organized groups or rings, crime that causes harm to a victim, like child pornography, and cyberattacks on European Union infrastructure, such as government Web sites, databases, and storage centers. The EC3 launched with 43 anti-cybercrime experts, but may need to increase its staff in the future along with its budget. It also established a 12-member Advisory group on Internet security that includes Internet security experts from a variety of different fields and backgrounds, including Raj Samani, Chief Technology Officer for EMEA at McAfee, Eugene Kaspersky, founder of Kaspersky Labs, and Rik Ferguson, Vice President of Security Research for Trend Micro. In 2014, EC3's funding was increased by €1.7 million, with an additional budget increase slated for 2015. The additional funds will help EC3 to add both temporary and contracted staff. Still, concerns remain as to whether the current level of funding will be enough to keep pace with the projected increase in cybercrime over this period.

The EC3 describes its operations as having five main functions. First is data fusion, which involves gathering and processing information on cybercrime. The EC3 hopes to function as a central repository for statistics on cybercrime and its apprehension. Its second function will be cybercrime prevention operations, including conducting cybercrime investigations within individual EU states or facilitating joint investigations across multiple EU states. The third major function of the EC3 will be developing strategies for fighting cybercrime, analyzing crime trends, and forecasting future trends in cybercrime. The fourth function will be research and development as well as training of law enforcement agencies in the skills required to effectively investigate and combat cybercrime. The organization will also educate judges and prosecutors on cybercrime. Lastly, the EC3 will conduct outreach, working with the private sector, academia, and society at large to better handle cybercrime.

The majority of credit card numbers used in cybercrime in the EU have historically originated from United States data breaches, so a major focus of the EC3 has been preventing card-not-present (CNP) fraud. Europol reports that organized crime makes €1.5 billion from credit card fraud, 900 million of which originate from CNP fraud. As technological infrastructure improves in developing nations, it is expected that incidences of online credit card fraud originating in Africa and other similar countries will increase. The EC3 will need to be prepared for this type of cybercrime becoming more prevalent.

The early results of the EC3 have been positive. In 2013, it took down the largest ransomware cybercrime network in Russia, Operation Ransom, which spanned 33 countries, including 22 in the EU. Operation Ransom infected computers with police ransomware, which is a type of malware that blocks a computer completely and warns the user that they have visited illegal websites, such as child pornography, and requests payment of a fine to unblock it. The leader of the ring was arrested in Dubai by Spanish police and Europol along with at least ten more members of the group. In September 2013, in an operation code-named "Operation Ransom II," EC3 and Spanish police arrested two Ukranian cybercriminals who sold access to a botnet with over 21,000 compromised servers located in 80 different countries. They also operated a sophisticated money laundering scheme that processed around €10,000 a day through various electronic payment systems and virtual currencies. These two investigations were part of EC3's "Focal Point Cyborg," which assisted in a total of 19 cybercrime operations in the EC3's first year of existence.

As part of its "Focal Point Terminal" division, the EC3 busted an Asian criminal network responsible for the theft of 15,000 credit card numbers and for conducting illegal Internet transactions and purchases of airline tickets. In July, the EC3 held a 'day of action' to target criminals using stolen credit cards to buy airline tickets as part of a different ring. Europol and individual law enforcement officers worked in concert in each country to make the arrests, which are expected to yield further links to other criminal organizations. A third area, "Focal Point Twins," focused on nine sophisticated online child sexual exploitation rings in EC3's first year.

The EC3 is currently focused on fighting "cybercrime-as-a-service." Experienced cybercriminals are selling programs and services that buyers can use to commit cybercrime without the same knowledge of criminal techniques. When cybercrime is committed outside of the EU's jurisdiction, it is more difficult to police, so many skilled cybercriminals within EU borders have taken to cybercrime-as-a-service to reduce their risk, allowing others to execute the cybercrime instead. Criminals are also increasingly making use of legitimate tools to stay anonymous on the Web, such as encryption techniques, virtual currencies like Bitcoin, anonymization services such as Tor which are used to navigate areas on the Web known as the "Darknet," private networks where connections are made without sharing IP addresses.

Troels Oerting, head of the EC3, noted that although these obstacles are daunting, worldwide cybercrime is driven by a small number of talented programmers, and that focusing on these "top-level" criminals is the best way to combat cybercrime going forward. To that end, EC3 has launched a cybercrime task force in tandem with other law enforcement agencies called the Joint Cybercrime Action Task Force, which will focus on developing strategies for handling newer cybercrime techniques, pursuing the most dangerous cybercriminals, and further improving the flow of data between law enforcement agencies across borders. In November 2014, the EC3 demonstrated its ability to shut down sites on the Darknet, shutting down the second iteration of the underground black market Silk Road 2.0, and arresting its operator, a 26-year old former Google programmer. EC3's challenge will be to continue making these high-profile arrests while adapting to the ever-changing array of techniques cybercriminals use.

SOURCES: : "FBI, Europol Make Large 'Dark Web' Bust," Reuters, November 7, 2014; "Only 100 Cybercrime Brains Worldwide Says Europol Boss," BBC News, October 10, 2014; "Service Model Driving Cyber Crime, Says Europol Report," by Warwick Ashford, Computerweekly.com, September 29, 2014; "Europol's EC3 Launches Pan-Euro Cybercrime Taskforce J-CAT," by Phil Muncaster, Info Security, September 2, 2014; "Europol Launches Taskforce to Fight World's Top Cybercriminals," by Tom Brewster, Theguardian.com, September 1, 2014; "First Year Report," EC3, February 9, 2014; "Brian Honan Appointed Special Advisor to Europol Cybercrime Centre," Net-security.org, October 10, 2013; "Europol Appoints McAfee's Raj Samani as Cybercrime Advisor at EC3," The Security Lion, October 8, 2013; "Spanish Police and Europol Arrest Cybercrime 'Service Providers,' Europol, September 27, 2013; "Europol-Interpol Cybercrime Conference Steps Up Policing in Cyberspace," Europol, September 25, 2013; "European Cybercrime Center Targets Airline Ticket Fraud," by Jeff Goldman, esecurityplanet.com, July 2, 2013; "International Network of On-Line Card Fraudsters Dismantled," Europol, March 8, 2013; "European Cybercrime Centre Dismantles its First Criminal Network," by Nerea Rial, neurope. eu, February 14, 2013; "Opening of the European Cybercrime Center — A Journey Begins," by Neil Robinson, rand.org, January 11, 2013; "Europe's Cybercrime Fighters Get New Digs...Complete with Faraday Room," by John Leyden, theregister.co.uk, January 11, 2013;"Europe's New Cybercrime Center to Open Its Doors This Week: EC3 To Act As Hub for EU-Wide Collaboration to Combat E-Crime," by Natasha Lomas, TechCrunch, January 9, 2013.

A s *Europol Takes on Cybercrime with EC3* illustrates, the Internet and Web are increasingly vulnerable to large-scale attacks and potentially large-scale failure. Increasingly, these attacks are led by organized gangs of criminals operating globally—an unintended consequence of globalization. Even more worrisome is the growing number of large-scale attacks that are funded, organized, and led by various nations against the Internet resources of other nations. Currently there are few if any steps that individuals or businesses can take to prevent these kinds of attacks. However, there are several steps you can take to protect your business Web sites, your mobile devices, and your personal information from routine security attacks. Reading this chapter, you should also start thinking about how your business could survive in the event of a large-scale "outage" of the Internet.

In this chapter, we will examine e-commerce security and payment issues. First, we will identify the major security risks and their costs, and describe the variety of solutions currently available. Then, we will look at the major payment methods and consider how to achieve a secure payment environment. **Table 4.1** highlights some of the major trends in online security in 2014–2015.

TABLE 4.1	WHAT'S NEW IN E-COMMERCE SECURITY 2014–2015

- Large-scale data breaches continue to expose data about individuals to hackers and other cybercriminals.
- Mobile malware presents a tangible threat as smartphones and other mobile devices become more common targets of cybercriminals.
- Malware creation continues to skyrocket and ransomware attacks rise.
- Nations continue to engage in cyberwarfare and cyberespionage.
- Hackers and cybercriminals continue to focus their efforts on social network sites to exploit potential victims through social engineering and hacking attacks.
- Politically motivated, targeted attacks by hacktivist groups continue, in some cases merging with financially motivated cybercriminals to target financial systems with advanced persistent threats.
- Software vulnerabilities, such as the Heartbleed bug and other zero day vulnerabilities, continue to create security threats.
- Incidents involving celebrities raise awareness of cloud security issues.

4.1   THE E-COMMERCE SECURITY ENVIRONMENT

For most law-abiding citizens, the Internet holds the promise of a huge and convenient global marketplace, providing access to people, goods, services, and businesses worldwide, all at a bargain price. For criminals, the Internet has created entirely new—and lucrative—ways to steal from the more than 1.2 billion Internet consumers worldwide in 2014. From products and services, to cash, to information, it's all there for the taking on the Internet.

It's also less risky to steal online. Rather than rob a bank in person, the Internet makes it possible to rob people remotely and almost anonymously. Rather than steal a CD at a local record store, you can download the same music for free and almost without risk from the Internet. The potential for anonymity on the Internet cloaks many criminals in legitimate-looking identities, allowing them to place fraudulent orders with online merchants, steal information by intercepting e-mail, or simply shut down e-commerce sites by using software viruses and swarm attacks. The Internet was never designed to be a global marketplace with billions of users and lacks many basic security features found in older networks such as the telephone system or broadcast television networks. By comparison, the Internet is an open, vulnerable-design network. The actions of cybercriminals are costly for both businesses and consumers, who are then subjected to higher prices and additional security measures. The costs of malicious cyberactivity include not just the cost of the actual crime, but also the additional costs that are required to secure networks and recover from cyberattacks, the potential reputational damage to the affected company, as well as reduced trust in online activities, the loss of potentially sensitive business information, including intellectual property and confidential business information, and the cost of opportunities lost due to service disruptions. Ponemon Institute estimates that the average loss to U.S. corporations for a breach of data security in 2013 was $5.9 million (Ponemon Institute, 2014).

THE SCOPE OF THE PROBLEM

Cybercrime is becoming a more significant problem for both organizations and consumers. Bot networks, DDoS attacks, Trojans, phishing, ransomware, data theft, identity fraud, credit card fraud, and spyware are just some of the threats that are making daily headlines. Social networks also have had security breaches. But despite the increasing attention being paid to cybercrime, it is difficult to accurately estimate the actual amount of such crime, in part because many companies are hesitant to report it due to the fear of losing the trust of their customers, and because even if crime is reported, it may be difficult to quantify the actual dollar amount of the loss. A study by the Center for Strategic and International Studies examined the difficulties in accurately estimating the economic impact of cybercrime and cyberespionage, with its initial research indicating a range of between €240 to €800 billion. Further research is planned to try to help determine an even more accurate estimate (Center for Strategic and International Studies, 2013).

One source of information is a survey conducted by Ponemon Institute. Ponemon's 2014 survey included 46 companies in Germany, 29 in France, 38 in the United Kingdom, 24 in the Russian Federation, 30 in Australia, and 31 in Japan, as well as 59 in the United States. There were 1,717 total attacks reported, a 10.4% increase from the previous year. The total cost of the attacks was over €48 million, with the average annualized cost around €6.1 million. In all countries, virtually all organizations experienced an attack involving viruses, worms, Trojans, and malware. More than 50% of the companies also suffered attacks involving botnets, Web-based attacks, phishing and social engineering, and malicious code. The most costly types of attacks, however, were those by malicious insiders and denial of service (Ponemon Institute, 2014).

Reports issued by security product providers, such as Symantec, are another source of data. Symantec issues a semi-annual *Internet Security Threat Report*, based on 40 million sensors monitoring Internet activity in more than 150 countries. Advances in technology have greatly reduced the entry costs and skills required to enter the cybercrime business. Low-cost and readily available Web attack kits enable hackers to create malware without having to write software from scratch. In addition, there has been a surge in polymorphic malware, which enables attackers to generate a unique version of the malware for each victim, making it much more difficult for pattern-matching software used by security firms to detect. Symantec dubbed 2013 as the year of the mega data breach, with over 250 different breaches being identified, a more than 60% rise compared to 2012, exposing over 550 million identities. Other findings indicate that targeted attacks, spear phishing, and ransomware are all increasing; social networks are helping criminals identify individual targets; and mobile platforms and applications are increasingly vulnerable (Symantec, 2014a). However, Symantec does not attempt to quantify actual crimes and/or losses related to these threats.

Online credit card fraud is one of the most high-profile forms of e-commerce crime. Although the average amount of credit card fraud loss experienced by any one individual is typically relatively small, the overall amount is substantial. The global cost of payment card fraud in 2013 is estimated to have been around €11 billion, a 19% increase over the previous year. The United States accounted for more credit card fraud than the rest of the world combined, in part because EMV chip cards, which are standard outside the United States and are more difficult to copy, have not yet been widely adopted in United States (Heggestuen, 2014). The nature of credit card fraud has changed greatly from the theft of a single credit card number and efforts to purchase goods at a few sites, to the simultaneous theft of millions of credit card numbers and their distributions to thousands of criminals operating as gangs of thieves. The emergence of identity fraud, described in detail later in this chapter, as a major online/offline type of fraud may well increase markedly the incidence and amount of credit card fraud, because identity fraud often includes the use of stolen credit card information and the creation of phony credit card accounts.

The Underground Economy Marketplace: The Value of Stolen Information

Criminals who steal information on the Internet do not always use this information themselves, but instead derive value by selling the information to others on the so-called underground or shadow economy market. Data is currency to cybercriminals and has a "street value" that can be monetized. For example, in 2013, Vladislav Horohorin (alias "BadB") was sentenced to over 7 years in U.S. federal prison for using online criminal forums to sell stolen credit and debit card information (referred to as "dumps"). At the time of his arrest, Horohorin possessed over 2.5 million stolen credit and debit card numbers. There are several thousand known underground economy marketplaces around the world that sell stolen information. **Table 4.2** lists some recently observed prices, which typically vary depending on the quantity being purchased, supply available and "freshness." For example, when credit card information

TABLE 4.2	THE CYBER BLACK MARKET FOR STOLEN DATA
Individual credit card	$1–$120
A full identity (date of birth, social security number, etc.)	$1–$200
Bank account	$80–$700
Online accounts (PayPal, eBay, Facebook, Twitter, etc.)	$10–$1500
E-mail accounts	$5–$12
Botnet rental	$15
A single compromised computer	$6–$20
Social security number	$5–$7
Exploit kits	Varies depending on type, $500–$1,800/month
1,000 fake Instagram "followers"	$15
Zero-day vulnerability	$2,000–$200,000, depending on severity of vulnerability, product involved, buyer location.

SOURCES: Based on data from RAND Corporation, 2014; Finkle, 2013; Panda Security, 2012.

from the Target data breach first appeared on the market, individual card numbers went for up to $120 each. After a few weeks, however, the price dropped dramatically (Leger, 2014). Experts believe the cost of stolen information has generally fallen as the tools of harvesting have increased the supply. On the demand side, the same efficiencies and opportunities provided by new technology have increased the number of people who want to use stolen information. It's a robust marketplace.

Finding these marketplaces and the servers that host them can be difficult for the average user (and for law enforcement agencies), and prospective participants are typically vetted by other criminals before access is granted. This vetting process takes place through Twitter, Tor and VPN services, and sometimes e-mail exchanges of information, money (often Bitcoins, a virtual currency that we discuss further in Section 4.5 and in the *Insight on Technology* case study on pages 295–296), and reputation. There is a general hierarchy of cybercriminals in the marketplace, with low-level, nontechnical criminals who frequent "carder forums," where stolen credit and debit card data is sold, aiming to make money, a political statement, or both at the bottom; resellers in the middle acting as intermediaries; and the technical masterminds who create malicious code at the top.

So, what can we can conclude about the overall size of cybercrime? Cybercrime against e-commerce sites is dynamic and changing all the time, with new risks appearing often. The amount of losses to businesses is significant and growing. The managers of e-commerce sites must prepare for an ever-changing variety of criminal assaults, and keep current in the latest security techniques.

WHAT IS GOOD E-COMMERCE SECURITY?

What is a secure commercial transaction? Anytime you go into a marketplace you take risks, including the loss of privacy (information about what you purchased). Your prime risk as a consumer is that you do not get what you paid for. As a merchant in the market, your risk is that you don't get paid for what you sell. Thieves take merchandise and then either walk off without paying anything, or pay you with a fraudulent instrument, stolen credit card, or forged currency.

E-commerce merchants and consumers face many of the same risks as participants in traditional commerce, albeit in a new digital environment. Theft is theft, regardless of whether it is digital theft or traditional theft. Burglary, breaking and entering, embezzlement, trespass, malicious destruction, vandalism—all crimes in a traditional commercial environment—are also present in e-commerce. However, reducing risks in e-commerce is a complex process that involves new technologies, organizational policies and procedures, and new laws and industry standards that empower law enforcement officials to investigate and prosecute offenders. **Figure 4.1** illustrates the multi-layered nature of e-commerce security.

To achieve the highest degree of security possible, new technologies are available and should be used. But these technologies by themselves do not solve the problem. Organizational policies and procedures are required to ensure the technologies are not subverted. Finally, industry standards and government laws are required to enforce payment mechanisms, as well as to investigate and prosecute violators of laws designed to protect the transfer of property in commercial transactions.

FIGURE 4.1	THE E-COMMERCE SECURITY ENVIRONMENT

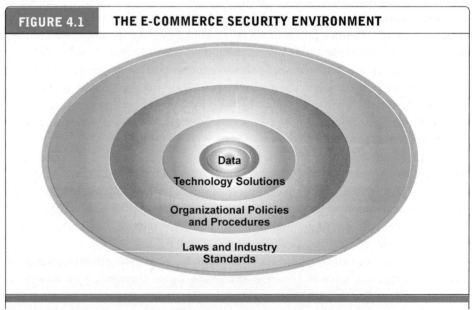

E-commerce security is multi-layered, and must take into account new technology, policies and procedures, and laws and industry standards.

The history of security in commercial transactions teaches that any security system can be broken if enough resources are put against it. Security is not absolute. In addition, perfect security of every item is not needed forever, especially in the information age. There is a time value to information—just as there is to money. Sometimes it is sufficient to protect a message for a few hours, days, or years. Also, because security is costly, we always have to weigh the cost against the potential loss. Finally, we have also learned that security is a chain that breaks most often at the weakest link. Our locks are often much stronger than our management of the keys.

We can conclude then that good e-commerce security requires a set of laws, procedures, policies, and technologies that, to the extent feasible, protect individuals and organizations from unexpected behavior in the e-commerce marketplace.

DIMENSIONS OF E-COMMERCE SECURITY

There are six key dimensions to e-commerce security: integrity, nonrepudiation, authenticity, confidentiality, privacy, and availability.

Integrity refers to the ability to ensure that information being displayed on a Web site, or transmitted or received over the Internet, has not been altered in any way by an unauthorized party. For example, if an unauthorized person intercepts and changes the contents of an online communication, such as by redirecting a bank wire transfer into a different account, the integrity of the message has been compromised because the communication no longer represents what the original sender intended.

Nonrepudiation refers to the ability to ensure that e-commerce participants do not deny (i.e., repudiate) their online actions. For instance, the availability of free e-mail accounts with alias names makes it easy for a person to post comments or send a message and perhaps later deny doing so. Even when a customer uses a real name and e-mail address, it is easy for that customer to order merchandise online and then later deny doing so. In most cases, because merchants typically do not obtain a physical copy of a signature, the credit card issuer will side with the customer because the merchant has no legally valid proof that the customer ordered the merchandise.

Authenticity refers to the ability to identify the identity of a person or entity with whom you are dealing on the Internet. How does the customer know that the Web site operator is who it claims to be? How can the merchant be assured that the customer is really who she says she is? Someone who claims to be someone he is not is "spoofing" or misrepresenting himself.

Confidentiality refers to the ability to ensure that messages and data are available only to those who are authorized to view them. Confidentiality is sometimes confused with **privacy**, which refers to the ability to control the use of information a customer provides about himself or herself to an e-commerce merchant.

E-commerce merchants have two concerns related to privacy. They must establish internal policies that govern their own use of customer information, and they must protect that information from illegitimate or unauthorized use. For example, if hackers break into an e-commerce site and gain access to credit card or other information, this violates not only the confidentiality of the data, but also the privacy of the individuals who supplied the information.

integrity
the ability to ensure that information being displayed on a Web site or transmitted or received over the Internet has not been altered in any way by an unauthorized party

nonrepudiation
the ability to ensure that e-commerce participants do not deny (i.e., repudiate) their online actions

authenticity
the ability to identify the identity of a person or entity with whom you are dealing on the Internet

confidentiality
the ability to ensure that messages and data are available only to those who are authorized to view them

privacy
the ability to control the use of information about oneself

TABLE 4.3	CUSTOMER AND MERCHANT PERSPECTIVES ON THE DIFFERENT DIMENSIONS OF E-COMMERCE SECURITY	
DIMENSION	CUSTOMER'S PERSPECTIVE	MERCHANT'S PERSPECTIVE
Integrity	Has information I transmitted or received been altered?	Has data on the site been altered without authorization? Is data being received from customers valid?
Nonrepudiation	Can a party to an action with me later deny taking the action?	Can a customer deny ordering products?
Authenticity	Who am I dealing with? How can I be assured that the person or entity is who they claim to be?	What is the real identity of the customer?
Confidentiality	Can someone other than the intended recipient read my messages?	Are messages or confidential data accessible to anyone other than those authorized to view them?
Privacy	Can I control the use of information about myself transmitted to an e-commerce merchant?	What use, if any, can be made of personal data collected as part of an e-commerce transaction? Is the personal information of customers being used in an unauthorized manner?
Availability	Can I get access to the site?	Is the site operational?

availability

the ability to ensure that an e-commerce site continues to function as intended

Availability refers to the ability to ensure that an e-commerce site continues to function as intended.

Table 4.3 summarizes these dimensions from both the merchants' and customers' perspectives. E-commerce security is designed to protect these six dimensions. When any one of them is compromised, overall security suffers.

THE TENSION BETWEEN SECURITY AND OTHER VALUES

Can there be too much security? The answer is yes. Contrary to what some may believe, security is not an unmitigated good. Computer security adds overhead and expense to business operations, and also gives criminals new opportunities to hide their intentions and their crimes.

Ease of Use

There are inevitable tensions between security and ease of use. When traditional merchants are so fearful of robbers that they do business in shops locked behind security gates, ordinary customers are discouraged from walking in. The same can be true with respect to e-commerce. In general, the more security measures added to an e-commerce site, the more difficult it is to use and the slower the site becomes. As you will discover reading this chapter, digital security is purchased at the price of slowing down processors and adding significantly to data storage demands on storage devices. Security is a technological and business overhead that can detract from doing business. Too much security can harm profitability, while not enough security can potentially put you out of business.

Public Safety and the Criminal Uses of the Internet

There is also an inevitable tension between the desires of individuals to act anonymously (to hide their identity) and the needs of public officials to maintain public safety that can be threatened by criminals or terrorists. This is not a new problem, or even new to the electronic era. The U.S. government began informal tapping of telegraph wires during the Civil War in the mid-1860s in order to trap conspirators and terrorists, and the first police wiretaps of local telephone systems were in place by the 1890s—20 years after the invention of the phone (Schwartz, 2001). No nation-state has ever permitted a technological haven to exist where criminals can plan crimes or threaten the nation-state without fear of official surveillance or investigation. In this sense, the Internet is no different from any other communication system. Drug cartels make extensive use of voice, fax, the Internet, and encrypted e-mail; a number of large international organized crime groups steal information from commercial Web sites and resell it to other criminals who use it for financial fraud. Over the years, the U.S. government has successfully pursued various "carding forums" (Web sites that facilitate the sale of stolen credit card and debit card numbers), such as Shadowcrew, Carderplanet, and Cardersmarket resulting in the arrest and prosecution of a number of their members and the closing of the sites. However, other criminal organizations have emerged to take their place.

The Internet and mobile platform also provide terrorists with convenient communications channels. Encrypted files sent via e-mail were used by Ramzi Yousef—a member of the terrorist group responsible for bombing the World Trade Center in 1993—to hide plans for bombing 11 U.S. airliners. The Internet was also used to plan and coordinate the subsequent attacks on the World Trade Center on September 11, 2001. The case of Umar Farouk Abdulmutallab further illustrates how terrorists make effective use of the Internet to radicalize, recruit, train, and coordinate youthful terrorists. Abdulmutallab allegedly attempted to blow up an American airliner in Detroit on Christmas Day 2009. He was identified, contacted, recruited, and trained, all within six weeks, according to a Pentagon counterterrorism official. In an effort to combat such terrorism, the U.S. government has significantly ramped up its surveillance of communications delivered via the Internet over the past several years. The extent of that surveillance has created a major controversy with National Security Administration contractor Edward Snowden's release of classified NSA documents that revealed that the NSA had obtained access to the servers of major Internet companies such as Facebook, Google, Apple, Microsoft, and others, as well as that NSA analysts have been searching e-mail, online chats, and browsing histories of U.S. citizens without any court approval. The proper balance between public safety and privacy in the effort against terrorism has proven to be a very thorny problem for the U.S. government.

4.2 SECURITY THREATS IN THE E-COMMERCE ENVIRONMENT

From a technology perspective, there are three key points of vulnerability when dealing with e-commerce: the client, the server, and the communications pipeline. **Figure 4.2** illustrates a typical e-commerce transaction with a consumer using a credit card to purchase a product. **Figure 4.3** illustrates some of the things that can go wrong at each major vulnerability point in the transaction—over Internet communications channels, at the server level, and at the client level.

In this section, we describe a number of the most common and most damaging forms of security threats to e-commerce consumers and site operators: malicious code, potentially unwanted programs, phishing, hacking and cybervandalism, credit card fraud/theft, spoofing, pharming, and spam (junk) Web sites (link farms), iden-

---

FIGURE 4.2	A TYPICAL E-COMMERCE TRANSACTION

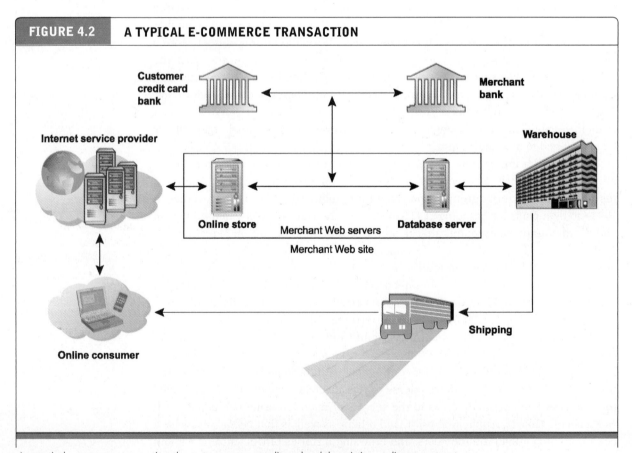

In a typical e-commerce transaction, the customer uses a credit card and the existing credit payment system.

FIGURE 4.3	VULNERABLE POINTS IN AN E-COMMERCE TRANSACTION

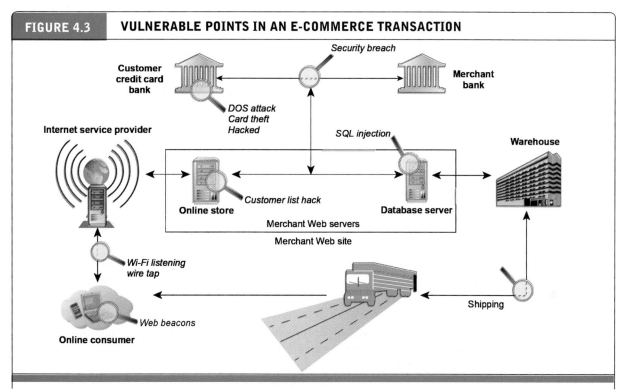

There are three major vulnerable points in e-commerce transactions: Internet communications, servers, and clients.

tity fraud, Denial of Service (DoS) and DDoS attacks, sniffing, insider attacks, poorly designed server and client software, social network security issues, mobile platform security issues, and finally, cloud security issues.

MALICIOUS CODE

Malicious code (sometimes referred to as "malware") includes a variety of threats such as viruses, worms, Trojan horses, ransomware, and bots. Some malicious code, sometimes referred to as an *exploit,* is designed to take advantage of software vulnerabilities in a computer's operating system, Web browser, applications, or other software components. **Exploit kits** are collections of exploits bundled together and rented or sold as a commercial product, often with slick user interfaces and in-depth analytics functionality. Use of an exploit kit typically does not require much technical skill, enabling novices to become cybercriminals. Exploit kits typically target software that is widely deployed, such as Microsoft Windows, Internet Explorer, Adobe Flash and Reader, and Oracle Java. Recently, vulnerabilities in out-of-data versions of the Java Runtime Environment (JRE), which is installed on desktops and laptops as a browser add-on, have been a frequent target. In 2013, JRE exploits accounted for between 85–99% of exploit kit-related detections each month (Microsoft, 2014). According to Panda Security, 30 million new strains of malware were created in 2012–13, an average

malicious code (malware)

includes a variety of threats such as viruses, worms, Trojan horses, and bots

exploit kit

collection of exploits bundled together and rented or sold as a commercial product

of about 82,000 every day (PandaLabs, 2014). In the past, malicious code was often intended to simply impair computers, and was often authored by a lone hacker, but increasingly the intent is to steal e-mail addresses, logon credentials, personal data, and financial information. Malicious code is also used to develop integrated malware networks that organize the theft of information and money.

In the early days of the Internet, malicious code was often delivered by e-mail, and this remains a popular distribution method, with 1 in about every 200 e-mails containing a malicious attachment (Symantec, 2014). One of the latest innovations in malicious code distribution is to embed it in the online advertising chain, including in Google and other ad networks. As the ad network chain becomes more complicated, it becomes more and more difficult for Web sites to vet ads placed on their sites to ensure they are malware-free. Favorite targets are social media sites and large government agencies. More than 12.4 billion malicious ads were served in 2013 in over 200,000 separate incidents, including "drive-by downloads" and fake anti-virus campaigns (Online Trust Alliance, 2014). A **drive-by download** is malware that comes with a downloaded file that a user intentionally or unintentionally requests. Drive-by is now one of the most common methods of infecting computers. For instance, Web sites as disparate as eWeek (a technology site), to MLB (Major League Baseball), and Yahoo have experienced instances where ads placed on their sites either had malicious code embedded or directed clickers to malicious sites (RAND Corporation, 2014). Malicious code embedded in PDF files also is common. Malware authors are also increasingly using links embedded within e-mail instead of the more traditional file attachments to infect computers. The links lead directly to a malicious code download or Web sites that include malicious JavaScript code. Equally important, there has been a major shift in the writers of malware from amateur hackers and adventurers to organized criminal efforts to defraud companies and individuals. In other words, it's now more about the money than ever before.

A **virus** is a computer program that has the ability to replicate or make copies of itself, and spread to other files. In addition to the ability to replicate, most computer viruses deliver a "payload." The payload may be relatively benign, such as the display of a message or image, or it may be highly destructive—destroying files, reformatting the computer's hard drive, or causing programs to run improperly.

Viruses are often combined with a worm. Instead of just spreading from file to file, a **worm** is designed to spread from computer to computer. A worm does not necessarily need to be activated by a user or program in order for it to replicate itself. The Slammer worm is one of the most notorious. Slammer targeted a known vulnerability in Microsoft's SQL Server database software and infected more than 90% of vulnerable computers worldwide within 10 minutes of its release on the Internet; crashed Bank of America cash machines, especially in the southwestern part of the United States; affected cash registers at supermarkets such as the Publix chain in Atlanta, where staff could not dispense cash to frustrated buyers; and took down most Internet connections in South Korea, causing a dip in the stock market there. The Conficker worm, which first appeared in November 2008, is the most significant worm since Slammer, and reportedly infected 9 to 15 million computers worldwide (Symantec, 2010).

drive-by download
malware that comes with a downloaded file that a user requests

virus
a computer program that has the ability to replicate or make copies of itself, and spread to other files

worm
malware that is designed to spread from computer to computer

Ransomware (scareware) is a type of malware (often a worm) that locks your computer or files to stop you from accessing them. Ransomware will often display a notice that says an authority such as the FBI, Department of Justice, or IRS has detected illegal activity on your computer and demands that you pay a fine in order to unlock the computer and avoid prosecution. In 2013, a new type of ransomware named CryptoLocker emerged. CryptoLocker encrypts victims' files with a virtually unbreakable asymmetric encryption and demands a ransom to decrypt them. If the victim does not comply within the time allowed, the files will not ever be able to be decrypted. Ransomware attacks increased by 500% in 2013, according to Symantec (Symantec, 2014).

A **Trojan horse** appears to be benign, but then does something other than expected. The Trojan horse is not itself a virus because it does not replicate, but is often a way for viruses or other malicious code such as bots or *rootkits* (a program whose aim is to subvert control of the computer's operating system) to be introduced into a computer system. The term *Trojan horse* refers to the huge wooden horse in Homer's *Iliad* that the Greeks gave their opponents, the Trojans—a gift that actually contained hundreds of Greek soldiers. Once the people of Troy let the massive horse within their gates, the soldiers revealed themselves and captured the city. In today's world, a Trojan horse may masquerade as a game, but actually hide a program to steal your passwords and e-mail them to another person. Miscellaneous Trojans and Trojan downloaders and droppers (Trojans that install malicious files to a computer they have infected by either downloading them from a remote computer or from a copy contained in their own code) are the most common type of malware, accounting for 64% of the malware threats in 2013, according to Cisco (Cisco, 2014). According to Panda Security, Trojans accounted for over 70% of all malware created in 2013, and almost 80% of all malware infections. In May 2011, Sony experienced the largest data breach in history up to that time when a Trojan horse took over the administrative computers of Sony's PlayStation game center and downloaded personal and credit card information involving 77 million registered users (Wakabayashi, 2011). Zeus is another example of a Trojan horse. Zeus steals information from users by keystroke logging. It is distributed through the Zeus botnet, which has millions of slave computers, and utilizes drive-by downloads and phishing tactics to persuade users to download files with the Trojan horse.

A **backdoor** is a feature of viruses, worms, and Trojans that allows an attacker to remotely access a compromised computer. Downadup is an example of a worm with a backdoor, while Virut, a virus that infects various file types, also includes a backdoor that can be used to download and install additional threats.

Bots (short for robots) are a type of malicious code that can be covertly installed on your computer when attached to the Internet. Around 75% of the world's spam, and 80% of the world's malware, is delivered by botnets. Once installed, the bot responds to external commands sent by the attacker; your computer becomes a "zombie" and is able to be controlled by an external third party (the "bot-herder"). **Botnets** are collections of captured computers used for malicious activities such as sending spam, participating in a DDoS attack, stealing information from computers, and storing network traffic for later analysis. The number of botnets operating world-

ransomware (scareware)
malware that prevents you from accessing your computer or files and demands that you pay a fine

Trojan horse
appears to be benign, but then does something other than expected. Often a way for viruses or other malicious code to be introduced into a computer system

backdoor
feature of viruses, worms, and Trojans that allows an attacker to remotely access a compromised computer

bot
type of malicious code that can be covertly installed on a computer when connected to the Internet. Once installed, the bot responds to external commands sent by the attacker

botnet
collection of captured bot computers

wide is not known but is estimated to be well into the thousands, controlling millions of computers. Bots and bot networks are an important threat to the Internet and e-commerce because they can be used to launch very large-scale attacks using many different techniques. In 2011, federal marshals accompanied members of Microsoft's digital crimes unit in raids designed to disable the Rustock botnet, the leading source of spam in the world with nearly 500,000 slave PCs under the control of its command and control servers located at six Internet hosting services in the United States. Officials confiscated the Rustock control servers at the hosting sites, which claimed they had no idea what the Rustock servers were doing. The actual spam e-mails were sent by the slave PCs under the command of the Rustock servers (Wingfield, 2011). In 2013, Microsoft and the FBI engaged in another aggressive botnet operation, targeting 1,400 of Zeus-derived Citadel botnets, which had been used in 2012 to raid bank accounts at major banks around the world, netting over $500 million (Chirgwin, 2013). However, illustrating the difficulty of the task, new Citadel botnets resurfaced within several months, once again stealing banking credentials, this time from Japanese banks (Muncaster, 2013).

Malicious code is a threat at both the client and the server levels, although servers generally engage in much more thorough anti-virus activities than do consumers. At the server level, malicious code can bring down an entire Web site, preventing millions of people from using the site. Such incidents are infrequent. Much more frequent malicious code attacks occur at the client level, and the damage can quickly spread to millions of other computers connected to the Internet. **Table 4.4** lists some well-known examples of malicious code.

POTENTIALLY UNWANTED PROGRAMS (PUPS)

potentially unwanted program (PUP)
program that installs itself on a computer, typically without the user's informed consent

In addition to malicious code, the e-commerce security environment is further challenged by **potentially unwanted programs (PUPs)** such as adware, browser parasites, spyware, and other applications that install themselves on a computer, such as rogue security software, typically without the user's informed consent. Such programs are increasingly found on social network and user-generated content sites where users are fooled into downloading them. Once installed, these applications are usually exceedingly difficult to remove from the computer. One example of a PUP is System Doctor 2014, which infects PCs running Windows operating systems. System Doctor 2014 poses as a legitimate anti-spyware program when in fact it is malware that, when installed, disables the user's security software, alters the user's Web browser, and diverts users to scam Web sites where more malware is downloaded.

adware
a PUP that serves pop-up ads to your computer

Adware is typically used to call for pop-up ads to display when the user visits certain sites. While annoying, adware is not typically used for criminal activities. ZangoSearch and PurityScan are examples of adware programs that open a partner site's Web pages or display the partner's pop-up ads when certain keywords are used in Internet searches. A **browser parasite** is a program that can monitor and change the settings of a user's browser, for instance, changing the browser's home page, or sending information about the sites visited to a remote computer. Browser parasites are often a component of adware. For example, Websearch is an adware component that modifies Internet Explorer's default home page and search settings.

browser parasite
a program that can monitor and change the settings of a user's browser

TABLE 4.4	NOTABLE EXAMPLES OF MALICIOUS CODE	
NAME	TYPE	DESCRIPTION
Cryptolocker	Ransomware/ Trojan	Hijacks users' photos, videos, and text documents, encrypts them with virtually unbreakable asymmetric encryption, and demands ransom payment for them.
Citadel	Trojan/botnet	Variant of Zeus Trojan, focuses on the theft of authentication credentials and financial fraud. Botnets spreading Citadel were targets of Microsoft/FBI action in 2012.
Zeus	Trojan/botnet	Sometimes referred to as king of financial malware. May install via drive-by download and evades detection by taking control of Web browser and stealing data that is exchanged with bank servers.
Reventon	Ransomware worm/Trojan	Based on Citadel/Zeus Trojans. Locks computer and displays warning from local police alleging illegal activity on computer; demands payment of fine to unlock.
Ramnit	Virus/worm	One of the most prevalent malicious code families still active in 2013. Infects various file types, including executable files, and copies itself to removable drives, executing via AutoPlay when the drive is accessed on other computers
Sality.AE	Virus/worm	Most common virus in 2012; still active in 2013. Disables security applications and services, connects to a botnet, then downloads and installs additional threats. Uses polymorphism to evade detection.
Conficker	Worm	First appeared November 2008. Targets Microsoft operating systems. Uses advanced malware techniques. Largest worm infection since Slammer in 2003. Still considered a major threat.
Netsky.P	Worm/Trojan horse	First appeared in early 2003. It spreads by gathering target e-mail addresses from the computers, then infects and sends e-mail to all recipients from the infected computer. It is commonly used by bot networks to launch spam and DoS attacks.
Storm (Peacomm, NuWar)	Worm/Trojan horse	First appeared in January 2007. It spreads in a manner similar to the Netsky.P worm. May also download and run other Trojan programs and worms.
Nymex	Worm	First discovered in January 2006. Spreads by mass mailing; activates on the 3rd of every month, and attempts to destroy files of certain types.
Zotob	Worm	First appeared in August 2005. Well-known worm that infected a number of U.S. media companies.
Mydoom	Worm	First appeared in January 2004. One of the fastest spreading mass-mailer worms.
Slammer	Worm	Launched in January 2003. Caused widespread problems.
CodeRed	Worm	Appeared in 2001. It achieved an infection rate of over 20,000 systems within 10 minutes of release and ultimately spread to hundreds of thousands of systems.
Melissa	Macro virus/ worm	First spotted in March 1999. At the time, the fastest spreading infectious program ever discovered. It attacked Microsoft Word's Normal.dot global template, ensuring infection of all newly created documents. It also mailed an infected Word file to the first 50 entries in each user's Microsoft Outlook Address Book.
Chernobyl	File-infecting virus	First appeared in 1998. It wipes out the first megabyte of data on a hard disk (making the rest useless) every April 26, the anniversary of the nuclear disaster at Chernobyl.

spyware

a program used to obtain information such as a user's keystrokes, e-mail, instant messages, and so on

social engineering

exploitation of human fallibility and gullibility to distribute malware

phishing

any deceptive, online attempt by a third party to obtain confidential information for financial gain

Spyware, on the other hand, can be used to obtain information such as a user's keystrokes, copies of e-mail and instant messages, and even take screenshots (and thereby capture passwords or other confidential data).

PHISHING

Social engineering relies on human curiosity, greed, and gullibility in order to trick people into taking an action that will result in the downloading of malware. Kevin Mitnick, until his capture and imprisonment in 1999, was one of America's most wanted computer criminals. Mitnick used simple deceptive techniques to obtain passwords, social security, and police records all without the use of any sophisticated technology (Mitnick, 2011).

Phishing is any deceptive, online attempt by a third party to obtain confidential information for financial gain. Phishing attacks typically do not involve malicious code but instead rely on straightforward misrepresentation and fraud, so-called "social engineering" techniques. One of the most popular phishing attacks is the e-mail scam letter. The scam begins with an e-mail: a rich former oil minister of Nigeria is seeking a bank account to stash millions of dollars for a short period of time, and requests your bank account number where the money can be deposited. In return, you will receive a million dollars. This type of e-mail scam is popularly known as a "Nigerian letter" scam (see **Figure 4.4**).

Thousands of other phishing attacks use other scams, some pretending to be eBay, PayPal, or Citibank writing to you for account verification (known as *spear*

| FIGURE 4.4 | AN EXAMPLE OF A NIGERIAN LETTER E-MAIL SCAM |

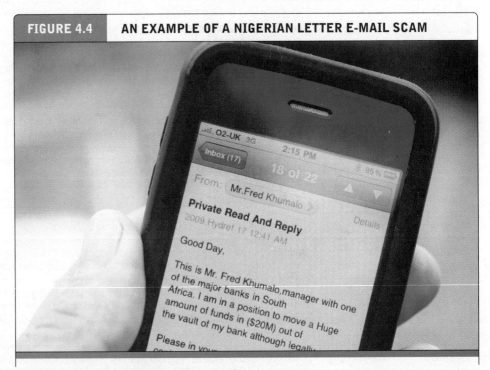

This is an example of a typical Nigerian letter e-mail scam.
© keith morris / Alamy

phishing, or targeting a known customer of a specific bank or other type of business). Click on a link in the e-mail and you will be taken to a Web site controlled by the scammer, and prompted to enter confidential information about your accounts, such as your account number and PIN codes. On any given day, millions of these phishing attack e-mails are sent, and, unfortunately, some people are fooled and disclose their personal account information.

Phishers rely on traditional "con man" tactics, but use e-mail to trick recipients into voluntarily giving up financial access codes, bank account numbers, credit card numbers, and other personal information. Often, phishers create (or "spoof") a Web site that purports to be a legitimate financial institution and cons users into entering financial information, or the site downloads malware such as a keylogger to the victim's computer. Phishers use the information they gather to commit fraudulent acts such as charging items to your credit cards or withdrawing funds from your bank account, or in other ways "steal your identity" (identity fraud). Phishing attacks are a common form of e-commerce crime and 2013 was one of the most active years on record for phishing, according to the Anti-Phishing Working Group (APWG, 2014). Symantec reported that in 2013, about 1 in every 390 e-mails contained a phishing attack. The number of spear-phishing e-mail campaigns increased by 91% in 2013, with the average duration of campaigns reaching 8 days (three times longer than in 2012) (Symantec, 2014). In 2013, two Romanians and one Nigerian who were found to have servers containing the details of over 30,000 bank customers in 14 different countries, and 70 million customer e-mail addresses to be used in phishing scams, were sentenced to jail terms in the United Kingdom totaling 21 years (Dunn, 2013). In the United States, men from Romania, Bulgaria, Croatia, and Canada also were sentenced to federal prison terms for their involvement in a phishing scheme that targeted customers of a number of banks, eBay, and PayPal (Federal Bureau of Investigation, 2013).

To combat phishing, in January 2012, leading e-mail service providers, including Google, Microsoft, Yahoo, and AOL, as well as financial services companies such as PayPal, Bank of America, and others, joined together to form DMARC.org, an organization aimed at dramatically reducing phishing e-mail. By January 2013, e-mail providers who had implemented DMARC represented around 60% of consumer in-boxes worldwide (DMARC.org, 2013). It appears as if some of this effort is having an effect, as organizations who have implemented DMARC standards are reporting a significant reduction in customer reports of suspicious e-mail (DMARG.org, 2014).

HACKING, CYBERVANDALISM, AND HACKTIVISM

A **hacker** is an individual who intends to gain unauthorized access to a computer system. Within the hacking community, the term **cracker** is typically used to denote a hacker with criminal intent, although in the public press, the terms hacker and cracker tend to be used interchangeably. Hackers and crackers gain unauthorized access by finding weaknesses in the security procedures of Web sites and computer systems, often taking advantage of various features of the Internet that make it an open system that is easy to use. In the past, hackers and crackers typically were computer aficionados excited by the challenge of breaking into corporate and government Web sites. Sometimes they were satisfied merely by breaking into the files of an e-commerce site. Today,

hacker
an individual who intends to gain unauthorized access to a computer system

cracker
within the hacking community, a term typically used to denote a hacker with criminal intent

cybervandalism

intentionally disrupting, defacing, or even destroying a site

hackers have malicious intentions to disrupt, deface, or destroy sites (**cybervandalism**) or to steal personal or corporate information they can use for financial gain (data breach). In one of the most brazen hacking crimes to occur to date, hackers on two separate occasions infiltrated the systems of credit-card processing companies that handle prepaid debit cards, raised the withdrawal limits on the cards, and were able to steal over $45 million from automated teller machines (Santora, 2013).

hacktivism

cybervandalism and data theft for political purposes

Hacktivism adds a political twist. Hacktivists typically attack governments, organizations, and even individuals for political purposes, employing the tactics of cybervandalism, distributed denial of service attacks, data thefts, doxing (gathering and exposing personal information of public figures, originating from the term "documents" or "docx"), and more. LulzSec and Anonymous are two prominent hacktivist groups.

Groups of hackers called *tiger teams* are sometimes used by corporate security departments to test their own security measures. By hiring hackers to break into the system from the outside, the company can identify weaknesses in the computer system's armor. These "good hackers" became known as **white hats** because of their role in helping organizations locate and fix security flaws. White hats do their work under contract, with agreement from clients that they will not be prosecuted for their efforts to break in.

white hats

"good" hackers who help organizations locate and fix security flaws

black hats

hackers who act with the intention of causing harm

In contrast, **black hats** are hackers who engage in the same kinds of activities but without pay or any buy-in from the targeted organization, and with the intention of causing harm. They break into Web sites and reveal the confidential or proprietary information they find. These hackers believe strongly that information should be free, so sharing previously secret information is part of their mission.

grey hats

hackers who believe they are pursuing some greater good by breaking in and revealing system flaws

Somewhere in the middle are the **grey hats**, hackers who believe they are pursuing some greater good by breaking in and revealing system flaws. Grey hats discover weaknesses in a system's security, and then publish the weakness without disrupting the site or attempting to profit from their finds. Their only reward is the prestige of discovering the weakness. Grey hat actions are suspect, however, especially when the hackers reveal security flaws that make it easier for other criminals to gain access to a system.

DATA BREACHES

data breach

occurs when an organization loses control over its information to outsiders

A **data breach** occurs whenever organizations lose control over corporate information to outsiders. According to Symantec, the total number of data breaches in 2013 grew by over 60% compared to 2012. Breaches caused by hacker attacks were responsible for exposing more than 550 million identities. Hackers are the leading cause of data breaches and were responsible for about 35% the data breaches that occurred in 2013 and 75% of the identities disposed. Accidental disclosures were the second most common cause, accounting for about 30% of breaches, while the theft or loss of a computer or hard drive ranked third, causing 27% of breaches. Among the high profile breaches that occurred were those affecting Evernote (50 million identities), Adobe (150 million identities), and perhaps the most publicized data breach of the year, involving Target, affecting over 110 million consumers. See the *Insight on Business* case, *Hackers Infiltrate Target,* for a closer look at the Target data breach and its aftermath. The trend is continuing in 2014, with eBay announcing a breach involving user names, passwords, phone numbers, and addresses in May 2014 affecting over 40 million of its users. In September 2014, Home Depot also announced that it

INSIGHT ON BUSINESS

HACKERS INFILTRATE TARGET

In today's marketing and advertising landscape, companies spend billions building goodwill with their customers and improving perceptions of their brand. When data breaches occur, the short-term monetary losses can sometimes pale in comparison to the damage to their reputations and to the brands that they work so tirelessly to build. In 2014, retailing giant Target learned this firsthand when the company experienced a data breach rivaling some of the biggest on record. Renowned for its positive reputation among customers, Target is still suffering the financial and reputational consequences for the breach. The company has been heavily criticized for its response to the breach while it was still in progress, and to a lesser extent for its handling of the breach in its aftermath.

In late 2013, in response to speculation from industry experts and security professionals, Target confirmed that it had been the victim of a data breach that had compromised approximately 40 million consumer credit and debit cards. Target later admitted that other personal information such as mailing addresses, phone numbers, and e-mail addresses had been stolen for an additional 70 million people, bringing the total of affected customers to 110 million. Hackers had reportedly gained access to the full set of information corresponding to each stolen credit card, including names, card numbers, expiration dates, and CVV codes, as well as the PIN data for debit cards. Although Target claimed that these PIN numbers were encrypted and were still secure, the company advised customers who had shopped at Target during the time frame of the attack to monitor their credit and debit cards for suspicious activity. In the immediate wake of the breach, customers

quickly reported fraudulent charges from Russia and other countries across the world.

The attack took place over the course of several weeks during November and December of 2013, after hackers used network credentials stolen from a heating and air conditioning company that was a Target subcontractor, and installed malware within Target's security and payments system. The malware was a simplistic program that was created to steal card information and to reroute it to external servers. Anytime a customer swiped their card, the malware would grab the card's identifying information and store it on an internal Target server controlled by hackers.

This type of attack should not have taken Target by surprise. The company had just contracted with computer security firm FireEye to install a system intended to detect these types of malware attacks. On one of the first days of the attack, FireEye spotted suspicious activity and notified Target. Amazingly, Target's security team did nothing in response to the alert, preferring instead to just monitor the situation. Had they responded in a timely manner, they could have neutralized the threat well before any customer data left Target's network. In fact, a FireEye security feature would even have neutralized the malware automatically, but Target had opted to turn that feature off.

When Target finally acted to stop the breach in mid-December, the breach had grown to such size and scope that it was the second-largest retail cyberattack ever, rivaling past breaches of Heartland Payment Systems and TJX Companies. Security experts have expressed shock that Target could have allowed such a simplistic attack to do so much damage, characterizing both the attack and the attackers as amateurish at best.

(continued)

Target initially gave customers a 10% storewide discount in the aftermath of the crisis to try and resurrect its reputation with its customers. It also offered free credit monitoring to affected customers, and CEO Gregg Steinhafel promised that no Target customer would have to pay fraudulent charges as a result of the data breach. Nevertheless, the data breach severely damaged Target's holiday sales, as the company experienced a drop of 46% from the previous year's figures, and that malaise continued into the first quarter of 2014, with sales figures declining 16% over the same period from 2013. Target plans to spend another $100 million upgrading its payment terminals, and customers and banks have filed nearly 100 lawsuits against Target for negligence and compensation for damages related to identity theft. Combine that with over $60 million and counting in costs to the company from promotions like the store discount and free credit monitoring, and the extent of the damage to Target becomes clearer. Some analysts estimate that the total damage to Target is between $1 and $2 billion dollars.

The data breach has also caused customers to have a crisis of confidence with respect to its brand. Before the day of the breach, Target's BrandIndex score was an excellent 25.8. In the week after the breach, its score was a negative 19.1, representing a whopping 44.8 drop in consumer perception. For reference, Citibank and Playstation suffered only 11- and 15-point drops in consumer perception, respectively, after the two companies each experienced a data breach in 2011. Midway through 2014, Target is still struggling to rebound from plummeting consumer sentiment towards its brand, with its scores measuring at approximately half of their levels prior to the breach.

Target has certainly been doing whatever it can to undo the damage. In March 2014, Target's CIO resigned, and the company announced an overhaul of its information security procedures. For many disgruntled customers and concerned analysts, this was an insufficient response, and more sweeping changes followed. In May 2014, CEO Steinhafel resigned as well, facing mounting pressure. Ironically, Target had already been bolstering its security, increasing the number of information security employees to 300 and opening a 24-hour operations center in charge of reviewing suspicious activity. Target selected Bob DeRodes, formerly a senior IT advisor for the Department of Homeland Security and CIO at Home Depot and Citibank NY Global Card Products Group, further indicating its commitment to information security. Ironically, just a few months later, Home Depot announced that it had also suffered a major data breach, extending from April to September 2014, the extent of which is not yet known, but perhaps may even surpass Target's.

Studies have shown that the average cost of a data breach has risen to $3.5 million in 2014, and that number may continue to escalate unless companies improve their safeguards against these events. One issue for Target was that its manager of security operations had stepped down in the months preceding the attack and had not yet been replaced. If Target had had someone in that position, that person might have taken a more active role in neutralizing the breach. More than continuing to increase its level of investment in IT security, Target and other companies need to improve their internal processes so that when warnings and alarms are sounded, security teams take action, instead of sit idly by as Target did.

SOURCES: "After the Big Data Breach, Has Target Learned Its Lesson?" by Adam Levin, Abcnews.go.com, June 15, 2014; "The Target Breach, By the Numbers," by Brian Krebs, Krebsonsecurity.com, May 14, 2014; "Lessons from Target's Data Breach Fumble," by Jennifer Schlesinger, CNBC.com, May 11, 2014; "Introducing Target's New CIO Bob DeRodes," Abullseyeview.com, April 29, 2014; "Missed Alarms and 40 Million Stolen Credit Card Numbers: How Target Blew It," by Michael Riley, Ben Elgin, Dune Lawrence, and Carol Matlack, Bloomberg Businessweek, March 13, 2014; "Target Missed Signs of a Data Breach," by Elizabeth A. Harris and Nicole Perlroth, New York Times, March 13, 2014; "Target Hackers Broke in Via HVAC Company," by Brian Krebs, Krebsonsecurity.com, February 14, 2014; "Target Perception Falls After Data Breach," by Ted Marzilli, BrandIndex.com, December 23, 2013.

was investigating a data breach that could potentially be even larger than Target's. Even more chilling was the disclosure in August 2014 that a Russian crime ring had amassed 1.2 billion unique user name and password combinations and almost 550 million different e-mail addresses, from over 420,000 different Web sites, by using botnets and SQL injection attacks. The group appeared to be using the stolen data to send spam on social networks (Perlroth and Gelles, 2014).

CREDIT CARD FRAUD/THEFT

Theft of credit card data is one of the most feared occurrences on the Internet. Fear that credit card information will be stolen prevents users from making online purchases in many cases. Interestingly, this fear appears to be largely unfounded. Incidences of stolen credit card information are actually much lower than users think, around 0.8% of all online card transactions (CyberSource, 2013). Several surveys have documented a slow drift downwards in the frequency and value of online credit card fraud due to better merchant screening systems and security improvements. Nevertheless, online credit card fraud is twice as common as offline card fraud.

There is substantial credit card fraud in traditional commerce, but the consumer is largely insured against losses by U.S. federal law. In the past, the most common cause of credit card fraud was a lost or stolen card that was used by someone else, followed by employee theft of customer numbers and stolen identities (criminals applying for credit cards using false identities). U.S. federal law limits the liability of individuals to $50 for a stolen credit card. For amounts more than $50, the credit card company generally pays the amount, although in some cases, the merchant may be held liable if it failed to verify the account or consult published lists of invalid cards. Banks recoup the cost of credit card fraud by charging higher interest rates on unpaid balances, and by merchants who raise prices to cover the losses.

But today, the most frequent cause of stolen cards and card information is the systematic hacking and looting of a corporate server where the information on millions of credit card purchases is stored. For instance, in 2010, Albert Gonzalez was sentenced to 20 years in prison for organizing one of the largest thefts of credit card numbers in American history. Along with several Russian co-conspirators, Gonzalez broke into the central computer systems of TJX, BJs, Barnes & Noble, and other companies, stealing over 160 million card numbers and costing these firms over $200 million in losses (Fox and Botelho, 2013).

International orders have been particularly prone to repudiation. If an international customer places an order and then later disputes it, online merchants often have no way to verify that the package was actually delivered and that the credit card holder is the person who placed the order. Most online merchants will not process international orders.

A central security issue of e-commerce is the difficulty of establishing the customer's identity. Currently there is no technology that can identify a person with absolute certainty. Until a customer's identity can be guaranteed, online companies are at a higher risk of loss than traditional offline companies. The federal government has attempted to address this issue through the Electronic Signatures in Global and National Commerce Act (the "E-Sign" law), which gives digital signatures the same authority as hand-written signatures in commerce. This law also intended to make digital signatures more commonplace and easier to use. Although the use of e-signatures is still uncommon in the B2C retail e-commerce arena, many businesses are starting to implement e-signature solutions, particularly for B2B contracting, financial services, insurance, health care, and government and professional services. DocuSign, Adobe EchoSign, RightSignature, and Silanis e-SignLive are currently the most widely adopted e-signature solutions (Ombud, Inc., 2013). They use a variety of techniques, such as remote user identification through third-party databases or personal information verification such as a photo of a driver's license; multi-factor user authentication methods (user ID and password, e-mail address verification, secret question and answer); and public/private key encryption to create a digital signature and embedded audit trail that can be used to verify the e-signature's integrity (Silanas Technology, 2014).

IDENTITY FRAUD

identity fraud

involves the unauthorized use of another person's personal data for illegal financial benefit

Identity fraud involves the unauthorized use of another person's personal data, such as social security, driver's license, and/or credit card numbers, as well as user names and passwords, for illegal financial benefit. Criminals can use such data to obtain loans, purchase merchandise, or obtain other services, such as mobile phone or other utility services. Cybercriminals employ many of the techniques described previously, such as spyware, phishing, data breaches, and credit card theft, for the purpose of identity fraud. Data breaches, in particular, often lead to identity fraud.

Identity fraud is a significant problem around the world. For instance, a European Commission study reported that as much as 2% of the EU's population (over 8 million people) are affected by identity fraud, with an average loss of around €2,500 (European Commission, 2012).

SPOOFING, PHARMING, AND SPAM (JUNK) WEB SITES

spoofing

involves attempting to hide a true identity by using someone else's e-mail or IP address

pharming

automatically redirecting a Web link to an address different from the intended one, with the site masquerading as the intended destination

Spoofing involves attempting to hide a true identity by using someone else's e-mail or IP address. For instance, a spoofed e-mail will have a forged sender e-mail address designed to mislead the receiver about who sent the e-mail. IP spoofing involves the creation of TCP/IP packets that use someone else's source IP address, indicating that the packets are coming from a trusted host. Most current routers and firewalls can offer protection against IP spoofing. Spoofing a Web site sometimes involves **pharming**, automatically redirecting a Web link to an address different from the intended one, with the site masquerading as the intended destination. Links that are designed to lead to one site can be reset to send users to a totally unrelated site—one that benefits the hacker.

Although spoofing and pharming do not directly damage files or network servers, they threaten the integrity of a site. For example, if hackers redirect customers to a fake Web site that looks almost exactly like the true site, they can then collect and process orders, effectively stealing business from the true site. Or, if the intent is to disrupt rather than steal, hackers can alter orders—inflating them or changing products ordered—and then send them on to the true site for processing and delivery. Customers become dissatisfied with the improper order shipment, and the company may have huge inventory fluctuations that impact its operations.

In addition to threatening integrity, spoofing also threatens authenticity by making it difficult to discern the true sender of a message. Clever hackers can make it almost impossible to distinguish between a true and a fake identity or Web address.

Spam (junk) Web sites (also sometimes referred to as *link farms*) are a little different. These are sites that promise to offer some product or service, but in fact are just a collection of advertisements for other sites, some of which contain malicious code. For instance, you may search for "[name of town] weather," and then click on a link that promises your local weather, but then discover that all the site does is display ads for weather-related products or other Web sites. Junk or spam Web sites typically appear on search results, and do not involve e-mail. These sites cloak their identities by using domain names similar to legitimate firm names, and redirect traffic to known spammer-redirection domains such as topsearch10.com.

> **spam (junk) Web sites**
> also referred to as link farms; promise to offer products or services, but in fact are just collections of advertisements

DENIAL OF SERVICE (DOS) AND DISTRIBUTED DENIAL OF SERVICE (DDOS) ATTACKS

In a **Denial of Service (DoS) attack**, hackers flood a Web site with useless pings or page requests that inundate and overwhelm the site's Web servers. Increasingly, DoS attacks involve the use of bot networks and so-called "distributed attacks" built from thousands of compromised client computers. DoS attacks typically cause a Web site to shut down, making it impossible for users to access the site. For busy e-commerce sites, these attacks are costly; while the site is shut down, customers cannot make purchases. And the longer a site is shut down, the more damage is done to a site's reputation. Although such attacks do not destroy information or access restricted areas of the server, they can destroy a firm's online business. Often, DoS attacks are accompanied by attempts at blackmailing site owners to pay tens or hundreds of thousands of dollars to the hackers in return for stopping the DoS attack.

> **Denial of Service (DoS) attack**
> flooding a Web site with useless traffic to inundate and overwhelm the network

A **Distributed Denial of Service (DDoS) attack** uses hundreds or even thousands of computers to attack the target network from numerous launch points. DoS and DDoS attacks are threats to a system's operation because they can shut it down indefinitely. Major Web sites have experienced such attacks, making the companies aware of their vulnerability and the need to continually introduce new measures to prevent future attacks. All told, over 1,150 separate DDoS attacks were reported to Akamai in 2013, an over 50% increase compared to 2012 (Akamai, 2014), and Akamai anticipates that this number will continue to grow in 2014 (Akamai Technologies Inc., 2014). In another measure of the prevalence of DDoS attacks, in an Arbor Networks survey of 220 ISP and network operators around the world, about two-thirds of participants reported that customers had experienced DDoS attacks in the previous year, with over 50% experiencing actual infrastructure outages as a result. Arbor Networks also reported that the size of reported DDoS attacks in terms of bandwidth consumed increased dramatically in 2013, with multiple companies reporting attacks in excess of 100 gigabits per second (Arbor Networks, 2014). Another trend is DDoS smoke-screening, in which attackers use DDoS as a distraction while they also insert malware or viruses or steal data. Almost 50% of the 440 North American companies surveyed by Neustar in 2014 who experienced a DDoS attack reported that viruses or malware were also installed or data stolen at the same time (Neustar, 2014).

> **Distributed Denial of Service (DDoS) attack**
> using numerous computers to attack the target network from numerous launch points

SNIFFING

A **sniffer** is a type of eavesdropping program that monitors information traveling over a network. When used legitimately, sniffers can help identify potential network trouble-spots, but when used for criminal purposes, they can be damaging and very difficult to detect. Sniffers enable hackers to steal proprietary information from anywhere on a network, including passwords, e-mail messages, company files, and confidential reports. For instance, in July 2013, five hackers were charged in another worldwide hacking scheme that targeted the corporate networks of retail chains such as 7-Eleven and the French retailer Carrefour SA, using sniffer programs to steal more than 160 million credit card numbers (Voreacos, 2013).

E-mail wiretaps are a variation on the sniffing threat. An e-mail wiretap is a method for recording or journaling e-mail traffic generally at the mail server level from any individual. E-mail wiretaps are used by employers to track employee messages, and by government agencies to surveil individuals or groups. E-mail wiretaps can be installed on servers and client computers. In the United States, the USA PATRIOT Act permits the FBI to compel ISPs to install a black box on their mail servers that can impound the e-mail of a single person or group of persons for later analysis. In the case of American citizens communicating with other citizens, an FBI agent or government lawyer need only certify to a judge on the secret 11-member U.S. Foreign Intelligence Surveillance Court (FISC) that the information sought is relevant to an ongoing criminal investigation to get permission to install the program. Judges have no discretion. They must approve wiretaps based on government agents' unsubstantiated assertions. In the case of suspected terrorist activity, law enforcement does not have to inform a court prior to installing a wire or e-mail tap. A 2007 amendment to the 1978 Foreign Intelligence Surveillance Act, known as FISA, provided new powers to the National Security Agency to monitor international e-mail and telephone communications where one person is in the United States, and where the purpose of such interception is to collect foreign intelligence (Foreign Intelligence Surveillance Act of 1978; Protect America Act of 2007). The FISA Amendments Reauthorization Act of 2012 extends the provisions of FISA for five more years, until 2017. NSA's XKeyscore program, revealed by Edward Snowden, is a form of "wiretap" that allows NSA analysts to search through vast databases containing not only e-mail, but online chats, and browsing histories of millions of individuals (Wills, 2013).

The U.S. Communications Assistance for Law Enforcement Act (CALEA) requires all communications carriers (including ISPs) to provide near-instant access to law enforcement agencies to their message traffic. Many Internet services (such as Facebook and LinkedIn) that have built-in ISP services technically are not covered by CALEA. One can only assume these non-ISP e-mail operators cooperate with law enforcement. Unlike the past where wiretaps required many hours to physically tap into phone lines, in today's digital phone systems, taps are arranged in a few minutes by the large carriers at their expense.

INSIDER ATTACKS

We tend to think of security threats to a business as originating outside the organization. In fact, the largest financial threats to business institutions come not from robberies but from embezzlement by insiders. Bank employees steal far more money than bank robbers. The same is true for e-commerce sites. Some of the largest disruptions to service, destruction to sites, and diversion of customer credit data and personal information have come from insiders—once trusted employees. Employees have access to privileged information, and, in the presence of sloppy internal security procedures, they are often able to roam throughout an organization's systems without leaving a trace. Research from Carnegie Mellon University documents the significant damage insiders have done to both private and public organizations. (Software Engineering Institute, 2012). Survey results also indicate that insiders are more likely to be the source of cyberattacks than outsiders, and to cause more damage to an organization than external attacks (PWC, 2014). In some instances, the insider might not have criminal intent, but inadvertently exposes data that can then be exploited by others. For instance, a Ponemon Institute study found that negligent insiders are a top cause of data breaches (Ponemon Institute, 2014).

POORLY DESIGNED SOFTWARE

Many security threats prey on poorly designed software, sometimes in the operating system and sometimes in the application software, including browsers. The increase in complexity and size of software programs, coupled with demands for timely delivery to markets, has contributed to an increase in software flaws or vulnerabilities that hackers can exploit. For instance, **SQL injection attacks** take advantage of vulnerabilities in poorly coded Web application software that fails to properly validate or filter data entered by a user on a Web page to introduce malicious program code into a company's systems and networks. An attacker can use this input validation error to send a rogue SQL query to the underlying database to access the database, plant malicious code, or access other systems on the network. Large Web applications have hundreds of places for inputting user data, each of which creates an opportunity for an SQL injection attack. A large number of Web-facing applications are believed to have SQL injection vulnerabilities, and tools are available for hackers to check Web applications for these vulnerabilities.

SQL injection attack
takes advantage of poorly coded Web application software that fails to properly validate or filter data entered by a user on a Web page

Each year, security firms identify thousands of software vulnerabilities in Internet browsers, PC, Macintosh, and Linux software, as well as mobile device operating systems and applications. According to Microsoft, vulnerability disclosures across the software industry in the second half of 2013 were up about 13% from 2012 (Microsoft, 2014). For instance, in its most recent *Internet Security Threat Report,* Symantec identified over 6,700 different software vulnerabilities, an almost 30% increase over 2012. Browser vulnerabilities in particular are a popular target, as well as browser plug-ins such as for Adobe Reader. According to Kaspersky Labs, the number of browser-based attacks in 2013 increased to over 1.7 billion. Java vulnerabilities on both PC and Mac computers accounted for 90% of detected attacks (Kaspersky Labs, 2013). A **zero-day vulnerability** is one that has been previously unreported and for which no patch yet exists. In 2013, 23 zero-day vulnerabilities were reported, up from 14 in 2012. The trend continues in 2014. Not surprisingly, Java was the target of a number of zero-day attacks during 2013. For instance, in January 2013, just a day after Oracle had patched two previous zero-day vulnerabilities, it learned that an exploit kit for yet another zero-day vulnerability was being marketed on a hacker forum (Schwartz, 2013). The

zero-day vulnerability
software vulnerability that has been previously unreported and for which no patch yet exists

very design of the personal computer includes many open communication ports that can be used, and indeed are designed to be used, by external computers to send and receive messages. The port most frequently attacked is TCP port 445 (Microsoft-DS); attacks on port 80 (WWW/HTTP) and 443 (SSL/HTTPS) also are common. Given their complexity and design objectives, all operating systems and application software, including Linux and Macintosh, have vulnerabilities.

Heartbleed bug

flaw in OpenSSL encryption system that allowed hackers to decrypt an SSL session and discover user names, passwords, and other user data

In April 2014, a flaw in the OpenSSL encryption system, used by millions of Web sites, known as the **Heartbleed bug**, was discovered (see Section 4.3 for a further discussion of SSL). The vulnerability allowed hackers to decrypt an SSL session and discover user names, passwords, and other user data, by using OpenSSL in combination with a communications protocol called the RFC6520 heartbeat that helps a remote user remain in touch after connecting with a Web site server. In the process a small chunk of the server's memory content can leak out (hence the name heartbleed), potentially large enough to hold a password or encyrption key that would allow a hacker to exploit the server further. Most of the world's top 1,000 Web sites were either unaffected or moved quickly to fix the problem, but as of June 2014, more than 300,000 servers remain vulnerable. The Heartbleed bug also affected over 1,300 Android apps (TrendMicros, 2014).

SOCIAL NETWORK SECURITY ISSUES

Social networks like Facebook, Twitter, LinkedIn, Pinterest, and Tumblr provide a rich and rewarding environment for hackers. Viruses, site takeovers, identity fraud, malware-loaded apps, click hijacking, phishing, and spam are all found on social networks. For instance, the Syrian Electronic Army hacked the Twitter accounts of a number of news organizations, including NPR, Fox News, the Associated Press, and The Financial Times, throughout 2013. According to Symantec, fake offers are the most common type of scam on social media sites, with victims being asked to share their credentials, send a text to a premium rate number, or share the scam with a friend. Other techniques include fake Like buttons that, when clicked, install malware and post updates to the user's Newsfeed, further spreading the attack, and fake apps (Symantec, 2014). By sneaking in among our friends, hackers can masquerade as friends and dupe users into scams.

Social network firms have thus far been relatively poor policemen because they have failed to aggressively weed out accounts that send visitors to malware sites (unlike Google, which maintains a list of known malware sites and patrols its search results looking for links to malware sites). Social networks are open: anyone can set up a personal page, even criminals. Most attacks are social engineering attacks that tempt visitors to click on links that sound reasonable. Social apps downloaded from either the social network or a foreign site are not certified by the social network to be clean of malware. It's "clicker beware."

MOBILE PLATFORM SECURITY ISSUES

The explosion in mobile devices has broadened opportunities for hackers. Mobile users are filling their devices with personal and financial information, and using them to conduct an increasing number of transactions, from retail purchases to mobile banking, making them excellent targets for hackers. In general, mobile devices face all the same risks as any Internet device as well as some new risks associated with wireless network security. For instance, public Wi-Fi networks that are not secured are very susceptible to hacking. While most PC users are aware their computers and Web sites may be hacked and contain malware, most cell phone users believe their cell phone is as secure as a traditional landline phone. As with social network members, mobile users are prone to think they are in a shared, trustworthy environment.

Mobile cell phone malware (sometimes referred to as malicious mobile apps (MMAs) or rogue mobile apps) was developed as early as 2004 with Cabir, a Bluetooth worm affecting Symbian operating systems (Nokia phones) and causing the phone to continuously seek out other Bluetooth-enabled devices, quickly draining the battery. The iKee.B worm infected jailbroken iPhones, turning the phones into botnet-controlled devices. An iPhone in Europe could be hacked by an iPhone in the United States, and all its private data sent to a server in Poland. Ikee.B established the feasibility of cell phone botnets. The first malicious iPhone app was discovered and removed from the iTunes Store. Many—if not most—apps written for Android phones have poor protection for user information, and the number of malicious and high-risk Android apps detected by TrendMicro has skyrocketed to over 2.7 million as of July 2014, compared to just 1,000 in 2011. Examples include rogue version or "trojanized" versions of popular apps such as Angry Birds and Bad Piggies (TrendMicro Incorporated, 2014). And it is not just rogue applications that are dangerous, but also popular legitimate applications that simply have little protection from hackers. ViaForensics, a mobile security firm in Chicago, found in a study of 50 popular iPhone apps that only three had adequate protection for usernames, passwords, and other sensitive data. Another survey by Webroot found that almost 80% of the top free iOS and Android apps were associated with security or privacy issues (Webroot, 2013). For instance, in January 2014, security researchers revealed that the Starbucks mobile app, the most used mobile payment app in the United States, was storing user names, e-mail addresses, and passwords in clear text, in such a way that anyone with access to the phone could see the passwords and user names by connecting the phone to a computer. According to researchers, Starbucks erred in emphasizing convenience and ease to use in the design of the app over security concerns (Schuman, 2014).

Vishing attacks target gullible cell phone users with verbal messages to call a certain number and, for example, donate money to starving children in Haiti. *Smishing* attacks exploit SMS/text messages. Compromised text messages can contain e-mail and Web site addresses that can lead the innocent user to a malware site. Criminal SMS spoofing services have emerged, which conceal the cybercriminal's true phone number, replacing it with a false alpha-numeric name. SMS spoofing can also be used by cybercriminals to lure mobile users to a malicious Web site by sending a text that appears to be from a legitimate organization in the From field, and suggesting the receiver click on a malicious URL hyperlink to update an account or obtain a gift card. A small number of downloaded apps from app stores have also contained malware. *Madware*—innocent-looking apps that contain adware that launches pop-up ads and text messages on your mobile device—is also becoming an increasing problem.

Read the *Insight on Technology* case, *Think Your Smartphone Is Secure?* for a further discussion of some of the issues surrounding smartphone security.

INSIGHT ON TECHNOLOGY

THINK YOUR SMARTPHONE IS SECURE?

So far, there have been few publicly identified, large-scale, smartphone security breaches, but just because it hasn't happened yet doesn't mean it won't. With about 164 million smartphone users in the United States, 167 million people accessing the Internet from mobile devices, business firms increasingly switching their employees to the mobile platform, and consumers using their phones for financial transactions and even paying bills, the size and richness of the smartphone target for hackers is growing.

Have you ever purchased anti-virus software for your smartphone? Probably not. Many users believe their smartphones are unlikely to be hacked because Apple and Google are protecting them from malware, and that Verizon and AT&T can keep the cell phone network secure just as they do the land-line phone system. Telephone systems are "closed" and therefore not subject to the kinds of attacks that occur on the open Internet.

Hackers can do to a smartphone just about anything they can do to any Internet device: request malicious files without user intervention, delete files, transmit files, install programs running in the background that can monitor user actions, and potentially convert the smartphone into a robot that can be used in a botnet to send e-mail and text messages to anyone.

Apps are one avenue for potential security breaches. Apple, Google, and RIM (BlackBerry) now offer over 2.5 million apps collectively. Apple claims that it examines each and every app to ensure that it plays by Apple's iTunes rules, but risks remain. Most of the known cases that occurred thus far have involved jailbroken phones. The first iPhone app confirmed to have embedded malware made it past Apple into the iTunes store in July 2012. However, security company Kaspersky expects the iPhone to face an onslaught of malware over the course of the next year. Apple iTunes app rules make some user information available to all apps by default, including the user's GPS position and name. However, a rogue app could easily do much more. Nicolas Seriot, a Swiss researcher, built a test app called SpyPhone that was capable of tracking users and all their activities, then transmitting this data to remote servers, all without user knowledge. The app harvested geolocation data, passwords, address book entries, and e-mail account information. Apple removed the app once it was identified. That this proof-of-concept app was accepted by the iTunes staff of reviewers suggests Apple cannot effectively review new apps prior to their use. Thousands of apps arrive each week. Also, Apple's 'walled garden' approach means that only Apple is truly qualified to defend iOS devices from attacks. Until it changes this policy, third parties won't be able to develop services to protect Apple devices as they may be able to with Android.

The amount of malware on the Android platform has skyrocketed over the past year. According to Cisco, 99% of all mobile malware in 2013 targeted Android devices. In part this is due to the fact that security on that platform is much less under the control of Google because it employs an "open" app model compared to Apple's "walled garden" approach. In addition, in the past, Google did not review Android apps, instead relying on user input and technical hurdles to limit malware. However, in 2013, in response to the growing malware problem, Google launched a universal app-scanning system that instantly checks each app for malicious code at the device level.

Android apps run in a "sandbox," where they cannot affect one another or manipulate device features without user permission. Android apps can use any personal information found on a Droid phone but they must also inform the user what each app is capable of doing, and what personal data it requires. Google removes any apps that break its rules against malicious activity. One problem: users may not pay attention to permission requests and simply click "Yes" when asked to grant permissions. Apple's iPhone does not inform users what information apps are using, but does restrict the information that can be collected by any app.

Google can perform a remote wipe of offending apps from all Droid phones without user intervention. This is a wonderful capability, but is itself a security threat if hackers gain access to the remote wipe capability at Google. In one incident, Google pulled down dozens of mobile banking apps made by a developer called 09Droid. The apps claimed to give users access to their accounts at many banks throughout the world. In fact, the apps were unable to connect users to any bank, and were removed before they could do much harm. Google does take preventive steps to reduce malware apps such as vetting the backgrounds of developers, and requiring developers to register with its Google Wallet payment service (both to encourage users to pay for apps using their service as well as to force developers to reveal their identities and financial information).

Beyond the threat of rogue apps, smartphones of all stripes are susceptible to browser-based malware that takes advantage of vulnerabilities in all browsers. In addition, most smartphones, including the iPhone, permit the manufacturers to remotely download configuration files to update operating systems and security protections. Unfortunately, flaws in the public key encryption procedures that permit remote server access to iPhones have been discovered, raising further questions about the security of such operations. Attackers have also developed methods of hijacking phones using weaknesses in SIM cards. There are at least 500 million vulnerable SIM cards in use today, and the defects allow hackers to obtain the encryption key that guards users' personal information, granting them nearly complete access over the phone in the process.

In 2013, internal NSA documents indicated that the law enforcement agency had developed the capability to tap into sensitive personal data held on all major smartphone devices, even the BlackBerry mail system, which is considered the most secure of any smartphone. In 2011, the NSA was also granted the ability to conduct warrantless searches of American communications in a way that had previously been reserved only for foreigners. While the NSA had devoted entire teams to individual smartphone operating systems in order to make this breakthrough, their success is proof-of-concept for other more malicious organizations to develop similar capabilities.

Suddenly, our smartphones and tablets don't seem quite as safe anymore. Some commentators dismiss these concerns as more hype than reality. But reality is catching up with the hype.

SOURCES: "Cisco 2014 Annual Security Report," 2014; "NSA Secretly Broke Smartphone Security," by Cory Doctorow, BoingBoing.com, September 8, 2013; "Obama Administration Had Restrictions on NSA Reversed in 2011," by Ellen Nakashima, September 7, 2013; "How Google Just Quietly Made Your Android Phone More Secure," by JR Raphael, *Computerworld*, July 26, 2013; "Crypto Flaw Makes Millions of Smartphone Susceptible to Hijacking," by Dan Goodin, ArsTechnica.com, July 22, 2013; "Android Will Account for 58% of Smartphone App Downloads in 2013, with iOS Commanding a Market Share of 75% in Tablet Apps," ABI Research, March 4, 2013; "Smartphone Cyberattacks to Grow This Year," by David Goldman, money.cnn.com, January 8, 2013; "iPhone Malware: Spam App 'Find and Call' Invades App Store," by Zach Epstein, BGR.com, July 5, 2012; "iPhone Malware: Kaspersky Expects Apple's iOS to be Under Attack by Next Year," by Sara Gates, Huffington Post, May 15, 2012; "Android, Apple Face Growing Cyberattacks," by Byron Acohido, *USA Today*, June 3, 2011; "Security to Ward Off Crime on Phones," by Riva Richmond, *New York Times*, February 23, 2011; "AT&T Plans Smartphone Security Service for 2012," "Smartphone Security Follies: A Brief History," by Brad Reed, *Network World*, April 18, 2011.

CLOUD SECURITY ISSUES

The move of so many Internet services into the cloud also raises security risks. From an infrastructure standpoint, DDoS attacks threaten the availability of cloud services on which more and more companies are relying. Safeguarding data being maintained in a cloud environment is also a major concern. For example, researchers identified several ways data could be accessed without authorization on Dropbox, which offers a popular cloud file-sharing service. In March 2013, an unknown intruder gained access to usernames, e-mail addresses, and encrypted passwords used by customers of Evernote, a cloud note-taking service. Evernote was forced to reset 50 million passwords. In September 2014, compromising photos of as many as 100 celebrities such as Jennifer Lawrence were posted online, reportedly stolen from Apple's iCloud. Although initially it was thought that the breach was made possible by a vulnerability in Apple's Find My iPhone API. it instead apparently resulted from lower-tech phishing attacks that yielded passwords that could be used to connect to iCloud. A similar hack into writer Mat Honan's Apple iCloud account using social engineering tactics in 2012 allowed the hackers to wipe everything from his Mac computer, iPhone, and iPad, which were linked to the cloud service, as well as take over his Twitter and Gmail accounts (Honan, 2012). These incidents highlight the risks involved as devices, identities, and data become more and more interconnected in the cloud. A June 2014 Ponemon Insititute study found that the majority of IT and IT security practitioners surveyed felt that the likelihood of a data breach increases due to the cloud, in part due to the fact that many organizations do not thoroughly examine cloud security before deploying cloud services (Ponemon Institute, 2014b).

4.3   TECHNOLOGY SOLUTIONS

At first glance, it might seem like there is not much that can be done about the onslaught of security breaches on the Internet. Reviewing the security threats in the previous section, it is clear that the threats to e-commerce are very real, potentially devastating for individuals, businesses, and entire nations, and likely to be increasing in intensity along with the growth in e-commerce. But in fact a great deal of progress has been made by private security firms, corporate and home users, network administrators, technology firms, and government agencies. There are two lines of defense: technology solutions and policy solutions. In this section, we consider some technology solutions, and in the following section, we look at some policy solutions that work.

The first line of defense against the wide variety of security threats to an e-commerce site is a set of tools that can make it difficult for outsiders to invade or destroy a site. **Figure 4.5** illustrates the major tools available to achieve site security.

PROTECTING INTERNET COMMUNICATIONS

Because e-commerce transactions must flow over the public Internet, and therefore involve thousands of routers and servers through which the transaction packets flow, security experts believe the greatest security threats occur at the level of Internet

FIGURE 4.5	TOOLS AVAILABLE TO ACHIEVE SITE SECURITY

There are a number of tools available to achieve site security.

communications. This is very different from a private network where a dedicated communication line is established between two parties. A number of tools are available to protect the security of Internet communications, the most basic of which is message encryption.

ENCRYPTION

Encryption is the process of transforming plain text or data into **cipher text** that cannot be read by anyone other than the sender and the receiver. The purpose of encryption is (a) to secure stored information and (b) to secure information transmission. Encryption can provide four of the six key dimensions of e-commerce security referred to in Table 4.3 on page 244:

- *Message integrity*—provides assurance that the message has not been altered.
- *Nonrepudiation*—prevents the user from denying he or she sent the message.
- *Authentication*—provides verification of the identity of the person (or computer) sending the message.
- *Confidentiality*—gives assurance that the message was not read by others.

This transformation of plain text to cipher text is accomplished by using a key or cipher. A **key** (or **cipher**) is any method for transforming plain text to cipher text.

encryption
the process of transforming plain text or data into cipher text that cannot be read by anyone other than the sender and the receiver. The purpose of encryption is (a) to secure stored information and (b) to secure information transmission

cipher text
text that has been encrypted and thus cannot be read by anyone other than the sender and the receiver

key (cipher)
any method for transforming plain text to cipher text

Encryption has been practiced since the earliest forms of writing and commercial transactions. Ancient Egyptian and Phoenician commercial records were encrypted using substitution and transposition ciphers. In a **substitution cipher**, every occurrence of a given letter is replaced systematically by another letter. For instance, if we used the cipher "letter plus two"—meaning replace every letter in a word with a new letter two places forward—then the word "Hello" in plain text would be transformed into the following cipher text: "JGNNQ." In a **transposition cipher**, the ordering of the letters in each word is changed in some systematic way. Leonardo Da Vinci recorded his shop notes in reverse order, making them readable only with a mirror. The word "Hello" can be written backwards as "OLLEH." A more complicated cipher would (a) break all words into two words and (b) spell the first word with every other letter beginning with the first letter, and then spell the second word with all the remaining letters. In this cipher, "HELLO" would be written as "HLO EL."

Symmetric Key Cryptography

In order to decipher (decrypt) these messages, the receiver would have to know the secret cipher that was used to encrypt the plain text. This is called **symmetric key cryptography** or **secret key cryptography**. In symmetric key cryptography, both the sender and the receiver use the same key to encrypt and decrypt the message. How do the sender and the receiver have the same key? They have to send it over some communication media or exchange the key in person. Symmetric key cryptography was used extensively throughout World War II and is still a part of Internet cryptography.

The possibilities for simple substitution and transposition ciphers are endless, but they all suffer from common flaws. First, in the digital age, computers are so powerful and fast that these ancient means of encryption can be broken quickly. Second, symmetric key cryptography requires that both parties share the same key. In order to share the same key, they must send the key over a presumably *insecure* medium where it could be stolen and used to decipher messages. If the secret key is lost or stolen, the entire encryption system fails. Third, in commercial use, where we are not all part of the same team, you would need a secret key for each of the parties with whom you transacted, that is, one key for the bank, another for the department store, and another for the government. In a large population of users, this could result in as many as $n^{(n-1)}$ keys. In a population of billions of Internet users, billions of keys would be needed to accommodate all e-commerce customers. Clearly this situation would be too unwieldy to work in practice.

Modern encryption systems are digital. The ciphers or keys used to transform plain text into cipher text are digital strings. Computers store text or other data as binary strings composed of 0s and 1s. For instance, the binary representation of the capital letter "A" in ASCII computer code is accomplished with eight binary digits (bits): 01000001. One way in which digital strings can be transformed into cipher text is by multiplying each letter by another binary number, say, an eight-bit key number 0101 0101. If we multiplied every digital character in our text messages by this eight-bit key

---

substitution cipher

every occurrence of a given letter is replaced systematically by another letter

transposition cipher

the ordering of the letters in each word is changed in some systematic way

symmetric key cryptography (secret key cryptography)

both the sender and the receiver use the same key to encrypt and decrypt the message

and sent the encrypted message to a friend along with the secret eight-bit key, the friend could decode the message easily.

The strength of modern security protection is measured in terms of the length of the binary key used to encrypt the data. In the preceding example, the eight-bit key is easily deciphered because there are only 2^8 or 256 possibilities. If the intruder knows you are using an eight-bit key, then he or she could decode the message in a few seconds using a modern desktop PC just by using the brute force method of checking each of the 256 possible keys. For this reason, modern digital encryption systems use keys with 56, 128, 256, or 512 binary digits. With encryption keys of 512 digits, there are 2^{512} possibilities to check out. It is estimated that all the computers in the world would need to work for 10 years before stumbling upon the answer.

The **Data Encryption Standard (DES)** was developed by the National Security Agency (NSA) and IBM in the 1950s. DES uses a 56-bit encryption key. To cope with much faster computers, it has been improved by *Triple DES*—essentially encrypting the message three times, each with a separate key. Today, the most widely used symmetric key algorithm is **Advanced Encryption Standard (AES)**, which offers key sizes of 128, 192, and 256 bits. AES had been considered to be relatively secure, but in 2011, researchers from Microsoft and a Belgian university announced that they had discovered a way to break the algorithm, and with this work, the "safety margin" of AES continues to erode. There are also many other symmetric key systems that are currently less widely used, with keys up to 2,048 bits.[1] In November 2013, Google upgraded the security of its SSL certificates to 2,048-bit keys and has reportedly accelerated other programs to encrypt data in the wake of the controversy over the NSA's PRISM program (Mimoso, 2013; Rosenblatt, 2013).

Public Key Cryptography

In 1976, a new way of encrypting messages called **public key cryptography** was invented by Whitfield Diffie and Martin Hellman. Public key cryptography (also referred to as *asymmetric cryptography*) solves the problem of exchanging keys. In this method, two mathematically related digital keys are used: a public key and a private key. The private key is kept secret by the owner, and the public key is widely disseminated. Both keys can be used to encrypt and decrypt a message. However, once the keys are used to encrypt a message, the same key cannot be used to unencrypt the message. The mathematical algorithms used to produce the keys are one-way functions. A *one-way irreversible mathematical function* is one in which, once the algorithm is applied, the input cannot be subsequently derived from the output. Most food recipes are like this. For instance, it is easy to make scrambled eggs, but impossible to retrieve whole eggs from the scrambled eggs. Public key cryptography is based on the idea of irreversible mathematical functions. The keys are sufficiently long (128, 256, and 512 bits) that it would take enormous computing power to derive one key from

Data Encryption Standard (DES)
developed by the National Security Agency (NSA) and IBM. Uses a 56-bit encryption key

Advanced Encryption Standard (AES)
the most widely used symmetric key algorithm, offering 128-, 192-, and 256-bit keys

public key cryptography
two mathematically related digital keys are used: a public key and a private key. The private key is kept secret by the owner, and the public key is widely disseminated. Both keys can be used to encrypt and decrypt a message. However, once the keys are used to encrypt a message, that same key cannot be used to unencrypt the message

[1] For instance: DESX and RDES with 168-bit keys; the RC Series: RC2, RC4, and RC5 with keys up to 2,048 bits; and the IDEA algorithm, the basis of PGP, e-mail public key encryption software described later in this chapter, which uses 128-bit keys.

the other using the largest and fastest computers available. **Figure 4.6** illustrates a simple use of public key cryptography and takes you through the important steps in using public and private keys.

Public Key Cryptography Using Digital Signatures and Hash Digests

In public key cryptography, some elements of security are missing. Although we can be quite sure the message was not understood or read by a third party (message confidentiality), there is no guarantee the sender really is the sender; that is, there is no authentication of the sender. This means the sender could deny ever sending the message (repudiation). And there is no assurance the message was not altered somehow in transit. For example, the message "Buy Cisco @ $16" could have been accidentally or intentionally altered to read "Sell Cisco @ $16." This suggests a potential lack of integrity in the system.

A more sophisticated use of public key cryptography can achieve authentication, nonrepudiation, and integrity. **Figure 4.7** illustrates this more powerful approach.

hash function
an algorithm that produces a fixed-length number called a hash or message digest

To check the integrity of a message and ensure it has not been altered in transit, a hash function is used first to create a digest of the message. A **hash function** is an algorithm that produces a fixed-length number called a *hash* or *message digest*. A hash function can be simple, and count the number of digital 1s in a message, or it can be more complex, and produce a 128-bit number that reflects the number of 0s and 1s, the number of 00s and 11s, and so on. Standard hash functions are available (MD4 and MD5 produce 128- and 160-bit hashes) (Stein, 1998). These more complex hash functions produce hashes or hash results that are unique to every message. The results of applying the hash function are sent by the sender to the recipient. Upon receipt, the recipient applies the hash function to the received message and checks to verify the same result is produced. If so, the message has not been altered. The sender then encrypts both the hash result and the original message using the recipient's public key (as in Figure 4.6 on page 271), producing a single block of cipher text.

**digital signature
(e-signature)**
"signed" cipher text that can be sent over the Internet

One more step is required. To ensure the authenticity of the message and to ensure nonrepudiation, the sender encrypts the entire block of cipher text one more time using the sender's private key. This produces a **digital signature** (also called an *e-signature*) or "signed" cipher text that can be sent over the Internet.

A digital signature is a close parallel to a handwritten signature. Like a handwritten signature, a digital signature is unique—only one person presumably possesses the private key. When used with a hash function, the digital signature is even more unique than a handwritten signature. In addition to being exclusive to a particular individual, when used to sign a hashed document, the digital signature is also unique to the document, and changes for every document.

The recipient of this signed cipher text first uses the sender's public key to authenticate the message. Once authenticated, the recipient uses his or her private key to obtain the hash result and original message. As a final step, the recipient applies the same hash function to the original text, and compares the result with the result sent by the sender. If the results are the same, the recipient now knows the message has not been changed during transmission. The message has integrity.

FIGURE 4.6	PUBLIC KEY CRYPTOGRAPHY—A SIMPLE CASE

STEP	DESCRIPTION
1. The sender creates a digital message.	The message could be a document, spreadsheet, or any digital object.
2. The sender obtains the recipient's public key from a public directory and applies it to the message.	Public keys are distributed widely and can be obtained from recipients directly.
3. Application of the recipient's key produces an encrypted cipher text message.	Once encrypted using the public key, the message cannot be reverse-engineered or unencrypted using the same public key. The process is irreversible.
4. The encrypted message is sent over the Internet.	The encrypted message is broken into packets and sent through several different pathways, making interception of the entire message difficult (but not impossible).
5. The recipient uses his/her private key to decrypt the message.	The only person who can decrypt the message is the person who has possession of the recipient's private key. Hopefully, this is the legitimate recipient.

In the simplest use of public key cryptography, the sender encrypts a message using the recipient's public key, and then sends it over the Internet. The only person who can decrypt this message is the recipient, using his or her private key. However, this simple case does not ensure integrity or an authentic message.

Early digital signature programs required the user to have a digital certificate, and were far too difficult for an individual to use. Newer programs are Internet-based and do not require users to install software, or understand digital certificate technology. DocuSign, Adobe EchoSign, and Sertifi are among a number of companies offering online digital signature solutions. Many insurance, finance, and surety companies now permit customers to electronically sign documents.

FIGURE 4.7	PUBLIC KEY CRYPTOGRAPHY WITH DIGITAL SIGNATURES
STEP	**DESCRIPTION**
1. The sender creates an original message.	The message can be any digital file.
2. The sender applies a hash function, producing a 128-bit hash result.	Hash functions create a unique digest of the message based on the message contents.
3. The sender encrypts the message and hash result using the recipient's public key.	This irreversible process creates a cipher text that can be read only by the recipient using his or her private key.
4. The sender encrypts the result, again using his or her private key.	The sender's private key is a digital signature. There is only one person who can create this digital mark.
5. The result of this double encryption is sent over the Internet.	The message traverses the Internet as a series of independent packets.
6. The receiver uses the sender's public key to authenticate the message.	Only one person can send this message, namely, the sender.
7. The receiver uses his or her private key to decrypt the hash function and the original message. The receiver checks to ensure the original message and the hash function results conform to one another.	The hash function is used here to check the original message. This ensures the message was not changed in transit.

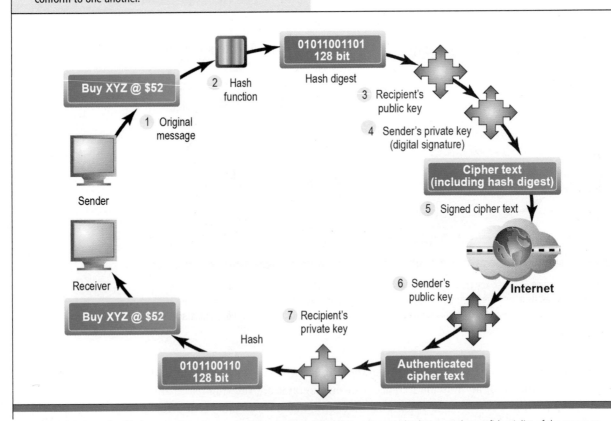

A more realistic use of public key cryptography uses hash functions and digital signatures to both ensure the confidentiality of the message and authenticate the sender. The only person who could have sent the above message is the owner or the sender using his/her private key. This authenticates the message. The hash function ensures the message was not altered in transit. As before, the only person who can decipher the message is the recipient, using his/her private key.

Digital Envelopes

Public key cryptography is computationally slow. If one used 128- or 256-bit keys to encode large documents—such as this chapter or the entire book—significant declines in transmission speeds and increases in processing time would occur. Symmetric key cryptography is computationally faster, but as we pointed out previously, it has a weakness—namely, the symmetric key must be sent to the recipient over insecure transmission lines. One solution is to use the more efficient symmetric encryption and decryption for large documents, but public key cryptography to encrypt and send the symmetric key. This technique is called using a **digital envelope**. See **Figure 4.8** for an illustration of how a digital envelope works.

In Figure 4.8, a diplomatic document is encrypted using a symmetric key. The symmetric key—which the recipient will require to decrypt the document—is itself encrypted, using the recipient's public key. So we have a "key within a key" (a *digital envelope*). The encrypted report and the digital envelope are sent across the Web. The recipient first uses his/her private key to decrypt the symmetric key, and then the recipient uses the symmetric key to decrypt the report. This method saves time because both encryption and decryption are faster with symmetric keys.

digital envelope
a technique that uses symmetric encryption for large documents, but public key cryptography to encrypt and send the symmetric key

FIGURE 4.8	**PUBLIC KEY CRYPTOGRAPHY: CREATING A DIGITAL ENVELOPE**

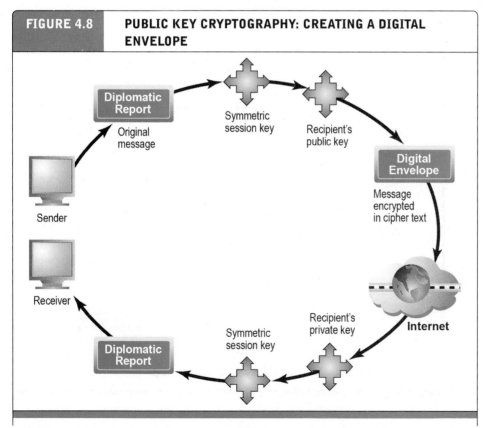

A digital envelope can be created to transmit a symmetric key that will permit the recipient to decrypt the message and be assured the message was not intercepted in transit.

Digital Certificates and Public Key Infrastructure (PKI)

There are still some deficiencies in the message security regime described previously. How do we know that people and institutions are who they claim to be? Anyone can make up a private and public key combination and claim to be someone they are not. Before you place an order with an online merchant such as Amazon, you want to be sure it really is Amazon you have on the screen and not a spoofer masquerading as Amazon. In the physical world, if someone asks who you are and you show a social security number, they may well ask to see a picture ID or a second form of certifiable or acceptable identification. If they really doubt who you are, they may ask for references to other authorities and actually interview these other authorities. Similarly, in the digital world, we need a way to know who people and institutions really are.

Digital certificates, and the supporting public key infrastructure, are an attempt to solve this problem of digital identity. A **digital certificate** is a digital document issued by a trusted third-party institution known as a **certification authority (CA)** that contains the name of the subject or company, the subject's public key, a digital certificate serial number, an expiration date, an issuance date, the digital signature of the certification authority (the name of the CA encrypted using the CA's private key), and other identifying information (see **Figure 4.9**).

digital certificate

a digital document issued by a certification authority that contains the name of the subject or company, the subject's public key, a digital certificate serial number, an expiration date, an issuance date, the digital signature of the certification authority, and other identifying information

certification authority (CA)

a trusted third party that issues digital certificates

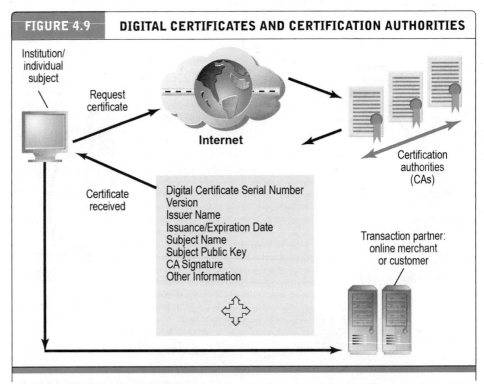

| FIGURE 4.9 | DIGITAL CERTIFICATES AND CERTIFICATION AUTHORITIES |

The PKI includes certification authorities that issue, verify, and guarantee digital certificates that are used in e-commerce to assure the identity of transaction partners.

Worldwide, thousands of organizations issue CAs. GlobalSign was the first certification authority created in Europe. EU member states and other European nations maintain lists of approved CAs. A hierarchy of CAs has emerged with less-well-known CAs being certified by larger and better-known CAs, creating a community of mutually verifying institutions. **Public key infrastructure (PKI)** refers to the CAs and digital certificate procedures that are accepted by all parties. When you sign into a "secure" site, the URL will begin with "https" and a closed lock icon will appear on your browser. This means the site has a digital certificate issued by a trusted CA. It is not, presumably, a spoof site.

To create a digital certificate, the user generates a public/private key pair and sends a request for certification to a CA along with the user's public key. The CA verifies the information (how this is accomplished differs from CA to CA). The CA issues a certificate containing the user's public key and other related information. Finally, the CA creates a message digest from the certificate itself (just like a hash digest) and signs it with the CA's private key. This signed digest is called the *signed certificate*. We end up with a totally unique cipher text document—there can be only one signed certificate like this in the world.

There are several ways the certificates are used in commerce. Before initiating a transaction, the customer can request the signed digital certificate of the merchant and decrypt it using the merchant's public key to obtain both the message digest and the certificate as issued. If the message digest matches the certificate, then the merchant and the public key are authenticated. The merchant may in return request certification of the user, in which case the user would send the merchant his or her individual certificate. There are many types of certificates: personal, institutional, Web server, software publisher, and CAs themselves.

PKI and CAs can also be used to secure software code and content for applications that are directly downloaded to mobile devices from the Internet. Using a technique referred to as code signing, mobile application developers use their private key to encrypt a digital signature. When end users decrypt the signature with the corresponding public key, it confirms the developer's identity and the integrity of the code.

You can easily obtain a public and private key for personal, noncommercial use at the International PGP Home Page Web site, Pgpi.org. **Pretty Good Privacy (PGP)** was invented in 1991 by Phil Zimmerman, and has become one of the most widely used e-mail public key encryption software tools in the world. Using PGP software installed on your computer, you can compress and encrypt your messages as well as authenticate both yourself and the recipient. There are also a number of Firefox, Chrome, Internet Explorer, and Safari add-ons, extensions, or plug-ins that enable you to encrypt your e-mail.

Limitations to Encryption Solutions

PKI is a powerful technological solution to security issues, but it has many limitations, especially concerning CAs. PKI applies mainly to protecting messages in transit on the Internet and is not effective against insiders—employees—who have legitimate access to corporate systems including customer information. Most e-commerce sites

public key infrastructure (PKI)
CAs and digital certificate procedures that are accepted by all parties

Pretty Good Privacy (PGP)
a widely used e-mail public key encryption software program

do not store customer information in encrypted form. Other limitations are apparent. For one, how is your private key to be protected? Most private keys will be stored on insecure desktop or laptop computers.

There is no guarantee the person using your computer—and your private key—is really you. For instance, you may lose your laptop or smartphone, and therefore lose the private key. Likewise, there is no assurance that someone else in the world cannot use your personal ID papers, such as a social security card, to obtain a PKI authenticated online ID in your name. If there's no real world identification system, there can be no Internet identification system. Under many digital signature laws, you are responsible for whatever your private key does even if you were not the person using the key. This is very different from mail-order or telephone order credit card rules, where you have a right to dispute the credit card charge. Second, there is no guarantee the verifying computer of the merchant is secure. Third, CAs are self-selected organizations seeking to gain access to the business of authorization. They may not be authorities on the corporations or individuals they certify. For instance, how can a CA know about all the corporations within an industry to determine who is or is not legitimate? A related question concerns the method used by the CA to identify the certificate holder. Was this an e-mail transaction verified only by claims of the applicants who filled out an online form? For instance, VeriSign acknowledged in one case that it had mistakenly issued two digital certificates to someone fraudulently claiming to represent Microsoft. Digital certificates have been hijacked by hackers, tricking consumers into giving up personal information. For example, in July 2014, India's National Informatics Centre, an intermediate CA that was trusted by the Indian Controller of Certifying Authorities, whose certificates are included in the Microsoft Root Store and thus trusted by the vast majority of programs running on Windows, including Internet Explorer and Chrome, was hacked and a number of unauthorized digital certificates were issued for domains operated by Google and Yahoo (Datta, 2014). Last, what are the policies for revoking or renewing certificates? The expected life of a digital certificate or private key is a function of the frequency of use and the vulnerability of systems that use the certificate. Yet most CAs have no policy or just an annual policy for reissuing certificates. If Microsoft, Apple, or Cisco ever rescinded a number of CAs, millions of users would not be able to access sites. The CA system is difficult and costly to police.

SECURING CHANNELS OF COMMUNICATION

The concepts of public key cryptography are used routinely for securing channels of communication.

Secure Sockets Layer (SSL) and Transport Layer Security (TLS)

secure negotiated session
a client-server session in which the URL of the requested document, along with the contents, contents of forms, and the cookies exchanged, are encrypted

The most common form of securing channels is through the *Secure Sockets Layer (SSL)* and *Transport Layer Security (TLS)* protocols. When you receive a message from a server on the Web with which you will be communicating through a secure channel, this means you will be using SSL/TLS to establish a secure negotiated session. (Notice that the URL changes from HTTP to HTTPS.) A **secure negotiated session** is a client-

FIGURE 4.10   SECURE NEGOTIATED SESSIONS USING SSL/TLS

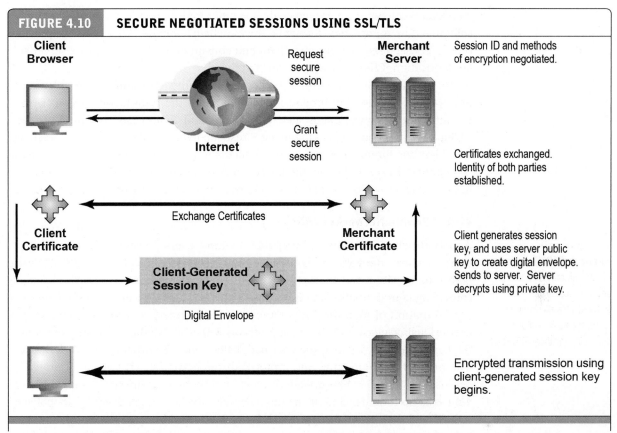

Certificates play a key role in using SSL/TLS to establish a secure communications channel.

server session in which the URL of the requested document, along with the contents, contents of forms, and the cookies exchanged, are encrypted (see **Figure 4.10**). For instance, your credit card number that you entered into a form would be encrypted. Through a series of handshakes and communications, the browser and the server establish one another's identity by exchanging digital certificates, decide on the strongest shared form of encryption, and then proceed to communicate using an agreed-upon session key. A **session key** is a unique symmetric encryption key chosen just for this single secure session. Once used, it is gone forever. Figure 4.10 shows how this works.

session key
a unique symmetric encryption key chosen for a single secure session

In practice, most private individuals do not have a digital certificate. In this case, the merchant server will not request a certificate, but the client browser will request the merchant certificate once a secure session is called for by the server.

SSL/TLS provides data encryption, server authentication, optional client authentication, and message integrity for TCP/IP connections. SSL/TLS addresses the issue of authenticity by allowing users to verify another user's identity or the identity of a server. It also protects the integrity of the messages exchanged. However, once the merchant receives the encrypted credit and order information, that information is typically stored in unencrypted format on the merchant's servers. While SSL/TLS provides secure transactions between merchant and consumer, it only guarantees server-side authentication. Client authentication is optional.

In addition, SSL/TLS cannot provide irrefutability—consumers can order goods or download information products, and then claim the transaction never occurred. Recently, social network sites such as Facebook and Twitter have begun to use SSL/TLS to thwart account hijacking using Firesheep over wireless networks. Firesheep, an add-on for Firefox, can be used by hackers to grab unencrypted cookies used to "remember" a user and allow the hacker to immediately log on to a Web site as that user. SSL/TLS can thwart such an attack because it encrypts the cookie.

Virtual Private Networks (VPNs)

virtual private network (VPN)
allows remote users to securely access internal networks via the Internet, using the Point-to-Point Tunneling Protocol (PPTP)

A **virtual private network (VPN)** allows remote users to securely access a corporation's local area network via the Internet, using a variety of VPN protocols. VPNs use both authentication and encryption to secure information from unauthorized persons (providing confidentiality and integrity). Authentication prevents spoofing and misrepresentation of identities. A remote user can connect to a remote private local network using a local ISP. The VPN protocols will establish the link from the client to the corporate network as if the user had dialed into the corporate network directly. The process of connecting one protocol through another (IP) is called *tunneling,* because the VPN creates a private connection by adding an invisible wrapper around a message to hide its content. As the message travels through the Internet between the ISP and the corporate network, it is shielded from prying eyes by an encrypted wrapper.

A VPN is "virtual" in the sense that it appears to users as a dedicated secure line when in fact it is a temporary secure line. The primary use of VPNs is to establish secure communications among business partners—larger suppliers or customers, and employees working remotely. A dedicated connection to a business partner can be very expensive. Using the Internet and VPN as the connection method significantly reduces the cost of secure communications.

Wireless (Wi-Fi) Networks

Accessing the Internet via a wireless (Wi-Fi) network has its own particular security issues. Early Wi-Fi networks used a security standard called Wired Equivalent Privacy (WEP) to encrypt information. WEP was very weak, and easy for hackers to crack. A new standard, Wi-Fi Protected Access (WPA), was developed that provided a higher standard of protection, but this too soon became vulnerable to intrusion. Today, the current standard is **WPA2**, which uses the AES algorithm for encryption and CCMP, a more advanced authentication code protocol.

WPA2
wireless security standard that uses the AES algorithm for encryption and CCMP, a more advanced authentication code protocol

PROTECTING NETWORKS

Once you have protected communications as well as possible, the next set of tools to consider are those that can protect your networks, as well as the servers and clients on those networks.

Firewalls

Firewalls and proxy servers are intended to build a wall around your network and the attached servers and clients, just like physical-world firewalls protect you from fires for a limited period of time. Firewalls and proxy servers share some similar functions, but they are quite different.

A **firewall** refers to either hardware or software that filters communication packets and prevents some packets from entering or exiting the network based on a security policy. The firewall controls traffic to and from servers and clients, forbidding communications from untrustworthy sources, and allowing other communications from trusted sources to proceed. Every message that is to be sent or received from the network is processed by the firewall, which determines if the message meets security guidelines established by the business. If it does, it is permitted to be distributed, and if it doesn't, the message is blocked. Firewalls can filter traffic based on packet attributes such as source IP address, destination port or IP address, type of service (such as WWW or HTTP), the domain name of the source, and many other dimensions. Most hardware firewalls that protect local area networks connected to the Internet have default settings that require little if any administrator intervention and employ simple but effective rules that deny incoming packets from a connection that does not originate from an internal request—the firewall only allows connections from servers that you requested service from. A common default setting on hardware firewalls (DSL and cable modem routers) simply ignores efforts to communicate with TCP port 445, the most commonly attacked port. The increasing use of firewalls by home and business Internet users has greatly reduced the effectiveness of attacks, and forced hackers to focus more on e-mail attachments to distribute worms and viruses.

There are two major methods firewalls use to validate traffic: packet filters and application gateways. *Packet filters* examine data packets to determine whether they are destined for a prohibited port or originate from a prohibited IP address (as specified by the security administrator). The filter specifically looks at the source and destination information, as well as the port and packet type, when determining whether the information may be transmitted. One downside of the packet filtering method is that it is susceptible to spoofing, because authentication is not one of its roles.

Application gateways are a type of firewall that filters communications based on the application being requested, rather than the source or destination of the message. Such firewalls also process requests at the application level, farther away from the client computer than packet filters. By providing a central filtering point, application gateways provide greater security than packet filters but can compromise system performance.

Next-generation firewalls use an application-centric approach to firewall control. They are able to identify applications regardless of the port, protocol, or security evasion tools used; identify users regardless of device or IP address; decrypt outbound SSL; and protect in real-time against threats embedded in applications.

Proxy Servers

Proxy servers (proxies) are software servers (often a dedicated computer) that handle all communications originating from or being sent to the Internet by local

firewall
refers to either hardware or software that filters communication packets and prevents some packets from entering the network based on a security policy

proxy server (proxy)
software server that handles all communications originating from or being sent to the Internet, acting as a spokesperson or bodyguard for the organization

FIGURE 4.11	FIREWALLS AND PROXY SERVERS

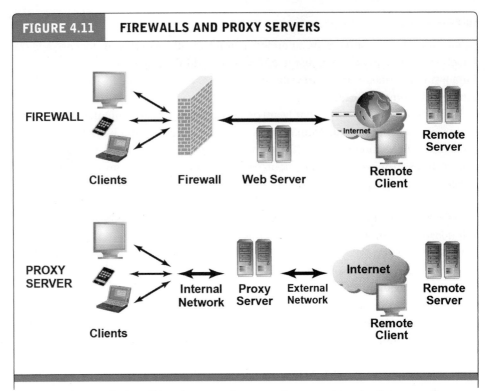

The primary function of a firewall is to deny access by remote client computers to local computers. The primary purpose of a proxy server is to provide controlled access from local computers to remote computers.

clients, acting as a spokesperson or bodyguard for the organization. Proxies act primarily to limit access of internal clients to external Internet servers, although some proxy servers act as firewalls as well. Proxy servers are sometimes called *dual-home systems* because they have two network interfaces. To internal computers, a proxy server is known as the *gateway*, while to external computers it is known as a *mail server* or *numeric address*.

When a user on an internal network requests a Web page, the request is routed first to the proxy server. The proxy server validates the user and the nature of the request, and then sends the request onto the Internet. A Web page sent by an external Internet server first passes to the proxy server. If acceptable, the Web page passes onto the internal network Web server and then to the client desktop. By prohibiting users from communicating directly with the Internet, companies can restrict access to certain types of sites, such as pornographic, auction, or stock-trading sites. Proxy servers also improve Web performance by storing frequently requested Web pages locally, reducing upload times, and hiding the internal network's address, thus making it more difficult for hackers to monitor. **Figure 4.11** illustrates how firewalls and proxy servers protect a local area network from Internet intruders and prevent internal clients from reaching prohibited Web servers.

Intrusion Detection and Prevention Systems

In addition to a firewall and proxy server, an intrusion detection and/or prevention system can be installed. An **intrusion detection system (IDS)** examines network traffic, watching to see if it matches certain patterns or preconfigured rules indicative of an attack. If it detects suspicious activity, the IDS will set off an alarm alerting administrators and log the event in a database. An IDS is useful for detecting malicious activity that a firewall might miss. An **intrusion prevention system (IPS)** has all the functionality of an IDS, with the additional ability to take steps to prevent and block suspicious activities. For instance, an IPS can terminate a session and reset a connection, block traffic from a suspicious IP address, or reconfigure firewall or router security controls.

PROTECTING SERVERS AND CLIENTS

Operating system features and anti-virus software can help further protect servers and clients from certain types of attacks.

Operating System Security Enhancements

The most obvious way to protect servers and clients is to take advantage of automatic computer security upgrades. The Microsoft, Apple, and Linux/Unix operating systems are continuously updated to patch vulnerabilities discovered by hackers. These patches are autonomic; that is, when using these operating systems on the Internet, you are prompted and informed that operating system enhancements are available. Users can easily download these security patches for free. The most common known worms and viruses can be prevented by simply keeping your server and client operating systems and applications up to date. In April 2014, Microsoft ended security support and updates for its Windows XP operating system. Despite this, many organizations continue to use XP-based systems, and as a result, many security experts anticipate a wave of strikes against such systems. Application vulnerabilities are fixed in the same manner. For instance, most popular Internet browsers are updated automatically with little user intervention.

Anti-Virus Software

The easiest and least-expensive way to prevent threats to system integrity is to install anti-virus software. Programs by McAfee, Symantec (Norton AntiVirus), and many others provide inexpensive tools to identify and eradicate the most common types of malicious code as they enter a computer, as well as destroy those already lurking on a hard drive. Anti-virus programs can be set up so that e-mail attachments are inspected before you click on them, and the attachments are eliminated if they contain a known virus or worm. It is not enough, however, to simply install the software once. Because new viruses are developed and released every day, daily routine updates are needed in order to prevent new threats from being loaded. Some premium-level anti-virus software is updated hourly.

Anti-virus suite packages and stand-alone programs are available to eliminate intruders such as bot programs, adware, and other security risks. Such programs work

intrusion detection system (IDS) examines network traffic, watching to see if it matches certain patterns or preconfigured rules indicative of an attack

intrusion prevention system (IPS) has all the functionality of an IDS, with the additional ability to take steps to prevent and block suspicious activities

much like anti-virus software in that they look for recognized hacker tools or signature actions of known intruders.

| 4.4 | **MANAGEMENT POLICIES, BUSINESS PROCEDURES, AND PUBLIC LAWS** |

Worldwide, in 2014, companies are expected to spend over €56 billion on security hardware, software, and services (Gartner, 2014). However, most CEOs and CIOs believe that technology is not the sole answer to managing the risk of e-commerce. The technology provides a foundation, but in the absence of intelligent management policies, even the best technology can be easily defeated. Public laws and active enforcement of cybercrime statutes also are required to both raise the costs of illegal behavior on the Internet and guard against corporate abuse of information. Let's consider briefly the development of management policy.

A SECURITY PLAN: MANAGEMENT POLICIES

In order to minimize security threats, e-commerce firms must develop a coherent corporate policy that takes into account the nature of the risks, the information assets that need protecting, and the procedures and technologies required to address the risk, as well as implementation and auditing mechanisms. **Figure 4.12** illustrates the key steps in developing a solid security plan.

risk assessment

an assessment of the risks and points of vulnerability

A security plan begins with **risk assessment**—an assessment of the risks and points of vulnerability. The first step is to inventory the information and knowledge assets of the e-commerce site and company. What information is at risk? Is it customer information, proprietary designs, business activities, secret processes, or other internal information, such as price schedules, executive compensation, or payroll? For each type of information asset, try to estimate the dollar value to the firm if this information were compromised, and then multiply that amount by the probability of the loss occurring. Once you have done so, rank order the results. You now have a list of information assets prioritized by their value to the firm.

security policy

a set of statements prioritizing the information risks, identifying acceptable risk targets, and identifying the mechanisms for achieving these targets

Based on your quantified list of risks, you can start to develop a **security policy**—a set of statements prioritizing the information risks, identifying acceptable risk targets, and identifying the mechanisms for achieving these targets. You will obviously want to start with the information assets that you determined to be the highest priority in your risk assessment. Who generates and controls this information in the firm? What existing security policies are in place to protect the information? What enhancements can you recommend to improve security of these most valuable assets? What level of risk are you willing to accept for each of these assets? Are you willing, for instance, to lose customer credit card data once every 10 years? Or will you pursue a 100-year hurricane strategy by building a security edifice for credit card data that can withstand the once-in-100-year disaster? You will need to estimate how much it will cost to achieve this level of acceptable risk. Remember, total and complete security may require extraordinary financial resources. By answering these questions, you will have the beginnings of a security policy.

FIGURE 4.12   DEVELOPING AN E-COMMERCE SECURITY PLAN

There are five steps involved in building an e-commerce security plan.

Next, consider an **implementation plan**—the steps you will take to achieve the security plan goals. Specifically, you must determine how you will translate the levels of acceptable risk into a set of tools, technologies, policies, and procedures. What new technologies will you deploy to achieve the goals, and what new employee procedures will be needed?

To implement your plan, you will need an organizational unit in charge of security, and a security officer—someone who is in charge of security on a daily basis. For a small e-commerce site, the security officer will likely be the person in charge of Internet services or the site manager, whereas for larger firms, there typically is a dedicated team with a supporting budget. The **security organization** educates and trains users, keeps management aware of security threats and breakdowns, and maintains the tools chosen to implement security.

The security organization typically administers access controls, authentication procedures, and authorization policies. **Access controls** determine which outsiders and insiders can gain legitimate access to your networks. Outsider access controls include firewalls and proxy servers, while insider access controls typically consist of login procedures (usernames, passwords, and access codes).

Authentication procedures include the use of digital signatures, certificates of authority, and PKI. Now that e-signatures have been given the same legal weight as an original pen-and-ink version, companies are in the process of devising ways to test and confirm a signer's identity. Companies frequently have signers type their full

implementation plan
the action steps you will take to achieve the security plan goals

security organization
educates and trains users, keeps management aware of security threats and breakdowns, and maintains the tools chosen to implement security

access controls
determine who can gain legitimate access to a network

authentication procedures
include the use of digital signatures, certificates of authority, and public key infrastructure

name and click on a button indicating their understanding that they have just signed a contract or document.

Biometric devices can also be used to verify physical attributes associated with an individual, such as a fingerprint or retina (eye) scan or speech recognition system. (**Biometrics** is the study of measurable biological, or physical, characteristics.) A company could require, for example, that an individual undergo a fingerprint scan before being allowed access to a Web site, or before being allowed to pay for merchandise with a credit card. Biometric devices make it even more difficult for hackers to break into sites or facilities, significantly reducing the opportunity for spoofing. Security tokens are used by millions of corporation and government workers to log on to corporate clients and servers. Apple's new iPhone 5S features a unique fingerprint sensor called the Touch ID built into the iPhone's home button to unlock the phone and authorize purchases from the iTunes, iBooks, and App Stores without requiring users to enter a PIN or other security code. According to Apple, the system does not store an actual fingerprint, but rather biometric data, which will be encrypted and stored only on a chip within the iPhone, and will not be made available to third parties.

Security tokens are physical devices or software that generate an identifier that can be used in addition to or in place of a password. One example is RSA's SecurID token, which continuously generates six-digit passwords.

Authorization policies determine differing levels of access to information assets for differing levels of users. **Authorization management systems** establish where and when a user is permitted to access certain parts of a Web site. Their primary function is to restrict access to private information within a company's Internet infrastructure. Although there are several authorization management products currently available, most operate in the same way: the system encrypts a user session to function like a passkey that follows the user from page to page, allowing access only to those areas that the user is permitted to enter, based on information set at the system database. By establishing entry rules up front for each user, the authorization management system knows who is permitted to go where at all times.

The last step in developing an e-commerce security plan is performing a security audit. A **security audit** involves the routine review of access logs (identifying how outsiders are using the site as well as how insiders are accessing the site's assets). A monthly report should be produced that establishes the routine and nonroutine accesses to the systems and identifies unusual patterns of activities. As previously noted, tiger teams are often used by large corporate sites to evaluate the strength of existing security procedures. Many small firms have sprung up in the last five years to provide these services to large corporate sites.

THE ROLE OF LAWS AND PUBLIC POLICY

The public policy environment today is very different from the early days of e-commerce. The net result is that the Internet is no longer an ungoverned, unsupervised, self-controlled technology juggernaut. Just as with financial markets in the last 70 years, there is a growing awareness that e-commerce markets work only when a powerful institutional set of laws and enforcement mechanisms are in place. These laws help ensure orderly, rational, and fair markets. This growing public policy envi-

---

biometrics

the study of measurable biological or physical characteristics

security token

physical device or software that generates an identifier that can be used in addition to or in place of a password

authorization policies

determine differing levels of access to information assets for differing levels of users

authorization management system

establishes where and when a user is permitted to access certain parts of a Web site

security audit

involves the routine review of access logs (identifying how outsiders are using the site as well as how insiders are accessing the site's assets)

ronment is becoming just as global as e-commerce itself. Despite some spectacular internationally based attacks on U.S. e-commerce sites, the sources and persons involved in major harmful attacks have almost always been uncovered and, where possible, prosecuted.

Voluntary and private efforts have played a very large role in identifying criminal hackers and assisting law enforcement. Since 1995, as e-commerce has grown in significance, national and local law enforcement activities have expanded greatly. New laws have been passed that grant local and national authorities new tools and mechanisms for identifying, tracing, and prosecuting cybercriminals. For instance, a majority of states now require companies that maintain personal data on their residents to publicly disclose when a security breach affecting those residents has occurred. **Table 4.5** on page 286 lists the most significant federal e-commerce security legislation and regulation.

By increasing the punishment for cybercrimes, the U.S. government is attempting to create a deterrent to further hacker actions. And by making such actions federal crimes, the government is able to extradite international hackers and prosecute them within the United States.

After September 11, 2001, Congress passed the USA PATRIOT Act, which broadly expanded law enforcement's investigative and surveillance powers. The act has provisions for monitoring e-mail and Internet use. The Homeland Security Act of 2002 also attempts to fight cyberterrorism and increases the government's ability to compel information disclosure by computer and ISP sources. Recent proposed legislation that focuses on requiring firms to report data breaches to the FTC, protection of the national electric grid, and cybersecurity has all failed to pass.

Private and Private-Public Cooperation Efforts

The good news is that e-commerce sites are not alone in their battle to achieve security on the Internet. Several organizations—some public and some private—are devoted to tracking down criminal organizations and individuals engaged in attacks against Internet and e-commerce sites. On the federal level, the Office of Cybersecurity and Communications (CS&C) within the U.S. Department of Homeland Security (DHS), is responsible for overseeing the security, resilience, and reliability of the United States' cyber and communications infrastructure. The National Cybersecurity and Communications Integration Center (NCCIC) acts as a 24/7 cyber monitoring, incident response, and management center. In addition, the DHS also operates the **United States Computer Emergency Readiness Team (US-CERT)**, which coordinates cyber incident warnings and responses across both the government and private sectors. One of the better-known private organizations is the **CERT Coordination Center** (formerly known as the Computer Emergency Response Team) at Carnegie Mellon University. CERT monitors and tracks online criminal activity reported to it by private corporations and government agencies that seek out its help. CERT is composed of full-time and part-time computer experts who can trace the origins of attacks against sites despite the complexity of the Internet. Its staff members also assist organizations in identifying security problems, developing solutions, and communicating with the public about widespread hacker threats. The CERT Coordination Center also provides

US-CERT
division of the U.S. Department of Homeland Security that coordinates cyber incident warnings and responses across government and private sectors

CERT Coordination Center
monitors and tracks online criminal activity reported to it by private corporations and government agencies that seek out its help

TABLE 4.5	U.S. E-COMMERCE SECURITY LEGISLATION AND REGULATION
LEGISLATION/REGULATION	SIGNIFICANCE
Computer Fraud and Abuse Act (1986)	Primary federal statute used to combat computer crime.
Electronic Communications Privacy Act (1986)	Imposes fines and imprisonment for individuals who access, intercept, or disclose the private e-mail communications of others.
National Information Infrastructure Protection Act (1996)	Makes DoS attacks illegal; creates NIPC in the FBI.
Health Insurance Portability and Accountability Act (1996)	Requires certain health care facilities to report data breaches.
Financial Modernization Act (Gramm-Leach-Bliley Act) (1999)	Requires certain financial institutions to report data breaches.
Cyberspace Electronic Security Act (2000)	Reduces export restrictions.
Computer Security Enhancement Act (2000)	Protects federal government systems from hacking.
Electronic Signatures in Global and National Commerce Act (the "E-Sign Law") (2000)	Authorizes the use of electronic signatures in legal documents.
USA PATRIOT Act (2001)	Authorizes use of computer-based surveillance of suspected terrorists.
Homeland Security Act (2002)	Authorizes establishment of the Department of Homeland Security, which is responsible for developing a comprehensive national plan for security of the key resources and critical infrastructures of the United States; DHS becomes the central coordinator for all cyberspace security efforts.
CAN-SPAM Act (2003)	Although primarily a mechanism for civil and regulatory lawsuits against spammers, the CAN-SPAM Act also creates several new criminal offenses intended to address situations in which the perpetrator has taken steps to hide his or her identity or the source of the spam from recipients, ISPs, or law enforcement agencies. Also contains criminal sanctions for sending sexually explicit e-mail without designating it as such.
U.S. SAFE WEB Act (2006)	Enhances FTC's ability to obtain monetary redress for consumers in cases involving spyware, spam, Internet fraud, and deception; also improves FTC's ability to gather information and coordinate investigations with foreign counterparts.
Improving Critical Infrastructure Cybersecurity Executive Order (2013)	After Congress failed to pass cybersecurity legislation in 2012, this executive order issued by the Obama administration directs federal agenices to share cybersecurity threat intelligence with private sector companies that may be targets, and the development and implementation of a cybersecurity framework for private industry, incorporating best practices and voluntary standards.

TABLE 4.6	GOVERNMENT EFFORTS TO REGULATE AND CONTROL ENCRYPTION	
REGULATORY EFFORT	IMPACT
Restricted export of strong security systems	Supported primarily by the United States. Widespread distribution of encryption schemes weakens this policy. The policy is changing to permit exports except to pariah countries.
Key escrow/key recovery schemes	France, the United Kingdom, and the United States supported this effort in the late 1990s but now have largely abandoned it. There are few trusted third parties.
Lawful access and forced disclosure	Growing support in U.S. legislation and in OECD countries.
Official hacking	All countries are rapidly expanding budgets and training for law enforcement "technical centers" aimed at monitoring and cracking computer-based encryption activities of suspected criminals.

product assessments, reports, and training in order to improve the public's knowledge and understanding of security threats and solutions.

Government Policies and Controls on Encryption Software

In the United States, both Congress and the executive branch have sought to regulate the uses of encryption and to restrict availability and export of encryption systems as a means of preventing crime and terrorism. At the international level, four organizations have influenced the international traffic in encryption software: the Organization for Economic Cooperation and Development (OECD), G-7/G-8 (the heads of state of the top eight industrialized countries in the world), the Council of Europe, and the Wassenar Arrangement (law enforcement personnel from the top 33 industrialized counties in the world). Various governments have proposed schemes for controlling encryption software or at least preventing criminals from obtaining strong encryption tools (see **Table 4.6**). The U.S. and U.K. governments are also devoting a large amount of resources to cryptography-related programs that will enable them to break encrypted communications collected on the Internet. Documents leaked by former NSA contractor Edward Snowden indicate that both the NSA and its U.K. counterpart, the GCHQ, may be able to break encryption schemes used by SSL/TLS, VPNs, and on 4G smartphones (Vaughan-Nichols, 2013).

4.5   E-COMMERCE PAYMENT SYSTEMS

For the most part, existing payment mechanisms such as cash, credit cards, checking accounts, and stored value accounts have been able to be adapted to the online environment, albeit with some significant limitations that have led to efforts to develop alternatives. In addition, new types of purchasing relationships, such as between

TABLE 4.7	MAJOR TRENDS IN E-COMMERCE PAYMENTS 2014–2015

- Payment by credit and/or debit card remains the dominant form of online payment.
- Mobile retail payment volume skyrockets.
- PayPal remains the most popular alternative payment method online.
- Apple introduces Apple Pay, a mobile payment service that uses near field communication (NFC) chips, with strong support from banks and credit card companies
- Square begins to gain traction with a smartphone app, credit card reader, and credit card processing service that permits anyone to accept credit card payments.
- Google Wallet, a mobile payment system based on NFC chips, struggles to find acceptance.

individuals online, and new technologies, such as the development of the mobile platform, have also created both a need and an opportunity for the development of new payment systems. In this section, we provide an overview of the major e-commerce payment systems in use today. **Table 4.7** lists some of the major trends in e-commerce payments in 2014–2015.

Worldwide, online payments by consumers represent a market of almost €1.2 billion in 2014. Institutions and business firms that can handle this volume of transactions (mostly the large banking and credit firms) generally extract 2%–3% of the transactions in the form of fees. Given the size of the market, competition for online payments is spirited.

In the United States, the primary form of online payment is still the existing credit and debit card system. According to Javelin Strategy & Research, credit cards accounted for about 46% of the e-commerce payments market and debit cards about 32%. Alternative payment methods such as PayPal, Google Wallet, Amazon Payments, and Bill Me Later currently account for about 15% and are expected to continue to make inroads into traditional payment methods, growing to around 20% of all online payment transactions by 2018. Mobile payments are also expected to grow significantly (Javelin Strategy & Research, 2014). **Figure 4.13** illustrates the percentage of consumers that use various alternative payment methods.

In other parts of the world, e-commerce payments can be very different depending on traditions and infrastructure. Credit cards are not nearly as dominant a form of online payment as they are in the United States. If you plan on operating a Web site in Europe, Asia, or Latin America, you will need to develop different payment systems for each region. For instance, consumers in the various Nordic countries of Europe differ in their preferred payment methods. Those in Denmark, Norway, and Finland pay primarily with credit or debit cards, while in Sweden, the most preferred payment method is payment after being tendered an invoice and by bank transfer (eMarketer, Inc., 2014a). In Italy, PayPal is the most popular payment method, followed by prepaid cards, and credit cards (eMarketer, Inc. 2014b). In Japan, although

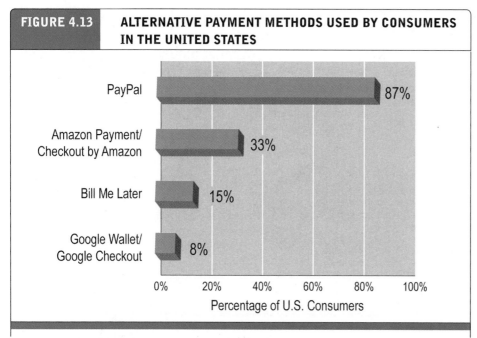

| FIGURE 4.13 | **ALTERNATIVE PAYMENT METHODS USED BY CONSUMERS IN THE UNITED STATES** |

PayPal is, by far, the most popular alternative payment method.
SOURCES: Based on data from Javelin Strategy & Research, 2014; Daly, 2014.

credit card is the primary payment method, many consumers still use cash on delivery (COD) or pick up and pay for goods at local convenience stores (konbini). Japanese consumers also use accumulated balance accounts with the telephone company for Internet purchases (eMarketer, Inc., 2014c).

ONLINE CREDIT CARD TRANSACTIONS

Because credit and debit cards are the dominant form of online payment, it is important to understand how they work and to recognize the strengths and weaknesses of this payment system. Online credit card transactions are processed in much the same way that in-store purchases are, with the major differences being that online merchants never see the actual card being used, no card impression is taken, and no signature is available. Online credit card transactions most closely resemble Mail Order-Telephone Order (MOTO) transactions. These types of purchases are also called Cardholder Not Present (CNP) transactions and are the major reason that charges can be disputed later by consumers. Because the merchant never sees the credit card, nor receives a hand-signed agreement to pay from the customer, when disputes arise, the merchant faces the risk that the transaction may be disallowed and reversed, even though he has already shipped the goods or the user has downloaded a digital product.

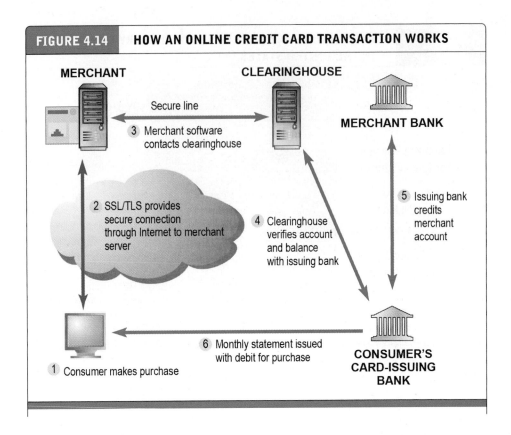

Figure 4.14 illustrates the online credit card purchasing cycle. There are five parties involved in an online credit card purchase: consumer, merchant, clearinghouse, merchant bank (sometimes called the "acquiring bank"), and the consumer's card-issuing bank. In order to accept payments by credit card, online merchants must have a merchant account established with a bank or financial institution. A **merchant account** is simply a bank account that allows companies to process credit card payments and receive funds from those transactions.

As shown in Figure 4.14, an online credit card transaction begins with a purchase (1). When a consumer wants to make a purchase, he or she adds the item to the merchant's shopping cart. When the consumer wants to pay for the items in the shopping cart, a secure tunnel through the Internet is created using SSL/TLS. Using encryption, SSL/TLS secures the session during which credit card information will be sent to the merchant and protects the information from interlopers on the Internet (2). SSL does not authenticate either the merchant or the consumer. The transacting parties have to trust one another.

Once the consumer credit card information is received by the merchant, the merchant software contacts a clearinghouse (3). As previously noted, a clearinghouse is a financial intermediary that authenticates credit cards and verifies account balances. The clearinghouse contacts the issuing bank to verify the account information (4). Once verified, the issuing bank credits the account of the merchant at the merchant's

merchant account
a bank account that allows companies to process credit card payments and receive funds from those transactions

bank (usually this occurs at night in a batch process) (5). The debit to the consumer account is transmitted to the consumer in a monthly statement (6).

Credit Card E-commerce Enablers

Companies that have a merchant account still need to buy or build a means of handling the online transaction; securing the merchant account is only step one in a two-part process. Today, Internet payment service providers (sometimes referred to as payment gateways) can provide both a merchant account and the software tools needed to process credit card purchases online.

For instance, Authorize.net is an Internet payment service provider. The company helps a merchant secure an account with one of its merchant account provider partners and then provides payment processing software for installation on the merchant's server. The software collects the transaction information from the merchant's site and then routes it via the Authorize.net "payment gateway" to the appropriate bank, ensuring that customers are authorized to make their purchases. The funds for the transaction are then transferred to the merchant's merchant account. CyberSource is another well-known Internet payment service provider.

Limitations of Online Credit Card Payment Systems

There are a number of limitations to the existing credit card payment system. The most important limitations involve security, merchant risk, administrative and transaction costs, and social equity.

The existing system offers poor security. Neither the merchant nor the consumer can be fully authenticated. The merchant could be a criminal organization designed to collect credit card numbers, and the consumer could be a thief using stolen or fraudulent cards. The risk facing merchants is high: consumers can repudiate charges even though the goods have been shipped or the product downloaded. The banking industry attempted to develop a secure electronic transaction (SET) protocol, but this effort failed because it was too complex for consumers and merchants alike.

The administrative costs of setting up an online credit card system and becoming authorized to accept credit cards are high. Transaction costs for merchants also are significant—roughly 3.5% of the purchase plus a transaction fee of 20–30 cents per transaction, plus other setup fees.

Credit cards are not very democratic, even though they seem ubiquitous. Millions of young adults do not have credit cards, along with millions of older adults who cannot afford cards or who are considered poor risks because of low incomes.

ALTERNATIVE ONLINE PAYMENT SYSTEMS

The limitations of the online credit card system have opened the way for the development of a number of alternative online payment systems. Chief among them is PayPal. PayPal (purchased by eBay in 2002) enables individuals and businesses with e-mail accounts to make and receive payments up to a specified limit. Paypal is an example of an **online stored value payment system**, which permits consumers to make instant, online payments to merchants and other individuals based on value

online stored value payment system
permits consumers to make instant, online payments to merchants and other individuals based on value stored in an online account

stored in an online account. PayPal operates in 193 countries around the world, in 26 different currencies. In 2013, PayPal processed $180 billion in payments ($54 billion of which were generated on eBay, and $126 billion elsewhere), and had 143 million active registered users as of the end of the year. PayPal builds on the existing financial infrastructure of the countries in which it operates. You establish a PayPal account by specifying a credit, debit, or checking account you wish to have charged or paid when conducting online transactions. When you make a payment using PayPal, you e-mail the payment to the merchant's PayPal account. PayPal transfers the amount from your credit or checking account to the merchant's bank account. The beauty of PayPal is that no personal credit information has to be shared among the users, and the service can be used by individuals to pay one another even in small amounts. Issues with PayPal include its high cost (in addition to paying the credit card fee of 3.5%, PayPal tacks on a variable fee of 1.5%–3% depending on the size of the transaction) and its lack of consumer protections when a fraud occurs or a charge is repudiated. PayPal is discussed in further depth in the case study at the end of the chapter.

Although PayPal is by far the most well-known and commonly used online credit/debit card alternative, there are a number of other alternatives as well. Amazon Payments is aimed at consumers who have concerns about entrusting their credit card information to unfamiliar online retailers. Consumers can purchase goods and services at non-Amazon Web sites using the payment methods stored in their Amazon accounts, without having to reenter their payment information at the merchant's site. Amazon provides the payment processing. Google Wallet, described further in the following section on mobile payment systems, offers similar functionality, enabling consumers to sign in once and then shop online at thousands of different stores without having to reenter account information. Visa Checkout (formerly V.me) and MasterCard's MasterPass substitute a user name and password for an actual payment card number during online checkout. Both MasterPass and Visa Checkout are supported by a number of large payment processors and online retailers. However, they have not yet achieved the usage of Paypal.

Bill Me Later (owned by eBay as well) also appeals to consumers who do not wish to enter their credit card information online. Bill Me Later describes itself as an open-ended credit account. Users select the Bill Me Later option at checkout and are asked to provide their birth date and the last four digits of their social security number. They are then billed for the purchase by Bill Me Later within 10 to 14 days. Bill Me Later is currently offered by more than 1,000 online merchants.

WUPay (formerly eBillme, and now operated by Western Union) offers a similar service. WUPay customers who select the WUPay option at firms such as Sears, Kmart, Buy.com, and other retailers do not have to provide any credit card information. Instead they are e-mailed a bill, which they can pay via their bank's online bill payment service, or in person at any Western Union location. Dwolla is a similar cash-based payment network for both individuals and merchants. It bypasses the credit card network and instead connects directly into a bank account. Dwolla is free for transactions under $10 and only 25 cents per transaction for those over $10, and is currently available at more than 15,000 merchants.

Like Dwolla, Stripe is another company that is attempting to provide an alternative to the traditional online credit card system. Stripe focuses on the merchant side of the process. It provides simple software code that enables companies to bypass much of the administrative costs involved in setting up an online credit card system, and instead lets companies begin accepting credit card payments almost immediately without the need to obtain a merchant account or use a gateway provider. Unlike PayPal, the customer doesn't need a Stripe account to pay, and all payments are made directly to the company rather than being routed through a third party.

MOBILE PAYMENT SYSTEMS: YOUR SMARTPHONE WALLET

The use of mobile devices as payment mechanisms is already well established in Europe and Asia and is now exploding in the United States, where the infrastructure to support mobile payment is finally being put in place.

Near field communication (NFC) is one of the enabling technologies for mobile payment systems. **Near field communication (NFC)** is a set of short-range wireless technologies used to share information among devices within about 2 inches of each other (50 mm). NFC devices are either powered or passive. A connection requires one powered unit (the initiator), and one target unpowered unit that can respond to requests from the powered unit. NFC targets can be very simple forms such as tags, stickers, key fobs, or readers. NFC peer-to-peer communication is possible where both devices are powered. An NFC-equipped smartphone, for instance, can be swiped by a merchant's reader to record a payment wirelessly and without contact. In 2011, Google introduced Google Wallet, a mobile app designed to work with NFC chips. Google Wallet currently works with the MasterCard PayPass contactless payment card system. It is also designed to work with Android smartphones that are equipped with NFC chips. About 275 million NFC-enabled phones were sold worldwide in 2013, and that number is expected to almost double in 2014 (IHS Technology, 2014). Prior to September 2014, Apple's failure to include an NFC chip in the iPhone had slowed the adoption of NFC-based mobile wallet technology. However, in September 2014, Apple introduced the iPhone 6, which will be equipped with NFC chips designed to work with Apple's new mobile payments platform, Apple Pay. Building on Apple Passbook and Touch ID biometric fingerprint scanning and encryption that Apple previously introduced in September 2012, Apple Pay will be able to be used for mobile payments at the point of sale at a physical store as well as online. It is supported by the major credit card networks and card issuing banks responsible for over 80% of all credit card transactions, as well as many national retailers. PayPal and Square are also attacking the mobile payment market from a different direction, with apps and credit card readers that attach to smartphones.

The promise of riches beyond description to a firm that is able to dominate the mobile payments marketplace has set off what one commentator has called a goat rodeo surrounding the development of new technologies and methods of mobile payment. The end-of-chapter case study, *Online Payment Marketplace: Goat Rodeo,* provides a further look at the future of online and mobile payment, including the efforts of PayPal, Apple, Google, Square, and others.

near field communication (NFC)
a set of short-range wireless technologies used to share information among devices

DIGITAL CASH AND VIRTUAL CURRENCIES

digital cash
an alternative payment system in which unique, authenticated tokens represent cash value

Although the terms digital cash and virtual currencies are often used synonymously, they actually refer to two separate types of alternative payment systems. **Digital cash** typically is based on an algorithm that generates unique authenticated tokens representing cash value that can be used "in the real world." Examples of digital cash include Bitcoin and Ukash. Bitcoins are encrypted numbers (sometimes referred to as cryptocurrency) that are generated by a complex algorithm using a peer-to-peer network in a process referred to as "mining," that requires extensive computing power. Like real currency, Bitcoins have a fluctuating value tied to open-market trading. Like cash, Bitcoins are anonymous—they are exchanged via a 34-character alphanumeric address that the user has, and do not require any other identifying information. Bitcoins have recently attracted a lot of attention as a potential money laundering tool for cybercriminals, and have also been plagued by security issues, with some high-profile heists. Nonetheless, there are companies now using Bitcoins as a legitimate alternative payment system. Read the *Insight on Society* case, *Bitcoin*, for a further look at Bitcoin and some of the issues surrounding it. Ukash is another digital cash system that uses a unique 19-digit code, and can be stored online in an eWallet. Ukash can be purchased at more than 460,000 retail locations around the globe, and used wherever it is accepted.

virtual currency
typically circulates within an internal virtual world community or is issued by a specific corporate entity, and used to purchase virtual goods

Virtual currencies, on the other hand, typically circulate primarily within an internal virtual world community, such as Linden Dollars, created by Linden Lab for use in its virtual world, Second Life, or are associated with a specific corporation, such as Facebook Credits, which can be used to purchase Facebook gift cards. Both types are typically used for purchasing virtual goods.

4.6 ELECTRONIC BILLING PRESENTMENT AND PAYMENT

In 2007, for the first time, the number of bill payments made online exceeded the number of physical checks written in the United States (Fiserv, 2007). In the $17 trillion U.S. economy with an $11.8 trillion consumer sector for goods and services, there are a lot of bills to pay—around 30 billion of them a year. No one knows for sure, but some experts believe the life-cycle cost of a paper bill for a business, from point of issuance to point of payment, ranges from $3 to $7. This calculation does not include the value of time to consumers, who must open bills, read them, write checks, address envelopes, stamp, and then mail remittances. The billing market represents an extraordinary opportunity for using the Internet as an electronic billing and payment system that potentially could greatly reduce both the cost of paying bills and the time consumers spend paying them. Estimates vary, but online payments are believed to cost between only 20 to 30 cents to process.

electronic billing presentment and payment (EBPP) system
form of online payment system for monthly bills

Electronic billing presentment and payment (EBPP) systems are systems that enable the online delivery and payment of monthly bills. EBPP services allow consumers to view bills electronically and pay them through electronic funds transfers from bank or credit card accounts. More and more companies are choosing to issue

INSIGHT ON SOCIETY

BITCOIN

In recent years, a number of countries around the world have experienced banking crises, eroding trust in the system. Enter Bitcoin, a form of electronic currency that does not exist in physical form and can be transferred from one person to another via peer-to-peer networks, without the need for a bank or other financial institution as intermediary.

Because Bitcoin requires no intermediaries to conduct transactions, it is out of the control of bankers and politicians. Bitcoin is a decentralized currency, and its supporters believe that it requires less trust than traditional currency. There is no need to trust the qualifications of central banks to monitor the currency, to hold money and transfer it, to lend money responsibly, and to safeguard personal information.

Bitcoin also allows businesses to take and make payments much more easily than through channels like PayPal and credit cards. Bitcoin allows merchants to avoid the fees associated with these services, enabling frictionless transactions. On the other hand, with Bitcoin, all transactions are irreversible, and if Bitcoins are somehow stolen, the victim has no recourse. Still, purchasers who use Bitcoin receive other benefits, such as not being required to provide personal information to merchants. With the proliferation of security breaches experienced by major companies seemingly every week, this has become an important advantage. Bitcoin also allows people without access to traditional banking services to conduct financial transactions more easily.

Bitcoin has many unique attributes that differentiate it from traditional currencies. For starters, Bitcoins are not physically minted, but have been generated at a predetermined rate beginning in 2009. A finite amount of coins are "built into the software," such that in the year 2140, all of the coins will be mined and present in the market. The program that is used to generate Bitcoins runs on a peer-to-peer network and requires very powerful computer systems to operate. "Mining" a Bitcoin is the result of these powerful computers solving cryptographic problems in tandem with other similar computers—the computer that hits upon the solution is awarded the coin, and a record of all of the involved computers' attempts at mining the coin is logged jointly, as "proof-of-work." Bitcoin holders believe Bitcoins have value because of the time and computational effort required to mine them.

Despite these advantages, there are many reasons to be skeptical of Bitcoin. Law enforcement agencies and governments are justifiably concerned about the emergence of a new currency whose purpose is to avoid regulation. A newly mined Bitcoin has no origin, purchase history, or any data associated with it, and can be used with nearly complete anonymity. Many supporters of Bitcoin are using it for criminal or illegal purposes. One report found that a full 5% percent of Bitcoins that were in circulation were collected by the online black market Silk Road, which sells illegal drugs. Still, studies of Bitcoin released in 2013 indicate that once a user attempts to spend or cash out his Bitcoin holdings, remaining anonymous becomes more difficult. By using Bitcoin addresses in tandem with the services used by the individuals in charge of those addresses, law enforcement may in fact be able to catch thieves and apprehend anyone making illegal purchases. For instance, in January 2014, Charlie Shrem, the founding member of a foundation to promote Bitcoin, was arrested for selling $1 million in Bitcoin to Silk Road and for purchasing illegal drugs on the site.

Traditionally regulated currencies make it difficult to launder money or to engage in criminal

(continued)

activities with complete anonymity. From a law enforcement perspective, the increasing popularity of Bitcoin is a troubling development. For now, regulatory agencies only require that "virtual currency" trading entities register as Money Services Businesses and be subject to the regulations required of those businesses—using Bitcoins to buy products and services is fully legal. However, in the future, governments might see fit to take a firmer stand against virtual currencies. In 2014, for instance, China's government announced that it had ordered banks to close their Bitcoin trading accounts. Denmark has also banned virtual currency deposits, and other countries like Russia and Israel have warned their citizens that similar regulations may be forthcoming. In July 2014, New York became the first U.S. state to propose regulations for virtual currencies, including a BitLicense for Bitcoin exchanges and companies that store Bitcoins.

Economists also are skeptical of Bitcoin for several reasons. Many critics observe that for a system intended to reduce the need for trust in external institutions like banks, Bitcoin requires an awful lot of trust itself. Bitcoin users must accept the risks that the currency will not catch on with a significant enough number of individuals and businesses, and that governments may eventually intervene to halt the proliferation and use of Bitcoins. There is also the risk that Bitcoins could be replaced by superior virtual currencies in the future, rendering Bitcoins nearly worthless. Bitcoin has also demonstrated tremendous volatility in value in its first few years of use, which hinders its chances for widespread adoption. The way Bitcoins are generated also encourages hoarding, because the computing power required to mine Bitcoins is likely to increase, making each coin worth more.

"Man in the middle" attacks may also be effective for stealing Bitcoins, and the perpetrators may be difficult to apprehend. In 2014, for instance, Mt. Gox, the largest online Bitcoin exchange at the time, was hacked, resulting in the theft of $425 million worth of Bitcoins. Another smaller exchange, Flexcoin, was hacked a week later, resulting in $600,000 worth of stolen Bitcoins. These breaches and concerns about stronger regulations from governments worldwide drove Bitcoin prices down from nearly $1,000 per coin at the beginning of 2014 all the way to the $400–$500 range by September. However, these prices still represent significant gains from the $13 price per coin at the start of 2013. Many Bitcoin experts point to critical security flaws with these exchanges as the reason for the breaches. These flaws are less likely to persist in future exchanges that are more legitimate as Bitcoin grows in popularity.

Nevertheless, the number of high-profile online businesses accepting them is growing, including well-known companies such as Expedia, Dell, Dish Network, Overstock, Lord & Taylor, and reportedly over 80,000 other merchants around the world. In September 2014, Braintree, a payments processing company owned by eBay, announced that its customers, which include companies such as OpenTable, Uber, Airbnb, and TaskRabbit, would soon be able to accept Bitcoins. Despite all of the issues surrounding Bitcoin in 2014, developments such as these may help push the currency further toward legitimacy and universal acceptance.

SOURCES: "Braintree, Popular Payments Processor, to Accept Bitcoin," by Mike Isaac, *New York Times*, September 8, 2014; "Bitcoin's Price Falls 12%, to Lowest Value Since May," by Sydney Ember, *New York Times*, August 18, 2014; "Tokyo Court: Bitcoin Exchange Mt. Gox Will Liquidate," by Donna Leinwand, *USA Today*, April 16, 2014; "China Cracks Down on Bitcoin," by Chao Deng and Lingling Wei, *Wall Street Journal*, April 1, 2014; "The Mt. Gox Bitcoin Scandal is the Best Thing to Happen to Bitcoin In Years," by Heidi Moore, Theguardian.com, February 26, 2014; "Israel's Central Bank Warns on Potential Fraud With Bitcoin," by Calev Ben-David, Bloomberg.com, February 19, 2014; "Russian Authorities Say Bitcoin Illegal," by Gabriela Baczynska, Reuters.com, February 9, 2014; "Bitcoin Pitchman Busted for 'Selling $1M in Currency to Silk Road,'" by Kaja Whitehouse and Rich Calder, *New York Post*, January 27, 2014; "How Bitcoin Spreads Violate Fundamental Economic Laws," by Donald Marron, Forbes.com, September 3, 2013; "Bitcoin Offers Privacy—As Long As You Don't Cash Out or Spend It," by Jeremy Kirk, Pcworld.com, August 28, 2013; "Following the Bitcoin Trail," Economist.com, August 28, 2013; "Government Eyes Regulation of 'Bitcoins,'" by Kavya Sukumar, *USA Today*, August 26, 2013; "Nine Trust-Based Problems with Bitcoin," by Steven Strauss, HuffingtonPost.com, April 4, 2013; "The Bitcoin Boom," by Maria Bustillos, *The New Yorker*, April 2, 2013.

statements and bills electronically, rather than mailing out paper versions. But even those businesses that do mail paper bills are increasingly offering online bill payment as an option to customers, allowing them to immediately transfer funds from a bank or credit card account to pay a bill somewhere else.

MARKET SIZE AND GROWTH

In 2002, 61% of bill payments in the United States were made by check, and only 12% by online bill payments. In 2014, in contrast, online bill payments now account for more than half of all bill payments, while paper checks now account for less than 25%. Among online households, almost three-quarters pay at least one bill online each month, and almost half receive at least one bill electronically each month. Mobile bill payments are surging, with 16% of households now paying at least one bill on a mobile device, double the percentage in the previous year. Most consumers cited the convenience and time saved by using mobile bill payment (Fiserv, 2014).

One major reason for the surge in EBPP usage is that companies are starting to realize how much money they can save through online billing. Not only is there the savings in postage and processing, but payments can be received more quickly (3 to 12 days faster, compared to paper bills sent via regular mail), thereby improving cash flow. In order to realize these savings, many companies are becoming more aggressive in encouraging their customers to move to EBPP by instituting a charge for the privilege of continuing to receive a paper bill.

Financials don't tell the whole story, however. Companies are discovering that a bill is both a sales opportunity and a customer retention opportunity, and that the electronic medium provides many more options when it comes to marketing and promotion. Rebates, savings offers, cross-selling, and upselling are all possible in the digital realm.

EBPP BUSINESS MODELS

There are two main competing business models in the EBPP marketspace: biller-direct and consolidator. The biller-direct system was originally created by utility companies that send millions of bills each month. Their purpose is to make it easier for their customers to pay their utility bills routinely online. Today, telephone and credit card companies also frequently offer this service, as well as a number of individual stores. Companies implementing a biller-direct system can either develop their own system in-house (usually only an option for the very largest companies), install a system acquired from a third-party EBPP software vendor, use a third-party EBPP service bureau (the service bureau hosts a biller-branded Web site that enables consumers to view and pay bills and handles all customer enrollment, bill presentment, and payment processing), or use an application service provider (similar to a service bureau, but runs on the biller's Web site rather than being hosted on the service provider's Web site).

In the consolidator model, a third party, such as a financial institution or a focused portal such as Intuit's Paytrust, Fiserv's MyCheckFree, Check (formerly named Pageonce), and others, aggregates all bills for consumers and ideally permits one-stop

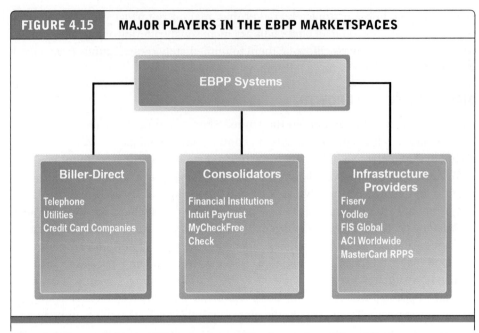

FIGURE 4.15   **MAJOR PLAYERS IN THE EBPP MARKETSPACES**

The main business models in the EBPP marketspace are biller-direct and consolidator. Infrastructure providers support both of these competing models and sometimes operate their own online payment portals.

bill payment (pay anyone). Currently, financial institutions have been more successful than portals in attracting online bill payers. The consolidator model faces several challenges. For billers, using the consolidator model means an increased time lag between billing and payment, and also inserts an intermediary between the company and its customer. For consumers, security continues to be a major issue. Most consumers are unwilling to pay any kind of fee to pay bills online, and many are concerned about sharing personal financial information with nonfinancial institutions. Today, more and more banks are offering online bill payment free to some or all of their customers as an enticement.

Supporting these two primary business models are infrastructure providers such as Fiserv, Yodlee, FIS Global, ACI Worldwide, MasterCard RPPS (Remote Payment and Presentment Service), and others that provide the software to create the EBPP system or handle billing and payment collection for the biller. **Figure 4.15** categorizes the major players in the EBPP marketspace.

4.7	CASE STUDY

The Mobile Payment Marketplace: Goat Rodeo

Nearly every day, it seems, a new online or mobile payment system is announced. The online payment marketplace is experiencing an explosion of innovative ideas, plans, and announcements, which one commentator has likened to a goat rodeo, a chaotic situation in which powerful players with different agendas compete with one another for public acceptance, and above all, huge potential revenues. Others liken the payment marketplace to a battle among the titans of online payment and retailing: PayPal, credit card companies like Visa and MasterCard, Google, Apple, start-up tech companies like Square that offer mobile credit card swiping backed by millions in venture capital, and even large retailers like Walmart, Best Buy, and Target, all of which are developing their own mobile payment systems that they control. For a variety of reasons, new digital mobile payment systems have been the next big thing for over five years, but none have come near success. Consumers still prefer to pay with credit cards while on the go, and even cash.

Apple entered the fray on September 9, 2014 with its announcement of Apple Pay for iPhone 6 smartphones, joining other titans like Google who already had developed a mobile payment system using Near Field Communications (NFC), a short-range radio communications protocol that operates within a range of a few inches, and allows consumers to bump, swipe, or just come close to a merchant's NFC reader to pay for goods and services. What's different about Apple's announcement of a new NFC-based payment system is that it's Apple—the firm that revolutionized five different industries and introduced the first smartphones, and which has changed forever how people shop and communicate with one another. Apple is also the most valuable company in the United States and is widely considered to be one of the most innovative firms in the world. To make the story even more interesting, Apple's iTunes store has the credit cards of 800 million users, arguably the largest such collection on earth.

Apple Pay is not just an app, a feature of a smartphone, or a device like the new EMV smart credit cards being pushed by the card-issuing banks, but instead is an entire ecosystem within an ecosystem. Apple has developed relationships with many of the key players in the payment ecosystem, which is the larger world in which Apple Pay needs to be understood. The credit giants Visa, MasterCard, American Express, and Discover have signed on, as well as 11 large bank credit card issuers including JP Morgan Chase, Bank America, Citigroup, and Well Fargo, which together account for 83% of U.S. credit card payment volume. Apple has also signed up national merchants such as Walgreen's, Duane Reade, McDonald's, Disney, Macys, Bloomingdales, Staples, and Whole Foods. Groupon and Uber are planning to integrate Apple Pay into their systems. Unlike the introductions of other mobile payment systems, which tended to reflect the self-interest of those making the introduction, Apple's approach is much more inclusive of the major stakeholders in the marketplace. Target, Walmart, and Best Buy are missing the Apple party because they are developing their own mobile payment systems.

Security is a central issue for all payment systems, and given the evident lack of security for Internet-connected devices and databases, payment security is a major concern for consumers and banks and merchants. The Apple announcement came on the heels of news in August 2014 that several celebrities had their personal iCloud accounts hacked, resulting in the distribution of provocative pictures on social media and the Web. In 2014, Target, Home Depot, and major banks reported their customer databases and point of sale terminals had been hacked, resulting in hackers gaining access to millions of credit card numbers and pin codes. A security firm claimed that Russian hackers had stolen 1.2 billion user name and password combinations, and 500 million e-mail addresses in the last year. For this reason, the emphasis at Apply Pay's introduction was security.

The Apple Pay system uses several levels of security to avoid the loss of customer information. Apple Pay relies on the customer having a credit card on file with Apple's iTunes, and that card is the financial vehicle for payment. When a customer wants to make a payment, they press the iPhone Touch ID button, which reads their fingerprint and ensures the phone does indeed belong to the person. Next, the consumer swipes the device near a merchant's NFC point-of-sale terminal, which begins the transaction process. The iPhone 6 comes with a hardware-defined secure area on a chip that contains a unique device number and the ability to generate a one-time 16-digit code. Together they form a digital token. The token information is encrypted and sent to Apple servers to verify the authenticity of the device and the person. Credit card issuers verify the account owner and available credit. In about one second, the transaction is approved or denied. Credit card information is not shared with the merchant and not transmitted from the iPhone. The 800 million credit cards stored on Apple's servers are also encrypted. If hackers intercept the NFC communication at the point of sale, or intercept the stream of data moving over the cellular network, it would be useless, and incapable of supporting additional transactions because the message is encrypted, and involves a one-time only code.

Privacy is also an issue of payment systems. Traditional credit card payment systems gather extensive information on user charges, recording what is purchased, where, and when. Selling credit card purchase information to credit agencies and data brokers is an important income stream for banks that issue credit cards. Apple Pay will not be playing that game. Timothy Cook, Apple's CEO, pointed out in an interview in September 2014 that Apple Pay gathers no consumer information, and that Apple is a technology company and not an advertising company. Apple Pay will not gather any consumer information that could be used to target or track consumers, or expose them to additional targeted advertising. In contrast, Google Wallet's Tap & Pay system (discussed below) is paid for by placing ads on the screen as users make mobile payments, and Google gathers the purchase information and point of payment.

How will Apple make money from Apple Pay? Credit card companies charge merchants a fee of 2% to 3% of the amount for each transaction. Apple Pay will not charge the merchant or the consumer an additional fee. Instead Apple will charge the credit card issuer bank a .15% fee in return for guaranteeing the authenticity of the transaction. In essence, Apple is providing an insurance policy for the issuers of credit cards. If the transaction is fraudulent, Apple will pay the issuer. How much is this worth to the issuers? According to the U.S. Federal Reserve, in 2012, there were 31 million fraudulent credit card transactions worth $6.1 billion. Because of the outdated magnetic strip cards used in the United States, more than half of the world's credit card fraud occurs here (twice as much as anywhere else in the world), and about 25% of user fees are used to make up for these losses. Apple Pay could significantly reduce credit card fraud in the United States, benefiting the issuing banks directly.

Apple's .15% fee is a very small charge, but Apple reasons the risk is quite small and it is willing to invest in their own technology. Assuming Apple Pay rings up $1 billion in transactions, how much will the banks and Apple receive as revenue? The banks on average will collect 3%, which works out to $30 million. Apple will receive just .15% or $1.5 million for every $1 billion in transactions, which probably will not clear the costs of operating Apple Pay. The real value to Apple is not the revenue from Apple Pay, but its contribution to the sales of Apple products like the iPhone and iPad, as well as the entire Apple ecosystem of services provided by iTunes. Apple becomes not just your source for music, videos, movies, television, books, and over 1.2 million apps, but also your wallet.

There are some obvious drawbacks to Apple Pay. It works only on Apple devices (and only on the latest iPhone 6); merchants need to buy NFC-enabled point-of-sale terminals, and consumers need to change their behaviors to achieve widespread acceptance. Finally, merchants lose some of their control over the point-of-payment/purchase moment when they could be up-selling customers, offering coupons, ads, and loyalty points.

The overall online payment market in the United States is estimated to be worth about $470 billion in 2014 and is growing at more than 12% a year. While small compared to the total e-commerce picture, mobile commerce, driven by smartphones, tablets, and cellular networks, is growing at more than 30% a year. While most of these mobile commerce transactions are occurring through the use of credit cards (just as with desktop e-commerce), there is a rapidly growing segment of contactless payments, which amounted to an estimated $240 million in 2013 but is expected to grow to $58 billion by 2018. And according to the Federal Reserve, U.S. consumers spent an estimated $3.3 trillion on 60 billion credit and debit card transactions in 2012 (the latest year for which data is available). Even if a small percentage of these transactions move from plastic to mobile payments, the potential revenue is very large. This is enough to drive even old goats into a frenzy.

Apple has several competitors in mobile payment. The most popular alternative mobile payment systems are offered by PayPal and Square, which do not use NFC. PayPal was late to the mobile payment market, beaten to the punch by Square. Square started in 2009 with Square Reader, a square plastic device that plugged into a iPhone or iPad. Using the Square app, it allows merchants to easily accept credit card payments from customers on the go. Square also developed Square Register, which is a software app that turns a tablet into a point-of-sale terminal and cash register. Square has been very popular with small businesses like coffee shops, news stands, small retailers, and farmers' market merchants, as well as piano teachers, baby sitters, and taxi drivers, allowing them to accept credit card payments. The company claims it processes billions of transactions a year, and has over 1 million merchants using its system in North America. Square is a private company and there is no way to verify these claims. Analysts do not believe the company has ever posted a profit.

PayPal is currently the most successful and profitable mobile payment system. PayPal currently enables mobile payments in three ways. First, PayPal sells to merchants a device that allows them to swipe credit cards using a smartphone or tablet, just like the Square device. Second, the most common mobile PayPal mobile payment occurs when customers use their mobile device browser to make a purchase or payment at a Web site. This is not very helpful for merchants like Starbucks, Macys, or local restaurants, who would like customers to be able to purchase goods in their stores and outlets on the fly without keying in information to a smartphone. A third method is PayPal's updated app for iOS and Android devices. On entering a merchant's store that accepts PayPal app payments, the app establishes a link using Bluetooth with the merchant's app that is also running on an iOS or Android device. This step authenticates the user's PayPal account. On checkout, the customer tells the merchant

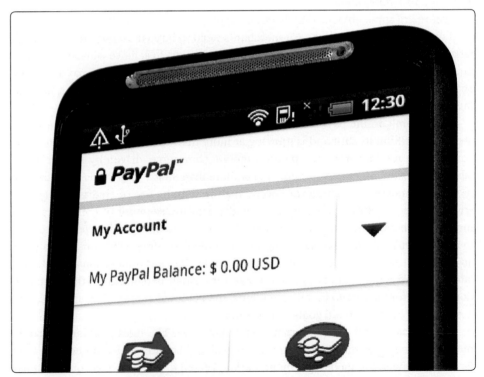

© Ian Dagnall / Alamy

he or she will pay with PayPal. The merchant device charges the customer's PayPal account. After the payment is authorized, a message is sent to the customer's phone. No credit card information is being transmitted or shared with the merchant or the issuing bank. Users do not have to enter a pin code or swipe their phone at a special merchant device, so merchants are not required to purchase an expensive NFC point-of-sale device.

PayPal is currently the largest alternative (non-credit card) online payment service, processing $180 billion in transactions in 2013. PayPal processed $27 billion in mobile payments in 2013, up 99% over 2012. Most of this mobile payment volume involved customers using their mobile phones or tablet browsers to make payments, just as they use PayPal on their PCs at work or home. PayPal has not announced the performance of the PayPal app, but acceptance appears to be very limited in 2014, in part because neither merchants nor customers are familiar with the product.

Apple Pay is also not the only contactless mobile payment system hoping for widespread acceptance. The other two contenders in the NFC payment market are Google Wallet (sometimes called Tap & Pay) and CurrentC, a system being developed by Merchant Customer Exchange (MCX).

Google Wallet (also called Tap & Play) is an online NFC-based payment system that uses an Android app. Beginning in 2011, Google has included support for the operation of NFC chips into the latest version of its Android operating system. Samsung's Galaxy phones are the only phones sold in the United States that have a built-in NFC chip and are ready for NFC payment. Google claims that it is available at 150,000 merchants.

Google Wallet's online payment is enabled by a prepaid MasterCard. Users must keep a cash balance with the issuing bank to fund purchases, as with any debit card, and have a Google Wallet account. To use Google Wallet, customers hold their phone near the merchant's NFC terminal at checkout. Users are asked for their Google Wallet PIN. Users have a choice to pay with a MasterCard debit card or a balance they keep with Google Wallet. If the user chooses to pay with MasterCard, the app passes the credit information to the merchant's terminal, which then clears the transaction with MasterCard. Bancorp Bank is the issuing bank.

How does Google Wallet make money? Google Wallet is free to credit card companies and merchants, and does not take a slice of transactions like many other mobile payment systems. Instead, Google retains the right to display ads, coupons, loyalty programs, and daily deals by local merchants nearby on the user's mobile screen. So far, however, Google Wallet has not been a market success and has not gained traction with consumers or merchants.

Perhaps the strongest competition for both Apple Pay and Google Wallet will come from the Merchant Customer Exchange (MCX), a joint venture of 15 of the largest retailers, including Walmart, Target, Sears, 7-Eleven, Sunoco, and 10 other national pharmacies, supermarkets, and restaurant chains. Announced in March 2012, the backers of this effort have annual sales of more than $1 trillion dollars. That's enough to make everyone involved in mobile payments stand up and listen, even Google and Apple. The MCX system is called CurrentC, is being pilot tested in 2014, and will be

SOURCES: "What Apple Pay Means for Retailers," by Abby Callard, Internetretailer.com, September 12, 2014; "Apple Pay: No Charge for Merchants, But Transaction-Security Fees for Issuers," by Jim Daly, Digital-transaction.net, September 11, 2014; "Apple Pushes Digital Wallet with Apple Pay," by Associated Press, *Wall Street Journal*, September 10, 2014; "Will Stores Warm Up to Apple Pay," by Daisuke Wakabayashi and Greg Bensinger, *Wall Street Journal*, September 10, 2014; "With Apple Pay and Smartwatch, a Privacy Challenge," by Brian X. Chen and Steve Lohr, *New York Times*, September 10, 2014; "As Questions Linger, Discover Says 'Me Too' to Apple Pay," by Kevin Woodward, Digitaltransactions.net, September 10, 2014; "Apple Unveils an 'Entirely New Payment Process' with Apple Pay," by Jim Daly, Digitaltransactions.net, September 9, 2014; "Endpoint: Not All Mobile-Payment Systems Are Mobile Wallets," Digital-transactions.net, July 1, 2014; "Apple Pay Leaps Ahead of Mobile Payments Providers," by Spencer Soper, Bloomberg.com, September 10, 2014; "Easier Ways to Make Payments with Smartphones," by Molly Wood, *New York Times*, July 30, 2014; "For Square, Making Money Remains a Challenge," by William Alden, *New York Times*, April 21, 2014; "Few Consumers Are Buying Premise of Mobile Wallets," by Brian X. Chen, *New York Times*, April 27, 2014.

released in a national roll-out in 2015. It is the only merchant-owned mobile payment system.

CurrentC is an app-based mobile payment system for both iOS and Android devices that permits customers to pay at the point of sale from credit or debit cards, gift cards, or bank accounts using their smartphone. During the checkout process, merchants can offer coupons, rewards, and loyalty points on the user's payment screen. CurrentC works by allowing users to load value (pre-paid cards or credit cards) into the app. It then generates a QR code unique to each customer that is displayed on the phone screen. After swiping the QR code, an encrypted token is generated and sent to MCX cloud servers, which store the credit card information and make the approval decision. An acceptance token is returned to the merchant. Older point of sale systems can be modified to read this QR code, reducing the need for merchants to upgrade.

Why are these nationwide merchants willing to invest billions in a mobile payment system when financial service firms and technology players also are investing billions in competing systems? The answer is control over the customer during the transaction, and the information on customer purchase history that the apps will be recording. The merchants do not want this valuable marketing asset to flow to financial service firms or Google. To some extent, the coming mobile payment battle is one between tech companies like Apple and Google and traditional brick and mortar merchants. The banks and credit card companies will benefit no matter who wins.

The future for smartphone mobile payments is assured given the size of the players involved, the potential rewards for successful players, and the demands of consumers for a payment system that does not involve swiping plastic cards and dealing with slips of paper. But it is unlikely that all the payment systems described above will survive, and also quite likely that consumers will remain confused by all their payment options for some time yet to come.

Case Study Questions

1. What is the value proposition that Apple Pay offers consumers? How about merchants?

2. What are some of the limitations of Apple Pay that might prevent its widespread adoption?

3. What advantages do the Square and PayPal mobile card-swiping solutions have in the mobile payment market? What are their weaknesses?

4. What strategies would you recommend that Apple pursue to assure widespread consumer adoption of Apple Pay?

4.8   REVIEW

KEY CONCEPTS

■ **Understand the scope of e-commerce crime and security problems, the key dimensions of e-commerce security, and the tension between security and other values.**

- While the overall size of cybercrime is unclear, cybercrime against e-commerce sites is growing rapidly, the amount of losses is growing, and the management of e-commerce sites must prepare for a variety of criminal assaults.
- There are six key dimensions to e-commerce security: integrity, nonrepudiation, authenticity, confidentiality, privacy, and availability.
- Although computer security is considered necessary to protect e-commerce activities, it is not without a downside. Two major areas where there are tensions between security and Web site operations are:
  - *Ease of use*—The more security measures that are added to an e-commerce site, the more difficult it is to use and the slower the site becomes, hampering ease of use. Security is purchased at the price of slowing down processors and adding significantly to data storage demands. Too much security can harm profitability, while not enough can potentially put a company out of business.
  - *Public safety*—There is a tension between the claims of individuals to act anonymously and the needs of public officials to maintain public safety that can be threatened by criminals or terrorists.

■ **Identify the key security threats in the e-commerce environment**

- The most common and most damaging forms of security threats to e-commerce sites include:
  - *Malicious code*—viruses, worms, Trojan horses, ransomware, and bot networks are a threat to a system's integrity and continued operation, often changing how a system functions or altering documents created on the system.
  - *Potentially unwanted programs (adware, spyware, etc.)*—a kind of security threat that arises when programs are surreptitiously installed on your computer or computer network without your consent.
  - *Phishing*—any deceptive, online attempt by a third party to obtain confidential information for financial gain.
  - *Hacking and cybervandalism*—intentionally disrupting, defacing, or even destroying a site.
  - *Credit card fraud/theft*—one of the most-feared occurrences and one of the main reasons more consumers do not participate in e-commerce. The most common cause of credit card fraud is a lost or stolen card that is used by someone else, followed by employee theft of customer numbers and stolen identities (criminals applying for credit cards using false identities).
  - *Identity fraud*—involves the unauthorized use of another person's personal data, such as social security, driver's license, and/or credit card numbers, as well as user names and passwords, for illegal financial benefit.
  - *Spoofing*—occurs when hackers attempt to hide their true identities or misrepresent themselves by using fake e-mail addresses or masquerading as someone else.
  - *Pharming*—involves redirecting a Web link to an address different from the intended one, with the site masquerading as the intended destination.
  - *Denial of Service (DoS) and Distributed Denial of Service (DDoS) attacks*—hackers flood a Web site with useless traffic to inundate and overwhelm the network, frequently causing it to shut down and damaging a site's reputation and customer relationships.

- *Sniffing*—a type of eavesdropping program that monitors information traveling over a network, enabling hackers to steal proprietary information from anywhere on a network, including e-mail messages, company files, and confidential reports. The threat of sniffing is that confidential or personal information will be made public.
- *Insider jobs*—although the bulk of Internet security efforts are focused on keeping outsiders out, the biggest threat is from employees who have access to sensitive information and procedures.
- *Poorly designed server and client software*—the increase in complexity and size of software programs has contributed to an increase in software flaws or vulnerabilities that hackers can exploit.
- *Social network security issues*—malicious code, PUPs, phishing, data breaches, identity fraud, and other e-commerce security threats have all infiltrated social networks.
- *Mobile platform security issues*—the mobile platform presents an alluring target for hackers and cyber-criminals, and faces all the same risks as other Internet devices, as well as new risks associated with wireless network security.
- *Cloud security issues*—as devices, identities, and data become more and more intertwined in the cloud, safeguarding data in the cloud becomes a major concern.

■ **Describe how technology helps secure Internet communication channels and protect networks, servers, and clients.**

- Encryption is the process of transforming plain text or data into cipher text that cannot be read by anyone other than the sender and the receiver. Encryption can provide four of the six key dimensions of e-commerce security: message integrity, nonrepudiation, authentication, and confidentiality.
- There are a variety of different forms of encryption technology currently in use. They include:
  - *Symmetric key cryptography*—Both the sender and the receiver use the same key to encrypt and decrypt a message.
  - *Public key cryptography*—Two mathematically related digital keys are used: a public key and a private key. The private key is kept secret by the owner, and the public key is widely disseminated. Both keys can be used to encrypt and decrypt a message. Once the keys are used to encrypt a message, the same keys cannot be used to unencrypt the message.
  - *Public key cryptography using digital signatures and hash digests*—This method uses a mathematical algorithm called a hash function to produce a fixed-length number called a hash digest. The results of applying the hash function are sent by the sender to the recipient. Upon receipt, the recipient applies the hash function to the received message and checks to verify that the same result is produced. The sender then encrypts both the hash result and the original message using the recipient's public key, producing a single block of cipher text. To ensure both the authenticity of the message and nonrepudiation, the sender encrypts the entire block of cipher text one more time using the sender's private key. This produces a digital signature or "signed" cipher text that can be sent over the Internet to ensure the confidentiality of the message and authenticate the sender.
  - *Digital envelope*—This method uses symmetric cryptography to encrypt and decrypt the document, but public key cryptography to encrypt and send the symmetric key.
  - *Digital certificates and public key infrastructure*—This method relies on certification authorities who issue, verify, and guarantee digital certificates (a digital document that contains the name of the subject or company, the subject's public key, a digital certificate serial number, an expiration date, an issuance date, the digital signature of the certification authority, and other identifying information).
- In addition to encryption, there are several other tools that are used to secure Internet channels of communication, including: Secure Sockets Layer (SSL)/Transport Layer Security (TLS), virtual private networks (VPNs), and wireless security standards such as WPA2.
- After communications channels are secured, tools to protect networks, the servers, and clients should be implemented. These include: firewalls, proxies, intrusion detection and prevention systems (IDS/IDP), operating system controls, and anti-virus software.

■ Appreciate the importance of policies, procedures, and laws in creating security.

- In order to minimize security threats, e-commerce firms must develop a coherent corporate policy that takes into account the nature of the risks, the information assets that need protecting, and the procedures and technologies required to address the risk, as well as implementation and auditing mechanisms.
- Public laws and active enforcement of cybercrime statutes also are required to both raise the costs of illegal behavior on the Internet and guard against corporate abuse of information.
- The key steps in developing a security plan are:
  - *Perform a risk assessment*—an assessment of the risks and points of vulnerability.
  - *Develop a security policy*—a set of statements prioritizing the information risks, identifying acceptable risk targets, and identifying the mechanisms for achieving these targets.
  - *Create an implementation plan*—a plan that determines how you will translate the levels of acceptable risk into a set of tools, technologies, policies, and procedures.
  - *Create a security team*—the individuals who will be responsible for ongoing maintenance, audits, and improvements.
  - *Perform periodic security audits*—routine reviews of access logs and any unusual patterns of activity.

■ Identify the major e-commerce payment systems in use today.

- The major types of e-commerce payment systems in use today include:
  - *Online credit card transactions,* which are the primary form of online payment system. There are five parties involved in an online credit card purchase: consumer, merchant, clearinghouse, merchant bank (sometimes called the "acquiring bank"), and the consumer's card-issuing bank. However, the online credit card system has a number of limitations involving security, merchant risk, cost, and social equity.
  - *PayPal,* which is an example of an online stored value payment system that permits consumers to make instant, online payments to merchants and other individuals based on value stored in an online account.
  - *Alternative payment services* such as Amazon Payments, Google Checkout/Google Wallet, and Bill Me Later, which enable consumers to shop online at a wide variety of merchants without having to provide credit card information each time they make a purchase.
  - *Mobile payment systems,* using either credit card readers attached to a smartphone (Square, PayPal Here) or near field communication (NFC) chips, which enable contactless payment.
  - *Digital cash* such as Bitcoin, which is based on an algorithm that generates unique authenticated tokens representing cash value, and virtual currencies, that typically circulate within an internal virtual world or are issued by a corporation, and usually used for the purchase of virtual goods.

■ Describe the features and functionality of electronic billing presentment and payment systems.

- Electronic billing presentment and payment (EBPP) systems are a form of online payment systems for monthly bills. EBPP services allow consumers to view bills electronically and pay them through electronic funds transfers from bank or credit card accounts. Major players in the EBPP marketspace include: biller-direct systems, consolidators, and infrastructure providers.

QUESTIONS

1. What is a VPN and what is its value to an organization?
2. What features or abilities does an intrusion prevention system use to protect a network?
3. Identify and describe the five main steps in establishing a company's security plan.
4. Describe the way that law and enforcement's role in Internet crime has changed along with the evolution of the Internet.

5. Outside of the United States, what types of payments are popular for online purchases?
6. What is the role that a consumer's card-issuing bank play in an online credit card transaction?
7. Why is the mobile payment industry in such a great state of flux today?
8. What are the general technologies and tools needed by merchants and users to implement a mobile payment system?
9. What risks do Bitcoin users face?
10. What are the challenges faced by the consolidator EBPP business model?
11. How are the SSL/TLS protocols used in securing Internet communications?
12. What is nonrepudiation and why is it an important dimension of e-commerce security? What technologies are used to establish nonrepudiation?
13. How are improvements to the overall e-commerce security environment achieved?
14. Explain why an e-commerce site might not want to report being the target of cybercriminals.
15. Give an example of security breaches as they relate to each of the six dimensions of e-commerce security. For instance, what would be a privacy incident?
16. Briefly explain how public key cryptography works.
17. Is a computer with anti-virus software protected from viruses? Why or why not?
18. What is the Heartbleed bug and how does it threaten security?
19. How does code signing protect a mobile app?
20. What is a next generation firewall?

PROJECTS

1. Imagine you are the owner of an e-commerce Web site. What are some of the signs that your site has been hacked? Discuss the major types of attacks you could expect to experience and the resulting damage to your site. Prepare a brief summary presentation.

2. Given the shift toward mobile commerce, do a search on "mobile commerce crime." Identify and discuss the security threats this type of technology creates. Prepare a presentation outlining your vision of the new opportunities for cybercrime that mobile commerce may provide.

3. Find three certification authorities and compare the features of each company's digital certificates. Provide a brief description of each company as well, including number of clients. Prepare a brief presentation of your findings.

4. Research the challenges associated with payments across international borders and prepare a brief presentation of your findings. Do most e-commerce companies conduct business internationally? How do they protect themselves from repudiation? How do exchange rates impact online purchases? What about shipping charges? Summarize by describing the differences between a U.S. customer and an international customer who each make a purchase from a U.S. e-commerce merchant.

REFERENCES

Akamai Technologies, Inc. "The State of the Internet, 1st Quarter, 2014 Report." Volume 7, Number 1 (2014).

APWG. "APWG Phishing Activity Trends Report, 4th Quarter 2013." (April 7, 2014).

Arbor Networks. "Worldwide Infrastructure Security Report Volume IX." (2014).

Center for Strategic and International Studies (James Lewis and Stewart Baker). "The Economic Impact of Cybercrime and Cyber Espionage." (2013).

Chirgwin, Richard. "Microsoft and FBI Storm Ramparts of Citadel Botnets." *The Register* (June 6, 2013).

Cisco. "2014 Cisco Annual Security Report." (2014).

Daly, Jim. "Report Documents the March of Online Alternatives to the Payments Mainstream." Digital-transactions.net (March 9, 2014).

Danchev, Dancho. "Exposing the Market for Stolen Credit Cards Data." DDanchev.blogspot.com (October 31, 2011).

Datta, Saikat. "Security Breach in NIC Allowed Hackers to Issue Fake Digital Certifcates—Hindustan Times." Medianama.com (August 14, 2014).

DMARC.org. "Prominent Brands Cut Email Abuse by More than 50% with DMARC." (February 18, 2014).

DMARC.org. "In First Year, DMARC Protects 60 Percent of Global Consumer Mailboxes." (February 6, 2013).

Dunn, John E. "Jailed Phishing Gang Targeted Banks in 14 Countries, Police Say." Techworld.com (June 18, 2013).

eMarketer, Inc. "Digital Buyers in the Nordic Countries Differ on Preferred Payment Methods." (August 15, 2014).

eMarketer, Inc. "Payment Method Share of B2C Ecommerce Transactions in Italy, Q1 2013 and Q1 2014." (May 9, 2014b)

eMarketer, Inc. "Payment Methods Used by Digital Buyers in Japan, 2012 & 2013." (June 27, 2014c).

European Commission. "Study for an Impact Assessment on a Proposal for a New Legal Framework on Identity Theft." (December 11, 2012).

Federal Bureau of Investigation. "Romanian Citizen Involved in Phishing Scheme Sentenced to Four Years in Federal Prison." FBI.gov (January 9, 2013).

Finkle, Jim, "Virus Targets the Social Network in New Fraud Twist." Reuters.com (August 16, 2013).

Fiserv. "The Mobile Bill Payment Surge: What Consumers Are Doing and How Billers Are Responding." (February 2014)

Fiserv. "Sixth Annual Billing Household Survey: The Gen Y Effect and Explosive Growth of the Mobile Channel Fuel Need for Billers to Support More Payment Channels Than Ever Before." (December 2013).

Fiserv. "2007 Consumer Bill Payments Trends Survey: Volume of Electronic Payments." (2007).

Fox, Emily Jane and Greg Botelho. "5 Charged in Credit Card Hacking Scheme Feds Call Largest Ever Prosecuted in the U.S." Cnn.com (July 25, 2013).

Gartner. "Gartner Says Worldwide Information Security Spending Will Grow Almost 8 Percent in 2014 as Organizations Become More Threat-Aware." (August 22, 2014).

Heggestuen, John. "The US Sees More Money Lost to Credit Card Fraud Than the Rest of the World Combined." Businessinsider.com. (March 5, 2014).

Honan, Mat. "How Apple and Amazon Security Flaws Led to My Epic Hacking." Wired.com (August 6, 2012).

IHS Technology. "World Shipments of NFC-enabled Cellular Handsets." (February 2014).

Javelin Strategy & Research. "Online Retail Payments Forecast 2013–2018: Alternative Payments Go Main

Kaspersky Lab. "Kapersky Security Bulletin. 2013." (December 10, 2013).

Leger, Donna Leinwand. "Credit Card Info Sold on Hacker Sites." *USA Today* (September 4, 2014).

Microsoft. "Microsoft Security Intelligence Report Volume 16: July–December 2013." (2014).

Mimoso, Michael. "Google Completes Upgrade of Its SSL Certificates to 2048-Bit RSA." Threatpost.com (November 18, 2013).

Mitnick, Kevin. *Ghost in the Wires.* Little, Brown & Co. (2011).

Muncaster, Phi. "Citadel Botnet Resurges to Storm Japanese PCs." *The Register* (September 4, 2013).

Neustar. "2014 Neustar DDoS Attacks and Impact Report." (June 3, 2014).

Ombud, Inc. "Ombud Open Research: eSignature Solutions." (June 27, 2013).

Online Trust Alliance. "Emerging Threats to Consumers with the Online Advertising Industry: Testimony of Craig D. Spiezle before the Senate Committee on Homeland Security & Government Affairs." (May 15, 2014).

Panda Security. "PandaLabs Annual Report 2013 Summary." (2014).

Panda Security, "Cyber-Crime Files." http://cybercrime.pandasecurity.com/blackmarket/how_works.php (accessed September 15, 2012).

Perlroth, Nicole and David Gelles. "Russian Hackers Amass Over a Billion Passwords." *New York Times* (August 5, 2014).

Ponemon Institute. "2014 Global Report on the Cost of Cyber Crime: United States." (October 2014).

Ponemon Institute. "2014 Cost of Data Breach Study: Global Analysis." (May 2014a).

Ponemon Institute. "Data Breach: The Cloud Multiplier Effect." (June 2014).

PWC. "Key Findings from the 2014 US State of Cybercrime Survey." (June 2014).

RAND Corporation. "Markets for Cybercrime Tools and Stolen Data: Hackers' Bazaar." (2014).

Rosenblatt, Seth. "Google Accelerates Encryption Project." News.cnet.com (September 6, 2013).

Santora, Marc. "In Hours, Thieves Took $45 Million in A.T.M. Scheme." *New York Times* (May 9, 2013).

Schuman, Evan. "Starbucks Caught Storing Mobile Passwords in Clear Text." *Computerworld* (January 15, 2014).

Schwartz, Mathew J. "Another Java Zero-Day

Vulnerability Hits Black Market." Informationweek.com (January 16, 2013).

Schwartz, John. "Fighting Crime Online: Who is in Harm's Way?" *New York Times* (February 8, 2001).

Silanas Technology. "Security for E-Signatures and E-Transactions: What to Look for in a Vendor." (2014).

Software Engineering Institute. "Common Sense Guide to Mitigating Insider Threats, 4th Edition." Sei.cmu.edu (December 2012).

Stein, Lincoln D. *Web Security: A Step-by-Step Reference Guide*. Reading, MA: Addison-Wesley (1998).

Symantec, Inc. "Internet Security Threat Report 2014 Volume 19." (April 2014).

Symantec, Inc. "Internet Security Threat Report Volume XVII: May 2012." (May 2012a).

Symantec. "Symantec Intelligence Report: August 2012." (September 2012b).

Symantec, Inc. "Internet Security Threat Report: Trends for 2010, Volume 16: April 2011." (April 2011).

Symantec, Inc. "Internet Security Threat Report Volume XV: April 2010." (April 2010).

TrendMicro, Incorporated. "TrendLabs 2Q 2014 Security Roundup: Turning the Tables on Cyber Attacks." (August 12, 2014).

Vaughan-Nichols, Steven J. "Has the NSA Broken SSL? TLS? AES?" Zdnet.com (September 6, 2013).

Voreacos, David. "5 Hackers Charged in Largest Data Breach Scheme in U.S." Bloomberg.com (July 26, 2013).

Wakabayashi, Daisuke. "A Contrite Sony Vows Tighter Security." *Wall Street Journal* (May 1, 2011).

Webroot. "Malicious Mobile Apps: A Growing Threat in 2013 and Beyond." (2013).

Wills, Amanda. "New Snowden Leak: NSA Program Taps All You Do Online." Mashable.com (August 1, 2013).

Wingfield, Nick. "Spam Network Shut Down." *Wall Street Journal* (March 18, 2011).

CHAPTER 5

E-commerce Business Strategies

After reading this chapter, you will be able to:

- Identify the key components of e-commerce business models.
- Describe the major B2C business models.
- Describe the major B2B business models.
- Understand key business concepts and strategies applicable to e-commerce.

Beatguide:

Turning a Passion into a Business

Timo Ehrich had a problem. He loved electronic music, but when he went out on the town while abroad in London, he was faced with the prospect of paying a high entrance fee to enter clubs without even knowing what type of music was playing inside. Feeling that this was a pity and a problem in need of a solution, he founded Beatguide: a music event platform for electronic music and clubbing events that combines listings of events with rich media content to provide electronic music enthusiasts a full-service experience for selecting their next event.

As music streaming services like Pandora, Spotify, and iTunes Radio have grown in popularity, more highly-focused apps and services have sprung up to serve specific subsets of music enthusiasts. Many event platforms focus on concerts and bands, or all music, but electronic music events tend to have more artists and events assembled at the last minute as opposed to a long time in advance. Not only are the events different, but many DJs play music from other artists spanning a variety of styles, unlike most musicians, who play their own music. Beatguide was designed to accommodate these differences.

© grasycho/Fotolia.com

Ehrich and his other cofounders, Brendon Blackwell and Stefan Baumschlager, are electronic music enthusiasts with backgrounds in other tech startups, and their knowledge of the genre as well as their experiences with other startup companies helped them create an app that they hope other fans of the genre love to use. They have also developed a strong team, including a chief operating officer, a chief technology officer and Web front-end developer, an Android developer, a head of content and several content managers, a press and community manager, serveral artist relations managers, as well as representatives in each location where Beatguide has a presence. The events and the associated music help to promote one another on the app and Web site. Music enhances the experience of searching for nearby shows and clubs, and the event calendar allows fans of an artist to find out where he's performing next. Beatguide boasts a simple, easily-navigated design format, and the music streaming service is provided by SoundCloud, an audio platform that allows sound creators to upload, record, promote, and share their originally-created sounds. Beatguide syncs with users' Soundcloud accounts to suggest various events of DJs and clubs that they follow on each service. The app also notifies users when those artists are playing in their home cities, and displays maps that show where the closest events to them are taking place. Beatguide is available in six languages—English, German, Dutch, French, Italian, and Spanish. It currently has more than 30,000 electronic music artists in its database.

Other event planning sites like Facebook have upcoming events for users' favorite artists, but they lack any kind of compatibility with music. Other sites offer music streaming, but have no facility to create events for performers to promote or for fans to find. With Beatguide, you start with a city, and then view events by date, cost, and genre – and you can then listen to the music you'd be likely to hear at each event. It's no wonder that the app has rapidly grown in popularity with electronic music fans in Berlin and across Europe. As many music companies are trying to wring as much money out of streaming music as possible, Beatguide has focused on making it easier for music lovers to go and see live performances and events.

Beatguide's founders know that confining the app to electronic music might limit its ability to grow. The service currently focuses only on electronic music because the founders are passionate about that genre and know it best, but technology could be applied to other genres as well with minimal effort. Blackwell is unsure whether Beatguide should fully integrate with Facebook beyond maintaining its existing Facebook page. While having such a large and already-established group of music fans and artists readily available would make it easier to access and create successful events, Beatguide would lose control over their content. In addition to its apps for iPhone and Android, Beatguide also maintains a Web site with all of the functionality of its apps, as well as an active presence on social media sites such as Twitter, Tumblr, Instagram, Pinterest, YouTube, Google+, and LinkedIn, in addition to Facebook.

In the meantime, Beatguide has a lot of room for growth even within the electronic music scene. Beatguide is focused on reaching more cities and attracting more artists and fans to their service. Lost in all of these plans is the possibility of actually making money from the service someday. The founders of the service are open about their lack of concern about monetization for the time being, insisting that this will come afterwards, once the business is larger. Blackwell points to mobile ticketing as an option for easy monetization in the future, allowing users to purchase tickets via Beatguide for events, with Beatguide presumably taking a small cut.

In 2014, Beatguide is available in 19 cities. In addition to representation in the major cities of Europe (Berlin, Paris, Colgone, Frankurt, Hamburg, Munich, Milan, Amsterdam, Barcelona, Madrid, London, and Moscow), it has also branched out to other continents, including South America (Buenos Aires), North America (San Francisco), and Africa (Johannesburg and Cape Town). Beatguide's main competition is Resident Advisor, a site that offers reviews and guides to upcoming events, but has a somewhat dated approach with all text and no images. Resident Advisor was founded in 2001 and focused on electronic music as well, but the site reads more like a newsletter, with exclusive interviews with artists, as opposed to a multimedia experience like Beatguide.

Beatguide has not had much trouble obtaining capital thus far, some of which has come from cofounder Baumschlager. In August 2013, Beatguide was selected as a finalist by Red Bull Amplifier, a music technology accelerator. Red Bull will make its network and marketing resources available to Beatguide. Beatguide has displayed the type of explosive growth that investors hope to see in startup companies, and its prospects for monetization appear brighter than usual with tech startups. In September 2013, it was one of ten chosen startups featured in the Berliner Morgenpost from over 70 startups participating in one of Europe's biggest startup events, Berlin's Startup Night. Nevertheless, the company would do well to plan for a future move into other genres of music if it hopes to reach its full potential.

SOURCES: Beatguide.me, accessed December 3, 2014; "Calling all Electro Fans/Beatguide," by Jenny Hoff, Deutsche Well, September 24, 2013; "Geschlafen wird Spater!-Lange Nacht der Start-ups," by Anne Onken, Berliner Morgenpost, September 3, 2013; "Beatguide Arrives in Cape Town," Therelevantmusicblog.com, September 9, 2013; "Beatguide, GigDropper and Makelight are Finalists for Red Bull Amplifier," Hypebot.com, August 27, 2013; "Startup of the Week – Beatguide, Your Local Electro Party Guide," by Michelle Kuepper, June 5, 2013; "Beatguide Combines Club and Concert Calendar Listings with Streaming Music," by Bruce Houghton, Hypebot.com, June 4, 2013; "With Beatguide, Listening Connects to Live Events: New Electronic Music Startup," by Peter Kirn, createdigitalmusic.com, May 13, 2013;

T he story of Beatguide illustrates the difficulties of turning a good business idea into a successful business model that produces revenues and even profits.

Thousands of firms have discovered that they can spend other people's invested capital much faster than they can get customers to pay for their products or services. In most instances of failure, the business model of the firm is faulty from the beginning. In contrast, successful e-commerce firms have business models that are able to leverage the unique qualities of the Internet, the Web, and the mobile platform, provide customers real value, develop highly effective and efficient operations, avoid legal and social entanglements that can harm the firm, and produce profitable business results. In addition, successful business models must scale. The business must be able to achieve efficiencies as it grows in volume. But what is a business model, and how can you tell if a firm's business model is going to produce a profit?

In this chapter, we focus on business models and basic business concepts that you must be familiar with in order to understand e-commerce.

5.1 E-COMMERCE BUSINESS MODELS

INTRODUCTION

business model
a set of planned activities designed to result in a profit in a marketplace

business plan
a document that describes a firm's business model

e-commerce business model
a business model that aims to use and leverage the unique qualities of the Internet and the World Wide Web

A **business model** is a set of planned activities (sometimes referred to as *business processes*) designed to result in a profit in a marketplace. A business model is not always the same as a business strategy, although in some cases they are very close insofar as the business model explicitly takes into account the competitive environment (Magretta, 2002). The business model is at the center of the business plan. A **business plan** is a document that describes a firm's business model. A business plan always takes into account the competitive environment. An **e-commerce business model** aims to use and leverage the unique qualities of the Internet, the Web, and the mobile platform.

EIGHT KEY ELEMENTS OF A BUSINESS MODEL

If you hope to develop a successful business model in any arena, not just e-commerce, you must make sure that the model effectively addresses the eight elements listed in **Figure 5.1**. These elements are value proposition, revenue model, market opportunity, competitive environment, competitive advantage, market strategy, organizational development, and management team. Many writers focus on a firm's value proposition and revenue model. While these may be the most important and most easily identifiable aspects of a company's business model, the other elements are equally important when evaluating business models and plans, or when attempting to understand why a particular company has succeeded or failed (Kim and Mauborgne, 2000). In the following sections, we describe each of the key business model elements more fully.

FIGURE 5.1	THE EIGHT KEY ELEMENTS OF A BUSINESS MODEL

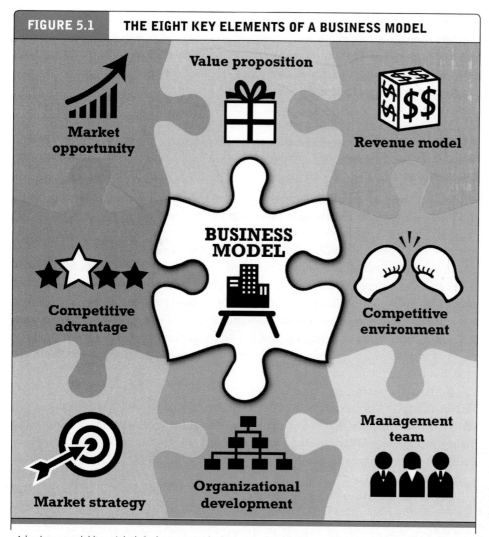

A business model has eight key elements. Each element must be addressed if you hope to be successful.

Value Proposition

A company's value proposition is at the very heart of its business model. A **value proposition** defines how a company's product or service fulfills the needs of customers (Kambil, Ginsberg, and Bloch, 1998). To develop and/or analyze a firm's value proposition, you need to understand why customers will choose to do business with the firm instead of another company and what the firm provides that other firms do not and cannot. From the consumer point of view, successful e-commerce value propositions include personalization and customization of product offerings, reduction of product search costs, reduction of price discovery costs, and facilitation of transactions by managing product delivery (Kambil, 1997; Bakos, 1998).

value proposition
defines how a company's product or service fulfills the needs of customers

For instance, before Amazon existed, most customers personally traveled to book retailers to place an order. In some cases, the desired book might not be available, and the customer would have to wait several days or weeks, and then return to the bookstore to pick it up. Amazon makes it possible for book lovers to shop for virtually any book in print from the comfort of their home or office, 24 hours a day, and to know immediately whether a book is in stock. Amazon's Kindle takes this one step further by making e-books instantly available with no shipping wait. Amazon's primary value propositions are unparalleled selection and convenience.

Revenue Model

revenue model

describes how the firm will earn revenue, produce profits, and produce a superior return on invested capital

A firm's **revenue model** describes how the firm will earn revenue, generate profits, and produce a superior return on invested capital. We use the terms *revenue model* and *financial model* interchangeably. The function of business organizations is both to generate profits and to produce returns on invested capital that exceed alternative investments. Profits alone are not sufficient to make a company "successful" (Porter, 1985). In order to be considered successful, a firm must produce returns greater than alternative investments. Firms that fail this test go out of existence.

Although there are many different e-commerce revenue models that have been developed, most companies rely on one, or some combination, of the following major revenue models: the advertising model, the subscription model, the transaction fee model, the sales model, and the affiliate model.

advertising revenue model

a company provides a forum for advertisements and receives fees from advertisers

In the **advertising revenue model**, a company that offers content, services, and/or products also provides a forum for advertisements and receives fees from advertisers. Companies that are able to attract the greatest viewership or that have a highly specialized, differentiated viewership and are able to retain user attention ("stickiness") are able to charge higher advertising rates. Yahoo, for instance, derives a significant amount of revenue from display and video advertising.

subscription revenue model

a company offers its users content or services and charges a subscription fee for access to some or all of its offerings

In the **subscription revenue model**, a company that offers content or services charges a subscription fee for access to some or all of its offerings. For instance, the digital version of *Consumer Reports* provides online and mobile access to premium content, such as detailed ratings, reviews, and recommendations, only to subscribers, who have a choice of paying a $6.95 monthly subscription fee or a $30.00 annual fee. Experience with the subscription revenue model indicates that to successfully overcome the disinclination of users to pay for content, the content offered must be perceived as a high-value-added, premium offering that is not readily available elsewhere nor easily replicated. Companies successfully offering content or services online on a subscription basis include eHarmony (dating services), Ancestry (genealogy research), Microsoft's Xboxlive (video games), Pandora, Spotify, and Rhapsody (music), Scribd, Oyster and Amazon's Kindle Unlimited program (ebooks), and Netflix and Hulu (television and movies). See **Table 5.1** for examples of various subscription services.

freemium strategy

companies give away a certain level of product or services for free, but then charge a subscription fee for premium levels of the product or service

Recently, a number of companies have been combining a subscription revenue model with a freemium strategy. In a **freemium strategy**, the companies give away a certain level of product or services for free, but then charge a subscription fee for premium levels of the product or service. See the case study, *Freemium Takes Pandora Public*, at the end of the chapter, for a further look at the freemium strategy.

TABLE 5.1	EXAMPLES OF SUBSCRIPTION SERVICES
NAME	**DESCRIPTION**
eHarmony.co.uk (dating)	• Free: Create profile and view profiles of matches. • Basic (see photos, send and receive messages): £44.95 for 1 month; £65.85 for 3 months; £113.7 for 6 months; £119.4 for 12 months • Total Connect (Basic plus additional services such as identification validation): £44.95 for 1 month; £68.85 for 3 months; £119.7 for 6 months; £155.4 for 12 months
Ancestry.co.uk (genealogical research)	• All U.K. records: £12.95 for 1 month; £107.4 for 12 months • Unlimited access to entire library: £18.95 for 1 month; £234 for 12 months • Pay as you go: 12 record views for 14 days, £6.95
Kindle Unlimited UK	• Unlimited books for £7.99/month (over 700,000 books from which to choose)
Spotify (music)	• Many different permutations, depending on device (mobile, tablet, or desktop) and plan chosen (Free, Unlimited, or Premium).

In the **transaction fee revenue model**, a company receives a fee for enabling or executing a transaction. For example, eBay provides an auction marketplace and receives a small transaction fee from a seller if the seller is successful in selling the item. E*Trade, a financial services provider, receives transaction fees each time it executes a stock transaction on behalf of a customer.

In the **sales revenue model**, companies derive revenue by selling goods, content, or services to customers. Companies such as Amazon (which sells books, music, and other products), LLBean, and Gap all have sales revenue models.

In the **affiliate revenue model**, companies that steer business to an "affiliate" receive a referral fee or percentage of the revenue from any resulting sales. For example, MyPoints makes money by connecting companies with potential customers by offering special deals to its members. When they take advantage of an offer and make a purchase, members earn "points" they can redeem for freebies, and MyPoints receives a fee. Community feedback companies such as Epinions receive much of their revenue from steering potential customers to Web sites where they make a purchase.

Table 5.2 on page 322 summarizes these major revenue models. The *Insight on Society* case, *Foursquare: Check Your Privacy at the Door*, examines some of the issues associated with Foursquare's business and revenue model.

transaction fee revenue model
a company receives a fee for enabling or executing a transaction

sales revenue model
a company derives revenue by selling goods, information, or services

affiliate revenue model
a company steers business to an affiliate and receives a referral fee or percentage of the revenue from any resulting sales

INSIGHT ON SOCIETY

FOURSQUARE: CHECK YOUR PRIVACY AT THE DOOR

Foursquare is one of a host of companies that combine a social network business model with location-based technology. Foursquare offers mobile social applications that know where you are located and can provide you with information about popular spots near by, in North America, Europe, South America, and Asia, as well as reviews from other Foursquare users, and that allow you to check in to a restaurant or other location, and automatically let friends on Facebook and other social networks learn where you are.

Foursquare was founded by Dennis Crowley and Naveen Selvadurai. They began building the first version of the Foursquare application in 2008, originally working in the kitchen of Crowley's East Village New York apartment. They debuted the application at the South by Southwest Interactive Festival in 2009, and soon attracted venture capital. As of July 2014, Foursquare had over 50 million members worldwide, split fairly evenly between the United States and the rest of the world, who have checked in over 6 billion times.

Foursquare shares many similarities with other social networks like Facebook and Twitter that began operating without a revenue model in place. Like those companies, Foursquare has been able to command high valuations from venture capital investors (with its latest round of funding fetching $35 million at a valuation of over $600 million), despite unimpressive revenue and profits. How is this possible? The answer lies in the coupling of its social network business model with smartphone-based technology that can identify where you are located within a few yards. There's potentially a great deal of money to be made from knowing where you are. Location-based data has extraordinary commercial value

because advertisers can then send you advertisements, coupons, and flash bargains, based on where you are located.

Just as Facebook and Twitter are monetizing their user bases with an advertising-based, social retail-based revenue model, so too is Foursquare. In one of its first efforts, Foursquare partnered with American Express to offer discounts to cardholders when they check in on their cell phone to certain shops and restaurants. In July 2012, Foursquare announced the next steps in the monetization of its business model: Local Updates and Promoted Updates (now called Foursquare Ads). Local Updates allow retailers to deliver geo-targeted offers and messages to customers, while Foursquare Ads, similar to Twitter's Promoted Tweets, are geo-targeted paid advertisements. People are shown ads based on their location and how likely they are to become customers, based on their previous check-in behavior. In June 2013, Foursquare launched two new ad products. The first, Check-In Retargeting, uses location and behavioral data to retarget ads to users on third-party Web sites. Foursquare claims it will not target users on an individual basis, but rather place users into various consumer segments, such as "luxury" or "business traveler," allowing advertisers to serve those users display and video ads based on those segments. The second, Post Check-In Units, serves contextual ads within the Foursquare app based on where the user has just checked in. Analysts estimated that it made between $15 and $20 million in 2013, a significant increase over the $2 million it earned in 2012. In 2014, Foursquare has begun to wring more revenue from its location data. For instance, Foursquare struck a multiyear data licensing agreement with Microsoft, which may use the data to customize Bing on a user-by-user basis with specific search results and advertisements based on their location data. In June 2014, Foursquare said it would also begin to charge outside developers for access to its database.

As the popularity of location-based services like Foursquare has grown, so too have concerns about privacy. Privacy advocates point out that many apps have no privacy policy, that most of the popular apps transmit location data to their developers after which the information is not well controlled, and that these services are creating a situation where government, marketers, creditors, and telecommunications firms will end up knowing nearly everything about citizens, including their whereabouts.

As a case in point, in April 2012, Foursquare was hit by a privacy landmine when an app called Girls Around Me surfaced that used Foursquare's application programming interface to show photos of women currently checked in around a particular neighborhood by pulling public photos of the women from their Facebook profiles linked to their Foursquare accounts. Foursquare quickly shut down the app and shortly thereafter made changes to its API to eliminate the ability of users to see strangers checked into a venue without being checked into the same place themselves. Illustrating the continuing issues Foursquare faces on the privacy front, the version of its mobile app introduced in June 2012 allowed users to see all of their friends' check-ins from the prior two weeks. As the ACLU noted, historical location data can reveal far more about a person than can individual location records. Many users may not truly understand how much of their location history is available to their friends. One advantage Foursquare does have, though, is that many of its users are actually interested in having their location tracked and their data collected – users are less likely to revolt when they find that Foursquare is collecting and sharing their data.

In 2014, Foursquare made a major change to its business model, spinning off its "check-in" feature to a new separate app called Swarm. It launched a redesigned version of its flagship Foursquare app in August 2014. The redesigned app continues to build around passive location-tracking and its business value, with CEO Dennis Crowley envisioning it as a service that lets you know what places you might enjoy when you travel somewhere new. The redesigned app asks the user to identify things he or she likes from over 10,000 possibilities (ranging from barbecue to museums to board games), and then provides recommendations. Rather than earn badges, users are encouraged to add tips to work toward becoming an "expert." But the redesigned app raises privacy concerns once again. The app tracks a user's location even when the app is not open. Instead, by default, the app automatically provides Foursquare with the phone's GPS coordinates any time the phone is turned on, unless the user specifically opts out of such tracking. Persistent location tracking of this sort could provide Foursquare with an even more valuable data stream that it can sell. Foursquare claims that the services it provides are a fair trade for the data it collects; privacy experts, on the other hand, fault Foursquare for requiring that users opt out of being tracked rather than opt in.

SOURCES: "Foursquare Launches Its Redesigned Mobile App Focused on Location-based Recommendations," by Nick Summers, Thenextweb.com, August 6, 2014; "Foursquare Now Tracks Users Even When the App is Closed," by Douglas Macmillan, *Wall Street Journal*, August 6, 2014; "About Foursquare," Foursquare.com, accessed July 31, 2014; "Foursquare Updates Swarm to Soothe Check-in Blues," by Caitlin McGarry, Techhive.com, July 8, 2014; "Foursquare to Begin Charging Fees," by Douglas Macmillan and Lisa Fleisher, *Wall Street Journal*, June 26, 2014; "Foursquare's CEO: We Want People to Open Their Eyes," by Matthew Zeitlin, Buzzfeed.com, May 6, 2014; "How Foursquare Uses Location Data to Target Ads on PCs, Phones," by Cotton Delo, AdAge.com, February 27, 2014; "With Foursquare Deal, Microsoft Aims for Supremacy in Hyper-Local Search," by Ryan Tate, Wired.com, February 5, 2014; "Foursquare Raises a $35 Million Round and Adds DFJ's Schuler to the Board," by Kara Swisher, Allthingsd.com, December 19, 2013; "Foursquare Goes Beyond the Check-in with Passive Tracking," by John McDermott, Digiday.com, December 18, 2013; "As Foursquare Concentrates on Demonstrating Value, It No Longer Allows Private Check-Ins on iOS7," by Matthew Panzarino, TechCrunch.com, December 9, 2013; "Foursquare Selling Its Location Data Through Ad Targeting Firm Turn," Adage.com, July 31, 2013; "Foursquare Initiates Ad-Retargeting and In-App Ads," by Ally Reis, Tier10lab.com, June 17, 2013; "Location-Based Advertising and Marketing—2nd Edition, by Berg Insight AB, April 18, 2013; "Three Reasons Why Foursquare's New Advertising Model Might Work," by Anne Marie Kelly, *Forbes*, August 22, 2012; "A Start-Up Matures, Working With AmEx," by Jenna Wortham, *New York Times*, June 22, 2011; "Telling Friends Where You Are (or Not)," by Jenna Wortham, *New York Times,* March 14, 2010.

TABLE 5.2	**FIVE PRIMARY REVENUE MODELS**	
REVENUE MODEL	EXAMPLES	REVENUE SOURCE
Advertising	Yahoo	Fees from advertisers in exchange for advertisements
Subscription	Wall Street Journal Consumer Reports Online	Fees from subscribers in exchange for access to content or services
Transaction Fee	eBay E*Trade	Fees (commissions) for enabling or executing a transaction
Sales	Amazon L.L.Bean Gap iTunes	Sales of goods, information, or services
Affiliate	MyPoints	Fees for business referrals

Market Opportunity

market opportunity
refers to the company's intended marketspace and the overall potential financial opportunities available to the firm in that marketspace

The term **market opportunity** refers to the company's intended **marketspace** (i.e., an area of actual or potential commercial value) and the overall potential financial opportunities available to the firm in that marketspace. The market opportunity is usually divided into smaller market niches. The realistic market opportunity is defined by the revenue potential in each of the market niches where you hope to compete.

For instance, let's assume you are analyzing a software training company that creates online software-learning systems for sale to businesses. The overall size of the software training market for all market segments is approximately €56 billion. The overall market can be broken down, however, into two major market segments: instructor-led training products, which comprise about 70% of the market (€39.2 billion in revenue), and computer-based training, which accounts for 30% (€16.8 billion). There are further market niches within each of those major market segments, such as the FT 500 computer-based training market and the small business computer-based training market. Because the firm is a start-up firm, it cannot compete effectively in the large business, computer-based training market (about €12 billion). Large brand-name training firms dominate this niche. The start-up firm's real market opportunity is to sell to the thousands of small business firms that spend about €4.8 billion on computer-based software training. This is the size of the firm's realistic market opportunity (see **Figure 5.2**).

marketspace
the area of actual or potential commercial value in which a company intends to operate

competitive environment
refers to the other companies operating in the same marketspace selling similar products

Competitive Environment

A firm's **competitive environment** refers to the other companies selling similar products and operating in the same marketspace. It also refers to the presence of substitute products and potential new entrants to the market, as well as the power of customers and suppliers over your business. We discuss the firm's environment

---

FIGURE 5.2 **MARKETSPACE AND MARKET OPPORTUNITY IN THE SOFTWARE TRAINING MARKET**

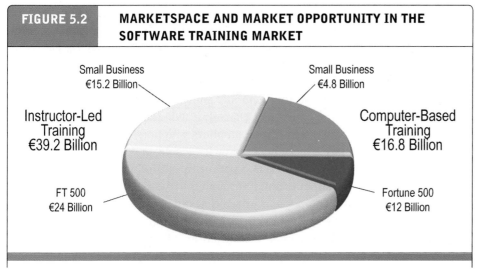

Small Business €15.2 Billion

Instructor-Led Training €39.2 Billion

FT 500 €24 Billion

Small Business €4.8 Billion

Computer-Based Training €16.8 Billion

Fortune 500 €12 Billion

Marketspaces are composed of many market segments. Your realistic market opportunity will typically focus on one or a few market segments.

---

later in the chapter. The competitive environment for a company is influenced by several factors: how many competitors are active, how large their operations are, what the market share of each competitor is, how profitable these firms are, and how they price their products.

Firms typically have both direct and indirect competitors. Direct competitors are companies that sell products and services that are very similar and into the same market segment. For example, Priceline and Travelocity, both of whom sell discount airline tickets online, are direct competitors because both companies sell identical products—cheap tickets. Indirect competitors are companies that may be in different industries but still compete indirectly because their products can substitute for one another. For instance, automobile manufacturers and airline companies operate in different industries, but they still compete indirectly because they offer consumers alternative means of transportation. CNN, a news outlet, is an indirect competitor of ESPN, not because they sell identical products, but because they both compete for consumers' time online.

The existence of a large number of competitors in any one segment may be a sign that the market is saturated and that it may be difficult to become profitable. On the other hand, a lack of competitors could either signal an untapped market niche ripe for the picking, or a market that has already been tried without success because there is no money to be made. Analysis of the competitive environment can help you decide which it is.

Competitive Advantage

Firms achieve a **competitive advantage** when they can produce a superior product and/or bring the product to market at a lower price than most, or all, of their

competitive advantage
achieved by a firm when it can produce a superior product and/or bring the product to market at a lower price than most, or all, of its competitors

competitors (Porter, 1985). Firms also compete on scope. Some firms can develop global markets, while other firms can develop only a national or regional market. Firms that can provide superior products at the lowest cost on a global basis are truly advantaged.

Firms achieve competitive advantages because they have somehow been able to obtain differential access to the factors of production that are denied to their competitors—at least in the short term (Barney, 1991). Perhaps the firm has been able to obtain very favorable terms from suppliers, shippers, or sources of labor. Or perhaps the firm has more experienced, knowledgeable, and loyal employees than any competitors. Maybe the firm has a patent on a product that others cannot imitate, or access to investment capital through a network of former business colleagues or a brand name and popular image that other firms cannot duplicate. An **asymmetry** exists whenever one participant in a market has more resources—financial backing, knowledge, information, and/or power—than other participants. Asymmetries lead to some firms having an edge over others, permitting them to come to market with better products, faster than competitors, and sometimes at lower cost.

For instance, when Apple announced iTunes, a service offering legal, downloadable individual song tracks for 99 cents a track that would be playable on any digital device with iTunes software, the company had better-than-average odds of success simply because of Apple's prior success with innovative hardware designs, and the large stable of music firms that Apple had meticulously lined up to support its online music catalog. Few competitors could match the combination of cheap, legal songs and powerful hardware to play them on.

One rather unique competitive advantage derives from being a first mover. A **first-mover advantage** is a competitive market advantage for a firm that results from being the first into a marketplace with a serviceable product or service. If first movers develop a loyal following or a unique interface that is difficult to imitate, they can sustain their first-mover advantage for long periods (Arthur, 1996). Amazon provides a good example. However, in the history of technology-driven business innovation, most first movers often lack the **complementary resources** needed to sustain their advantages, and often follower firms reap the largest rewards (Rigdon, 2000; Teece, 1986). Indeed, many of the success stories we discuss in this book are those of companies that were slow followers—businesses that gained knowledge from failure of pioneering firms and entered into the market late.

Some competitive advantages are called "unfair." An **unfair competitive advantage** occurs when one firm develops an advantage based on a factor that other firms cannot purchase (Barney, 1991). For instance, a brand name cannot be purchased and is in that sense an "unfair" advantage. Brands are built upon loyalty, trust, reliability, and quality. Once obtained, they are difficult to copy or imitate, and they permit firms to charge premium prices for their products.

In **perfect markets**, there are no competitive advantages or asymmetries because all firms have access to all the factors of production (including information and knowledge) equally. However, real markets are imperfect, and asymmetries leading to competitive advantages do exist, at least in the short term. Most competitive

---

asymmetry

exists whenever one participant in a market has more resources than other participants

first-mover advantage

a competitive market advantage for a firm that results from being the first into a marketplace with a serviceable product or service

complementary resources

resources and assets not directly involved in the production of the product but required for success, such as marketing, management, financial assets, and reputation

unfair competitive advantage

occurs when one firm develops an advantage based on a factor that other firms cannot purchase

perfect market

a market in which there are no competitive advantages or asymmetries because all firms have equal access to all the factors of production

advantages are short term, although some can be sustained for very long periods. But not forever. In fact, many respected brands fail every year.

Companies are said to **leverage** their competitive assets when they use their competitive advantages to achieve more advantage in surrounding markets. For instance, Amazon's move into the online grocery business leverages the company's huge customer database and years of e-commerce experience.

Market Strategy

No matter how tremendous a firm's qualities, its marketing strategy and execution are often just as important. The best business concept, or idea, will fail if it is not properly marketed to potential customers.

Everything you do to promote your company's products and services to potential customers is known as marketing. **Market strategy** is the plan you put together that details exactly how you intend to enter a new market and attract new customers.

For instance, Twitter, YouTube, and Pinterest have a social network marketing strategy that encourages users to post their content on the sites for free, build personal profile pages, contact their friends, and build a community. In these cases, the customer becomes part of the marketing staff!

Organizational Development

Although many entrepreneurial ventures are started by one visionary individual, it is rare that one person alone can grow an idea into a multi-million dollar company. In most cases, fast-growth companies—especially e-commerce businesses—need employees and a set of business procedures. In short, all firms—new ones in particular—need an organization to efficiently implement their business plans and strategies. Many e-commerce firms and many traditional firms that attempt an e-commerce strategy have failed because they lacked the organizational structures and supportive cultural values required to support new forms of commerce (Kanter, 2001).

Companies that hope to grow and thrive need to have a plan for **organizational development** that describes how the company will organize the work that needs to be accomplished. Typically, work is divided into functional departments, such as production, shipping, marketing, customer support, and finance. Jobs within these functional areas are defined, and then recruitment begins for specific job titles and responsibilities. Typically, in the beginning, generalists who can perform multiple tasks are hired. As the company grows, recruiting becomes more specialized. For instance, at the outset, a business may have one marketing manager. But after two or three years of steady growth, that one marketing position may be broken down into seven separate jobs done by seven individuals.

For instance, eBay founder Pierre Omidyar started an online auction site, according to some sources, to help his girlfriend trade Pez dispensers with other collectors, but within a few months the volume of business had far exceeded what he alone could handle. So he began hiring people with more business experience to help out. Soon the company had many employees, departments, and managers who were responsible for overseeing the various aspects of the organization.

leverage
when a company uses its competitive advantages to achieve more advantage in surrounding markets

market strategy
the plan you put together that details exactly how you intend to enter a new market and attract new customers

organizational development
plan describes how the company will organize the work that needs to be accomplished

Management Team

management team

employees of the company responsible for making the business model work

Arguably, the single most important element of a business model is the **management team** responsible for making the model work. A strong management team gives a model instant credibility to outside investors, immediate market-specific knowledge, and experience in implementing business plans. A strong management team may not be able to salvage a weak business model, but the team should be able to change the model and redefine the business as it becomes necessary.

Eventually, most companies get to the point of having several senior executives or managers. How skilled managers are, however, can be a source of competitive advantage or disadvantage. The challenge is to find people who have both the experience and the ability to apply that experience to new situations.

To be able to identify good managers for a business start-up, first consider the kinds of experiences that would be helpful to a manager joining your company. What kind of technical background is desirable? What kind of supervisory experience is necessary? How many years in a particular function should be required? What job functions should be fulfilled first: marketing, production, finance, or operations? Especially in situations where financing will be needed to get a company off the ground, do prospective senior managers have experience and contacts for raising financing from outside investors?

Table 5.3 summarizes the eight key elements of a business model and the key questions that must be answered in order to successfully develop each element.

RAISING CAPITAL

Raising capital is one of the most important functions for a founder of a start-up business and its management team. Not having enough capital to operate effectively is a primary reason why so many start-up businesses fail. Many entrepreneurs initially

TABLE 5.3	KEY ELEMENTS OF A BUSINESS MODEL
COMPONENTS	KEY QUESTIONS
Value proposition	Why should the customer buy from you?
Revenue model	How will you earn money?
Market opportunity	What marketspace do you intend to serve, and what is its size?
Competitive environment	Who else occupies your intended marketspace?
Competitive advantage	What special advantages does your firm bring to the marketspace?
Market strategy	How do you plan to promote your products or services to attract your target audience?
Organizational development	What types of organizational structures within the firm are necessary to carry out the business plan?
Management team	What kinds of experiences and background are important for the company's leaders to have?

"bootstrap" to get a business off the ground, using personal funds derived from savings, credit card advances, home equity loans, or from family and friends. Funds of this type are often referred to as **seed capital**. Once such funds are exhausted, if the company is not generating enough revenue to cover operating costs, additional capital will be needed. Traditional sources of capital include incubators, commercial banks, angel investors, venture capital firms, and strategic partners.

Incubators (sometimes also referred to as accelerators) such as Y-Combinator typically provide a small amount of funding, but more importantly, also provide an array of services to start-up companies that they select to participate in their programs, such as business, technical, and marketing assistance, as well as introductions to other sources of capital. Well-known incubator programs include TechStars, DreamIt Ventures, and Capital Factory.

Obtaining a loan from a commercial bank is often difficult for a start-up company without much revenue, but it may be worthwhile to investigate programs offered by microfinance programs provided by the European Union. The advantage of obtaining capital in the form of a loan (debt) is that, although it must be repaid, it does not require an entrepreneur to give up any ownership of the company.

Angel investors are typically wealthy individuals (or a group of individuals) who invest their own money in an exchange for an equity share in the stock in the business. In general, angel investors make smaller investments (typically €1 million or less) than venture capital firms, are interested in helping a company grow and succeed, and invest on relatively favorable terms compared to later stage investors. The first round of external investment in a company is sometimes referred to as Series A financing.

Venture capital investors typically become more interested in a start-up company once it has begun generating some revenue, even if it is not profitable. **Venture capital investors** invest funds they manage for other investors such as investment banks, pension funds, insurance companies, or other businesses, and usually want to obtain a larger stake in the business and exercise more control over the operation of the business. Venture capital investors also typically want a well-defined "exit strategy," such as a plan for an initial public offering or acquisition of the company by a more established business within a relatively short period of time (typically 3 to 7 years), that will enable them to obtain an adequate return on their investment. Venture capital investment often ultimately means that the founder(s) and initial investors will no longer control the company at some point in the future.

Crowdfunding involves using the Internet to enable individuals to collectively contribute money to support a project. The concepts behind crowdfunding have been popularized by Kickstarter and Indiegogo (see the *Insight on Business* case, *Crowdfunding Takes Off*), but in the past, they have not been able to be used for equity investments in for-profit companies due to various legal regulations. However, this is changing in the United States with the passage of the JOBS Act. In Europe, the European Commission has indicated an intention to support crowdfunding and in October 2013, started a public consultation exploring how the EU might promote crowdfunding through the creation of a harmonised single market regulation.

seed capital
typically, an entrepreneur's personal funds derived from savings, credit card advances, home equity loans, or from family and friends

incubators
typically provide a small amount of funding and also an array of services to start-up companies

angel investors
typically wealthy individuals or a group of individuals who invest their own money in exchange for an equity share in the stock of a business; often are the first outside investors in a start-up

venture capital investors
typically invest funds they manage for other investors; usually later-stage investors

crowdfunding
involves using the Internet to enable individuals to collectively contribute money to support a project

INSIGHT ON BUSINESS

CROWDFUNDING TAKES OFF

Think you have the next big idea but lack the resources to make it happen? Crowdfunding sites might be your best shot. Sites such as Kickstarter, Indiegogo, RocketHub, and Crowdtilt have led the growth of crowdfunding. A World Bank study predicts that capital raised via crowdfunding will exceed around €75 billion by 2025. The Internet is the ideal medium for crowdfunding because it allows individuals and organizations in need of funds and potential backers to find one another around the globe. For instance, Kickstarter has localized sites for the United Kingdom, Canada, Australia, and New Zealand. Kickstarter is also now available for projects from Sweden, Denmark, Norway and Ireland. In the past year, Indiegogo has also focused on international growth, growing over 300% in Europe, and with international funding now accounting for over 30% of its funding activity.

How do sites like Kickstarter and Indiegogo work? The idea is simple—an inventor, artist, or activist looking to raise money for a project uses the site to create a page for that project. People can pledge to support the project, but at Kickstarter, money actually only changes hands once the project fully reaches its funding goal (other sites, such as Indiegogo and RocketHub, allow project creators to keep the money they raise even if they do not achieve their goal). The sites take a small commission, usually about 5%, on completed projects. Backers do not receive any ownership interest in the project, but typically receive some type of reward, often corresponding to the size of their contribution to the project.

Crowdfunding projects are diverse, ranging from inventions to art installations, movies, video games, and political action projects. All you need is an idea that captures the attention of the crowd and for which people are willing to contribute funds. Crowdfunding is quickly becoming a mainstay in nearly all of these fields. For instance, in Australia, one of top projects funded in the past year was Ninja Sphere, a device that maps the locations of objects in the home, and which raised over $700,000 Australian dollars. In the United Kingdom, a company located in Pembrokeshire County raised over £460,000 for ZANO, an autonomous, intelligent, swarming, nano drone. In New Zealand, clothing company Opus Fresh raised over $165,000 New Zealand dollars for their merino clothing line, many times its initial target of $16,000. The applications for crowdfunding are limited only by the imagination.

In addition to the general sites like Kickstarter and Indiegogo, there are a number of niche sites and regional sites. For instance, Pubslush is a crowdfunding site for authors. Seed&Spark is a niche site focused on filmmaking. Appbackr focuses on app developers. Niche sites often have a higher success rate than the more general sites.

Successful crowdfunding projects typically share some common elements. One of the most important is a clear and concise presentation of the idea, especially through the use of video. One major crowdfunding site reports that campaigns with great videos get significantly more investment than those without. The crowdfunding campaign is in many ways similar to presenting a business plan, and should touch on the same eight elements of a business model, such as the project's value proposition, its target market, and so on. A whole ecosystem of video producers, editors, and other services has sprung up to support crowdfunding projects. Not every crowdfunding project gets off the ground—Kickstarter reports that only about 44% of its approximately 145,000 projects thus far have reached their funding goals. Sometimes projects that do get off the ground simply flame out, disappointing their backers. Although this is no different than investing in stocks, Kickstarter has sought to ease concerns by improving communication with respect to the risk inherent in the projects posted on its site. For instance, it now requires fundraisers to disclose the risks associated with their project, and for inventions, now requires photos of prototype products instead of simply drawings, simulations, or renderings.

There also is some worry that the lack of privacy involved with donating to crowdfunding sites has a negative effect on the process. In the art world, many artists are concerned that they will make enemies within their industry if they ignore requests for crowdfunding donations, not to mention the possibility of the focus on fundraising corrupting the artistic process. Another common criticism is that those who need Kickstarter the least, such as projects launched by established Hollywood actors and producers, are the ones benefitting the most. Kickstarter counters that a high-profile project draws attention to the site and helps lesser-known artists in their own fundraising efforts.

A new use of crowdfunding is to provide seed capital for startup companies. Under the JOBS Act passed by the U.S. Congress in 2012, a company will be able to crowdfund up to $1 million over a 12-month period. Many expect the use of crowdfunding for this purpose to skyrocket once regulations allowing it are fully implemented. However, some critics worry that there will be a steep learning curve and that a period of chaos is likely to ensue, until all participants (entrepreneurs, investors, crowdfunding platforms, and regulators)

become familiar with all the potential benefits and risks of equity crowdfunding.

In Europe, the situation is more complicated. Although the European Commission is considering how best to promote equity crowdfunding, currently national laws in countries throughout Europe vary widely, with the United Kingdom, Italy, and France each taking their own unique approaches. Italy is leading the way, with one of the first set of rules that regulates equity crowdfunding. In the United Kingdom, as of April 2014, crowdfunding is regulated by the Financial Conduct Authority, which is in the process of developing new rules. In France, new regulations are also in the planning stage, with the French Ministry of Economy and Finance announcing the creation of a crowdfunding investment service provider for crowdfunding in September 2013. In Europe, much of the crowdfunding still takes the form of peer-to-peer lending rather than equity investment. Some of the leading companies in this area include Zopa and Ratesetter, both London-based P2P lenders. Funding Circle is also one of the biggest crowdfunding platforms in the United Kingdom, and has facilitated loans to over 5,000 small and medium-sized businesses totalling more than £300 million since its launch in 2010. In Germany, Auxmoney, has facilitated more than 20,000 loans, worth more than €100 million, since its launch in 2013. Over 25% of all crowdfunding transactions currently come from Europe, but that percentage is expected to increase once equity crowdfunding becomes permissible in more jurisdictions.

SOURCES: "The Regulation of Crowd-Funding in Europe," by Perle Kruger and Assia Belaid, Acc.com, accessed December 2, 2014; "Here Are Australia's Most Successful Kickstarter Projects," by Junglist, Gizmodo,.com.au, November 13, 2014; "Kickstarter Opens Up to Projects from Scandinavia and Ireland," by Ben Woods, Thenextweb.com, September 15, 2014; "The Ultimate Guide to Crowdfunding in New Zealand," by Vaughn Davis, Idealog.co.nz, February 7, 2014; "Indiegogo's European Presence Grew 300% Last Year, 30% of Funding Now Outside U.S.," by Darrell Etherington, Techcrunch.com, October 29, 2013; "Leverage Video to Cut Through the Crowdfunding Clutter," by Ben Chodor, Entrepeneur.com, August 13, 2014; "Kickstarter Basics," Kickstarter.com, accessed July 22, 2014; "FAQ," Indiegogo.com, accessed July 22, 2014; "Why Investors Are Pouring Millions into Crowdfunding," by Katherine Noyes, Fortune, April 17, 2014; "Invest in Next Facebook...For a Few Bucks," by Patrick M. Sheridan, CNNMoney.com, April 14, 2014; "Crowdfunding Tips for Turning Inspiration into Reality," by Kate Murphy, New York Times, January 22, 2014; "World Bank: Crowdfunding Investment Market to Hit $93 Billion by 2025," by Richard Swart, PBS.org, December 10, 2013; "Review of Crowdfunding Regulation," by European Crowdfunding Network, October 2013; "SEC Finally Moves on Equity Crowdfunding, Phase 1," by Chance Barnett, Forbes.com, July 19, 2013; "Preparing for the Chaos of Equity Crowdfunding," Phys.org, July 18, 2013; "Why Crowdfunding Hasn't Caught on in Asia," by Kurt Wagner, Tech.Fortune.com, July 8, 2013; "SeedInvest Raises $1M to Help Angels Invest Online – Privately," by Lora Kolodny, Wall Street Journal, June 28, 2013; "Equity Crowdfunding in Europe: Where It Stands," by Charles Luzar, Crowdfundinsider.com, June 13, 2013; "The Trouble with Kickstarter," by Ellen Gamerman, Wall Street Journal, June 21, 2013; "Crowdfunding Finds a Creative Outlet," by Ella Delany, New York Times, June 11, 2013; "Top 10 Crowdfunding Sites for Fundraising," by Chance Barnett, Forbes.com, May 8, 2013; "Crowdfunding in Europe: The Top 10 'Peer-to-Peer' Lenders," by David Drake, Forbes.com, April 23, 2013; "AngelList Commits to Crowdfunding," by Lora Kolodny, Wall Street Journal, April 24, 2013.

CATEGORIZING E-COMMERCE BUSINESS MODELS: SOME DIFFICULTIES

There are many e-commerce business models, and more are being invented every day. The number of such models is limited only by the human imagination, and our list of different business models is certainly not exhaustive. However, despite the abundance of potential models, it is possible to identify the major generic types (and subtle variations) of business models that have been developed for the e-commerce arena and describe their key features. It is important to realize, however, that there is no one correct way to categorize these business models.

Our approach is to categorize business models according to the different major e-commerce sectors—B2C and B2B—in which they are utilized. You will note, however, that fundamentally similar business models may appear in more than one sector. For example, the business models of online retailers (often called e-tailers) and e-distributors are quite similar. However, they are distinguished by the market focus of the sector in which they are used. In the case of e-tailers in the B2C sector, the business model focuses on sales to the individual consumer, while in the case of the e-distributor, the business model focuses on sales to another business. Many companies use a variety of different business models as they attempt to extend into as many areas of e-commerce as possible. We look at B2C business models in Section 5.2 and B2B business models in Section 5.3.

A business's technology platform is sometimes confused with its business model. For instance, "mobile e-commerce" refers to the use of mobile devices and cellular and wide area networks to support a variety of business models. Commentators sometimes confuse matters by referring to mobile e-commerce as a distinct business model, which it is not. All of the basic business models we discuss below can be implemented on both the traditional Internet/Web and mobile platforms. Likewise, although they are sometimes referred to as such, social e-commerce and local e-commerce are not business models in and of themselves, but rather subsectors of B2C and B2B e-commerce in which different business models can operate.

You will also note that some companies use multiple business models. For instance, Amazon has multiple business models: it is an e-retailer, content provider, market creator, e-commerce infrastructure provider, and more. eBay is a market creator in the B2C and C2C e-commerce sectors, using both the traditional Internet/Web and mobile platforms, as well as an e-commerce infrastructure provider. Firms often seek out multiple business models as a way to leverage their brands, infrastructure investments, and assets developed with one business model into new business models.

Finally, no discussion of e-commerce business models would be complete without mention of a group of companies whose business model is focused on providing the infrastructure necessary for e-commerce companies to exist, grow, and prosper. These are the e-commerce enablers: the Internet infrastructure companies. They provide the hardware, operating system software, networks and communications technology, applications software, Web design, consulting services, and other tools that make e-commerce (see **Table 5.4**). While these firms may not be conducting e-commerce per se (although in many instances, e-commerce in its traditional sense is in fact one of their sales channels), as a group they have perhaps profited the most from the development of e-commerce. We discuss many of these players in the following chapters.

TABLE 5.4	**E-COMMERCE ENABLERS**
INFRASTRUCTURE	PLAYERS
Hardware: Web Servers	IBM • HP • Dell • Lenovo
Software: Server Software	Microsoft • IBM • Red Hat Linux (Apache) • Oracle
Cloud Providers	Amazon Web Services • Google • IBM • Rackspace
Hosting Services	Rackspace • WebIntellects • 1&1 • HostGator • Hostway
Domain Name Registration	Go Daddy • Network Solutions • Dotster
Content Delivery Networks	Akamai • Limelight
Site Design	eBay Enterprise • Fry • Oracle
E-commerce Platform Providers	eBay Enterprise • Magento • IBM • Oracle • Demandware
Mobile Commerce Hardware Platform	Apple • Samsung • LG
Mobile Commerce Software Platform	Apple • Google • Adobe • Usablenet • Unbound Commerce
Streaming, Rich Media, Online Video	Adobe • Apple • Easy2 Technologies • ChannelAdvisor
Security and Encryption	VeriSign • Checkpoint • GeoTrust • Entrust • Thawte • McAfee
Payment Systems	PayPal • Authorize.net • Chase Paymentech • Cybersource
Web Performance Management	Compuware • SmartBear • Keynote
Comparison Engine Feeds/Marketplace Management	Channel Advisor • Mercent • CPC Strategy
Customer Relationship Management	Oracle • SAP • eBay Enterprise • Salesforce • NetSuite
Order Management	JDA Software • eBay Enterprise • Monsoon Commerce
Fulfillment	JDA Software • eBay Enterprise • CommerceHub
Social Marketing	Buffer • HootSuite • SocialFlow
Search Engine Marketing	iProspect • ChannelAdvisor • RKG
E-mail Marketing	Constant Contact • Experian CheetahMail • Bronto Software • MailChimp
Affiliate Marketing	Conversant • Rakuten LinkShare
Customer Reviews and Forums	Bazaarvoice • PowerReviews • BizRate
Live Chat/Click-to-Call	LivePerson • BoldChat • Oracle
Web Analytics	Google Analytics • Adobe Analytics • IBM Digital Analytics • Webtrends

5.2 **MAJOR BUSINESS-TO-CONSUMER (B2C) BUSINESS MODELS**

Business-to-consumer (B2C) e-commerce, in which online businesses seek to reach individual consumers, is the most well-known and familiar type of e-commerce. **Table 5.5** illustrates the major business models utilized in the B2C arena.

E-TAILER

e-tailer
online retail store

Online retail stores, often called **e-tailers**, come in all sizes, from giant Amazon to tiny local stores that have Web sites. E-tailers are similar to the typical bricks-and-mortar storefront, except that customers only have to connect to the Internet or use their smartphone to place an order. Some e-tailers, which are referred to as "bricks-and-clicks," are subsidiaries or divisions of existing physical stores and carry the same products. REI, JCPenney, Barnes & Noble, Walmart, and Staples are examples of companies with complementary online stores. Others, however, operate only in the virtual world, without any ties to physical locations. Amazon, Blue Nile, and Bluefly are examples of this type of e-tailer. Several other variations of e-tailers—such as online versions of direct mail catalogs, online malls, and manufacturer-direct online sales—also exist.

Given that the overall global retail market in 2014 is estimated to be around €16.1 trillion, the market opportunity for e-tailers is very large. Every Internet and smartphone user is a potential customer. Customers who feel time-starved are even better prospects, because they want shopping solutions that will eliminate the need to drive to the mall or store (Bellman, Lohse, and Johnson, 1999). The e-tail revenue model is product-based, with customers paying for the purchase of a particular item.

barriers to entry
the total cost of entering a new marketplace

This sector, however, is extremely competitive. Because **barriers to entry** (the total cost of entering a new marketplace) into the e-tail market are low, tens of thousands of small e-tail shops have sprung up. Becoming profitable and surviving is very difficult, however, for e-tailers with no prior brand name or experience. The e-tailer's challenge is differentiating its business from existing competitors.

Companies that try to reach every online consumer are likely to deplete their resources quickly. Those that develop a niche strategy, clearly identifying their target market and its needs, are best prepared to make a profit. Keeping expenses low, selection broad, and inventory controlled is key to success in e-tailing, with inventory being the most difficult to gauge. Online retail is covered in more depth in Chapter 11.

COMMUNITY PROVIDER

community provider
creates an online environment where people with similar interests can transact (buy and sell goods); share interests, photos, and videos; communicate with like-minded people; and receive interest-related information

Although community providers are not a new phenomenon, the Internet has made such sites for like-minded individuals to meet and converse much easier, without the limitations of geography and time to hinder participation. **Community providers** create an online environment where people with similar interests can transact (buy and sell goods); share interests, photos, videos; communicate with like-minded people; receive interest-related information; and even play out fantasies by adopting online personalities called avatars. The social network sites Facebook, LinkedIn, Twitter, and

TABLE 5.5	B2C BUSINESS MODELS			
BUSINESS MODEL	**VARIATIONS**	**EXAMPLES**	**DESCRIPTION**	**REVENUE MODEL**
E-tailer	Virtual Merchant	Amazon iTunes Bluefly	Online version of retail store, where customers can shop at any hour of the day or night without leaving their home or office	Sales of goods
	Bricks-and-Clicks	Walmart Sears	Online distribution channel for a company that also has physical stores	Sales of goods
	Catalog Merchant	LLBean LillianVernon	Online version of direct mail catalog	Sales of goods
	Manufacturer-Direct	Dell Mattel SonyStyle	Manufacturer uses online channel to sell direct to customer	Sales of goods
Community Provider		Facebook LinkedIn Twitter Pinterest	Sites where individuals with particular interests, hobbies, common experiences, or social networks can come together and "meet" online	Advertising, subscription, affiliate referral fees
Content Provider		Wall Street Journal CBSSports CNN ESPN Rhapsody	Information and entertainment providers such as newspapers, sports sites, and other online sources that offer customers up-to-date news and special interest how-to guidance and tips and/or information sales	Advertising, subscription fees, sales of digital goods
Portal	Horizontal/General	Yahoo AOL MSN Facebook	Offers an integrated package of content, content-search, and social network services: news, e-mail, chat, music downloads, video streaming, calendars, etc. Seeks to be a user's home base	Advertising, subscription fees, transaction fees
	Vertical/Specialized (Vortal)	Sailnet	Offers services and products to specialized marketplace	Advertising, subscription fees, transaction fees
	Search	Google Bing . Ask	Focuses primarily on offering search services	Advertising, affiliate referral
Transaction Broker		E*Trade Expedia Monster Travelocity Orbitz	Processors of online sales transactions, such as stockbrokers and travel agents, that increase customers' productivity by helping them get things done faster and more cheaply	Transaction fees
Market Creator		eBay Etsy Amazon Priceline	Businesses that use Internet technology to create markets that bring buyers and sellers together	Transaction fees
Service Provider		VisaNow Carbonite RocketLawyer	Companies that make money by selling users a service, rather than a product	Sales of services

Pinterest, and hundreds of other smaller, niche sites all offer users community-building tools and services.

The basic value proposition of community providers is to create a fast, convenient, one-stop site where users can focus on their most important concerns and interests, share the experience with friends, and learn more about their own interests. Community providers typically rely on a hybrid revenue model that includes subscription fees, sales revenues, transaction fees, affiliate fees, and advertising fees from other firms that are attracted by a tightly focused audience.

Community sites such as iVillage make money through affiliate relationships with retailers and from advertising. For instance, a parent might visit RightStart's Web site for tips on diapering a baby and be presented with a link to Huggies' Web site; if the parent clicks the link and then makes a purchase from Huggies, RightStart gets a commission. Likewise, banner ads also generate revenue. Some of the oldest online communities are The Well, which provides a forum for technology and Internet-related discussions, and The Motley Fool, which provides financial advice, news, and opinions. The Well offers various membership plans ranging from $10 to $15 a month. Motley Fool supports itself through ads and selling products that start out "free" but turn into annual subscriptions.

Consumers' interest in communities is mushrooming. Community is, arguably, the fastest growing online activity. While many community sites have had a difficult time becoming profitable, many have succeeded over time, with advertising as their main source of revenue. Both the very large social network sites such as Facebook, Twitter, and LinkedIn, as well as niche sites with smaller dedicated audiences, are ideal marketing and advertising territories. Traditional online communities such as The Well, iVillage, and WebMD (which provides medical information to members) find that breadth and depth of knowledge at a site is an important factor. Community members frequently request knowledge, guidance, and advice. Lack of experienced personnel can severely hamper the growth of a community, which needs facilitators and managers to keep discussions on course and relevant. For the newer community social network sites, the most important ingredients of success appear to be ease and flexibility of use, and a strong customer value proposition. For instance, Facebook leapfrogged over its rival MySpace by encouraging the development of third-party revenue-producing applications.

Online communities benefit significantly from offline word-of-mouth, viral marketing. Online communities tend to reflect offline relationships. When your friends say they have a profile on Facebook, and ask you to "friend" them, you are encouraged to build your own online profile.

CONTENT PROVIDER

content provider
distributes information content, such as digital news, music, photos, video, and artwork

Content providers distribute information content, such as digital video, music, photos, text, and artwork. Content providers can make money via a variety of different revenue models, including advertising, subscription fees, and sales of digital goods. For instance, in the case of Rhapsody, a monthly subscription fee provides users with access to thousands of music tracks. Other content providers, such as the *Wall Street*

Journal online newspaper, *Harvard Business Review*, and many others, charge customers for content downloads in addition to, or in place of, a subscription fee.

Of course, not all online content providers charge for their information: just look at the Web sites for CBSSports, CIO, CNN, and the online versions of many newspapers and magazines. Users can access news and information at these sites without paying a cent, although sometimes they may be required to register as a member. These popular sites make money in other ways, such as through advertising and partner promotions on the site. Increasingly, however, "free content" may be limited to headlines and text, whereas premium content—in-depth articles or videos—is sold for a fee.

Generally, the key to becoming a successful content provider is owning the content. Traditional owners of copyrighted content—publishers of books and newspapers, broadcasters of radio and television content, music publishers, and movie studios—have powerful advantages over newcomers who simply offer distribution channels and must pay for content, often at very high prices.

Some content providers, however, do not own content, but syndicate (aggregate) and then distribute content produced by others. *Syndication* is a major variation of the standard content provider model. Aggregators, who collect information from a wide variety of sources and then add value to that information through post-aggregation services, are another variation. For instance, Shopzilla collects information on the prices of thousands of goods online, analyzes the information, and presents users with tables showing the range of prices and links to the sites where the products can be purchased. Shopzilla adds value to content it aggregates, and resells this value to advertisers who advertise on its site.

Any e-commerce start-up that intends to make money by providing content is likely to face difficulties unless it has a unique information source that others cannot access. For the most part, this business category is dominated by traditional content providers. The *Insight on Technology* case, *Battle of the Titans: Music in the Cloud*, discusses how changes in Internet technology are driving the development of new business models in the online content market by Internet titans Apple, Google, and Amazon.

Online content is discussed in further depth in Chapter 9.

PORTAL

Portals such as Yahoo, MSN, and AOL offer users powerful search tools as well as an integrated package of content and services, such as news, e-mail, instant messaging, calendars, shopping, music downloads, video streaming, and more, all in one place. Initially, portals sought to be viewed as "gateways" to the Internet. Today, however, the portal business model is to be a destination site. They are marketed as places where consumers will hopefully stay a long time to read news, find entertainment, and meet other people (think of destination resorts). Portals do not sell anything directly—or so it seems—and in that sense they can present themselves as unbiased. Portals generate revenue primarily by charging advertisers for ad placement, collecting referral fees for steering customers to other sites, and charging for premium services.

portal
offers users powerful search tools as well as an integrated package of content and services all in one place

INSIGHT ON TECHNOLOGY

BATTLE OF THE TITANS: MUSIC IN THE CLOUD

Business models are closely related to the technologies available to produce and distribute products and services. Nowhere is this more apparent than the recorded music business, whose foundations since the early 20th century have been based on the technology on hand, from sheet music, to records, tape cassettes, CDs, and DVDs. And now, the Internet has enabled two new business models: the online store download-and-own model used by Amazon and Apple's iTunes, where you purchase songs and store them on a computer or devices, and the subscription service model used by Rhapsody, Pandora, Spotify, and many others, where for a monthly fee you can listen to an online library of songs streamed to your devices. In this business model you don't own the music, and if you miss a payment, it's gone.

Both the download-and-own and subscription service models have significant shortcomings that detract from the customer experience. If you download music to a computer, you need cables and software to get the music to your smartphone, and you will be limited as to how many devices you can use. You may download using different devices and then face a problem coordinating them. Subscription services have confusing pricing schemes, typically cost $15 a month or more, and require you to have Internet access. Many services don't allow you to store songs locally on a device for off-the-Net play, while others allow local storage of music that will not be playable if you miss the monthly payment. Many of the inconveniences of these existing business models were created by record companies who feared, legitimately, that their music would be ripped off and their revenue decimated.

Changes in technology have introduced yet a third recorded music business model: cloud streaming. Here, you own the music and you can store it on a single online cloud drive and play it from any device you choose—one music collection, no coordination issues, and local storage for offline playback. The technology behind this business model is cloud computing, a model of computing where software and files are stored on servers located on the Internet rather than on local devices like PCs and local servers in an office or corporate headquarters. While cloud computing started out as a new and less-expensive method of information processing for large corporations, it is spreading to consumer services such as music, file storage, productivity software, and calendars. What makes cloud computing possible is mammoth data centers stocked with hundreds of thousands of computer processors, and cheap broadband networks that can move files and software instructions rapidly back and forth from local devices to cloud servers.

In 2012, Apple, Amazon, and Google, three of the largest Internet players, introduced their cloud-based music models. The resulting competition is a battle royale among Internet titans to preserve existing advantages for each firm, and to dominate the future of music distribution.

Amazon was the first to announce its cloud music service, in March 2011. Using a "music locker" business model, Amazon Music (previously called Amazon Cloud Player) allows you to upload MP3 and ACC music files, store the music in Amazon's cloud, and play the music on any number of supported digital devices, such as your PC, Mac, Kindle Fire, Android Phone, iPhone, or iPod Touch. All Amazon customers can store their Amazon Digital Music purchases and 250 imported songs for free. Storage for additional imported songs (up to 250,000) costs $24.99 a year. Presto: your music is no longer tied to a single digital device or platform. Amazon also sells music; it is the second largest music retailer in the world, with more than 20 million songs for sale.

Amazon's announcement was followed by Google's announcement in May 2011 of its own music locker service, now known as Google Play. This is another music locker service based on cloud computing. You download a Google music uploader app called Music Manager and it searches your hard drive or smartphone for music files, and automatically uploads them to the Google cloud. You get free storage for 20,000 songs, for $9.99 a month, and you can enjoy unlimited listening to millions of songs and create a personalized radio station similar to that offered by Pandora based on any song or artist. In addition, the Google Play store has over 22 million songs available for purchase.

In June 2011, Apple also joined the party, announcing its own cloud service player and storage system, iCloud. Apple is the largest retailer of music in the world with an inventory of more than 37 million songs. Apple's iCloud service allows you to store all your digital files, including music files, on Apple's cloud drive, and then play your music on any Apple device or PC connected to the Internet. Apple's approach is a "matching service" where you do not need to upload any of your music files. In a unique agreement with the four largest music firms, Apple's iCloud software identifies the music titles stored on your device and places high-quality copies into your iCloud drive automatically. iTunes Match is available on a subscription basis for the same price as Amazon Music, $24.99 a year. Without it, you are limited only to the music you have purchased through iTunes. You can also upload digital documents, from photos and calendars to spreadsheets and papers, to the iCloud. Apple provides 5 gigabytes of storage for free, with additional amounts available for purchase. Apple's iCloud drive service is coordinated with its iOS operating system for smartphones and i-devices. The operating system does not require a PC or Mac base station, and you can manage all your digital content online using just an iPhone.

It's still too early to tell which of these giants will prevail in the music distribution business, but all will continue to be the dominant players. While there are mostly similarities among the various cloud services (they all play on any device you choose), some differences may have business significance. For instance, Google and Amazon require users to upload their music, which can take many hours or even days, and some of your music tracks might be very low quality. Apple's service matches your local collection and places high-quality versions of the music online automatically. It's unclear if this is a permanent advantage because both Google and Amazon could negotiate similar deals with the music companies. Google and Apple can sell users expensive smartphones to play cloud music, whereas Amazon has no proprietary music player.

Music is just the first online content to go onto cloud servers. It will soon be followed by movies, television shows, books, and magazines. In addition, the presence of all this content will drive consumers to buy mobile devices. None of the titans plan to miss out on this opportunity. There's also money for the content producers. The streaming music cloud services promise to provide a rich and stable stream of revenue for the content producers and artists. Instead of fighting each other, for once it appears the content owners and the Internet content distributors have reached a consensus on a mutually profitable business model for content.

SOURCES: "iTunes Match," Apple.com, accessed July 15, 2014; "Google Play/Music," Play.google.com, accessed July 15, 2014; "Amazon Music," Amazon.com, accessed July 15, 2014; "Now Streaming on Sonos: Google Play Music's 22 Million Songs," by Eric Blattberg, Venturebeat.com, April 10, 2014; "Web Services to Drive Future Growth for Amazon," by Trefis Team, Forbes.com, August 21, 2012; "Top Cloud Services for Storing and Streaming Music," by Paul Lilly, *PCWorld*, July 29, 2012; "The Cloud That Ate Your Music," by Jon Pareles, *New York Times*, June 22, 2011; "Amazon's and Google's Cloud Services Compared," by Paul Boutin, *New York Times*, June 6, 2011; "For a Song, Online Giants Offer Music in a Cloud," by Walter Mossberg, *Wall Street Journal*, May 19, 2011; "Apple's Cloud Music Service Might Crush the Competition," by Mikko Torikka, VentureBeat.com, May 19, 2011; "Amazon Beats Apple and Google to Cloud Music," by Dean Takahashi, VentureBeat.com, March 28, 2011.

Although there are numerous portal/search engine sites, the top five sites (Google, Microsoft (Bing), Yahoo, Ask, and AOL) gather more than 95% of the search engine traffic because of their superior brand recognition (comScore, 2014). Many of the top sites were among the first to appear on the Web and therefore had first-mover advantages. Being first confers advantage because customers come to trust a reliable provider and experience switching costs if they change to late arrivals in the market. By garnering a large chunk of the marketplace, first movers—just like a single telephone network—can offer customers access to commonly shared ideas, standards, and experiences (something called *network externalities* that we describe in later chapters).

The traditional portals have company: Facebook and other social network sites are now the initial start or home page (portal) for millions of Internet users in the United States.

Yahoo, AOL, and others like them are considered to be horizontal portals because they define their marketspace to include all users of the Internet. Vertical portals (sometimes called vortals) attempt to provide similar services as horizontal portals, but are focused around a particular subject matter or market segment. For instance, Sailnet focuses on the world's sailing community, and provides sailing news, articles, discussion groups, free e-mail, and a retail store. Although the total number of vortal users may be much lower than the number of portal users, if the market segment is attractive enough, advertisers are willing to pay a premium in order to reach a targeted audience. Also, visitors to specialized niche vortals spend more money than the average Yahoo visitor. Google and Ask can also be considered portals of a sort, but focus primarily on offering search and advertising services. They generate revenues primarily from search engine advertising sales and also from affiliate referral fees.

TRANSACTION BROKER

transaction broker

site that processes transactions for consumers that are normally handled in person, by phone, or by mail

Companies that process transactions for consumers normally handled in person, by phone, or by mail are **transaction brokers**. The largest industries using this model are financial services, travel services, and job placement services. The online transaction broker's primary value propositions are savings of money and time. In addition, most transaction brokers provide timely information and opinions. Companies such as Monster offer job searchers a national marketplace for their talents and employers a national resource for that talent. Both employers and job seekers are attracted by the convenience and currency of information. Online stock brokers charge commissions that are considerably less than traditional brokers, with many offering substantial deals, such as cash and a certain number of free trades, to lure new customers.

Given rising consumer interest in financial planning and the stock market, the market opportunity for online transaction brokers appears to be large. However, while millions of customers have shifted to online brokers, some are still wary about switching from their traditional broker who provides personal advice and a brand name. Fears of privacy invasion and the loss of control over personal financial information also contribute to market resistance. Consequently, the challenge for online brokers is to overcome consumer fears by emphasizing the security and privacy measures in place, and, like physical banks and brokerage firms, providing a broad range of financial services and not just stock trading. This industry is covered in greater depth in Chapter 11.

Transaction brokers make money each time a transaction occurs. Each stock trade, for example, nets the company a fee, based on either a flat rate or a sliding scale related to the size of the transaction. Attracting new customers and encouraging them to trade frequently are the keys to generating more revenue for these companies. Travel sites generate commissions from travel books and job sites generate listing fees from employers up front, rather than charging a fee when a position is filled.

MARKET CREATOR

Market creators build a digital environment in which buyers and sellers can meet, display and search for products and services, and establish prices. Prior to the Internet and the Web, market creators relied on physical places to establish a market. Beginning with the medieval marketplace and extending to today's New York Stock Exchange, a market has meant a physical space for transacting business. There were few private digital network marketplaces prior to the Web. The Web changed this by making it possible to separate markets from physical space. Prime examples are Priceline, which allows consumers to set the price they are willing to pay for various travel accommodations and other products (sometimes referred to as a reverse auction), and eBay, the online auction site utilized by both businesses and consumers. Market creators make money by either charging a percentage of every transaction made, or charging merchants for access to the market.

For example, eBay's auction business model is to create a digital environment for buyers and sellers to meet, agree on a price, and transact. This is different from transaction brokers who actually carry out the transaction for their customers, acting as agents in larger markets. At eBay, the buyers and sellers are their own agents. Each sale on eBay nets the company a commission based on the percentage of the item's sales price, in addition to a listing fee. eBay is one of the few e-commerce companies that has been profitable virtually from the beginning. Why? One answer is that eBay has no inventory or production costs. It is simply a middleman.

The market opportunity for market creators is potentially vast, but only if the firm has the financial resources and marketing plan to attract sufficient sellers and buyers to the marketplace. As of June 30, 2014, eBay had more than 149 million active buyers, and this makes for an efficient market (eBay Inc., 2014). There are many sellers and buyers for each type of product, sometimes for the same product, for example, laptop computer models. Many other digital auctions have sprung up in smaller, more specialized vertical market segments such as jewelry and automobiles.

Uber, Airbnb, and Lyft are another example of the market creator business model. **Sharing economy (mesh economy)** companies are market creators that have developed online platforms that allow people to sell services, such as transportation or spare rooms, in a marketplace that operates in the cloud and relies on the Web or smartphone apps to conduct transactions. It is important to note that, although referred to as sharing economy or mesh economy companies, these companies do not in fact share resources. Users of these services are either selling something or buying something, and the companies produce revenue by extracting fees for each transaction.

market creator
builds a digital environment where buyers and sellers can meet, display products, search for products, and establish a price for products

sharing economy (mesh economy)
online platforms that allow people to sell services in a marketplace that operates in the cloud and relies on the Web or smartphone apps

However, they do unlock the economic value in spare resources (personal cars and rooms) that might otherwise have been lost. In the process they have created huge online markets. For instance, Uber (founded in 2009) currently operates in 100 countries and 70 cities. Airbnb, founded in 2008, operates in 190 countries and 34,000 cities, lists over 800,000 rooms available for rent, and has arranged for 17 million visits around the world. Airbnb has raised around $800 million in funding thus far and is valued at over $10 billion; Uber has raised $1.5 billion and is valued at $18 billion.

SERVICE PROVIDER

service provider
offers services online

While e-tailers sell products online, **service providers** offer services online. There's been an explosion in online services that is often unrecognized. Web 2.0 applications such as photo sharing, video sharing, and user-generated content (in blogs and social network sites) are all services provided to customers. Google has led the way in developing online applications such as Google Maps, Google Docs, and Gmail. Other personal services such as online medical bill management, financial and pension planning, and travel recommendation are showing strong growth.

Service providers use a variety of revenue models. Some charge a fee, or monthly subscriptions, while others generate revenue from other sources, such as through advertising and by collecting personal information that is useful in direct marketing. Some services are free but are not complete. For instance, Google Apps' basic edition is free, but a business edition with advanced tools costs $5/user/month or $50/user/year. Much like retailers who trade products for cash, service providers trade knowledge, expertise, and capabilities for revenue.

Obviously, some services cannot be provided online. For example, dentistry, plumbing, and car repair cannot be completed via the Internet. However, online arrangements can be made for these services. Online service providers may offer computer services, such as information storage (as does Carbonite), provide legal services (RocketLawyer), or bookkeeping services (Bench). Grocery shopping sites such as FreshDirect and Peapod are also providing services.[1] To complicate matters a bit, most financial transaction brokers (described previously) provide services such as college tuition and pension planning. Travel brokers also provide vacation-planning services, not just transactions with airlines and hotels. Indeed, mixing services with your products is a powerful business strategy pursued by many hard-goods companies (for example, warranties are services).

The basic value proposition of service providers is that they offer consumers valuable, convenient, time-saving, and low-cost alternatives to traditional service providers or—in the case of search engines and most Web 2.0 applications—they provide services that are truly unique. Where else can you search billions of Web pages, or share photos with as many people instantly? Research has found, for instance, that a major factor in predicting online buying behavior is *time starvation*. Time-starved people tend to be busy professionals who work long hours and simply do not have the time to pick up packages, buy groceries, send photos, or visit with financial planners (Bellman,

---

[1] FreshDirect and other e-commerce businesses can also be classified as online retailers insofar as they warehouse commonly purchased items and make a profit based on the spread between their buy and sell prices.

Lohse, and Johnson, 1999). The market opportunity for service providers is as large as the variety of services that can be provided and potentially is much larger than the market opportunity for physical goods. We live in a service-based economy and society; witness the growth of fast-food restaurants, package delivery services, and wireless cellular phone services. Consumers' increasing demand for convenience products and services bodes well for current and future online service providers.

Marketing of service providers must allay consumer fears about hiring a vendor online, as well as build confidence and familiarity among current and potential customers. Building confidence and trust is critical for service providers just as it is for retail product merchants.

5.3 MAJOR BUSINESS-TO-BUSINESS (B2B) BUSINESS MODELS

In Chapter 1, we noted that business-to-business (B2B) e-commerce, in which businesses sell to other businesses, is more than 10 times the size of B2C e-commerce, even though most of the public attention has focused on B2C. For instance, it is estimated that revenues for all types of B2B e-commerce worldwide will total around €12.4 trillion in 2014, compared to about €1.18 trillion for all types of B2C e-commerce. Clearly, most of the dollar revenues in e-commerce involve B2B e-commerce. Much of this activity is unseen and unknown to the average consumer.

Table 5.6 lists the major business models utilized in the B2B arena.

TABLE 5.6	B2B BUSINESS MODELS		
BUSINESS MODEL	EXAMPLES	DESCRIPTION	REVENUE MODEL
(1) NET MARKETPLACE			
E-distributor	Grainger AmazonSupply	Single-firm online version of retail and wholesale store; supply maintenance, repair, operation goods; indirect inputs	Sales of goods
E-procurement	Ariba Supplier Network PerfectCommerce	Single firm creating digital markets where sellers and buyers transact for indirect inputs	Fees for market-making services, supply chain management, and fulfillment services
Exchange	Go2Paper	Independently owned vertical digital marketplace for direct inputs	Fees and commissions on transactions
Industry Consortium	TheSeam SupplyOn	Industry-owned vertical digital market open to select suppliers	Fees and commissions on transactions
(2) PRIVATE INDUSTRIAL NETWORK			
	Walmart Procter & Gamble	Company-owned network that coordinates supply chains with a limited set of partners	Cost absorbed by network owner and recovered through production and distribution efficiencies

E-DISTRIBUTOR

e-distributor
a company that supplies products and services directly to individual businesses

Companies that supply products and services directly to individual businesses are **e-distributors**. W.W. Grainger, for example, is the largest distributor of maintenance, repair, and operations (MRO) supplies. In the past, Grainger relied on catalog sales and physical distribution centers in metropolitan areas. Its catalog of equipment went online in 1995. Today, Grainger's e-commerce platform, which includes Web sites and mobile apps, produces over $3 billion in sales (one-third of total sales) for the company.

E-distributors are owned by one company seeking to serve many customers. However, as with exchanges (described on the next page), critical mass is a factor. With e-distributors, the more products and services a company makes available on its site, the more attractive that site is to potential customers. One-stop shopping is always preferable to having to visit numerous sites to locate a particular part or product.

E-PROCUREMENT

e-procurement firm
creates and sells access to digital markets

Just as e-distributors provide products to other companies, **e-procurement firms** create and sell access to digital markets. Firms such as Ariba, for instance, have created software that helps large firms organize their procurement process by creating mini-digital markets for a single firm. Ariba creates custom-integrated online catalogs (where supplier firms can list their offerings) for purchasing firms. On the sell side, Ariba helps vendors sell to large purchasers by providing software to handle catalog creation, shipping, insurance, and finance. Both the buy and sell side software is referred to generically as "value chain management" software.

B2B service provider
sells business services to other firms

scale economies
efficiencies that arise from increasing the size of a business

B2B service providers make money through transaction fees, fees based on the number of workstations using the service, or annual licensing fees. They offer purchasing firms a sophisticated set of sourcing and supply chain management tools that permit firms to reduce supply chain costs. In the software world, firms such as Ariba are sometimes also called Software as a Service (SaaS) or Platform as a Service (PaaS) providers; they are able to offer firms much lower costs of software by achieving scale economies. **Scale economies** are efficiencies that result from increasing the size of a business, for instance, when large, fixed-cost production systems (such as factories or software systems) can be operated at full capacity with no idle time. In the case of software, the marginal cost of a digital copy of a software program is nearly zero, and finding additional buyers for an expensive software program is exceptionally profitable. This is much more efficient than having every firm build its own supply chain management system, and it permits firms such as Ariba to specialize and offer their software to firms at a cost far less than the cost of developing it.

EXCHANGES

exchange
an independent digital marketplace where suppliers and commercial purchasers can conduct transactions

Exchanges have garnered most of the B2B attention and early funding because of their potential market size even though today they are a small part of the overall B2B picture. An **exchange** is an independent digital marketplace where hundreds of suppliers meet a smaller number of very large commercial purchasers (Kaplan and Sawhney, 2000). Exchanges are owned by independent, usually entrepreneurial start-up firms whose business is making a market, and they generate revenue by charging a commission or fee based on the size of the transactions conducted among trading parties. They usually serve a single vertical industry such as steel, polymers, or aluminum, and focus on the exchange of direct inputs to production and short-term contracts or spot purchasing. For buyers, B2B exchanges make it possible to gather information, check out suppliers, collect prices, and keep up to date on the latest happenings all in one place. Sellers, on the other hand, benefit from expanded access to buyers. The greater the number of sellers and buyers, the lower the sales cost and the higher the chances of making a sale. The ease, speed, and volume of transactions are summarily referred to as *market liquidity*.

In theory, exchanges make it significantly less expensive and time-consuming to identify potential suppliers, customers, and partners, and to do business with each other. As a result, they can lower transaction costs—the cost of making a sale or purchase. Exchanges can also lower product costs and inventory-carrying costs—the cost of keeping a product on hand in a warehouse. In reality, as will be discussed in Chapter 12, B2B exchanges have had a difficult time convincing thousands of suppliers to move into singular digital markets where they face powerful price competition, and an equally difficult time convincing businesses to change their purchasing behavior away from trusted long-term trading partners. As a result, the number of exchanges has fallen significantly.

INDUSTRY CONSORTIA

Industry consortia are industry-owned *vertical marketplaces* that serve specific industries, such as the automobile, aerospace, chemical, floral, or logging industries. In contrast, *horizontal marketplaces* sell specific products and services to a wide range of companies. Vertical marketplaces supply a smaller number of companies with products and services of specific interest to their industry, while horizontal marketplaces supply companies in different industries with a particular type of product and service, such as marketing-related, financial, or computing services. For example, SupplyOn, founded in 2000 and owned by industrial giants Bosch (one of the world's largest suppliers of automotive components), Continental (a leading automotive manufacturing company), and Schaeffler (a global manufacturer of various types of bearings), among others, provides a shared supply chain collaboration platform for companies in various manufacturing industries. In 2013, in addition to its shareholders, its customers include Airbus, BMW, BordWarner, Siemens, Thales, and many other major global manufacturing companies.

Industry consortia have tended to be more successful than independent exchanges in part because they are sponsored by powerful, deep-pocketed industry players, and also because they strengthen traditional purchasing behavior rather than seek to transform it.

PRIVATE INDUSTRIAL NETWORKS

Private industrial networks constitute about 75% of all B2B expenditures by large firms and far exceed the expenditures for all forms of Net marketplaces. A **private**

industry consortia
industry-owned vertical marketplaces that serve specific industries

private industrial network
digital network designed to coordinate the flow of communications among firms engaged in business together

industrial network (sometimes referred to as a private trading exchange or PTX) is a digital network (often but not always Internet-based) designed to coordinate the flow of communications among firms engaged in business together. The network is owned by a single large purchasing firm. Participation is by invitation only to trusted long-term suppliers of direct inputs. These networks typically evolve out of a firm's own enterprise resource planning (ERP) system, and are an effort to include key suppliers in the firm's own business decision making. For instance, Walmart operates one of the largest private industrial networks in the world for its suppliers, who on a daily basis use Walmart's network to monitor the sales of their goods, the status of shipments, and the actual inventory level of their goods.

We discuss the nuances of B2B e-commerce in more detail in Chapter 12.

5.4 HOW E-COMMERCE CHANGES BUSINESS: STRATEGY, STRUCTURE, AND PROCESS

Now that you have a clear grasp of the variety of business models used by e-commerce firms, you also need to understand how e-commerce has changed the business environment in the last decade, including industry structures, business strategies, and industry and firm operations (business processes and value chains). We return to these concepts throughout the book as we explore the e-commerce phenomenon. In general, the Internet is an open standards system available to all players, and this fact inherently makes it easy for new competitors to enter the marketplace and offer substitute products or channels of delivery. The Internet tends to intensify competition. Because information becomes available to everyone, the Internet inherently shifts power to buyers who can quickly discover the lowest-cost provider. On the other hand, the Internet presents many new opportunities for creating value, for branding products and charging premium prices, and for enlarging an already powerful offline physical business such as Walmart or Sears.

Recall Table 1.2 in Chapter 1 that describes the truly unique features of e-commerce technology. **Table 5.7** suggests some of the implications of each unique feature for the overall business environment—industry structure, business strategies, and operations.

INDUSTRY STRUCTURE

industry structure
refers to the nature of the players in an industry and their relative bargaining power

E-commerce changes industry structure, in some industries more than others. **Industry structure** refers to the nature of the players in an industry and their relative bargaining power. An industry's structure is characterized by five forces: *rivalry among existing competitors,* the *threat of substitute products, barriers to entry into the industry,* the *bargaining power of suppliers,* and the *bargaining power of buyers* (Porter, 1985). When you describe an industry's structure, you are describing the general business environment in an industry and the overall profitability of doing business in that environment. E-commerce has the potential to change the relative strength of these competitive forces (see **Figure 5.3** on page 346).

TABLE 5.7	EIGHT UNIQUE FEATURES OF E-COMMERCE TECHNOLOGY
FEATURE	SELECTED IMPACTS ON BUSINESS ENVIRONMENT
Ubiquity	Alters industry structure by creating new marketing channels and expanding size of overall market. Creates new efficiencies in industry operations and lowers costs of firms' sales operations. Enables new differentiation strategies.
Global reach	Changes industry structure by lowering barriers to entry, but greatly expands market at same time. Lowers cost of industry and firm operations through production and sales efficiencies. Enables competition on a global scale.
Universal standards	Changes industry structure by lowering barriers to entry and intensifying competition within an industry. Lowers costs of industry and firm operations by lowering computing and communications costs. Enables broad scope strategies.
Richness	Alters industry structure by reducing strength of powerful distribution channels. Changes industry and firm operations costs by reducing reliance on sales forces. Enhances post-sales support strategies.
Interactivity	Alters industry structure by reducing threat of substitutes through enhanced customization. Reduces industry and firm costs by reducing reliance on sales forces. Enables differentiation strategies.
Personalization/ Customization	Alters industry structure by reducing threats of substitutes, raising barriers to entry. Reduces value chain costs in industry and firms by lessening reliance on sales forces. Enables personalized marketing strategies.
Information density	Changes industry structure by weakening powerful sales channels, shifting bargaining power to consumers. Reduces industry and firm operations costs by lowering costs of obtaining, processing, and distributing information about suppliers and consumers.
Social technologies	Changes industry structure by shifting programming and editorial decisions to consumers. Creates substitute entertainment products. Energizes a large group of new suppliers.

When you consider a business model and its potential long-term profitability, you should always perform an industry structural analysis. An **industry structural analysis** is an effort to understand and describe the nature of competition in an industry, the nature of substitute products, the barriers to entry, and the relative strength of consumers and suppliers.

E-commerce can affect the structure and dynamics of industries in very different ways. Consider the recorded music industry, an industry that has experienced

industry structural analysis

an effort to understand and describe the nature of competition in an industry, the nature of substitute products, the barriers to entry, and the relative strength of consumers and suppliers

significant change because of e-commerce. Historically, the major record companies owned the exclusive rights to the recorded music of various artists. With the entrance into the marketplace of substitute providers such as Napster and Kazaa, millions of consumers began to use the Internet to bypass traditional music labels and their distributors entirely. In the travel industry, entirely new middlemen such as Travelocity entered the market to compete with traditional travel agents. After Travelocity, Expedia, CheapTickets, and other travel services demonstrated the power of e-commerce marketing for airline tickets, the actual owners of the airline seats—the major airlines—banded together to form their own Internet outlet for tickets, Orbitz, for direct sales to consumers (although ultimately selling the company to a

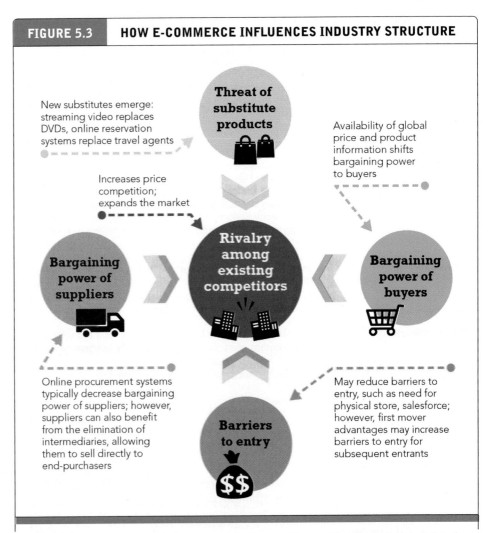

FIGURE 5.3   **HOW E-COMMERCE INFLUENCES INDUSTRY STRUCTURE**

Threat of substitute products

New substitutes emerge: streaming video replaces DVDs, online reservation systems replace travel agents

Availability of global price and product information shifts bargaining power to buyers

Increases price competition; expands the market

Bargaining power of suppliers

Rivalry among existing competitors

Bargaining power of buyers

Online procurement systems typically decrease bargaining power of suppliers; however, suppliers can also benefit from the elimination of intermediaries, allowing them to sell directly to end-purchasers

Barriers to entry

May reduce barriers to entry, such as need for physical store, salesforce; however, first mover advantages may increase barriers to entry for subsequent entrants

E-commerce has many impacts on industry structure and competitive conditions. From the perspective of a single firm, these changes can have negative or positive implications depending on the situation. In some cases, an entire industry can be disrupted, while at the same time, a new industry is born. Individual firms can either prosper or be devastated.

private investor group). Clearly, e-commerce creates *new industry dynamics* that can best be described as the give and take of the marketplace, the changing fortunes of competitors.

Yet, in other industries, e-commerce has strengthened existing players. In the chemical and automobile industries, e-commerce is being used effectively by manufacturers to strengthen their traditional distributors. In these industries, e-commerce technology has not fundamentally altered the competitive forces—bargaining power of suppliers, barriers to entry, bargaining power of buyers, threat of substitutes, or rivalry among competitors—within the industry. Hence, each industry is different and you need to examine each one carefully to understand the impacts of e-commerce on competition and strategy.

New forms of distribution created by new market entrants can completely change the competitive forces in an industry. For instance, consumers gladly substituted free access to Wikipedia for a $699 set of World Book encyclopedias, or a $40 DVD, radically changing the competitive forces in the encyclopedia industry. As we describe in Chapter 9, the content industries of newspapers, books, movies, games, and television have been transformed by the emergence of new distribution platforms.

Inter-firm rivalry (competition) is one area of the business environment where e-commerce technologies have had an impact on most industries. In general, e-commerce has increased price competition in nearly all markets. It has been relatively easy for existing firms to adopt e-commerce technology and attempt to use it to achieve competitive advantage vis-à-vis rivals. For instance, e-commerce inherently changes the scope of competition from local and regional to national and global. Because consumers have access to global price information, e-commerce produces pressures on firms to compete by lowering prices (and lowering profits). On the other hand, e-commerce has made it possible for some firms to differentiate their products or services from others. Amazon patented one-click purchasing, for instance, while eBay created a unique, easy-to-use interface and a differentiating brand name. Therefore, although e-commerce has increased emphasis on price competition, it has also enabled businesses to create new strategies for differentiation and branding so that they can retain higher prices.

It is impossible to determine if e-commerce technologies have had an overall positive or negative impact on firm profitability in general. Each industry is unique, so it is necessary to perform a separate analysis for each one. Clearly, e-commerce has shaken the foundations of some industries, in particular, information product industries (such as the music, newspaper, book, and software industries) as well as other information-intense industries such as financial services. In these industries, the power of consumers has grown relative to providers, prices have fallen, and overall profitability has been challenged. In other industries, especially manufacturing, e-commerce has not greatly changed relationships with buyers, but has changed relationships with suppliers. Increasingly, manufacturing firms in entire industries have banded together to aggregate purchases, create industry exchanges or marketplaces, and outsource industrial processes in order to obtain better prices from suppliers. Throughout this book, we document these changes in industry structure and market dynamics introduced by e-commerce.

INDUSTRY VALUE CHAINS

While an industry structural analysis helps you understand the impact of e-commerce technology on the overall business environment in an industry, a more detailed industry value chain analysis can help identify more precisely just how e-commerce may change business operations at the industry level. One of the basic tools for understanding the impact of information technology on industry and firm operations is the value chain. The concept is quite simple. A **value chain** is the set of activities performed in an industry or in a firm that transforms raw inputs into final products and services. Each of these activities adds economic value to the final product; hence, the term *value chain* as an interconnected set of value-adding activities. **Figure 5.4** illustrates the six generic players in an industry value chain: suppliers, manufacturers, transporters, distributors, retailers, and customers.

> **value chain**
>
> the set of activities performed in an industry or in a firm that transforms raw inputs into final products and services

By reducing the cost of information, e-commerce offers each of the key players in an industry value chain new opportunities to maximize their positions by lowering costs and/or raising prices. For instance, manufacturers can reduce the costs they pay for goods by developing Internet-based B2B exchanges with their suppliers. Manufacturers can develop direct relationships with their customers, bypassing the costs of distributors and retailers. Distributors can develop highly efficient inventory management systems to reduce their costs, and retailers can develop highly efficient customer relationship management systems to strengthen their service to customers. Customers in turn can search for the best quality, fastest delivery, and lowest prices, thereby lowering their transaction costs and reducing prices they pay for final goods. Finally, the operational efficiency of the entire industry can increase, lowering prices and adding value for consumers, and helping the industry to compete with alternative industries.

FIGURE 5.4   E-COMMERCE AND INDUSTRY VALUE CHAINS

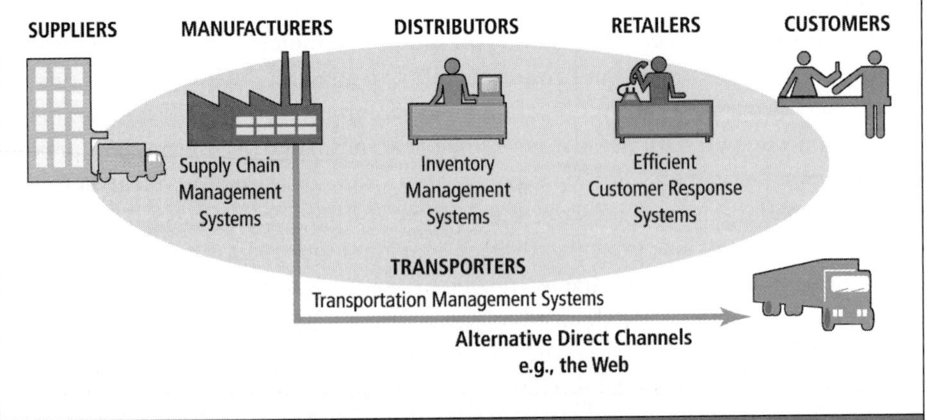

Every industry can be characterized by a set of value-adding activities performed by a variety of actors. E-commerce potentially affects the capabilities of each player as well as the overall operational efficiency of the industry.

FIRM VALUE CHAINS

The concept of value chain can be used to analyze a single firm's operational efficiency as well. The question here is: How does e-commerce technology potentially affect the value chains of firms within an industry? A **firm value chain** is the set of activities a firm engages in to create final products from raw inputs. Each step in the process of production adds value to the final product. In addition, firms develop support activities that coordinate the production process and contribute to overall operational efficiency. **Figure 5.5** illustrates the key steps and support activities in a firm's value chain.

E-commerce offers firms many opportunities to increase their operational efficiency and differentiate their products. For instance, firms can use the Internet's communications efficiency to outsource some primary and secondary activities to specialized, more efficient providers without such outsourcing being visible to the consumer. In addition, firms can use e-commerce to more precisely coordinate the steps in the value chains and reduce their costs. Finally, firms can use e-commerce to provide users with more differentiated and high-value products. For instance, Amazon provides consumers with a much larger inventory of books to choose from, at a lower cost, than traditional book stores. It also provides many services—such as instantly available professional and consumer reviews, and information on buying patterns of other consumers—that traditional bookstores cannot.

firm value chain
the set of activities a firm engages in to create final products from raw inputs

FIRM VALUE WEBS

While firms produce value through their value chains, they also rely on the value chains of their partners—their suppliers, distributors, and delivery firms. E-commerce creates new opportunities for firms to cooperate and create a value web. A **value web** is a networked business ecosystem that uses e-commerce technology to coordinate

value web
networked business ecosystem that coordinates the value chains of several firms

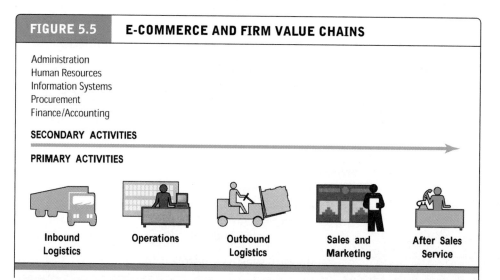

| FIGURE 5.5 | E-COMMERCE AND FIRM VALUE CHAINS |

Administration
Human Resources
Information Systems
Procurement
Finance/Accounting

SECONDARY ACTIVITIES

PRIMARY ACTIVITIES

| Inbound Logistics | Operations | Outbound Logistics | Sales and Marketing | After Sales Service |

Every firm can be characterized by a set of value-adding primary and secondary activities performed by a variety of actors in the firm. A simple firm value chain performs five primary value-adding steps: inbound logistics, operations, outbound logistics, sales and marketing, and after sales service.

the value chains of business partners within an industry, or at the first level, to coordinate the value chains of a group of firms. **Figure 5.6** illustrates a value web.

A value web coordinates a firm's suppliers with its own production needs using an Internet-based supply chain management system. We discuss these B2B systems in Chapter 12. Firms also use the Internet to develop close relationships with their logistics partners. For instance, Amazon relies on UPS tracking systems to provide its customers with online package tracking, and it relies on the U.S. Postal Service systems to insert packages directly into the mail stream. Amazon has partnership relations with hundreds of firms to generate customers and to manage relationships with customers. In fact, when you examine Amazon closely, you realize that the value it delivers to customers is in large part the result of coordination with other firms and not simply the result of activities internal to Amazon. The value of Amazon is, in large part, the value delivered by its value web partners. This is difficult for other firms to imitate in the short run.

business strategy
a set of plans for achieving superior long-term returns on the capital invested in a business firm

profit
the difference between the price a firm is able to charge for its products and the cost of producing and distributing goods

BUSINESS STRATEGY

A **business strategy** is a set of plans for achieving superior long-term returns on the capital invested in a business firm. A business strategy is therefore a plan for making profits in a competitive environment over the long term. **Profit** is simply the differ-

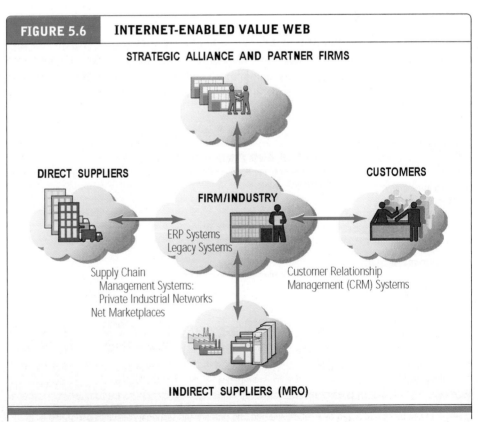

| FIGURE 5.6 | **INTERNET-ENABLED VALUE WEB** |

STRATEGIC ALLIANCE AND PARTNER FIRMS

DIRECT SUPPLIERS

FIRM/INDUSTRY

CUSTOMERS

ERP Systems
Legacy Systems

Supply Chain
Management Systems:
Private Industrial Networks
Net Marketplaces

Customer Relationship
Management (CRM) Systems

INDIRECT SUPPLIERS (MRO)

Internet technology enables firms to create an enhanced value web in cooperation with their strategic alliance and partner firms, customers, and direct and indirect suppliers.

ence between the price a firm is able to charge for its products and the cost of producing and distributing goods. Profit represents economic value. Economic value is created anytime customers are willing to pay more for a product than it costs to produce. Why would anyone pay more for a product than it costs to produce? There are multiple answers. The product may be unique (there are no other suppliers), it may be the least costly product of its type available, consumers may be able to purchase the product anywhere in the world, or it may satisfy some unique needs that other products do not. Each of these sources of economic value defines a firm's strategy for positioning its products in the marketplace. There are four generic strategies for achieving a profitable business: differentiation, cost, scope, and focus. We describe each of these below. The specific strategies that a firm follows will depend on the product, the industry, and the marketplace where competition is encountered.

Although the Internet is a unique marketplace, the same principles of strategy and business apply. As you will see throughout the book, successful e-commerce strategies involve using the Internet and mobile platform to leverage and strengthen existing business (rather than destroy your business), and to provide products and services your competitors cannot copy (in the short term anyway). That means developing unique products, proprietary content, distinguishing processes (such as Amazon's one-click shopping), and personalized or customized services and products (Porter, 2001). There are five generic business strategies: product/service differentiation, cost competition, scope, focus, and customer/supplier intimacy. Let's examine these ideas more closely.

Differentiation refers to all the ways producers can make their products or services unique and distinguish them from those of competitors. The opposite of differentiation is **commoditization**—a situation where there are no differences among products or services, and the only basis of choosing is price. As economists tell us, when price alone becomes the basis of competition and there are many suppliers and many customers, eventually the price of the good/service falls to the cost to produce it (marginal revenues from the nth unit equal marginal costs). And then profits are zero! This is an unacceptable situation for any business person. The solution is to differentiate your product or service and to create a monopoly-like situation where you are the only supplier.

There are many ways businesses differentiate their products or services. A business may start with a core generic product or service, but then create expectations among users about the "experience" of consuming the product or using the service—"Nothing equals the experience of driving a BMW." Businesses may also augment products and services by adding features to make them different from those of competitors. And businesses can differentiate their products and services further by enhancing their abilities to solve related consumer problems. For instance, tax programs such as TurboTax can import data from spreadsheet programs, as well as be used to file tax returns online. These capabilities are enhancements to the product that solve a customer's problems. The purpose of marketing is to create these differentiation features and to make the consumer aware of the unique qualities of products and services, creating in the process a "brand" that stands for these features. We discuss marketing and branding in Chapters 6 and 7.

In their totality, the differentiation features of a product or service constitute the customer value proposition we described in earlier sections of this chapter.

differentiation
refers to all the ways producers can make their products or services unique and different to distinguish them from those of competitors

commoditization
a situation where there are no differences among products or services, and the only basis of choosing is price

E-commerce offers some unique ways to differentiate products and services, such as the ability to personalize the shopping experience and to customize the product or service to the particular demands of each consumer. E-commerce businesses can also differentiate products and services by making it possible to purchase the product from home, work, or on the road (ubiquity); by making it possible to purchase anywhere in the world (global reach); by creating unique interactive content, videos, stories about users, and reviews by users (richness and interactivity); and by storing and processing information for consumers of the product or service, such as warranty information on all products purchased through a site or income tax information online (information density).

strategy of cost competition

offering products and services at a lower cost than competitors

Adopting a **strategy of cost competition** means a business has discovered some unique set of business processes or resources that other firms cannot obtain in the marketplace. Business processes are the atomic units of the value chain. For instance, the set of value-creating activities called Inbound Logistics in Figure 5.6 is in reality composed of many different collections of activities performed by people on the loading docks and in the warehouses. These different collections of activities are called *business processes*—the set of steps or procedures required to perform the various elements of the value chain.

When a firm discovers a new, more efficient set of business processes, it can obtain a cost advantage over competitors. Then it can attract customers by charging a lower price, while still making a handsome profit. Eventually, its competitors go out of business as the market decisively tilts toward the lowest-cost provider. Or, when a business discovers a unique resource, or lower-cost supplier, it can also compete effectively on cost. For instance, switching production to low-wage-cost areas of the world is one way to lower costs.

Competing on cost can be a short-lived affair and very tricky. Competitors can also discover the same or different efficiencies in production. And competitors can also move production to low-cost areas of the world. Also, competitors may decide to lose money for a period as they compete on cost.

E-commerce offers some ways to compete on cost, at least in the short term. Firms can leverage ubiquity by lowering the costs of order entry (the customer fills out all the forms, so there is no order entry department); leverage global reach and universal standards by having a single order entry system worldwide; and leverage richness, interactivity, and personalization by creating customer profiles online and treating each individual consumer differently—without the use of an expensive sales force that performed these functions in the past. Finally, firms can leverage information intensity by providing consumers with detailed information on products, without maintaining either expensive catalogs or a sales force.

While e-commerce offers powerful capabilities for intensifying cost competition, which makes cost competition appear to be a viable strategy, the danger is that competitors have access to the same technology. The *factor markets*—where producers buy supplies—are open to all. Assuming they have the skills and organizational will to use the technology, competitors can buy many of the same cost-reducing techniques in the marketplace. Even a skilled labor force can be purchased, ultimately. However, self-knowledge, proprietary tacit knowledge (knowledge that is not published or codified), and a loyal, skilled workforce are in the short term difficult to purchase in factor markets. Therefore, cost competition remains a viable strategy.

Two other generic business strategies are scope and focus. A **scope strategy** is a strategy to compete in all markets around the globe, rather than merely in local, regional, or national markets. The Internet's global reach, universal standards, and ubiquity can certainly be leveraged to assist businesses in becoming global competitors. Yahoo, for instance, along with all of the other top 20 e-commerce companies, has readily attained a global presence. A **focus/market niche strategy** is a strategy to compete within a narrow market segment or product segment. This is a specialization strategy with the goal of becoming the premier provider in a narrow market. For instance, L.L.Bean uses e-commerce to continue its historic focus on outdoor sports apparel; and W.W. Grainger—the Web's most frequently visited B2B site—focuses on the narrow MRO market segment. E-commerce offers some obvious capabilities that enable a focus strategy. Firms can leverage richness and interactivity to create highly focused messages to different market segments; information intensity makes it possible to focus e-mail and other marketing campaigns on small market segments; personalization—and related customization—means the same product can be customized and personalized to fulfill the very focused needs of specific market segments and consumers.

Another generic strategy is **customer intimacy**, which focuses on developing strong ties with customers. Strong linkages with customers increase *switching costs* (the costs of switching from one product or service to a competing product or service) and thereby enhance a firm's competitive advantage. For example, Amazon's one-click shopping that retains customer details and recommendation services based on previous purchases makes it more likely that customers will return to make subsequent purchases.

Table 5.8 summarizes the five basic business strategies.

scope strategy
competing in all markets around the globe, rather than just local, regional, or national markets

focus/market niche strategy
competing within a narrow market or product segment

customer intimacy
focuses on developing strong ties with customers in order to increase switching costs

TABLE 5.8	BUSINESS STRATEGIES	
STRATEGY	DESCRIPTION	EXAMPLE
Differentiation	Making products and services unique and different in order to distinguish them from those of competitors	Warby Parker (Vintage-inspired prescription eyeglasses)
Cost competition	Offering products and services at a lower cost than competitors	Walmart
Scope	Competing in all markets around the globe, rather than merely in local, regional, or national markets	Apple iDevices
Focus/market niche	Competing within a narrow market or product segment	Bonobos (Men's clothing)
Customer intimacy	Developing strong ties with customers	Amazon; Netflix

Industry structure, industry and firm value chains, value webs, and business strategy are central business concepts used throughout this book to analyze the viability of and prospects for e-commerce sites. In particular, the signature case studies found at the end of each chapter are followed by questions that may ask you to identify the competitive forces in the case, or analyze how the case illustrates changes in industry structure, industry and firm value chains, and business strategy.

E-COMMERCE TECHNOLOGY AND BUSINESS MODEL DISRUPTION

disruptive technologies

technologies that underpin a business model disruption

digital disruption

a business model disruption that is driven by changes in information technology

While e-commerce has changed most industries in terms of their structure, processes, and strategies, in some cases e-commerce has radically changed entire industries, driving incumbent firms out of business, greatly altering the economics of an industry, and spawning entirely new firms and value chains (Schumpeter, 1942). When new technologies are at the core of a change in the way business is done, they are referred to as **disruptive technologies**. When the technology involved is digital, the term **digital disruption** is used. Usually it is not the technology per se that is disruptive—in fact, it can be rather ordinary and commonplace. Instead, the disruption occurs when an innovative firm applies the technology to pursue a different business model and strategy than existing firms, perhaps discovering a whole new market that existing firms did not even know existed (Bower and Christensen, 1995; Christensen and Leslie, 2000). For instance, personal computers using off-the-shelf inexpensive processors and technologies disrupted the market for mainframe and mini-computers. All the eight elements of a business model identified previously can be affected by disruptive technologies, from the business value proposition to the revenue model, market opportunity, competitive environment, competitive advantage, market strategy, organizational development, and management. In short, it's a whole new world that often confuses and surprises successful companies who tend to dismiss and mock the early disruptive products. For instance, the entrepreneurs who introduced personal computers identified an entire new market of customers that had been ignored by the large computer firms, along with new price points, competitive factors, and market strategy, using new organizational and management teams. Many existing firms could not compete, and dissolved. Similar dynamics can be found in communications (disrupted by e-mail), data storage, music, photography, publishing, and transportation (Lepore, 2014). In 2014, firms like Uber and Airbnb are beginning to have an impact on the taxi and lodging industries, which may be disrupted in several years if these newer firms succeed.

sustaining technologies

technologies that enable the incremental improvement of products and services

disruptors

the entrepreneurs and their business firms that lead a business model disruption

Not all technologies are disruptive. In fact, most successful companies use technology to sustain their current business models, industry structre, processes, and strategies. This use of technology is referred to as **sustaining technology** because it helps companies to cope with competitive pressures and improve their products, and serve their customers with less expensive, more powerful, or unique products. But the same technology can be used by innovative entrepreneurs (**disruptors**) to destroy existing business models. Here's how it works.

Successful companies use whatever technology is available to incrementally improve their products, focusing on the customer by improving quality, price, and service. The incumbent and dominant firms seek to maintain the status quo in an industry, and their firms. In the first disruptive stage, disruptors, often funded by new sources of finance, introduce new products that are less expensive, less capable, and of poorer quality. The first personal computers used relatively unsophisticated technology compared to mainframe computers of the 1970s. These early products nevertheless find a niche in a market that incumbents do not serve or are unaware of. In the second stage, disruptors improve their products at a rapid pace, taking advantage of newer technologies at a faster pace than incumbents, expanding their niche market, and eventually attracting a larger customer base from the incumbents' market. When word processors, and eventually Microsoft Office, were married to the more powerful PC of the 1980s, they attracted a new market of business managers and professionals that was not served by incumbents. The concept was entirely new at the time. The successful incumbents never thought business professionals, let alone people working at home, would like to have a computer at their desk to create documents, build spreadsheets, and make presentation slides. The people and companies that developed personal computers were outsiders to the mainframe computer industry. They were disruptors. They had the vision.

In the third stage, the new products and business model become good enough, and even superior to products offered by incumbents. In the fourth stage, incumbent companies lose market share, and either go out of business or are consolidated into other more successful firms that serve a much more limited customer base. Some incumbents survive by finding new customers for their existing product, adopting some of the newer products and business models in separate divisions of their firms, or moving into other often nearby markets. For instance, mainframe computers are still made by IBM, but they are one of the few survivors. They survived by sustaining innovation in their traditional market of large-scale computing for Fortune 500 firms, moving into computing services, data centers, enterprise software, and most recently cloud computing, business analytics, data mining, and machine learning. As for the PC industry, it is currently being disrupted by smartphones and tablet computers, created by outsiders who played a small role in the personal computer world, and who have identified huge consumer markets that incumbent PC manufacturers did not realize even existed. They have the vision, for now, but they face new digital disruptors sure to follow.

Why don't the existing companies realize the changes that are coming, and take steps to compete directly with the disruptors? Successful incumbents usually have enormous capital reserves, in-depth technology and intellectual skills, and access to prestigious management consulting firms. Why didn't Kodak see the transition to digital photography? Why didn't Canon see the smartphone camera as a powerful competitor to digital cameras? Why don't firms disrupt their own business models? The answers are complex. Incumbent technologists and professionals may be trained in an *unfit fitness*, having the wrong skills for the current environment. Shareholders expect returns on investment, not destruction of a firm's historic and cherished profitable products. The existing customer base comes to expect continuous improvement in existing products—not a business disruption, but business as usual. These powerful practices, all of which make good business sense, prevent incumbent firms from meeting the challenges of business model disruption. It is unclear at this time if the two most innovative firms in the current e-commerce environment, Apple and Google, will prove any different from previous incumbents.

CASE STUDY

Freemium
Takes Pandora Public

Pandora is the Internet's most successful radio service. As of May 2014, it had over 250 million registered users (200 million of which access the service via a mobile device) and 77 million active listeners. Pandora now accounts for more than 70% of all Internet radio listening hours and a 9% share of total U.S. radio listening (both traditional and Internet).

At Pandora, users select a genre of music based on a favorite musician, and a computer algorithm puts together a personal radio station that plays not only the music of the selected artist but also closely related music by different artists. A team of professional musicians listens to new songs each day and classifies the music according to more than 450 musical criteria. These criteria are used in a computer algorithm to classify new songs into various genres. Within each of these genres are hundreds of subgenres. Altogether, Pandora has a database of over 1 million analyzed songs from over 100,000 artists.

Pandora's founders, Will Glaser and Tim Westergren, launched Pandora in 2005. Their biggest challenge was how to make a business out of a totally new kind of online

© NetPhotos / Alamy

radio station when competing online stations were making music available for free, many without advertising, and online subscription services were streaming music for a monthly fee and finding some advertising support as well. Online music illegally downloaded from P2P networks for free was also a significant factor, as was iTunes, which by 2005 was a roaring success, charging 99 cents a song. The idea of a "personal" radio station playing your kind of music was very new.

Facing stiff odds, Pandora's first business model was to give away 10 hours of free access, and then ask subscribers to pay $36 a month for a year after they used up their free 10 hours. The result: 100,000 people listened to their 10 hours for free and then refused to pay for the annual service. People loved Pandora but were unwilling to pay for it, or so it seemed in the early years.

Facing financial collapse, in November 2005 Pandora introduced an ad-supported option. Subscribers could listen to a maximum of 40 hours of music in a calendar month for free. After the 40 hours were used up, subscribers had three choices: (a) pay 99 cents for the rest of the month, (b) sign up for a premium service offering unlimited usage, or (c) do nothing. If they chose (c), the music would stop, but users could sign up again the next month. The ad-supported business model was a risky move because Pandora had no ad server or accounting system, but it attracted so many users that in a few weeks it had a sufficient number of advertisers (including Apple) to pay for its infrastructure. In 2006, Pandora added a "Buy" button to each song being played and struck deals with Amazon, iTunes, and other online retail sites. Pandora now gets an affiliate fee for directing listeners to Amazon where users can buy the music. In 2008, Pandora added an iPhone app to allow users to sign up from their smartphones and listen all day if they wanted. By 2009, this "free" ad-supported model had attracted 20 million users.

Still not giving up on its premium service, in late 2009, the company launched Pandora One, a premium service that offered no advertising, higher-quality streaming music, a desktop app, and fewer usage limits. The service cost $36 a year. This time around they met with much more success, so much so that Pandora went public in June 2011. By 2013, it had over $600 million in revenue with about 80% coming from advertising and the remainder from subscriptions and other sources. However, Pandora has not yet shown a profit, and does face competition from services such as Spotify, which also is using the freemium strategy.

Pandora is an example of the freemium business strategy. A freemium strategy is based on giving away some products or services for free while relying on a certain percentage of customers to pay for premium versions of the same product or service. As Chris Anderson, author of *Free: The Future of a Radical Price,* has pointed out, because the marginal cost of digital products is typically close to zero, providing free product does not cost much, and potentially enables you to reach many more people, and if the market is very large, even getting just 1% of that market to purchase could be very lucrative. There are many other examples of successful freemium strategy companies. Other notable success stories include LinkedIn, a social network for career-oriented and job networking that offers some basic services for free, such as creating a profile and making connections, but which charges for premium services, and Dropbox, a cloud storage and file sharing service that provides 2 gigabytes of cloud storage for free, but charges for additional storage. Freemium has been the standard business model for most apps, with over 65% of the top 100 apps in Apple's App Store using a freemium strategy. But it won't work for every online business.

While freemium clearly has worked for Pandora, LinkedIn, and Dropbox, there is ongoing debate among e-commerce CEOs and venture capitalists about the effectiveness of the freemium strategy. The crux of the issue is that while freemium can be an efficient way to gather a large group of potential customers, companies have found that it's a challenge to convert eyeballs into those willing to pay. Absent subscriber revenue, firms need to rely on advertising revenues.

MailChimp's story is both a success and a cautionary tale. The company lets anyone send e-mail to customers, manage subscriber lists, and track the performance of an e-mail marketing campaign. Despite the powerful tools it gives marketers, and its open applications programming interface, after 10 years in business, the company had only 85,000 paid subscribers.

In 2009, CEO Ben Chestnut decided that it was time to implement new strategies to attract additional customers. MailChimp began giving away its basic tools and charging subscription fees for special features. The concept was that as those customers' e-mail lists grew, they would continue using MailChimp and be willing to pay for enhanced services. These services included more than just the ability to send e-mails to a greater number of people. Clients would pay to use sophisticated analytics to help them target their e-marketing campaigns more efficiently and effectively.

In just over a year, MailChimp went from 85,000 to 450,000 users. E-mail volume went from 200 million a month to around 700 million. Most importantly, the number of paying customers increased more than 150%, while profit increased more than 650%! Sounds great, but there was also a price to pay. The company also saw a significant increase in abuse of its system. As a result, they were forced to develop an algorithm to help them to find and eliminate spammers using their service.

For MailChimp, freemium has been worth the price. It currently supports more than 6 million subscribers worldwide, sending about 10 billion e-mails a month. However, Ning, a company originally founded to enable users to create their own social networks, tried freemium and came to a different conclusion.

Marc Andreessen, co-author of Mosaic, the first Web browser, and founder of Netscape, launched Ning in 2004. With his assistance, the company has raised $119 million in funding. Despite being the market's leading social network infrastructure platform, Ning was having a common problem—converting eyeballs into paying customers. While 13% of customers were paying for some premium services, the revenue was not enough. The more free users Ning acquired, the more it cost the company.

In May 2010, Ning announced the impending end of its freemium strategy. The company shed staff, going from 167 to 98, and began using 100% of its resources to capture premium users. Since shifting to a three-tier paid subscription model, Ning has experienced explosive growth, increasing the number of paying customers from 17,000 to more than 100,000 and growing revenue by more than 500%. By September 2011, Ning had more than 100 million registered user social profiles and its social networks reached more than 60 million monthly unique users. In December 2011, Ning was

SOURCES: "Pandora Announces May 2014 Audience Metrics," June 4, 2014; "Making 'Freemium' Work," by Vineet Kumar, *Harvard Business Review*, May 2014; "Pandora's Improved Algorithms Yield More Listening Hours," *Wall Street Journal*, April 1, 2014; Annual Report on Form 10-K, February 5, 2014; "How MailChimp Learned to Treat Data Like Orange Juice and Rethink the Email in the Process," by Derrick Harris, Gigaom.com, May 5, 2013; "Remember Ning? Once-buzzy Social Network Has Relaunched Again as a Publishing Platform," by Eliza Kern, Gigaom.com, March 25, 2013; "When Freemium Fails," by Sarah E. Needleman and Angus Loten, *Wall Street Journal*, August 22, 2012; "Glam Media Completes Ning Acquisition," press release, December 5, 2011; "Pandora IPO Prices at $16; Valuation $2.6 Billion," by Eric Savitz, Blogs.forbes.com, June 14, 2011; "Social-Networking Site Ning: Charging Users Works for Us," by Jennifer Valentino-DeVries, *Wall Street Journal*, April 13, 2011; "Explainer: What Is the Freemium Business Model," by Pascal-Emmanuel Gobry, *San Francisco Chronicle*, April 8, 2011; "Shattering Myths About 'Freemium' Services: Mobility is Key," by Martin Scott, *WirelessWeek*, April 7, 2011; "Going Freemium: One Year Later," by Ben Chestnut, Blog.mailchimp.com, September 27, 2010; "How To Avoid The Traps and Make a 'Freemium' Business Model Pay," Anna Johnson, Kikabink.com, June 14th, 2010; "6 Ways for Online Business Directories to Convert More Freemium to Premium," BusinessWeek.com, April 14, 2010; "Case Studies in Freemium: Pandora, Dropbox, Evernote, Automattic and MailChimp," by Liz Gannes, Gigacom.com, March 26, 2010; *Free: The Future of a Radical Price*, by Chris Anderson, Hyperion, 2009.

acquired by Glam Media, a leading social media company, for $200 million. In March 2013, Glam relaunched Ning as a personal blogging platform for brands and individuals to bring all of their social media followers together in one place. This version of Ning will attempt to intertwine content publishing with community. Glam intends to charge users a fee, rather than returning to a free or freemium strategy.

So when does it make sense to include freemium in a business plan? It makes sense when the product is easy to use and has a very large potential audience, preferably in the millions. Using a freemium strategy can be a very success marketing tool, because free features can help attract a user base, and are more attractive to most consumers than 30-day free trials that require a cancellation process. A solid customer value proposition is critical. It's helpful if a large user network increases the perceived value of the product (i.e., a dating service such as Match). Freemium may work when a company has good long-term customer retention rates and the product produces more value over time. An extremely important part of the equation is that the variable costs of providing the product or service to additional customers for free must be low.

Companies also face challenges in terms of determining what products and/or services to offer for free versus what to charge for (this may change over time), the cost of supporting free customers, and how to price premium services. Further, it is difficult to predict attrition rates, which are highly variable at companies using freemium. So, while freemium can be a great way to get early users and to provide a company with a built-in pool for upgrades, it's tough to determine how many users will be willing to pay and willing to stay.

A freemium strategy makes sense for companies such as Pandora, where there is a very low marginal cost, approaching zero, to support free users. It also makes sense for a company where the value to its potential customers depends on a large network, like LinkedIn. Freemium also works when a business can be supported by the percentage of customers who are willing to pay, like Pandora, especially when there are other revenues like advertising fees that can make up for shortfalls in subscriber revenues.

Case Study Questions

1. Compare Pandora's original business model with its current business model. What's the difference between "free" and "freemium" revenue models?

2. What is the customer value proposition that Pandora offers?

3. Why did MailChimp ultimately succeed with a freemium model but Ning did not?

4. What's the most important consideration when considering a freemium revenue model?

5.6 REVIEW

KEY CONCEPTS

■ **Identify the key components of e-commerce business models.**

A successful business model effectively addresses eight key elements:
- *Value proposition*—how a company's product or service fulfills the needs of customers. Typical e-commerce value propositions include personalization, customization, convenience, and reduction of product search and price delivery costs.
- *Revenue model*—how the company plans to make money from its operations. Major e-commerce revenue models include the advertising model, subscription model, transaction fee model, sales model, and affiliate model.
- *Market opportunity*—the revenue potential within a company's intended marketspace.
- *Competitive environment*—the direct and indirect competitors doing business in the same marketspace, including how many there are and how profitable they are.
- *Competitive advantage*—the factors that differentiate the business from its competition, enabling it to provide a superior product at a lower cost.
- *Market strategy*—the plan a company develops that outlines how it will enter a market and attract customers.
- *Organizational development*—the process of defining all the functions within a business and the skills necessary to perform each job, as well as the process of recruiting and hiring strong employees.
- *Management team*—the group of individuals retained to guide the company's growth and expansion.

■ **Describe the major B2C business models.**

There are a number of different business models being used in the B2C e-commerce arena. The major models include the following:
- *Portal*—offers powerful search tools plus an integrated package of content and services; typically utilizes a combined subscription/advertising revenue/transaction fee model; may be general or specialized (vortal).
- *E-tailer*—online version of traditional retailer; includes virtual merchants (online retail store only), bricks-and-clicks e-tailers (online distribution channel for a company that also has physical stores), catalog merchants (online version of direct mail catalog), and manufacturers selling directly to the consumer.
- *Content provider*—information and entertainment companies that provide digital content; typically utilizes an advertising, subscription, or affiliate referral fee revenue model.
- *Transaction broker*—processes online sales transactions; typically utilizes a transaction fee revenue model.
- *Market creator*—uses Internet technology to create markets that bring buyers and sellers together; typically utilizes a transaction fee revenue model.
- *Service provider*—offers services online.
- *Community provider*—provides an online community of like-minded individuals for networking and information sharing; revenue is generated by advertising, referral fees, and subscriptions.

■ **Describe the major B2B business models.**

The major business models used to date in the B2B arena include:
- *E-distributor*—supplies products directly to individual businesses.
- *E-procurement*—single firms create digital markets for thousands of sellers and buyers.

- *Exchange*—independently owned digital marketplace for direct inputs, usually for a vertical industry group.
- *Industry consortium*—industry-owned vertical digital market.
- *Private industrial network*—industry-owned private industrial network that coordinates supply chains with a limited set of partners.

■ Understand key business concepts and strategies applicable to e-commerce.

E-commerce has had a major impact on the business environment in the last decade, and have affected:

- *Industry structure*—the nature of players in an industry and their relative bargaining power by changing the basis of competition among rivals, the barriers to entry, the threat of new substitute products, the strength of suppliers, and the bargaining power of buyers.
- *Industry value chains*—the set of activities performed in an industry by suppliers, manufacturers, transporters, distributors, and retailers that transforms raw inputs into final products and services by reducing the cost of information and other transaction costs.
- *Firm value chains*—the set of activities performed within an individual firm to create final products from raw inputs by increasing operational efficiency.
- *Business strategy*—a set of plans for achieving superior long-term returns on the capital invested in a firm by offering unique ways to differentiate products, obtain cost advantages, compete globally, or compete in a narrow market or product segment.

QUESTIONS

1. What distinguishes an e-commerce business plan from a traditional business plan?
2. Identify and describe the business model element that specifies how the company's product will fulfill the needs of its customers.
3. How can e-commerce technologies be used to improve a firm's value web?
4. What is a freemium strategy?
5. What is a disruptive technology, and how does it differ from a sustaining technology?
6. What types of services does Amazon provide for businesses? Which e-commerce business models do Amazon's services fall into?
7. What is a sharing economy company?
8. Why would a firm decide to engage in a strategy of cost competition?
9. What are the benefits offered by incubator investor firms over other traditional sources of capital?
10. Why is it difficult to categorize e-commerce business models?
11. What is an industry structural analysis and what is its place in the e-commerce business plan?
12. What has been the effect of e-commerce technologies on general interfirm rivalry?
13. What revenue models do content providers use, and what is the key to becoming a successful content provider?
14. What disadvantages are faced by "first-mover" companies entering a marketspace?
15. What are the major similarities and differences between exchanges and e-distributors?
16. Describe the feature of information density as it applies to e-commerce technology and describe how it has affected the business environment over the past decade.
17. Who are the major players in an industry value chain and how are they impacted by e-commerce technology?
18. What are five generic business strategies for achieving a profitable business?
19. Define market opportunity and describe how you would determine a new company's realistic market opportunity.

20. What is crowdfunding and how does it help e-commerce companies raise capital?

PROJECTS

1. Select an e-commerce company. Visit its Web site and describe its business model based on the information you find there. Identify its customer value proposition, its revenue model, the marketspace it operates in, who its main competitors are, any comparative advantages you believe the company possesses, and what its market strategy appears to be. Also try to locate information about the company's management team and organizational structure. (Check for a page labeled "the Company," "About Us," or something similar.)

2. Examine the experience of shopping online versus shopping in a traditional environment. Imagine that you have decided to purchase a digital camera (or any other item of your choosing). First, shop for the camera in a traditional manner. Describe how you would do so (for example, how you would gather the necessary information you would need to choose a particular item, what stores you would visit, how long it would take, prices, etc.). Next, shop for the item on the Web or via a mobile app. Compare and contrast your experiences. What were the advantages and disadvantages of each? Which did you prefer and why?

3. Visit eBay and look at the many types of auctions available. If you were considering establishing a rival specialized online auction business, what are the top three market opportunities you would pursue, based on the goods and auction community in evidence at eBay? Prepare a report or slide presentation to support your analysis and approach.

4. During the early days of e-commerce, first-mover advantage was touted as one way to success. On the other hand, some suggest that being a market follower can yield rewards as well. Which approach has proven to be more successful—first mover or follower? Choose two e-commerce companies that prove your point, and prepare a brief presentation to explain your analysis and position.

5. Select an e-commerce company that has participated in an incubator program such as Y-Combinator, TechStars, DreamIt Ventures, Capital Factory, or another of your choosing, and write a short report on its business model and the amount and sources of capital it has raised thus far. Include your views on the company's future prospects for success.

6. Select a B2C e-commerce retail industry segment such as pet products, sporting goods, or toys, and analyze its value chain and industry value chain. Prepare a short presentation that identifies the major industry participants in that business and illustrates the move from raw materials to finished product.

REFERENCES

Arthur, W. Brian. "Increasing Returns and the New World of Business." *Harvard Business Review* (July-August 1996).

Bakos, Yannis. "The Emerging Role of Electronic Marketplaces on the Internet." *Communications of the ACM* (August 1998).

Barney, J. B. "Firm Resources and Sustained Competitive Advantage." *Journal of Management* Vol. 17, No. 1 (1991).

Bellman, Steven; Gerald L. Lohse; and Eric J. Johnson. "Predictors of Online Buying Behavior." *Communications of the ACM* (December 1999).

comScore, "comScore Releases July 2014 U.S. Top 50 Web Property, Search and Online Video Rankings." (August 18, 2014).

eBay, Inc. "eBay Inc. Reports Second Quarter Results." (July 16, 2014).

Kambil, Ajit. "Doing Business in the Wired World." *IEEE Computer* (May 1997).

Kambil, Ajit; Ari Ginsberg; and Michael Bloch. "Reinventing Value Propositions." Working Paper, NYU Center for Research on Information Systems (1998).

Kanter, Elizabeth Ross. "The Ten Deadly Mistakes of Wanna-Dots." *Harvard Business Review* (January 2001).

Kaplan, Steven, and Mohanbir Sawhney. "E-Hubs: The New B2B Marketplaces." *Harvard Business Review* (May-June 2000).

Kim, W. Chan, and Renee Mauborgne. "Knowing a Winning Business Idea When You See One." *Harvard Business Review* (September-October 2000).

Magretta, Joan. "Why Business Models Matter." *Harvard Business Review* (May 2002).

Porter, Michael E. "Strategy and the Internet." *Harvard Business Review* (March 2001).

Porter, Michael E. *Competitive Advantage: Creating and Sustaining Superior Performance.* New York: Free Press (1985).

Rigdon, Joan I. "The Second-Mover Advantage." *Red Herring* (September 1, 2000).

Teece, David J. "Profiting from Technological Innovation: Implications for Integration, Collaboration, Licensing and Public Policy." *Research Policy* 15 (1986).

E-commerce Marketing and Advertising

After reading this chapter, you will be able to:

- Understand the key features of the Internet audience, the basic concepts of consumer behavior and purchasing, and how consumers behave online.
- Identify and describe the basic digital commerce marketing and advertising strategies and tools.
- Identify and describe the main technologies that support online marketing.
- Understand the costs and benefits of online marketing communications.

InMobi's

Global Mobile Ad Network

Watch out tech titans! An innovative Bangalore, India-based startup, InMobi, is making some serious waves in the global mobile advertising network marketplace currently dominated by Google, Facebook, and Twitter. InMobi was founded in early 2007 by four graduates of the Indian Institute of Technology, including Naveen Tewari. After unsuccessful attempts at SMS-based mobile search and a mobile-based deals company specifically for Mumbai, Tewari and his co-founders scrambled to come up with a new idea. With the last of their personal funds, they honed in on mobile advertising. Apple had just introduced the iPhone in

© fotografiedk/Fotolia.com

early 2007, and few companies were focusing yet on the cellphone as a mobile advertising platform. This new idea proved to be the company's golden ticket, and in 2008, Tewari convinced venture firm Kleiner Perkins Caufield & Byers, and Sherpalo Investments to make an $8 million investment in the company. They then moved to Bangalore, deeming it a better location from which to attract talent, and later changed the name of the company to InMobi.

InMobi bills itself as a mobile advertising platform and solutions provider. It acts as an intermediary between companies that want to advertise and content owners/publishers that offer mobile content, often in the form of apps. For instance, if you've seen the advertisements that appear when you play the Angry Birds games on an Android smartphone, you've seen InMobi's mobile ad platform at work. InMobi serves almost 140 billion mobile ads a month to over 870 million consumers in over 200 countries. There are over 30,000 apps and mobile sites on the inMobi network, and its mobile app install ads have led to over 50 million downloads. Although it is a private company, InMobi's revenues in 2013 are believed to have been over $500 million, although it has not yet shown a profit. It makes money by keeping a percentage of the revenue per ad, typically 30–40%. Increasingly, InMobi has focused on native advertising as the marketplace abandons banner ads and moves towards more creative and interactive formats. Native advertising appears seamlessly within an app and often appears as if it were a post from a friend. InMobi's customers include Unilever, Samsung, Microsoft, Adidas, and countless other prominent companies and brands.

SOURCES: "InMobi in Numbers: Close to 138B Ad Impressions, Reaching 872M Users a Month," by Anand Rai, Techcircle.in, November 10, 2014; "InMobi Claims That It Reaches 872 Million Active Unique Users," by Aparajita Saxena, Medianama.com, November 7, 2014; "Think They're Tracking You Now? Wait Till InMobi's Unveiling Next Month," by Richard Byrne Reilly, Venturebeat.com, October 16, 2014; "InMobi Takes a Bold Stand: But How Much Can They Really Guarantee?" by Michael Essany, Mobilemarketing-watch.com, October 14, 2014; "InMobi Has Positioned Itself as the Go-To Company In Mobile Advertising," by Deepak Ajwani, *Forbes India*, October 10, 2014; "InMobi and Rubicon Project Unveil Exchange for Mobile Native Ads," by Lauren Johnson, *AdWeek*, May 29, 2014; "InMobi decoded: How Bangalore-based firm is taking on Google and Facebook," by Peerzada Abrar & Krithika Krishnamurthy, *The Economic Times*, March 7, 2014; "The Next Infosys - Tapping the Mobile Entertainment Space - InMobi," by Anirban Sen, LiveMint.com, January 10, 2014; "inMobi Launches New AppGalleries, a White Label Web App Store for Publishers to Curate Apps, and Boost Mobile Ads," by Ingrid Lunden, techcrunch.com, October 22, 2013; "InMobi and Mindshare Win Top Awards for Innovation and In-App Advertising," inMobi, October 14, 2013; "InMobi Claims New IAB Ad Formats Prompt Tenfold Spike to Interactions," by Zen Terrelonge, mobile-ent.biz, September 23, 2013; "InMobi Australia's Latest Mobile Insights Report for Q2 Reveals Mobile Advertising has Doubled," campaignbrief.com, August 15, 2013; "InMobi in the IPO Wings," sramanamitra.com, August 2nd, 2013; "How inMobil Grew from a Startup to a Giant Mobile Ad Network," by Willis Wee, Techinasia.com, May 16, 2013; "InMobi Now Serves Ads to 691m Unique Users a Month," by Zen Terrelonge, mobile-ent.biz, May 1, 2013; "InMobi Named to MIT Technology Review's 2013 50 Disruptive Companies List Recog-

From the very beginning, CEO Tewari and his co-founders knew that they wanted to have a global presence. It used a "reverse market strategy," establishing leadership positions in Asia and Africa first and then tackling the European Union and U.S. markets. Today it employs 800 people and has offices around the world, including in India, Asia (China, Singapore, Malaysia, Korea, Taiwan, Japan), Australia, the European Union (Germany, the United Kingdom, Spain, France, Sweden), the Middle East (U.A.E.), and the United States (San Francisco). Fueled in part by a $200 million investment from Japanese media and telecommunications giant Softbank that valued InMobi at over $1 billion, InMobi is focusing on growth in the U.S. currently and plans to focus next on Russia and Latin America, where growth in mobile users is expected to rise the fastest. Softbank believes that its partnership with InMobi will help Softbank become the lead Internet company in Asia. InMobi has also used funds to make some strategic purchases, including MMTG Labs, a developer of an application market for Facebook pages, Appstores.com, and Overlay Media, which helps to deliver more highly targeted and context-sensitive ads.

Can InMobi truly hope to challenge Google, which currently is the dominant leader with about a 60% market share? Its $500 million in revenues still trails behind Google's $1 billion in revenue from mobile advertising. Nonetheless, Tewari thinks so, claiming that InMobi is currently second, with a market share of more than 10%, and that the company is on a trajectory to become one of the top 10 Internet companies by 2020. InMobi boasts a multi-million dollar partnership with Amobee, which services a large portfolio of Fortune 500 brands that will now be using InMobi's ad network. Tewari also points to InMobi's primary focus on mobile, compared to Google, which is involved in many different areas. InMobi also claims that its technology is superior and that its data on customers is richer and more granular. Tewari boldly claims that inMobi is one of the largest players on the planet that understands user behavior.

Tewari's confidence stems from InMobi's appographic targeting system, which uses algorithms and data on how users interact with apps to determine very precise trends and preferences of those users. To develop the system, InMobi studied over 100,000 apps and how different types of consumers used them. The result is a system so accurate that InMobi has guaranteed 2–3% increases in engagement by app developers using InMobi's services. In 2014, InMobi continued to innovate, honing the Geo Context Targeting system used in its Smart Ads, which it says generate ten times the interaction compared to traditional ads, and more than three times the conversion rate of traditional ads. SmartAds support rich media and are tailored based on users' personal details and geographic conditions in the area, such as location and weather nearby. For example, if you're strolling city streets on a hot summer afternoon, you'll be given advertisements for cold beverages from nearby food chains. InMobi's emphasis on data drives its product offerings, prompting Tewari to describe InMobi as "a data company," not an advertising company.

InMobi also launched several new advertising platforms in 2014, including an interactive video ad platform as well as a native ad exchange, to help advertisers boost their sales on mobile beyond Facebook and Google. InMobi's video ad platform focuses on contextualized mobile video ads using its advanced targeting system. InMobi's native ad exchange, developed in tandem with programmatic advertising service provider Rubicon Project, is the first that allows buying and selling of mobile native advertising on a global scale.

Tewari realizes that the competition is about to get a lot tougher, but believes his company is well-positioned, particularly due to its global scope. Although InMobi is at a disadvantage because Google, Facebook and Twitter have major social media platforms and services with which they can provide mobile advertising, the market for independent native ad networks which are not affiliated with these companies is estimated to be between $8 and $10 billion annually. For many advertisers, advertising with InMobi may be more cost effective than developing individual advertisements for Google, Facebook, Twitter, and other services of sufficient size. On the other hand, users spend much more time on these bigger sites than they do anywhere else, which complicates things for inMobi. The mobile advertising marketplace is expected to become so large (it is estimated that over $500 billion will be spent by mobile advertisers over the next 10 years) that there is plenty of room for more than just one company to benefit. InMobi also claims that its margins are a whopping 40% compared to just 5–10% in the TV and print advertising industry, and when asked whether users are tired of all the advertising, Tewari counters that users are tired of irrelevant ads, not advertising in general. Many analysts believe that InMobi is close to launching an IPO, as the global mobile advertising market continues to grow rapidly and InMobi's future prospects get brighter.

nizing World's Most Innovative Companies," InMobi.com, February 20, 2013; "InMobi Acquires Overlay Media," InMobi, January 8, 2013; "Desi Software Product Company Takes Global Tech Giants Head-on," by Bibhu Ranjan Mishra, Business-standard.com, November 19, 2012; "InMobi Names Ex-Google Exec as North America Head," by Mark Walsh, Media-post.com, October 30, 2012; "Softbank-backed Mobile Ad Giant InMobi Pulls Out of Africa and Russia Over Its Poor Performance," by Jon Russell, Thenextweb.com, October 30, 2012; "Smart Mobile Ads 'Turn to the Sun' by Tracking Conversions," Marketingmag.com/au, October 23, 2012; "InMobi Wins Three Smartie Awards for Excellence in Mobile Advertising," InMobi, October 16, 2012; "InMobi Voted Number One Mobile Advertising Network in Malaysia," InMobi, October 11, 2012; "Make Your Dream a Success," InMobi, September 3, 2012; "Mobile Ad Network InMobi Continues Buying Spree, Picks Up Metaflow Solutions for App Distribution," by Ingrid Lunden, Techcrunch.con, July 31, 2012; "The New Poster Boys of Start-Ups," by Kushan Mitra, *Business Today*, November 1, 2011; "Softbank Invests $200M in InMobi," by Jamie Yap, ZDnet.com, September 15, 2011; "InMobi Raises Massive $200M to Overtake Google in Mobile Ads," by Matt Marshall, Venturebeat.com, September 15, 2011; "HTML Ad Builder Sprout Acquired by InMobi," by Jason Kincaid, Techcrunch.com, August 2, 2011; "InMobi Signs "Multi-million Dollar" Mobile Ad Partnership with Amobee," by Steve O'Hear, Techcrunch.com, May 11, 2011.

Perhaps no area of business has been more affected by Internet and mobile platform technologies than marketing and marketing communications. As a communications tool, the Internet affords marketers new ways of contacting millions of potential customers at costs far lower than traditional media. The Internet also provides new ways—often instantaneous and spontaneous—to gather information from customers, adjust product offerings, and increase customer value. The Internet has spawned entirely new ways to identify and communicate with customers, including search engine marketing, social network marketing, behavioral targeting, and targeted e-mail, among others.

The Internet was just the first transformation. Today, the mobile platform based on smartphones and tablet computers is transforming online marketing and communications yet again. The key changes in 2014 involve social networks, mobile marketing, and location-based services, including local marketing, as well as the increasing prevalence of digital video ads, as discussed in the opening case. **Table 6.1** summarizes some of the significant new developments in online marketing and advertising for 2014–2015.

The subject of online marketing, branding, and market communications is very broad and deep. We have created two chapters to cover the material. In this chapter, we begin by examining consumer behavior on the Web, the major types of online marketing and branding, and the technologies that support advances in online marketing. We then focus on understanding the costs and benefits of online marketing communications. In Chapter 7, we focus on the social, mobile, and local marketing phenomenon in greater depth.

6.1   CONSUMERS ONLINE: THE INTERNET AUDIENCE AND CONSUMER BEHAVIOR

Before firms can begin to sell their products online, they must first understand what kinds of people they will find online and how those people behave in the online marketplace. In this section, we focus primarily on individual consumers in the business-to-consumer (B2C) arena. However, many of the factors discussed apply to the B2B arena as well, insofar as purchasing decisions by firms are made by individuals. For readers who have no background in marketing, we have created an online Learning Track, Learning Track 6.1, that discusses basic marketing and branding concepts.

INTERNET TRAFFIC PATTERNS: THE ONLINE CONSUMER PROFILE

We will start with an analysis of some basic background demographics of Web consumers. The first principle of marketing and sales is "know thy customer." Who is online, who shops online and why, and what do they buy? In 2014, around 2.8 billion people of all ages had access to the Internet. An estimated 640 million households worldwide (about 30% of all households) have broadband access to the Internet.

TABLE 6.1	**WHAT'S NEW IN ONLINE MARKETING AND ADVERTISING 2014–2015**

BUSINESS

- Worldwide online marketing and advertising spending continues to increase (by almost 17% in 2014), compared to only about 1%–2% for traditional media marketing and advertising.
- Mobile marketing and advertising spending continues to grow at a rate of more than 50%.
- Social media marketing and advertising channels expand, but search and display marketing remains dominant.
- Local marketing and advertising based on geolocation services like Groupon and LivingSocial take off.
- Video advertising continues to be one of the fastest growing formats.
- Search engine marketing and advertising continues its dominance, but its rate of growth is slowing somewhat compared to other formats.
- Native advertising and other forms content marketing rise.

TECHNOLOGY

- Mobile devices challenge the PC as the major online marketing and advertising platform. Smartphones and tablet computers become prevalent Web access devices.
- Big Data: online tracking produces oceans of data, challenging business analytics programs.
- Cloud computing makes rich marketing content and multi-channel, cross-platform marketing a reality.
- The Facebook, Twitter, and Pinterest platforms grow into valuable social customer relationship management tools, enabling businesses to connect with customers on social network sites.
- Programmatic advertising (automated, technology-driven method of buying and selling display ads) takes off.

SOCIETY

- Targeted advertising based on behavioral tracking on leads to growing privacy awareness and fears.
- Social network sites are accused of abusing customer profile information without providing sufficient user controls over profile distribution.
- Mobile GPS tracking of individual location information built into smartphones and other mobile devices raises privacy concerns.

Although the number of new online users increased at a rate of 30% a year or higher in the early 2000s, over the last several years, this growth rate has slowed in most parts of the world. E-commerce businesses can no longer count on a double-digit growth rate in the online population to fuel their revenues. The days of extremely rapid growth in the Internet population are over.

Intensity and Scope of Usage

The slowing rate of growth in the Internet population is compensated for, in part, by an increasing intensity and scope of use. In the United States, 71% of all adults report logging on on a typical day (Pew Research Center, 2014a). Several studies also show that a greater amount of time is being spent online by Internet users—over 2 hours a day. In 2014, mobile smartphones and tablets are major access points to the Internet and online commerce. About 2.25 billion people, about 80% of all Internet users, access the Internet using a mobile device. Owners of mobile devices spend almost 3 hours a day using them for nontelephone activities such as playing games, viewing videos, and visiting social networks (eMarketer, Inc., 2014a). Engaging in such activities is widespread—in 2014, around 147 million mobile users in the United States played games, about 90 million watched videos, 137 million visited a social network, and millions of others listened to music or shopped (eMarketer, 2014b). The more time users spend online, becoming more comfortable and familiar with Internet features and services, the more services they are likely to explore, according to the Pew Research Center.

Demographics and Access

In the United States, the demographic profile of the Internet—and e-commerce—has changed greatly since 1995. Up until 2000, single, white, young, college-educated males with high incomes dominated the Internet. This inequality in access and usage led to concerns about a possible "digital divide." However, in recent years, there has been a marked increase in Internet usage by females, minorities, seniors, and families with modest incomes, resulting in a notable decrease—but not elimination—in the earlier inequality of access and usage.

A roughly equal percentage (about 87%) of men and 86% women use the Internet today. Young adults (18–29) form the age group with the highest percentage of Internet use, at 97%. Adults in the 30–49 group (93%) are also strongly represented. Another fast-growing group online is the 65 and over segment, 57% of whom now use the Internet. Teens (12–17) also have a very high percentage of their age group online (97%). The percentage of very young children (0–11 years) online has also spurted, to 49% of that age group (eMarketer, Inc., 2014c). Variation across ethnic groups is not as wide as across age groups. Ten years ago, there were significant differences among ethnic groups, but this has receded. In 2014, user participation by whites is 85%, Hispanics, 83%, and African-Americans, 81%.

About 99% of households with income levels above $75,000 have Internet access, compared to only 77% of households earning less than $30,000. Over time, income differences have declined but they remain significant with a 22% gap between the highest category of household income and the lowest. Amount of education also makes a significant difference when it comes to online access. Of those individuals with less than a high school education, only 76% were online in 2014, compared to 97% of individuals with a college degree or more. Even some college education boosted Internet usage, with that segment reaching 91% (Pew Research Center, 2014b).

Overall, there remains a strong relationship between age, income, ethnicity, and education on one hand and Internet usage on the other. The so-called "digital divide" has indeed moderated, but it still persists along the income, education, age, and ethnic dimensions. Gender, income, education, age, and ethnicity also impact online behavior. According to the Pew Research Center, adults over the age of 65, those who have not completed high school, those who make less than $30,000 a year, and Hispanics are all less likely to purchase products online. Women are slightly more likely to purchase online than men, but not significantly so. With respect to online banking, the demographics are similar—those 65 and older are less likely than any age group to bank online, while those with at least some college are more likely than those with a high school diploma or less. Online banking is also more popular with men than women. No significant differences were found in terms of ethnicity (Pew Research Center, 2012). Other commentators have observed that children of poorer and less educated families are spending considerably more time using their access devices for entertainment (movies, games, Facebook, and texting) than children from wealthier households. For all children and teenagers, the majority of time spent on the Internet has been labeled "wasted time" because the majority of online use is for entertainment, and not education or learning (Richtel, 2012).

Type of Internet Connection: Broadband and Mobile Impacts

While a great deal of progress has been made in reducing glaring gaps in access to the Internet, there are significant inequalities in access to broadband service. In 2014, around 90 million households had broadband service in their homes—74% of all households (eMarketer, Inc., 2014d). Research by the Pew Research Center indicates that broadband adoption levels are especially low for older adults, those with low levels of education, and those with low household incomes. Rural residents, African Americans, and Latinos are also less likely to have a home broadband connection (Pew Research Center, 2013a). For marketers, the broadband audience offers unique opportunities for the use of multimedia marketing campaigns, and for the positioning of products especially suited for this more educated and affluent audience. It is also important to note that just because a household does not have broadband access, it does not mean that household members do not use the Internet. About 50% of the non-broadband adopters do use the Internet, either from another location or via a smartphone (Pew Research Center, 2013a, 2013b). The explosive growth of smart-phones and tablet computers connected to broadband cellular and Wi-Fi networks is the foundation for a truly mobile e-commerce and marketing platform, which did not exist a few years ago. Marketers are now beginning to use this new platform for brand development.

Community Effects: Social Contagion in Social Networks

For a physical retail store, the most important factor in shaping sales is location, location, location. If you are located where thousands of people pass by every day, you will tend to do well. But for Internet retailers, physical location has almost no consequence as long as customers can be served by shipping services such as UPS or the post office or their services can be downloaded to anywhere. What does make a difference for consumer purchases on the Internet is whether or not the consumer is located in "neighborhoods" where others purchase on the Internet. These neighborhoods can be either face-to-face and truly personal, or digital. These so-called neighborhood effects, and the role of social emulation in consumption decisions, are well known for goods such as personal computers. In general, there is a relationship between being a member of a social network and purchasing decisions. Yet the relationship between "connectedness" (either offline or online) and purchase decisions is not straightforward or simple. People who score in the top 10%–15% of connectedness "do their own thing" to differentiate themselves and often do not share purchase decisions with friends. In fact, highly connected users often stop purchasing what their friends purchase. One can think of them as iconoclasts. The middle 50% of connected people very often share purchase patterns of their friends.

One can think of these people as "keeping up with the Joneses" (Iyengar et al., 2009). A recent study of 6,000 social network users found that social networks have a powerful influence on shopping and purchasing behavior. An estimated 40% of social media users have purchased an item after sharing or favoriting it on Facebook, Pinterest, or Twitter. Facebook is the network most likely to drive customers to purchase, followed by Pinterest and Twitter. Unexpectedly, social networks increase research online, followed by purchase offline (sometimes referred to as ROPO), driving purchase traffic into physical stores where the product can be seen, tried, and then purchased. This is the opposite of the showrooming effect where consumers shop in stores, and then purchase online. The ROPO effect was found to be as large as the research offline-and-purchase-on-line effect (Vision Critical, 2013; Schleiger, 2013; Sevitt and Samuel, 2013).

Membership in social networks has a large influence on discovering new independent music, but less influence on already well-known products (Garg, 2009). Membership in an online brand community like Ford's Facebook page and community has a direct effect on sales (Adjei et al., 2009). Amazon's recommender systems ("Consumers who bought this item also bought ...") create co-purchase networks where people do not know one another personally, but nevertheless triple the influence of complementary products (Oestreicher-Singer and Sundararajan, 2008). The value of social networks to marketers rests on the proposition that brand strength and purchase decisions are closely related to network membership, rank, prominence, and centrality. At this point, the strength and scope of the relationship between social network membership, brand awareness, and purchase decisions is not completely understood, although all researchers agree that it exists in a variety of contexts and in varying degrees (Guo et al., 2011).

CONSUMER BEHAVIOR MODELS

consumer behavior
a social science discipline that attempts to model and understand the behavior of humans in a marketplace

Once firms have an understanding of who is online, they need to focus on how consumers behave online. The study of **consumer behavior** is a social science discipline that attempts to model and understand the behavior of humans in a marketplace. Several social science disciplines play roles in this study, including sociology, psychology, and economics. Models of consumer behavior attempt to predict or "explain" what consumers purchase and where, when, how much, and why they buy. The expectation is that if the consumer decision-making process can be understood, firms will have a much better idea how to market and sell their products. **Figure 6.1** illustrates a general consumer behavior model that takes into account a wide range of factors that influence a consumer's marketplace decisions. Learning Track 6.2 contains further information about the cultural, social, and psychological background factors that influence consumer behavior.

PROFILES OF ONLINE CONSUMERS

Online consumer behavior parallels that of offline consumer behavior with some obvious differences. It is important to first understand why people choose the Internet channel to conduct transactions. **Table 6.2** lists the main reasons consumers choose the online channel.

While price is an important consideration, consumers also shop online because of convenience, which in turn is produced largely by saving them time. Overall transaction cost reduction appears to be a major motivator for choosing the online channel.

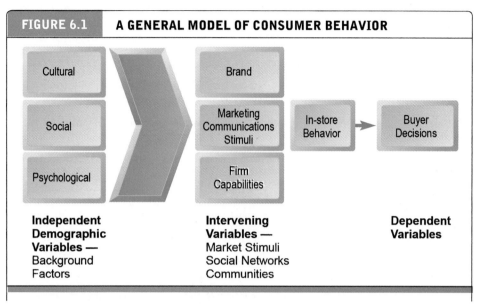

FIGURE 6.1 | **A GENERAL MODEL OF CONSUMER BEHAVIOR**

Consumer behavior models try to predict the decisions that consumers make in the marketplace.
SOURCE: Adapted from Kotler and Armstrong, 2009.

THE ONLINE PURCHASING DECISION

Once online, why do consumers actually purchase a product or service at a specific site? Among the most important reasons are price and the availability of free shipping. That the seller is someone whom the purchaser trusts is also a very important factor. The ability to make a purchase without paying tax and the availability of an online coupon are also significant factors.

TABLE 6.2 | **WHY CONSUMERS CHOOSE THE ONLINE CHANNEL**

REASON	PERCENTAGE OF RESPONDENTS
Lower prices	59%
Shop from home	53%
Shop 24/7	44%
Wider variety of products available	29%
Easier to compare and research products and offers	27%
Products only available online	22%
Online customer reviews	18%
Better product information available	7%
Promotion via e-mail or text	7%
Social media influence	1%

SOURCE: Based on data from eMarketer, Inc., 2014e

| FIGURE 6.2 | THE CONSUMER DECISION PROCESS AND SUPPORTING COMMUNICATIONS |

MARKET COMMUNICATIONS	Awareness— Need Recognition	Search	Evaluation of Alternatives	Purchase	Post-purchase Behavior— Loyalty
Offline Communications	Mass media TV Radio Print media Social networks	Catalogs Print ads Mass media Sales people Product raters Store visits Social networks	Reference groups Opinion leaders Mass media Product raters Store visits Social networks	Promotions Direct mail Mass media Print media	Warranties Service calls Parts and repair Consumer groups Social networks
Online Communications	Targeted banner ads Interstitials Targeted event promotions Social networks	Search engines Online catalogs Site visits Targeted e-mail Social networks	Search engines Online catalogs Site visits Product reviews User evaluations Social networks	Online promotions Lotteries Discounts Targeted e-mail Flash sales	Communities of consumption Newsletters Customer e-mail Online updates Social networks

You also need to consider the process that buyers follow when making a purchase decision, and how the Internet environment affects consumers' decisions. There are five stages in the consumer decision process: awareness of need, search for more information, evaluation of alternatives, the actual purchase decision, and post-purchase contact with the firm. **Figure 6.2** shows the consumer decision process and the types of offline and online marketing communications that support this process and seek to influence the consumer before, during, and after the purchase decision.

The stages of the consumer decision process are basically the same whether the consumer is offline or online. On the other hand, the general model of consumer behavior requires modification to take into account new factors, and the unique features of the Internet that allow new opportunities to interact with the customer online also need to be accounted for. In **Figure 6.3**, we have modified the general model of consumer behavior to focus on user characteristics, product characteristics, and Web site features, along with traditional factors such as brand strength and specific market communications (advertising) and the influence of both online and offline social networks.

In the online model, Web site features, along with consumer skills, product characteristics, attitudes towards online purchasing, and perceptions about control over the Web environment come to the fore. Web site features include latency (delay in downloads), navigability, and confidence in a Web site's security. There are parallels in the analog world. For instance, it is well known that consumer behavior can be influenced by store design, and that understanding the precise movements of consumers through a physical store can enhance sales if goods and promotions are arranged along the most likely consumer tracks. Consumer skills refers to the knowledge that consumers have about how to conduct online transactions (which increases with experience). Product characteristics refers to the fact that some products can be easily

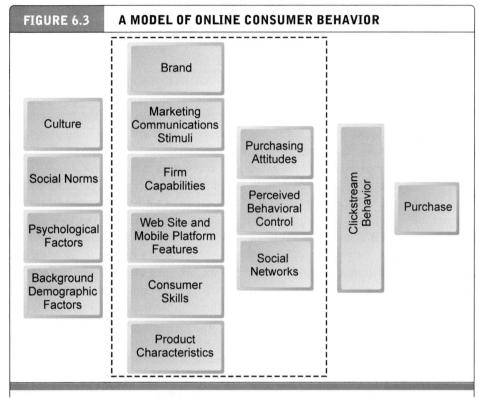

| FIGURE 6.3 | **A MODEL OF ONLINE CONSUMER BEHAVIOR** |

In this general model of online consumer behavior, the decision to purchase is shaped by background demographic factors, several intervening factors, and, finally, influenced greatly by clickstream behavior very near to the precise moment of purchase.

described, packaged, and shipped over the Internet, whereas others cannot. Combined with traditional factors, such as brand, advertising, and firm capabilities, these factors lead to specific attitudes about purchasing at a Web site (trust in the Web site and favorable customer experience) and a sense that the consumer can control his or her environment on the Web site.

Clickstream behavior refers to the transaction log that consumers establish as they move about the Web, from search engine to a variety of sites, then to a single site, then to a single page, and then, finally, to a decision to purchase. These precious moments are similar to "point-of-purchase" moments in traditional retail. A study of over 10,000 visits to an online wine store found that detailed and general clickstream behavior were as important as customer demographics and prior purchase behavior in predicting a current purchase (Van den Poel and Buckinx, 2005). Clickstream marketing takes maximum advantage of the Internet environment. It presupposes no prior "deep" knowledge of the customer (and in that sense is "privacy-regarding"), and can be developed dynamically as customers use the Internet. For instance, the success of search engine marketing (the display of paid advertisements on Web search pages) is based in large part on what the consumer is looking for at the moment and how they go about looking (detailed clickstream data). After examining the detailed data, general

clickstream behavior
the transaction log that consumers establish as they move about the Web

clickstream data is used (days since last visit, past purchases). If available, demographic data is used (region, city, and gender).

SHOPPERS: BROWSERS AND BUYERS

The picture of Internet use sketched in the previous section emphasizes the complexity of behavior online. Although the Internet audience still tends to be concentrated among the well educated, affluent, and youthful, the audience is increasingly becoming more diverse. Clickstream analysis shows us that people go online for many different reasons. Online shopping is similarly complex. Beneath the surface of the €1.18 trillion B2C e-commerce market in 2014 are substantial differences in how users shop online.

Worldwide, around 1.2 billion people (about 40% of the Internet population) are "buyers" who actually purchase something online. In the United States, about 74% of Internet users, age 14 and older, are "buyers." Another 16% research products online ("browsers"), but purchase them offline (see **Figure 6.4**). With the teen and adult U.S. Internet audience (14 years or older) estimated at about 219 million in 2014, online shoppers (the combination of buyers and browsers, totalling almost 90%) add up to a market size of almost 197 million consumers. Most marketers find this number exciting.

The significance of online browsing for offline purchasing should not be underestimated. Although it is difficult to precisely measure the amount of offline sales that occur because of online product research, several different studies have found that about one-third of all offline retail purchasing is influenced by online product research, blogs, banner ads, and other Internet exposure. The offline influence varies by product. This amounts to about $1.4 trillion in annual U.S. retail sales, a truly extraordinary number. By 2018, Forrester predicts that U.S. Web-influenced retail sales will generate more than $1.8 trillion (Forrester Research, 2014).

E-commerce is a major conduit and generator of offline commerce. The reverse is also true: online traffic is driven by offline brands and shopping. While online

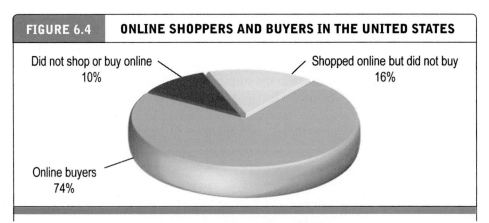

| FIGURE 6.4 | ONLINE SHOPPERS AND BUYERS IN THE UNITED STATES |

Did not shop or buy online
10%

Shopped online but did not buy
16%

Online buyers
74%

About 90% of U.S Internet users, age 14 and older, shop online on desktop computers and mobile devices, either by researching products or by purchasing products online. The percentage of those actually purchasing has increased to about 74%. Only about 10% do not buy or shop online.
SOURCE: Based on data from eMarketer, Inc., 2014f.

research influences offline purchases, it is also the case that offline marketing media heavily influence online behavior including sales. Traditional print media (magazines and newspapers) and television are by far the most powerful media for reaching and engaging consumers with information about new products and directing them to the Web. Online communities and blogging are also very influential but not yet as powerful as traditional media. This may be surprising to many given the attention to social networks as marketing vehicles, but it reflects the diversity of influences on consumer behavior and the real-world marketing budgets of firms that are still heavily dominated by traditional media. Even more surprising in the era of Facebook, face-to-face interactions are a more powerful influence than participation in online social communities.

These considerations strongly suggest that e-commerce and traditional commerce are coupled and should be viewed by merchants (and researchers) as part of a continuum of consuming behavior and not as radical alternatives to one another. Commerce is commerce; the customers are often the same people. Customers use a wide variety of media, sometimes multiple media at once. The significance of these findings for marketers is very clear. Online merchants should build the information content of their sites to attract browsers looking for information, build content to rank high in search engines, put less attention on selling per se, and promote services and products (especially new products) in offline media settings in order to support their online stores.

WHAT CONSUMERS SHOP FOR AND BUY ONLINE

You can look at online sales as divided roughly into two groups: small-ticket and big-ticket items. Big-ticket items include computer equipment and consumer electronics, where orders can easily be more than $1,000. Small-ticket items include apparel, books, health and beauty supplies, office supplies, music, software, videos, and toys, where the average purchase is typically less than $100. In the early days of e-commerce, sales of small-ticket items vastly outnumbered those of large-ticket items. But the recent growth of big-ticket items such as computer hardware, consumer electronics, furniture, and jewelry has changed the overall sales mix. Consumers are now much more confident spending online for big-ticket items. Although furniture and large appliances were initially perceived as too bulky to sell online, these categories have rapidly expanded in the last few years. Free shipping offered by Amazon and other large retailers has also contributed to consumers buying many more expensive and large items online such as air conditioners. The types of purchases made also depend on levels of experience with the Web. New Web users tend primarily to buy small-ticket items, while experienced Web users are more willing to buy large-ticket items in addition to small-ticket items. Refer to Figure 1.10 to see how much consumers spent online for various categories of goods in 2013.

INTENTIONAL ACTS: HOW SHOPPERS FIND VENDORS ONLINE

Given the prevalence of "click here" banner ads, one might think customers are "driven" to online vendors by spur-of-the-moment decisions. In fact, only a tiny percentage of shoppers click on banners to find vendors. E-commerce shoppers are highly intentional. Typically, they are focused browsers looking for specific products, companies, and services. Once they are online, a majority of consumers use a search engine as their preferred method of research for purchasing a product. Many will go directly to a online marketplace, such as Amazon or eBay, and some will go directly to a specific retail Web site. Merchants can convert these "goal-oriented," intentional shoppers into buyers if the merchants can target their communications to the shoppers and design their sites in such a way as to provide easy-to-access and useful product information, full selection, and customer service, and do this at the very moment the customer is searching for the product. This is no small task.

WHY MORE PEOPLE DON'T SHOP ONLINE

A final consumer behavior question to address is: Why don't more online Web users shop online? About 10% of Internet users do not shop or buy online. Why not?

One of the most important factors preventing people from shopping online is the "trust factor," the fear that online merchants will cheat you, lose your credit card information, or use personal information you give them to invade your personal privacy, bombarding you with unwanted e-mail and pop-up ads. Secondary factors can be summarized as "hassle factors," like shipping costs, returns, and inability to touch and feel the product.

TRUST, UTILITY, AND OPPORTUNISM IN ONLINE MARKETS

A long tradition of research shows that the two most important factors shaping the decision to purchase online are utility and trust (Brookings Institute, 2011; Kim et al., 2009; Ba and Pavlou, 2002). Consumers want good deals, bargains, convenience, and speed of delivery. In short, consumers are looking for utility. On the other hand, in any seller-buyer relationship, there is an asymmetry of information. The seller usually knows a lot more than the consumer about the quality of goods and terms of sale. This can lead to opportunistic behavior by sellers (Akerlof, 1970; Williamson, 1985; Mishra, 1998). Consumers need to trust a merchant before they make a purchase. Sellers can develop trust among online consumers by building strong reputations of honesty, fairness, and delivery of quality products—the basic elements of a brand. Feedback forums such as Epinions.com (now part of Shopping.com), Amazon's book reviews from reviewers, and eBay's feedback forum are examples of trust-building online mechanisms (NielsenWire, 2012; Opinion Research Corporation, 2009). Online sellers who develop trust among consumers are able to charge a premium price for their online products and services (Kim and Benbasat, 2006, 2007; Pavlou, 2002). A review of the literature suggests that the most important factors leading to a trusting online relationship are perception of Web site credibility, ease of use, and perceived risk (Corritore et al., 2006). An important brake on the growth of e-commerce is lack of trust. Newspaper and television ads are far more trusted than online ads (Nielsen, 2011). Personal friends and family are far more powerful determinants of online purchases than membership in social networks (eMarketer, Inc., 2010a). These attitudes have grown more positive over time, but new concerns about the use of personal information by Web marketers is raising trust issues among consumers again.

6.2 DIGITAL COMMERCE MARKETING AND ADVERTISING STRATEGIES AND TOOLS

Internet marketing has many similarities to, and differences from, ordinary marketing. (For more information on basic marketing concepts, see Learning Tracks 6.1 and 6.2). The objective of Internet marketing—as in all marketing—is to build customer relationships so that the firm can achieve above-average returns (both by offering superior products or services and by communicating the brand's features to the consumer). These relationships are a foundation for the firm's brand. But Internet marketing, including all forms of digital marketing, is also very different from ordinary marketing because the nature of the medium and its capabilities are so different from anything that has come before.

There are four features of Internet marketing that distinguish it from traditional marketing channels. Compared to traditional print and television marketing, Internet marketing can be more personalized, participatory, peer-to-peer, and communal. Not all types of Internet marketing have these four features. For instance, there's not much difference between a marketing video splashed on your computer screen without your consent and watching a television commercial. However, the same marketing video can be targeted to your personal interests, community memberships, and allow you to share it with others using a Like or + tag. Marketers are learning that the most effective Internet marketing has all four of these features.

STRATEGIC ISSUES AND QUESTIONS

In the past, from 2000 to 2010, the first step in building an online brand was to build a Web site, and then try to attract an audience. The most common "traditional" marketing techniques for establishing a brand and attracting customers were search engine marketing, display ads, e-mail campaigns, and affiliate programs. This is still the case: building a Web site is still a first step, and the "traditional" online marketing techniques are still the main powerhouses of brand creation and online sales revenue in 2014. But today, marketers need to take a much broader view of the online marketing challenge, and to consider other media channels for attracting an audience such as social network sites and mobile devices, in concert with traditional Web sites.

The five main elements of a comprehensive multi-channel marketing plan are: Web site, traditional online marketing, social marketing, mobile marketing, and offline marketing. **Table 6.3** illustrates these five main platforms, central elements within each type, some examples, and the primary function of marketing in each situation. Each of the main types of online marketing is discussed in this section and throughout the chapter in greater detail.

Immediately, by examining Table 6.3, you can understand the management complexity of building brands online. There are five major types of marketing, and a variety of different platforms that perform different functions. If you're a manager of a start-up, or the Web site manager of an existing commercial Web site, you face a number of strategic questions. Where should you focus first? Build a Web site, develop a blog, or jump into developing a Facebook presence? If you have a successful Web

TABLE 6.3	THE DIGITAL MARKETING ROADMAP		
TYPE OF MARKETING	**PLATFORMS**	**EXAMPLES**	**FUNCTION**
Web Site	Traditional Web site	Ford.com	Anchor site
Traditional Online Marketing	Search engine marketing	Google; Bing; Yahoo	Query-based intention marketing
	Display advertising	Yahoo; Google; MSN	Interest- and context-based marketing; targeted marketing
	E-mail	Major retailers	Permission marketing
	Affiliates	Amazon	Brand extension
Social Marketing	Social networks	Facebook/Google +1	Conversations; sharing
	Micro blogging sites	Twitter	News, quick updates
	Blogs/forums	Tumblr	Communities of interest; sharing
	Video marketing	YouTube	Engage; inform
	Game marketing	You Don't Know Jack	Identification
Mobile Marketing	Smartphone site	m.ford.com	Quick access; news; updates
	Tablet site	t.ford.com	Visual engagement
	Apps	Ford Mustang Customerizer	Visual engagement
		Vehicle Brochure Apps	Visual engagement
Offline Marketing	Television	FIFA World Cup 2014	Brand anchoring; inform
	Newspapers	Apple Perspective campaign	Brand anchoring; inform
	Magazines	BMW Expression of Joy print and video campaign	Brand anchoring; inform

site that already uses search engine marketing and display ads, where should you go next: develop a social network presence or use offline media? Does your firm have the resources to maintain a social media marketing campaign?

A second strategic management issue involves the integration of all these different marketing platforms into a single coherent branding message. Often, there are different groups with different skill sets involved in Web site design, search engine and display marketing, social media marketing, and offline marketing. Getting all these different specialties to work together and coordinate their campaigns can be very difficult. The danger is that a firm ends up with different teams managing each of the four platforms rather than a single team managing the digital online presence, or for that matter, marketing for the entire firm including retail outlets.

A third strategic management question involves resource allocation. There are actually two problems here. Each of the different major types of marketing, and each of the different platforms, has different metrics to measure its effectiveness. In some cases, for new social marketing platforms, there is no commonly accepted metric, and few that have withstood critical scrutiny or have a deep experience base providing empirical data. For instance, in Facebook marketing, an important metric is how many Likes your Facebook page produces. The connection between Likes and sales is still being explored. In search engine marketing, effectiveness is measured by how many clicks your ads are receiving; in display advertising, by how many impressions of your ads are served. Second, each of these platforms has different costs for Likes, impressions, and clicks. In order to choose where your marketing resources should be deployed, you will have to link each of these activities to sales revenue. You will need to determine how much clicks, Likes, and impressions are worth. We address these questions in greater detail in Chapter 7.

THE WEB SITE AS A MARKETING PLATFORM: ESTABLISHING THE CUSTOMER RELATIONSHIP

A firm's Web site is a major tool for establishing the initial relationship with the customer. The Web site performs four important functions: establishing the brand identity and consumer expectations, informing and educating the consumer, shaping the customer experience, and anchoring the brand in an ocean of marketing messages coming from different sources. The Web site is the one place the consumer can turn to find the complete story. This is not true of apps, e-mails, or search engine ads.

The first function of a Web site is to establish the brand's identity and to act as an anchor for the firm's other Web marketing activities, thereby driving sales revenue. This involves identifying for the consumer the differentiating features of the product or service in terms of quality, price, product support, and reliability. Identifying the differentiating features of the product on the Web site's home page is intended to create expectations in the user of what it will be like to consume the product. For instance, Snapple's Web site creates the expectation that the product is a delicious, refreshing drink made from high quality, natural ingredients. Ford's Web site focuses on automobile technology and high miles per gallon. The expectation created by Ford's Web site is that if you buy a Ford, you'll be experiencing the latest automotive technology and the highest mileage. At the location-based social network Web site for Foursquare, the focus is on meeting friends, discovering local places, and saving money with coupons and rewards.

Web sites also function to anchor the brand online, acting as a central point where all the branding messages that emanate from the firm's multiple digital presences, such as Facebook, Twitter, mobile apps, or e-mail, come together at a single online location. Aside from branding, Web sites also perform the typical functions of any commercial establishment by informing customers of the company's products and services. Web sites, with their online catalogs and associated shopping carts, are important elements of the online customer experience. **Customer experience** refers to the totality of experiences that a customer has with a firm, including the search, informing, purchase, consumption, and after-sales support for the product. The concept "customer experience" is broader than the traditional concept of "customer satisfaction" in that a much broader range of

customer experience
the totality of experiences that a customer has with a firm, including the search, informing, purchase, consumption, and after-sales support for its products, services, and various retail channels

impacts is considered, including the customer's cognitive, affective, emotional, social, and physical relationship to the firm and its products. The totality of customer experiences will generally involve multiple retail channels. This means that, in the customer's mind, the Web site, Facebook page, Twitter feed, physical store, and television advertisements are all connected as part of his or her experience with the company.

TRADITIONAL ONLINE MARKETING AND ADVERTISING TOOLS

Below we describe the basic marketing and advertising tools for attracting e-commerce consumers: search engine marketing, display ad marketing (including banner ads, rich media ads, video ads, and sponsorships), e-mail and permission marketing, affiliate marketing, viral marketing, and lead generation marketing.

online advertising

a paid message on a Web site, online service, or other interactive medium

Companies will spend an estimated €436 billion on advertising worldwide in 2014, and an estimated €113 billion of that amount on **online advertising**, which includes display (banners, video, and rich media), search, mobile messaging, sponsorships, classifieds, lead generation, and e-mail, on desktop, laptop, and tablet computers, as well as mobile phones (see **Figure 6.5**) (eMarketer, Inc., 2014y).

In the last five years, advertisers have aggressively increased online spending and cut outlays on traditional channels such as newspapers and magazines while outdoor,

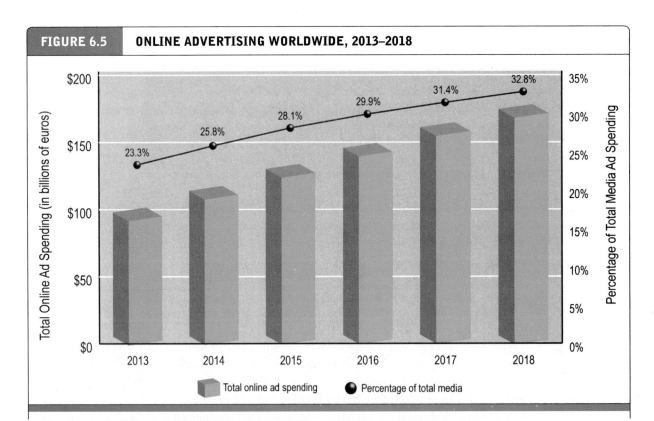

FIGURE 6.5 | **ONLINE ADVERTISING WORLDWIDE, 2013–2018**

Spending on online advertising is expected to grow from €113 billion in 2014 to over €175 billion by 2018, and comprise an increasing percentage of total media ad spending.

SOURCES: Based on data from eMarketer, Inc., 2014y.

TABLE 6.4	ONLINE ADVERTISING SPENDING IN THE UNITED STATES FOR SELECTED FORMATS (IN BILLIONS)		
FORMAT	2014	2018	AVERAGE GROWTH RATE
Search	$22.9	$33.1	10.6%
Banner ads	$10.9	$16.0	10.5%
Video	$6.0	$12.7	25.2%
Rich media	$3.1	$9.5	35.7%
Classifieds	$3.0	$3.7	6.1%
Sponsorships	$2.4	$4.2	17.1%
Lead generation	$2.0	$2.5	5.4%
E-mail	$0.25	$0.32	6.6%

SOURCES: Based on data from eMarketer, Inc., 2014g.

television, and radio advertising have shown modest growth. Over the next five years, online advertising is expected to continue to be the fastest growing form of advertising, and by 2018, it is expected to be the second largest ad channel with over a 32% share.

Table 6.4 provides some comparative data on the amount of spending for certain advertising formats in the United States. The online advertising format that currently produces the highest revenue is paid search, followed by banner ads, but the fastest growing online ad formats are rich media and video ads. Note, however, that this does not include mobile ads, which are growing fastest of all.

Spending on U.S. online advertising among different industries is somewhat skewed. Retail accounts for the highest percentage (21%), followed by financial services (13%), automotive (12%), telecommunications (9%), leisure travel (8%), consumer packaged goods (7%), computing products (6%), pharmaceuticals and healthcare (5%), media (5%), and entertainment (4%) (Interactive Advertising Bureau/ PricewaterhouseCoopers, 2014). Online advertising has both advantages and disadvantages when compared to advertising in traditional media, such as television, radio, and print (magazines and newspapers). One big advantage for online advertising is that the Internet is where the audience has moved, especially the very desirable 18–34 age group. A second big advantage for online advertising is the ability to target ads to individuals and small groups and to track performance of advertisements in almost real time. **Ad targeting**, the sending of market messages to specific subgroups in the population in an effort to increase the likelihood of a purchase, is as old as advertising itself, but prior to the Internet, it could only be done with much less precision, certainly not down to the level of individuals. Ad targeting is also the foundation of price discrimination: the ability to charge different types of consumers different prices for

ad targeting
the sending of market messages to specific subgroups in the population

the same product or service. With online advertising, it's theoretically possible to charge every customer a different price.

Theoretically, online advertising can personalize every ad message to precisely fit the needs, interests, and values of each consumer. In practice, as we all know from spam and constant exposure to pop-up ads that are of little interest, the reality is very different. Online advertisements also provide greater opportunities for interactivity—two-way communication between advertisers and potential customers. The primary disadvantages of online advertising are concerns about its cost versus its benefits, how to adequately measure its results, and the supply of good venues to display ads. For instance, the owners of Web sites who sell advertising space ("publishers") do not have agreed-upon standards or routine audits to verify their claimed numbers as do traditional media outlets. We examine the costs and benefits of online advertising as well as research on its effectiveness in Section 6.4.

Search Engine Marketing and Advertising

In 2014, companies in Western Europe will spend an estimated €12 billion on search engine marketing and advertising, about 45% of all spending for digital marketing. Briefly, this is where the eyeballs are (at least for a few moments) and this is where advertising can be very effective by responding with ads that match the interests and intentions of the user. The click-through rate for search engine advertising is generally 1%–4% and has been fairly steady over the years. The top search engine provider throughout Western Europe is Google, with over a 90% market share in the U.K., France, Germany, and Spain. **Search engine marketing (SEM)** refers to the use of search engines to build and sustain brands. **Search engine advertising** refers to the use of search engines to support direct sales to online consumers.

Search engines are often thought of as mostly direct sales channels focused on making sales in response to advertisements. While this is a major use of search engines, they are also used more subtly to strengthen brand awareness, drive traffic to other Web sites or blogs to support customer engagement, to gain deeper insight into customers' perceptions of the brand, to support other related advertising (for instance, sending consumers to local dealer sites), and to support the brand indirectly. Search engines can also provide marketers insight into customer search patterns, opinions customers hold about their products, top trending search keywords, and what their competitors are using as keywords and the customer response. For example, Pepsico, home of mega brands like Pepsi and Doritos, makes no sales on the Web, but has several branding Web sites aimed at consumers, investors, and shareholders. The focus is on building, sustaining, and updating the Pepsi collection of branded consumer goods. A search on Pepsi will generate numerous search results that link to Pepsi marketing materials.

Types of Search Engine Advertising There are at least three different types of search engine advertising: keyword paid inclusion (so-called "sponsored links"), advertising keywords (such as Google's AdWords), and search engine context ads (such as Google's AdSense). Search engine sites originally performed unbiased searches of the Web's

---

search engine marketing (SEM)

involves the use of search engines to build and sustain brands

search engine advertising

involves the use of search engines to support direct sales to online

huge collection of Web pages and derived most of their revenue from banner advertisements. This form of search engine results is often called **organic search** because the inclusion and ranking of Web sites depends on a more or less "unbiased" application of a set of rules (an algorithm) imposed by the search engine. Since 1998, search engine sites slowly transformed themselves into digital yellow pages, where firms pay for inclusion in the search engine index, pay for keywords to show up in search results, or pay for keywords to show up in other vendors' ads.

Most search engines offer **paid inclusion** (also called sponsored link) programs, which, for a fee, guarantee a Web site's inclusion in its list of search results, more frequent visits by its Web crawler, and suggestions for improving the results of organic searching. Search engines claim that these payments—costing some merchants hundreds of thousands a year—do not influence the organic ranking of a Web site in search results, just inclusion in the results. However, it is the case that page inclusion ads get more hits, and the rank of the page appreciates, causing the organic search algorithm to rank it higher in the organic results.

Google claims that it does not permit firms to pay for their rank in the organic results, although it does allocate two to three sponsored links at the very top of their pages, albeit labeling them as "Sponsored Links." Merchants who refuse to pay for inclusion or for keywords typically fall far down on the list of results, and off the first page of results, which is akin to commercial death.

The two other types of search engine advertising rely on selling keywords in online auctions. In **keyword advertising**, merchants purchase keywords through a bidding process at search sites, and whenever a consumer searches for that word, their advertisement shows up somewhere on the page, usually as a small text-based advertisement on the right, but also as a listing on the very top of the page. The more merchants pay, the higher the rank and greater the visibility of their ads on the page. Generally, the search engines do not exercise editorial judgment about quality or content of the ads although they do monitor the use of language. In addition, some search engines rank the ads in terms of their popularity rather than merely the money paid by the advertiser so that the rank of the ad depends on both the amount paid and the number of clicks per unit time. Google's keyword advertising program is called AdWords, Yahoo's is called Sponsored Search, and Microsoft's is called adCenter.

Network keyword advertising (**context advertising**), introduced by Google as its AdSense product in 2002, differs from the ordinary keyword advertising described previously. Publishers (Web sites that want to show ads) join these networks and allow the search engine to place "relevant" ads on their sites. The ads are paid for by advertisers who want their messages to appear across the Web. Google-like text messages are the most common. The revenue from the resulting clicks is split between the search engine and the site publisher, although the publisher gets much more than half in some cases. About half of Google's revenue comes from AdWords and the rest comes from AdSense.

Search engine advertising is nearly an ideal targeted marketing technique: at precisely the moment that a consumer is looking for a product, an advertisement for that product is presented. Consumers benefit from search engine advertising because ads for merchants appear only when consumers are looking for a specific product.

---

organic search
inclusion and ranking of sites depends on a more or less unbiased application of a set of rules imposed by the search engine

paid inclusion
for a fee, guarantees a Web site's inclusion in its list of sites, more frequent visits by its Web crawler, and suggestions for improving the results of organic searching

keyword advertising
merchants purchase keywords through a bidding process at search sites, and whenever a consumer searches for that word, their advertisement shows up somewhere on the page

network keyword advertising (context advertising)
publishers accept ads placed by Google on their Web sites, and receive a fee for any click-throughs from those ads

search engine optimization

techniques to improve the ranking of Web pages generated by search engine algorithms

There are no pop-ups, Flash animations, videos, interstitials, e-mails, or other irrelevant communications to deal with. Thus, search engine advertising saves consumers cognitive energy and reduces search costs (including the cost of cars or trains needed to do physical searches for products).

Because search engine marketing can be very effective, companies optimize their Web sites for search engine recognition. The better optimized the page is, the higher a ranking it will achieve in search engine result listings, and the more likely it will appear on the top of the page in search engine results. **Search engine optimization** is the process of improving the ranking of Web pages with search engines by altering the content and design of the Web pages and site. By carefully selecting key words used on the Web pages, updating content frequently, and designing the site so it can be easily read by search engine programs, marketers can improve the impact and return on investment in their Web marketing programs.

Panda

change in the Google algorithm to eliminate low-quality sites from search results

Penguin

change in the Google algorithm to eliminate sites with low-quality back links

Google and other search engine firms make frequent changes to their search algorithms in order to improve the search results and user experience. Google, for instance, reportedly makes over 600 search engine changes in a year. Most are small unannounced tweaks. Recent major changes have included Panda, Penguin, Hummingbird, and Knowledge Graph. **Panda** was introduced in 2011 in an effort to weed out low quality sites from search results. Those sites with thin content, duplicate content, content copied from elsewhere on the Web, and content that did not attract high-quality hits from other sources were systematically pushed down in the search results. Google introduced **Penguin** in 2012 in an effort to punish Web sites and their SEO marketing firms who were manipulating links to their site in order to improve their rankings. The Google search engine rewards sites that have links from many other sites. What some marketers discovered is that Google could not tell the quality of these back links, and they began to manufacture links by putting their clients onto list sites, creating multiple blogs to link to their clients site, and paying others to link to their clients' sites. Penguin evaluates the quality of links to a site, and pushes down in the rankings those sites that have poor-quality back links.

Hummingbird

semantic search component of Google's search algorithm

Many search engines are attempting to capture more of what the user intended, or might like to know about a search subject. This is often referred to as semantic search. Google introduced **Hummingbird**, its new search algorithm in September 2013. Rather than evaluate each word separately in a search, Google's semantically informed Hummingbird will try to evaluate an entire sentence. Semantic search more closely follows conversational search, or search as you would ordinarily speak it to another human being.

Knowledge Graph

function in Google's search engine that displays a selection of facts related to your search term that you may be interested in knowing more about

Google introduced **Knowledge Graph** in 2012 as an effort to anticipate what you might want to know more about as you search on a topic or answer questions you might not thought of asking. Since 2013, results of Knowledge Graph appear on the right of the screen and contain more information about the topic or person you are searching on. Not all search terms have a Knowledge Graph result. Google displays information based on what other users have searched for in the past, as well as its database on over 500 million objects (people, places, and things), and some 18 billion facts.

Social Search **Social search** is an attempt to use your social contacts (and your entire social graph) to provide search results. In contrast to the top search engines that use a mathematical algorithm to find pages that satisfy your query, social search reviews your friends' (and their friends') recommendations, past Web visits, and use of Like buttons. One problem with Google and mechanical search engines is that they are so thorough: enter a search for "smartphone" and in .28 second you will receive 504 million results, some of them providing helpful information and others that are suspect. Social search is an effort to provide fewer, more relevant, and trustworthy results based on the social graph. For instance, Google has developed Google + 1 as a social layer on top of its existing search engine. Users can place a + 1 next to Web sites they found helpful, and their friends will be automatically notified. Subsequent searches by their friends would list the + 1 sites recommended by friends higher up on the page. Facebook's Like button is a similar social search tool. Facebook's Graph Search is a social search engine introduced by Facebook in March 2013. Graph Search produces information from within a user's network of friends supplemented with additional results provided by Bing.

social search
effort to provide fewer, more relevant, and trustworthy results based on the social graph

Search Engine Issues While search engines have provided significant benefits to merchants and customers, they also present risks and costs. For instance, search engines have the power to crush a small business by placing its ads on the back pages of search results. Merchants are at the mercy of search engines for access to the online marketplace, and this access is dominated by a single firm, Google. How Google decides to rank one company over another in search results is not known. No one really knows how to improve in its rankings (although there are hundreds of firms who claim otherwise). Google editors intervene in unknown ways to punish certain Web sites and reward others. Using paid sponsored listings, as opposed to relying on organic search results, eliminates some, but not all, of this uncertainty.

Other practices that degrade the results and usefulness of search engines include:

- **Link farms** are groups of Web sites that link to one another, thereby boosting their ranking in search engines that use a PageRank algorithm to judge the "usefulness" of a site. For instance, in the 2010 holiday season, JCPenney was found to be the highest ranked merchant for a large number of clothing products. On examination, it was discovered that this resulted from Penney's hiring a search engine optimization company to create thousands of Web sites that linked to JCPenney's Web site. As a result, JCPenney's Web site became the most popular (most linked-to) Web site for products like dresses, shirts, and pants. No matter what popular clothing item people searched for, JCPenney came out on top. Experts believe this was the largest search engine fraud in history. Google's Panda series of updates to its search algorithms were aimed in part at eliminating link farms (Castell, 2014).

link farms
groups of Web sites that link to one another, thereby boosting their ranking in search engines

- **Content farms** are companies that generate large volumes of textual content for multiple Web sites designed to attract viewers and search engines. Content farms profit by attracting large numbers of readers to their sites and exposing them to ads. The content typically is not original but is artfully copied or summarized from legitimate content sites.

content farms
companies that generate large volumes of textual content for multiple Web sites designed to attract viewers and search engines

click fraud

occurs when a competitor clicks on search engine results and ads, forcing the advertiser to pay for the click even though the click is not legitimate

- **Click fraud** occurs when a competitor clicks on search engine results and ads, forcing the advertiser to pay for the click even though the click is not legitimate. Competitors can hire offshore firms to perform fraudulent clicks or hire botnets to automate the process. Click fraud can quickly run up a large bill for merchants, and not result in any growth in sales.

Display Ad Marketing

In 2014, companies in Western Europe spent around €9.25 billion on display ad marketing, about 36% of all spending for digital marketing. Over 5.3 trillion display ad impressions were served in 2012 (comScore, 2013a). The top five display ad companies in the United States are Facebook, Google, Yahoo, AOL, and Twitter, and together they account for about 50% of U.S. display ad revenue. The Interactive Advertising Bureau (IAB), an industry organization, has established voluntary industry guidelines for display ads. Publishers are not required to use these guidelines, but many do. One objective of IAB is to give the consumer a consistent experience across all Web sites. The various types of ads are designed to help advertisers break through the "noise" and clutter created by the high number of display ad impressions that a typical user is exposed to within a given day. **Figure 6.6** shows examples of the seven core standard ad units, as specified by the IAB. According to Google, the top performing ad formats are the medium rectangle, the large rectangle, the leaderboard, and the half-page (Google, 2014). Eye-tracking research has found that for both desktop and tablet computers, leaderboard ads are the most effective in grabbing a user's attention and holding it (Tobii/Mediative, 2012). Display ads consist of four different kinds of ads: banner ads, rich media ads (animated ads), sponsorships, and video ads.

banner ad

displays a promotional message in a rectangular box at the top or bottom of a computer screen

Banner Ads Banner ads are the oldest and most familiar form of display marketing. They are also the least effective and the lowest cost form of online marketing. A banner ad displays a promotional message in a rectangular box at the top or bottom of a computer screen. A **banner ad** is similar to a traditional ad in a printed publication but has some added advantages. When clicked, it brings potential customers directly to the advertiser's Web site, and the site where the ad appears can observe the user's behavior on the site. The ability to identify and track the user is a key feature of online advertising. Banner ads feature Flash video and other animations. It's important to note, although the terms banner ad and display ad are often used interchangeably, that banner ads are just one form of display ad.

rich media ad

ad employing animation, sound, and interactivity, using Flash, HTML5, Java, and JavaScript

Rich Media Ads **Rich media ads** are ads that employ animation, sound, and interactivity, using Flash, HTML5, Java, and JavaScript. They are far more effective than simple banner ads. For instance, one research report that analyzed 24,000 different rich media ads with more than 12 billion impressions served in North America over a six-month period found that exposure to rich media ads boosted advertiser site visits by nearly 300% compared to standard banner ads. Viewers of rich media ads that included video were six times more likely to visit the advertiser's Web site, by either

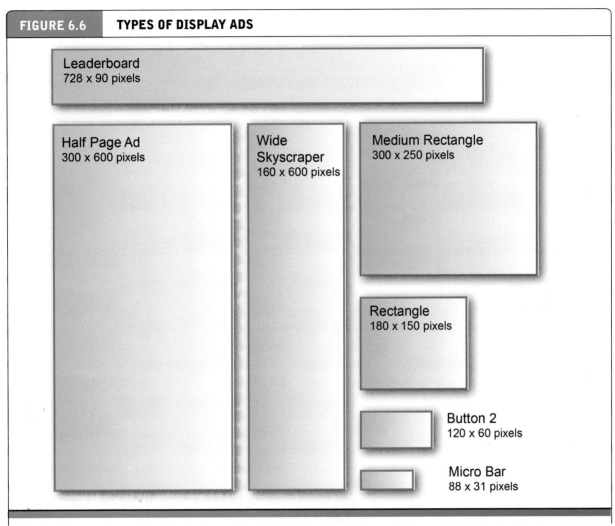

FIGURE 6.6 **TYPES OF DISPLAY ADS**

In addition to the various display ads shown above, IAB also provides standards for six new formats called "Rising Star" display ad units.

SOURCE: Based on data from Interactive Advertising Bureau, 2011.

directly clicking on the ad, typing the advertiser's URL, or searching (MediaMind, 2012a).

The IAB provides guidance for a number of different types of rich media ads, such as those that contain in-banner video, those that are expandable/retractable, pop-ups, floating versions, and interstitials. An **interstitial ad** (interstitial means "in between") is a way of placing a full-page message between the current and destination pages of a user. Interstitials are usually inserted within a single Web site, and displayed as the user moves from one page to the next. The interstitial is typically contained in its own browser window and moves automatically to the page the user requested after allowing enough time for the ad to be read. Interstitials can also be deployed over an advertising network and appear as users move among Web sites.

interstitial ad
a way of placing a full-page message between the current and destination pages of a user

TABLE 6.5	TYPES OF VIDEO ADS		
FORMAT	DESCRIPTION	WHEN USED	USED WITH
Linear video ad	Pre-roll; takeover; ad takes over video for a certain period of time	Before, between, or after video	Text, banners, rich media video player skins
Nonlinear video ad	Overlay; ad runs at same time as video content and does not take over full screen	During, over, or within video	
In-banner video ad	Rich media; ad is triggered within banner, may expand outside banner	Within Web page, generally surrounded by content	None
In-text video ad	Rich media; ad is delivered when user mouses over relevant text	Within Web page, identified as a highlighted word within relevant content	None

Because the Web is such a busy place, people have to find ways to cope with over-stimulation. One means of coping is known as *sensory input filtering*. This means that people learn to filter out the vast majority of the messages coming at them. Internet users quickly learn at some level to recognize banner ads or anything that looks like a banner ad and to filter out most of the ads that are not exceptionally relevant. Interstitial messages, like TV commercials, attempt to make viewers a captive of the message. Typical interstitials last 10 seconds or less and force the user to look at the ad for that time period. IAB standards for pre-roll ads also limit their length. To avoid boring users, ads typically use animated graphics and music to entertain and inform them. A good interstitial will also have a "skip through" or "stop" option for users who have no interest in the message.

The IAB also provides mobile rich media ad interface definitions (MRAID) in an effort to provide a set of standards designed to work with HTML5 and JavaScript that developers can use to create rich media ads to work with apps running on different mobile devices. The hope is make it easier to display ads across a wide variety of devices without having to rewrite code (Interactive Advertising Bureau, 2012).

video ad
TV-like advertisement that appears as an in-page video commercial or before, during, or after content

Video Ads **Video ads** are TV-like advertisements that appear as in-page video commercials or before, during, or after a variety of content. **Table 6.5** describes some of the IAB standards for video ads.

Although from a total spending standpoint, online video ads are still very small when compared to the amount spent on search engine advertising, video ads are another fast growing form of online advertisement. The rapid growth in video ads is due in part to the fact that video ads are far more effective than other display ad formats. For instance, according to research analyzing a variety of ad formats, in-stream video ads had click-through rates 12 times that of rich media and 27 times that of standard banner ads (MediaMind, 2012b). Exactly how to best take advantage of this opportunity is still somewhat of a puzzle. Internet users are apparently willing to tolerate advertising in order to watch online as long as the ads are not too long and don't interfere too much with the viewing experience.

There are many formats for displaying ads with videos. The most widely used format is the "pre-roll" (followed by the mid-roll and the post-roll) where users are forced to watch a video ad either before, in the middle of, or at the end of the video they originally clicked on.

There are many specialized video advertising networks such as SAY Media, Advertising.com, and others who run video advertising campaigns for national advertisers and place these videos on their respective networks of Web sites. Firms can also establish their own video and television sites to promote their products. Retail sites are among the largest users of advertising videos. For instance, Zappos, the largest online shoe retailer, has a video for every one of its over 100,000 products.

Sponsorships A **sponsorship** is a paid effort to tie an advertiser's name to particular information, an event, or a venue in a way that reinforces its brand in a positive yet not overtly commercial manner. In 2014, companies will spend about $2.4 billion for sponsorship marketing. Sponsorships typically are more about branding than immediate sales. A common form of sponsorship is targeted content (or advertorials), in which editorial content is combined with an ad message to make the message more valuable and attractive to its intended audience. For instance, WebMD.com, the leading medical information Web site in the United States, offers "sponsorship sites" on the WebMD Web site to companies such as Phillips to describe its home defibrillators, and Lilly to describe its pharmaceutical solutions for attention deficit disorders among children. Social media sponsorships, in which marketers pay for mentions in social media, such as blogs, tweets, or in online video, have also become a popular tactic. Sponsorships have also moved onto the mobile platform. For instance, Subaru sponsors an app called MapMyDogwalk, a GPS-enabled dog walking tool.

sponsorship
a paid effort to tie an advertiser's name to information, an event, or a venue in a way that reinforces its brand in a positive yet not overtly commercial manner

Native Advertising **Native advertising** is advertising that looks similar to editorial content. Native advertising is not new. Traditional native advertising includes television infomercials, newspaper advertorials, and entire sections of newspapers and magazines that are given over to advertisers, where the advertising looks similar to the rest of the publication. In the online world, native ads are most often found on social media, especially mobile social media, as part of a Facebook Newsfeed, Twitter Timeline, or Pinterest Promoted Pin. Mobile social networks do not have room for ads on the right side of the screen (the sidebar or right rail), and therefore native ads in the form of posts that look like other posts are the favored option.

native advertising
advertising that looks similar to editorial content

Typically, native ads mimic the editorial content around them. They appear outside the normal or expected area for ads and are labeled to indicate they are not editorial content, although in most cases the word "ad" is not used. On the Web or mobile screens, native ads are usually distinguished by a "sponsored" tag underneath the headline, often in a different color. Online native advertising is growing rapidly, especially on social networks. In 2014, native ad spending is expected to reach $3.1 billion (eMarketer, Inc., 2014x). F.T.C. researchers found that 73% of online publishers offer native advertising, including the New York Times, which began the practice in 2014.

Researchers have found that 35% of online consumers cannot distinguish between editorial content and sponsored ads that look like editorial content, even if the ads are labelled as sponsored or promoted. Most consumers do not know what sponsored or promoted means. In a survey of 10,000 consumers, researchers found that consumers skip over labels like sponsored, and many do not understand the difference between paid and unpaid content (Franklin, 2013). Yet market researchers have found that native ads are far more influential with consumers. Consumers look at native ads 53% more frequently than display ads; native ads raise purchase intent by 18%; and consumers are twice as likely to share a native ad with a family member as a regular ad. Marketers and advertisers are opposed to labeling native advertising with the word "ad" and instead prefer other tags.

Native advertising is controversial. Critics contend that the purpose of native ads is to deceive or fool the consumer into thinking the ad has the same validity as the editorial content in media. The FTC held a conference in December 2013 to explore the native advertising phenomenon because of the potential to deceive consumers. Supporters argue that native ads add value by helping consumers, advertisers, and the media in which they are used (FTC, 2013).

Advertising Networks   In the early years of e-commerce, firms placed ads on the few popular Web sites in existence, but by early 2000, there were hundreds of thousands of sites where ads could be displayed, and it became very inefficient for a single firm to purchase ads on each individual Web site. Most firms, even very large firms, did not have the capability by themselves to place banner ads and marketing messages on thousands of Web sites and monitor the results. Specialized marketing firms called **advertising networks** appeared to help firms take advantage of the powerful marketing potential of the Internet, and to make the entire process of buying and selling online ads more efficient and transparent. These ad networks have proliferated and have greatly increased the scale and liquidity of online marketing.

advertising networks

connect online marketers with publishers by displaying ads to consumers based on detailed customer information

Advertising networks represent the most sophisticated application of Internet database capabilities to date, and illustrate just how different Internet marketing is from traditional marketing. Advertising networks sell advertising and marketing opportunities (slots) to companies who wish to buy exposure to an online audience (advertisers). Advertising networks obtain their inventory of ad opportunities from a network of participating sites that want to display ads on their sites in return for receiving a payment from advertisers everytime a visitor clicks on an ad. These sites are usually referred to as Web publishers. Marketers buy audiences and publishers sell audiences by attracting an audience and capturing audience information. Ad networks are the intermediaries who make this market work efficiently.

Figure 6.7 illustrates how these systems work. Advertising networks begin with a consumer requesting a page from a member of the advertising network (1). A connection is established with the third-party ad server (2). The ad server identifies the user by reading the cookie file on the user's hard drive and checks its user profile database for the user's profile (3). The ad server selects an appropriate banner ad based on the user's previous purchases, interests, demographics, or other data in the profile (4). Whenever the user later goes online and visits any of the network member sites, the

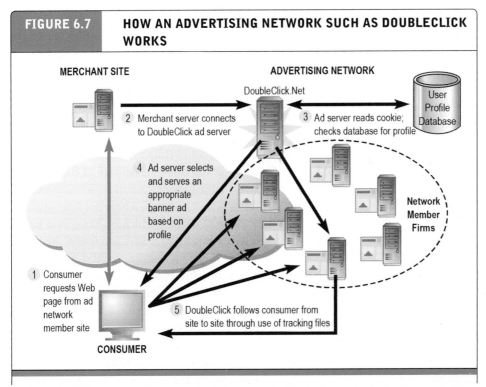

| FIGURE 6.7 | HOW AN ADVERTISING NETWORK SUCH AS DOUBLECLICK WORKS |

Millions of publishers have audiences to sell, and pages to fill with ads. Thousands of advertisers are looking for audiences. Ad networks are intermediaries that connect publishers with marketers.

ad server recognizes the user and serves up the same or different ads regardless of the site content. The advertising network follows users from site to site through the use of Web tracking files (5).

Programmatic Advertising, Real-Time Bidding and Advertising Exchanges. **Programmatic advertising** is an automated, auction-based method implemented via markets known as **ad exchanges** that match demand and supply of online display ads. Programmatic advertising uses a **real-time bidding process (RTB)** to match advertiser demand for display ads with publisher supply of Web page space. Publishers are able to sell their inventory of empty Web pages, often excess inventory that could not be sold directly. Want to contact males age 18 to 34, recent visitors to a car site, unmarried, high risk-taking profile, located in New York or California, urban home, and financial service industry employment? An ad exchange will allow you to bid in real time on this audience against other advertisers, and then manage the placement of ads, accounting, and measurement for your firm. Ad exchanges offer tremendous global scale and efficiency. One of the best known is Google's DoubleClick Ad Exchange, which is based on more than 100 ad networks (the supply side), and provides a computer-based market for buyers to purchase audiences (the demand side). This exchange sells audiences sliced into 1,600 interest categories. It displays more than 250 billion ad impressions a month across 2 million Web sites worldwide,

programmatic advertising
An automated, auction-based method for matching demand and supply for online display ads

ad exchanges
auction-based markets where ad networks sell ad space to marketers

real-time bidding process (RTB)
used to match advertiser demand for display ads with publisher supply of Web page space

and maintains or distributes more than 500 million user profiles of Internet users (Kantrowitz, 2013). These profiles are based on Web tracking files, offline purchase information, and social network data. Marketing firms, the buyers from publishers of Web sites, can target their audience and control the frequency and timing of ads during the day. The case study at the end of the chapter, *Programmatic Advertising: Real Time Marketing*, provides you with a further look at ad exchanges and real-time bidding.

Display Advertising Issues

Ad Fraud.   According to Interactive Advertising Bureau estimates, about 36% of all Web traffic is fake, and by extension, about the same percentage of clicks on ads are fake as well (Vranica, 2014). Display advertising expenditure in 2014 is expected to be about €9.25 billion, so possibly €3.3 billion is being wasted. There are four primary sources of ad fraud. Botnets can be hired by publishers to click on their Web pages to create phony traffic. Second, a browser extension can insert ads into a premium publisher's Web site, and then list the ads as available on a programmatic ad exchange. Third, ad targeting firms can create bots that imitate the behavior of real shoppers, and then charge advertisers for successfully targeting consumers. Fourth, if you are a publisher looking to attract ads to your site, the simplest technique is simply to hire people in low-wage countries to click on your ads using a proxy server (Kantrowitz, 2014).

Large advertisers have begun to hire online fraud detection firms (a growth industry) to determine the extent of fraud in their campaigns. Verizon Wireless, L'Oreal, and Kellogg are among the firms in 2014 that found millions of dollars of ad fraud in recent campaigns, and have demanded advertising networks to either reimburse them or generate real Web traffic in the amount of the fraud.

Viewability.   Research by comScore has revealed that 54% of display ads, and 57% of video ads, are not in fact seen by people, even though advertisers are charged for generating ad impressions and serving ads (comScore, 2013b). There are a number of reasons for this situation. First, there is no mechanism for measuring how many people actually see an online ad that has been served. The same is true of most offline print and TV advertising, although several methods and certifications have been developed over decades to accurately measure audience exposure. There are no such mechanisms for online advertising. Second, a large percentage of ads served appear lower down on the screen where users are less likely to go, or video ads on auto-play are playing in areas the user cannot see. Advertisers are still charged for ads that are served but not viewed. Unscrupulous publishers can place multiple ads on top of each other and charge multiple times for the same page space (Segal, 2014). Third, bot nets can be programmed to click on ads on fraudulent Web sites, generating impressions and ad serves, but no one actually sees the ads. The Media Rating Council, an advertising industry group, released a very low standard for "viewability" in 2014: an ad is considered viewable if half of the ad can be viewed for at least one second (Hof, 2014). For video ads, half of the video needs to be viewable for two seconds. The advertisers who pay for online ads are beginning to demand guarantees of viewability. Several companies, including comScore, are offering tagging technology that can partially measure viewability

(Vranica, 2014). Unviewed ads are just as profitable as viewed ads for Web publishers and advertising agencies. For advertisers, they represent the half of marketing expenditures that is wasted.

E-mail Marketing

When e-mail marketing began, unsolicited e-mail was not common. **Direct e-mail marketing** (e-mail marketing messages sent directly to interested users) was one of the first and most effective forms of online marketing communications. Direct e-mail marketing messages are sent to an opt-in audience of Internet users who, at one time or another, have expressed an interest in receiving messages from the advertiser. By sending e-mail to an opt-in audience, advertisers are targeting interested consumers. Response rates to legitimate, opt-in e-mail campaigns average just over 6%, depending on the targeting and freshness of the list. By far, in-house e-mail lists are more effective than purchased e-mail lists. Because of the comparatively high response rates and low cost, direct e-mail marketing remains a common form of online marketing communications. Other benefits of e-mail marketing include its mass reach, the ability to track and measure response, the ability to personalize content and tailor offers, the ability to drive traffic to Web sites for more interaction, the ability to test and optimize content and offers, and the ability to target by region, demographic, time of day, or other criteria. In 2014, although companies will spend a relatively small amount on e-mail marketing when compared to search and display ad marketing, e-mail marketing still packs a punch with solid customer response. Click-through rates for legitimate e-mail depend on the promotion (the offer), the product, and the amount of targeting, but average around 4%. Despite the deluge of spam mail, e-mail remains a highly cost-effective way of communicating with existing customers, and to a lesser extent, finding new customers. E-mail is also increasingly being accessed via mobile devices, which has the potential to create both opportunities and issues for marketers. Between 40%–50% of e-mails are opened on mobile devices, and mobile users have much higher e-mail utilization rates than do desktop users (eMarketer, Inc., 2014h).

E-mail marketing and advertising is inexpensive and somewhat invariant to the number of mails sent. The cost of sending 1,000 mails is about the same as the cost to send 1 million. The primary cost of e-mail marketing is for the purchase of the list of names to which the e-mail will be sent. This generally costs anywhere from 5 to 20 cents a name, depending on how targeted the list is. Sending the e-mail is virtually cost-free. In contrast, the cost to send a direct mail 5 x 7-inch post card is about 15 cents per name, but printing and mailing costs raise the overall cost to around 75 to 80 cents a name. While the cost of legitimate e-mail messages based on high-quality commercial opt-in e-mail lists is $5 to $10 per thousand, the direct mail cost is $500 to $700 per thousand.

While e-mail marketing often is sales oriented, it can also be used as an integral feature of a multi-channel marketing campaign designed to strengthen brand recognition. For instance, Jeep created an e-mail campaign to a targeted audience of people who had searched on SUVs, and visited Chrysler and Jeep Facebook pages. The e-mail campaign announced a contest based on a game users could play online that involved

direct e-mail marketing
e-mail marketing messages sent directly to interested users

tracking an arctic beast with a Jeep. Recipients could sign up on Facebook, Twitter, or the Jeep blog.

Although e-mail can still be an effective marketing and advertising tool, it faces three main challenges: spam, software tools used to control spam that eliminate much e-mail from user inboxes, and poorly targeted purchased e-mail lists. **Spam** is unsolicited commercial e-mail (sometimes referred to as "junk" e-mail) and *spammers* are people who send unsolicited e-mail to a mass audience that has not expressed any interest in the product. Spammers tend to market pornography, fraudulent deals and services, scams, and other products not widely approved in most civilized societies. Legitimate direct opt-in e-mail marketing is not growing as fast as behaviorally targeted banners, pop-ups, and search engine advertising because of the explosion in spam. Consumer response to even legitimate e-mail campaigns has become more sophisticated. In general, e-mail works well for maintaining customer relationships but poorly for acquiring new customers.

While click fraud may be the Achilles' heel of search engine advertising, spam is the nemesis of effective e-mail marketing and advertising. The percentage of all e-mail that is spam averaged around 62% in the first 8 months of 2014 (Symantec, 2014). Most spam originates from bot networks, which consist of thousands of captured PCs that can initiate and relay spam messages (see Chapter 4). Spam volume has declined somewhat since authorities took down the Rustock botnet in 2011. Spam is seasonally cyclical, and varies monthly due to the impact of new technologies (both supportive and discouraging of spammers), new prosecutions, and seasonal demand for products and services.

Legislative attempts in the United States to control spam have been mostly unsuccessful. Thirty-seven states have laws regulating or prohibiting spam (National Conference of State Legislatures, 2013). State legislation typically requires that unsolicited mail (spam) contain a label in the subject line ("ADV") indicating the message is an advertisement, requires a clear opt-out choice for consumers, and prohibits e-mail that contains false routing and domain name information (nearly all spammers hide their own domain, ISP, and IP address).

The U.S. Congress passed the first national anti-spam law ("Controlling the Assault of Non-Solicited Pornography and Marketing" or CAN-SPAM Act) in 2003, and it went into effect in January 2004. The act does not prohibit unsolicited e-mail (spam) but instead requires unsolicited commercial e-mail messages to be labeled (though not by a standard method) and to include opt-out instructions and the sender's physical address. It prohibits the use of deceptive subject lines and false headers in such messages. The FTC is authorized (but not required) to establish a "Do Not E-mail" registry. State laws that require labels on unsolicited commercial e-mail or prohibit such messages entirely are pre-empted, although provisions merely addressing falsity and deception may remain in place. The act imposes fines of $10 for each unsolicited pornographic e-mail and authorizes state attorneys general to bring lawsuits against spammers. The act obviously makes lawful legitimate bulk mailing of unsolicited e-mail messages (what most people call spam), yet seeks to prohibit certain deceptive practices and provide a small measure of consumer control

spam

unsolicited commercial e-mail

by requiring opt-out notices. In this sense, critics point out, CAN-SPAM ironically legalizes spam as long as spammers follow the rules. For this reason, large spammers have been among the bill's biggest supporters, and consumer groups have been the act's most vociferous critics.

In contrast, Canada's anti-spam law is one of the toughest in the world. Unlike the CAN-SPAM Act, Canada's law is based on an opt-in model and prohibits the sending of commercial e-mail, texts, and social media messaging unless the recipient has given his or her consent. Violations of the law can lead to penalties of up to $1 million for individuals and $10 million for organizations. The first phase of the law went into effect in July 2014. The law applies anytime a computer within Canada is used to send or access an electronic message, so companies located within the United States that send e-mail to Canada must comply with the law (French, 2014).

There have been a number of state and federal prosecutions of spammers, and private civil suits by large ISPs such as Microsoft. Volunteer efforts by industry are another potential control point. Notably, the Direct Marketing Association (DMA), an industry trade group that represents companies that use the postal mail system as well as e-mail for solicitations, is now strongly supporting legislative controls over spam, in addition to its voluntary guidelines. The DMA would like to preserve the legitimate use of e-mail as a marketing technique. The DMA has formed a 15-person anti-spam group and spends $500,000 a year trying to identify spammers. The DMA is also a supporter of the National Cyber-Forensics & Training Alliance (NCFTA), a nonprofit organization with "close ties" to the FBI. NCFTA operates a variety of initiatives aimed at combating cybercrime, including digital phishing via spam.

Affiliate Marketing

Affiliate marketing is a form of marketing where a firm pays a commission, typically anywhere between 4% to 20%, to other Web sites (including blogs) for sending customers to their Web site. Affiliate marketing generally involves pay-for-performance: the affiliate or affiliate network gets paid only if users click on a link or purchase a product (Robinson, 2014). Industry experts estimate that around 10% of all retail online sales are generated through affiliate programs (as compared to search engine ads, which account for more than 30% of online sales).

Visitors to an affiliate Web site typically click on ads and are taken to the advertiser's Web site. In return, the advertiser pays the affiliate a fee, either on a per-click basis or as a percentage of whatever the customer spends on the advertiser's site. Paying commissions for referrals or recommendations long predated the Web.

For instance, Amazon has a strong affiliate program consisting of more than 1 million participant sites, called Associates, which receive up to 15% on sales their referrals generate. Affiliates attract people to their blogs or Web sites where they can click on ads for products at Amazon. Amazon pays affiliates a percentage on the sales generated within 24 hours of a visitor's click. Members of eBay's Affiliates Program can earn between $20 and $35 for each active registered user sent to eBay. Amazon, eBay, and other large e-commerce companies with affiliate programs typically administer such programs themselves. Smaller e-commerce firms who wish to

affiliate marketing
commissions paid by advertisers to affiliate Web sites for referring potential customers to their Web site

use affiliate marketing often decide to join an affiliate network (sometimes called an affiliate broker), such as Commission Junction and Rakuten Linkshare, which acts as an intermediary. Bloggers often sign up for Google's AdSense program to attract advertisers to their sites. They are paid for each click on an ad and sometimes for subsequent purchases made by visitors.

Viral Marketing

viral marketing

the process of getting customers to pass along a company's marketing message to friends, family, and colleagues

Just as affiliate marketing involves using a trusted Web site to encourage users to visit other sites, **viral marketing** is a form of social marketing that involves getting customers to pass along a company's marketing message to friends, family, and colleagues. It's the online version of word-of-mouth advertising, which spreads even faster and further than in the real world. In the offline world, next to television, word of mouth is the second most important means by which consumers find out about new products. And the most important factor in the decision to purchase is the face-to-face recommendations of parents, friends, and colleagues. Millions of online adults in the United States are "influencers" who share their opinions about products in a variety of online settings. In addition to increasing the size of a company's customer base, customer referrals also have other advantages: they are less expensive to acquire because existing customers do all the acquisition work, and they tend to use online support services less, preferring to turn back to the person who referred them for advice. Also, because they cost so little to acquire and keep, referred customers begin to generate profits for a company much earlier than customers acquired through other marketing methods. There are a number of online venues where viral marketing appears. E-mail used to be the primary online venue for viral marketing ("please forward this e-mail to your friends"), but venues such as Facebook, Google+, YouTube, blogs, and social game sites now play a major role. For example, the most viral video ad of 2013 was Dove's Real Beauty Sketches, with over 135 million views (Russell, 2013).

Lead Generation Marketing

lead generation marketing

uses multiple e-commerce presences to generate leads for businesses who later can be contacted and converted into customers

Lead generation marketing uses multiple e-commerce presences to generate leads for businesses who later can be contacted and converted into customers through sales calls, e-mails, or other means. In one sense, all Internet marketing campaigns attempt to develop leads. But lead generation marketing is a specialized subset of the Internet marketing industry that provides consulting services and software tools to collect and manage leads for firms, and to convert these leads to customers. Companies will spend an estimated $2 billion on lead generation marketing in 2014. Sometimes called "inbound marketing," lead generation marketing firms help other firms build Web sites, launch e-mail campaigns, use social network sites and blogs to optimize the generation of leads, and then manage those leads by initiating further contacts, tracking interactions, and interfacing with customer relationship management systems to keep track of customer-firm interactions. One of the foremost lead generation marketing firms is Hubspot.com, which has developed a software suite for generating and managing leads.

SOCIAL, MOBILE, AND LOCAL MARKETING AND ADVERTISING

In this section we provide a brief overview of the social, mobile, and local marketing and advertising landscape. Then, in Chapter 7, we provide a much more in-depth examination of social, mobile, and local marketing and advertising tools.

Social Marketing and Advertising

Social marketing/advertising involves the use of online social networks and communities to build brands and drive sales revenues. There are several kinds of social networks, from Facebook and Twitter, to social apps, social games, blogs, and forums (Web sites that attract people who share a community of interests or skills). In 2013, companies spent about €8.9 billion on social marketing and advertising worldwide, and this is expected to grow to about €21 billion by 2016. Next to mobile marketing, it is the fastest growing type of online marketing. Nevertheless, in 2014, it represents only about 11.5% of all online marketing and is still dwarfed by the amount spent on search engine advertising and display advertising (eMarketer, Inc., 2014z).

Marketers cannot ignore the huge audiences that social networks such as Facebook, Twitter, and LinkedIn are gathering, which rival television and radio in size. In 2014, there were over 1.3 billion Facebook members, 270 million active Twitter users, 310 million who have joined LinkedIn, and around 70 million Pinterest members worldwide. It's little wonder that marketers and advertisers are joyous at the prospect of connecting with this large audience, and research has found that social network users are more likely to talk about and recommend a company or product they follow on Facebook or Twitter.

Features of social marketing and advertising that are driving its growth include:

- *Social sign-on:* Signing in to various Web sites through a social network like Facebook. This allows Web sites to receive valuable social profile information from Facebook and use it in their own marketing efforts.

- *Collaborative shopping:* Creating an environment where consumers can share their shopping experiences with one another by viewing products, chatting, or texting. Instead of talking about the weather, friends can chat online about brands, products, and services.

- *Network notification:* Creating an environment where consumers can share their approval (or disapproval) of products, services, or content, or share their geolocation, perhaps a restaurant or club, with friends. Facebook's ubiquitous "Like" button is an example. Twitter tweets and followers are another example.

- *Social search (recommendation):* Enabling an environment where consumers can ask their friends for advice on purchases of products, services, and content. While Google can help you find things, social search can help you evaluate the quality of things by listening to the evaluations of your friends or their friends. For instance, Amazon's social recommender system can use your Facebook profile to recommend products.

Social networks offer advertisers all the formats found on portal and search sites including banner ads (the most common), short pre-roll and post-roll ads associated with videos, and sponsorship of content. Having a corporate Facebook page is in itself a marketing tool for brands just like a Web page. Many firms, such as Coca-Cola, have shut down product-specific Web pages and instead use Facebook pages.

Blogs and online games can also be used for social marketing. Blogs have been around for a decade and are a part of the mainstream online culture (see Chapter 2 for a description of blogs). Around 27 million people write blogs, and around 76 million read blogs in the United States. Blogs play a vital role in online marketing. Over 60% of companies used blogs for marketing in 2014 (ExactTarget, 2014). Although more firms use Twitter and Facebook, these sites have not replaced blogs, and in fact often point to blogs for long-form content. Because blog readers and creators tend to be more educated, have higher incomes, and be opinion leaders, blogs are ideal platforms for ads for many products and services that cater to this kind of audience. Because blogs are based on the personal opinions of the writers, they are also an ideal platform to start a viral marketing campaign. Advertising networks that specialize in blogs provide some efficiency in placing ads, as do blog networks, which are collections of a small number of popular blogs, coordinated by a central management team, and which can deliver a larger audience to advertisers. For more information on social marketing using blogs, see Learning Track 6.3.

The online gaming marketplace continues to expand rapidly as users increasingly play games on smartphones and tablets, as well as PCs and consoles. The story of game advertising in 2014 is social, local, and mobile: social games are ascendant, mobile devices are the high-growth platform, and location-based advertising is starting to show real traction. The objective of game advertising is both branding and driving customers to purchase moments at restaurants and retail stores. In 2014, in the United States, over 125 million people played games on their mobile devices, another 46 million on consoles, and another 101 million played online games with a PC. Of the online gamers, about 85 million play social games, such as Jackbox Games' You Don't Know Jack (eMarketer, Inc., 2014j).

Mobile Marketing and Advertising

Marketing on the mobile platform is growing rapidly and becoming a significant part (26%) of the overall €113 billion online marketing spending. In 2014, spending on all forms of mobile marketing is estimated to be about €28 billion, and it is growing at over 50% a year (eMarketer, Inc., 2014x). A number of factors are driving advertisers to the mobile platform, including much more powerful devices, faster networks, wireless local networks, rich media and video ads, and growing demand for local advertising by small business and consumers. Most important, mobile is where the eyeballs are now and increasingly will be in the future: 2.25 billion people access the Internet at least some of the time from mobile devices.

Mobile marketing includes the use of display banner ads, rich media, video, games, e-mail, text messaging, in-store messaging, Quick Response (QR) codes, and couponing. Mobile is now a required part of the standard marketing budget. In 2014, search engine advertising is expected to remain the most popular mobile advertising format in the

United States,, accounting for over 50% of all mobile ad spending. Search engine ads can be further optimized for the mobile platform by showing ads based on the physical location of the user. Display ads are also a popular format, and are expected to account for over 35% of mobile ad spending in 2014. Display ads can be served as a part of a mobile Web site or inside apps and games. Facebook is the leader in mobile display ad revenues, followed by Google, Twitter, Pandora, and Apple. Mobile messaging generally involves SMS text messaging to consumers offering coupons or flash marketing messages. Messaging is especially effective for local advertising because consumers can be sent messages and coupons as they pass by or visit locations. Video advertising currently accounts for the smallest percentage of mobile ad spending, but it is one of the fastest growing formats. Ad networks such as Google's AdMob, Apple's iAd, Twitter's MoPub, InMobi (see the opening case), and Millennial Media are also important players in the mobile advertising market.

Apps on mobile devices constitute a new marketing platform that did not exist a few years ago. Apps are a nonbrowser pathway for users to experience the Web and perform a number of tasks from reading the newspaper to shopping, searching, and buying. Apps provide users much faster access to content than do multi-purpose browsers. Apps are also starting to influence the design and function of traditional Web sites as consumers are attracted to the look and feel of apps, and their speed of operation. There are over 2.5 million apps available on Apple's App Store and Google Play and another million apps provided by Internet carriers and third-party storefronts like GetJar and PocketGear, app portals like dev.appia.com, and the Amazon Appstore. An estimated 1.2 billion people used apps in 2013 worldwide and downloaded more than 100 billion apps (SocialMediaToday.com, 2013).

Local Marketing: The Social-Mobile-Local Nexus

Along with social marketing and mobile marketing, local marketing is the third major trend in e-commerce marketing in 2014–2015. The growth of mobile devices has accelerated the growth of local search and purchasing since 2007. New marketing tools like local advertisements on social networks and daily deal sites are also contributing to local marketing growth.

Spending on online local ads in the United States is estimated at around $32 billion in 2014 and is expected to grow to around $53 billion by 2018. The mobile portion of local advertising spending is expected to reach $4.5 billion in 2014, and is projected to almost triple over the next 5 years, growing to to $15.7 billion by 2018 (BIA/Kelsey, 2014a, 2014b). In contrast, spending on traditional local advertising is expected to be flat during the same time period. The most common local marketing tools are geotargeting using Google Maps (local stores appearing on a Google map), display ads in hyperlocal publications like those created by Patch Properties, daily deals, and coupons.

The most commonly used venues include Facebook, Google, Amazon Local, LinkedIn, Yahoo, Bing, and Twitter, as well as more specific location-based offerings such as Google Places, Yahoo Local, Citysearch, YP, SuperPages, and Yelp. The "daily deal" coupon sites, Groupon and LivingSocial, and location-based mobile firms such as Foursquare are also a significant part of this trend.

We examine social, mobile, and local marketing in greater depth in Chapter 7.

MULTI-CHANNEL MARKETING: INTEGRATING ONLINE AND OFFLINE MARKETING

Without an audience, marketing is not possible. With the rapid growth of the Internet, media consumption patterns have changed greatly as consumers are more and more likely to engage with online media, from videos and news sites, to blogs, Twitter feeds, Facebook friends, and Pinterest posts. Increasingly, marketers are using multiple online channels to "touch" customers, from e-mail to Facebook, search ads, display ads on mobile devices, and affiliate programs. Forrester Research reports, for instance, that most customers purchased online following some Web marketing influence, and nearly half of online purchases followed multiple exposures to Web marketing efforts (Forrester Research, 2014).

In 2013, for the first time ever, the average U.K. adult spent more time with digital media per day than the amount viewing TV. In 2014, in the United States, the average adult will spend almost 6 hours a day online and using a mobile device for something other than telephone calls, compared to about 4 and a half hours watching television (see **Figure 6.8**) (eMarketer, Inc., 2014a). An increasing percentage of American media consumers multitask by using several media at once in order to increase the total media exposure. In this environment, marketers increasingly are developing multi-channel marketing programs that can take advantage of the strengths of various media, and reinforce branding messages across media. Online marketing is not the only way,

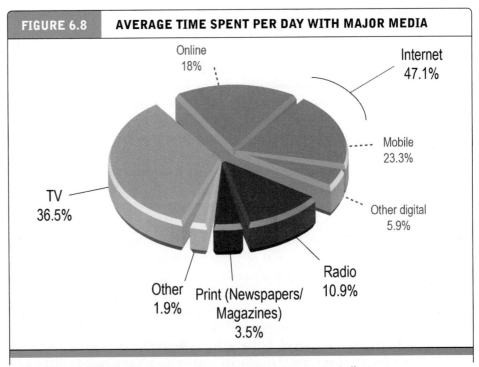

FIGURE 6.8 | AVERAGE TIME SPENT PER DAY WITH MAJOR MEDIA

Online 18%
Internet 47.1%
Mobile 23.3%
Other digital 5.9%
Radio 10.9%
Print (Newspapers/Magazines) 3.5%
Other 1.9%
TV 36.5%

Online marketing should be coupled with offline marketing to achieve optimal effectiveness.
SOURCE: Based on data from eMarketer, Inc., 2014a.

or by itself the best way, to engage consumers. Internet campaigns can be significantly strengthened by also using e-mail, TV, print, and radio. The marketing communications campaigns most successful at driving traffic to a Web site have incorporated both online and offline tactics, rather than relying solely on one or the other. Several research studies have shown that the most effective online advertisements are those that use consistent imagery with campaigns running in other media at the same time.

Insight on Business: Are the Very Rich Different from You and Me? examines how luxury goods providers use online marketing in conjunction with their offline marketing efforts.

OTHER ONLINE MARKETING STRATEGIES

In addition to the "traditional" online marketing and advertising tools we have previously discussed, such as search engine, display, and e-mail marketing, and the newer social, mobile, and local marketing and advertising tools, there are also a number of other, more focused online marketing strategies. Here we examine tools aimed at customer retention, pricing, and a strategy known as the "long tail."

Customer Retention Strategies

The Internet offers several extraordinary marketing techniques for building a strong relationship with customers and for differentiating products and services.

Personalization, One-to-One Marketing, and Interest-based Advertising (Behavioral Targeting)
No Internet-based marketing technique has received more popular and academic comment than "one-to-one" or "personalized marketing." **One-to-one marketing (personalization)** segments the market on the basis of individuals (not groups), based on a precise and timely understanding of their needs, targeting specific marketing messages to these individuals, and then positioning the product vis-à-vis competitors to be truly unique. One-to-one marketing is the ultimate form of market segmentation, targeting, and positioning—where the segments are individuals.

one-to-one marketing (personalization)
segmenting the market based on a precise and timely understanding of an individual's needs, targeting specific marketing messages to these individuals, and then positioning the product vis-à-vis competitors to be truly unique

The movement toward market segmentation has been ongoing since the development of systematic market research and mass media in the 1930s. However, e-commerce and the Internet are different in that they enable personalized one-to-one marketing to occur on a mass scale.

The Amazon and Barnes & Noble Web sites are good examples of personalization at work. Both sites greet registered visitors (based on cookie files), recommend recent books based on user preferences (stored in a user profile in their database) as well as what other consumers purchased, and expedite checkout procedures based on prior purchases.

Behavioral targeting of ads involves using the online and offline behavior of consumers to adjust the advertising message delivered online, often in real time (milliseconds from the consumer's first URL entry). The intent is to increase the efficiency of marketing and advertising, and to increase the revenue streams of firms who are in a position to behaviorally target visitors. Because "behavioral targeting" as a label has somewhat unfavorable connotations, the online advertising industry, led by

INSIGHT ON BUSINESS

ARE THE VERY RICH DIFFERENT FROM YOU AND ME?

"Let me tell you about the very rich. They are different from you and me." So observed F. Scott Fitzgerald in the short story, "The Rich Boy." Palm Beach has its Worth Avenue, New York has its Fifth Avenue, Los Angeles has its Rodeo Drive, and Chicago has the Magnificent Mile. So where do the rich go on the Web to get that $5,000 cocktail dress or that $3,000 Italian suit? Well, today, it turns out they may not be so different from the rest of us: they look for online deals and situations where quality can be had at a bargain. At Net-a-Porter, a leading fashion site that combines an online magazine with a strong sales component, you can find a Gucci two-tone silk wrap dress for $1,750 that looks smashing with a pair of Gucci horse bit-detailed patent-leather knee boots for $1,595. There's free shipping too!

Even experts find it hard to define what it means to be affluent and who is affluent. After all, how high is up? There are 24 million households (20% of all U.S. households) where household income is in the $100,000 to $250,000 range. These are often referred to as HENRYs (High Earnings, Not Yet Rich). But the really affluent are those 2.4 million (the top 2% of U.S. households) that earn more than $250,000 a year. And then there are the 9 million households (.7% of households) that earn more than a million a year. These are the real one-percenters. Finally, we have arrived at a reasonable understanding of affluence: there are the "sort of rich" HENRYs, the affluent, and what the experts call "ultra rich."

Retail consumption in general is highly skewed: the wealthiest top 10% of households account for 50% of all retail spending and 37% of all e-commerce retail spending. The recovery in consumer spending since the recession of 2009 has been largely driven by the 24 million affluent households, the top 20%, and this is especially true of luxury goods. Luxury goods markets worldwide expanded by 10% in 2012, but have since slowed down to flat or even declined slightly as the incomes of the rich have fluctuated and fallen on average. Just like the rest of us, the wealthy are shopping online more and more frequently: in 2013, online luxury goods sales are up 28%. The economy has bounced back for some, the stock market is touching new highs, and home sale prices have improved. According to Realtor.com, in 2014, homes selling for more than $15 million are being quickly snapped up. Wealthy Americans are opening their wallets to spend on expensive clothing, accessories, jewelry, and beauty products. In fact, in 2014, the United States has replaced China as the leader in luxury spending around the world, according to Bain & Company research.

Yet even the rich are not immune to the lure of a good deal. The problem is that luxury retailers are typically loath to offer sales because they believe sales detract from their reputations. However, change is in the air (or online, as it were). LVMH, the world's largest luxury brand holding company, has launched Nowness, a Web site featuring all manner of daily specials. Times are changing when Lacoste (the polo shirts with the crocodile logo) pulls the plug on print advertising and puts all its U.S. marketing dollars on the Internet. You know something is different when Faberge introduces its first new line of luxury jewelry in 90 years with a Web-only marketing effort on a single Web site. The site offers 100 pieces of jewelry ranging in price from $48,000 to $10 million. A Faberge marketing report found that what the rich really respond to is the personal attention of a salesperson. An online shopping cart? Please, are you kidding? Instead many luxury sites are now offering a personal sales rep to walk customers through the Web site.

One of the largest fashion destinations on the Web is Net-a-Porter, an online luxury brand store for women that sells into 170 countries. Launched as an online store in 2000, initially luxury goods designers would not even consider selling to the site. Affluent women in that period only bought clothes they had seen, touched and tried on. That all changed in the last decade, and now Net-a-Porter sells over 100 of the world's most fashionable high-end brands from Gucci to Tory Burch and Burberry. The Web site has 6 million visitors a month, 2.6 million followers on social media, and the company now has over 100 physical retail stores. The average customer at the site is 39 years old, has an average income of $278,000, and spends $21,000 a year on clothing. On balance, these customers are at the low end of the truly affluent or at the top end of the HENRYs (High Earnings, Not Yet Rich).

Luxury retailers are in fact offering discounts— but they're secret. How can a sale be secret? Whispered discounts at the physical stores ("Shhhh! There's a special sale in the dress department!") have their online counterpart in flash e-mail campaigns and "private online sales" in which selected online customers are e-mailed alerts such as "A $3,000 handbag on sale for the next two hours for $800." Neiman Marcus calls them Midday Dash sales. Two-hour online-only sales promise 50% off on luxury goods that can be purchased only by clicking on a link in the e-mail. One week's "dash sale" featured a $697 Burberry handbag, marked down from $1,395.

But not all is well among the HENRYs and the affluent. Since 2010, the average income of the affluent has declined, and shown greater volatility than in the past. In past recessions, the top 1% of earners experienced the greatest shocks to their income. It's a wild ride. As it turns, being on top is not permanent, but temporary. Only 27% of America's top 400 income earners have made the list more than one year. One result is that the affluent have entered a new age of austerity. Affluents

spent nearly 25% less on luxury in 2013 than in 2012, according to the latest Luxury Report from Unity Marketing. For luxury goods stores, this means it's important to have plenty of goods for sale that represent quality, at a reasonable price, for those rich who are not doing so well.

Luxury retailers have a dilemma: they need to attract not just the ultra-affluent, but also the aspirational HENRYs who are far more numerous and anxious to display their wealth. They need to be both exclusive and accessible. One solution is the so-called Mercedes Benz strategy: build luxurious but affordable cars for the HENRYs while maintaining a focus on high-end truly luxury models for the ultra-affluent. Mercedes Benz combines a dual level product strategy with effective use of social and mobile media. Mercedes' Facebook page is a main hub of interaction between the brand and its customers, with 2.3 million followers entertained with sweepstakes, videos, images, news, and links to its blog, the Mercedes Reporter, for additional insight into why Mercedes is unique and worth all that money. Mercedes also uses Twitter and a dozen iPhone apps to engage a broader range of customers by providing personalized video tours of its cars.

While luxury retails still rely on upscale retail stores offering personal attention and an unparalleled consumer experience, the action has moved to the Internet in part because that's where the wealthy shop. Wealthy consumers are much more likely to own iPads, spend on average twice as much, and aren't afraid to lay down serious money on a whim. In addition, luxury retailers can offer discreet sales to a select group of customers without tarnishing the brand, preserving exclusivity, and creating a sense of urgency by limiting the time to purchase. At the same time, they can deny they discount their items. If prices were public, customers would know that the $800 Marni skirt they bought today was on sale the next day for $400. They might conclude that none of these goods are worth the price charged, certainly not the retail price, no matter what it is. Online dash sales are sort of like impulse buying at

(continued)

Walmart, but instead of 20 batteries for $5, it's more like one Burberry bag for $1,000. Rich people can indulge bigger impulses. But like the rest of us, the rich just can't seem to get enough of a good thing, especially if it's half price.

The explosion of social media and the increasing investments in the online channel by luxury companies has reinforced and enlarged the community of those who explore, comment upon, and eventually purchase luxury goods. Luxury companies are more than doubling their "friends" on Facebook annually in recognition of the link between online and offline purchases. Burberry Group, the United Kingdom's largest luxury goods maker, reports that it obtains the most reach and most response from digital initiatives compared with other media. To promote the Burberry Body fragrance, the London-based company offered exclusive samples to its Facebook fans. It received more than 225,000 requests in little more than a week.

Tiffany, the quintessential luxury firm, experienced lower profits in the recession of 2008–2009, but never experienced a loss. Since then, however, revenues have expanded sharply worldwide, increasing by 8% in 2013, four times as fast as the economy as a whole. Revenues have accelerated in 2014 as the economy recovers. Tiffany's strategy is not to lower prices but to add more lower-priced items to the marketing mix. For instance, pendants are going for as little as $150 to "only" $15,000 (those are the ones with the big diamonds). Online jewelry has plenty of sterling as well as gold pieces.

Developing an online marketing approach that increases a company's access to consumers while retaining an image of exclusivity was the challenge faced by Tiffany & Co. The company is in the enviable position of being perhaps the most famous jewelry company in the United States. Tiffany's offline marketing communications seek to engender feelings of beauty, quality, and timeless style—all hallmarks of the Tiffany brand. How could Tiffany maintain its approach on the Web, a medium that often emphasizes speed and flashy graphics over grace and elegance, and low-cost bargains over high-priced exclusive fashion? The Web, for the most part, is all about low prices and great deals—concepts that are anathema to the high-fashion merchants like Tiffany. The answer is apparent in a visit to the Tiffany Web site. The site features limited inventory, with a focus on high-resolution images of its exclusive and original designs in jewelry and apparel. There are no sales, coupons, discounts, or other offers although visitors can choose jewelry in lower price ranges (less than $250 for instance). The Web site and Facebook brand page reflect custom service and design, calm, and simplicity. The prices are equally exclusive: an exquisite Atlas Hinged Bangle in 18k rose gold and round brilliant diamonds for $9,000, and sunglasses for $500.

Today, Tiffany has shifted more of its direct marketing effort from the offline catalog to the online catalog, a YouTube Channel, and a Facebook brand page with 4 million Likes. It has Web sites in 13 different countries, including Canada, the United Kingdom, Japan, and Australia. Tiffany sites carry over 2,100 products in six categories of goods: engagement, jewelry, watches, designers and collections, gifts, and accessories. In 2013, Tiffany's online sales were over $241 million, 6% of its $4 billion worldwide sales, placing it in second place in the online jewelry industry. (Blue Nile is first with $450 million in online sales.)

SOURCES: "Luxury Homes: Priced to Sell at $30 Million," by Stefanos Chen, *Wall Street Journal*, September 10, 2014; "Luxury Goods Worldwide Market Study Spring 2014," by Bain & Company, May 19, 2014; Tiffany & Co. Annual Report on Form 10-K, filed with the Securities and Exchange Commission, April 1, 2014; "Luxury Report 2014: Ultimate Six-Year Guide to the Luxury Consumer Market," by Unity Marketing Inc., January 2014; "The Luxury Consumer," by Patricia Orsini, eMarketer, Inc., November 2013; "Louis Vuitton Walks the Fine Luxury Line," by Renee Schultes, *Wall Street Journal*, April 14, 2013; "What Recession? Americans Regain a Craving for Luxury," by Nadya Masidlover, *Wall Street Journal*, February 13, 2013; "Luxury Marketing: Recreating the One-on-One Experience With Mobile," [Patricia Orsini], eMarketer, Inc., September 2012; "Affluents: Demographic Profile and Marketing Approach," eMarketer, Inc. (Mark Dolliver), January 2012; "Affluent Shoppers and Luxury Brand Retailers Online," eMarketer, Inc. (Jeffrey Grau), September 2011; "High Fashion Relents to Web's Pull," by Stephanie Clifford, *New York Times*, July 11, 2010; "Luxury Brands Warming to the Web," by Mark Porter, Reuters, June 3, 2011; "Mr Porter to Test Men's Urge to Shop Online," by Ray Smith, *Wall Street Journal*, February 10, 2011.

Google, has introduced a new name for behavioral targeting. They call it **interest-based advertising**.

One of the original promises of the Web has been that it can deliver a marketing message tailored to each consumer based on this data, and then measure the results in terms of click-throughs and purchases. If you are visiting a jewelry site, you would be shown jewelry ads. If you entered a search query like "diamonds," you would be shown text ads for diamonds and other jewelry. This was taken one step further by advertising networks composed of several thousand sites. An advertising network could follow you across thousands of Web sites and come up with an idea of what you are interested in as you browse, and then display ads related to those interests. For instance, if you visit a few men's clothing sites in the course of a few hours, you will be shown ads for men's clothing on most other sites you visit subsequently, regardless of their subject content. If you search for a certain pair of shoes at Zappos, and Like them to your friends on Facebook, you will be shown ads for the exact same shoes at other sites (including Facebook). Behavioral targeting combines nearly all of your online behavioral data into a collection of interest areas, and then shows you ads based on those interests, as well as the interests of your friends. What's new about today's behavioral targeting is the breadth of data collected: your e-mail content, social network page content, friends, purchases online, books read or purchased, newspaper sites visited, and many other behaviors. And finally, ad exchanges take the marketing of all this information one step further. Most popular Web sites have more than 100 tracking programs on their home pages that are owned by third-party data collector firms who then sell this information in real time to the highest bidding advertiser in real-time online auctions. Ad exchanges make it possible for advertisers to retarget ads at individuals as they roam across the Internet. **Retargeting ads** involves showing the same or similar ads to individuals across multiple Web sites. Retargeted ads are nearly as effective as the original ad (eMarketer, Inc., 2013a).

There are four methods that online advertisers use to behaviorally target ads: search engine queries, the collection of data on individual browsing history online (monitoring the clickstream), the collection of data from social network sites, and increasingly, the integration of this online data with offline data like income, education, address, purchase patterns, credit records, driving records, and hundreds of other personal descriptors tied to specific, identifiable persons. This level of integration of both "anonymous" as well as identifiable information is routinely engaged in by Google, Microsoft, Yahoo, Facebook, and legions of small and medium-sized marketing firms that use their data, or collect data from thousands of Web sites using Web beacons and cookies. On average, online information bureaus maintain 2,000 data elements on each adult person in their database. The currency and accuracy of this data are never examined, and the retention periods are not known. Currently, there are no federal laws or regulations governing this data.

Earlier in the chapter we described search engine advertising in some detail. Search engine advertising has turned out to be the most effective online advertising format by several orders of magnitude, and provides more than 95% of the revenue of Google, the world's largest online advertising agency. Why is search engine advertising so effective? Most agree that when users enter a query into a search engine, it reveals a

interest-based advertising (behavioral targeting)
using search queries and clicks on results to behaviorally target consumers

retargeting ads
showing the same ad to individuals across multiple Web sites

very specific intention to shop, compare, and possibly purchase. When ads are shown at these very moments of customer behavior, they are 4 to 10 times as effective as other formats. The author John Battelle coined the phrase and the notion that the Web is a database of intentions composed of the results from every search ever made and every path that searchers have followed, since the beginning of the Web. In total, this database contains the intentions of all mankind. This treasure trove of intentions, desires, likes, wants, and needs is owned by only a few private business firms, namely, Google, Microsoft, and to a lesser extent, Yahoo, in massive, global databases (Battelle, 2003). Batelle later extended the concept of a database of intentions beyond search to include the social graph (Facebook and Google+), status updates (Twitter and Facebook), and the "check-in" (Foursquare and Yelp) (Battelle, 2010). The database of intentions can be exploited to track and target individuals and groups. Not only is this capability unprecedented, but it's growing exponentially into the foreseeable future. The potential for abuse is also growing exponentially.

The decline in the growth rate of search engine advertising, from the early days of double-digit growth to today's growth of high single digits, has caused the major search engine firms to seek out alternative forms of future growth, which include display, rich media, and video advertising on millions of Web publisher sites. Web publishers have responded by producing billions of pages of content. In this environment, the effectiveness of display ads has been falling in terms of response rates and prices for ads. Behavioral targeting is an effective way to solve this problem and increase response rates. Behavioral targeting of both search and display advertising is currently driving the expansion in online advertising.

Behavioral targeting seeks to optimize consumer response by using information that Web visitors reveal about themselves online, and if possible, to combine this with offline identity and consumption information gathered by companies such as Acxiom. Behavioral targeting is based on real-time information about visitors' use of Web sites, including pages visited, content viewed, search queries, ads clicked, videos watched, content shared, and products they purchased. Once this information is collected and analyzed on the fly, behavioral targeting programs attempt to develop profiles of individual users, and then show advertisements most likely to be of interest to the user. More than 80% of North American advertisers use some form of targeting in their online display ads (Forrester Research, 2014b).

For a variety of technical and other reasons, this vision has, thus far, not been widely achieved. The percentage of ads that are actually targeted is unknown, but most display ads are not targeted. Instead, advertisers use less expensive context ads displayed to a general audience without any targeting, or very minimal demographic targeting. The quality of the data, largely owned by the online advertising networks, is quite good but hardly perfect. The ability to understand and respond—the business intelligence and real-time analytics—is still weak, preventing companies from being able to respond quickly in meaningful ways when the consumer is online. The firms who sell targeted ads to their clients claim the targeted ads are two or three times more effective than general ads. There is not very good data to support these claims from independent sources. Generally these claims confound the impact of brands on targeted audiences, and the impact of the ads placed to this targeted audience.

Advertisers target groups that are most likely to buy their product even in the absence of targeting ads at them. The additional impact of a targeted ad is much smaller than ad platforms claim. A recent research report based on real data from 18 ad campaigns on Yahoo, involving 18.4 million users, found that brand interest is the largest single factor in determining targeted ad effectiveness, and not the targeted ad itself (Farahat and Bailey, 2012). And marketing companies are not yet prepared to accept the idea that there needs to be several hundred or a thousand variations on the same display ad depending on the customer's profile. Such a move would raise costs. Last, consumer resistance to targeting continues. A recent survey found that nearly 70% of Americans are opposed to having companies track their online behavior even if they receive a free service or product. Over 60% of consumers do not believe that viewing more relevant ads is fair trade off for being tracked. Almost 90% say people should have the right to control what information is collected online and a significant majority would like to turn tracking off (Consumer-action.org, 2013). These results are consistent with earlier polls in 2012 (TRUSTe, 2012; Gigaom, 2012).

Nevertheless, firms are experimenting with more precise targeting methods, and ad budgets for targeting are expanding rapidly. Snapple used behavioral targeting methods (with the help of online ad firm Tacoda) to identify the types of people attracted to Snapple Green Tea. Answer: people who like the arts and literature, travel internationally, and visit health sites. Some advertisers have reported more than 50% increases in click-through rates. General Motors used Digitas (a Boston-based online ad firm) to create several hundred versions of a single ad for its Acadia crossover vehicle. Viewers were initially shown ads that emphasize brand, features, and communities. On subsequent viewings, they were shown different ads based on demographics, lifestyle, and behavioral considerations. Men were shown versions of the ads emphasizing engines, specifications, and performance, while women were shown versions that emphasize comfort, accessibility, and families.

The growth of targeting continues to raise privacy issues. The public and congressional reaction to behavioral targeting is described more fully in Chapter 8.

Customization and Customer Co-Production

Customization is an extension of personalization. **Customization** means changing the product—not just the marketing message—according to user preferences. **Customer co-production** means the users actually think up the innovation and help create the new product.

Many leading companies now offer "build-to-order" customized products on the Internet on a large scale, creating product differentiation and, hopefully, customer loyalty. Customers appear to be willing to pay a little more for a unique product. The key to making the process affordable is to build a standardized architecture that lets consumers combine a variety of options. For example, Nike offers customized sneakers through its Nike iD program on its Web site. Consumers can choose the type of shoe, colors, material, and even a logo of up to eight characters. Nike transmits the orders via computers to specially equipped plants in China and Korea. The sneakers cost only $10 extra and take about three weeks to reach the customer. At the Shop M&M's Web site, customers can get their own message printed on custom-made M&Ms; Timberland. com also offers online customization of its boots.

customization
changing the product, not just the marketing message, according to user preferences

customer co-production
in the Web environment, takes customization one step further by allowing the customer to interactively create the product

Information goods—goods whose value is based on information content—are also ideal for this level of differentiation. For instance, the New York Times—and many other content distributors—allows customers to select the news they want to see on a daily basis. Many Web sites, particularly portal sites such as Yahoo, MSN, and AOL, allow customers to create their own customized version of the Web site. Such pages frequently require security measures such as usernames and passwords to ensure privacy and confidentiality.

Customer Service A Web site's approach to customer service can significantly help or hurt its marketing efforts. Online customer service is more than simply following through on order fulfillment; it has to do with users' ability to communicate with a company and obtain desired information in a timely manner. Customer service can help reduce consumer frustration, cut the number of abandoned shopping carts, and increase sales.

Most consumers want to, and will, serve themselves as long as the information they need to do so is relatively easy to find. Online buyers largely do not expect or desire "high-touch" service unless they have questions or problems, in which case they want relatively speedy answers that are responsive to their individual issue. Researchers have found that online consumers strongly attach to brands when they have a problem with an order. Customer loyalty increases substantially when online buyers learn that customer service representatives are available online or at an 800-number and were willing and able to resolve the situation quickly. Conversely, online buyers who do not receive satisfaction at these critical moments often terminate their relationship with the business and switch to merchants that may charge more but deliver superior customer service (Ba et al., 2010; Wolfinbarger and Gilly, 2001).

There are a number of tools that companies can use to encourage interaction with prospects and customers and provide customer service—FAQs, customer service chat systems, intelligent agents, and automated response systems—in addition to the customer relationship management systems described in the preceding section.

frequently asked questions (FAQs)
a text-based listing of common questions and answers

Frequently asked questions (**FAQs**), a text-based listing of common questions and answers, provide an inexpensive way to anticipate and address customer concerns. Adding an FAQ page on a Web site linked to a search engine helps users track down needed information more quickly, enabling them to help themselves resolve questions and concerns. By directing customers to the FAQs page first, Web sites can give customers answers to common questions. If a question and answer do not appear, it is important for sites to make contact with a live person simple and easy. Offering an e-mail link to customer service at the bottom of the FAQs page is one solution.

real-time customer service chat systems
a company's customer service representatives interactively exchange text-based messages with one or more customers on a real-time basis

Real-time customer service chat systems (in which a company's customer service representatives interactively exchange text-based messages with one or more customers on a real-time basis) are an increasingly popular way for companies to assist online shoppers during a purchase. Chats with online customer service representatives can provide direction, answer questions, and troubleshoot technical glitches that can kill a sale. Leading vendors of customer service chat systems include LivePerson and InstantService. Vendors claim that chat is significantly less expensive than telephone-based customer service. However, critics point out this conclusion may be based on optimistic assumptions that chat representatives can assist three or four customers at once, and that chat sessions are shorter than phone sessions. Also, chat sessions are text sessions, and not as rich as talking with a human being over the phone. On the plus side, chat has been reported to raise per-order sales figures, providing sales assistance by allowing companies to "touch" customers during the decision-making process. Evidence suggests that chat can lower shopping cart abandonment rates, increase the number of items purchased per transaction, and increase the dollar value of transactions. "Click to call" or "live call" is another version of a real-time online customer service system, in which the customer clicks a link or accepts an invitation to have a customer service representative call them on the telephone.

Intelligent agent technology is another way customers are providing assistance to online shoppers. Intelligent agents are part of an effort to reduce costly contact with customer service representatives. **Automated response systems** send e-mail order confirmations and acknowledgments of e-mailed inquiries, in some cases letting the customer know that it may take a day or two to actually research an answer to their question. Automating shipping confirmations and order status reports are also common.

automated response system
sends e-mail order confirmations and acknowledgments of e-mailed inquiries

Pricing Strategies

As we noted in Chapter 1, during the early years of e-commerce, many academics and business consultants predicted that the Web would lead to a new world of information symmetry and "frictionless" commerce. In this world, newly empowered customers, using intelligent shopping agents and the nearly infinite product and price information available on the Internet, would shop around the world (and around the clock) with minimal effort, driving prices down to their marginal cost and driving intermediaries out of the market as customers began to deal directly with producers (Wigand and Benjamin, 1995; Rayport and Sviokla, 1995; Evans and Wurster, 1999; Sinha, 2000). The result was supposed to be an instance of the **"Law of One Price"**: with complete price transparency in a perfect information marketplace, one world price for every product would emerge. "Frictionless commerce" would, of course, mean the end of marketing based on brands.

Law of One Price
with complete price transparency in a perfect information marketplace, there will be one world price for every product

But it didn't work out this way. Firms still compete for customers through price as well as product features, scope of operations, and focus. **Pricing** (putting a value on goods and services) is an integral part of marketing strategy. Together, price and quality determine customer value. Pricing of e-commerce goods has proved very difficult for both entrepreneurs and investors to understand.

pricing
putting a value on goods and services

In traditional firms, the prices of traditional goods—such as books, drugs, and automobiles—are usually based on their fixed and variable costs as well as the market's **demand curve** (the quantity of goods that can be sold at various prices). *Fixed costs* are the costs of building the production facility. *Variable costs* are costs involved in running the production facility—mostly labor. In a competitive market, with undifferentiated goods, prices tend toward their *marginal costs* (the incremental cost of

demand curve
the quantity of goods that can be sold at various prices

producing the next unit) once manufacturers have paid the fixed costs to enter the business.

Firms usually "discover" their demand curves by testing various price and volume bundles, while closely watching their cost structure. Normally, prices are set to maximize profits. A profit-maximizing company sets its prices so that the *marginal revenue* (the revenue a company receives from the next unit sold) from a product just equals its marginal costs. If a firm's marginal revenue is higher than its marginal costs, it would want to lower prices a bit and sell more product (why leave money on the table when you can sell a few more units?). If its marginal revenue for selling a product is lower than its marginal costs, then the company would want to reduce volume a bit and charge a higher price (why lose money on each additional sale?).

In the early years of e-commerce, something unusual happened. Sellers were pricing their products far below their marginal costs. Some sites were losing money on every sale. How could this be? New economics? New technology? The Internet age? No. Internet merchants could sell below their marginal costs (even giving away products for free) simply because a large number of entrepreneurs and their venture capitalist backers thought this was a worthwhile activity, at least in the short term. The idea was to attract "eyeballs" with free goods and services, and then later, once the consumer was part of a large, committed audience, charge advertisers enough money to make a profit, and (maybe) charge customers subscription fees for value-added services (the so-called *"piggyback" strategy* in which a small number of users can be convinced to pay for premium services that are piggybacked upon a larger audience that receives standard or reduced value services). To a large extent, social networking sites and user-generated content sites have resurrected this revenue model with a focus on the growth in audience size and not short-term profits. To understand the behavior of entrepreneurial firms, it is helpful to examine a traditional demand curve (see **Figure 6.9**).

A small number of customers are willing to pay a great deal for the product—far above P_1. A larger number of customers would happily pay P_1, and an even larger number of customers would pay less than P_1. If the price were zero, the demand might approach infinity! Ideally, in order to maximize sales and profits, a firm would like to pick up all the money in the market by selling the product at the price each customer is willing to pay. This is called **price discrimination**—selling products to different people and groups based on their willingness to pay. If some people really want the product, sell it to them at a high price. But sell it to indifferent people at a much lower price; otherwise, they will not buy. This only works if the firm can (a) identify the price each individual would be willing to pay, and (b) segregate the customers from one another so they cannot find out what the others are paying. Therefore, most firms adopt a fixed price for their goods (P_1), or a small number of prices for different versions of their products.

What if the marginal cost of producing a good is zero? What should the price be for these goods? It would be impossible then to set prices based on equalizing marginal revenue and marginal cost—because marginal cost is zero. The Internet is primarily filled with information goods—from music to research reports, to stock quotes, stories, weather reports, articles, pictures, and opinions—whose marginal cost of production

price discrimination
selling products to different people and groups based on their willingness to pay

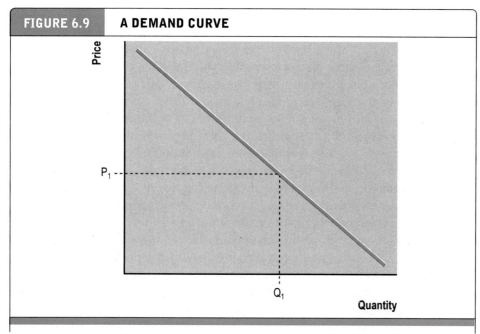

FIGURE 6.9	A DEMAND CURVE

A demand curve shows the quantity of product (Q) that could be sold at various prices (P).

is zero when distributed over the Internet. Thus, another reason certain goods, such as some information goods, may be free on the Internet is that they are "selling" for what it costs to produce them—next to nothing. Content that is stolen from television, CDs, and Hollywood movies has zero production costs. Content that is contributed by users also has zero production costs for the Web sites themselves.

Free and Freemium Everyone likes a bargain, and the best bargain is something for free. Businesses give away free PCs, free data storage, free music, free Web sites, free photo storage, and free Internet connections. Free is not new: banks used to give away "free" toasters to depositors in the 1950s. Google offers free office apps, free e-mail, and free collaboration sites. There can be a sensible economic logic to giving things away. Free content can help build market awareness (such as the free online *New York Times* that contains only the daily stories—not the archived stories) and can lead to sales of other follow-on products. Finally, free products and services knock out potential and actual competitors (the free browser Internet Explorer from Microsoft spoiled the market for Netscape's browser) (Shapiro and Varian, 1999).

Today, online "free" is increasingly being implemented as "freemium" to borrow a phrase from Chris Anderson's book *Free: The Future of a Radical Price.* The freemium pricing model is a cross-subsidy online marketing strategy where users are offered a basic service for free, but must pay for premium or add-on services. The people who pay for the premium services hopefully will pay for all the free riders on the service. Skype uses a freemium model: millions of users can call other Skype users on the

Internet for free, but there's a charge for calling a land line or cell phone. Flickr, Google Sites, Yahoo, and a host of others offer premium services at a price in order to support "free" services. Pandora offers free Internet radio, but it is restricted to a few hours a month. Premium unlimited service costs $36 a year. (See the Chapter 5 case study, *Freemium Takes Pandora Public,* for more information on Pandora and the freemium pricing strategy.)

"Free" and "freemium" as pricing strategies do have limits. In the past, many e-commerce businesses found it difficult to convert the eyeballs into paying customers. YouTube is still not profitable. Free sites attract hundreds of millions of price-sensitive "free loaders" who have no intention of ever paying for anything, and who switch from one free service to another at the very mention of charges. The piggyback strategy has not been a universal success. "Free" eliminates a rich price discrimination strategy. Clearly some of the free loaders would indeed pay a small amount each month, and this revenue is lost to the firms who offer significant services for free. Some argue that everything digital will one day be free in part because Internet users expect it to be so. But the history of "free" includes broadcast television, which used to be "free" (it was advertising-supported), but the public eventually had no problem moving to cable television and DVDs as paid services. The exceptions to "free" are really valuable streams of information that are exclusive, expensive to produce, not widely distributed, unique, and have immediate consumption or investment value. Even in the age of the Internet, these digital streams will sell for a price greater than zero. There probably is no free lunch after all, at least not one that's worth eating.

versioning

creating multiple versions of information goods and selling essentially the same product to different market segments at different prices

Versioning One solution to the problem of free information goods is **versioning**—creating multiple versions of the goods and selling essentially the same product to different market segments at different prices. In this situation, the price depends on the value to the consumer. Consumers will segment themselves into groups that are willing to pay different amounts for various versions (Shapiro and Varian, 1998). Versioning fits well with a modified "free" strategy. A reduced-value version can be offered for free, while premium versions can be offered at higher prices. What are characteristics of a "reduced-value version?" Low-priced—or in the case of information goods, even "free"—versions might be less convenient to use, less comprehensive, slower, less powerful, and offer less support than the high-priced versions. Just as there are different General Motors car brands appealing to different market segments (Cadillac, Buick, Chevrolet, and GMC), and within these divisions, hundreds of models from the most basic to the more powerful and functional, so can information goods be "versioned" in order to segment and target the market and position the products. In the realm of information goods, online magazines, music companies, and book publishers offer sample content for free, but charge for more powerful content. The *New York Times,* for instance, offers free daily content for several days after publication, but then charges per article for access to the more powerful archive of past issues. Writers, editors, and analysts are more than willing to pay for access to archived, organized content. Some Web sites offer "free services" with annoying advertising, but turn off the ads for a monthly fee.

Bundling "Ziggy" Ziegfeld, a vaudeville entrepreneur at the turn of the twentieth century in New York, noticed that nearly one-third of his theater seats were empty on some Friday nights, and during the week, matinee shows were often half empty. He came up with an idea for bundling tickets into "twofers": pay for one full-price ticket and get the next ticket free. Twofers are still a Broadway theater tradition in New York. They are based on the idea that (a) the marginal cost of seating another patron is zero, and (b) a great many people who would not otherwise buy a single ticket would buy a "bundle" of tickets for the same or even a slightly higher price.

Bundling of information goods online extends the concept of a twofer. **Bundling** offers consumers two or more goods for a price that is less than the goods would cost when purchased individually. The key idea behind the concept of bundling is that although consumers typically have very diverse ideas about the value of a single product, they tend to agree much more on the value of a bundle of products offered at a fixed price. In fact, the per-product price people are willing to pay for the bundle is often higher than when the products are sold separately. Bundling reduces the variance (dispersion) in market demand for goods.

bundling
offers consumers two or more goods for a reduced price

Examples of bundling abound in the information goods marketplace. Microsoft bundles its separate Office tools (Word, Excel, PowerPoint, and Access) into a single Microsoft Office package. Even though many people want to use Word and Excel, far fewer want Access or PowerPoint. However, when all products are put into a single bundle, a very large number of people will agree that about $399 (or around $100 per tool) is a "fair" price for so many products. Likewise, the more software applications that Microsoft bundles with its basic operating system, the more the marketplace agrees that as a package of functionality, it is reasonably priced. On the Web, many content sites bundle as opposed to charging individual prices. Theoretically, bundlers have distinct competitive advantages over those who do not or cannot bundle. Specifically, on the supply side, bundler firms can pay higher prices for content, and on the demand side, bundlers can charge higher prices for their bundles than can single-good firms (Bakos and Brynjolfsson, 2000).

However, bundling of digital goods does not always work. It depends on the bundle and the price. For instance, Reed Elsevier, the world's largest publisher of scientific journals, created a bundle of 1,500 digital scientific journals for American universities, and priced the bundle at a substantial markup to what universities were paying for a much smaller number of journals. It then raised the price to universities that did not want the bundle. The result was a marketplace rebellion shaped in part by the fact that much of the research in these journals was paid for by taxpayers through government grants.

Dynamic Pricing and Flash Marketing The pricing strategies we have discussed so far are all fixed-price strategies. Versions and bundles are sold for fixed prices based on the firm's best effort at maximizing its profits. But what if there is product still left on the shelf along with the knowledge that someone, somewhere, would be willing to pay something for it? It might be better to obtain at least some revenue from the product, rather than let it sit on the shelf, or even perish. Imagine also that there are some people in every market who would pay a hefty premium for a product if they could have it right away. In other situations, such as for an antique, the value of the product has to be discovered in the marketplace (usually because there is a belief that the marketplace would value the product at a much higher price than its owner paid as a cost). In other cases, the value of a good is equal to what the market is willing to pay (and has nothing to do with its cost). Or let's say you want to build frequent visits to your site and offer some really great bargains for a few minutes each day, or the whole day with a set time limit. Here is where dynamic pricing mechanisms come to the fore, and where the strengths of the Internet can be seen. With **dynamic pricing**, the price of the product varies, depending on the demand characteristics of the customer and the supply situation of the seller.

dynamic pricing
the price of the product varies, depending on the demand characteristics of the customer and the supply situation of the seller

There are a number of different kinds of dynamic pricing mechanisms. For instance, *auctions* have been used for centuries to establish the instant market price for goods. Auctions are flexible and efficient market mechanisms for pricing unique or unusual goods, as well as commonplace goods such as computers, flower bundles, and cameras.

Yield management is quite different from auctions. In auctions, thousands of consumers establish a price by bidding against one another. In *yield management*, managers set prices in different markets, appealing to different segments, in order to sell excess capacity. Airlines exemplify yield management techniques. Every few minutes during the day, they adjust prices of empty airline seats to ensure at least some of the 50,000 empty airline seats are sold at some reasonable price—even below marginal cost of production. Amazon and other large online retailers frequently use yield management techniques that involve changing prices hourly to stimulate demand and maximize revenues. Amazon can also track shopping behavior of individuals seeking a specific product, such as a laser printer. As the consumer searches for the best price, Amazon can observe the offering prices on other Web sites, and then adjust its prices dynamically so that when the user visits Amazon again, a lower price will be displayed than all other sites visited.

Yield management works under a limited set of conditions. Generally, the product is perishable (an empty airline seat perishes when the plane takes off without a full load); there are seasonal variations in demand; market segments are clearly defined; markets are competitive; and market conditions change rapidly (Cross, 1997). In general, only very large firms with extensive monitoring and database systems in place have been able to afford yield management techniques.

Surge pricing is a kind of dynamic pricing used by sharing economy companies such as Uber. Uber uses a dynamic pricing algorithm to optimize its revenue, or as the company claims, to balance supply and demand. Prices have surged from two to ten times or higher during storms and popular holiday periods. Uber was sharply criticized for using this scheme in New York City during Hurricane Sandy in 2012. Critics claim the practice amounts to price gouging, which during an emergency, is illegal in some states like New York. Uber counters that the higher prices bring more livery cars onto the streets, increasing supply just when needed. But surge pricing, like most dynamic pricing schemes, is not the same as an open auction, where price movements are transparent to all. Uber does not make its data on supply and demand available to the public. Therefore it is impossible to know if Uber prices go up during holidays and storms because demand exceeds supply or because Uber wants to increase profits. In July 2014, Uber reached an agreement with the New York State Attorney General to limit pricing surges during emergencies (Isaac, 2014).

A third dynamic pricing technique is *flash marketing*, which has proved extraordinarily effective for travel services, luxury clothing goods, and other goods. Using e-mail or dedicated Web site features to notify loyal customers (repeat purchasers), merchants offer goods and services for a limited time (usually hours) at very low prices. JetBlue has offered $14 flights between New York and Los Angeles. Deluxe hotel rooms are flash marketed at $1 a night. Companies like Rue La La, HauteLook, and Gilt Groupe are based on flash marketing techniques. Blink and you can easily miss these great prices. Gilt purchases overstocked items from major fashion brands and then offers them to their subscribers at discounted prices via daily e-mail and SMS flash messages. Typically, the sale of an item lasts for two hours or until the inventory is depleted. On many occasions, Gilt rises to the top of most frequently visited Web sites when it conducts a sale. Critics point out that these sites take advantage of compulsive shoppers and lead to overshopping for unneeded goods. In another example of mass retail dynamic pricing, in 2011, Amazon used its new cloud music service to offer a flash one-day sale of Lady Gaga's latest album for 99 cents. Response was so great that Amazon's cloud servers could not meet the demand, and the offer has not been repeated.

The Internet has truly revolutionized the possibilities to engage in dynamic, and even misleading, pricing strategies. With millions of consumers using a site every hour, and access to powerful databases, merchants can raise prices one minute and drop them another minute when a competitor threatens. Bait-and-switch tactics become more common: a really low price on one product is used to attract people to a site when in fact the product is not available.

Long Tail Marketing

Consider that Amazon sells a larger number of obscure books than it does of "hit" books (defined as the top 20% of books sold). Nevertheless, the hit books generate 80% of Amazon's revenues. Consumers distribute themselves in many markets according to a power curve where 80% of the demand is for the hit products, and demand for nonhits quickly recedes to a small number of units sold. In a traditional market, niche products are so obscure no one ever hears about them. One impact of the Internet and e-commerce on sales of obscure products with little demand is that obscure products become more visible to consumers through search engines, recommendation engines, and social networks. Hence, online retailers can earn substantial revenue selling products for which demand and price are low. In fact, with near zero inventory costs, and a good search engine, the sales of obscure products can become a much larger percentage of total revenue. Amazon, for instance, has millions of book titles for sale at $2.99 or less, many written by obscure authors. Because of its search and recommendation engines, Amazon is able to generate profits from the sale of this large number of obscure titles. This is called the "**long tail**" effect. See *Insight on Technology: The Long Tail: Big Hits and Big Misses.*

long tail
a colloquial name given to various statistical distributions characterized by a small number of events of high amplitude and a very large number of events with low amplitude

INSIGHT ON TECHNOLOGY

THE LONG TAIL: BIG HITS AND BIG MISSES

The "Long Tail" is a name given to various statistical distributions characterized by a small group of events of high amplitude and a large group of events with low amplitude. Coined by *Wired Magazine* writer Chris Anderson in 2004, the Web's Long Tail has since gone on to fascinate academics and challenge online marketers. The concept is straightforward. Think Hollywood movies: there are a few big hits and also thousands of films that no one ever hears about. In economics, it's the Pareto principle: 20% of anything produces 80% of the effects. That means 20% of a product line produces 80% of the revenue, and by extension, 80% of the product line only returns 20% of the revenue. It's the legion of misses that make up the Long Tail. Anderson claims to have discovered a new rule: no matter how much content you put online, someone, somewhere will show up to buy it. Rather than 20:80, Anderson suggests the Internet changes the Pareto principle. Internet search, recommendation engines, and online social networks all enable niche products to be discovered and purchased. eBay would seem to be a perfect example. The online tag sale contains millions of items drawn from every Aunt Tilly's closet in the world and still seems to find a buyer somewhere for just about anything, revenue that would not be realized without an online marketplace.

On the Internet, where search costs are tiny, and storage and distribution costs are near zero, Amazon is able to offer millions of books for sale compared to a typical large bookstore. The same is true of DVDs, digital cameras, e-books, and streaming videos. Wherever you look on the Web, you find huge inventories, and a great many items that few people are interested in buying. But someone is almost always searching for something. With 2.8 billion people online, even a one-in-a-million product could find over 2,000 buyers. Researchers

note that it isn't just that some people search for strange things, but rather that most shoppers have a taste for both popular as well as niche products. The strength of "infinite inventory" online retailers like Amazon and China-based Alibaba is that they can satisfy the broadest range of individual tastes. Unlike physical stores, such as Walmart and Sears, online merchants have much lower overhead costs because they do not have physical stores and have lower labor costs. Therefore, they can load up on inventory, including items that rarely sell.

There are several implications of the Long Tail phenomenon for Internet marketing. Some writers such as Anderson claim that the Internet revolutionizes digital content by making even niche products highly profitable, and that the revenues produced by small niche products will ultimately outweigh the revenues of hit movies, songs, and books. For content producers, this means less focus on the blockbusters that bust the budget, and more emphasis on the steady base, focusing on creating a quantity of titles that have at least some audience. The Long Tail is a democratizing phenomenon: even less well-known movies, songs, books, and apps can now find a market. For economists, the Long Tail represents a net gain for social welfare because customers can find exactly the niche content they really want rather than just accept the "big hits" on the shelf. The Long Tail makes more customers happy, and the possibility of making money on niche products should encourage more production of "indie" music and film.

One problem with the Long Tail in the past is that people sometimes have had difficulty finding these niche products because they are—by definition—largely unknown. In their native state, the revenue value of low-demand products is locked up in collective ignorance. Here's where recommender systems come into play: they can guide consumers to obscure but wonderful works based on the recommendations of others. Netflix has spent millions in recent years on improving its recommender system.

Long-Tail keywords are another way marketers are trying to unlock the power of the Long Tail. Long-Tail keywords are phrases that a small but significant number of people might use to find products. For instance, instead of investing in keywords such as "shoes" or "men's shoes," a marketer focused on the Long Tail might choose a keyword like "purple Adidas running shoes." Google has also rolled out an update to its search algorithm called Hummingbird that improves Long Tail searches. According to Google, Long Tail searches comprise as much as 50% of all Web queries, with approximately 20% of searches being extremely unique or never seen before. Hummingbird uses textual analysis to deliver better, more focused results for these searches. Another way marketers tap into the Long Tail is to create highly specific blog or other content, which they then promote through social media.

Social networks also make the Long Tail phenomenon even stronger. One online person discovers an unheard-of niche product and shares his or her feelings with others. A recent study found that popularity information of the sort produced in a social network spurs sales of niche products more than mainstream products because of the higher perceived quality of the niche product. If a lot of people say they like an obscure product, it means more to consumers than if the same popularity attaches to a mainstream product.

But some research casts some doubt on the revenue potential in the Long Tail. Solid best sellers have expanded and produce the vast part of online media revenues. A study of millions of digital downloads in England found that 75% of the digital titles were not downloaded even once. The Long Tail is a very lonely, quiet place. In reality, there seems to be more selling of less (the hits) than less selling of more (the misses). In 2013, 20% of Spotify's 20 million tracks were never played, and the top 1% of music artists accounted for 77% of all income. As music services compete to offer increasingly large catalogs of songs, the well-known artists do better, while each individual member of the growing Long Tail finds it harder to stand out amidst lesser-known peers. On mobile devices especially, "front end display" for music services is smaller than on desktop screens, and only the superstars get this valuable marketing real estate. On the other hand, up-and-coming artists have more avenues than ever to promote themselves without the aid of major labels. Artists like violinist Lindsey Stirling started out in the Long Tail; she has put up her own videos on YouTube, and has since become a major commercial success.

Both the Long Tail and the winner-take-all approaches have implications for marketers and product designers. In the Long Tail approach, online merchants, especially those selling digital goods such as content, should build up huge libraries of content because they can make significant revenues from niche products that have small audiences. In the winner-take-all approach, the niche products produce little revenue, and firms should concentrate on hugely popular titles and services. Surprisingly, contrary to what Anderson originally theorized, the evidence for online digital content increasingly supports a winner-take-all perspective.

SOURCES: "Tales of Long Tail's Death Greatly Exaggerated," by Tracy Maddux, Billboard.com, June 17, 2014; "Why Alibaba's Long Tail Makes Amazon's Look Like a Bobcat's," by Matt Schifrin, *Forbes*, May 8, 2014; "The Death of the Long Tail," Musicindustryblog.com, March 4, 2014; "Winners Take All, But Can't We Still Dream," by Robert H. Frank, *New York Times*, February 22, 2014; "Blockbusters: Why The Long Tail is Dead and Go-Big Strategies Pay Off," by Ginny Marvin, Marketingland.com, October 23, 2013; "How Google Is Changing Long-Tail Search with Efforts Like Hummingbird," by Rand Fishkin, Moz.com, October 18, 2013; "Microsoft, Apps and the Long Tail," by Ben Bajarin, Time.com, July 8, 2013; "Goodbye Pareto Principle, Hello Long Tail: The Effect of Search Costs on the Concentration of Product Sales," by Eric Brynjolfsson et al., *Management Science*, July 2012; "Recommendation Networks and the Long Tail of Electronic Commerce," by Gail Oestreicher-Singer, New York University, 2012; "Research Commentary—Long Tails vs. Superstars: The Effect of Information Technology on Product Variety and Sales Concentration Patterns," by Erik Brynjolfsson et al., *Information Systems Research*, December 2010; "How Does Popularity Affect Choices? A Field Experiment," by Catherine Tucker and Juanjuan Zhang, *Management Science*, May 2011; "From Niches to Riches: Anatomy of the Long Tail," by Eric Brynjolfsson et al., *MIT Sloan Management Review*, Summer 2006; "The Long Tail," by Chris Anderson, *Wired Magazine*, October 2004.

| **6.3** | **INTERNET MARKETING TECHNOLOGIES** |

Internet marketing has many similarities to and differences from ordinary marketing. The objective of Internet marketing—as in all marketing—is to build customer relationships so that the firm can achieve above-average returns (both by offering superior products or services and by communicating the product's features to the consumer). But Internet marketing is also very different from ordinary marketing because the nature of the medium and its capabilities are so different from anything that has come before. In order to understand just how different Internet marketing can be and in what ways, you first need to become familiar with some basic Internet marketing technologies.

THE REVOLUTION IN INTERNET MARKETING TECHNOLOGIES

In Chapter 1, we listed eight unique features of e-commerce technology. **Table 6.6** on page 423 describes how marketing has changed as a result of these new technical capabilities.

On balance, the Internet has had four very powerful impacts on marketing. First, the Internet, as a communications medium, has broadened the scope of marketing communications—in the sense of the number of people who can be easily reached as well as the locations where they can be reached, from desktops to mobile smartphones (in short, everywhere). Second, the Internet has increased the richness of marketing communications by combining text, video, and audio content into rich messages. Arguably, the Web is richer as a medium than even television or video because of the complexity of messages available, the enormous content accessible on a wide range of subjects, and the ability of users to interactively control the experience. Third, the Internet has greatly expanded the information intensity of the marketplace by providing marketers (and customers) with unparalleled fine-grained, detailed, real-time information about consumers as they transact in the marketplace.

Fourth, the always-on, always-attached, environment created by mobile devices results in consumers being much more available to receive marketing messages. One result is an extraordinary expansion in marketing opportunities for firms.

WEB TRANSACTION LOGS

transaction log
records user activity at a Web site

registration forms
gather personal data on name, address, phone, zip code, e-mail address, and other optional self-confessed information on interests and tastes

How can e-commerce sites know more than a department store or the local grocery store does about consumer behavior? A primary source of consumer information on the Web is the transaction log maintained by all Web servers. A **transaction log** records user activity at a Web site. The transaction log is built into Web server software. Transaction log data becomes even more useful when combined with two other visitor-generated data trails: registration forms and the shopping cart database. Users are enticed through various means (such as free gifts or special services) to fill out registration forms. **Registration forms** gather personal data on name, address, phone, zip code, e-mail address (usually required), and other optional self-confessed information on interests and tastes. When users make a purchase, they also enter additional

TABLE 6.6	IMPACT OF UNIQUE FEATURES OF E-COMMERCE TECHNOLOGY ON MARKETING
E-COMMERCE TECHNOLOGY DIMENSION	SIGNIFICANCE FOR MARKETING
Ubiquity	Marketing communications have been extended to the home, work, and mobile platforms; geographic limits on marketing have been reduced. The marketplace has been replaced by "marketspace" and is removed from a temporal and geographic location. Customer convenience has been enhanced, and shopping costs have been reduced.
Global reach	Worldwide customer service and marketing communications have been enabled. Potentially hundreds of millions of consumers can be reached with marketing messages.
Universal standards	The cost of delivering marketing messages and receiving feedback from users is reduced because of shared, global standards of the Internet.
Richness	Video, audio, and text marketing messages can be integrated into a single marketing message and consuming experience.
Interactivity	Consumers can be engaged in a dialog, dynamically adjusting the experience to the consumer, and making the consumer a co-producer of the goods and services being sold.
Information density	Fine-grained, highly detailed information on consumers' real-time behavior can be gathered and analyzed for the first time. "Data mining" Internet technology permits the analysis of terabytes of consumer data every day for marketing purposes.
Personalization/ Customization	This feature potentially enables product and service differentiation down to the level of the individual, thus strengthening the ability of marketers to create brands.
Social technology	User-generated content and social networking sites, along with blogs, have created new, large, online audiences where the content is provided by users. These audiences have greatly expanded the opportunity for marketers to reach new potential customers in a nontraditional media format. Entirely new kinds of marketing techniques are evolving. These same technologies expose marketers to the risk of falling afoul of popular opinion by providing more market power to users who now can "talk back."

information into the shopping cart database. The **shopping cart database** captures all the item selection, purchase, and payment data. Other potential additional sources of data are information users submit on product forms, contribute to chat groups, or send via e-mail messages using the "Contact Us" option on most sites.

For a Web site that has a million visitors per month, and where, on average, a visitor makes 15 page requests per visit, there will be 15 million entries in the log each month. These transaction logs, coupled with data from the registration forms

shopping cart database
captures all the item selection, purchase, and payment data

and shopping cart database, represent a treasure trove of marketing information for both individual sites and the online industry as a whole. Nearly all the new Internet marketing capabilities are based on these data-gathering tools. For instance, here are just a few of the interesting marketing questions that can be answered by examining a site's Web transaction logs, registration forms, and shopping cart database:

- What are the major patterns of interest and purchase for groups and individuals?
- After the home page, where do most users go first, and then second and third?
- What are the interests of specific individuals (those we can identify)?
- How can we make it easier for people to use our site so they can find what they want?
- How can we change the design of the site to encourage visitors to purchase our high-margin products?
- Where are visitors coming from (and how can we optimize our presence on these referral sites)?
- How can we personalize our messages, offerings, and products to individual users?

Businesses can choke on the massive quantity of information found in a typical site's log file. We describe some technologies that help firms more effectively utilize this information below.

SUPPLEMENTING THE LOGS: TRACKING FILES

While transaction logs create the foundation of online data collection at a single Web site, marketers use tracking files to follow users across the entire Web as they visit other sites. There are four kinds of tracking files: cookies, beacons, Flash cookies, and apps (software programs used on smartphones and Web sites). As described in Chapter 2, a cookie is a small text file that Web sites place on the hard disk of visitors' client computers every time they visit, and during the visit, as specific pages are visited. Cookies allow a Web site to store data on a user's computer and then later retrieve it. The cookie typically includes a name, a unique ID number for each visitor that is stored on the user's computer, the domain (which specifies the Web server/domain that can access the cookie), a path (if a cookie comes from a particular part of a Web site instead of the main page, a path will be given), a security setting that provides whether the cookie can only be transmitted by a secure server, and an expiration date (not required). First-party cookies come from the same domain name as the page the user is visiting, while third-party cookies come from another domain, such as ad serving or adware companies, affiliate marketers, or spyware servers. On some Web sites, there are literally hundreds of tracking files on the main pages.

A cookie provides Web marketers with a very quick means of identifying the customer and understanding his or her prior behavior at the site. Web sites use cookies to determine how many people are visiting the site, whether they are new or repeat visitors, and how often they have visited, although this data may be somewhat inaccurate because people share computers, they often use more than one computer, and cookies may have been inadvertently or intentionally erased. Cookies make shopping carts and "quick checkout" options possible by allowing a site to keep track of a user as he or she adds to the shopping cart. Each item added to the shopping cart is stored in the site's database along with the visitor's unique ID value.

Ordinary cookies are easy to spot using your browser, but Flash cookies, beacons, and tracking codes are not easily visible. All common browsers allow users to see the cookies placed in their cookies file. Users can delete cookies, or adjust their settings so that third-party cookies are blocked, while first-party cookies are allowed.

With growing privacy concerns, over time the percentage of people deleting cookies has risen. The more cookies are deleted, the less accurate are Web page and ad server metrics, and the less likely marketers will be able to understand who is visiting their sites or where they came from. As a result, advertisers have sought other methods. One way is using Adobe Flash software, which creates its own cookie files, known as Flash cookies. Flash cookies can be set to never expire, and can store about 5 MB of information compared to the 1,024 bytes stored by regular cookies. A study by researchers at the University of California-Berkeley analyzed the use of Flash cookies at the top 100 Web sites, and found that 98% used regular cookies and 54% used Flash cookies, many to store the same information as the regular cookie. Some used the Flash cookies to re-create cookies that consumers had previously deleted.

Although cookies are site-specific (a Web site can only receive the data it has stored on a client computer and cannot look at any other cookie), when combined with Web beacons (also called "bugs"), they can be used to create cross-site profiles. Web beacons are tiny (1-pixel) graphic files embedded in e-mail messages and on Web sites. Web beacons are used to automatically transmit information about the user and the page being viewed to a monitoring server in order to collect personal browsing behavior and other personal information. For instance, when a recipient opens an e-mail in HTML format or opens a Web page, a message is sent to a server calling for graphic information. This tells the marketer that the e-mail was opened, indicating that the recipient was at least interested in the subject header. Web beacons are not visible to users. They are often clear or colored white so they are not visible to the recipient. You may be able to determine if a Web page is using Web beacons by using the View Source option of your browser and examining the IMG (image) tags on the page. As noted above, Web beacons are typically 1 pixel in size and contain the URL of a server that differs from the one that served the page itself. *Insight on Society: Every Move You Take, Every Click You Make, We'll Be Tracking You* examines the use of Web tracking files.

DATABASES, DATA WAREHOUSES, DATA MINING, AND BIG DATA

Databases, data warehouses, data mining, and the variety of marketing decision-making techniques loosely called *profiling* are at the heart of the revolution in Internet marketing. **Profiling** uses a variety of tools to create a digital image for each consumer. This image can be quite inexact, even primitive, but it can also be as detailed as a character in a novel. The quality of a consumer profile depends on the amount of data used to create it, and the analytical power of the firm's software and hardware.

profiling
profiling uses a variety of tools to create a digital image for each consumer

INSIGHT ON SOCIETY

EVERY MOVE YOU TAKE, EVERY CLICK YOU MAKE, WE'LL BE TRACKING YOU

Advertising-supported Web sites depend on knowing as much personal information as possible about you. One of the main ways ad firms discover your personal information is by placing so-called "tracking files" on your computer's browser. There are several kinds of third-party tracking files on Web pages. Cookies are the best known. These simple text files are placed in your browser and assign a unique number to your computer, which is then used by advertisers to track you across the Web as you move from one site to another (without telling you). Web beacons (sometimes also referred to as Web bugs) are a little more pernicious. Beacons are small software files that track your clicks, choices, and purchases, and even location data from mobile devices, and then send that information, often in real time, to advertisers tracking you. Beacons can also assign your computer a unique number and track you across the Web. Tracking may also occur as you watch Adobe Flash-enabled videos, visit Web sites equipped with HTML5 local storage, and use apps on smartphones. Most Facebook apps, for instance, send personal information, including names, to dozens of advertising and Internet tracking companies.

So how common is Web tracking? In a recent study, researchers found a very widespread surveillance system. Only one site, Wikipedia, had no tracking files. Two-thirds of the tracking files came from companies whose primary business is identifying and tracking Internet users to create consumer profiles that can be sold to advertising firms looking for specific types of customers. The other third came from database firms that gather and bundle the information and then sell it to marketers. Many of the tracking tools gather personal information such as age, gender, race, income, marital status, health concerns, TV shows and movies viewed, magazines and newspapers read, and books purchased. While tracking firms claim the information they gather is anonymous, this is true in name only. Scholars have shown that with just a few pieces of information, such as age, gender, zip code, and marital status, specific individuals can be easily identified. In 2012, a Web Privacy Census conducted by the University of California Berkeley Center for Law and Technology found that the total number of cookies on the top 100 Web sites had increased by 80%, from 3,600 when first measured in 2009 to over 6,400. The vast majority of these cookies (about 85%) were third-party tracking cookies, from over 450 different third-party hosts. Google's DoubleClick was the top tracker, and the most frequently appearing cookie keys were those associated with Google Analytics. Similar results were observed when looking at the top 1,000 and top 25,000 Web sites. One cause: growth of online ad auctions where advertisers buy data about users' Web browsing behavior. When you visit a site, your visit is auctioned and the winner gets to show you some ads. All this takes place in a few milliseconds so you don't know its happening. Welcome to the brave new world of Internet marketing!

The Privacy Foundation has issued guidelines for Web beacon usage. The guidelines suggest that Web beacons should be visible as an icon on the screen, the icon should be labeled to indicate its function, and it should identify the name of the company that placed the Web beacon on the page. In addition, if a user clicks on the Web beacon, it should display a disclosure statement indicating what data is being collected, how the data is used after it is collected, what companies receive the data, what other data the Web beacon is combined with, and whether or not a cookie is associated with the Web beacon. Users should be able to opt out of any data collection done by the Web beacon, and the Web beacon should not be used to collect information from Web pages of a sensitive nature, such as medical, financial, job-related, or sexual matters. Many sites have adopted the Network Advertising Initiative (NAI)'s self-regulatory guidelines, but these are only voluntary, and these guidelines have done little to assuage fears from Web users that their privacy is at risk.

One roadblock involves the meaning of Do Not Track. Industry wants an opt-in, default Track Me feature on all Web sites, while the government and privacy groups are pushing for an opt-out Do Not Track feature in which the default is Do Not Track, and which users can switch off for all sites at ones In July 2013, a working group commissioned by the W3C proposed that Web users should be able to tell advertising networks not to show them targeted advertisements. In 2014, the W3C announced that it had made major progress, advancing its work to the "last call" phase of review from the outside world.

Nearly all browsers now offer users the option of using a Do Not Track feature. But users have to remember to turn it on. In addition, not all Web sites honor the Do Not Track request, because they are not legally obligated to do so. Major Web sites and the online advertising industry insist their industry can self-regulate and preserve individual privacy. However, this solution has not worked in the past. In 2014, major companies like Yahoo and AOL abandoned the Do Not Track standard, citing the lack of traction that Do Not Track has encountered across the rest of the Web. Although some bigger Web sites like Twitter and Pinterest do follow the Do Not Track guidelines, these defections are setbacks for the standard.

The situation in Europe is somewhat different. EU Directive 2009/136/EC, also known as the E-Privacy Directive, or more familiarly as the EU cookie law, provides that Web sites must ask visitors for their consent before they can install most cookies (although not cookies considered necessary for the basic function of a Web site, such as session cookies that are used to track a shopping cart). The directive also applies to Flash and HTML5 local storage. The Directive was first passed in 2009, and by 2013, many countries in the EU, including the U.K., had enacted legislation enabling it. However, compliance with the law remains spotty, with consultants KPMG finding that more than half of the organizations it analyzed in the U.K were still not compliant.

▬ **SOURCES:** "Do Not Track – The Privacy Standard That's Melting Away," by Mark Stockley, Nakedsecurity.sophos.com, August 26, 2014; "California Urges Websites to Disclose Online Tracking," by Vindu Goel, *New York Times*, May 21, 2014; "Yahoo Is the Latest Company Ignoring Web Users' Requests for Privacy," by Jon Brodkin, Arstechnica.com, May 1, 2014; "At Last, Some Progress on Do Not Track," Justin Brookman, Cdt.org, April 24, 2014; "'Do Not Track' Rules Come a Step Closer to an Agreement," by Somini Sengupta and Natasha Singer, *New York Times*, July 15, 2013; "Half of UK Organisations Not Compliant with EU Cookie Law," by Sooraj Shah, Computing.co.uk, May 29, 2013; "What You Need to Know About the EU Cookie Law," by Bobbie Johnson, Gigaom.com, May 25, 2013; "What Firefox's New Privacy Settings Mean for You," by Sarah A. Downey, Abine.com, March 29, 2013; "The Web Privacy Census," by Chris Jay Hoofnagle and Nathan Good, law.berkeley.edu/privacycensus.htm, October 2012; "Online Data Collection Explodes Year Over Year in US," eMarketer, Inc., July 19, 2012; "Online Tracking Ramps Up," by Julia Angwin, *Wall Street Journal*, June 17, 2012; "Microsoft's 'Do Not Track' Move Angers Advertising Industry," by Julia Angwin, *Wall Street Journal*, May 31, 2012; "Websites Using 14 Tracking Tools to Take Our Private Data, Says Truste Research," News.com.au, April 20, 2012; "Opt-Out Provision Would Halt Some, but Not All, Web Tracking," by Tanzina Vega, *New York Times*, February 28, 2012; "How Companies Learn Your Secrets," by Charles Duhigg, *New York Times Magazine*, February 16, 2012; "Latest in Web Tracking: Stealthy 'Supercookies,'" by Julia Angwin, *Wall Street Journal*, August 18, 2011; "WPP Ad Unit Has Your Profile," by Emily Steel, *Wall Street Journal*, June 27, 2011; "Not Me Dot Com," by Luke O'Neil, *Wall Street Journal*, June 18, 2011; "Show Us the Data. (It's Ours, After All)," by Richard Thaler, *New York Times*, April 23, 2011; "What They Know About You," by Jennfier Valentino-Devries, *Wall Street Journal*, July 31, 2010; "Sites Feed Personal Details to New Tracking Industry," Julia Angwin and Tom McGinty, *Wall Street Journal*, July 30, 2010; "Study Finds Behaviorally-Targeted Ads More Than Twice As Valuable, Twice as Effective As Non-targeted Online Ads," Network Advertising Initiative, March 24, 2010.

database

a software application that stores records and attributes

database management system (DBMS)

a software application used by organizations to create, maintain, and access databases

structured query language (SQL)

industry-standard database query language used in relational databases

relational databases

represent data as two-dimensional tables with records organized in rows and attributes in columns; data within different tables can be flexibly related as long as the tables share a common data element

data warehouse

a database that collects a firm's transactional and customer data in a single location for offline analysis

data mining

a set of analytical techniques that look for patterns in the data of a database or data warehouse, or seek to model the behavior of customers

Together, these techniques attempt to identify precisely who the online customer is and what they want, and then, to fulfill the customer's criteria exactly. These techniques are more powerful, far more precise, and more fine-grained than the gross levels of demographic and market segmentation techniques used in mass marketing media or by telemarketing.

In order to understand the data in transaction logs, registration forms, shopping carts, cookies, Web bugs, and other unstructured data sources like e-mails, Tweets, and Likes, Internet marketers need massively powerful and capacious databases, database management systems, and analytic tools.

Databases

The first step in interpreting huge transaction streams is to store the information systematically. A **database** is a software application that stores records and attributes. A telephone book is a physical database that stores records of individuals and their attributes such as names, addresses, and phone numbers. A **database management system** (**DBMS**) is a software application used by organizations to create, maintain, and access databases. The most common DBMS are DB2 from IBM and a variety of SQL databases from Oracle, Sybase, and other providers. **Structured query language (SQL)** is an industry-standard database query and manipulation language used in relational databases. **Relational databases** such as DB2 and SQL represent data as two-dimensional tables with records organized in rows, and attributes in columns, much like a spreadsheet. The tables—and all the data in them—can be flexibly related to one another as long as the tables share a common data element.

Relational databases are extraordinarily flexible and allow marketers and other managers to view and analyze data from different perspectives very quickly.

Data Warehouses and Data Mining

A **data warehouse** is a database that collects a firm's transactional and customer data in a single location for offline analysis by marketers and site managers. The data originate in many core operational areas of the firm, such as Web site transaction logs, shopping carts, point-of-sale terminals (product scanners) in stores, warehouse inventory levels, field sales reports, external scanner data supplied by third parties, and financial payment data. The purpose of a data warehouse is to gather all the firm's transaction and customer data into one logical repository where it can be analyzed and modeled by managers without disrupting or taxing the firm's primary transactional systems and databases. Data warehouses grow quickly into storage repositories containing terabytes (trillions of bytes) of data on consumer behavior at a firm's stores and Web sites. With a data warehouse, firms can answer such questions as: What products are the most profitable by region and city? What regional marketing campaigns are working? How effective is store promotion of the firm's Web site? Data warehouses can provide business managers with a more complete awareness of customers through data that can be accessed quickly.

Data mining is a set of analytical techniques that look for patterns in the data of a database or data warehouse, or seek to model the behavior of customers. Web site data can be "mined" to develop profiles of visitors and customers. A **customer profile** is simply a set of rules that describe the typical behavior of a customer or a group of customers at a Web site. Customer profiles help to identify the patterns in group and individual behavior that occur online as millions of visitors use a firm's Web site. For example, almost every financial transaction you engage in is processed by a data mining application to detect fraud. Phone companies closely monitor your cell phone use as well to detect stolen phones and unusual calling patterns. Financial institutions and cell phone firms use data mining to develop fraud profiles. When a user's behavior conforms to a fraud profile, the transaction is not allowed or is terminated (Mobasher, 2007).

There are many different types of data mining. The simplest type is **query-driven data mining**, which is based on specific queries. For instance, based on hunches of marketers who suspect a relationship in the database or who need to answer a specific question, such as "What is the relationship between time of day and purchases of various products at the Web site?", marketers can easily query the data warehouse and produce a database table that rank-orders the top 10 products sold at a Web site by each hour of the day. Marketers can then change the content of the Web site to stimulate more sales by highlighting different products over time or placing particular products on the home page at certain times of day or night.

Another form of data mining is model-driven. **Model-driven data mining** involves the use of a model that analyzes the key variables of interest to decision makers. For example, marketers may want to reduce the inventory carried on the Web site by removing unprofitable items that do not sell well. A financial model can be built showing the profitability of each product on the site so that an informed decision can be made.

A more fine-grained behavioral approach that seeks to deal with individuals as opposed to market segments derives rules from individual consumer behavior (along with some demographic information) (Adomavicius and Tuzhilin, 2001a; Chan, 1999; Fawcett and Provost, 1996, 1997). Here, the pages actually visited by specific users are stored as a set of conjunctive rules. For example, if an individual visits a site and typically ("as a rule") moves from the home page to the financial news section to the Asian report section, and then often purchases articles from the "Recent Developments in Banking" section, this person—based on purely past behavioral patterns—might be shown an advertisement for a book on Asian money markets. These rules can be constructed to follow an individual across many different Web sites.

There are many drawbacks to all these techniques, not least of which is that there may be millions of rules, many of them nonsensical, and many others of short-term duration. Hence, the rules need extensive validation and culling (Adomavicius and Tuzhilin, 2001b). Also, there can be millions of affinity groups and other patterns in the data that are temporal or meaningless. The difficulty is isolating the valid, powerful (profitable) patterns in the data and then acting on the observed pattern fast enough to make a sale that otherwise would not have been made. As we see later, there are practical difficulties and trade-offs involved in achieving these levels of granularity, precision, and speed.

customer profile
a description of the typical behavior of a customer or a group of customers at a Web site

query-driven data mining
data mining based on specific queries

model-driven data mining
involves the use of a model that analyzes the key variables of interest to decision makers

Hadoop and the Challenge of Big Data

Up until about five years ago, most data collected by organizations consisted of structured transaction data that could easily fit into rows and columns of relational database management systems. Since then, there has been an explosion of data from Web traffic, e-mail messages, and social media content (tweets, status messages), even music playlists, as well as machine-generated data from sensors. This data may be unstructured or semi-structured and thus not suitable for relational database products that organize data in the form of columns and rows. The popular term "Big Data" refers to this avalanche of digital data flowing into firms around the world largely from Web sites and Internet click stream data. The volumes of data are so large that traditional DBMS cannot capture, store, and analyze the data in a reasonable time. Some examples of Big Data challenges are analyzing 12 terabytes of tweets created each day to improve your understanding of consumer sentiment towards your products; 100 million e-mails in order to place appropriate ads alongside the e-mail messages; or 500 million call detail records to find patterns of fraud and churn. Big Data and the tools needed to deal with it really started with Google and other search engines. Google's problem: it has to deal with 3.5 billion searches a day, and within milliseconds, display search results and place ads. For fun, do a search on "Big Data" and you'll see Google respond with more than 6 million results in .42 seconds. That's much faster than you can read this sentence!

Big Data

Big Data refers to very large data sets in the petabyte and exabyte range

Big Data usually refers to data in the petabyte and exabyte range—in other words, billions to trillions of records, often from different sources. Big Data is produced in much larger quantities and much more rapidly than traditional data collection mechanisms. Even though tweets are limited to 140 characters each, Twitter generates more than 8 terabytes of data daily. According to the IDC technology research firm, data is more than doubling every two years, so the amount of data available to organizations is skyrocketing. Making sense out of it quickly in order to gain a market advantage is critical.

Marketers are interested in Big Data because it can be mined for patterns of consumer behavior and contain more interesting anomalies than smaller data sets, with the potential to provide new insights into customer behavior, weather patterns, financial market activity, or other phenomena. However, to derive business value from this data, organizations need new technologies and analytic tools capable of managing and analyzing nontraditional data along with their traditional enterprise data.

Hadoop

a software framework for working with various big data sets

To handle unstructured and semi-structured data in vast quantities, as well as structured data, organizations are using Hadoop. **Hadoop** is an open source software framework managed by the Apache Software Foundation that enables distributed parallel processing of huge amounts of data across inexpensive computers. It breaks a Big Data problem down into subproblems, distributes them among up to thousands of inexpensive computer processing nodes, and then combines the result into a smaller data set that is easier to analyze. You've probably used Hadoop to find the best airfare on the Internet, get directions to a restaurant, search on Google, or connect with a friend on Facebook.

Hadoop can process large quantities of any kind of data, including structured transactional data, loosely structured data such as Facebook and Twitter feeds, complex data such as Web server log files, and unstructured audio and video data. Hadoop runs on a cluster of inexpensive servers, and processors can be added or removed as needed. Companies use Hadoop to analyze very large volumes of data as well as for a staging area for unstructured and semi-structured data before it is loaded into a data warehouse. Facebook stores much of its data on its massive Hadoop cluster, which holds an estimated 300 petabytes, about 30,000 times more information than the Library of Congress. Yahoo uses Hadoop to track user behavior so it can modify its home page to fit user interests. Life sciences research firm NextBio uses Hadoop and HBase to process data for pharmaceutical companies conducting genomic research. Top database vendors such as IBM, Hewlett-Packard, Oracle, and Microsoft have their own Hadoop software distributions. Other vendors offer tools for moving data into and out of Hadoop or for analyzing data within Hadoop.

MARKETING AUTOMATION AND CUSTOMER RELATIONSHIP MANAGEMENT (CRM) SYSTEMS

Marketing automation systems are software tools that marketers use to track all the steps in the lead generation part of the marketing process. The marketing process begins with making the potential customer aware of the firm and product, and recognizing the need for the product. This is the beginning of a lead—someone who might buy. From there, consumers need to find you as they search for products; they will compare your products with your competitors' offerings and at some point, choose to purchase. Software can help in each of these stages of the marketing process. A number of firms sell software packages that can visualize most of the online marketing activities of a firm and then track the progression from exposure to display ads, finding your firm on a search engine, directing follow-up e-mail and communications, and finally a purchase. Once leads become customers, customer relationship management systems take over the maintenance of the relationship.

Customer relationship management systems are another important Internet marketing technology. A **customer relationship management (CRM) system** is a repository of customer information that records all of the contacts that a customer has with a firm (including Web sites) and generates a customer profile available to everyone in the firm with a need to "know the customer." CRM systems also supply the analytical software required to analyze and use customer information. Customers come to firms not just over the Web but also through telephone call centers, customer service representatives, sales representatives, automated voice response systems, ATMs and kiosks, in-store point-of-sale terminals, and mobile devices (m-commerce). Collectively, these are referred to as "**customer touchpoints**." In the past, firms generally did not maintain a single repository of customer information, but instead were organized along product lines, with each product line maintaining a customer list (and often not sharing it with others in the same firm).

In general, firms did not know who their customers were, how profitable they were, or how they responded to marketing campaigns. For instance, a bank customer might see a television advertisement for a low-cost auto loan that included an 800-number to call. However, if the customer came to the bank's Web site instead, rather than calling the 800-number, marketers would have no idea how effective the television campaign was because this Web customer contact data was not related to the

marketing automation systems
software tools that marketers use to track all the steps in the lead generation part of the marketing process

customer relationship management (CRM) system
a repository of customer information that records all of the contacts that a customer has with a firm and generates a customer profile available to everyone in the firm with a need to "know the customer"

customer touchpoints
the ways in which customers interact with the firm

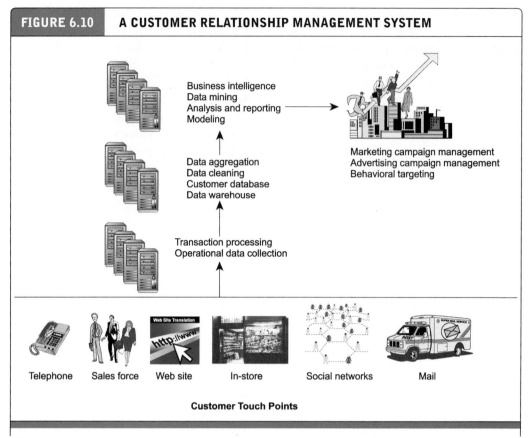

| FIGURE 6.10 | A CUSTOMER RELATIONSHIP MANAGEMENT SYSTEM |

This is an example of a CRM system for a financial services institution. The system captures customer information from all customer touchpoints as well as other data sources, merges the data, and aggregates it into a single customer data repository or data warehouse where it can be used to provide better service, as well as to construct customer profiles for marketing purposes. Online analytical processing (OLAP) allows managers to dynamically analyze customer activities to spot trends or problems involving customers. Other analytical software programs analyze aggregate customer behavior to identify profitable and unprofitable customers as well as customer activities.

800-number call center data. **Figure 6.10** illustrates how a CRM system integrates customer contact data into a single system.

CRMs are part of the evolution of firms toward a customer-centric and marketing-segment–based business, and away from a product-line–centered business. CRMs are essentially a database technology with extraordinary capabilities for addressing the needs of each customer and differentiating the product or service on the basis of treating each customer as a unique person. Customer profiles can contain the following information:

- A map of the customer's relationship with the institution
- Product and usage summary data
- Demographic and psychographic data
- Profitability measures

- Contact history summarizing the customer's contacts with the institution across most delivery channels
- Marketing and sales information containing programs received by the customer and the customer's responses
- E-mail campaign responses
- Web site visits

With these profiles, CRMs can be used to sell additional products and services, develop new products, increase product utilization, reduce marketing costs, identify and retain profitable customers, optimize service delivery costs, retain high lifetime value customers, enable personal communications, improve customer loyalty, and increase product profitability.

For instance, Home Depot saw increased competition from online hardware stores and decided to emphasize e-commerce as part of its business strategy. The company sought a comprehensive CRM solution that could organize and analyze information from both clicks and mortar. They used a CRM software package called Epiphany Insight to gain a better understanding of which Home Depot products were selling on the Web and enabled their customer service focus from their stores to exist on the Web as well. Epiphany has since been acquired by Infor. Other leading CRM vendors include SAP, SalesForce.com, Oracle, Kana, and eGain.

6.4 UNDERSTANDING THE COSTS AND BENEFITS OF ONLINE MARKETING COMMUNICATIONS

As we noted earlier, online marketing communications still comprise only a small part of the total marketing communications universe. While there are several reasons why this is the case, two of the main ones are concerns about how well online advertising really works and about how to adequately measure the costs and benefits of online advertising. We will address both of these topics in this section. But first, we will define some important terms used when examining the effectiveness of online marketing.

ONLINE MARKETING METRICS: LEXICON

In order to understand the process of attracting prospects to your firm's Web site or Facebook page via marketing communications and converting them into customers, you will need to be familiar with Web marketing terminology. **Table 6.7** lists some terms commonly used to describe the impacts and results of online marketing for display ads, social network ads, and e-mail campaigns.

The first nine metrics focus primarily on the success of a Web site in achieving audience or market share by "driving" shoppers to the site. These measures often substitute for solid information on sales revenue as e-commerce entrepreneurs seek to have investors and the public focus on the success of the Web site in "attracting eyeballs" (viewers).

Impressions are the number of times an ad is served. **Click-through rate (CTR)** measures the percentage of people exposed to an online advertisement who actually

impressions
number of times an ad is served

click-through rate (CTR)
the percentage of people exposed to an online advertisement who actually click on the banner

TABLE 6.7	MARKETING METRICS LEXICON
COMMON MARKETING DISPLAY AD METRICS	**DESCRIPTION**
Impressions	Number of times an ad is served
Click-through rate (CTR)	Percentage of times an ad is clicked
View-through rate (VTR)	Percentage of times an ad is not clicked immediately but the Web site is visited within 30 days
Hits	Number of HTTP requests
Page views	Number of pages viewed
Stickiness (duration)	Average length of stay at a Web site
Unique visitors	Number of unique visitors in a period
Loyalty	Measured variously as the number of page views, frequency of single-user visits to the Web site, or percentage of customers who return to the site in a year to make additional purchases
Reach	Percentage of Web site visitors who are potential buyers; or the percentage of total market buyers who buy at a site
Recency	Time elapsed since the last action taken by a buyer, such as a Web site visit or purchase
Acquisition rate	Percentage of visitors who indicate an interest in the Web site's products by registering or visiting product pages
Conversion rate	Percentage of visitors who become customers
Browse-to-buy ratio	Ratio of items purchased to product views
View-to-cart ratio	Ratio of "Add to cart" clicks to product views
Cart conversion rate	Ratio of actual orders to "Add to cart" clicks
Checkout conversion rate	Ratio of actual orders to checkouts started
Abandonment rate	Percentage of shoppers who begin a shopping cart purchase but then leave the Web site without completing a purchase (similar to above)
Retention rate	Percentage of existing customers who continue to buy on a regular basis (similar to loyalty)
Attrition rate	Percentage of customers who do not return during the next year after an initial purchase
SOCIAL MARKETING METRICS	
Gross rating points	Audience size times frequency of views (audience reach)
Applause ratio	Number of Likes per post
Conversation ratio	Ratio of number of comments per post
Amplification	Number of shares (or re-tweets) per post
Sentiment ratio	Ratio of positive comments to total comments
Duration of engagement	Average time on site
E-MAIL METRICS	
Open rate	Percentage of e-mail recipients who open the e-mail and are exposed to the message
Delivery rate	Percentage of e-mail recipients who received the e-mail
Click-through rate (e-mail)	Percentage of recipients who clicked through to offers
Bounce-back rate	Percentage of e-mails that could not be delivered
Unsubscribe rate	Percentage of recipients who click unsubscribe
Conversion rate (e-mail)	Percentage of recipients who actually buy

click on the advertisement. Because not all ads lead to an immediate click, the industry has invented a new term for a long-term hit called **view-through rate (VTR)**, which measures the 30-day response rate to an ad. **Hits** are the number of HTTP requests received by a firm's server. Hits can be misleading as a measure of Web site activity because a "hit" does not equal a page. A single page may account for several hits if the page contains multiple images or graphics. A single Web site visitor can generate hundreds of hits. For this reason, hits are not an accurate representation of Web traffic or visits, even though they are generally easy to measure; the sheer volume of hits can be huge—and sound impressive—but not be a true measure of activity. **Page views** are the number of pages requested by visitors. However, with increased usage of Web frames that divide pages into separate sections, a single page that has three frames will generate three page views. Hence, page views per se are also not a very useful metric.

Viewability rate is the percentage of ads (either display or video) that are actually seen by people online. See page 396 for a further discussion of the issue of viewability.

Stickiness (sometimes called *duration*) is the average length of time visitors remain at a Web site. Stickiness is important to marketers because the longer the amount of time a visitor spends at a Web site, the greater the probability of a purchase. For instance, while Facebook generates a great deal of stickiness, it's not the case that this translates directly into more sales and more revenue. Equally important is what people do when they visit a Web site and not just how much time they spend there. People don't go to Facebook to buy or research goods, whereas Google visitors are more likely to visit because they are searching for something to buy (Nielsen, 2012).

The number of unique visitors is perhaps the most widely used measure of a Web site's popularity. The measurement of **unique visitors** counts the number of distinct, unique visitors to a Web site, regardless of how many pages they view. **Loyalty** measures the percentage of visitors who return in a year. This can be a good indicator of a site's Web following, and perhaps the trust shoppers place in a site. **Reach** is typically a percentage of the total number of consumers in a market who visit a Web site; for example, 10% of all book purchasers in a year will visit Amazon at least once to shop for a book. This provides an idea of the power of a Web site to attract market share. **Recency**—like loyalty—measures the power of a Web site to produce repeat visits and is generally measured as the average number of days elapsed between shopper or customer visits. For example, a recency value of 25 days means the average customer will return once every 25 days.

The metrics described so far do not say much about commercial activity nor help you understand the conversion from visitor to customer. Several other measures are more helpful in this regard. **Acquisition rate** measures the percentage of visitors who register or visit product pages (indicating interest in the product). **Conversion rate** measures the percentage of visitors who actually purchase something. Conversion rates can vary widely, depending on the success of the site. Fireclick, a provider of Web analytics software, publishes conversion rate statistics, and cites a global conversion rate of around 3%–5% (Fireclick, 2014). The **browse-to-buy ratio** measures the ratio of items purchased to product views. The **view-to-cart ratio** calculates the ratio

view-through rate (VTR)
measures the 30-day response rate to an ad

hits
number of http requests received by a firm's server

page views
number of pages requested by visitors

viewability rate
percentage of ads that are actually seen by people online

stickiness (duration)
average length of time visitors remain at a site

unique visitors
the number of distinct, unique visitors to a site

loyalty
percentage of purchasers who return in a year

reach
percentage of the total number of consumers in a market who will visit a site

recency
average number of days elapsed between visits

acquisition rate
percentage of visitors who register or visit product pages

conversion rate
percentage of visitors who purchase something

browse-to-buy ratio
ratio of items purchased to product views

view-to-cart ratio
ratio of "Add to cart" clicks to product views

cart conversion rate
ratio of actual orders to "Add to cart" clicks

checkout conversion rate
ratio of actual orders to checkouts started

abandonment rate
% of shoppers who begin a shopping cart, but then fail to complete it

retention rate
% of existing customers who continue to buy

attrition rate
% of customers who purchase once, but do not return within a year

conversation ratio
number of comments produced per post

applause ratio
number of Likes or Shares per post

amplification
number of re-tweets or re-shares per post

sentiment ratio
ratio of positive comments to total comments

open rate
% of customers who open e-mail

delivery rate
% of e-mail recipients who received e-mail

click-through rate (e-mail)
% of e-mail recipients who clicked through to the offer

bounce-back rate
percentage of e-mails that could not be delivered

of "Add to cart" clicks to product views. **Cart conversion rate** measures the ratio of actual orders to "Add to cart" clicks. **Checkout conversion rate** calculates the ratio of actual orders to checkouts started. **Abandonment rate** measures the percentage of shoppers who begin a shopping cart form but then fail to complete the form and leave the Web site. Abandonment rates can signal a number of potential problems—poor form design, lack of consumer trust, or consumer purchase uncertainty caused by other factors. A recent study on shopping cart abandonment found that, on average, 68% of carts are abandoned (Baymard, 2014). Among the reasons for abandonment were security concerns, customer just checking prices, couldn't find customer support, couldn't find preferred payment option, and the item being unavailable at checkout. Given that more than 80% of online shoppers generally have a purchase in mind when they visit a Web site, a high abandonment rate signals many lost sales. **Retention rate** indicates the percentage of existing customers who continue to buy on a regular basis. **Attrition rate** measures the percentage of customers who purchase once but never return within a year (the opposite of loyalty and retention rates).

Social network marketing differs from display ad marketing because the objective is to create word-of-mouth impact and alter the interaction among your visitors, and between your visitors and your brand. While unique visitors is important, it's even more important what they do when they arrive on-site. **Conversation ratio** measures the number of comments produced per post to your site. **Applause ratio** measures the number of Likes or Shares per post. **Amplification** measures the number of re-tweets or re-shares per post. All three of these measures are different dimensions of "word of mouth" advertising on social network sites. **Sentiment ratio** is the ratio of positive comments to total comments.

Facebook, Nielsen, and comScore are also measuring Facebook exposure using gross rating points, a traditional ad metric that multiplies the reach, or size, of an audience by the frequency with which that audience sees a brand. By using this metric, marketers can discuss online advertising in the same terms that they already use for TV, print, or outdoor ads (Raice, 2011; Nielsen, 2011). Facebook's application software development package provides extensive measures of user interactions and demographics. On the other hand, this metric does not measure dimensions of consumer engagement, which is the main strength of social network advertising. You will learn more about measuring the effectiveness of social, mobile, and local advertising in Chapter 7.

E-mail campaigns have their own set of metrics. **Open rate** measures the percentage of customers who open the e-mail and are exposed to the message. Generally, open rates are quite high, in the area of 50% or greater. However, some browsers open mail as soon as the mouse cursor moves over the subject line, and therefore this measure can be difficult to interpret. **Delivery rate** measures the percentage of e-mail recipients who received the e-mail. **Click-through rate (e-mail)** measures the percentage of e-mail recipients who clicked through to the offer. Finally, **bounce-back rate** measures the percentage of e-mails that could not be delivered.

There is a lengthy path from simple online ad impressions, Web site visits, and page views to the purchase of a product and the company making a profit (see **Figure 6.11**). You first need to make customers aware of their needs for your product and somehow drive them to your Web site. Once there, you need to convince them you have the best value—quality and price—when compared to alternative providers. You then must persuade them to trust your firm to handle the transaction (by providing a secure environment and fast fulfillment). Based on your success, a percentage of customers will remain loyal and purchase again or recommend your Web site to others.

HOW WELL DOES ONLINE ADVERTISING WORK?

What is the most effective kind of online advertising? How does online advertising compare to offline advertising? The answers depend on the goals of the campaign, the nature of the product, and the quality of the Web site you direct customers toward. The answers also depend on what you measure. Click-through rates are interesting, but ultimately it's the return on the investment in the ad campaign that counts. A broader understanding of the matter requires that you consider the cost of purchasing the promotional materials and mailing lists, and the studio production costs for radio and TV ads. Also, each media has a different revenue-per-contact potential because the products advertised differ. For instance, online purchases tend to be for smaller items when compared to newspaper, magazine, and television ads (although this too seems to be changing).

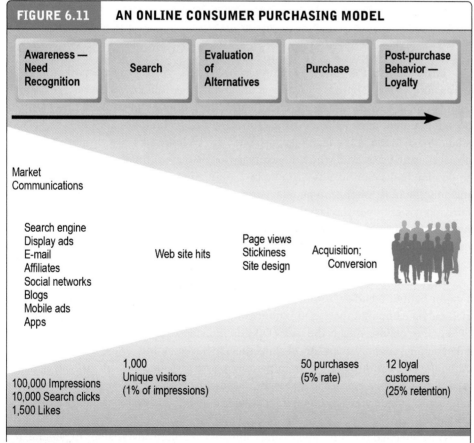

| FIGURE 6.11 | AN ONLINE CONSUMER PURCHASING MODEL |

The conversion of visitors into customers, and then loyal customers, is a complex and long-term process that may take several months.

TABLE 6.8	ONLINE MARKETING COMMUNICATIONS: TYPICAL CLICK-THROUGH RATES	
MARKETING METHODS	TYPICAL CLICK-THROUGH RATES
Banner ads	.03%–.30%
Google enhanced search ads (Product Listing Ads)	1.66%
Search engine keyword purchase	.70–5.0%
Video	.50%–1.5%
Rich media	.10–2.0%
Sponsorships	1.50%–3.00%
Affiliate relationships	.20%–.40%
E-mail marketing in-house list	3.0–5.0%
E-mail marketing purchased list	.01%–1.50%
Social site display ads	.15%–.25%
Mobile display ads	.15%–.50%

SOURCES: Based on data from The Search Agency, 2014; eMarketer, Inc., 2014h; PointRoll, 2014; VINDICO, 2014; industry sources; authors' estimates.

Table 6.8 lists the click-through rates for various types of online marketing communications tools. There is a great deal of variability within any of these types, so the figures should be viewed as general estimates. Click-through rates on all these formats are a function of personalization and other targeting techniques. For instance, several studies have found that e-mail response rates can be increased 20% or more by adding social sharing links. And while the average Google click-through rate is less than 1%, some merchants can hit 10% or more by making their ads more specific and attracting only the most interested people. Permission e-mail click-through rates have been fairly consistent over the last five years, in the 3%–5% range. Putting the recipient's name in the subject line can double the click-through rate. (For unsolicited e-mail and outright spam, response rates are much lower, even though about 20% of U.S. e-mail users report clicking occasionally on an unsolicited e-mail.)

The click-through rate for video ads may seem low, but it is twice as high as the rate for banner ads. For instance, research by PointRoll found that adding video to a rich media campaign increased interaction rates by over 17% on average (PointRoll, 2014). "Interaction" means the user clicks on the video, plays it, stops it, or takes some other action (possibly skips the ad altogether) (eMarketer, Inc., 2009; Eyeblaster, 2009). Although click-through rate is an important metric for video ads, advertising agencies also focus on other metrics to assess the success of an online video campaign, such as number of unique viewers, target impressions, brand lift, sales impact, and conversions (Brightroll, 2013).

How effective is online advertising compared to offline advertising? In general, the online channels (e-mail, search engine, display ads, video, and social, mobile, and local marketing) compare very favorably with traditional channels. This explains in large part why online advertising has grown so rapidly in the last five years. Search engine advertising over the last five years has grown to be one of the most cost-effective forms of marketing communications and accounts for, in large part, the growth of Google, as well as other search engines. Surprisingly, direct opt-in e-mail is nearly twice as cost-effective as search engine advertising. This is, in part, because e-mail lists are so inexpensive compared to keywords, and because opt-in e-mail is a form of targeting people who are already interested in receiving more information.

A study of the comparative impacts of offline and online marketing concluded that the most powerful marketing campaigns used multiple forms of marketing, including online, catalog, television, radio, newspapers, and retail store. Traditional media like television and print media remain the primary means for consumers to find out about new products even though advertisers have reduced their budgets for print media ads. The consensus conclusion is that consumers who shop multiple channels are spending more than consumers who shop only with a single channel, in part because they have more discretionary income but also because of the combined number of "touchpoints" that marketers are making with the consumers. The fastest growing channel in consumer marketing is the multi-channel shopper.

THE COSTS OF ONLINE ADVERTISING

Effectiveness cannot be considered without an analysis of costs. Initially, most online ads were sold on a barter or **cost per thousand (CPM)** impressions basis, with advertisers purchasing impressions in 1,000-unit lots. Today, other pricing models have developed, including **cost per click (CPC)**, where the advertiser pays a prenegotiated fee for each click an ad receives; **cost per action (CPA)**, where the advertiser pays a prenegotiated amount only when a user performs a specific action, such as a registration or a purchase; and hybrid arrangements, combining two or more of these models (see **Table 6.9**).

cost per thousand (CPM)
advertiser pays for impressions in 1,000-unit lots

cost per click (CPC)
advertiser pays prenegotiated fee for each click an ad receives

cost per action (CPA)
advertiser pays only for those users who perform a specific action

TABLE 6.9	DIFFERENT PRICING MODELS FOR ONLINE ADVERTISEMENTS
PRICING MODEL	**DESCRIPTION**
Barter	Exchange of ad space for something of equal value
Cost per thousand (CPM)	Advertiser pays for impressions in 1,000-unit lots
Cost per click (CPC)	Advertiser pays prenegotiated fee for each click ad received
Cost per action (CPA)	Advertiser pays only for those users who perform a specific action, such as registering, purchasing, etc.
Hybrid	Two or more of the above models used together
Sponsorship	Term-based; advertiser pays fixed fee for a slot on a Web site

While in the early days of e-commerce, a few online sites spent as much as $400 on marketing and advertising to acquire one customer, the average cost was never that high. While the costs for offline customer acquisition are higher than online, the offline items are typically far more expensive. If you advertise in the *Wall Street Journal,* you are tapping into a wealthy demographic that may be interested in buying islands, jets, other corporations, and expensive homes in France. A full-page black and white ad in the *Wall Street Journal* National Edition costs about $350,000, whereas other papers are in the $10,000 to $100,000 range. For these kinds of prices, you will need to either sell quite a few apples or a small number of corporate jet lease agreements.

One of the advantages of online marketing is that online sales can generally be directly correlated with online marketing efforts. If online merchants can obtain offline purchase data from a data broker, the merchants can measure precisely just how much revenue is generated by specific banners or e-mail messages sent to prospective customers. One way to measure the effectiveness of online marketing is by looking at the ratio of additional revenue received divided by the cost of the campaign (Revenue/Cost). Any positive whole number means the campaign was worthwhile.

A more complex situation arises when both online and offline sales revenues are affected by an online marketing effort. A large percentage of the online audience uses the Web to "shop" but not buy. These shoppers buy at physical stores. Merchants such as Sears and Walmart use e-mail to inform their registered customers of special offers available for purchase either online or at stores. Unfortunately, purchases at physical stores cannot be tied precisely with the online e-mail campaign. In these cases, merchants have to rely on less precise measures such as customer surveys at store locations to determine the effectiveness of online campaigns.

In either case, measuring the effectiveness of online marketing communications—and specifying precisely the objective (branding versus sales)—is critical to profitability. To measure marketing effectiveness, you need to understand the costs of various marketing media and the process of converting online prospects into online customers.

In general, online marketing communications are more costly on a CPM basis than traditional mass media marketing, but are more efficient in producing sales. **Table 6.10** shows costs for typical online and offline marketing communications. For instance, a local television spot (30 seconds) can cost $4,000–$40,000 to run the ad and an additional $40,000 to produce the ad, for a total cost of $44,000–$80,000. The ad may be seen by a population of, say, 2 million persons (impressions) in a local area for a CPM ranging from 2 to 4 cents, which makes television very inexpensive for reaching large audiences quickly. A Web site banner ad costs virtually nothing to produce and can be purchased at Web sites for a cost of from $2–$15 per thousand impressions. Direct postal mail can cost 80 cents to $1 per household drop for a post card, but e-mail can be sent for virtually nothing and costs only $5–$15 per thousand targeted names. Hence, e-mail is far less expensive than postal mail on a CPM basis.

TABLE 6.10	TRADITIONAL AND ONLINE ADVERTISING COSTS COMPARED
TRADITIONAL ADVERTISING	
Local television	$4,000 for a 30-second commercial during a movie; $45,000 for a highly rated show
Network television	$80,000–$600,000 for a 30-second spot during prime time; the average is $120,000 to $140,000
Cable television	$5,000–$8,000 for a 30-second ad during prime time
Radio	$200–$1,000 for a 60-second spot, depending on the time of day and program ratings
Newspaper	$120 per 1,000 circulation for a full-page ad
Magazine	$50 per 1,000 circulation for an ad in a regional edition of a national magazine, versus $120 per 1,000 for a local magazine
Direct mail	$15–$20 per 1,000 delivered for coupon mailings; $25–$40 per 1,000 for simple newspaper inserts
Billboard	$5,000–$25,000 for a 1–3 month rental of a freeway sign
ONLINE ADVERTISING	
Banner ads	$2–$15 per 1,000 impressions on a Web site, depending on how targeted the ad is (the more targeted, the higher the price)
Video and rich media	$20–$25 per 1,000 ads, depending on the Web site's demographics
E-mail	$5–$15 per 1,000 targeted e-mail addresses
Sponsorships	$30–$75 per 1,000 viewers, depending on the exclusivity of the sponsorship (the more exclusive, the higher the price)
Social network ads	$0.50–$3.00 per 1,000 impressions, with news feed ads at the high end of the range

WEB ANALYTICS: SOFTWARE FOR MEASURING ONLINE MARKETING RESULTS

A number of software programs are available to automatically calculate activities at a Web site or on a mobile device. Tracking the viewing and behavior of consumers on three screens—PC, mobile, and television—is a more difficult task.. Other software programs and services assist marketing managers in identifying exactly which marketing initiatives are paying off and which are not.

The purpose of marketing is to convert shoppers into customers who purchase what you sell. The process of converting shoppers into customers is often called a "purchasing funnel." We have characterized this as a process rather than a funnel that is composed of several stages: awareness, engagement, interaction, purchase, and post-purchase service and loyalty. **Web analytics** is a software package that collects,

Web analytics
software package that collects, stores, analyzes, and graphically presents data on each of the stages in the conversion of shoppers to customers process on e-commerce sites

| FIGURE 6.12 | WEB ANALYTICS AND THE ONLINE PURCHASING PROCESS |

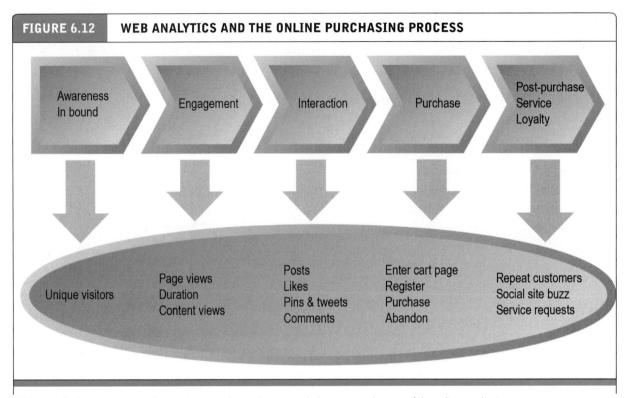

Web analytics help e-commerce firms to better understand consumer behavior at each stage of the online purchasing process.

stores, analyzes, and graphically presents data on each of the stages in the conversion of shoppers to customers process on e-commerce sites (see **Figure 6.12**).

Web analytics packages can tell business managers how people become *aware* of their site, and where they come from (e.g., search, self-entered URL, e-mail, social campaigns, or off-line traditional print and TV ads), along with demographic, behavioral, and geographic information. Are shoppers coming from mobile devices, from Facebook or Pinterest? This information can help managers decide the best ways to drive traffic to their sites, the so-called "in-bound" links to a site. Once on the Web site, analytics packages can record how *engaged* visitors are with the site's content, measured in terms of pages viewed and duration on site. This information can allow managers to change the design or their sites, or change the content viewers are seeing. For instance, video testimonials from product users may be much more engaging than expert reviews or user text comments. In a social network marketing world, where consumers' opinions and behavior can be harvested and broadcast to their friends, an important intermediate step in the consumer conversion process is to encourage visitors to *interact* with your content and share their experiences, opinions, preferences, and behaviors with their friends, as well as other visitors to the site. Web analytics packages can track visitor interaction and help managers decide what content leads to higher levels of visitor interaction with friends and other visitors. The *purchase activity* on the shopping cart page is a major focus of analytics tools not just because this is where the revenue is generated, but also because this is where the customer frequently exits the entire site and the firm loses a potential sale. Current shopping cart abandonment is about 70% in the United States, with little change over the last few years, and higher in other countries (eMarketer, Inc., 2014k). This seems like an extraordinary rate but, like most of the indicators discussed in this chapter, abandonment is a complex phenomenon and often not what it seems. Consumers use carts like a shopping list, and don't complete the transaction immediately; they use it for price comparison and to know shipping costs, or taxes; they complete transactions later on a different device, such as a mobile phone. Another measure of near-purchase activity is the add-to-cart rate. Web analytics software can help managers tease out the meaning of behavior on a Web site's shopping cart page. Finally, Web analytics can help managers discover customer *loyalty and post-purchase* behavior. In an increasingly social marketing environment, marketing managers need to know how their products and services are being talked about on other sites, Facebook pages, or Twitter tweets, often called "buzz" or sentiment analysis. Are the comments positive or negative? What is the source of negative comments? Possible candidates are poor quality, high costs, poor warranty service, and shipping issues.

The end objective of Web analytics packages is to help business managers optimize the return on investment on their Web sites and social marketing efforts, and to do this by building a detailed understanding of how consumers behave when visiting their Web sites. Web analytics also allows managers to measure the impact of specific marketing campaigns involving, say, discounts, loyalty points, and special offers, as well as regional, or demographic-based campaigns. Aside from its role in enhancing management decision making, and optimizing the effectiveness of building a Web presence, Web analytics packages also enable a near real-time marketing capability where managers are able to change the content of a Web site, respond to customer complaints and comments, and align campaigns with trending topics or news developments, all in a near real-time manner (real-time may be a matter of minutes or at most 24 hours) (eMarketer, Inc., 2013b).

While there are a great many Web analytics firms and software packages on the market, the leaders are Google Analytics with an estimated 65% market share of the Internet Retailer top 500 sites, followed by Adobe Analytics (10%), IBM Digital Analytics (20%), and Webtrends, 2%. Very little is known about the size of the Web analytics market, but analysts believe it is on the order of $1.5 to $2 billion in annual revenues (Belisle, 2013). Web analytics is typically part of a much larger package sold to corporations from hardware, to Web design tools, cloud services, and management expertise.

Programmatic Advertising:
Real-Time Marketing

The holy grail of advertising and marketing is to deliver the right message to the right person at the right time. If this were possible, no one would receive ads they did not want to see, and then no advertising dollars would be wasted, reducing the costs to end users and increasing the efficiency of each ad dollar. In the physical world, only a very rough approximation of this ideal is possible. Advertisers can buy television and radio spots, newspaper ads, and billboards based on broad demographics and interests of likely potential customers. The Internet promised to change this. On the Internet, ads supposedly could be targeted to individual consumers based on their personal characteristics, interests, and recent clickstream behavior. One early vision of e-commerce was a trade-off between privacy and efficiency: let us know more about you, and we will show you only the advertising and products you are interested in seeing, and even offer free content. E-commerce was supposed to end the mass advertising that exploded in the television era.

But contrary to popular impressions and the fears of privacy advocates, most of the display ads shown to site visitors are marvelously irrelevant to visitors' interests, both short-term and long-term. For this reason, the click-through rate for banner advertising is a stunningly low 0.03%, and the price of display ads has fallen to a few cents because of their poor performance. Check this out: point your browser at Yahoo (the largest display advertiser on earth), look at the prominent ads shown on the right,

and ask yourself if you are really interested in the ad content at this moment in time. How about ever? Chances are slim you are interested at this moment, even if the ad is somewhat appropriate to your demographics. Often, it is an ad for something you are totally not interested in and never have been. Researchers have found that only 20% of Internet users find that display ads on Web sites are relevant to their interests. Programmatic advertising promises to improve the targeting of ads, decreasing costs for advertisers, and making the Web less annoying to consumers by showing them ads that really are of interest to them.

Programmatic advertising is an automated method that publishers use to sell their inventory (empty slots on their Web pages) to advertisers who want to buy ad space for their customers (brand and product owners looking to market their products and services). There are two kinds of programmatic advertising: auction-based real time bidding (RTB), and programmatic direct, where advertisers deal directly with publishers in a semi-automated environment.

Programmatic advertising platforms use Big Data repositories that contain personal information on hundreds of millions of online shoppers and consumers; analytic software to classify and search the database for shoppers with the desired characteristics; and machine learning techniques to test out combinations of consumer characteristics that optimize the chance of a purchase resulting from exposure to an ad. All of this technology is designed to lower the cost, increase the speed, and increase the efficiency of advertising in an environment where there are hundreds of millions of Web pages to fill with ads, and millions of online consumers looking to buy at any given moment. Programmatic advertising allows advertisers to potentially show the right ad, at the right time, to just the right person, in a matter of milliseconds. To the extent this is true, display advertising becomes more effective, and perhaps could become as effective as search-based advertising, where it is much more obvious what the searcher is looking for, or interested in, at the moment of search. In 2014, programmatic digital display advertising worldwide will total an estimated €16.8 billion and analysts believe it will grow to over €43 billion by 2018.

Currently, 80% of online display advertising is done in a non-automated, traditional environment that involves e-mail, fax, phone, and text messaging. This is the world of the traditional insertion order: if you want to advertise in a newspaper or magazine, call the ad department and fill out an insertion order. In this environment, firms who want to sell products and services online hire advertising agencies to develop a marketing plan. The ad agencies learn from the firms what kinds of people they would like to contact online. The ad agencies pay data brokers or advertising networks like DoubleClick to help them identify where the online ads should be placed given the nature of the product and the specific characteristics the producer firms are looking for. For instance, let's say a firm wants to market a new mountain bike to men and women, ages 24–35, who live in zip codes where mountain biking is a popular activity. Ad networks traditionally would direct the agency to direct purchases of ad space from Web sites that attract the mountain biking audience.

This traditional environment is expensive, imprecise, and slow, in part because of the number of people involved in the decision about where to place ads. Also, the technology used is slow, and the process of learning which of several ads is optimal could take weeks or months. The ads could be targeted to a more precise group of potential customers. While context advertising on sites dedicated to a niche product is very effective, there are many other Web sites visited by bikers that might be equally effective, and cost much less.

The process is very different in a programmatic environment. Ad agencies have access to any of several programmatic ad platforms offered by Google, Yahoo, AOL, Facebook, and many smaller firms. Working with their clients, the ad agency more precisely defines the target audience to include men and women, ages 24–35, who live in zip codes where mountain biking is a popular activity, have mentioned biking topics on social network sites, have e-mail where mountain biking is discussed, make more than $70,000 a year, and currently do not own a mountain bike. The ad agency enters a bid expressed in dollars per thousand impressions for 200,000 impressions to people who meet the characteristics being sought. The platform returns a quote for access to this population of 200,000 people who meet the characteristics required. The quote is based on what other advertisers are willing to pay for that demographic and characteristics. The quote is accepted or denied. If accepted, the ads are shown to people as they move about the Web, in real-time. As people come on to various Web sites they visit, the automated program assesses whether they meet the desired characteristics, and displays the mountain bike ad with milliseconds to that person. The programmatic platforms also track the responses to the ads in real time, and can change to different ads and test for effectiveness based on the platform's experience. Once the system learns from experience, it will focus on showing the most effective ads on the most productive Web sites. Programmatic direct (or premium) advertising uses the same platform, but publishers sell blocks of inventory to ad agencies rather than single impressions. This stabilizes their income, and puts them in closer contact with advertisers who can also exercise greater oversight over the publishers.

The auto industry is a large user of programmatic advertising. Toyota, General Motors, Ford, and Chrysler are among the top 10 programmatic spenders in 2014. Car brands are highly focused on specific demographic groups, income levels, and aspirations. A programmatic campaign begins with the advertiser picking a demographic target, establishing a total budget for the campaign, and then choosing an RTB platform and competing for the delivery of an ad to that audience against other advertisers who may be other auto companies, retailers, or telecommunications providers. The ads are awarded and served automatically in millisecond-quick transactions handled by machines.

Despite its clear advantages, there are also several risks involved for all parties. Advertisers lose control over where their ads will appear on the Web. This is a threat to a brand if its products are shown on inappropriate sites. Advertisers lose some accountability for their expenditures because they cannot verify that their ads are actually being shown, and they must take the ad platform's word that indeed the ads are being shown to real people. This is a transparency issue. Ghost sites and ad fraud complicate the picture as well. There are thousands of ghost sites on the Web that do nothing but attract clicks using various ruses. Ad networks record this traffic and have little capability to determine if it is legitimate, and may show ads on these sites, which will generate fraudulent clicks that are paid for by the ad network and the advertising firm.

Given the risks, many of the largest advertisers do not use programmatic advertising. It was initially used by publishers to sell inventory that was left over after the major ad campaigns had purchased the premium slots on Web pages. Today, a significant portion of programmatically traded inventory is discount inventory that sells for a fraction of premium inventory. Programmatic platforms were inexpensive places to sell excess inventory. However, that is beginning to change as advertisers gain confidence and the platforms themselves improve their abilities to avoid inappropriate Web sites, purge ghost sites, and learn how to detect click fraud.

For instance, in 2014, Proctor & Gamble plans to buy 70% of its U.S. digital media using programmatic methods. In the following year, it intends to shift 70% of its mobile advertising to programmatic platforms. P&G is the largest advertiser in the country, with a $3.2 billion budget. It spends $235 million on Internet display ads. In the past, P&G purchased premium online inventory at the top 100 ComScore sites through several different ad agencies and tracked performance using its internal staff. Most consumer brand firms have held back, however, because of issues like brand safety, fraud prevention, ensuring the target actually receives the ads, and transparency. However, several firms have stepped into this market with tools addressing these concerns.

SOURCES: "Get With the Programmatic: A Primer on Programmatic Advertising," by Or Shani, Marketingland.com, August 22, 2014; "Programmatic Advertising Spreads Quickly Despite Nagging Problems, Says AOL Survey," by Robert Hof, Adage.com, August 13, 2014; "How Big Media is Adapting to Automated Ad Buying," *Wall Street Journal*, June 27, 2014; "Proctor & Gamble Aims to Buy 70% of Digital Ads Programmatically," Adage.com, June 4, 2014; "Programmatic Buying Roundup," by Lauren Fisher, eMarketer, Inc., June 2014; "Programmatic Guaranteed," by Lauren Fisher, eMarketer Inc., May 2014; "Driving Programmatic Buying: Automotive Industry Will Invest Big in 2014," by Mike Hudson et al., eMarketer, Inc., January 2014; "Programmatic Everywhere? Data, Technology and the Future of Audience Engagement," IAB, November 4, 2013; "RTB Is the Most Overhyped Technology Ever: It's Useful for Extending the Reach of Mediocre Content, but Not for Subtle, Thoughtful Buys," by Joe Mohen, Adage.com, May 30, 2013.

Case Study Questions

1. Pay a visit to your favorite portal and count the total ads on the opening page. Count how many of these ads are (a) immediately of interest and relevant to you, (b) sort of interesting or relevant but not now, and (c) not interesting or relevant. Do this 10 times and calculate the percentage of the three kinds of situations. Describe what you find and explain the results using this case.

2. Advertisers use different kinds of "profiles" in the decision to display ads to customers. Identify the different kinds of profiles described in this case, and explain why they are relevant to online display advertising.

3. How can display ads achieve search-engine–like results?

4. Do you think instant display ads based on your immediately prior clickstream will be as effective as search engine marketing techniques? Why or why not?

6.6   REVIEW

KEY CONCEPTS

- ■ **Understand the key features of the Internet audience, the basic concepts of consumer behavior and purchasing, and how consumers behave online.**
  - Key features of the Internet audience include the number of users online, the intensity and scope of use, demographics and aspects, the type of Internet connection, and community effects.
  - Models of consumer behavior attempt to predict or explain what consumers purchase, and where, when, how much, and why they buy. Factors that impact buying behavior include cultural, social, and psychological factors.
  - There are five stages in the consumer decision process: awareness of need, search for more information, evaluation of alternatives, the actual purchase decision, and post-purchase contact with the firm.
  - The online consumer decision process is basically the same, with the addition of two new factors: Web site and mobile platform capabilities and consumer clickstream behavior.

- ■ **Identify and describe the basic digital commerce marketing and advertising strategies and tools.**
  - A *Web site* is the major tool for establishing the initial relationship with the customer.
  - *Search engine marketing and advertising* allows firms to pay search engines for inclusion in the search engine index (formerly free and based on "objective" criteria), receiving a guarantee that their firm will appear in the results of relevant searches.
  - *Display ads* are promotional messages that users can respond to by clicking on the banner and following the link to a product description or offering. Display ads include banner ads, rich media, video ads, and sponsorships.
  - *E-mail marketing* sends e-mail directly to interested users, and has proven to be one of the most effective forms of marketing communications.
  - *Lead generation marketing* uses multiple e-commerce presences to generate leads for businesses who later can be contacted and converted into customers.
  - *Affiliate marketing* involves a firm putting its logo or banner ad on another firm's Web site from which users of that site can click through to the affiliate's site.
  - *Viral marketing* is a form of social marketing that involves getting customers to pass along a company's marketing message to friends, family, and colleagues.
  - *Social marketing and advertising* involves using the social graph to communicate brand images and directly promote sales of products and services.
  - *Mobile and local marketing and advertising* involves using display ads, search engine advertising, video ads, and mobile messaging on mobile devices such as smartphones and tablet computers, often using the geographic location of the user.
  - *Multi-channel marketing* (combining offline and online marketing efforts) is typically the most effective. Although many e-commerce ventures want to rely heavily on online communications, marketing communications campaigns most successful at driving traffic have incorporated both online and offline tactics.
  - *Customer retention techniques* for strengthening customer relationships include personalization, one-to-one marketing, and interest-based advertising, customization and customer co-production, and customer service (such as CRMs, FAQs, live chat, intelligent agents, and automated response systems).
  - *Online pricing strategies* include offering products and services for free, versioning, bundling, and dynamic pricing.

- ■ Identify and describe the main technologies that support online marketing.

- *Web transaction logs*—records that document user activity at a Web site. Coupled with data from the registration forms and shopping cart database, these represent a treasure trove of marketing information for both individual sites and the online industry as a whole.
- *Tracking files*—Various files, like cookies, Web beacons, Flash cookies, and apps, that follow users and track their behavior as they visit sites across the entire Web.
- *Databases, data warehouses, data mining, and profiling*—technologies that allow marketers to identify exactly who the online customer is and what they want, and then to present the customer with exactly what they want, when they want it, for the right price.
- *CRM systems*—a repository of customer information that records all of the contacts a customer has with a firm and generates a customer profile available to everyone in the firm who has a need to "know the customer."

- ■ Understand the costs and benefits of online marketing communications.

- Key terms that one must know in order to understand evaluations of online marketing communications' effectiveness and its costs and benefits include:
  - *Impressions*—the number of times an ad is served.
  - *Click-through rate*—the number of times an ad is clicked.
  - *View-through rate*—the 30-day response rate to an ad.
  - *Hits*—the number of http requests received by a firm's server.
  - *Page views*—the number of pages viewed by visitors.
  - *Stickiness (duration)*—the average length of time visitors remain at a site.
  - *Unique visitors*—the number of distinct, unique visitors to a site.
  - *Loyalty*—the percentage of purchasers who return in a year.
  - *Reach*—the percentage of total consumers in a market who will visit a site.
  - *Recency*—the average number of days elapsed between visits.
  - *Acquisition rate*—the percentage of visitors who indicate an interest in the site's product by registering or visiting product pages.
  - *Conversion rate*—the percentage of visitors who purchase something.
  - *Browse-to-buy ratio*—the ratio of items purchased to product views.
  - *View-to-cart ratio*—the ratio of "Add to cart" clicks to product views.
  - *Cart conversion rate*—the ratio of actual orders to "Add to cart" clicks.
  - *Checkout conversion rate*—the ratio of actual orders to checkouts started.
  - *Abandonment rate*—the percentage of shoppers who begin a shopping cart form, but then fail to complete the form.
  - *Retention rate*—the percentage of existing customers who continue to buy on a regular basis.
  - *Attrition rate*—the percentage of customers who purchase once, but do not return within a year.
  - *Conversation ratio*—the number of comments produced per post to a site.
  - *Applause ratio*—the number of Likes or Shares per post.
  - *Amplification*—the number of re-tweets or re-shares per post.
  - *Sentiment ratio*—the ratio of positive comments to total comments.
  - *Open rate*—the percentage of customers who open the mail and are exposed to the message.
  - *Delivery rate*—the percentage of e-mail recipients who received the e-mail.
  - *Click-through rate (e-mail)*—the percentage of e-mail recipients who clicked through to the offer.
  - *Bounce-back rate*—the percentage of e-mails that could not be delivered.
- Studies have shown that low click-through rates are not indicative of a lack of commercial impact of online advertising, and that advertising communication does occur even when users do not directly

respond by clicking. Online advertising in its various forms has been shown to boost brand awareness and brand recall, create positive brand perceptions, and increase intent to purchase.

- Effectiveness cannot be considered without analysis of cost. Typical pricing models for online marketing communications include barter, cost per thousand (CPM), cost per click (CPC), cost per action (CPA), hybrid models, and sponsorships.
- Online marketing communications are typically less costly than traditional mass media marketing. Also, online sales can generally be directly correlated with online marketing efforts, unlike traditional marketing communications tactics.

QUESTIONS

1. What are some of the ways that gender, income, education, age, and ethnicity impact online purchasing behavior?
2. What are the primary differences between online and offline consumer behavior?
3. What is clickstream behavior and how is it used by marketers?
4. Research has shown that many consumers use the Internet to investigate purchases before actually buying, which is often done in a physical storefront. What implication does this have for online merchants? What can they do to entice more online buying, rather than pure research?
5. What are Web analytics and how do they help e-commerce firms better understand consumer behavior at the various stages of the online purchasing process?
6. Why have advertising networks become controversial? What, if anything, can be done to overcome any resistance to this technique?
7. What are the five main elements of a comprehensive marketing plan? What are some different platforms used for each?
8. List the differences among databases, data warehouses, and data mining.
9. What are three strategic questions that online marketing managers need to address?
10. What are the primary marketing functions of a Web site?
11. Name and describe three different types of search engine advertising.
12. What are some issues associated with the use of search engine advertising?
13. What is lead generation marketing?
14. What are the four features of social marketing and advertising that are driving its growth?
15. Explain why author John Battelle calls the Web a database of intentions.
16. What are some of the advantages of direct e-mail marketing?
17. What are four methods that online advertisers use to behaviorally target ads?
18. Shopping cart abandonment rates are typically 70% or higher. Why is this rate so high and what techniques can help improve this rate?
19. Define CTR, CPM, CPC, CPA, and VTR.
20. What advantages do rich media ads have over static display ads?

PROJECTS

1. Go to www.strategicbusinessinsights.com/vals/presurvey.shtml. Take the survey to determine which lifestyle category you fit into. Then write a two-page paper describing how your lifestyle and values impact your use of e-commerce. How is your online consumer behavior affected by your lifestyle?

2. Visit Net-a-porter.com and create an Internet marketing plan for it that includes each of the following:
   - One-to-one marketing
   - Affiliate marketing

- Viral marketing
- Blog marketing
- Social network marketing

Describe how each plays a role in growing the business, and create a slide presentation of your marketing plan.

3. Use the Online Consumer Purchasing Model (Figure 6.11) to assess the effectiveness of an e-mail campaign at a small Web site devoted to the sales of apparel to the ages 18–26 young adult market in the United States. Assume a marketing campaign of 100,000 e-mails (at 25 cents per e-mail address). The expected click-through rate is 5%, the customer conversion rate is 10%, and the loyal customer retention rate is 25%. The average sale is $60, and the profit margin is 50% (the cost of the goods is $30). Does the campaign produce a profit? What would you advise doing to increase the number of purchases and loyal customers? What Web design factors? What communications messages?

4. Surf the Web for at least 15 minutes. Visit at least two different e-commerce sites. Make a list describing in detail all the different marketing communication tools you see being used. Which do you believe is the most effective and why?

5. Do a search for a product of your choice on at least three search engines. Examine the results page carefully. Can you discern which results, if any, are a result of a paid placement? If so, how did you determine this? What other marketing communications related to your search appear on the page?

6. Examine the use of rich media and video in advertising. Find and describe at least two examples of advertising using streaming video, sound, or other rich media technologies. (Hint: Check the sites of Internet advertising agencies for case studies or examples of their work.) What are the advantages and/ or disadvantages of this kind of advertising? Prepare a 3- to 5-page report on your findings.

7. Visit your Facebook page and examine the ads shown in the right margin. What is being advertised and how do you believe it is relevant to your interests or online behavior? You could also search on a retail product on Google several times, and related products, then visit Yahoo or another popular site to see if your past behavior is helping advertisers track you.

REFERENCES

Adjei, Mavis, and Stephanie Noble. "The Influence of C2C Communications in Online Brand Communities On Purchase Behavior." *Journal of the Academy of Marketing Science*, Vol. 38, No. 5 (2009).

Adomavicius, Gediminas, and Alexander Tuzhilin. "Using Data Mining Methods to Build Customer Profiles." *IEEE Computer* (February 2001a).

Adomavicius, Gediminas, and Alexander Tuzhilin. "Expert-Driven Validation of Rule-Based User Models in Personalization Applications." *Data Mining and Knowledge Discovery* (January 2001b).

Akerlof, G. "The Market for 'Lemons' Quality Under Uncertainty and the Market Mechanism." *Quarterly Journal of Economics* (August 1970).

Ba, Sulin, Jan Stallaert, and Zhang. "Balancing IT with the Human Touch: Optimal Investment in IT-Based Customer Service." *Information Systems Research* (September 2010).

Ba, Sulin, and Paul Pavlou. "Evidence on the Effect of Trust Building Technology in Electronic Markets: Price Premiums and Buyer Behavior." *MIS Quarterly* (September 2002).

Bakos, J. Y., and Erik Brynjolfsson. "Bundling and Competition on the Internet: Aggregation Strategies for Information Goods." *Marketing Science* (January 2000).

Battelle, John. "The Database of Intentions is Far Larger Than I Thought." Battellemedia.com (March 5, 2010).

Battelle, John. "Search Blog." Battellemedia.com (November 13, 2003).

Baymard Research, "27 Cart Abandonment Rate Statistics." Baymard.com (March 14, 2014).

Belisle, Jean Francois. "The Battle of Web Analytics Solutions in 2013." Jfbelisle.com (January 21, 2013).

BIA/Kelsey. "U.S. Local Media Ad Revenues to Grow from $133.2B in 2013 to $158.6B in 2018." (April 28, 2014a).

BIA/Kelsey. "U.S. Mobile Local Ad Revenues to Reach $4.5 Billion in 2014." (April 10, 2014b).

Brightroll. "2013 US Video Advertising Report." (April 30, 2013).

Brookings Institute. "Online Identity and Consumer Trust: Assessing Online Risk." (January 2011).

Calvert, Mary F. "As Online Ads Look More Like News Articles, F.T.C. Warns Against Deception." *New York Times* (December 4, 2013).

Castell, John. "Google Panda Explained for Website Owners." Linkedin.com (June 12, 2014).

Chan, P. K. "A Non-Invasive Learning Approach to Building Web User Profiles." In *Proceedings of ACM SIGKDD International Conference* (1999).

comScore. "2013 U.S. Digital Future in Focus." (February 14, 2013).

comScore (Andrea Vollman). "Viewability Benchmarks Show Many Ads Are Not In-View but Rates Vary by Publisher." (June 28, 2013).

Consumer-action.org. "Consumer Action 'Do Not Track' Survey Results." (May 5, 2013).

Corritore, C. L., B. Kracher, and S. Wiedenbeck, "On-line trust: concepts, evolving themes, a model," *International Journal of Human-Computer Studies* (2006).

Cross, Robert. "Launching the Revenue Rocket: How Revenue Management Can Work For Your Business." *Cornell Hotel and Restaurant Administration Quarterly* (April 1997).

Dyer, Pam. "Social Networks Have Little Influence on What You Buy Online." Pamarama.net (April 2011).

eMarketer, Inc. "US Time Spent with Media: The Complete eMarketer Forecast for 2014." (April 2014a).

eMarketer, Inc. (Alison McCarthy). "US Mobile Users: 2014 Complete Forecast." (April 2014b).

eMarketer, Inc. (Alison McCarthy) "US Internet Users: 2014 Complete Forecast." (March 20, 2014c).

eMarketer, Inc. "US Fixed Broadband Households, 2012–2018." (February 2014d).

eMarketer, Inc. "Reasons US Internet Users Buy Products Digitally Rather Than In-Store." (February 23, 2014e).

eMarketer, Inc. "US Digital Shoppers and Buyers, 2013–2018." (September 2014f).

eMarketer, Inc. (Alison McCarthy) "US Ad Spending: Q2 2014 Forecast and Comparative Estimates." (July 8, 2014g).

eMarketer, Inc. (Lauren Fisher). "Email Benchmarks 2014: Richer Data, Mobile Optimization Crucial for Greater Relevancy." (August 4, 2014h).

eMarketer, Inc. "US Social Network Ad Revenues, 2013–2016." (September 1, 2014i)

eMarketer, Inc. "US Social Network Ad Revenues, by Venue, 2013–2016." (September 2014j).

eMarketer, Inc. "What's the Upside to Shopping Cart Abandonment." (March 3, 2014k).

eMarketer, Inc. (Paul Verna) "Native Advertising: Difficult to Define, but Definitely Growing." (March 2014x).

eMarketer, Inc. (Alison McCarthy). "Worldwide Ad Spending: Q3 2014 Forecast and Comparative Estimates." (October 2014y).

eMarketer, Inc. (Alison McCarthy). "Worldwide Social Network Ad Spending: Midyear 2014 Complete Forecast." (August 2014z).

eMarketer, Inc. "Online Buyers Notice Retargeted Ads." (August 12, 2013a).

eMarketer, Inc. (Debra Aho Williamson). "Meeting the Needs for Speed: How Social Analytics Support Real-time Marketing." (February 2013b).

eMarketer, Inc. (Paul Verna). "Word of Mouth Marketing" (October 2010a).

Evans, P., and T. S. Wurster. "Getting Real About Virtual Commerce." *Harvard Business Review* (November-December 1999).

ExactTarget. "2014 State of Marketing." (January 8, 2014).

Farahat, Ayman and Michael Bailey. "How Effective is Targeted Advertising." International World Wide Web Conference Committee (April 26–20, 2012).

Fawcett, Tom, and Foster Provost. "Adaptive Fraud Detection." *Data Mining and Knowledge Discovery* (1997).

Fawcett, Tom, and Foster Provost. "Combining Data Mining and Machine Learning for Effective User Profiling." In *Proceedings of the Second International Conference on Knowledge Discovery and Data Mining* (1996).

Federal Trade Commission. "Blurred Lines: Advertising or Content?—An FTC Workshop on Native Advertising." (December 4, 2013).

Fenn, Donna. "Some Businesses Go Creative on Prices, Applying Technology." *New York Times* (January 22, 2014).

Fireclick. "Fireclick Index/Top Line Growth." Index.Fireclick.com (accessed September 18, 2014).

Forrester Research. "US Cross-Channel Retail Sales Forecast, 2014 to 2018." (July 24, 2014a).

Forrester Research. "Refresh Your Approach to 1:1 Marketing: How Real-Time Automation Elevates Personalization." (August 18, 2014b)

Forrester Research. (Sucharita Mulpuru). "Will Facebook Ever Drive eCommerce?" (April 7, 2011a).

Franklin, David J. "Consumer Recognition and Understanding of Native Advertisements." Federal Trade Commission (December 4, 2013).

French, Violet. "Canada's Tough New Anti-Spam Legislation: Beware Its Extra-Territorial Reach." Americanbar.org (January 2014).

Garg, Rajiv. "Peer Influence and Information Difusion in Online Networks: An Empricial Analysis." Carnegie Mellon University, School of Information Systems and Management, Working Paper, 2009.

Gigaom.com, "Survey: Percentage of Users Saying They Opt Out of Targeted Ads Has Nearly Doubled." Gigaom.com (July 16, 2012).

Google, Inc. "Guide to Ad Sizes." (accessed September 17, 2014).

Guo, Stephen, M. Wang, and J. Leskovec. "The Role of Social Networks in Online Shopping Choice: Information Passing, Price of Trust, and Consumer Choice." Stanford University (June 2011).

Hanes, Marle. "Your Google Algorithm Cheat Sheet: Panda, Penguin, and Hummingbird." Themozblog.com (June 11, 2014).

Hof, Robert. "The One Second Rule: New Viewability Metrics Exposes How Low Online Advertising Standards Still Are." *Forbes* (March 3, 2014).

Interactive Advertising Bureau. "Mobile Rich Media Ad Definitions (MRAID)" (September 2012).

Interactive Advertising Bureau. "IAB Standards and Guidelines." Iab.net (September 2011).

Interactive Advertising Bureau (IAB)/PriceWaterhouse-Coopers. "IAB Internet Advertising Revenue Report: 2013 Full Year Results." (April 2014).

Isaac, Mike. "Uber Reaches Deal With New York on Surge Pricing in Emergencies." *New York Times* (July 8, 2014).

Iyengar, Raghuram, S. Han, and S. Gupta. "Do Friends Influence Purchases in a Social Network." Harvard Business School. Working Paper, 2009.

Kantrowitz, Alex. "Digital Ad Fraud is Rampant. Here's Why So Little Has Been Done about It." Adage.com (March 24, 2014).

Kantrowitz, Alex. "Just Look At How Google Dominates Ad Tech." Adage.com (October 18, 2013).

Kim, D., and I. Benbasat. "The Effects of Trust-Assuring Arguments on Consumer Trust in Internet Stores," *Information Systems Research* (2006).

Kim, D., and I. Benbasat. "Designs for Effective Implementation of Trust Assurances in Internet Stores," *Communications of the ACM* (July 2007).

Kim, Dan, Donald Ferrin, and Raghav Rao. "Trust and Satisfaction, Two Stepping Stones for Successful E-Commerce Relationships: A Longitudinal Exploration." *Journal of Information Systems Research* (June 2009).

Kotler, Philip, and Gary Armstrong. *Principles of Marketing, 13th Edition.* Upper Saddle River, NJ: Prentice Hall (2009).

Lowreyjan, Annie. "Is Uber's Surge-Pricing an Example of High-Tech Gouging?" *New York Times* (January 10, 2014).

MediaMind Inc. "The Rich and the Powerful." (March 2012a).

MediaMind Inc. "Consumers 27 Times More Likely to Click-Through Online Video Ads than Standard Banners." (September 12, 2012b).

Mishra, D. P., J. B. Heide, and S. G. Cort. "Information Asymmetry and Levels of Agency Relationships." *Journal of Marketing Research.* (1998).

Mobasher, Bamshad. "Data Mining for Web Personalization." Center for Web Intelligence, School of Computer Science, Telecommunication, and Information Systems, DePaul University, Chicago, Illinois. (2007).

National Conference of State Legislatures. "State Laws Relating to Unsolicited Commercial of Bulk E-mail (SPAM)." (January 2, 2013).

Nielsen Company. "December 2011—Top U.S. Web Brands." (January 25, 2012).

Nielsen Company. "Nielsen Receives MRC Accreditation for Nielsen Online Campaign Ratings." (September 7, 2011).

Nielsen Company. "Global Online Consumer Survey." (May 2011).

Oestreicher-Singer, Gail and Arun Sundararajan. "The Visible Hand of Social Networks." *Electronic Commerce Research* (2008).

O'Malley, Gavin. "IAB Issues Traffic Fraud Best Practices." Mediapost.com (December 6, 2013).

Opinion Research Corporation. "Online Consumer Product Reviews Have Big Influence." Opinion Research Corporation (April 16, 2009).

Pavlou, Paul. "Institution-Based Trust in Interorganizational Exchange Relationships: The Role of Online B2B Marketplaces on Trust Formation." *Journal of Strategic Information Systems* (2002).

Pew Research Center. "Part 1: How the Internet Has Woven Itself into American Life." (February 27, 2014a).

Pew Research Center. "Internet User Demographics." (accessed September 16, 2014b).

Pew Research Center. (Lee Rainie) "The State of the Digital Divides." (November 5, 2013a).

Pew Research Center. "Broadband Adoption: The Next Mile—Senate Testimony." (October 29, 2013b).

Pew Research Center. (Kathryn Zickuhr and Aaron Smith) "Digital Differences." (April 13, 2012).

PointRoll. "2013 Benchmark Report." (April 4, 2014).

Powell, Tracie. "Native Ads Aren't As Clear As Outlets Think." *Columbia Journalism Review* (December 5, 2013).

Rayport, J. F., and J. J. Sviokla. "Exploiting the Virtual Value Chain." *Harvard Business Review* (November–December 1995).

Reuter, Thad. "The Price is Right. Then It's Not." Internetretailer.com (August 4, 2014).

Richtel, Matt. "Wasting Time Is Divide in Digital Era." *New York Times* (May 29, 2012).

Robinson, Jim. "What You Need to Know About the Changing Affiliate Landscape." Marketingprofs.com (August 8, 2014).

Russell, Mallory. "What the Top 10 Viral Videos of 2013 Taught Us." Visiblemeasures.com (December 24, 2013).

Schleifer, Dan. "Which Social Network Makes Your Customers Buy?" *Harvard Business Review* (April 2, 2013).

Schwartz, Barry. "Google Made 890 Improvements To Search Over The Past Year." Searchengineland.com (August 19, 2014).

Segal, David. "Web Display Ads Often Not Visible." *New York Times* (May 3, 2014).

Sevitt, David, and Alexandra Samuel. "Vision Statement: How Pinterest Puts People in Stores." *Harvard Business Review* (July–August, 2013).

Shapiro, Carl, and Hal Varian. *Information Rules: A Strategic Guide to the Network Economy.* Cambridge, MA: Harvard Business School Press (1999).

Shapiro, Carl, and Hal Varian. "Versioning: The Smart Way to Sell Information." *Harvard Business Review* (November–December 1998).

Sinha, Indrajit. "Cost Transparency: The Net's Real Threat to Prices and Brands." *Harvard Business Review* (March-April 2000).

Socialmediatoday.com. "Mobile Apps: How Many People Use Apps?" (September 3, 2013).

Symantec. "Symantec Intelligence Report." (August 2014).

The Search Agency. "State of Paid Search Report—Q2 2014." (2014).

Tobii/Mediative. "The Effectiveness of Display Advertising on a Desktop PC vs. a Tablet Device." (August 2012).

TRUSTe. "U.S. Consumer Privacy Attitudes and Business Implications." (July 16, 2012).

Van den Poel, Dirk, and Wouter Buckinx. "Predicting Online Purchasing Behavior." *European Journal of Operations Research*, Vol. 166, Issue 2 (2005).

VINDICO. "2013 Annual Report." (May 1, 2014).

VisionCritical Corporation. "From Social to Sale: 8 Questions to Ask Your Customers." (June 2013).

Vranica, Suzanne. "A 'Crisis' in Online Ads: One-Third of Traffic is Bogus." *Wall Street Journal* (March 23, 2014).

Wigand, R. T., and R. I. Benjamin. "Electronic Commerce: Effects on Electronic Markets." *Journal of Computer Mediated Communication* (December 1995).

Williamson, O. E. *The Economic Institutions of Capitalism.* New York: Free Press (1985).

Wolfinbarger, Mary, and Mary Gilly. "Shopping Online for Freedom, Control and Fun." *California Management Review* (Winter 2001).

CHAPTER 7

Social, Mobile, and Local Marketing

LEARNING OBJECTIVES

After reading this chapter, you will be able to:

- Understand the difference between traditional online marketing and the new social-mobile-local marketing platforms and the relationships between social, mobile, and local marketing.
- Understand the social marketing process from fan acquisition to sales and the marketing capabilities of social marketing platforms such as Facebook, Twitter, and Pinterest.
- Identify the key elements of a mobile marketing campaign.
- Understand the capabilities of location-based local marketing.

Just Falafel

Soars with Social Media

When Reema Shetty and her longtime friend from high school, Alia Al Mazrouei, were kicking around ideas for a healthy fast food outlet in the United Arab Emirates, their mutual friend, Mohamad Bitar, suggested promoting Middle Eastern and Lebanese delicacies. By the time the trio was ready to open their first restaurant in Abu Dhabi in 2007, they were already dreaming big. They believed they could take a 1000 year-old vegetarian staple, whose main marketplace incarnation had been as street vendor food, to mall food courts and compete head to head with the likes of McDonald's, Subway, and Sbarro.

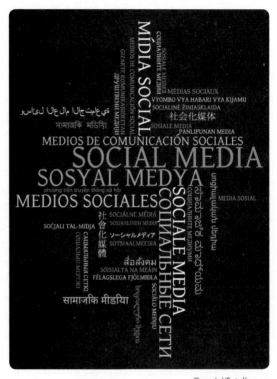

© maigi/Fotolia.com

Falafel, they thought, had a number of propitious characteristics. Made from either ground chick peas or fava beans, it could be marketed as a wholesome alternative to typical preservative- and fat-laden food court fare. It had never been adapted for food court distribution, so they would have first mover advantage. By using the best ingredients, they would create a superior, more delicious product than the competition, and by diversifying condiments and breads, they could internationalize the fried patties, appealing to a wide range of palates. A falafel aficionado, Bitar believed that with the proper attention, this poor man's food could be elevated to equal standing with its competitors.

To start, Just Falafel offered the Original, served with tahini and pickles in pita bread, a Greek version with Tzatziki dressing and olives on tortilla bread, and an Indian version with spicy Indian dressing and cucumber pickles, also on tortilla bread. By 2010, it had five locations and had gained acclaim as the caterer for some of the UAE's biggest sporting events. Bitar and Shetty, now married, believed that Just Falafel's business proposition—from a menu standpoint—was nearing completion. Mexican, Italian, Lebanese, American, and Japanese flavors were offered, and Just Falafel began soliciting suggestions for an Emirati version on its Facebook page. A YouTube channel was launched shortly thereafter. Though not quite sure yet how to leverage their social media channels, the founders had a new dream: global expansion.

As 2011 began, they set a goal to have 75 stores in the UAE within the next five years. Franchising was the only way to achieve this. Just Falafel would need partners on the retail front-end so that it could reinvest on the back-end. Fadi Malas was brought on board as CEO in March and the official start of Just Falafel's franchising plan was trumpeted on Facebook: Falafill Your Ambitions. Become a Franchisee.

Five new franchises were quickly sold through the Just Falafel Web site for 60,000 dirhams (Dhs) each. Franchisees need approximately an additional 300,000 to 500,000 Dhs to set up shop, for a total investment of between $100,000 and $150,000 US. The Web site was garnering ten to fifteen franchise inquiries a day, and by year end, 25 had been sold. Success offline was translating to Facebook fans online, supported by more active management of the page. By communicating how Just Falafel was growing, where new stores were opening, what new menu items were being considered, and numerous other facets of the business, Just Falafel began building an online community. By December 2011, it celebrated its 100,000th fan just as its first outlet outside the UAE opened in Amman, Jordan. On December 30, Just Falafel capped off the year by signing a master franchising contract with Centurion Holding to serve as the sub-franchisor for over 200 outlets in the U.K. by 2017.

Just Falafel's franchising efforts snowballed once the company launched a Facebook advertising campaign linking to a franchise application page. Applications began pouring in from across the Gulf region and from as far afield as India and Canada. Bitar, now the Managing Director, quickly realized that Facebook could give Just Falafel the highest possible exposure and serve as its main communication highway—and an economical one at that. The total advertising outlay was between US $300,000-$400,000, a pittance compared to established fast food operators. CEO Malas believed Facebook was Just Falafel's best chance of reaching both local markets and a global audience. Bitar estimated that Just Falafel achieved a nineteen times return on investment from the media spend (over US $8 million in sales). Using Facebook's built-in measurement tools, it targeted people over the age of 25 with disposable income over US $200,000. It placed Just Falafel franchising ads on pages of interest to those in its demographic target groups. But recognizing the power of word-of-mouth referrals, general consumer targeting was not ignored. The over 7 million Facebook impressions Just Falafel now records daily would otherwise have been unattainable. Traditional marketing and media channels would have cost millions of dollars per month. In 2014, Malas said that approximately 90% of its advertising and digital media budgets are focused on Facebook, yielding 1.5 billion impressions for Just Falafel over the previous year.

Facebook is also used to prime new markets, educating prospective consumers about falafel in general and Just Falafel's unique spin. Before a single outlet has opened, country pages are created to actively seek followers. Location pages follow after a franchise has opened. Just Falafel averages 25,000 fans per outlet, ten times more than all other quick service restaurants (QSR) globally. To help build its fan base, Just Falafel sponsors local sporting, fashion, and film events. Once there is a sufficient following, it shares its franchising ambitions and invites interested parties to submit a form. And of course, Facebook is used to launch marketing campaigns and drive customers to its locations. Just Falafel is one of very few companies to have had case studies conducted on its use of social media by Facebook more than once. The fruitful synergy between Just Falafel and Facebook was

SOURCES: "Just Falafel Slows Down Franchising," by Sarah Algethami, Gulfnews.com, November 17, 2014; "Just Falafel Franchise Refocuses On The Food," by Lianne Gutcher, Thenational.ae, November 10, 2014; "UAE's Just

fueled by Just Falafel's exceptionally responsive fan base and its engaging trailers, many featuring animated falafel balls sporting either the national headwear for their flavor or suitable head and eyewear for excursions to a polo match, film festival, boat show or shopping excursion. The Just Falafel logo and tagline, *I Fell for Falafel*, closes each video.

By March 2013, Just Falafel was averaging 100 franchise information requests per day, with the total number of inquiries exceeding 12,000. It had 650 signed contracts for franchises in 15 countries. The menu had been steadily broadened to complement Just Falafel's healthful vegetarian niche. Mexican-style falafel burritos and quesadillas and a baked version of the bean patty were joined in 2013 by three organic salads made from locally grown produce. Each introduction was, of course, trumpeted on Facebook—and Twitter, which had been added into the mix. The hashtag #JustTryIt encourages people to try its offerings, while other tweets drive customers to specific locations, give directions, solicit meal choice input, and highlight health benefits. Twitter is used as a tactical tool to reach influencers and provide customer service. In its own case study of the social network marketing phenomenon, Netizency found that Just Falafel used Twitter's location-based, follower-based, and interest-based targeting tools to achieve nearly 9 million impressions, 170,000 engagements, and over 10,000 followers. Over 10% of the sales fluctuations at its London location were attributed to changes in Just Falafel's Twitter ad spend, and a targeted franchising campaign in Turkey yielded 455,000 impressions, 4,000 Web site visits, and 43 applications.

The bulk of its 2 million Facebook fans hail from 45 nations targeted for expansion, including Ireland, Australia, Brazil, and the United States. More than a quarter of its fans are from India. With vegetarians comprising 60% of its population, India is a natural fit for Just Falafel. In 2014, Just Falafel opened stores in India, Egypt, Australia, Canada, and the United States, where it hopes to open 160 new outlets within the next five years. The company also continued its expansion throughout the Middle East, announcing 10 new restaurants in Oman, 7 in Kuwait, and continued expansion throughout the UAE. All together, the company has 45 stores in 10 different countries, with signed franchise contracts to develop over 720 additional stores in 18 countries.

Although the company has continued its rapid expansion, Just Falafel rededicated itself to its food in 2014, hoping to improve its selection beyond falafel and to improve its recipes. After sampling items from the menu and detecting a dip in quality, Bitar hired a new chef and led an effort to improve its offerings. Just Falafel totally revamped its menu, dropping fava beans and using exclusively chickpeas in its falafel recipe, improving its hummus using techniques from street vendors, and offering choices of sweet potato wedges, among many other changes. The new menu is devoid of preservatives and boasts reduced calorie counts. Admitting that perhaps the company had focused too much on expansion and growth at the expense of core elements of its business, Just Falafel closed stores in some of its peripheral markets like Lebanon and Jordan and announced that it would slow its growth slightly going forward, focusing more on company owned and operated outlets, and shelving plans to launch an initial public offering of shares until it matures a bit more as a company.

Falafel Announces Expansion Plan in Kuwait," by Andy Sambidge, Arabianbusiness.com, August 22, 2014; "UAE's Just Falafel Enters India, Opens First Restaurant in Bangalore," by Aarti Nagraj, Gulfbusiness.com, July 27, 2014; "Just Falafel to Open 10 New Outlets in Oman," by Mary Sophia, Gulfbusiness.com, July 24, 2014; "The Franchise Story: CEO Fadi Malas On Just Falafel's Lucrative Business Model," by Kareem Chehayeb, Entrepreneurmiddleeast.com, June 24, 2014; "Just Falafel Says Not Planning IPO In Next Few Months," by Samuel Potter, Stefania Bianchi, and Zahra Hankir, Bloomberg.com, June 16, 2014; "A Look at Just Falafel's Recipe as It (Potentially) Readies for an IPO," by Nina Curley, Wamda.com, October 2, 2013; "Just Falafel CEO and Founder Discuss Developing a Global Food Franchise in the Middle East," Justfalafel.com/blog, July 1, 2013; "Just Falafel Video Case Study English," Facebook.com/video/, June 19, 2013; "How Just Falafel's Facebook Campaign Drives 100 Daily Franchising Requests," Digibuzzme.com, March 25, 2013; "Twitter Case Study: Just Falafel," by Fadi Khater, Netizency, Slideshare.net, March 22, 2013; "Just Falafel's Taste for Fast Expansion," by Simeon Kerr, FT.com, February 7, 2013; "Just Falafel Gets 3K Franchise Queries on Facebook," Hoteliermiddleeast.com, October 4, 2012; "Just Falafel Gets 3,500 Franchising Requests," Tradearabia.com, September 25, 2012; "Just Falafel Growth Demonstrates Power of Social Media Becoming Facebook's First GCC Case Study," Ameinfo.com/blog/company-news/, September 25, 2012; "Interview: Just Falafel-With love, from UAE to the World," by Priyanka Pradhan, Kippreport.com, August 8, 2012; "Making a Social Phenomenon of Streetfood," by Ola Diab, Qatartoday.tumblr.com, May 11, 2012; "Just Falafel Aims to Have 25 Outlets in Two Years," by Derek Baldwin, Gulfnews.com, March 15, 2011; "With More than One Million Falafels Sold in 2010, Just Falafel Aims to Become the Largest Falafel Franchise Globally," Albawaba.com, January 13th, 2011.

> ## 7.1 INTRODUCTION TO SOCIAL, MOBILE, AND LOCAL MARKETING

Social, mobile, and local marketing have transformed the online marketing landscape. Before 2007, Facebook was a fledgling company limited to college students. Apple had not yet announced the iPhone. Online marketing consisted largely of creating a corporate Web site, buying display ads on Yahoo, purchasing Ad Words on Google, and sending e-mail. The workhorse of online marketing was the display ad that flashed brand messages to millions of users who were not expected to respond immediately, ask questions, or make observations. The primary measure of success was how many "eyeballs" (unique visitors) a Web site produced, and how many "impressions" a marketing campaign generated. An impression was one ad shown to one person. Both of these measures were carryovers from the world of television, which measures marketing in terms of audience size and ad views.

FROM EYEBALLS TO CONVERSATIONS

After 2007, everything began to change, with the rapid growth of Facebook and other social network sites, the explosive growth of smartphones beginning with Apple iPhone in 2007, and the growing interest in local marketing. What's different about the new world of social-mobile-local marketing and advertising are the related concepts of "conversations" and "engagement." Marketing today is based on businesses marketing themselves as partners in multiple online conversations with their customers, potential customers, and even critics. Your brand is being talked about on the Web and social media (that's the conversation part). Today, marketing your firm and brands requires you to locate, identify, and participate in these conversations. Social marketing means all things social: listening, discussing, interacting, empathizing, and engaging. Rather than bombarding your audience with fancier, louder ads, instead have a conversation with them and engage them in your brand. The emphasis in online marketing has shifted from a focus on eyeballs to a focus on participating in customer-oriented conversations. In this sense, social marketing and advertising is not simply a "new ad channel," but a collection of technology-based tools for communicating with shoppers.

In the past, businesses could tightly control their brand messaging and lead consumers down a funnel of cues that ended in a purchase. That is not true of social marketing. Consumer purchase decisions are increasingly driven by the conversations, choices, tastes, and opinions of the consumer's social network. Social marketing is all about businesses participating in and shaping this social process.

FROM THE DESKTOP TO THE SMARTPHONE AND TABLET

Today, social, mobile, and local marketing are the fastest growing forms of online marketing. It's taken five years for this new landscape to emerge, and firms are still learning how to use the new social and mobile marketing technologies.

By 2012, mobile marketing had already overtaken social marketing using traditional Web browsers on the Web. In 2015, spending on mobile marketing worldwide will be more than double the amount spent on social marketing. By 2016, it is estimated

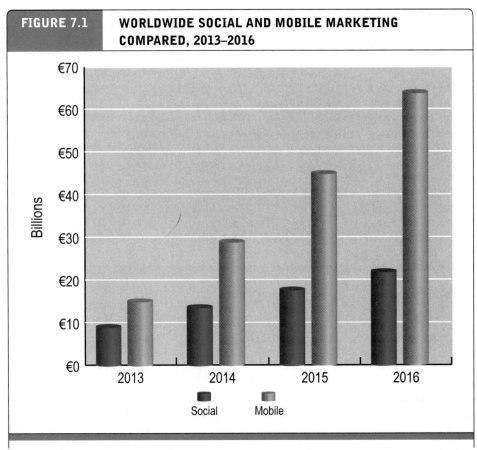

| FIGURE 7.1 | **WORLDWIDE SOCIAL AND MOBILE MARKETING COMPARED, 2013–2016** |

In 2015, marketers are expected to spend more than double on mobile marketing worldwide as they do on social marketing.

SOURCE: Based on data from eMarketer, Inc., 2014a, 2014v, 2014w

that mobile marketing spending will account for around €64 billion annually, while social marketing will be about €22 billion (see **Figure 7.1**). While social marketing is expected to grow by around 35% a year for the next several years, mobile will be growing at over 60% in the same time period (eMarketer, Inc., 2014v, w). This figure underestimates the total social marketing spending because of the high percentage of visits to social networks that originate from a mobile device. For instance, Twitter reports that over 75% of their monthly active users access Twitter from a mobile device; about 30% of Facebook's active user base are mobile-only members (Twitter, Inc., 2014; Ong, 2014). A substantial part of the mobile marketing spending should be counted as "social" marketing. Nevertheless, the figure indicates the extraordinary impact that mobile devices are having on marketing expenditures. Local online marketing in the United States was almost three times the amount of mobile marketing in 2013, but mobile is expected to close the gap significantly by 2016. As with social and mobile, there is significant overlap between local and mobile and social marketing, with much of local marketing also either social or mobile or both.

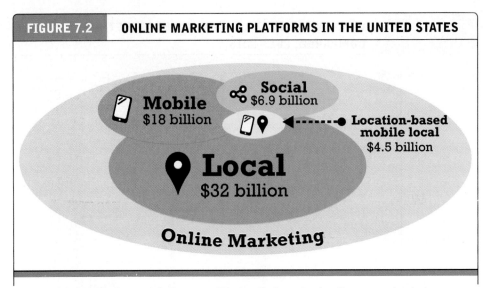

FIGURE 7.2 | **ONLINE MARKETING PLATFORMS IN THE UNITED STATES**

Traditional desktop marketing, including most of local marketing to local audiences, remains the largest part of all online marketing. Mobile marketing is aimed often at local audiences and is the fastest growing form of online marketing, followed closely by social marketing on social networks. Mobile local is in its infancy but it is also growing far faster than traditional desktop marketing.
SOURCE: Based on data from eMarketer, 2014a; BIA/Kelsey, 2014a, 2014b.

Figure 7.2 puts the social-mobile-local forms of advertising into the context of the total U.S. online advertising market. Here you can see that traditional online marketing (browser-based search and display ads, and e-mail marketing) still constitutes the majority of all online marketing, but it is growing much more slowly than social-mobile-local marketing. By 2016, it is expected that social-mobile-local marketing will be more than 50% of all online marketing. The marketing dollars are following customers and shoppers from the desktop PC to mobile devices.

THE SOCIAL, MOBILE, LOCAL NEXUS

Social, mobile, and local digital marketing are self-reinforcing and connected. For instance, as mobile devices become more powerful, they are more useful for accessing Facebook and other social sites. As mobile devices become more widely adopted, they can be used by customers to find local merchants, and for merchants to alert customers in their neighborhood to special offers. Over time, these will become more overlapped as the three platforms become more tightly coupled.

Over 60% of Facebook's ad revenue is generated by its mobile audience. Mobile constitutes an even larger share of Twitter's ad revenues—over 80%! Local marketing and mobile are highly related: local advertisers most often target mobile devices. And a considerable amount of mobile ad spending comes from local advertisers. The strong ties among social, mobile, and local marketing has significant implications for managing your own marketing campaign in this new environment. The message is that when you design a social marketing campaign, you must also consider that your customers will be accessing the campaign using mobile devices, and often they will also be looking for local content. Social-mobile-local must be seen in an integrated management framework (comScore, 2013a).

In the sections that follow we will examine social, mobile, and local marketing more closely. The focus will be on describing the primary marketing tools of each platform and how to envision and manage a marketing campaign on each platform.

7.2 SOCIAL MARKETING

Social marketing differs markedly from traditional online marketing. The objectives of traditional online marketing are to put your business's message in front of as many visitors as possible and hopefully encourage them to come to your Web site to buy products and services, or to find out more information. The more "impressions" (ad views) you get, and the more unique visitors to your site, the better. Traditional online marketing never expected to listen to customers, much less have a conversation with them, any more than TV advertisers expected to hear from viewers.

In social marketing, the objective is to encourage your potential customers to become fans of your company's products and services, and engage with your business by entering into a conversation with it. Your further objective is to encourage your business's fans to share their enthusiasm with their friends, and in so doing create a community of fans online. Ultimately, the point is to strengthen the brand and drive sales, and to do this by increasing your "share of online conversation." There is some reason to believe that social marketing is more cost effective than traditional marketing although this is still being explored.

SOCIAL MARKETING PLAYERS

There are hundreds of social network sites worldwide, but the most popular sites (Facebook, Google+, Twitter, LinkedIn, Pinterest, Instagram, and Tumblr) account for over 90% of all visits. (See Chapter 10, Section 10.1 for a full discussion of social networks.)

While the number of monthly unique visitors is a good measure of market reach, it is not helpful in understanding engagement—the amount and intensity of user involvement in a site. One measure of engagement is the amount of time users spend on a site. **Figure 7.3** illustrates engagement at the top social network sites.

On measures of engagement, Facebook once again dominates, accounting for 60% of user engagement with the average visitor spending 336 minutes on the site, followed by the blogging site Tumblr. In May 2013 Yahoo purchased Tumblr for $1 billion and picked up a 22% share of social marketing site engagement.

For a manager of a social marketing campaign, these findings suggest that in terms of reach and engagement, the place to start a social campaign is Facebook. Yet visitors to the other leading social sites collectively account for more reach and engagement than Facebook, and therefore, a social marketing campaign also has to include them at some point. It helps that social network users use multiple social sites. Facebook users are likely to be users at Twitter, Pinterest, LinkedIn, and Instagram. In addition,

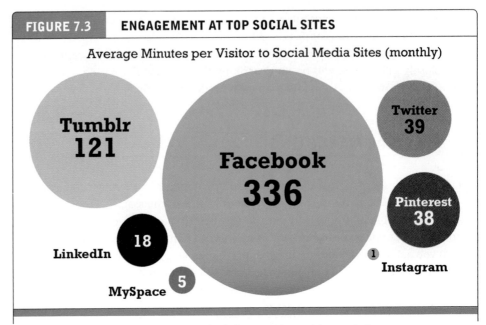

FIGURE 7.3 **ENGAGEMENT AT TOP SOCIAL SITES**

Average Minutes per Visitor to Social Media Sites (monthly)

Tumblr 121
Facebook 336
Twitter 39
Pinterest 38
LinkedIn 18
MySpace 5
Instagram 1

Visitors spend significantly more time on Facebook than any other social network site.
SOURCE: Based on data from Miller, 2014a; eMarketer, Inc., 2013a.

dark social
those forms of social sharing that occur off the major social networks, through alternative communication tools such as e-mail, instant messages, texts, and mobile messaging apps

marketers need to be aware of what has come to be known as dark social. **Dark social** refers to those forms of social sharing that occur off the major social networks, through alternative communication tools such as e-mail, instant messages, texts, and mobile messaging apps such as WhatsApp, WeChat and Snapchat.

THE SOCIAL MARKETING PROCESS

At first glance the large number of different social sites is confusing, each with a unique user experience to offer, from Twitter's micro blogging text messaging service, to Tumblr's blogging capability, and to graphical social sites like Pinterest and Instagram. Yet they can all be approached with a common framework. **Figure 7.4** illustrates a social marketing framework that can be applied to all social, mobile, and local marketing efforts.

There are five steps in the social marketing process: Fan acquisition, engagement, amplification, community, and brand strength (sales). Each of these steps in the process can be measured. The metrics of social marketing are quite different from those of traditional Web marketing or television marketing. This is what makes social marketing so different—the objectives and the measures. This will become more apparent as we describe marketing on specific social sites.

fan acquisition
attracting people to your marketing messages

Social marketing campaigns begin with **fan acquisition**, which involves using any of a variety of means, from display ads to News Feed and page pop-ups, to attract people to your Facebook page, Twitter feed, or other platform like a Web page. It's getting your brand "out there" in the stream of social messages. Display ads on social sites have a social dimension (sometimes called "display ads with social features" or

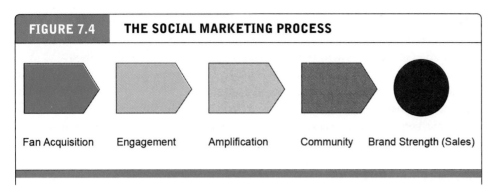

FIGURE 7.4   **THE SOCIAL MARKETING PROCESS**

Fan Acquisition   Engagement   Amplification   Community   Brand Strength (Sales)

The social marketing process has five steps.

simply "social ads"). Social ads encourage visitors to interact and do something social, such as participate in a contest, obtain a coupon, or obtain free services for attracting friends.

The next step is to generate **engagement,** which involves using a variety of tools to encourage users to interact with your content and brand located on your Facebook or Web pages. You can think of this as "starting the conversation" around your brand. You want your fans to talk about your content and products. You can generate engagement through attractive photos, interesting text content, and blogger reports, with plenty of opportunities for users to express opinions. You can also provide links to Pinterest photos of your products or fan comments on blog sites like Tumblr.

Once you have engaged visitors, you can begin to use social site features to amplify your messages by encouraging users to tell their friends by clicking a Like or +1 button, or by sending a message to their followers on Twitter. **Amplification** involves using the inherent strength of social networks. On Facebook, the average user has 120 "friends." This includes all people they have ever friended, including people whom they don't really know (and who don't really know them). Facebook users typically have only three to four close friends with whom they can discuss confidential matters, and a larger set of around 20 friends with whom they have two-way communications (mutual friends). Let's use 20 as a reasonable number of mutual friends for marketing purposes. For marketers, this means that if they can attract one fan and encourage that fan to share his or her approval with his or her friends, the message can be amplified twenty times: 20 friends of the one fan can be influenced. Best of all: the friends of fans are free. Marketers pay to attract only the initial fan and they are not charged by social sites (currently) for the amplification that can result.

Once you have gathered enough engaged fans, you will have created the foundation for a **community**—a more or less stable group of fans who are engaged and communicating with one another over a substantial period of time (say several months or more). Marketers have a number of tactics to nurture these communities, including inside information on new products, price breaks for loyalty, and free gifts for bringing in new members. The ultimate goal is to enlarge your firm's "share of the online conversation." The process ends with strengthening the brand and, hopefully,

engagement
encouraging visitors to interact with your content and brand

amplification
encouraging visitors to share their Likes and comments with their friends

community
a stable group of fans engaged and communicating with one another over a substantial period of time about your brand

additional sales of products and services. Brand strength can be measured in a variety of ways both online and offline, a subject that is beyond the boundaries of this text (Ailawadi et al., 2003; Aaker, 1996; Simon and Sullivan, 1993; Keller, 1993).

Ultimately, the point of marketing is to drive sales revenue. Measuring the impact of a social marketing campaign on brand strength and sales is still being explored by marketers, social site managers, and researchers, but generally the results are positive: social marketing campaigns drive sales. Whether they drive sales better than alternative online marketing measures is still a matter of research.

FACEBOOK MARKETING

Nearly everyone reading this book has a Facebook page. There are power users who spend hours a day on the site, some with thousands of "friends," and there are casual users who have a small set of perhaps 20 friends and relatives. While most have a basic understanding of Facebook, it's worthwhile to review the major features of Facebook before discussing its marketing potential.

Basic Facebook Features

Facebook describes itself as having three pillars: News Feed, Timeline (Profile), and the recently added Graph Search. Facebook also has many other features that are equally important to its potential as a marketing platform. **Table 7.1** describes these features.

Reviewing Table 7.1, it is clear that Facebook is built to encourage people to reveal as much personal information about themselves as feasible, including activities, behavior, photos, music, movies, purchases, and preferences. One result is that Facebook is the world's largest repository of deeply personal behavioral information on the Internet. Facebook knows a great deal more about its users than Google does about its users. Second, Facebook's features are built to maximize the connections among people in the form of notifications, tagging, messaging, posting, and sharing. In many instances, the movement of personal information is so widespread that it is beyond the understanding of users and outside observers. The effect of these two factors is to greatly

social density
refers to the number of interactions among members of a group and reflects the "connectedness" of a group, even if these connections are forced on users

magnify the social density of the Facebook audience. **Social density** refers to the number of interactions among members of a group and reflects the "connectedness" of a group, even if these connections are forced on users. For instance, some natural groups of people are not very "social" and few messages flow among members. Other natural groups are loquacious and chatty with many messages flowing among members. The scope, intensity, and depth of Facebook's repository of personal information and rich social network present extraordinary marketing opportunities.

Facebook Marketing Tools

Facebook offers a number of marketing and advertising opportunities and tools for branding and developing community on its site.

Like Button The Like and Share buttons on Facebook, and similar buttons such as +1 on other social sites, are perhaps the single most important element in the rise of

TABLE 7.1	BASIC FACEBOOK FEATURES
FEATURE	**DESCRIPTION**
Profile	As part of account creation, you create a profile that includes certain personal information. The profile may also include photos and other media. Establishes baseline information that will be shared with friends.
Friend search	Helps you find friends who are already using Facebook, as well as friends who are not, typically by searching your e-mail contact list. Creates your baseline social network based on prior contacts.
Timeline	A history of your actions on Facebook, including photos, history of posts, and comments to your News Feed, as well as life events that you post and want others to see as a part of your profile. Additions you make to your Timeline may appear on your friends' News Feed. Creates additional links with friends.
Tagging	Ability to tag photos, status updates, check-ins, or comments with the names of friends. Tagging links to that person's Timeline and News Feed. Your friends are notified they have been tagged, and you are linked to their Timeline. Friends of your friends may also be notified. Whenever Facebook detects the person in a new image, it notifies all those who have tagged the photo that this friend appears in a new photo that you can link to. The tagging tool is designed to create additional connections among users.
News Feed	The center of the action on Facebook Home pages, News Feed is a continuously updated list of stories from friends and Pages that you have liked on Facebook. News Feed stories include status updates, photos, videos, links, app activity, and Likes. Provides a continual stream of messages from friends and others.
Trending	Facebook's version of trending topics; appears at top of right-hand column next to News Feed
Status update	A way to post your comments, observations, and location to all your friends.
Like button	The ubiquitous Like button communicates your support of comments, photos, activities, brands, articles, and products to your friends, and also to the Facebook social graph and third-party marketers. The Like button lives on virtually all Facebook content including status updates, photos, comments, brands, timelines, apps, and even ads. The Like button also appears on external sites, mobile and social apps, and ads. These sites are utilizing Facebook's Like social plug-in, and when you Like something outside of Facebook, it appears on your Timeline, where friends can comment on the activity.
Apps	Facebook apps are built by third-party developers, and add functionality to Facebook. Apps run the gamut from games (Candy Crush Saga; FarmVille) to photos (Instagram, now part of Facebook), music (Spotify), and publications (Washington Post Social Reader). Your personal information and that of your friends is shared with apps that you install. Most Facebook apps are free, and most rely on revenues from advertising that they expose you to.
Open Graph	A feature used by app developers to integrate their apps into the Facebook pages of users who sign up for the app, and in that sense, it opens the Facebook social graph to the developer, who can then use all the features of Facebook in the app. For instance, this feature allows your performance on game apps to be sent to your Friend's News Feeds. Supports the development of social apps and increases links among users.
Graph Search	A "social" search engine introduced in July 2013 that searches your social network, and potentially the entire Facebook social graph, for answers to your queries. It is a "semantic" search engine insofar as it provides a single answer rather than a list of links based on an algorithm's estimate of user intentions. It is also a "hybrid" search engine that relies on Bing to supplement results when your social network comes up empty. Graph Search indexes everyone's public posts, Likes, photos, and interests, and makes them available to all users of Facebook, friends or not. All of your information is available to Graph Search, and there is no opting out, and no editing of content is allowed. However, privacy controls can limit distribution, and you can delete personal information and photos from Facebook's social graph.

Like button

gives users a chance to share their feelings about content and other objects they are viewing

social marketing. "Like" is the engine of social marketing. The Like button was introduced by Facebook on its own Web site in 2009 and rolled out as a plug-in to other Web sites in 2010. Unlike traditional Web advertising, the **Like button** gives users a chance to share their feelings about content and other objects they are viewing and Web sites they are visiting. It's a way for users to express their opinions to their friends about their Web experience. With Like buttons on millions of Web sites, Facebook can track user behavior on other sites and then sell this information to marketers.

Like gives Big Data real meaning. Industry analysts estimate that there are 4.5 billion Likes, 4.75 billion content items shared, 350 million photos uploaded, and 500 TB (terabytes) of data received, every day. This breaks down to each user Liking something three times a day and posting a photo every three days. Facebook's Like and Share buttons are embedded in more than 7.5 million Web sites, and are viewed over 22 billion times a day (Taylor, 2013).

Brand Pages Facebook's early efforts at brand marketing focused on the development of brand pages as a means for firms to establish a direct relationship with their current and potential customers. Nearly all Fortune 1000 companies, and hundreds of thousands of smaller firms, have Facebook brand pages, similar to brand Web sites, on Facebook as an adjunct to their main Web site. The purpose of a brand page is to develop fans of the brand by providing users opportunities to interact with the brand through comments, contests, and offerings. Using social calls to action, such as "Like us on Facebook" and "Share," brand pages can escape their isolation and make it more easily into users' social networks, where friends can hear the message.

Social brand pages have many more social opportunities for fans to like and comment than are typical of traditional Web pages. However, corporate Web sites have, over time, adopted many social features and the two are now often indistinguishable. Brand pages on Facebook typically attract more visitors than a brand's Web site. For instance, the Skittles brand page on Facebook has attracted over 26 million Likes, while its Web site attracts only around 160,000 monthly unique visitors.

Brands can get exposure on Facebook either organically or via paid advertisements. Organic reach is free, and happens when fans see the brand's updates and posts in their News Feed, or when others who are not fans see that content because a fan liked, commented, or shared the post (viral reach). In order to ensure that they get the exposure that they want for their marketing messages, most companies choose one of the paid advertising formats discussed below.

Facebook enables you to choose from a variety of different marketing objectives, including promoting your Page posts/ads (Page Post Engagement); obtaining Likes for your Facebook page to grow your company's audience and brand (Page Likes); getting people to click through to your Web site (Clicks to Web sites); getting people to take certain actions on your Web site (Web site Conversions); getting people to install an app (App Installs), getting people to use an app (App Engagement); creating offers for people to redeem (Offer Claims); and getting people to watch a video (Video Views).

Once you have chosen a marketing objective, the next decision is to whom you want to target the advertisement. Facebook ads can be targeted based on location, age, interest, gender, education level, relationship status, and political views, as well as to custom audiences defined by the marketer. Facebook can also create what it calls a "lookalike audience" based on demographics shared with the custom audience identified by the marketer.

Once the marketing objectives and audience have been determined, the next decision is where to place the advertisement. Facebook has four basic locations from which to choose: the News Feed, the right-hand column or sidebar section of Facebook pages, and the mobile News Feed. Ads can also be placed within apps.

News Feed Page Post Ads The News Feed is the most prominent place for advertisements. The News Feed is the center of the action for Facebook users and where Facebook users spend most of their time because that is where posts from their friends appear. Page Post Ads appear in a user's News Feed along with all of the other posts and status updates that normally appear from friends. Page Post Ads have a tiny tag that indicates that they are sponsored (i.e., are advertisements) but otherwise look very similar to posts from friends. They have social context ("John Smith and Jane Doe like Pottery Barn") and can be liked, shared, and commented on, just like any other post. Page Post Ads can contain text, photos, video, and links. They can be used for many of the marketing objectives mentioned above, such as increasing brand engagement, obtaining Likes for the brand's Facebook page, and encouraging app installs and engagement. Companies pay to promote or boost Page Post Ads in order to extend their reach. This has become increasingly important as Facebook has reportedly reduced the organic reach that brands previously enjoyed for free in an effort to increase advertising revenues (Vahl, 2014; Ernoult, 2014).

Right-Hand Column Sidebar Ads These display ads are located in the right-hand column or sidebar of Facebook pages. They are often used to direct users to off-Facebook content such as Web site landing pages and content offers. Facebook has recently reduced the number of ads that appear in the right-hand column sidebar from seven to two, increased their size, and made them consistent with the format of News Feed Page Post Ads in an effort to enhance their performance.

Mobile Ads Facebook introduced Facebook for Mobile in 2006. It now has over 1 billion mobile monthly active users as of June 2014, of which over 650 million use their mobile devices to visit Facebook daily (Facebook, 2014). Users download a Facebook app to their mobile devices to gain access to the mobile interface. Users can also access Facebook using their mobile browser although it is slower. In 2014, almost 50% of Facebook ad revenue will come from its mobile ad platform, and it is its fastest growing revenue stream. Mobile app install ads are those paid for by mobile app developers to persuade users to install their app.

Because the smartphone screen is much smaller than regular computer screens, there is no room for sidebar ads on the right-hand column, so all mobile ads need to be displayed in the users' News Feed. Mobile ads can include many of the ad formats described above. Critics complain that the number of ads in the mobile News Feed becomes distracting and annoying. Mobile ads often take up the entire screen. There also is far less targeting of mobile ads, which increases the likelihood users will see

TABLE 7.2	BASIC FACEBOOK MARKETING TOOLS
MARKETING TOOL	DESCRIPTION
Like Button	Amplification. A feature that allows users to express support for content on social sites to their friends, and friends of friends. The one tool that marketers cannot control. Currently free.
Brand Pages	Engagement and community building. Similar to a business Web page, but much more social by encouraging user interaction and response; ongoing discussions among the community of fans. Brand pages are currently free.
News Feed Page Post Ads	Fan acquisition. Paid brand messages can be inserted into the News Feed. Requires payment.
Right-Hand Sidebar Ads	Fan acquisition. Display ads in the right-hand column (sidebar) similar to display ads elsewhere on the Web. Requires payment.
Mobile Ads	Fan acquisition and engagement. Mobile News Feed Page Post Ads are delivered to smartphones and tablets. Requires payment.
Facebook Exchange (FBX)	Facebook's real-time ad exchange, which sells ads and retargets ads through online bidding. Advertisers place cookies on user browsers when they visit a site, and when they return to Facebook, they are shown ads on the right side from the site they visited. Requires payment.

irrelevant ads. So far, despite the annoyance, Facebook mobile users continue to sign up and view.

Facebook Exchange (FBX)

a real-time bidding system that allows advertisers to target their ads based on personal information provided by Facebook.

Facebook Exchange (FBX). Facebook Exchange (FBX) is a real-time bidding system that allows advertisers to target their ads based on personal information provided by Facebook. FBX competes with Google's display ad system DoubleClick and other real-time exchanges. Visitors to third-party Web sites are marked with a cookie, and can then be shown ads related to their Web browsing when they return to Facebook.

Table 7.2 summarizes the major tools used by marketers to build their brands on Facebook.

Starting a Facebook Marketing Campaign

Prior to starting a Facebook marketing campaign, there are some basic strategy questions you need to address. While every product presumably could benefit from a social marketing campaign, how is this true of your products? Who is your audience? How can you reach them? How have real-world social networks been used in the past to support sales in your industry? Can you be a "thought leader?" Once you have

TABLE 7.3	SELECTED FACEBOOK MARKETING CAMPAIGNS
COMPANY	MARKETING CAMPAIGN
Target Stores	Promotes discounts across Facebook, Twitter, and mobile platforms providing access to the Cartwheel.Target.com Web site. Shoppers' Cartwheel interactions shared with their Facebook friends.
Domino's Pizza	Uses Marketplace Ads to offer discounts, along with Premium Ads in News Feeds on the day of the discounts to drive sales.
Expedia	Uses its fan base to enlist friends' help to win a free vacation package using both Marketplace and Premium Ads.
Jackson Hewitt	Tax preparation service anchored in Walmart stores used Facebook to increase engagement with its brand by placing Marketplace Ads promoting a dancing game. Winners were given a $25 gift certificate to use at Walmart.

identified your audience, what content will get them excited and interested? Where are you going to get the content? What will it cost and what impact do you expect it to have on your brand and sales? At this point you do not need a detailed budget, but you should be able to develop estimates of the cost of such a campaign, as well as anticipated revenues.

If you're new to Facebook marketing, start simple and build on your fan base based on experience. A typical marketing campaign for Facebook might include the following elements:

- Establish a Facebook page for your brand. Content is king: have interesting, original content that visitors can be enthusiastic about. Acquire fans.
- Use comment and feedback tools to develop fan comments. You want visitors to engage with your content. You can also encourage bloggers to develop content for your page.
- Develop a community of users. Try to encourage fans to talk with one another, and develop new (free) content for your page.
- Encourage brand involvement through videos and rich media showing products being used by real customers.
- Use contests and competitions to deepen fan involvement.
- Develop display ads for use on Facebook.
- Develop display ads for use in response to social search queries.
- Liberally display the Like button so fans share the experience with their friends.

For more information on social marketing using Facebook, see Learning Track 7.1. **Table 7.3** provides some examples of Facebook marketing campaigns.

Measuring Facebook Marketing Results

There are many ways to measure the success of a Facebook marketing campaign, some very sophisticated. This is a very new field that changes daily. Making matters more complicated is that industry sources sometimes use different names to refer to the same thing! Where this occurs we try to give both the most reasonable name and alternative names you might find in trade literature.

Table 7.4 describes some of the basic metrics to use when evaluating a social marketing campaign. It uses the five steps of the social marketing process found in Figure 7.4—fan acquisition, engagement, amplification, community, and ultimately brand strengthening and sales—as an organizing schema.

TABLE 7.4	MEASURING FACEBOOK MARKETING RESULTS
SOCIAL MARKETING PROCESS	MEASUREMENT
Fan acquisition (impressions)	The number of people exposed to your Facebook brand page posts and paid ads (impressions). The percentage of those exposed who become fans based on Likes or comments. The ratio of impressions to fans.
Engagement (conversation rate)	The number of posts, comments, and responses. The number of views of brand page content. The number of Likes generated per visitor. The number of users who responded to games, contests, and coupons (participation). The number of minutes on average that visitors stay on your page (duration). The rate of Likes per post or other content (applause rate).
Amplification (reach)	The percentage of Likes, shares, or posts to other sites (the rate at which fans share your content).
Community	The monthly interaction rate with your content (i.e., the monthly total of posts, comments, and actions on your Facebook brand page). The average monthly on-site minutes for all fans. The ratio of positive to negative comments.
Brand Strength/Sales	The percentage (or revenue) of your online sales that is generated by Facebook links compared to other platforms, such as e-mail, search engines, and display ads. The percentage of Facebook-sourced customer purchases compared to other sources of customers (conversion ratio). The conversion ratio for friends of fans.

While the ultimate goal of Facebook marketing is to drive sales (which typically will take place on your Web site), it is very important to understand what the elements of social marketing that produce these sales are, and how they can be improved.

At the most elementary level, the number of fans (or followers) generated is the beginning of all social marketing. Visitors become fans when they like your content. In the early days of social marketing, firms put a great deal of emphasis on the size of the fan base, and collecting Likes. This is less important today, as social marketing managers have become more sophisticated. Fan engagement in your content and brand is the first step towards developing a truly social experience, and arguably is more important than simply the number of impressions or the number of fans. Fans that you never hear from are not valuable. Engagement relates to how your fans are interacting with your content, how intensely, and how often. Understanding the kinds of content (videos, text, photos, or posts from fans) that create the highest levels of engagement is also very important.

The ability to amplify your marketing message by tapping into the social network of your fans is also at the core of social marketing. This can be measured very simply as the rate at which fans recommend your content to their friends, and how many of their friends further recommend your content to their friends.

Measuring the strength of a Facebook community is not that much different from measuring the strength of an offline community. In both cases you attempt to measure the collective activities of all in the community. Among your fans, how many actively participate? What is the total number of actions taken by fans in a month? How many minutes of involvement are generated each month? What is the percentage of favorable comments?

Finally, measuring sales that result from social campaigns is also straightforward. First, measure the percentage of sales you receive from the Facebook channel. You can easily measure the number of visits to your Web site that originate on Facebook, and the sales these visits generate. In addition, you can compare purchase rates (conversion rate) for fans and compare these to conversion rates for non-fans from Facebook. More important, you can compare the Facebook conversion rate to other visitors who come from different marketing channels, such as e-mail, display ads, and blogs.

Facebook marketing has entered its second generation even though it's only four years old. The emphasis today in social marketing has gone beyond collecting Likes and more towards building engagement with high-quality content that fans want to share with their friends; nurturing stable communities of intensely involved fans and friends of fans; and ultimately turning these communities of fans into communities of purchasers.

The experience of marketers is tantalizing but still unclear. E-mail and search easily drive more sales than Facebook or any social marketing today (eMarketer, Inc., 2013b). Facebook ads are much less likely to be clicked on than display ads on the Web, and sell for less than half the price of Web display ads. Facebook users join social networks to be social, not to buy or even shop. Despite these limitations, in the space of a few years, Facebook has been able to create a multi-billion dollar business selling ads. Rather than replace other ad venues, Facebook may be creating a whole new venue that it dominates and that has unique value, but nevertheless does not diminish the role of e-mail or search in the marketing mix. However, Facebook still faces the challenge of monetizing its billion-person network and convincing marketers.

There are a variety of Facebook analytics tools that provide valuable information about your Facebook marketing efforts. Facebook Page Insights, provided by Facebook, tracks total Page Likes, People Talking About This (PTAT) (which tracks the number of unique people who have clicked on, Liked, commented on, or shared a post), Page Tags and Mentions, Page Checkins, and other interactions on a page. It also tracks something it calls Engagement Rate. People are considered to have engaged with a post if they Like it, comment on it, share it, or click it.

Social media management system HootSuite enables teams to execute marketing campaigns across multiple networks from one dashboard, and also provides custom reports. Major analytics providers, such as Google Analytics, Webtrends, and IBM Digital Analytics, also provide Facebook reporting modules. Read the *Insight on Technology* case study *Fairmont Hotels: Using Google Analytics to Optimize Social and Mobile Marketing* for a further look at how one organization is using analytics tools to help them better understand social marketing.

TWITTER MARKETING

Twitter is a micro-blogging social network site that allows users to send and receive 140-character messages, as well as article previews, photos, and videos. Twitter has an estimated 270 million active users worldwide as of June 2014, and its 2013 revenue was $665 million, more than double its 2012 revenue. Over 75% of Twitter's users access the service on mobile devices. Almost all of Twitter's revenue comes from pop-ads that appear in users' timelines (tweet stream), but Twitter also has many other marketing tools in its quiver. The real magic of Twitter, like Facebook, is that Twitter does not pay for the 500 million tweets sent each day. They are supplied for free by active users. Twitter sells ads based on the content of these user messages. Some analysts believe Twitter could easily become the next Google. See the opening case in Chapter 2 for more information on Twitter.

Twitter was designed from the start as a real-time text messaging service. Twitter offers advertisers and marketers a chance to interact and engage with their customers in real time and in a fairly intimate, one-on-one manner. Advertisers can buy ads that look like organic tweets (the kind you receive from friends), and these ads can tie into and enhance marketing events like new product announcements or pricing changes. Twitter is announcing new marketing tools every quarter in an effort to boost its revenues. On the other hand, there may be a limit to how many ads Twitter users will tolerate.

Basic Twitter Features

While most people probably know what a tweet is, Twitter offers marketers many other ways of communicating using Twitter. In fact, Twitter has introduced a whole

INSIGHT ON TECHNOLOGY

FAIRMONT HOTELS: USING GOOGLE ANALYTICS TO OPTIMIZE SOCIAL AND MOBILE MARKETING

In the global hotel business, customer acquisition and customer loyalty are the keys to success. Major hotel chains report that about 30% of bookings come from repeat customers. Identifying these loyal customers and targeting them with marketing messages has a very high return on investment. In the new world of multiple access points on different platforms, tracking visitors to digital properties is a herculean task. Visitors may come from a traditional Web site, from a social network, or from a mobile site or app. Complicating matters, visitors to any of these presence points can share their initial contact and engagement with your content, resulting in secondary and tertiary traffic to your site. The result is a flood of data points of moments when individuals are engaging with your content.

Fairmont Raffles Hotels International (FRHI) is a global operator of over 100 high-end hotels. The first Fairmont Hotel, the iconic Fairmont Hotel in San Francisco, is known for its luxury accommodations and wealthy clientele and is located on Nob Hill overlooking San Francisco Bay.

FRHI receives bookings requests from four different places: its branded Web site, merchant Web sites (such as Expedia), "opaque" Web sites where users do not know the hotel until they pay for the booking (Priceline), and retail Web sites (third-party distributors or portals like Hotel Reservation System's HRS). Fairmont was an early Internet adopter, creating its first Web site in 1995, when marketing essentially involved putting the existing reservation system on the Internet to handle transactions, and posting pictures and other features of the hotel. Tracking visitors to the Web site was straightforward: visitors entered the site with a browser that revealed the customer's IP address, and interaction with online content was easily observable as page views. Cookies were used to identify frequent visitors and former customers, who could be offered discounts for their loyalty.

With the advent of mobile devices and social sites, the marketing equation has become much more complicated. Fairmont has branded content pages on the Web, as well as on Facebook, Twitter, and Pinterest. When a visitor Likes the firm's Facebook page, the message is sent to all the visitor's friends. The same is true for the company's Twitter and Pinterest pages. In addition, the Fairmont iPhone app replicates much of the functionality of the firm's Web site. Because marketing messages placed on Facebook, Twitter, Pinterest, or any social site can easily ricochet across a number of other social networks, or get passed from one individual to another by SMS text messaging or Facebook Chat, it's difficult for marketers to measure exactly how their social messaging is generating traffic. Who was the first visitor to click on the link, who did he or she share it with, and how did the first click lead to additional clicks, or posts, either on the original site or another platform entirely? The person who ultimately clicks on a post and ends up on the firm's Web site is often not the first person to receive the post.

The problem for Fairmont was how to integrate all these visitor touch points and interactions to enable marketing managers to understand which of their digital efforts were attracting visitors, how visitors were engaging with content once they entered the various sites, and if these diverse digital efforts were leading to sales. In

(continued)

2010, Fairmont turned to Google Analytics to find solutions.

Google Analytics is an analytics product that is used by an estimated 60% of the top 1 million Web sites. Basic service is free and a premium package is available for a fee. Another option, Google Analytics for Mobile, was introduced in 2010. Mobile analytics is a subset of Web analytics that seeks to understand how potential customers use a firm's apps and mobile Web sites—from discovery of the app, to download, and engagement. The service works across both tablets and smartphones, and is fully integrated with the regular Google Analytics package designed originally for analyzing Web site traffic. Google also provides custom variables that allow site owners to collect data that is unique to individual businesses.

Google cloud servers run the databases needed to process the streams of information produced by users on all platforms. At participating Web sites, Google Analytics downloads to every visitor's browser a short piece of code (also known as a beacon) that records user behavior and identifies the user by the IP address of the user's computer, and then sends this information back to Google's servers without user visibility, and without placing a noticeable load on a firm's own Web servers.

With this trove of information, Google Analytics can track visitors from all referral sources including direct visits to the Web site, social networks, search engines, referral sites, and mobile devices. Marketers can identify key performance indicators, establish goals, optimize content and pages, and track users' from initial visit to online behavior to, ultimately, sales. Google Analytics provides dashboards and reports for marketing analysts that can be viewed on desktops and mobile devices; provides a single source of data on visitors; tracks the impact of various marketing campaigns; and develops information on the impact of marketing on key performance indicators including purchases, site visits, length of time on site, and engagement with all pieces of content such as downloading content or sharing content on social networks.

Fairmont uses Google Analytics to track all the platforms users use to discover Fairmont and ultimately book a room. For instance, for visitors from Twitter's Web interface, the source is identified as a direct source "twitter.com." Visitors using one of several Twitter mobile apps are identified as other Twitter sources, or as referral traffic when, say, a user visits Fairmont from a Twitter referral site (Expedia). Fairmont also uses Google Analytics Campaign Tracking. Tracking tells marketers the source of the visitor (Facebook app); the medium (unpaid or paid search; referral site; or direct organic search engine); keywords the user may be responding to; the campaign name; and content features. Users can identify a specific link in a campaign.

Google Analytics allows Fairmont marketers to understand the growth in its social media campaigns and the viral traffic generated by visitors who post comments. Each Twitter tweet, Pinterest photo, or Facebook post is uniquely tagged, allowing Fairmont marketers to measure and compare the effectiveness of its campaigns. Fairmont can now identify the most successful ads, campaigns, channels, and paths to conversion and then make faster and better investments with its marketing budget. The result has been overwhelmingly positive—bookings and revenue from social media doubled in the year after the adoption of Google Analytics.

SOURCES: "In-Depth: Interview with Barbara Pezzi, Director Analytics & Search Optimization, Fairmont Raffles Hotels International," by Ritesh Gupta, Eyefortravel.com, accessed September 2014; "How To Turn Data Analysis Into Action," by Harvey Chipkin, Hotelnewsnow.com, February 17, 2014; "Google Analytics Summit 2013 Keynote Liveblog – The Data Opportunity," by Jeff Sauer, Jeffalytics.com, October 1, 2013; "Fairmont Gets Deeper Understanding of Social Interactions for Real Results," Analytics.blogspot.com, December 5, 2013; "Fairmont Hotels Harness the Power of Google Analytics to Optimize Social Media Marketing," Google Analytics, January 2013; "Mobile Analytics and Reporting," by Google, Google.com/analytics/features/mobile.html, undated.

TABLE 7.5	TWITTER FEATURES
FEATURE	DESCRIPTION
Tweet	140-character text message. Messages can be private (to a single person or one to one), public (to everyone, one to many), or to a group of followers.
Followers	You can follow someone's tweets and receive them as soon as they are made. Others can follow your tweets.
Message (DM)	A direct private message (DM) is like an e-mail that only you and the recipient can read.
Hashtag #<word>	Like a Twitter search engine, #<word> organizes the conversations on Twitter around a specific topic. Click on a hashtag and you are taken to the search results for that term.
Mention	A public Tweet that includes another user's name "@username." You can click on mentions and link back to that person's profile. As a public tweet, your followers will be alerted as well.
Reply	A public response to a tweet using the Reply button. Replies show up on your timeline and that of the person you are responding to.
Timeline	Your timeline is your home page on Twitter listing the tweets you have received in chronological order, the most recent first. Click on a tweet in the timeline and it expands to reveal videos, and photos. Place your mouse over a tweet to reply, retweet, or make it a favorite (which is passed to your followers).
Retweet	Allows you to send along a tweet to all of your followers.
Links	Twitter has a link-shortening feature that allows you to paste in a URL of any link and it will be automatically shortened.

new vocabulary that is specific to Twitter's platform. **Table 7.5** describes the most common Twitter features.

Twitter Marketing Tools

There are many kinds of Twitter marketing products, and the firm is creating new ones every few months. The current major Twitter marketing tools include the following.

Promoted Tweets. Advertisers pay to have their tweets appear in users' search results. Promoted Tweets are Twitter's version of Google's Ad Words. The tweets appear as "promoted" in the search results. Pricing is on a "cost-per-click" basis of between $.50 to $2.00 per click, and based on an auction run by Twitter on the Twitter ad platform. Promoted Tweets can be geo-targeted and also offer keyword targeting that enables advertisers to send the tweets to specific users based on keywords in their recent tweets or tweets with which they have interacted. For instance, if you are tweeting with a friend about a really cool new album, and the band has scheduled a concert in your area, Twitter can pass this information to marketers who will send a Promoted Tweet offering tickets. Twitter says this will not lead to more ads, but much better targeted ads close to the point of consumer purchase.

Promoted Trends. Advertisers pay to move their hashtags (# symbol used to mark keywords in a tweet) to the top of Twitter's Trends List. Otherwise, hashtags are found by the Twitter search engine, and only those that are organically popular make it to the Trends List. Promoted Trends cost about $200,000 a day in the United States in 2014, and are also available for purchase in 50 different countries.

Promoted Accounts. Advertisers pay to have their branded account suggested to users who are likely to be interested in the account in the "Who to Follow" list, Twitter's account recommendation engine, on the Twitter home page. Promoted Accounts can be targeted by interest, geography, and gender, and are priced on a cost-per-follower basis, with advertisers paying only for new followers gained. Prices range from $.50 to $2.50.

Enhanced Profile Pages. Companies get their own banner and the ability to pin a tweet to the top of the company's timeline. The price reportedly ranges from $15,000 to $25,000.

Amplify. The Twitter Amplify program provides marketers with a real-time digital dashboard so they can see the resulting tweet activity about the show or the brand. Based on this information, marketers can send Promoted Tweets to users who tweeted about a show. They can alter the copy as well based on other information about the tweeters. For example, Jim Beam used Amplify in 2013 to promote its new Jim Beam Red Stag brand of premium bourbon. The intent was to increase brand awareness, purchase intent, and user engagement. The strength of Twitter, according to Jim Beam marketers, is that it allows the brand to be a part of a real-time conversation, as opposed to Facebook, which is better at reaching a mass audience but not at engaging consumers in real time. The power of social media, including Facebook, is finding consumer advocates who will speak on behalf of the brand. In August 2014, building on the Amplify program, Twitter announced a beta test of Promoted Video, which will allow advertisers to distribute videos on the Twitter platform.

Television Ad Retargeting. Millions of users tweet with their friends while watching television, and Twitter can follow the conversation to identify who is watching a particular show. Marketers displaying TV ads can retarget those ads or other messages to tweeters in real time to reinforce their marketing message. Advertisers with video content, like the National Basketball Association, insert in-tweet video clips, which are video replays. Advertisers can precede the video with an ad, or place an ad just below the video on screen. Companies can follow up with a Promoted Tweet.

Lead Generation Cards. Marketers can embed a "card" into business tweeters' standard Twitter messages. When users click on the message, a promotional offer appears and users are asked to sign up. Cards are different from display ads because they are used only by businesses who want to develop new leads, and they always include an offer, such as 50% off your next cup of coffee. This is a one-click process. The users' e-mail and Twitter account names are automatically obtained by Twitter and sent to marketers, who can then follow up with a tweet or an e-mail.

Table 7.6 summarizes these Twitter marketing tools.

TABLE 7.6	TWITTER MARKETING TOOLS
TWITTER MARKETING TOOLS	DESCRIPTION
Promoted Tweets	Advertisers pay to have their tweets appear in users' search results and timelines. The tweets appear as "promoted", and the pricing is on a per-click basis, based on an auction run on the Twitter ad platform. Promoted Tweets can be both keyword- and geo-targeted.
Promoted Trends	Advertisers pay to move their hashtags (# symbol used to mark keywords in a tweet) to the top of Twitter's Trends List. Otherwise, hashtags are found by the Twitter search engine, and only those that are organically popular make it to the Trends List.
Promoted Accounts	Advertisers pay to have their branded account suggested to users likely to be interested in the account in the "Who to Follow" list, Twitter's account recommendation engine, available on the Twitter home page. Promoted Accounts can be specifically targeted and are priced on a cost-per-follower basis.
Enhanced Profile Pages	Companies can get their own banner to display images and the ability to pin a tweet to the top of the company's timeline.
Amplify	A real-time digital dashboard connecting television commercials and tweet activity.
TV Ad Retargeting	Tweeting viewers of TV shows with the same ads targeted at them on a show they are watching.
Lead Generation Card	Promotional offers that appear in users' Twitter timeline of messages with a coupon or other offer. Used for lead generation.
Mobile ads	All of the above formats delivered on mobile devices, as well as mobile app install and app engagement ads

Mobile Ads Because over 75% of Twitter users access Twitter on a mobile device, most of the above referenced marketing tools can be considered mobile ads. Mobile is also proving to be the primary driver of Twitter's business and the source of most of its revenue. In addition to all of the above formats, in April 2014, Twitter added mobile app install and app engagement ads, which have been lucrative formats for Facebook as well.

Starting a Twitter Marketing Campaign

If you're new to Twitter marketing, start simple and build on your follower base using experience as a guide for what works. A typical marketing campaign for Twitter may include the following elements:

- Establish a Twitter account. Start following others you are interested in or conversations that you might want to participate with # < topic >. Don't expect any followers at first. Your visibility rises as you follow others, who will begin to tweet back or retweet interesting content. Then start retweeting content you think the group would be interested in, and start encouraging ongoing conversations.

- Try a simple Promoted Tweet. Twitter has a very good online ad facility that will allow you to define an ad, establish the groups you would like to target, and understand the costs. You might start with a regional or metropolitan Promoted Tweet.

Test various formats. You don't have to pay for Promoted Tweets unless someone clicks on the tweet, so it is up to you to make those clicks count. Direct users to your Web site and offer a coupon or discount.

- Promoted Trends can be very expensive—around $200,000. If your budget will allow, and your topic is of general interest to a large audience, you can try this tool. Geo-targeting is possible.
- TV ad retargeting is obviously a big business tool for media companies that have television content and television ads. Retargeting these to the Twitter community strengthens the overall brand image, and can direct people to the firm's Web site.
- Lead Generation Cards are something that small and medium-sized businesses can use. If you sell anything locally, from pizza to stationery, make up an offer and build a Lead Generation Card specifying the geo-location where your business is located.

As with Facebook, the objective is to establish your brand identity online and seek out engagement with users, not immediate sales. Encourage others to retweet your content and offers to their friends.

Table 7.7 describes some selected Twitter marketing campaigns.

Measuring Twitter Marketing Results

Measuring the results of Twitter marketing is similar to measuring the results of Facebook and other social marketing platforms, with some minor changes to account for the unique qualities of Twitter. Table 7.8 describes some basic ways to measure the results of a Twitter marketing campaign.

TABLE 7.7	SELECTED TWITTER MARKETING CAMPAIGNS
COMPANY	**MARKETING CAMPAIGN**
ESPN/Ford	Used embedded replays of football games in posts sent to Twitter users who have shown an interest in sports. Ads for Ford shown before the video roll.
Starbucks	Used both Promoted Tweets and Lead Generation Cards. Users only need to hit the Submit button and their personal information flows to Starbucks to sign them up for special offers or coupons.
LG Electronics	Used hashtags and Promoted Tweets to promote a treasure hunt and drive awareness of a new smartphone.
Porsche	Used hashtags and Promoted Tweets to enhance awareness of its new 911 sports car launch and support television, newspaper, and magazine campaigns.
Airbnb	The community marketplace for unique accommodations used Promoted Tweets to stimulate interest in a new sublet program with a $200 discount offer.
HubSpot	The online marketing firm used Promoted Accounts and Promoted Tweets to target B2B decision-makers in online marketing.
Lord & Taylor	The luxury goods retail chain used Twitter to promote a giveaway of Rihanna tickets at one of its store locations, and in the process, drive traffic to its stores.

TABLE 7.8	MEASURING TWITTER MARKETING RESULTS
SOCIAL MARKETING PROCESS	MEASUREMENT
Fan acquisition (impressions)	The number of people exposed to your Promoted Tweets, Promoted Trends, etc. (impressions). The number of followers and monthly growth.
Engagement (conversation rate)	The number of comments, responses to, and retweets of, your tweets. The number of views of brand page content. The number of users that responded to games, contests, and coupons (participation). The number of minutes on average that followers stay on your page (duration).
Amplification (reach)	The rate at which fans retweet or otherwise share your tweets.
Community	The monthly interaction rate (i.e., the monthly total of comments and responses to, and retweets of, your content). The average monthly onsite minutes for all followers. The ratio of positive to negative tweets.
Brand Strength/Sales	The number of leads generated (people who sign up for news or content). Visitor/lead rate: the number of visitors that become leads to compare campaigns. The percentage (or revenue) of your online sales generated by Twitter links compared to other platforms, such as e-mail, search engines, and display ads. The percentage of Twitter-sourced customer purchases compared to other sources of customers (conversion ratio).

Tools provided by Twitter include a dashboard that provides real-time information on impressions, retweets, clicks, replies, and follows for Promoted Tweets and Promoted Accounts. Twitter's Timeline activity dashboard provides data on how every tweet performs in terms of mentions, follows, and reach. Twitter's Followers dashboard enables marketers to track the growth of the follower base, as well as information about their interests, geography, and engagement.

Third-party tools include TweetDeck, which enables you to track mentions, people, and keywords; Twitalyzer, which provides one-click access to Twitter metrics that analyze followers, mentions, retweets, influencers, and their locations; and Back-Tweets, which allows you to search through a tweet archive for URLs sent via Twitter.

PINTEREST MARKETING

Pinterest is the social network site that provides users with an online board to which they can "pin" interesting pictures (see also the Chapter 1 opening case, *Pinterest: A Picture is Worth a Thousand Words*). The success of Pinterest is based in part on a shift in consumer behavior enabled by new technologies: people talk about brands using pictures rather than words. Large numbers of Web users are pinning and instagramming about their lives using pictures.

You can think of Pinterest as a highly interactive and social online magazine or "zine." One difference, of course, is that users (including business firms) contribute all the photos. The site currently has 36 categories of boards from gifts, animals, art, cars, and motorcycles to crafts, food, and men's and women's fashion. Users can pin to these boards, create their own boards, and follow other pinners and boards as well. Firms can create their own brand boards and product pins. See the opening case in Chapter 1 for more information on Pinterest.

Users who pin photos can alert Facebook and Twitter friends and followers who can access their pictures and boards on Pinterest. Pinned photos and photo boards are available to all Pinterest users at this time, although many marketers are pushing Pinterest to develop private boards that can allow marketers to require registration (customer information) as a condition of access to content. But the point of Pinterest, according to its cofounder Ben Silberman, is to share beautiful, interesting photos and graphics as widely as possible across the Web. Everyone can repin images they like to their own boards as well. Pinterest is therefore one of the largest image sharing sites on the Internet.

Pinterest is also one of the fastest growing sites in Web history. In 2010, Pinterest had 10,000 users, then 12 million by the end of 2011, and 70 million by July 2014. It has around 40 million monthly unique visitors. Today, about 15%–20% of online adults in the United States use Pinterest. Pinterest's visitors are overwhelmingly female: over 80% are women, but users cover a broad demographic range from grandparents to teenagers, with the largest segment (27%) between 25 and 34. The hope for marketers, and Pinterest, is that its "referral capacity" (the ability to direct users to retail Web sites where they can purchase something) will rapidly increase as its audience grows and intensity of use grows.

One way to look at the millions of pictures on Pinterest is as disguised display ads—click, and off you go to a brand Web site for a purchase. Pinterest pins are much better than display ads because they are unobtrusive, and because they don't look like display ads. Instead, they look like sumptuous catalog or magazine photos. In the future, analysts believe, Pinterest could charge an affiliate fee for any subsequent purchases. Pinterest could also charge businesses for creating brand sites or boards, which currently are free.

Basic Pinterest Features

Marketing on Pinterest requires that you understand the basic features and capabilities of Pinterest. While all users of Pinterest understand how to pin photos to an online scrapbook, many other capabilities are less well understood or used. **Table 7.9** provides a list of Pinterest features.

Pinterest Marketing Tools

Pinterest marketing tools are still in an early stage of development. The company is adding new tools every month as Pinterest begins the journey towards monetizing its large user audience. In 2014, Pinterest, following in Facebook's and Twitter's footsteps,

TABLE 7.9	PINTEREST FEATURES
FEATURE	**DESCRIPTION**
Pins	Used to post a photo to a Pinterest board.
Board	An online scrapbook where photos are organized by the user.
Repins	The ability to pin the photos of other users to your own boards, and to share with your friends.
Hashtags and keywords	Use <#hashtags> in the description of your pins, e.g., #style, #cars, #sports cars. Use keywords people are likely to use when searching for specific content.
Share	Sharing your pinned photos with friends. Options: Twitter, Facebook, e-mail, embed.
Image Hover	A widget you can add to your browser. When your mouse hovers over an online image, the Pin It button pops up and you can pin the photo automatically to your Pinterest boards.
Embed	Code that allows you to embed your pinned photos into your blog automatically.
Me+ Contributors	Allows others to contribute to your boards (only if they are already a follower of yours).
Follow	Users can choose to follow other pinners and boards and receive e-mail updates.
Number of Pins and Followers	A count of the number of pins and the number of followers visible at the top of the brand page.
Link to URL; Link to pinner	Click on the URL of the company who pinned a photo; click on a link to the person who pinned a photo.
Price display	Hover over a product and a display pops up with the price and model information.
Integration with Facebook and Twitter	Login from Facebook, Twitter, and other social sites. Your personal profile (but not your photo) information from Facebook comes over to Pinterest; your pins go onto your Facebook Timeline. Twitter and Pinterest profile pages are also integrated.
Pin It browser button (bookmarklet)	Browsers' red Pin It button. Users drag the button onto their browser screen, allowing them to instantly pin photos they see on the Web.
Pinterest app	Smartphone app that allows users to pin photos, browse pins and boards, get ideas while shopping, and display pins.
Pinterest widget	Pin It button on your brand page that makes it easy for people to pin images from your site.

took the official leap into paid advertising. It launched Promoted Pins with a select group of national brands and also announced a trial of a Do It Yourself version of Promoted Pins for small and medium-sized businesses, to be paid for on a cost per click basis, similar to the Google AdWords platform. Promoted Pins will appear in search results and category feeds.

TABLE 7.10	PINTEREST MARKETING TOOLS
MARKETING TOOL	DESCRIPTION
Promoted Pins	A way to promote pins to a targeted audience, and pay for click through to your Web site.
Add Pin It or Follow button to your Web site (Pinterest widget)	Makes it easy for visitors to pin photos from your Web site, and be notified when you post new photos to your site.
Pin as display ad	The Pinned photo acts as a display ad by directing users back to a firm's Web site.
Create theme-based boards to reflect your brand messaging	Pinterest recommends that business boards not be strictly sales-oriented, but lifestyle-oriented instead.
Brand page	A new Pinterest feature that allows companies to create a corporate brand page. In the past, Pinterest did not distinguish between a personal page and a corporate brand page.
URL Link to stores	Makes it easier for consumers to click through links on brand pages and product pins so they can reliably purchase what they see. The goal is to integrate photos of inventory with Pinterest to make items more easily tracked. What this means is retailers can see a definite link between a sale and a photo they pinned. Currently, after thousands of repins, clicking on the URL sometimes leads to a broken link.
Retail brand Pins (Product Pin; Enhanced Pin)	A new kind of pin for food, retail, and movies. Click on a Retail Pin and you will see the price and where to buy it. Food Pins reveal recipes.
Integration with other social sites	Ask your Facebook fans and Twitter followers to pin photos of your products and tag you. Repin these photos to your brand page on Pinterest. Give a shout-out to your loyal users and fans to show potential customers how much current users like using your product.
Network with users, followers, and others	As with Facebook and Twitter, comment, mention, and communicate with others using Pinterest. Participate in the community and you will become better known, and learn more about potential customers and what they believe and to what they aspire.

Table 7.10 identifies and describes some of the primary Pinterest marketing tools.

For instance, Lands' End has several brand pages on Pinterest, one of which is Lands' End Canvas. Search for Lands' End Canvas and it takes you to the page that Lands' End Canvas created and where Lands' End has pinned some of its catalog photos. On this brand page, only Lands' End Canvas products are pinned, and the company is identified. You can see the number of people who have pinned these photos elsewhere, and the total number of others who follow this line of clothing and have posted their own photos. When you click on a photo, you get a larger version of the photo (sometimes called a photo landing page), and the chance to link to the Web site (canvas.landsend.com) where you can purchase the product and find similar ones. You will also see on this photo landing page a picture of the person who pinned the photo, other boards where it was pinned, and recommendations for related photos and products in a section titled "People who pinned this also pinned ...."

Table 7.11 provides a brief description of Pinterest marketing campaigns of selected retailers.

Starting a Pinterest Marketing Campaign

Before leaping into a Pinterest campaign, ask yourself some questions about your products and services, and then identify some strategic objectives for your Pinterest presence. First, sketch out a vision of what you hope to accomplish with a Pinterest presence. Are you an established brand trying to strengthen your brand? Are you the new kid on the block that no one knows and you want to start a marketing campaign? Are your products visual and can your brand be expressed in a set of pictures? Most products have a visual component, some more compelling than others. Today, most Pinterest marketing campaigns involve clothing, jewelry, home furnishings, food, and art/crafts. If your product is hip implants, for instance, it might be hard to portray your products to likely consumers (but not impossible if you are creative). Is the consumer accustomed to seeing the products in your industry expressed through photos? Food is increasingly a visual experience with the growth of food magazines and Web sites.

Next, consider the target demographic for your products and services, and compare it to the Pinterest demographic. Currently, Pinterest visitors are over 80% women, and while this might change over time, your offerings will have to be attractive to women. Do your products or services appeal to this demographic?

Think about strategy in your marketspace. What are your competitors doing? Are they on Pinterest? Do they have an effective presence? What types of people follow your competitors and what are the users pinning? How many followers, re-pinners, brand pages, and product pins are there? Because photos are central to a Pinterest presence, where will the photos for your brand pages come from? Are you, or a member

TABLE 7.11	SELECTED PINTEREST MARKETING CAMPAIGNS
COMPANY	CAMPAIGN
Whole Foods	Natural and organic food stores with 60 boards, over 4,000 pinned photos, and over 200,000 followers.
West Elm	Home furnishing company emphasizing simple and elegant designs. 70 boards, almost 10,000 Pins, and over 255,000 followers.
Bergdorf Goodman	New York's Fifth Avenue luxury goods department store. 43 boards, over 5,000 pins, and 78,000 followers.
Lands' End	A clothing retailer that started as a mail order business and is now a successful multi-channel retailer of outerwear, footwear, home furnishings, and apparel. 34 boards, 1,295 pins, and over 7,000 followers.
Etsy	Online-only Web site that sells handmade craft objects, vintage items, and arts and crafts supplies. Provides a platform for small firms to sell their goods on their own storefronts. 100 boards, over 10,500 pins, over 464,000 followers. Arts and Crafts Pinterest boards show both its products and how to use them in everyday life. The emphasis is on attaining a life style, and humanizing the Etsy products to form a deeper bond with their customers.

of your team, a skilled photographer? You can pin photos from all over the Web, and from other Pinterest boards, but then you're just sharing content, not creating unique and unusual content.

Pinterest is an adjunct to a fully developed marketing plan, both online and offline. You will want to integrate your social and online marketing efforts with a Facebook and Twitter presence. You can share photos from your Web site, and send Web photos to your brand pages. The same photos can be used on your Facebook page and on Twitter. Your customers will be using all these platforms and you will have to follow them to keep up.

Once you have envisioned your Pinterest campaign and developed a marketing plan, you can start implementing your plan. In order to implement your Pinterest plan, you should have a traditional Web site where your products are displayed (a catalog) and can be purchased. Second, you should also have a Facebook brand page to develop followers and a method for informing your followers of new Pins. Once these are in place, you can begin your Pinterest campaign:

- Create a Pinterest brand page and start pinning photos of your products. Grow, and change your pins and board regularly. Be sure your photos are the same quality level or higher than those of your competitors. If necessary, hire a skilled photographer. Brand pages generally do not allow followers to pin photos but only to follow and comment. The idea here is to control the content of your brand page, and develop other boards where followers can pin pictures.

- Improve the quality of your photos. Computer screens limit the resolution that can be displayed to users, but the lighting, composition, and color in your pinned photos are under your control.

- Use URL links and keywords. Make sure your pins have a URL link to your store, or to vendor stores, so followers can easily buy as well as "see." Be sure to use keywords and hashtags to classify each of your photos so they show up in Pinterest searches. Remember, Pinterest cannot "see" a photo or understand its content. It only "knows" the content based on your tags.

- Create a Pinterest product pin. If you are in the food, retail, or movie distribution business, product pins are worth a try if you have a popular product at an attractive price, or if you want to use a specific product as a loss-leader to motivate people to come to your Web site (where you can expose them to your entire catalog of products).

- Use Pin It buttons. Add a Pin It button to your Web site and Facebook page to encourage fans and followers to pin your photos to their own boards, and to recommend them to friends.

- Create multiple theme-based life style boards. Develop several theme-based boards that emphasize life styles or fashions. Pinterest is not just, or even primarily, a selling site. It is also an entertainment and branding site. You want followers to adore your photos. On theme-based boards you will want others besides yourself to be able to pin.

- Use your Facebook and Twitter networks. Start using your Facebook and Twitter networks by adding a Pin It button to Facebook (also called a Pinterest tab), and start sharing your pinned photos with your followers.

- Integrate with Facebook and Twitter. Create Facebook and Twitter logins so that users can go to your pins and boards without leaving the Facebook and Twitter sites.

- Be social. Join the conversation. It's all about being social. Follow other pinners and boards and ask to receive e-mail and Facebook updates.

Measuring Pinterest Marketing Results

Because Pinterest is just beginning to introduce and test its marketing tools, learning how to measure the results of a Pinterest marketing campaign is also in the early stages. Nevertheless, like any social marketing platform, the key dimensions to measure are fan (follower) acquisition, engagement, amplification, community, and sales. **Table 7.12** describes some basic ways to measure the results of a Pinterest marketing campaign.

TABLE 7.12	MEASURING PINTEREST MARKETING RESULTS
SOCIAL MARKETING PROCESS	**MEASUREMENT**
Fan acquisition (impressions)	The number of people exposed to your pins. The number of followers and the rate of growth. The number of people that have pinned your product photos. The percentage of those exposed to your pins who also pin them to their own or other boards.
Engagement (conversation rate)	The number of posts, comments, and responses to your brand or pins on Pinterest. The number of users who are responding to games, contests, and coupons (participation). The number of minutes on average fans stay on your brand or product pages (duration). The rate of pins per post or other content (applause rate).
Amplification	The rate at which fans share your pinned photos by sharing or repinning to their own or others' boards.
Community	The monthly interaction rate with your content (i.e., the monthly total of pins, comments, and actions on your Pinterest brand page). The average monthly onsite minutes for all fans. The ratio of positive to negative comments.
Brand Strength/Sales	The percentage of your online sales that are generated by Pinterest links (referrals) compared to other platforms, such as e-mail, search engines, and display ads. The percentage of Pinterest-sourced customer purchases, compared to other sources of customers (conversion ratio). The conversion ratio for users receiving repinned photos (friends of followers).

Pinterest provides a built-in Web Analytics service that offers insights into how people are interacting with pins that originate from their Web sites. There are several firms that will help produce the metrics referred to in Table 7.12. For instance, Curalate is an online service to measure the impact of Pinterest and other visual social media. It listens and measures visual conversations by seeing what pictures users pin and repin, and also analyzes the colors in the picture. Curalate currently has over 450 brands using its platform.

THE DOWNSIDE OF SOCIAL MARKETING

Social marketing is not without its disadvantages. One problem is that brands lose a substantial amount of control over where their ads appear in terms of other content and what people say about their brands on social sites. Ads placed on Facebook according to an algorithm can be placed near content that does not represent the values of the brand. This is not peculiar to social marketing, as advertising using Google's advertising platform faces the same problem. This is very different, however, from TV ads where brands maintain near complete control. Social sites are unique in that disgruntled consumers, or just malicious people, can post material that is inaccurate and/or embarrassing (Vega and Kaufman, 2013).

The *Insight on Society* case, *Marketing to Children of the Web in the Age of Social Networks,* illustrates some additional issues with respect to social marketing.

7.3 MOBILE MARKETING

Although still in its infancy, mobile marketing involves the use of mobile devices such as smartphones and tablet computers to display banner ads, rich media, video, games, e-mail, text messaging, in-store messaging, QuickResponse (QR) codes, and couponing. Mobile is now a required part of the standard marketing budget. Mobile devices represent a radical departure from previous marketing technologies simply because the devices integrate so many human and consumer activities from telephoning or texting friends, to listening to music, watching videos, and using the Web to shop and purchase goods. The more mobile devices can do, the more people rely on them in daily life. More than 4.6 billion people worldwide are now using mobile phones, while over 1.7 billion of these use smartphones. Over 100 million in the EU-5 also use tablet computers (eMarketer, Inc., 2014x). One report found that people look at their mobile devices at least 40 times a day. Most mobile phone users keep their phone within arm's length 24 hours a day. For many, it's the first thing they check in the morning, the last thing they check at night, and the first tool to use when there's a question of where to go, what to do, and where to meet up.

OVERVIEW: M-COMMERCE TODAY

It's a short number of steps from owning a smartphone or tablet, to searching for products and services, browsing, and then purchasing. The rate of growth of mobile

INSIGHT ON SOCIETY

MARKETING TO CHILDREN OF THE WEB IN THE AGE OF SOCIAL NETWORKS

In the United States, children influence over $1 trillion in overall family spending. In order to capture a portion of this spending and position themselves for future purchases as the child ages, marketers are becoming increasingly interested in advertising aimed at children.

Today, 93% of all U.S. 5- to 15-year-olds use the Internet. Once children reach 12 years of age, nearly 99% of them are online. Social and mobile marketing provides advertisers with an entirely new arsenal to influence children. Using custom banner ads, product characters, videos, games, virtual worlds, and surveys, marketers are both influencing behaviors and gathering valuable data about purchasing preferences and family members. A children's digital culture has been created with built-in avenues to the psyche of young minds—in some cases, minds that are so young they are unlikely to know when they are being marketed to and when they are being given misleading or even harmful information.

Marketers have also moved aggressively to use online social networks and viral marketing to get kids hooked on brands early in life. For instance, Red Bull does little TV advertising and instead uses Web-based contests, games, and apps such as Urban Futbol, an Angry Birds-like game app. Using social networks, blogs, and YouTube, in a way much more powerful than earlier Web marketing to children, marketers are able to circumvent what few restrictions exist on marketing to children.

While such moves may be savvy marketing, are they ethical? Some people say no. Research has shown that young children cannot understand the potential effects of revealing their personal information; neither can they distinguish between

substantive material on Web sites and the advertisements surrounding it. Experts argue that since children don't understand persuasive intent until they are eight or nine years old, it is unethical to advertise to them before they can distinguish between advertising and the real world. Others believe that fair advertising is an important and necessary part of the maturation process for future adults in today's society.

In 1998, Congress passed the Children's Online Privacy Protection Act (COPPA) after the FTC discovered that 80% of Web sites were collecting personal information from children, but only 1% required their parents' permission. Under COPPA, companies must post a privacy policy on their Web sites, detailing exactly how they collect information from consumers, how they'll use it, and the degrees to which they'll protect consumer privacy. Companies are not permitted to use personal information collected from children under 13 years of age without the prior, verifiable consent of parents.

Since the law took effect, the FTC has obtained a number of settlements and fined a number of companies for violations of COPPA. In 2012, the operator of fan sites for Justin Bieber, Selena Gomez, Rihanna, and others agreed to pay a $1 million penalty for collecting personal information from children such as names, e-mail addresses, street addresses, and cell phone numbers without their parents' permission. Previously, in 2011, Disney's Playdom was fined $3 million, the largest penalty to date, for collecting and disclosing children's information without parental approval.

In 2011, the FTC announced its first-ever COPPA enforcement action involving mobile

(continued)

apps. W3 Innovations was fined $50,000 for collecting personal information such as e-mail addresses from children in connection with numerous apps, such as Emily's Girl World and Emily's Dress Up. Shortly thereafter, in response to the explosion in children's use of mobile devices, the proliferation of online social networks, and interactive gaming, the FTC announced long-awaited proposed revisions to its COPPA regulations , which finally took effect in July 2013. The revisions expanded the definition of personal information to include a child's location, along with any personal data collected through the use of cookies for the purpose of targeted advertising, and require that Web sites that collect a child's information to ensure that they can protect it, hold on to it for only as long as reasonably necessary, and to thereafter delete the information. If firms want to use the personal information of children for internal uses only, the FTC requires an e-mail from the parent plus one other form of verification (such as a credit card or phone number). A stricter standard is required of firms who want to sell personal information about children. These firms are required to use one of the following means of verification in addition to an e-mail: a print-and-send consent form, credit card transaction, a toll-free number or video conference staffed by trained personnel, or verification of a parent's identity by checking a form of government-issued identification. Privacy groups applaud the effort, but whether the new regulations will really affect the way Internet companies

do business is not yet clear, and enforcement is likely to continue to be an issue. For example, in 2014, the FTC fined Snapchat for COPPA violations. Snapchat had falsely claimed that its messages were deleted forever after they were sent and also collected users' contact information without their consent, despite the fact that many of its users were younger than 12 years old. In addition to the fine, Snapchat was required to implement a comprehensive privacy program and will be monitored for 20 years.

Major technology companies have also recently been fined and required to adjust their policies with regard to children signing up for their services. Google settled with the FTC in 2014 and agreed to refund $19 million worth of in-app purchases that were made unwittingly by children. Apple had also agreed to refund $32.5 million in similar purchases earlier in the year, and Amazon is likely to follow suit shortly despite its claim that parents are to blame for these purchases. Yelp was hit with a $450,000 fine despite not having much vested interest in collecting children's information, and even game developers like TinyCo have fallen into the FTC crosshairs and incurred a $300,000 fine for violating children's privacy. The question is whether these FTC fines will be enough to discourage bigger companies from gathering valuable data on future consumers from such a young age. Yelp and TinyCo released statements suggesting their products were now fully COPPA-compliant, but the giants might not budge so easily.

SOURCES: "FTC Fines Tech Giants for Violating Kids' Privacy," by Bill Snyder, Cio.com, September 18, 2014; "Games Developer TinyCo Fined for Illegally Collecting Children's Data," by Dominic Rushe, *The Guardian,* September 18, 2014; "Amazon Blames Parents for Kids' App Store Purchases," by Jonathan Randles, Law360.com, September 9, 2014; "Google to Refund $19 Million of Children's In-App Purchases," Mashable.com, September 4, 2014; "Round Two for Snapchat: Agreement with the Maryland Attorney General Settling Claims of Consumer Deception and COPPA Violations," by Julia M. Siripurapu, Lexology.com, June 19, 2014; "FTC to Better Define New COPPA 'Actual Knowledge' Standards," by John Eggerton, Broadcastingcable.com, July 8, 2013; "Child Privacy Online: FTC Updates COPPA Rules," by Mathew Schwartz, Informationweek.com, July 5, 2013; "Revised Children's Online Privacy Protection Rule Goes Into Effect Today," FTC.gov, July 1, 2013; "The Ripple Effects of Stricter Privacy Rules for Kids," by Bryon Acohido, *USA Today,* July 1, 2013; "Fan Sites for Pop Stars Settle Children's Privacy Charges," by Natasha Singer, *New York Times,* October 3, 2012; "FTC Announces First-Ever COPPA Enforcement Action Against Mobile Apps," by David Silverman, Privsecblog.com, August 17, 2011; "FTC Fine on App Developer Prompts Calls for Updated Privacy Policies," by Josh Smith, *National Journal,* August 15, 2011; "FTC: Disney's Playdom Violated Child Protection Act," by Don Reisinger, News.cnet.com, May 13, 2011.

| FIGURE 7.5 | **THE GROWTH OF MOBILE COMMERCE IN THE UNITED STATES** |

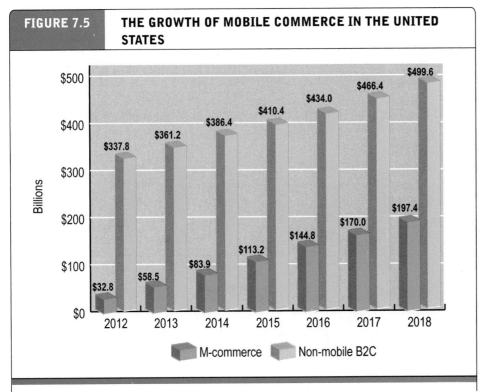

Mobile commerce in the United States is expected to grow to almost $200 billion by 2018.
SOURCE: Based on data from eMarketer, Inc., 2014e; authors' estimates.

commerce has skyrocketed over the last several years, and is expected to continue growing by over 30% in the next few years. Analysts estimate that by 2018, mobile commerce will account for almost 30% of all B2C e-commerce. **Figure 7.5** describes the expected growth of mobile commerce in the United States to 2018.

Initially, m-commerce was focused primarily on digital goods, such as music, videos, games, and e-books. Today, however, traditional retail products are the source of much of the growth in m-commerce, and eMarketer projects that physical retail goods will account for nearly 85% of U.S. m-commerce sales in 2014 (eMarketer, 2014d). **Figure 7.6** lists the top ten companies in terms of mobile sales in 2014. Not surprisingly, the giant is Amazon, with an expected $16.8 billion in sales through its mobile Web site and Amazon app (Walmart is ranked #5 with an expected $1 billion in sales). Apple is second, primarily due to music and app sales for mobile devices.

Increasingly, consumers are using their mobile devices to search for people, places, and things—like restaurants and deals on products they saw in a retail store. The rapid switch of consumers from desktop platforms to mobile devices is driving a surge in mobile marketing expenditures. Because search is so important for directing

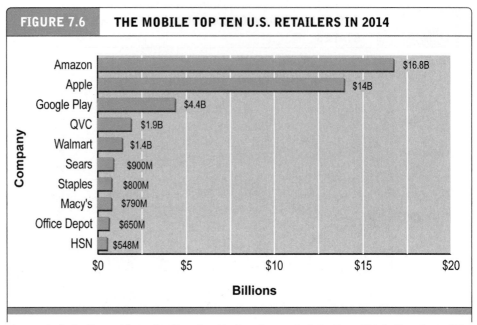

FIGURE 7.6 | **THE MOBILE TOP TEN U.S. RETAILERS IN 2014**

Amazon is the leading mobile retailer. Note that this chart does not include eBay, which facilitated over $20 billion in mobile commerce transactions.

SOURCE: Based on data from Internet Retailer, 2014.

consumers to purchase situations, the mobile search advertising market is very important for search engines like Google and Bing. Desktop search revenues are slowing for both. Google's mobile ad business is growing rapidly, but the prices it can charge for mobile ads are far less than for desktop PC ads. The challenge facing Google and other mobile marketing firms is how to get more consumers to click on mobile ads, and how to charge marketers more for each click. And the answer lies with the consumer who decides what and when to click.

How People Actually Use Mobile Devices

If you plan a mobile marketing campaign, it's important to understand how people actually use their mobile devices (which may be different from what you do or think others do) For instance, most of us think people use their mobile devices on the go, but in fact, according to one of the very few studies of actual mobile behavior, almost 70% of all mobile minutes actually occur in the home. **Figure 7.7** describes how consumers actually use their mobile devices in terms of broad categories of activity.

On average, U.S. mobile users spend an estimated 1660 minutes per month using their devices (excluding phone calls, text messages, and e-mail). Entertainment is the largest single use, at 52% of user time (860 minutes). This includes viewing movies, television shows, shorter videos, or reading a gossip column, as well as just browsing. Users spend 25% of their mobile time (410 minutes) socializing with others on social

| FIGURE 7.7 | **HOW PEOPLE USE THEIR MOBILE DEVICES** |

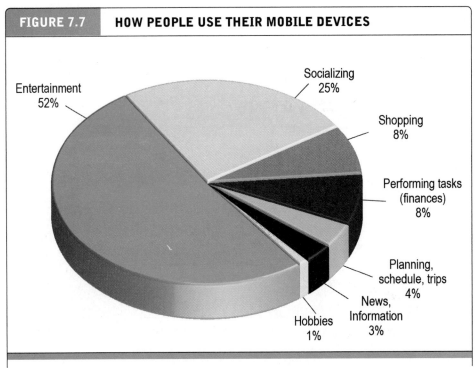

The predominant use of mobile devices is for entertainment and relaxation.

Source: Based on data from AOL/BBDO, 2012.

network sites or blogs. Shopping (looking for specific goods to buy) accounts for only 7% of users' time (126 minutes). Actual purchasing of goods and services using mobile devices involves an estimated 3% of user time. Other uses include performing tasks such as online banking and investing (8%), planning trips (4%), reading news and magazines (3%), and hobbies (1%).

The mobile platform has changed over the past few years, and there are now almost as many tablet users as smartphone users in the United Kingdom: around 30 million use tablets, compared to 36 million who have a smartphone. Tablets, with their larger screens, are the fastest growing and largest source of mobile commerce revenues (**Figure 7.8**).

In-App Experiences and In-App Ads

You may think that using a browser to access the Web on your smartphone is a typical mobile activity. In reality, however, mobile users spend over 85% of their smartphone time using apps, and about 15% using their browsers (eMarketer, Inc., 2014d). On average, users regularly use only about 25 apps a month (Nielsen, 2014a). Over 40% of all app time is spent on the user's single most used apps, and 75% of all app time spent is focused on the user's top 4 apps (comScore, 2014a). There may be millions of apps on the iOS and Android cloud servers, but just a tiny handful are actually generating sufficient user traffic to be of interest to advertisers. Almost 50% of users' time

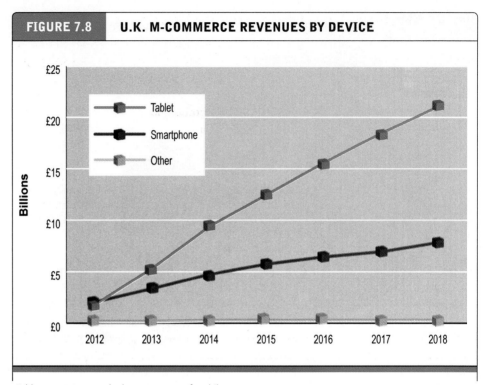

FIGURE 7.8 | **U.K. M-COMMERCE REVENUES BY DEVICE**

Tablet computers are the largest source of mobile commerce revenues.

SOURCE: Based on data from eMarketer, Inc., 2014y.

is spent on social networking apps (25%), games (16%), and radio (8%). Facebook is the top app both in audience size and share of time spent. Other top 25 apps in terms of unique visitors include those from Google (YouTube, Google Play, Google Search, Google Maps, Gmail, and Google+), Apple (iTunes, Apple Maps), Pandora Radio, Yahoo (Stocks, Weather and Mail), Instagram (owned by Facebook), Twitter, Netflix, Snapchat, and Pinterest. Only two retail-oriented apps are in the top 25: Amazon Mobile and eBay (comScore, 2014a).

The implications for marketers are quite clear: if consumers are primarily using apps rather than browsing the Web on their mobile devices, marketers need to place ads in apps where most of the action is for attracting consumers. Second, if mobile consumers only use, on average, 25 apps, then marketers need to concentrate their marketing in these popular apps, let's say, the top 100. Niche marketers, on the other hand, can concentrate their ads in apps that support that niche. A distributor of diving equipment, for instance, could place ads in apps devoted to the diving community.

Another implication for marketers is that rather than focus on mobile display ads that are difficult to read, the best ad may be an app that directly serves customer interest or an ad in an app that is precisely targeted to the consumer's current activities and interests.

How the Multi-Screen Environment Changes the Marketing Funnel

Along with the growth of smartphones and tablets comes a multi-screen world: smartphones, tablets, desktops, and television. The reality, and the future, of computing devices is that consumers will be multi-platform: using desktops and laptops at work and home, and smartphones and tablets at home as well as when moving about. Television will be available all the time, both at home and on the go via tablets and smartphones. Consumer purchasing behavior changes in a multi-screen world. Consumers will often be using two or more screens at once, tweeting when watching a TV show, or moving seamlessly from a TV ad, to a mobile search for more information, to a later tablet purchase screen. Several research studies have found that 90% of multi-device users switch among screens to complete tasks, for instance, viewing an ad on TV, searching on a smartphone for the product, and then purchasing it with a tablet. Consumers move seamlessly among devices, either sequentially or simultaneously. Also, the more screens people use, the more shopping and purchasing they do. One conclusion is that the more screens consumers have, the more consumer touchpoints or marketing opportunities exist (Google, Inc., 2012).

The implications of the multi-device platform, or screen diversity environment, are that marketing needs to be designed for whatever device the consumer is using, and consistent branding across platforms will be important. Screen diversity means that one ad size, for instance, will not fit all situations, and that branding images will need to be adjusted automatically based on the device the consumer is using. From a design perspective, graphics and creative elements will appear differently depending on the screen. This is called responsive design or responsive creative design. Responsive design is a Web design process that allows your marketing content to resize, reformat, and reorganize itself so that it looks good on any screen. You can see responsive design in action if you look at any portal on a desktop, and then compare the screen to that same portal viewed on a smartphone or tablet. You are likely to find there are three versions of the screen, one for each platform (IAB, 2012).

But even beyond screen adaptability, a multi-screen world means merchants need to be on all platforms, and to be integrated across platforms, in order to send a coherent message and to create a convenient consumer platform. The marketing environment today is much more complex than placing banner ads on pages or on search engine results pages on the Web.

BASIC MOBILE MARKETING FEATURES

As millions of consumers adopt mobile devices, mobile marketing expenditures have rapidly grown and in the next five years will equal marketing on desktop PCs. **Figure 7.9** illustrates how rapidly mobile marketing expenditures in the United Kingdom is growing, while marketing on desktops is slowing and will eventually decline.

In 2015, mobile marketing will be about 40% of all online marketing in the United Kingdom, which is extraordinary given that smartphones appeared only seven years ago, in 2007, and tablets not until 2010. Analysts believe that if current mobile marketing growth rates continue, by 2018, mobile marketing will be over 70% of all online advertising.

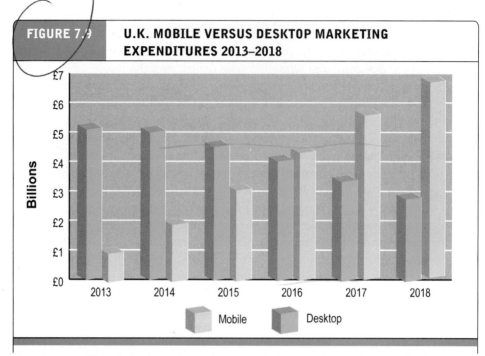

FIGURE 7.9 **U.K. MOBILE VERSUS DESKTOP MARKETING EXPENDITURES 2013–2018**

Spending on mobile marketing is growing much more rapidly than spending on advertising aimed at desktop computers.

SOURCE: Based on data from eMarketer, Inc. 2014z.

Mobile advertising is dominated by Google, with an expected $7.1 billion in mobile ad revenues, constituting about 40% of the entire market. On the mobile platform, Google is king of search, garnering almost $6 billion in mobile search ad revenues in 2014. Google is also the largest distributor of video ads on the mobile platform because of YouTube, and is expected to earn about $1.1 billion in video ad revenues in 2014. Facebook is second with $3.3 billion in mobile ad revenues, of which over 95% ($3.2 billion) is generated by mobile display ads. Facebook is the leading display ad site on mobile devices.

Other players in the mobile marketing marketplace are Twitter (with a 3.7% share), Pandora (3%), YP (2.9%) (previously known as the Yellow Pages, an AT&T telephone directory and online marketing business), and Apple (iAd), with 2.7% (see **Figure 7.10**).

The Technology: Basic Mobile Device Features

Everybody knows the capabilities of smartphones and tablets. But what is it about mobile platforms that make them any different from desktops? Are there any features that make them especially suitable for marketing? **Table 7.13** describes these basic features.

Smartphones today play a much more central role in the personal life of consumers than desktops and laptops in large part because smartphones are always physically with us, or close by. In this sense, they are more personal, and almost "wearable." The "always on, always with us" nature of smartphones has several implications for marketers.

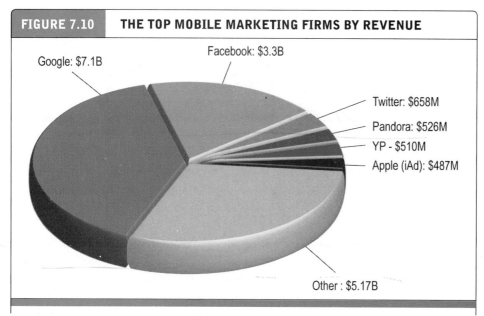

FIGURE 7.10 | **THE TOP MOBILE MARKETING FIRMS BY REVENUE**

Google: $7.1B

Facebook: $3.3B

Twitter: $658M

Pandora: $526M

YP - $510M

Apple (iAd): $487M

Other : $5.17B

Mobile advertising is dominated by Google.
SOURCE: Based on data from eMarketer, Inc. 2014a.

Because they are perceived as "personal appendages," consumers are less tolerant of commercial intrusion. Have you ever had a telephone conversation interrupted by an advertisement? You probably have not, and if so, you most likely would be annoyed at the interference with a personal conversation. These attitudes extend to any use of the phone or tablet, from reading e-mail, visiting Facebook, or watching a video. Consumers are simply less tolerant of advertising on the small screens of smartphones. Second, the around-the-clock physical proximity of smartphones to our persons greatly expands the time available for marketing materials and increases the supply of screens for marketing

TABLE 7.13 | **FEATURES OF MOBILE DEVICES**

FEATURE	DESCRIPTION
Personal communicator and organizer	Telephone plus calendars and clocks to coordinate life on a personal scale.
Screen size and resolution	Resolution of both tablets and phones is high enough to support vibrant graphics and video.
GPS location	Self-locating GPS capability.
Web browser	Standard browsers will operate all Web sites and applications.
Apps	Over a million specialized applications running in native code and extending the functionality of mobile devices.
Ultraportable and personal	Fits into a pocket, or a briefcase for tablets, able to be used anywhere and on the go.
Multimedia capable: video, audio, text	Fully capable of displaying all common media from video to text and sound.

materials. This excess supply decreases the price of mobile marketing messages. In turn, there is a tension between marketers and consumers: marketers want to increase the number of mobile ads, while consumers want to see fewer ads, not more, on their mobile devices. Ads inside apps are treated differently by consumers: in return for a free game, consumers are more accepting of ads.

But perhaps the most unique feature of smartphones is that they know users' precise location by virtue of their built-in GPS. This allows marketing messages to be targeted to consumers on the basis of their location, and supports the introduction of location-based marketing and local marketing (described in Section 7.4). While Web sites may know a desktop's general location, it is a very imprecise fix, and the position of the desktop does not change as the user moves about.

MOBILE MARKETING TOOLS: AD FORMATS

Unlike social marketing, mobile marketing does not require much of a new marketing vocabulary. All the marketing formats available on the desktop are also available on mobile devices. With few exceptions, mobile marketing is very much like desktop marketing—except it is smaller. The major marketing opportunities in mobile marketing are search ads, display ads, videos and rich media, messaging (SMS/MMS/PPS), and some familiar other formats like e-mail, classified, and lead generation. **Figure 7.11** illustrates the relative size of U.S. mobile marketing expenditures by format. The marketing formats on mobile devices are search ads, display, video, text/video messaging, and other (including e-mail, classifieds, and lead generation).

In 2013, search engine advertising was the most popular mobile marketing format, accounting for over 50% of all mobile ad spending, not surprising given that search is the second most common smartphone application (after voice and text

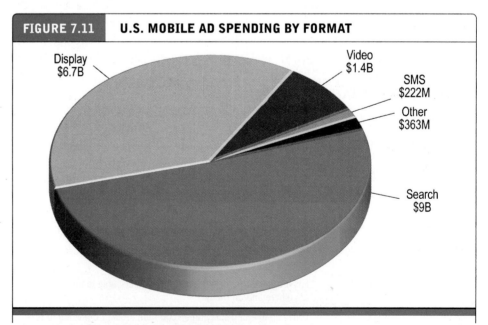

| FIGURE 7.11 | U.S. MOBILE AD SPENDING BY FORMAT |

Display $6.7B
Video $1.4B
SMS $222M
Other $363M
Search $9B

Search engine advertising is the most popular mobile marketing format.
SOURCE: Based on data from eMarketer, Inc. 2014a.

TABLE 7.14	SELECTED MOBILE MARKETING CAMPAIGNS
COMPANY	CAMPAIGN
Walmart	Company-wide mobile strategy using mobile applications, mobile Web, augmented reality, mobile advertising, mobile bar codes, social media, location-based services, and push notifications.
eBay	Multiple apps for deals, clothing, and flagship brand app eBay Mobile. $10 billion in mobile sales and $10 billion in mobile PayPal transactions.
OfficeMax	Uses iPhone and Android platforms for loyalty marketing and daily deals.
RueLaLa	Flash sales site for luxury clothing using SMS and Facebook mobile ads saw mobile sales increase to 40% of all online sales.
Ikea	Uses the Apple iAd platform to display banner ads promoting the Ikea catalog.
Starbucks	Early adopter of mobile marketing, now using a number of apps (company app, augmented reality app, and the Square Wallet mobile payment app) along with SMS and QR code campaigns to reach out to customers.

communication). Search engine ads can be further optimized for the mobile platform by showing ads based on the physical location of the user. Display ads (banner ads, rich media, and sponsorships) are the second leading ad format, accounting for about 38% of mobile ad spending. Display ads can be served as a part of a mobile Web site or inside apps and games. Ad networks such as Google's AdMob, Facebook, Apple's iAd, Twitter's MoPub, and MillennialMedia are some of the largest providers of mobile display advertising. Video ads are only about 8% of mobile marketing, but are a fast growing segment because of their very high click rates. Most desktop video ads can be resized for use on mobile phones and tablets. Mobile messaging generally involves SMS text messaging to consumers, with coupons or flash marketing messages. Messaging is especially effective for local advertising because consumers can be sent messages and coupons as they pass by or visit locations (see Section 7.4).

Social networks such as Facebook, Twitter, and Pinterest have generally brought their desktop advertising techniques over to the mobile platform, with some alterations of the interface for use on small-screen smartphones. In the process, social networks have brought real innovation to the mobile marketing experience, including News Feed posts on Facebook and Promoted Tweets in Twitter. **Table 7.14** provides selected examples of mobile marketing campaigns and techniques used by several well-known firms.

Mobile marketing is uniquely suited for branding purposes, raising awareness through the use of video and rich interactive media such as games. Read the *Insight on Business* case, *Mobile Marketing: Land Rover Seeks Engagement on the Small Screen*, for a further look.

STARTING A MOBILE MARKETING CAMPAIGN

As with all marketing campaigns, start by identifying your objectives and understanding just how a mobile marketing campaign might help your firm. Are you a new unknown start-up seeking to develop a brand image, or an already existing brand looking to strengthen your presence and sell products? Is there something about your products that makes them especially attractive to a mobile audience? For instance, if

INSIGHT ON BUSINESS

MOBILE MARKETING: LAND ROVER SEEKS ENGAGEMENT ON THE SMALL SCREEN

Why is mobile marketing any different from ordinary online marketing? In one sense, it isn't. The same kinds of ad formats you find on Web sites are also used on smartphones—in order of importance, search, display, video, and text messages. In another sense, mobile marketing can be very different from other types of online marketing because of the unique features of the smartphone, which include a built-in GPS, a gyroscope, and an accelerometer. This means marketers can know the location of the user, and they can present rich media and video ads where the user can control the action in a way not possible with an ordinary PC. Smartphones use a touch interface, which increases user involvement. Mobile ads can therefore be more engaging and interactive than traditional PC ads. Location information can be used to market local businesses at the very point of consumer purchase, namely, on the street or in the store while browsing. Other unique smartphone features are that people almost always carry them and keep them turned on while moving about. This means that smartphone users can be exposed to marketing messages throughout the day (and sometimes the night).

Mobile devices are used by consumers throughout the purchase cycle: 45% of the population uses a mobile device to research products online before purchasing. The use of mobile devices to actually purchase products or services online (as opposed to just shopping and browsing online) is also growing: in 2014, U.S. mobile commerce is expected to generate around $84 billion, and grow to almost $200 million by 2018. About 70% of the 145 million U.S. mobile online shoppers buy something using their devices. For certain goods that the consumer is familiar with, for sites that have an easy-to-use one-click shopping capability, and for purchases of content like books and movies, mobile purchasing is particularly convenient. Also, for local marketing, mobile is an ideal platform for merchants to attract consumers in the neighborhood. Restaurants, museums, and entertainment venues are ideal candidates to use mobile marketing aimed at local consumers. What attracts users to mobile purchasing is the ability to access product information now, find deals, and buy all with the swipe of a finger. But mobile is also good for introducing new products and building brand recognition, with sales taking place elsewhere and offline.

A good example of the use of mobile devices for marketing is Land Rover's use of Apple's iAd platform to introduce the Range Rover Evoque. The Evoque (pronounced "evoke") is a compact SUV aimed at young urban buyers. Land Rover is known for its line of very luxurious and expensive SUVs that appeal to an older consumer. The Evoque is a smaller, more fuel-efficient, "greener" SUV than its much larger luxury SUV cousins. Land Rover wanted to introduce the car to an entirely new demographic: young affluent urban consumers. The problem was how to introduce this new concept for Land Rover to an audience that most likely never intended to buy a Land Rover.

Land Rover worked with Mindshare (an Internet marketing firm), Y&R Group (a New York-based marketing firm), and Apple's iAd Network team to build an immersive and engaging interactive app that would allow consumers to explore and configure the interior and exterior of the car using the finger gestures of the iPhone. Users are shown a mobile ad on their cell phones, and tapping the ad, they are taken to the Land Rover app to explore the car. iAd used iTunes-based targeting to pinpoint the right audience based on the kinds of music they liked to listen to.

Using Land Rover's configuration app, customers can change the Evoque's body style, color, and wheels. They can take a photo of the car and send it to others by e-mail or SMS. There's an immersive 360-degree view of the interior that puts viewers inside the car. Using the iPhone's built-in gyroscope and accelerometer, viewers can tilt and turn the device to see a 360-view of the interior.

According to Land Rover, the iAd mobile marketing effort has been a success. As one Land Rover marketer noted, there's a difference between looking at a 30-second TV commercial, and someone using their iPhone to explore a new product. With the mobile ad, people are more engaged, in control, and attentive to the message. On average, people spent on average nearly 80 seconds whenever they engaged with the ad, nearly three times longer than a typical TV commercial.

In 2013, Land Rover built on its mobile platform by adding a mobile application called The Trail Less Traveled to showcase its new Range Rover through an interactive online journey using four synced camera angles. Users can select their own route through an interactive map, advance to different stages of the journey, and even pause the experience to explore pictures and videos of the latest engineering advancements in the vehicle.

Spurred onward by the success of these campaigns, Land Rover has continued its digital media marketing efforts. In 2013, they began promoting the 2014 Range Rover Sport with an interactive film called "Race the Sun." Users get a 360-degree view of the car's interior and then use their phone as a game controller to control the car in various situations like going through water or down a hill or speeding down a desert highway. The action sequences are interspersed with cinematic segments.

Land Rover also launched an advertisement using Blippar augmented reality technology that allows users to use their mobile device to experience the Range Rover Sport in different ways. Users can scan several images on the print advertisement to see and "feel" the car as it goes off-road, with accompanying phone vibrations, or use the phone as a pedal by tilting it to accelerate the car. The ad quickly reached the top five of Blippar's most shared and most popular augmented reality ads. Other components of the marketing campaign for the Range Rover Sport included more traditional interactive banner ads and rich media mobile ads. Land Rover also added an Instagram element to its campaign, asking users to create a series of photos or a video that shows what "drives" them to new heights, using the hashtag #IAmDriven.

SOURCES: "Mobile Commerce Deep Dive: The Products, Channels, and Tactics Fueling Growth," by Cathy Boyle, eMarketer, Inc., July 2014; "Land Rover: Blippar Powered Sensory Overdrive," Digitalbuzzblog.com, January 22, 2014; "Land Rover Celebrates Personal Ambitions in Instagram Campaign," by Joe McCarthy, Luxurydaily.com, November 7, 2013; "Land Rover Targets Affluent Car Buyers in 'Race the Sun,'" by Matt Kapko, Clickz.com, October 18, 2013; "Land Rover Unveils Marketing Campaign to Launch All-New 2014 Range Rover Sport," Yahoo! Finance, September 6, 2013; "Land Rover Unveils Huge TV and Digital Push," by Christopher Heine, Adweek.com, September 4, 2013; "Land Rover Flaunts New Range Rover Vehicle via Interactive Mobile App," by Rimma Kats, Luxurydaily.com, May 6, 2013; "Land Rover Reaches New Audience with iAd for Brands," Apple Inc., 2012; "Land Rover iAd Campaign Delivers Highest Engagement Levels," by Chantal Tode, *Mobile Marketer*, August 8, 2012.

you sell to local customers walking by your shop, then you might want to use the GPS capabilities of smartphones to target consumers who are nearby.

Next, consider the target demographic for your campaign and products. The most active purchasers on mobile devices are men, and they are more likely to buy consumer electronics equipment and digital content. Women are more likely to cash in coupons and respond to flash sales and deals. Younger consumers are more likely to research products and price on mobile devices, and more likely to share experiences using social media. Mobile shoppers and buyers are more affluent than the online population in general. These demographics are averages, and mobile marketing campaigns do not need to restrict themselves to these averages. Find out where your mobile customers are congregating. Are your mobile customers likely to be using apps, and if so, what are they? Are your customers likely to be on Facebook or use Twitter? Or are your customers most likely to find you on a Google mobile search page?

Finally, consider the marketspace where you hope to succeed. What are your competitors doing on the mobile platform? Is their presence effective? Where do they place their marketing efforts: display ads on Web portals, or display ads in Google search results? Or can they be found as in-app ads? What apps are they advertising in? How are they represented on Facebook Mobile? Do they also have a Twitter and/or Pinterest brand page? Do your competitors have an app that users can easily download? You'll want to be able to meet your competitors on each of the platforms they have adopted. Once you've developed an initial vision for your marketing campaign, you can develop a timeline and an action plan of how to meet the milestones identified in your timeline.

Once you have envisioned your marketing campaign and identified your market, it is time to start implementing your mobile campaign. Here are some steps to follow:

- Develop a mobile Web site so mobile consumers can see and buy your products. Make your mobile Web site social by including Facebook, Twitter, Pinterest, and other social site links.

- Develop a Facebook brand page so your social and mobile marketing efforts are integrated.

- Develop a Twitter brand page so customers can follow your posts.

- If you already use a display advertising program like Google's AdWords or a Facebook display ad account, you can create a new campaign using the same ads designed specifically for mobile platforms.

- Consider opening an iAd account and using Apple's iAd network or Google's AdMob in part because these ad networks can publish and track your ads on multiple platforms simultaneously.

- Develop marketing content that is aimed specifically at the mobile user, with videos and high levels of interactivity designed for the mobile screen.

- Measure and manage your campaign. iAd and AdWords, along with many other ad networks, will host and manage your mobile campaigns. In addition, they can provide you with a host of campaign measures that will allow you to see which mobile ads and techniques are attracting the most followers, comments, and social activity concerning your brand. With this basic data you can start to manage the mobile marketing campaign by reducing expenditures on ads that do not work and increasing the budget of ads that do work.

MEASURING MOBILE MARKETING RESULTS

There are many different mobile marketing objectives, and therefore different types of mobile marketing campaigns. Some campaigns are sales-oriented, based on display and search ads, offering coupons or discounts, and taking users directly to a Web site where they can buy something. Measuring the results of these mobile campaigns follows similar campaigns launched on desktops. Other campaigns focus on branding, where the objective is to engage consumers in a conversation, acquire them as fans, and spread the word among their friends. You can use the framework from Figure 7.4 on page 425 to measure the results of these campaigns. The key dimensions to measure for mobile social campaigns are fan acquisition, engagement, amplification, community, brand strength (center of conversation), and sales.

Figure 7.12 illustrates how a brand-oriented marketing campaign utilizing the mobile platform and social marketing might present its effectiveness measures over a six-month period. In a branding campaign, the object is not so much sales as it is strengthening consumers' engagement with the brand. In the example provided in Figure 7.12, acquiring fans is measured by the number of unique visitors. Here you can see that over six months, visitors have risen over 60%. Engagement is reflected in the time on-site (in thousands of minutes); amplification is measured by the number of Likes, and this has expanded threefold. Community is measured by the number of

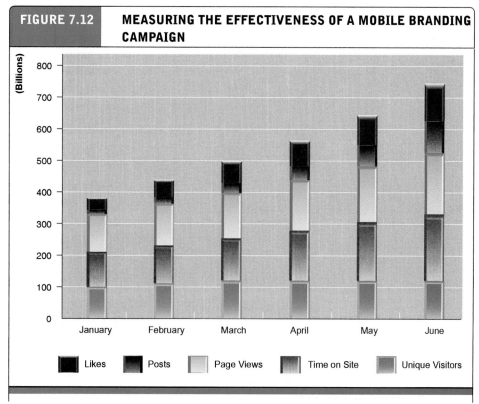

FIGURE 7.12 MEASURING THE EFFECTIVENESS OF A MOBILE BRANDING CAMPAIGN

The effectiveness of a branding campaign utilizing the mobile platform and social marketing can be measured by examining the number of Likes, posts, page views, time on site, and unique visitors.

posts, suggesting fans are actively engaging with one another and the brand. Posts have risen eightfold in the period. Brand strength is best summarized in this figure as the composite picture of fan acquisition, engagement, amplification, and community measures. Measuring the impacts of this mobile campaign on ultimate sales requires going a step further and measuring which sales can be attributed to this mobile campaign.

7.4   LOCAL AND LOCATION-BASED MOBILE MARKETING

location-based marketing

targets marketing messages to users based on their location

location-based services

involve providing services to users based on their location

Location-based marketing is one of the fastest growing segments of the digital marketing universe. **Location-based marketing** targets marketing messages to users based on their location. Generally, location-based marketing involves marketing of location-based services. **Location-based services** involve providing services to users based on their location. Examples of location-based services are: personal navigation (How do I get there?), point-of-interest (What's that?), reviews (What's the best restaurant in the neighborhood?), friend-finder (Where are you? Where's the crowd?), and family-tracker services (Where is my child?). There is a connection of course: the more people use their mobile devices to search for and obtain local services, the more opportunities there are for marketers to target consumers with messages at just the right moment, at just the right location, and in just the right way—not too pushy and annoying, but in a way to improve the consumer experience at the moment of local shopping and buying. This is the ideal in any event. Location-based marketing can take place on a desktop as well because browsers and marketers know your approximate location. But in this section we focus primarily on location-based mobile marketing, which is where the greatest growth and opportunities lie.

Experience and market research suggest that consumers want local ads, offers, information, and content. Consumers have a high likelihood of acting on local ads and purchasing the products and services offered. Because it has evolved so rapidly in the last five years, experience and research with respect to location-based marketing is a work in progress with many different platforms, providers, and techniques. Measures of effectiveness and returns on investment are being developed.

THE GROWTH OF LOCAL MARKETING

Prior to the release of Google Maps in 2005, nearly all local advertising was nondigital and provided by local newspapers, radio and television stations, local yellow pages, and billboards. Of course, some was digital, involving the Web sites of local merchants. Today, total media ad spending in the United States is $180 billion, and approximately $138 billion of this is local media spending by both national and local brands. An estimated 40% of this local advertising (about $54 billion) involves truly local firms like restaurants, grocery stores, theaters, and shoe stores marketing to their local audience. The remaining 60% of local media marketing involves large national firms marketing to local audiences, such as an ad for Coca-Cola in a local newspaper or Web sites created for local auto dealers by national firms. Of the $138 billion of local media spending, about 23% ($32 billion) will be spent on online marketing, and this amount is expected to grow at a rate of about 14% to about $53 billion by 2018, which will constitute about 33% of all local advertising spending at that point (BIA/Kelsey, 2014a).

After the introduction of Google Maps in 2005 and smartphones in 2007, online local marketing began to rapidly expand. Google Maps on desktop computers enabled the targeting of ads to users based on a general sense of their IP address and enabled merchants to display ads to users based on the general location of potential customers, usually within a several square-mile radius. IP addresses can be used to identify a city, and a neighborhood within the city, but not a zip code, street, or building. Google Maps helped users answer the question "Where can I find an Italian restaurant" in a city or section of a city from their desktop. The arrival of smartphones in 2007, and Google's mobile maps app, took this one step further. The GPS receivers in second-generation smartphones introduced in 2008 (Apple's 3G iPhone), along with other techniques, meant that a user's location (latitude and longitude) could be fairly well known by cell phone manufacturers, marketers, service providers, and carriers like AT&T and Verizon. These developments opened an entirely new growth path for local online advertising that heretofore had been confined to the desktop. In this new world, a local food market could shout out to mobile phone users as they walked by the store, offering discounts to responders, and users in turn could search for specific retail stores nearby, even checking their inventory before walking into the store.

THE GROWTH OF LOCATION-BASED (LOCAL) MOBILE MARKETING

Location-based (local) mobile marketing is currently a small part of the online marketing environment, but it is expected to triple over the next 5 years. **Figure 7.13** helps put the location-based mobile market in perspective. In 2014, total U.S. online marketing will be about $51 billion and local online marketing is expected to be a healthy and

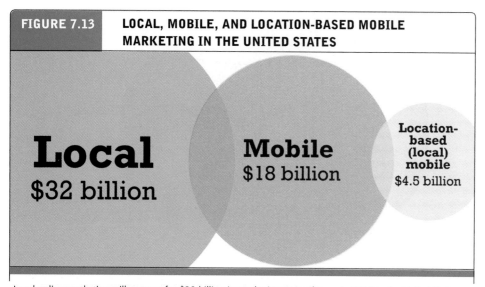

| FIGURE 7.13 | LOCAL, MOBILE, AND LOCATION-BASED MOBILE MARKETING IN THE UNITED STATES |

Local
$32 billion

Mobile
$18 billion

Location-based (local) mobile
$4.5 billion

Local online marketing will account for $32 billion in marketing expenditures in 2014 in the United States, with location-based mobile expected to account for $4.5 billion of that amount..

surprisingly large $32 billion. The part of local online that is location-based mobile is expected to generate an estimated $4.5 billion.

The ad formats used in local mobile marketing are familiar—search ads, display, native/social, videos, and SMS text messages. Search ads displayed as a part of user search results comprise the largest location-based mobile ad format, with U.S. marketers expected to spend an estimated $2.5 billion in 2014. This amount is expected to more than triple to $7.5 billion in 2018. The local mobile search market is dominated by Google. Display ads are the second largest format, and are expected to account for $1.1 billion in spending in 2014, and to also triple to $3.2 billion by 2018. Social/native ads are the fastest growing format, generating an estimated $500 billion in spending in 2014, but expected to increase by over six times that, to $3.4 billion by 2018. Here the main players are Facebook and Google. Together, Google and Facebook account for 70% of location-based mobile marketing. Videos are currently a relatively small part of the location-based mobile market, accounting for only about $317 billion in spending in 2014, but they too are expected to triple, to over $1 billion, by 2018. The primary platform for video ads today is Google'sYouTube. SMS text messages only play a small role in local mobile marketing, in part due to consumer resistance to "text spam," which has made such ads ineffective and of little market value. **Figure 7.14** illustrates the relative shares of location-based mobile ad format spending in the United States in 2014 (eMarketer, Inc., 2014f).

LOCATION-BASED MARKETING PLATFORMS

The key players in location-based mobile marketing are the same giants who dominate the mobile marketing environment described in a previous section, namely, Google,

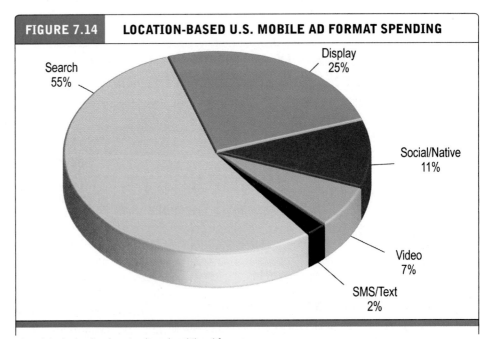

FIGURE 7.14   **LOCATION-BASED U.S. MOBILE AD FORMAT SPENDING**

Search 55%
Display 25%
Social/Native 11%
Video 7%
SMS/Text 2%

Search is the leading location-based mobile ad format.
SOURCE: Based on data from eMarketer, Inc., 2014f.

Facebook, Apple, Twitter, YP (formerly Yellow Pages), Pandora, and Millenial. Google is clearly the leading location-based marketer largely because of its widely used Google Maps app on smartphones. When a consumer searches for a location on Google Maps, it is an ideal marketing moment to pop an ad before the consumer's eyes. Google Places is a simple but effective service that provides short business profiles when users search for a specific business. Google's Android operating system has location functionality built into the system, and Google apps, like Google Maps, continuously update the user's location. Google purchased a mobile advertising firm called AdMob in 2009 and claims to be the world's largest mobile advertising firm for both Android and Apple's iOS operating systems. App developers use AdMob to provide their apps with consumer and user location information. Google also sells location information to independent marketing firms. Marketing firms use AdMob to develop full-screen rich media ads. Google's main revenue stream comes from its AdWords service, where marketers bid for keywords on Google's search engine. AdWords used to be the same whether displayed on a PC or a mobile device. Google has upgraded its AdWords service to optimize ads for user contexts and devices, and to provide management of campaigns across all mobile and desktop devices. The new service is called Enhanced AdWords. For instance, if a customer searches for "pizza" on a desktop PC from work at 1 PM, he or she would be shown restaurants nearby and a quick order form. If the customer searched for "pizza" at 8 PM on a smartphone within a half-mile of a pizza restaurant, he or she might be shown a click-to-call phone number and directions to the restaurant. Pizza restaurants pay Google for the chance to show up in these searches.

Google and Apple have advantages in the location-based market: they both have developed extensive maps of Wi-Fi networks throughout the world, allowing them to develop much more precise location information than competitors.

Apple's mobile platform iAd provides location data to iOS app developers and mobile marketing firms. Like AdMob, when users click on an iAd ad, a full-screen ad appears within the app they are using. The ad can be targeted to the user's location. Facebook was late to the mobile marketing but in three years it has gone from zero mobile advertising to an expected $7.4 billion worldwide in 2014. Facebook's strength is showing display ads to its over 1 billion mobile users worldwide.

LOCATION-BASED MOBILE MARKETING: THE TECHNOLOGIES

Location-based services and marketing require marketers and local service providers to have a fairly precise idea of where consumer mobile devices are located. There are two general types of location-based marketing techniques: geo-aware and proximity marketing. **Geo-aware** techniques identify the location of a user's device and then target marketing to the device, recommending actions within reach (which, in itself, requires the marketer to know where relevant things like stores are located). For instance, a marketer may target smartphones within several square city blocks to alert them to available offers from participating merchants. **Proximity marketing** techniques identify a perimeter around a physical location, and then target ads to users within that perimeter, recommending actions possible within the fenced-in area. The

geo-aware
techniques that identify the location of a user's device and then target marketing to the device

proximity marketing
techniques that identify a perimeter around a physical location, and then target ads to users within that perimeter, recommending actions possible within the fenced-in area

TABLE 7.15	MAJOR LOCATING TECHNOLOGIES
TECHNOLOGY	**DESCRIPTION**
GPS	The user's device downloads GPS data from a GPS satellite. First introduced with the Apple 3G iPhone in 2008. Today, cellphones are required to broadcast their GPS location for emergency assistance purposes.
Wi-Fi	Estimates user's location within a radius of a known Wi-Fi access point.
Bluetooth low energy (BLE)	Used by Apple in iBeacon. Uses less battery power than traditional Bluetooth or GPS and more accurate than targeting through Wi-Fi triangulation.
Geo-search	Uses location information based on the user's search queries.
Cell tower	AT&T, Verizon, and other carriers are in constant contact with their devices, which allows approximation of location by triangulation and refinement of the unit's GPS location. Wireless carriers use a cell phone's MAC address to identify the phone and the location.
Sign in/registration	Estimates users' location when they self-identify their location using sign-in services or social network posts.

perimeter can be from hundreds of feet (in urban areas) to several miles (in suburban locations). For instance, if users walk into the geo-fenced perimeter of a store, restaurant, or retail shop, they will receive ads from these businesses. Both of these techniques utilize the same locating technologies.

Ad networks, local-mobile marketing firms, providers of devices and services like Google and Apple, as well as phone companies use several methods for locating mobile devices, none of which are perfect, and all of which have varying degrees of accuracy. **Table 7.15** describes the major locating technologies used to enable location-based services and marketing.

GPS (Global Positioning System) location is the most accurate positioning method in theory. In practice, the signal can be weak in urban areas, nonexistent inside buildings, signals can be deflected, and it can take a long time (30–60 seconds) for the device to acquire the signal and calculate a position. When a clear signal is obtained, GPS can be accurate to within 3–10 meters under ideal conditions, but more frequently, a cell phone's GPS is accurate only to within 50 meters—half a football field. Also, users have to activate the feature, and many do not for privacy reasons. Assisted GPS (A-GPS) supplements GPS information with other information from the phone network to speed up acquisition. Nearly all smartphones use A-GPS. In Apple's iOS, users can decide whether to turn Location Services on or off. When turned on, the iOS uses GPS, cellular, and Wi-Fi networks to determine the user's approximate location to within 10 meters (30 feet). The user's iPhone continuously reports its position and reports to Apple servers.

Cell tower location is used by wireless telephone carriers to track the location of their devices, which is required to complete phone calls as devices pass from the range of one tower into the range of another. Cell tower location is also the basis of the wireless emergency response system in the United States. The FCC's wireless Enhanced 9-1-1 (E9-1-1) rules require wireless carriers to track cellphone locations whether or not the user has turned on location services in order to assist emergency responders in locating users who make 911 calls.

Wi-Fi location is used in conjunction with GPS signals to more accurately locate a user based on the known location of Wi-Fi transmitters, which are fairly ubiquitous in urban and suburban locations. Apple, Google, and other mobile service providers have developed global databases of wireless access points simply by driving cars around urban areas in much of the world. Google uses Street View cars to build a global database of wireless access points and their geographic location. Android applications can use this database to determine the approximate location of individuals based on the Wi-Fi networks detected by their mobile devices. All Wi-Fi devices continuously monitor the presence of local Wi-Fi networks, and mobile devices report back this data to Apple and Microsoft, along with other device manufacturers, who use similar methods. The goal of these technologies is to provide consumers and marketers with "micro-location data" accurate to within a few feet to support truly real-time, accurate, local marketing at the personal level. For instance, if you are looking at a rack of dress shirts in a retail store, an accurate positioning system could detect this, and direct you to appropriate accessories like socks and ties on surrounding shelves.

WHY IS LOCAL MOBILE ATTRACTIVE TO MARKETERS?

Consumers who seek information about local businesses using mobile devices are much more active and ready to purchase than desktop users. In part this is because desktop searchers for local information are not in as close proximity to merchants as are mobile searchers. A recent Google survey found that over 80% of U.S. consumers use smartphones and tablet computers to conduct local searches on search engines for a variety of local information such as business hours, local store addresses and directions, and availability of products at local stores. The survey found that consumers search for local information through the purchase process, and 50% of smartphone users visited a store within a day of their local search, and 18% made a purchase within a day. The survey also found that over 60% of smartphone users wanted ads customized both to their city/zip code and to their immediate surroundings (Google, 2014a).

LOCATION-BASED MARKETING TOOLS

Location-based digital marketing, like social marketing, presents students of digital marketing with a confusing array of new services, platforms, and firms that provide these services. While some local-based marketing techniques, like placing ads on Google's AdSense platform aimed at mobile customers, are relatively easy to establish for the small business owner, others require the help of mobile marketing provider firms.

A New Lexicon: Location-Based Digital Marketing Features

Location-based services involve providing services to users based on their location. Examples include personal navigation, point-of-interest, reviews, friend-finder, and

TABLE 7.16	LOCATION-BASED MARKETING TOOLS AND CAMPAIGNS
LOCATION-BASED MARKETING TOOLS	**DESCRIPTION**
Geo-social-based services marketing	Users share their location with friends. Can be used for check-in services like Foursquare; friend finders; transportation services.
Location-based services marketing	Provides services to consumers looking for local services and products.
Mobile-local social network marketing based on users' location	Facebook expands local offerings of deals by local firms, display ads using News Feed. Discount offers from a Gap store when claimed are broadcast to friends.
	Google+ Local. Connecting users with local businesses. Users can conduct searches within a local area and get Zagat reviews.
	Upgraded Foursquare app focuses on social updates but also recommendations and deals.
	Social network monitoring: sends messages within an app based on mentions of interest in products in Facebook and Twitter posts. Used by H&M.
	Intent marketing: scanning social networks for indications of real-time consumer interest in specific products. H&M partnered with LocalResponse to promote clothing inspired by the movie "Girl With the Dragon Tattoo."
Proximity marketing	Send messages to consumers in the area of a store or outlet to generate sales using a virtual fence around a retail location (could also be an airport, train station, or arena). Generally opt in. Miller Coors created a geo-fence around 28 U.S. airports to alert Blue Moon beer fans on where it could be purchased.
In-store messaging	Messaging consumers while entering or browsing in a store.
	Retailers collect, analyze, and respond to customers' real-time shopping behavior.
Location-based app messaging	American Express MyOffersapp presents cardholders with personalized deals based on their location.

family-tracker services. **Table 7.16** describes how some of these features can be used for marketing.

Proximity Marketing with Beacons

While all location-based marketing is in some sense proximity marketing, when Apple introduced iBeacon in 2013 with its iOS 7, it made it possible for retail store retailers to communicate directly and quite precisely with customers as they passed within a few feet of in-store beacons. There are many close proximity technologies such as QR codes, Wi-Fi, and NFC (Near Field Communication), but each has drawbacks in terms of precision, cost, and widespread availability. Now that Apple has adopted NFC in its hardware for Apple Pay, NFC will become a good candidate technology for close proximity marketing. Apple's iBeacon uses a different technology called Bluetooth

Low Energy (BLE). Android phones also have this capability. BLE is inexpensive to implement, and uses much less power than traditional Blue Tooth. Unlike QR codes, BLE has a two-way, push-pull communication capability. Using QR codes, consumers need to show the code to a QR scanner, and then they see information on a product. With iBeacon, consumers can be contacted as soon as they walk into a store and exposed to special offers, and then when browsing the store, contacted as they pass specific areas, like the jewelry department. This all takes place automatically on the user's iPhone. Consumers can respond to these messages as well.

In 2013, physical store retailers got only about half the holiday traffic they had in 2010, in large part because of the growth of e-commerce, and also lingering effects of the recession. Yet in-store sales in 2013 were flat or slightly up. The consumers who did go to stores bought more than in the past (eMarketer, Inc., 2014g). All the large national retailers have active e-commerce Web sites. At first glance, for retail stores, it makes no difference if the sale takes place online or offline in a store. One exception to this is impulse sales: in a retail store, impulse sales account for a significant amount of sales, but online, there are very limited impulse sales. Hence, getting consumers into the store where they can be engaged is very important to retailers. In a store, consumers can be surrounded by a brand and can spend time thinking about the brand without interruption (eMarketer, Inc., 2014h).

In 2014, Macy's will deploy iBeacon in all its retail stores after a successful test of the system in San Francisco and New York. Using an app from Shopkick (a marketing firm) called shopBeacon, Macy's customers who have downloaded the app receive notifications to open the app when they enter a Macy's store. Customers receive promotions, deals, and discounts. In a few months, Macy's and Shopkick will be able to more precisely tailor the system to departments within Macy's. The hope is that by using proximity marketing, retail stores will be able to attract more consumers to their stores, and increase purchases from those who come to their stores (Macy's, 2014).

STARTING A LOCATION-BASED MARKETING CAMPAIGN

As with all marketing campaigns, start by identifying your objectives and understand just how a location-based mobile marketing campaign might help your business. Location-based marketing is generally much more action-oriented than other forms of online marketing. A person is in a given location only for a short time, measured in minutes and hours, rarely days or weeks. If you want the consumer to do something, it's now. Does your product or service have this quality? Is there something related to a person's location that fits with your product? Is there something about your products that makes them especially attractive to a mobile audience at a specific location and time? There are very few products and services that don't have a location connection.

Next, consider the target demographic for your campaign and products. Location-aware consumers (those with mobile devices and familiar with location-based services) tend to be a younger, more educated, and wealthier demographic. They have many of the same characteristics as all mobile shoppers.

A strategic analysis of your marketspace is very important. The same questions that you would seek to answer if you were doing a nonlocation-aware mobile marketing campaign apply to a location-based marketing effort, such as examining what your competitors are doing.

Once you have envisioned your marketing campaign and identified your market, it is time to start implementing your mobile campaign. The same steps that you would follow in implementing a mobile campaign apply to location-based marketing as well. Note that you can't do everything at once—mobile-centric and location-based. Start by doing something simple like local search. Then consider more sophisticated local-based marketing tactics.

MEASURING LOCATION-BASED MARKETING RESULTS

There are a great many ways to measure the success of a mobile location-based campaign, some very sophisticated. The measures of success will vary depending on the objective of the campaign, which might be to raise the awareness of your brand among consumers, to bring customers to your retail store, or a click-to-call campaign where you want people to make reservations for a concert.

Because mobile local campaigns use the same marketing ad formats as both traditional and mobile Web marketing, the basic measures of effectiveness are similar (see Figure 7.13). For instance, the number of impressions (people who see an ad), click-through rate, and unique visitors are basic measures for a mobile local campaign. But mobile location-based marketing is much more personal and social than traditional Web marketing or even simple mobile marketing: it's a marketing message directed to a consumer's personal mobile device based on that person's location. Local mobile marketers hope consumers will take follow-on action almost immediately—inquire, reserve, click-to-call, friend, and ultimately purchase. **Table 7.17** describes some of the basic dimensions and metrics to use when evaluating a mobile marketing campaign. The nature of the location-based campaign makes a difference for how you measure success. For instance, in a click-to-call campaign, you want to measure the volume of calls, duration of call, new versus existing customers, and the number of accidental or hostile calls.

TABLE 7.17	MOBILE LOCATION-BASED MARKETING EFFECTIVENESS
SOCIAL MARKETING PROCESS	MEASUREMENT
Acquisition	Impressions; click-through; unique visitors to a mobile or desktop Web site; pages viewed; time on site.
Engagement	Inquire; reserve; visit a physical store; click-to-call; check maps for directions; register; request more information; posts and comments; responders to offers; Likes generated per visitor; click-to-call rate.
Amplification	SMS to friends; notify friends of location; share location or offers with friends.
Community	Content generated by visitors or responders; reviews; posts; positive comments generated.
Sales	Purchases; percentage increase in sales due to local mobile campaign; percentage of customers from local mobile.

ExchangeHunterJumper.com:
Building a Brand with Social Marketing

The Internet and Web have enabled thousands of business ideas to become online realities. The Internet has reduced the costs of starting a small business, and allowed small players to effectively use the same marketing and selling tools as major corporations. Small businesses usually occupy a market niche not occupied by big players or corporations. One such market niche in America, comprising about 10,000 to 30,000 players, is the high-end horse show circuit. These are people who are willing to drop $200,000 on a horse that can jump a five-foot fence with ease. This may be a very small market, but its members are highly motivated to both buy and sell horses, and they are willing to spend in the process. ExchangeHunterJumper.com is one example of how a small business focusing on a tiny niche market was able to successfully build an online brand.

According to Dagny Amber Aslin, founder and owner of ExchangeHunterJumper. com (The Exchange), a Web site created to help owners and professional trainers sell high-end competition horses, it's hard to "get rich" or even make money on the Internet. She adds, "There are a lot of preconceived notions … I beat down a path

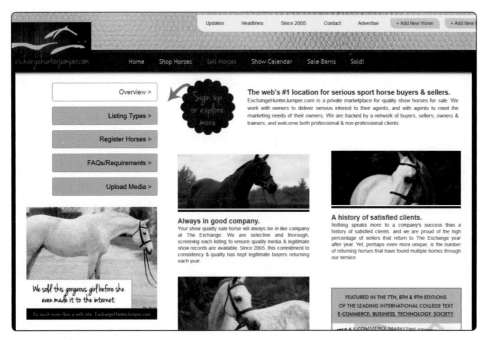

previously unplowed. It cost us a lot of money and we suffered many setbacks from our mistakes." Yet the site is still growing and has succeeded where others failed. How did Aslin break through and develop a site that works for professionals buying and selling alike? How did she build trust? How did she market her services?

Experience helped. Aslin started with applicable experience—in the horse world and in the world of Internet marketing. In addition to riding and competing as a child, Aslin spent several years working as a professional trainer. Working six-day weeks, including weekends, and spending most of her time outdoors riding, teaching, and competing, she saw first-hand the challenges facing professional horsemen, and she gained valuable credibility with those who would become her audience.

While working in the horse business, and learning how difficult it was to make a living, she took a part-time job as an assistant to a top California real estate agent, helping him market and sell high-end real estate in the Santa Barbara area. Among other activities, she helped him develop and expand his Web site. Through that experience, she realized that "selling six-figure horses and seven-figure houses are ridiculously similar—both tend to be overpriced, have emotional strings attached, require vettings and exhaustive negotiations, involve agents, and the list goes on." In 2005, when she moved from California back to the Midwest, where she had spent her childhood, The Exchange was born. Seven years later, the equine marketing model she has built is "a customized copy" of the real estate program she assisted with in Santa Barbara.

Aslin knew that busy horse professionals needed a high-quality, reliable source of suitable mounts for their clients, but their day-to-day business lives left them little time to thoroughly search the market, and they often lacked a good grasp of modern media technology. The same dilemma applied when it came to selling high-end horses. In response, she created an organized, professional process for preparing online horse sale advertisements. It included detailed forms for sellers to fill out, and she insisted that quality photos and video be provided for each horse advertised, enabling her to turn the descriptions into accurate portrayals of each animal and its capabilities. She created a fee structure that was reasonable and affordable, and she developed a multi-channel marketing program.

Aslin understood that her business plan needed to be a living document, evolving over time based on what the market was telling her. This helped her make inroads in a traditional industry that is very resistant to change. Most horse professionals spend their days outside, and tend to do business only with those they know personally—the level of trust is very low. Most existing horse sale Web sites were little more than online classifieds cluttered with unreliable information. Although professional horsemen have been slow to use computers and the Internet, the rise of smartphones and tablet computers has helped increase their comfort level with technology.

The Exchange took all of these things into account, and Aslin went further. In order to remain true to her business goal of providing a *reliable* service to professionals in the horse industry that would become a source of good horses described accurately, Aslin personally reviewed all potential advertisers. In some cases she went back to sellers and insisted on higher quality photographs and video, and in other cases where she determined the horse was not as represented, she turned down their business. The initial business plan process involved strict screening, and it meant turning away money and valuing quality over quantity in every area—horses, buyers, traffic, and ads. It was a hard and expensive premise to adhere to when building a reputation from scratch, but through persistence and dedication it has worked, and today, The Exchange's reputation and "brand" has become one of its most valuable assets.

In discussing some of the obstacles she faced in getting The Exchange up and running, Aslin starts with education—her own or lack thereof, specifically in the areas of graphic design and Web technology. While she knew what professional horsemen needed, she did not know how to translate that into graphic design or onto the Web. She says that looking back on the original logo and print designs is "a painful exercise," but she is happy with the current direction.

The budget was also an initial obstacle, as there wasn't a lot of money to spend up front. However, in hindsight, she believes that gave her an advantage because she had to learn what her market wanted and was able to do so without breaking the bank. Conversely, her main competitor took an opposite track, spent big up front, missed the mark with customers, and is now defunct.

In addition, she faced the negative perception among industry professionals and prospective buyers that equine Internet advertising was "worthless." Further, much of her target audience barely knew how to use a computer, didn't have e-mail addresses, and had been doing business in the same old-school manner for decades. For a few key players this worked very well, but it left a void for those outside that inner circle to move horses. Through a combination of knowledge of the marketplace, on-the-job training, perseverance, and listening to what the market was telling her, The Exchange has successfully begun to fill that void.

Here's how it works. The Exchange handles advertising for sellers and trainers across the country. In 2014, show horses advertised on The Exchange are typically priced from $15,000 to $250,000. The recession caused prices to fall significantly, but the prices in certain parts of the market have started to rebound. The Exchange specializes strictly in hunter-jumper show horses, and specifically those suited for high-level competition.

Trainers/sellers who sign up for a premium listing pay a flat $250 fee for the initial advertisement and a subscription fee of $35/month, which includes a listing on The Exchange's Web site featuring the horse's details, photos, show record, lineage, and videos. The Exchange provides copy-writing services and professionally edits all videos supplied by sellers, hosting them on its private server and making them available to download, embed, and share. Each listing typically takes 8–10 hours to prepare. In 2012, The Exchange added a second listing alternative—a Sale Barn listing for $300 a month or $3,000 a year, that allows for listing of up to 10 horses. A three-month commitment is required, but there are no initial or other fees. Aimed at high-volume operations with frequent turnover, the Sale Barn page can link to the seller's Web site, YouTube, Facebook, and Twitter feeds, if available, with the goal of increasing overall brand awareness for the seller's business. Aslin designed the Sale Barn as an affordable option for professionals who might otherwise be reluctant to spend on marketing. International sellers are given a slight additional discount.

Statistics show that a horse's first month online is most successful in terms of the number of Web page visits. With the addition of monthly campaign management, The Exchange helps keep each horse's marketing fresh and up to date. Updates can immediately escalate a horse's popularity as much as 30% and attract new potential buyers. Sellers are encouraged to provide updates as frequently as possible. Online videos add to the brand of the horse for sale and are especially important for young horses or those "growing into" their price tags. Updates are added to the Web site and promoted through various media outlets including Facebook and e-mail campaigns.

Sellers currently fill out two separate forms: a credit card registration form and an equine fact sheet. The fact sheet includes a long series of checkboxes from which sellers select preworded traits, coupled with space for additional written descriptions. This saves some production time, although writing the actual copy is still a major part of the value that The Exchange provides. To implement this option, Aslin spent time investigating form-building tools. Custom-built form solutions were likely to be too expensive, so she played with numerous online form generators and ultimately was able to find some that offered great functionality at a relatively low cost. So, for example, a seller can indicate that the horse is a "jumper" and questions specific to jumpers will be displayed.

The Exchange develops a specific marketing strategy for each horse listed. This includes reviewing information submitted, combing through a horse's official show record, considering impartial impressions, and identifying the most likely buyers. If The Exchange thinks that the photos or videos don't help to sell the horse, they advise the seller on how to improve them. This advice stems from experience in marketing all types of horses from coast to coast, and an understanding of varied buyer profiles and geographic trends that exist in the market.

Social marketing forms the core of the Exchange's marketing efforts. Starting in 2009, The Exchange began experimenting with social media including RSS feeds, YouTube, Facebook, Twitter, and now, Pinterest. Aslin notes that when she began The Exchange, social media was not yet the phenomenon that it is today, but when its significance started to became apparent, she had no choice but to jump in and begin using it, learning as she went. The Exchange has experienced varying success with social media. For instance, The Exchange runs multiple RSS feeds through the free service, FeedBurner, although thus far, the equestrian set does not appear to be particularly interested in RSS feed subscriptions. The company's YouTube channel has been largely supplanted by a professional video management system from Vzaar that hosts all of its videos, serves to most smartphones, and provides more control, branding, and flexibility than YouTube without any annoying advertisements. Facebook has been the most resounding social media success. For the first nine months of 2014, Facebook generated over 50,000 visits to The Exchange's Web site, 57% from desktop users and 43% from mobile users (traffic from Facebook's mobile site was up 200% during the first six months of 2014, compared to the first six months of 2013). About 18% of visitors from Facebook were new visitors. Aslin reports good results using Facebook's Boost Page Post Ads option. The Exchange now has almost 7,500 Likes on Facebook. In addition, Aslin's personal Facebook friends, which number over 1,400, extend her cumulative Facebook reach to almost 9,000 friends and fans, and make her online marketing efforts even more personal. The Exchange's Twitter account has more than 1,800 followers, and links with both The Exchange's

Facebook page and its YouTube channel. The YouTube channel has over 300 subscribers, and almost 40,000 views. The latest social media platform now in The Exchange's sights is Pinterest, which Aslin believes may be very beneficial, because visuals such as photos and video play such an important role in the marketing of show horses. Because every business is different, The Exchange's experience suggests it's important for e-commerce sites to experiment with social media to determine which outlets are most effective in reaching their specific target audiences. The Exchange's successful use of social media in the equestrian industry was recognized when it was named one of 10 finalists for the 2012 PagePlay Equestrian Social Media Awards for best use of social media in North America.

To track the effectiveness of her social marketing efforts, Aslin uses various tracking systems. For instance, Google Analytics allows her to track exactly how many people are on the ExchangeHunterJumper site in real time and how they got there. Aslin has found that focusing solely on Likes is not sufficient. For example, she notes that a photo she posted advertising a horse on Facebook generated only 10 Likes, but that actually almost 150 people followed the link associated with the photo to the ExchangeHunterJumper Web site. She also uses a short URL service, bit.ly, to create unique URLs associated with Facebook and other social media posts that have built-in click trackers. This enables her to quickly see the collective success of her social marketing efforts; in a good month, bit.ly stats show around 5,000 click-throughs to the ExchangeHunterJumper site.

Another challenge is developing the actual social media content, which needs to be presented in such as way as to attract attention, and determining the optimal amount and timing of new content to post each day. Aslin notes that if she posts too many times a day, or posts too much content too close together, the reach of her posts seems to drop off.

Although Facebook is currently the primary social marketing platform for ExchangeHunterJumper, the firm also has loyal followers on Twitter. Although Aslin doubts that many of these followers are actual buyers or sellers at this time, she notes that in the future they probably will be. Her site has grown up along with her clientele, and children who once drooled over ponies on her site are now, 8 years later, soon-to-be adults and, possibly, young professionals.

The firm's Web site is also a key element of its e-commerce presence. Aslin continually reviews the design of the Web site with an eye to making it the most effective marketing tool possible. She built the original site herself in 2005 and updated it almost yearly in response to her target market's needs. In 2012, Aslin relaunched the site for a fifth time, and for the first time ever hired a professional Web development team to convert the static HTML site into a dynamically driven content management system on the Expression Engine platform. While she was able to keep costs low by designing and developing the site's CSS layout, the advanced functionality that was desired, such as the sale horse filter that enables shoppers to sort horses based on price, location, gender, type, and size, still required a hefty five-figure investment. Aslin believes the ability to get to know the market and update the site accordingly has kept The Exchange fresh and innovative. Every iteration of the Web site has been focused on meeting the target market's needs. For instance, she has also spent considerable time

SOURCES: Exchangehunterjumper. com, accessed September 21, 2014; Interview with Amber Aslin, founder of ExchangeHunterJumper, September 2014, September 2013, and September 2012.

and expense to make sure The Exchange's Web site, including video, works just as well on mobile devices as it does on a traditional laptop or desktop computer. Aslin has scrapped plans to create a stand-alone mobile site in favor of using responsive design techniques for The Exchange's site. And possibly on the horizon—browser-friendly 30-inch TV screens! Although potentially representing a whole new environment that would need to be designed for, Aslin believes it would actually be a great tool for her particular industry, given that it is so video reliant.

In addition to the Web site, The Exchange uses a variety of other marketing strategies, including e-mail campaigns, magazine advertising, and word of mouth. It recently ceased distributing its four-color, printed National Sales List booklet due to its high cost, and now relies almost totally on various types of online marketing. Aslin has found it has been extremely helpful to have the Web development experience she has honed over the years. Here are some of her words of wisdom: She feels that entrepreneurs don't necessarily have to know how to build sites, but do need to be familiar with what is and what is not possible in site construction. It is important to understand which functions are complicated and which are not, so that overly complicated add-ons that don't really add to the user experience can be eliminated from tight budgets. It's also important to know what technology is popular now and what technology is just around the corner. Even if you think you are proficient in all the tasks you will need to launch your business, with the rapid pace of technology, you inevitably spend much of your time learning something totally new, whether you want to or not.

By paying attention to these words of wisdom, as well as to detail at every step of the marketing process, The Exchange has managed to build a successful brand, one the horse community has come to rely upon.

Case Study Questions

1. Find a site on the Web that offers classified ads for horses. Compare this site to exchangehunterjumper.com in terms of the services offered (the customer value proposition). What does The Exchange offer that other sites do not?

2. In what ways were social media effective in promoting The Exchange brand? Which media led to the highest increase in sales and inquiries? Why?

3. Make a list of all the ways The Exchange attempts to personalize its services to both buyers and sellers.

7.6 REVIEW

KEY CONCEPTS

■ Understand the difference between traditional online marketing and the new social-mobile-local marketing platforms and the relationships between social, mobile, and local marketing.

- Social, mobile, and local marketing have transformed the online marketing landscape. The major trends and concepts include:
  - The emphasis in online marketing has shifted from exposing consumers to messages towards engaging them in conversations about your brand.
  - Social marketing means all things social: listening, discussing, interacting, empathizing, and engaging the consumer.
  - Social marketing and advertising is not simply a "new ad channel," but a collection of technology-based tools for communicating with shoppers.
  - In the past, businesses could tightly control their brand messaging and lead consumers down a funnel of cues that ended in a purchase. This is no longer the case. Instead, consumer purchase decisions are increasingly driven by the conversations, choices, tastes, and opinions of the consumer's social network.
  - Social, mobile, and local marketing are the fastest growing forms of online marketing.
- Social, mobile, and local digital marketing are self-reinforcing and connected.
- As mobile devices become more powerful, they are more useful for accessing Facebook and other social sites.
- Local and mobile marketing are highly related: local advertisers most often target mobile devices.
- The strong ties among social, mobile, and local marketing have significant implications for managing a marketing campaign in this new environment. When you design a social marketing campaign, you must also consider that your customers will be accessing the campaign using mobile devices, and often they will also be looking for local content.

■ Understand the social marketing process from fan acquisition to sales and the marketing capabilities of social marketing platforms such as Facebook, Twitter, and Pinterest.

- In social marketing, the objective is to encourage your potential customers to become fans of your company's products and services and engage with your business by entering into a conversation with it.
- There are five steps in the social marketing process model: fan acquisition, engagement, amplification, community, and brand strength and sales.
- Facebook is a social network with over 1.3 billion members. Facebook is designed to encourage people to reveal as much personal information about themselves as feasible, including activities, behavior, photos, music, movies, and purchases.
- Facebook's features are built to maximize the connections among people in the form of notifications, tagging, messaging, posting, and sharing. In many instances, the movement of personal information is so widespread that it is beyond the understanding of users.
- Social density refers to the number of interactions among members of a group and reflects the "connectedness" of a group, even if these connections are forced on users.
- Facebook has many marketing tools, including the Like button, Brand Pages, News Feed ads, Right-hand sidebar ads, mobile ads, and Facebook Exchange.
- The effectiveness of Facebook ads can be measured using five stages of social marketing model: fan acquisition, engagement, amplification, community, and ultimately brand strengthening and sales.
- Twitter is a micro-blogging social network site that allows users to send and receive 140-character messages as well as videos, photos, and article previews.

- Twitter marketing tools include Promoted Tweets, Promoted Trends, Promoted Accounts, Enhanced Profile Pages, the Twitter Amplify program, television ad retargeting, Lead Generation Cards, and app install and app engagement ads.
- Measuring the results of Twitter marketing is similar to measuring the results of Facebook and other social marketing platforms, with some minor changes to account for the unique qualities of Twitter.
- Pinterest is the social network site that provides users with an online board to which they can "pin" interesting pictures. The success of Pinterest is based in part on a shift in consumer behavior enabled by new technologies: people talk about brands using pictures rather than words.
- Pinterest marketing tools include Promoted Pins; adding a Pin It logo to your Web site; pinning photos to Pinterest and direct users to your Web site; creating theme-based Pin It boards; placing URLs to stores that you support and receive lead generation fees from; integrating your pins and boards with other social sites; networking with users and followers.
- Pinterest campaigns can be measured using the same procedures as for Facebook and Twitter. The key dimensions to measure are fan (follower) acquisition, engagement, amplification, community, and sales.
- One downside of social marketing is that brands lose a substantial amount of control over where their ads appear in terms of other content and what people say about their brands on social sites.

■ **Identify the key elements of a mobile marketing campaign.**

- Although still in its infancy, mobile marketing involves the use of mobile devices such as smartphones and tablet computers to display banner ads, rich media, video, games, e-mail, text messaging, in-store messaging, QuickResponse (QR) codes, and couponing.
- Mobile devices represent a radical departure from previous marketing technologies simply because the devices integrate so many human and consumer activities from telephoning or texting friends, to listening to music, watching videos, and using the Web to shop and purchase goods.
- The mobile platform has changed over the past few years, and there are now almost as many tablet users as smartphone users in the United States.
- Mobile users spend over 85% of their mobile minutes using apps, and only 15% using their browsers. Marketers need to place ads in apps where consumers spend most of their time.
- Mobile devices create a multi-screen world: smartphones, tablets, desktops, and television. The reality, and the future, of computing devices is that consumers will be multi-platform: using desktops and laptops at work and home, and smartphones and tablets at home as well as when moving about.
- The implications of the multi-device platform, or screen diversity, environment are that marketing needs to be designed for whatever device the consumer is using, and consistent branding across platforms will be important.
- Unlike social marketing, mobile marketing does not require a great deal of new marketing vocabulary. All the marketing formats available on the desktop are also available on mobile devices. With few exceptions, mobile marketing is very much like desktop marketing—except it is smaller, mobile, and with the user all the time.
- The major marketing opportunities in mobile marketing are search ads, display ads, videos and rich media, messaging (SMS/MMS/PPS), and other familiar formats like e-mail, classified, and lead generation.
- The effectiveness of mobile marketing can be measured using the dimensions of the social marketing process model: fan acquisition, engagement, amplification, community, brand strength, and sales. Traditional Web-browser based metrics also can be used when measuring mobile campaigns.

■ **Understand the capabilities of location-based local marketing.**

- Location-based marketing is the targeting of marketing messages to users based on their location. Generally, location-based marketing involves marketing of location-based services.

- Examples of location-based services are personal navigation, point-of-interest, reviews, friend-finder, and family-tracker services.
- Location-based marketing is dependent on two technologies: accurate mapping software and mobile device geo-positioning technologies like GPS, Wi-Fi network location data, and Bluetooth low energy (BLE) technology.
- Location-based mobile marketing is currently a small part of the online marketing environment, but is expected to double over the next two years, and is growing far faster than any other form of digital advertising.
- The ad formats used in local mobile marketing are familiar—search ads, display, social/native advertising, video, and SMS text messages. A very large percentage of these local mobile ads will be delivered by search engines such as Google, and social sites such as Facebook.
- The key players in location-based mobile marketing are the same giants of advertising who dominate the mobile marketing environment: Google, Facebook, Apple, Twitter, YP (formerly Yellow Pages), Pandora, and Millenial.
- Geo-aware techniques identify the location of a user's device and then target marketing to the device, recommending actions within reach.
- Geo-targeting of ads involves sending ads based on the user's location.
- Proximity marketing techniques identify a perimeter around a physical location, and then target ads to users within that perimeter, recommending actions possible within the fenced-in area.
- In-store messaging involves messaging consumers while entering and browsing in a retail store. This requires a very precise calculation of location.
- Consumers who seek information about local businesses using mobile devices are much more active and ready to purchase than desktop users.
- Measuring the effectiveness of location-based mobile campaigns involves using the same techniques used for browser-based search and display ads (impressions), but also should include the dimensions of the social marketing process model such as acquisition, engagement, amplification, community, and brand strength and sales.

QUESTIONS

1. How and why has online marketing changed since 2007?
2. What are the difficulties in differentiating the social, local, and mobile marketing channels?
3. What is meant by the social marketing term *amplification,* and how is it created and measured?
4. What is meant by the term *conversation* as it applies to online marketing and how do businesses engage in a conversation?
5. What does the term *dark social* refer to?
6. Identify and describe the first step in a social marketing campaign.
7. How would you measure the brand strength of a Facebook marketing campaign?
8. What marketing opportunities does Facebook's News Feed feature offer?
9. Which of Facebook's various marketing tools is the most important to social marketing, and why?
10. How would you measure engagement for your Twitter marketing campaign?
11. From a business perspective, what are the disadvantages or challenges in social marketing?
12. How has Lands' End used Pinterest for marketing?
13. List and briefly describe some of Pinterest's marketing tools.
14. How effective are Facebook ads in comparison to other traditional online marketing channels?
15. Describe Twitter's Lead Generation Card feature and how it differs from a display ad.
16. Why are in-app ads so important to marketers?
17. What are social ads?
18. What kinds of ad formats are found on mobile devices?

19. What is the effect of the growing "multi-screen environment" on e-commerce and marketing?
20. What is Apple's iBeacon technology and how does it differ from using QR codes?

PROJECTS

1. Visit the Web sites of at least two different online companies. Make a list of the social, mobile, and local marketing efforts you see on the Web site. Do their pages display Like it! plug-ins, and/or Google +1 logos? Do they have a Facebook page? If so, visit the pages to see how they use their Facebook pages. Is it different from their Web site pages? Can you identify how the firms use mobile marketing? Use your smartphone or tablet to access their Web sites. Are their Web sites designed specifically for each platform? In conclusion, compare and critically contrast these firms, and make recommendations for how you, as a marketing manager, would improve their effectiveness.

2. Visit your Facebook page and examine the ads shown in the right margin. What is being advertised and how do you believe it is relevant to your interests or online behavior? Make a list of ads appearing in your News Feed. Are these ads appropriately targeted to you in terms of your demographics, interests, and past purchases? Go to at least two Web sites, and Like it or Like a product. In the next 24 hours, do you see marketing messages on Facebook related to your Likes?

3. Visit two Web sites of your choice and apply the social marketing process model to both. Critically compare and contrast the effectiveness of these sites in terms of the dimensions of the social marketing process. How well do these sites acquire fans, generate engagement, amplify responses, create a community, and strengthen their brands? What recommendations can you make for these sites to improve their effectiveness?

4. Identify two Pinterest brand pages. Identify how they use Pinterest marketing tools described in this chapter. Are there some tools they are not using? What recommendations can you make for these sites to improve their Pinterest marketing campaigns?

REFERENCES

Aaker, D. A. "Measuring Brand Equity across products and markets." *California Management Review*, Vol 38, No. 3, pp. 102–20. (1996).

Ailawadi, Kusum L., Donald R. Lehmann, and Scott A Neslin. "Revenue Premium as an Outcome Measure of Brand Equity." *Journal of Marketing*, 67 (October), 1–17 (October 2003).

AOL/BBDO/Insights Now. "Seven Shades of Mobile: The Hidden Motivations of Mobile Users." (October 2012).

BIA/Kelsey. "US Local Media Ad Revenues to Grow from $133.2B in 2013 to $158.6B in 2018." (April 28, 2014a).

BIA/Kelsey. "U.S. Mobile Local Ad Revenues to Reach $4.5 Billion in 2014." (April 10, 2014b).

comScore. "The U.S. Mobile App Report." (2014).

comScore. "U.S. Digital Future in Focus 2013." (February 2013).

comScore/Facebook. "The Power of Like: How Brands Reach and Influence Fans Through Social Marketing." White Paper (October 21, 2012).

eMarketer, Inc. "US Ad Spending: Q2 2014 Forecast and Comparative Estimates." (July 8, 2014a).

eMarketer, Inc. (Alison McCarthy). "US Mobile Users: 2014 Complete Forecast." (April 2014b).

eMarketer, Inc. (Alison McCarthy). "US Tablet Users: Q1 2014 Forecast and Comparative Estimates." (May 7, 2014c)

eMarketer, Inc. (Catherine Boyle). "Mcommerce Deep Dive: The Products and Tactics Fueling Growth." (July 15, 2014d).

eMarketer, Inc. "US B2C Mcommerce Sales, 2012–2018." (April 2014e).

eMarketer, Inc. "After Success, More Spending on Mobile Local Ads." (April 17, 2014f).

eMarketer, Inc. (Krista Garcia) "How Beacons Are Changing Mobile Marketing." (July 2014g).

eMarketer, Inc. (Yory Wurmser) "Proximity Marketing in Retail." (April 2014h).

eMarketer, Inc. (Alison McCarthy) "Worldwide Ad Spending: Q3 2014 Forecast and Comparative Estimates. (October 2014v).

eMarketer, Inc. (Karin von Abrams) "Western Europe Digital Ad Spending: Steady Overall Gains Mask Slower Progress in Italy and Spain. (November 2014w).

eMarketer, Inc. "eMarketer Estimates for Mobile Phone Users, Smartphone Users and Tablet Users." (Accessed December 6, 2014x)

eMarketer, Inc. "UK B2C Ecommerce 2014 Midyear Update: Digital Purchasing Thrives Amidst an Improving Economy." (June 2014y).

eMarketer, Inc. (Robert Andrews) "UK Mobile Ad Spending 2014: On Course to Dent Desktop and Topple TV as Leading Channel." (September 2014z).

eMarketer, Inc. "Time Spent on Social Network Sites by US Internet Users, Nov 2012 (millions of minutes)." (January 16, 2013a).

eMarketer, Inc. (Krista Garcia). "Facebook Commerce: Evolving, Not Extinct." (April 2013b).

eMarketer, Inc. "Net US Mobile Internet Ad Revenue Share, by Company, 2011–2015." (June 1, 2013c).

Ernoult Emeric. "Guide to Facebook Reach: What Marketers Need to Know." Socialmediaexaminer.com (March 3, 2014).

Google, Inc. "Understanding Consumers' Local Search Behavior." (May 2014).

Google, Inc. "The New Multiscreen World." (August 2012).

IAB (Interactive Advertising Bureau). "Response Design and Ad Creative: An IAB Perspective." (September 2012).

Internet Retailer. "The Mobile 200 2015 Edition." (2014).

Keller, K. L. (1993), "Conceptualizing, Measuring and Managing Customer-Based Brand Equity." *Journal of Marketing*, Vol 57, January, pp 1–22.

Macy's. "Macy's Outlines New Omnichannel Strategy and Tech." Internetretailer.com (September 18, 2014).

Nielsen. "Smartphones: So Many Apps, So Much Time." Nielsen (July 1, 2014).

Ong, Josh. "Facebook Now Has 399 Million Users Who Login Only From Mobile Devices." Thenextweb.com (July 23, 3014).

Simon, C. J., and M. J. Sullivan. The Measurement and Determinants of Brand Equity: A Financial Approach, *Marketing Science*, Vol. 12, No 1, pp. 28–52. (1993).

Taylor, Chris. "The Thumb Is Gone: Facebook Like Button Gets a Makeover." Mashable.com (November 6, 2013).

Twitter, Inc. "Report on Form 10-k for the fiscal year ended December 31, 2014 filed with the Securities and Exchange Commission." (March 6, 2014).

Vahl, Andrea. "Boost Posts or Promoted Posts on Facebook: Which is Better?" Socialexaminer.com (May 5, 2014).

Vega, Tanzina, and Leslie Kaufman. "The Distasteful Side of Social Media Puts Advertisers on Their Guard." *New York Times* (June 3, 2013).

CHAPTER 8

Ethics, Law, and E-commerce

LEARNING OBJECTIVES

After reading this chapter, you will be able to:

- Understand why e-commerce raises ethical, social, and political issues.
- Understand basic concepts related to privacy and information rights, the practices of e-commerce companies that threaten privacy, and the different methods that can be used to protect online privacy.
- Understand the various forms of intellectual property and the challenges involved in protecting it.
- Understand how the Internet is governed and why taxation of e-commerce raises governance and jurisdiction issues.
- Identify major public safety and welfare issues raised by e-commerce.

The EU Objects

to Google's New Privacy Policy

Google, by all accounts, is the largest collector of personal private information on earth by virtue of its search engine, which is used by an estimated 1.2 billion searchers who generate about 115 billion searches each month. Arguably, Google's collection of personal information dwarfs that of any national government. In addition, Google offers over 60 other products and services to Internet users, from Google Maps, the Google+ social network, YouTube, Gmail, to Google Voice. Every hour

© fotodo/Fotolia.com

of every day, users of Google's many services generate thousands of data points that are stored in Google's computers somewhere in the world. For instance, the videos users watch on YouTube (over one billion visitors a month); the phone calls made on Google Voice; the emails sent via Gmail (425 million users worldwide); the Web sites users visit using Chrome, Google's browser (now with a 60% market share, and over 400 million mobile users alone); the personal news and opinions users share with friends using Google+ (350 million active users); and the places they visit that are recorded by the Google Maps app (the most popular smartphone app with a 43% market share and about 250 million mobile users).

In prior years, each of Google's products and services had its own login and maintained its own silo of personal information. Each product and service had its own privacy policy. In part this reflects the fact that some of Google's growth had come through the acquisition of companies with their own logins and privacy policies. In part, the "silo" nature of Google also fit in with Google's privacy policies in its early years, when it purportedly sought to avoid an integrated, all-encompassing "Big Brother" Web presence. Initially, for instance, Google did not use the content of users' Gmail for advertising purposes. On the other hand, for a user trying to understand how Google used personal private information, having over 60 different products and services, each with its own logins, privacy and information use policies, complicated the lives of consumers and diminished the consumer experience. This prior policy also made it difficult to Google to formulate a single coherent privacy policy.

In 2012, Google announced a new worldwide privacy policy that eliminated all the separate policies. The new policy also made clear that Google was doing something that it had in fact been doing since 2011: combining the information collected on individuals by its separate products and services into a virtual single file so customer information generated at one service, say YouTube, could be used by all other Google services.

The change in privacy policy was also coordinated with a change in login procedures that had been in the works for several years as Google management sought to rationalize its array of services from a multiple-login ID process to a single Google account login that would give users access to all Google services. Since 2011, for instance, YouTube users have been required to login to a separate Google+ account if they want to login into YouTube services. When users create a user account, they automatically create a Gmail account and automatically join Google+. In this sense, the new emphasis on a single point of entry to Google's services mirrors that of Facebook where there is a single login to a variety of services that Facebook has added to over time. In addition, a single login allows Google to cross-sell its services by automatically enrolling new accounts into various services. At the same time, the new pooling of personal information into a single account allows Google to sell more and better-targeted advertising based on a more detailed, fine-grained understanding of its users.

Despite its earlier statements supporting separate and unique services and accounts, by January 2012 Google had arrived at a position of becoming an all-encompassing, integrated Web presence that surrounded its users with a bevy of services, but also collected an extraordinary amount of personal information from multiple consumer activities.

Within days of Google announcing its new privacy policy, EU authorities announced an investigation into the changes. France's data protection agency, CNIL, took the lead in a Europe-wide investigation of Google's pooling data on users gathered at any of its Web service sites. The CNIL expressed doubts about the lawfulness and fairness of Google's processing of information from all its sites, and doubted it was in compliance with European data protection legislation. The European Commission had just recently overhauled its 17-year-old data protection rules in January 2012. Under the proposed new EU privacy rules (the General Data Protection Regulation), firms like Facebook, Google, Apple, and others that gather personal information would be required to ask users for their permission to store and sell their data to other businesses and advertisers. Firms are required to be transparent about how they use personal information. This is anathema to firms whose entire business model is based on the ability to use whatever personal information can be collected for business purposes, such as selling advertising or products and services.

In February 2012, CNIL requested that Google delay implementing its new privacy policy. Google claimed its new policy was in compliance with EU laws, and implemented the policy on March 1, 2012 despite objections from EU authorities. In the United States, a similar reaction occurred, with eight lawmakers sending a letter to Google management objecting to the consolidation of user information and the potential for endangering consumers' privacy. Google has argued that users can search anonymously or while logged out of any Google service to avoid being tracked by Google, and they can use separate accounts on different Google services to keep their personal data in separate silos and avoid it falling into a pooled set of data. Users can control their ad preferences to some extent, and turn off their Web history.

In October 2012, 27 EU national privacy regulators sent a letter to Larry Page, the CEO of Google, asking Google to modify its privacy policy and bring it into compliance with EU data protection laws and concerns. Claiming Google's new policy permitted an unprecedented combination of data across different Google services, the regulators asked Google to modify its policy so that users would have a clearer understanding of what personal data is being collected, and can better control how that information will be used by Google and advertising firms. The regulators claimed that Google's new privacy policy did not give users any idea about how the information is being used or processed, or stored. On the matter of consent, the regulators disagreed with Google's claim that it was collecting personal data with the users' consent, only when users "opted in." The regulators pointed out that "opting in" for Google meant clicking the "I Agree" button before using a service. If the user wants to use the service, there is no option to opt out of Google's use of their personal information. The only way to maintain their privacy is to not use the service. By clicking "I Agree," users have to agree to allow Google to use their personal information without limitations and without really knowing how that information will be used or treated. The regulators gave Google three months to respond to their requests for a change in policy. Google responded by saying that it already complied with EU law and that it had worked closely with the CNIL to ensure its policies were lawful.

In February 2013, privacy regulators from France and other EU nations escalated their efforts by calling for "repressive actions," mostly fines. In June, the CNIL issued a 15-page order finding that Google's use of personal data violated French law, and ordered six remedies, including disclosing how long it retains each type of user data, providing user consent to gather data, and stopping the combination of data from different Google services without a legal basis. It once again gave Google three months to make changes in its policy. Google, as it had previously, responded by issuing a statement claiming that it was fully compliant with EU and French law. In September 2013, the CNIL initiated a court-like proceeding against Google seeking fines for failure to comply with the law. The agency can impose fines of up to €150,000, which is a pittance for a $50 billion firm like Google. However, the agency is considering classifying every Google user in France as an infraction. This would multiply the fine to a size that Google would likely take seriously.

European privacy authorities are pressing their case against Google's privacy policies. In September 2014, the main European agency for privacy regulation wrote a letter to Larry Page warning the company that it was failing to meet its privacy obligations throughout Europe. The regulators suggested Google offer users a simple switch that would allow them to turn off Google's ability to mix data from its many services. The letter also claimed Google had failed to properly implement the decision of Europe's highest court, the European Court of Justice in Luxembourg, which in June 2014 supported a Spanish lower court decision declaring that individuals have the "right to be forgotten" and can request search services like Google to expunge their personal information from Google's search engine. Google initially resisted this idea, but began implementing the policy in Europe only, and by November 2014, had processed over 180,000 requests from individuals to remove their records. In December 2014, the French data protection authority declared that Google must implement the right to be forgotten across the globe and not just in Europe.

SOURCES: "French Official Campaigns to Make 'Right to be Forgotten' Global, by Mark Scott, *New York Times*, December 3, 2014; "E.U. Parliament Passes Measure to Break Up Google in Symbolic Vote," by James Kanter, *New York Times*, November 27, 2014; "The Solace of Oblivion: In Europe, the Right to Be Forgotten Trumps the Internet," by Jeffrey Toobin, *The New Yorker*, September 29, 2014; European Court Lets Users Erase Records on Web," by David Streitfeld, *New York Times*, May 13, 2014; "Google Plus Creates Uproar Over Forced YouTube Integration," by Paul Tassal, *Forbes*, November 9, 2013; French Privacy Agency Moves to Sanction Google," by Sam Schneider, *Wall Street Journal*, September 27, 2013; Google Spain SL and Google Inc. v Agencia Española de Protección de Datos (AEPD), Case C-131/12, June 25, 2013; "Privacy Policy," Google.com/policies/privacy, June 24, 2013; "Google Privacy Comes Under Fire From European Watchdogs," by Sam Schechner, *Wall Street Journal*, June 20, 2013; "Google Faces More Inquiries in Europe Over Privacy," by Eric Pfanner, *Wall Street Journal*, April 2, 2013; "EU Regulators Weigh New Google Crackdown," by Sam Schechner, *Wall Street Journal*, February 18, 2013; "Europe Presses Google to Change Privacy Policy," by Eric Pfanner and Kevin O'Brien, *New York Times*, October 16, 2012; "Updating Our Privacy Policies and Terms of Service," January 24, 2012;. Googleblog. blogspot.com.

D etermining how or whether personal information should be retained or deleted on the Internet is just one of many ethical, social, and political issues raised by the rapid evolution of the Internet and e-commerce. For instance, as discussed in the opening case, should Google be allowed to go business in such a way that the EU feels it threatens citizens' privacy? These questions are not just ethical questions that we as individuals have to answer; they also involve social institutions such as family, schools, business firms, and in some cases, entire nation-states. And these questions have obvious political dimensions because they involve collective choices about how we should live and what laws we would like to live under.

In this chapter, we discuss the ethical, social, and political issues raised in e-commerce, provide a framework for organizing the issues, and make recommendations for managers who are given the responsibility of operating e-commerce companies within commonly accepted standards of appropriateness.

8.1   UNDERSTANDING ETHICAL, SOCIAL, AND POLITICAL ISSUES IN E-COMMERCE

The Internet and its use in e-commerce have raised pervasive ethical, social, and political issues on a scale unprecedented for computer technology. Entire sections of daily newspapers and weekly magazines are devoted to the social impact of the Internet. But why is this so? Why is the Internet at the root of so many contemporary controversies? Part of the answer lies in the underlying features of Internet technology itself, and the ways in which it has been exploited by business firms. Internet technology and its use in e-commerce disrupt existing social and business relationships and understandings.

Consider for instance Table 1.2 (in Chapter 1), which lists the unique features of Internet technology. Instead of considering the business consequences of each unique feature, **Table 8.1** examines the actual or potential ethical, social, and/or political consequences of the technology.

We live in an "information society," where power and wealth increasingly depend on information and knowledge as central assets. Controversies over information are often disagreements over power, wealth, influence, and other things thought to be valuable. Like other technologies, such as steam, electricity, telephones, and television, the Internet and e-commerce can be used to achieve social progress, and for the most part, this has occurred. However, the same technologies can be used to commit crimes, despoil the environment, and threaten cherished social values. Before automobiles, there was very little interstate crime and very little federal jurisdiction over crime. Likewise with the Internet: before the Internet, there was very little "cybercrime."

Many business firms and individuals are benefiting from the commercial development of the Internet, but this development also exacts a price from individuals, organizations, and societies. These costs and benefits must be carefully considered by those seeking to make ethical and socially responsible decisions in this new envi-

TABLE 8.1	UNIQUE FEATURES OF E-COMMERCE TECHNOLOGY AND THEIR POTENTIAL ETHICAL, SOCIAL, AND/OR POLITICAL IMPLICATIONS
E-COMMERCE TECHNOLOGY DIMENSION	**POTENTIAL ETHICAL, SOCIAL, AND POLITICAL SIGNIFICANCE**
Ubiquity—Internet/Web technology is available everywhere: at work, at home, and elsewhere via mobile devices, anytime.	Work and shopping can invade family life; shopping can distract workers at work, lowering productivity; use of mobile devices can lead to automobile and industrial accidents. Presents confusing issues of "nexus" to taxation authorities.
Global reach—The technology reaches across national boundaries, around the Earth.	Reduces cultural diversity in products; weakens local small firms while strengthening large global firms; moves manufacturing production to low-wage areas of the world; weakens the ability of all nations—large and small—to control their information destiny.
Universal standards—There is one set of technology standards, namely Internet standards.	Increases vulnerability to viruses and hacking attacks worldwide, affecting millions of people at once. Increases the likelihood of "information" crime, crimes against systems, and deception.
Richness—Video, audio, and text messages are possible.	A "screen technology" that reduces use of text and potentially the ability to read by focusing instead on video and audio messages. Potentially very persuasive messages that may reduce reliance on multiple independent sources of information.
Interactivity—The technology works through interaction with the user.	The nature of interactivity at commercial sites can be shallow and meaningless. Customer e-mails are frequently not read by human beings. Customers do not really "co-produce" the product as much as they "co-produce" the sale. The amount of "customization" of products that occurs is minimal, occurring within predefined platforms and plug-in options.
Information density—The technology reduces information costs, and raises quality.	While the total amount of information available to all parties increases, so does the possibility of false and misleading information, unwanted information, and invasion of solitude. Trust, authenticity, accuracy, completeness, and other quality features of information can be degraded. The ability of individuals and organizations to make sense out of this plethora of information is limited.
Personalization/Customization—The technology allows personalized messages to be delivered to individuals as well as groups.	Opens up the possibility of intensive invasion of privacy for commercial and governmental purposes that is unprecedented.
Social technology—The technology enables user content generation and social networking.	Creates opportunities for cyberbullying, abusive language, and predation; challenges concepts of privacy, fair use, and consent to use posted information; creates new opportunities for surveillance by authorities and corporations into private lives.

ronment. The question is: How can you as a manager make reasoned judgments about what your firm should do in a number of e-commerce areas—from securing the privacy of your customer's clickstream to ensuring the integrity of your company's domain name?

A MODEL FOR ORGANIZING THE ISSUES

E-commerce—and the Internet—have raised so many ethical, social, and political issues that it is difficult to classify them all, and hence, complicated to see their relationship to one another. Clearly, ethical, social, and political issues are interrelated. One way to organize the ethical, social, and political dimensions surrounding e-commerce is shown in **Figure 8.1**. At the individual level, what appears as an ethical issue—"What should I do?"—is reflected at the social and political levels—"What should we as a society and government do?" The ethical dilemmas you face as a manager of a business using the Web reverberate and are reflected in social and political debates. The major ethical, social, and political issues that have developed around e-commerce over the past 10 years can be loosely categorized into four major dimensions: information rights, property rights, governance, and public safety and welfare.

Some of the ethical, social, and political issues raised in each of these areas include the following:

- **Information rights:** What rights to their own personal information do individuals have in a public marketplace, or in their private homes, when Internet technologies make information collection so pervasive and efficient? What rights do individuals have to access information about business firms and other organizations?
- **Property rights:** How can traditional intellectual property rights be enforced in an Internet world where perfect copies of protected works can be made and easily distributed worldwide in seconds?
- **Governance:** Should the Internet and e-commerce be subject to public laws? And if so, what law-making bodies have jurisdiction—state, federal, and/or international?

FIGURE 8.1	THE MORAL DIMENSIONS OF AN INTERNET SOCIETY

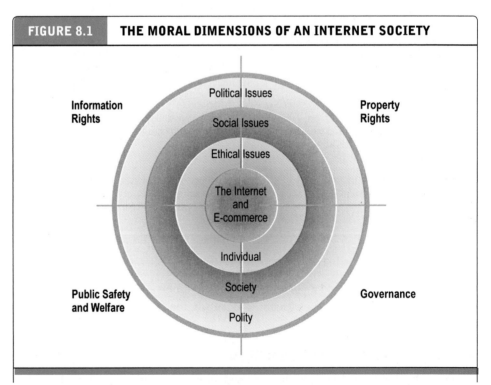

The introduction of the Internet and e-commerce impacts individuals, societies, and political institutions. These impacts can be classified into four moral dimensions: property rights, information rights, governance, and public safety and welfare.

- **Public safety and welfare:** What efforts should be undertaken to ensure equitable access to the Internet and e-commerce channels? Should governments be responsible for ensuring that schools and colleges have access to the Internet? Are certain online content and activities—such as pornography and gambling—a threat to public safety and welfare? Should mobile commerce be allowed from moving vehicles?

To illustrate, imagine that at any given moment, society and individuals are more or less in an ethical equilibrium brought about by a delicate balancing of individuals, social organizations, and political institutions. Individuals know what is expected of them, social organizations such as business firms know their limits, capabilities, and roles, and political institutions provide a supportive framework of market regulation, banking, and commercial law that provides sanctions against violators.

Now, imagine we drop into the middle of this calm setting a powerful new technology such as the Internet and e-commerce. Suddenly, individuals, business firms, and political institutions are confronted by new possibilities of behavior. For instance, individuals discover that they can download perfect digital copies of music tracks from Web sites without paying anyone, something that, under the old technology of CDs, would have been impossible. This can be done, despite the fact that these music tracks still legally belong to the owners of the copyright—musicians and record label companies. Then, business firms discover that they can make a business out of aggregating these digital musical tracks—or creating a mechanism for sharing musical tracks—even though they do not "own" them in the traditional sense. The record companies, courts, and Congress were not prepared at first to cope with the onslaught of online digital copying. Courts and legislative bodies will have to make new laws and reach new judgments about who owns digital copies of copyrighted works and under what conditions such works can be "shared." It may take years to develop new understandings, laws, and acceptable behavior in just this one area of social impact. In the meantime, as an individual and a manager, you will have to decide what you and your firm should do in legal "gray" areas, where there is conflict between ethical principles but no clear-cut legal or cultural guidelines. How can you make good decisions in this type of situation?

Before examining the four moral dimensions of e-commerce in greater depth, we will briefly review some basic concepts of ethical reasoning that you can use as a guide to ethical decision making, and provide general reasoning principles about the social and political issues of the Internet that you will face in the future.

BASIC ETHICAL CONCEPTS: RESPONSIBILITY, ACCOUNTABILITY, AND LIABILITY

Ethics is at the heart of social and political debates about the Internet. **Ethics** is the study of principles that individuals and organizations can use to determine right and wrong courses of action. It is assumed in ethics that individuals are free moral agents who are in a position to make choices. When faced with alternative courses of action, what is the correct moral choice? Extending ethics from individuals to business firms and even entire societies can be difficult, but it is not impossible. As long as there is a decision-making body or individual (such as a board of directors or CEO in a business

ethics

the study of principles that individuals and organizations can use to determine right and wrong courses of action

firm, or a governmental body in a society), their decisions can be judged against a variety of ethical principles.

If you understand some basic ethical principles, your ability to reason about larger social and political debates will be improved. In western culture, there are four basic principles that all ethical schools of thought share: responsibility, accountability, liability, and due process. **Responsibility** means that as free moral agents, individuals, organizations, and societies are responsible for the actions they take. **Accountability** means that individuals, organizations, and societies should be held accountable to others for the consequences of their actions. The third principle—liability—extends the concepts of responsibility and accountability to the area of law. **Liability** is a feature of political systems in which a body of law is in place that permits individuals to recover the damages done to them by other actors, systems, or organizations. **Due process** is a feature of law-governed societies and refers to a process in which laws are known and understood, and there is an ability to appeal to higher authorities to ensure that the laws have been correctly applied.

You can use these concepts immediately to understand some contemporary Internet debates. For instance, consider the 2005 U.S. Supreme Court decision in the case of *Metro-Goldwyn-Mayer Studios v. Grokster, et al.* MGM had sued Grokster and other P2P networks for copyright infringement. The court decided that because the primary and intended use of Internet P2P file-sharing services such as Grokster, StreamCast, and Kazaa was the swapping of copyright-protected music and video files, the file-sharing services should be held accountable and shut down. Although Grokster and the other networks acknowledged that the most common use of the software was for illegal digital music file-swapping, they argued that there were substantial, nontrivial uses of the same networks for legally sharing files. They also argued they should not be held accountable for what individuals do with their software, any more than Sony could be held accountable for how people use VCRs, or Xerox for how people use copying machines. Ultimately, the Supreme Court ruled that Grokster and other P2P networks could be held accountable for the illegal actions of their users if it could be shown that they intended their software to be used for illegal downloading and sharing, and had marketed the software for that purpose. The court relied on copyright laws to arrive at its decisions, but these laws reflect some basic underlying ethical principles of responsibility, accountability, and liability.

Underlying the *Grokster* Supreme Court decision is a fundamental rejection of the notion that the Internet is an ungoverned "Wild West" environment that cannot be controlled. Under certain defined circumstances, the courts will intervene into the uses of the Internet. No organized civilized society has ever accepted the proposition that technology can flaunt basic underlying social and cultural values. Through all of the industrial and technological developments that have taken place, societies have intervened by means of legal and political decisions to ensure that the technology serves socially acceptable ends without stifling the positive consequences of innovation and wealth creation. The Internet in this sense is no different, and we can expect societies around the world to exercise more regulatory control over the

responsibility
as free moral agents, individuals, organizations, and societies are responsible for the actions they take

accountability
individuals, organizations, and societies should be held accountable to others for the consequences of their actions

liability
a feature of political systems in which a body of law is in place that permits individuals to recover the damages done to them by other actors, systems, or organizations

due process
a process in which laws are known and understood and there is an ability to appeal to higher authorities to ensure that the laws have been correctly applied

Internet and e-commerce in an effort to arrive at a new balance between innovation and wealth creation, on the one hand, and other socially desirable objectives on the other. This is a difficult balancing act, and reasonable people will arrive at different conclusions.

ANALYZING ETHICAL DILEMMAS

Ethical, social, and political controversies usually present themselves as dilemmas. A **dilemma** is a situation in which there are at least two diametrically opposed actions, each of which supports a desirable outcome. When confronted with a situation that seems to present an ethical dilemma, how can you analyze and reason about the situation? The following is a five-step process that should help:

dilemma
a situation in which there are at least two diametrically opposed actions, each of which supports a desirable outcome

1. **Identify and clearly describe the facts.** Find out who did what to whom, and where, when, and how. In many instances, you will be surprised at the errors in the initially reported facts, and often you will find that simply getting the facts straight helps define the solution. It also helps to get the opposing parties involved in an ethical dilemma to agree on the facts.

2. **Define the conflict or dilemma and identify the higher-order values involved.** Ethical, social, and political issues always reference higher values. Otherwise, there would be no debate. The parties to a dispute all claim to be pursuing higher values (e.g., freedom, privacy, protection of property, and the free enterprise system). For example, supporters of the use of advertising networks such as DoubleClick argue that the tracking of consumer movements on the Web increases market efficiency and the wealth of the entire society. Opponents argue this claimed efficiency comes at the expense of individual privacy, and advertising networks should cease their activities or offer Web users the option of not participating in such tracking.

3. **Identify the stakeholders.** Every ethical, social, and political issue has stakeholders: players in the game who have an interest in the outcome, who have invested in the situation, and usually who have vocal opinions. Find out the identity of these groups and what they want. This will be useful later when designing a solution.

4. **Identify the options that you can reasonably take.** You may find that none of the options satisfies all the interests involved, but that some options do a better job than others. Sometimes, arriving at a "good" or ethical solution may not always be a balancing of consequences to stakeholders.

5. **Identify the potential consequences of your options.** Some options may be ethically correct but disastrous from other points of view. Other options may work in this one instance but not in other similar instances. Always ask yourself, "What if I choose this option consistently over time?"

Once your analysis is complete, you can refer to the following well-established ethical principles to help decide the matter.

CANDIDATE ETHICAL PRINCIPLES

Although you are the only one who can decide which ethical principles you will follow and how you will prioritize them, it is helpful to consider some ethical principles with deep roots in many cultures that have survived throughout recorded history:

- **The Golden Rule:** Do unto others as you would have them do unto you. Putting yourself into the place of others and thinking of yourself as the object of the decision can help you think about fairness in decision making.

- **Universalism:** If an action is not right for all situations, then it is not right for any specific situation (Immanuel Kant's categorical imperative). Ask yourself, "If we adopted this rule in every case, could the organization, or society, survive?"

- **Slippery Slope:** If an action cannot be taken repeatedly, then it is not right to take at all. An action may appear to work in one instance to solve a problem, but if repeated, would result in a negative outcome. In plain English, this rule might be stated as "once started down a slippery path, you may not be able to stop."

- **Collective Utilitarian Principle:** Take the action that achieves the greater value for all of society. This rule assumes you can prioritize values in a rank order and understand the consequences of various courses of action.

- **Risk Aversion:** Take the action that produces the least harm, or the least potential cost. Some actions have extremely high failure costs of very low probability (e.g., building a nuclear generating facility in an urban area) or extremely high failure costs of moderate probability (speeding and automobile accidents). Avoid the high-failure cost actions and choose those actions whose consequences would not be catastrophic, even if there were a failure.

- **No Free Lunch:** Assume that virtually all tangible and intangible objects are owned by someone else unless there is a specific declaration otherwise. (This is the ethical "no free lunch" rule.) If something someone else has created is useful to you, it has value and you should assume the creator wants compensation for this work.

- **The New York Times Test (Perfect Information Rule):** Assume that the results of your decision on a matter will be the subject of the lead article in the *New York Times* the next day. Will the reaction of readers be positive or negative? Would your parents, friends, and children be proud of your decision? Most criminals and unethical actors assume imperfect information, and therefore they assume their decisions and actions will never be revealed. When making decisions involving ethical dilemmas, it is wise to assume perfect information markets.

- **The Social Contract Rule:** Would you like to live in a society where the principle you are supporting would become an organizing principle of the entire society? For instance, you might think it is wonderful to download illegal copies of Hollywood movies, but you might not want to live in a society that does not respect property rights, such as your property rights to the car in your driveway, or your rights to a term paper or original art.

None of these rules is an absolute guide, and there are exceptions and logical difficulties with all of them. Nevertheless, actions that do not easily pass these guidelines deserve some very close attention and a great deal of caution because the appearance of unethical behavior may do as much harm to you and your company as the actual behavior.

Now that you have an understanding of some basic ethical reasoning concepts, let's take a closer look at each of the major types of ethical, social, and political debates that have arisen in e-commerce.

8.2 PRIVACY AND INFORMATION RIGHTS

Privacy is the moral right of individuals to be left alone, free from surveillance or interference from other individuals or organizations, including the state. Privacy is a girder supporting freedom: Without the privacy required to think, write, plan, and associate independently and without fear, social and political freedom is weakened, and perhaps destroyed. **Information privacy** is a subset of privacy. The right to information privacy includes both the claim that certain information should not be collected at all by governments or business firms, and the claim of individuals to control the use of whatever information is collected about them. Individual control over personal information is at the core of the privacy concept. Implicit in the claim to control one's own personal information is the claim to be able to edit and even delete personal information from the Web. This is often called "**the right to be forgotten**," as discussed in the opening case (Rosen, 2012).

Due process also plays an important role in defining privacy. The best statement of due process in record keeping is given by the Fair Information Practices doctrine developed in the early 1970s and extended to the online privacy debate in the late 1990s (described later in this section).

There are two kinds of threats to individual privacy posed by the Internet. One threat originates in the private sector and concerns how much personal information is collected by commercial Web sites and how it will be used. A second threat originates in the public sector and concerns how much personal information federal, state, and local government authorities collect, and how they use it. While these threats are conceptually distinct, in practice they are related as the federal government increasingly relies on Internet companies to provide intelligence on specific individuals and groups, and as Internet records held by search engine companies and others (like Amazon) are sought by legal authorities and attornies.

In 2014, the public discussion of privacy has broadened from a concern about tracking the behavior of individuals while they use the Internet, especially on social networks, to include the impact of mobile devices for tracking the location of people via their smartphones, and collecting information on their personal behavior including the shops, churches, political rallies, bars, and other locations they have visited. There is increasing public attention and criticism of the entire ecosystem of data brokerage firms called data brokers that collect and re-sell this personal information to advertisers. These concerns about tracking and surveilling people throughout their daily lives have been heightened by the revelation that the federal government's National Security Agency has been logging virtually all cell phone calls of all residents for many years. Smartphone apps that tap user information have also received criti-

privacy
the moral right of individuals to be left alone, free from surveillance or interference from other individuals or organizations, including the state

information privacy
includes both the claim that certain information should not be collected at all by governments or business firms, and the claim of individuals to control the use of whatever information is collected about them

right to be forgotten
the claim of individuals to be able to edit and delete personal information online

cal attention. The falling costs of personal tracking technology like mobile cameras, the ubiquitous use of always-on smartphones fitted out with GPS, and the growth of powerful storage and analytic capabilities, have resulted in a torrent of data, referred to as Big Data, pouring into marketing and law enforcement databases. Private and government investigations have found both Apple and Google are collecting personal location and behavior data, and sharing this information with marketers and government agencies. The cell phone carriers receive more than a million requests each year from law enforcement agencies for call data (Maass and Rajagopalen, 2012). Apart from smartphone surveillance, new wireless cameras mounted on cars (a kind of remote sensing device) have led to a new industry of license plate tracking, resulting in hundreds of millions of license plate photos collected by private firms and police forces, regardless of whether or not the car's owners have done anything wrong (Angwin and Valentino-Devries, 2012). Facial recognition technology employed by Facebook and others simply adds to public anxiety over the loss of personal privacy.

In general, the Internet and the Web provide an ideal environment for both business and government to invade the personal privacy of millions of users on a scale unprecedented in history. Perhaps no other recent issue has raised as much widespread social and political concern as protecting the privacy of Internet users.

INFORMATION COLLECTED AT E-COMMERCE SITES

personally identifiable information (PII)
any data that can be used to identify, locate, or contact an individual

anonymous information
demographic and behavioral information that does not include any personal identifiers

As you have learned in previous chapters, e-commerce sites routinely collect a variety of information from or about consumers who visit their site and/or make purchases. Some of this data constitutes **personally identifiable information (PII)**, which is defined as any data that can be used to identify, locate, or contact an individual (Federal Trade Commission, 2000a). Other data is **anonymous information**, composed of demographic and behavioral information, such as age, occupation, income, zip code, ethnicity, and other data that characterizes your life such as Web browsing behavior without identifying who you are. **Table 8.2** lists just a few of the personal identifiers routinely collected by online e-commerce sites including mobile sites and apps. This is not an exhaustive list, and in fact many Web sites collect hundreds of different data points on visitors. A study of nine data brokers identified twelve broad categories of information collected by brokers, and 240 data elements from address

TABLE 8.2	PERSONAL INFORMATION COLLECTED BY E-COMMERCE SITES	
Name	Gender	Education
Address	Age	Preference data
Phone number	Occupation	Transaction data
E-mail address	Location	Clickstream data
Social security number	Location history	Device used for access
Bank accounts	Likes	Browser type
Credit card accounts	Photograph	

history, to liens and political leanings, to vehicle and travel data (Federal Trade Commission, 2014).

Advertising networks and search engines also track the behavior of consumers across thousands of popular sites, not just at one site, via cookies, Web beacons, tracking software, spyware, and other techniques

Table 8.3 illustrates some of the major ways online firms gather information about consumers.

TABLE 8.3	THE INTERNET'S MAJOR INFORMATION-GATHERING TOOLS AND THEIR IMPACT ON PRIVACY
INTERNET CAPABILITY	**IMPACT ON PRIVACY**
Smartphones and apps	Used to track location and share photos, addresses, phone numbers, search, and other behavior to marketers.
Advertising networks	Used to track individuals as they move among thousands of Web sites.
Social networks	Used to gather information on user-provided content such as books, music, friends, and other interests, preferences, and lifestyles.
Cookies and Super Cookies	Used to track individuals at a single site. Super Cookies are nearly impossible to identify or remove.
Third-party cookies	Cookies placed by third-party advertising networks. Used to monitor and track online behavior, searches, and sites visited across thousands of sites that belong to the advertising network for the purpose of displaying "relevant" advertising.
Spyware	Can be used to record all the keyboard activity of a user, including Web sites visited and security codes used; also used to display advertisements to users based on their searches or other behavior.
Search engine behavioral targeting (Google and other search engines)	Uses prior search history, demographics, expressed interests, geographic, or other user-entered data to target advertising.
Deep packet inspection	Uses software installed at the ISP level to track all user clickstream behavior.
Shopping carts	Can be used to collect detailed payment and purchase information.
Forms	Online forms that users voluntarily fill out in return for a promised benefit or reward that are linked with clickstream or other behavioral data to create a personal profile.
Site transaction logs	Can be used to collect and analyze detailed information on page content viewed by users.
Search engines	Can be used to trace user statements and views on newsgroups, chat groups, and other public forums on the Web, and profile users' social and political views. Google returns name, address, and links to a map with directions to the address when a phone number is entered.
Digital wallets (single sign-on services)	Client-side wallets and software that reveal personal information to Web sites verifying the identity of the consumer.
Digital Rights Management (DRM)	Software (Windows Media Player) that requires users of online media to identify themselves before viewing copyrighted content.
Trusted Computing Environments	Hardware and software that controls the viewing of copyrighted content and requires users' identification, e.g., Amazon Kindle.

SOCIAL NETWORKS AND PRIVACY

Social networks pose a unique challenge for the maintenance of personal privacy because they encourage people to reveal details about their personal lives (passions, loves, favorites, photos, videos, and personal interests), and to share them with their friends. Social networks have greatly enlarged the depth, scope, and richness of information collected by private corporations. While Google's search engine is a massive database of personal intentions, Facebook has created a massive database of friends, preferences, Likes, posts, and activities. An Austrian researcher was able to obtain his Facebook file (possible under European laws) and received a 1,222 page document of messages, photos, posts, and friends (Sengupta, 2012). Some social networkers share these personal details with everyone on the social network. On the face of it, this would seem to indicate that people who participate in social networks voluntarily give up their rights to personal privacy. How could they claim an expectation of privacy? When everything is shared, what's private?

But the reality is that many adult (18 or over) participants in social networks have a very keen sense of their personal privacy. Facebook is a prime example of senior management pushing the envelope of privacy, and experiencing a number of public relations reversals and growing government concern. For instance, Facebook deployed facial recognition technology without any previous notice, which compromised its users' privacy by allowing them to be tagged in photos without their consent. Researchers at Carnegie Mellon found that it is possible to identify people, even their social security numbers, based on a single Facebook photograph and using facial recognition programs (Angwin, 2011; Acquisti et al., 2011). After consumer uproar and challenges from various state attorneys general, Facebook reversed course and made it easier for users to opt out of the technology. In 2012, Facebook began pushing ads on its users based on their use of apps, and offering advertisers the ability to serve ads to Facebook users even while not using Facebook. In 2013, Facebook announced a new privacy policy that it claimed clarified its use of personal information. In the new policy, Facebook claimed it could use any personal information for any purpose it wanted to. After howls of protest from users, privacy groups, and congressmen, the policy was temporarily withdrawn. In 2014, Facebook changed its default privacy settings to reveal information only to friends, and allowed users to see some of the data Facebook collects about them and to edit that data. Actually performing these tasks is quite difficult. For a review of Facebook's various positions on online privacy over the years, and public and congressional reaction to these issues, refer back to the *Insight on Society* case, *Facebook and the Age of Privacy*, in Chapter 1.

The result of these conflicts suggests that social network participants do indeed have a strong expectation of privacy in the sense that they want to control how "their" information is used. People who contribute user-generated content have a strong sense of ownership over the content that is not diminished by posting the information on a social network for one's friends. As for members who post information to everyone, not just friends, these should be seen as "public performances" where the contributors voluntarily publish their performances, just as writers or other artists do. This does not mean they want the entirety of their personal lives thrown open to every Web tracking automaton on the Internet.

MOBILE AND LOCATION-BASED PRIVACY ISSUES

As the mobile platform becomes more and more important, issues about mobile and location-based privacy are also becoming a major concern. In 2012, investigators discovered that iOS and Android apps were funneling location information to mobile advertisers, along with users' address books and photos (Bilton, 2012). As a result, Congress opened an investigation into the privacy policies of smartphone manufacturers, along with Facebook, Pinterest, Yahoo, Google, and 30 others in the app marketplace. Twitter announced that anyone using its "Find Friends" feature on smartphones was also sending every phone number and e-mail address in their address books to the company (Sarno, 2012).

In 2011, a furor erupted over news that Apple iPhones and iPads and Google Android smartphones were able to track and store user location information. In 2012, Facebook launched a new mobile advertising service that tracks what apps people use on their smartphones, and what they do while using the apps. Apple and Google track users' apps also. Apple disclosed that it can target ads based on the apps that a person has downloaded, while Google does not currently do this. Google and Apple do not track what users do on apps, while the Facebook program goes this additional step. For instance, Facebook can target a frequent player of Zynga games with ads using the player's Facebook News Feed, which is a major channel for Facebook ads (the other being display ads on the user's page) (Raice, 2012). In 2012, investigators discovered that some cell phone companies had installed tracking devices inside phones to improve customer service. This ignited a flurry of criticism.

In June 2014, the U.S. Supreme Court, in a pathbreaking unanimous decision, ruled that police needed a warrant prior to searching a person's cell phone for informaton. All mobile devices will likely receive this protection against general, warrantless police searches (Savage, 2014). An earlier decision in 2012 requires police to obtain a warrant prior to attaching GPS tracking devices to a suspect's car. In both cases, the Supreme Court found that cell phones held extensive detailed personal information, retained information for many years, and stored many different types of information. Much of a person's intimate and personal life can be stored on cell phones, making them the modern equivalent of personal papers, which are protected under the Fourth Amendment to the Constitution, which protects the "right of the people to be secure in their persons, houses, papers, and effects, against unreasonable searches and seizures." The U.S. Senate held hearings in June 2014 on the Consumer Location Privacy Protection Act, which requires firms to notify cell phone users and obtain their consent if they want to gather location data. The FTC signed a 20-year consent order with Snapchat after discovering the app was collecting location data contrary to Snapchat's own privacy policy.

A backlash against the privacy-invading practices of Internet firms and the online advertising industry is gaining momentum, as reflected in opinion polls. Both attitudes and behavior are changing. According to a recent survey, Americans' privacy concerns about online invasions of privacy are growing stronger, leading to people taking concrete actions to protect themselves (Pew Research Center, 2013). Over 50% are very concerned about the wealth of personal data online; 86% have taken steps to mask their online behavior; 25% of Web users use ad-blocking software (see **Table 8.4**). Next

TABLE 8.4	INTERNET USERS' EFFORTS TO PRESERVE PRIVACY	
ACTION	**PERCENTAGE WHO HAVE DONE THIS**	
Cleared Web browser history and cookies	64%	
Deleted or edited something previously posted	41%	
Used Web browser settings to turn off or disable cookies	41%	
Refused to use Web site that required user to provide his or her real name	36%	
Used a temporary user name or e-mail address	26%	
Posted comments online anonymously	25%	
Attempted to get something posted online about them removed	21%	
Attempted to mask identity	18%	
Browsed anonymously on a public computer	18%	
Used a fake or untraceable user name	18%	
Encrypted communications	14%	
Used anonymous Web browsing service	14%	
Provided false or inaccurate information about self	13%	

SOURCE: Based on data from Pew Research Center, 2013.

to hackers, Americans try to avoid advertisers pursuing them while online, and 64% block cookies to make tracking more difficult. Refer back to the *Insight on Society* case, *Foursquare: Check Your Privacy at the Door*, in Chapter 5, for more discussion of some of the issues associated with mobile and location-based privacy.

PROFILING AND BEHAVIORAL TARGETING

On an average day, billions of people around the world go online. Marketers would like to know who these people are, what they are interested in, and what they buy. The more precise the information, the more complete the information, and the more valuable it is as a predictive and marketing tool. Armed with this information, marketers can make their ad campaigns more efficient by targeting specific ads at specific groups or individuals, and they can even adjust the ads for specific groups.

profiling
the creation of digital images that characterize online individual and group behavior

anonymous profiles
identify people as belonging to highly specific and targeted groups

Many Web sites allow third parties—including online advertising networks such as Microsoft Advertising, DoubleClick, and others—to place "third-party" cookies and Web tracking software on a visitor's computer in order to engage in profiling the user's behavior across thousands of Web sites. A third-party cookie is used to track users across hundreds or thousands of other Web sites who are members of the advertising network. **Profiling** is the creation of digital images that characterize online individual and group behavior. **Anonymous profiles** identify people as belonging to highly specific and targeted groups, for example, 20- to 30-year-old males, with college degrees and incomes greater than €40,000 a year, and interested in high-fashion clothing (based on recent search engine use). **Personal profiles** add a personal e-mail address, postal address, and/or phone number to behavioral data. Increasingly, online firms are linking their online profiles to personal offline consumer data collected by database firms tracking credit card purchases, as well as established retail and catalog firms.

The online advertising networks such as DoubleClick and 24/7 Real Media have added several new dimensions to established offline marketing techniques. First, they have the ability to precisely track not just consumer purchases, but all browsing behavior on the Web at thousands of the most popular member sites, including browsing book lists, filling out preference forms, and viewing content pages. Second, they can dynamically adjust what the shopper sees on screen—including prices. Third, they can build and continually refresh high-resolution data images or behavioral profiles of consumers. Other advertising firms have created spyware software that, when placed on a consumer's computer, can report back to the advertiser's server on all consumer Internet use, and is also used to display advertising on the consumer's computer.

A different kind of profiling and a more recent form of behavioral targeting is Google's results-based personalization of advertising. Google has a patent on a program that allows advertisers using Google's AdWords program to target ads to users based on their prior search histories and profiles, which Google constructs based on user searches, along with any other information the user submits to Google or that Google can obtain, such as age, demographics, region, and other Web activities (such as blogging). Google also applied for a second patent on a program that allows Google to help advertisers select keywords and design ads for various market segments based on search histories, such as helping a clothing Web site create and test ads targeted at teenage females. Google uses behavioral targeting to help it display more relevant ads based on keywords. According to Google, the feature is aimed at capturing a more robust understanding of user intent, and thereby delivering a better ad. Google's Gmail, a free e-mail service, offers a powerful interface, and more than 7 gigabytes of free storage. In return, Google computers read all incoming and outgoing e-mail and place "relevant" advertising in the margins of the mail. Profiles are developed on individual users based on the content in their e-mail.

Both American and European regulators have objected to Google's integration of personal information from all of its services into a single personal profile, and second, failing to let users know what it is doing with their personal information (Charlton, 2013). Google is claiming that people who send mail to a friend's Gmail account do not have an expectation of privacy, and that anyone who sends information to a third party does not have an expectation of privacy. Privacy groups expressed concerns when Google announced in 2014 that it was purchasing Nest, the maker of digital home thermostats and smoke detection devices that are connected to the Internet. Critics fear that Google will monitor the personal whereabouts of people in their own homes, and use this information for its online advertising business (Crum, 2014).

Facial recognition tools add a new dimension to profiling and behavioral targeting. In 2014, several uses of facial recognition are already commonplace. Facebook and Google+ use the software to automatically suggest name tags for members or their friends in photographs. The technology is evolving rapidly: Google has applied

personal profiles
add a personal e-mail address, postal address, and/or phone number to behavioral data

for a patent to identify faces in online videos, and Facebook has developed a highly accurate facial recognition system called DeepFace (Singer, 2014a). It is difficult for people to detect if they are being stalked or followed by persons using facial recognition technology, and currently there are no controls over its use.

deep packet inspection

a technology for recording every key stroke at the ISP level

Deep packet inspection is another technology for recording every keystroke at the ISP level of every Internet user (no matter where they ultimately go on the Web), and then using that information to make suggestions, and target ads. While advertising networks are limited, and even Google does not constitute the universe of search, deep packet inspection at the ISP level really does capture the universe of all Internet users. In 2014, deep packet inspection is not used in the United States by advertising firms because of it is likely a violation of the Electronic Communications Privacy Act of 1986. However, it is used as a network management and law enforcement tool (Kuehn and Mueller, 2012).

Network advertising firms argue that Web profiling benefits both consumers and businesses. Profiling permits targeting of ads, ensuring that consumers see advertisements mostly for products and services in which they are actually interested. Businesses benefit by not paying for wasted advertising sent to consumers who have no interest in their product or service. The industry argues that by increasing the effectiveness of advertising, more advertising revenues go to the Internet, which in turn subsidizes free content on the Internet. Last, product designers and entrepreneurs benefit by sensing demand for new products and services by examining user searches and profiles.

Critics argue that profiling undermines the expectation of anonymity and privacy that most people have when using the Internet, and changes what should be a private experience into one where an individual's every move is recorded. As people become aware that their every move is being watched, they will be far less likely to explore sensitive topics, browse pages, or read about controversial issues. How can people experience freedom if they believe their every move on the Internet is being watched? In most cases, the profiling is invisible to users, and even hidden. Consumers are not notified that profiling is occurring. Profiling permits data aggregation on hundreds or even thousands of unrelated sites on the Web. The cookies placed by ad networks are persistent, and they can be set to last days, months, years, or even forever. Their tracking occurs over an extended period of time and resumes each time the individual logs on to the Internet. This clickstream data is used to create profiles that can include hundreds of distinct data fields for each consumer. Associating so-called anonymous profiles with personal information is fairly easy, and companies can change policies quickly without informing the consumer. Although the information gathered by network advertisers is often anonymous (non-PII data), in many cases, the profiles derived from tracking consumers' activities on the Web are linked or merged with personally identifiable information. Anonymous behavioral data is far more valuable if it can be linked with offline consumer behavior, e-mail addresses, and postal addresses.

THE INTERNET AND GOVERNMENT INVASIONS OF PRIVACY: E-COMMERCE SURVEILLANCE

Today, the online and mobile behavior, profiles, and transactions of consumers are routinely available to a wide range of government agencies and law enforcement authorities, contributing to rising fears among online consumers, and in some cases, their withdrawal from the online marketplace. The last few years have not been good for advocates of privacy, with revelations that U.S. federal government agencies have been routinely gathering cell phone call data on Americans and foreigners in the United States for a period of several years with scant judicial oversight. In June 2013, Edward Snowden, a security contractor for the U.S. National Security Agency (NSA), began releasing NSA documents to *The Guardian*, a U.K. newspaper, providing a detailed description of NSA surveillance programs of both U.S. and foreign citizens. These programs were unprecedented in scope and involved wholesale collection of cell phone metadata around the world, tapping communications lines of Google, Yahoo, and other Internet services, and tapping cell phones of foreign leaders. The NSA enlisted the support of the major telecommunications carriers to give it information about Americans' phone calls and e-mail in a program called Prism. These programs were conceived in the aftermath of the terrorist attack on the United States on September 11, 2001, and were envisaged as necessary to protect the country. The programs were authorized by the USA PATRIOT Act of 2001, and subsequent amendments, and were reviewed by relevant Congressional committees. Many in the computer science academic community were aware of these programs, in part because they participated in the development of techniques for discovering patterns in large data sets, as well as so-called machine learning programs. Nevertheless, the revelations alarmed average citizens who previously believed that if they did nothing wrong, surely the government would not be collecting information about them. The revelations also heightened public awareness and criticism of Internet firms like Google and Facebook, and others engaging in extensive tracking and consumer surveillance.

Advances in technology for storing, processing, and analyzing unimaginable quantities of personal data, referred to as Big Data and business analytics (data mining and representation software), have further heightened perceptions that privacy is increasingly difficult to define and protect in the age of e-commerce and social networks (Kakutani, 2013; Mayer-Schonberger and Cukier, 2013).

Striking a balance between security and liberty is at the center of the privacy debate (Ford, 2013). While the Internet used to be thought of as impossible for governments to control or monitor, nothing could be actually further from the truth. Law enforcement authorities have long claimed the right under numerous statutes to monitor any form of electronic communication pursuant to a court order and judicial review and based on the reasonable belief that a crime is being committed. This includes the surveillance of consumers engaged in e-commerce. The Communications Assistance for Law Enforcement Act (CALEA), the USA PATRIOT Act, the Cyber Security Enhancement Act, and the Homeland Security Act all strengthen the ability of U.S. law enforcement agencies to monitor Internet users without their knowledge and, under certain circumstances when life is purportedly at stake, without judicial oversight. The USA PATRIOT Act, designed to combat terrorism inside the borders of the United States, permits nearly unlimited government surveillance without court oversight, according to several senators (Savage, 2012).

Partly in response to the Snowden revelations, and to the growing concerns about the decline in online privacy, in May 2014, the Obama administration released a report,

Big Data: Seizing Opportunities and Preserving Values, that focused on the role of technology, including e-commerce and mobile phones, in expanding the amount and depth of information on citizens. A supporting report of the President's Council of Advisors on Science and Technology (PCAST) was also released, calling for a consumer privacy bill of rights, a data breach law requiring firms to report losses of consumer data, extension of these privacy rights to non-citizens, use of technologies to enhance privacy, restriction of the use of data that might cause discrimination against various groups in America, and the amendment of the Electronic Communications Privacy Act to strengthen protections against government surveillance of the sort uncovered by Snowden. A survey of 24,000 individuals found a majority of Americans were concerned with data storage security, transparency about data use, legal standards, collection of location data, and collection of communications data. This major report had little to say about reforming laws governing the NSA, however (Executive Office of the President, 2014; PCAST, 2014).

There have been several Congressional initiatives to strengthen the privacy protections for electronic communications and personal location data, although thus far, none have passed. In 2014, the Email Privacy Act (H.R. 1852) has gained strong support in the U.S. House of Representatives. The Act would amend the Electronic Communications Privacy Act to prohibit a provider of remote computing service or electronic communication service to the public from knowingly divulging to any governmental entity the contents of any communication that is in electronic storage or otherwise maintained by the provider in the absence of a valid warrant. As of September 2014, however, the bill has not yet been passed in the House or Senate.

Taking matters into its own hands, in September 2014, Apple introduced the iPhone 6, which offers the ability for users to encrypt e-mail, photos, and contacts stored on the phone using a strong encryption algorithm. The data can only be decrypted by using a passcode that only the user possesses. Google is expected to make similar ecryption available as the default setting on Android phones in October 2014. As a result, the NSA will no longer be able to force Apple and Google to reveal such user data. Not surprisingly, the NSA and law enforcement officials are not happy with this prospect and fear that it will enable criminals and terrorists to evade surveillance. Apple and Google contend that in order for them to compete globally, they must be able to convince consumers that their data is secure, a task made more difficult as a result of the Snowden revelations (Sanger and Chen, 2014).

Government agencies are among the largest users of private sector commercial data brokers, such as ChoicePoint, Acxiom, Experian, and TransUnion Corporation, that collect a vast amount of information about consumers from various offline and online public sources, such as public records and the telephone directory, and non-public sources, such as "credit header" information from credit bureaus (which typically contains name, aliases, birth date, social security number, current and prior addresses, and phone numbers). Acxiom is the largest private personal database in the world with records on more than 500,000 people and about 1,500 data points per person (Singer, 2012). Information contained in individual reference services' databases ranges from purely identifying information (e.g., name and phone number) to much more extensive data (e.g., driving records, criminal and civil court records, property records, and licensing records). This information can be linked to online behavior information collected from other commercial sources to compile an extensive profile of an individual's online and offline behavior.

When you use a search engine, the IP address of your computer is typically recorded, and cookies are placed on your browser to record the search terms of the current session, time of visit, and links you actually chose. This information is stored in a database where it can be related to previous searches and other personal identifiers that the search engine may have gleaned from those previous searches. Search engine data provides a comprehensive picture of a person's intentions and actions on the Internet. The amount of time such data is retained is not governed by U.S. law, but the European Union has indicated that it should not be retained for more than six months. The three major search engines (Google, Bing, and Yahoo) have varying policies. Data can be de-identified by purposely storing search queries separate from personal identifiers (name, address, zip code, and gender), and it can be completely anonymized by not storing or removing the IP address and any cross-session identifiers. In 2010, Microsoft agreed to reduce the amount of time that it retains certain data, such as IP addresses, to six months to comply with the E.U. standard, although it retains other data, such as cookie IDs and cross-session IDs, for 18 months. Google has refused, however, and retains search records for 18 months with IP address and cookies, claiming that this amount of time is necessary for it to improve services and prevent fraud. In 2011, Yahoo, which had previously prided itself for retaining search records for only three months, announced that it too would extend that time to 18 months, for competitive reasons. Some search engines like Startpage and Ixquick do not keep any IP information or use cookies, and usage of such search engines has greatly increased since the Snowden revelations. Recent research has found that the claim that retaining search data for longer periods, such as 18 months, improves the accuracy of searches is not supported by empirical data (Chiou and Tucker, 2014).

LEGAL PROTECTIONS

In the United States, Canada, and Germany, rights to privacy are explicitly granted in, or can be derived from, founding documents such as constitutions, as well as in specific statutes. In England and the United States, there is also protection of privacy in the common law, a body of court decisions involving torts or personal injuries. For instance, in the United States, four privacy-related torts have been defined in court decisions involving claims of injury to individuals caused by other private parties: intrusion on solitude, public disclosure of private facts, publicity placing a person in a false light, and appropriation of a person's name or likeness (mostly concerning celebrities) for a commercial purpose (Laudon, 1996). In the United States, the claim to privacy against government intrusion is protected primarily by the First Amendment guarantees of freedom of speech and association, the Fourth Amendment protections against unreasonable search and seizure of one's personal documents or home, and the Fourteenth Amendment's guarantee of due process. It's important to remember that these protections apply to government intrusions of privacy, not private firms' intrusions.

In addition to common law and the U.S. Constitution, there are both federal laws and state laws that protect individuals against government intrusion and in some cases define privacy rights vis-à-vis private organizations such as financial, educational, and media institutions (cable television and video rentals) (see **Table 8.5**).

Informed Consent and Notice

The conceptual basis of American privacy law is notification and consent. It is assumed that consumers can read Terms of Use notices (or privacy policies) concerning how a Web site will use their personal information, and then make a rational choice to either consent to the terms of use, opt out of the data collection (if that is an option), or stop using the site. The concept of **informed consent** (defined as consent given with knowledge of all material facts needed to make a rational decision) also plays an important role in protecting privacy. In the United States, business firms can gather transaction information generated in the marketplace and then use that information for other purposes, without obtaining the explicit affirmative informed consent of the individual. For instance, in the United States, if a shopper purchases books about baseball from an e-commerce company that participates in an advertising network such as DoubleClick, a cookie can be placed on the consumer's hard drive and used by other member companies to sell the shopper sports clothing without the explicit permission or even knowledge of the user. This online preference information may also be linked with personally identifying information. In Europe, this would be illegal. A business in Europe cannot use marketplace transaction information for any purpose other than supporting the current transaction, unless it obtains the individual's consent in writing or by filling out an on-screen form.

There are traditionally two models for informed consent: opt-in and opt-out. The **opt-in** model requires an affirmative action by the consumer to allow collection and use of information. For instance, using opt-in, consumers would first be asked if they approved of the collection and use of information, and then directed to check a selection box if they agreed. Otherwise, the default is not to approve the collection of data. In the **opt-out** model, the default is to collect information unless the consumer takes an affirmative action to prevent the collection of data by checking a box or by filling out a form.

Until recently, many U.S. e-commerce companies rejected the concept of informed consent and instead simply published their information use policy on their site. Nearly all Web sites have Terms of Use policies that users can find if they look carefully. These Terms of Use policies are sometimes called privacy policies, and they describe how the firms will use information collected on their sites. These policies are notices, and as noted above, it is assumed that anyone who uses the site has implicitly agreed to the Terms of Use policy. A recent study reviewed 30 popular social network and community sites and found that it would take the average reader about eight hours to simply read the policy. The longest policy was SoundCloud's, with 7,961 words. Obviously a critical flaw with informed consent as the basis of privacy protections is that it assumes the average user can understand what privacy they may be giving up by using a site (Singer, 2014b; Fiesler and Bruckman, 2014). For instance, Yahoo's privacy policy begins by stating that Yahoo takes the user's privacy seriously and Yahoo does not rent, sell, or share personal information about users with others or non-affiliated companies. However, there are a number of exceptions that significantly weaken this statement. For instance, Yahoo may share the information with "trusted

---

informed consent

consent given with knowledge of all material facts needed to make a rational decision

opt-in

requires an affirmative action by the consumer to allow collection and use of consumer information

opt-out

the default is to collect information unless the consumer takes an affirmative action to prevent the collection of data

TABLE 8.5	U.S. FEDERAL AND STATE PRIVACY LAWS
NAME	**DESCRIPTION**
GENERAL FEDERAL PRIVACY LAWS	
Freedom of Information Act of 1966	Gives people the right to inspect information about themselves held in government files; also allows other individuals and organizations the right to request disclosure of government records based on the public's right to know.
Privacy Act of 1974, as amended	Regulates the federal government's collection, use, and disclosure of data collected by federal agencies. Gives individuals a right to inspect and correct records.
Electronic Communications Privacy Act of 1986	Makes conduct that would infringe on the security of electronic communications illegal.
Computer Security Act of 1987	Makes conduct that would infringe on the security of computer-based files illegal.
Computer Matching and Privacy Protection Act of 1988	Regulates computerized matching of files held by different government agencies.
Driver's Privacy Protection Act of 1994	Limits access to personal information maintained by state motor vehicle departments to those with legitimate business purposes. Also gives drivers the option to prevent disclosure of driver's license information to marketers and the general public.
E-Government Act of 2002	Regulates the collection and use of personal information by federal agencies.
FEDERAL PRIVACY LAWS AFFECTING PRIVATE INSTITUTIONS	
Fair Credit Reporting Act of 1970	Regulates the credit investigating and reporting industry. Gives people the right to inspect credit records if they have been denied credit and provides procedures for correcting information.
Family Educational Rights and Privacy Act of 1974	Requires schools and colleges to give students and their parents access to student records and to allow them to challenge and correct information; limits disclosure of such records to third parties.
Right to Financial Privacy Act of 1978	Regulates the financial industry's use of personal financial records; establishes procedures that federal agencies must follow to gain access to such records.
Privacy Protection Act of 1980	Prohibits government agents from conducting unannounced searches of press offices and files if no one in the office is suspected of committing a crime.
Cable Communications Policy Act of 1984	Regulates the cable industry's collection and disclosure of information concerning subscribers.
Video Privacy Protection Act of 1988	Prevents disclosure of a person's video rental records without court order or consent.
Children's Online Privacy Protection Act (1998)	Prohibits deceptive practices in connection with the collection, use, and/or disclosure of personal information from and about children on the Internet.
Health Insurance Portability and Accountability Act of 1996 (HIPAA)	Requires healthcare providers and insurers and other third parties to promulgate privacy policies to consumers and establishes due process procedures.
Financial Modernization Act (Gramm-Leach-Bliley Act) (1999)	Requires financial institutions to inform consumers of their privacy policies and permits consumers some control over their records.

TABLE 8.5	U.S. FEDERAL AND STATE PRIVACY LAWS (CONT'D)
NAME	DESCRIPTION
SELECTED STATE PRIVACY LAWS	
Online privacy policies	The California Online Privacy Protection Act of 2003 was the first state law in the United States requiring owners of commercial Web sites or online services to post a privacy policy. The policy must, among other things, identify the categories of PII collected about site visitors and categories of third parties with whom the information may be shared. Failure to comply can result in a civil suit for unfair business practices. Nebraska and Pennsylvania prohibit false and misleading statements in online privacy policies. At least 16 states require government Web sites to establish privacy policies or procedures or incorporate machine-readable privacy policies into their Web sites.
Spyware legislation	A number of states, including California, Utah, Arizona, Arkansas, and Virginia, among others, have passed laws that outlaw the installation of spyware on a user's computer without consent.
Disclosure of security breaches	In 2002, California enacted legislation that requires state agencies or businesses that own or license computer data with personal information to notify state residents if they experience a security breach involving that information; today, nearly every state has enacted similar legislation.
Privacy of personal information	Two states, Nevada and Minnesota, require ISPs to keep their customers' PII private unless the customer consents to disclose the information. Minnesota also requires ISPs to get permission from subscribers before disclosing information about subscribers' online surfing habits.
Data encryption	In October 2007, Nevada passed the first law that requires encryption for the transmission of customer personal information. The law took effect October 1, 2008.

partners," which could be anyone that Yahoo does business with, although perhaps not a company that the user might choose to do business with. In its privacy policy, Yahoo also says it uses cookies, device identifiers, and Web beacons in order to track user clickstream behavior across the Web. To opt-out of interest-based advertising, a user must sign into his or her Yahoo account and allow cookies from Yahoo. U.S. businesses argue that informing consumers about how the information will be used is sufficient to obtain the users' informed consent. Privacy advocates argue that many Terms of Use/privacy policy statements on U.S. Web sites are obscure and difficult to read, and legitimate just about any use of personal information. For instance, in 2014, a furor erupted when it was revealed that both Facebook and OKCupid (a dating site) had conducted undisclosed social experiments involving user behavior on their sites. Facebook secretly manipulated the News Feeds of almost 700,000 users to see if negative posts on users' News Feeds made them more likely to make negative posts as well. Facebook claimed that such research was covered by its Terms of Use; critics argued that conducting such research without explicit informed consent is both unethical and illegal (Storm, 2014). In the United States, most e-commerce companies that offer informed consent use the opt-out model, and collect information unless the consumer specifically declines by checking a box on the site. Often, the selection box is at the very bottom of the Web page, where the consumer is unlikely to see it.

The Federal Trade Commission's Fair Information Practices Principles

In the United States, the Federal Trade Commission (FTC) has taken the lead in conducting research on online privacy and recommending legislation to Congress. The FTC is a cabinet-level agency charged with promoting the efficient functioning of the marketplace by protecting consumers from unfair or deceptive practices and increasing consumer choice by promoting competition. In addition to reports and recommendations, the FTC enforces existing legislation by suing corporations it believes are in violation of federal fair trade laws.

In 1998, the FTC issued its Fair Information Practice (FIP) principles, on which it has based its assessments and recommendations for online privacy. **Table 8.6** describes these principles. Two of the five are designated as basic, "core" principles that must be present to protect privacy, whereas the other practices are less central. The FTC's FIP principles restate and strengthen in a form suitable to deal with online privacy the Fair Information Practices doctrine developed in 1973 by a government study group (U.S. Department of Health, Education and Welfare, 1973).

The FTC's FIP principles set the ground rules for what constitutes due process privacy protection procedures at e-commerce and all other Web sites—including government and nonprofit Web sites—in the United States.

The FTC's FIP principles are guidelines, not laws. They have stimulated private firms and industry associations to develop their own private guidelines (discussed next). However, the FTC's FIP guidelines are often used as the basis of legislation. The most important online privacy legislation to date that has been directly influenced by the FTC's FIP principles is the Children's Online Privacy Protection Act (COPPA)

TABLE 8.6	FEDERAL TRADE COMMISSION'S FAIR INFORMATION PRACTICE PRINCIPLES
Notice/Awareness (core principle)	Sites must disclose their information practices before collecting data. Includes identification of collector, uses of data, other recipients of data, nature of collection (active/inactive), voluntary or required, consequences of refusal, and steps taken to protect confidentiality, integrity, and quality of the data.
Choice/Consent (core principle)	There must be a choice regime in place allowing consumers to choose how their information will be used for secondary purposes other than supporting the transaction, including internal use and transfer to third parties. Opt-in/opt-out must be available.
Access/Participation	Consumers should be able to review and contest the accuracy and completeness of data collected about them in a timely, inexpensive process.
Security	Data collectors must take reasonable steps to assure that consumer information is accurate and secure from unauthorized use.
Enforcement	There must be a mechanism to enforce FIP principles in place. This can involve self-regulation, legislation giving consumers legal remedies for violations, or federal statutes and regulation.

SOURCE: Based on data from Federal Trade Commission, 1998, 2000a.

TABLE 8.7	FTC RECOMMENDATIONS REGARDING ONLINE PROFILING
PRINCIPLE	DESCRIPTION OF RECOMMENDATION
Notice	Complete transparency to user by providing disclosure and choice options on the host Web site. "Robust" notice for PII (time/place of collection; before collection begins). Clear and conspicuous notice for non-PII.
Choice	Opt-in for PII, opt-out for non-PII. No conversion of non-PII to PII without consent. Opt-out from any or all network advertisers from a single page provided by the host Web site.
Access	Reasonable provisions to allow inspection and correction.
Security	Reasonable efforts to secure information from loss, misuse, or improper access.
Enforcement	Done by independent third parties, such as seal programs and accounting firms.
Restricted collection	Advertising networks will not collect information about sensitive financial or medical topics, sexual behavior or sexual orientation, or use social security numbers for profiling.

SOURCE: Based on data from Federal Trade Commission, 2000b.

(1998), which requires Web sites to obtain parental permission before collecting information on children under 13 years of age.

In 2000, the FTC recommended legislation to Congress to protect online consumer privacy from the threat posed by advertising networks. **Table 8.7** summarizes the commission's recommendations. The FTC profiling recommendations significantly strengthened the FIP principles of notification and choice, while also including restrictions on information that may be collected.[1] Although the FTC supported industry efforts at self-regulation, it nevertheless recommended legislation to ensure that all Web sites using network advertising and all network advertisers complied.

In the last decade, the FTC's privacy approach has shifted somewhat, away from notice and choice requirements and into a harm-based approach targeting practices that are likely to cause harm or unwarranted intrusion in consumers' daily lives. However, in recent years, the FTC has recognized the limitations of both the notice-and-choice and harm-based models. In 2009, the FTC held a series of three public roundtables to explore the effectiveness of these approaches in light of rapidly evolving technology and the market for consumer data. The major concepts that emerged from these roundtables were:

• The increasing collection and use of consumer data

• Consumers' lack of understanding about the collection and use of their personal data, and the resulting inability to make informed choices

---

[1] Much general privacy legislation affecting government, e.g., the Privacy Act of 1974, precludes the government from collecting information on political and social behavior of citizens. The FTC restrictions are significant because they are the FTC's first effort at limiting the collection of certain information.

- Consumers' interest in and concern about their privacy
- Benefits of data collection and use to both businesses and consumers
- Decreasing relevance of the distinction between PII and non-PII.

As a result of the roundtables, the FTC has now developed a new framework to address consumer privacy. **Table 8.8** summarizes the important aspects of this framework. Among the most noteworthy is the call for a "Do Not Track" mechanism for online behavioral advertising. The mechanism would involve placing a persistent cookie on a consumer's browser and conveying its setting to sites that the browser

TABLE 8.8	THE FTC'S NEW PRIVACY FRAMEWORK
PRINCIPLE	APPLICATION
Scope	Applies to all commercial entities that collect or use consumer data; not limited to those that just collect PII.
Privacy by Design	Companies should promote consumer privacy throughout the organization and at every stage of development of products and services: • Data security • Reasonable collection limits • Reasonable and appropriate data retention policies • Data accuracy • Comprehensive data management procedures
Simplified Choice	Companies should simplify consumer choice. Need not provide choice before collecting and using data for commonly accepted practices: • Product and fulfillment • Internal operations, fraud prevention • Legal compliance • First-party marketing For all other commercial data collection and use, choice is required, and should be clearly and conspicuously offered at a time and in context in which consumer is providing data. Some types of information or practices (children, financial, and medical information, deep packet inspection) may require additional protection through enhanced consent. Special choice mechanism for online behavioral advertising: "Do Not Track."
Greater Transparency	Increase transparency of data practices by: • Making privacy notices clearer, shorter, and more standardized to enable better comprehension and comparison • Providing consumers with reasonable access to data about themselves • Providing prominent disclosures and obtaining express affirmative consent before using consumer data in a materially different manner than claimed when data was collected • Educating consumers about commercial data privacy practices

SOURCE: Based on data from Federal Trade Commission, 2010.

visits to signal whether or not the consumer wants to be tracked or receive targeted advertisements. A number of bills have been introduced in Congress to implement Do Not Track, but as yet none have been passed.

In response to growing public and congressional concern with online and mobile privacy violations, the FTC has begun taking a much more aggressive stance based on its new privacy policies developed over several years. In 2011, the FTC reached an agreement with Google concerning charges it used deceptive tactics and violated its own privacy policies when it launched its Google Buzz social network, forcing people to join the network even if they selected not to join. Under the settlement, Google agreed to start a privacy program, permit independent privacy audits for 20 years, and face $16,000 fines for every future privacy misrepresentation. This was the first time the FTC had charged a company with such violations and ordered it to start a privacy program (Federal Trade Commission, 2011). In 2012, the FTC fined Google $22.5 million to settle charges that it had bypassed privacy settings in Apple's Safari browser to be able to track users of the browser and show them advertisements, and violated the earlier privacy settlement with the agency. This fine is the largest civil penalty levied by the FTC to date, which has been cracking down on tech companies for privacy violations and is also investigating Google for antitrust violations (Federal Trade Commission, 2012a). In 2012, the FTC also reached a settlement with Facebook resolving charges that Facebook deceived its users by telling them they could keep their information on Facebook private, but then repeatedly allowing it to be shared and made public. The settlement requires Facebook to live up to its promises by giving consumers clear and prominent notice and obtaining their express consent before sharing their information beyond the user's privacy settings. It also requires Facebook to develop a comprehensive privacy program, and obtain independent biennial privacy audits for a period of 20 years (Federal Trade Commission, 2012b).

In 2012, the FTC released a final report based on its work in the previous two years. The report describes industry best practices for protecting the privacy of Americans and focuses on five areas: Do Not Track, mobile privacy, data brokers, large platform providers (advertising networks, operating systems, browsers, and social media companies), and the development of self-regulatory codes. The report called for implementation of an easy to use, persistent, and effective Do Not Track system; improved disclosures for use of mobile data; making it easier for people to see the files about themselves compiled by data brokers; development of a central Web site where data brokers identify themselves; development of a privacy policy by large platform providers to regulate comprehensive tracking across the Internet; and enforcement of self-regulatory rules to ensure firms adhere to industry codes of conduct (Federal Trade Commission, 2012c).

In 2014, the FTC issued a report on the data broker industry, which is at the heart of the online and offline privacy debate in the United States. The report found that data brokers operate without transparency, and most users have no idea how their information is being used. The report found that data brokers collect and store billions of data elements covering nearly every U.S. consumer. One of the nine data brokers studied had information on more than 1.4 billion consumer transactions and 700 billion data elements and another broker adds more than 3 billion new data points to its database each month. The report called for legislation giving consumers more control over their personal information by creating a centralized portal where data brokers would identify themselves, describe their information collection and use practices, and provide links to access tools and opt-outs; require brokers to give consumers access to their data; provide opportunities to opt-out of data collection; describe where they get information and what inferences they make from the data; and require retailers to notify customers when they share information with data brokers (Federal Trade Commission, 2014). The emphasis in recent FTC privacy reports is not on restricting the collection of information (as in previous eras of privacy regulation), but instead on giving consumers rights with respect to the information collected about them in large databases and its use by various businesses and agencies.

Facing fines, congressional investigations, and public embarrassment over their privacy invading behaviors, with the potential loss of some business and credibility, the major players in the e-commerce industry in the United States are beginning to change some of their policies regarding the treatment of consumer data. Large Internet firms that rely on personal information (Google, Facebook, Microsoft, and many others), along with privacy advocates, are calling on Washington to develop comprehensive consumer privacy protection legislation that would clarify for consumers and business firms the meaning of privacy in the current online commercial environment (Singer, 2013). The Obama administration has proposed a Consumer Privacy Bill of Rights that emphasizes transparency (how personal information is being used and distributed) and user control over personal information. This represents a change in the meaning of privacy from "leave me alone" to "I want to know and control how my personal information is being used." Invoking a Bill of Rights perspective is shifting the privacy debate towards a rights-based privacy policy, similar to the European model described below.

The European Data Protection Directive

In Europe, privacy protection is much stronger than it is in the United States. In the United States, private organizations and businesses are permitted to use PII gathered in commercial transactions for other business purposes without the prior consent of the consumer (so-called secondary uses of PII). In the United States, there is no federal agency charged with enforcing privacy laws. Instead, privacy laws are enforced largely through self-regulation by businesses, and by individuals who must sue agencies or companies in court to recover damages. This is expensive and rarely done. The European approach to privacy protection is more comprehensive and regulatory in nature. European countries do not allow business firms to use PII without the prior consent of consumers. They enforce their privacy laws by creating data protection agencies to pursue complaints brought by citizens and actively enforce privacy laws.

In 1998, the European Commission's Data Protection Directive went into effect, standardizing and broadening privacy protection in the E.U. nations. The Directive is based on the Fair Information Practices doctrine but extends the control individuals can exercise over their personal information. The Directive requires companies to inform people when they collect information about them and to disclose how it will be stored and used. Customers must provide their informed consent before any company can legally use data about them, and they have the right to access that information, correct it, and request that no further data be collected. Further, the Directive prohibits the transfer of PII to organizations or countries that do not have similarly strong privacy protection policies. This means that data collected in Europe by American business firms cannot be transferred or processed in the United States (which has weaker privacy protection laws). This would potentially interfere with a $3.5 trillion annual trade flow in goods, services, and investment between the United States and Europe.

safe harbor

a private self-regulating policy and enforcement mechanism that meets the objectives of government regulators and legislation but does not involve government regulation or enforcement

The U.S. Department of Commerce, working with the European Commission, developed a safe harbor framework for U.S. firms. A **safe harbor** is a private self-regulating policy and enforcement mechanism that meets the objectives of government regulators and legislation, but does not involve government regulation or enforcement. The government plays a role in certifying safe harbors, however. Organizations that decide to participate in the safe harbor program must develop policies that meet European standards, and they must publicly sign on to a Web-based register maintained by the Department of Commerce. Enforcement occurs in the United States and relies to a large extent on self-policing and regulation, backed up by government enforcement of fair trade statutes. For more information on the safe harbor procedures and the E.U. Data Protection Directive, see www.export.gov/safeharbor.

In 2012, the European Union issued significant proposed changes to its data protection rules (European Commission, 2012). The new rules would apply to all companies providing services in Europe, and require Internet companies like Amazon, Facebook, Apple, Google, and others to obtain explicit consent from consumers about the use of their personal data, delete information at the user's request (based on the "right to be forgotten," as discussed in the opening case), and retain information only as long as absolutely necessary. The regulations also give users the right to transfer text, photo, and video files in usable formats from one online service provider to another. American consumers do not have such a national right to data portability, and have to depend on the largesse of companies like Google, which permits them to download their own YouTube videos or Picasa photo albums. The proposed rules provide for fines up to 2% of the annual gross revenue of offending firms. In the case of Google, for instance, with 2013 revenue of over $57 billion, a maximum fine would amount to over $1.1 billion. The requirement for user consent includes the use of cookies and super cookies used for tracking purposes across the Web (third-party cookies), and not for cookies used on a Web site. In March 2014, the European Parliment gave a strong endorsement to the proposed data protection rules. In order to become law, the next step is for the proposed regulations to be adopted by the E.U.'s Council of Ministers, which is expected to occur by the end of 2015 (European Commission, 2014; Pearce and Clarke, 2014).

PRIVATE INDUSTRY SELF-REGULATION

The online industry in the United States has historically opposed online privacy legislation, arguing that industry can do a better job of protecting privacy than government.

However, individual firms such as Facebook, Apple, Yahoo, and Google have adopted policies on their own in an effort to address the concerns of the public about personal privacy on the Internet. The online industry formed the Online Privacy Alliance (OPA) in 1998 to encourage self-regulation in part as a reaction to growing public concerns and the threat of legislation being proposed by FTC and privacy advocacy groups.

The FTC and private industry in the United States has created the idea of safe harbors from government regulation. For instance, COPPA includes a provision enabling industry groups or others to submit for the FTC's approval self-regulatory guidelines that implement the protections of the FIP principles and FTC rules. In May 2001, the FTC approved the TRUSTe Internet privacy protection program under the terms of COPPA as a safe harbor.

OPA has developed a set of privacy guidelines that members are required to implement. The primary focus of industry efforts has been the development of online "seals" that attest to the privacy policies on a site. The Better Business Bureau (BBB), TRUSTe, WebTrust, and major accounting firms—among them PricewaterhouseCoopers' BetterWeb—have established seals for Web sites. To display a seal, Web site operators must conform to certain privacy principles, a complaint resolution process, and monitoring by the seal originator. More than 5,000 companies subscribe to TRUSTe and display the TRUSTe seal, while more than 140,000 display the BBB's Accredited Business seal. Nevertheless, online privacy seal programs have had a limited impact on Web privacy practices. Critics argue that the seal programs are not particularly effective in safeguarding privacy. For these reasons, the FTC has not deemed the seal programs as "safe harbors" yet (with the exception of TRUSTe's children's privacy seal under COPPA), and the agency continues to push for legislation to enforce privacy protection principles.

The advertising network industry has also formed an industry association, the Network Advertising Initiative (NAI), to develop privacy policies. The NAI policies have two objectives: to offer consumers a chance to opt out of advertising network programs (including e-mail campaigns), and to provide consumers redress from abuses. In order to opt out, the NAI has created a Web site—Networkadvertising.org—where consumers can use a global opt-out feature to prevent network advertising agencies from placing their cookies on a user's computer. If a consumer has a complaint, the NAI has a link to the Truste.org Web site where the complaints can be filed. Consumers still receive Internet advertising just as before, but the ads will not be targeted to their browsing behavior (Network Advertising Initiative, 2010; 2011).

The AdChoices program is an industry-sponsored initiative to encourage Web sites to be more transparent about how they use personal information and to make it more likely that appropriate ads are shown to users by asking users themselves. An AdChoices icon appears next to ads, and clicking on this icon provides more information and the opportunity to provide feedback to the advertiser. There is no data available yet to indicate how well this program is working.

In general, industry efforts at self-regulation in online privacy have not succeeded in reducing American fears of privacy invasion during online transactions, or in reducing the level of privacy invasion. At best, self-regulation has offered consumers notice about whether a privacy policy exists, but usually says little about the actual use of

TABLE 8.9	PRIVACY ADVOCACY GROUPS
ADVOCACY GROUP	**FOCUS**
Electronic Privacy Information Center (EPIC)	Washington, DC–based watch-dog group
Privacy International	Watch-dog organization focused on privacy intrusions by government and businesses
Center for Democracy and Technology	Foundation- and business-supported group with a legislative focus
Privacy.org	Clearinghouse sponsored by EPIC and Privacy International
Privacy Rights Clearinghouse	Educational clearinghouse
Online Privacy Alliance	Industry-supported clearinghouse

the information, does not offer consumers a chance to see and correct the information or control its use in any significant way, offers no promises for the security of that information, and offers no enforcement mechanism (Hoofnagle, 2005).

PRIVACY ADVOCACY GROUPS

There are a number of privacy advocacy groups on the Web that monitor developments in privacy. Some of these sites are industry-supported, while others rely on private foundations and contributions. Some of the better-known sites are listed in **Table 8.9**.

THE EMERGING PRIVACY PROTECTION BUSINESS

As Web sites become more invasive and aggressive in their use of personal information, and as public concern grows, a number of firms have sprung up to sell products that they claim will help people protect their privacy. Venture capital firms have picked up the scent and are investing millions in small start-up companies based on the premise that people will pay to protect their reputations. For instance, Reputation.com has received over $67 million in funding as of 2014. Other firms in the business of reputation protection include Avira Social Network Protection and Abine. For as little as $14.95 a month, you can monitor what people are saying about you, or about your children, on social Web sites. A small number of firms are trying to help users put a price on their personal information, and sell it to the highest bidders if they want (Laudon, 1996). Personal.com creates a personal data locker for users that stores all their online behavioral information in a single location. Users can then decide who they want to give access to, and how much to charge. The idea is to make it possible for people to control the uses of their information. Personal.com has raised $22 million as of 2014. However, these types of firms can succeed only if people are willing to pay out of pocket for privacy protection. Economists studying this issue have found that people are not willing to pay much to protect their privacy (at most about $30), and many are willing to give up their privacy for small discounts (Brustein, 2012; Acquisti et al., 2009).

TECHNOLOGICAL SOLUTIONS

A number of privacy-enhancing technologies have been developed for protecting user privacy during interactions with Web sites such as spyware blockers, pop-up blockers, cookie managers, and secure e-mail (see **Table 8.10**). However, the most powerful tools for protecting privacy need to be built into browsers. Responding to pressure from privacy advocates, browsers now have a number of tools that can help users protect their privacy, such as eliminating third-party cookies. One of the most powerful browser-based protections is a built-in Do Not Track capability. Microsoft, Mozilla, Google, and Apple have all introduced a default Do Not Track capability. However, refer to the *Insight on Technology* case, *Every Move You Take, Every Click You Make, We'll be Tracking You*, in Chapter 6 for a discussion of the difficulties that have developed in implementing Do Not Track. Most of these tools emphasize security—the ability of individuals to protect their communications and files from illegitimate snoopers.

TABLE 8.10	TECHNOLOGICAL PROTECTIONS FOR ONLINE PRIVACY	
TECHNOLOGY	**PRODUCTS**	**PROTECTION**
Spyware blockers	Spyware Doctor, ZoneAlarm, Ad-Aware, and Spybot—Search & Destroy (Spybot-S&D) (freeware)	Detects and removes spyware, adware, keyloggers, and other malware
Pop-up blockers	Browsers: Firefox, IE, Safari, Opera Toolbars: Google, Yahoo, MSN Add-on programs: Adblock, PopupMaster	Prevents calls to ad servers that push pop-up, pop-under, and leave-behind ads; restricts downloading of images at user request
Secure e-mail	ZL Technologies; SafeMessage.com, Hushmail.com, Pretty Good Privacy (PGP)	E-mail and document encryption
Anonymous remailers	Jack B. Nymble, Java Anonymous Proxy, QuickSilver, Mixmaster	Send e-mail without trace
Anonymous surfing	Freedom Websecure, Anonymizer.com, Tor, GhostSurf	Surf without a trace
Cookie managers	Cookie Monster and most browsers	Prevents client computer from accepting cookies
Disk/file erasing programs	Mutilate File Wiper, Eraser, WipeFile	Completely erases hard drive and floppy files
Policy generators	OECD Privacy Policy Generator	Automates the development of an OECD privacy compliance policy
Public Key Encryption	PGP Desktop	Program that encrypts your mail and documents

| 8.3 | **INTELLECTUAL PROPERTY RIGHTS** |

Congress shall have the power to "promote the progress of science and useful arts, by securing for limited times to authors and inventors the exclusive right to their respective writings and discoveries."

—Article I, Section 8, Constitution of the United States, 1788.

Next to privacy, the most controversial ethical, social, and political issue related to e-commerce is the fate of intellectual property rights. Intellectual property encompasses all the tangible and intangible products of the human mind. As a general rule, in the United States, the creator of intellectual property owns it. For instance, if you personally create an e-commerce site, it belongs entirely to you, and you have exclusive rights to use this "property" in any lawful way you see fit. But the Internet potentially changes things. Once intellectual works become digital, it becomes difficult to control access, use, distribution, and copying. These are precisely the areas that intellectual property seeks to control.

Digital media differ from books, periodicals, and other media in terms of ease of replication, transmission, and alteration; difficulty in classifying a software work as a program, book, or even music; compactness—making theft easy; and difficulty in establishing uniqueness. Before widespread use of the Internet, copies of software, books, magazine articles, or films had to be stored on physical media, such as paper, computer disks, or videotape, creating hurdles to distribution.

The Internet technically permits millions of people to make perfect digital copies of various works—from music to plays, poems, and journal articles—and then to distribute them nearly cost-free to hundreds of millions of Web users. The proliferation of innovation has occurred so rapidly that few entrepreneurs have stopped to consider who owns the patent on a business technique or method that they are using on their site. The spirit of the Web has been so free-wheeling that many entrepreneurs ignored trademark law and registered domain names that could easily be confused with another company's registered trademarks. In short, the Internet has demonstrated the potential to disrupt traditional conceptions and implementations of intellectual property law developed over the last two centuries.

The major ethical issue related to e-commerce and intellectual property concerns how we (both as individuals and as business professionals) should treat property that belongs to others. From a social point of view, the main questions are: Is there continued value in protecting intellectual property in the Internet age? In what ways is society better off, or worse off, for having the concept of property apply to intangible ideas? Should society make certain technology illegal just because it has an adverse impact on some intellectual property owners? From a political perspective, we need to ask how the Internet and e-commerce can be regulated or governed to protect the institution of intellectual property while at the same time encouraging the growth of e-commerce and the Internet.

TYPES OF INTELLECTUAL PROPERTY PROTECTION

There are three main types of intellectual property protection: copyright, patent, and trademark law. In the United States, the development of intellectual property law begins in the U.S. Constitution in 1788, which mandated Congress to devise a system of laws to promote "the progress of science and the useful arts." Congress passed the first copyright law in 1790 to protect original written works for a period of 14 years, with a 14-year renewal if the author was still alive. Since then, the idea of copyright has been extended to include music, films, translations, photographs, and most recently the designs of vessels under 200 feet (Fisher, 1999). The copyright law has been amended (mostly extended) 11 times in the last 40 years.

The goal of intellectual property law is to balance two competing interests—the public and the private. The public interest is served by the creation and distribution of inventions, works of art, music, literature, and other forms of intellectual expression. The private interest is served by rewarding people for creating these works through the creation of a time-limited monopoly granting exclusive use to the creator.

Maintaining this balance of interests is always challenged by the invention of new technologies. In general, the information technologies of the last century—from radio and television to CD-ROMs, DVDs, and the Internet—have at first tended to weaken the protections afforded by intellectual property law. Owners of intellectual property have often, but not always, been successful in pressuring Congress and the courts to strengthen the intellectual property laws to compensate for any technological threat, and even to extend protection for longer periods of time and to entirely new areas of expression. In the case of the Internet and e-commerce technologies, once again, intellectual property rights are severely challenged. In the next few sections, we discuss the significant developments in each area: copyright, patent, and trademark.

COPYRIGHT: THE PROBLEM OF PERFECT COPIES AND ENCRYPTION

In the United States, **copyright law** protects original forms of expression such as writings (books, periodicals, lecture notes), art, drawings, photographs, music, motion pictures, performances, and computer programs from being copied by others for a period of time. Up until 1998, the copyright law protected works of individuals for their lifetime plus 50 years beyond their life, and works created for hire and owned by corporations, such as Mickey Mouse of the Disney Corporation, for 75 years after initial creation. Copyright does not protect ideas—just their expression in a tangible medium such as paper, cassette tape, or handwritten notes.

In 1998, the U.S. Congress extended the period of copyright protection for an additional 20 years, for a total of 95 years for corporate-owned works, and life plus 70 years of protection for works created by individuals (the Copyright Term Extension Act, also known as CTEA). In *Eldred v. Ashcroft*, the U.S. Supreme Court ruled that CTEA was constitutional, over the objections of groups arguing that Congress

copyright law
protects original forms of expression such as writings, art, drawings, photographs, music, motion pictures, performances, and computer programs from being copied by others for a minimum of 70 years

had given copyright holders a permanent monopoly over the expression of ideas, which ultimately would work to inhibit the flow of ideas and creation of new works by making existing works too expensive (*Eldred v. Ashcroft*, 2003; Greenhouse, 2003a). Librarians, academics, and others who depend on inexpensive access to copyrighted material opposed the legislation.

In the mid-1960s, the Copyright Office began registering software programs, and in 1980, Congress passed the Computer Software Copyright Act, which clearly provides protection for source and object code and for copies of the original sold in commerce, and sets forth the rights of the purchaser to use the software while the creator retains legal title. For instance, the HTML code for a Web page—even though easily available to every browser—cannot be lawfully copied and used for a commercial purpose, say, to create a new Web site that looks identical.

Copyright protection is clear-cut: it protects against copying of entire programs or their parts. Damages and relief are readily obtained for infringement. The drawback to copyright protection is that the underlying ideas behind a work are not protected, only their expression in a work. A competitor can view the source code on your Web site to see how various effects were created and then reuse those techniques to create a different Web site without infringing on your copyright.

Look and Feel

"Look and feel" copyright infringement lawsuits are precisely about the distinction between an idea and its expression. For instance, in 1988, Apple Computer sued Microsoft Corporation and Hewlett-Packard Inc. for infringing Apple's copyright on the Macintosh interface. Among other claims, Apple claimed that the defendants copied the expression of overlapping windows. Apple failed to patent the idea of overlapping windows when it invented this method of presenting information on a computer screen in the late 1960s. The defendants counterclaimed that the idea of overlapping windows could only be expressed in a single way and, therefore, was not protectable under the "merger" doctrine of copyright law. When ideas and their expression merge (i.e., if there is only one way to express an idea), the expression cannot be copyrighted, although the method of producing the expression might be patentable (*Apple Computer, Inc. v. Microsoft*, 1989). In general, courts appear to be following the reasoning of a 1992 case—*Brown Bag Software vs. Symantec Corp.*—in which the court dissected the elements of software alleged to be infringing. There, the Federal Circuit Court of Appeals found that neither similar concept, function, general functional features (e.g., drop-down menus), nor colors were protectable by copyright law (*Brown Bag vs. Symantec Corp.*, 1992).

Fair Use Doctrine

doctrine of fair use
under certain circumstances, permits use of copyrighted material without permission

Copyrights, like all rights, are not absolute. There are situations where strict copyright observance could be harmful to society, potentially inhibiting other rights such as the right to freedom of expression and thought. As a result, the doctrine of fair use has been created. The **doctrine of fair use** permits teachers and writers to use copyrighted materials without permission under certain circumstances. **Table 8.11**

TABLE 8.11	FAIR USE CONSIDERATIONS TO COPYRIGHT PROTECTIONS
FAIR USE FACTOR	INTERPRETATION
Character of use	Nonprofit or educational use versus for-profit use.
Nature of the work	Creative works such as plays or novels receive greater protection than factual accounts, e.g., newspaper accounts.
Amount of work used	A stanza from a poem or a single page from a book would be allowed, but not the entire poem or a book chapter.
Market effect of use	Will the use harm the marketability of the original product? Has it already harmed the product in the marketplace?
Context of use	A last-minute, unplanned use in a classroom versus a planned infringement.

describes the five factors that courts consider when assessing what constitutes fair use.

The fair use doctrine draws upon the First Amendment's protection of freedom of speech (and writing). Journalists, writers, and academics must be able to refer to, and cite from, copyrighted works in order to criticize, or even discuss them. Professors are allowed to clip a contemporary article just before class, copy it, and hand it out to students as an example of a topic under discussion. However, they are not permitted to add this article to the class syllabus for the next semester without compensating the copyright holder.

What constitutes fair use has been at issue in a number of recent cases, including the Google Books Library Project described in the case study at the end of the chapter, and in several recent lawsuits. In *Kelly v. Arriba Soft* (2003) and *Perfect 10, Inc. v. Amazon.com, Inc. et al.,* (2007), the Federal Circuit Court of Appeals for the 9th Circuit held that the display of thumbnail images in response to search requests constituted fair use. A similar result was reached by the district court for the District of Nevada with respect to Google's storage and display of Web sites from cache memory, in *Field v. Google, Inc.* (2006). In all of these cases, the courts accepted the argument that caching the material and displaying it in response to a search request was not only a public benefit, but also a form of marketing of the material on behalf of its copyright owner, thereby enhancing the material's commercial value. Fair use is also at issue in the lawsuit filed by Viacom against Google and YouTube described further in the next section.

The Digital Millennium Copyright Act of 1998

The **Digital Millennium Copyright Act (DMCA)** of 1998 was the first major effort to adjust the copyright laws to the Internet age. This legislation was the result of a confrontation between the major copyright holders in the United States (publishing, sheet music, record label, and commercial film industries), ISPs, and users of copy-

Digital Millennium Copyright Act (DMCA)
the first major effort to adjust the copyright laws to the Internet age

righted materials such as libraries, universities, and consumers. While social and political institutions are sometimes thought of as "slow" and the Internet as "fast," in this instance, powerful groups of copyright owners anticipated Web music services such as Napster by several years. Napster was formed in 1999, but work by the World Intellectual Property Organization (WIPO)—a worldwide body formed by the major copyright-holding nations of North America, Europe, and Japan—began in 1995. **Table 8.12** summarizes the major provisions of the DMCA.

The penalties for willfully violating the DMCA include restitution to the injured parties of any losses due to infringement. Criminal remedies may include fines up to $500,000 or five years imprisonment for a first offense, and up to $1 million in fines and 10 years in prison for repeat offenders. These are serious remedies.

The DMCA attempts to answer two vexing questions in the Internet age. First, how can society protect copyrights online when any practical encryption scheme imaginable can be broken by hackers and the results distributed worldwide? Second, how can society control the behavior of thousands of ISPs, who often host infringing Web sites or who provide Internet service to individuals who are routine infringers? ISPs claim to be like telephone utilities—just carrying messages—and they do not want to put their users under surveillance or invade the privacy of users. The DMCA recognizes that ISPs have some control over how their customers use their facilities.

The DMCA implements the WIPO Copyright Treaty of 1996, which declares it illegal to make, distribute, or use devices that circumvent technology-based protections of copyrighted materials, and attaches stiff fines and prison sentences for violations. WIPO is an organization within the United Nations. Recognizing that these provisions alone cannot stop hackers from devising circumventions, the DMCA makes it difficult for such inventors to reap the fruits of their labors by making the ISPs (including universities) responsible and accountable for hosting Web sites or providing services

TABLE 8.12	THE DIGITAL MILLENNIUM COPYRIGHT ACT
SECTION	IMPORTANCE
Title I, WIPO Copyright and Performances and Phonograms Treaties Implementation	Makes it illegal to circumvent technological measures to protect works for either access or copying or to circumvent any electronic rights management information.
Title II, Online Copyright Infringement Liability Limitation	Requires ISPs to "take down" sites they host if they are infringing copyrights, and requires search engines to block access to infringing sites. Limits liability of ISPs and search engines.
Title III, Computer Maintenance Competition Assurance	Permits users to make a copy of a computer program for maintenance or repair of the computer.
Title IV, Miscellaneous Provisions	Requires the Copyright Office to report to Congress on the use of copyright materials for distance education; allows libraries to make digital copies of works for internal use only; extends musical copyrights to include "webcasting."

SOURCE: Based on data from United States Copyright Office, 1998.

to infringers once the ISP has been notified. ISPs are not required to intrude on their users. However, after copyright holders inform the ISP that a hosted site or individual users are infringing, they must "take down" the site immediately to avoid liability and potential fines. ISPs must also inform their subscribers of the ISP's copyright management policies. Copyright owners can subpoena the personal identities of any infringers using an ISP. There are important limitations on these ISP prohibitions that are mostly concerned with the transitory caching of materials for short periods without the knowledge of the ISP. However, should the ISP be deriving revenues from the infringement, it is as liable as the infringer, and is subject to the same penalties.

Title I of the DMCA provides a partial answer to the dilemma of hacking. It is probably true that skilled hackers can easily break any usable encryption scheme, and the means to do so on a large scale through distribution of decryption programs already exists. The WIPO provisions accept this possibility and simply make it illegal to do so, or to disseminate or enable such dissemination, or even store and transmit decrypted products or tools. These provisions put large ISPs on legal notice.

There are a number of exceptions to the strong prohibitions against defeating a copyright protection scheme outlined above. There are exceptions for libraries to examine works for adoption, for reverse engineering to achieve interoperability with other software, for encryption research, for privacy protection purposes, and for security testing. Many companies, such as YouTube and Google, have latched on to the provision of the DMCA that relates to removing infringing material upon request of the copyright owner as a "safe harbor" that precludes them from being held responsible for copyright infringement. This position was tested in a $1 billion lawsuit originally brought by Viacom in 2007 against Google and YouTube for willful copyright infringement.

In the Viacom case, Viacom alleged that YouTube and Google engaged in massive copyright infringement by deliberately and knowingly building up a library of infringing works to draw traffic to the YouTube site and enhance its commercial value. Entire episodes of shows like SpongeBob SquarePants and the Jon Stewart show were appearing on YouTube without permission or payment. In response, Google and YouTube claim that they are protected by the DMCA's safe harbor and fair use, and that it is often impossible to know whether a video is infringing or not. YouTube also does not display ads on pages where consumers can view videos unless it has an agreement with the content owner. In 2007, Google announced a filtering system (ContentID) aimed at addressing the problem. It requires content owners to give Google a copy of their content so Google can load it into an auto-identification system. The copyright owner can specify whether it will allow others to post the material. Then after a video is uploaded to YouTube, the system attempts to match it with its database of copyrighted material and removes any unauthorized material. Whether content owners will be satisfied with this system is unknown, particularly because guidelines issued by a coalition of major media and Internet companies with respect to the handling of copyrighted videos on user-generated Web sites call for the use of filtering technology that can block infringing material before it is posted online. In June 2010, the federal district court ruled against Viacom, on the grounds that YouTube had taken down more than 100,000 videos requested by Viacom, as required by the DMCA, and that YouTube was protected by the safe harbor provisions of DMCA. Viacom continued to appeal the case. In 2012, a U.S. appeals court reversed the lower court decision, allowing the case to move forward. The court ruled that YouTube had specific knowledge or awareness of the infringing activity, and ample ability to prevent it. In 2013, the lower court ruled against Viacom's claim that Google knew it was infringing copyrighted material, and encouraged infringement. In March 2014, seven years after the billion dollar suit was filed, Google and Viacom settled out of court. Google's efforts to take down copyrighted material had become very effective, and Google agreed to rent hundreds of Viacom shows (Kaufman, 2014).

The entertainment industry continues to be aggressive in pursuing online copyright infringement. In 2011, in a suit brought by the Motion Picture Association of America, a federal judge ordered DVD-streaming service Zediva to shut down. Zediva had argued that its service was just like one person lending a physical DVD to another, but just using the Web to accomplish the task. The court did not agree and said that the service threatened the growing Internet-based video-on-demand market. In 2012, the Department of Justice seized the domain megaupload.com, one of the largest cyberlockers on the Internet dedicated to storing and sharing copyrighted movies and music. A **cyberlocker** is an online file storage service dedicated to sharing copyrighted material (often movies) illegally. Megaupload's founder Kim Dotcom was arrested in New Zealand at his home, and $17 million in assets were confiscated, and later, $37 million in cash in Hong Kong was confiscated. Since the Megaupload case, other cyberlockers have restricted their activities to avoid a similar fate as Megaupload.

In 2013, the Center for Copyright Information (CCI), along with 5 of the largest ISPs, major entertainment industry companies, and the Consumer Advisory Board launched the Copyright Alert System (CAS)—a tiered notice and response system aimed at reducing copyright infringement over P2P networks. During its first 10 months of operation, the CAS sent out over 1.3 million alerts to 720,000 ISP account holders of alleged copyright infringement. If the account holder ignores repeated alerts, their ISP may impose consequences, such as a downgrade of the customer's Internet service. The CCI believes that the CAS has great promise for its ability to move user behavior away from copyright infringement and toward legal sources of content (Center for Copyright Information, 2014). Refer to the case study at the end of Chapter 1, *The Pirate Bay: Searching for a Safe Harbor,* for further discussion of copyright issues in e-commerce.

cyberlocker

an online file storage service dedicated to sharing copyrighted material illegally

PATENTS: BUSINESS METHODS AND PROCESSES

> "Whoever invents or discovers any new and useful process, machine, manufacture, or composition of matter, or any new and useful improvement thereof, may obtain a patent therefore, subject to the conditions and requirements of this title."
>
> —Section 101, U.S. Patent Act

patent

grants the owner an exclusive monopoly on the ideas behind an invention for 20 years

A **patent** grants the owner a 20-year exclusive monopoly on the ideas behind an invention. The congressional intent behind patent law was to ensure that inventors of new machines, devices, or industrial methods would receive the full financial and other rewards of their labor and still make widespread use of the invention possible by providing detailed diagrams for those wishing to use the idea under license from the patent's owner. Patents are obtained from the United States Patent and Trademark Office (USPTO), which was created in 1812. Obtaining a patent is much more difficult and time-consuming than obtaining copyright protection (which is automatic with the creation of the work). Patents must be formally applied for, and the granting of a patent is determined by Patent Office examiners who follow a set of rigorous rules. Ultimately, federal courts decide when patents are valid and when infringement occurs.

Patents are very different from copyrights because patents protect the ideas themselves and not merely the expression of ideas. There are four types of inventions for which patents are granted under patent law: machines, man-made products, compositions of matter, and processing methods. The Supreme Court has determined that patents extend to "anything under the sun that is made by man" (*Diamond v. Chakrabarty*, 1980) as long as the other requirements of the Patent Act are met. There are three things that cannot be patented: laws of nature, natural phenomena, and abstract ideas. For instance, a mathematical algorithm cannot be patented unless it is realized in a tangible machine or process that has a "useful" result (the mathematical algorithm exception).

In order to be granted a patent, the applicant must show that the invention is new, original, novel, nonobvious, and not evident in prior arts and practice. As with copyrights, the granting of patents has moved far beyond the original intent of Congress's first patent statute, which sought to protect industrial designs and machines. Patent protection has been extended to articles of manufacture (1842), plants (1930), surgical and medical procedures (1950), and software (1981). The Patent Office did not accept applications for software patents until a 1981 Supreme Court decision that held that computer programs could be a part of a patentable process. Since that time, thousands of software patents have been granted. Virtually any software program can be patented as long as it is novel and not obvious.

Essentially, as technology and industrial arts progress, patents have been extended to both encourage entrepreneurs to invent useful devices and promote widespread dissemination of the new techniques through licensing and artful imitation of the published patents (the creation of devices that provide the same functionality as the invention but use different methods) (Winston, 1998). Patents encourage inventors to come up with unique ways of achieving the same functionality as existing patents. For instance, Amazon's patent on one-click purchasing caused Barnesandnoble.com to invent a simplified two-click method of purchasing.

The danger of patents is that they stifle competition by raising barriers to entry into an industry. Patents force new entrants to pay licensing fees to incumbents, and thus slow down the development of technical applications of new ideas by creating lengthy licensing applications and delays. The *Insight on Technology* case, *Apple and Samsung Fight a Patent Battle Around the Globe,*, examines these issues in the context of the Apple-Samsung lawsuit with respect to infringement of Apple's patents for the iPhone.

E-commerce Patents

Much of the Internet's infrastructure and software was developed under the auspices of publicly funded scientific and military programs in the United States and Europe.

INSIGHT ON TECHNOLOGY

APPLE AND SAMSUNG FIGHT A PATENT BATTLE AROUND THE GLOBE

Imagine you have just bought the car of your dreams, one with an unmistakable, unique look and some very unique features. You drive the car home to discover that your neighbor's newly purchased car is strikingly similar, although manufactured by a different company. It has all the features that your car dealer claimed were unique to your car, but cost substantially less. You might feel "cheated" as a consumer, paying so much more for an identical product. How would you feel if you were the manufacturer?

Apple found itself in a similar situation when Samsung introduced its line of Galaxy smartphones in 2010, phones that Apple claimed were nearly identical in design and functionality to Apple's iPhone, right down to the icons that bounced when clicked and the polished metal band around the phone.

Apple introduced the first iPhone in 2007. The iPhone was the first device that combined the functionality of a phone with a music player and an Internet browser. It quickly captured the lion's share of the smartphone market worldwide. In the same year, Google introduced the Android operating system and licensed it free of charge to other smartphone manufacturers. The Open Handset Alliance, also formed in 2007 and spearheaded by Google, represented a coordinated effort by firms like Samsung to compete with the iPhone.

The first HTC Android phones were sold in 2008, followed shortly by a Samsung Android phone. In 2014, over 1.75 billion people around the world use smartphones. In the United States, Android phones now account for about 50% of the market, while the iPhone has about 40%. Android phones have also swallowed up market share in developing countries, because they typically cost

less than iPhones. Nevertheless, Apple is still the largest single manufacturer of smartphones.

Samsung introduced the Galaxy S in 2010. While the early Samsung smartphones of 2008–2010 did not look like Apple's iPhones or have the same functionality, the Galaxy S was clearly designed to compete against the iPhone, with similar functionality, and it looked strikingly like an iPhone—so much so that Apple sued Samsung in 2011 for trademark and patent infringement, unfair competition, and other violations of law.

Apple alleged in its complaint that Samsung had quite literally copied the functionality and design of the iPhone. Apple claimed that Samsung violated Apple's so-called "utility patents" like the multi-touch interface (which enables gestures such as selecting, scrolling, pinching, and zooming); arrangement of text on screen; arrangement and actions of images (such as bounce-back when the user scrolls down too far), and the movement of buttons when pressed. Apple had been granted patents for these "fundamental features" that the world has come to associate with Apple products. Apple also claimed infringement of its "trade dress" patents. Trade dress patents cover non-functional design elements of physical devices such as the unique appearance of the iPhone.

In a counter-complaint, Samsung denied infringing any Apple patents, and questioned the integrity of the patents issued by the U.S. Patent Office on the grounds that the functionality of the utility patents had already been prior art that Apple itself had copied. Samsung simply denied the trade dress and trademark infringement claims. Samsung claimed as well that Apple had violated its patents on various electronic components that perform critical functions in cell and smartphones. Samsung asked for $422 million in damages. Usually patent and trademark cases are settled out of court after a fair amount of posturing. But in this case, the parties could not come to an agreement, and the case went to a jury trial, a rare, risky, and expensive endeavor.

The jury found in over 700 determinations that Samsung had violated Apple's utility patents covering things like the "bounce back" effect at the end of lists and the ability to distinguish between one-finger scrolling and two-finger scrolling. The jury also found that Samsung had violated Apple's trade dress patents protecting the physical design of the iPhone, and the trademarked icons as well. The $1 billion in damages awarded to Apple (later reduced to $930 million) represented a crushing blow to Samsung, not only in the moment, but also to its future chances of winning similar court cases. The jury flatly denied Samsung's claims that Apple violated its patents on various components and rejected Samsung's claim for $422 million in damages. The same court also ruled that Samsung could not sell its Galaxy 10.1 tablet computer in the United States. This was not just a loss for Samsung, but a warning shot across the bow for Google, the developer of the Android operating system used by Samsung.

In 2013, the war between Apple and Samsung raged on around the globe. Samsung won patent lawsuits in the Netherlands and Germany over the Galaxy Tab 10.1's general design and Samsung's "slide-to-unlock" feature, respectively, but lost them in Japan and the UK over Samsung's "bounce-back" feature and technology allowing phones to send and receive information over third-generation mobile networks. European Union regulators also accused Samsung's lawsuits of breaking antitrust rules. In response, Samsung offered to stop suing Apple over patent disputes as long as Apple agreed to a "particular licensing framework," according to the European Commission. In the United States, although the federal judge in charge of the case entered a final

judgment that Samsung owed Apple $930 million in damages, the judge also permitted Samsung to continue selling 26 different products that were found to infringe on Apple patents. Not surprisingly, both Apple and Samsung proceeded to appeal. Apple was also the beneficiary of a U.S. trade agency ruling preventing Samsung from selling any devices infringing two particular patents covering the detection of headphone jacks and touchscreen operation. Still, Samsung was cleared of infringing on other Apple design patents, which according to Samsung, will prevent Apple from attempting to monopolize rectangles and rounded corners. Samsung also claims that more recent devices have features that differentiate them more clearly from Apple's offerings.

In 2014, Google is expected to take a more central role in Samsung's battle against Apple. Google is one of the few companies with the size and resources to battle Apple as an equal. In its defenses against Apple's latest round of U.S. patent infringement lawsuits, Samsung has argued that Google had been working on Android well before Apple filed its software patents. Google engineers like Andy Rubin, the former head of Google's mobile business, are likely to take the stand and confirm this timeline. Apple is seeking $2 billion from Samsung in this latest series of U.S. lawsuits, more than double what it received in the 2012 jury verdict, but experts are skeptical that Apple can justify such a large figure, noting that there are 250,000 different patents in smartphones like the latest iPhone or Samsung offerings, and proving that a small number of those are worth such a large amount will be difficult. In May 2014, the federal jury hearing the case ruled that Samsung did infringe on Apple's patents in two cases, but that it did not in two others, and awarded Apple just $119.6 million dollars, a far cry from the $2.2 billion that it had originally sought. Still, the dollar amounts aren't as important as the principle of the matter to Apple, which plans to continue to

(continued)

attack Android itself. This latest ruling is still only the latest verdict in what promises to be a protracted battle between Apple and Samsung/Google.

In August 2014, Apple and Samsung decided to end their patent fights outside the United States. The companies agreed to drop all suits against each other in Australia, Japan, South Korea, Germany, the Netherlands, the United Kingdom, France, and Italy. However, they will continue to battle within the United States and have not entered into any cross-licensing agreements. The Apple vs. Samsung battle raises several issues for manufacturers of smartphones, consumers, and the development of the smartphone market. But it also raises ethical issues having to do with what's right and what's wrong. Few, if any, would argue that it's ethically acceptable to copy another person's work (their intellectual property), claim it is your own, and be well rewarded by the marketplace for the theft. In a society that respects property rights, this would seem to be a contradiction: people could take your house or car if they wanted and sell them. Nobody wants this outcome. Copycat designs challenge one of the foundations of intellectual (and other property), which argues that people (and companies) deserve the rewards of their investments and efforts—the "sweat of the brow" theory.

Business critics of the decision argue that innovation in the marketplace will be harmed and slowed down because the inventions of one firm cannot be built upon, but will have to be designed around, slowing the introduction of innovations. They also argue that some of the features Apple claims to own are part of the "standard design" of a smartphone without which a contemporary smartphone can't be built, or only built by the one firm that owns the patents. This would include features of Apple's multi-touch interface like pinching, zooming, and active icons. This is the "steering wheel" argument: you can't build a car without a steering wheel because it's become the standard design in the market. Owners of the steering wheel patent must therefore license the steering wheel patent for a reasonable fee. If smartphone makers could not use some of Apple's patented features, the smartphone market would become fractionated into a plethora of designs, and some phones would have missing features that consumers expect (like pinch to zoom).

Supporters of the decision argue that it provides incentives for firms to invest in design, and come up with new innovations, rather than just copy existing state-of-the-art designs. They point to Windows Phone, Microsoft's operating system for smartphones, which looks nothing like the iOS interface and has received praise for its distinctive design. Moreover, innovative firms like Apple deserve to be rewarded for their research and successful designs and products. Without financial incentives, innovation will decline or disappear. Why should firms innovate if they cannot be rewarded in the marketplace?

▬▬ **SOURCES:** "Apple, Samsung Agree to End Patent Suits Outside U.S.," by Adam Satariano and Joel Rosenblatt, Bloomberg.com, August 6, 2014; "Apple Tells Fed. Circ. to OK $930M Samsung Patent Verdict," by Vin Gurrieri, Law360.com, July 30, 2014; "Apple-Samsung Legal Outcome Won't Likely End Feud," by Mike Snider and Jon Swartz, *USA Today*, May 5, 2014; "Federal Jury Says Samsung Infringed Two Apple Patents," by Jon Swartz and Mike Snider, *USA Today*, May 5, 2014; "Mixed Verdict in Apple-Samsung Patent Fight," by Brian X. Chen, *New York Times*, May 2, 2014; "Apple's War on Samsung Has Google in Crossfire," by Brian X. Chen, *New York Times*, March 30, 2014; "Google is Central to Latest Apple-Samsung Case," by Daisuke Wakabayashi, *Wall Street Journal*, March 30, 2014; "EU Says Samsung Offers to Stop Patent Lawsuits in Europe," Foo Yun Chee, Reuters.com, October 17, 2013; "Apple's Legal Wins Show No Clear Victor in Patent War," by Susan Decker, Bloomberg.com, August 11, 2013; "Apple-Samsung Patent Battle Heads for Next Round," by Ashby Jones, *Wall Street Journal*, August 8, 2013; "Intelligent Automated Assistant," Apple Inc., United States Patent Application, 20120245944, September 27, 2012; "Apple Seeks U.S. Samsung Sales Ban, $707 Million More in Damages," *Reuters*, September 22, 2012; "Samsung Fails to Defeat Galaxy Tablet Sale Ban in Apple Case," by Joel Rosenblatt, Bloomberg.com, September 19, 2012; "Apple Did Not Violate Samsung Patents: U.S. Trade Judge," by Diane Bartz, *Reuters*, September 14, 2012; "Apple Case Muddies the Future of Innovations," by Nick Wingfield, *New York Times*, August 26, 2012; "Apple-Samsung Case Shows Smartphone as Legal Magnet," by Steve Lohr, *New York Times*, August 25, 2012; "Jury Awards $1 Billion to Apple in Samsung Patent Case," by Nick Wingfield, *New York Times*, August 24, 2012; "Apple v. Samsung: The Patent Trial of the Century," by Ashby Jones and Jessica Vascellaro, *Wall Street Journal*, July 24, 2012; *Apple v. Samsung*, Complaint, United States District Court, Northern District of California, Case No. 11-cv-01846-LHK, June 16, 2011.

Unlike Samuel F. B. Morse, who patented the idea of Morse code and made the telegraph useful, most of the inventions that make the Internet and e-commerce possible were not patented by their inventors. The early Internet was characterized by a spirit of worldwide community development and sharing of ideas without consideration of personal wealth (Winston, 1998). This early Internet spirit changed in the mid-1990s with the commercial development of the World Wide Web.

In 1998, a landmark legal decision, *State Street Bank & Trust v. Signature Financial Group, Inc.*, paved the way for business firms to begin applying for "business methods" patents. In this case, a Federal Circuit Court of Appeals upheld the claims of Signature Financial to a valid patent for a business method that allows managers to monitor and record financial information flows generated by a partner fund. Previously, it was thought business methods could not be patented. However, the court ruled there was no reason to disallow business methods from patent protection, or any "step by step process, be it electronic or chemical or mechanical, [that] involves an algorithm in the broad sense of the term" (*State Street Bank & Trust Co. v. Signature Financial Group*, 1998). The State Street decision led to an explosion in applications for e-commerce "business methods" patents. In June 2010, the U.S. Supreme Court issued a divided opinion on business methods patents in the *Bilski et al. v. Kappos* case (*Bilski et al. v. Kappos*, 2010). The majority argued that business methods patents were allowable even though they did not meet the traditional "machine or transformation test," in which patents are granted to devices that are tied to a particular machine, are a machine, or transform articles from one state to another. The minority wanted to flatly declare that business methods are not patentable in part because any series of steps could be considered a business method (Schwartz, 2010). The Supreme Court struck another blow against business method patents in 2014, with its decision in *Alice Corporation vs. CLS Bank International*. The Court ruled that basic business methods cannot be patented and that while software can be patented, implementing an abstract idea that otherwise could not be patented by using software does not transform the idea into a patentable innovation (*Alice Corporation Pty. Ltd. v. CLS Bank International*, 2014).

Table 8.13 on page 530 lists some of the better-known e-commerce patents. Some are controversial. Reviewing these, you can understand the concerns of commentators and corporations. Some of the patent claims are very broad (for example, "name your price" sales methods), have historical precedents in the pre-Internet era (shopping carts), and seem "obvious" (one-click purchasing). Critics of online business methods patents argue that the Patent Office has been too lenient in granting such patents, and that in most instances, the supposed inventions merely copy pre-Internet business methods and thus do not constitute "inventions" (Harmon, 2003; Thurm, 2000; Chiappetta, 2001). The Patent Office argues, on the contrary, that its Internet inventions staff is composed of engineers, lawyers, and specialists with many years of experience with Internet and network technologies, and that it consults with outside technology experts before granting patents. To complicate matters, the European Patent Convention and the patent laws of most European countries do not recognize business methods per se unless the method is implemented through some technology (Takenaka, 2001).

TABLE 8.13	SELECTED E-COMMERCE PATENTS	
COMPANY	SUBJECT	UPDATE
Amazon	One-click purchasing	Amazon attempted to use patent originally granted to it in 1999 to force changes to Barnes & Noble's Web site, but a federal court overturned a previously issued injunction. Eventually settled out of court. In 2007, a USPTO panel rejected some of the patent because of evidence another patent predated it. Amazon amended the patent, and the revised version was confirmed in 2010.
Priceline	Buyer-driven "name your price" sales	Originally filed by Walker Digital, an intellectual property laboratory, and then assigned to Priceline. Granted by the USPTO in 1999. Shortly thereafter, Priceline sued Microsoft and Expedia for copying its patented business method.
Sightsound	Music downloads	Sightsound won a settlement in 2004 against Bertelsmann subsidiaries CDNow and N2K music sites for infringing its patent.
Akamai	Internet content delivery global hosting system	A broad patent granted in 2000 covering techniques for expediting the flow of information over the Internet. Akamai sued Digital Island for violating the patent and, in 2001, a jury found in its favor.
DoubleClick	Dynamic delivery of online advertising	The patent underlying DoubleClick's business of online banner ad delivery, originally granted in 2000. DoubleClick sued competitors 24/7 Media and L90 for violating the patent and ultimately reached a settlement with them.
Overture	Pay for performance search	System and method for influencing position on search result list generated by computer search engine, granted in 2001. Competitor FindWhat sued Overture, charging that patent was obtained illegally; Overture countered by suing both FindWhat and Google for violating patent. Google agreed to pay a license fee to Overture in 2004 to settle.
Acacia Technologies	Streaming video media transmission	Patents for the receipt and transmission of streaming digital audio and or video content originally granted to founders of Greenwich Information Technologies in 1990s. Patents were purchased by Acacia, a firm founded solely to enforce the patents, in 2001.
Soverain Software	Purchase technology	The so-called "shopping cart" patent for network-based systems, which involves any transaction over a network involving a seller, buyer, and payment system. In other words, e-commerce! Soverain filed suit against Amazon for patent infringement, which Amazon paid $40 million to settle. In 2013 a federal district court ruled Soverain's claims against Newegg in part invalid.
MercExchange (Thomas Woolston)	Auction technology	Patents on person-to-person auctions and database search, originally granted in 1995. eBay ordered to pay $25 million in 2003 for infringing on patent. In July 2007, a motion for permanent patent injunction against eBay was denied. MercExchange and eBay settled the dispute in 2008 on confidential terms.
Google	Search technology	Google PageRank patent filed in 1998 and granted in 2001. Became non-exclusive in 2011 and expires in 2017.
Google	Location technology	Patent for a method of using location information in an advertising system issued to Google in 2010.
Apple	Social technology	Apple applied for a patent in 2010 that allows groups of friends attending events to stay in communication with each other and share reactions to live events as they are occurring.
PersonalWeb	Cloud computing, distributed search engine file systems, storage systems	Claims patents are being infringed by Facebook, Yahoo, Google, Apple, Microsoft, and others.

TRADEMARKS: ONLINE INFRINGEMENT AND DILUTION

A trademark is "any word, name, symbol, or device, or any combination thereof ... used in commerce ... to identify and distinguish ... goods ... from those manufactured or sold by others and to indicate the source of the goods."

—The Trademark Act, 1946

Trademark law is a form of intellectual property protection for **trademarks**—a mark used to identify and distinguish goods and indicate their source. Trademark protections exist at both the federal and state levels in the United States. The purpose of trademark law is twofold. First, trademark law protects the public in the marketplace by ensuring that it gets what it pays for and wants to receive. Second, trademark law protects the owner—who has spent time, money, and energy bringing the product to the marketplace—against piracy and misappropriation. Trademarks have been extended from single words to pictures, shapes, packaging, and colors. Some things may not be trademarked such as common words that are merely descriptive ("clock"). Federal trademarks are obtained, first, by use in interstate commerce, and second, by registration with the U.S. Patent and Trademark Office (USPTO). Federal trademarks are granted for a period of 10 years and can be renewed indefinitely.

Disputes over federal trademarks involve establishing infringement. The test for infringement is twofold: market confusion and bad faith. Use of a trademark that creates confusion with existing trademarks, causes consumers to make market mistakes, or misrepresents the origins of goods is an infringement. In addition, the intentional misuse of words and symbols in the marketplace to extort revenue from legitimate trademark owners ("bad faith") is proscribed.

In 1995, the U.S. Congress passed the Federal Trademark Dilution Act (FTDA), which created a federal cause of action for dilution of famous marks. This legislation dispenses with the test of market confusion (although that is still required to claim infringement), and extends protection to owners of famous trademarks against **dilution**, which is defined as any behavior that would weaken the connection between the trademark and the product. In 2006, the FTDA was amended by the Trademark Dilution Revision Act (TDRA), which allows a trademark owner to file a claim based on a "likelihood of dilution" standard, rather than having to provide evidence of actual dilution. The TDRA also expressly provides that dilution may occur through blurring (weakening the connection between the trademark and the goods) and tarnishment (using the trademark in a way that makes the underlying products appear unsavory or unwholesome). Internationally, WIPO handles many cybersquatting cases under its Uniform Dispute Resolution Procedures. In 2014, WIPO warned that the expansion of generic top-level domains recently authorized by ICANN is likely to be very disruptive in terms of trademark protection (New, 2014).

Trademarks and the Internet

The rapid growth and commercialization of the Internet have provided unusual opportunities for existing firms with distinctive and famous trademarks to extend their

trademark
a mark used to identify and distinguish goods and indicate their source

dilution
any behavior that would weaken the connection between the trademark and the product

Anticybersquatting Consumer Protection Act (ACPA)

creates civil liabilities for anyone who attempts in bad faith to profit from an existing famous or distinctive trademark by registering an Internet domain name that is identical or confusingly similar to, or "dilutive" of, that trademark

cybersquatting

involves the registration of an infringing domain name, or other Internet use of an existing trademark, for the purpose of extorting payments from the legitimate owners

cyberpiracy

involves the same behavior as cybersquatting, but with the intent of diverting traffic from the legitimate site to an infringing site

brands to the Internet. These same developments have provided malicious individuals and firms the opportunity to squat on Internet domain names built upon famous marks, as well as attempt to confuse consumers and dilute famous or distinctive marks (including your personal name or a movie star's name). The conflict between legitimate trademark owners and malicious firms was allowed to fester and grow because Network Solutions Inc. (NSI), originally the Internet's sole agency for domain name registration for many years, had a policy of "first come, first served." This meant anyone could register any domain name that had not already been registered, regardless of the trademark status of the domain name. NSI was not authorized to decide trademark issues (Nash, 1997).

In response to a growing number of complaints from owners of famous trademarks who found their trademark names being appropriated by Web entrepreneurs, Congress passed the **Anticybersquatting Consumer Protection Act (ACPA)** in November 1999. The ACPA creates civil liabilities for anyone who attempts in bad faith to profit from an existing famous or distinctive trademark by registering an Internet domain name that is identical or confusingly similar to, or "dilutive" of, that trademark. The act does not establish criminal sanctions. It proscribes using "bad-faith" domain names to extort money from the owners of the existing trademark **(cybersquatting)**, or using the bad-faith domain to divert Web traffic to the bad-faith domain that could harm the good will represented by the trademark, create market confusion, or tarnish or disparage the mark **(cyberpiracy)**. The act also proscribes the use of a domain name that consists of the name of a living person, or a name confusingly similar to an existing personal name, without that person's consent, if the registrant is registering the name with the intent to profit by selling the domain name to that person.

Trademark abuse can take many forms on the Web. **Table 8.14** lists the major behaviors on the Internet that have run afoul of trademark law, and some of the court cases that resulted.

Cybersquatting and Brandjacking

In one of the first cases involving the ACPA, E. & J. Gallo Winery, owner of the registered mark "Ernest and Julio Gallo" for alcoholic beverages, sued Spider Webs Ltd. for using the domain name Ernestandjuliogallo.com. Spider Webs Ltd. was a domain name speculator that owned numerous domain names consisting of famous company names. The Ernestandjuliogallo.com Web site contained information on the risks of alcohol use, anti-corporate articles about E. & J. Gallo Winery, and was poorly constructed. The court concluded that Spider Webs Ltd. was in violation of the ACPA and that its actions constituted dilution by blurring because the Ernestandjuliogallo.com domain name appeared on every page printed off the Web site accessed by that name, and that Spider Webs Ltd. was not free to use this particular mark as a domain name (*E. & J. Gallo Winery v. Spider Webs Ltd.*, 2001). In August 2009, a court upheld the largest cybersquatting judgment to date: a $33 million verdict in favor of Verizon against OnlineNIC, an Internet domain registration company that had used over 660 names that could easily be confused with legitimate Verizon domain names. Although there have not been many cases decided under the ACPA, that does not mean the problem has gone away. Impersonation of individuals and brands on social network sites adds

TABLE 8.14	**INTERNET AND TRADEMARK LAW EXAMPLES**	
ACTIVITY	DESCRIPTION	EXAMPLE CASE
Cybersquatting	Registering domain names similar or identical to trademarks of others to extort profits from legitimate holders	*E. & J. Gallo Winery v. Spider Webs Ltd.*, 129 F. Supp. 2d 1033 (S.D. Tex., 2001) aff'd 286 F. 3d 270 (5th Cir., 2002)
Cyberpiracy	Registering domain names similar or identical to trademarks of others to divert Web traffic to their own sites	*Ford Motor Co. v. Lapertosa*, 2001 U.S. Dist. LEXIS 253 (E.D. Mich., 2001); *PaineWebber Inc. v. Fortuny*, Civ. A. No. 99-0456-A (E.D. Va., 1999); *Playboy Enterprises, Inc. v. Global Site Designs, Inc.*, 1999 WL 311707 (S.D. Fla., 1999); *Audi AG and Volkswagen of America Inc. v. Bob D'Amato* (No. 05-2359; 6th Cir., November 27, 2006)
Metatagging	Using trademarked words in a site's metatags	*Bernina of America, Inc. v. Fashion Fabrics Int'l, Inc.*, 2001 U.S. Dist. LEXIS 1211 (N.D. Ill., 2001); *Nissan Motor Co., Ltd. v. Nissan Computer Corp.*, 289 F. Supp. 2d 1154 (C.D. Cal., 2000), aff'd, 246 F. 3rd 675 (9th Cir., 2000)
Keywording	Placing trademarked keywords on Web pages, either visible or invisible	*Playboy Enterprises, Inc. v. Netscape Communications, Inc.*, 354 F. 3rd 1020 (9th Cir., 2004); *Nettis Environment Ltd. v. IWI, Inc.*, 46 F. Supp. 2d 722 (N.D. Ohio, 1999); *Government Employees Insurance Company v. Google, Inc.*, Civ. Action No. 1:04cv507 (E.D. VA, 2004); *Google, Inc. v. American Blind & Wallpaper Factory, Inc.*, Case No. 03-5340 JF (RS) (N.D. Cal., April 18, 2007)
Linking	Linking to content pages on other sites, bypassing the home page	*Ticketmaster Corp. v. Tickets.com*, 2000 U.S. Dist. Lexis 4553 (C.D. Cal., 2000)
Framing	Placing the content of other sites in a frame on the infringer's site	*The Washington Post, et al. v. TotalNews, Inc., et al*, (S.D.N.Y., Civil Action Number 97-1190)

another dimension to the problem. Both Twitter and Facebook make cybersquatting and impersonation a violation of their terms of service. ICANN's authorization of hundreds of new top-level domains is also expected to make it even harder for companies to track cybersquatters.

Cyberpiracy

Cyberpiracy involves the same behavior as cybersquatting, but with the intent of diverting traffic from the legitimate site to an infringing site. In *Ford Motor Co. v. Lapertosa*, Lapertosa had registered and used a Web site called Fordrecalls.com as an adult entertainment Web site. The court ruled that Fordrecalls.com was in violation of the ACPA in that it was a bad-faith attempt to divert traffic to the Lapertosa site and diluted Ford's wholesome trademark (*Ford Motor Co. v. Lapertosa*, 2001).

The Ford decision reflects two other famous cases of cyberpiracy. In the *Paine Webber Inc. v. Fortuny* case, the court enjoined Fortuny from using the domain name wwwpainewebber.com—a site that specialized in pornographic materials—because it diluted and tarnished Paine Webber's trademark and diverted Web traffic from Paine Webber's legitimate site—Painewebber.com (*Paine Webber Inc. v. Fortuny*, 1999). In the *Playboy Enterprises, Inc. v. Global Site Designs, Inc.* case, the court enjoined the defendants from using the Playboy and Playmate marks in their domain names Playboyonline.net and Playmatesearch.net and from including the Playboy trademark in their metatags. In these cases, the defendants' intention was diversion for financial gain (*Playboy Enterprises, Inc. v. Global Site Designs, Inc.*, 1999).

Typosquatting is a form of cyberpiracy in which a domain name contains a common misspelling of another site's name. These domains are sometimes referred to as "doppelganger" domains. Often the user ends up at a site very different from one they intended to visit. For instance, John Zuccarini is an infamous typosquatter who was jailed in 2002 for setting up pornographic Web sites with URLs based on misspellings of popular children's brands, such as Bob the Builder and Teletubbies. The FTC fined him again in October 2007 for engaging in similar practices (McMillan, 2007). Harvard Business School professor Ben Edelman conducted a study that found that there were at least 938,000 domains typosquatting on the top 3,264 ".com" Web sites, and that 57% of these domains included Google pay-per click ads. In July 2011, Facebook filed a lawsuit against 25 typosquatters who established Web sites with such domain names as Faceboook, Facemook, Faceboik, and Facebooki. In 2013, Facebook was awarded $2.8 milion in damages.

Metatagging

The legal status of using famous or distinctive marks as metatags is more complex and subtle. The use of trademarks in metatags is permitted if the use does not mislead or confuse consumers. Usually this depends on the content of the site. A car dealer would be permitted to use a famous automobile trademark in its metatags if the dealer sold this brand of automobiles, but a pornography site could not use the same trademark, nor a dealer for a rival manufacturer. A Ford dealer would most likely be infringing if it used "Honda" in its metatags, but would not be infringing if it used "Ford" in its metatags. (Ford Motor Company would be unlikely to seek an injunction against one of its dealers.)

In the *Bernina of America, Inc. v. Fashion Fabrics Int'l, Inc.* case, the court enjoined Fashion Fabrics, an independent dealer of sewing machines, from using the trademarks "Bernina" and "Bernette," which belonged to the manufacturer Bernina, as metatags. The court found the defendant's site contained misleading claims about Fashion Fabrics' knowledge of Bernina products that were likely to confuse customers. The use of the Bernina trademarks as metatags per se was not a violation of ACPA, according to the court, but in combination with the misleading claims on the site would cause confusion and hence infringement (*Bernina of America, Inc. v. Fashion Fabrics Int'l, Inc.*, 2001).

In the *Nissan Motor Co., Ltd. v. Nissan Computer Corp.* case, Uzi Nissan had used his surname "Nissan" as a trade name for various businesses since 1980, including Nissan

Computer Corp. Nissan.com had no relationship with Nissan Motor, but over the years began selling auto parts that competed with Nissan Motor. The court ruled that Nissan Computer's behavior did indeed infringe on Nissan Motor's trademarks, but it refused to shut the site down. Instead, the court ruled Nissan Computer could continue to use the Nissan name, and metatags, but must post notices on its site that it was not affiliated with Nissan Motor (*Nissan Motor Co., Ltd. v. Nissan Computer Corp.*, 2000).

Keywording

The permissibility of using trademarks as keywords on search engines is also subtle and depends (1) on the extent to which such use is considered to be a "use in commerce" and causes "initial customer confusion" and (2) on the content of the search results.

In *Playboy Enterprises, Inc. v. Netscape Communications, Inc.*, Playboy objected to the practice of Netscape's and Excite's search engines displaying banner ads unrelated to *Playboy Magazine* when users entered search arguments such as "playboy," "playmate," and "playgirl." The Ninth Circuit Court of Appeals denied the defendant's motion for a summary judgment and held that when an advertiser's banner ad is not labeled so as to identify its source, the practice could result in trademark infringement due to consumer confusion (*Playboy Enterprises, Inc. v. Netscape Communications, Inc.*, 2004).

Google has also faced lawsuits alleging that its advertising network illegally exploits others' trademarks. For instance, insurance company GEICO challenged Google's practice of allowing competitors' ads to appear when a searcher types "Geico" as the search query. A U.S. district court ruled that this practice did not violate federal trademark laws as long as the word "Geico" was not used in the ads' text (*Government Employees Insurance Company v. Google, Inc.*, 2004). Google quickly discontinued allowing the latter, and settled the case (Associated Press, 2005). In July 2009, Rosetta Stone, the language-learning software firm, filed a lawsuit against Google for trademark infringement, alleging its AdWords program allowed other companies to use Rosetta Stone's trademarks for online advertisements without permission. In April 2012, the 4th Circuit Court of Appeals held that a jury might hold Google liable for trademark infringement, pointing to evidence that an internal Google study found that even sophisticated users were sometimes unaware that sponsored links were advertisements. In November 2012, Rosetta Stone and Google settled, which was seen as a strategic win for Google because it eliminated one of the last major cases challenging the legitimacy of its AdWords program. Currently Google allows anyone to buy anyone else's trademark as a keyword. In 2011, Microsoft decided to follow this practice as well with Bing and Yahoo Search.

Linking

Linking refers to building hypertext links from one site to another site. This is obviously a major design feature and benefit of the Web. **Deep linking** involves bypassing the target site's home page and going directly to a content page. In *Ticketmaster Corp. v. Tickets.com*, Tickets.com—owned by Microsoft—competed directly against Ticketmaster in the events ticket market. When Tickets.com did not have tickets for an

linking
building hypertext links from one site to another site

deep linking
involves bypassing the target site's home page, and going directly to a content page

event, it would direct users to Ticketmaster's internal pages, bypassing the Ticketmaster home page. Even though its logo was displayed on the internal pages, Ticketmaster objected on the grounds that such "deep linking" violated the terms and conditions of use for its site (stated on a separate page altogether and construed by Ticketmaster as equivalent to a shrink-wrap license), and constituted false advertising, as well as the violation of copyright. The court found, however, that deep linking per se is not illegal, no violation of copyright occurred because no copies were made, the terms and conditions of use were not obvious to users, and users were not required to read the page on which the terms and conditions of use appeared in any event. The court refused to rule in favor of Ticketmaster, but left open further argument on the licensing issue. In an out-of-court settlement, Tickets.com nevertheless agreed to stop the practice of deep linking (*Ticketmaster v. Tickets.com*, 2000).

Framing

framing

involves displaying the content of another Web site inside your own Web site within a frame or window

Framing involves displaying the content of another Web site inside your own Web site within a frame or window. The user never leaves the framer's site and can be exposed to advertising while the target site's advertising is distorted or eliminated. Framers may or may not acknowledge the source of the content. In *The Washington Post, et al. v. TotalNews, Inc.* case, The Washington Post Company, CNN, Reuters, and several other news organizations filed suit against TotalNews, Inc., claiming that Total-News's use of frames on its Web site, TotalNews.com, infringed upon the respective plaintiffs' copyrights and trademarks, and diluted the content of their individual Web sites. The plaintiffs claimed additionally that TotalNews's framing practice effectively deprived the plaintiffs' Web sites of advertising revenue.

TotalNews's Web site employed four frames. The TotalNews logo appeared in the lower left frame, various links were located in a vertical frame on the left side of the screen, TotalNews's advertising was framed across the screen bottom, and the "news frame," the largest frame, appeared in the center and right. Clicking on a specific news organization's link allowed the reader to view the content of that particular organization's Web site, including any related advertising, within the context of the "news frame." In some instances, the framing distorted or modified the appearance of the linked Web site, including the advertisements, while the appearance of Total-News's advertisements, in a separate frame, remained unchanged. In addition, the URL remained fixed on the TotalNews address, even though the content in the largest frame on the Web site was from the linked Web site. The "news frame" did not, however, eliminate the linked Web site's identifying features.

The case was settled out of court. The news organizations allowed TotalNews to link to their Web sites, but prohibited framing and any attempt to imply affiliation with the news organizations (*The Washington Post, et al. v. TotalNews, Inc.*, 1997).

CHALLENGE: BALANCING THE PROTECTION OF PROPERTY WITH OTHER VALUES

The challenge in intellectual property ethics and law is to ensure that creators of intellectual property can receive the benefits of their inventions and works, while also making it possible for their works and designs to be disseminated and used by the widest possible audience. Protections from rampant theft of intellectual property inevitably lead to restrictions on distribution, and the payments to creators for the use of their works—which in itself can slow down the distribution process. Without these protections, however, and without the benefits that flow to creators of intellectual property, the pace of innovation could decline. In the early years of e-commerce, up to 2005, the balance has been struck more towards Internet distributors and their claim to be free from restrictions on intellectual content, particularly music. Since the development of the iTunes store, smartphones, and tablets, after 2005, the balance has swung back towards content owners, largely because Internet distributors depend on high-quality content to attract audiences, but also partly due to the effectiveness of lawsuits in raising the costs to Internet firms that fail to protect intellectual property.

8.4 GOVERNANCE

Governance has to do with social control: Who will control the Internet? Who will control the processes of e-commerce, the content, and the activities? What elements will be controlled, and how will the controls be implemented? A natural question arises and needs to be answered: Why do we as a society need to "control" e-commerce? Because e-commerce and the Internet are so closely intertwined (though not identical), controlling e-commerce also involves regulating the Internet.

governance
has to do with social control: who will control e-commerce, what elements will be controlled, and how will the controls be implemented

CAN THE INTERNET BE CONTROLLED?

Early Internet advocates argued that the Internet was different from all previous technologies. They contended that the Internet could not be controlled, given its inherent decentralized design, its ability to cross borders, and its underlying packet-switching technology that made monitoring and controlling message content impossible. Many still believe this to be true today. The implication is that the content and behavior of e-commerce sites—indeed Internet sites of any kind—cannot be "controlled" in the same way. Content issues such as pornography, gambling, and offensive written expressions and graphics, along with commercial issue of intellectual property protection, ushered in the current era of growing governmental regulation of the Internet and e-commerce throughout the world. Currently, we are in a mixed-mode policy environment where self-regulation through a variety of Internet policy and technical bodies co-exists with limited government regulation (Stone, 2010). See Chapter 2 for a review of the different governing bodies involved in overseeing the Internet, including ICANN and IANA, and proposed changes in the United States' authority over IANA (see pages 136–137).

In fact, as you learned in the Chapter 2 *Insight on Society* case, *Government Regulation and Surveillance of the Internet*, the Internet is technically very easily controlled, monitored, and regulated from central locations (such as network access points, telecommunication firm or agency fiber trunk lines, as well as servers and routers throughout the network). For instance, in China, Saudi Arabia, Iran, North Korea, Thailand, Singapore, and many other countries, access to the Web is controlled from government-owned centralized routers that direct traffic across their borders and within the country (such as China's "Great Firewall of China," which permits the government to block access to certain U.S. or European Web sites), or via tightly regulated ISPs operating within the countries. In China, for instance, all ISPs need a license from the Ministry of Information Industry (MII), and are prohibited from disseminating any information that may harm the state or permit pornography, gambling, or the advocacy of cults. In addition, ISPs and search engines such as Google, Yahoo, and Bing typically self-censor their Asian content by using only government-approved news sources or, in the case of Google, exit the country altogether. Twitter is not planning any Chinese presence. China has also recently instituted new regulations that require cafes, restaurants, hotels, and bookstores to install Web monitoring software that identifies those using wireless services and monitors Web activity. Because of the design of the Internet, a substantial part of global Internet traffic flows through U.S. telecommunication facilities.

Following the outbreak of street demonstrations in 2009 protesting a rigged election, the Iranian government unleashed one of the world's most sophisticated mechanisms for controlling and censoring the Web. Built with the assistance of Western companies like Siemens and Nokia, the system uses deep packet inspection to open every packet, look for keywords, reseal it, and send it on the network. In Great Britain, Prime Minister David Cameron suggested that he might temporarily block social network sites such as Facebook and Twitter during periods of social unrest such as the rioting that hit the country in 2011.

In the United States, as we have seen in our discussion of intellectual property, e-commerce sites can be put out of business for violating existing laws, and ISPs can be forced to "take down" offending or stolen content. Government security agencies such as the NSA and the FBI can obtain court orders to monitor ISP traffic and engage in widespread monitoring of millions of e-mail messages. Under the USA PATRIOT Act, American intelligence authorities are permitted to tap into whatever Internet traffic they believe is relevant to the campaign against terrorism, in some circumstances without judicial review. Working with the large ISP firms such as AT&T, Verizon, and others, U.S. security agencies have access to nearly all Internet communications throughout the country. And many American corporations are developing restrictions on their employees' at-work use of the Web to prevent gambling, shopping, and other activities not related to a business purpose.

In the United States, efforts to control media content on the Web have run up against equally powerful social and political values that protect freedom of expression, including several rulings by the Supreme Court that have struck down laws attempting to limit Web content in the United States. The U.S. Constitution's First Amendment says, "Congress shall make no law ... abridging the freedom of speech, or of the press." As it turns out, the 200-year-old Bill of Rights has been a powerful brake on efforts to control twenty-first-century online content.

TAXATION

Few questions illustrate the complexity of governance and jurisdiction more potently than taxation of e-commerce sales. In both Europe and the United States, governments rely on sales taxes based on the type and value of goods sold. In Europe, these taxes are collected along the entire value chain, including the final sale to the consumer, and are called "value-added taxes" (VAT). See the *Insight on Business* case, *New Rules Extend EU Taxation of E-commerce*, for a further look at this topic. In the United States, in contrast, taxes are collected by states and localities on final sales to consumers and are called consumption and use taxes. In the United States, there are 50 states, 3,000 counties, and 12,000 municipalities, each with unique tax rates and policies. Cheese may be taxable in one state as a "snack food" but not taxable in another state (such as Wisconsin), where it is considered a basic food. Consumption taxes are generally recognized to be regressive because they disproportionately tax poorer people, for whom consumption is a larger part of total income.

Sales taxes were first implemented in the United States in the late 1930s as a Depression-era method of raising money for localities. Ostensibly, the money was to be used to build infrastructure such as roads, schools, and utilities to support business development, but over the years the funds have been used for general government purposes of the states and localities. In most states, there is a state-based sales tax, and a smaller local sales tax. The total sales tax ranges from zero in some states (North Dakota) to as much as 13% in New York City.

The development of "remote sales" such as mail order/telephone order (MOTO) retail in the United States in the 1970s broke the relationship between physical presence and commerce, complicating the plans of state and local tax authorities to tax all retail commerce. States sought to force MOTO retailers to collect sales taxes for them based on the address of the recipient, but Supreme Court decisions in 1967 and 1992 established that states had no authority to force MOTO retailers to collect state taxes unless the businesses had a "nexus" of operations (physical presence) in the state.

The explosive growth of e-commerce, the latest type of "remote sales," has once again raised the issue of how—and if—to tax remote sales. Since its inception, e-commerce has benefited from a tax subsidy of up to 13% for goods shipped to high sales-tax areas. Local retail merchants have complained bitterly about the e-commerce tax subsidy. E-commerce merchants have argued that this form of commerce needs to be nurtured and encouraged, and that in any event, the crazy quilt of sales and use tax regimes would be difficult to administer for Internet merchants. Online giants like Amazon claim they should not have to pay taxes in states where they have no operations because they do not benefit from local schools, police, fire, and other governmental services. State and local governments meanwhile see billions of tax dollars slipping from their reach. As Amazon's business model has changed with its building of large distribution centers close to urban areas to enable next-day delivery, so has its opposition to paying sales taxes softened.

In 1998, Congress passed the Internet Tax Freedom Act, which placed a moratorium on "multiple or discriminatory taxes on electronic commerce," as well as on taxes on Internet access, for three years until October 2001. Since that time, the moratorium has been extended several times, most currently until November 2014.

The taxation situation in Europe, and trade between Europe and the United States, is similarly complex. The Organization for Economic Cooperation and Development (OECD), the economic policy coordinating body of European, American, and Japanese governments, is currently investigating different schemes for applying consumption

INSIGHT ON BUSINESS

NEW RULES EXTEND EU TAXATION OF E-COMMERCE

Most people are happy when they discover they don't have to pay any sales tax on a purchase they make online. However, few stop to consider the implications that this may have. National and local governments in the last few years have been suffering a persistent budget crunch. Focused on balancing budgets, starved for revenue, and simultaneously facing increased demand for public services, many countries and states that levy sales taxes have been eyeing the lost revenue from e-commerce sales, estimated to be in the billions in 2014. Internet retail kingpin Amazon has been at the center of that battle for years, but as e-commerce establishes itself as an ever-increasing percentage of the retail economy, governments worldwide are putting their collective feet down and demanding tax revenue from all online transactions.

The EU and the U.S. have a combined population of more than 800 million people. In both areas, the tax code is changing to reflect the new online landscape, where goods and services are sold without a physical presence or local representative in the countries where they are purchased. In 2013, the EU standardized its tax collection practices for e-businesses, bringing them more in line with businesses which are not situated in the EU. In the U.S., however, e-commerce retailers were initially granted special protections in the form of nonexistent or relaxed sales tax requirements, in an effort to protect them from bricks-and-mortar retailers. This is no longer necessary in today's world. The EU never seriously considered a similar strategy for e-commerce retailers, believing exemptions of this type to be unfair to existing businesses.

In 2014, any company providing online services to EU customers is bound by new EU regulations to collect a value added tax, or VAT, regardless of whether it has a physical presence in that area or not. The customer's location is the determinant of whether the new EU rules apply. Currently, VAT is due at the location of the seller, but it will now be due at the location of the buyer. This was already the case for non-EU companies selling to EU B2C customers, but will also become policy for EU companies selling to EU B2C customers starting in 2015.

VAT becoming due at the location of customers as opposed to sellers will force EU-based businesses to register in every EU country where their customers reside and charge VAT at local rates. Because non-EU businesses selling to EU customers are already subject to these regulations, in 2015, there will be no distinction between the two as far as VAT collection in EU countries. Another option for these companies will be to register for VAT in one EU country, and electronically submit quarterly returns in that country, still determining amounts based on the VAT of their customers' residencies, and pay their full VAT amount in that country, which would be distributed to the rest of the EU countries. Some analysts predict that Ireland will be a popular registration jurisdiction for this purpose.

These new rules have created some additional requirements to be followed by e-businesses that service the EU. These businesses will need to distinguish between B2C and B2B customers, classify customers by country of residence, begin charging VAT at variable rates depending upon where they are from, report and remit payment of VAT to individual countries, and to create systems that avoid charging EU VAT to B2C customers outside the EU. Companies that fail to do all of these things would theoretically be tax evaders, and EU tax authorities should easily be able to discipline any offenders.

The US is one of the rare countries that does not levy a VAT. State and local taxing jurisdictions are responsible for their own taxes, and there is no national sales tax. Also, sales taxes apply mostly to end consumers, not intermediaries like wholesalers and the retailers themselves. Five out of the fifty states do not currently levy sales taxes, and within those states, there are 7,600 taxing jurisdictions, each with their own set of rules. Before taxation laws were changed and exemptions for online businesses were eliminated, Amazon would move its manufacturing operations from state to state depending on the tax laws of that area. With the adjustments to the EU's tax collection procedures, it's possible that at some point, the US will follow suit, perhaps as the result of pressure from retailers forced to navigate the confusing patchwork of local regulations.

VAT standard percentages in EU countries vary from the high teens, such as in Germany, Spain, and the U.K., to the mid-twenties, such as in Sweden, Denmark, and Hungary, though the reduced percentages are closer to ten percent and below for certain goods and services. The majority of countries have a 20% VAT, and the highest rate is 27%. The EU has also stipulated that wherever the Internet is used solely as a means of communication, this does not necessarily create a taxable good. However, whereas it was once the case in the US that e-commerce businesses received special protections against taxation, the EU is considering adjusting its rate reductions to reflect the fact that digital information services may in some cases actually be more valuable than the direct equivalent of traditional products. For example, e-books have

search facilities, hyperlinks, and archives, and should perhaps not be sold with a steeply reduced VAT rate. The EU has also simplified VAT compliance by creating a "distance selling" threshold for companies—if companies do not cross the sales threshold, they can use local taxation rates as opposed to the rates in places where they seldom send goods. This reduces the regulatory burden of dealing with VAT compliance and administration in those countries. More countries even outside the EU are toying with adding VAT, including Mexico, the Bahamas, and many more.

The EU is helping countries and businesses to adjust to the new rules by posting guidelines and FAQs for businesses hoping to comply with the changes before 2015. Additional guidelines will be available in 2014. Still, for many smaller online business, the regulatory costs involved in compliance with 28 countries in the EU with 75 different VAT rates are a major concern. Even smaller companies are required to store personal data for ten years, adding even more costs. Business owners have bristled at the changes. For example, many of the approximately 34,000 small online business owners in England have rallied behind the Twitter hashtag #VATMESS in protest.

Other countries outside the EU and the United States are also grappling with the issue of e-commerce taxes. In China, the Chinese government reportedly lost over $15.9 billion in potential taxes on e-commerce in 2012, and is now studying the feasibility of levying a 5% tax on e-commerce sales. And some academics are even suggesting the possibility of a global tax on cross-border e-commerce, with funds spend to finance global public goods.

▬ **SOURCES:** "How New VAT Regulations Will Affect SMEs – and How to Prepare," by Carol Tricks, *The Guardian*, December 8, 2014; "#VATMess: UK's Army of Start-Up Firms Protest Over New European VAT Rules Aimed At Curbing Tax Dodging by Web Giants," by Vicki Owen, Thisismoney.co.uk, November 29, 2014; "New EU VAT Regulations Could Threaten Micro-businesses, by Kitty Dann and Eleanor Ross, *The Guardian*, November 25, 2014; "European VAT: 10 Things Online Sellers Need To Know About Taxes On Digital Goods And Services," by Rick Minor, Forbes.com, May 15, 2014; "Frequently Asked Questions," European Commission Taxation and Customs Union, accessed November 2013; "EU Prepares Businesses for VAT Place of Supply Changes," by Ulrika Lomas, Tax-news.com, October 31, 2013; "Chinese Govt is Mulling E-commerce Tax," Chinadaily.com.cn, by Wang Ying, June 5, 2013; "A World of Difference: How the EU and US Tax E-commerce," Tmagazine.ey.com, March 15, 2013; "China E-commerce Evaded $15.9B in tax in 2012," by Liau Yun Qing, Zdnet.com, March 6, 2013; "EU: 2015 VAT Changes to E-services – the "Keep It Simple" Edition, by Tom Borec, Ebiz.pwc.com, January 17, 2013; "Cross-border E-commerce Within the EU," by Tom Borec, Ebiz.pwc.com, November 2012; "Global Taxation of Cross Border E-commerce Income," by Rifat Azam, 31 Virginia Taxation Review 639 (2012).

and business profit taxes for digitally downloaded goods. The European Union began collecting a VAT on digital goods such as music and software delivered to consumers by foreign companies in 2003. Previously, E.U. companies were required to collect the VAT on sales to E.U. customers, but U.S. companies were not. This gave American companies a huge tax edge. European countries have other tax issues with Internet companies like Google, Apple, Yahoo, and others, that sell goods to consumers in one country, but book the sales in a low-tax country like Ireland.

NET NEUTRALITY

net neutrality

the concept that Internet backbone owners should treat all Internet traffic equally (or "neutrally") in the sense that usage is charged the same flat rate regardless of how much bandwidth is used

Net neutrality is more a political slogan than a concept. It means different things to different people. "Open Internet" is an equivalent slogan. Both of these ideas refer to the principle that the Internet should be a publicly available service that anyone can access and all traffic that flows across the network should be treated in roughly the same way (Federal Communications Commission, 2014). Currently, in the United States, this is the case: all Internet traffic is treated equally (or "neutrally") by Internet backbone owners in the sense that all activities and files—word processing, e-mailing, video downloading, music and video files, etc.—are charged the same flat rate regardless of how much bandwidth is used. No matter how many Netflix movies your neighbor watches, he or she will pay the same amount for Internet service as you. Moreover, Netflix, which consumes over 33% of Internet bandwidth in 2014, does not pay any more than other Web sites that consume little bandwidth. However, the telephone and cable companies (the ISPs) that provide the Internet backbone and which have spent billions of dollars developing the Internet's facilities, would like to be able to charge differentiated prices based on the amount of bandwidth consumed by content being delivered over the Internet, much like a utility company charges according to how much electricity consumers use. The ISPs claim they need to introduce differential pricing in order to properly manage and finance their networks. Critics respond that this really means giant content providers like Google and Netflix will receive faster Internet connections from equally giant ISPs like Comcast, while smaller start-up Web sites and ordinary consumers will receive much slower service.

cap pricing

Putting caps on bandwidth usage, charging more for additional usage in tiers of prices

speed tiers

charging more for higher-speed Internet service

usage-based billing

charging on the basis of metered units of Internet service

congestion pricing

charging more for peak hour Internet service

There are three basic ways to achieve a rationing of bandwidth using the pricing mechanism: cap plans (also known as "tiered plans"), usage metering, and "highway" or "toll" pricing. Each of these plans have historical precedents in highway, electrical, and telephone pricing. **Cap pricing** plans place a cap on usage, say 300 gigabytes a month in a basic plan, with more bandwidth available in 50-gigabyte chunks for, say, an additional $50 a month. The additional increments can also be formalized as tiers where users agree to purchase, say, 400 gigabytes each month as a Tier II plan. Additional tiers could be offered.

A variation on tier pricing is to offer **speed tiers**. Comcast offers its Xfinity Platinum Internet plan with download speeds of 300 megabits per second for $300, and Verizon offers its FiOS high-speed tier for $204 a month. An alternative to cap plans is metered or **usage-based billing**. Time Warner is testing usage plans that start at five gigabytes a month (the equivalent of two high-definition movie downloads) and charge $1 for every additional gigabyte (much like an electric usage meter in a home). One variation on metering is **congestion pricing**, where, as with electric "demand pricing," the price of bandwidth goes up at peak times, say, Saturday and Sunday evening from 6:00 P.M. to 12 midnight—just when everyone wants to watch a movie! Still a third pricing model is **highway (toll) pricing** where the firms that use high levels of bandwidth for their business pay a toll based on their usage of the Internet. Highway pricing is a common way for governments to charge trucking companies based on the weight of their vehicles to compensate for the damage that heavy vehicles inflict on roadways. In the case of the Internet, YouTube, Netflix, Hulu, and other heavy bandwidth providers would pay fees to the Internet carriers based on their utilization of the networks in order to compensate the carriers for the additional capacity they are required to supply to these heavy user firms. Presumably, these fees would be passed on to customers by the industry players by charging users a distribution expense. The only way to do this fairly is to charge fees to users based on how much they download (e.g., a short YouTube video might cost 10 cents, a feature-length movie might cost $1).

> **highway (toll) pricing**
> charging service providers like Netflix for their use of the Internet based on their bandwidth use

Plans to ration bandwidth are controversial, and in some cases bring legal, regulatory, and political scrutiny. For instance, in 2007, Comcast, the largest ISP in the United States, began to slow down traffic and specific Web sites using the BitTorrent protocol not because the content was pirated, but because these video users were consuming huge chunks of the Comcast network capacity during peak load times. In this case Comcast was restricting certain file types. Comcast claims its policy was a legitimate effort to manage capacity. In 2008 the Federal Communications Commission (FCC) disagreed and ordered Comcast to stop discriminating against certain Web sites. Comcast filed suit and in 2010, a federal appeals court ruled against the FCC and for Comcast, arguing that Comcast had the right to manage its own network, including charging some users more for bandwidth or slowing down certain traffic such as BitTorrent files (Watt, 2010).

In 2009, the FCC began developing a national broadband strategy. In 2010, the FCC released the Open Internet Order, which established high-level rules requiring transparency and prohibiting blocking and unreasonable discrimination to protect Internet openness. This order meant that ISPs could not charge for premium access to their Internet pipelines. Verizon sued the FCC arguing that the FCC had no jurisdiction to impose such rules. In January 2014, a federal appeals court threw out the FCC proscriptions on blocking and price discrimination, but retained the idea that the FCC has some jurisdiction over Internet providers, and it upheld transparency rules (e.g., ISPs are required to make public their network management practices). In May 2014, the FCC issued a new proposed regulation that would reinstitute the no-blocking rule, with certain changes to conform to the federal appeals court decision, bar commercially unreasonable actions from threatening Internet openness, and enhance the transparency rule that it had previously adopted. The proposed regulations have elicited over 3.7 million comments as of September 2014, many of which argue that the plan does not adequately protect net neutrality. Many of these critics would like the FCC to regulate broadband ISP service as if it were a utility, and subject it to strict operating rules and even rate controls.

In February 2014, Comcast, the country's largest cable and broadband provider, and Netflix, the giant television and movie streaming service, announced an agreement in which Netflix will pay Comcast for faster and more reliable access to Comcast's subscribers. The deal is a milestone in the history of the Internet. But the growing power of broadband companies like Comcast, Verizon, and AT&T has given those companies increased leverage over companies whose traffic gobbles up large chunks of a network's capacity. Netflix is one of those companies, accounting for nearly 30% of all Internet traffic at peak hours. One fear is that if such deals become common, only the wealthiest content companies will be able to afford to pay for them, which could stifle the next Netflix from ever getting off the ground. The agreement came ten days after Comcast agreed to buy Time Warner Cable for $45 billion, an acquisition that would make Comcast the cable provider to nearly one-third of American homes and the high-speed Internet company for close to 40%. Federal regulators are expected to scrutinize whether that deal would thwart competition among cable and Internet providers. Just to demonstrate its power to discriminate against big Internet bandwidth users, in the months leading up to the agreement, the speed of Netflix delivery over Comcast networks fell 20% from previous levels in the year. Netflix customers experienced gaps in their videos and dropped frames. After the agreement, Netflix speeds on the Comcast network spurted upwards by about 50% above previous levels. Similarly, AT&T is planning to acquire the satellite ISP DirecTV. Critics fear that consolidation in the ISP marketplace will result in just a few firms controlling the entire U.S. Internet service market, and these firms will exercise their power to extract higher fees for premium access from firms like Netflix, fees that ultimately will be passed onto consumers.

How the net neutrality debate impacts the use of the mobile platform in the future is anyone's guess. Will consumers be less likely to want to use the mobile platform once they start to bump up against the data limits of their plans and have to pay additional fees? For instance, in 2012, AT&T restricted FaceTime calls on Apple's iPhones to customers signed up to a premium data plan. After several public interest groups threatened to file a complaint with the FCC, AT&T reversed its policy. Currently, the FCC's proposed net neutrality rules do not cover mobile broadband, enabling cellphone service providers to provide different levels of service and charge different rates for different data plans, but the FCC has indicated that it may be reconsidering that position. Large Internet companies such as Google and Microsoft argue that wireless Internet service should be subject to the same rules and regulations as other types of service. Cellphone companies, not surprisingly, object, and point to the growth of mobile broadband as evidence that the current approach should be maintained.

8.5 PUBLIC SAFETY AND WELFARE

Governments everywhere claim to pursue public safety, health, and welfare. This effort produces laws governing everything from weights and measures to national highways, to the content of radio and television programs. Electronic media of all kinds (telegraph, telephone, radio, and television) have historically been regulated by governments seeking to develop a rational commercial telecommunications environment and to control the content of the media—which may be critical of government or offensive to powerful groups in a society. Historically, in the United States, newspapers and print media have been beyond government controls because of constitutional guarantees of freedom of speech. Electronic media such as radio and television have, on the other hand, always been subject to content regulation because they use the publicly owned frequency spectrum. Telephones have also been regulated as public utilities and "common carriers," with special social burdens to provide service and access, but with no limitations on content.

In the United States, critical issues in e-commerce center around the protection of children, strong sentiments against pornography in any public media, efforts to control gambling, and the protection of public health through restricting sales of drugs and cigarettes.

PROTECTING CHILDREN

Pornography is an immensely successful Internet business. Statistics with respect to revenues generated by online pornography range widely. However, it is probably safe to estimate that the online pornography industry generates somewhere between $5–$10 billion in revenue in the United States. Adult Web sites reportedly attract around 75 million unique visitors a month and make up 12% of the Internet (Rosen, 2013).

To control the Web as a distribution medium for pornography, in 1996, Congress passed the Communications Decency Act (CDA). This act made it a felony criminal offense to use any telecommunications device to transmit "any comment, request, suggestion, proposal, image, or other communications which is obscene, lewd, lascivious, filthy, or indecent" to anyone, and in particular, to persons under 18 years of age (Section 502, Communications Decency Act of 1996). (One section of the CDA that did survive scrutiny, Section 230, provides immunity for providers and users of interactive computer services (such as ISPs and Web sites) from being considered a publisher that might be liable for harmful content posted by others. This is the law that allows social networks, blogs, and online bulletin boards to operate without fear of being held liable for online defamation or libel.) In 1997, the Supreme Court struck down most of the CDA as an unconstitutional abridgement of freedom of speech protected by the First Amendment. While the government argued the CDA was like a zoning ordinance designed to allow "adult" Web sites for people 18 years of age or over, the Court found the CDA was a blanket proscription on content and rejected the "cyberzoning" argument as impossible to administer. In 2002, the Supreme Court struck down another law, the Child Pornography Prevention Act of 1996, which made it a crime to create, distribute, or possess "virtual" child pornography that uses computer-generated images or young adults rather than real children, as overly broad (*Ashcroft v. Free Speech Coalition*). The Children's Online Protection Act (COPA) of 1998 met with a similar fate.

In 2001, Congress passed the Children's Internet Protection Act (CIPA), which requires schools and libraries in the United States to install "technology protection measures" (filtering software) in an effort to shield children from pornography. In June 2003, the Supreme Court upheld CIPA, overturning a federal district court that found the law interfered with the First Amendment guarantee of freedom of expression. The Supreme Court, in a 6–3 opinion, held that the law's limitations on access to the

Internet posed no more a threat to freedom of expression than limitations on access to books that librarians choose for whatever reason not to acquire. The dissenting justices found this analogy inappropriate and instead argued the proper analogy was if librarians were to purchase encyclopedias and then rip out pages they thought were or might be offensive to patrons. All the justices agreed that existing blocking software was overly blunt, unable to distinguish child pornography from sexually explicit material (which is protected by the First Amendment), and generally unreliable (Greenhouse, 2003b). Other legislation such as the 2002 Domain Names Act seeks to prevent unscrupulous Web site operators from luring children to pornography using misleading domain names or characters known to children. A plan to create an .xxx domain for adult Web site content was approved by ICANN in June 2010, and in September 2011, limited registration for .xxx domains began. Trademark holders who do not wish their brand to be associated with an .xxx domain can block requests by other companies for domain names that include their brand name. The 2003 Protect Act is an omnibus law intended to prevent child abuse that includes prohibitions against computer-generated child pornography. Part of that statute was previously held to be unconstitutional by the Eleventh Circuit Court of Appeals, but in May 2008, the Supreme Court reversed the circuit court and upheld the provision (Greenhouse, 2008).

The Children's Online Privacy Protection Act (COPPA) (1998) prohibits Web sites from collecting information on children under the age of 13. It does permit such data collection if parental consent is obtained. Because COPPA does not interfere with speech or expression, it has not been challenged in the courts. However, since 1998, entirely new technologies like social networks, online tracking, advertising networks, online gaming, and mobile apps have appeared that are now being used to gather data on children and which were not specifically addressed in COPPA or FTC regulations. Responding to these changes in technology and public pressure, the FTC announced a new set of rules that are now in effect. The new rules prohibit online tracking of children across the Web with cookies or any other technology such as persistent identifiers; prohibit ad networks from following children across the Web and advertising to them without parental consent; make clear that mobile devices are subject to COPPA, including games and software apps; and make clear that third-party data collection firms that collect data on Web sites are responsible for any unlawful data collection. See the Chapter 7 *Insight on Society* case, *Marketing to Children of the Web in the Age of Social Networks*, for more information.

CIGARETTES, GAMBLING, AND DRUGS: IS THE WEB REALLY BORDERLESS?

In the United States, and around the world, governments have adopted legislation to control certain activities and products in order to protect public health and welfare. Cigarettes, gambling, medical drugs, and of course addictive recreational drugs, are either banned or tightly regulated (see *Insight on Society: The Internet Drug Bazaar Operates Around the Globe*). Yet these products and services are ideal for distribution over the Internet through e-commerce sites. Because the sites can be located offshore, they can operate beyond the jurisdiction of state and federal prosecutors. Or so it seemed until recently. In the case of cigarettes, state and federal authorities have been quite successful in shutting down tax-free cigarette Web sites within the

INSIGHT ON SOCIETY

THE INTERNET DRUG BAZAAR OPERATES AROUND THE GLOBE

In June 2014, Interpol announced the latest round of arrests and seizures as part of its Operation Pangea effort to combat sales of illegal drugs online. The operation shut down 10,600 fake online pharmacies, removed 19,000 advertisements from social media, seized 9.4 million doses of illegal drugs worth more than $36 million, and resulted in 237 arrests. Despite successes such as this, however, the Internet drug bazaar operated by rogue Internet drug outlets remains a continuing public health and safety issue. According to a study done by the Treatment Research Institute at the University of Pennsylvania, addictive and potentially lethal medications are available without prescription from more than 2 million Web sites around the world, with many sites based in countries that impose little if any regulation on pharmaceuticals. A Google search on "drugs no prescription" in 2014 returns more than 57 million results. Although this number is down significantly from 94 million the previous year, it still represents a significant problem.

The International Narcotics Control Board, a U.N. narcotics watchdog agency, has provided guidelines and a framework for governments struggling to contain growing abuse of prescription drugs on the Internet. According to the report, only two of 365 so-called Internet pharmacies it surveyed were legitimate. In many countries, the report said, trafficking in illegal prescription drugs now equals or exceeds the sale of heroin, cocaine, and amphetamines. While properly regulated Internet pharmacies offer a valuable service by increasing competition and access to treatments in underserved regions, Web pharmacies are a long way from proper regulation.

The sale of drugs without a prescription is not the only danger posed by the Internet drug bazaar.

Rogue online pharmacy sites may be selling counterfeit drugs or unapproved drugs. For instance, in the past, the U.S. Food and Drug Administration has issued warnings that a number of consumers who had purchased Ambien, Xanax, and Lexapro online had instead received a product containing haloperial, a powerful anti-psychotic drug. Drug pushers on the Internet also include legitimate pharmaceutical firms who have discovered search engine advertising. Google and other search engines have come under fire for its relationships with purveyors of illegal drugs and other unlawful products like stolen credit cards and fake IDs. In 2014, Google announced a settlement in a shareholder lawsuit over accusations that it had allowed advertising from illegal drug sellers outside the United States. As part of the settlement, Google agreed to allocate $50 million per year to an internal effort to sever ties with and disrupt the operations of illegal online pharmacies. Fedex was also indicted in 2014 for knowingly shipping packages from illegal online pharmacies. Fedex claims that it has requested lists of illegal pharmacies from the U.S. Drug Enforcement Agency to help them identify problematic packages, but has never received that information.

Despite these dangers, online pharmacies remain alluring and are one of the fastest growing business models with, oddly, senior citizens—usually some of the most law-abiding citizens—leading the charge for cheaper drugs. The main attraction of online drug sites is price. Typically, online pharmacies are located in countries where prescription drugs are price-controlled, or where the price structure is much lower, such as Canada, the United Kingdom, and European countries, as well as India and Mexico. Citizens can save quite a bit of money by purchasing from online pharmacies located in other countries.

(continued)

Another haven for online purveyors of illegal drugs is the "Dark" or "Deep" Web, which consists of sites that are not accessible by search engines and often feature security measures designed to allow complete anonymity or to mask illegal activity. In 2013, the most prominent online drug marketplace on the Deep Web was the Silk Road, which was estimated to attract as much as $45 million a year in illegal drug purchases and $1.2 billion worth of total transactions. The Silk Road requires users to run the Tor anonymity software and accepts the virtual currency Bitcoin (see the *Insight on Society* case *Bitcoin* in Chapter 4), allowing online drug buyers an unprecedented level of protection. The Silk Road is not so much a pharmacy as it is a sort of eBay for illegal drugs. But in 2013, the Silk Road's founder and chief operator, a shadowy figure formerly known as "Dread Pirate Roberts," was revealed to be a former Eagle Scout named Ross Ulbricht, who was arrested and charged with drug trafficking and money laundering. U.S. federal agents also seized $33.6 million in Bitcoins from Ulbricht. Although the Silk Road still operates today, the arrest was a major blow for the continued operation of the Web's most prominent online drug marketplace. And though many Bitcoin exchanges are forcing users to provide their identities, law enforcement agencies have not developed reliable methods for tracking virtual currencies. While law enforcement agencies grapple with sites like the Silk Road, traditional illegal pharmacies continue to proliferate. Although the demise of the Silk Road was a breakthrough for law enforcement, not all of the news has been good. In 2013, the EU released a report detailing the increase in number and availability of illegal drugs in the EU and beyond. Citing globalization, technology advances, and the Internet as primary causes, the report stated that European law enforcement authorities have encountered over 70 new drugs in the past year, and that drugs are more potent and even cheaper than ever before. A record 1.2 million Europeans were treated for addiction in 2011, which is positive in that people are receiving help, but negative in that they had been addicted in the first place. European law enforcement agencies also report that the illicit drug market has become increasingly dynamic and innovative, and that Europe has become a major drug production hub. Although cocaine comes primarily from the Andes and is smuggled into Europe, Europe is now one of the world's biggest methamphetamines and cannabis producers. A 2014 follow-up report raised continued concerns over the increasingly innovative and global drug marketplace.

These reports also suggest that drug regulation enforcement needs to adapt with the times. A 2013 report from the International Centre for Science in Drug Policy has gone even further, suggesting that the war on drugs as we know it has failed. The Centre found that the average price of opiates and cocaine have decreased by 74% and 51%, respectively, between 1990 and 2010, and that these drugs had become much more potent in that time. Among the alternative approaches recommended by the report were decriminalization and strict legal regulation, and emphasizing the problem as a public health issue as opposed to a criminal justice issue. Skeptics of this strategy insist that drugs are illegal because they are dangerous and a threat to society.

SOURCES: "European Drug Report," European Monitoring Centre for Drugs and Drug Addiction, 2014; "Silk Road's Alleged Mastermind Faces More U.S. Charges," by Erik Larson and Bob Van Voris, Bloomberg.com, August 22, 2014; "Google Settles Shareholder Suit Over Online Drug Ads," Dan Levine, Reuters, August 8, 2014; "FedEx Indicted for Shipping Drugs Sold Online," by Katie Lobosco, Money.cnn.com, July 17, 2014; "Operation Pangea VII Shuts Down Thousands of Fake Online Pharmacies in Largest Operation Yet," Safemedicines.org, May 28, 2014; "Cyber Bust: Illegal Online Pharmacies Suffer Massive Blow," by Brian Wu, Thedishdaily.com, May 26, 2014; "Digital Citizens Alliance Report Strongly Critical of Google," Stevenimmons.org, March 12, 2014; "Eagle Scout. Idealist. Drug Trafficker?," by David Segal, *New York Times*, January 18, 2014; "War on Illegal Drugs Failing, Medical Researchers Warn," Bbc.co.uk, October 1, 2013; "Meet the Dread Pirate Roberts, The Man Behind Booming Black Market Drug Website Silk Road," by Andy Greenberg, *Forbes*, September 2, 2013; "New Drugs Require Flexible Response, Says EU Report," European Commission, June 6, 2013; "Europe Is a Major Illicit Drug Producer", by Jennifer Fraczek, Dw.de, January 2, 2013; "UN Cracks Down on International Drug Fraudsters," by Natalie Morrison, In-pharmatechnologist.com, March 1, 2012.

United States by pressuring PayPal and credit card firms to drop cigarette merchants from their systems. The major shipping companies—UPS, FedEx, and DHL—have been pressured into refusing shipment of untaxed cigarettes. Philip Morris has also agreed not to ship cigarettes to any resellers that have been found to be engaging in illegal Internet and mail order sales. However, a few off-shore Web sites continue to operate using checks and money orders as payments and the postal system as a logistics partner, but their level of business has plummeted as consumers fear state tax authorities will present them with huge tax bills if they are discovered using these sites. In 2010, President Obama signed the Prevent All Cigarette Trafficking Act. The law restricts the sale of untaxed cigarettes and other tobacco products over the Internet and bans the delivery of tobacco products through the U.S. mail.

Gambling also provides an interesting example of the clash between traditional jurisdictional boundaries and claims to a borderless, uncontrollable Web. The online gambling market, based almost entirely offshore—primarily in the United Kingdom and various Caribbean Islands—grew by leaps and bounds between 2000 and 2006, with much of the action (some estimate up to 50%) coming from customers based in the United States. Online gambling is still banned in most of the United States even though the global market is now a \$35.5 billion dollar business, almost entirely offshore, and roughly half the size of the entire U.S. casino business (O'Keefe, 2014). Congress initially outlawed online gambling and the payment systems including credit cards used to support it in 2006 (the Unlawful Internet Gambling Enforcement Act of 2006 and the Wire Act) and the U.S. Department of Justice enforced the law vigorously, denying offshore operators access to American payment systems, crippling their U.S. business, and arresting several executives. However, the mood has changed in the last five years. State revenue needs have grown, and many in the casino gambling industry have switched sides and now support online gambling, seeing it as a revenue growth opportunity. The federal government has also changed its position and reversed its stance against Internet gambling, removing a major obstacle for states (Wyatt, 2011). The ethical issues surrounding online gambling may have less influence on the public debate than the need for new tax revenues, and for firms, the hope for additional revenues.

In June 2012, Delaware became the first state to legalize online gambling in all its forms (Berzo, 2012). Since then, two other states (Nevada and New Jersey) have joined Delaware and seven states including California, Mississippi, New York, and Pennsylvania have legislation under consideration to approve it (NCSL, 2014).

In 2013, Station Casinos, a local Las Vegas company, opened the nation's first legal, pay-to-play poker Web site. The site claims it can use geo-location technology to ensure that the players are in the State of Nevada and over the age of 21, a condition of its operation insofar as the federal government does not yet permit online poker whereas it is legal in Nevada and supported by the large casinos as an extension of their brands.

However, so far, legal online gambling has disappointed expectations: New Jersey expected to make \$160 million in state revenue from online gambling in 2014, but had collected only \$9 million by June 2014.

The Google Books Settlement:
Is It Fair?

In the Internet age, books are supposed to die off and go away. Who wants to read books when 100 hours of new video are uploaded to YouTube every minute, covering most topics known to man, and Google can provide online access to the world's information? Steve Jobs once noted in an interview about the Kindle e-book reader that people don't read anymore. However, in 2013, the U.S. book and journal publishing industry generated $27 billion with over 2.6 billion books sold. Books continue to be a very hot topic in 2014 as e-readers and tablets have exploded in popularity and Google battles the major heavy-hitter tech companies, authors, publishing firms, the United States Congress, the Department of Justice, and the European Commission over the future of online digital books.

Google is on a tear to put everything digital on its servers and then, as the founders promise in ceaseless self-congratulatory announcements, provide access to "all the world's information" through its efforts. And make a buck, as it turns out, by selling ads aimed at you that are "relevant" to your searches. A problem arises, however, when what Google wants to put on its servers does not belong to them. We're all familiar

© Cyberstock / Alamy

with the copyrighted music and video situation, where firms often operate offshore, beyond the law (or so they think), and enable, induce, and encourage Internet users to illegally download copyrighted material without paying a dime for it, while in the meantime raking in millions of advertising dollars from companies willing to advertise on their networks.

But Google is no criminal organization. For a firm whose informal motto is don't be evil, it seems out of character for it to initiate a program of scanning millions of copyrighted books it does not own and then, without permission, providing its search engine users with access to those books without charge, while selling ad space and pocketing millions for its own account without sharing that revenue with publishers or authors. One major difference between Google and most offshore file-sharing firms is that Google has very deep pockets filled with cash, and they are based in the United States, making it an excellent legal target.

It all started with Google's secret 2002 project to scan all the books in libraries and make parts ("snippets") available online, and of course, display ads next to the results of book searches, even on the pages of snippets. In 2004, Google announced a program it first called Google Print and now just calls Google Books. There are two parts to the project. Under the Partner Program, publishers give permission to Google to scan their books, or make scans available, and then make parts of the work, or simply bibliographic information (title, author, and publisher), available on Google's search engine. No problem there: publishers and authors get a chance to find a wider market, and Google sells more ads. Publishers may even choose to sell online editions of their books on their own Web sites. And publishers were promised a hefty 70% of the display ad revenues and book sales (far better than Amazon's cut of book sales, which is about 50%).

It's the second part of the project that became controversial. Under the Library Project, Google proposed to scan millions of books in university and public libraries, allow users to search for key phrases, and then display "relevant" portions of the text ("snippets"), all without contacting the publisher or seeking permission or paying a royalty fee. Google said it would "never show a full page without the right from the copyright holder," just the "relevant" portion. Google gave the publishing industry until November 2005 to opt out by providing Google with a list of books they did not want included. In addition, Google proposed to scan millions of books for which the copyright has lapsed and make those available on its servers for free. In these early days, Google's public stance towards authors and publishers was, "Stop us if you can."

Google has the backing of a number of prestigious libraries, such as the University of Michigan, Harvard University, Stanford University, the New York Public Library, and Oxford University. Libraries would benefit from the Library Project because Google planned to give libraries free access to the database of over 20 million books for no charge. But not all librarians agree. Some believe this is a marvelous extension of public access to library collections, while other librarians fear it is harmful to book authors and publishers. A number of well-known libraries, such as the Smithsonian Institution and the Boston Public Library, as well as a consortium of 19 research and academic libraries in the Northeast, refused to participate, in part because of restrictions that Google wants to place on the collection. Libraries that work with Google must agree to make the material unavailable to other commercial search services. Google claims it is performing a public service by making an index of books, and relevant portions, available to millions on the Internet, and perhaps even helping publishers sell new copies of books that currently sit on dusty library shelves. Google wants a monopoly on the books it has scanned (which is pretty much the universe of all books).

In 2005, the publishing industry struck back at Google's book-scanning program and two lawsuits were filed in federal court in New York, one a class-action suit by the Authors Guild and the second by five major publishing companies (McGraw-Hill, Pearson Education, Penguin Group, Simon & Schuster, and John Wiley & Sons), claiming copyright infringement. Patricia Schroeder, president of the publishers' consortium, the American Association of Publishers (AAP), alleged that Google was claiming the right to unilaterally change copyright law and copy anything unless somebody told them "No." Schroeder noted that Google keeps talking about how what it is doing is good for the world, but that in her view, they are just stealing people's property. Or, as one commentator put it, it's like having a thief break into your house and clean the kitchen—it's still breaking and entering.

Google, on the other hand, claimed its use was "fair" under the "fair use" doctrine that has emerged from a number of court decisions issued over the years, and which is codified in the Copyright Act of 1976. The copying and lending of books by libraries has been considered a fair use since the late 1930s under a "gentleman's agreement" between libraries and publishers, and a library exemption was codified as Section 108 of the Copyright Act of 1976. Libraries loan books to patrons for a limited period, and must purchase at least one copy. Many people read books borrowed from libraries and recommend them to friends, who often buy the books rather than take the time and effort to go to a library. Libraries are also considered by many in the publishing industry as helping to market a book to a larger public, and libraries are believed to be performing a public service by increasing literacy and education. Google argued that its Library Project was just making it easier for libraries to do what they always have done, namely, allow the public to access books.

In 2008, Google agreed to a settlement of the lawsuit with the authors and publishers. In return for the nonexclusive right to sell books scanned into its database, place advertisements on those pages, display snippets, and make other commercial uses of its database of scanned books, Google agreed to pay about $125 million to the parties. All books that Google digitizes will be listed in the central registry available to the public on the Internet. In 2009, a group of companies and organizations, including Microsoft, Yahoo, and Amazon, the American Association of Publishers, members of the Authors Guild, and publishers in the European Union all filed briefs with the court disputing the settlement. The technology companies formed the Open Book Alliance to oppose the settlement. They were joined by privacy protection groups who claimed that Google would be able to track whatever e-books people accessed and read. In September 2009, representatives of those groups spoke out at a hearing sponsored by the European Commission against the proposed deal. They said it would give Google too much power, including exclusive rights to sell out-of-print works that remain under copyright, a category that includes millions of books.

The Justice Department continued its investigation into the antitrust implications of the settlement. Critics argued the settlement would create a de facto monopoly position for Google, making it difficult for competitors to enter the field, and would give Google broad copyright immunity. The settlement provided that Google's access to publishers' books is "non-exclusive," but competitors would have to scan all the same books over again in order to establish a competitive position, something that experts believe is financially prohibitive. Google, they argued, would end up owning the digital book, which is like owning the libraries of the future. Google countered that the settlement would expand digital access to millions of books that are gathering dust on library shelves.

Currently, Google has reportedly scanned about 30 million of the estimated 130 million books in the libraries participating in the program. About 2 million of those are in the public domain and can be viewed for free through Google's Book Search. Google Book users can also view previews of another 2 million books that are in copyright and in print, under agreements with various publishers. The remainder of the scanned books are out of print but still in copyright. These are currently available only in short "snippet view." The settlement would have allowed users to preview longer parts of those works and potentially purchase them in their entirety, but in March 2011, Federal Judge Denny Chin rejected the settlement, throwing the project into legal limbo once again. Citing copyright, antitrust, and other concerns, Chin said that the settlement went too far, and agreed with critics that it would give Google a "de facto monopoly" and the right to exploit and profit from books without the permission of copyright owners, particularly the authors of "orphaned" works whose content owners Google could not identify. The judge said that he would consider a revised settlement that addressed these concerns, suggesting that copyright owners be given the right to "opt in" to the settlement rather than "opt out" as originally proposed. An "opt in" structure had previously been rejected by Google as unworkable.

In May 2012, Judge Chin granted class-action certification to the lawsuit, allowing authors to sue Google as a group. In July 2013, however, a federal Circuit Court of Appeals ruled that before the court could consider the Authors Guild's desire to convert the lawsuit into a class action, whether Google's actions constitute fair use must first be determined. The Authors Guild had suffered a previous setback in October 2012, when Google and the publishers reached an out-of-court settlement (after seven years of litigation) that allows the publishers to choose whether to permit Google to scan their out-of-print books that are still under copyright. If Google scans these permitted books, it must provide the publishers with a digital copy for their own use.

In November 2013, a federal court finally found in favor of Google without reservation by ruling that Google's scanning and making snippets of text available to the public was "fair use" under U.S. copyright law. The judge believed the project had a broad public purpose of making it easier for students, researchers, teachers, and the general public to find books, while also preserving consideration for author and publisher rights. The Google project was "transformative" in the court's view, giving books a new character and purpose, making it easier to discover old books, and leading to increased sales.

SOURCES: "Settlement Announced in 2010 Lawsuit Against Google Books by Photographers and Artists," by Michael Cader, PublishersLunch, September 5, 2014; "Second Circuit Decision on Authors Guild v. HathiTrust," by Sofia Castillo, Copyrightalliance.org, June 13, 2014; *Authors Guild v. HathiTrust* (S.D.N.Y 2012, 2nd Cir. 2014)."U.S. Appeals Court Rules Against Authors in Book-Scanning Lawsuit," by Joseph Ax, Reuters.com, June 10, 2014; "Authors Guild Vows Appeal of Google Fair Use Ruling," by Michael Cader, November 14, 2013; "Google Defeats Authors in U.S. Book-scanning Lawsuit," by Jonathan Stempel, Reuters, November 14, 2013; "Judge Chin Finds Google's Book Scanning is Fair Use, First Ruling in Eight-Year Case," by Michael Cader, PublishersLunch, November 14, 2013; *Authors Guild v. Google, Inc.*, No. 05 Civ. 8136 (DC) (S.D.N.Y. Nov. 14, 2013); "Google Seeks Ruling Copying Books Without Permission Is Fair," by Don Jeffrey, Businessweek.com, September 23, 2013; "Appeals Court Hints Strongly That Google Books Project Is Fair Use," by Emma Woollacott, Forbes.com, July 1, 2013; "Google Scanning Is Fair Use Says Judge," by Andrew Albanese, October 11, 2012; "Google Deal Gives Publishers a Choice: Digitize or Not," by Claire Cain Miller, *New York Times*, October 4, 2012; "Suit Over Google Book Scanning Delayed on Appeal," by Chad Bray, *Wall Street Journal*, September 17, 2012; "Book Sales Fell 2.5% in 2011," by Jim Milliot, *Publishers Weekly*, July 18, 2012; "Google Suit Gets Class-Action Status," by Jeffrey A. Trachtenberg, *Wall Street Journal*, May 31, 2012; "Authors Organizations File Fresh Lawsuit Challenging Google Library Scans and Pending 'Orphan Works' Access," by Michael Cader, PublishersLunch, September 13, 2011; "New Publishing Industry Survey Details Strong Three-Year Growth in Net Revenue Unit," by Andi Sporkin, Publishers.org, August 9, 2011; "Judge Rejects Google Books Settlement," by Amir Efrati and Jeffrey A. Trachtenberg, *Wall Street Journal*, March 23, 2011; "Judge

Rejects Google's Deal to Digitize Books," by Miguel Helft, *New York Times,* March 22, 2011; "What Is Google Editions?" by Peter Osnos, Theatlantic.com, July 10, 2010; "11th Hour Filings Oppose Google's Book Settlement," by Miguel Helft, *New York Times,* September 9, 2009; "Congress to Weigh Google Books Settlement," *New York Times,* September 9, 2009; "Tech Heavyweights Put Google's Books Deal in Cross-hairs," by Jessica Vascellaro and Geoffrey Fowler, *Wall Street Journal,* August 21, 2009; "Probe of Google Book Deal Heats Up," by Elizabeth Williamson, J. Trachten-berg, and J. Vascellaro, *Wall Street Journal,* June 10, 2009; "Justice Department Opens Antitrust Inquiry Into Google Books Deal," by Miguel Helft, *New York Times,* April 29, 2009; *The Authors Guild, Inc., Association of American Publishers, Inc., et al., v. Google Inc.,* Preliminary Settlement, Case 1:05-cv-08136-JES Document 56, Filed 10/28/2008; "Publishers Sue Google to Stop Scanning," by David A. Vise, *Washington Post,* October 20, 2005; *The McGraw-Hill Companies, et al., v. Google Inc.,* United States Southern District Court, Southern District of New York, October 19, 2005.

Previously, in 2011, in a related action, the Authors Guild had also filed a second lawsuit related to the Library Project, suing Google, the university consortium HathiTrust, and five universities that were participating in the book-scanning project. The suit charged that the scanning of 9.5 million works in the HathiTrust repository constituted massive copyright infringement, and also took issue with HathiTrust's planned Orphan Works Project, which would make available scans of books it had concluded were available after failing to locate valid copyright holders. (Interestingly, as soon as the list was made public, a crowdsourcing effort quickly located some of the authors that purportedly could not be found.) In October 2012, the U.S. District Court for the Southern District of New York dismissed the Authors Guild case against HathiTrust, finding that HathiTrust's use of Google's scanning program was fair use under copyright law, and that in particular, the scanning of books for the purpose of indexing was a transformative act. The Authors Guild appealed the decision and in June 2014, the appeals court also ruled in Google's favor by finding the HathiTrust Digital Library was "fair use" under U.S. copyright law. The ruling allows HathiTrust to maintain a database of digitized books (essentially a digital card catalog), and approved two uses of the database: word search for every user and the display of the complete book to the visually disabled. According to the Authors Guild, the ruling did not authorize universal display of snippets or the display of full text to all HathiTrust users. In the process, HathiTrust and Google abandoned the Orphan Works Project entirely. Future cases coming before the courts will answer the question of whether Google can make commercial use of the full text of copyrighted works without compensation to the authors. If allowed, this would result in much more than a digital card catalog with snippets of books, but instead a full blown commercial exploitation of copyrighted works. This case will continue.

Case Study Questions

1. Who is harmed by the Library Project? Make a list of harmed groups, and for each group, try to devise a solution that would eliminate or lessen the harm.

2. Why is Google pursuing the Library Project? What is in it for Google? Make a list of benefits to Google.

3. If you were a librarian, would you support the Library Project? Why or why not?

4. Why have firms like Amazon, Yahoo, and Microsoft opposed the Library Project? Why would a firm like Sony support Google?

5. Do you think the Library Project will result in a de facto monopoly in e-books, or will there be other competitors?

6. Why did the courts decide that Google's scanning of copyrighted books was a "fair use?"

8.7 REVIEW

KEY CONCEPTS

■ **Understand why e-commerce raises ethical, social, and political issues.**

• Internet technology and its use in e-commerce disrupts existing social and business relationships and understandings. Suddenly, individuals, business firms, and political institutions are confronted by new possibilities of behavior for which understandings, laws, and rules of acceptable behavior have not yet been developed. Many business firms and individuals are benefiting from the commercial development of the Internet, but this development also has costs for individuals, organizations, and societies. These costs and benefits must be carefully considered by those seeking to make ethical and socially responsible decisions in this new environment, particularly where there are as yet no clear-cut legal or cultural guidelines.

• The major issues raised by e-commerce can be loosely categorized into four major dimensions:
  • *Information rights*—What rights do individuals have to control their own personal information when Internet technologies make information collection so pervasive and efficient?
  • *Property rights*—How can traditional intellectual property rights be enforced when perfect copies of protected works can be made and easily distributed worldwide via the Internet?
  • *Governance*—Should the Internet and e-commerce be subject to public laws? If so, what law-making bodies have jurisdiction—state, federal, and/or international?
  • *Public safety and welfare*—What efforts should be undertaken to ensure equitable access to the Internet and e-commerce channels? Do certain online content and activities pose a threat to public safety and welfare?

• Ethical, social, and political controversies usually present themselves as dilemmas. Ethical dilemmas can be analyzed via the following process:
  • Identify and clearly describe the facts.
  • Define the conflict or dilemma and identify the higher-order values involved.
  • Identify the stakeholders.
  • Identify the options that you can reasonably take.
  • Identify the potential consequences of your options.
  • Refer to well-established ethical principles, such as the Golden Rule, Universalism, the Slippery Slope, the Collective Utilitarian Principle, Risk Aversion, the No Free Lunch Rule, the *New York Times* Test, and the Social Contract Rule to help you decide the matter.

■ **Understand basic concepts related to privacy and information rights, the practices of e-commerce companies that threaten privacy, and the different methods that can be used to protect online privacy.**

• To understand the issues concerning online privacy, you must first understand some basic concepts:
  • *Privacy* is the moral right of individuals to be left alone, free from surveillance or interference from others.
  • *Information privacy* includes both the claim that certain information should not be collected at all by governments or business firms, and the claim of individuals to control the use of information about themselves.
  • *Due process* as embodied by the Fair Information Practices doctrine, informed consent, and opt-in/opt-out policies also plays an important role in privacy.

• Almost all e-commerce companies collect some personally identifiable information in addition to anonymous information and use cookies to track clickstream behavior of visitors. Advertising networks and search engines also track the behavior of consumers across thousands of popular sites, not just at one site, via cookies, spyware, search engine behavioral targeting, and other techniques.

- There are a number of different methods used to protect online privacy. They include:
  - Legal protections deriving from constitutions, common law, federal law, state laws, and government regulations. In the United States, rights to online privacy may be derived from the U.S. Constitution, tort law, federal laws such as the Children's Online Privacy Protection Act (COPPA), the Federal Trade Commission's Fair Information Practice principles, and a variety of state laws. In Europe, the European Commission's Data Protection Directive has standardized and broadened privacy protection in the European Union nations.
  - Industry self-regulation via industry alliances, such as the Online Privacy Alliance and the Network Advertising Initiative, that seek to gain voluntary adherence to industry privacy guidelines and safe harbors. Some firms also hire chief privacy officers.
  - Privacy-enhancing technological solutions include spyware and pop-up blockers, secure e-mail, anonymous remailers, anonymous surfing, cookie managers, disk file-erasing programs, policy generators, and public key encryption programs.

■ **Understand the various forms of intellectual property and the challenges involved in protecting it.**

- *Copyright law* protects original forms of expression such as writings, drawings, and computer programs from being copied by others for a minimum of 70 years. It does not protect ideas—just their expression in a tangible medium. Copyrights, like all rights, are not absolute. The doctrine of fair use permits certain parties under certain circumstances to use copyrighted material without permission. The Digital Millennium Copyright Act (DMCA) was the first major effort to adjust copyright law to the Internet age. The DMCA implements a World Intellectual Property Organization treaty, which declares it illegal to make, distribute, or use devices that circumvent technology-based protections of copyrighted materials, and attaches stiff fines and prison sentences for violations.

- *Patent law* grants the owner of a patent an exclusive monopoly to the ideas behind an invention for 20 years. Patents are very different from copyrights in that they protect the ideas themselves and not merely the expression of ideas. There are four types of inventions for which patents are granted under patent law: machines, man-made products, compositions of matter, and processing methods. In order to be granted a patent, the applicant must show that the invention is new, original, novel, nonobvious, and not evident in prior arts and practice. Most of the inventions that make the Internet and e-commerce possible were not patented by their inventors. This changed in the mid-1990s with the commercial development of the World Wide Web. Business firms began applying for "business methods" and software patents.

- *Trademark protections* exist at both the federal and state levels in the United States. The purpose of trademark law is twofold. First, trademark law protects the public in the marketplace by ensuring that it gets what it pays for and wants to receive. Second, trademark law protects the owner who has spent time, money, and energy bringing the product to market against piracy and misappropriation. Federal trademarks are obtained, first, by use in interstate commerce, and second, by registration with the U.S. Patent and Trademark Office (USPTO). Trademarks are granted for a period of 10 years and can be renewed indefinitely. Use of a trademark that creates confusion with existing trademarks, causes consumers to make market mistakes, or misrepresents the origins of goods is an infringement. In addition, the intentional misuse of words and symbols in the marketplace to extort revenue from legitimate trademark owners ("bad faith") is proscribed. The Anticybersquatting Consumer Protection Act (ACPA) creates civil liabilities for anyone who attempts in bad faith to profit from an existing famous or distinctive trademark by registering an Internet domain name that is identical or confusingly similar to, or "dilutive" of, that trademark. The major behaviors on the Internet that have run afoul of trademark law include cybersquatting, cyberpiracy, metatagging, keywording, linking, and framing.

■ **Understand how the Internet is governed and why taxation of e-commerce raises governance and jurisdiction issues.**

- Governance has to do with social control: who will control e-commerce, what elements will be controlled, and how the controls will be implemented. We are currently in a mixed-mode policy environment where self-regulation, through a variety of Internet policy and technical bodies, co-exists with limited government regulation.

- E-commerce raises the issue of how—and if—to tax remote sales. The national and international character of Internet sales has wreaked havoc on taxation schemes in the United States that were built in the 1930s and based on local commerce and local jurisdictions. E-commerce has benefited from a tax subsidy since its inception. E-commerce merchants have argued that this new form of commerce needs to be nurtured and encouraged, and that in any event, the crazy quilt of sales and use tax regimes would be difficult to administer for Internet merchants. In 1998, Congress passed the Internet Tax Freedom Act, which placed a moratorium on multiple or discriminatory taxes on electronic commerce, and any taxation of Internet access, and since that time has extended the moratorium several times, most recently until November 2014. Federal legislation to implement a uniform set of rules for collecting taxes on e-commerce sales is currently pending in Congress.

■ **Identify major public safety and welfare issues raised by e-commerce.**

- Critical public safety and welfare issues in e-commerce include:
    - The protection of children and strong sentiments against pornography. Several attempts by Congress to legislate in this area have been struck down as unconstitutional. The Children's Internet Protection Act (CIPA), which requires schools and libraries in the United States to install "technology protection measures" (filtering software) in an effort to shield children from pornography, has, however, been upheld by the Supreme Court.
    - Efforts to control gambling and restrict sales of cigarettes and drugs. In the United States, cigarettes, gambling, medical drugs, and addictive recreational drugs are either banned or tightly regulated by federal and state laws. Yet these products and services are often distributed via offshore e-commerce sites operating beyond the jurisdiction of federal and state prosecutors. At this point, it is not clear that the Web will remain borderless or that e-commerce can continue to flaunt national, state, and local laws with impunity.

QUESTIONS

1. Identify the four main dimensions that e-commerce ethical, political, and social issues fall into and provide an example of how each dimension might apply to an individual.
2. Define the ethical principle of accountability and describe two ways in which Internet technologies have raised accountability issues.
3. What concerns does the use of mobile devices bring to the issue of information privacy?
4. What is an ethical dilemma? Describe the two tactics you can use to resolve or reach a greater understanding of the dilemma.
5. Explain why someone with a serious medical condition might be concerned about researching his or her condition online, through medical search engines or pharmaceutical sites, for example. What is one technology that could prevent one's identity from being revealed?
6. Why has the development of the Internet brought about so many ethical, political, and social issues?
7. How does information collected through online forms differ from site transaction logs? Which potentially provides a more complete consumer profile?
8. What are some of the ethical, social, or political issues raised by the information density created by e-commerce technology?
9. What is the FTC and what has its role been in consumer privacy protection? How has its role evolved?
10. What are the primary differences between consumer data privacy protection in Europe and the United States, and how do these differences affect U.S. e-commerce firms?
11. Why do social networks pose a unique problem to the issue of information privacy, and how might sharing personal information on a social site adversely affect a user?

12. What are the overall social benefits that network ad agencies claim derive from the practice of online profiling?
13. Identify and describe the main issues that the Internet and digital content have brought to the wider concerns of protecting intellectual property.
14. Identify the five steps outlined in the text you can use to analyze ethical conflicts.
15. What implications does the Internet's quality of information density have on societal needs?
16. What is deep linking and why is it a trademark issue? Compare it to framing—how is it similar and different?
17. What are some of the tactics that illegal businesses, such as betting parlors and casinos, successfully use to operate outside the law on the Internet?
18. Define cybersquatting. How is it different from cyberpiracy? What type of intellectual property violation does cybersquatting entail?
19. What is the "right to be forgotten"? What are some of the risks and benefits of establishing this right?
20. What is the doctrine of "fair use"?

PROJECTS

1. Go to Google and find the Advanced Search link. Examine its SafeSearch filtering options. Surf the Web in search of content that could be considered objectionable for children using each of the options. What are the pros and cons of such restrictions? Are there terms that could be considered inappropriate to the filtering software but be approved by parents? Name five questionable terms. Prepare a brief presentation to report on your experiences and to explain the positive and negative aspects of such filtering software.

2. Develop a list of privacy protection features that should be present if a Web site is serious about protecting privacy. Then, visit at least four well-known Web sites and examine their privacy policies. Write a report that rates each of the Web sites on the criteria you have developed.

3. Review the provisions of the Digital Millennium Copyright Act of 1998. Examine each of the major sections of the legislation and make a list of the protections afforded property owners and users of copyrighted materials. Do you believe this legislation balances the interests of owners and users appropriately? Do you have suggestions for strengthening "fair use" provisions in this legislation?

4. Visit at least four Web sites that take a position on e-commerce taxation, beginning with the National Conference of State Legislatures (Ncsl.org) and the National Governors Association (Nga.org). You might also include national associations of local businesses or citizen groups opposed to e-commerce taxation. Develop a reasoned argument for, or against, taxation of e-commerce.

REFERENCES

Acquisti, Alessandro, Ralph Gross, and Fred Stutzman. "Faces of Facebook: Privacy in the Age of Augmented Reality," Heinz College & CyLab Carnegie Mellon University (August 4, 2011).

Acquisti, Alessandro, Leslie John, and George Loewenstein. "What is Privacy Worth?" Twenty First Workshop on Information Systems and Economics (WISE) (December 14–15, 2009).

Alice Corporation Pty. Ltd. v. CLS Bank International, et al., Supreme Court of the United States, No. 13-298. June 19, 2014.

Angwin, Julia, and Jennifer Valentino-Devries. "New Tracking Frontier: Your License Plates." *Wall Street Journal* (September 28, 2012).

Angwin, Julia. "Face-ID Tools Pose New Risk." *Wall Street Journal* (August 1, 2011).

Apple Computer, Inc. v. Microsoft Corp. 709 F. Supp. 925, 926 (N. D. Cal. 1989); 799 F. Supp. 1006, 1017 (N. D. Cal., 1992); 35 F. 3d 1435 (9th Cir.); cert. denied, 63 U. S. L. W. 3518 (U.S., Feb. 21, 1995) (No. 94-1121).

Ashcroft v. Free Speech Coalition, 535 U.S. 234 (2002).

Associated Press. "Google Settles Final Piece of Geico Case." BizReport.com (September 8, 2005).

Bernina of America, Inc. v. Fashion Fabrics Int'l., Inc. 2001 U. S. Dist. LEXIS 1211 (N. D. Ill., Feb. 8, 2001).

Berzo, Alexandra. "Delaware Lawmakers Clear Online Gambling." *Wall Street Journal* (June 27, 2012).

Bilski et al. v. Kappos, 177 L. Ed. 2d 792, 130 S. Ct. 3218, 561 U.S. 593 (2010).

Bilton, Nick. "Apple Loophole Gives Developers Access to Photos." *New York Times* (February 28, 2012).

Brown Bag vs. Symantec Corp., 960 F. 2d 1465 (9th Cir. 1992).

Brustein, Joshua. "Start-Ups Seek to Help Users Put a Price on Their Personal Data." *New York Times* (February 12, 2012).

Center for Copyright Information. "The Copyright Alert System: Phase One and Beyond." (May 28, 2014).

Charlton, Angela. "France Threatens Google with Privacy Fines." *New York Times* (June 20, 2013).

Chiappetta, Vincent. "Defining the Proper Scope of Internet Patents: If We Don't Know Where We Want to Go, We're Unlikely to Get There." *Michigan Telecommunications Technology Law Review* (May 2001).

Chiou, Lesley, and Catherine Tucker. "Search Engines and Data Retention: Implications for Privacy and Antitrust." MIT Sloan School Working Paper 5094-14 (May 27, 2014).

Crum, Rex. "Google Raises Some Privacy Issues with Nest Buy," Marketwatch.com (January 13, 2014).

Diamond v. Chakrabarty, 447 US 303 (1980).

E. & J. Gallo Winery v. Spider Webs Ltd. 129 F. Supp. 2d 1033 (S.D. Tex., 2001) aff'd 286 F. 3d 270 (5th Cir., 2002).

Eldred v. Ashcroft, 537 U.S. 186 (2003).

European Commission. "Progress on EU Data Protection Reform Now Irreversible Following European Parliament Vote." (March 12, 2014).

European Commission. "Commission Proposes a Comprehensive Reform of the Data Protection Rules." (January 26, 2012).

Executive Office of the President. "Big Data: Seizing Opportunities, Preserving Values." (May 1, 2014).

Federal Communications Commission. "Guide: The Open Internet." (July 23, 2014).

Federal Trade Commission. "Data Brokers: A Call for Transparency and Accountability." (May 27, 2014).

Federal Trade Commission. "Google Will Pay $22.5 Million to Settle FTC Charges It Misrepresented Privacy Assurance to Users of Apple's Safari Internet Browser." (August 9, 2012a).

Federal Trade Commission. "Facebook Must Obtain Consumers' Consent Before Sharing Their Information Beyond Established Privacy Settings." (August 10, 2012b).

Federal Trade Commission. "Protecting Consumer Privacy in an Era of Rapid Change." (March 26, 2012c).

Federal Trade Commission. "FTC Charges Deceptive Privacy Practices in Google's Rollout of Its Buzz Network." (March 3, 2011).

Federal Trade Commission. "Privacy Online: Fair Information Practices in the Electronic Marketplace." (May 2000a).

Federal Trade Commission. "Online Profiling: A Report to Congress." (June 2000b).

Federal Trade Commission. "Privacy Online: A Report to Congress." (June 1998).

Field v. Google, Inc. 412 F.Supp. 2nd 1106 (D. Nev., 2006).

Fiesler, Casey, and Amy Bruckman. "Copyright Terms in Online Creative Communities." Georgia Institute of Technology, Working Paper (April 26, 2014).

Fisher, William W. III. "The Growth of Intellectual Property: A History of the Ownership of Ideas in the United States." Law.harvard.edu/Academic_Affairs/coursepages/tfisher/iphistory.html (1999).

Ford, Paul. "Balancing Security and Liberty in the Age of Big Data." Businessweek.com (June 13, 2013)

Ford Motor Co. v. Lapertosa 2001 U.S. Dist. LEXIS 253 (E. D. Mich. Jan. 3, 2001).

Government Employees Insurance Company v. Google, Inc. Civ. Action No. 1:04cv507 (E.D. VA, December 15, 2004).

Greenhouse, Linda. "Supreme Court Upholds Child Pornography Law." *New York Times* (May 20, 2008).

Greenhouse, Linda. "20 Year Extension of Existing Copyrights Is Upheld." *New York Times* (January 16, 2003a).

Greenhouse, Linda. "Justices Back Law to Make Libraries Use Internet Filters." *New York Times* (June 24, 2003b).

Harmon, Amy. "Pondering Value of Copyright vs. Innovation." *New York Times* (March 3, 2003).

Hoofnagle, Chris Jay. "Privacy Self-Regulation: A Decade of Disappointment." Electronic Privacy Information Center (Epic.org) (March 4, 2005).

Kakutani, Michiko. "Watched by the Web: Surveillance Is Reborn." *New York Times* (June 10, 2013).

Kaufman, Leslie. "Viacom and YouTube Settle Suit Over Copyright Violations." *New York Times* (March 18, 2014).

Kelly v. ArribaSoft. 336 F3rd 811 (CA 9th, 2003).

Kuehn, Andreas, and Milton Mueller. "Profiling the Profilers: Deep Packet Inspection and Behavioral Advertising in Europe and the United States." Available at SSRN: http://ssrn.com/abstract=2014181. (September 1, 2012).

Laudon, Kenneth. "Markets and Privacy." *Communications of the ACM* (September 1996).

Mayer-Schonberger, Viktor, and Kenneth Cukier. *Big Data: A Revolution That Will Transform How We Live, Work, and Think*. Eamon Dolan/Houghton Mifflin Harcourt (2013).

Maass, Peter, and Megha Rajagopalen. "That's No Phone. That's My Tracker." *New York Times* (July 13, 2012).

McMillan, Robert. "Porn Typosquatter Fined Again by FTC." *InfoWorld* (October 16, 2007).

Nash, David B. "Orderly Expansion of the International Top-Level Domains: Concurrent Trademark Users Need a Way Out of the Internet Trademark Quagmire." *The John Marshall Journal of Computer and Information Law* Vol. 15, No. 3 (1997).

Nathanson, John. "Gambling is the Next Wave in Mobile Gaming," Salon.com (March 13, 2014).

Network Advertising Initiative. "Network Advertising Initiative Releases 2010 Compliance Report." Networkadvertising.org (February 18, 2011).

Network Advertising Initiative. "Major Marketing/Media Trade Groups Launch Program to Give Consumers Enhanced Control over Collection and Use of Web Viewing Data for Online Behavioral Advertising." (October 4, 2010).

New, William. "WIPO: Internet Domain Expansion Disruptive to Trademark Strategies." Ip-watch.com (March 17, 2014).

Nissan Motor Co., Ltd. v. Nissan Computer Corp. 289 F. Supp. 2d 1154 (C. D. Cal.), aff'd, 2000 U. S. App. LEXIS 33937 (9th Cir. Dec. 26, 2000).

PaineWebber Inc. v. Fortuny, Civ. A. No. 99-0456-A (E. D. Va. Apr. 9, 1999).

Pearce, Sarah, and Annie Clarke. "EU: European Commission Commits to Finalising Negotiations on the EU Data Protection Regulation in 2015." Lexology.com (September 15, 2014).

Perfect 10, Inc. v. Amazon.com, Inc. 487 F3rd 701 (CA 9th, 2007).

Pew Internet & American Life Project. "Daily Internet Activities." (September 2013).

Pew Research Center (Lee Rainie). "Anonymity, Privacy, and Security Online." (September 5, 2013).

Playboy Enterprises, Inc. v. Global Site Designs, Inc. 1999 WL 311707 (S. D. Fla. May 15, 1999).

Playboy Enterprises, Inc. v. Netscape Communications, Inc. 354 F. 3rd 1020 (9th Cir., 2004).

Presidents Council of Advisors on Science and Technology. "PCAST Report on Big Data and Privacy: A Technological Perspective" (May 1, 2014).

Raice, Shayndi. "Facebook to Target Ads Based on App Usage." *New York Times* (July 6, 2012).

Rosen, Jeffrey. "The Right to be Forgotten." *Stanford Law Review*, 64. Stan. L. Rev. Online 88 (February 13, 2012).

Rosen, David. "Is Success Killing the Porn Industry." Alternet.org (May 27, 2013).

Sarno, David. "SmartPhone Apps Dial Up Privacy Worries." *Los Angeles Times* (February 16, 2012).

Savage, Charlie. "Between the Lines of the Cellphone Privacy Ruling." *New York Times* (June 25, 2014).

Savage, Charlie. "Democratic Senators Issue Strong Warning About Use of the Patriot Act." *New York Times* (March 16, 2012).

Schwartz, John. "Justices Take Broad View of Business Methods Patents." *New York Times* (June 28, 2010).

Sengupta, Somini. "Europe Weighs Tough Law on Online Privacy." *New York Times* (January 23, 2012).

Singer, Natasha. "Never Forgetting a Face," *New York Times* (May 17, 2014a).

Singer, Natasha. "Didn't Read Those Terms of Service? Here's What You Agreed to Give Up," *New York Times* (April 28, 2014b).

Singer, Natasha. "An American Quilt of Privacy Laws, Incomplete." *New York Times* (March 30, 2013).

Singer, Natasha. "Consumer Data, But Not For Consumers." *New York Times* (July 21, 2012).

State Street Bank & Trust Co. v. Signature Financial Group, 149 F. 3d 1368 (1998).

Stelter, Brian. "Sweeping Effects as Broadband Moves to Meters." *New York Times* (June 26, 2012).

Stone, Brad. "Scaling the Digital Wall in China." *New York Times* (January 15, 2010).

Storm, Darlene. "Was Facebook & OKCupid's Research Treating Users Like Guinea Pigs Illegal?," Computerworld.com (September 24, 2014).

Takenaka, Toshiko. "International and Comparative Law Perspective on Internet Patents." Michigan Telecommunications Technology Law Review (May 15, 2001).

Thurm, Scott. "The Ultimate Weapon: It's the Patent." Wall Street Journal (April 17, 2000).

Ticketmaster v. Tickets.com. 2000 U.S. Dist. Lexis 4553 (C.D. Cal., August 2000).

United States Copyright Office. "Digital Millennium Copyright Act of 1998: U.S. Copyright Office Summary." (December 1998).

Washington Post, The et al. v. TotalNews, Inc., et al., S.D.N.Y., Civil Action Number 97-1190 (February 1997).

Watt, Edward. "U.S. Court Curbs F.C.C. Authority on Web Traffic." New York Times (April 6, 2010).

Winston, Brian. Media Technology and Society: A History From the Telegraph to the Internet. Routledge (1998).

Wyatt, Edward. "Rule by Justice Department Opens a Door on Online Gambling." *New York Times* (December 24, 2011).

CHAPTER 9

Online Media

Spotify and Deezer:

European Streaming Music Services
Spread Around the Globe

The global music business has been in a state of steep revenue decline for the last decade, ever since the Internet and alternative music distribution channels became widespread. Alternative digital channels include piracy as well as legitimate channels such as iTunes, Google Play, and others, along with the more recent growth in digital streaming channels such as Spotify, Deezer, and Pandora. The rise of legal digital channels has slowed the fall in music industry revenues, and according to many analysts, its future looks positive for the first time in decades.

Global music sales fell 3.9% in 2013 to a total of €12 billion. By comparison, in 2002, global music sales were estimated to be around €25 billion, at which time widespread downloading of music tracks from unauthorized file sharing sites, along with the growing use of CD-burning consumer technologies, began to cause a

© Kit Wai Chan/Fotolia.com

major decline in the sale of CDs on a global basis. In 2013, digital accounted for over 43% of recorded music revenues worldwide, but in 2014, the percentage of revenues from streaming music services continues to grow at the expense of digital downloads.

Globally, the digital music business is expanding rapidly because of convenient new legal channels and stronger enforcement of copyright laws. Digital services such as iTunes, Spotify, and Deezer are now operating in well over 100 countries, up from 23 countries in 2011. The introduction of new laws like France's Hadopi graduated response law, which allows a criminal court to suspend Internet access for up to a month and fine individuals around $2,000, has resulted in a 26% decrease in piracy.

The two leading European streaming music services are Spotify and Deezer. Spotify was founded in Sweden by Daniel Ek and Martin Lorentzon in 2006. Spotify is an on-demand, interactive service. Users can choose the artists and music they want to hear, create and share playlists, and control the music while it plays. In this sense, Spotify is very different from traditional broadcast radio, webcasting, and digital streaming services such as Pandora, which are not on-demand and do not allow users to control what they play. Available on mobile devices, Facebook, and other social network sites, Spotify is a vibrant music community with a focus on user-generated content, playlists, blogs, and commentary.

Spotify launched its service in October 2008, after reaching licensing agreements with several major record companies in Europe (but not the United States). Now headquartered in London, Spotify quickly rose to become the leading streaming music service in the United Kingdom and Europe. In 2009, Spotify adopted a global expansion business strategy and currently operates throughout the European Union, as well as Australia, Poland, and Greece. Spotify uses a freemium business model: consumers can listen to up to a certain number of hours of advertising-supported free music each month. Unlimited service without ads is available on computers and mobile phones for an additional cost. In Europe, Spotify originally offered 40 hours of free streaming music but found this business model did not generate enough paying subscribers. It now offers 20 hours for free.

In 2011, Spotify launched its service in the United States after reaching agreements with three major record companies. The companies refused to license their music unless Spotify radically reduced the amount of free play available. As a result, in the United States, consumers can stream only 10 hours of advertising-supported free music each month. Spotify has simplified its pricing options, offering Free and Premium plans. The Premium plan allows users to play any song, anywhere across a wide array of devices without advertising. In the United States, Spotify says its paying subscribers are a much larger percentage of its total listener base. Spotify is also pursuing deals with ISPs and mobile operators to enable it to offer discounted premium services. For instance, it recently entered into an agreement with Telefonica in Spain to offer premium service to customers there at a 50% discount. In 2014, streaming subscriptions throughout the industry increased by 57%, with Spotify leading the way. Spotify reached 50 million active users in 2014, 12.5 million of whom are subscribers, representing more than double the 6 million subscribers they had in 2013.

In 2012, Spotify raised $100 million in a financing that valued the company at about $3 billion. However, Wall Street analysts have taken a negative view of Spotify's business model and long-term prospects, just as they have for the U.S.-based streaming service Pandora. As a private company, Spotify does not report financial data, but analysts estimate that the company will bring in nearly $700 million in 2013, up from just $97 million in 2010. But content costs have also risen over that time frame, and Spotify has struggled to show a profit. In 2014, analysts have estimated that the company has lost approximately $200 million over its lifespan. Spotify is negotiating new deals for 2015 and beyond with major music labels, including Warner Music, Sony Music, and Universal Music Group. Spotify is believed to currently have enough capital to continue investing in its service and pay for the rights to music for the time being. Investors include major New York investment banks and Silicon Valley firms, along with Russia-based DST Global. Spotify also faces strong competition in the United States and globally: Apple, Google, and Amazon have all announced or started streaming music services, not to mention smaller but entrenched subscription services like Rhapsody, Pandora, and Rdio. In 2014, Apple acquired Beats Electronics, maker of popular headphones and, more importantly, a fledgling music service called Beats Music. The cost was $3 billion, a testament to the bright future of streaming music.

In 2014, pop superstar Taylor Swift made waves in the music industry when she announced that she had pulled the entirety of her music catalog down from Spotify, citing inadequate compensation and opining that valuable things should be paid for. Other prominent musicians such as Radiohead's Thom Yorke have voiced displeasure with the service. Spotify has countered that as its platform continues to grow in size, payouts to artists will improve, and that by the end of 2014, the company had paid nearly $2 billion back to the music industry, and pays 70% of its revenues back to musicians. In Europe, the latest sales figures from 2014 support Spotify's defense of its business model, as Spotify royalties have overtaken iTunes Music Store revenues by 13% in 2014. As recently as 2013, iTunes had a commanding lead of 32% over Spotify in earnings. Many industry veterans associated with record labels report satisfaction with the royalties their artists receive. Taylor Swift's music was earning $500,000 per month before her label removed it.

As the market for streaming music services grows, other companies also stand to benefit. Deezer is a French-based startup firm and the second-largest streaming music service in Europe behind Spotify. It is a direct competitor to Spotify around the world and operates in over 180 countries, including the United States. Like Spotify, Deezer is an interactive streaming service, offering its users unlimited access to a catalog of artists and songs, a recommendation engine, substantial background information on artists, and connections to Facebook and Twitter, along with a lively social community.

Deezer was founded by Jonathan Benassaya and Daniel Marhely in 2007. In 2008, it received an $8.5 million angel investment from several sources and rapidly expanded to dominate the French streaming music market in 2009 and 2010. In 2011, Deezer reached agreement with Facebook to allow its users to sign into Deezer from their Facebook accounts. Deezer has also partnered with telecommunications carriers Orange and French Telecom to include the Deezer service as part of mobile phone contracts. It has partnerships with 25 mobile operators and ISPs around the world. Deezer currently has more than 35 million licensed tracks, 100 million playlists, and over 30 million users, 16 million of whom are active monthly, and 5 million paying subscribers, who listen around 60 hours a week. In France, it is the dominant streaming music service. It has doubled its number of paying subscribers within the last year, trailing only Spotify. Like other streaming services, such as Spotify that have freemium business models, Deezer offers free unlimited access for two weeks for registered users, who thereafter can continue to listen for free for 10 hours a month. For premium service without ads, Deezer charges $4.99 per PC-only use, and $9.99 for full mobile and PC access. Deezer has tried to avoid growing its advertiser-supported free music option. According to Deezer's chief executive officer, the free advertiser-supported model is too expensive because advertising revenues do not cover the cost of musical content. In 2012, Deezer received an investment of $130 million from Access Industries, which is the new owner of the Warner Music Group, one of the big three U.S. record compa-

SOURCES: "Revenue Streams," by John Seabrook, *The New Yorker*, November 24, 2014; "In Europe, Spotify Royalties Overtake iTunes By 13%," by Ingrid Lunden, Techcrunch.com, November 4, 2014; "Taylor Swift Abruptly Pulls Entire Catalog From Spotify," by Steve Knopper, *Rolling Stone*, November 3, 2014; "Deezer Buys Stitcher, Adds 35K Talk Radio Shows And Podcasts To Its Music Platform," by Ingrid Lunden, TechCrunch.com, October 24, 2014; "Deezer, Entering US, Will Sound Like Spotify, Act Like Netflix," by Joan E. Solsman, Cnet. com, October 11, 2014; "Digital Music Sales Are in a Free Fall, as Spotify Does to iTunes What iTunes did to CDs," by David Holmes, Pandodaily.com, July 3, 2014; "Spotify Hits 10 Million Paid Users. Now Can It Make Money?" by Joshua Brustein, Businessweek.

com, May 21, 2014; "IFPI Music Report 2014: Global Record Revenues Fall 4%, Streaming and Subs Hit $1 Billion," by Richard Smirke, Billboard.com, March 18, 2014; "Deezer Takes on Spotify with 5M Paying Subscribers and New Discovery Features," by Stuart Dredge, Theguardian.com, November 6, 2013; "Music Sales at Mid-Year: Vinyl, Streams, and the Digital Album Are Doing Just Fine," Spin.com, July 19, 2013; "Subscriptions Rising: Four Million People Pay Deezer for Music," Evolver.fm, May 23, 2013; "Deezer: 'We See the End of Music Downloads as Coming This Year,'" Theguardiran.com, March 25, 2013; by Spotify: Growing Like Mad, Yet So Far To Go," by Paul Sloan, News.cnet.com, March 12, 2013; "Global Music Sales Up 0.3% in 2012, First Increase in 13 Years," by Randy Lewis, Los Angeles Times, February 26, 2013; "iTunes Music Store Launches in 56 New Countries, Movies Arrive in Four," by Eric Slivka, MacRumors. com, December 3, 2012; "Spotify Valued at $3 Billion, but Where is the Missing Billion," by Ben Rooney, *Wall Street Journal*, November 15, 2012; "French Music Streaming Service Is Taking On the World, but Omitting America," by Eric Pfanner, *New York Times*, October 21, 2012; "Deezer's CEO Axel Dauchez On Cracking Into the U.S. and Why It's Not Just Another Spotify," by Ingrid Lunden, Techcrunch.com, October 9, 2012; "Is Spotify's Business Model Broken?" by Greg Sandoval, Techcrunch.com, October 5, 2012; "Streaming Music Won't Stem Industry Slow Down," by Ben Rooney, *Wall Street Journal*, August 15, 2012; "Spotify Launch U.S. Music Service ," by Ethan Smith, *Wall Street Journal*, July 15, 2011.

nies. Record companies have invested in Deezer and Spotify as a way to diversify their distribution chain and to avoid dependence on Apple, Google, and Amazon.

In 2013, Deezer unveiled some new features. The first feature is called Hear This, that will recommend albums, artists, and playlists, similar to Spotify's Discover tab. Hear This will be available both as an iOS and Android app, as well as on Deezer's Web site. Another new feature, called Explore, allows users to filter by region and genre. A third new feature, still in beta, is a Mac desktop app that will synchronize users' iTunes accounts with Deezer's catalog, making those files available on different devices. Deezer's management hopes that these new apps will further encourage people to switch from downloading to streaming.

Deezer is a private company and does not publish its financial results. It has plans to reach $1.3 billion in revenues by 2016. Deezer sees its future growth taking place in China, Asia, and the Middle East. It has recently expanded in the MENA region (Algeria, Bahrain, Egypt, Iraq, Jordan, Kuwait, Lebanon, Morocco, Oman, Qatar, Saudi Arabia, Tunisia, the United Arab Emirates), Latin America (Brazil and Venezuela), Asia (Hong Kong, the Philippines, the Republic of Korea, and Taiwan), as well as Pakistan, South Africa, Turkey, the Netherlands, and Poland. In 2014, Deezer began its first attempts to gain a foothold in the United States. Analysts believe the competition in the United States is too potent and well-financed for Deezer to make a direct assault on the market, whereas in the developing countries it is a more of a wide open market. To that end, Deezer has partnered with speaker manufacturers Sonos and Bose to offer high quality music streams at discounted pricing plans. Instead of launching a service available to everyone in the United States, Deezer is opting to tackle individual segments of the marketplace to gain traction and establish a loyal base. Deezer's main global competitor is, of course, Spotify. Deezer is trying to differentiate itself from Spotify and others by focusing on its social and editorial content, including reviews and user comments. In 2013, Deezer incorporated third-party apps into its mobile platforms, and Spotify appears to be planning on doing the same. In 2014, Deezer acquired Stitcher, an aggregator of podcasts and radio shows, an area where Spotify isn't an unquestioned leader. Stitcher's catalog of 35,000 shows and podcasts will help to differentiate Deezer from Spotify and its other competitors. At this time, it is unclear to analysts if either Spotify or Deezer will ever attain profitable operations as they expand into global markets. Spotify and Deezer, on the other hand, have faith in their business models and do not agree. Who is right remains to be seen.

The opening case illustrates how online content distributors like Spotify and Deezer are challenging both traditional and newer digital music distribution channels. If consumers can stream any song whenever they want to whatever device they want, the demand for physical CDs, as well as iTunes downloads, is reduced. On the other hand, it is not clear that Spotify or Deezer have viable business models. The case also illustrates how a traditional content business like recorded music has survived the initial digital disruption of its business and begun to develop new innovative digital distribution channels that replace revenues from earlier products like CDs. As Internet users increasingly change their habits, spurred on by the growth of mobile devices, they are challenging existing business models that worked for decades to support newspapers, books, magazines, television, and Hollywood movies. Clearly, the future of content—news, music, and video—is online. Today, the print industry, including newspapers, books, and magazines, is having a difficult time coping with the movement of their readership to digital alternatives. Broadcast and cable television, along with Hollywood and the music labels, are also wrestling with outdated business models based on physical media. Established media giants are continuing to make extraordinary investments in unique online content, new technology, new digital distribution channels, and entirely new business models. Internet giants like Apple, Google, Amazon, and Facebook are competing to dominate online content distribution. In this chapter, we focus primarily on the publishing and entertainment industries as they attempt to transform their traditional media into digitally deliverable forms and experiences for consumers, while at the same time earning profits.

9.1 ONLINE CONTENT

No other sector has been so challenged by the Internet and the Web than the content industries. The online content industries are organized into two major categories: the print industries (newspapers, magazines, and books), and the entertainment industries, which includes television, movies, music (including radio), and games. Together, the online content industries in the United States are expected to generate revenues of about $28 billion in 2014.

As a communications medium, the Web is, by definition, a source of online content as well as a powerful distribution platform. In this chapter, we will look closely at publishing (newspapers, magazines, and books) and entertainment (television and movies, music and radio, and games). These industries make up the largest share of the commercial content marketplace, both offline and online. In each of these industries, there are powerful offline brands, significant new pure-play online providers and distributors, consumer constraints and opportunities, a variety of legal issues, and new mobile technology platforms that offer an entirely new content distribution system in the form of smartphones and tablet computers.

Table 9.1 describes the most recent trends in online content and media for 2014–2015.

TABLE 9.1	WHAT'S NEW IN ONLINE CONTENT AND MEDIA, 2014–2015

BUSINESS

- The mobile platform of smartphones and tablets accelerates the transition to digital content.
- Vertical integration: Amazon, Google (YouTube), Hulu, and Netflix (owners of the distribution channel) enter the content production business for video, books, and online TV-like video channels.
- YouTube offers over 100 entertainment channels offering TV-like amateur productions aimed at the twenty-something marketplace.
- Internet video begins to challenge cable TV for the home viewing audience.
- Music: digital music sales top physical sales; streaming surpasses downloading.
- TV: the number of Americans watching TV online continues to grow, to over 120 million (about 50% of the U.S. Internet population).
- E-book sales growth slows but represents one-third of all book revenues.
- Movies: Americans continue to spend more on online movies than for DVDs.
- Newspapers: online readership exceeds print readership. Online ad revenues grow but not enough to offset declining print ad revenues.
- Gaming market: console game sales stagnate as mobile gaming soars.
- The four Internet Titans compete: Apple, Google, Amazon, and Facebook vie for ownership of the online entertainment and content ecosystem, selling experiences as well as content.
- Cable companies consolidate: Comcast offers $45 billion for Time Warner that may create the largest cable provider in the nation.

TECHNOLOGY

- Smartphones, tablet computers, and e-readers together create a totally mobile multimedia entertainment environment.
- Netflix remains the largest consumer of bandwidth, consuming about 35% of Internet traffic.
- Apps become the foundation for an app economy as they morph into content-distribution platforms that are proprietary, where users can be charged for content.
- Cloud storage services grow to serve the huge market for mobile device content. Apple launches iCloud video service that allows users to watch purchased videos on multiple Apple devices (iPhones, iPads, and Macs). Amazon and Google develop similar cloud services.

SOCIETY

- Media consumption: Americans spend around 4,100 hours a year consuming various types of media, more than twice as many hours as they work.
- Time spent using digital media exceeds time spent with television; time spent on mobile devices exceeds time spent on desktops.
- With federal net neutrality rules still undecided, Netflix, and other heavy bandwidth users, agree to pay higher fees to broadband providers for faster delivery of their content.

CONTENT AUDIENCE AND MARKET: WHERE ARE THE EYEBALLS AND THE MONEY?

The average American adult spends around 4,100 hours each year consuming various media, twice the amount of time spent at work (2,000 hours/year) (see **Figure 9.1**). U.S. entertainment and media (E & M) revenues (both online and offline) in 2014 are estimated to be $564 billion, and they are expected to grow at a compound rate of 6% to a total of $680 billion in 2018. Sales of tablets and smartphones have created new revenue streams for entertainment and media firms as consumer behavior changes in response to the new technologies. Content is no longer tied to physical products and can be delivered over the Internet to multiple mobile devices, reducing costs for consumers. Currently, online digital E&M revenue is 31% of total E&M revenue, or an estimated $175 billion in 2014. Analysts believe that by 2018, digital E&M revenue will be 43% of E&M revenue, or about $292 billion (PricewaterhouseCoopers (PWC), 2014).

Media Utilization: A Converging Digital Stream

The proliferation of mobile devices—tablets and smartphones—has led to an increase in the total amount of time spent listening to radio, watching TV and movies, and reading books, newspapers, and even magazines. Together, TV, the Internet, and radio account for more than 77% of the hours spent consuming various media. While the

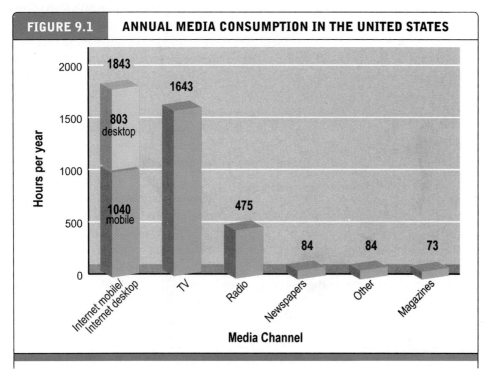

FIGURE 9.1 **ANNUAL MEDIA CONSUMPTION IN THE UNITED STATES**

Each American spends around 4,100 hours annually on various types of media. Time spent on the Internet (both mobile and desktop) is expected to exceed time spent on television for the first time in 2014.

SOURCES: Based on data from eMarketer, Inc., 2014a; authors' estimates.

number of hours of TV viewing used to be far larger than Internet usage, since the development of mobile devices, time spent on desktops plus the mobile Internet is now expected to consume 5 hours and 45 minutes compared to 4.5 hours spent watching television on a TV in 2014, marking the first time that total Internet media usage will surpass television. On the other hand, a great deal of Internet usage is watching time-shifted television shows! In 2014, an estimated 130 million Americans will use their computers and mobile devices to watch television shows, over 40% of the general population. Therefore, the distinction between Internet usage and television usage is not easy to make. The Internet, television, and movies are converging into a single digital stream. This convergence is described later in the chapter. Well over 50% of younger television viewers multitask while watching television, usually using a smartphone or tablet computer, texting with friends, reading e-mail, searching the Web, or visiting social network sites (eMarketer, Inc., 2014b). During the 2014 FIFA Soccer World Cup, about 30% of Internet users were multitasking as they watched the games, often on multiple devices (eMarketer, Inc., 2014c).

Internet and Traditional Media: Cannibalization versus Complementarity

Several studies reveal that time spent on the Internet reduces consumer time available for other media (Pew Research Center, 2013). This is referred to as cannibalization. The alternative argument is that the Internet and traditional media are complementary and mutually supportive rather than substitutive. True, there has been a massive shift of the general audience to the Web, tablets, and smartphones, and once there, a large percentage of time is spent on viewing content. Yet more recent data finds a more complex picture. Despite the availability of the Internet on high-resolution tablet computers, television viewing remains strong, video viewing on all devices has increased, and the reading of all kinds of books, including physical books, has increased. Total music consumption measured in hours a day listening to music has increased even as CDs decline, and movie consumption has increased even as DVD sales decline markedly. Music streaming has doubled in 2014 compared to 2013. The impact of the Internet on media appears to be increasing the total demand for media, including stimulating demand for traditional products like books. The overall pattern is that physical products are being replaced by digital versions delivered on computers, tablets, and smartphones. Even as consumers reduce consumption of traditional physical content products, they maintain and often increase their exposure to content on digital platforms.

Consumers are spending about 20% of their time online on social networks, 16% of their time doing e-mail, 12% of their time watching online video, 12% of their time searching, and 10% of their time playing online games. The remainder of the time is spent doing other activities, such as reading online newspapers, magazines, and blogs, and listening to online radio (eMarketer, Inc., 2014a).

Media Revenues

An examination of U.S. media revenues reveals a somewhat different pattern when compared to media consumption (see **Figure 9.2**). In 2014, media of all kinds is expected to generate $217 billion in revenue (not including transmission fees for content). Television accounts for 30% of media revenues, print media (books, newspapers, and magazines) accounts for 40%, Internet media (online music and video), 4.5%, music media (radio and recorded music), 7.5%, box office, 6%, and video games, 7%. Internet media, while relatively small now, is growing at 12% annually, far faster than traditional media revenues.

Three Revenue Models for Digital Content Delivery: Subscription, A La Carte, and Advertising-Supported (Free and Freemium)

There are three revenue models for delivering content on the Internet. The two pay models are subscriptions (usually "all you can eat") and a la carte (pay for what you use). The third model uses advertising revenue to provide content for free, usually with a freemium (higher price) option. There is also completely free, user-generated content, which we will discuss later. Contrary to early analysts' projections that "free" would drive "paid" out of business, it turns out that both models are viable now and in the near future. Consumers increasingly choose to pay for high-quality, convenient, and unique content, and they have gladly accepted free advertiser-supported content when that content is deemed not worth paying for but entertaining nevertheless. There's nothing contradictory about all three models working in tandem and cooperatively: free content can drive customers to paid content, as the recorded music firms have discovered with services like Pandora and Spotify.

| FIGURE 9.2 | **U.S. MEDIA REVENUES BY CHANNEL** |

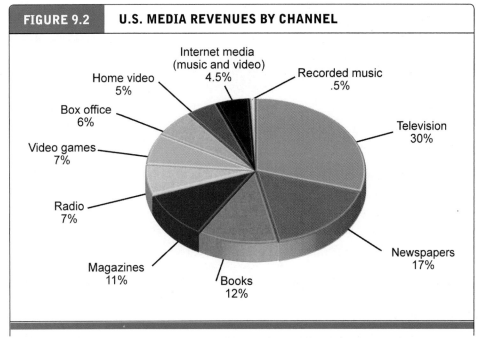

Traditional media (television, print, and radio) still dominate the entertainment and media market, but Internet media (streaming videos, music, and content) is the fastest growing segment.

SOURCES: Based on data from industry sources; authors' estimates.

Online Content Consumption

Now let's look at what kinds of online content U.S. Internet users purchase or view online (**Figure 9.3**). It's not a surprise that 77% of U.S. Internet users watch online videos of many kinds, but it is a surprise that 74% read newspapers. Listening to online radio and watching TV shows and movies online are the next most popular, followed by playing online games and listening to music on mobile devices. E-book consumption (31%) has grown at triple-digit rates since the Kindle was introduced in 2007 and the iPad in 2010 but has slowed to around 12% annual growth in 2014. What this reveals is that Internet users retain their affinity to traditional formats—newspapers, radio, TV shows, books, and music tracks and albums—and bring these tastes to the Internet and their mobile phones and tablets.

Figure 9.4 shows the estimated revenues from the U.S. online entertainment and media industries, projected to 2017. In 2014, total paid online entertainment content is estimated to be $13 billion, and is expected to reach $18 billion by 2017. Online TV and movies is the largest and fastest growing online entertainment form, growing at 25% in 2014. Online music sales are no longer growing at double digits in 2014, but music remains the second largest revenue generator of online entertainment content.

The U.S. online video audience is huge, estimated at around 190 million Americans who watch around 45–50 billion videos monthly in 2014. **Figure 9.5** shows the top U.S. online video sites in May 2014. The most popular site remains Google (YouTube) with

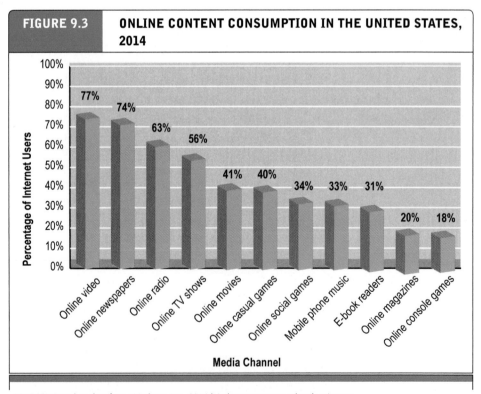

FIGURE 9.3 **ONLINE CONTENT CONSUMPTION IN THE UNITED STATES, 2014**

SOURCES: Based on data from eMarketer, Inc., 2014d; industry sources; authors' estimates.

FIGURE 9.4	**PAID ONLINE ENTERTAINMENT CONTENT REVENUES IN THE UNITED STATES, 2012–2017**

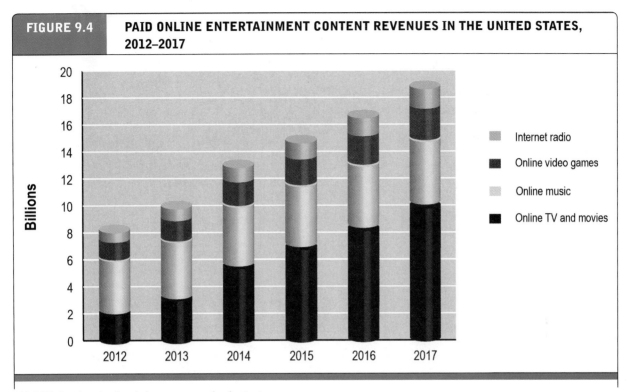

SOURCES: Based on data from industry sources; authors' estimates.

around 155 million viewers, followed by Facebook, AOL, and the fast growing video syndication service NDN. NDN distributes video content produced by advertisers (such as Major League Baseball) and distributes it across a network of publishers who are looking for video content to show ads against. The monetary value of all these videos is that they attract large audiences that can be shown ads.

The overall size of the online video audience is about the same size as the traditional television audience. There are 115 million households with televisions, representing about 200 million individuals who tune in every month. However, major TV events tend to draw a much higher one-time viewership. For instance, 111 million people watched Super Bowl XLVIII in 2014, the most widely viewed television program in history. In comparison, the FIFA World Cup Soccer tournament drew an average audience in America of about 25 million per game. No Internet video draws such large audiences during a single time period.

Free or Fee: Attitudes About Paying for Content and the Tolerance for Advertising

In the early years of online content, multiple surveys found that large majorities of the Internet audience expected to pay nothing for online content although equally large majorities were willing to accept advertising as a way to pay for free content. In reality, on the early Web, there wasn't much high-quality content. By 2014, con-

FIGURE 9.5 | **TOP 10 U.S. ONLINE VIDEO SITES, 2014**

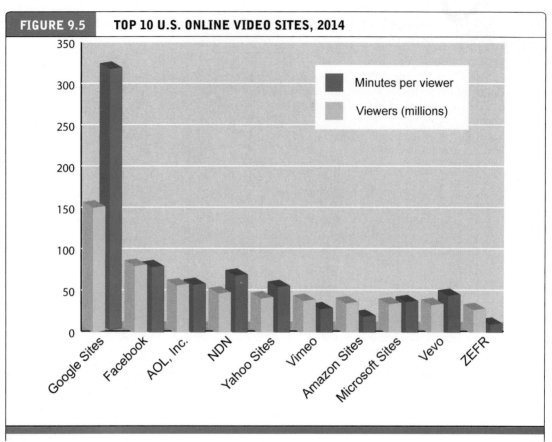

SOURCE: Based on data from comScore, 2014.

sumer behavior and attitudes towards paying for content had greatly changed. Until Internet services such as iTunes arrived in 2007, few thought the "fee" model could compete with the "free" model, and most Internet aficionados and experts concluded that information on the Internet wants to be free. Cable TV systems (networks themselves) offer a totally different history: they always charged for service and content, and cable executives, investors, and TV experts never thought information wanted to be free. Neither did the Hollywood and New York media companies that paid for and provided the content to television and movie theaters. In 2014, millions of Internet users pay for high-quality content delivered on a convenient device such as a smartphone, tablet computer, or e-reader or using Internet TV services like Netflix, Apple TV, or Amazon. Like cable TV, Apple iTunes charges for service and content as well. In a demonstration of just how much quality online content is worth paying for, by 2014, Apple had sold an estimated 35 billion songs, over 700 million TV shows, and more than 200 million movies. Worldwide, iTunes has more than 800 million credit cards on file. iTunes accounts for 67% of TV show downloads, 65% of movies, and 63% of music downloads (Kahn, 2014; NPD Group, 2013a). Pandora, the second largest source of Internet music with 250 million subscribers, and the largest streaming service, has 77 million monthly unique visitors. While an estimated 21 million Internet users in the United States still download songs from illegal P2P sites (down from 33 million in 2005), over 100 million buy music in various formats from legal sites in 2014, and over 160 million listen to online radio (all of which are difficult to pirate), generating about $4.4 billion in digital music sales (eMarketer, Inc., 2014e), about 60% of the music industry's revenues.

The culture of the Internet changed when firms such as YouTube (and its parent Google), which started out with a business model based on amateur videos and illegally uploaded music videos, began cooperating closely with Hollywood and New York production studios for premium content. As it turns out, free content isn't worth very much and should be free, especially if producers give it away. Premium content is worth a great deal, and should be priced accordingly.

DIGITAL RIGHTS MANAGEMENT (DRM) AND WALLED GARDENS

Content producers—newspapers, book publishers, television, movie, and music producers—generate revenue and profits from their creations, and they protect these revenue streams through copyright. Created by Congress in Article I, Section 8 of the United States Constitution, Congress granted authors and inventors copyrights and patent rights to "the progress of science and useful arts." The first Copyright Act was passed in 1790. In the digital age, when exact copies and widescale distribution of works are possible, protecting the copyrights to content is a major challenge.

Digital rights management (DRM) refers to a combination of technical (both hardware and software) and legal means for protecting digital content from unlimited reproduction and distribution without permission. DRM hardware and software encrypts content so that it cannot used without some form of authorization typically based on a payment. The objective is to control the uses of content after it has been sold or rented to consumers. Essentially, DRM can prevent users from purchasing and making copies for widespread distribution over the Internet without compensating the content owners. While music tracks in the iTunes Store were originally protected by DRM, in 2009, Apple abandoned the practice because of user objections, and because Amazon had opened an online music store in 2007 without any DRM protections, with the support of music label firms, who came to realize that DRM prevented them from exploiting the opportunities of the Internet and perhaps encouraged an illegal market. Most music firms with subscription services use technologies that limit the time period that a song can be played without resubscribing. For instance, songs downloaded from Rhapsody, the largest music subscription service, will not play after 30 days unless the user pays the monthly subscription fee. And if you don't pay, you will lose access to all your songs. Movies streamed from Netflix are technically difficult for the average user to capture and share. Likewise, music streamed from Pandora is cumbersome to record and share. Streaming services, including both Apple and Amazon, use a kind of DRM called a **walled garden** to restrict the widespread sharing of content. They do this by tying the content to the hardware, operating system, or streaming environment. E-books purchased from Amazon can only be read on Kindles or Kindle apps running on smartphones, tablets, computers, or browsers. Kindle books cannot be converted to other formats, like EPUB or Adobe PDF files. By locking the content to a physical device, or a digital stream with no local storage, the appliance

digital rights management (DRM)
refers to the combination of technical and legal means for protecting digital content from unlimited reproduction without permission

walled garden
refers to a kind of DRM that uses proprietary file formats, operating systems, and hardware to control the use of content after initial sale

makers derive additional revenues and profits by locking customers into their service or device. Streaming content from a cloud server also offers publishers some protection from piracy when compared to selling a physical product like a CD, or DVD.

While the issue of DRM is often cast as a moral contest between content owners and hackers bent on distributing and using free music, films, and books, the industry titans themselves are divided on DRM. The telecommunications and digital device industries directly benefit from the illegal and unfettered downloading of music and other content. For instance, Apple, Intel, Sony, and Microsoft all benefited from the explosion in illegal sharing of intellectual property simply because users will buy more devices. A mantra voiced first by Steve Jobs as Rip. Mix. Burn became an Apple advertising slogan and popular rationale for copying CDs and sharing or posting the music online for commercial purposes. [In subsequent interviews, Jobs said he did not intend this remark to encourage people to steal music, and in fact, he was a strong supporter of protecting the intellectual property rights of all artists and their production firms (Isaacson, 2011). Likewise, Verizon, SBC Communications, and Time Warner Cable (and the major Internet trunk line owners) also depend on their networks being kept as busy as possible. In 2014, an estimated 24% of global Internet bandwidth consists of unauthorized stolen material. BitTorrent traffic—mostly pirated video, but music and books as well—has fallen drastically from its high of 35% in 2005 to about 10% of Internet traffic in the United States. Netflix has replaced BitTorrent as the leading bandwidth user with 35% of all Internet traffic in the United States (Sandvine, 2014). Internet service providers, telecom providers, and even search engines like Google derive revenue from an environment where users can share any content whether or not it is legally obtained content. In contrast, content creators and owners often insist on DRM and are supportive of walled gardens that make their content unusable on more general purpose platforms such as PCs, using Adobe Flash or PDF files. Content producers make nothing on the delivery devices or the telecommunications infrastructure. To understand all this, you need to keep your eye on the money.

In 2003, Apple provided a game-changing solution to illegal downloading and sharing by creating iTunes, and has managed to make it a popular alternative to illegal file-sharing services like Megaupload, Pirate Bay, Kazaa, eDonkey, and Limewire. Google Play, Amazon, Pandora, Spotify, and Netflix have followed in iTunes' footsteps by providing an environment where users can conveniently download or stream legal content for a very low cost. By 2014, it is clear to the major online content distributors and device makers that more revenue can be generated from legal distribution of paid content than distribution of stolen content.

MEDIA INDUSTRY STRUCTURE

The media content industry prior to 1990 was composed of many smaller independent corporations specializing in content creation and distribution in the separate industries of film, television, book and magazine publishing, and newspaper publishing. During the 1990s and into this century, after an extensive period of consolidation, huge entertainment and publishing media conglomerates emerged.

The media industry is still organized largely into three separate vertical stovepipes: print, movies, and music. Each segment is dominated by a few key players.

We do not include the delivery platform firms here, such as AT&T, Verizon, Sprint, Dish Network, or Comcast, because in general they do not create content but instead move content across cable, satellite, and telephone lines. The transmission industry is itself highly oligopolistic, with two dominant players in each distribution market. In telephony and wireless distribution, AT&T and Verizon dominate. In cable distribution, Comcast and Time Warner dominate. Generally, there is very little crossover from one segment to another. Newspapers do not also produce Hollywood films, and publishing firms do not own newspapers or film production studios. The purchase of the *Washington Post* in 2013 by Jeff Bezos, the founder of Amazon, and an Internet mogul in his own right, was an anomaly. Even within media conglomerates that span several different media segments, separate divisions control each media segment. The competition between corporate divisions in mega-sized corporations is often more severe than with marketplace competitors.

While the commercial media industry is highly concentrated within each segment, the much larger media ecosystem includes literally millions of individuals and independent entrepreneurs creating content in the form of blogs, videos on YouTube and Vevo, and music on indie sites like Madeloud. At times, the viewership (or readership) of these much smaller but numerous players exceeds that of the media titans.

MEDIA CONVERGENCE: TECHNOLOGY, CONTENT, AND INDUSTRY STRUCTURE

Media convergence is a much used but poorly defined term. There are at least three dimensions of media where the term convergence has been applied: technology, content (artistic design, production, and distribution), and the industry's structure as a whole. Ultimately for the consumer, convergence means being able to get any content you want, when you want it, on whatever platform you want it—from an iPod to an iPad, Android phone, or home PC, or set-top device like Apple TV.

Technological Convergence

Convergence from a technology perspective **(technological convergence)** has to do with the development of hybrid devices that can combine the functionality of two or more existing media platforms, such as books, newspapers, television, movies, radio, and games, into a single device. Examples of technological convergence include the iPad, iPhone, and Android ("smartphones") that combine print, music, pictures, and video in a single device.

Content Convergence

A second dimension of convergence is **content convergence**. There are three aspects to content convergence: design, production, and distribution.

There is a historical pattern in which content created in an older media technology migrates to the new technology largely intact, with little artistic change. Slowly, the different media are integrated so that consumers can move seamlessly back and forth among them, and artists (and producers) learn more about how to deliver content in the new media. Later, the content itself is transformed by the new media as artists learn how

technological convergence
development of hybrid devices that can combine the functionality of two or more existing media platforms into a single device

content convergence
convergence in the design, production, and distribution of content

to fully exploit the capabilities in the creation process. At this point, content convergence and transformation has occurred—the art is different because of the new capabilities inherent to new tools. For instance, European master painters of the fifteenth century in Italy, France, and the Netherlands (such as van Eyck, Caravaggio, Lotto, and Vermeer) quickly adopted new optical devices such as lenses, mirrors, and early projectors called *camera obscura* that could cast near-photographic quality images on canvases, and in the process they developed new theories of perspective and new techniques of painting landscapes and portraits. Suddenly, paintings took on the qualities of precision, detail, and realism found later in photographs (Boxer, 2001). A similar process is occurring today as artists and writers assimilate new digital and Internet tools into their toolkits. For instance, GarageBand from Apple enables low-budget independent bands (literally working in garages) to mix and control eight different digital music tracks to produce professional sounding recordings on a shoestring budget. Writers of books are beginning to think about video and interactive versions of their books. Online newspapers are changing the news cycle to a 24-hour stream, producing their own video channels, and expanding user comment opportunities on their Web sites.

On the production side, tools for digital editing and processing (for film and television) are driving content convergence. Given that the most significant cost of content is its creation, if there is a wide diversity of target delivery platforms, then it is wise to develop and produce only once using technology that can deliver to multiple platforms. Generally, this means creating content on digital devices (hardware and software) so that it can be delivered on multiple digital platforms.

On the distribution side, it is important that distributors and the ultimate consumers have the devices needed to receive, store, and experience the product. While for the most part technology companies have succeeded in giving consumers portable devices to receive online content, it has been more difficult for the content owners to come up with new, profitable business models.

Figure 9.6 depicts the process of media convergence and transformation using the example of books. For example, consider this book. In 2014, this book was written with a view to appearing on iPads and Kindle e-book readers, and is moving closer to the media maturity stage, in which the book will be available mostly as a purely digital product with substantial visual and aural content that can be displayed on many different digital devices. By that time, the learning experience will be transformed by greater use of interactive graphics, videos, as well as an integrated testing system that monitors student performance during the semester. Even the number of pages read by students, and the time on page, will be accounted for by this near-future digital learning system. Traditional bound books will probably still be available (books have many advantages), but most likely, print editions will be printed on demand by customers using their own print facilities.

Industry Structure Convergence

industry convergence
merger of media enterprises into synergistic combinations that create and cross-market content on different platforms

A third dimension of convergence is the structure of the various media industries. **Industry convergence** refers to the merger of media enterprises into powerful, synergistic combinations that can cross-market content on many different platforms and create new works that use multiple platforms. This can take place either through pur-

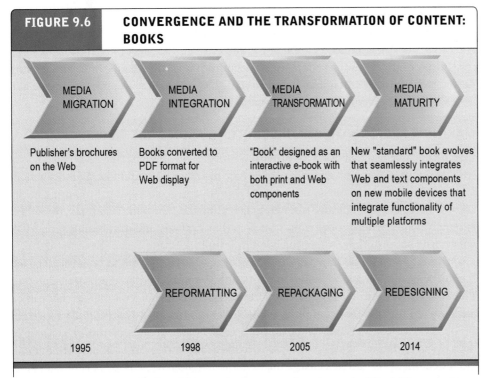

| **FIGURE 9.6** | **CONVERGENCE AND THE TRANSFORMATION OF CONTENT: BOOKS** |

MEDIA MIGRATION

MEDIA INTEGRATION

MEDIA TRANSFORMATION

MEDIA MATURITY

Publisher's brochures on the Web

Books converted to PDF format for Web display

"Book" designed as an interactive e-book with both print and Web components

New "standard" book evolves that seamlessly integrates Web and text components on new mobile devices that integrate functionality of multiple platforms

REFORMATTING

REPACKAGING

REDESIGNING

1995   1998   2005   2014

The Internet is making it possible for publishers and writers to transform the standard "book" into a new form that integrates features of both text and the Internet, and also transforms the content of the book itself.

chases or through strategic alliances. Traditionally, each type of media—film, text, music, television—had its own separate industry, typically composed of very large players. For instance, the entertainment film industry has been dominated by a few large Hollywood-based production studios, book publication is dominated by a few large book publishers, and music production is dominated by four global record label firms.

However, the Internet has created forces that make mergers and partnerships among media and Internet firms a necessary business proposition. Media industry convergence may be necessary to finance the substantial changes in both the technology platform and the content. Traditional media firms who create the content generally do not possess the core competencies or financial heft to distribute it on the Internet. Technology companies that dominate the Internet (Google, Apple, Amazon, and Facebook) have the competency and wealth to pursue Internet channel strategies, but do not currently have the competencies needed to create content. Business combinations and partnerships are made to solve these issues.

While traditional media companies have not done well in purchases of Internet platform companies, the technology owners such as Apple, Amazon, Facebook, Microsoft, and Google have generally avoided merging with media companies, and instead rely on contractual arrangements with media companies to protect intellectual property rights and to create a business pricing model that both parties can accept. However, this pattern may be changing. For instance, CBS Inc., a movie and television content producer, produces television shows for Netflix; Netflix and Hulu have begun production and distribution of their own original TV shows; Google is producing original content designed for Internet distribution on YouTube. Amazon created its own book imprint, Amazon Books Publishing, and entered the book publishing business.

In the end, consumers' demands for content anywhere, anytime, and on any device is pushing the technology and content companies towards both strategic alliances and strategic conflicts in their search for advantage.

MAKING A PROFIT WITH ONLINE CONTENT: FROM FREE TO FEE

Despite the resistance of users in the early years of e-commerce, there is broad consensus that online consumers are willing to pay for high-quality content, at their discretion, and that sites offering a mix of free and fee content can be successful. Streaming music sites like Pandora and Spotify, and newspapers like the *New York Times*, use freemium revenue models where some content is free (but limited) and advertising supported, versus paid subscriptions where the content is unlimited and free of advertising.

There appear to be four factors required to charge for online content: focused market, specialized content, sole-source monopoly, and high perceived net value (see **Figure 9.7**). **Net value** refers to that portion of perceived customer value that can be attributed to the fact that content is available on the Internet. Net value derives from the ability of consumers to instantaneously access the information on the Web or mobile device, search large and deep historical archives, and move the online information to other documents or devices easily. Customer convenience is a large part of net value.

net value

that portion of perceived customer value that can be attributed to the fact that content is available on the Internet

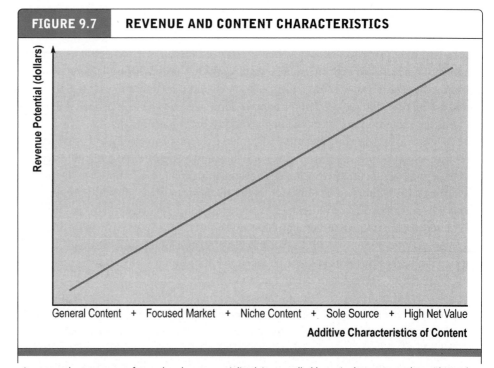

| FIGURE 9.7 | REVENUE AND CONTENT CHARACTERISTICS |

General Content + Focused Market + Niche Content + Sole Source + High Net Value

Additive Characteristics of Content

As content becomes more focused and more specialized, is controlled by a single source, and provides real value to consumers for an Internet delivery (i.e., speed, searchability, and portability), the prospects for charging fees for access increase.

For instance, the business information services firm Hoover's provides four different subscriptions ranging from $75 a month to $2,995 for a professional subscription. Hoover's content addresses a focused market (business analysts and executive search firms); it has specialized content (data gathered by its own reporters and other sources); it is the sole source for some of this information; and it has high perceived value because it can be quickly accessed, searched, and downloaded into other documents and made a part of business decision making. And the consumers are in a hurry to get the information. In general, the opportunity for paid content varies by the scarcity and time value of the content, and the urgency of the audience to access the content.

9.2 THE ONLINE PUBLISHING INDUSTRY

Nothing is quite so fundamental to a civilized society as reading text. Text is the way we record our history, current events, thoughts, and aspirations, and transmit them to all others in the civilization who can read. Even television shows and movies require scripts. Today, the publishing industry (composed of books, newspapers, magazines, and periodicals) is a $102 billion media sector based originally on print, and now moving rapidly to the Internet and mobile delivery. The Internet offers the text publishing industry an opportunity to move toward a new generation of newspapers, magazines, and books that are produced, processed, stored, distributed, and sold over the Web, available anytime, anywhere, and on any device. The same Internet offers the possibility of destroying many existing print-based businesses that may not be able to make this transition and remain profitable.

ONLINE NEWSPAPERS

Newspapers: Searching for a Digital Business Model

Newspapers in 2014 are the most troubled segment of the print publishing industry. A free fall in revenues that accelerated with the recession of 2008–2010 has stabilized. Newspaper industry revenues have shrunk from their high of $60 billion in 2000 to $32 billion in 2013 (down 2.6% from 2012). See **Figure 9.8**. The newspaper labor force has roughly been cut in half over this period. The newspaper industry has been in an extended period of digital disruption since the rise of the Web in 2000 and the emergence of powerful search engines like Google, which allow consumers to search for news on any subject without having to browse a physical newspaper or an online edition. Social media sites have become a major source of unique visitors, who, unfortunately, do not browse for news and usually stay on the newspaper's site for only a few moments to read a single article. These fleeting visitors typically do not engage with the newspaper as a whole or with its online ads. Even before the Internet and Web, newspaper revenue was falling due the influence of earlier technologies like broadcast and cable television. In 2014, three of the largest newspaper organizations (Gannett, Tribune Company, and E.W. Scripps) spun off their newspaper operations as independent firms so they could focus on television and other media assets, including in some cases, successful digital

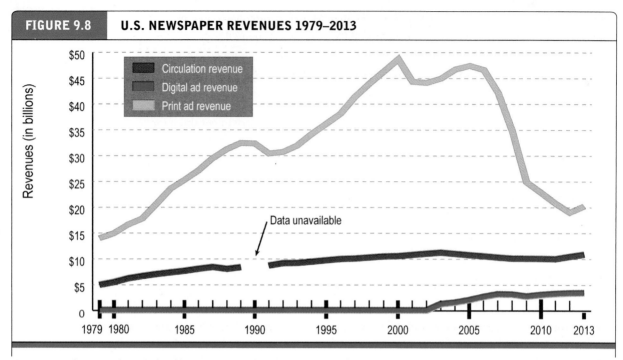

| FIGURE 9.8 | **U.S. NEWSPAPER REVENUES 1979–2013** |

Newspaper ad revenues have declined by 50% since 1980. As a percentage of total revenues, circulation subscription revenues have become more important. Digital is a small source of revenue but growing up until recently.

SOURCE: Based on data from Newspaper Association of America, 2014.

properties. Newspapers will now be pure-play print enterprises and will have to make it on their own without the protection of television or other media assets (Carr, 2014).

The striking growth of alternative pure digital news sources in the last five years, from Twitter and Facebook, to BuzzFeed and Huffington Post, poses additional challenges in 2014. Online news sources like Yahoo and Google News, and many others, are attracting millions of consumers everyday, and steer potential newspaper readers—both online and offline—away from the most valuable front page of print and digital edition newspapers. The shift of consumers towards the mobile platform and social media deepens the potential for disruption in the newspaper industry. Social media sites are playing a significant factor in directing traffic directly to specific newspaper articles, bypassing the newspaper's valuable front page, and increasingly, are providing their own original reporting and commentary by hiring professional journalists away from troubled newspapers. Newspaper survival will depend on how fast newspaper organizations can transform themselves from print to digital, and how fast they can monetize the expanding audience for news all the time, anywhere, on all devices.

As can be seen from Figure 9.8, while newspaper circulation revenues (subscriptions plus newsstand sales) have declined 10% since 2000 to around $10 billion, print advertising, which includes display ads, classified ads, and legal notices, has fallen precipitously from a high of $50 billion in 2000 to $19 billion in 2013. Online advertising in newspapers in the last year has shown weak growth, and newspapers' revenues from online ads are still only 15% of print ad revenue, and only 10% of total revenue. The gains in online ad revenue are not large enough to compensate for the loss of print revenue. Only the music industry has suffered a similar devastating decline in revenue. The 15-year decline in newspaper revenues has resulted from four factors:

- The growth of the Web and mobile devices as an alternative medium for news and advertising. The Web and apps generate billions of pages used to create ad impressions and page views and attract large audiences. The movement of consumers to an online life style has drained billions of ad dollars (including classified ads) from newspapers. The same has not been true of television advertising as we will discuss later in the chapter.
- The rise of alternative digital sources for news, commentary, feature stories, and articles.
- The difficulty of traditional newspaper firms and their managers to develop suitable business and revenue models that could survive and even prosper on the Internet, and the mobile/social platform.
- The rise of social media, and its role in directing traffic to newspaper content, has challenged newspapers to change their business model to accommodate changes in consumer behavior and technology.

From Print-centric to Digital First: The Evolution of Newspaper Online Business Models, 1995–2014

Since 1995, when e-commerce and digital advertising began, through to the present, newspapers have developed three distinct business models in an effort to adapt to the Internet, and more recently, the mobile and social platform (see **Figure 9.9**). The

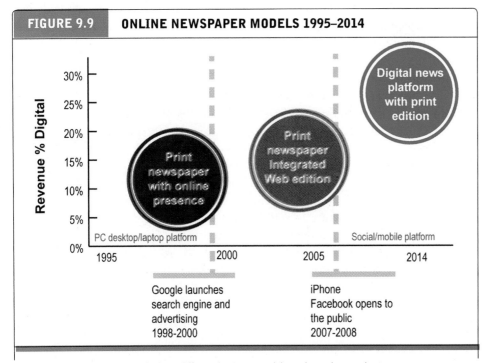

FIGURE 9.9   ONLINE NEWSPAPER MODELS 1995–2014

Newspapers have gone through three different business models as they adapt to the Internet.

three models are: Print-centric (1995–2000), Integrated Print/Web (2000–2010), and the most current model, Digital First (2010–present). You can compare these models on four dimensions:

- **Search and discovery:** How do readers find the news?
- **Awareness:** How are potential readers made aware of news?
- **Engagement:** how are readers engaged with the news and journalists?
- **Technology platform:** how, when, and where is the news delivered to readers? (New York Times, 2014).

The milestones reflect important dates in the evolution of the Web and the mobile-social platform. In 1998 to 2000, Google launched its search engine with 60 million pages indexed, and introduced search engine paid advertising based on its Page Rank algorithm. In 2007, Apple introduced its iPhone, creating a truly mobile and universal Web device, and Facebook opened its site to the public, and in 2008 signed up over 100 million users, creating the first large-scale, online social network.

Prior to the development of the Web, search engines, mobile devices, and social media platforms, readers discovered the news by browsing (a form of searching) the printed paper. They became aware of stories by reading the front page, section pages, and article titles. Readers did not engage with journalists, editors, or other contributors, except for the few who wrote letters to the editor (less than 1% of all readers). Journalism was considered a profession, and readers were not expected to do much more than read and be fascinated, enlightened, and entertained by people who obviously were more informed than they. Journalists worked all day on their articles and filed them at 5 PM; professional editors revised the copy, and compositors put it on the page for the presses, which ran after midnight. The news stream ended at 5 PM. The technology platform was print, sometimes with color (a major innovation and expense in this period).

With the introduction of the Web and its growing popularity, newspapers retained their existing print-centric strategy and culture. In the Print-centric period from 1995 to 2000, newspapers created digital copies of their print editions and posted them online. Readers discovered stories as they did before, by reading the front page online, following links to stories, and clicking on topic areas or sections (e.g. Sports or Technology). Stories were promoted by a business department that sought to enlarge the print audience and to attract advertisers based on readership and online visitors. Digital advertising was very limited, in part because advertisers did not believe it was effective. Readers were not engaged with journalists except insofar as they read the stories and could identify with the subjects of stories. The business process of creating journalism did not change: articles were filed at 5 PM and went to print editors, and then were sent to the Web team and the print group. There was little difference, if any, between the print and online versions. The technology platform for the digital edition was the desktop or laptop, and news was consumed at home and work.

In the Integrated Print/Web period, from 2000 to 2010, newspapers adopted multimedia elements such as video, added more interactive elements like crossword puzzles and contests, and provided more reader feedback opportunities, especially on opinion and editorial pages. There were opportunities to personalize the news using RSS feeds and push news to the reader. Nevertheless, news was discovered by the reader visiting the Web site; promoting content online was limited, primarily to RSS feeds. Readers were somewhat more engaged. The technology platform remained the desktop or laptop platform.

In the Digital First period, from 2010 to the present, two developments in the technology and popular audience platform occurred: the rapid adoption of smartphones and tablets, and the equally astounding growth of social media sites like Facebook and Twitter, which have come to dominate consumer time on the Web and mobile devices. The rise of start-up news sites specifically focused on using the new technology and platforms has spurred newspapers to radically transform their business—or go out of business. The new platform is not based on personal computers using a browser, but on mobile devices and apps, with desktops and laptops now just one pillar of the delivery platform. In this new environment, the news does not stop at 5 PM, but goes on 24 × 7. Stories might start with a tweet, or from a Facebook post, followed by thousands of tweets, then millions of shares on multiple social sites. Often amateurs on scene know more about the news in the first hours of a story than any collection of journalists in their offices. Amateurs provide video feeds, commentary, and opinion.

The Digital First business model inverts previous models: the top priority is producing the most engaging, continually updated digital edition, and then producing a print product based on the news developed in the digital edition. In the case of pure digital start-ups, there is no print edition, and the news is just a continuous stream of updates, blogs, tweets, and posts, rather than a fixed article. News articles are time-stamped, indicating an update is on the way and the reader should return to follow the story. Instead of waiting for readers to discover the news, or search for the news on a search engine, the news is pushed to readers on any of a variety of venues where they happen to be—social media sites, mobile news feeds, Twitter, or Yahoo or Google News. Journalists remain professionals, but they follow Twitter feeds and social media sites, and promote their stories and personas on social media sites. Their job is no longer simply reporting and writing, but promoting and engaging readers on a personal level through their own efforts. Superior reporting and writing is no longer the sole criterion for hiring and advancement. More emphasis is put on reporters' abilities to attract audiences on their own social media pages and Twitter feeds.

The Digital First business model is not yet a reality for traditional newspapers. The largest print newspaper organizations, such as *The Wall Street Journal*, *New York Times*, *Washington Post*, and others, have begun the journey towards becoming Digital First news organizations. In 2014 *The Wall Street Journal* launched its Real-Time news desk, a headquarters group of 60 editors aiming to produce a continuous and lively flow of digital news and commentary to social media sites, mobile followers, and its online sites (Romenesko, 2014). *The New York Times* also initiated a Digital First in January 2014. Another example of newspaper innovation along the path of a Digital First strategy is provided by *The Financial Times,* discussed in the Chapter 3 opening case.

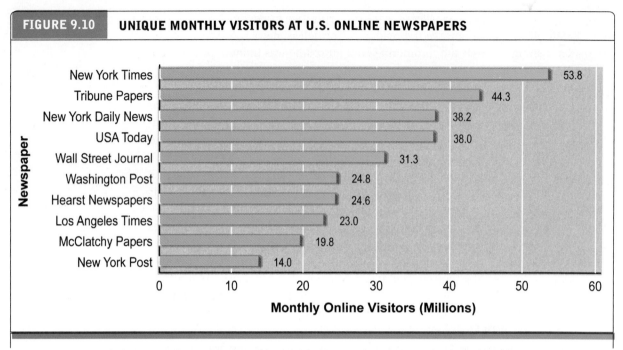

FIGURE 9.10   **UNIQUE MONTHLY VISITORS AT U.S. ONLINE NEWSPAPERS**

Online newspaper readership is expanding as consumers shift to mobile devices and participate in social networks.

SOURCES: Based on data from Compete.com; various newspaper Web sites.

Assets: Newspaper Audience Size and Growth

But there is some good news for traditional newspapers too. Online readership of newspapers is growing at more than 10% a year. About 74% of Internet users (about 161 million people) read newspaper content online, making it the second most popular online activity behind watching video, and is about 20% higher than 2013. See **Figure 9.10** for a list of the top ten online newspapers in the United States. The online newspaper is one of the most successful of all online media in terms of audience size. Mobile newspaper readership is especially strong among young persons due to their greater usage of smartphones and tablet computers.

Newspapers have responded to the changing audience by providing access to their content on all digital platforms (see **Figure 9.11**). With 58% of Americans having a smartphone, 42% a tablet, and 55% accessing the Internet through mobile devices, in a few short years newspapers have become truly multi-platform by developing apps and Web sites optimized for mobile devices (Pew Research Center, 2014a). Only 55% of newspaper readers are exclusively print readers, 45% use a combination of Web, print, or mobile. Mobile and tablet engagement is growing at more than 70% annually, especially among 18–34 year olds (Newspaper Association of America, 2014c).

Online newspapers also attract a wealthy and consumer-intense demographic, reaching 64% of 25- to 34-year-olds and 75% of individuals in households earning more than $100,000 a year on average throughout the quarter. Given the large online newspaper audience, it is clear that the future of newspapers lies in the online and mobile market even as readership and subscriptions to the traditional print newspapers continue to decline at a steady pace.

| FIGURE 9.11 | **U.S. NEWSPAPER AUDIENCE PLATFORM** |

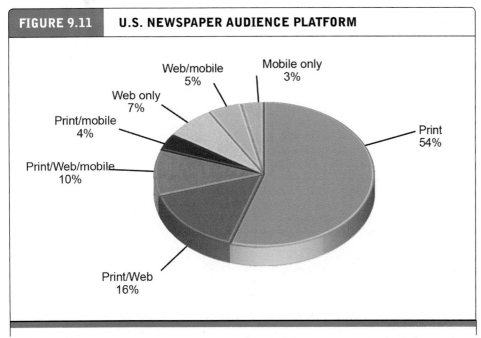

Web-only readership of newspapers remains quite small compared to print only and multi-platform reading.

SOURCE: Based on data from Newspaper Association of America, 2014c.

Challenge: Digital Ad Revenue

Newspapers hope that the digital ad revolution and revenue will hit their shores, and lift total ad revenues. But here's the problem: while unique visitors to newspaper Web sites are expanding, increasingly this traffic is less valuable for two reasons. First, the audience is increasingly coming from social media sites and search engines in order to find specific articles, rather than coming directly to the newspaper's home page. As a result, newspaper home page visits have fallen dramatically since 2011. Today's newspaper Web site visitors are fleeting, view fewer pages, and are far less likely to return (see **Figure 9.12**).

The less engaged visitors are in terms of pages viewed, minutes on site, and return visits, the less time there is to show them ads and earn revenue. Direct visitors are therefore much more valuable. Ironically, as a result, growth in digital ad revenues at online newspapers has been tepid despite increasing unique visitors. While print ad revenue continued to decline in 2013 by 8%, newspaper digital ad revenue grew only 1.5%. In comparison, total Internet digital ad revenue (search, social, and display ads) grew at a robust 25% (Doctor, 2014; Benton, 2014). If current trends continue, it is unlikely newspapers can rely on growing unique visitors, or growing digital ad revenues, to reverse the revenue declines of the past decade.

Strength: Content Is King

The oft-repeated bon mot that "content is king" appears to be true in the case of print as well as online content of all kinds, including news and pure digital news sites. As

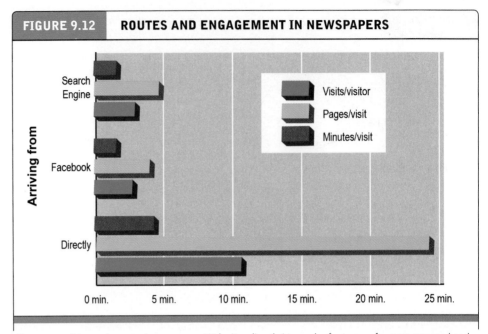

FIGURE 9.12 **ROUTES AND ENGAGEMENT IN NEWSPAPERS**

Newspaper visitors who come to newspaper Web sites directly in search of news are far more engaged and generate more digital ad revenue.
SOURCE: Based on data from Pew Research Center, 2014b.

in competitive sports, in general, quality counts. The reason why online newspapers attract exceptionally large and loyal audiences who are deeply engaged is simple: quality of content. Compared to other media, newspapers are the most trusted source of news and commentary on local, national, and international stories (Nielsen, 2013). Local newspapers produce the highest levels of ad engagement: 35% of consumers report making purchases on the basis of local newspaper ads. Online banner ads, e-mail campaigns, and fleeting mobile ads in a Facebook Newsfeed do not even come close to these engagement levels. Newspapers employ about 40,000 full-time professional editorial staff, down from about 60,000 in 2000, but still much larger than television, radio, or newer pure digital news sources, which obtain most of their content from unpaid bloggers, cellphone photographers, and bloggers (Pew Research Center, 2014c).

Amateur blogs and tweets may be wonderful for expressing opinions, or making instant reports on newsworthy events as they occur, but they are no substitute for professional reporters and editors, who make sense out of the constant stream of reports, and they are not a place for brand-conscious advertisers who do not want their products associated with low-quality content. Therefore, Internet distributors of news content are recognizing they have a vested interest in keeping the newspaper content industry alive and in working order. Google, Apple, Yahoo, and other large online news distributors are working with newspapers to attract bigger audiences and generate more ad revenue. In 2014, Google is offering Google Journalism Fellowships to journalism students in the stated belief that quality journalism is a key ingredient of a vibrant and functioning society (Wingfield, 2013a). While Internet news giants are dependent on newspapers to provide them with content to search and index, newspapers are equally dependent on Internet giants for visitors: in 2013, Google sent an estimated 6 billion visitors to news sites, mostly newspapers, because they have the most authoritative content.

High-quality content translates into strong brand identification with readers. This in turn results in consumer engagement with news sites and printed content, which in turn means that news readers stay around on news Web sites, and spend a fair amount of time reading printed news content. Americans on average spend about 30 minutes a day reading print newspapers (eMarketer, Inc., 2014a). As online newspaper sites have grown in terms of unique visits, many visitors engage only for a short time, say, to read an article recommended by a friend. In large part this is because reading news online is a work or commuting activity on trains and buses where there isn't time to read lengthy stories or entire sections of a paper. Reading the print newspaper is more of a leisure time activity where people can take the time to read in greater depth (Grabowicz, 2014; Varian, 2010). Nevertheless, total page views at online newspaper sites have grown to over four billion pages per year, offering advertisers a large opportunity to engage the online readership. Finally, the more time on site, the more ads can be shown to readers, and the more revenue generated (Pew Research Center, 2014c). Quality content drives revenue. This relationship is not lost on venture capital firms and wealthy investors, who are buying up journalistic assets and print newspapers at a record pace.

Challenge: Finding a Revenue Model

In 1995, when the first newspaper Web sites appeared, newspapers offered their content for free, with registration. The hope was that advertising would support the Web site's operation and provide a new revenue stream for the print edition content. In some cases, free content was limited to the most popular articles and did not include the classified ads, a lucrative newspaper franchise. At that time, print advertising provided over 75% of revenues and subscription revenue generated about 25%. The *New York Times* charged only for archived content, a valuable research tool for business. But new ad revenue from digital publication did not cover the cost of digital production, and was completely unable to replace the drastic fall in print ad revenues that occurred beginning in 2000.

Charging for general newspaper content was an obvious answer, but publications that tried this during the 1995–2005 period were punished by an Internet culture that expected online content such as music and news to be free. For instance, in 1998, Slate, an online magazine owned by Microsoft, began charging its 140,000 readers a $19.95 annual subscription fee (a so-called **paywall**). There was a free Front Porch section with a few articles. In 1999, Slate dropped its subscription fee after only 20,000 readers signed up. Some specialized content newspapers, like the *Wall Street Journal*, were able to charge an annual subscription fee ($50 annually) and survive. In a year the *Journal* had 200,000 paid subscribers. Similarly, the *Financial Times* (London) introduced a subscription service in 2001, and in 2007 adopted a **metered subscription** model where readers got ten free articles but were asked to pay a $395 subscription fee after that. Both the *Journal* and *Financial Times* were exceptions to consumer resistance to paying for news, and based on a wealthy, focused readership interested in high-value information.

paywall
paid subscription service

metered subscription
paid subscription service where some content is offered for free, similar to a freemium revenue model

The introduction of the iTunes store in 2003 and the iPhone in 2007 changed the public perception of paid content. While plenty of pirated music was available, Apple devices (iPods and later iPhones and iPads) and iTunes provided a high-quality, convenient, and legal alternative that users were willing to pay for. In 2014, paying a subscription fee for content is the foundation of streaming video and music services from Netflix to Pandora.

Newspapers and online magazines have benefited from this change in popular culture. An estimated 450 of the country's 1,380 daily newspapers now charge for online access (Edmunds, 2013). These plans have three key elements: a paywall for heavy users; considerable free content for casual or link traffic (visitors from social media sites, for instance, who stay for a few moments and then move on); and a bundled price for both print and digital subscriptions, in some cases offering the digital version free with a print subscription, allowing users to read the paper on any digital device.

In 2011, the *Times* introduced a metered subscription model where casual readers could read 20 articles for free, and unlimited reading of current archived content for $35 annually. Print subscribers received the digital subscription for free. The free-to-print subscribers policy put the emphasis on subscription to the *Times* content, and not to any particular platform. This is important because today's newspaper readers are multi-platform: they read the content with a variety of devices depending on the context. A metered subscription model is identical to a freemium model: some content is free but ad-supported, while unlimited content is only through a subscription (advertising is still shown in the newspaper world). In 2013, the number of free articles was reduced to 10, given the success of the metered model. In 2013, the *New York Times* subscription revenue exceeded ad revenue for the first time. In 2014, the *Times* has over 760,000 digital subscribers. With 30 million online visitors and 20 million mobile readers, there's plenty of room for the *Times* to grow its subscriber base.

Challenge: Growth of Pure Digital Competitors

The Web has provided an opportunity for newspapers to extend their print brands, but at the same time it has given digital entrepreneurs the opportunity to disaggregate newspaper content by creating specialized Web sites for popular content such as weather, classified ads (Craigslist), restaurant and product reviews (Yelp), as well as topical national and international news sites and apps that compete with online newspapers. Despite the declining revenues of the traditional print newspaper industry, entrepreneurs have poured money into news sites, and even newspapers. Since 2011, Warren Buffet has purchased 28 newspapers for an estimated $344 million in a belief that newspapers delivering comprehensive and reliable information to small tightly bound communities, and that have a reasonable Internet strategy, will be viable for a long time (Berkshire Hathaway, 2013). In August 2013, Jeffrey Bezos purchased the iconic *Washington Post* for $250 million in the belief that newspapers are not just papers but news gathering and distribution businesses independent of any technology or platform (Hagey and Bensinger, 2013).

While actual print newspapers are attracting wealthy individual investors, venture capital investors have poured over $1 billion dollars into purely digital online news sites. In 2013, Pierre Omidyar, co-founder of eBay, pledged $250 million to create an online news and political commentary site called First Look Media, and began hiring name-brand journalists from print newspapers. BuzzFeed took a $50 million investment in 2014 from a venture firm. **Table 9.2** describes several leading pure digital start-up news sites and their investment profile. Huffington Post and Buzzfeed are growing at over 100% a year although this growth is expected to slow in coming years (Fischer, 2014; Isaac, 2014). Within the last five years, both sites have surpassed the *New York*

TABLE 9.2	START-UP DIGITAL NEWS SITES
START UP	**DESCRIPTION**
Huffington Post	Founded in 2005, sold to AOL for $350 million in 2011. Aggregates content from traditional news outlets, invited paid bloggers, legions of unpaid bloggers, and original reporting.
Buzzfeed	Founded in 2006. Focus on using social media to generate viral stories. Buzzfeed focuses on shareable content like quizzes and listicles ("The five most important people"), and photos and gifs. This Digital First media organization also includes more traditional news topics like politics, business, and technology. Originally a news aggregator but now hiring journalists for traditional news reporting. In the top 50 Web sites in terms of traffic, exceeding *Wall Street Journal* and *Forbes*. Has raised $35 million in venture funding since 2012, with an estimated valuation of $200 million.
Flipboard	Founded in 2010. News aggregator app organizes stories in a magazine format that user flips through. Content drawn from traditional media and social sites, such as Twitter and Facebook datastreams, and then reassembled in an easy-to-navigate, personalized format in a mobile—and now a desktop—touchscreen environment. Apple's app of the year. *Time, New York Times*, and book publishers joining up to push content. Has raised $110 million in venture funding since 2011 and is now valued at $800 million.
Vox	Founded in 2014. A property of Vox Media (2008) along with six other specialty brands, 300 Web sites, and 400 unpaid bloggers. The brands are deep verticals including SBNation (sports), The Verge (tech), Polygon (games), Curbed (real estate), Eater (food), and Racked (retail shopping). Vox covers politics and general news. Hired Ezra Klein (ex-*Washington Post* writer) to be editor-in-chief. Eschews banner ads for sponsored videos and stories. Vox Media has raised over $75 million since 2010, $34 million in 2013, and is now valued at $200 million.
Reddit	Founded in 2005. Purchased by Conde Nast in 2006 and operated as an independent company. A bulletin board of user generated posts made up of 185,000 forums from science trivia, politics, videogames, humor, and photos. Registered community members can submit content, such as text posts or direct links. Mostly male, college-educated members contribute content. Limited advertising on the main pages. Unprofitable, but with 18 million unique visitors. Estimated market value $240 million.
Vice	Founded as a magazine in 1994 and moved on to Web sites in 2000 as Vice Media. Vice is a bulletin board of user generated articles, aggregated content, and photos. Focuses on irreverent content appealing to young readers, and reporting from dangerous locations. Vice's YouTube channel is a video-based news site. Reportedly valued by suitor Time Warner at $1 billion in 2014. Seven million unique visitors, but little advertising revenue.

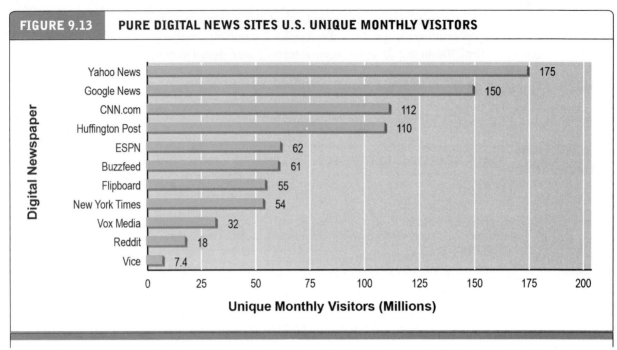

Pure digital news sites have greatly expanded their unique visitor count although many of these visits link back to traditional newspaper articles.

SOURCE: Based on data from Compete.com; Newspaper Association of America, 2014c.

Times in terms of unique visitors, and currently BuzzFeed has 150 million unique visitors a month. Other more traditional pure online news sites like Yahoo, Google, ESPN, and CNN have also shown extraordinary growth (see **Figure 9.13**).

Not all digital news services succeed, and none are profitable so far. For instance, Digg, a news aggregator site, failed in 2011 despite having 230 million unique visitors at one point.

Can Newspapers Survive Digital Disruption?

The newspaper industry would appear at first glance to be a classic case of a disruptive technology—the Internet, mobile devices, and apps—destroying a traditional business model based on physical products and physical distribution. Incumbents (the existing print newspapers) slowly and incrementally improve their products over time. New firms—disruptors—introduce new products (Huffington Post, Buzzfeed, Vox), which are not as good as the incumbents' products, but are based on newer and more powerful technologies. The new products are less expensive, or free, and target underserved or entirely new markets. They often are founded and promoted by people new to the industry. Eventually the disruptor's products are improved and become more acceptable, or good enough. At this point, the new products and the disruptors start draining significant market share from the incumbents who eventually fail. Incumbents fail for a variety of reasons, from an expensive legacy production process, large human capital investments, a contrary culture, and an inability to perceive rapid changes in the business and technology environment. For a description of a news industry start-up that may have a disruptive impact on traditional newspapers, see the *Insight on Society* case, *Vox: The All-Digital News Site*.

Pure digital news sites have many advantages over print newspapers. They don't have the cost of printing papers; they can create new work flows and business processes that are more efficient and timely; they have a lower cost structure, often relying on user generated content and minimal payments to reporters and bloggers, with lower pension costs; and they can take advantage of newer technologies for producing the news. While the quality of journalism on these pure digital sites is not as good as traditional print newspapers, this situation is changing rapidly as the pure digital sites hire talented journalists and editors from print newspapers that are experiencing financial difficulties.

What online news sites often do not have is credibility and trust. For instance, Buzzfeed has been the subject of many lawsuits accusing it of copying content from competing newspapers and sites without attribution, claiming the content as its own. Without trust and quality, online news sites are simply distractions filled with celebrity photos, and there is significant competition for this kind of content.

At this point, it is too early to predict the demise of print newspapers or the newspaper industry. The Web has a long history of news sites that have come and gone. Profit is necessary for a digital disruption. Closely held by venture firms, it is not clear that any of the new pure digital news sites are profitable, and all live off the largesse of exceptionally wealthy individuals and venture funds. The new pure digital news sites rely heavily on social media to drive visitors to their sites. As a result, they face the same problem as online newspapers: so-called **link visitors** stay for a few seconds, and are not very responsive to ads. As online news sites proliferate, the supply of ad pages expands, and prices of ads fall, and the market is very thin and unprofitable (Launder, 2014). It is not clear if any of the new pure digital news sites will be profitable in the near future. In contrast, *The Guardian* (U.K.'s largest online newspaper), the *Wall Street Journal*, and the *New York Times* are profitable businesses in 2014, along with many other traditional newspapers, most of whom have significant Web presence.

link visitor
a person who comes to a news site following a link from another site

If the newspaper industry has a future, it will be online and multiplatform. The challenge for newspapers is to create value by focusing on differentiated, timely, and exclusive content available nowhere else; to transform its culture of journalism to provide a continuous news stream just as its pure digital competitors; and to make this content available anywhere, anytime, anyplace, on any device. In short, newspapers will have to become Digital First publications, while maintaining their historic quality edge, and meeting the challenge from their pure digital competitors.

MAGAZINES REBOUND ON THE TABLET PLATFORM

Magazines in the United States reached their peak circulation in the early 1980s, with more than 40 million people reading some kind of weekly or monthly magazine. Most Americans at that time got their national and international news from the three weekly news magazines, *Time*, *Newsweek*, and *U.S. News and World Report*. The "glossies," as general-interest magazines were known, attracted readers with superb writing, short-form articles, and stunning photography brought to life by very high-resolution color printing (Vega, 2012).

INSIGHT ON SOCIETY

VOX: THE ALL-DIGITAL NEWS SITE

It's surprising that anyone is reading news and news commentary in the age of the smartphone, texting, social networks, and online movies, not to mention the continuing strength of television. With so much entertainment and just plain time-wasting joy available at the click of a mouse, who has time for reading news, or reading much of anything beyond short text messages of 140 characters? But contrary to expectations, people are reading more news online than ever before. In fact, reading news online is the second most popular activity online with over 160 million people doing so in 2014. They aren't just reading either: an estimated 12 million write comments on the news sites they follow (compared to less than 1% of print newspaper readers who write letters to the editor). Digital news readers are highly engaged with the content and the journalists who put the words on the screen. All of this is not lost on investors and venture capital firms, which have poured over $1 billion dollars into digital native news sites in the last few years.

What is a digital native news site? It's a news site without a print edition or a television franchise, populated by young journalists (so-called digital natives) who grew up with the Web, including Facebook, Twitter, texting, chatting, and digital-fast news streams. The term digital native was coined in 2001 as a metaphor for people who were born in the digital age, sometime after 1995, and who have grown up with the technology of e-mail, the Web, and later, mobile devices and social networks. Presumably, digital natives are more comfortable than their elders with all things digital, and come to see and think about the world with a digital mind set.

Vox Media is a prime example of a start-up media firm grounded in the digital news stream that originated on the Internet and has since moved to a mobile social platform as well. The company was founded in 2003 by Jim Bankoff and is a privately held company based in Washington D.C. with 330 employees. Bankoff got his start at CNN, the public television station WETA in Washington D.C., and later AOL, where he was the Programing Chief. Vox Media is a private firm and does not reveal revenue figures although the company claims it is profitable in 2014. The real money comes from over $100 million in venture capital raised since 2008, and the company is currently valued at about $200 million after raising $34 million in 2013.

Vox Media has pursued a unique strategy from the beginning. Rather than creating a single digital news site, as, say, traditional newspapers have done, and showing tabs for various areas of interest (sports, business, or entertainment), it instead has unbundled the general news site into a number of focused news sites, populating them with content from hundreds of different blogs that it has created or purchased. It started with SBNation (SportsBlogNation), a sports news site that is a collection of 306 blogs, each with its own name, URL, brand, and writer/bloggers. For instance, when you go to the SBNation Web site, you will see a tab for NFL. Click that, and you will see a list of teams. Click on, say, the Pittsburgh Steelers, and you will be taken to a Web site devoted to the Steelers (Behindthesteelcurtain). There you will find blog posts (stories) and pictures from external photo vendors. The bloggers typically are contract writers (work-for-hire) who are generally paid by the number and length of posts, rather than regular employees with benefits. For SBNation's main Web site, Vox does hire some full-time journalists, some with strong reputations from previous assignments with print newspapers.

Covering just about every popular sport, from football, baseball, and basketball, to soccer, skiing, and boxing, with hundreds of teams, it is easy to see how 306 blogs are needed. Compared to a national newspaper like the *New York Times*, SBNation can provide new content on just about any team you choose. And the intensity of engagement is much greater when readers find commentary on their home team. It seems to be working: Vox Media is reaching 75 million visitors at all its sites, and it was the fastest growing digital media site in a recent report, with the typical visitor being an individual under 35 with income over $100,000 a year.

Vox Media has built on the success of SBNation and currently owns seven specialty sites, which themselves are often collections of blogs or Web sites. Vox verticals include Eater (food), Curbed (real estate), Verge (culture), Polygon (game), Racked (fashion), and most recently, a general news and commentary site, Vox.com.

Vox.com was created in January 2014 when Vox hired Ezra Klein from the *Washington Post*. At the *Post*, Klein was the editor of Wonkblog, a data-dense and political policy-intense blog that Klein had created at the *Post*. Klein, 29 in 2014, had built Wonkblog into one of the most successful online *Washington Post* sites, with 2.4 million unique visitors. Klein left when the *Post* refused to back his proposal to expand Wonkblog into a full-time news streaming service, which would have required a major investment in new technology by the *Post*. He left with two colleagues to join Vox Media, reportedly because of Vox Media's technology for delivering online news and its commitment to digital news. Vox.com launched in April 2014. At Vox, Klein is aiming to create a new kind of digital journalism that will keep readers up to date with the news, but also provide background understanding and context to the news stream.

Vox Media is often regarded as the future of digital news publishing because of its technology, culture, and business organization. Traditional newspaper firms typically have a melange of technologies, built at different times, to coordi-nate the flow of news with both print and Web versions. At Vox, millions of dollars were invested in Chorus from the very beginning of the firm. Chorus is a unique content management system (CMS). As you learned in Chapter 3, a CMS is essentially a database that stores content, with front-end word processing, and back-end page composition templates (what the reader actually sees on the Web site or print page). A CMS allows content creators, writers, and educators to create text products that can seamlessly and artfully integrate other objects like photos, videos, tweets, blog posts, and Web links, to the text they are writing. Unlike a word processor on a desktop, a CMS can run on local or cloud servers so multiple people in any location can work on the same documents in collaborative fashion. Chorus goes beyond content creation and management because it provides the publishing environment as well. When reporters and editors are done, they can use Chorus to publish format-ted content to various Web sites and social media. They can also read comments back from readers and eliminate inappropriate comments in real time.

Chorus is an evolving tool chest created by technologists who call themselves journal-ists, and who work with journalists to develop new tools as needed. For instance, they created a word recognition tool that helps journalists police reader comments more efficiently. They also created Story Stream, a tool that allows journalists to click and drag content from pre-vious stories, tweets, user comments, and Web pages, and pull them into a coherent document. In this way, Vox can create running stories that continuously evolve as new developments occur. Chorus is a comprehensive digital publishing environment that includes not only the journal-ists, editors, photographers, and social market-ers, but also the readers! You can experience the results on Vox Web sites. The resulting Web pages are virtually the same across all sites, and there is a limited range of page layout schemes,

(continued)

usually two-column pages with large photos introducing the articles.

Vox also has a unique organizational structure when compared to traditional newspapers. At Vox, the organization is flat, with fewer middle and senior managers. This gives extraordinary discretion to reporters compared to the lengthy editorial review process that can take hours at a traditional paper. According to some commentators, digital journalists consume and produce content at the same time, constantly publishing and/or republishing what they are reading on Twitter, Facebook, bloggers, and newsmakers. It's a much faster, quick-draw form of journalism that reports on the digital stream, aggregates content from elsewhere, and maybe adds some commentary to create a new stream.

The journalistic process at digital news sites is also different from traditional newspapers. The discrete stages of a traditional print news site move in serial order (research, first draft, copy-edit, fact check, second draft, proofread, composite, print). In a pure digital environment these steps are greatly compressed into a continuous process, with some stages running in parallel. For instance, research and drafting takes place with light editing, using a collaborative software environment that allows these steps to occur nearly simultaneously. Later, more in-depth editing and fact checking, re-drafting, and proofing all occur together, with publishing the last step. The published version will then be revised as facts change or errors become apparent. Publishing, in other words, is continuous, whereas printing is final in the traditional world. Nothing can change once the press is running.

Whether or not Vox will ultimately succeed depends on whether it is able to attract a large audience and enough advertisers to the site. The key elements are unbundling the news into narrow, dedicated, vertical Web sites; using a less expensive labor force composed of bloggers and contract writers; using technology to reduce the cost; increasing the speed of creating and distributing content and interacting with readers; and finally, building sufficient audience size and demographics to attract advertisers.

But there still is one missing ingredient that traditional journalists point to: quality reporting. It's unclear to critics that journalists can read and write the news at anything near the same time, just aggregating tweets and user comments, without spending time interviewing newsmakers, doing background research, and taking the time to write an original article. Simply repeating tweets, repeating content taken from traditional news sources, and aggregating user comments adds fluff but no real economic value to the news stream. Listicles and so-called link bait (bold headline teasers designed to generate clicks) produce only fleeting visitors, not serious consumers. Business critics also point out that none of the digital news sites, including the most famous Huffington Post, has turned a profit. All the digital news sites, with the exception of Yahoo, are private and do not report revenues or profits. Yahoo is reporting 7% declines in ad revenue for 2014. The average price for Yahoo ads has dropped 24% in the second quarter of 2014. The pure digital news sites face the same problems online as traditional newspapers do, namely, the declining revenues from digital advertising. The costs of generating traffic to these sites far exceeds the revenues being produced. What really would be news is a report that digital news sites make money. Tweet that!

SOURCES: "Vox Media Ventures into General News and News Analysis With Vox.com," by Paul Farhi, *Washington Post*, April 7, 2014; "Vox Takes Melding of Journalism and Technology to a New Level," by Leslie Kaufman, *New York Times*, April 6, 2014; "Putting Journalism Cart Before Advertising Horse," by Michael Wolf, USAToday.com, February 26, 2014; "Telling Storys About the Future of Journalism," by George Packer, *New York Magazine*, January 27, 2014; "Ezra Klein Is Joining Vox Media as Web Journalism Asserts Itself," *New York Times*, January 26, 2014.

Circulation fell after 2000 in part because of the Internet. At first, the Internet and the Web did not have much impact on magazine sales, in part because the PC was no match for the high-resolution, large-format pictures found in, say, *Life* or *Time*. Eventually, as screens improved, as video on the Web became common, and the economics of color publishing changed, magazine circulation began to plummet and advertisers turned their attention to the digital platform on the Web, where readers were increasingly getting their news, general-interest journalism, and photographic accounts of events (Pew Research Center, 2014c).

Magazine newsstand sales dropped from 22 million units weekly in 2001 to 12 million in 2013. Yet special-interest, celebrity, homemaking, and automobile magazines remained stable. The largest monthly subscription magazine for several decades has been the *AARP* (American Association of Retired Persons) magazine, with a paid circulation of over 20 million readers.

While newstand sales are falling at 10% a year, and subscription sales are flat, magazines have responded by developing digital replica magazines—fairly close copies of the physical magazine. Currently, there are about 300 digital replica magazines, and about 8 million units are sold each year. Total revenues from subscriptions and newstand sales of magazine are expected to be around $25 billion in 2014, and this is expected to remain flat through 2018. The fall-off in total revenues has stopped. Ad revenues will constitute $15 billion of the total, and are expected to remain at that level through 2018. This, in itself, is good news, but even better is that growth in digital ad revenues is over 22% a year, around $4 billion in 2013. Print ad revenue is of course shrinking, at around 4% a year. The increasing digital revenue is not quite enough to compensate for the decline in print ad revenue (eMarketer, Inc., 2014f; Sebastian, 2014). The magazine industry parallels closely the newspaper industry: newstand sales are down, circulation and subscription revenues are flat, print ads are down, digital ads are up (Magazine Publishers Association, 2014). One possible solution is to begin charging a subscription fee for access to the digital editions, which currently are often free. The *New Yorker*, perhaps the most prestigious magazine in the country, is also one of the most widely read, with 1 million print subscribers and 12 million unique visitors to its Web site. In 2014, the magazine introduced a metered paywall. Some articles are free, but frequent readers will be charged an annual subscription fee (Somaiya, 2014). Like newspapers, magazines are experimenting with different revenue models in an effort to monetize the rapidly growing tablet audience. Most magazines participate in Apple's iPad Subscription Service, which allows magazines to offer subscriptions from within their app and have the transaction processed by the App Store billing system. Publishers set the price, and customers can subscribe with one click. Apple keeps 30% of the transaction. Publishers can also direct app readers to their Web site for a subscription, in which case Apple does not make any fee. Virtual storefronts such as Apple's iOS Newstand and Google Play have helped publishers grow their digital subscriber base.

Despite the shrinkage of print subscription and newsstand sales, the growth of digital magazine sales has been extraordinary. Almost one-third of the Internet population in the United States (about 74 million people) read magazines online. More than 35% of tablet computer owners read magazine content once a week, and there are an estimated 1,200 magazine apps for mobile readers (eMarketer, Inc., 2013).

Popular Web sites like Pinterest, an image-collecting site that attracts millions of women, and Facebook, Yahoo, and Twitter are among the largest drivers of traffic to digital magazines. The widespread adoption of tablet computers has helped create the visual Internet, where glossy magazine publishers, who are inherently oriented to richly detailed color photography, can display their works and advertisements to great advantage. Social reader apps are another way magazines are trying to engage digital readers. Social reader apps allow Facebook users to share with their friends what they read in online newspapers and magazines. However, using these apps requires readers to share their personal information with Facebook, and many have decided they do not want their reading habits that widely distributed.

With hundreds of popular online magazines to choose from, magazine aggregators like Zinio, Flipboard, and Pulse make it possible for customers to find their favorite magazines using a single app. A **magazine aggregator** is a Web site or app that offers users online subscriptions and sales of many digital magazines. See the *Insight On Business* case, *Digital Newsstands Grow.*

magazine aggregator
a Web site or app that provides subscriptions and sales of many digital magazines

E-BOOKS AND ONLINE BOOK PUBLISHING

In April 2000, Stephen King, one of America's most popular writers, published a novella called *Riding the Bullet.* This novella was only available as an e-book. King was the first major fiction writer to create an e-book-only volume of a new work. King's publisher, Simon & Schuster, arranged for sales online through online retailers such as Amazon. In the first day, there were 400,000 downloads, so many that Amazon's servers crashed several times. More than 600,000 downloads occurred in the first week. While Amazon gave the book away for free in the first two weeks, when it began charging $2.50 for a 66-page novella—about the same price per page as a standard King hardcover novel—sales continued to be brisk. This experiment showed Simon & Schuster, and Amazon, that there was a mass market for popular fiction, and maybe other titles as well. For publishers, it meant their entire back list of older books suddenly had monetary value if they could be sold as e-book editions.

Ten years later, on April 15, 2010, Amanda Hocking, an unknown and unpublished writer from Austin, Minnesota, uploaded one of her vampire novels, *My Blood Approves*, to Amazon's self-publishing site, and later to the Barnes & Noble e-book store. Her novels had been rejected by many of the publishing houses in New York. By March 2011, she had sold more than 1 million copies of her e-books, which generally sell for 99 cents to $2.99, and earned more than $2 million. Starting out with sales of 5 to 10 books a day, Hocking's sales have reached as many as 100,000 a day when she first publishes a novel. In the same month, she signed a traditional publishing contract worth $2 million with St. Martin's Press. In 2012, Hocking was listed as one of the Amazon 99 cent millionaires. In 2013, Hugh Howey's self-published science fiction e-book *Wool* sold more than 500,000 copies and earned him more than $1 million dollars in royalties and film rights. Howey began publishing *Wool* as an online serial novel in 2011, developing a large group of readers on Amazon. In 2013, he refused to sell the electronic rights to Simon & Schuster, but did sell the print rights for a mid-six-figures advance. Around 25% of Amazon's top 100 selling books are now self published. Twenty-three so-called Indie (independently published) books have sold more than

INSIGHT ON BUSINESS

DIGITAL NEWSSTANDS GROW

Newsstands, the shop on the corner hawking magazines, newspapers, soda, candy, cigarettes, and chewing gum, are a pillar of magazine sales. The other pillar of magazine sales is paid subscriptions. Despite declines in magazine advertising dollars and circulation, despite the threatened and actual digital disruption of new digital platforms for news and photos, magazines still attract a huge monthly audience of over 120 million readers. This is an audience worth fighting for—it's a more educated, wealthier, and aspirational audience than television or newspapers attract.

What really made magazines such a popular form of mass communication in the past was high-resolution photography, resulting in stunning, often full-page photos. In addition, magazines had longer, in-depth articles, written by some of the best writers in the business. Personal computer displays didn't stand a chance against the color photography available in magazines. But with the introduction of high-resolution tablet computers, connected to an online content store, it was a short hop to the idea of a digital newsstand, where high-quality photography and long-form magazine articles could easily be presented and consumed. This short hop has turned into a fight among several start-ups, the owners of the content stores and devices (Apple, Google, Amazon, etc.), and the magazine publishers themselves.

The largest digital newsstand, Zinio, has been a mainstay on the list of top grossing apps for iOS devices for years. Zinio is an online magazine newsstand where users can find over 5,500 magazine titles, 2,500 of them exclusive to the platform. Among the available titles are *Rolling Stone, Road & Track, Seventeen,* and *The Economist*. In addition to iOS devices, Zinio is available on Android devices and Kindle. Zinio

has partnerships with nearly all the largest magazine publishers including McGraw-Hill Companies, Wiley, Ziff Davis, Hearst Corporation, and Playboy Enterprises, Inc. The advantage of using Zinio, the company claims, is that a single app provides interface consistency across all the different magazines and makes it easier for consumers to manage their subscriptions at one site. In August 2013, Zinio introduced a subscription model that it calls Z-pass that allows users to access any three of the magazines available on its platform for just $5 a month—a great option for users interested only in a small number of titles. Zinio has also boosted its selection of offerings for libraries in 2014, adding 1,000 magazine titles to the existing 800 in its Zinio for Libraries service, and the company purchased mobile app developer Audience Media to translate print publications into mobile apps that work seamlessly with tablets.

Notably absent from Zinio's list is Time Inc., the largest U.S. magazine publisher with titles like *Time, Fortune,* and *People*; Condé Nast; the New York Times Company; and Wall Street Journal/Dow Jones. These publishers have their own proprietary apps available to consumers on the two largest mobile platforms, Apple's iOS and Android tablets and smartphones. Their message is clear: why sell to digital newsstand distributors at a discount when they can sell directly to the consumer using apps available for tablet computers? This works for readers who want to buy single issues (as a traditional newsstand) and pay the same price as they would for the physical magazine. Digital doesn't mean cheap. According to Hearst Publications, readers are willing to pay more for a tablet version than a physical version of its magazine simply because of its greater ease of use, portability, high resolution, and the inclusion of videos in some issues.

(continued)

Adding to the competition for tablet magazine readers, the five largest publishers have launched their own newsstand called Next Issue Media with some of the most popular magazine titles in the United States, including *Better Homes and Gardens*, *Condé Nast Traveler*, *Esquire*, *Elle*, *Fortune*, *Glamour*, *Parents*, *People*, *Popular Mechanics*, *Real Simple*, *Sports Illustrated*, *Time*, *The New Yorker*, *Vanity Fair*, and many more. The top five publishers are Condé Nast, Meredith, Hearst, News Corp., and Time. Next Issue offers 132 magazines at $9.99 per month with its basic plan, and 143 magazines at $14.99 per month with its premium plan, which includes weeklies like *Time*, *Sports Illustrated*, and *The New Yorker*. With Next Issue, like Hulu in the television and film industry, the major publishers are building their own digital distribution platform rather than ceding the customer relationship and revenues to start-up intermediaries like Zinio.

Another powerful player in the fight for the digital newsstand is the owners of the distribution platform (the tablet), and that means Apple and Google. Each has its own newsstand. Apple's Newsstand organizes magazine and newspaper subscriptions into a single app, provides a point of purchase for new subscriptions on iTunes, and sends the user notices as new issues become available. Google has also launched a similar service. Publishers are wary of Apple because it wants a 30% cut of subscription revenue, and worse, will not allow publishers to send users outside the Apple iOS sandbox to purchase subscriptions. Everything has to be purchased through the iTunes Store, and Apple retains ownership and personal data on the customer. The publishers and Apple are working on a compromise solution. Both need each other: Apple's Newsstand without magazines is a loser, and magazines want to sell digital subscriptions to iTunes' millions of users. Not to be outdone, Amazon also has a newsstand offering available to users of the Amazon Kindle Fire tablet.

New entrants into the digital newsstand marketplace include Magzter, which has struck deals with high-profile publishers like Hearst, Conde Nast, and Newsweek. Magzter has an emphasis on publishing several different international editions of a magazine concurrently and on a single platform. Magzter and Zinio are both trying to overcome Apple, Google, and Amazon's advantage of owning the content distribution platform. Another company, Magvault, hopes to solve the growing problem of finding less popular magazines or magazines not offered in consumers' geographical area.

Whether or not digital newsstands can produce enough revenue to overcome the decline in physical magazine sales and advertising is not clear at this time. Although the unique features of tablets offer opportunities for publishers and writers, some industry predictions suggest that by 2017, the U.S. consumer magazine market will be worth $23 billion, down from $25 billion in 2012. The increase in digital advertising is unlikely to keep up with the decline in print advertising. In the short term, magazines have rebounded from recession-year lows, but the industry has more work to do to continue its growth in the future. Nevertheless, the tablet is a friend of magazines by enhancing the consumer experience of viewing high-quality photos and videos.

SOURCES: "Zinio Adds 1,000 New International Magazines with New Language Content to Libraries," *Publishing Executive*, May 14, 2014; "Zinio Acquires Audience Media to Become Mobile First Leader in Digital Magazines," *Publishing Executive*, April 29, 2014; "Print Magazine Sales Decline in 1st Half of 2014," by Tess Stynes, *Wall Street Journal*, August 7, 2014; "Digital Magazine Startup Magzter Raises $10M To Fuel Global Growth," by Darrell Etherington, Techcrunch.com, December 11, 2013; "Magvault Seeks to Address the Growing Issue of Discoverability of Digital Magazines," by D. B. Hebbard, Talkingnewmedia.com, November 8, 2013; "Zinio: App Now Offers Any 3 Magazines for $5 a Month," by Marc Saltzman, *USA Today*, August 22, 2013; "Magazine Newsstand Sales Plummet, but Digital Editions Thrive," by Christine Haughney, *New York Times*, August 6, 2013; "Consumer Magazine Market Predicted to Shed $1.3B by 2017," Adweek.com, June 4, 2013; "eMarketer: Magazines to See Positive Ad Spending Growth in 2012," eMarketer, Inc., September 25, 2012; "Hearst Hails the Age of the Tablet, Says Readers Are Willing to Pay More for Tablet Editions," by Doug Drinkwater, *Editor & Publisher*, May 15, 2012; "A Buffet of Magazines on a Tablet," by David Pogue, *New York Times*, April 11, 2012; "Zinio Makes the iPad a Viable Magazine Platform," by Jason O'Grady, Zdnet.com, April 4, 2012.

250,000 copies, and four Indie authors have sold more than a million copies of their books, according to Amazon (Alter, 2013).

The book publishing industry's experience with the Internet is very different from the newspaper and magazine industries. E-book editions of fiction and non-fiction books (so-called trade books) have been very successful, yet printed book sales have not collapsed and have remained about the same over time. Professional books, which includes college textbooks, remain almost entirely printed for a variety of reasons. Book publishing revenues have been stable over the last five years. In 2013, the book publishing industry generated $27 billion in revenue and sold 2.5 billion books (both e-books and printed books). Trade books (general fiction and non-fiction) generated $14.6 billion in revenue on sales of 2.3 billion books (AAP, 2014a). These numbers are slightly higher than 2012, a boom year in publishing because of the explosive growth of e-books.

In the space of a decade, e-books have gone from an unusual experiment by a major author, to an everyday experience for millions of Americans, and an exciting new market for authors. Sales of e-books have exploded in a few short years, and the process of writing, selling, and distributing books has radically changed. E-book sales in 2014 are expected to be $6.1 billion dollars, 32% of all consumer book sales. By 2017, this percentage is expected to grow to 42% (see **Figure 9.14**). An entire new channel for self-published authors now exists, a channel not controlled by the

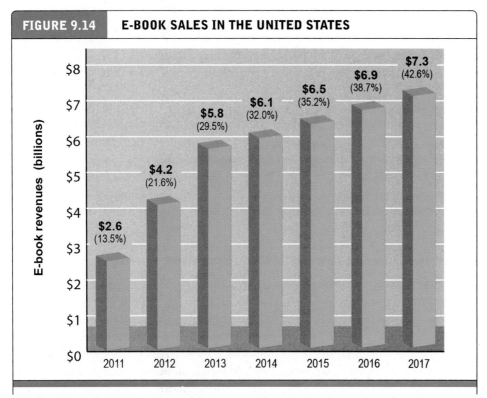

FIGURE 9.14   **E-BOOK SALES IN THE UNITED STATES**

This figure shows both total revenues and the percentage that e-books sales constitute of total book sales revenues. The growth rate of e-books has markedly slowed in 2014.

SOURCE: Based on data from Association of American Publishers, 2014a, 2014b; authors' estimates.

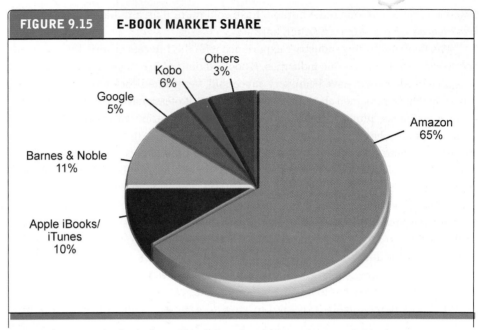

FIGURE 9.15 **E-BOOK MARKET SHARE**

Amazon dominates e-book sales by a wide margin and uses this margin to set e-book prices.

SOURCE: Based on data from various company filings with Securities and Exchange Commission.

major New York publishing companies and their professional editors. Bypassing professional editors and publishers, authors can now crowdsource the distribution of their books, relying on reader recommendations and social networks to market their books. Recognizing the booming e-book self-publishing market, Penguin (the second largest trade book publisher in the world after Random House) purchased the self-publishing company Author Solutions in 2012. Author Solutions has published 150,000 authors and more than 190,000 books. Other publishers have made similar purchases in the hope that successful books and authors will emerge from the burgeoning online author crowd (Bosman, 2012). The e-book market in the United States is dominated by three players: Amazon, Apple, and Barnes & Noble (see **Figure 9.15**). Kobo is a Toronto-based e-reader manufacturer and e-book store that is widely adopted outside the United States.

Amazon and Apple: The New Digital Media Ecosystems

Although precursors of e-books and e-book readers began to be introduced in the 1990s and early 2000s, it was not until 2007 that the future of e-books was firmly established. In that year, Apple released the first iPhone and Amazon introduced the Kindle. The early Kindle readers used electronic ink technology, providing a higher resolution than PCs and a longer battery life than portable book readers. The early Kindle had 16 megabytes of memory and could store 200 books. More important, the reader was linked to the Internet through AT&T's cell network, permitting users to access Amazon's bookstore, where they could browse, search, and purchase e-books. Amazon's bookstore is the largest online bookstore on the Internet. The first Kindle readers sold out in a few days and were on backorder for five months until Amazon caught up with demand. The Kindle is now available in a variety of different formats, such as the Kindle Fire, a small tablet computer that is no longer just an e-book reader, but rather a portable media and entertainment device connected to the Internet.

In 2014, Amazon's e-book and media store contains an estimated 1 million e-book titles. Although Amazon does not release Kindle sales numbers, it is estimated that more than 800 million Kindles of all types have been sold in the United States, and there are 80 million adults who use e-readers like the Kindle and tablet computers like the iPad. Industry analysts believe that Amazon is racking up Kindle unit sales of over 30 million units a year, selling an estimated 400 million e-books worldwide, and generating $8.1 billion in Kindle-related revenue, 11% of Amazon's total revenue in 2013. For Amazon and Apple's iBooks Store, books are a big business. For every sale of 100 print books, Amazon sells over 115 e-books. Kindle users are avid readers and typically purchase a book a week. Prior to the introduction of the iPad tablet computers, Amazon accounted for 90% of the e-book market. This did not last long: Apple's entry into the e-book marketspace temporarily reduced this share to 60% up until recently, when Amazon's share of the e-book market returned to near 70%.

E-books received another large boost in 2010 when Apple introduced its first iPad tablet computer. With its large 11.7" screen and access to the iTunes Store of online music, video, TV, and book content, the iPad was an ideal media entertainment device. And with its high-resolution screen, the iPad was an even better e-book reader than the Kindle, albeit not easily slipped into a purse. While Amazon got the jump on Apple in dedicated e-book readers, Apple's approach from the beginning was a multipurpose device that could handle movies, music, magazines, and books, as well having a Wi-Fi connection to the Internet. Apple's iBooks Store at launch in 2010 had 60,000 titles, and is estimated to have about 2 million titles in 2014 (much smaller than Amazon's store). Apple has sold over 200 million iPads since 2007. It has a 59% market share of tablet computers, but only an estimated 20% of the e-book market, although it is gaining ground on Amazon's market share (NPD Group, 2013b). The Google Play online store in 2014 is not a large book media and entertainment player yet, and is unlikely to challenge Amazon and Apple for the online e-book consumer, preferring to focus on a much more lucrative video-based entertainment market.

The result of the Amazon and Apple ecosystems, combining hardware, software, and online mega stores, is an explosion in online book content, readership, authorship, marketing, and at least a partial upending of the traditional book publishing and marketing channels. Increasingly, social networks play an important role in all book marketing as millions of social network members tell their friends about their favorite books. Traditional book publishing has similarly been altered. In the traditional process, authors worked with agents, who sold book manuscripts to editors and publishers, who sold books through bookstores, at prices determined largely by the publishers. Because bookstores had a vested interest in selling books at a profit, there was only limited discounting during clearance sales. In the new publishing model, authors still write books, but then bypass traditional agent and publisher channels and instead publish digital books that are sold on Amazon or the iTunes Store. Prices are determined by the author, usually much lower than traditional books depending on the popularity of the author, and the digital distributor takes a percentage of the sale (usually 30%). New self-published authors typically give away their early works to develop an audience, and then, when an audience appears, charge a small amount for their books, typically 99 cents to $2.99. Marketing occurs by word of mouth on social networks, author blogs, and public readings. While a small percentage of all books are produced this way, it is a growing and popular form of publishing and some authors are able to strike it rich. They're called "99 cent millionaires," and there's enough around to arouse the passions of thousands of potential writers of the great American novel, as well as lesser genres from police procedurals to paranormal romance writers.

The book publishing industry has become generally comfortable with the security and intellectual property protections offered by online distributors. Both Amazon and Apple offer publishers walled gardens and tight controls over proprietary formats, devices, and files, thus preventing the large-scale theft of copyrighted book content. This is very different from the music industry, where the music files can be easily copied and distributed. Apple and Amazon e-books are difficult to copy and upload to cyberlockers or to distribute on the Internet.

E-Book Business Models

The e-book industry is composed of intermediary retailers (both brick-and-mortar stores and online merchants), traditional publishers, technology developers, device makers (e-readers), and vanity presses (self-publishing service companies). Together, these players have pursued a wide variety of business models and developed many alliances in an effort to move text onto the computer screen.

There are five very large publishers that dominate trade book, education, and religious book publishing. These traditional publishers have the largest content libraries for conversion to e-books and they produce over 80% of new book titles in a year. In the e-book marketplace, the large publishers started out using a **wholesale model** of distribution and pricing, in part because this is the same model they used with hard cover books. In this model, the retail store pays a wholesale price for the book and then decides at what price to sell it to the consumer. The retailer sets the price with, of course, some kind of understanding with the publisher that the book will not be given away for free. In the past, the wholesale price was 50% of the retail price. A retailer would pay the publisher a $10 wholesale price and mark it up to a $20 retail price. However, retailers could also determine to sell the book at a much lower sale price, say $5, as a way to attract readers to the store or as a close-out sale. Brick-and-mortar stores had a vested interest in selling most books above their wholesale cost. With e-books, publishers discovered that some online retailers like Amazon and Apple might sell books below cost in order to encourage customers to purchase their e-book reader devices or to sell them other goods.

In the case of e-books, publishers sought to keep their prices high enough so as not to discourage sales of hard cover books, which typically sell for $26. Generally, this meant publishers wanted e-books to sell at a retail price of $12.99 to $14.99, depending on the popularity of the book and the stage in the product life cycle (months since first publication). E-book distributors like Amazon were charged a wholesale price of about $9 and were expected to mark up the product to around $12.99 to $14.99 or more.

wholesale model
prices are determined by the retailer

Instead, Amazon chose to sell e-books for $9.99, at or below cost, in order to attract buyers to its content store to buy Kindles, and to attract new customers to its online retail store. Amazon lost $1 to $3 on every e-book sold, but recouped the money by selling Kindles for hundreds of dollars, and from additional sales of other products. With Amazon selling e-books at $9.99, the lowest prices on the Web, publishers were forced to sell their e-books on all other Web sites at the $9.99 Amazon price. Using this strategy, Amazon not only sold millions of Kindles but also sold 90% of all e-book titles on the Web in 2010 and 2011. Amazon had a near monopoly on e-books.

Publishers opposed Amazon's policy as debasing the perceived value of both physical and digital books, and as a mortal threat to the publishers who could not survive if their e-books were priced at $9.99 across the Web. They claimed Amazon was engaging in predatory pricing, designed to destroy traditional book publishers. In 2010, five of the largest publishers secretly met with Steve Jobs and Apple. They agreed to a new pricing model called the agency model. In the **agency model**, the distributor is an agent of the publisher, and can be directed to sell e-books at a price determined by the publisher, around $14.99 and higher for certain titles. In return for a 30% commission, Apple agreed to support this model, as did Google, neither of whom were comfortable watching as Amazon dominated one of the hottest areas of Web content sales. In these meetings, publishing executives discussed a common pricing strategy.

agency model
the retailer is an agent and prices are set by the manufacturer

The agency model temporarily turned the tables on Amazon: it now had to charge whatever price the publishers wanted or the publishers would not sell Amazon any books (they would not choose Amazon as an agent for their products). A result of the agency model was that Amazon's prices on e-books rose to the publisher desired levels, and its market share fell to 60% in 2012. Apple, Google, Barnes & Noble, and the five major publishers were delighted. The Justice Department was not delighted: it sued the five publishers and Apple for price fixing in violation of antitrust laws. All five of the publishers settled, but Apple refused to settle and asked for a trial before a judge. In 2013, the United States District Court found that Apple had engaged in price fixing, not because of its agency pricing model, which is quite common throughout retail trade, but because of its "most favored seller" clause in its agreements with publishers, which had the effect of discouraging other sites (like Amazon) from selling e-books for less than Apple's iBooks Store price. In addition, the publishers and Apple conspired to act in concert, rather than as individual publishers. Under the agreements, the publishers, not Amazon, would determine prices on Amazon. If publishers sold their books on Amazon for $9.95, then publishers would have to sell their e-books at the iBooks Store for $9.95. The court found that Apple and the book publishers' plan would result in less price competition, and higher prices, by enforcing a single higher price on all online distributors and e-books. In the field of antitrust, less competition and higher prices for all is considered a cardinal violation of the law. After the ruling, e-book prices on Amazon have fallen to an average of $9.99, with some older titles far less, with limited discounting, and its market share rose to 65%. In August 2014, Apple agreed to pay a $450 million fine to compensate consumers for its price fixing behavior. While the ruling prevents Apple from fixing prices of e-books, it does nothing to solve the issues surrounding Amazon's dominance of the e-book marketplace. Publishers will need to each reach independent marketing agreements with Amazon, one by one. Critics of the court case believe Amazon's market power will force publishers to submit to Amazon's price terms.

The Challenges of the Digital E-Book Platform

Because of the rapid growth in e-books, the book publishing industry is in stable condition. Yet the industry faces a number of challenges. The early fear of cannibalization, namely inexpensive and less profitable e-books replacing more expensive and profitable print books, has mostly been put to rest. Unlike the newspaper and magazine industries, printed books are surviving in large part because purchasers of e-book readers continue to purchase printed books, and switch back and forth from digital to print as circumstances merit, and because more than 50% of book readers continue to prefer the physical format, while only 6% of book readers use e-books exclusively (eMarketer, 2014g). In the professional and educational book markets, e-books have not yet made substantial inroads. E-books may be like audio books, a useful alternative but not a substitute. The falling growth rate of e-books from double-digit to single-digit growth in the last year may reflect this reality.

The biggest challenge facing the book publishing industry is control over pricing on the digital e-book platforms of Amazon, Apple, and others. Currently, Amazon controls the largest market share, about 65%, which, while not a monopoly, nevertheless gives Amazon extraordinary market power (refer back to Figure 9.15 on page 668).

For critics, Amazon threatens to decimate the traditional book publishing industry, replacing the old print world of a small number of publishers, limited numbers of titles, several thousand independent bookstores, elitist editors in New York, and newspaper book critics, with a new digital world of publishing where content is shaped by algorithms identifying what the consumer wants to read about, writers are their own editors, critics are replaced by reader comments, and distribution is controlled by one or a few online stores (Packer, 2014). Efforts by Amazon to create its own book publishing brand, circumventing the traditional book publishers, have only worsened relations between the world's largest book store and the world's largest publishers (Streitfield, 2014).

Amazon, as the largest player in the e-book market, offers the biggest challenge. This is ironic because Amazon, through its online store and Kindle e-book marketplace and reader, has helped the publishing industry to survive the transition to a digital marketplace, both by providing the largest book store on earth, and by creating the Kindle e-book platform. While the expansion of e-book revenues has offset a small decline in print sales, the industry has lost pricing power vis-à-vis its largest distribution partner, Amazon. Amazon, if not a monopoly, nevertheless exercises extraordinary market power over the publishers. In 2014, Amazon got into a trade dispute with one of the world's largest publishers, British-based Hachette, over the pricing of e-books. To encourage Hachette to agree with the $9.99 price and the wholesaler model, Amazon removed the Buy buttons from Hachette books on its Web site, and refused to accept pre-publication orders for forthcoming books (Greenfield, 2014).

A second serious challenge is the further evolution of the digital distribution platform. In July 2014, Amazon announced Kindle Unlimited, a subscription service where for $9.95 a month, customers can read all the books they want. Over 600,000 titles are available, according to Amazon, but this Netflix for books does not include any books from the big five publishers—Hachette, HarperCollins, Simon & Schuster, Macmillan, and Penguin Random House. How the revenue of $9.95 subscriptions is split up has not been announced, but publishing firms (and authors) would surely want a substantial part of that revenue before signing up. Major publishers believe subscription e-book services would negatively impact book publisher and author revenues. Control over pricing is again the key issue.

Close behind subscription e-book plans is the idea of a digital marketplace where people could exchange any of their digital media, from books to music tracks. Both Amazon and Apple have filed patents for digital media exchanges, where, for instance, someone who purchased an e-book could swap that book for another e-book. These plans do not involve making copies of consumer purchased content in part because consumers do not purchase e-books but instead licenses for their use, and second, making copies to re-sell would potentially involve a violation of copyright. Instead the digital exchanges are based on the notion that only one copy of a purchased file is in existence, and no copies are made. A consumer could swap one e-book for another, or one music file for another, but no new copies would be made (Streitfield, 2013a). So far no publishers have commented on digital exchanges.

While the book publishing industry has survived, even prospered, in the first era of e-books and the digital distribution platform provided by Amazon, Apple, and others, the long-term prospects for book publishing revenues and profits remains an open question.

Interactive Books: Converging Technologies

The future of e-books may depend in part on changes in the concept and design of a book. The modern e-book is not really very different from the first two-facing page, bound books that began to appear in seventeenth-century Europe and had already appeared in the fourth century BCE in ancient China. The traditional Western book has a very simple, nondigital operating system: text appears left to right, pages are numbered, there is a front and a back cover, and text pages are bound together by stitching or glue. In educational and reference books, there is an alphabetical index in the back of the book that permits direct access to the book's content. While these traditional books will be with us for many years given their portability, ease of use, and flexibility, a parallel new world of interactive e-books is expected to emerge in the next five years. Interactive books combine audio, video, and photography with text, providing the reader with a multimedia experience thought to be more powerful than simply reading a book. In 2012, Apple released iBook Author, an app to help authors create interactive books. Hundreds of children's books are already built as interactive books. In 2012, Apple also introduced iBook Textbooks, a line of interactive textbooks created by several of the largest textbook publishing firms. Some experts believe that traditional print books will be curiosities by 2020. Yet as of 2014 these newer multimedia textbooks have not yet been successful in the marketplace (Streitfield, 2013b). Among the failures are Social Books, Push Pop Press, Copia, and Small Demons.

9.3 THE ONLINE ENTERTAINMENT INDUSTRY

The entertainment industry is generally considered to be composed of four traditional, commercial players and one new arrival: television, radio broadcasting, Hollywood films, music, and games (the new arrival). Together, these largely separate entertainment players generate $137 billion in annual revenue. This includes both digital and traditional format revenues. **Figure 9.16** illustrates the estimated relative sizes of these commercial entertainment markets in the United States as of 2014. By far, the largest entertainment producer is television (broadcast, satellite, and cable), and then motion pictures, followed by music, radio, and games (both stand-alone and online games). While online, computer, and console games have grown to be larger than film box office revenues (about $10 billion), total Hollywood film revenues dwarf the game industry when DVD sales and rentals, licensing, and ancillary products are added. Radio remains a strong revenue producer aided in part by the growth of Internet radio services like Spotify and Pandora, but is still largely reliant on FM and AM broadcast technologies, especially in automobiles. Recorded music is the smallest of the major players at $8 billion, half of its size ten years ago.

Along with the other content industries, the entertainment segment is undergoing a transformation brought about by the Internet and the extraordinary growth of mobile devices. Several forces are at work. Accelerated platform development such as the iPhone/iPad video and music platform, other smartphones and tablets, the Amazon music and video platform, not to mention the Netflix streaming platform, have changed consumer preferences and increased demand for music, video, television, and game entertainment delivered over Internet devices, whether in subscription or a la carte pay-per-view forms. Social network platforms are also spurring the deliv-

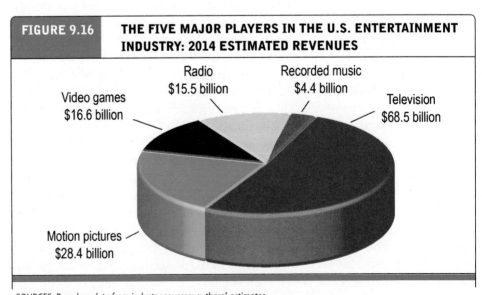

FIGURE 9.16 | **THE FIVE MAJOR PLAYERS IN THE U.S. ENTERTAINMENT INDUSTRY: 2014 ESTIMATED REVENUES**

Video games
$16.6 billion

Radio
$15.5 billion

Recorded music
$4.4 billion

Television
$68.5 billion

Motion pictures
$28.4 billion

SOURCES: Based on data from industry sources; authors' estimates.

ery of entertainment content to desktop and mobile devices. Their role is not content delivery, but rather social interaction with friends while watching or listening to online content and linking consumers to sites selling entertainment. The iTunes store and Amazon have demonstrated successful download music services where users pay for tracks and albums. Music subscription services like Pandora, Spotify, and Rhapsody have never made a profit and bleed cash despite having millions of subscribers. Both kinds of services—download and streaming—have demonstrated that millions of consumers are willing to pay reasonable prices for high-quality content, portability, and convenience. The growth in broadband has obviously made possible both wired and wireless delivery of all forms of entertainment over the Internet, potentially displacing cable and broadcast television networks. The development of high-quality customer experiences at online entertainment sites has made it convenient and easy to obtain high-quality entertainment. Closed platforms, like the Kindle and iBooks and streaming, also work to reduce the need for DRM. Subscription services for streaming music and video are inherently copyright-protected because the content is never downloaded to a computer (similar to cable TV). All of these forces have combined in 2014 to bring about a transformation in the entertainment industries.

In an ideal world, consumers would be able to watch any movie, listen to any music, watch any TV show, and play any game, when they want, and where they want, using whatever Internet-connected device is convenient. Consumers would be billed monthly for these services by a single provider of Internet service. This idealized version of a convergent media world is many years away, but clearly this is the direction of the Internet-enabled entertainment industry, in part because technology will enable this outcome, but also because of the emergence of very large-scale, integrated technology media companies like Amazon, Google, and Apple. Many analysts believe the large entertainment media giants of the future will be technology companies that have moved into the production of content.

When we think of the producers of entertainment in the offline world, we tend to think about television networks such as ABC, Fox, NBC, HBO, or CBS; Hollywood film studios such as MGM, Disney, Paramount, and Twentieth Century Fox; and music labels such as Sony BMG, Atlantic Records, Columbia Records, and Warner Records. Interestingly, none of these international brand names have a significant entertainment presence on the Internet. Although traditional forms of entertainment such as television shows and Hollywood movies are now commonplace on the Web, neither the television nor film industries have built an industry-wide delivery system. Instead, they are building relationships with tech-based Internet distributors like Netflix, Yahoo, Google, Amazon, Facebook, MSN, and Apple, all of whom have become significant players in media distribution.

While industry titans waiver, online consumers are redefining and considerably broadening the concept of entertainment. We refer to this development as nontraditional entertainment or what most refer to as user-generated content that also has entertainment value, such as user videos uploaded to YouTube, photos uploaded to Instagram, as well as blogs. User-generated content reflects some of the same shifts in consumer preferences experienced by traditional media: people want to participate in the creation and distribution of content.

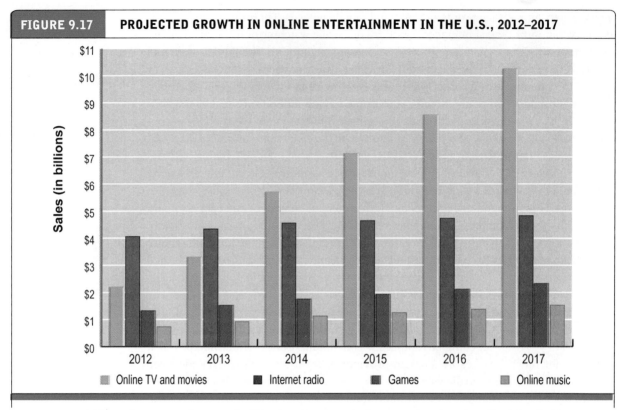

FIGURE 9.17   **PROJECTED GROWTH IN ONLINE ENTERTAINMENT IN THE U.S., 2012–2017**

Legend: Online TV and movies ■ Internet radio ■ Games ■ Online music

Among commercial forms of mass entertainment, online TV and movies engage the largest number of people and generate the largest revenues on the Web in 2014. By 2017, TV and movies will engage more people and generate more revenue than all other forms of digital media, including music.

SOURCES: Based on data from industry sources; authors' estimates.

ONLINE ENTERTAINMENT AUDIENCE SIZE AND GROWTH

Measuring the size and growth of the Internet content audience is far less precise than measuring a television audience. In fact, one of the issues facing television producers is an inability to count Internet viewing, or time-delayed viewing. Recognizing the difficulties of measuring an Internet audience, let's first examine the use of traditional entertainment content, such as feature-length movies, music, online TV, online radio, and games. **Figure 9.17** shows the current and projected growth for U.S. commercial online entertainment revenues for the major players: music, Internet radio, online TV, online games, and online video. Most noticeable is the extraordinary growth of online TV and movies, driven in large part by adoption of mobile devices, as well as the success of TV and movie streaming sites. Other forms of online entertainment will also continue to grow, but at single-digit rates.

There will be some interesting changes by 2017. Movies will surpass music as the largest form of online entertainment. Online TV will grow very rapidly (by more than 15% annually), while online games and radio remain relatively smaller generators of revenue, declining in significance when compared to movies, music, and TV.

TELEVISION AND PREMIUM VIDEO

In the television industry in 2014, viewers have gone mobile, Internet distributors have gained market power vis-à-vis TV and movie production firms, and cable television systems are losing ground to Internet and mobile app delivery of content. New streaming services provided by firms like Netflix, and convenient downloading of movies and entire TV series, have created powerful alternatives to traditional cable television delivery systems. Cable distribution systems are challenged as the Internet offers alternative, unbundled, a la carte access to TV programs. Contrary to expectations, the big TV screen in the home is as popular as ever, supported by social networks that buzz with chat about what's on TV right now. In 2014, over 140 million Americans watch TV online, about 55% of the Internet population (eMarketer, Inc., 2014d). Increasingly, the TV household is a cross-platform phenomenon. Every day, Americans watch about 4½ hours of TV on traditional TV sets, but 5¾ hours online using a computer or mobile device. While teens continue to spend more time texting than ever, over 75% of millennials (ages 16–34 in 2014) report watching streamed television shows and movies (eMarketer, Inc., 2014h). Apple's iTunes (which provides downloads or cloud storage and rentals, but not until recently a streaming service) has 67% of the digital TV download market and 65% of the movie download market. No competitor comes close to producing Apple's combined TV plus movie download revenue of $1.75 billion annually (NPD Group, 2013a). It's a different story with streaming video: Netflix is the market leader in streaming movies and TV shows, producing $14.4 billion in revenue in 2013. While streaming has not replaced downloading (either purchasing or renting), it has grown faster and today produces more revenue.

The television industry, the major source of premium video on the Internet, is beginning a transition to a new delivery platform—the Internet and mobile smartphones and tablet computers. Over 90 million consumers use a mobile phone to watch movies and television (eMarketer, Inc., 2014d). This transition closely follows an earlier but related transition to DVRs and time-shifting by consumers who no longer were constrained by television executives' programming and scheduling decisions. The current transition to Internet and especially mobile delivery of television is not leading to a decline in traditional television viewing, which has in fact increased slightly. The new platform is changing how, when, and where consumers can watch TV. Cloud computing, the storage and streaming of content from large Internet datacenters rather than on individual personal devices, has created a large shift away from ownership of content, and a focus instead on access to content anywhere, anytime, from any device. Streaming of movies from subscription services has expanded more rapidly than buying and downloading of movies. Social networks have enabled a new kind of **social TV**, where consumers share comments while viewing television shows. The most important activity in today's television household may not be what's on screen, but instead what's being said about what's on screen. Television rating agencies today do not have a methodology for measuring this kind of engagement.

Expansion of broadband networks, especially those serving mobile devices such as Wi-Fi and high-speed cellular networks, and the growth of cloud servers, has enabled the growth of a whole new class of television distributors. Cloud distributors, like

social TV
involves consumers sharing comments via social networks while viewing television

Apple's iCloud service, allow users to purchase video and movies, store them in iCloud, and view the entertainment from any device, anywhere. Whereas the dominant way consumers obtained a TV signal in the past was from over-the-air broadcasters, cable TV, or satellite distributors, a new "over-the-top" channel has developed led by powerful technology companies such as Apple, Google, Hulu, VUDU, Netflix, and many others, all of whom offer consumers access to television shows and some full-length feature movies using the household Internet service rather than the cable TV service.

over-the-top (OTT)
use of the Internet to deliver entertainment services to the home on cable TV or FiOS networks

Over-the-top (OTT) entertainment services refers to the use of the Internet to deliver online entertainment services to the home. "Over-the-top" refers to the fact that the entertainment service rides "on top" of other network services like cable TV and telephone service. It's as if we have a new Internet Broadcasting System with many new players. This new network is obviously a threat to cable television and the other distributors, who, in turn, have their on-demand services for television series and movies. If customers switch to Internet delivery of TV shows and movies, they have less incentive to continue paying for cable TV service.

While the Internet has not diminished TV viewing, it has transformed how, when, and where TV shows are watched. Alongside traditional television viewing, and the traditional TV household, is a whole new digital household with broadband connections to the Internet, and new mobile viewing devices: the smartphone, tablet, and game console (Carr, 2011). While TV might be the biggest screen in the house, it has to compete with other digital devices. The living room where the TV used to be located is now a digital living room that moves along with the viewer from place to place. Increasingly, the television industry is providing high-quality content in the form of older versions of television series and some sporting events. These three factors—broadband penetration, mobile platforms, and a willing industry that wants to monetize its library of high-quality content—are the leading factors in changing the television industry.

The Internet and the mobile platform have also changed the viewing experience. The best screen when commuting or traveling is the smartphone and tablet. More importantly, Internet-enabled social networks like Facebook and Twitter have made TV viewing a social experience shared among neighbors, friends, and colleagues. In the past, television was often a social event involving family and friends in the same room watching a single TV show. In 2014, the social circle has expanded to include Facebook and Twitter friends in different locations, changing television from a "lean back and enjoy" experience into a "lean forward and engage" experience. TV viewers are multitasking: co-viewing shows while texting, commenting, and chatting online while the show unfolds. Around 32% of Internet users will use social media while watching TV, and this jumps to 64% for users who own smartphones and tablets (eMarketer, Inc., 2014i).

While the Internet so far has had an expansive and positive impact on the television industry, challenges lie ahead. The largest providers of television in virtually all countries are cable television systems that charge consumers a monthly service fee for providing service, often accompanied by Internet and/or telephone service. This service in the United States costs, on average, about $125 per month per household. Cable systems also generate advertising revenues from local and national advertisers.

The revenues generated are used to maintain the physical cable network, and pay program producers (often called cable networks) for their content. For instance, HBO (Home Box Office network) creates a variety of television shows for the nearly 11,000 local cable systems in the United States, and collects fees from the local cable systems and their subscribers. ESPN, the largest sports network on TV and the Internet, charges local and national cable systems per-viewer fees. But with so much video available online for free, many users are thinking about "cutting the cable cord" and just relying on the Internet for their video entertainment. Other viewers are "cord shavers," who have reduced their subscriptions to digital channels. Likewise, the improvement in over-the-air digital broadcasting of television signals has resulted in a slight increase in over-the-air viewers (about 15% of all television viewers). So far, cord cutting and shaving has been very limited, but the high service fees for cable television service, and expanding Internet capabilities, suggest the future of traditional cable systems, and their ungainly set-top boxes, may be challenged.

MOVIES

In Hollywood, box office revenues are stable, DVDs are down but not out, sales of digital movies online are soaring, and Internet downloading and streaming is way up, offering many different and competing online distribution alternatives. As a result, prices for movie content charged by Hollywood are rising, pinching the profitability of distributors like Netflix, Amazon, Apple, and Google. For the first time in a decade, both box office theater receipts and attendance are up. Filmed entertainment revenue worldwide for 2014 is expected to reach almost €73 billion, up about 3% over 2013 (Statistica, 2014). Overall movie revenue in the United States was $28 billion. Movie box office revenues in the United States hit $10.9 billion, up slightly from 2012. Attendance dropped a bit, but prices went up making up for the loss. Home movie sales of DVDs and Blue Ray were nearly $8 billion, down 6% from the previous year. Online spending soared with streaming sales (Netflix, Hulu, and others) rising 45%, while download sales of movies (Apple and Amazon) rose 35%. The sales of digital movies that can be downloaded for home viewing (either purchased or rented) soared 47% in 2013. Hollywood created a new product called Digital HD, recent releases that viewers can download up to four weeks prior to their release on DVD. Instead of waiting to rent the DVD, consumers are downloading the movies soon after release. Total digital movie spending was up 28% in 2013, and accounted for $5.7 billion, 30% of the home entertainment market (Fritz, 2014). On average, Hollywood receives 50 cents from every streamed movie, about $2 for each downloaded movie, and $4.50 for each DVD/Blu-ray sale. The challenge for Hollywood is that its fastest growing sales are its least profitable, and its most profitable products are declining in sales (NPD Group, 2013b).

The Hollywood movie industry is going through a difficult transition from a reliance on DVDs, its primary revenue generator over the last decade, to a new marketplace where consumers want to watch movies on their PCs, tablet computers, and their smartphones. In 2014, Americans spent more money on online videos (both streaming and purchased films) than they did on DVDs. Consumers downloaded or

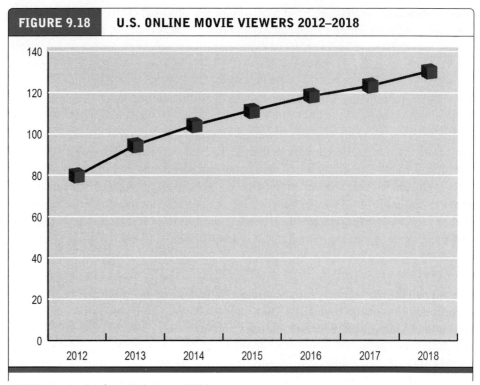

FIGURE 9.18   **U.S. ONLINE MOVIE VIEWERS 2012–2018**

SOURCE: Based on data from eMarketer, Inc., 2014d.

streamed 4 billion movies in 2013, versus renting or purchasing 2.4 billion DVDs. A little over 104 million Americans will watch movies online in 2014 (see **Figure 9.18**). Digital preferences are changing: consumers increasingly want access to cloud-stored movies rather than downloading entire movies to their devices. There are many parallels with the television industry: a very rapid growth in the mobile platform, expansion of cloud computing to support instant streaming of movies, and a change in consumer behavior in which movie viewing becomes both more individualized (watch whatever you want on your phone) and more social (let's text or tweet as we watch the movie). Both the television and movie industries are concentrated oligopolies with little competition. Pundits may write about the "indie" television movement, along with indie films built for the Internet, and the hundreds of millions of nonpremium movies on YouTube. But these subpremium efforts produce subpremium revenues or no revenues at all.

Hollywood is weathering the digital onslaught far better than is the music industry. Hollywood has a potent weapon in its corner: no one goes online to see zeroes and ones. Instead, they download or stream movies to be happy, sad, awed, romantically stimulated, or agitated. Hollywood has few competitors. Also, movies are more difficult to illegally download and move around the Web without detection. And unlike the music labels, which allowed a single distributor (Apple iTunes) to dominate online sales, the movie producers have Apple, Google (YouTube), Amazon, Netflix, Hulu, VUDU, and others competing for distribution rights.

Major studios and production groups in Hollywood and New York still dominate profit-making movie and television content production. But the movie industry faces a more challenging environment than does television because, unlike TV, it heavily depended for several decades on physical DVDs, which are rapidly losing favor with consumers who want to watch movies they can download or stream on any of several digital devices. DVD sales were cut in half from 2006 to 2012.

The size of the online movie business is difficult to ascertain because TV show rentals and movies are often lumped together. Nevertheless, industry observers estimate the total digital online movie market at about $5.7 billion in 2013. To put this in perspective, the total annual revenues of Hollywood studios when all revenue streams are combined is about $28 billion in the United States. So at this point, the Internet and online distribution is an important but not the largest part of the overall picture, although it is growing very rapidly. Netflix is the largest Internet video distributor (44% of online video and movie revenues), followed by Apple, and then a host of smaller services (Chen, 2013; NPD Group, 2013a) (see **Figure 9.19**).

There are two kinds of online movie sales and business models: iVOD (Internet video on demand), and EST (electronic sell-through). Streaming video services such as Netflix, for instance, are considered **iVOD (Internet video on demand)** services, and they are the largest, and fastest growing segment of Internet video, about 44%

iVOD (Internet video on demand)
streaming video to consumers for a subscription fee

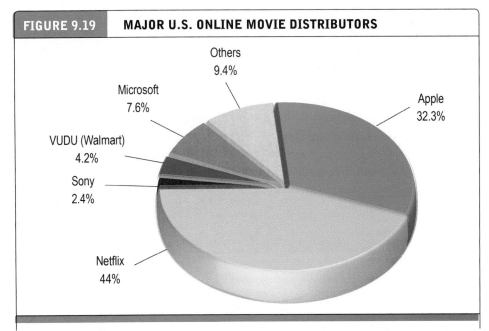

| FIGURE 9.19 | **MAJOR U.S. ONLINE MOVIE DISTRIBUTORS** |

Others 9.4%
Microsoft 7.6%
VUDU (Walmart) 4.2%
Sony 2.4%
Apple 32.3%
Netflix 44%

Apple dominates downloading and purchasing of movies, while Netflix leads in streaming movies and TV shows.
SOURCE: Based on data from industry sources.

EST (electronic sell-through)

downloading movies to consumers for home or cloud storage

(about $4 billion) of the Internet TV and movie market. Cable video on demand (pay TV) is another kind of iVOD where customers rent movies for viewing. iTunes is the leading example of **EST (electronic sell-through)**, with a business model of consumers downloading movies to their home storage devices or to a cloud server where they can be watched at any time, from any device. The video downloading EST market is declining as video streaming services grow in popularity. Currently, the EST market generates about $2.5 billion in revenue.

The online movie industry is a complex web of competing forces with conflicting interests. The existing Hollywood movie industry, which creates the products that produce the revenues, is threatened by the piracy of its products, loss of control over its traditional and very profitable distribution channels (largely movie theaters, television networks, and sales retailers of its DVD products), and the growth of powerful technology players such as Apple, Google, and Amazon, who own online movie stores and also sell the physical devices used to watch movies.

Piracy remains a threat to the movie and television industry despite years of effort by the industry and government to reduce piracy. Nevertheless, industry studies find that 24% of Internet traffic worldwide involves infringing content (illegal copies of movies and music), and about half of this involves bit torrent traffic (Envisional, 2013). In the United States, only 17% of Internet content is infringing. These numbers have declined in the last five years. BitTorrent is the most common illegal file transfer system. Other forms on Internet piracy include cyberlockers/file hosting sites (like Megaupload, now shut down), and third-party portals like MovieWatch and Movie2k, which link users to illegitimate streaming video and movie sites.

In the past, the movie industry estimated that it lost over $6 billion a year in pirated movies distributed over the Internet, copied from DVDs, early production copies, and in-theater videoing (Bialik, 2013). More recent academic research now estimates the loss is closer to $2 to $3 billion in the United States, roughly 10% of the $30 billion movie industry in the United States (Danaher et al., 2013a). Critics argue the industry has exaggerated the losses. The emergence of multiple legitimate sources for streaming and downloading movies in a convenient and safe manner appears to have reduced the overall amount of piracy, both for movies and music. A Google research paper found that searches for pirated movies peaked in 2008, and have been dropping steadily, while searches for online rentals and streaming are up (Google, 2011). Insofar as searches are an indicator of consumer interest and intent, the public interest in pirated movies is declining. Services like Netflix and iTunes that permit access to streams of movies for $8 a month, or download rentals for a few dollars, have arguably reduced the motivation to pirate movies for many potential pirates.

In countries like France, which has passed strong laws to protect artists and discourage illegal downloading (the HADOPI laws), once the laws were implemented, sales of movies on DVDs and legitimate downloading sites increased by 25% in the following twelve months (Danaher et al., 2013a).

Government actions to close down cyberlockers also can have a powerful impact on movie sales. In January 2012, the U.S. government, along with other governments, closed down the world's largest cyberlocker, Megaupload. In a few days, 25 petabytes of music and movies disappeared from the Internet. In 12 countries where Megaupload was the most widely used, digital revenues for two movie studios in the study were 6–12% higher in the 18 weeks following the shutdown (Danaher and Smith, 2013; Fritz, 2013b). With few exceptions, the academic literature produced since 2000 shows that piracy causes a significant reduction in sales of legitimate movies (Danaher et al., 2013a).

In 2014, the movie and Internet industries are both cooperative and competitive, with an explosion in alliances. In 2012, Apple, the leading digital-movie downloading site, reached an agreement with five movie studios that allows consumers to buy their films on Apple's iTunes Store on one Apple device, store them on Apple's iCloud movie service, and then watch the same film on any Apple device (Vascellaro et al., 2012). The revenue split was not announced but movie studios much prefer users to own movies rather than rent because ownership generates more revenue. Meanwhile, 70 movie studios spent three years coming up with a cyberlocker service called Ultra-Violet that performs many of the same functions as iCloud. **UltraViolet** is a proof-of-purchase system where users enter a code into their UltraViolet online account attached to purchased DVDs, or online-purchased movies, which gives them access to that movie from any device, including Android and Apple smartphones. Walmart and other DVD retailers are offering their customers in-store assistance in setting up Ultra-Violet accounts, and storing their DVDs in the cloud. In 2014, there were 15 million subscribers using UltraViolet, and the service was expanded to allow sharing of movies among five friends.

Insight on Technology: Hollywood and the Internet: Let's Cut a Deal describes how Hollywood studios and Internet distributors are cutting deals to provide more video and movie content online.

UltraViolet
movie industry proof of DVD purchase program that allows playback of DVDs to any digital device

MUSIC

Perhaps no other industry has been so severely disrupted by the Internet and new business models as the recorded music industry. Revenues for the industry have been cut by more than half since 1999. By 2010, revenues stabilized and since then, have remained relatively flat, although global sales of music fell around 4% in 2013, down to about €12 billion, compared to around €25 billion in 2002 (IFPI, 2014).

Digital revenues now make up about 64% of all U.S. music revenues (about $4.5 billion), and are expected to rise slowly to $5.4 billion by 2016 (see **Figure 9.20** on page 687). Revenues from CDs are declining but are still a strong performer, accounting for 35% of the industry's revenue (about $1.35 billion). Digital revenues have obviously not made up for the loss of revenue caused by the drastic decline in CD sales. While CD sales declined 14.5% last year, vinyl sales grew 32% from 4.5 million units sold in 2012 to 6 million sold in 2013, according to Nielsen SoundScan. Vinyl is escaping the niche market of hobbyists, and growing number of groups are issuing vinyl editions alongside CD editions although these are only 2% of industry revenues.

INSIGHT ON TECHNOLOGY

HOLLYWOOD AND THE INTERNET: LET'S CUT A DEAL

In tough times, people go to the movies. All things considered, 2013 was a good year for the movie industry. Despite the continuing effects of the recession, or because of it, box office receipts were $10.9 billion in North America, up slightly from the previous year. Global box office sales were also up, to $35.9 billion in 2013, a record, and 4% higher than the previous year. Admissions were actually down slightly, reaching 1.3 billion in the United States, and ticket prices were up slightly, making up for the loss in admissions. The number of films released in 2013 was up to 714 new films. And online revenues from downloading and streaming exploded to $5.7 billion (about 30% of the home entertainment market). In 2014, users are downloading 800,000 TV shows and 350,000 movies from iTunes every day. By any measure, the Hollywood money machine has been transformed by the Internet as DVD physical unit sales declined to half of what they were in 2005. But, unlike the music business, the movie business has so far avoided the kind of disruption that occurred in the music business. The reasons why are complex.

Continuing sales of DVDs, and revenues from online streaming services and sales at the iTunes Store, drive revenues higher for even older movies. *Avatar*, originally released in 2009, now has grossed over $3 billion; *Titanic*, released in 1997, $2.2 billion. More recent blockbusters include *The Avengers* (2012), generating $1.5 billion, and *Frozen* (2013), which hit $1.2 billion in its first year. If only all movies could produce results like these, Hollywood would be golden again. One impact of the Internet on Hollywood revenues is that consumers can easily and inex-

pensively watch older movies that they did not see or that they want to revisit years after their release. The Internet has made Hollywood's backlist much more valuable.

But all is not well in Tinseltown. Once movies are shown in theaters, where Hollywood generates only 20% of its revenue, they move on to less-profitable venues, from DVDs (which are very profitable) to cable television video-on-demand services, and then to Internet distributors like Netflix and Apple for either purchase, rental downloads, or streaming. Internet streaming services like Netflix pay the least, and therefore, Hollywood does not sell current content to Netflix, preferring to deal with Apple, who charges its customers $5–$12 for recently released movies for download. Eventually, movies end up with cable networks' broadcast television stations years after they were released. Even cable networks have greatly reduced their feature length movies and replaced them with much less expensive unscripted reality shows. Netflix and other online services have become the place to go for older movies. This "release window" differs for various films based on the studio's estimate of the revenue potential for each film. A very popular film will be delayed all along the release window.

Hollywood is facing several problems moving forward to a world where most people will be watching movies on the Internet, either at home, or on the go, using tablet computers and smartphones. One problem is that the fastest growing segment of its business, the Internet, is also the least profitable. A second problem is that Hollywood does not control its own Internet distribution network, but instead is forced to rely on the likes of Netflix, Apple, Amazon, and Google, each of whom attract large online audiences. Likewise, the big Internet distributors face a content problem: they cannot attract large audiences without recently made movies. Old movies and movie libraries on Netflix have a limited appeal, and consumers are looking for the latest releases.

Initially, Hollywood was highly dependent on Amazon's sales of DVDs as rental revenue from physical stores declined. iTunes is still the largest downloading service of movies a la carte (so-called electronic sell-through, or EST). In the last two years, the market dynamics have changed, in large part because of Netflix's success with its streaming video model. Why download to own when you can subscribe to anything you want? Hollywood is in the enviable position of being pursued by Internet distributors who are short of high-quality content. This is so different from what happened in the music business over the last decade. Multiple buyers of movies have appeared, not just Amazon or iTunes. Google is developing its own home TV device (like Apple TV) that may be a platform for movie streaming. Hulu is ramping up again as a studio-owned distribution platform.

Netflix continues to dominate online movie revenues, with a 44% market share compared to Apple at 32%. At one time, Apple had a 70% share of Internet movie revenue, and Hollywood studios feared Apple would be able to dominate Internet distribution and dictate prices. Now with Netflix dominating the streaming market, Hollywood fears it will be forced to sell its product for a pittance compared to DVD prices. For this reason, Hollywood has been restricting the release of movies to Netflix, doling out access to recent movies very carefully. Hollywood would much prefer that fans download movies from Apple rather than wait to rent or stream them. To encourage this, Hollywood, has created a new product called Digital HD where fans can download high definition copies of movies three weeks prior to their release on DVD or video on demand

services. This is the first time Hollywood has changed its release window strategy in order to drive digital download sales. The studios can charge a premium price for new movie digital downloads, making this outlet more valuable than either the DVD channel or the video on demand channel offered by cable networks.

More and more large firms are entering the premium video downloading and streaming market, and competing with one another for Hollywood movies, driving up prices. Google is expanding its movie service beyond rentals to include sales of digital movies; Walmart's VUDU, and Best Buy's CinemaNow are promoting their movie rentals and sales. VUDU cut a deal with several major studios to supply rentals of movies on the same day they are released on DVDs, months before they become available on Netflix. Amazon is seeking to strike deals with the studios for digital a la carte purchases and streaming of recent movies. Amazon has struck a deal with Viacom to purchase TV episodes and movies to stock its forthcoming streaming service. In 2013, Amazon announced it would produce five original TV series for streaming to its Amazon Prime subscribers for no additional cost. Amazon produced 14 pilot series, and allowed user feedback to determine which to finally produce. Amazon may not charge for these series in the future, seeing the investment as a way to sell diapers and other other consumer goods on its retail site, or to populate its growing Kindle library and a future Kindle movie store.

Google's YouTube announced the expansion of its movie rental service by adding 3,000 new films. YouTube finally signed deals with the major Hollywood studios including Warner Brothers, Sony, Universal, and Lionsgate. Most movies will be priced at $2.99. No subscriptions are required, it's a la carte. In addition, Google is spending $300 million to produce its own content, making deals with Hollywood and New

(continued)

York production companies as a way to avoid hefty commissions paid to these same studios for their content. Imagine, *The Google Comedy Hour*!

One result of all this competition for Hollywood content is rising prices paid by the distributors, and a feeling in Hollywood that they can maintain some semblance of control over their fate, unlike the music industry. In fact, the prices being paid by Netflix and others exceed those paid by cable television video-on-demand services. For instance, Netflix cut a multi-year deal with the Weinstein Company for exclusive display of *The Artist* (an Academy Award–winning movie), and other films, before the films are released to leading pay-TV channels. The estimated size of this deal is over $200 million. Dreamworks, a Hollywood studio, has signed a deal with Netflix for exclusive access to films for $30 million a movie. Netflix spent nearly $3 billion in 2013 for content to stream to its 50 million worldwide subscribers, and produced only $112 million in earnings.

The movie industry itself has launched a new movie service that would possibly give new life to DVDs. The new service is called Ultra-Violet. Designed to cut down on piracy, and make it possible for consumers to watch their movies on multiple devices, customers will purchase DVDs in retail stores and register the DVD serial number at the same time on the Ultra-Violet service. Once registered, consumers can watch a digital version of their movies stored on Walmart cloud servers streamed to their smartphones, tablets, or PCs. Apple's iCloud movie service avoids DVDs altogether. Can you imagine Steve Jobs wanting to preserve DVDs? iCloud offers a cyberlocker that allows consumers to purchase digital movies at iTunes and play them on other Apple devices, including Macs. Apple has struck deals with five major studios (Lionsgate, Sony Pictures, Walt Disney, Paramount, and Warner Brothers).

In the end, Hollywood and the Internet need each other, and the only question is how to find the price, define the terms of trade, and cut a deal where both parties come out winners. The flurry of deals in 2013 and 2014 bodes well for consumers, and probably for both Internet distributors and Hollywood studios. Consumers are finding multiple services that will allow them to watch movies on whatever device is convenient, and move from one device to another with a lot less effort than in the past. Given the shift of eyeballs to online entertainment, Hollywood is expanding its audience, maintaining and even enhancing its prices. With lots of Internet distributors competing, Hollywood gains in power from the competition among alternative distributors. And Internet companies are coming up with even more reasons why consumers should forget about cable TV and watch the Internet, which means more ad revenues for Internet distributors. How all these calculations will work out remains to be determined. Tune in next year on the same channel.

SOURCES: "NPD Reports Movies Drive EST Growth with Strong Revenue Increases Continuing," NPD.com, June 3, 2014; Netflix Inc., "SEC Form 10K," filed for the period ending December 31, 2013, February 3, 2014; "Sales of Digital Movies Surge," by Ben Fritz, *Wall Street Journal*, January 7, 2014; "Electronic Sell Through Spending Soars 50%," Digital Entertainment Group, January 7, 2014; "How the New iPhone Helps Hollywood," by Andy Lewis, *Hollywood Reporter*, September 6, 2013; "Amazon Invests Millions in Original TV Shows to Get You to Buy More Diapers," by Timothy Senovac, *Huffington Post*, May 31, 2013; "Google Goes Hollywood with the Internship," by Ronald Grover and Alexei Oreskovic, Reuters.com, May 28, 2013; "Netflix Passes Apple to Take Lead in Online Movie Business," by Dan Graziano, BGR.com, June 6, 2012; "Hollywood Studios Warm to Apple's iCloud Effort," by Jessica Vascellaro and Erica Ordern, *Wall Street Journal*, March 12, 2012; "Theatrical Market Statistics," Motion Picture Industry Association, March 2012; "Walmart to Give Hollywood a Hand," by Michelle Kung, *Wall Street Journal*, February 28, 2012; "Web Deals Cheer Hollywood, Despite Drop in Moviegoers," by Brooks Barnes, *New York Times*, February 24, 2012; Netflix Secures Streaming Deal With DreamWorks," by Brooks Barnes and Brian Stelter, *New York Times*, September 25, 2011; "For Wal-Mart, a Rare Online Success," by Miguel Bustillo and Karen Talley, *Wall Street Journal*, August 20, 2011; "Painful Profits From Web Video," by Sam Schechner, *Wall Street Journal*, August 15, 2011; "YouTube Is Said to Be Near a Major Film Rental Deal," by Brooks Barnes and Claire Cain Miller, *New York Times*, April 26, 2011; "YouTube Recasts for New Profits," by Jessica Vascellaro, *Wall Street Journal*, April 7, 2011.

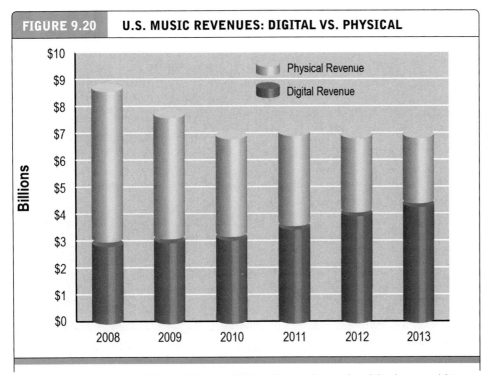

FIGURE 9.20 **U.S. MUSIC REVENUES: DIGITAL VS. PHYSICAL**

Music industry revenues have fallen by 50% since 2000, and have only recently stabilized at around $7 billion. Digital music now makes up 64% of all music revenues.

SOURCE: Based on data from Recording Industry of America (RIAA), 2014; industry sources.

For most of its history, the music industry depended on a variety of physical media to distribute music—acetate records, vinyl recordings, cassette tapes, and finally CD-ROMs. At the core of its revenue was a physical product. Since the 1950s, that physical product was an album—a collection of bundled songs that sold for a much higher price than singles. The Internet changed all that when, in 2000, a music service called Napster begin distributing pirated music tracks over the Internet to consumers using their PCs as record players. Despite the collapse of Napster due to legal challenges, hundreds of other illegal sites showed up, resulting in music industry revenues falling from $14 billion in 1999 to an estimated $7.1 billion in 2013. The appearance of powerful mobile media players beginning in 2001 that could be connected to the Internet, like Apple's iPod, and later iPhone and iPad, further eroded sales of CD albums.

The music industry initially resisted the development of legal digital channels of distribution, but ultimately and reluctantly struck deals with Apple's new iTunes Store in 2003, as well as with several small subscription music services, for online distribution. Today, digital downloads of tracks and albums are widely perceived as the saviour of the music industry, which was losing sales to piracy and file sharing. Nevertheless, revenues from the sales of digital downloads of individual songs from iTunes selling for 99 cents pale in comparison to revenues produced by CD albums.

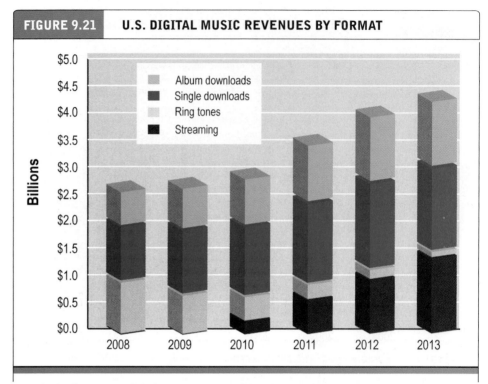

FIGURE 9.21 | **U.S. DIGITAL MUSIC REVENUES BY FORMAT**

Downloads of songs are still the largest component of digital music, but streaming digital music is the fastest growing format.

SOURCE: Based on data from Recording Industry of America (RIAA), 2014; eMarketer, Inc., 2014e.

Figure 9.21 shows consumer spending on digital music in four different formats: single songs, albums, streaming, and ringtones.

While some have argued that Apple's iTunes music service offering single tracks for 99 cents destroyed the sales of albums, this clearly is not the case. Album downloads have held up well against single downloads, and actually have grown faster than single downloads. For instance, in 2013, Justin Timberlake's *The 20/20 Experience* was the most popular album and sold almost over 2.4 million downloaded albums, and about 1.4 million CDs. By 2014, Adele's *21* had sold a record 11 million CDs and 3 million digital albums, becoming one of the most popular albums in history. Sales of digital or CD albums appears to be a function more of the music quality and popularity than the format.

There are two kinds of digital music services, each with a different business model: digital download and streaming subscription services. Digital download services (also known as download to own) are exemplified by iTunes, Amazon, and Google Play, where users download tracks and albums a la carte and pay a fee for each song. Increasingly, the songs are stored on a cloud server so users can listen to the music from any of several personal devices. All revenue derives from the sale of music tracks. Streaming subscription services (also known as Internet radio) like Pandora, Lastfm, iHeart, and Spotify allow users access to free streamed music for a limited number of hours per month and rely on advertising to generate revenue for the free streams. The music is delivered to users from a cloud server and is not stored on user devices. Users can also subscribe for a monthly fee, but fewer than 10% of stream listeners pay for subscriptions, relying instead on the free service with ads. Sites like Pandora are curated sites where users select an artist they want to listen to, and then the site uses experts and algorithms to build a list of artists similar to the artist selected by the user. Users do not control what they hear and cannot repeat a selection. Users in this sense do not own the music or control it. Spotify allows users to specify artists and songs. While most subscription services use freemium revenue models, some like Rhapsody offer only a subscription service for a monthly fee ($10) that gives users access to millions of songs stored on the site's servers. Users can select specific artists and specific tracks, as if they owned the tracks. The music can be downloaded to user devices, and the user can have access to whatever songs they select using any device. However, once a user's subscription lapses, access to the music disappears (eMarketer, Inc., 2013b).

Digital download is the biggest part of the digital music industry. The largest players are iTunes and Amazon, followed by Google Play. While illegal pirated file sharing and downloads of music were the leading edge of a digital tide that deeply disrupted the music industry beginning in the 1990s, iTunes and similar legal download sites have saved the music label firms by generating solid revenues and profits, albeit not as generous as in the heyday of CDs. While music labels might make $7 on a CD sold at $16, they only make about 32 cents for a single track downloaded from iTunes for 99 cents. Digital albums produce about $3.00 for the music labels, roughly half of a CD album sale. Artists are similarly impacted, facing a halving of their incomes in the digital environment.

While digital downloads to own constitute the largest part of digital music revenues, growth in digital downloads from services like iTunes has declined, and the fastest growing segment is the streaming music services. It appears that the success of music streaming services is cannibalizing the sales of downloads, and in 2013 the sales of downloads declined for the first time in history. The leading players in streaming are Pandora, Yahoo Music, Last.fm, and Spotify. With the growth of cloud computing and cloud-based music services, the very concept of owning music began to shift instead to accessing music from any device, anywhere. Streaming music services are adding new listeners at a growth rate of 47.5% in 2014. Unfortunately, while streaming services are growing listeners at a torrid pace, they have not managed to earn a profit because of infrastructure costs, the costs of acquiring music content from the music labels, and freemium revenue models supported by advertising revenues. For artists and music label firms, streaming services have little to offer. While music labels might receive 32 cents for every iTunes track they sell, they receive only .63 of a penny on a streamed version of the same song. This revenue is split with the artists who receive .32 of a penny. Rolling Stone calculated that a very popular song selling 1 million streams would produce revenue of $3,166 for the artist and a similar amount for the music label. For this reason, many artists and groups refuse to allow streaming of their music; studios release only limited tracks of their popular musicians, and charge a fee for even free songs broadcast by the sites. Digital streaming for the music labels and artists is similar to traditional broadcast radio, which pays very little for the music it plays. Music labels allow the streaming services to stream music in the hope of interesting listeners to purchase a CD or download a track from iTunes. In fact this model does work somewhat, and a site like Pandora does receive referral fees from sites like Amazon for directing traffic to them, and artists do receive compensation from sales of CDs by Amazon.

None of the streaming subscription services has ever shown a profit. It is unclear if streaming music is a viable business model. Pandora and the other streaming services demonstrate negative scale: the bigger they become, the more money they lose. Investors have nevertheless poured money into Pandora and Spotify hoping that their large audiences can be monetized. Apple has also added an iTunes radio service. A curated service, iTunes radio is a direct competitor with Pandora, and has both free ad-supported options and a subscription service for $25 per year, undercutting Pandora's annual fee of $36. In 2014, Apple also launched its Beats Music streaming service, which competes with Pandora and Spotify. The music never stops.

GAMES

No Internet media content form has grown as explosively as online games. Well over 150 million Internet users play some kind of game online in the United States, and that number swells to over 300 million worldwide (eMarketer, Inc., 2014d; NPD Group, 2013d). In the United States, revenue from digital games (games, add-ons, subscriptions, and mobile and social games) in 2013 was over $7 billion. Gamers spent about $8 billion on new and used physical video and PC game software (NPD Group, 2014). There are four types of Internet gamers. Casual gamers play games on a PC or laptop computer. Social gamers play games using a Web browser on a social network like Facebook. Mobile gamers play games using their smartphones or tablet computers. Console gamers play games online (or offline) using a console like Xbox, PlayStation, or Wii. Often, console gamers are connected over the Internet to enable group play. Consoles were the heart of the game industry, but the market has changed with the introduction of smartphones, tablets, and Facebook, which offer games that change frequently, have greater variety for different demographics, and are much lower in price, often initially free and supported by ads. Consoles are also hampered by the expense of creating new models. In 2014, a new Sony PlayStation replaced a seven-year-old model, and a new Microsoft Xbox replaced an eight-year old model. In a fast-moving online world, such long replacement cycles inevitably lead to declines in hardware sales. Both consoles are integrated entertainment devices integrating cable TV, movies via Internet services, and games.

Console game makers, software, and content creators are scrambling to cope with the fact that millions of game players now play on smartphones and tablets (Wingfield, 2014; Wingfield 2013b). In 2013, half of smartphone owners, 40% of the population, played games on their phones. Mobile gaming revenues were about $1.8 billion. Nevertheless, console sales are still propelled by blockbuster titles. When the latest version

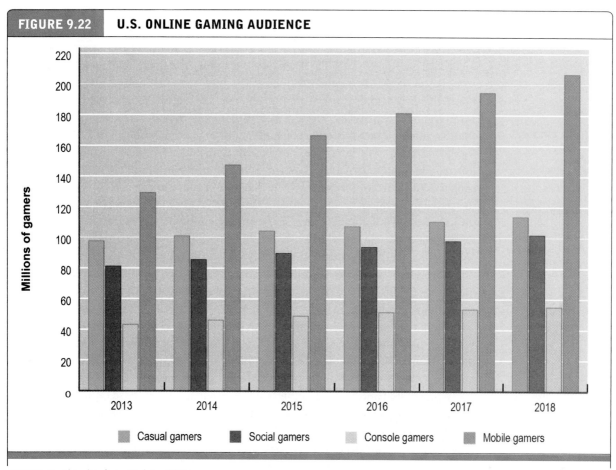

FIGURE 9.22 **U.S. ONLINE GAMING AUDIENCE**

SOURCE: Based on data from eMarketer, 2014d.

of Grand Theft Auto launched in late 2013, sales were over $1 billion within three days. The cost of developing Grand Theft Auto is estimated at $100 million.

Figure 9.22 illustrates the relative size of these four online gaming audiences and their future growth prospects. Because people play games in a variety of different venues, the total number of online gamers is on the order of 150 million, about 50% of all Internet users. One of the most widely played mobile casual games is Angry Birds. In Angry Birds, players launch birds at green pigs hiding inside buildings using a sling shot to blast away the pig and the building. As mindless as this sounds, Angry Birds had been downloaded in various editions more than 2 billion times by 2014.

In 2014, the mobile casual "free" gaming market, supported by advertising, remains the fastest growing form of online gaming; physical game console sales are down, and game software growth is slow. The growth of online games put a dent in the growth of console games sales, which fell 2% in 2013. Nevertheless, like DVDs in movies and CDs in music, the sale of video game hardware and boxed software generates nearly 70% of the video game industry's revenue. The challenge for the video game console and content market is to move onto the mobile platform and still make profits. Social and casual gaming—often lumped together in a single number—was growing at 10% in 2013, but is expected to slow over time to about 5% in 2018.

Social gaming on sites like Facebook have grown very rapidly since 2009 in large part due to the success of games like Farmville, CityVille, and Words With Friends offered by Zynga. Online social gaming enlarged the demographic of gamers to include women and older people, compared to console gamers who tend to be young and male. But like other game platforms, consumers tire of current games and are attracted to the latest market entrants. Users of various Zynga games fell in 2013 by up to 50%, down to 39 million active users (Rusli, 2013). Zynga cut its staff by 20% and its stock sank to $3 a share after reporting large declines in audience. Zynga had failed to make the move to mobile gaming, and its reliance on sales of virtual goods becomes more difficult in the mobile environment. Mobile gamers are the largest segment of the online gaming audience. There are almost 150 million mobile gamers in 2014. These games are sometimes social, but more often focus on individual performance of short duration. The possibilities of selling virtual goods or displaying ads on these mobile games is very limited and therefore these sites need to rely on in-app advertising to make their revenue targets.

The number of console gamers, about 46 million in 2014, has leveled off in recent years. In part this is due to the age of the platforms. The Xbox, PlayStation, and Wii are old, have not been able to expand much beyond the young male demographic, and the games typically have large initial sales that wane quickly.

While casual and social gaming rapidly grows, nearly all these online and mobile games are free and users do not stay in the games very long. These two features make it difficult for gaming firms to monetize their user base by showing advertisements and charging for services. The business model of social and casual gaming is still not settled. Marketers have just recently begun to build video marketing campaigns that increase a brand's engagement and interaction with customers who are playing at social mobile gaming sites.

CASE STUDY

Netflix:
How Does This Movie End?

I n the Netflix online television comedy-drama series, *Orange is the New Black*, the lead character is Piper Chapman (Taylor Schilling), a recently engaged blond New Yorker sent to a federal prison for a crime committed years before. Critically acclaimed, and widely followed, *Orange* follows in the foot steps of Netflix's earlier successful online TV series *House of Cards*, a political insider's tale of Washington politics starring Kevin Spacey. *House of Cards* was the first ever online television series to win an Emmy award (for best director). *Orange* won three Emmy creative awards in 2014. By producing its own content, Netflix is able to differentiate itself from cable TV shows, as well as obtain content for a lower price, and attract new subscribers.

While Netflix does not release the number of viewers for any of its original TV shows, executives do credit these two shows with driving the streaming service to a record 50 million worldwide subscribers by the second quarter of 2014 (40 million in the United States), with growth running at a blistering pace of 2.5 million new subscribers each quarter. For Netflix, orange is indeed the new "black," as in a positive bottom line and profits. Netflix shares have soared to over $400 a share (from its $15 offering price in 2002). Revenues in 2013 were $4.3 billion, but profits were a paltry $112 million. This gives Netflix a price earnings ratio of over 170 times earnings, one of the loftiest in the e-commerce arena.

Netflix got its start as a mail order company renting DVDs of older Hollywood movies using the postal system. Founded by two Silicon Valley entrepreneurs, Marc

© Digitallife/Alamy

Randolph and Reed Hastings, in 1997, the company started by renting individual copies of 900 DVD movie titles and delivering them to customers by postal mail. In 2000, it switched to a subscription model where customers could receive DVDs on a regular basis for a monthly fee. By 2006, it had delivered its billionth DVD and became the largest subscription provider of DVDs. In 2007, Netflix began a video-on-demand streaming service of movies although it still retains a DVD subscription business. In 2014, Netflix is the largest player in the movie and TV series streaming market, and consumes over 30% of the U.S. Internet bandwidth to serve its customers.

Netflix is one of those Silicon Valley stories that might make a good movie, or even a television series, because of its potential for disrupting the American television and movie landscape (or what's called premium video). It's a dream-come-true story of accomplishment, pluck, innovation, and Internet technology. In a few short years Netflix created the largest DVD rental business in the country, then created the largest streaming video service. Today Netflix accounts for over 90% of digital movie streaming, while its chief streaming competitors, Amazon and Hulu, make up the remaining market; Netflix has created the largest database on consumer video preferences and built a recommendation system that encourages consumers to see more movies; Netflix discovered that older TV series had strong niche followings and built a new model of "binge viewing" where consumers could watch all the episodes of a series in several sittings. Finally, Netflix has entered the content creation business by developing original TV series.

In the movie and TV business there are only two ways to make money: either own the content or own the pipes that deliver the content. All the better if you can do both. Netflix has turned itself into a major pipeline to 35 million Internet users in the United States and is increasingly recognized as an important pipeline to large audiences. For instance, in 2013, Netflix announced a deal with the Weinstein Company, a major American film studio and producer of ten Academy Award films, to become the exclusive subscription TV home for the film studios' content, beginning in 2016. Weinstein chose Netflix over its long-time cable network distributor Showtime. This move puts Netflix into the same league of premium channel distributors and in direct competition with other cable networks like HBO, Starz, Showtime, and A&E for the rights to show movies about eight months after their theater run is complete.

In one possible ending scenario for the Netflix movie, the company challenges the much larger cable television industry, which is based on an entirely different technology and business model, namely, selling expensive bundles of hundreds of TV channels that few people watch, then raising monthly fees faster than the rate of inflation. Given Netflix's large national audience of streamers, the company makes new friends in Hollywood and New York that are looking for ways to distribute their shows to a new online, mobile, and social world; Hollywood stretches the distribution window so that Internet distributors like Netflix get the same treatment as cable systems by allowing them to show the latest movies and shows at about the same time as cable systems. And the cable television industry is forced to retreat from its bundling practices and offer customers the ability to select just those channels they actually watch. Cable industry revenues would plunge as a result. In this dream scenario, Netflix goes on to challenge the cable networks by producing its own original TV dramas, and adds comedy and documentaries to the mix. A story with a happy ending! But happy endings happen mostly in Hollywood.

The outcome of this movie depends on how well Netflix can deal with some considerable challenges. For instance, one source of Netflix's poor profitability is that the costs of content are very high, both purchased older series as well as new content, which is far more risky. The owners of older cable TV series and Hollywood movies charge Netflix for the privilege of distributing their content as much as they do established cable TV networks. Netflix's cost of revenues was $3.9 billion in 2013, largely due to the cost of purchasing the cherished content that brings the customers. Netflix is, after all, just a delivery platform, and the company is in a constant bidding war with both cable and Internet giants all looking for the same thing—popular old TV series with a built-in audience, on the cheap. But content owners have wised up to the value of their backlist TV series and have raised their prices accordingly. For instance, in 2008, Netflix reached a $30 million deal with the Starz cable network for several popular TV series and movies. When the deal came up for renewal in 2012, Starz wanted $300 million. Netflix is paying hundreds of millions to Disney, Paramount, Lionsgate, and MGM to license hit shows and movies. As a result of content owners charging more, the costs of its large and frequently updated content library are rising more quickly than its revenues. To illustrate, streaming content obligations (current and future payments to content owners) ballooned from $3.9 billion in 2011 to $7.3 billion in 2013, roughly twice its gross revenues in 2013. New original content is not exactly a bargain either. The critically acclaimed *House of Cards* cost Netflix $100 million for 26 episodes, $4 million an episode. Older content like *Madmen* runs about $1 million an episode. It's possible that Netflix does not scale, and that the more subscribers it has, the less profit it makes because the cost of doing business rises faster than revenue.

A second challenge Netflix faces is the risk of creating new content. It's not as if wealthy Silicon Valley entrepreneurs can fly to Hollywood or New York with lots of cash and simply purchase new content. As one pundit noted, this might lead to a mugging, but not a successful TV series or movie. Silicon Valley is generally not the place to go if you're looking for story tellers, writers, producers, directors, talent agents, and cinematographers. Algorithms don't come up with new ideas for novels, plays, movies, or TV series. Netflix started out as a recycler of old TV and movie content, and like HBO in the cable world, is trying to expand into original content production both to reduce costs and to build a brand name as a content creator, not just a middle man. Content can be sold and re-sold to cable networks, or other Internet distributors. But there is considerable risk in original content, long-form TV or Hollywood quality video. Older series are proven series, and Netflix can identify which of its customers watched the series in previous years, and estimate the audience size, and whether new subscribers will be attracted by the re-plays. But when it comes to new TV series, Netflix has tried to use its algorithms to predict what new series its customers might be interested in with mixed results. Netflix has produced some real winners according to critics, like *House of Cards* and *Orange Is the New Black*. It has also produced some real losers that did not get critical acclaim like *Lillyhammer*, *Hemlock Grove*, and *Bad Samaritans*. While Netflix's *House of Cards* and *Orange Is the New Black* have garnered half a dozen Emmies, HBO (the cable-based network in business since 1972) has over 400 Emmies. There has been only one tech company in history that was successful with video content production for movies or television, and that is Pixar, Steve Job's firm, which pioneered animated feature length movies. Netflix does not make it easy

SOURCES: "Video Streaming Beats DVR and Video On Demand Viewing," eMarketer, Inc., September 6, 2013; "The Comedy Lineup Expands on Netflix," by Brian Stelter, *New York Times*, August 29, 2013; "Netflix Insiders Take the Money and Run," by Adam Levin-Weinberg, Motley Fool, August 29, 2013; "Netflix Expands Content Deal with Weinstein Co.," Amol Sharma and Ben Fritz, *Wall Street Journal*, August 20, 2013; "Form 10-Q Netflix Inc.," United States Securities and Exchange Commission, July 25, 2013; "Media Journal: Netflix Profit, Subscribers Rise, but Wall Street Underwhelmed," by William Launder, *Wall Street Journal*, July 23, 2013; "The State of Streaming TV, According to Netflix," by Tom Gara, *Wall Street Journal*, July 22, 2013; "Original Content Ever More Important to Netflix," Brian Fitzgerald, *Wall Street Journal*, July 22, 2013; "Inside Netflix's Historic 'House of Cards' Emmy Nods," Maria LaMagna, July 18, 2013; "How Netflix Is Shaking Up Hollywood," by Amol Sharma, *Wall Street Journal*, July 7, 2013; "Apple and Netflix Dominate Online Video," by Brian Chen, *New York Times*, June 19, 2013; "DreamWorks and Netflix in Deal for New TV Shows," by Brooks Barnes, *New York Times*, June 17, 2013; "Form 10-K Netflix Inc.," United States Securities and Exchange Commission, February 1, 2013; "Once Film Focused, Netflix Transitions to TV Shows," by Brian Stelter, February 27, 2012; "Will Qwikster, a Netflix Spinoff DVD-by-Mail Service, Damage Brand?," *Washington Post*, September 19, 2011; "Netflix Raises Price of DVD and Online Movies Package by 60%," by Brian Stelter and Sam Grobart, *New York Times*, July 12, 2011; "Amazon Adds Streaming-Video Service For Prime Members," by Nat Worden and Stu Woo, *Wall Street Journal*, February 23, 2011.

to understand which of its original series are winners or losers because it refuses to publish audience numbers.

While Netflix stands out as a powerful Internet brand today, Netflix has many powerful competitors. The success of Netflix's streaming model has attracted Amazon, Apple, Yahoo, and perhaps Google to the fray. All of these firms are tech firms with very large Internet audiences, strong brand names, and a good understanding of what their millions of online customers want.

Apple is the leader in downloaded movies where customers own or rent movies, and of course, it does own iTunes, the world's largest online media store for the purchase of music, videos, and TV series. HBO, founded in 1972, is the oldest and most successful pay television service in the United States with over 35 million cable TV subscribers, and the originator of a long list of highly successful original TV series and movies such as *Sex and the City, The Sopranos, The Wire, Game of Thrones,* and *True Blood.* If Netflix has a direct competitor on the creative front, it is HBO, a more traditional programmer that does not use computer algorithms to design its content, but instead relies on the hunches and gifts of editors, producers, and directors to produce its content.

Netflix's competitors have very deep pockets. This means Netflix also has competitors for talent and the production of new content, and perhaps price pressure as well. For instance, Amazon offers free streaming to Amazon Prime customers, and in 2014 has taken on HBO TV series to stream to Prime customers without additional fees. Google is actively pursuing long-form content creators for its video channel program. There is no cost to Google users because the service is ad supported.

Netflix's costs are likely to rise in the future for another reason besides the cost of content. Netflix (consuming 35% of Internet bandwidth), along with streaming services like Google (18% of bandwidth), is an Internet free rider, consuming orders of magnitude more bandwidth than what it pays for. Flying under the flag of net neutrality, Netflix in the past has opposed efforts by ISPs (cable owners like Time Warner, Comcast, ATT, Verizon, and others) to charge users on the basis of bandwidth actually used. It has been supported by the FCC, which has argued innovation would be inhibited if heavy bandwidth users like Netflix and Google actually paid for the amount of bandwidth they consume. In January 2014, a U.S. appeals court threw out federal rules to treat all Internet traffic equally, making it possible for Internet providers like Verizon and Comcast to charge higher fees for big bandwidth users, or slow down their streams until they agreed to higher fees. Shortly after the court ruling, Comcast slowed down Netflix videos. By April 2014, Netflix had signed agreements with nearly all the large ISPs to pay several million dollars a year to connect directly to provider networks and receive sufficient bandwidth speed to serve its customers. The net result is that Netflix production costs will go up, and more accurately reflect the cost of resources its service is consuming.

So another possible ending for the Netflix movie is that ultimately it can't compete with Apple, Google, Yahoo, and Amazon. Its shares are too expensive to purchase, but it can be imitated by its competitors, and its profitability reduced to less than shareholders can tolerate. Apple's 2013 revenue was a staggering $171 billion, fifty times larger than Netflix, and it has a cash reserve of $145 billion. It is entirely within Apple's capabilities, or Amazon's or Google's, to develop a competing streaming video service. This show is not over till the last episode is finished. Stay tuned.

Case Study Questions

1. What are three challenges that Netflix faces?

2. What are the key elements of Netflix's strategy in 2014?

3. What are the implications of Netflix's new strategy for the cable television systems like Comcast and TimeWarner?

4. Why is Netflix in competition with Apple, Amazon, and Google, and what strengths does Netflix bring to the market?

9.5 REVIEW

KEY CONCEPTS

■ **Understand the major trends in the consumption of media and online content, the major revenue models for digital content delivery, digital rights management, and the concept of media convergence.**

- Major trends in the consumption of media and online content include the following:
  - The average American adult spends around 4,100 hours per year consuming various media. The most hours are spent online, using a desktop or mobile device, followed by watching television and listening to the radio.
  - Although several studies indicate that time spent on the Internet reduces consumer time available for other media, recent data reveals a more complex picture, as Internet users multitask and consume more media of all types than do non-Internet users.
  - In terms of all media revenue, print media (newspapers, books, and magazines) together accounts for the most revenue (40%), followed by television (30%). Internet media (music and video) currently accounts for only 4.5% of all media revenue.
  - The three major revenue models for digital content delivery are the subscription, a la carte, and advertising-supported (free and freemium) models.
  - In terms of paid online content, online TV and movies is the largest and fastest growing form of online entertainment.
  - Digital rights management (DRM) refers to the combination of technical and legal means for protecting digital content from reproduction without permission. Walled gardens are a kind of DRM that restrict the widespread sharing of content.
- The concept of media convergence has three dimensions:
  - Technological convergence, which refers to the development of hybrid devices that can combine the functionality of two or more media platforms, such as books, newspapers, television, radio, and stereo equipment, into a single device.

- Content convergence, with respect to content design, production, and distribution.
- Industry convergence, which refers to the merger of media enterprises into powerful, synergistic combinations that can cross-market content on many different platforms and create works that use multiple platforms.
- In the early years of e-commerce, many believed that media convergence would occur quickly. However, many early efforts failed, and new efforts are just now appearing.

■ **Understand the key factors affecting the online publishing industry.**

- Key factors affecting online newspapers include:
  - *Audience size and growth.* Although the newspaper industry as a whole is the most troubled part of the publishing industry, online readership of newspapers is growing, fueled by smartphones, e-readers, and tablet computers.
  - *Revenue models and results.* Online newspapers predominantly rely on both advertising and subscription revenues.
- Key factors affecting online magazines include:
  - *Online audience and growth:* Digital magazine sales have soared, with almost a third of the Internet population now reading magazines online.
  - *Magazine aggregation:* Magazine aggregators (Web sites or apps) offer users online subscriptions and sales of many digital magazines.
- Key factors affecting e-books and online book publishing include:
  - *Audience size and growth.* E-book sales have exploded, fueled by the Amazon Kindle, Apple iPad, and smartphones. The mobile platform of smartphones and tablets has made millions of books available online at a lower price than print books. The future of the book will be digital although printed books will not disappear for many years.
  - *Challenges.* The two primary challenges of the digital e-book platform are control over pricing and the further evolution of the digital distribution platform.
  - *Competing business models.* E-book business models include the wholesale model and the agency model.
  - *Convergence.* The publishing industry is making steady progress toward media convergence. Newly authored e-books are appearing with interactive rich media, which allow the user to click on icons for videos or other material.

■ **Understand the key factors affecting the online entertainment industry.**

- There are five main players in the entertainment sector: television, motion pictures, music, games, and radio broadcasting. The entertainment segment is currently undergoing great change, brought about by the Internet and the mobile platform. Consumers have begun to accept paying for content and also to expect to be able to access online entertainment from any device at any time.
- Key factors include the following:
  - *Audience size and growth.* The audience for online movies and television is growing dramatically.
  - *The emergence of streaming services and the mobile platform.* In the movie and television industries, two major trends are the move to streaming services, from Amazon, Apple, to Hulu and other channels, and the continued increase in online purchases and downloads. Although physical sales of products (DVDs) are dropping significantly, more and more consumers are purchasing movies and television episodes on mobile devices.
  - The music industry is experiencing similar trends as the movie industry: the growth of streaming services, or Internet radio, the continued expansion of online purchases, and increased downloads on mobile devices. However, the unbundling of a traditional music product, the album, into individual songs, has decimated music industry revenues.

- Of the four types of gamers—casual, social, mobile, and console—the greatest growth is anticipated for mobile gamers, as the mobile market is rapidly expanding along all e-commerce fronts.

QUESTIONS

1. Does time spent on the Internet cannibalize or complement traditional media?
2. What are the basic revenue models for online content?
3. How have attitudes about paying for content changed since the early years of the Web?
4. What is DRM?
5. What are the three dimensions in which the term "convergence" has been applied? What does each of these areas of convergence entail?
6. What factors are needed to support successfully charging the consumer for online content?
7. What are the different revenue models that newspapers have used?
8. What are the two primary e-book business models?
9. What features make it difficult for gaming firms to monetize their user base?
10. How has the Internet transformed television viewing?
11. Why is the growth of cloud storage services important to the growth of mobile content delivery?
12. What impact did shutting down Megaupload have?
13. What are OTT entertainment services?
14. What are the two kinds of online movie sales and business models? Give an example of each type.
15. What are the four basic types of Internet gamers?
16. What type of convergence does the Kindle Fire represent?
17. What alternatives do magazine publishers have to using Apple and Google newsstands as distribution channels?
18. How has the book publishing industry's experience with the Internet differed from the newspaper and magazine industries' experience?
19. What are some of the challenges currently facing the book publishing industry?
20. What advantages do pure digital news sites have over print newspapers? What advantages do traditional newspapers have over pure digital sites?

PROJECTS

1. Research the issue of media convergence in the newspaper industry. Do you believe that convergence will be good for the practice of journalism? Develop a reasoned argument on either side of the issue and write a 3- to 5-page report on the topic. Include in your discussion the barriers to convergence and whether these restrictions should be eased.

2. Go to Amazon and explore the different digital media products that are available. For each kind of digital media product, describe how Amazon's presence has altered the industry that creates, produces, and distributes this content. Prepare a presentation to convey your findings to the class.

3. Identify three online sources of content that exemplify one of the three digital content revenue models (subscription, a la carte, and advertising-supported) discussed in the chapter. Describe how each site works, and how it generates revenue. Describe how each site provides value to the consumer. Which type of revenue model do you prefer, and why?

4. Identify a popular online magazine that also has an offline subscription or newsstand edition. What advantages (and disadvantages) does the online edition have when compared to the offline physical

edition? Has technology platform, content design, or industry structure convergence occurred in the online magazine industry? Prepare a short report discussing this issue.

5. In August 2014, Amazon announced that it was going to purchase Twitch, which lets users stream their video game sessions, for almost $1 billion. Why would Amazon spend so much money on Twitch? Create a short presentation either defending the purchase or explaining why you think it was a bad idea.

REFERENCES

Alter, Alexandra. "Sci-Fi's Underground Hit." *Wall Street Journal* (March 14, 2013).

Association of American Publishers. "US Publishing Industry Annual Survey Reports $27 Billion in Net Revenue." (June 26, 2014a).

Association of American Publishers. "Monthly StatShot." (January 2014b).

Benton, Joshua. "American Newspaper Revenue is Still Dropping, Just Not Quite as Much as Before." Nieman Journalism Lab. (April 21, 2014).

Berkshire Hathaway Corporation. "Annual Report 2013." (March 1, 2013).

Bialik, Carl. "Studios Struggle for Focus on Film Pirates Booty." *Wall Street Journal* (April 5, 2013).

Bosman, Julie. "Penguin Acquires Self-Publishing Company." New York Times (July 19, 2012).

Boxer, Sarah. "Paintings Too Perfect? The Great Optics Debate." *New York Times* (December 4, 2001).

Carr, David. "Print Is Down, and Now Out." *New York Times* (August 10, 2014).

Carr, David. "New Rules for the Ways We Watch." *New York Times* (December 24, 2011).

Chen, Brian. "Apple and Netflix Dominate Online Video." *New York Times* (June 19, 2013).

comScore. "comScore Releases January 2014 U.S. Online Video Rankings." (February 21, 2014).

Danaher, Brett, Michael D. Smith, and Rahul Tang. "Piracy and Copyright Enforcement Mechanisms," *Innovation Policy and the Economy*, Vol. 14 (May 3, 2013a).

Danaher, Brett, and Michael D. Smith. "Gone in 60 Seconds: The Impact of the Megaupload Shutdown on Movie Sales." Working Paper (April 2013b).

Doctor, Ken. "The Newsonomics of Newspapers' Slipping Digital Performance." Nieman Journalism Lab. (April 24, 2014).

Edmunds, Rick. "Newspapers Stabilizing, but Still Threatened." Poynter Institute and Pew Research Center. (July 18, 2013).

eMarketer, Inc. "US Time Spent With Media: The Complete eMarketer Forecast for 2014." (April 2014a).

eMarketer, Inc. "Activities Conducted Simultaneously While Watching TV According to US Internet Users, by Generation, 2013 & 2014." (June 18, 2014b).

eMarketer, Inc. "Digital Activities Conducted While Watching the 2014 World Cup According to US Internet Users, by Demographic." (June 11, 2014c).

eMarketer, Inc. (Alison McCarthy) "US Internet and Mobile Users: Midyear 2014 Complete Forecast (September 2014d).

eMarketer, Inc. "US Digital Music Shipments and Revenues, by Format, 2012 & 2013." (March 18, 2014e).

eMarketer, Inc. "Magazine Ad Spending, United States, 2012–2018." (June 2014f).

eMarketer, Inc., "Ebook Readers Use Devices to Supplement, Not Replace, Printed Media." (January 30, 2014g).

eMarketer, Inc. (Mark Dolliver). "Millennials' Media Usage: What's Distinctive, What's Not, and What Matters Most." (April 2014h).

eMarketer, Inc. (Debra Aho Williamson). Social TV: Marketers' Enthusiasm Cools a Bit, but Experimentation Continues." (August 2014i).

eMarketer, Inc. "US Digital Content Users, 2013." (March 2013a).

eMarketer, Inc. (Paul Verna). "Internet Radio." (February 2013b.)

Envisional, Inc. "An Estimate of Infringing Use of the Internet." (2013).

Fischer, Mary. "BuzzFeed and the Huffington Post Crush Legacy Outlets in Traffic Growth." *American Journalism Review* (May 21, 2014).

Fritz, Ben. "Sales of Digital Movies Surge," *Wall Street Journal*, (January 7, 2014).

Fritz, Ben. "Movie Sales Increase With Shutdown of Piracy Site." *Wall Street Journal* (March 7, 2013).

Google. (Deborah Schwartz) "A Window Into Film." (April 2011).

Grabowicz, Paul. "The Transition to Digital Journalism." UC Berkeley Graduate School of Journalism (July 22, 2014).

Greenfield, Jeremey. "How the Amazon–Hachette Fight Could Shape the Future of Ideas." *Atlantic Monthly* (May 28, 2014).

Hagey, Keach and Greg Bensinger. "Jeff Bezo's Tool Kit for the Post." *Wall Street Journal* (August 6, 2013).

IFPI. "Global Statistics." (August 6, 2014).

Isaac, Mike. "A Push to Go Beyond Lists for Content at BuzzFeed." *New York Times* (August 11, 2014).

Isaacson, Walter. *Steve Jobs.* Simon & Schuster (2011).

Kahn, Jordan. "Eddy Cue: Apple Passed 35 Billion Songs Sold on iTunes Last Week, 40 Million iTunes Radio Listeners." 9to5mac.com (May 28, 2014).

Launder, William. "News Websites Proliferate, Stretching Thin Ad Dollars." *Wall Street Journal* (January 27, 2014).

Magazine Publishers Association. "2013 A Growth Year for Magazine Media Across Platforms." (January 9, 2014).

New York Times. "Innovation." (May 2014).

Newspaper Association of America. "NAA Media Revenue 2013: Dollars Grow in Several Categories." (April 18, 2014a).

Newspaper Association of America. "Annual Daily and Sunday Newspaper Circulation Expenditures." (April 18, 2014b).

Newspaper Association of America. "Newspaper Web Audience." (July 7, 2014c).

Nielsen. "2013 Nielsen National Cross Media Engagement Study." (April 16, 2013).

NPD Group, "US Spent $15.39 Billion on Games in 2013," by Brendan Sincalir, Gamesindustry.biz. (February 11, 2014.)

NPD Group. "Apple iTunes Dominates Internet Video." (April 23, 2013a).

NPD Group. "U.S. Commercial Channel Computing Device Sales Set to End 2013 with Double-Digit Growth, According to NPD." (December 23, 2013b).

NPD Group, "DVDs Still Largest Revenue Source for Movies." (January 31, 2013c).

NPD Group. "Report Shows Increased Number of Online Gamers and Hours Spent." (May 2, 2013d).

Packer, George. "Cheap Words: Amazon Is Good for Customers. But Is It Good for Books?" *New Yorker* (February 17, 2014).

Pew Research Center (Kenneth Olmstead). "5 Key Findings About Digital News Audiences." (March 17, 2014a).

Pew Research Center (Amy Mitchell, Mark Jurkowitz, and Kenneth Olmstead). "Audience Routes: Direct, Search, and Facebook." (March 12, 2014b.)

Pew Research Center. "State of the News Media 2014." (2014c).

Pew Research Center. "The State of the News Media 2013." (March 18, 2013).

PriceWaterhouseCooper (PWC). "Global Entertainment and Media Outlook 2014–2018." (2014).

Recording Industry Association of America (RIAA). "News and Notes on 2013 RIAA Music Industry Shipments and Revenue Statistics." (March 18, 2014).

Romenesko, Jim. "Wall Street Journal Memo: Newsroom Changes Mean a Faster-moving, Digital First News Operation." Jimromenesko.com. (January 21, 2014.)

Rusli, Evelyn. "Zynga Business Erodes Further." *Wall Street Journal* (July 25, 2013).

Sandvine, Inc. "Global Internet Phenomena Report, 2014." (May 5, 2014).

Sebastian, Michael. "Digital Growth to Prop Up Magazine Revenue Amid Print Losses, PwC Forecasts." *Advertising Age* (June 3, 2014).

Somaiya, Ravi. "The New Yorker Alters Its Online Strategy." *New York Times* (July 8, 2014).

Statistica.com. "Facts on the Film Industry." (accessed September 30, 2014).

Streitfield, David. "Amazon, a Friendly Giant As Long As It's Fed." *New York Times* (July 12, 2014).

Streitfield, David. "Imagining a Swap Meet for E-Books and Music." *New York Times* (March 7, 2013a)

Streitfield, David. "Out of Print, but Not Out of Mind." *New York Times* (December 1, 2013b).

Varian, Hal. "Newspaper Economics: Online and Offline." Google Public Policy Blog (March 9, 2010).

Vascellaro, Jessica, Erica Order, and Sam Schechner. "Hollywood Studios Warm to Apple's iCloud Effort." *Wall Street Journal* (March 12, 2012).

Vega, Tanzina. "Marketers Find a Friend in Pinterest." *New York Times* (April 17, 2012).

Wingfield, Nick. "New Consoles on the Way but Gaming Isn't the Same." *New York Times* (November 11, 2013b).

Wingfield, Nick. "Shrinking List of Video Games Is Dominated by Blockbusters." *New York Times* (September 29, 2014).

Wingfield, Nick. "Technology Industry Extends a Hand to Struggling Print Media." *New York Times* (August 11, 2013a).

CHAPTER 10

Online Communities

After reading this chapter, you will be able to:

- Describe the different types of social networks and online communities and their business models.
- Describe the major types of auctions, their benefits and costs, how they operate, when to use them, and the potential for auction abuse and fraud.
- Describe the major types of Internet portals and their business models.

Viadeo Challenges LinkedIn

with a Multi-Local Approach

Viadeo is a French professional social network site with over 60 million members worldwide. It is the leading professional network in France and China and the second-largest professional social network after LinkedIn, which is based in the United States. A recent study found that in France, almost 80% of people contacted by recruiters using social media were contacted through Viadeo. In 2014, Viadeo launched a highly anticipated IPO after several successful rounds of venture capital financing in previous years. The IPO raised €24.4 million, raising the company's market capitalization to €171.1 million.

© gigra/Fotolia.com

Like LinkedIn, Viadeo attracts professionals who want to publish their resumes, establish relationships with other professionals, and discover new clients, potential employees, even business partners. Viadeo offers these services for free to individuals. It generates revenue from businesses that pay fees in order to search the professional database created by participating individuals. Viadeo claims that it adds more than 1 million new members and 10 million new connections are made each month. Over 100 million profiles are also viewed each month. Its business model is based on its ability to monetize its rapidly growing user audience by providing human resource and advertising opportunities to business firms worldwide. In 2014, Viadeo reached the 9-million-member milestone in France.

Viadeo's global strategy is twofold. First, it wants to be the top non-English speaking network in the world. The company employs over 400 staff members worldwide. In addition to its Paris headquarters, Viadeo has offices and teams in the rest of the EU-5, United States, Russia, China, India, Mexico, Senegal, and Morocco. In Africa as a whole, Viadeo has over 2 million members, including 1 million in the Maghreb region, and it has stated that Africa is a very important continent for the company. In China, it is the leading professional social network site, and it is also the dominant site in Europe and Latin America.

A second element in its global strategy is what the company calls a "multi-local" approach to social networks. In contrast to LinkedIn, Viadeo claims to uniquely adjust to, and honor, the language, business, and popular cultures of the countries in which it operates. It goes beyond simple translation and focuses on catering to, and understanding, the business and cultural needs of each market. The company points to its success in China, where its subsidiary Tianji now has over 20 million members. Tianji has experienced success in the local elite market with upper-level professionals who are graduates of China's top universities, and it also reaches out to business firms that want to meet local professionals and do

SOURCES: "The Shocking Reality of Viadeo's Current Market Cap," by Liam Boogar, Rudebaguette. com, October 30, 2014; "Viadeo Passes the 9 Million Member Mark in France," Viadeo.com, September 30, 2014; "French Start-up Viadeo Sets IPO Price at Bottom of Range," Reuters, July 1, 2014; "Viadeo Offering Native Advertising on Mobile Devices," Viadeo. com, June 6, 2014; "Viadeo App Now Available on Android Tablets," Viadeo.com, March 24, 2014; "Marketing on LinkedIn: New Opportunities, But Old Issues Remain," eMarketer, Inc., August 23, 2013; "More Employers Finding Reasons Not to Hire Candidates on Social Media, Finds CareerBuilder Survey," Careerbuilder.com, June 27, 2013; "LinkedIn Builds Its Publishing Presence," by Leslie Kaufman, New York Times, June 16, 2013; "Number of Active Users at Facebook Over the Years," Associated Press, October, 4, 2012; "How Professionals Use LinkedIn," eMarketer, August 5, 2011; "LinkedFA Offers Social Network for Financial Advisors," by David F. Carr, *Information Week*, June 1, 2011.

business in China. In China, use of the Internet is skewed towards young, urban professionals with a younger demographic than is served by Western professional networks.

Viadeo has also experienced an uptick in mobile usage that is driving its growth. After releasing its iOS app in 2013, the company launched an Android app in early 2014. Over half of Viadeo's users logged on using the company's mobile app in 2014, and unique visitors to the site were up 16% over the previous half-year, with overall site visits up a whopping 41% over that time frame. Viadeo also launched its first round of native app advertising, offering sponsored articles and suggested apps that are displayed unobtrusively to app users, with other options including companies that are hiring, and sponsored job offers. The company allows advertisers to offer extremely precise and granular advertising, with ads targeted towards very specific careers and skills, to an audience already interested in that type of content.

Viadeo's biggest competitor and potential impediment to its future prospects is LinkedIn, currently the world's leading professional network. LinkedIn is an online network with more than 300 million worldwide members in over 200 countries, representing 170 different industries. LinkedIn allows a member to create a profile, including a photo, to summarize his or her professional accomplishments. LinkedIn also has a multi-local strategy: the site has versions in English, French, German, Italian, Portuguese, Spanish, Dutch, Swedish, Romanian, Russian, Turkish, Japanese, Czech, Polish, Korean, Indonesian, and Malay. In 2011 LinkedIn went public in what was, at the time, the biggest Internet IPO since Google, raising more than $350 million and giving it a company valuation of $8.9 billion. Its stock has more than doubled since then, returning to all-time highs after dipping briefly in the second and third quarters of 2014. Viadeo's stock, on the other hand, has plummeted since its 2014 IPO. After opening at approximately €17 per share, the stock price is now down to just €6 in late 2014, and while analysts like the company's profitability to date, they are unsure of its prospects for growth given the strength of LinkedIn and more specialized local competitors such as Ushi in China.

LinkedIn also has a Chinese presence, and would, of course, also like to be the leading professional network in China. But company insiders note that doing business in China is quite different than elsewhere. First there is the question of whether a free-spirited social network can survive government censorship. For instance, both Facebook and Twitter have been banned in China. There is a strong popular sentiment in China to support Chinese companies. Also, the business culture is different in China: for instance, face-to-face meetings are preferred, and doing business with strangers is distrusted. In this sense, online social networks need to focus on facilitating offline connections, something that a site like MeetUp in the United States does quite well. Up until now, both Viadeo and LinkedIn have been allowed to operate in China. If Viadeo can make inroads with Tianji in China, that may represent the best path to dethroning LinkedIn in the professional social network market space.

I n this chapter, we discuss social networks, auctions, and portals. What do social networks, auctions, and portals have in common? They are all based on feelings of shared interest and self-identification—in short, a sense of community. Social networks and online communities explicitly attract people with shared affinities, such as ethnicity, gender, religion, and political views, or shared interests, such as hobbies, sports, and vacations. The auction site eBay started as a community of people interested in trading unwanted but functional items for which there was no ready commercial market. That community turned out to be huge—much larger than anyone expected. Portals also contain strong elements of community by providing access to community-fostering technologies such as e-mail, chat groups, bulletin boards, and discussion forums.

10.1 SOCIAL NETWORKS AND ONLINE COMMUNITIES

The Internet was designed originally as a communications medium to connect scientists in computer science departments around the continental United States. From the beginning, the Internet was intended, in part, as a community-building technology that would allow scientists to share data, knowledge, and opinions in a real-time online environment (see Chapter 2) (Hiltzik, 1999). The result of this early Internet was the first "virtual communities" (Rheingold, 1993). As the Internet grew in the late 1980s to include scientists from many disciplines and university campuses, thousands of virtual communities sprang up among small groups of scientists in very different disciplines that communicated regularly using Internet e-mail, listservs, and bulletin boards. The first articles and books on the new electronic communities began appearing in the mid- to late 1980s (Kiesler et al., 1984; Kiesler, 1986). One of the earliest online communities, The Well, was formed in San Francisco in 1985 by a small group of people who once shared an 1,800-acre commune in Tennessee. It is now a part of Salon.com, an online community and magazine. The Well (Whole Earth 'Lectronic Link) is an online community that now has thousands of members devoted to discussion, debate, advice, and help (Hafner, 1997; Rheingold, 1998). With the development of the Web in the early 1990s, millions of people began obtaining Internet accounts and Web e-mail, and the community-building impact of the Internet strengthened. By the late 1990s, the commercial value of online communities was recognized as a potential new business model (Hagel and Armstrong, 1997).

The early online communities involved a relatively small number of Web aficionados, and users with intense interests in technology, politics, literature, and ideas. The technology was largely limited to posting text messages on bulletin boards sponsored by the community, and one-to-one or one-to-many e-mails. In addition to The Well, early networks included GeoCities, a Web site hosting service based on neighborhoods. By 2002, however, the nature of online communities had begun to change. User-created Web sites called blogs became inexpensive and easy to set up without any technical expertise. Photo sites enabled convenient sharing of photos. Beginning in 2007, the growth of mobile devices like smartphones, tablet computers, digital cameras, and portable media devices enabled sharing of rich media such as photos, music, and videos. Suddenly there was a much wider audience for sharing interests and activities, and much more to share.

A new culture emerged as well. The broad democratization of the technology and its spread to the larger population meant that online social networks were no longer limited to a small group but instead broadened to include a much wider set of people and tastes, especially pre-teens, teens, and college students who were the fastest to adopt many of these new technologies. Entire families and friendship networks soon joined. The new social network culture is very personal and "me" centered, displaying photos and broadcasting personal activities, interests, hobbies, and relationships on social network profiles. In an online social network, the "news" is not something that happened somewhere else to other people; instead, the news is what happened to you today, and what's going on with your friends and colleagues. Today's social networks are as much a sociological phenomenon as they are a technology phenomenon.

Currently, social network participation is one of the most common usages of the Internet. Almost two-thirds of all Internet users—about 1.8 billion people—use social networks (eMarketer, Inc., 2014b). Facebook has over 1.3 billion active users of its Web site and a little over 1 billion mobile monthly users (Facebook, 2014). There is obviously an overlap between these two sets of users. The Google+ social network has over 540 million accounts worldwide, making it the second leading social network worldwide (Miller, 2014b). Other large social networks include LinkedIn (profiled in the opening case), Twitter, Pinterest, Instagram, and Tumblr.

Social network user numbers are notoriously inaccurate when assessing what exactly is an "active user." Both Facebook and Google+ have integrated their various services, forcing users to be "active" even if they did not intend to be active. Both networks routinely cause people to share personal information even if they did not intend to. People who "Like" a Web site, for instance, are considered "active users" by Facebook. In 2013, Google began automatically adding users of Gmail and its other services as members of Google+. The objective at both sites, as well as others, was to maximize the reported number of active users, and encourage potential users to sign up with the most popular service (Efrati, 2013). So while Google+, for instance, has a reported 540 million registered users, only a very small percentage (anywhere from 30 to 50 million, depending on which third-party measurement service data is being used) visit the Web site monthly, while around 40 million access the social network via its app. Facebook's user engagement and mindshare also trumps Google+'s by a long way—the average Facebook user spends over 6 hours on the Web site and nearly 7 hours using the Facebook app per month, compared to just 7 minutes on the Google+ Web site and 11 minutes on the Google+ app for the average Google+ user (Compete, Inc., 2014; Miller, 2014a). In September 2014, Google reversed its position on requiring new Gmail users to automatically sign up for Google+, leading analysts to wonder if Google is planning on de-emphasizing, or even abandoning, the social network in the future (Gaudin, 2014).

Worldwide, the social network phenomena is even stronger. Social networks are a top online destination in every country, accounting for the majority of time spent online, and reaching over 60% of active Internet users. Asia-Pacific has the largest social network audience (about 800 million), followed by Latin America (about 230 million), while North America has the highest penetration of social network usage among the general population (about 54%) (eMarketer, 2014b). Although Facebook dominates the global social network marketspace, in some countries, localized social networks are signficant, such as Orkut (owned by Google) in Brazil, Mixi and social messaging app LINE in Japan, Qzone, QQ, Sina Weibo, and RenRen in China, XING in Germany, Tuenti in Spain, and VK in Russia (eMarketer, 2014d). There is an online social network for you to join almost anywhere you go! Unfortunately, there's very little, if any, communication across social networks.

WHAT IS AN ONLINE SOCIAL NETWORK?

So exactly how do we define an online social network, and how is it any different from, say, an offline social network? Sociologists, who frequently criticize modern society for having destroyed traditional communities, unfortunately have not given us very good definitions of social networks and community. One study examined 94 different sociological definitions of community and found four areas of agreement. **Social networks** involve (a) a group of people, (b) shared social interaction, (c) common ties among members, and (d) people who share an area for some period of time (Hillery, 1955). This will be our working definition of a social network. Social networks do not necessarily have shared goals, purposes, or intentions. Indeed, social networks can be places where people just "hang out," share space, and communicate.

It's a short step to defining an **online social network** as an area online where people who share common ties can interact with one another. This definition is very close to that of Howard Rheingold's—one of The Well's early participants—who coined the term *virtual communities* as "cultural aggregations that emerge when enough people bump into each other often enough in cyberspace." It is a group of people who may or may not meet one another face to face, and who exchange words and ideas through the mediation of an online social meeting space. The Internet removes the geographic and time limitations of offline social networks. To be in an online network, you don't need to meet face to face, in a common room, at a common time.

THE GROWTH OF SOCIAL NETWORKS AND ONLINE COMMUNITIES

Figure 10.1 shows the top social network sites in the United States, which together account for well over 90% of the Internet's social network activity.

While social networks originally attracted mostly young Internet users, social networks today are not just about teens and college students, but a much larger social phenomenon. Almost 50% of Facebook's users are 35 and over. Likewise with Twitter. The service sees the most usage from 18- to 34-year olds, rather than younger teens (eMarketer, Inc., 2014d; 2014e).

social network
involves a group of people, shared social interaction, common ties among members, and people who share an area for some period of time

online social network
an area online, where people who share common ties can interact with one another

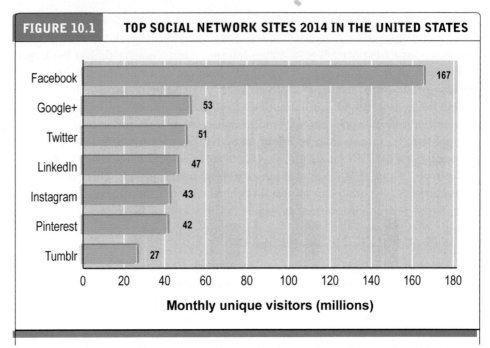

FIGURE 10.1   **TOP SOCIAL NETWORK SITES 2014 IN THE UNITED STATES**

Monthly unique visitors (millions)

Facebook is by far and away the dominant social network in the United States in terms of monthly unique visitors.

SOURCES: Based on data from Compete, Inc., 2014.

While Facebook and Twitter dominate the news, a new kind of social network is appearing, and growing much faster than Facebook with respect to unique visitors and subscribers. These new sites are attracting marketers and advertisers as well. For instance, Pinterest is a visually oriented site that allows users to curate their tastes and preferences, expressed in visual arts. You can think of Pinterest as a visual blog. Users post images to an online "pinboard." The images can come from any source. Users can also "re-pin" images they see on Pinterest. Pinterest's membership has skyrocketed since its launch and now has more than 40 million monthly unique visitors in the United States in July 2014. Instagram is another social network that focuses on images. A mobile app that enables a user to easily share images to social networks, Instagram was acquired by Facebook for $1 billion in 2012 and has over 200 million active users as of May 2014. Tumblr is an easy-to-use blogging site with tools for visual and text curating, sharing with others, and reblogging contents. Tumblr started in 2007, was acquired by Yahoo in 2013, and has around 30 million users in 2014.

Other social networks are not necessarily competing with Facebook, but adding to the social network mix and enlarging the total social network audience. **Table 10.1** describes some other popular social networks.

Contributing to the continued growth and commercial success of networks is the rapid adoption and intense use of mobile devices. About 75% of Facebook's users are multi-platform, using both mobile and desktop computers. Around 50% are desktop

TABLE 10.1	OTHER SOCIAL NETWORKS
SOCIAL NETWORK	DESCRIPTION
Myspace	Early leader in social networking was overtaken by Facebook; being reinvented as a music-oriented social network by pop star Justin Timberlake.
Meetup	Helps groups of people with shared interests plan events and meet offline.
Tagged	A network aimed at introducing members to one another through games, shared interests, friend suggestions, and browsing profiles.
MeetMe	Another social network aimed at meeting new people.
Polyvore	Topic-focused social network (fashion).
deviantART	Web site focused on art, sharing of images.
Vevo	Video and music sharing site.

only, and 41% are mobile only. Several of the largest newer social networks like Instagram, Snapchat, and Vine are almost entirely mobile (comScore, Inc., 2014b). In 2014, over 60% of Facebook's revenue comes from mobile users. See the *Insight on Technology* case, *The Appification of Facebook*, for more on the way apps are transforming Facebook.

A new crop of social networks launched since 2008 focus on messaging, either sending of text or photos. Snapchat (2009) lets users send photos to friends that self-extinguish in ten seconds. Slingshot (2014) lets Facebook users instant message photos and video to their Facebook friends. WhatsApp (2009; acquired by Facebook in 2014) is a messaging service that, for $1, lets users send text, photos, and videos to their friends' cellphones using the Internet and without having to pay telecommunications companies for use of cellphone SMS messaging services. It is unclear if these social networks based on messaging are economically viable.

It is easy to both overestimate and underestimate the significance of social networks. The top four social network sites in the United States (Facebook, Google+, Twitter, and LinkedIn) together have a total monthly unique U.S. audience of almost 320 million. In contrast, the top four portal/search engine sites (Google, Yahoo, MSN, and AOL) together have a total monthly unique U.S. audience of over 625 million. (Obviously, with 252 million people of all ages on the Internet in the United States, users are unique to more than one site.) Still, since 2008, Facebook has grown from a very small Internet audience of less than 20 million, to an Internet behemoth among the top three to four Web sites on the Internet.

The number of unique visitors is just one way to measure the influence of a site. Time on site is another important metric. The more time people spend on a site, called engagement, the more time to display ads and generate revenue. In this sense,

INSIGHT ON TECHNOLOGY

THE APPIFICATION OF FACEBOOK

When does an app get too big to manage, both for the developer and the user? This is a problem Facebook recently faced. Facebook's current app is itself a collection of apps and native functionalities developed separately over time, and mostly for the desktop. Now on the tiny smartphone screen, all this functionality gets crowded and hard for the user to navigate. Mark Zuckerberg, founder of Facebook, has decided it is time to split Facebook up into more manageable apps that are linked to the main Facebook app, but are not a part of it. In this new strategy, Facebook becomes an app platform, not just a social network, that contains a wide variety of linked capabilities, which may, or may not, be branded as Facebook apps. It's a risky strategy that has investors worried.

Zuckerberg first envisioned Facebook as a unitary experience, a place where all your social needs could be addressed. This approach fit with the branding strategy of Facebook connecting people all around the world. But Facebook is changing direction in 2014, and moving from having a single app that tries to be all things to all people, towards a collection of apps that are linked to the main Facebook app, but that stand alone and can compete with other apps. This will allow the main Facebook app to focus on what it does best—posting updates and displaying the Newsfeed and Timelines of users.

The first app to be split off is Messenger, previously a functionality within Facebook (and also a stand-alone app since 2011) used by hundreds of millions around the world. The Messenger function within Facebook's app will be turned off, and replaced by an icon. When users press the icon, the Messenger app will launch. The new Messenger app is faster and leaner than the original, and can be more easily customized by the user. As a result, messages can be delivered 20% faster than before. The new Messenger app will also contain a number of new features. For instance, the new Messenger can set up groups of contacts based on the user's cell phone contacts, create groups of contacts for different purposes (such as a party or trip), and deliver quick voice messages and photos. According to privacy advocates, the new Messenger will disregard users' privacy choices and will automatically attach the user's location to every message. The reason? Mobile advertisers will want to know where users are every time they message so marketers can send location-based ads.

To further the long-term strategy of developing Facebook as a collection of stand-alone apps, Facebook has created a new unit called Creative Labs, the purpose of which is to build apps, lots of apps. Equally important, Creative Labs will allow small, specialized groups of programmers to pursue new ideas, and to develop new apps without the distraction of maintaining the larger Facebook system, and integrating new apps into the existing Facebook interface. The idea is that apps that perform a single function can have a simpler interface, run faster, and can be more intuitive. Programmers working in Creative Labs say it gives them greater freedom to develop new products without worrying about Facebook's existing customers, and without shoehorning them into the already crowded main Facebook interface.

News that Facebook is adopting a new strategy, and developing apps that may not be branded as Facebook apps, has investors worried. They would prefer a simpler world where Facebook focuses on its knitting, its core customers, and its existing brand. Critics point to Paper, the first new app to come out of Creative Labs. Paper is an iPhone app that allows users to navigate Facebook's News Feed using touch gestures. So far in 2014, Paper has found little support from existing users.

Facebook's track record with apps is disappointing. Critics point out that the most innovative and popular products coming out of Facebook are those that it recently purchased, rather than any developed in-house. Facebook has launched a number of ho-hum apps that few people use. Home was an Android feature that locked your smartphone screen to your Facebook. Wasn't the Web, including smartphones, supposed to be a place where you could find new and different things? Instead, Home made the Internet and Web like a mirror of yourself and friends. Few adopted this app. Seeing the rapid growth of Instagram, the photo-based social site, Facebook developed a copycat app called Camera. Then it bought Instagram for in April 2012 for $1 billion before launching Camera. Instagram has since grown from 40 to 100 million users but does not yet generate any revenue. The rationale for the purchase was to attract young social network users who had gravitated to the site, rather than using Facebook's photo app, and of course to prevent it from becoming a rival. Facebook has continued to run Instagram as a separate, autonomous unit since its purchase.

In 2012, Facebook was rebuffed when it tried to buy SnapChat, the self-deleting messaging app, for $3 billion. Snapchat is one of several mobile messaging services that have become wildly popular, with twice as many messages sent over the mobile Internet than via traditional texts, according to Deloitte Research. These messages generate little revenue for anyone, and nearly all of the messaging industry's revenue is still driven by text messaging. In December 2012, Facebook cloned Snapchat with an app called Poke. However, Poke never took off. Instead, in 2014 Facebook bought the world's largest messaging service, WhatsApp, for a stunning $19 billion. Yes, that's right: $19 billion, possibly the largest acquisition in .com history! With 450 million users, and adding 1 million users a day, WhatsApp became the fastest growing app in history. It has about 55 employees. WhatsApp charges users $1 a year after their second year (the first year is free)

to send text messages to cell phone numbers using the Internet rather than the more expensive mobile cell networks like traditional SMS messaging. Facebook's own messaging app, Messenger, already was the second largest Internet messaging service with over 200 million users. For Facebook, the purchase of WhatsApp makes it the leader in Internet messaging, and permits it to attract a younger demographic, as well as eliminate its largest competitor in messaging. Like Instagram, WhatsApp will function as an autonomous unit within Facebook, with all the existing employees coming in as part of the deal. What's more, optimistic analysts argue that while the prices paid by Facebook for Instagram and WhatsApp cannot be justified by any current measures of revenue and earnings, they may be the foundation for a much larger social platform that includes new functionality like payments, retail sales, and media sales, which cannot be foreseen today.

Facebook does indeed face some serious long-term issues that Creative Labs, and recent purchases of Instagram and WhatsApp, are designed to solve. Its growth has flatlined in the United States and slowed markedly around the world. Engagement is falling with minutes spent on Facebook down 6% in the last year. Facebook demographics are going in the wrong direction: young teens and 18–24-year-olds are losing interest, joining niche social sites. A Piper Jaffray Teen Market Research report found 23% of teens claimed Facebook was their most important social network, while 26% chose Twitter. Creative Labs and the strategy of developing stand-alone apps that are linked to Facebook, but not integrated into its mobile app, may be a solution for these issues. But recent experience suggests that Facebook might be better off using its big checkbook to buy already market proven apps like Instagram and WhatsApp rather than trying to develop its own apps.

SOURCES: "Can Facebook Innovate? A Conversation With Mark Zuckerberg," by Farhad Manjo, *New York Times*, April 16, 2014; "The Future of Facebook May Not Say 'Facebook,'" by Farhad Manjoo, *New York Times*, April 16, 2014; "Facebook Requires Users to Install Separate Messaging App," by Vindu Goel, *New York Times*, April 15, 2014; "I Thought Facebook's WhatsApp Deal Was Crazy. Then I Did Some Math," by Dennis Berman, *Wall Street Journal*, February 24, 2014; "Facebook's Plot to Conquer Mobile: Shatter Itself Into Pieces," by Josh Constine, Techcrunch.com, January 29, 2014.

TABLE 10.2	TIME SPENT ON TOP WEB SITES
WEB SITE	**HOURS/MINUTES/MONTH PER VISITOR**
Facebook	6.68 hrs
Yahoo	2.53 hrs
AOL Media Network	2.15 hrs
Google	2.08 hrs
Tumblr	2.02 hrs
YouTube	1.95 hrs
MSN/WindowsLive/Bing	1.25 hrs
Twitter	39 minutes
Amazon	38 minutes
Pinterest	38 minutes
Wikipedia	24 minutes
LinkedIn	18 minutes
Ask Network	12 minutes
Google+	7 minutes
Myspace	5 minutes

SOURCES: Based on data from Miller, 2014b; Nielsen, 2013; eMarketer, Inc., 2013a.

Facebook is much more addictive and immersive than the other top sites on the Web. **Table 10.2** illustrates of the different levels of engagement with the top Web and social sites. In the United States, visitors spend almost seven hours a month on Facebook, a significantly higher amount of time compared to all other Web sites.

The amount of advertising revenue generated by sites is perhaps the ultimate metric for measuring the business potential of Web sites and brands. The top three search engine companies (Google, Yahoo, and Microsoft) are expected to generate about €42 billion in search and display advertising revenue worldwide in 2014 (eMarketer, Inc., 2014f). In contrast, social network sites in 2014 are expected to generate about €12.9 billion in advertising revenue worldwide (eMarketer, Inc., 2014g). Social network sites are the fastest growing form of Internet usage, but they are not yet as powerful as traditional search engines/portals in terms of ad dollars generated. A part of the problem is that subscribers do not go to social network sites to seek ads for relevant products, nor pay attention to the ads that are flashed before their eyes (see Chapters 6 and 7).

TURNING SOCIAL NETWORKS INTO BUSINESSES

While the early social networks had a difficult time raising capital and revenues, today's top social network sites are now learning how to monetize their huge audiences. Early social network sites relied on subscriptions, but today, most social networks rely on advertising or the investments of venture capitalists. Users of portals and search

| FIGURE 10.2 | WORLDWIDE AD SPENDING ON SOCIAL NETWORKS, 2014 |

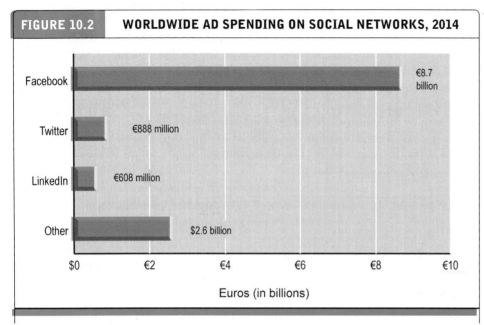

SOURCE: Based on data from eMarketer, 2014g.

engines have come to accept advertising as the preferred means of supporting Web experiences rather than paying for it. One important exception is LinkedIn, which offers free memberships to individual job seekers but charges professional recruiters and business firms for premium services. **Figure 10.2** shows the comparative amount of ad spending on various social networks.

[handwritten margin notes: average ad spend; users accept adverts rather than pay; LinkedIn except; challenges of mobile]

The rapid adoption of mobile devices has posed a challenge to Facebook and Google, two of the largest advertising firms on the Internet. Google dominated mobile ad revenues up until 2013 because its search engine and Google Maps were among the most popular apps. Facebook quickly developed its mobile app and within the space of two years has been able to capture a significant part of the mobile ad market, using its mobile News Feed to provide users a continual stream of ads.

Social networks have had a profound impact on how businesses operate, communicate, and serve their customers. The most visible business firm use of social networks is as a marketing and branding tool. The most popular social network tool for large corporate businesses is LinkedIn, with 97% of the Fortune 500 having a LinkedIn company page. Twitter is the second most popular, with 83% having corporate Twitter accounts, including 7 of the top 10 companies. About 80% have a Facebook page. Pinterest has the fastest growth rate among the Fortune 500, increasing from 9% in 2013 to 36% in 2014 (Nanji, 2014). A less visible marketing use of networks is as a powerful listening tool that has strengthened the role of customers and customer feedback systems inside a business. The software drink industry is a good example. Coca-Cola has built a fan base of 88 million on Facebook. Pepsi has 33 million Likes, Dr. Pepper 16 million, and Mountain Dew about 8.8 million.

Social networks are where corporate brands and reputations are formed, and firms today take very seriously the topic of "online reputation," as evidenced by social network posts, commentary, chat sessions, and Likes. In this sense, social network sites become an extension of corporate customer relationship management systems and extend existing market research programs. Beyond branding, social network sites are being used increasingly as advertising platforms to contact a somewhat younger audience than Web sites and e-mail, and as customers increasingly shift their eyeballs to social networks. Rosetta Stone, for instance, uses its Facebook page to display videos of its learning technology, encourage discussions and reviews, and post changes in its learning tools. Yet the business use of social networks does not always go well. The *Insight on Society* case, *The Dark Side of Social Networks*, discusses some of the risks associated with social networks.

TYPES OF SOCIAL NETWORKS AND THEIR BUSINESS MODELS

There are many types and many ways of classifying social networks and online communities. While the most popular general social networks have adopted an advertising model, other kinds of networks have different revenue sources. Social networks have different types of sponsors and different kinds of members. For instance, some are created by firms such as IBM for the exclusive use of their sales force or other employees (intra-firm communities or B2E [business-to-employee] communities); others are built for suppliers and resellers (inter-organizational or B2B communities); and others are built by dedicated individuals for other similar persons with shared interests (P2P [people-to-people] communities). In this chapter, we will discuss B2C communities for the most part, although we also discuss briefly P2P communities of practice.

Table 10.3 describes in greater detail the five generic types of social networks and online communities: general, practice, interest, affinity, and sponsored. Each type of

TABLE 10.3	TYPES OF SOCIAL NETWORKS AND ONLINE COMMUNITIES
TYPE OF SOCIAL NETWORK / COMMUNITY	DESCRIPTION
General	Online social gathering place to meet and socialize with friends, share content, schedules, and interests. Examples: Facebook, Pinterest, Tumblr, and Twitter.
Practice	Social network of professionals and practitioners, creators of artifacts such as computer code or music. Examples: Just Plain Folks (musicians' community), LinkedIn (business), and Doximity (physicians and health care professionals).
Interest	Community built around a common interest, such as games, sports, music, stock markets, politics, health, finance, foreign affairs, or lifestyle. Examples: E-democracy.org (political discussion group) and PredictWallStreet (stock market site).
Affinity	Community of members who self-identify with a demographic or geographic category, such as women, African Americans, or Arab Americans. Examples: BlackPlanet (African American community and social network site) and iVillage (focusing on women).
Sponsored	Network created by commercial, government, and nonprofit organizations for a variety of purposes. Examples: Nike, IBM, Cisco, and political candidates.

INSIGHT ON SOCIETY

THE DARK SIDE OF SOCIAL NETWORKS

ChapStick thought it had a great marketing idea when it decided to launch a new Facebook ad—a mildly provocative picture of a young woman on her disheveled sofa—derriere in the air—rummaging behind the couch. The ad proclaimed: WHERE DO LOST CHAPSTICKS GO? The subtitle—BE HEARD AT FACEBOOK.com/CHAPSTICK—invited user comment. Little did Chapstick realize that it was about to endure a social network advertising fiasco.

First, a blogger cited the ad in a post about the pervasiveness of sexist advertising. When she posted to ChapStick's Facebook page, her comment was deleted. Other Facebook posters followed suit. Their comments were also deleted. It wasn't long before a stream of comments mocking the "Be Heard" subtitle ensued.

ChapStick treated Facebook as simply another broadcast channel and lacked advertising policies specific to social networks. But social networks are interactive. When your customers have an immediate and visible "voice," you cannot simply stay silent, delete dissent, and, as ChapStick did, hope the whole thing will just go away on its own. While negative posts that can be clearly identified as trolling can either be ignored or quickly deleted, criticisms that have merit must be responded to with candor, admission of guilt when appropriate, and by outlining the steps that will be taken to remedy the problem.

ChapStick had an opportunity to begin a conversation with its customers that would have demonstrated its cognizance of and sensitivity to sexist advertising. Rather than a public relations nightmare, it could have created a public relations coup, stamping itself as a company that cares about its most loyal fans.

Finally, when it could no longer delete the negative posts quickly enough, ChapStick pulled the ad and responded. However, not only was its response anemic, it did not even fully own up to the mass deletions it had perpetrated. It offered regret if fans "felt" this had happened and essentially blamed posters for being uncivil or posting "menacing" comments.

When ChapStick finally tried to assure its fans that it valued them and was listening, it was hardly credible. In short, ChapStick presented us with a textbook case in how not to conduct social network advertising!

Attempts to control social media response on Twitter can be equally misguided. MasterCard's PR firm, House PR, was in charge of organizing a social media campaign to promote the 2014 Brit Awards event for British music. House demanded that journalists agree to very specific terms to obtain accreditation for the event, including guarantees from the journalists to use both official and personal accounts to live tweet the awards, to provide links to specific videos determined by House, and to use the #PricelessSurprises hashtag in these tweets. Journalists chafed at the attempts to micromanage their social media participation, with many tweeting their outrage at the terms. Forcing social media participants to respond in a predetermined way might work sometimes, but when it doesn't, as it didn't for MasterCard, it can be embarrassing and damaging to the company's brand.

Fast food giant McDonald's also confronted the dark side of social networks when it began a public relations campaign on Twitter. Using the hashtag #meetthefarmers, it inserted promotional tweets into the streams of Twitter users and paid for premium search engine results. The Supplier

(continued)

Stories campaign encouraged users to share stories about the farmers who sold their meat and produce to McDonald's. All was proceeding nicely until McDonald's replaced the hashtag with #McDStories. Now encouraging users to share their general consumer stories, McDonald's almost immediately lost control of its advertising campaign. The Twittersphere exploded with tweets comparing McDonald's fare to dog food and diarrhea, sprinkled with barbs about Type II diabetes, obesity, and food poisoning. The best that can be said for McDonald's is that it was prepared to pull the plug on the campaign should anything go amiss. Within two hours, the promotion was halted.

The ChapStick, MasterCard, and McDonald's fiascos are instructive. ChapStick had no policies in place for how to respond to an ad campaign gone wrong. MasterCard attempted to exert corporate control over a medium that users value for its ability to provide honest, unfiltered individual feedback. McDonald's failed to fully recognize the polarizing nature of its product, making soliciting general comments a risky proposition. Companies with controversial products need to tread carefully, and companies need to be prepared to handle negative comments appropriately and take responsibility for mistakes.

Not all companies are learning from the experience of other firms. In 2013, supermarket chain Tesco suffered a public relations nightmare when it unwittingly tweeted from its corporate account, "It's sleepy time so we're off to hit the hay!" shortly after it was discovered that horse meat had been found in its burgers labeled as beef. Allergy medicine Benadryl launched an initiative to crowdsource pollen count maps in users' neighborhoods; instead, the maps were defaced with vulgar language and images. Chrysler's social media account tweeted, "I find it ironic that Detroit is known as the #motorcity and yet no one here knows how to (expletive) drive"—clearly a case of an employee tweeting from the wrong account.

But in 2014, KFC set a good example when the news broke that a 3-year-old girl from Mississippi who had been mauled by her grandfather's dogs had subsequently been asked to leave a local KFC because she reportedly was scaring the other patrons. The visit to the restaurant had been a special treat for the girl from her family after a doctor's visit. When the news hit social media, KFC was caught in a firestorm of enraged customers. The company took the next several days to respond to as many individual comments as it could, posted a personal apology to the girl's Facebook page, and pledged $30,000 towards her medical bills.

But marketing is not the only social media hazard. For employees, privacy protection for Facebook posts is still being determined in the courts. For example, Danielle Mailhoit was the manager of a Home Depot store in Burbank, California. After she was fired, she filed suit claiming gender and disability discrimination due to her vertigo. The defense attorney filed a broad request for all of Mailhoit's social media activity. In September 2012, a federal judge ruled this request overly broad and limited discovery to only communications between the plaintiff and current or former Home Depot employees. Stating that they were unlikely to be relevant unless they were directly related to the lawsuit or her former employment, she also denied Home Depot's request for photos.

Employers must be careful with personal information gleaned from social networking sites. If it can be proven that membership in a protected group was discovered during the hiring process and used to reject a candidate or later used to terminate an employee, a claim can be filed under one of the Federal Equal Employment Opportunity (EEO) laws. These include Title VII of the Civil Rights Act of 1964, the Age Discrimination in Employment Act of 1967 (ADEA), Title I and Title V of the Americans with Disabilities Act of 1990 (ADA), and Title II of the Genetic Information

Nondiscrimination Act of 2008 (GINA), which prohibits employment discrimination based on genetic information about an applicant, employee, or former employee. GINA's regulations provide a distinction between whether genetic information is acquired purposefully or inadvertently. Inadvertent acquisition includes acquisition through social media sites, equating it to accidentally overhearing a conversation at work.

However, data on a social media site protected by privacy controls should not be able to be "inadvertently" acquired. The Stored Communications Act (SCA) covers privacy protection for e-mail and digital communications. The latest court rulings on its application to social network communications have held that Facebook wall postings and other social media comments are protected as long as they have not been made public.

Facebook, to protect its business model, is speaking out against recent hiring practices that have come to its attention—and threatening legal action. According to both Facebook and the American Civil Liberties Union (ACLU), some companies have been asking new hires either to friend the hiring manager or to submit their password. Facebook's Privacy Page condemns this practice, stating that it violates both individual users' and their friends' expectations of privacy, jeopardizes security, and could reveal a user's membership in a protected group.

Legislators in a growing number of states have decided to be proactive. In May 2012, a bill prohibiting employers from asking prospective employees for their social media user names and passwords unanimously passed the California State Assembly and was on its way to the Senate. In 2013, New Jersey became the 12th state to restrict employer access to employee social media accounts, although New Jersey–based employers are still granted some rights in the cases of companies dealing with public safety and workplace investigations. In 2014, Rhode Island passed its own legislation making it illegal for an employer or school to demand login information for social media accounts for prospective employees or students, and other states are expected to follow suit, such as Louisiana and Wisconsin.

Carefully crafted policies can help companies to avoid the dark side of social networking. Advertising and hiring are but two of the areas that must be monitored. The Human Resources department must also develop policies regarding employee use of social networks. Employee education programs must be implemented to apprise employees of infractions that can be grounds for disciplinary action. IT departments must develop stringent policies to protect proprietary data and defend company networks from cyberscams. Social networking is an exciting new tool, but one that requires safeguards.

SOURCES: "RI Passes Social Media Privacy Law," by Bill Tomison, Wpri.com, July 3, 2014; "Facebook's Facing a Losing Battle to Protect Users' Privacy," by Lisa Vaas, Nakedsecurity.sophos.com, June 30, 2014; "KFC Shows How to Handle a Social Media Disaster," by Mary Elizabeth Williams, Salon.com, June 17, 2014; "19 Horrific Social Media Fails from the First Half of 2014," by Christopher Ratcliff, Econsultancy.com, June 16, 2014; "States Continue Banning Employer Access to Social Media," by Brian Heaton, Govtech.com, May 21, 2014; "Brit Awards Sponsors in Priceless Twitter PR Fail," Theguardian.com, February 19, 2014; "NJ Passes a Business-Friendly Workplace Social Media Privacy Law," by Eric B. Meyer, Theemployerhandbook.com, September 3, 2013; "Top Social Media Mishaps of 2013," Blueclawsearch.co.uk, August 24, 2013; "19 Companies That Made Huge Social Media Fails," by Arielle Calderon, Buzzfeed.com, May 22, 2013; "Judge: Home Depot Went Too Far in Seeking Worker's Social Posts," by Declan McCullagh, News.cnet.com, September 17, 2012; "California May Ban Employers from Asking for Facebook Passwords," by Jessica Guynn, *Los Angeles Times,* May 11, 2012; "Facebook Speaks Out Against Employers Asking for Passwords," by Doug Gross, Cnn.com, March 23, 2012; "Why McDonald's Should Have Known Better," by Shelley DuBois, Cnnmoney. com, January 31, 2012; "McDonald's Social Media Director Explains Twitter Fiasco," by Jeff John Roberts, Paidcontent.org, January 24, 2012; "Lessons from the ChapStick Social Media Fiasco," by Ted Rubin, Tedrubin.com, December 3, 2011; "ChapStick Gets Itself in a Social Media Death Spiral: A Brand's Silent War Against Its Facebook Fans," by Tim Nudd, *Adweek,* October 26, 2011; "The Dangers of Using Social Media Data in Hiring," by Gregg Skall, *Radio Business Report,* June 6, 2011; "Stored Communications Act Protects Facebook and MySpace Users' Private Communication," by Kathryn Freund, Jolt. law.harvard.edu, June 11, 2010.

community can have a commercial intent or commercial consequence. We use this schema to explore the business models of commercial communities.

general communities

offer members opportunities to interact with a general audience organized into general topics

General communities offer members opportunities to interact with a general audience organized into general topics. Within the topics, members can find hundreds of specific discussion groups attended by thousands of like-minded members who share an interest in that topic. The purpose of the general community is to attract enough members to populate a wide range of topics and discussion groups. The business model of general communities is typically advertising supported by selling ad space on pages and videos.

practice networks

offer members focused discussion groups, help, information, and knowledge relating to an area of shared practice

Practice networks offer members focused discussion groups, help, information, and knowledge relating to an area of shared practice. For instance, Linux.org is a nonprofit community for the open source movement, a worldwide global effort involving thousands of programmers who develop computer code for the Linux operating system and share the results freely with all. Other online communities involve artists, educators, art dealers, photographers, and nurses. Practice networks can be either profit-based or nonprofit, and support themselves by advertising or user donations.

interest-based social networks

offer members focused discussion groups based on a shared interest in some specific topic

Interest-based social networks offer members focused discussion groups based on a shared interest in some specific subject, such as business careers, boats, horses, health, skiing, and thousands of other topics. Because the audience for interest communities is necessarily much smaller and more targeted, these communities have usually relied on advertising and tenancy/sponsorship deals. Sites such as Fool.com, Military.com, Sailing Anarchy, and Chronicle Forums all are examples of Web sites that attract people who share a common pursuit. Job markets and forums such as LinkedIn can be considered interest-based social networks as well.

affinity communities

offer members focused discussions and interaction with other people who share the same affinity

Affinity communities offer members focused discussions and interaction with other people who share the same affinity. "Affinity" refers to self- and group identification. For instance, people can self-identify themselves on the basis of religion, ethnicity, gender, sexual orientation, political beliefs, geographical location, and hundreds of other categories. For instance, iVillage, Oxygen, and NaturallyCurly are affinity sites designed to attract women. These sites offer women discussion and services that focus on topics such as babies, beauty, books, diet and fitness, entertainment, health, and home and garden. These sites are supported by advertising along with revenues from sales of products.

sponsored communities

online communities created for the purpose of pursuing organizational (and often commercial) goals

Sponsored communities are online communities created by government, nonprofit, or for-profit organizations for the purpose of pursuing organizational goals. These goals can be diverse, from increasing the information available to citizens; for instance, a local county government site such as Westchestergov.com, the Web site for Westchester County (New York) government; to an online auction site such as eBay; to a product site such as Tide.com, which is sponsored by an offline branded product company (Procter & Gamble). Cisco, IBM, HP, and hundreds of other companies have developed their internal corporate social networks as a way of sharing knowledge.

SOCIAL NETWORK FEATURES AND TECHNOLOGIES

Social networks have developed software applications that allow users to engage in a number of activities. Not all sites have the same features, but there is an emerging

TABLE 10.4	SOCIAL NETWORK FEATURES AND TECHNOLOGIES
FEATURE	**DESCRIPTION**
Profiles	User-created Web pages that describe themselves on a variety of dimensions
Friends network	Ability to create a linked group of friends
Network discovery	Ability to find other networks and find new groups and friends
Favorites	Ability to communicate favorite sites, bookmarks, content, and destinations
Games, widgets, and apps	Apps and games on the site, such as those offered by Facebook
E-mail	Ability to send e-mail within the social network site to friends
Storage	Storage space for network members' content
Instant messaging	Immediate one-to-one contact with friends through the community facility
Message boards	Posting of messages to groups of friends and other groups' members
Online polling	Polling of member opinion
Chat	Online immediate group discussion; Internet relay chat (IRC)
Discussion groups	Discussion groups and forums organized by topic
Experts online	Certified experts in selected areas respond to queries
Membership management tools	Ability of site managers to edit content, and dialog; remove objectionable material; protect security and privacy

feature set among the larger communities. Some of these software tools are built into the site, while others can be added by users to their profile pages as widgets (described in earlier chapters). **Table 10.4** describes several social network functionalities.

THE FUTURE OF SOCIAL NETWORKS   *Conclusion*

Social networking in 2014 is one of the most popular online activities. Will it stay that way or grow even more popular? Today's social network scene is highly concentrated with the top site, Facebook, attracting over 85% of the social network audience. However, Facebook's growth has slowed to only about 2%–3% a year, while other social networks, such as Twitter, LinkedIn, Instagram, Pinterest, and Tumblr, are still growing at double-digit rates. There has also been an explosion of social networks that are more focused on specific interests that tie members together, not some diffuse sense of "friendship." It may be more fun to network on a site dedicated to your central interests.

Many Facebook users also report "network fatigue" caused by spending too much time keeping up with their close and distant friends on many social networks. Fatigue grows as users increase the number of social networks to which they belong (Rosenblum, 2011). One result is avoiding Facebook (and other sites) or spending less and less time on the sites. A Pew survey found 42% of young users are spending less time on Facebook, in large part because they are bored. Over 60% of users said they

Bored!

had dropped using Facebook at one time or another; 20% of online adults used the site once, but no longer use it. The Facebook audience is highly fluid (Pew Internet, 2013b). The fears that many users have about the privacy of their posts and content is another factor in people either not joining Facebook, or pulling back from engagement. A new social network, Ello, designed to appeal to disgruntled Facebook users, made a splash when it launched a public beta in September 2014. Ello has positioned itself as an ad-free alternative that promises never to sell its users' information to third parties (DeMers, 2014).

The financial future of social networks hinges on them becoming successful advertising and sales platforms. But social networks are not yet proven advertising platforms that drive sales. The relationship between Likes and sales is not clear yet. Response rates to display ads on Facebook are still lower than on portal sites like Yahoo or search ads like Google. In part this reflects the sentiment of users who go onto social sites without the intention of purchasing anything.

10.2   ONLINE AUCTIONS

consumer-to-consumer (C2C) auctions
auction house acts as an intermediary market maker, providing a forum where consumers can discover prices and trade

Auctions are used throughout the e-commerce landscape. The most widely known auctions are **consumer-to-consumer (C2C) auctions**, in which the auction house is simply an intermediary market maker, providing a forum where consumers—buyers and sellers—can discover prices and trade. The market leader in C2C auctions is eBay, which, as of June 2014, had around 150 million active users and over 550 million items listed on any given day within thousands of different categories. In 2013, eBay had about $6.8 billion in net revenues from its Marketplaces segment, a 12% increase from 2012, and the total worth of goods sold or auctioned was around $83 billion (Gross Merchandise Value) (eBay, 2014). eBay is expanding rapidly in emerging markets and predicts that 25% of its users will be in developing countries by the end of 2015. eBay is further discussed in the case study at the end of this chapter. In the United States alone, there are several hundred auction sites, some specializing in unique collectible products such as stamps and coins, others adopting a more generalist approach in which almost any good can be found for sale.

business-to-consumer (B2C) auctions
business sells goods it owns, or controls, using various dynamic pricing models

Less well known are **business-to-consumer (B2C) auctions**, where a business owns or controls assets and uses dynamic pricing to establish the price. Increasingly, online retail sites, such as Sam's Club, are adding auctions to their sites. Auctions also constitute a significant part of B2B e-commerce in 2014, and more than a third of procurement officers use auctions to procure goods.

Some leading online auction sites are listed in **Table 10.5**. Auctions are not limited to goods and services. They can also be used to allocate resources, and bundles of resources, among any group of bidders. For instance, if you wanted to establish an optimal schedule for assigned tasks in an office among a group of clerical workers, an auction in which workers bid for assignments would come close to producing a nearly optimal solution in a short amount of time (Parkes and Ungar, 2000). In short, auctions—like all markets—are ways of allocating resources among independent agents (bidders).

BENEFITS AND COSTS OF AUCTIONS

The Internet is primarily responsible for the resurgence in auctions. The Internet provides a global environment and very low fixed and operational costs for the aggregation of huge buyer audiences, composed of millions of consumers worldwide, who can use a universally available technology (Internet browsers) to shop for goods.

Benefits of Auctions

Aside from the sheer game-like fun of participating in auctions, consumers, merchants, and society as a whole derive a number of economic benefits from participating in Internet auctions. These benefits include:

- **Liquidity:** Sellers can find willing buyers, and buyers can find sellers. Sellers and buyers can be located anywhere around the globe. Just as important, buyers and sellers can find a global market for rare items that would not have existed before the Internet.

- **Price discovery:** Buyers and sellers can quickly and efficiently develop prices for items that are difficult to assess, where the price depends on demand and supply, and where the product is rare.

TABLE 10.5	LEADING ONLINE AUCTION SITES
GENERAL	
eBay	The world market leader in auctions: 59 million visitors a month and hundreds of millions of products.
eBid	In business since 1998. Operates in 23 countries, including the United States. Currently, one of the top competitors to eBay. Offers much lower fees.
uBid	Marketplace for excess inventory from pre-approved merchants.
OnlineAuction	Allows sellers to list for a low monthly fee, without a per-item listing or additional fees when the item sells.
SPECIALIZED	
Racersauction	Specialized site for automobile racing parts.
Philatelicphantasies	Stamp site for professionals, monthly online stamp auction.
Stacksbowers	America's largest fully automated auction company of certified coins including ancient gold, silver, and copper coins. Also offers sports cards.
Bid4Assets	Liquidation of distressed real estate assets from government and the public sector, corporations, restructurings, and bankruptcies.
Oldandsold	Online auction service specializing in quality antiques. Dealers pay a 3% commission on merchandise sold.
B2C AUCTIONS	
Auctions.samsclub	Merchandise from Sam's Club in a variety of categories.
Shopgoodwill	Goodwill's online auction site. Offers a wide variety of collectibles, books, and antiques chosen from the goods donated to Goodwill.

- **Price transparency:** Public Internet auctions allow everyone in the world to see the asking and bidding prices for items.
- **Market efficiency:** Auctions can, and often do, lead to reduced prices, and hence reduced profits for merchants, leading to an increase in consumer welfare—one measure of market efficiency.
- **Lower transaction costs:** Online auctions can lower the cost of selling and purchasing products, benefiting both merchants and consumers. Like other Internet markets, such as retail markets, Internet auctions have very low (but not zero) transaction costs.
- **Consumer aggregation:** Sellers benefit from large auction sites' ability to aggregate a large number of consumers who are motivated to purchase something in one marketspace.
- **Network effects:** The larger an auction site becomes in terms of visitors and products for sale, the more valuable it becomes as a marketplace for everyone by providing liquidity and several other benefits listed previously, such as lower transaction costs, higher efficiency, and better price transparency.

Risks and Costs of Auctions

There are a number of risks and costs involved in participating in auctions. In some cases, auction markets can fail—like all markets at times. (We describe auction market failure in more detail later.) Some of the more important risks and costs to keep in mind are:

- **Delayed consumption costs:** Internet auctions can go on for days, and shipping will take additional time.
- **Monitoring costs:** Participation in auctions requires your time to monitor bidding.
- **Equipment costs:** Internet auctions require you to purchase a computer system and pay for Internet access.
- **Trust risks:** Online auctions are a significant source of Internet fraud. Using auctions increases the risk of experiencing a loss.
- **Fulfillment costs:** Typically, the buyer pays fulfillment costs of packing, shipping, and insurance, whereas at a physical store these costs are included in the retail price.

Auction sites such as eBay have taken a number of steps to reduce consumer participation costs and trust risk. For instance, auction sites attempt to solve the trust problem by providing a rating system in which previous customers rate sellers based on their overall experience with the merchant. Although helpful, this solution does not always work. Auction fraud is a leading source of e-commerce complaints to federal law enforcement officials. Another partial solution to high monitoring costs is, ironically, fixed pricing. At eBay, consumers can reduce the cost of monitoring and waiting for auctions to end by simply clicking on the Buy It Now! button and paying a premium price. The difference between the Buy It Now price and the auction price is the cost of monitoring.

Nevertheless, given the costs of participating in online auctions, the generally lower cost of goods on Internet auctions is in part a compensation for the other additional costs consumers experience. On the other hand, consumers experience lower search costs and transaction costs because there usually are no intermediaries (unless, of course, the seller is an online business operating on an auction site, in which case there is a middleman cost), and usually there are no local or state taxes.

Merchants face considerable risks and costs as well. At auctions, merchants may end up selling goods for prices far below what they might have achieved in conventional markets. Merchants also face risks of nonpayment, false bidding, bid rigging, monitoring, transaction fees charged by the auction site, credit card transaction processing fees, and the administration costs of entering price and product information.

AUCTIONS AS AN E-COMMERCE BUSINESS MODEL

Online auctions have been among the most successful business models in retail and B2B commerce. eBay, the Internet's most lucrative auction site, has been profitable nearly since its inception. The strategy for eBay has been to make money off every stage in the auction cycle. eBay earns revenue from auctions in several ways: transaction fees based on the amount of the sale, listing fees for display of goods, financial service fees from payment systems such as PayPal, and advertising or placement fees where sellers pay extra for special services such as particular display or listing services.

However, it is on the cost side that online auctions have extraordinary advantages over ordinary retail or catalog sites. Auction sites carry no inventory and do not perform any fulfillment activities—they need no warehouses, shipping, or logistical facilities. Sellers and consumers provide these services and bear these costs. In this sense, online auctions are an ideal digital business because they involve simply the transfer of information.

Even though eBay has been extraordinarily successful, the success of online auctions is qualified by the fact that the marketplace for online auctions is highly concentrated. eBay dominates the online auction market, followed by eBid and uBid. Many of the smaller auction sites are not profitable because they lack sufficient sellers and buyers to achieve liquidity. In auctions, network effects are highly influential, and the tendency is for one or two very large auction sites to dominate, with hundreds of smaller specialty auction sites (sites that sell specialized goods such as stamps) being barely profitable.

TYPES AND EXAMPLES OF AUCTIONS

The primary types of auctions found on the Internet are English auctions, Dutch Internet auctions, Name Your Own Price auctions, and so-called penny auctions.

The **English auction** is the easiest to understand and the most common form of auction on eBay. Typically, there is a single item up for sale from a single seller. There is a time limit when the auction ends, a reserve price below which the seller will not sell (usually secret), and a minimum incremental bid set. Multiple buyers bid against one another until the auction time limit is reached. The highest bidder wins the item (if the reserve price of the seller has been met or exceeded). English auctions are considered to be seller-biased because multiple buyers compete against one another—usually anonymously.

The **Dutch Internet auction** format is perfect for sellers that have many identical items to sell. Sellers start by listing a minimum price, or a starting bid for one item, and

English auction
most common form of auction; the highest bidder wins

Dutch Internet auction
public ascending price, multiple unit auction. Final price is lowest successful bid, which sets price for all higher bidders

the number of items for sale. Bidders specify both a bid price and the quantity they want to buy. The uniform price reigns. Winning bidders pay the same price per item, which is the lowest successful bid. This market clearing price can be less than some bids. If there are more buyers than items, the earliest successful bids get the goods. In general, high bidders get the quantity they want at the lowest successful price, whereas low successful bidders might not get the quantity they want (but they will get something).

Name Your Own Price auction

auction where users specify what they are willing to pay for goods or services

The **Name Your Own Price auction** was pioneered by Priceline, and is the second most-popular auction format on the Web. Although Priceline also acts as an intermediary, buying blocks of airline tickets, hotel rooms, and vacation packages at a discount and selling them at a reduced retail price or matching its inventory to bidders, it is best known for its Name Your Own Price auctions, where users specify what they are willing to pay for goods or services, and multiple providers bid for their business. Prices do not descend and are fixed: the initial consumer offer is a commitment to purchase at that price. In 2014, Priceline had more than $6.8 billion in revenues, and in 2013, attracts around 15 million unique visitors a month. It is one of the top-ranked travel sites in the United States.

But how can Priceline offer such steep discounts off prices for services provided by major brand-name providers? There are several answers. First, Priceline "shields the brand" by not publicizing the prices at which major brands sell. This reduces conflict with traditional channels, including direct sales. Second, the services being sold are perishable: if a Priceline customer did not pay something for the empty airline seat, rental car, or hotel room, sellers would not receive any revenue. Hence, sellers are highly motivated to at least cover the costs of their services by selling in a spot market at very low prices. The strategy for sellers is to sell as much as possible through more profitable channels and then unload excess capacity on spot markets such as Priceline. This works to the advantage of consumers, sellers, and Priceline, which charges a transaction fee to sellers.

penny (bidding fee) auction

bidder must pay a non-refundable fee to purchase bids

So-called penny auctions are really anything but. To participate in a **penny auction** (also known as a **bidding fee auction**), you typically must pay the penny auction site for bids ahead of time, typically 50 cents to $1 dollar, usually in packs costing $25-$50. Once you have purchased the bids, you can use them to bid on items listed by the penny auction site (unlike traditional auctions, items are owned by the site, not third parties). Items typically start at or near $0 and each bid raises the price by a fixed amount, usually just a penny. Auctions are timed, and when the time runs out, the last and highest bidder wins the item. Although the price of the item itself may not be that high, the successful bidder will typically have spent much more than that. Unlike a traditional auction, it costs money to bid and that money is gone even if the bidder does not win the auction. The bidder's cumulative cost of bidding must be added to the final price of a successful bid to determine the true cost of the item. The Federal Trade Commission has issued an alert about penny auctions, warning that bidders may find that they spend far more than they intended (Consumer Reports.org, 2013). Examples of penny auction sites include QuiBids, Beezid, and HappyBidDay.

WHEN TO USE AUCTIONS (AND FOR WHAT) IN BUSINESS

There are many different situations in which auctions are an appropriate channel for businesses to consider. For much of this chapter, we have looked at auctions from a

TABLE 10.6	**FACTORS TO CONSIDER WHEN CHOOSING AUCTIONS**
CONSIDERATIONS	DESCRIPTION
Type of product	Rare, unique, commodity, perishable
Stage of product life cycle	Early, mature, late
Channel-management issues	Conflict with retail distributors; differentiation
Type of auction	Seller vs. buyer bias
Initial pricing	Low vs. high
Bid increment amounts	Low vs. high
Auction length	Short vs. long
Number of items	Single vs. multiple
Price-allocation rule	Uniform vs. discriminatory
Information sharing	Closed vs. open bidding

consumer point of view. The objective of consumers is to receive the greatest value for the lowest cost. Now, switch your perspective to that of a business. Remember that the objective of businesses using auctions is to maximize their revenue (their share of consumer surplus) by finding the true market value of products and services, a market value that hopefully is higher in the auction channel than in fixed-price channels. **Table 10.6** provides an overview of factors to consider.

The factors are described as follows:

- **Type of product:** Online auctions are most commonly used for rare and unique products for which prices are difficult to discover, and there may have been no market for the goods. However, Priceline has succeeded in developing auctions for perishable commodities (such as airline seats) for which retail prices have already been established, and some B2B auctions involve commodities such as steel (often sold at distress prices). New clothing items, new digital cameras, and new computers are generally not sold at auction because their prices are easy to discover, catalog prices are high, sustainable, and profitable, they are not perishable, and there exists an efficient market channel in the form of retail stores (online and offline).

- **Product life cycle:** For the most part, businesses have traditionally used auctions for goods at the end of their product life cycle and for products where auctions yield a higher price than fixed-price liquidation sales. However, products at the beginning of their life cycle are increasingly being sold at auction. Early releases of music, books, videos, games, and digital appliances can be sold to highly motivated early adopters who want to be the first in their neighborhood with new products. Online sales of event tickets from music concerts to sports events now account for upwards of 25% of all event ticket sales in the United States.

- **Channel management:** Established retailers such as JCPenney and Walmart, and manufacturers in general, must be careful not to allow their auction activity to interfere with their existing profitable channels. For this reason, items found on established retail-site auctions tend to be late in their product life cycle or have quantity purchase requirements.

- **Type of auction:** Sellers obviously should choose auctions where there are many buyers and only a few, or even one, seller. English ascending-price auctions such as those at eBay are best for sellers because as the number of bidders increases, the price tends to move higher.

- **Initial pricing:** Research suggests that auction items should start out with low initial bid prices in order to encourage more bidders to bid (see "Bid increments" below). The lower the price, the larger the number of bidders will appear. The larger the number of bidders, the higher the prices move.

- **Bid increments:** It is generally safest to keep bid increments low so as to increase the number of bidders and the frequency of their bids. If bidders can be convinced that, for just a few more dollars, they can win the auction, then they will tend to make the higher bid and forget about the total amount they are bidding.

- **Auction length:** In general, the longer auctions are scheduled, the larger the number of bidders and the higher the prices can go. However, once the new bid arrival rate drops off and approaches zero, bid prices stabilize. Most eBay auctions are scheduled for seven days.

- **Number of items:** When a business has a number of items to sell, buyers usually expect a "volume discount," and this expectation can cause lower bids in return. Therefore, sellers should consider breaking up very large bundles into smaller bundles auctioned at different times.

- **Price allocation rule:** Most buyers believe it is "fair" that everyone pay the same price in a multi-unit auction, and a uniform pricing rule is recommended. eBay Dutch Internet auctions encourage this expectation. The idea that some buyers should pay more based on their differential need for the product is not widely supported. Therefore, sellers who want to price discriminate should do so by holding auctions for the same goods on different auction markets, or at different times, to prevent direct price comparison.

- **Closed vs. open bidding:** Closed bidding has many advantages for the seller, and sellers should use this approach whenever possible because it permits price discrimination without offending buyers. However, open bidding carries the advantage of "herd effects" and "winning effects" (described later in the chapter) in which consumers' competitive instincts to "win" drive prices higher than even secret bidding would achieve.

AUCTION PRICES: ARE THEY THE LOWEST?

It is widely assumed that auction prices are lower than prices in other fixed-price markets. Empirical evidence is mixed on this assumption. There are many reasons why auction prices might be higher than those in fixed-price markets for items of identical quality, and why auction prices in one auction market may be higher than those in other auction markets. Consumers are not driven solely by value maximization, but instead are influenced by many situational factors, irrelevant and wrong information, and misperceptions when they make market decisions (Simonson and Tversky, 1992). Auctions are social events—shared social environments, where bidders adjust to one another (Hanson and Putler, 1996). Briefly, bidders base their bids on what others previously bid, and this can lead to an upward cascading effect (Arkes and Hutzel, 2000). In a study of hundreds of eBay auctions for Sony PlayStations, CD players, Mexican pottery, and Italian silk ties, Dholakia and Soltysinski (2001) found that bidders exhibited **herd behavior** (the tendency to gravitate toward, and bid for, auction listings with one or more existing bids) by making multiple bids on some auctions (coveted comparables), and making no bids at auctions for comparable items (overlooked comparables). Herd behavior resulted in consumers paying higher prices than necessary for reasons having no foundation in economic reality.

The behavioral reality of participating in auctions can produce many unintended results. Winners can suffer **winner's regret**, the feeling after winning an auction that they paid too much for an item, which indicates that their winning bid does not reflect what they thought the item was worth but rather what the second bidder thought the item was worth. Sellers can experience **seller's lament**, reflecting the fact that they sold an item at a price just above the second place bidder, never knowing how much the ultimate winner might have paid or the true value to the final winner. Auction losers can experience **loser's lament**, the feeling of having been too cheap in bidding and failing to win. In summary, auctions can lead to both winners paying too much and sellers receiving too little. Both of these outcomes can be minimized when sellers and buyers have a very clear understanding of the prices for items in a variety of different online and offline markets.

herd behavior
the tendency to gravitate toward, and bid for, auction listings with one or more existing bids

winner's regret
the winner's feeling after an auction that he or she paid too much for an item

seller's lament
concern that one will never know how much the ultimate winner might have paid, or the true value to the final winner

loser's lament
the feeling of having been too cheap in bidding and failing to win

CONSUMER TRUST IN AUCTIONS

Auction sites have the same difficulties creating a sense of consumer trust as all other e-commerce Web sites, although in the case of auction sites, the operators of the marketplace do not directly control the quality of goods being offered and cannot directly vouch for the integrity of customers. This opens the possibility for criminal actors to appear as either sellers or buyers. Several studies have found that trust and credibility increase as users gain more experience, if trusted third-party seals are present, and if the site has a wide variety of consumer services for tracking purchases (or fraud), thus giving the user a sense of control (Krishnamurthy, 2001; Stanford-Makovsky, 2002; Nikander and Karnonen, 2002; Bailey et al., 2002; Kollock, 1999). Because of the powerful role that trust plays in online consumer behavior, eBay and most auction sites make considerable efforts to develop automated trust-enhancing mechanisms such as seller and buyer ratings, escrow services, and authenticity guarantees (see the next section).

WHEN AUCTION MARKETS FAIL: FRAUD AND ABUSE IN AUCTIONS

Online and offline auction markets can be prone to fraud, which produces information asymmetries between sellers and buyers and among buyers, which in turn causes auction markets to fail. Some of the possible abuses and frauds include:

- **Bid rigging:** Agreeing offline to limit bids or using shills to submit false bids that drive prices up.

- **Price matching:** Agreeing informally or formally to set floor prices on auction items below which sellers will not sell in open markets.
- **Shill feedback, defensive:** Using secondary IDs or other auction members to inflate seller ratings.
- **Shill feedback, offensive:** Using secondary IDs or other auction members to deflate ratings for another user (feedback bombs).
- **Feedback extortion:** Threatening negative feedback in return for a benefit.
- **Transaction interference:** E-mailing buyers to warn them away from a seller.
- **Bid manipulation:** Using the retraction option to make high bids, discovering the maximum bid of the current high bidder, and then retracting the bid.
- **Non-payment after winning:** Blocking legitimate buyers by bidding high, then not paying.
- **Shill bidding:** Using secondary user IDs or other auction members to artificially raise the price of an item.
- **Transaction non-performance:** Accepting payment and failing to deliver.
- **Non-selling seller:** Refusing payment or failing to deliver after a successful auction.
- **Bid siphoning:** E-mailing another seller's bidders and offering the same product for less.

Auction sites have sought to reduce these risks through various methods including:

- **Rating systems:** Previous customers rate sellers based on their experience with them and post them on the site for other buyers to see.
- **Watch lists:** These allow buyers to monitor specific auctions as they proceed over a number of days and only pay close attention in the last few minutes of bidding.
- **Proxy bidding:** Buyers can enter a maximum price they are willing to pay, and the auction software will automatically place incremental bids as their original bid is surpassed.

eBay and many other auction sites have investigation units that receive complaints from consumers and investigate reported abuses. Nevertheless, with millions of visitors per week and hundreds of thousands of auctions to monitor, eBay is highly dependent on the good faith of sellers and consumers to follow the rules.

10.3 E-COMMERCE PORTALS

Port: From the Latin porta, an entrance or gateway to a locality.

Portals are among the most frequently visited sites on the Web if only because they often are the first page to which many users point their browser on startup. The top portals such as Yahoo, MSN, and AOL have hundreds of millions of unique visitors worldwide each month. Web portal sites are gateways to the billions of Web pages available on the Internet. Millions of users have set Facebook as their home page, choosing to start their sessions with news from their friends. We have already discussed Facebook in Section 10.1. Perhaps the most important service provided by portals is that of helping people find the information they are looking for on the Web. The original portals in the early days of e-commerce were search engines. Consumers would pass through search engine portals on their way to rich, detailed, in-depth content on the Web. But portals evolved into much more complex Web sites that provide news, entertainment, maps, images, social networks, in-depth information, and education on a growing variety of topics all contained at the portal site. Portals today seek to be a sticky destination site, not merely a gateway through which visitors pass. In this respect, Web portals are very much like television networks: destination sites for content supported by advertising revenues. Portals today want visitors to stay a long time—the longer the better. For the most part they succeed: portals are places where people linger for a long time.

Portals also serve important functions within a business or organization. Most corporations, universities, churches, and other formal organizations have **enterprise portals** that help employees or members navigate to important content, such as human resources information, corporate news, or organizational announcements. For instance, your university has a portal through which you can register for courses, find classroom assignments, and perform a host of other important student activities. Increasingly, these enterprise portals also provide general-purpose news and real-time financial feeds provided by content providers outside the organization, such as MSNBC News and generalized Web search capabilities. Corporate portals and intranets are the subject of other textbooks focused on the corporate uses of Web technology and are beyond the scope of this book (see Laudon and Laudon, 2012). Our focus here is on e-commerce portals.

enterprise portals
help employees navigate to the enterprise's human resource and corporate content

THE GROWTH AND EVOLUTION OF PORTALS

Web portals have changed a great deal from their initial function and role. As noted above, most of today's well-known portals, such as Yahoo, MSN, and AOL, began as search engines. The initial function provided by portals was to index Web page content and make this content available to users in a convenient form. Early portals expected visitors to stay only a few minutes at the site. As millions of people signed on to the Internet in the early 2000s, the number of visitors to basic search engine sites exploded commensurately. At first, few people understood how a Web search site could make money by passing customers on to other destinations. But search sites attracted huge audiences, and therein lay the foundation for their success as vehicles for marketing and advertising. Search sites, recognizing the potential for commerce, expanded their offerings from simple navigation to include commerce (the sale of items directly from the Web site as well as advertising for other retail sites), content (in the form of news at first, and later in the form of weather, investments, games, health, and other subject matter), and distribution of others' content. These three characteristics have become the basic definition of portal sites, namely, sites that provide three functions: navigation of the Web, commerce, and content.

Because the value of portals to advertisers and content owners is largely a function of the size of the audience each portal reaches, and the length of time visitors stay on site, portals compete with one another on reach and unique visitors. *Reach* is defined as the percentage of the Web audience that visits the site in a month (or some other time period), and *unique visitors* is defined as the number of uniquely identified individuals who visit in a month. Portals are inevitably subject to network effects: The value of the portal to advertisers and consumers increases geometrically as reach increases, which, in turn, attracts still more customers. These effects have resulted in the differentiation of the portal marketspace into three tiers: a few general-purpose mega portal sites that garner 60%–80% of the Web audience, second-tier general-purpose sites that hover around 20%–30% reach, and third-tier specialized vertical market portals that attract 2%–10% of the audience. As described in Chapter 2, the top five portals/search engines (Google, Yahoo, MSN/Bing, AOL, and Ask) account for more than 95% of online searches in the United States. A similar pattern of concentration is observed when considering the audience share of portals/search engines as illustrated in **Figure 10.3**. However, this picture is changing as large audiences move to social network sites, and millions of users make these sites their opening or home pages. Web sites of companies that provide ISP services, such as Verizon, Comcast (Xfinity), and others are also common portal/home pages for millions of users.

For more insight into the nature of the competition and change among the top portals, read *Insight on Business: The Transformation of AOL.*

general-purpose portals

attempt to attract a very large general audience and then retain the audience on-site by providing in-depth vertical content

TYPES OF PORTALS: GENERAL-PURPOSE AND VERTICAL MARKET

There are two primary types of portals: general-purpose portals and vertical market portals. **General-purpose portals** attempt to attract a very large general audience and then retain the audience on-site by providing in-depth vertical content channels, such as information on news, finance, autos, movies, and weather. General-purpose portals typically offer Web search engines, free e-mail, personal home pages, chat

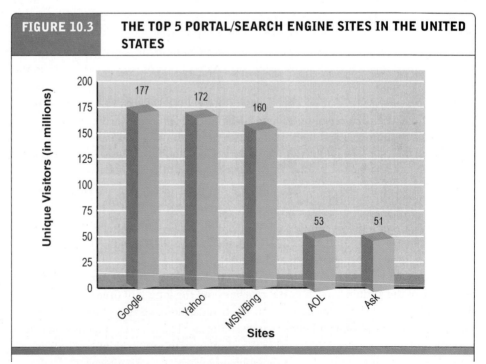

| FIGURE 10.3 | THE TOP 5 PORTAL/SEARCH ENGINE SITES IN THE UNITED STATES |

SOURCE: Based on data from Compete, Inc., 2014; comScore, 2014a.

INSIGHT ON BUSINESS

THE TRANSFORMATION OF AOL

You have to hand it to AOL; its corporate DNA must include a gene for tenacity. From its inauspicious beginnings as an online game server for the Atari 2600 video game console to its dizzying heights as the leading ISP in the United States—a time that even spawned a Meg Ryan/Tom Hanks movie entitled *You've Got Mail* after the ubiquitous greeting AOL users heard each time they signed on—to its equally staggering decline after its failed merger with Time Warner—somehow AOL has found a way to survive.

Started in the early 1980s as Control Video Corporation, it provided an online service called Gameline for the Atari 2600. The company didn't make enough money, and in 1983, it was reorganized as Quantum Computer Services, providing a dedicated online service for Commodore 64 and 128 computers called Quantum Link. In 1988, the company added online services called Apple Link and PC Link, and in 1989, its name was changed to America Online.

In 1991, AOL launched an online program for the DOS operating system (the early Microsoft operating system that used text commands) and one for Windows the following year. In contrast to CompuServe, which served the technical community, AOL positioned itself as the online service for people who weren't comfortable with technology, a shrewd move at the time. Initially, it provided proprietary software and charged users hefty hourly fees. In 1996, it switched to a subscription-based model, charging $19.99 per month. Mass distribution of AOL CD-ROMs through the mail spurred adoption—AOL was everywhere, giving over 10 million people their first exposure to the Web, e-mail, instant messaging, and chat rooms. However, the company was slow to provide access to the open Internet, and complaints erupted, in particular, about dropped connections and busy signals. Still, it continued to grow. In 1996, in another boon to its brand, AOL signed a five-year

agreement that it would be bundled with Windows on new PCs. The first major Web portal for the general public was on its way.

In 1999, CEO Steve Case said that Windows was in the past, and predicted that AOL would be the next Microsoft. This is not exactly how the story unfolded. When AOL tried to exploit its tremendous name recognition and brand prominence, it failed repeatedly. Its biggest failure, though not its only one, was not anticipating the broadband transformation. But that's getting ahead of the story.

In 2000, before the company's spectacular fall began, Time Warner bought AOL for $165 billion. Despite the media fanfare, there were problems from the start with what is now acknowledged by current CEO Tim Armstrong to be the worst merger in corporate history. In the first year, the merged company already had difficulty reaching growth targets, possibly because AOL had improperly inflated its premerger revenue. In 2002, advertising revenue declined sharply. The number of AOL ISP subscribers peaked that year at 26.7 million and has been declining ever since at about 9% per year. There are only around 2.3 million ISP subscribers today. However, these subscribers still generated $650 million in 2013, almost 30% of the company's revenue. Incredibly, these core dial-up holdouts have substantially helped to keep the company afloat.

Some people believe the merger did not have to turn out that way. Marrying one of the foremost providers of "old fashioned" content to one of the largest distributors of "online" content might have made sense if it had been managed differently. But it wasn't. Key players at Time Warner resented the merger and thought it was a waste of time and money. To make matters worse, corporate leadership did little to persuade brand/division heads that it was their responsibility to make the merged company work.

And then came broadband. AOL underestimated just how attractive broadband would become. By

(continued)

2004, broadband adoption was gathering speed. At the same time, Google's search engine advertising took off and banner advertising with it. Yahoo was successful with banner display ads, and it added content that drew the broadband audience. AOL was quickly perceived as stodgy, slow, and uncool. Even when AOL made its subscriber-only content freely available, it was too little, too late.

Between 2002 and 2007 the company occupied various positions on the continuum between misstep and turmoil. Its stock price plummeted, it was investigated by the SEC for several unorthodox advertising deals, the Justice Department conducted a criminal probe, financial reports had to be revised downward, and the positions of CEO and VP of Marketing became revolving doors.

In 2007, AOL began pursuing a new strategy, creating more than a dozen niche content sites. The following year, Time Warner negotiated with both Microsoft and Google in an attempt to sell AOL. When this was unsuccessful, it decided to spin off the company instead. First, it repurchased Google's 5% stake for $283 million. Google's purchase price in 2005 had been $1 billion.

When Tim Armstrong came on board in 2009, he added senior staff members from Google and Yahoo with an eye towards turning the company into the biggest creator of premium content on the Web and the largest seller of online display ads. Positioning AOL to be ready when the line between online and broadcast programming permanently blurred, he began assembling the infrastructure, acquiring a number of companies specializing in the delivery of online content, including Studio Now, 5Min Media, Thing Labs, and Pictela. The real blockbuster acquisition was the Huffington Post in 2011 for $315 million. Armstrong appeared to be betting big on its charismatic leader, Arianna Huffington, and its 25 million unique monthly visitors. Around 20% of AOL's workforce was eliminated following the purchase.

It soon became clear that the big bet was actually on online video, with HuffPost Live as one significant part of the wager. Launched in 2012, HuffPost Live features live discussions on current events 12 hours a day, five days a week. The unique twist and perceived draw is user interaction. Viewers submit chat comments as programs are airing and can also tweet and submit their own videos. Viewers will also increasingly be included in programming, so that they can engage with the host and his or her guest, creating a "social video" experience. Rather than scheduling specific programs at specific times of the day, or even for a set period of time, topics are conversational, not bound by timeframe, and not bound by the hot topic of the day—a sort of freeform television. To which Armstrong is of course hoping to add live advertising. Cadillac and Verizon are two of the main investors in the venture. Though HuffPost Live is not yet profitable, the site is on track to show a profit by the end of 2014.

AOL also has teams of video producers in both New York and Los Angeles that are creating branded entertainment video. Sometimes working with celebrities, these teams, as well as video partners from around the world, are producing hundreds of videos a day of an informational, how-to, or entertainment nature. Sources include wholly owned properties such as TechCrunch, one of the most popular tech blogs on the Internet. These videos will attempt to tread the line between branded infomercial and useful and sought-after information. In 2014, AOL has continued its efforts to develop original programming, primarily via its AOL On Channel. New features are on the way featuring James Franco, Steve Buscemi, and Morgan Spurlock, and AOL also struck a deal with Apple to allow the channel to be accessed via Apple TV. AOL is also not just relying on developing its own premium content. It recently reached a deal with Miramax to stream films on AOL On for free, supported by advertising, and it hopes to continue acquiring the rights to premium content from other studios as well.

AOL's latest big bet is on programmatic advertising, an automated form of ad buying that promises to cut out advertising middlemen and allow content providers and advertisers both to make more money. AOL announced that it had already struck deals with major ad agencies to participate in these automated ad exchanges, which it believes will begin a seismic shift of TV advertising dollars to online video. To that end, the company also bought video ad company Adap.tv to bolster its position in online video. In 2014, AOL unveiled its new automated advertising platform, named One, which it hopes will become the standard for automated purchases of digital media. However, other companies like Google and Adobe are challenging One with their own offerings. In 2014, AOL also rolled out a mobile native ad product across all of its sites that featured six times the conversion rate of traditional mobile banner ads and the participation of over 50 major brand advertisers. It also purchased the advertising company Gravity, which personalizes sites based on users' interests across Internet and social site searches, making them more engaging.

AOL's strategy to focus on video, content, and display advertising is risky. Around 30% of the company's revenue is still derived from its dwindling dial-up subscriptions. But its online video, and content and programmatic advertising initiatives appear to be moving in the right direction. AOL's second quarter 2014 results showed a whopping 60% growth in third-party display advertising revenues, up to $194 million, and analysts estimate that this now constitutes over 35% of AOL's value, and that it will be a key driver in boosting AOL's revenues going forward.

SOURCES: "AOL Earnings: Programmatic Platform Boosts Ad Revenues Yet Again," by Trefis Team, Forbes.com, August 8, 2014; AOL Inc. Form 10-Q for the quarterly period ending June 30, 2014, filed with the Securities and Exchange Commission, August 6, 2014; "AOL Strikes Deal to Distribute Original Video on Apple TV," by Mike Shields, *Wall Street Journal*, June 24, 2014; "AOL, Yahoo, YouTube, Each Take Unique Road to Video," by Steve Rosenbaum, HuffingtonPost, May 5, 2014; "AOL Still Has 2.4 Million Paying Subscribers," by Laura Northrup, Consumerist.com, May 7, 2014; "AOL Claims Huge Conversion Rates in Test Campaigns," by Christopher Heine, Adweek.com, April 24, 2014; "AOL, Microsoft Lure Advertisers with TV-Style Shows," by Jennifer Saba and Lisa Richwine, Reuters, April 23, 2014; "AOL Rolls out New Platform in Bid to Become Digital Ad Hub," by Jennifer Saba, Reuters, March 26, 2014; AOL Inc. Form 10-K for the year ended December 31, 2013, filed with the Securities and Exchange Commission, February 19, 2014; "AOL Buys Gravity, a Firm That Personalizes Web Searches," by Leslie Kaufman, *New York Times*, January 23, 2014; "AOL CEO Leads Charge to Pry Ad Dollars From TV," by Keach Hagey, *Wall Street Journal*, September 24, 2013; "comScore: AOL Climbs to Second Place in Online Video Content Ranking," by Greg Jarboe, Clickz.com, September 24, 2013; "AOL Urges Industry to Embrace Programmatic Buying," by Mike Shields, *Adweek*, September 23, 2013; "AOL to Launch Programmatic Upfront During Advertising Week," by Mike Shields, *Adweek*, July 24, 2013; "AOL: You've Got Apps," *New York Business Journal*, October 4, 2012; "AOL," Wikipedia.com, accessed September 26, 2012; "AOL CEO Tim Armstrong: 'We Haven't Won Yet'," by Daniel Terdiman, News.cnet.com, September 11, 2012; "AOL's Triple-Pronged Approach to Online Video," by Troy Dreier, Streamingmedia.com, August/September 2012; "$1.1B Microsoft Patent Deal Done, AOL Buys Back $600M In Stock, Offers Dividend of $5.15 Per Share," by Ingrid Lunden, Techcrunch.com, August 27th, 2012; "AOL's Ad Revenue Up; Armstrong Bullish on Video," by Tanzina Vega, *New York Times*, July 25, 2012; "AOL Buys TechCrunch, 5Min and Thing Labs," by Jessica E. Vascellaro and Emily Steel, *New York Times*, September 29, 2010; "Eleven Years of Ambition and Failure at AOL," by Saul Hansell, *New York Times*, July 24, 2009; "Daring to Dream of a Resurgent AOL," by Saul Hansell, *New York Times*, July 23, 2009; "Before Spin-off, AOL Tries for that Start-up Feeling," *New York Times*, July 20, 2009.

rooms, community-building software, and bulletin boards. Vertical content channels on general-purpose portal sites offer content such as sports scores, stock tickers, health tips, instant messaging, automobile information, and auctions.

Vertical market portals (sometimes also referred to as destination sites or vortals) attempt to attract highly focused, loyal audiences with a deep interest in either community or specialized content—from sports to the weather. In addition to their focused content, vertical market portals have recently begun adding many of the features found in general-purpose portals. For instance, in addition to being a social network, you can also think of Facebook as a portal—the home page for millions of users, and a gateway to the Internet. Facebook is an affinity group portal because it is based on friendships among people. Facebook offers e-mail, search (Bing), games, and apps. News is limited.

The concentration of audience share in the portal market reflects (in addition to network effects) the limited time budget of consumers. This limited time budget works to the advantage of general-purpose portals. Consumers have a finite amount of

vertical market portals
attempt to attract highly focused, loyal audiences with a deep interest in either community or specialized content

time to spend on the Web, and as a result, most consumers visit fewer than 30 unique domains each month. Facing limited time, consumers concentrate their visits at sites that can satisfy a broad range of interests, from weather and travel information, to stocks, sports, and entertainment content.

General-purpose sites such as Yahoo try to be all things to all people and attract a broad audience with both generalized navigation services and in-depth content and community efforts. For instance, Yahoo has become the Web's largest source of news: more people visit Yahoo News than any other news site including online newspapers. Yet recent changes in consumer behavior on the Web show that consumers are spending less time "surfing the Web" and on general browsing, and more time doing focused searches, research, and participating in social networks. These trends will advantage special-purpose, vertical market sites that can provide focused, in-depth community and content.

As a general matter, the general-purpose portals are very well-known brands, while the vertical content and affinity group portals tend to have less well-known brands. **Figure 10.4** lists examples of general-purpose portals and the two main types of vertical market portals.

PORTAL BUSINESS MODELS

Portals receive income from a number of different sources. The revenue base of portals is changing and dynamic, with some of the largest sources of revenue declining. **Table 10.7** summarizes the major portal revenue sources.

The business strategies of both general-purpose and vertical portals have changed greatly because of the rapid growth in search engine advertising and intelligent ad placement networks such as Google's AdSense, which can place ads on thousands of Web sites based on content. General portal sites such as AOL and Yahoo did not have well-developed search engines, and hence have not grown as fast as Google, which has a powerful search engine. Microsoft, for instance, has invested billions of dollars

FIGURE 10.4	TWO GENERAL TYPES OF PORTALS: GENERAL-PURPOSE AND VERTICAL MARKET PORTALS		
	GENERAL PURPOSE PORTALS	**VERTICAL MARKET PORTALS**	
		Affinity Group	**Focused Content**
	Yahoo!	Facebook	ESPN.com
	MSN	iVillage	Bloomberg.com
	AOL	Sina.com	NFL.com
	Ask.com	Sify.com	WebMD.com
		Law.com	Gamers.com
		Ceoexpress.com	Away.com
			Econline.com
			Sailnet.com

There are two general types of portals: general-purpose and vertical market. Vertical market portals may be based on affinity groups or on focused content.

TABLE 10.7	TYPICAL PORTAL REVENUE SOURCES
PORTAL REVENUE SOURCE	**DESCRIPTION**
General advertising	Charging for impressions delivered
Tenancy deals	Fixed charge for guaranteed number of impressions, exclusive partnerships, "sole providers"
Commissions on sales	Revenue based on sales at the site by independent providers
Subscription fees	Charging for premium content
Applications and games	Games and apps are sold to users; advertising is placed within apps

in its Bing search engine to catch up with Google. On the other hand, general portals have content, which Google did not originally have, although it added to its content by purchasing YouTube and adding Google sites devoted to news, financial information, images, and maps. Facebook users stay on-site and linger three times as long as visitors to traditional portals like Yahoo. For this reason social network sites, Facebook in particular, are direct competitors of Yahoo, Google, and the other portals. Yahoo has struggled in the last three years to grow revenues and earnings despite the fact that its unique visitor count has held steady with Google's. One part of the problem is the falling price of display ads, which are the mainstay of Yahoo's ad platform. Another key issue is declining user engagement with materials on the site and the amount of time spent on the site. To address these issues, Yahoo has made a number of acquisitions including Aviate, Tumblr, and Flickr, and launched digital magazines like Yahoo Food and Yahoo Tech that curate content from around the Web. The key to display ad revenue is content and engagement: the more you can show users, the longer they stay on your site, the more ad revenue can be generated. So far, Yahoo and the other general portal sites have not been able to compete with social network sites on these dimensions of engagement and time on site.

The survival strategy for general-purpose portals in the future is therefore to develop deep, rich vertical content in order to reach and engage customers at the site. The strategy for much smaller vertical market portals is to put together a collection of vertical portals to form a vertical portal network, a collection of deep, rich content sites. The strategy for search engine sites such as Google is to obtain more content to attract users for a long time and expose them to more ad pages (or screens).

eBay Evolves

With the unveiling of its new, more reserved logo in 2012, eBay announced its arrival to the mainstream. Gone are the jaunty, incongruent block letters that characterized the offbeat startup auction site founded by Pierre Omidyar in 1995. In their place, the bold primary colors intact, is a symmetrical set of block letters staidly observing the same parallel bottom line. With eBay now deriving 70% of its revenue from traditional e-commerce, and peer-to-peer auctions taking a backseat, the time had come. Since then, eBay has banned the sales of quirkier services like tarot card readings and magic spells, and has instituted a rewards program with prominent retail chains like Dick's Sporting Goods and Toys "R" Us. Eccentric was out; conventional in.

The transformation began in November 2007, when former CEO Meg Whitman exited and was replaced by former Bain & Company managing director, John Donahoe. The company had already begun to stall, and the trend continued through 2009. For many buyers, the novelty of online auctions had worn off, and they were returning to

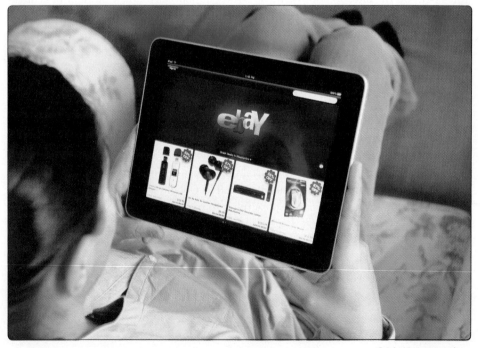

© Iain Masterton / Alamy

easier and simpler methods of buying fixed-price goods from fixed-price retailers such as Amazon, which, by comparison, had steady growth during the same time period. Search engines and comparison shopping sites were also taking away some of eBay's auction business by making items easier to find on the Web.

Donahoe quickly found that dramatically altering the business model of an Internet company is never easy, particularly one that is one of the most recognizable sites on the Web. His three-year revival plan moved eBay away from its origins as an online flea market, and at first it began to resemble an outlet mall where retailers sold out-of-season, overstocked, refurbished, or discontinued merchandise. From there it was a straightforward progression to partnering with retail chains to simply serve as another channel for current merchandise.

Small sellers were encouraged to shift away from the auction format and move toward the fixed-price sales model. The fee structure was adjusted, listing fees for fixed-price sales were lowered, improvements were made to the search engine, and rather than displaying ending auctions first, a formula was devised that took into account price and seller reputation so that highly rated merchants appeared first and received more exposure.

Unsurprisingly, the growing pains during this period included increasing complaints from sellers about excessive fees and eBay's favoritism toward big retailers. The hundreds of thousands of people who supported themselves by selling on eBay and many millions more who used eBay to supplement their income often felt slighted. With its stock continuing to drop, analysts' faith that Donahoe could turn things around dwindled. This pessimism discounted eBay's history of sensible growth marked by a number of canny purchases.

Its signature purchase is, of course, PayPal, whose payment services enable the exchange of money between individuals over the Internet. This acquisition was the key to eBay's endurance through the lean years, protecting it from weakness in its auction business, and the propeller that pushed it towards the future. PayPal has accounted for over 40% of eBay's revenues for some time, and has been a significant factor in eBay's growth. In 2014, PayPal has over 152 million active accounts and continues to grow at a steady pace.

eBay has continued to expand PayPal's presence into new aras. One of its biggest innovations has been a credit card processing device called PayPal Here that allows small businesses to use smartphones and tablets to accept credit cards. eBay has enabled consumers to "check in" so that they can be personally greeted, complete purchases without a mobile device or a credit card, and receive a text message as their receipt. In 2014, eBay released a development kit for PayPal Here, allowing developers to integrate the payment system into more areas of a business such as traditional POS systems.

The 2008 addition of Bill Me Later to the PayPal wallet, an instant credit product offered at checkout, has also proved, so far, to be prescient. BML, which lets online customers pay several months after they have made purchases, has been one of eBay's fastest growing business segments. BML can reduce funding costs for PayPal and help it to develop into a true financial product. Currently, more than 50% of PayPal purchases are funded using Visa and MasterCard credit and debit cards, which come

SOURCES: "PayPal Introduces an SDK for PayPal Here, Its Square-like Credit Card Reader," by Roberto Baldwin, Thenextweb.com, September 4, 2014; "eBay's 900 Million Dollar Question," by Chad Henage, Motley Fool, June 17, 2014; "Alibaba Takes on eBay, Etsy with U.S.-based Shopping Site," by Gail Sullivan, *Washington Post*, June 11, 2014; "Web? Store? Mobile? Shoppers Want It All," by Don Davis, Internetretailer.com, June 11, 2014; "Did Panda Really Beat Up On eBay?" by Thad Rueter, Interneretailer.com, June 9, 2014; "eBay Plays the Field," by Katie Evans, Internetretailer.com, June 2, 2014; "How the Once Impregnable eBay Fell Victim to Hackers (And You Can Too)," by Jeremy Quittner, Inc.com, May 30, 2014; "eBay Reports 13% Sales Growth and Rejects PayPal Spinoff," by Katie Evans, Internetretailer.com, January 22, 2014; "Behind eBay's $800M Buy: Braintree will Replace PayPal's Developer Platform," by Kevin Fitchard, Gigaom.com, September 26, 2013; "Amazon, eBay Lead Way as E-Commerce Sales Still Surge," by Brian Deagon, *Investor's Business Daily*, July 2, 2013; "eBay Hits 100m Mobile App Download Mark," by Dervedia Thomas, Dailydealmedia.com, September 29, 2012; "eBay: We Need to Behave More Like a Retailer," by Sarah Shearman, Tamebay.com, September 25, 2012; "eBay Logo Gets a Refresh; The Time Felt Right After 17 Years," by Mark Tyson, Hexus.com, September 14, 2012; "eBay Bans Magic Spells and Potions," by Katy Waldman, Slate.com, August 17, 2012; "Behind eBay's Comeback," by James B. Stewart, *New York Times*, July 27, 2012; "Bill Me Later, eBay's Credit Version of PayPal, Helps Company's Profits but Exposes It to Risk," by Alistair Barr, MercuryNews.com, July 12, 2012; "PayPal Strength Helps eBay Exceed Forecasts," by Somini Sengupta, *New York Times*, April 18, 2012; "eBay Favors Big-Box Retailers in Holiday Promotions," by Ina Steiner, eCommerce-Bytes.com, December, 16, 2011; "How Jack Abraham is Reinventing eBay," by Danielle Sacks, *Fast Company*, June 22, 2011; "Connecting the Dots on eBay's Local Shopping Strategy," by Leena Rao, Techcrunch.com, May 15, 2011; "eBay CEO Sees Opportunities in Online and Offline Commerce," by Scott Morrison, *Wall Street Journal*, February 10, 2011.

with substantial fees. Reducing this cost would naturally increase profit margins. In 2014, some analysts predict that BML will be the next big source of PayPal's growth. Although there was skepticism regarding the additional risk eBay was likely to incur as a result of increasing its profile as a lender via BML, those fears have not been realized to this point.

PayPal's success gave eBay's Marketplaces segment time to rebound. And recover it has. The Marketplaces segment has posted strong results from 2012 to 2014. In the second quarter of 2014, it grew 24% compared to the previous year.

As impressive and encouraging as the Marketplaces turnaround has been, eBay's investments in mobile technology have been at least as important in its resurgence. eBay's mobile investments began in 2010 with RedLaser, a barcode-scanning mobile application. This was followed by Critical Path, an industry leading mobile app developer, doubling the size of eBay's mobile team. eBay also purchased WHERE, a location-based media and advertising company with a local discovery mobile application, and Zong, a provider of mobile payments through mobile carrier billing. PayPal was used to purchase Fig Card, a small mobile payment startup. These outlays have borne fruit, supporting $47 billion in mobile transactions in 2013. Approximately 45% ($22 billion) of these transactions were mobile Marketplaces sales, while the other 55% ($27 billion) represented mobile PayPal transactions.

eBay recognized the coming mobile revolution even before the first iPhone or the establishment of the App Store, according to Olivier Ropars, senior director of Mobile Commerce. This prescience resulted in two significant milestones in 2012—the 100 millionth download of eBay mobile apps and the 100 millionth mobile listing. In 2013, eBay encountered increased competition in mobile commerce, and moved quickly to acquire mobile payment gateway Braintree for $800 million. Braintree's technology allows eBay consumers to more easily make payments on smartphones and tablets, and the acquisition also eliminates a major competitor in that space for PayPal.

While many other acquisitions through the years have also helped to transform eBay from an online garage sale to a mainstream competitor with Amazon, its adoption of the "social, mobile, local" driving theme has been central to its survival. Positioning itself at the center of the online—offline—mobile triangle by offering a wide variety of services that enable merchants to more easily integrate their cross-channel retailing has been the key to eBay's resurgence and to its continued success.

However, eBay's return to prominence is not without continuing challenges. In 2014, eBay was the victim of a hacking attack that compromised the information of nearly 150 million of its customers. Paypal was unaffected, and the company doesn't believe that any financial information was stolen, but the incident underscored the need for eBay to remain vigilant with its security measures. eBay sales decreased steeply in the wake of the breach, dropping 5.4% in the following 10 days. Also, Chinese Internet company Alibaba, which is larger than Amazon and eBay put together, announced a U.S.-based site to compete with eBay called 11 Main, which represents a real, credible threat in the online marketplace. And Google rolled out an update to its search algorithm, which reduced eBay's search traffic by as much as 33%. Will eBay be able to respond to these new challenges as well as it has to those in the past?

Case Study Questions

1. Contrast eBay's original business model with its current business model.

2. What are the problems that eBay is currently facing? How is eBay trying to solve these problems?

3. Are the solutions eBay is seeking to implement good solutions? Why or why not? Are there any other solutions that eBay should consider?

4. Who are eBay's top three competitors online, and how will eBay's strategy help it compete? Will eBay be providing a differentiated service to customers?

10.5 REVIEW

KEY CONCEPTS

■ **Describe the different types of social networks and online communities and their business models.**

- Social networks involve a group of people, shared social interaction, common times among members, and a shared area for some period of time. An online social network is one where people who share common ties can interact with one another online.

- The different types of social networks and communities and their business models include:
  - *General communities:* Members can interact with a general audience segmented into numerous different groups. Most general communities began as non-commercial subscription-based endeavors, but many have been purchased by larger community portal sites.
  - *Practice networks:* Members can participate in discussion groups and get help or information relating to an area of shared practice, such as art, education, or medicine. These generally have a nonprofit business model in which they simply attempt to collect enough in subscription fees, sales commissions, and limited advertising to cover the cost of operations.
  - *Interest-based communities:* Members can participate in focused discussion groups on a shared interest. The advertising business model has worked because the targeted audience is attractive to marketers. Tenancy and sponsorship deals provide another similar revenue stream.
  - *Affinity communities:* Members can participate in focused discussions with others who share the same affinity or group identification. The business model is a mixture of subscription revenue from premium content and services, advertising, tenancy/sponsorships, and distribution agreements.
  - *Sponsored communities:* Members can participate in online communities created by government, nonprofit, or for-profit organizations for the purpose of pursuing organizational goals. They use community technologies and techniques to distribute information or extend brand influence. The goal of a branded product site is to increase offline product sales. These sites do not seek to make a profit and are often cost centers.

■ **Describe the major types of auctions, their benefits and costs, how they operate, when to use them, and the potential for auction abuse and fraud.**

- Auctions are markets where prices vary (dynamic pricing) depending on the competition among the participants who are buying or selling products or services. They can be classified broadly as C2C or B2C, although generally the term C2C auction refers to the venue in which the sale takes place, for example, a consumer-oriented Web site such as eBay, which also auctions items from established merchants. A B2C *auction* refers to an established online merchant that offers its own auctions. There are also numerous B2B online auctions for buyers of industrial parts, raw materials, commodities, and services. Within these three broad categories of auctions are several major auction types classified based upon how the bidding mechanisms work in each system:
  - *English auctions:* A single item is up for sale from a single seller. Multiple buyers bid against one another within a specific time frame, with the highest bidder winning the object, as long as the high bid has exceeded the reserve bid set by the seller, below which he or she refuses to sell.
  - *Dutch Internet auctions:* Sellers with many identical items for sale list a minimum price or starting bid, and buyers indicate both a bid price and a quantity desired. The lowest winning bid that clears the available quantity is paid by all winning bidders. Those with the highest bid are assured of receiving the quantity they desire, but only pay the amount of the lowest successful bid (uniform pricing rule).

- *Name Your Own Price or reverse auctions:* Buyers specify the price they are willing to pay for an item, and multiple sellers bid for their business. This is one example of discriminatory pricing in which winners may pay different amounts for the same product or service depending on how much they have bid.
  - *Penny (bidding fee) auctions:* Bidder pay a non-refundable fee to purchase bids.
- Benefits of auctions include: liquidity, price discovery, price transparency, market efficiency, lower transaction costs, consumer aggregation, network effects, and market-maker benefits.
- Costs of auctions include: delayed consumption, monitoring costs, equipment costs, trust risks, and fulfillment costs.
- Auction sites have sought to reduce these risks through various methods including rating systems, watch lists, and proxy bidding.
- Auctions can be an appropriate channel for businesses to sell items in a variety of situations. The factors for businesses to consider include the type of product, the product life cycle, channel management, the type of auction, initial pricing, bid increments, auction length, number of items, price allocation, and closed vs. open bidding.
- Auctions are particularly prone to fraud, which produces information asymmetries between buyers and sellers. Some of the possible abuses and frauds include bid rigging, price matching, defensive shill feedback, offensive shill feedback, feedback extortion, transaction interference, bid manipulation, non-payment after winning, shill bidding, transaction non-performance, non-selling sellers, and bid siphoning.

- ■ Describe the major types of Internet portals and their business models.
- Web portals are gateways to billions of Web pages available on the Internet. Originally, their primary purpose was to help users find information on the Web, but they evolved into destination sites that provided a myriad of content from news to entertainment. Today, portals serve three main purposes: navigation of the Web, content, and commerce.
- Among the major portal types are:
  - *Enterprise portals:* Corporations, universities, churches, and other organizations create these sites to help employees or members navigate to important content such as corporate news or organizational announcements.
  - *General-purpose portals:* Examples are AOL, Yahoo, and MSN, which try to attract a very large general audience by providing many in-depth vertical content channels. Some also offer ISP services on a subscription basis, search engines, e-mail, chat, bulletin boards, and personal home pages.
  - *Vertical market portals:* Also called destination sites, they attempt to attract a highly focused, loyal audience with an intense interest in either a community they belong to or an interest they hold. Vertical market portals can be divided into two main classifications, although hybrids that overlap the two classifications also exist.
  - *Affinity groups:* Designed to serve aggregates of people who identify themselves by their attitudes, values, beliefs, and behavior.
  - *Focused content portals:* These sites contain in-depth information on a particular topic that all members are interested in. They can provide content on such broad topics as sports, news, weather, entertainment, finance, or business, or they can appeal to a much more focused interest group such as boat, horse, or video game enthusiasts.
- Portals receive revenue from a number of different sources. The business model is presently changing and adapting to declines in certain revenue streams, particularly advertising revenues. Revenue sources can include general advertising, tenancy deals, subscription fees, and commissions on sales.
- The survival strategy for general-purpose portals is to develop deep, rich vertical content in order to attract advertisers to various niche groups that they can target with focused ads. The strategy for the small vertical market portals is to build a collection of vertical portals, thereby creating a network of deep, rich content sites for the same reason.

QUESTIONS

1. What is an online social network?
2. How does a social network differ from a portal? How are the two similar?
3. What are some ways to measure the business potential and influence of a social network site?
4. List and describe the five generic types of social networks and online communities.
5. What is "network fatigue" and what impact may it have on social networks?
6. List and describe three social networks focused on messaging.
7. List and describe four different types of auctions.
8. What is trigger pricing and how is it used?
9. How does a Dutch Internet auction differ from an English auction?
10. Why is assessing the number of active users of social networks so difficult?
11. Name and describe five types of possible abuses and frauds that may occur with auctions.
12. What three characteristics define a portal site today?
13. What are the two main types of vertical market portals, and how are they distinguished from one another?
14. List and briefly explain the main revenue sources for the portal business model.
15. Why are mobile social networks growing so fast?
16. What is the difference between a C2C and a B2C auction?
17. How does a Name Your Own Price auction, such as Priceline's, work?
18. Why has the FTC warned consumers about penny (bidding fee) auctions?
19. What is herd behavior and how does it impact auctions?
20. Why has Yahoo struggled in the last three years?

PROJECTS

1. Find two examples of an affinity portal and two examples of a focused-content portal. Prepare a presentation explaining why each of your examples should be categorized as an affinity portal or a focused-content portal. For each example, surf the site and describe the services each site provides. Try to determine what revenue model each of your examples is using and, if possible, how many members or registered visitors the site has attracted.

2. Examine the use of auctions by businesses. Go to any auction site of your choosing and look for outlet auctions or auctions directly from merchants. Research at least three products for sale. What stage in the product life cycle do these products fall into? Are there quantity purchasing requirements? What was the opening bid price? What are the bid increments? What is the auction duration? Analyze why these firms have used the auction channel to sell these goods and prepare a short report on your findings.

3. Visit one for-profit-sponsored and one nonprofit-sponsored social network. Create a presentation to describe and demonstrate the offering at each site. What organizational objectives is each pursuing? How is the for-profit company using community-building technologies as a customer relations management tool?

4. Visit one of the social networks listed in Table 10.1 and compare it to Facebook. In what ways is it similar to Facebook, and in what ways is it different? Which do you prefer, and why?

REFERENCES

Arkes, H. R., and L. Hutzel. "The Role of Probability of Success Estimates in the Sunk Cost Effect." *Journal of Behavioral Decisionmaking* (2000).

Bailey, Brian P., Laura J. Gurak, and Joseph Konstan, "Do You Trust Me? An Examination of Trust in Computer-Mediated Exchange," In *Human Factors and Web Development*, 2nd Edition. Mahwah, NJ: Lawrence Erlbaum (2002).

Compete, Inc. "July 2014 Unique Visitors." (accessed September 14, 2014a).

comScore, Inc. "comScore Media Metrix Ranks Top 50 U.S. Desktop Web Properties for July 2014." (August 18, 2014).

comScore, Inc. "U.S. Digital Future in Focus 2014." (2014b). Consumerreports.org. "With Penny Auctions, You Can Spend a Bundle But Still Leave Empty-Handed." (June 30, 2014).

DeMers, Jayson. "Ello: What Is It and Why Does Everyone Want an Invite." Forbes.com (October, 2014).

Dholakia, Utpal, and Kerry Soltysinski. "Coveted or Overlooked? The Psychology of Bidding for Comparable Listings in Digital Auctions." *Marketing Letters* (2001).

eBay, Inc. "Form 10-K for the Fiscal Year Ended December 31, 2013." Filed with the Securities and Exchange Commission. (January 31, 2014).

Efrati, Amir. "There's No Avoiding Google +." *New York Times* (January 2, 2013).

eMarketer, Inc. "US Social Network Users and Penetration, 2012–2018." (February 2014a).

eMarketer, Inc. (Alison McCarthy). "Worldwide Internet, Social Network and Mobile Users: Q2 2014 Complete Forecast." (June 26, 2014b).

eMarketer, Inc. (Rahul Chadha) "The Global Social Network Landscape 2014: A Country-by-Country Guide to Social Network Usage." (July 14, 2014c).

eMarketer, Inc. "Demographic Profile of US Facebook Users." (July 1, 2014d).

eMarketer, Inc. "US Twitter User Base Begins to Mature." (February 27, 2014e).

eMarketer, Inc. "Net Digital Ad Revenues Worldwide, by Company, 2013 & 2014) (December 2, 2014f).

eMarketer, Inc. (Alison McCarthy) "Worldwide Social Network Ad Spending: Midyear 2014 Complete Forecast." (August 2014g).

eMarketer, Inc. "Time Spent on Social Network Sites by US Internet Users, Nov 2012 (millions of minutes)." (January 16, 2013a).

Facebook. "Newsroom/Company Info." (accessed September 14. 2014).

Gaudin, Sharon. "Without Mandatory Signups, Is Google + Adrift?" Computerworld.com (September 23, 2014).

Hafner, Katie. "The Epic Saga of The Well: The World's Most Influential Online Community (and It's Not AOL)." Wired (May 1997).

Hagel, John III, and Arthur G. Armstrong. *Net Gain: Expanding Markets Through Virtual Communities*. Cambridge, MA: Harvard Business School Press (1997).

Hanson, Ward, and D. S. Putler. "Hits and Misses: Herd Behavior and Online Product Popularity." Marketing Letters (1996).

Hillery, George A. "Definitions of Community: Areas of Agreement." Rural Sociology (1955).

Hiltzik, Michael. *Dealers of Lightning: Xerox PARC and the Dawn of the Computer Age*. New York: Harper Collins (1999).

Kiesler, Sara. "The Hidden Messages in Computer Networks." Harvard Business Review (January-February 1986).

Kiesler, Sara, Jane Siegel, and Timothy W. McGuire. "Social Psychological Aspects of Computer-Mediated Communication." *American Psychologist* (October 1984).

Kollock, Peter. "The Production of Trust in Online Markets." In *Advances in Group Processes* (Vol 16) edited by E. J. Lawler, M. Macy, S. Thyne, and H. A. Walker. Greenwich, CT: JAI Press (1999).

Krishnamurthy, Sandeep. "An Empirical Study of the Causal Antecedents of Customer Confidence in ETailers." *First Monday* (January 2001).

Laudon, Kenneth C., and Jane P. Laudon. *Management Information Systems: Managing the Digital Firm. 13th edition*. Upper Saddle River, NJ, Prentice Hall (2012).

Miller, Claire Cain. "The Loyal Users of Google Plus Say It Is No Ghost Town." *New York Times* (February 19, 2014a).

Miller, Claire Cain. "The Plus in Google Plus? It's Mostly for Google." *New York Times* (February 14, 2014b).

Nanji, Ayaz. "Blogs and Social Media Usage by Fortune 500 Companies." Marketingprofs.com (September 12, 2014).

Nielsen. "January 2013: Top U.S. Entertainment Sites and Web Brands." (March 22, 2013).

Nikander, Pekka, and Kristina Karvonen. "Users and Trust in Cyberspace." In the Proceedings of Cambridge Security Protocols Workshop 2000, April 3–5, 2000, Cambridge University (2002).

Parkes, David C., and Lyle Ungar. "Iterative Combinatorial Auctions: Theory and Practice." *Proceedings of the 17th National Conference on Artificial Intelligence* (AAAI-00) (2000).

Pew Internet &American Life Project. (Lee Rainie). "Coming and Going in Facebook." (February 5, 2013).

Rheingold, Howard. *Hosting Web Communities*. New York: John Wiley and Sons (1998). Also see Rheingold.com for more recent articles by Rheingold.

Rheingold, Howard. *The Virtual Community*. Cambridge MA: MIT Press (1993).

Rosenblum, Stephanie. "For the Plugged-In, Too Many Choices." *New York Times* (August 10, 2011).

Simonson, Itamar, and Amos Tversky. "Choice in Context: Tradeoff Contrast and Extremeness Aversion." *Journal of Marketing Research*, Vol. 20, 281–287 (1992).

Stanford Persuasive Technology Lab and Makovsky & Company. "Stanford-Makovsky Web Credibility Study 2002." Stanford Persuasive Technology Lab. (Spring 2002).

CHAPTER 11

E-commerce Retailing and Services

After reading this chapter, you will be able to:

- Understand the environment in which the online retail sector operates today.
- Explain how to analyze the economic viability of an online firm.
- Identify the challenges faced by the different types of online retailers.
- Describe the major features of the online service sector.
- Discuss the trends taking place in the online financial services industry.
- Describe the major trends in the online travel services industry today.
- Identify current trends in the online career services industry.
- Understand the business models of new sharing economy companies.

Souq.com:

The Amazon of the Middle East

When Souq.com was launched in 2005, e-commerce in the Middle East and North Africa (MENA) region was in its infancy. With no local roadmap to follow, its original parent company Maktoob, a 1998 Internet pioneer that provided the first free Arabic-supported e-mail service, Arabic chat, greeting card, and content channels, opted to follow the successful auction format forged ten years earlier in the West by eBay. A souq, or souk, is the traditional Arab marketplace at which a wide range of products from wood carvings and rugs to spices and food are exchanged through a bargaining process between buyer and seller. In spite of the apropos name, Souq, based in Dubai (United Arab Emirates), struggled to thrive. In 2009, Yahoo acquired Maktoob for its portal and news site, but decided against retaining its consumer e-commerce division, including Souq, which was spun off to Jabbar Internet Group, formed by the original founders of Maktoob.

© Fenton/Fotolia.com

Transactions between Gulf States with different currencies, laws, and regulations complicated trans-country shipping, often necessitating bank accounts in each country and requiring local business partners. Inventory management was likewise thorny. Even more challenging, customers were reluctant to use online payment systems, preferring cash on delivery (C.O.D.) to entering credit card details online. These problems have plagued MENA retail and service e-commerce.

While Souq initially sought to replicate the C2C business model, it soon began cultivating relationships with small businesses, encouraging them to enter online retailing in the cost-effective atmosphere of an online marketplace. Through trial and error, Souq discovered that the "Buy-It-Now" model was superior to the auction format in nations in which, although face-to-face bargaining was customary, auctions were not culturally accepted. Now considered the Amazon of the Middle East, Souq has outperformed the other clones in both securing investors and encouraging entrepreneurs to launch their businesses through its site.

In 2011, with auctions tailing off and a twelve-month analysis backing up the decision, Souq completed the switchover to the fixed-price model. Souq launched a revamped Web site in April 2012. Focusing on usability, better product placement, and enhanced search capabilities, the redesign aimed to support Souq's continued success and persistent growth. In addition to helping customers quickly find the best deals with the new storefront, Souq expanded its logistics capabilities by adding fulfillment centers and warehouses, and training delivery and warehouse personnel in modernized logistics systems. Data storage systems were also updated to ensure that consumers' personal data was secure.

The Fawry electronic bill payment service launched in Egypt in 2010 has helped to overcome consumer reluctance to shop online. Buyers can go to an ATM machine, post office, or one of 3,000 authorized retailers including grocery stores and pharmacies, to pay for online purchases. Amounts owed for purchases are debited from the customer's bank account and credited to a Fawry Payment Services account from which the payment to the vendor is submitted. If the customer does not have a bank account, as is common in the region (only 10% of the Egyptian population has a bank account), cash can be deposited into the Fawry network at the local corner store. The Fawry network in Egypt can also be used to replenish cashU prepaid online payment cards, another popular method of transacting business online in the MENA region.

In another 2012 move designed to attract female customers, Souq internally purchased another Jabbar Group property, Sukar.com, a high-fashion flash sales site, to bolster its burgeoning fashion division. Sukar benefitted from the use of Souq's logistics and delivery systems while Souq gained customer service and fashion expertise and reinforced its position as the leading e-commerce site in the region. While women have lagged behind men as e-commerce consumers in the MENA region, that is finally beginning to change with increased Internet access at home and increased mobile device usage.

The integration of Sukar with Souq and the launch of Souq Fashion position Souq to capitalize on this budding market segment. While in the West around 11% to 15% of fashion sales are derived from e-commerce, in the MENA region only a meager 1% of the $30 billion in fashion purchases are online. Supported by the new Web site design and advised by stylists for prominent stars including Jennifer Lopez and Rihanna, Souq Fashion provides the traditional counterpart to the daily flash sale specials offered on Sukar. High fashion from over 80 designers including Arabic designers such as Dina JSR, Ronald Abdala, and Dima Ayad are offered at reasonable price points with the additional benefit of advice from stylists. While men's fashion is also offered, the focus is on trendy, but affordable, labels popular with female celebrities in both the United States and the United Kingdom.

All of these improving conditions, investments, acquisitions, and upgrades likely contributed to Souq's October 2012 announcement that it had sold a portion of its business to Naspers, a South African Web and media group, and received further investment capital from a current shareholder, New York hedge fund Tiger Global Management. The company proudly likened the magnitude of the deal to the 2009 Yahoo-Maktoob purchase for $175 million which put the MENA region on the map as an emerging e-commerce force and spurred further venture capital investment and entrepreneurial initiatives. Naspers and Souq did not reveal the selling price, but Arabian Business magazine estimated that Souq had netted in the neighborhood of $40 million. Over the preceding 15 years, Naspers had grown from a print and broadcast media company in South Africa to a global Internet media and pay TV force in close to 130 countries. In 2014, Souq raised another $75 million from Naspers, representing the largest round of funding by any Arab startup and giving Souq a valuation of more than $500 million. Though the size of the stake was not disclosed, Naspers now owns significantly more of the company than its previous stake of approximately 36%.

With the influx of cash, Souq plans to further expand its distribution center network in the UAE, Saudi Arabia, and Egypt. It currently features more than 200,000 products. Souq also plans continued support for and expansion of its network of 75,000 entrepreneurial sellers such as KAF, a weaving company; NAS, a design-printed T-shirts company; the Joud Store, a company that creates home accessories, mugs, coaster-art and trays from tiles; and Skinzo, a laptop covers company.

Souq has embraced mobile technology and social media as it attempts to increase its worldwide visibility and bolster its branding and marketing efforts. Souq's Facebook page has over 4 million Likes, with its UAE- and Saudi Arabia-focused Facebook pages both having well over a million Likes as well, and the company began maintaining an active Twitter account with flash deals and other useful information. Souq CEO Ronaldo Mouchawar also noted that the company would use the latest funding to improve its customer relationship technology as well as to attract new talent as the company grows.

In 2013, Souq launched its first regional advertising campaigns across the MENA region, displaying colorful characters interrupted by Souq deliveries. Souq established Egypt's first Internet-based youth commerce training academy and has also entered agreements with universities like the Canadian University of Dubai to promote entrepreneurship and help a new wave of young people in the MENA region develop tech skills. The company also partnered with regional non-profit Manzil, which provides custom-made products for individuals with special needs. Souq has also focused on technology as well—NDOT Technologies developed a mobile app for Souq that allows users to shop on the go. In 2014, mobile customers represent 40% of all purchases on Souq.com, and Souq expects that mobile will quickly become the primary way most customers shop on the site. Souq has also hosted the launch of a new tablet computer developed in the United Arab Emirates, the QTAB, an eight-inch Wi-Fi Android tablet aimed at Arabic consumers. CEO Mouchawar indicated in 2014 that the demand for the QTAB has been strong in the company's target areas of Egypt and Saudi Arabia.

In 2014, Souq is hoping that the third time is the charm and that this infusion of financing takes it and its 2,000 current employees from the largest e-commerce site in the Arab world and Amazon of the Middle East to Amazon rival in market capitalization value. Given that online purchasing represents a much smaller fraction of total purchases in the MENA region than it does in the rest of the world, still checking in at about 1-2% compared to the mid- to high teens in England, Souq's potential for growth in 2014 and beyond remains strong—e-commerce is growing approximately 60% every year in the Middle East, indicating that the region is destined to catch up quickly. Souq has even outpaced those figures, growing by 170% in the last year alone and by 1000% in the last two years. On Black Friday in 2014, Souk reported 100,000 customers, sales of more than 250,000 units, and 10 million site visits.

SOURCES: "$500M E-Commerce Platforms Emerge in Africa, Middle East," by Elizabeth MacBride, *Forbes*, November 29, 2014; "Ronaldo Mouchawar: How I Created Souq.com," Arabianbusiness.com, by Ed Attwood, April 5, 2014; "Souq.com, Dubai-Based E-Commerce Site, Raises $75 Million," by Rory Jones, *Wall Street Journal,* March 24, 2014; What Souq Has to Say About Those Rumors, And Its New Mobile Strategy," by Nina Curley, Wamda.com, February 19, 2014; "Souq.com," ndottech.com case study, accessed October 15, 2013; "Souq.com Launches Low-cost QTAB Tablet in UAE," telecompaper.com, September 30, 2013; "Souq.com Partners with Manzil to Help Sell Products Made by Special Needs Students," mid-east.info, July 28, 2013; "Souq.com Launches New Regional Advertising Campaign," communicate.ae, June 20, 2013; "Souq.com Establishes Egypt's First Internet-Based Youth Commerce Training Academy," *Daily News Egypt*, February 24, 2013; "Souq.com Signs MOU with the Canadian University of Dubai to Promote Entrepreneurship," Canadian University of Dubai, February 6th, 2013; "About Jabbar," Jabbar.com, accessed November 16, 2012; "Maktoob Story," Jabbar.com, accessed November 16, 2012; "After Many Slip-Ups, Mideast E-Commerce Gains Its Footing," by Sara Hamdan, *New York Times*, November 7, 2012; "South Africa's Naspers Swoops on Middle East with Souq.com buy," by Lance Harris, ZDnet.com, October 31, 2012; "Souq Fashion Launches to Boost High-End Online Retail in the Arab World," by Rania Habib, Wamda.com, October 23, 2012; "Souq in Egypt: Not Relinquishing its Crown Anytime Soon," by Omar Aysha, Wamda.com, October 18, 2012; "Why Middle East E-Commerce Site Souq.com Acquired Sister Site Sukar.com," by Nina Curley, Wamda.com, April 29, 2012; "Souq.com launches its redesigned site with new retail-focused design," Zawya.com, April 25, 2012; "How to Launch an E-commerce Business," Wamda.com, April 14, 2011; "Refocus of Souq.com Will End Auction Service," by David George-Cosh, Thenational.ae, January 2, 2011.

The opening case illustrates some of the difficulties that a pure-play startup retail company such as Souq.com faces, particularly when starting out in a part of the world, such as North Africa and the Middle East, that has not already embraced e-commerce. Pure-play start-up companies often have razor-thin profit margins, lack a physical store network to bolster sales to the non-Internet audience, and often are based on unproven business assumptions that, in the long term, may not prove out. In contrast, large offline retailers have established brand names, a huge real estate investment, a loyal customer base, and established inventory control and fulfillment systems. In Souq's case, it originally adopted a business model based on the assumption that C2C auctions would find ready acceptance in its marketspace, when in fact they did not. Luckily for Souq, it was able to successfully transition to a B2C model, and take advantage of some of the benefits that this model offers. For instance, a pure-play B2C company can simplify the existing industry supply chain and instead develop a Web-based distribution system that may be more efficient than traditional retail outlets. As we shall see in this chapter, traditional offline catalog merchants are even more advantaged. We will also see that in order to leverage their assets and core competencies, established offline retailers need to cultivate new competencies and a carefully developed business plan to succeed on the Web.

As with retail goods, the promise of pure-online service providers is that they can deliver superior-quality service and greater convenience to millions of consumers at a lower cost than established bricks-and-mortar service providers, and still make a respectable return on invested capital. The service sector is one of the most natural avenues for e-commerce because so much of the value in services is based on collecting, storing, and exchanging information—something for which the Web is ideally suited. And, in fact, online services have been extraordinarily successful in attracting banking, brokerage, travel, and job-hunting customers. The quality and amount of information online to support consumer decisions in finance, travel, and career placement is extraordinary, especially when compared to what was available to consumers before e-commerce.

The online service sector—like online retail—has shown both explosive growth and some recent impressive failures. Despite the failures, online services have established a significant beachhead and are coming to play a large role in consumer time on the Internet. In areas such as brokerage, banking, and travel, online services are an extraordinary success story, and are transforming their industries. As with the retail sector, many of the early innovators—delivery services such as Kozmo and Webvan and consulting firms such as BizConsult.com—are gone. However, some early innovators, such as E*Trade, Schwab, Expedia, and Monster, have been successful, while many established service providers, such as Citigroup, JPMorgan Chase, Wells Fargo, Bank of America, and the large airlines, have developed successful online e-commerce service delivery sites. In Sections 11.5–11.7 of this chapter, we take a close look at three of the most successful online services: financial services (including insurance and real estate), travel services, and career services.

11.1 THE ONLINE RETAIL SECTOR

Table 11.1 summarizes some of these leading trends in online retailing for 2014–2015. Perhaps the most important theme in online retailing is the effort by retailers—both offline and online—to integrate their operations so they can serve customers in the various ways they want to be served.

By any measure, the size of the global retail market is huge: around €16.1 trillion in 2014.

TABLE 11.1	WHAT'S NEW IN ONLINE RETAIL 2014–2015

- Mobile commerce is exploding, increasing from around €10.5 billion in 2013 to an estimated €17.7 billion in 2014 in the United Kingdom.
- Social networks such as Facebook, Twitter, and Pinterest, together with online retailers, continue to try to understand how best to facilitate social commerce, with trials of Buy buttons on Facebook and Twitter.
- Local commerce, headlined by daily deal sites such as Groupon and LivingSocial, continues to be popular with consumers, increasing to an estimated $4.8 billion in 2014 in the United States.
- The number of online buyers continues to increase, to over 1.2 billion worldwide in 2014.
- Online retailers remain generally profitable by focusing on revenue growth, increasing the size of average purchase amounts, and improving efficiency of operations.
- Online retail remains the fastest growing retail channel.
- Buying online has become a normal, mainstream, everyday experience. Over 70% of Internet users in Western Europe are now online buyers.
- The selection of goods for purchase online continues to increase to include luxury goods, such as jewelry, gourmet groceries, furniture, and wine, as customer trust and experience increase.
- Informational shopping for big-ticket items such as cars and appliances continues to expand rapidly to include nearly all retail goods (both durables and non-durables).
- Specialty retail sites show rapid growth in online retail as they develop customized retail goods and customer online configuration of goods.
- Online retailers place an increased emphasis on providing an improved "shopping experience," including ease of navigation and use, online inventory updates, interactive tools, customer feedback and ratings, and social shopping opportunities.
- Online retailers increase the use of interactive marketing technologies and techniques such as blogs, user-generated content, and video that exploit the dominance of broadband connections and offer features such as zoom, color switch, product configuration, and virtual simulations of households and businesses.
- Retailers are increasingly becoming omni-channel retailers, integrating the multiple retail channels provided by physical stores, the Web, and the mobile platform.
- New virtual merchants such as Birchbox, Naturebox, and others emerge that are using a new subscription-based revenue model for retail.
- Big Data and powerful analytic programs begin to be used for predictive marketing by both large and small retailers.

THE RETAIL INDUSTRY

The retail industry is composed of many different types of firms. **Figure 11.1** illustrates the major segments of the U.S. retail industry: durable goods, general merchandise, food and beverage, specialty stores, gasoline and fuel, mail order/telephone order (MOTO), and online retail firms. Each of these segments offers opportunities for online retail, and yet in each segment, the uses of the Internet may differ. Some eating and drinking establishments use the Web to inform people of their physical locations and menus, while others offer delivery via Web orders (although this has not been a successful model). Retailers of durable goods typically use the Web primarily as an informational tool rather than as a direct purchasing tool, although this has begun to change.

The MOTO sector is the most similar to the online retail sales sector. In the absence of physical stores, MOTO retailers distribute millions of physical catalogs (their largest expense) and operate large telephone call centers to accept orders. They have developed extraordinarily efficient order fulfillment centers that generally ship customer orders within 24 hours of receipt. MOTO was the fastest growing retail segment throughout the 1970s and 1980s. It grew as a direct result of improvements in the national toll-free call system, the implementation of digital switching in telephone systems, falling long distance telecommunications prices, and of course, the expansion of the credit card industry and associated technologies, without which neither MOTO nor e-commerce would be possible on a large national scale. MOTO was the last "technological" retailing revolution that preceded e-commerce. Because

FIGURE 11.1   COMPOSITION OF THE U.S. RETAIL INDUSTRY

General Merchandise

Specialty Stores

MOTO

Online Retail

Consumer Durables

Gasoline and Fuel

Food and Beverage

The retail industry can be grouped into seven major segments.
SOURCE: Based on data from U.S. Census Bureau, 2012.

of their experience in fulfilling small orders rapidly, the transition to e-commerce was not difficult for these firms.

ONLINE RETAILING

Online retail is perhaps the most high-profile e-commerce sector. Over the past decade, this sector has experienced both explosive growth and spectacular failures. Many of the early pure-play online-only firms that pioneered the retail marketspace failed. Entrepreneurs and their investors seriously misjudged the factors needed to succeed in this market. But the survivors of this early period emerged much stronger, and along with traditional offline general and specialty merchants, as well as new start-ups, the e-tail space is growing very rapidly and is increasing its reach and size.

E-commerce Retail: The Vision

In the early years of e-commerce, literally thousands of entrepreneurial Web-based retailers were drawn to the marketplace for retail goods, simply because it was one of the largest market opportunities. Many entrepreneurs initially believed it was easy to enter the retail market. Early writers predicted that the retail industry would be revolutionized, literally "blown to bits"—as prophesized by two consultants in a famous Harvard Business School book (Evans and Wurster, 2000). The basis of this revolution would be fourfold. First, because the Internet greatly reduced both search costs and transaction costs, consumers would use the Web to find the lowest-cost products. Several results would follow. Consumers would increasingly drift to the Web for shopping and purchasing, and only low-cost, high-service, quality online retail merchants would survive. Economists assumed that the Web consumer was rational and cost-driven—not driven by perceived value or brand, both of which are nonrational factors.

Second, it was assumed that the entry costs to the online retail market were much less than those needed to establish physical storefronts, and that online merchants were inherently more efficient at marketing and order fulfillment than offline stores. The costs of establishing a powerful Web site were thought to be minuscule compared to the costs of warehouses, fulfillment centers, and physical stores. There would be no difficulty building sophisticated order entry, shopping cart, and fulfillment systems because this technology was well known, and the cost of technology was falling by 50% each year. Even the cost of acquiring consumers was thought to be much lower on the Web because of search engines that could almost instantly connect customers to online vendors.

Third, as prices fell, traditional offline physical store merchants would be forced out of business. New entrepreneurial companies—such as Amazon—would replace the traditional stores. It was thought that if online merchants grew very quickly, they would have first-mover advantages and lock out the older traditional firms that were too slow to enter the online market.

Fourth, in some industries—such as electronics, apparel, and digital content—the market would be disintermediated as manufacturers or their distributors entered to build a direct relationship with the consumer, destroying the retail intermediaries or middlemen. In this scenario, traditional retail channels—such as physical stores, sales clerks, and sales forces—would be replaced by a single dominant channel: the Web.

Many predicted, on the other hand, a kind of hypermediation based on the concept of a virtual firm in which online retailers would gain advantage over established offline merchants by building an online brand name that attracted millions of customers, and outsourcing the expensive warehousing and order fulfillment functions—the original concept of Amazon and Drugstore.com.

As it turned out, few of these assumptions and visions were correct, and the structure of the retail marketplace, with some notable exceptions, has not been blown to bits, disintermediated, or revolutionized in the traditional meaning of the word "revolution." With several notable exceptions, online retail has often not been successful as an independent platform on which to build a successful "pure-play" Web-only business. As it turns out, the consumer is not primarily price-driven when shopping on the Internet but instead considers brand name, trust, reliability, delivery time, convenience, ease of use, and above all "the experience," as at least as important as price (Brynjolfsson, Dick, and Smith, 2004).

omni-channel

retailers that sell products through a variety of channels and integrate their physical stores with their Web site and mobile platform

However, the Internet has created an entirely new venue for **omni-channel** firms (those that sell products through a variety of channels and integrate their physical stores with their Web sites and mobile platform), and in some cases, the Internet has supported the development of pure-play online-only merchants, both general merchandisers as well as specialty retailers. As predicted, online retail has indeed become the fastest growing and most dynamic retail channel in the sense of channel innovation. The Web has created a new marketplace for millions of consumers to conveniently shop. The Internet and Web have continued to provide new opportunities for entirely new firms using new business models and new online products—such as Blue Nile, as previously described. The online channel can conflict with a merchant's other channels, such as direct sales forces, physical stores, and mail order, but this multichannel conflict can be managed and turned into a strength.

The Online Retail Sector Today

Although online retailing is one of the smallest segments of the retail industry, constituting about 6% of the total retail market today, it is growing at a faster rate than its offline counterparts, with new functionality and product lines being added every day (see **Figure 11.2**). Due to the recession, online retail revenues were basically flat from 2008 to 2009, but they since have resumed their upward trajectory. When we refer to online retail, we will not be including online services revenues such as travel, job-hunting, or the purchase of digital downloads such as software applications and music. Instead, for the purposes of this chapter, online retail refers solely to sales of physical goods over the Internet. The Internet provides a number of unique advantages and challenges to online retailers. **Table 11.2** summarizes these advantages and challenges.

Despite the high failure rate of online retailers in the early years, more consumers than ever are shopping online. For most consumers, the advantages of shopping on the Web overcome the disadvantages. In 2014, it is estimated that around 70% of Internet users in Western Europe over the age of 14 (around 190 million people) will make at least one online purchase. While the number of new Internet users is not growing as

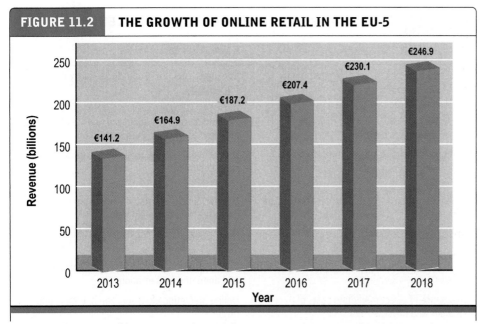

| FIGURE 11.2 | **THE GROWTH OF ONLINE RETAIL IN THE EU-5** |

Online retail revenues will be an estimated €165 billion in 2014, and are expected to increase to almost €250 billion by 2018.

SOURCES: Based on data from eMarketer, 2014a.

rapidly at it was, this slowdown will not necessarily slow the growth in online retail e-commerce because the average shopper is spending more on the Internet each year, and finding many new categories of items to buy. For instance, in 2003, the average annual amount spent online by users in the United States was $675, but by 2014, it had jumped to over $1,800 (eMarketer, Inc., 2014a, 2005). Also, as noted in Chapter 6, millions of additional consumers research products on the Web and are influenced in their purchase decisions at offline stores.

The primary beneficiaries of this growing consumer support are not only the pure online companies, but also the established offline retailers who have the brand-name recognition, supportive infrastructure, and financial resources to enter the online marketplace successfully. Table 1.5 on page 78 lists the top U.S. online retail firms ranked by online sales. The list contains pure-play online retailers for whom the Internet is the only sales channel, such as Amazon (in first place); omni-channel firms that have established brand names and for whom e-commerce plays a relatively small role when compared to their offline physical store channels, such as Staples (3rd), Walmart (4th), Sears (5th), Macy's (8th) Office Depot (9th), OfficeMax (12th), Costco (14th), and Best Buy (15th), and manufacturers of computer and electronic equipment, such as Apple (2nd) and Dell (10th) (although Apple's position on the list is also due to its sales of digital content on iTunes and the App Store). The top 500 retailers account for about 85% of all online retail. For pure-play firms heavily dependent on Web sales, the challenge is to turn visitors into customers, and to develop efficient operations that permit them to achieve long-term profitability. For traditional firms that are much

TABLE 11.2	ONLINE RETAIL: ADVANTAGES AND CHALLENGES	
ADVANTAGES		**CHALLENGES**
Lower supply chain costs by aggregating demand at a single site and increasing purchasing power		Consumer concerns about the security of transactions
Lower cost of distribution using Web sites rather than physical stores		Consumer concerns about the privacy of personal information given to Web sites
Ability to reach and serve a much larger geographically distributed group of customers		Delays in delivery of goods when compared to store shopping
Ability to react quickly to customer tastes and demand		Inconvenience associated with return of damaged or exchange goods
Ability to change prices nearly instantly		Overcoming lack of consumer trust in online brand names
Ability to rapidly change visual presentation of goods		Added expenses for online photography, video, and animated presentations
Avoidance of direct marketing costs of catalogs and physical mail		Online marketing costs for search, e-mail, and displays
Increased opportunities for personalization, customization		Added complexity to product offerings and customer service
Ability to greatly improve information and knowledge delivered to consumer		Greater customer information can translate into price competition and lower profits
Ability to lower consumers' overall market transaction costs		

less dependent on e-commerce sales, their challenge is to integrate the offline and online channels so customers can move seamlessly from one environment to another.

Clearly one of the most important e-commerce retail themes of 2014–2015, and into the future, is the ability of offline traditional firms such as Walmart, Target, JCPenney, Staples, and others to continue to integrate their Web and mobile operations with their physical store operations in order to provide an "integrated shopping customer experience," and leverage the value of their physical stores. **Table 11.3** illustrates some of the various ways in which traditional retailers have integrated the Web, the mobile platform, and store operations to develop nearly seamless omni-channel shopping. This list is not exclusive, and retailers continue to develop new links between channels.

Rather than demonstrate disintermediation, online retailing provides an example of the powerful role that intermediaries continue to play in retail trade. Established offline retailers have rapidly gained online market share. Increasingly, consumers are attracted to stable, well-known, trusted retail brands and retailers. The online audience is very sensitive to brand names and is not primarily cost-driven. Other factors such as reliability, trust, fulfillment, and customer service are equally important.

The most significant changes in retail e-commerce in 2014 are the explosive growth in social e-commerce, the growing ability of firms to market local services and products

TABLE 11.3	RETAIL E-COMMERCE: OMNI-CHANNEL INTEGRATION METHODS
INTEGRATION TYPE	**DESCRIPTION**
Online order, in-store pickup	Probably one of the first types of integration.
Online order, store directory, and inventory	When items are out of stock online, customer is directed to physical store network inventory and store location.
In-store kiosk Web order, home delivery	When retail store is out of stock, customer orders in store and receives at home. Presumes customer is Web familiar.
In-store retail clerk Web order, home delivery	Similar to above, but the retail clerk searches Web inventory if local store is out of stock as a normal part of the in-store checkout process.
Web order, in-store returns, and adjustments	Defective or rejected products ordered on the Web can be returned to any store location.
Online Web catalog	Online Web catalog supplements offline physical catalog and often the online catalog has substantially more product on display.
Manufacturers use online Web site promotions to drive customers to their distributors' retail stores	Consumer product manufacturers such as Colgate-Palmolive and Procter & Gamble use their Web channels to design new products and promote existing product retail sales.
Gift card, loyalty program points can be used in any channel	Recipient of gift card, loyalty program points can use it to purchase in-store, online, or via catalog, if offered by merchant.
Mobile order, Web site and physical store sales	Apps take users directly to specially formatted Web site for ordering, or to in-store bargains.
Geo-fencing mobile notification, in-store sales	Use of smartphone geo-location technology to target ads for nearby stores and restaurants.

through the use of location-based marketing, and not least, the rapidly growing mobile platform composed of smartphones and tablet computers. In retail circles, tablets are being called "the ultimate shopping machine," enabling consumers to browse media-rich online catalogs just like they used to do with physical catalogs, and then buy when they feel the urge.

Social e-commerce refers to marketing and purchasing on social network sites like Facebook, Twitter, Pinterest, Tumblr, and others. To date, these sites have not become major locations from which consumers actually purchase products, although both Facebook and Twitter have started trials of a Buy button that may begin to change that. Instead they have developed into major marketing and advertising platforms, directing consumers to external Web sites to purchase products. In 2013, the top 500 retailers in Internet Retailer's Social Media 500 earned about $2.7 billion from social commerce, a 60% increase over 2012. More than 7.5 million Web sites have integrated with Facebook by embedding Facebook's Like and Share buttons on their sites (He,

2013). Facebook has around 240 million North American members, and getting the marketing message out on the social graph can happen very quickly.

Whereas in the past only large firms could afford to run marketing and ad campaigns on the Web, this changed radically with the development of local marketing firms like Groupon and LivingSocial, and dozens of others, who make it possible for consumers to receive discount deals and coupons from local merchants based on their geographic location. Using billions of daily e-mails, these so-called daily deal sites have sold millions of coupons to purchase local goods and services at steep discounts. For the first time, local merchants can inexpensively use the Web to advertise their products and services. In 2014, local commerce in the United States is estimated to generate about $4.8 billion in revenues, and this is expected to grow to around $5.5 billion by 2016 (eMarketer, Inc., 2012a).

Social and local e-commerce are enabled by the tremendous growth in mobile Internet devices, both smartphones and tablet computers. In 2014, mobile commerce is expected to generate an estimated €17.7 billion in the United Kingdom. The United Kingdom also has the highest percentage in the EU-5 who use a mobile device to make a purchase, followed by Germany.

11.2 ANALYZING THE VIABILITY OF ONLINE FIRMS

economic viability
refers to the ability of firms to survive as profitable business firms during a specified period

In this and the following chapters, we analyze the viability of a number of online companies that exemplify specific e-commerce models. We are primarily interested in understanding the near-to-medium term (1–3 years) economic viability of these firms and their business models. **Economic viability** refers to the ability of firms to survive as profitable business firms during the specified period. To answer the question of economic viability, we take two business analysis approaches: strategic analysis and financial analysis.

STRATEGIC ANALYSIS

Strategic approaches to economic viability focus on both the industry in which a firm operates and the firm itself (see Chapter 2, Sections 2.2 and 2.5). The key industry strategic factors are:

- *Barriers to entry*: Can new entrants be barred from entering the industry through high capital costs or intellectual property barriers (such as patents and copyrights)?
- *Power of suppliers*: Can suppliers dictate high prices to the industry or can vendors choose from among many suppliers? Have firms achieved sufficient scale to bargain effectively for lower prices from suppliers?
- *Power of customers*: Can customers choose from many competing suppliers and hence challenge high prices and high margins?
- *Existence of substitute products*: Can the functionality of the product or service be obtained from alternative channels or competing products in different industries? Are substitute products and services likely to emerge in the near future?

- *Industry value chain*: Is the chain of production and distribution in the industry changing in ways that benefit or harm the firm?

- *Nature of intra-industry competition*: Is the basis of competition within the industry based on differentiated products and services, price, scope of offerings, or focus of offerings? How is the nature of competition changing? Will these changes benefit the firm?

The strategic factors that pertain specifically to the firm and its related businesses include:

- *Firm value chain*: Has the firm adopted business processes and methods of operation that allow it to achieve the most efficient operations in its industry? Will changes in technology force the firm to realign its business processes?

- *Core competencies*: Does the firm have unique competencies and skills that cannot be easily duplicated by other firms? Will changes in technology invalidate the firm's competencies or strengthen them?

- *Synergies*: Does the firm have access to the competencies and assets of related firms either owned outright or through strategic partnerships and alliances?

- *Technology*: Has the firm developed proprietary technologies that allow it to scale with demand? Has the firm developed the operational technologies (e.g., customer relationship management, fulfillment, supply chain management, inventory control, and human resource systems) to survive?

- *Social and legal challenges*: Has the firm put in place policies to address consumer trust issues (privacy and security of personal information)? Is the firm the subject of lawsuits challenging its business model, such as intellectual property ownership issues? Will the firm be affected by changes in Internet taxation laws or other foreseeable statutory developments?

FINANCIAL ANALYSIS

Strategic analysis helps us comprehend the competitive situation of the firm. Financial analysis helps us understand how in fact the firm is performing. There are two parts to a financial analysis: the statement of operations and the balance sheet. The statement of operations tells us how much money (or loss) the firm is achieving based on current sales and costs. The balance sheet tells us how many assets the firm has to support its current and future operations.

Here are some of the key factors to look for in a firm's statement of operations:

- *Revenues*: Are revenues growing and at what rate? Many e-commerce companies have experienced impressive, even explosive, revenue growth as an entirely new channel is created.

- *Cost of sales*: What is the cost of sales compared to revenues? Cost of sales typically includes the cost of the products sold and related costs. The lower the cost of sales compared to revenue, the higher the gross profit.

- *Gross margin*: What is the firm's gross margin, and is it increasing or decreasing? **Gross margin** is calculated by dividing gross profit by net sales revenues. Gross

gross margin
gross profit divided by net sales

margin can tell you if the firm is gaining or losing market power vis-à-vis its key suppliers.

- *Operating expenses*: What are the firm's operating expenses, and are they increasing or decreasing? Operating expenses typically include the cost of marketing, technology, and administrative overhead. They also include, in accordance with professional accounting standards (see below), stock-based compensation to employees and executives, amortization of goodwill and other intangibles, and impairment of investments. In e-commerce companies, these turn out to be very important expenses. Many e-commerce firms compensated their employees with stock shares (or options), and many e-commerce firms purchased other e-commerce firms as a part of their growth strategy. Many of the companies were purchased at extremely high values using company stock rather than cash; in numerous instances, the purchased companies fell dramatically in market value. All these items are counted as normal operating expenses.

operating margin
calculated by dividing operating income or loss by net sales revenue

- *Operating margin*: What did the firm earn from its current operations? **Operating margin** is calculated by dividing operating income or loss by net sales revenue. Operating margin is an indication of a company's ability to turn sales into pre-tax profit after operating expenses have been deducted. Operating margin tells us if the firm's current operations are covering its operating expenses, not including interest expenses and other non-operating expenses.

net margin
the percentage of its gross sales revenue the firm is able to retain after all expenses are deducted; calculated by dividing net income or loss by net sales revenue

- *Net margin*: **Net margin** tells us the percentage of its gross sales revenue the firm was able to retain after all expenses are deducted. Net margin is calculated by dividing net income or loss by net sales revenue. Net margin sums up in one number how successful a company has been at the business of making a profit on each dollar of sales revenues. Net margin also tells us something about the efficiency of the firm by measuring the percentage of sales revenue it is able to retain after all expenses are deducted from gross revenues, and within a single industry can be used to measure the relative efficiency of competing firms. Net margin takes into account many non-operating expenses such as interest and stock compensation plans.

When examining the financial announcements of e-commerce companies, it is important to realize that online firms often choose not to announce their net income according to generally accepted accounting principles (GAAP). These principles have been promulgated by the Financial Accounting Standards Board (FASB), a board of professional accountants that establishes accounting rules for the profession, and which has played a vital role since the 1934 Securities Act, which sought to improve financial accounting during the Great Depression. Many e-commerce firms in the early years instead reported an entirely new calculation called *pro forma earnings* (also called EBITDA—earnings before income taxes, depreciation, and amortization). Pro forma earnings generally do not deduct stock-based compensation, depreciation, or amortization. The result is that pro forma earnings are always better than GAAP earnings. The firms that report in this manner typically claim these expenses are non-recurring and special and "unusual." In 2002 and 2003, the SEC issued new guidelines (Regulation G) that prohibit firms from reporting pro forma earnings in official reports to the SEC, but still allow firms to announce pro forma earnings in public statements (Weil, 2003). Throughout this book, we consider a firm's income or loss based on GAAP accounting standards only.

A **balance sheet** provides a financial snapshot of a company's assets and liabilities (debts) on a given date. **Assets** refer to stored value. **Current assets** are those assets such as cash, securities, accounts receivable, inventory, or other investments that are likely to be able to be converted to cash within one year. **Liabilities** are outstanding obligations of the firm. **Current liabilities** are debts of the firm that will be due within one year. Liabilities that are not due until the passage of a year or more are characterized as **long-term debt**. For a quick check of a firm's short-term financial health, examine its **working capital** (the firm's current assets minus current liabilities). If working capital is only marginally positive, or negative, the firm will likely have trouble meeting its short-term obligations. Alternatively, if a firm has a large amount of current assets, it can sustain operational losses for a period of time.

11.3 E-COMMERCE IN ACTION: E-TAILING BUSINESS MODELS

So far, we have been discussing online retail as if it were a single entity. In fact, as we briefly discussed in Chapter 2, there are four main types of online retail business models: virtual merchants, omni-channel merchandisers (sometimes referred to as bricks-and-clicks or clicks-and-bricks), catalog merchants, and manufacturer-direct firms. In addition, there are small mom-and-pop retailers that use eBay, Amazon, and Yahoo Stores sales platforms, as well as affiliate merchants whose primary revenue derives from sending traffic to their "mother" sites. Each of these different types of online retailers faces a different strategic environment, as well as different industry and firm economics.

VIRTUAL MERCHANTS

Virtual merchants are single-channel e-commerce firms that generate almost all their revenue from online sales. Virtual merchants face extraordinary strategic challenges. They must build a business and brand name from scratch, quickly, in an entirely new channel and confront many virtual merchant competitors (especially in smaller niche areas). Because these firms typically do not have any physical stores, they do not have to bear the costs associated with developing and maintaining physical stores, but they face large costs in building and maintaining an e-commerce presence, building an order fulfillment infrastructure, and developing a brand name. Customer acquisition costs are high, and the learning curve is steep. Like all retail firms, their gross margins (the difference between the retail price of goods sold and the cost of goods to the retailer) are low. Therefore, virtual merchants must achieve highly efficient operations in order to preserve a profit, while building a brand name as quickly as possible in order to attract sufficient customers to cover their costs of operations. Most merchants in this category adopt low-cost and convenience strategies,

balance sheet
provides a financial snapshot of a company on a given date and shows its financial assets and liabilities

assets
refers to stored value

current assets
assets such as cash, securities, accounts receivable, inventory, or other investments that are likely to be able to be converted to cash within one year

liabilities
outstanding obligations of the firm

current liabilities
debts of the firm that will be due within one year

long-term debt
liabilities that are not due until the passage of a year or more

working capital
firm's current assets minus current liabilities

virtual merchants
single-channel Web firms that generate almost all of their revenue from online sales

coupled with extremely effective and efficient fulfillment processes to ensure customers receive what they ordered as fast as possible. In the following *E-commerce in Action* section, we take an in-depth look at the strategic and financial situation of Amazon, the leading online virtual merchant. In addition to Amazon, other successful virtual merchants include Newegg, Netflix, Overstock, Ratuken (Buy.com), Gilt Groupe, Zulily, Wayfair, Rue La La, Blue Nile (profiled in the opening case), Bluefly, Hayneedle, Net-a-Porter, and Shoebuy. Recently, a new group of virtual merchants have emerged that use a subscription revenue model. Examples include Birchbox (personalized beauty samples delivered monthly), Stitch Fix (clothing selected by a personal stylist) (see the *Insight on Technology* case, *Big Data and Predictive Marketing,* on pages 594–595 for more on Birchbox and Stitch Fix), Barkbox (pet supplies), Naturebox (healthy snacks), Bulu Box (supplements and vitamins), and hundreds more. According to Internet Retailer, overall, virtual merchants accounted for $122 billion (about 41%) of all online retail sales in the United States in 2013 (Internet Retailer, 2014a).

E-COMMERCE IN ACTION

AMAZON

Amazon, the Seattle-based pure-online merchant, is one of the most well-known names on the Web. As stated in its annual report filed with the U.S. Securities and Exchange Commission, Amazon's objective is to be Earth's most customer-centric company. Exactly what this means, and how it might be possible to achieve it, is a matter of speculation for both customers and investors. Yet this has not stopped Amazon's founder, Jeff Bezos, and his team from becoming the Web's most successful and innovative online retailer.

Few business enterprises have experienced the roller-coaster ride from explosive early growth, to huge losses, and then on to profitability that Amazon has. No Internet business has been both so widely reviled and so hotly praised throughout its development. Its stock reflects these changing fortunes, fluctuating over the past 10 years, from an early high of $106 in 1999, to a low of $6 a share in 2001, and then bouncing back and forth between $50–$90 in 2003–2009, then climbing above $400 in 2013 before settling down to closer to $300 in 2014. While controversial, Amazon has also been one of the most innovative online retailing stories in the history of e-commerce. From the earliest days of e-commerce, Amazon has continuously adapted its business model based on both its market experience and its insight into the online consumer.

The Vision

The original vision of founder Jeff Bezos and his friends was that the Internet was a revolutionary new form of commerce and that only companies that became really big early on (ignoring profitability) would survive. The path to success, according to founder Bezos, was to offer consumers three things: the lowest prices, the best selection, and convenience (which translates into feature-rich content, user-generated reviews of books and products, fast and reliable fulfillment, and ease of use). Currently, Amazon offers consumers millions of unique new, used, and collectible items in a variety of different categories, both physical and digital. Its physical goods include books; movies, music, and games; electronics and computers; home, garden, and tools; grocery, health, and beauty; toys, kids, and baby; clothing, shoes, and jewelry; sports and outdoors; and auto and industrial. Its digital products include unlimited instant videos, digital games and software, MP3s and Cloud Player, Audible audiobooks, and Kindle e-book reader products. And if Amazon does not carry it, they have created systems for helping you find it at online merchants who rent space from Amazon, or even at other places on the Web. In short, Amazon has become the largest, single one-stop merchant on the Web, a kind of combined "shopping portal" and "product search portal" that puts it in direct competition with other large online general merchants, eBay, and general portals such as Yahoo, MSN, and even Google. As Amazon succeeded in becoming the world's largest online store, it expanded its original vision to become one of the Web's largest suppliers of merchant and search services.

Business Model

Amazon's business is currently organized into two basic segments, North American and International. Within those segments, it serves not only retail customers but also merchants and developers. The retail component of the business sells physical and digital products that Amazon has purchased and then resells to consumers just like a traditional retailer. It also manufactures and sells a variety of versions of its Kindle e-reader and Kindle Fire tablet computer, as well as its new Fire phone and TV.

Another major component of Amazon's business is its third-party merchant segment. Amazon Services enables third parties to integrate their products into Amazon's Web site, and use Amazon's customer technologies. In the early years of its business, Amazon entered into partnerships with large merchants such as Toys"R"Us, Borders, and Target, and created storefronts for these companies within the larger Amazon site. Today, Amazon has increasingly left the enterprise-level business to competitors and instead it has focused its efforts on small and medium-sized retail merchants.

Thousands of these types of merchants have signed on with Amazon, offering products that in some instances even compete with those that Amazon itself sells. For instance, a single product on the Amazon Web site may be listed for sale simultaneously by Amazon, by a large branded merchant participant such as Target, and by a business or individual selling a new, used, or collectible version of the product through Amazon Marketplace or an Amazon Webstore created by the merchant. For these types of merchants, Amazon is not the seller of record, does not own these products, and the shipping of products is usually handled by the third party (although in some instances, Amazon provides fulfillment services as well). Amazon collects a monthly fixed fee, sales commission (generally estimated to be between 10% and 20% of the sale), per-unit activity fee, or some combination thereof from the third party. In this segment,

Amazon acts as an online shopping mall, collecting "rents" from other merchants and providing "site" services such as order entry and payment.

In many respects, Amazon's third-party seller segment is an effort to compete directly with eBay, the Web's most successful third-party merchant sales platform. eBay has a registered trading community of over 149 million active buyers and sellers. Amazon has even developed its own version of PayPal, Checkout by Amazon, as well as a mobile wallet application for consumers, Amazon Wallet, designed for use at the point of sale. At the same time, eBay itself has moved closer to Amazon's business model by encouraging merchants to sell rather than auction goods on its sites.

Another major part of Amazon's business is Amazon Web Services (AWS). Through this segment, Amazon offers a variety of Web services that provide developers with direct access to Amazon's technology platform, and allow them to build their own applications based on that platform. The company launched the program in 2002. Bezos, however, was not satisfied with only a slew of cool new applications for his company's Web site. In 2006, Amazon introduced the first of several services that Bezos hoped would transform the future of Amazon as a business. With Simple Storage Service (S3) and, later, Elastic Compute Cloud (EC2), Amazon entered the utility computing market. The company realized that the benefits of the billions it had invested in technology could also be valuable to other companies. Amazon has tremendous computing capacity, but like most companies, only uses a small portion of it at any one time. Moreover, the Amazon infrastructure is considered by many to be among the most robust in the world. Amazon began to sell its computing power on a per-usage basis, just like a power company sells electricity.

S3, for example, is a data storage service that is designed to make Web-scale computing easier and more affordable for developers. New customers get a certain amount of storage and services for free. Therafter, customers pay for exactly what they use and no more. Working in conjunction with S3, EC2 enables businesses to utilize Amazon's servers for computing tasks, such as testing software. **Table 11.4** lists some of the various Amazon Web Services that Amazon offers.

Amazon does not break out its revenues from AWS, but analysts believe it will generate over $5 billion in revenue in 2014, up from $3.1 billion the previous year, and that its revenue is likely to double every two years for the foreseeable future. Because AWS provides cloud computing to thousands of Web sites, one research firm concluded that one-third of all Internet users access an AWS cloud site once a day on average, and that 1% of all Internet traffic runs through AWS infrastructure. According to Gartner, AWS has more than five times the combined capacity of its next 14 rivals. These numbers place Amazon at the forefront of the "infrastructure as a service" market.

Even with the success of AWS, Amazon still continues to generate revenue primarily by selling products. While Amazon started out as an online merchant of books, CDs, and DVDs, since 2002, it has diversified into becoming a general merchandiser of millions of other products. Amazon has turned itself into a major online media and content firm and, following its success with Kindle e-books, has also made a strong move into the music and streaming video business, with Amazon Music and Amazon Instant Video. In 2013, 29% of its revenue came from the sales of media and 65% came from sales of electronics and general merchandise.

TABLE 11.4	AMAZON WEB SERVICES
NAME	**DESCRIPTION**
COMPUTING SERVICES	
Elastic Cloud Compute (EC2)	Scalable cloud computing services
Elastic Load Balancing (ELB)	Distributes incoming application traffic among multiple EC2 instances
STORAGE SERVICES	
Simple Storage Service (S3)	Data storage infrastructure
Glacier	Low-cost archival and backup storage
DATABASE SERVICES	
DynamoDB	NoSQL database service
Redshift	Petabyte-scale data warehouse service
Relational Database Service (RDB)	Relational database service for MySQL, Oracle, SQL Server, and PostgreSQL databases
ElastiCache	In-memory cache in the cloud
SimpleDB	Non-relational data store
NETWORKING AND CONTENT DELIVERY SERVICES	
Route 53	DNS service in the cloud, enabling business to direct Internet traffic to Web applications
Virtual Private Cloud (VPC)	Creates a VPN between the Amazon cloud and a company's existing IT infrastructure
CloudFront	Content delivery services
Direct Connect	Provides alternative to using the Internet to access AWS cloud services
ANALYTICS	
ElasticMapReduce (EMR)	Web service that enables users to perform data-intensive tasks
Kinesis	Big Data service for real-time data streaming ingestion and processing
APPLICATION SERVICES	
AppStream	Provides streaming services for applications and games from the cloud
CloudSearch	Search service that can be integrated by developers into applications
Messaging Services	
Simple Email Service (SES)	Cloud e-mail sending service
Simple Notification Service (SNS)	Push messaging service
Simple Queue Service (SQS)	Queue for storing messages as they travel between computers

(continued)

TABLE 11.4	AMAZON WEB SERVICES (CONT.)
DEPLOYMENT AND MANAGEMENT SERVICES	
Identity and Access Management (IAM)	Enables securely controlled access to AWS services
CloudWatch	Monitoring service
Elastic Beanstalk	Service for deploying and scaling Web application and services developed with Java, .Net, PHP, Python, Ruby, and Node.js
CloudFormation	Service that allows developers an easy way to create a collection of related AWS resources
MOBILE	
Cognito	Allows developers to securely manage and synchronize app data for users across mobile devices
Mobile Analytics	Can collect and process billions of events from millions of users a day
PAYMENT SERVICES	
Flexible Payment Service (FPS)	Payment services for developers
DevPay	Online billing and account management service for developers who create an Amazon cloud application
MISCELLANEOUS	
Amazon Mechanical Turk	Marketplace for work that requires human intelligence
Alexa Web Information Service	Provides Web traffic data and information for developers

In addition to Amazon.com in the United States, Amazon also operates a number of localized sites in Europe, Asia, and Canada. The success of its international business often does not attract much attention. For instance, in 2013, Amazon derived over $29 billion, or about 38%, of its $74.4 billion of gross revenue offshore, and international sales grew by 14% for the year.

Financial Analysis

Amazon's revenues have increased from about $600 million in 1998 to an astounding $74.4 billion in 2013 (see **Table 11.5**). From 2010 to 2013, Amazon's revenues have almost doubled. This is very impressive, explosive revenue growth. However, Amazon's growth strategies have made it difficult for the company from a net income perspective. Although it showed a profit of $631 million in 2011, in 2012, Amazon experienced a net loss of $39 million, in large part due to increased operating expenses, which almost doubled during the period, from $33 billion in 2010 to $60 billion in 2012. In 2013, Amazon did reverse that loss and reported net income of $274 million, but fell short of analysts' estimates. Even though investors are generally unhappy with Amazon's poor

TABLE 11.5	AMAZON'S CONSOLIDATED STATEMENTS OF OPERATIONS AND SUMMARY BALANCE SHEET DATA 2011–2013

CONSOLIDATED STATEMENTS OF OPERATIONS (in millions)

For the fiscal year ended December 31,	2013	2012	2011
Revenue			
Net sales/products.	$ 60,903	$ 51,733	$ 42,000
Net sales/services	13,549	9,360	6,077
Cost of sales	$ 54,181	$ 45,971	$37,288
Gross profit	**20,271**	**15,122**	**10,789**
Gross margin	**27.2%**	**24.8%**	**22.4%**
Operating expenses			
Marketing.	3,133	2,408	1,630
Fulfillment.	8,585	6,419	4,576
Technology and content.	6,565	4,564	2,909
General and administrative	1,129	896	658
Other operating expense (income), net. . .	114	159	154
Total operating expenses.	19,526	14,446	9,927
Income from operations	**745**	**676**	**862**
Operating margin	**1%**	**1.1%**	**1.8%**
Total non-operating income (expense) . .	(239)	(132)	72
Income before income taxes	506	544	934
Provision for income taxes.	(161)	(428)	(291)
Equity-method investment activity, net of tax	(71)	(155)	(12)
Net income (loss).	**274**	**(39)**	**631**
Net margin	**.03%**	**−0.06%**	**1.3%**

SUMMARY BALANCE SHEET DATA (in millions)

At December 31,	2013	2012	2011
Assets			
Cash, cash equivalents, and marketable securities.	12,447	11,448	9,576
Total current assets.	24,625	21,296	17,490
Total assets.	40,159	32,555	25,278
Liabilities			
Total current liabilities.	22,980	19,002	14,896
Long-term liabilities.	7,433	5,361	2,625
Working capital.	1,645	2,294	2,594
Stockholders' Equity (Deficit)	9,746	8,192	7,757

SOURCE: Amazon.com, Inc, 2014a.

earnings record, they drove the price of the stock to as high as $400 a share in early 2014, although since then it has dropped down to closer to $300. What this means is that investors are still betting that Amazon will keep growing for a long time and that ultimately, it will be able to show a significant profit.

At the end of December 2013, Amazon had about $12.4 billion in cash and marketable securities. The cash and securities were obtained from sales, sales of stock and notes to the public, venture capital investors, and institutional investors in return for equity (shares) in the company or debt securities. Total assets are listed at about $40 billion. The company emphasizes the strength of its "free cash flow" as a sign of financial strength, suggesting it has more than enough cash available to cover short-term liabilities (such as financing holiday season purchasing). Amazon's cash assets should certainly be enough to cover future short-term deficits should they occur.

Strategic Analysis—Business Strategy

Amazon engages in a number of business strategies that seek to maximize growth in sales volume, while cutting prices to the bare bones. Its revenue growth strategies include driving the growth of e-book sales by offering continuing enhancements of its Kindle e-reader and Kindle Fire tablet computer, both in the United States and internationally, as well as new e-book publishing initiatives; expanding into the cell phone and TV business with its Amazon Fire phone and TV, expanding into the music and streaming video business, with its Amazon Music and Instant Video services; expanding its Amazon Web Services offerings and extending their geographic reach; moving towards a broader trading platform by expanding the third-party seller segment; and moving towards greater product focus by grouping its offerings into major categories called stores. Amazon is still following Walmart's and eBay's examples by attempting to be a mass-market, low-price, high-volume online supermarket where you can get just about anything. To achieve profitability in this environment, Amazon has invested heavily in supply chain management and fulfillment strategies to reduce its costs to the bare minimum while providing excellent customer service and even free shipping.

Specific programs to increase retail revenues are the continuation of free shipping from Amazon Retail (a strategy that has increased order sizes by 25%), Amazon Prime (which for $99 a year provides free two-day shipping and one-day delivery upgrades for $3.99, as well as free access to Amazon Music and Instant Videos), greater product selection, and shorter order fulfillment times. Amazon offers customers same-day shipping in a number of major cities without charging additional fees. Internet customers have long been frustrated both by high shipping and handling charges as well as long delays in receiving goods. A ticking clock can be seen next to some Amazon sale items indicating the hours remaining for an order to make it to the customer by the next day.

Amazon has moved strongly into the mobile shopping space as well, with shopping apps for the iPhone, BlackBerry, Android, Windows Phone 7, and iPad. It also has Deals, Price Check, and Student apps for the iPhone and has opened an Appstore for Android applications. In 2013, Amazon earned around $8 billion from mobile commerce and analyts expect it to more than double that, to $16.8 billion, in 2014. In 2014, Amazon launched its Fire smartphone, which opened to underwhelming sales.

In response, Amazon cut the price of the phone to $0.99 as long as users sign a two-year contract with AT&T. The phone boasts features such as Firefly, which allows you to identify items you see in the world and quickly purchase them via Amazon from your phone.

Amazon has continued to build on the rousing success of its Kindle e-book reader platform, which Amazon has touted as the best-selling product in its history. It has continued to release iterations of the Kindle Fire HD, with the latest, the HDX 8.9-inch selling for $379, while the original Fire HD now sells for just $154. In September 2013, it introduced an all new version of the Kindle Paperwhite, with new higher contrast display technology, a 25% faster processor, a next generation built-in light, and new touch technology that allows the Kindle to respond more accurately. According to Amazon, it now sells more Kindle books than all print books combined.

In 2012, Amazon increased its efforts in the entertainment business, with an expanded content licensing agreement with NBC Universal to add content to Amazon's Instant Video library, and similar agreements with CBS, Viacom and nearly every major Hollywood studio. In 2013, Amazon continued these efforts, with further agreements with Viacom, PBS, A + E, Scripps Networks, and FX. In 2014, they added HBO to the group, and have also developed a series of original shows of their own, in response to Netflix's similar efforts.

On the cost side, Amazon increasingly uses "postal injection" for shipping, in which Amazon trucks deliver pre-posted packages to U.S. Postal System centers. In 2012, Amazon began an aggressive strategy to build warehouses all across the country to improve its delivery speeds, which it has continued through 2014, opening new fulfillment centers in New Jersey, Texas, and North Carolina. Many of Amazon's customers who had previously not paid sales taxes are now being required to pay them due to legislation in various states, so Amazon has prepared by seeking an insurmountable advantage in the entirely different area of delivery speeds. The ultimate goal for Bezos and Amazon: same-day delivery in many areas of the country, perhaps even via airborne delivery drones, which Amazon is reportedly testing.

Strategic Analysis—Competition

Amazon's competitors are general merchandisers who are both offline and online, and increasingly both. This includes the largest online competitor, eBay, and omni-channel retailers such as Walmart, Sears, and JCPenney. Amazon also competes with catalog merchants such as L.L.Bean and Lands' End in a number of product areas. As the Web's largest bookseller, Amazon is in competition with bookstores such as Barnesandnoble.com. Insofar as other portal sites such as MSN and Yahoo are involved in operating online stores or auctions, or selling their own products, Amazon also competes with these portals. Amazon also has a growing rival in China-based Alibaba, which handled more business than eBay and Amazon combined in 2012 and announced its IPO in 2014. In addition, Amazon competes with other firms who sell Web services such as hosting, shopping cart, and fulfillment services. Amazon has also engaged iTunes and Netflix in competition by offering video and audio downloads and Amazon Music, which allows users to store and play music on the Web. Amazon offers over

25 million DRM-free MP3 songs from the major music labels, as well as thousands of independent labels, that can be played on virtually any hardware device and managed with any music software. Amazon also offers Amazon Instant Video, which offers over 150,000 movies and TV shows to rent or buy, and in 2014 launched Amazon Prime Music, which offers over 1 million tracks that users can stream for free, to counter similar offerings from its competitors.

Strategic Analysis—Technology

The person who said that "IT doesn't make a difference" clearly does not know much about Amazon. Amazon arguably has the largest and most sophisticated collection of online retailing technologies available at any single site on the Web. Amazon has implemented numerous Web site management, search, customer interaction, recommendation, transaction processing, and fulfillment services and systems using a combination of its own proprietary technologies and commercially available, licensed technologies. Amazon's transaction-processing systems handle millions of items, a number of different status inquiries, gift-wrapping requests, and multiple shipment methods. These systems allow customers to choose whether to receive single or several shipments based on availability and to track the progress of each order. Amazon's technology extends to its employees as well. Every warehouse worker carries a shoehorn-size device that combines a bar code scanner, a display screen, and a two-way data transmitter. It continues to invest heavily in AWS and the new versions of the Kindle e-reader, and in consumer electronics, with the Kindle Fire tablet and the Kindle Fire smartphone. In 2013, Amazon spent over $6.5 billion on technology and new content, and is on track to spend even more in 2014.

Strategic Analysis—Social and Legal Challenges

Amazon faces a number of lawsuits concerning various aspects of its business. Amazon is frequently sued for patent infringement, which it typically settles out of court. Currently, there are a number of pending patent suits, including some involving Amazon's Kindle.

In recent years, Amazon faced increased challenges from states who were eager to begin collecting sales taxes from Amazon's sales. In the past, only customers in five states were required to pay sales taxes, but at least 23 states have now enacted legislation that will force companies like Amazon to begin charging sales tax. Amazon has already lost several legal battles involving the imposition of sales taxes. Many states had offered Amazon sweetened deals with tax breaks several years ago to lure Amazon's business, perhaps not expecting that Amazon would grow so large that the untaxed sales amount to billions of dollars in lost tax revenue. As many of those deals expire, Amazon has already begun, as mentioned previously, an aggressive (and costly) expansion of its warehousing infrastructure across the United States. In 2014, Amazon settled many of these disputes, agreeing to collect and remit taxes in many states.

Future Prospects

For the first six months of 2014, Amazon registered over $39 billion in sales, as opposed to $31 billion for the same period in 2013, paced by increases in third-party sales, retail, and mobile sales. Amazon believes the increased sales were driven largely by its continued efforts to reduce prices, including shipping offers, by increased in-stock availability, and by an increased selection of products. After posting earnings of $0.23 per share in the first quarter of 2014, up 27% from the previous year, the company took a $0.27 per share loss in the second quarter, due primarily to increased spending on new technology initiatives, such as the Fire phone, new warehouses, buying up video content in competition with Netflix, and creating original programming, as well as introducing new product categories, opening up marketplaces in new territories such as India, and continuing to introduce innovations and new content on the Kindle platform. Amazon's leadership claims to be taking a long-term view, and believes significant profits in the future will result from the investments it is currently making (Amazon, 2014a, 2014b; Kepes, 2014; McGrath, 2014; Perez, 2014; Somaiya, 2014; Portillo, 2014; McIntyre, 2014; Ovide, 2014; Demos and Jarzemsky, 2014).

OMNI-CHANNEL MERCHANTS: BRICKS-AND-CLICKS

Also called omni-channel merchants, **bricks-and-clicks** companies have a network of physical stores as their primary retail channel, but also have online offerings. These are omni-channel firms such as Walmart, Macy's, Sears, JCPenney, Staples, OfficeMax, Costco, Target, and other brand-name merchants. While bricks-and-clicks merchants face high costs of physical buildings and large sales staffs, they also have many advantages such as a brand name, a national customer base, warehouses, large scale (giving them leverage with suppliers), and a trained staff. Acquiring customers is less expensive because of their brand names, but these firms face challenges in coordinating prices across channels and handling returns of Web purchases at their retail outlets. However, these retail players are used to operating on very thin margins and have invested heavily in purchasing and inventory control systems to control costs, and in coordinating returns from multiple locations. Bricks-and-clicks companies face the challenge of leveraging their strengths and assets to the Web, building a credible Web site, hiring new skilled staff, and building rapid-response order entry and fulfillment systems. According to Internet Retailer, in 2013, the chain retailers accounted for around $113 billion (around 35%) of all online retail sales in the United States. In addition, 8 out of the top 10 fastest-growing U.S. merchants over a 10-year period tracked by Internet Retailer from 2003 to 2013 were retail chains (Internet Retailer, 2014a, 2013a).

bricks-and-clicks
companies that have a network of physical stores as their primary retail channel, but have also introduced online offerings

Macy's is a prime example of a traditional merchant based on physical stores moving successfully to become an omni-channel retailer. Rowland H. Macy opened the first R.H. Macy & Co. store in New York City in 1858, and moved the flagship store (now the site of the famous Macy's Thanksgiving parade) to Herald Square at 34th Street and Broadway in 1902. Today, Macy's is one of the largest national department store chains, with around 800 Macy's department stores throughout the United States.

Like many traditional retailers, Macy's has had to change its business model to accommodate the Internet. Macy's (then called Federated Department Stores Inc.) jumped into e-commerce in 1995 with the creation of the Macys.com Web site. In

1999, Federated bought Fingerhut, at that time a leading catalog and direct marketer, in part for its expertise in e-commerce fulfillment and database management. Although the Fingerhut acquisition did not prove to be a financial success, Macy's e-commerce efforts benefitted from the acquisition.

In 2013, Macy's ranked 8th on Internet Retailer's list of the top 500 retail Web sites ranked by annual sales, with about $4.15 billion in online sales, representing over 30% growth over 2012, and more than tripling since 2009. Growth of its physical store sales pales by comparison.

The Macy's Web site receives around 14 million monthly unique visitors. Web site features and functions include an interactive catalog, enlarged product views, ability to see products in different colors and from alternate views, including via zoom, and videos. It also offers product comparisons, product ratings, and product recommendations, as well as a real-time inventory check system. Macy's ranked 6th in the 2013 National Retail Federation Favorite 50 2014 survey of companies with respect to the best e-commerce sites for convenience, safety, and customer service.

Macy's has jumped into social media as well, with a Facebook page that has over 14 million Likes, a Twitter feed with over 390,000 followers, a Pinterest page with 44 different boards and almost 13,000 pins, and a YouTube channel with almost 4 million views. A shopping widget allows shoppers to create polls on Facebook.

Mobile sales at Macy's are booming, and will reach an estimated $790 million in 2014, according to Internet Retailer, 13th on their list of the top 500 mobile retailers for 2014. It has iPhone and Android apps, new versions of which it launched in 2014, and an HMTL5 mobile Web site powered by Usablenet. It currently gets most of its mobile sales from tablets (65%) and via its mobile Web site (also 65%). It has also tried QR codes, SMS marketing, and augmented reality. In a trial run into mobile game advertising, Macy's ran an ad in the Pandora iPhone application that encouraged users to play a game while listening to music. The top of the ad promoted a one-day sale, and after playing the game, users could click through to visit the Macy's mobile site, where the sale was promoted. Previously, Macy's had partnered with Spotify as one of Spotify's first mobile advertisers. Macy's ran audio ads inside Spotify's iPhone app to promote its MStyleLab, targeted at Millennials. In 2014, Macy's is focused on refining its omni-channel approach, encompassing its physical stores, its Web site, and the mobile platform. It will be among the first retailers to support Apple Pay, Apple's new mobile payment system, offering it in addition to Macy's own mobile wallet that allows shoppers to virtually store and access offers and coupons. It is piloting same-day delivery of products ordered online in 8 major U.S. markets, using Deliv, a crowd-sourced delivery provider. Its Buy Online Pickup In Store program, piloted in 2013, also rolled out to all Macy's stores nationwide. It is also piloting new point-of-sale technology that will enable shoppers to purchase with mobile devices while in the store, as well as iBeacon technology (see Chapter 7) (Macy's, 2014; Internet Retailer, 2014a; Kroll, 2014; Kats, 2013; Love, 2013; Johnson, 2012).

CATALOG MERCHANTS

catalog merchants
established companies that have a national offline catalog operation that is their largest retail channel, but who have recently developed online capabilities

Catalog merchants such as Lands' End, L.L.Bean, CDW Corp., PC Connection, and Cabela's are established companies that have a national offline catalog operation, but who have also developed online capabilities. Catalog merchants face very high costs for printing and mailing millions of catalogs each year—many of which have a half-life of 30 seconds after the customer receives them. Catalog merchants typically have developed centralized fulfillment and call centers, extraordinary service, and excellent fulfillment in partnership with package delivery firms such as FedEx and UPS. Catalog firms have suffered in recent years as catalog sales growth rates have fallen. As a result, catalog merchants have had to diversify their channels either by building stores (L.L.Bean), being bought by store-based firms (Sears purchased Lands' End), or by building a strong Web presence.

Catalog firms are uniquely advantaged because they already possess very efficient order entry and fulfillment systems. However, they face many of the same challenges as bricks-and-mortar stores—they must leverage their existing assets and competencies to a new technology environment, build a credible Web presence, and hire new staff. Nevertheless, according to Internet Retailer, in 2013, catalog merchants generated combined Web sales of about $31 billion in the United States (Internet Retailer, 2014a).

Arguably one of the most successful online catalog merchants is LandsEnd.com. Lands' End started out in 1963 in a basement of Chicago's tannery district selling sailboat equipment and clothing, handling 15 orders on a good day. Since then it expanded into a direct catalog merchant, distributing over 200 million catalogs annually and selling a much expanded line of "traditionally" styled sport clothing, soft luggage, and products for the home. Lands' End was the first apparel retailer to have an e-commerce-enabled Web site, launching in 1995 with 100 products and travelogue essays. Located in Dodgeville, Wisconsin, it has since grown into one of the Web's most successful apparel sites.

Lands' End has always been on the leading edge of online retailing technologies, most of which emphasize personal marketing and customized products. Lands' End was the first e-commerce Web site to allow customers to create a 3-D model of themselves to "try on" clothing. Lands' End "Get Live Help" enables customers to chat online with customer service representatives; Lands' End Custom allows customers to create custom-crafted clothing built for their personal measurements. While customized clothing built online was thought to be a gimmick in the early years of online retailing, today, 40% of Lands' End clothing sold online is customized. In 2003, Lands' End was purchased by Sears (which itself was purchased by Kmart in 2004) and then was spun off as an independent company again in 2014. In 2014, Lands' End was 13th on the National Retail Foundation's Favorite 50 survey (Kroll, 2014). Features that garner praise include live video chat, product recommendations that reflect a shopper's preferences, content display based on the shopper's location and referral source, and iPhone and iPad apps that deliver Lands' End catalogs to mobile users. The digital catalogs contain exclusive content, including stories written by Lands' End employees. Shoppers can also visit Lands' End on Facebook, where it has over 1 million Likes. Shoppers can send Lands' End e-gift cards directly from Facebook. Lands' End also has a Twitter presence, where it has over 55,000 followers, and 34 different Pinterest boards (Landsend.com, 2014).

MANUFACTURER-DIRECT

Manufacturer-direct firms are either single- or multi-channel manufacturers that sell directly online to consumers without the intervention of retailers. Manufacturer-

manufacturer-direct
single- or multi-channel manufacturers who sell directly online to consumers without the intervention of retailers

direct firms were predicted to play a very large role in e-commerce manufacturers, but this has generally not happened. The primary exceptions are computer hardware, such as Apple, Dell, Sony, and Hewlett-Packard, and apparel manufacturers, such as Ralph Lauren, Nike, Under Armour, Carter's, Tory Burch, Deckers, Kate Spade, Jones Retail, and Vera Bradley. Most consumer products manufacturers do not sell directly online, although this has started to change. For instance, Procter & Gamble offers PGeStore, which carries over 50 different Procter & Gamble brands. Overall, according to Internet Retailer, consumer brand manufacturers account for about $38 billion in online retail sales in the United States (Internet Retailer, 2014a).

channel conflict
occurs when retailers of products must compete on price and currency of inventory directly against the manufacturers

supply-push model
products are made prior to orders received based on estimated demand

demand-pull model
products are not built until an order is received

Manufacturer-direct firms sometimes face channel conflict challenges. **Channel conflict** occurs when retailers of products must compete on price and currency of inventory directly against the manufacturer, who does not face the cost of maintaining inventory, physical stores, or sales staffs. Firms with no prior direct marketing experience face the additional challenges of developing a fast-response online order and fulfillment system, acquiring customers, and coordinating their supply chains with market demand. Switching from a **supply-push model** (where products are made prior to orders received based on estimated demand and then stored in warehouses awaiting sale) to a **demand-pull model** (where products are not built until an order is received) has proved extremely difficult for traditional manufacturers. Yet for many products, manufacturer-direct firms have the advantage of an established national brand name, an existing large customer base, and a lower cost structure than even catalog merchants because they are the manufacturer of the goods and thus do not pay profits to anyone else. Therefore, manufacturer-direct firms should have higher margins.

One of the most frequently cited manufacturer-direct retailers is Dell Inc., the world's largest direct computer systems supplier, providing corporations, government agencies, small-to-medium businesses, and individuals with computer products and services ordered straight from the manufacturer's headquarters in Austin, Texas. Although sales representatives support corporate customers, individuals and smaller businesses buy direct from Dell by phone, fax, and via the Internet, with about $3.6 billion in sales generated online in 2013 (ranking 2nd only to Apple among consumer brand manufacturers and 10th on Internet Retailer's list of top 500 online retailers) (Internet Retailer, 2014a).

When Michael Dell started the company in 1984 in his college dorm room, his idea was to custom-build computers for customers, to eliminate the middleman, and more effectively meet the technology needs of his customers. Today, the company sells much more than individual computer systems; it also offers enterprise systems, desktop, and laptop computers, as well as installation, financing, repair, and management services. By relying on a build-to-order manufacturing process, the company achieves faster inventory turnover (five days), and reduced component and finished goods inventory levels; this strategy virtually eliminates the chance of product obsolescence.

The direct model simplifies the company's operations, eliminating the need to support a wholesale and retail sales network, as well as cutting out the costly associated markup, and gives Dell complete control over its customer database. In addition, Dell can build and ship custom computers nearly as fast as a mail-order supplier can pull a computer out of inventory and ship it to the customer.

To extend the benefits of its direct sales model, Dell has aggressively moved sales, service, and support online. Each month, the company typically has about 7 million unique visitors at the Dell Web site, where it maintains an estimated 80 country-specific Web sites. Dell's Premier service enables companies to investigate product offerings, complete order forms and purchase orders, track orders in real time, and review order histories all online. For its small business customers, it has created an online virtual account executive, as well as a spare-parts ordering system and virtual help desk with direct access to technical support data. Dell has also continued to broaden its offerings beyond pure hardware product sales, adding warranty services, product integration and installation services, Internet access, software, and technology consulting, referring to them as "beyond the box" offerings. These include nearly 30,000 software and peripheral products from leading manufacturers that can be bundled with Dell products. Dell has also embraced social media. It has a corporate blog, called Direct2Dell, and a presence on Facebook (with almost 7 million Likes), Pinterest (with 10 boards, including boards on entrepreneurship, infographics, and tech tips), and Twitter (with almost 400,000 followers). It posts Twitter-exclusive sales for those who follow Dell Outlet. It also has a channel on YouTube that it calls the Dell Vlog Channel, with almost 40,000 subscribers and almost 70 million views. In 2011, it released mobile apps for the iPhone and Android that featured in-app purchasing, customer ratings and reviews, product comparison, order tracking, a Shopping Advisor, and easy access to various customer support options. Dell promoted the release of the app via both a standard e-mail campaign and one optimized for mobile viewing, and discovered that the open rate for the mobile e-mail was twice that of the standard version, and the clickthrough rate was more than five times higher. In 2012, Dell redesigned its two-year-old mobile site, with a new layout, updated HTML5 navigation, and a host of new functionalities, including shopping assistance, Dell's full product image gallery, social sharing, mobile live chat, a product comparison tool, and simpler, more intuitive purchase process, as well as a more robust set of mobile analytics tools. By 2013, it was reaping the benefits, with an almost 80% increase in mobile revenue (Dell, Inc.; Internet Retailer, 2014a, 2014b; Dusto, 2012).

COMMON THEMES IN ONLINE RETAILING

We have looked at some very different companies in the preceding section, from entrepreneurial Web-only merchants to established offline giants. Online retail is the fastest growing channel in retail commerce, has the fastest growing consumer base, and has growing penetration across many categories of goods. On the other hand, profits for many start-up ventures have been difficult to achieve, and it took even Amazon eight years to show its first profit.

The reasons for the difficulties experienced by many online retailers in achieving profits are also now clear. The path to success in any form of retail involves having a central location in order to attract a larger number of shoppers, charging high enough prices to cover the costs of goods as well as marketing, and developing highly efficient inventory and fulfillment systems so that the company can offer goods at lower costs than competitors and still make a profit. Many online merchants failed to follow these fundamental ideas, lowering prices below the total costs of goods and operations, failing to develop efficient business processes, failing to attract a large enough audience to their Web sites, and spending far too much on customer acquisition and marketing. By 2013, the lessons of the past have been learned, and far fewer online merchants are selling below cost, especially if they are start-up companies. There's also been a change in consumer culture and attitudes. Whereas in the past consumers looked to the Web for really cheap prices, in 2014, they look to online purchasing for convenience, time savings, and time shifting (buying retail goods at night from the sofa). Consumers have been willing to accept higher prices in return for the convenience of shopping online and avoiding the inconvenience of shopping at stores and malls. This allows online merchants more pricing freedom.

A second common theme in retail e-commerce is that, for the most part, disintermediation did not occur and the retail middleman did not disappear. Indeed, virtual merchants, along with powerful offline merchants who moved online, maintained their powerful grip on the retail customer, with some notable exceptions in electronics and software. Manufacturers—with the exception of electronic goods—have used the Web primarily as an informational resource, driving consumers to the traditional retail channels for transactions. Leaving Amazon aside, the most significant online growth has been that of offline general merchandiser giant intermediaries such as Walmart, Sears, Costco, JCPenney, Macy's, Target, and Nordstrom. Many of the first-mover, Web pure-play merchants (online intermediaries) failed to achieve profitability and closed their doors en masse as their venture capital funds were depleted. Traditional retailers have been the fast followers (although many of them cannot be characterized as particularly "fast") and are most likely to succeed on the Web by extending their traditional brands, competencies, and assets. In this sense, e-commerce technological innovation is following the historical pattern of other technology-driven commercial changes, from automobiles to radio and television, where an explosion of start-up firms attracts significant investment, but quickly fail, and are consolidated into larger existing firms.

A third theme is that in order to succeed online, established merchants need to create an integrated shopping environment that combines their catalog, store, and online experiences into one. Customers want to shop wherever they want, using any device, and at any time. Established retailers have significant fulfillment, inventory management, supply chain management, and other competencies that apply directly to the online channel. To succeed online, established retailers need to extend their brands, provide incentives to consumers to use the online channel (which given the same prices for goods is more efficient to operate than a physical store), avoid channel conflict, and build advertising campaigns using online search engines such as Google, Yahoo, and Bing, and shopping comparison sites.

A fourth theme is the growth of online specialty merchants selling high-end, fashionable and luxury goods such as diamonds (Blue Nile), jewelry (Tiffany), and high fashion (Emporio Armani and Gilt) or selling discounted electronics (BestBuy), apparel (Gap), or office products (OfficeDepot). These firms are demonstrating the vitality and openness of the Internet for innovation and extending the range of products available on the Web. Many virtual merchants have developed large, online customer bases, as well as the online tools required to market to their customer base. These online brands can be strengthened further through alliances and partnerships that add the required competencies in inventory management and fulfillment services. Virtual merchants need to build operational strength and efficiency before they can become profitable.

Another theme in 2014 is the continuing extraordinary growth in social commerce, local marketing and commerce, and mobile commerce. In the space of seven years since the first iPhone appeared, the mobile platform has emerged as a retail marketing and shopping tool, which will greatly expand e-commerce, potentially driving e-commerce to 20% of all commerce in the next five years. Local merchants will be a major benefactor of the growing mobile commerce platform. In an equally short time, people have begun to spend an increasing amount of their Internet time on social network sites where they share attitudes and experiences about business firms, products, and services. In a few years, social sites may turn into large purchasing venues.

A final theme in 2014 is the increasing use by retailers, large and small, of Big Data in their marketing efforts. The *Insight on Technology* case, *Big Data and Predictive Marketing*, examines this development.

11.4 THE SERVICE SECTOR: OFFLINE AND ONLINE

The service sector is typically the largest and most rapidly expanding part of the economies in advanced industrial nations such as the United States, and many European and some Asian countries. E-commerce in the service sector offers extraordinary opportunities to deliver information, knowledge, and transaction efficiencies.

The major service industry groups are finance, insurance, real estate, travel, professional services such as legal and accounting, business services, health services, and educational services. Business services include activities such as consulting, advertising and marketing, and information processing. Within these service industry groups, companies can be further categorized into those that involve **transaction brokering** (acting as an intermediary to facilitate a transaction) and those that involve providing a "hands-on" service. For instance, one type of financial service involves stockbrokers who act as the middle person in a transaction between buyers and sellers. Online mortgage companies such as LendingTree.com refer customers to mortgage companies that actually issue the mortgage. Employment agencies put a seller of labor in contact with a buyer of labor. The service involved in all these examples is brokering a transaction.

transaction brokering
acting as an intermediary to facilitate a transaction

In contrast, some industries perform specific hands-on activities for consumers. In order to provide their service, these professionals need to interact directly and personally with the "client." For these service industries, the opportunities for e-commerce are somewhat different. Currently, doctors and dentists cannot treat patients over the Internet. However, the Internet can assist their services by providing consumers with information, knowledge, and communication.

With some exceptions (for example, providers of physical services, such as cleaning, gardening, and so on), perhaps the most important feature of service industries

INSIGHT ON TECHNOLOGY

BIG DATA AND PREDICTIVE MARKETING

Big Data is a phrase that refers to the deluge of digital data that is being produced by 2.8 billion people using the Internet, 1.5 billion using smartphones, over 1 billion people on social networks, and an explosion of data sensors from home thermostats, RFID tags on goods in stores, wearable computing devices like Apple Watch, to retail store cameras and traffic counters. Estimates vary, but an IBM report claimed Big Data amounts to 2.5 billion gigabytes a day. It is estimated that 80% of the world's digital data has been created in the last two years. But Big Data is more than about volume, It is also about velocity: data comes in real time torrents, loses value quickly, and requires rapid responses; variety: the data deluge contains both structured numeric data and unstructured text documents, e-mail, video, audio, stock ticker data and financial transactions; variability: the flow of data is event driven and leads to peak loads, followed by relative calm; and complexity: the data comes from different sources and requires cleansing, matching, and reformatting in order to be useful. Storing all this data requires new kinds of database technologies, and analyzing all this data involves software called business analytics.

Big Data is important for business because it can lead to better decisions and competitive advantages for firms that get it right. Nowhere is this more true than retailing where a great deal of consumer information is now being generated, new products are continually arriving on the scene, and customers have a lot of choices about where to buy. Big Data is influencing the design and marketing of retail products and in-store sales efforts. Big Data and powerful analytics programs make possible predictive marketing, the ability to

send personalized messages to customers recommending products before they ask. The hope for retail firms is that Big Data will make us all into big spenders.

Predictive marketing is not entirely new. Skilled salespeople have always been able to size up a customer and predict how much a customer is willing to spend, informing what they decide to show a customer. It's called salesmanship. Predictive marketing is different because it is not based on traditional sales skills but instead on the collection of data and the use of software programs to maximize the likelihood of a sale. Predictive marketing can scale to millions of customers and make decisions in milliseconds.

Big Data and predictive marketing are not just for huge national retailers, but now can be used by much smaller firms as well. One such firm is Stitch Fix, a women's clothing retailer who is using the monthly subscription revenue model popularized by Birchbox (discussed below). Stitch Fix blends expert styling advice, software, and unique products to deliver a personalized shopping experience. Customers fill out a Style Profile online, which is then analyzed by the firm's proprietary software to identify products that the customer is likely to purchase. Personal stylists interpret the output of the system and then handpick five clothing items and accessories each month that are unique to the customer's taste, budget, and life style. The customer is not required to purchase the items until they have been received and accepted; they can be returned if they do not suit. Over time, the software it uses keeps track of what the customer purchased, and learns to make better predictions in the future based on what customers actually keep (as opposed to what they say they want, a key difference). The better Stitch Fix can make the right choices about what its customers will likely buy, the more revenue it generates. The key to the success of this system is the data collected in the Style Profile online questionnaire that has about 20 questions involving basic demographic information, plus a photo section that depicts seven different styles. Customers can respond to each style suggestion to anchor themselves in the Stitch Fix software. Based on the customer's demographic information and selections of preferred styles, the software predicts which of several thousand products the customer would like.

Birchbox is another subscription-based retailer using predictive marketing and Big Data. Birchbox calls itself a discovery commerce platform and claims to be redefining the retail process by offering consumers a unique and personalized way to discover, learn about, and shop for the best beauty, grooming, and lifestyle products. Headquartered in New York City, Birchbox launched in 2010 and extended into men's products in 2012 with Birchbox Man. Customers fill out a survey telling the company their skin color, hair type, age, and favorite grooming products. The company uses software to match that personal information with profiles of other customers, observes what these other customers have purchased, and makes an educated guess about the beauty products new customers will purchase. The software program analyzes a 15-page profile of each customer, with over 66 characteristics tracked. For each product in inventory, a predictive heat score is produced that is, in essence, the probability that the customer will purchase a product. Birchbox Fix then fills a box each month with beauty samples that match the customer's

profile. If this sounds similar to Netflix's movie recommendation service, that may be because Birchbox's chief analytics officer is Eric Colson, who formerly headed up that firm's recommendation system.

At the other end of the spectrum Walmart, the world's largest retailer with over $470 billion in revenue, is using Big Data and predictive marketing both online and in its stores. About one-third of Walmart's Web traffic comes from mobile devices. Walmart's strategy is to turn mobile devices into shopping instruments for both online and offline shopping. Its mobile app generates shopping lists automatically for customers based on what they and other customers purchase each week. When the customer is in the store, a proximity marketing feature prompts the user to switch into store mode, and then customers are sent discounts and loyalty offers.

Experience with Big Data and predictive marketing in retail is still somewhat limited in 2014. There are many pilot projects, but little information on how well these systems really work for online or offline retail firms. The ability of Big Data to reverse the reduction in shoppers at physical retail stores that has occurred in the last few years (store visits are down at least 5% in the last year) is not certain. So far, there appears to be more data than there is analysis and strategy in predictive marketing. In opinion surveys, firms identify getting value from the data they have as the most challenging aspect of predictive marketing. A key limitation is the scarcity of data scientists who can bring meaning to the data, and managers who can translate these results into sales tactics and strategies.

▬ **SOURCES:** "A New Kind of E-Commerce Adds a Personal Touch," by Molly Wood, *New York Times,* August 13, 2014; "Big Data's High-Priests of Algorithms," by Elizabeth Dwoskin, *Wall Street Journal,* August 8, 2014; "Shoppers Are Fleeing Physical Stores," by Shelly Banjo and Paul Ziobro, *Wall Street Journal,* August 5, 2014; "Retailers Use Big Data to Turn You into a Big Spender," by Mark Milian, Bloomberg.com, June 3, 2014; "How Big Data Helps Stores Like Macy's and Kohl's Track You Like Never Before," by Barbara Thau, *Forbes,* January 24, 2014; "The Risks of Big Data for Companies," by John Jordan, *Wall Street Journal,* October 20, 2013; "Fashion Industry Meets Big Data," by Kathy Gordon, *Wall Street Journal,* September 8, 2013; "Wal-Mart Puts Its Faith in Big Data foir Mobile Strategy," by Cadie Thompson, Cnbc.com, May 22, 2013.

(and occupations) is that they are knowledge- and information-intense. In order to provide value, service industries process a great deal of information and employ a highly skilled, educated workforce. For instance, to provide legal services, you need lawyers with law degrees. Law firms are required to process enormous amounts of textual information. Likewise with medical services. Financial services are not so knowledge-intensive, but require much larger investments in information processing just to keep track of transactions and investments. In fact, the financial services sector is the largest investor in information technology, with over 80% of invested capital going to information technology equipment and services.

Services differ in the amount of personalization and customization required, although just about all services entail some personalization or customization. Some services, such as legal, medical, and accounting services, require extensive personalization—the adjustment of a service to the precise needs of a single individual or object. Others, such as financial services, benefit from customization by allowing individuals to choose from a restricted menu. The ability of Internet and e-commerce technology to personalize and customize service, or components of service, is a major factor undergirding the extremely rapid growth of e-commerce services. Future expansion of e-services will depend in part on the ability of e-commerce firms to transform their customized services—choosing from a list—into truly personalized services, such as providing unique advice and consultation based on a digital yet intimate understanding of the client (at least as intimate as professional service providers).

11.5 ONLINE FINANCIAL SERVICES

The online financial services sector is a shining example of an e-commerce success story, but one with many twists and turns. While the innovative, pure-online firms such as E*Trade have been instrumental in transforming the brokerage industry, the impacts of e-commerce on the large, powerful banking, insurance, and real estate firms have been delayed by consumer resistance and the lack of industry innovation. For instance, online-only banks have not displaced or transformed the large national banks or even regional and local banks. But e-commerce has nevertheless transformed the banking and financial industries, as the major institutions have deployed their own online applications to service an increasingly connected online customer base. Insurance has become more standardized and easier to purchase on the Web. Although security is still a concern, consumers are much more willing to trust online sites with their financial information than in the past. Firms such as Mint (now owned by Quicken), SmartyPig, Credit Karma, Moven, and Simple (now owned by Spanish banking giant BBVA) continue to show growth. Multi-channel, established financial services firms—the slow followers—also continue to show modest gains in online transactions.

ONLINE FINANCIAL CONSUMER BEHAVIOR

Surveys show that consumers are attracted to financial sites because of their desire to save time and access information rather than save money, although saving money is an important goal among the most sophisticated online financial households. Most online consumers use financial services sites for mundane financial management, such as checking balances of existing accounts, and paying bills, most of which were established offline. Once accustomed to performing mundane financial management activities, consumers move on to more sophisticated capabilities such as using personal financial management tools, making loan payments, and considering offers from online institutions. The number of people using mobile devices for financial service needs is also surging. According to research from Mojiva, 70% of survey respondents used a mobile device to access a financial app or site four or more times a week. Over 70% accessed banks accounts, more than 50% used credit card apps and sites, over 40% looked at financial news and stock market information, 35% accessed budgeting apps or sites, and 27% brokerage accounts (Mojiva, 2013).

ONLINE BANKING AND BROKERAGE

NetBank and Wingspan Bank pioneered online banking in the United States in 1996 and 1997, respectively. Although late by a year or two, the established brand-name national banks have taken a substantial lead in market share as the percentage of their customers who bank online has grown rapidly. The top banks are all large, national banks that also offer online banking: Bank of America, JPMorgan Chase, Citigroup, Wells Fargo, and Capital One. The major direct banks (those that operate without a network of branches or branded ATMs), include Ally, Discover, Capital One 360, State Farm, and USAA. These direct banks have seen customer deposits grow faster than regular banks, indicating their growing popularity, particularly with younger customers. Several start-ups have also moved into the online banking and financial services spaces. For instance, Moven offers debit account services linked with online and mobile financial management tools. Simple, recently acquired by Spanish bank BBVA, provides checking accounts linked to debit cards in addition to financial management tools.

In 2014, more than two-thirds of the Internet users in Germany (around 37 million) used online banking. In France the percentage is even higher—around 70% of Internet users. Mobile banking has become an important banking channel for all age groups. For instance, in the U.K, banking transactions conducted via mobile apps more than doubled between 2012 and 2013. According to comScore, U.S. banking Web sites had around 100 million monthly unique visitors in 2013, via both desktop and mobile devices. Top mobile banking activities include checking balances and bank statements, viewing recent transactions, transferring money from one account to another, paying bills, making bill payments, and depositing checks using smartphone apps that snap a photo of the check. Security issues still deter some. A survey by Javelin Strategy & Research found that about 45% of those surveyed cited security concerns as the reason why they did not use mobile banking services (eMarketer, 2014d; Chaudhuri, 2014; Bruene, 2013).

From the bank's perspective, online and mobile banking can provide significant cost savings. According to Javelin Strategy & Research, the average in-person transaction at a bank branch costs $4.25, while an online transaction costs 19 cents, and a mobile transaction, just 10 cents (Javelin Strategy & Research, 2013).

TABLE 11.6	TOP U.S. ONLINE BROKERAGES, 2014
FIRM	NUMBER OF UNIQUE VISITORS (IN MILLIONS)
Fidelity	8.23
Schwab	2.96
Vanguard	2.75
Scottrade	2.36
E*Trade	1.73
TD Ameritrade	1.71
ML (Merrill Lynch)	1.65
Troweprice	0.85
ShareBuilder	0.83

SOURCES: Based on data from Compete.com, 2014

The history of online brokerage has been similar to that of online banking. Early innovators such as E*Trade have been displaced from their leadership positions in terms of numbers of online accounts by discount broker pioneer Charles Schwab and financial industry giant Fidelity (which has more mutual fund customers and more funds under management than any other U.S. firm).

According to comScore, almost 50 million U.S. Internet users have access to an online brokerage account and online trading sites averaged about 10.8 million visitors a month. Over 33% of visitors use a mobile device, or both a mobile device and a computer (comScore, 2014a, 2014b). The top trading Web site among U.S. Internet users in 2014 is Fidelity Investments, with around 8.2 million monthly unique visitors (see **Table 11.6**). The major online brokerage firms are investing significantly in search engine marketing, and are among the biggest spenders in the paid search market. They are also increasingly using social media to engage with customers, although they must be careful to comply with all regulations and rules as they do so. For instance, some brokerage firms use Twitter to deliver commentary, company information, marketing, and customer service.

Multi-Channel vs. Pure Online Financial Services Firms

Online consumers prefer to visit financial services sites that have physical outlets or branches. In general, multi-channel financial services firms that have both physical branches or offices and solid online offerings are growing faster than pure-online firms that have no physical presence, and they are assuming market leadership as well. Traditional banking firms have literally thousands of branches where customers can open accounts, deposit money, take out loans, find home mortgages, and rent a safety deposit box. Top online brokerage firms do not have the same physical foot-print as the banks do, but each has a strong physical presence or telephone presence to strengthen its online presence. Fidelity has walk-in service center branches, but it relies primarily on the telephone for interacting with investors. Charles Schwab has investment centers around the country as an integral part of its online strategy. Pure-online banks and brokerages cannot provide customers with some services that still require a face-to-face interaction.

Financial Portals and Account Aggregators

Financial portals are sites that provide consumers with comparison shopping services, independent financial advice, and financial planning. Independent portals do not themselves offer financial services, but act as steering mechanisms to online providers. They generate revenue from advertising, referral fees, and subscription fees. For example, Yahoo's financial portal, Yahoo Finance, offers consumers the ability to track their stock portfolio, market overviews, real-time stock quotes, news, financial advice, and streaming video interviews with financial leaders. Other independent financial portals include Intuit's Quicken, MSN's MSN Money, and CNNMoney. A host of financial portal sites have sprung up to help consumers with financial management and planning such as Mint (owned by Quicken), SmartPiggy, and Credit Karma.

Account aggregation is the process of pulling together all of a customer's financial (and even nonfinancial) data at a single personalized Web site, including brokerage, banking, insurance, loans, frequent flyer miles, personalized news, and much more. For example, a consumer can see his or her TD Ameritrade brokerage account, Fidelity 401(k) account, Travelers Insurance annuity account, and American Airlines frequent flyer miles all displayed on a single site. The idea is to provide consumers with a holistic view of their entire portfolio of assets, no matter what financial institution actually holds those assets.

The leading provider of account aggregation technology is Yodlee. It uses screen-scraping and other techniques to pull information from over 12,500 different data sources. A smart-mapping technology is also used so that if the underlying Web sites change, the scraping software can adapt and still find the relevant information. Today, Yodlee has more than 40 million personal financial management (PFM) users worldwide and is used by 750 leading financial institutions and companies, including 9 of the 15 largest U.S. banks (Yodlee, 2014).

ONLINE MORTGAGE AND LENDING SERVICES

During the early days of e-commerce, hundreds of firms launched pure-play online mortgage sites to capture the U.S. home mortgage market. Early entrants hoped to radically simplify and transform the traditional mortgage value chain process, dramatically speed up the loan closing process, and share the economies with consumers by offering lower rates.

By 2003, over half of these early-entry, pure-online firms had failed. Early pure-play online mortgage institutions had difficulties developing a brand name at an affordable price and failed to simplify the mortgage generation process. They ended up suffering from high start-up and administrative costs, high customer acquisition costs, rising interest rates, and poor execution of their strategies.

financial portals
sites that provide consumers with comparison shopping services, independent financial advice, and financial planning

account aggregation
the process of pulling together all of a customer's financial (and even nonfinancial) data at a single personalized Web site

Despite this rocky start, the online mortgage market is slowly growing; it is dominated by established online banks and other online financial services firms, traditional mortgage vendors, and a few successful online mortgage firms.

Many mortgage shoppers research mortgages online, but few actually apply online because of the complexity of mortgages. Most mortgages today are written by intermediary mortgage brokers, with banks still playing an important origination role but generally not servicing mortgages they originate.

Although online mortgage originations currently represent a small percentage of all mortgages, their number is expected to continue to grow slowly but surely over the next several years.

Consumer benefits from online mortgages include reduced application times, market interest rate intelligence, and process simplification that occurs when participants in the mortgage process (title, insurance, and lending companies) share a common information base. Mortgage lenders benefit from the cost reduction involved in online processing of applications, while charging rates marginally lower than traditional bricks-and-mortar institutions.

Nevertheless, the online mortgage industry has not transformed the process of obtaining a mortgage. A significant brake on market expansion is the complexity of the mortgage process, which requires physical signatures and documents, multiple institutions, and complex financing details—such as closing costs and points—that are difficult for shoppers to compare across vendors. Nevertheless, as in other areas, the ability of shoppers to find low mortgage rates on the Web has helped reduce the fees and interest rates charged by traditional mortgage lenders.

ONLINE INSURANCE SERVICES

In 1995, the price of a $500,000 20-year term life policy for a healthy 40-year-old male was $995 a year. In 2014, the same policy could be had for around $350—a decline of about 65%—while other prices have risen 15% in the same period. In a study of the term life insurance business, Brown and Goolsbee discovered that Internet usage led to an 8%–15% decline in term life insurance prices industry-wide (both offline and online), and increased consumer surplus by about $115 million per year (and hence reduced industry profits by the same amount) (Brown and Goolsbee, 2000). Price dispersion for term life policies initially increased, but then fell as more and more people began using the Internet to obtain insurance quotes.

Unlike books and CDs, where online price dispersion is higher than offline, and in many cases online prices are higher than offline, term life insurance stands out as one product group supporting the conventional wisdom that the Internet will lower search costs, increase price comparison, and lower prices to consumers. Term life insurance is a commodity product, however, and in other insurance product lines, the Web offers insurance companies new opportunities for product and service differentiation and price discrimination.

The insurance industry forms a major part of the financial services sector. It has four major segments: automobile, life, health, and property and casualty. Insurance products can be very complex. For example, there are many different types of non-automotive property and casualty insurance: liability, fire, homeowners, commercial, workers' compensation, marine, accident, and other lines such as vacation insurance. Writing an insurance policy in any of these areas is very information-intense, often necessitating personal inspection of the properties, and it requires considerable actuarial experience and data. The life insurance industry has also developed life insurance policies that defy easy comparison and can only be explained and sold by an experienced sales agent. Historically, the insurance industry has relied on thousands of local insurance offices and agents to sell complex products uniquely suited to the circumstances of the insured person and the property. Complicating the insurance marketplace is the fact that the insurance industry is not federally regulated, but rather is regulated by 50 different state insurance commissions that are strongly influenced by local insurance agents. Before a Web site can offer quotations on insurance, it must obtain a license to enter the insurance business in all the states where it provides quotation services or sells insurance.

Like the online mortgage industry, the online insurance industry has been very successful in attracting visitors who are looking to obtain prices and terms of insurance policies. While many national insurance underwriting companies initially did not offer competitive products directly on the Web because it might injure the business operations of their traditional local agents, the Web sites of almost all of the major firms now provide the ability to obtain an online quote. Even if consumers do not actually purchase insurance policies online, the Internet has proven to have a powerful influence on consumer insurance decisions by dramatically reducing search costs and changing the price discovery process. According to a 2013 survey by Accenture, 47% of respondents preferred to obtain auto and home insurance quotes online or via a mobile app. However, conversely, most still preferred to meet in person with an agent to set up and proceed with payment for such policies (Accenture, 2013). Another survey found that over 60% of consumers surveyed would use the Internet to conduct research if they were to make a life insurance purchase, although they ultimately would buy from an insurance agent, and an additional 23% said they would both research and buy life insurance online (LIMRA and Life and Health Insurance Foundation for Education, 2013). Another survey found that nearly 2 in 3 consumers who own a mobile device said they already have or plan to use those devices to access services to their life insurance policies, although currently only about 30% of life insurance services have such capabilities (LIMRA, 2014a). Other forms of insurance are more likely to be purchased online. For instance, according to a 2013 comScore study, the online channel continues to be consumers' preferred method for shopping for auto insurance policies, with over two-thirds of shoppers getting an online quote (comScore, 2013a). Insurance companies are also making increased use of social media. For instance, a LIMRA survey found that over 90% of life insurance companies had social media programs, up from 60% in 2010. Facebook and LinkedIn are the most popular platforms, both used by over 90% (LIMRA, 2014b). All of the major insurers, such as GEICO, Allstate, State Farm, Progressive, and Travelers, have a significant online presence. Some of the leading online insurance services companies include InsWeb, Insure.com, Insurance.com, QuickQuote, and NetQuote.

ONLINE REAL ESTATE SERVICES

During the early days of e-commerce, real estate seemed ripe for an Internet revolution that would rationalize this historically local, complex, and local agent-driven industry that monopolized the flow of consumer information. Potentially, the Internet and e-commerce might have disintermediated this huge marketspace, allowing buyers and sellers, renters and owners, to transact directly, lower search costs to near zero, and dramatically reduce prices. However, this did not happen. What did happen is extremely beneficial to buyers and sellers, as well as to real estate agents. At one point, there were an estimated 100,000 real estate sites on the Internet worldwide. Many of these sites have disappeared. However, the remaining online sites have started to make headway toward transforming the industry. In addition, most local real estate brokers in the United States have their own agency Web sites to deal with clients, in addition to participating with thousands of other agencies in multiple listing services that list homes online. Some of the major online real estate sites are Realtor.com, HomeGain, RealEstate.com, ZipRealty, Move.com, Craigslist, Redfin, Zillow, and Trulia. In July 2014, Zillow agreed to buy Trulia for $3.5 billion. Together, they account for over 60% of Web and mobile traffic to online real estate sites (De La Merced, 2014).

Real estate differs from other types of online financial services because it is impossible to complete a property transaction online. Clearly, the major impact of Internet real estate sites is in influencing offline decisions. The Internet has become a compelling method for real estate professionals, homebuilders, property managers and owners, and ancillary service providers to communicate with and provide information to consumers. According to the National Association of Realtors, 90% of buyers surf the Internet to search for a home. Although buyers also use other resources, most start the search process online and then contact an agent, with about 89% purchasing through an agent. Over 40% of buyers said that they first learned of the home that they ultimately purchased via the Internet (Stone, 2013).

The primary service offered by real estate sites is a listing of houses available. In August 2014, Realtor.com, the official site of the National Association of Realtors, listed over 4 million homes and had over 11 million unique visitors. Listings typically feature detailed property descriptions, multiple photographs, and virtual 360-degree tours. Consumers can link to mortgage lenders, credit reporting agencies, house inspectors, and surveyors. There are also online loan calculators, appraisal reports, sales price histories by neighborhood, school district data, crime reports, and social and historical information on neighborhoods. Some online real estate brokers now charge substantially less than traditional offline brokers who typically charge 6% of the sale price. They can do this because the buyers (and in some cases, the sellers) do much of the work of traditional real estate agents, such as prospecting, choosing neighborhoods, and identifying houses of interest prior to contacting an online agent. For instance, Move (the parent company of Realtor.com) also offers a "Find a Neighborhood" feature that allows users to choose the type of neighborhood they want to live in by weighing factors such as the quality (and tax costs) of schools, age of the population, number of families with children nearby, and available social and recreational services. Move also offers mobile apps for the iPad and iPhone, Android, and Windows phones. For instance, the Area Scout function allows users to see the list prices of all homes in a neighborhood on the street level.

Despite the revolution in available information, there has not been a revolution in the industry value chain. The listings available on Web sites are provided by local multiple listing services supported by local real estate agents. Sometimes, addresses of the houses are not available, and online users are directed to the local listing agent who is hired by the seller. Traditional hands-on real estate brokers will show the house and handle all transactions with the owner to preserve their fees, typically ranging from 5% to 6% of the transaction.

11.6 | ONLINE TRAVEL SERVICES

Online travel is one of the most successful B2C e-commerce segments, and accounts for about one-third of all U.S. B2C ecommerce revenues in 2014. The Internet has become the most common channel used by consumers to research travel options, seek the best possible prices, and book reservations for airline tickets, hotel rooms, rental cars, cruises, and tours. Today, more travel is booked online than offline. Online travel services revenues in the EU-5 are expected to reach almost €60 billion in 2014, and continue growing to over €75 billion by 2018 in the EU-5 (see **Figure 11.3**) (eMarketer, Inc., 2014e).

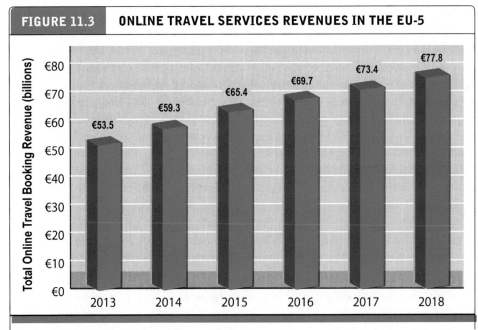

FIGURE 11.3 | **ONLINE TRAVEL SERVICES REVENUES IN THE EU-5**

Online travel service revenues in the EU-5 are expected to reach over €75 billion by 2018.

SOURCE: Based on data from eMarketer, Inc., 2014e.

WHY ARE ONLINE TRAVEL SERVICES SO POPULAR?

Online travel sites offer consumers a one-stop, convenient, leisure and business travel experience where travelers can find content (descriptions of vacations and facilities), community (chat groups and bulletin boards), commerce (purchase of all travel elements), and customer service (usually through call centers). Online sites offer much more information and many more travel options than traditional travel agents. For suppliers—the owners of hotels, rental cars, and airlines—the online sites aggregate millions of consumers into singular, focused customer pools that can be efficiently reached through on-site advertising and promotions. Online sites create a much more efficient marketplace, bringing consumers and suppliers together in a low-transaction cost environment.

Travel services appear to be an ideal service for the Internet, and therefore e-commerce business models should work well for this product. Travel is an information-intensive product requiring significant consumer research. It is a digital product in the sense that travel requirements—planning, researching, comparison shopping, reserving, and payment—can be accomplished for the most part online in a digital environment. On the travel reservation side, travel does not require any "inventory": there are no physical assets. And the suppliers of the product— owners of hotels, airlines, rental cars, vacation rooms, and tour guides—are highly fragmented and often have excess capacity. Always looking for customers to fill vacant rooms and rent idle cars, suppliers will be anxious to lower prices and willing to advertise on Web sites that can attract millions of consumers. The online agencies—such as Travelocity, Expedia, and others—do not have to deploy thousands of travel agents in physical offices across the country but can instead concentrate on a single interface with a national consumer audience. Travel services may not require the kind of expensive multi-channel "physical presence" strategy required of financial services (although they generally operate centralized call centers to provide personal customer service). Therefore, travel services might "scale" better, permitting earnings to grow faster than costs. But these efficiencies also make it hard for reservation sites to make a profit.

THE ONLINE TRAVEL MARKET

There are four major sectors in the travel market: airline tickets, hotel reservations, car rentals, and travel packages. Airline tickets are the source of the greatest amount of revenue in online travel. Airline reservations are largely a commodity. They can be easily described over the Web. The same is true with car rentals; most people can reliably rent a car over the phone or the Web and expect to obtain what they ordered. Although hotels are somewhat more difficult to describe, hotel branding, supplemented by Web sites that include descriptions, photographs, and virtual tours, typically provides enough information to most consumers to allow them to feel as if they know what they are purchasing, making them comfortable enough to make hotel reservations online. Travel packages purchased online constituted the smallest percentage of travel sales.

Increasingly, corporations are outsourcing their travel offices entirely to vendors who can provide Web-based solutions, high-quality service, and lower costs. Online vendors to corporations provide **corporate online booking solutions (COBS)** that provide integrated airline, hotel, conference center, and auto rental services at a single site.

ONLINE TRAVEL INDUSTRY DYNAMICS

Because much of what travel agency sites offer is a commodity, and thus they face the same costs, competition among online providers is intense. Price competition is difficult because shoppers, as well as online site managers, can comparison shop easily. Therefore, competition among sites tends to focus on scope of offerings, ease of use, payment options, and personalization. Some well-known travel sites are listed in **Table 11.7**.

The online travel services industry has gone through a period of consolidation with stronger offline, established firms such as Sabre Corporation (which owns Travelocity,

corporate online booking solutions (COBS)

provide integrated airline, hotel, conference center, and auto rental services at a single site

TABLE 11.7	MAJOR ONLINE TRAVEL SITES
NAME	**DESCRIPTION**
LEISURE/UNMANAGED BUSINESS TRAVEL	
OdeigO	One of Europe's largest online travel groups, formed by merger of eDreams, Go Voyages, Opodo, and Travelink.
Expedia	Largest online travel service; leisure focus.
Orbitz	Second-largest online travel service. Began as supplier-owned reservation system; now part of Orbitz Worldwide, a public company.
Priceline	Name Your Price model; leisure focus. Also owns Travelweb and Lowestfare.com.
Travelocity	Part of global technology company Sabre Corporation. Leisure focus.
TripAdvisor	Travel shopping bot that searches for the lowest fares across all other sites. Owned by Expedia.
Booking.com	Owned by Priceline. Leading European hotel booking service.
TUI AG	German multinational travel and tourism company
MANAGED BUSINESS TRAVEL	
GetThere	Corporate online booking solution (COBS). Owned by Sabre Corporation.
BCD Travel	Full-service corporate travel agency (acquired Travelocity Business (TBiz) in 2013).

Lastminute, and Site59, among others) purchasing weaker and relatively inexpensive online travel agencies in order to build stronger multi-channel travel sites. Orbitz and Expedia have also been involved in the industry consolidation. Orbitz was initially an industry consortium, then went public, then was purchased by Cendant (along with other travel firms such as CheapTickets and Trip.com), then sold by Cendant to Blackstone Group, and finally went public again in 2007. Expedia, originally begun by Microsoft, was purchased by Barry Diller's conglomerate IAC/InterActiveCorp, but has now been spun off as an independent company once again, picking up IAC's Hotels.com, Hotwire, TripAdvisor, and TravelNow in the process. In 2013, Expedia entered into a long-term strategic marketing agreement with Travelocity in which it agreed to provide the technology platform for Travelocity's U.S. and Canadian Web sites, as well as provide Travelocity with access to Expedia's supply and customer service platforms, further consolidating the online travel industry.

In addition to industry consolidation, the online travel industry has been roiled by meta-search engines that scour the Web for the best prices on travel and lodging, and then collect finder or affiliate fees for sending consumers to the lowest-price sites. For instance, TripAdvisor has created a one-stop Web site where consumers can find the lowest price airfares and hotels by searching over 100 other Web travel sites and presenting the fares in rank order. Similar "travel aggregator" sites are Kayak, Fly.com, and Mobissimo. These sites, in the eyes of many industry leaders, commoditize the online travel industry even further, cause excessive price competition, and divert revenues from the leading, branded firms who have made extensive investments in inventory and systems.

Mobile devices and apps used for pre-trip planning, booking, check-in, and context and location-based destination information are also transforming the online travel industry (see also the case study on Orbitz's mobile strategy in Chapter 3). For instance, in 2014, research by comScore found that almost 50% of all UK Internet owners who own a mobile device had used a smartphone or tablet, or both, to research and plan their trips. About 25% used a mobile device to book a hotel or flight (eMarketer, Inc., 2014g). Most of the major airlines now have apps for a variety of mobile platforms to enable flight research, booking, and management. Apps from hotels and car rental companies are available from most of the major players such as Hertz and Avis for car rentals, and Best Western, Choice Hotels, Hilton, and Starwood for hotels. Apps may sometimes target specific consumer behavior. For instance, Expedia reports that 25% of its mobile hotel sales are made at properties within 10 miles of the user's current location, indicating that they are searching for and booking rooms on-the-go, as they travel. Mobile devices are also proving to be quite popular for booking at the last minute. Marriott says that 35% of its smartphone bookings are for same-day travel (eMarketer, Inc., 2014f).

Social media is also having a big impact on the online travel industry. User-generated content and online reviews are having an increasing influence on travel-buying decisions. The *Insight on Society* story, *Phony Reviews,* examines some of the issues this presents for the industry.

INSIGHT ON SOCIETY

PHONY REVIEWS

People used to rely on travel agents for professional recommendations about travel destinations and hotels. Today, however, that function has been largely usurped by sites like TripAdvisor, which aggregates consumer reviews. TripAdvisor has been a smashing success, with more than 100 million user-generated reviews, and is often one of the first places consumers go as they try to decide where to travel and what hotels to book. A good rating can be worth thousands of dollars in bookings. But are all those reviews for real? Can they be trusted?

In the United Kingdom, TripAdvisor was investigated by the U.K. Advertising Standards Authority as a result of complaints. According to online reputation management firm KwikChex, hotels pay people to create false identities and post favorable reviews on their properties, and also to slam competing venues. Known as "astroturfing," the practice of submitting fake favorable reviews to sites like TripAdvisor is becoming more common. In 2013, astroturfing began to draw attention from the legal system, including the New York State Attorney General's office, which began cracking down on astroturfing by businesses giving themselves or paying for positive reviews, and a Virginia court, which ruled in 2014 that anonymous reviews aren't protected by the First Amendment unless the reviewer was a customer.

Astroturfing is just one of several types of problems with online reviews. A disgruntled consumer with an axe to grind can do a lot of damage on online review sites. For instance, Dancing Deer Mountain, a small wedding venue in Junction City, Oregon, had steady business until one wedding went horribly wrong. The proprietors said that rules about bringing in outside alcohol were broken; the situation with the wedding-goers purportedly became combative as a result. Afterwards, scathing online reviews were posted. As a result, business dropped off precipitously. The owners tried suing the reviewers but lost under Oregon law that protects free speech.

Businesses can also damage their reputations by mishandling bad reviews, phony or otherwise. An Arizona bakery went viral in 2013 after an unflattering appearance on a reality show drew negative social media attention. The bakery's owners used Facebook, Yelp, and Reddit to make personal attacks against anyone who had posted a negative review and quickly gained unwanted notoriety. Other businesses offering "reputation management" services have also come under scrutiny for using underhanded tactics and loopholes to artificially manipulate online business ratings.

For sites such as TripAdvisor and Yelp, the growth in phony reviews presents a considerable challenge. The authenticity and accuracy of reviews are critically important to their success, but garnering a high review score is equally important to the businesses listed on the site. Studies have found that if a business can increase its Yelp rating by one star, its revenues will increase anywhere from 5% to 9%, and in March 2014, an industry study found that small businesses using Yelp experienced annual revenue increases of $8,000. This gives businesses ample incentive to post phony reviews praising their own business and slamming their competitors. A 2013 study concluded that approximately 16% of Yelp reviews are fraudulent. If the reviews cannot be trusted, there isn't much incentive for visitors to use the site. With this in mind, Yelp continues to develop ways to remove suspect reviews, including those from rings of businesses who work together to fraudulently increase the ratings of each business in the group. Yelp is also developing its own algorithms, which are intended to detect phony reviews. The company also conducts sting opera-

(continued)

tions to infiltrate these rings, determines which businesses are working together, and outs those businesses publicly.

In 2012, Yelp introduced Consumer Alerts, which inform readers when a review is likely to be fraudulent. The alerts are generated via an algorithm that monitors the site for suspicious posting patterns. While this helps to combat phony reviews, it also increases the risk that legitimate positive reviews will be flagged and removed, hurting both the reputation of the business and the reputation of the review. Since then, Yelp has released additional rounds of Consumer Alerts for over 150 businesses. Still, this is only a fraction of the total number of businesses likely committing fraud on Yelp.

TripAdvisor also claims it uses an algorithm to help filter out false reviews, although it rejects requiring would-be reviewers to supply a reservation number in order to prove that they have actually stayed at the property that they are reviewing. According to TripAdvisor, it takes the authenticity of its reviews very seriously, and has numerous methods to ensure their legitimacy, including automated site tools and a team of review integrity experts. It also relies on the review community itself to identify suspicious content and trolls the sites where businesses advertise for fake reviewers.

There may soon be another tool in TripAdvisor's toolbox. Researchers at Cornell University have developed an algorithm that they say can identify language features specific to fake and truthful reviews. To train the algorithm, they created a database of 20 truthful and 20 fake reviews for 20 hotels, for a total of 800 reviews. According to the researchers, the algorithm accurately identified fake reviews 90% of the time. The truthful reviews tended to talk about the specific details, using specific nouns and adjectives as descriptors. Because those who wrote the fake reviews were not necessarily familiar with the physical location they were reviewing, the fake reviewers, not surprisingly, tended to talk more about themselves, reasons for the trip, and traveling companions. The algorithm has attracted the attention of a number of companies, including TripAdvisor, Hilton, and several specialist travel sites. A new competitor named TripExpert also plans to enter the fray, using aggregated scores from hotels from a variety of sources, instead of customer reviews. The site claims that this will avoid many of the pitfalls of user reviews, but travel writers may be prone to bias and influence to similar degrees.

Will the days of phony reviews come to an end thanks to these advances? Probably not. But review sites and regulators are cracking down on phony reviews with increasing vigor. In 2013, for instance, 19 companies received fines from New York regulators totaling $350,000 for buying and selling fraudulent reviews. Investigators posed as a Brooklyn yogurt shop supposedly seeking help from reputation management firms to increase their rating. Other states are likely to follow suit. So it's best to take what you read with a grain of salt, discarding both the overwhelmingly positive and the unrelentingly negative reviews.

SOURCES: "How TripExpert, a New Review Site, Is Doing Things Differently Than TripAdvisor," Hotelchatter.com, June 12, 2014; A Virginia Court Slams Phony Reviews," by Jill Krasny, Inc.com, January 10, 2014; "Leaving Negative Reviews Online Is Not as Safe as It Used to Be," by Alex Goldman, Onthemedia.org, January 9, 2014; "Fake It Till You Make It: Reputation, Competition, and Yelp Review Fraud," by Michael Luca and Georgios Zervas, Harvard Business School, November 8, 2013; "Fake Yelp Reviews: Anatomy of an 'Astroturfing' Post," by Dhiya Kuriakose, *The Guardian*, September 25, 2013; "Amy's Baking Co. Meltdown Begs the Question: Is Yelp Bad for Small Business?" by Caitlin Dewey, *Washington Post*, May 17, 2013; "Companies To Pay $350,000 Fine Over Fake Online Reviews," by Lance Whitney, Cnetnews.com, September 23, 2013; "Give Yourself 5 Stars? Online, It Might Cost You," by David Streitfeld, *New York Times*, September 22, 2013; "TripAdvisor: Can Users Be Sued for Bad Reviews?" by Natalie Paris, Telegraph.co.uk, September 12, 2013; "Why Yelp Will Never Be Rid of Phony Reviews," by Joshua Brustein, Businessweek.com, August 13, 2013; "Yelp Consumer Alerts: Letting You Know Before You Spend Your Dough," Yelp Official Blog, August 12, 2013; "Deceptive Reviews: The Influential Tail," Eric Anderson and Duncan Simester, MIT, May 2013; "Buy Reviews on Yelp, Get Black Mark," by David Streitfeld, *New York Times*, October 18, 2012; "Yelp Reviews: Can You Trust Them? Some Firms Game the System," by Jessica Guynn and Andrea Chang, *Los Angeles Times*, July 4, 2012; "TripAdvisor Told to Stop Claiming Reviews are 'Trusted and Honest,'" *Daily Mail*, February 1, 2012; "A Lie Detector Test for Online Reviewers," by Karen Weise, *BusinessWeek*, September 29, 2011; "Cornell Researchers Work to Spot Fake Reviews," by Emma Court, *The Cornell Daily Sun*, September 23, 2011; "The Yelp Wars: False Reviews, Anti-SLAPP, and Slander – What's Ethical in Online Reviewing?", by Kathleen Miles, Scpr.org, August 25, 2011.

11.7 ONLINE CAREER SERVICES

Next to travel services, one of the Internet's most successful online services has been job services (recruitment sites) that provide a free posting of individual resumes, plus many other related career services; for a fee, they also list job openings posted by companies. Career services sites collect revenue from other sources as well, by providing value-added services to users and collecting fees from related service providers.

The U.S. online job market is dominated by two large players: Monster, with about 13 million unique monthly visitors, and CareerBuilder, with about 9.5 million. Other popular sites include Indeed (25 million unique visitors), Glassdoor (6.5 Million), SimplyHired (5 million), and SnagAJob (4 million). These top sites generate more than $1 billion annually in revenue from employers' fees and consumer fees. A 2013 survey found that around 70% of U.S. Internet users surveyed had looked for jobs online, and that it was the primary form of job hunting for over 25% (Pilon, 2013). The professional social network site LinkedIn is also becoming an increasingly important player in this market.

Traditionally, companies have relied on five employee recruitment tools: classified and print advertising, career expos (or trade shows), on-campus recruiting, private employment agencies (now called "staffing firms"), and internal referral programs. In comparison to online recruiting, these tools have severe limitations. Print advertising usually includes a per-word charge that limits the amount of detail employers provide about a job opening, as well as a limited time period within which the job is posted. Career expos do not allow for pre-screening of attendees and are limited by the amount of time a recruiter can spend with each candidate. Staffing firms charge high fees and have a limited, usually local, selection of job hunters. On-campus recruiting also restricts the number of candidates a recruiter can speak with during a normal visit and requires that employers visit numerous campuses. And internal referral programs may encourage employees to propose unqualified candidates for openings in order to qualify for rewards or incentives offered.

Online recruiting overcomes these limitations, providing a more efficient and cost-effective means of linking employers and potential employees, while reducing the total time to hire. Online recruiting enables job hunters to more easily build, update, and distribute their resumes while gathering information about prospective employers and conducting job searches.

IT'S JUST INFORMATION: THE IDEAL WEB BUSINESS?

Online recruitment is ideally suited for the Web. The hiring process is an information-intense business process that involves discovering the skills and salary requirements of individuals and matching them with available jobs. In order to accomplish this matchup, there does not initially need to be face-to-face interaction, or a great deal of personalization. Prior to the Internet, this information sharing was accomplished locally by human networks of friends, acquaintances, former employers, and relatives, in addition to employment agencies that developed paper files on job hunters.

TABLE 11.8	POPULAR U.S. ONLINE RECRUITMENT SITES
RECRUITMENT SITE	BRIEF DESCRIPTION
GENERAL RECRUITMENT SITES	
Monster	One of the first commercial sites on the Web in 1994. Today, a public company offering general job searches in 50 countries. Acquired Yahoo HotJobs in 2010 for $225 million.
CareerBuilder	Owned by Gannett, Tribune, and McClatchy (all newspaper companies). Provides job search for more than 10,000 Web sites, including AOL and MSN, and 140 newspapers; over 1 million jobs listed.
Indeed	Job site aggregator
SimplyHired	Job site aggregator
Craigslist	Popular classified listing service focused on local recruiting
EXECUTIVE SEARCH SITES	
Futurestep	Korn/Ferry site, low-end executive recruiting
Spencerstuart	Middle-level executive recruiting
ExecuNet	Executive search firm
NICHE JOB SITES	
SnagAJob	Part-time and hourly jobs
USAJobs	Federal government jobs
HigherEdJobs	Education industry
EngineerJobs	Engineering jobs
Medzilla	Biotechnology, pharmaceutical, medical, and healthcare industry
Showbizjobs	Entertainment industry
Salesjobs	Sales and marketing
Dice	Information technology jobs
MBAGlobalNet	MBA-oriented community site

The Internet can clearly automate this flow of information, reducing search time and costs for all parties.

Table 11.8 lists some of the most popular recruitment sites.

Why are so many job hunters and employers using Internet job sites? Recruitment sites are popular largely because they save time and money for both job hunters and employers seeking recruits. For employers, the job boards expand the geographical reach of their searches, lower costs, and result in faster hiring decisions.

For job seekers, online sites are popular not only because their resumes can be made widely available to recruiters but also because of a variety of other related job-hunting services. The services delivered by online recruitment sites have greatly expanded since their emergence in 1996. Originally, online recruitment sites just provided a digital version of newspaper classified ads. Today's sites offer many other services, including skills assessment, personality assessment questionnaires, personalized account management for job hunters, organizational culture assessments, job search tools, employer blocking (prevents your employer from seeing your posting), employee blocking (prevents your employees from seeing your listings if you are their employer), and e-mail notification. Online sites also provide a number of educational services such as resume writing advice, software skills preparation, and interview tips.

For the most part, online recruitment sites work, in the sense of linking job hunters with jobs, but they are just one of many ways people actually find jobs. A survey by The Conference Board found that the majority (70%) of job seekers rely equally on both the Internet and newspapers to look for jobs, with about half relying on word-of-mouth leads, and about a quarter on employment agencies. Given that the cost of posting a resume online is zero, the marginal returns are very high.

The ease with which resumes can be posted online has also raised new issues for both job recruiters and job seekers. If you are an employer, how do you sort through the thousands of resumes you may receive when posting an open job? If you are a job seeker, how do you stand out among the thousands or even millions of others? Perhaps one way is to post a video resume. In a survey by Vault, nearly nine in 10 employers said they would watch a video resume if it were submitted to them, in part because it would help them better assess a candidate's professional presentation and demeanor, and over half said they believed video would become a common addition to future job applications. CareerBuilder became the first major online job site to implement a video resume tool for job candidates, following a previous launch for an online video brand-building tool for employers.

Perhaps the most important function of online recruitment sites is not so much their capacity to actually match employers with job hunters but their ability to establish market prices and terms, as well as trends in the labor market. Online recruitment sites identify salary levels for both employers and job hunters and categorize the skill sets required to achieve those salary levels. In this sense, online recruitment sites are online national marketplaces that establish the terms of trade in labor markets. For instance, Monster.com offers its U.S. Monster Employment Index. This index is based on a large, representative selection of corporate career sites and job boards, and calculates employment demand for the nation, regions, and specific occupations. The existence of these online national job sites should lead to a rationalization of wages, greater labor mobility, and higher efficiency in recruitment and operations because employers will be able to quickly find the people they need.

ONLINE RECRUITMENT INDUSTRY TRENDS

Trends for 2014–2015 in the online recruitment services industry include the following:

- **Social networking:** According to a survey of recruiters and executives in North America, 98% of recruiting professionals used social networks to find new employees, with over 97% of them using LinkedIn (eMarketer, Inc., 2013). LinkedIn, probably the most well-known business-oriented social network, has grown significantly to over 310 million members representing over 170 different industries in over 200 countries as of September 2014. LinkedIn's corporate hiring solutions are used by over 90 of the Fortune 100 companies, and more than 3 million companies have a LinkedIn page. Consumers are using sites such as LinkedIn to establish business contacts and networks. For instance, according to LinkedIn, its members do almost 6 billion professionally-oriented searches on LinkedIn a year. Employers are also using LinkedIn to conduct searches to find potential job candidates that may not be actively job hunting. For instance, LinkedIn offers companies a feature called LinkedIn Talent Solutions that includes tools that help corporate recruiters find "passive talent" (people who are not actively looking for a new job), as well as custom company profiles that are specifically designed for recruitment. Career-Builder offers a job and internship matching application on Facebook that allows users to receive continuously updated listings based on the information found in their profiles. Social network sites are also being used by employers to "check up" on the background of job candidates. A study by Harris Interactive of over 2,000 managers and human resource employees found that over 40% are using social networks to screen job candidates, and over 50% have rejected candidates because of content on a social site. Employers typically search Facebook, Twitter, and LinkedIn. Provocative photos were the biggest negative factor followed by drinking and drug references (Careerbuilder, 2014).

- **Mobile:** As with other forms of services, career services firms have also moved onto the mobile platform. A 2011 study found that around 20% of job seekers who are 18 to 34 years old reported that they searched for jobs and researched companies using mobile devices. To reach this audience, CareerBuilder, Monster, LinkedIn, and most of the other major sites all have a mobile Web site, as well as apps that allow job seekers to create and upload resumes, search jobs by keyword, location, and company, e-mail jobs, browse and apply, and more. LinkedIn's app, for instance, can also recommend jobs based on data you provide on your profile page. In 2014, mobile accounts for 45% of the unique members visiting LinkedIn.

- **Job search engines/aggregators:** As with travel services, search engines that focus specifically on jobs are posing a new threat to established online career sites. For instance, Indeed, SimplyHired, and Us.jobs "scrape" listings from thousands of online job sites such as Monster, CareerBuilder, specialty recruiting services, and the sites of individual employers to provide a free, searchable index of thousands of job listings in one spot. Because these firms do not charge employers a listing fee, they are currently using a pay-per-click or other advertising revenue model.

- **Consolidation:** The two major job services are CareerBuilder and Monster. In 2014, these two sites continue to dominate the market, and are expected to do so for some time to come.

- **Diversification:** While the national online market is becoming larger and consolidating into a few general sites, there is an explosion in specialty niche employment sites that focus on specific occupations. This is creating greater online job market diversity and choice.

- **Localization:** While local classified ads in newspapers remain a significant source of jobs, the large national online sites are also developing local boards in large metropolitan areas that compete more directly against local newspapers. The local newspapers themselves have responded by building Web sites that focus on local job markets, especially hourly and contract jobs that often do not appear on the large national job boards. Craigslist is another source of local job listings. Hence there is a growing focus on local job markets by all participants in the marketplace because this is where so many new jobs first appear.

11.8 SHARING ECONOMY COMPANIES

The phrase "sharing economy" refers to the explosion of online firms that provide a platform for users to share assets and resources like bikes, cars, rooms with beds, entire homes, jet planes, and even high fashion clothes (Friedman, 2014; Rosenberg, 2013). Other common phrases used to describe these online businesses are "collaborative commerce," "peer to peer consumption," "mesh economy," and "we-commerce." Unlike traditional sharing where there is no fee charged in the transaction, in today's so-called sharing economy, firms collect a fee from both sellers and buyers for using the platform (Rosenberg, 2013). In the last four years, hundreds of start-ups, funded by nearly $2 billion in venture capital, have created online platforms where owners of resources that are underutilized can sell access to those resources to consumers who would prefer not to, or are unable to, buy those resources themselves. It's a tradeoff between owning versus accessing (Needleman and Loten, 2014; Friedman, 2014).

Several sharing economy firms have grown exponentially over the last five years. If eBay liberated the economic value of stuff in the attics of America, the new sharing economy sites are emptying the garages filled with cars at rest, and the houses and apartments filled with rarely used spare beds. **Table 11.9** describes just a few of the hundreds of firms whose business model is to provide transaction platforms for asset owners and consumers.

TABLE 11.9	EXAMPLES OF SHARING ECONOMY FIRMS
FIRM	BUSINESS MODEL
Airbnb	Property owners rent out lodging
Uber	Car owners rent their cars
Lyft	Car owners rent their cars
CitiBike	New York City bike sharing service
Rent the Runway	High fashion dresses and accessories
Task Rabbit	Errand service platform rents labor
RelayRides	Peer-to-peer car rental service
Guidehop	Guide service connects travelers to local guides
PeerSpace	Business space owners rent creative space for short periods

Collaborative commerce, trading platforms, sharing firms, and peer-to-peer commerce are not new. While eBay involves the sale of items at auction or for fixed prices, most of the new sharing sites sell access to cars, beds, room, spaces, and even skilled people. What is new about these firms is their use of mobile and Internet technology to enable transactions on their platforms. This is especially true of the car and room rental services where transactions are local and mobile. Second, the growth of these firms is supported by the use of online reputation systems based on peer review, to establish a trusted environment where sellers and consumers can feel confident transacting with one another. Online peer review of both the owners and the consumers help to ensure that both parties have acceptable reputations, and that a high quality of service is provided. These firms have learned from eBay and Netflix the importance of peer reviews and ratings. A third factor in the growth of the sharing economy is that successful firms lower the cost of services like urban transportation, lodging, office space, and personal errand services. Firms that can do this are highly disruptive of existing firms and business models.

Uber and Airbnb are among the most successful peer-to-peer sharing platforms. Uber operates in 92 U.S. cities and 72 outside the United States. Uber was founded in 2009 as a car service with professional drivers and Lincoln Town Cars. It added a low cost service, UberX, in 2012. In June 2014, it took an investment from investment giant Fidelity for $1.2 billion, one of the largest venture investments of the year, and has raised a total of $1.6 billion in its first four years of operation (Rusli and Macmillan, 2014). In October 2014, Uber was valued by investors at about $18 billion. It is said to be the fastest expanding e-commerce company in history. It has estimated revenues of $1 billion, and earnings of over $200 million in 2013 although it is a private company and does not release revenue or earning numbers (Panzarino, 2014).

Airbnb was founded in 2008 as a way to find lodging for attendees at a business convention. Since then, Airbnb has expanded to the entire lodging marketplace, and has grown exponentially. Airbnb now operates in 34,000 cities in 190 countries, and lists over 800,000 properties for rent, including 600 castles and dozens of yurts in Mongolia. In the six years since its founding, Airbnb has grown to be larger than the Intercontinental, the world's largest private hotel chain, which has 4,600 hotels, and more than 674,000 rooms in 100 countries.

In April 2014, Airbnb took an investment of $475 million, which valued the company at $10 billion. People with spaces to rent, which can range from a single sofa to an entire apartment or house, create an account and a profile, and then list their properties on the site. The amount charged depends on the host and is usually based on the host's assessment of similar listings nearby and market demand. Travelers seeking to rent spaces register and create an account, which includes a profile. They then consult the Web site listings, read reviews of the host, and contact the host to arrange for the rental. After the rental period, hosts rate their renters, and vice versa. Renters pay through their Airbnb account, which must be funded by a credit card. Airbnb charges guests a sliding fee of 6% to 12%, depending on the price of the booking, and charges the host 3%. The hosts are issued a 1099 form at the end of the year to report taxes due on the income. See the *Insight on Business* case, *Airbnb Takes Off*, for a further discussion of Airbnb and other similar services, such as Wimdu and 9flats.

INSIGHT ON BUSINESS

AIRBNB TAKES OFF

Wouldn't it be nice if every time you went on vacation, you could make a little extra money by renting your apartment to responsible tenants? Or if you had a second property that you could use to make a little extra money without having to make six-month or year-long sublet agreements? And wouldn't it be even better if every time you traveled somewhere, you could find one of these types of apartments for yourself for a deep discount compared to area hotels? This is the inefficiency that short-term C2C real estate rental companies such as Airbnb, Wimdu, and a host of others have attempted to solve with the aid of the new mobile platform. So far, these fledgling "private accommodation service" companies are still finding their footing with regard to profits and losses, but the industry has grown steadily since Airbnb's founding in 2008.

Airbnb is regarded as the biggest player in this emerging field, but it does have some competition. One such competitor is Wimdu. Funded by Rocket Internet and the Samwer brothers, Wimdu is very closely modeled after Airbnb, but tailors its business tactics from country to country. Travelers log onto Wimdu, type in their destination and specify their travel dates, and site filters display locations that meet those criteria. Currently, travelers can choose from over 300,000 properties in over 140 countries worldwide. Its portal is available in 26 different languages. Users can add places to their "favorites" list and submit reviews of hosts and properties. Wimdu also offers insurance against damages to properties up to €500,000 and offers travelers free customer service. Wimdu and 9flats, another European-based C2C rental company, have both struggled

to show profits in the early going. Wimdu, in particular, has raised almost $100 million in an effort to grow its user base rapidly (currently totalling over 3 million people) and reach profitability, but they have not reached that point as of yet. 9flats has not received anywhere near as much venture capital, though it is supported by eVenture Capital Partners, Redpoint Ventures, and T-venture. Potential challenges to the business model include preventing guests from damaging apartments and challenges from local and national governments, as will be subsequently discussed.

With many clone companies like Wimdu, the end goal is to sell the business to the established leader, which in this case is Airbnb. Although Airbnb founder Brian Chesky admitted coming close to purchasing Wimdu in 2011, the company ultimately decided against it, reportedly due to concerns about Wimdu's business culture and operating style. To date, Airbnb has continued to spurn Wimdu and has instead opted to enter the German market and compete directly against Wimdu. Airbnb is valued at $10 billion, operates in 34,000 cities in 190 countries, and raised almost $800 million in venture funding. Its eventual initial public offering is highly anticipated, but the company is determined to solidify its business operations before going public.

Wimdu's management rejects the idea that it is struggling with its bottom line figures and growth prospects, instead focusing on Wimdu's increased selection of properties. Wimdu has been recognized by media outlets for its superior customer marketing. Also, because the private accommodation services are business platforms more so than a social network, the existing power of Airbnb is not an insurmountable obstacle for

(continued)

Wimdu, 9flats, and other European-based C2C real estate rental companies, such as Homeaway and HouseTrip.

Perhaps the biggest current problem for the private accommodation service industry is governmental interference. Both city and national governments are cracking down on short-term rental services, which could enable residents to elude restrictions that would preclude them from securing permanent housing. In Singapore, law enforcement is imposing stiff penalties on any homeowner renting their home via these services. The minimum subletting period is six months. This only applies if money is exchanged. Homeowners can allow friends and relatives to stay over. Berlin is another city that has decided to regulate short-term holiday rentals, hoping to curb the notable increase in cost of living and scarcity of affordable apartments available for rent in the city dating back to 2007. Munich and Hamburg already have similar laws.

In Amsterdam, where individuals are allowed to rent out their property only if they follow certain regulations, the city government has used Airbnb and its competitors to investigate illegal rental properties, by combining its own data with listings. An initial government scan found that about 700 of the almost 4,000 listings on Airbnb were illegal hotels. The government also believes that Airbnb and similar businesses fail to comply with local tax legislation. Airbnb contends that it is simply a marketplace, and that its users are the ones responsible for complying with local laws.

New York City is another battleground, initially ruling in 2013 that a host using Airbnb was violating a 2010 law preventing individuals from renting out properties for fewer than 29 days. The host faced the possibility of over $40,000 in fines, but those fines were reduced and then eventually overturned by a New York City regulatory board. This represented a big win for Airbnb, but many other New York City regulations curtail hosts' ability to rent their apartments on services like Airbnb. Naturally, C2C rental companies argue that their services don't contribute to increases in costs of living, and evidence of this is scarce.

Airbnb has continued to exercise influence in New York to overturn similar rulings and to change legislative opinion. The Internet Association, a coalition whose members include industry leaders such as Amazon, eBay, Google, and Facebook, joined with Airbnb to fight an attempt by the New York State Attorney General to obtain data on 15,000 New York State residents who have hosted guests using Airbnb since 2010. New York is one of the prime battlegrounds for short-term rental services. In the same vein, 9flats, Wimdu, and HouseTrip, another Swiss-based rental service, have formed a network to lobby European governments with a unified voice as these services become a more important part of the tourism industry there. Airbnb is not a part of that group, perhaps an effort by the European-based companies to compete together against a common enemy. The European network hopes to support tenants and landlords with legal matters and participate in creating regulations and developing solutions to current issues. Still, Airbnb, Wimdu, and their counterparts are united in their desire to see C2C short-term home rental become commonplace, and there are signs that it just might happen.

SOURCES: "Two-thirds of Berlin's Tourist Flats Now Illegal," Thelocal.de, August 1, 2014; "Internet Association Sides with Airbnb in NY Privacy Battle," by Wendy Davis, Mediapost.com, November 8, 2013; "9Flats, Wimdu, and HouseTrip Form Lobby Group," by Michelle Kuepper, Venturevillage.eu, October 31, 2013; "Rocket Internet's Wimdu Missed Out on Dream Takover by Airbnb – Here's Why," by Georg Rath, Venturevillage.eu, October 14, 2013; "Tenant's Fine for Renting to Tourist is Overturned," by Ann Carrns, *New York Times*, September 30, 2013; "Short Term Home Rentals Illegal in Singapore – Airbnb, Roomorama, Travelmob, and Wimdu Affected." Asia-travel-notes.com, September 13, 2013; "Sharing Verboten: Berlin Puts Kibosh on Airbnb and Co.," by Janko Tietz, Spiegal.de, August 14, 2013; "Airbnb is Shifting Its Strategy So It Doesn't Crash and Burn," by Megan Rose Dickey, Businessinsider.com, July 16, 2013; "Will Berlin Follow New York and Rule Airbnb-style Sites Illegal?" by Nina Fowler, Venturevillage.eu, May 30, 2013; "Airbnb Deemed Illegal in New York City in Landmark Ruling," by Linsey Fryatt, Venturevillage.eu, May 21, 2013; "Amsterdam Airbnb Listings Set to Decline Sharply in Illegal Rental Crack Down," by Loek Essers, Cio.com.au, February 19, 2013; "Airbnb Could Be Banned in Amsterdam: Local Authorities are Now Hunting for Illegal Hotels," by Harrison Weber, Thenextweb.com, February 2, 2013; "Are Wimdu and 9flats.com Weighing Down Their Investors?" by Alexander Husing, Deutsche-startups.com, January 2, 2013.

Not all peer-to-peer sharing economy platforms are successful. Among the dozens of failures are BlackJet, a Florida-based jet rental service that could not develop a stable demand; RideJoy, a carpooling site; DogVacy, a site that matched pet owners with sitters; Neighborrow, a site that helped neighbors share tools; and HiGear, a luxury rental car business. While the reasons for their failure are several, one cause of failure is choosing a marketspace that is too small to generate sufficient and steady demand throughout the year. The infrastructure required to service a market with 100,000 potential customers costs nearly as much as the infrastructure needed to serve 10 million customers.

Uber and Airbnb stand out not only as the most successful of sharing economy firms, but also as the most disruptive and controversial. For instance, with Airbnb, property renters do not have the regulatory or tax burdens that hotel owners have. It is possible that the success of Airbnb could greatly reduce the demand for regulated hotels. There is little research on this topic, but an early paper found that Airbnb had a small impact on rental income at lower-end tourist hotels, but little empirical impact on business traveler hotels (Zervas and Buyers, 2014). The possibility of negative outcomes from transactions on these sharing economy sites (e.g., a driver robs or harms a passenger, or an apartment is destroyed by renters), is leading both firms to require liability insurance, or to offer such insurance for free. It is unlikely that sharing economy firms will escape regulation altogether, but due to their popularity and success, it is likely that regulation will be minimal.

OpenTable:
Your Reservation Is Waiting

OpenTable is the leading supplier of reservation, table management, and guest management software for restaurants. In addition, the company operates OpenTable.com, the world's most popular Web site for making restaurant reservations online. In 15 years, OpenTable has gone from a start-up to a successful and growing public company that counts around two-thirds of the nation's reservation-taking restaurants as clients.

Today, more than 31,000 restaurants in the United States, Canada, Mexico, the United Kingdom, Germany, and Japan use the OpenTable hardware and software system. This system automates the reservation-taking and table management process, while allowing restaurants to build diner databases for improved guest recognition and targeted e-mail marketing. The OpenTable Web site, OpenTable for Mobile Web (its mobile Web site), and OpenTable Mobile (its mobile app) provide a fast, efficient way for diners to find available tables in real time. The Web sites and app connect directly to the thousands of computerized reservation systems at OpenTable restaurants, and reservations are immediately recorded in a restaurant's electronic reservation book.

© Justin Sullivan/Getty Images

Restaurants subscribe to the OpenTable Electronic Reservation Book (ERB), the company's proprietary software, which is installed on a touch-screen computer system and supported by asset-protection and security tools. The ERB software provides a real-time map of the restaurant floor and enables the restaurant to retain meal patterns of all parties, serving as a customer relationship management (CRM) system for restaurants. The software is upgraded periodically, and the latest version, introduced in April 2012, was designed to provide increased ease of use and a more thorough view of table availability to help turn more tables, enhance guest service, personalize responses to diners, coordinate the seating process, and maximize guest seating. The ERBs at OpenTable's customer restaurants connect via the Internet to form an online network of restaurant reservation books. For restaurants that rely less heavily on reservations, OpenTable offers Connect, a web-based service that lets restaurants accept online reservations.

OpenTable's revenue comes from two sources. Restaurants pay a one-time fee for on-site installation and training, a monthly subscription fee for software and hardware, and a transaction fee for each restaurant guest seated through online reservations. The online reservation service is free to diners. The business model encourages diners to assist in viral marketing. When an individual makes a reservation, the site "suggests" that they send e-vites to their dinner companions directly from OpenTable.com. The e-vites include a link back to the OpenTable site.

OpenTable is a service-based (software as service, or SaaS) e-commerce company. In other words, customers don't buy software and install it on their computers, but instead go online and get the software functionality through subscriptions. OpenTable is also an online service that does not sell goods, but instead enables diners to make reservations, like social networking sites provide services.

The restaurant industry was slow to leverage the power of the Internet. This was in part because the industry was, and continues to be, highly fragmented and local—made up of more than 30,000 small, independent businesses or local restaurant-owning groups.

The founders of OpenTable knew that dealing with these restaurants as a single market would be difficult. They also realized that the Internet was changing things for diners by providing them with instant access to reviews, menus, and other information about dining options. And there was no method for making reservations online—we all know reserving by phone is time-consuming, inefficient, and prone to errors. In order to make the system work, reach and scale were very important. For diners to use an online reservation system, they would need real-time access to a number of local restaurants, and the ability to instantly book confirmed reservations around the clock. If customers were planning a trip to another city, OpenTable would need participating restaurants in those cities.

The company was originally incorporated in San Francisco in 1998 as Easy-eats.com, morphing into OpenTable.com, Inc. a year later. When the company was founded, most restaurants did not have computers, let alone systems that would allow online reservations made through a central Web site. OpenTable's initial strategy was to pay online restaurant reviewers for links to its Web site and target national chains in order to quickly expand its reach. This got the company into 50 cities, but it was spending $1 million a month and bringing in only $100,000 in revenue. Not exactly a formula for success. The original investors still felt there was a viable business to be built, and they made a number of management changes, including installing investor and board member Thomas Layton, founder of CitySearch.com, as OpenTable's CEO. Layton cut staff, shut down marketing efforts, and got the company out of all but four cities: Chicago, New York, San Francisco, and Washington, D.C.

The company retooled its hardware and software to create the user-friendly ERB system and deployed a door-to-door sales force to solicit subscriptions from high-end restaurants. The combination of e-commerce, user-friendly technology, and the personal touch worked. The four markets OpenTable targeted initially developed into active, local networks of restaurants and diners that continue to grow. OpenTable has implemented the same strategy across the country, and now includes approximately 31,000 OpenTable restaurant customers. In 15 years, the company has seated approximately 575 million diners, and it is currently averaging 14 million diners per month.

As the company grew, investors began making plans for it to go public. Layton stepped down from his position as CEO in 2007, though he remains a board member. He was replaced by Jeffrey Jordan, former president of PayPal. Jordan had some experience with public companies from working with eBay on its acquisition of PayPal. In 2009, he chose an aggressive strategy—going ahead with an initial public offering (IPO) despite a terrible economy and worse financial markets. So far, the gamble has paid off. On its first day of trading, OpenTable's shares climbed 59%. The share price in July 2013 was over $100, more than five times the $20 IPO price.

Despite the challenging economy, OpenTable's numbers at the time of the IPO were strong, and since then, it has continued to grow. In 2013, the company's total revenues were $190 million, up 18% from the $161 million recorded in 2012, with no signs of slowing in 2014.

The company has benefited from having e-commerce revenue streams from subscription fees and per-transaction charges, rather than depending on advertising. Further, more than 50% of OpenTable's revenue comes from B2B subscriptions, which are typically part of long-term contracts. Restaurants that have invested in OpenTable's software package are less likely to want to incur the switching costs associated with changing to a different reservation management package.

Another reason for its success is that OpenTable has a large number of satisfied customers. Restaurant owners report that they and their staff members find the software easy to use, and it helps them manage their business better. Specifically, it streamlines operations, helps fill additional seats, and improves quality of service, providing a concrete return on investment. This has led to both high customer satisfaction and high retention rates.

OpenTable has also taken advantage of the interconnected needs of restaurants and diners. Restaurants want cost-effective ways to attract guests and manage their reservations, while diners want convenient ways to find available restaurants, choose among them, and make reservations. By creating an online network of restaurants and diners that transact with each other through real-time reservations, OpenTable has figured out how to successfully address the needs of both.

OpenTable's market is susceptible to network effects: the more people use it, the more utility the system delivers. More diners discover the benefits of using the online reservation system, which in turn delivers value to restaurant customers, and helps attract more restaurants to the network. Diners serve as a source of viral marketing, as the OpenTable Web site encourages them to e-vite their dinner companions to the meal. When they do so, the e-mail provides links back to the OpenTable Web site. And the OpenTable link appears on the restaurant's Web site, linking directly to the reservation page. OpenTable has been able to improve its efficiency even as diners are staying home more often.

While OpenTable is the biggest, most successful online player in the restaurant reservations market, it does have competitors. MenuPages.com offers access to restaurant menus and reviews, but visitors to the site can't make reservations, and the site covers only eight U.S. cities. In 2012, OpenTable partnered with onetime competitor Urbanspoon, acquiring its reservation management system, Rezbook, and becoming Urbanspoon's reservation provider. Looming on the horizon is Google, which purchased online restaurant guide Zagat in September 2011, raising the specter that it might try to compete with OpenTable, although Zagat does not yet possess that functionality. Competitors in other countries where OpenTable does not yet operate, such as Restalo in Spain and Italy, and in markets like casual dining, such as NoWait, represent challenges to OpenTable.

While some may argue that there are better ways to make reservations that don't take visitors away from restaurant's Web sites (once someone clicks on the OpenTable link, they navigate away), restaurant owners like the OpenTable software, and diners have an enormous range of dining choices. Those two factors make this argument a relatively weak one.

The company is committed to shrewd technological investments to advance its position. It has a mobile Web site, mobile applications that work on just about every smartphone platform, and an iPad app that fully integrates with its ERB software. GPS enables mobile users to locate and make reservations at nearby venues.

OpenTable is attempting to shift its relationship with both diners and restaurants from a "transactional" relationship to an "experiential" relationship, which enhances the experience of dining more so than allowing diners to enjoy the traditional dining experience more conveniently. OpenTable launched a payments feature that allows users to pay for meals completely within the OpenTable app. OpenTable has employed its tried-and-true business model, combining technology with old-fashioned door-to-door sales, to expand its North American markets over time. Growth is projected to continue in the United States, Canada, and Mexico despite considerable market penetration. Selective international expansion is planned beyond its current operations in Germany, Japan, and the United Kingdom. OpenTable supports each of these locations with a direct sales force servicing approximately 1,000 restaurants.

The company's international strategy is to replicate the successful U.S. model by focusing initially on building a restaurant customer base. OpenTable believes the

SOURCES: "Priceline Agrees to Buy OpenTable for $2.6 Billion," by Drew FitzGerald, *Wall Street Journal*, June 13, 2014; "Open-Table Is Moving From 'Transactional' to 'Experiential'," by Ava Seave, Forbes.com, April 22, 2014; "OpenTable's Media Play: Before, During and After Dining," by Ava Seave, Forbes.com, April 21, 2014; "OpenTable Launches Pilot Mobile Payment Program in San Francisco," by Emily Price, Engadget.com, February 7th, 2014; "Open-Table, Inc. Announces 4Q and Full Year 2013 Financial Results," Opentable.com, February 6, 2014; "European OpenTable Competitor Restalo Raises $10M Series B Led By Seaya Ventures," by Steve O'Hear, Techcrunch.com, September 17, 2013; "Pittsburg Startup NoWait Could Overtake OpenTable's Volume in 2014," by Louis Bedigan, Benzinga.com, August 20, 2013; "Forget Flagging the Waiter: OpenTable Testing App That Lets You Pay," by Teresa Novellino, Upstart.bizjournals.com, July 31, 2013; "OpenTable Partners with Urbanspoon; Acquires Rezbook," Opentable.com, July 31, 2013; "OpenTable Releases New Electronic Reservation Book and iPad App for Restaurants," Opentable.com, April 4, 2012; "Google Buys Zagat to View the OpenTable, Yelp," by Alexei Oreskovic, Reuters, September 8, 2011; "Behind OpenTable's Success," Kevin Kelleher, Cnnmoney.com, September 23, 2010; "OpenTable Introduces the Next Generation of Its Electronic Reservation Book Software," Restaurantnews.com, August 17, 2010; "OpenTable Unveils Version 2.0 of its iPhone App," AppScout.com, August 14, 2009; Open Table S-1/A Amendment #6, filed with the Securities and Exchange Commission, May 19, 2009.

localized versions of its software will compare favorably against competitive software offerings, enabling them to expand across a broad selection of local restaurants.

In 2014, Priceline announced that it would acquire OpenTable for $2.6 billion. Priceline had long been rumored to be interested in OpenTable. OpenTable will benefit from Priceline's global reach as it continues to expand its business beyond the United States, which accounted for 80% of its revenues in 2013. Priceline plans to allow OpenTable to operate autonomously. Although OpenTable's revenues of $190 million in 2013 pale in comparison to Priceline's $6.8 billion over the same span, Priceline has a strong track record of acquisitions, including Booking.com, which propelled Priceline's revenue from the millions to the billions. Clearly, Priceline believes OpenTable can help it grow even further, this time into restaurant reservations. They might be right: OpenTable is well-positioned for future growth. Its size, track record of growth, and high customer satisfaction rates should continue to work in its favor.

Case Study Questions

1. Why will OpenTable competitors have a difficult time competing against Open-Table?

2. What characteristics of the restaurant market make it difficult for a reservation system to work?

3. How did OpenTable change its marketing strategy to succeed?

4. Why would restaurants find the SaaS model very attractive?

11.10 REVIEW

KEY CONCEPTS

■ **Understand the environment in which the online retail sector operates today.**

- The retail industry can be divided into seven major firm types: general merchandise, durable goods, specialty stores, food and beverage, gasoline and fuel, MOTO, and online retail firms. Each type offers opportunities for online retail. The MOTO sector is the most similar to the online retail sales sector.
- During the early days of e-commerce, some predicted that the retail industry would be revolutionized, based on reduced search costs, lower marketing entry costs, the replacement of physical store merchants by online companies, elimination of middlemen (distintermediation), and hypermediation.
- Today, it has become clear that few of the initial assumptions about the future of online retail were correct. Also, the structure of the retail marketplace in the United States has not been revolutionized. The reality is that:
  - Online consumers are not primarily cost-driven—instead, they are as brand-driven and influenced by perceived value as their offline counterparts.
  - Online market entry costs were underestimated, as was the cost of acquiring new customers.
  - Older traditional firms, such as the general merchandising giants and the established catalog-based retailers, are taking over as the top online retail sites.
  - Disintermediation did not occur. On the contrary, online retailing has become an example of the powerful role that intermediaries play in retail trade.

■ **Explain how to analyze the economic viability of an online firm.**

- The economic viability, or ability of a firm to survive during a specified time period, can be analyzed by examining the key industry strategic factors, the strategic factors that pertain specifically to the firm, and the financial statements for the firm.
- The key industry strategic factors include barriers to entry, the power of suppliers, the power of customers, the existence of substitute products, the industry value chain, and the nature of intra-industry competition.
- The key firm strategic factors include the firm value chain, core competencies, synergies, the firm's current technology, and the social and legal challenges facing the firm.
- The key financial factors include revenues, cost of sales, gross margin, operating expenses, operating margin, net margin, and the firm's balance sheet.

■ **Identify the challenges faced by the different types of online retailers.**

- *Virtual merchants* are single-channel Web firms that generate all of their revenues from online sales. Their challenges include building a business and a brand name quickly, many competitors in the virtual marketplace, substantial costs to build and maintain an e-commerce presence, considerable marketing expenses, large customer acquisition costs, a steep learning curve, and the need to quickly achieve operating efficiencies in order to preserve a profit. Amazon is the most well-known example of a virtual merchant.
- *Multi-channel merchants* (bricks-and-clicks) have a network of physical stores as their primary retail channel, but also have online operations. Their challenges include high cost of physical buildings, high cost of large sales staffs, the need to coordinate prices across channels, the need to develop methods of handling cross-channel returns from multiple locations, building a credible e-commerce presence, hiring new skilled staff, and building rapid-response order entry and fulfillment systems. Macy's is an example of a bricks-and-clicks company.

- *Catalog merchants* are established companies that have a national offline catalog operation as their largest retail channel, but who also have online capabilities. Their challenges include high costs for printing and mailing, the need to leverage their existing assets and competencies to the new technology environment, the need to develop methods of handling cross-channel returns, building a e-commerce presence, and hiring new skilled staff. Lands' End is an example of a catalog merchant.
- *Manufacturer-direct merchants* are either single- or multi-channel manufacturers who sell to consumers directly online without the intervention of retailers. Their challenges include channel conflict, quickly developing a rapid-response online order and fulfillment system; switching from a supply-push (products are made prior to orders being received based on estimated demand) to a demand-pull model (products are not built until an order is received); and creating sales, service, and support operations online. Dell is an example of a manufacturer-direct merchant.

■ Describe the major features of the online service sector.

- The service sector is the largest and most rapidly expanding part of the economy of advanced industrial nations.
- The major service industry groups are financial services, insurance, real estate, business services, and health services.
- Within these service industry groups, companies can be further categorized into those that involve transaction brokering and those that involve providing a "hands-on" service.
- With some exceptions, the service sector is by and large a knowledge- and information-intense industry. For this reason, many services are uniquely suited to e-commerce and the strengths of the Internet.
- E-commerce offers extraordinary opportunities to improve transaction efficiencies and thus productivity in a sector where productivity has so far not been markedly affected by the explosion in information technology.

■ Discuss the trends taking place in the online financial services industry.

- The online financial services sector is a good example of an e-commerce success story, but the success is somewhat different than what had been predicted in the early days of e-commerce. Today, the multi-channel established financial firms are growing the most rapidly and have the best prospects for long-term viability.
- Multi-channel firms that have both physical branches and solid online offerings have assumed market leadership over pure-online firms.
- Financial portals provide comparison shopping services and steer consumers to online providers for independent financial advice and financial planning.
- Account aggregation is another rapidly growing online financial service, which pulls together all of a customer's financial data on a single personalized Web site.
- Despite a rocky start, the online mortgage market is slowly growing; it is dominated by established online banks and other online financial services firms, traditional mortgage vendors, and a few successful online mortgage firms.
- Term life insurance stands out as one product group supporting the early visions of lower search costs, increased price transparency, and the resulting consumer savings. However, in other insurance product lines, the Web offers insurance companies new opportunities for product and service differentiation and price discrimination.
- The early vision that the historically local, complex, and agent-driven real estate industry would be transformed into a disintermediated marketplace where buyers and sellers could transact directly has not been realized.
- The major impact of the online real estate industry is in influencing offline purchases and the primary service is a listing of available houses, with secondary links to mortgage lenders, credit reporting agen-

cies, neighborhood information, loan calculators, appraisal reports, sales price histories by neighborhood, school district data, and crime reports.

- **Discuss the major trends in the online travel services industry today.**
- The Internet has become the most common channel used by consumers to research travel options and book reservations for airline tickets, rental cars, hotel rooms, and tours.
- The major trends in online travel services include consolidation, the rise of meta-search engines, mobile devices, and social media.

- **Identify current trends in the online career services industry.**
- Next to travel services, job-hunting services have been one of the Internet's most successful online services because they save money for both job hunters and employers.
- Online recruiting can also serve to establish market prices and terms, thereby identifying both the salary levels for specific jobs and the skill sets required to achieve those salary levels.
- The major trends in the online career services industry are social networking, mobile, job search engines, consolidation, diversification, and localization.

- **Understand the business models of new sharing economy companies.**
- Sharing economy companies are firms that provide a platform for users to share assets and resources. The companies collect a fee both from sellers and buyers for using the platform.
- Uber, a car rental service, and Airbnb, a room rental service, are the most well-known sharing economy companies. They are also among the most disruptive and controversial.

QUESTIONS

1. Why is the slowdown in new Internet users not causing a slowdown in the growth of online retail sales?
2. What frequently makes the difference between profitable and unprofitable online businesses today?
3. What enabled firms in the MOTO retail sector to transition more easily to e-commerce than other sectors?
4. Describe three techniques retail merchants use to integrate their online and offline sales channels, beyond having an online retail store.
5. Why did economists speculate that e-commerce would result in only low-cost, high-service, quality online retail merchants surviving?
6. What is an intermediator? Provide an example of one. What effect has e-commerce had on retail intermediators?
7. What is Amazon's chief business strategy, and what tactics does it use to achieve these strategies?
8. What unique challenges do manufacturer-direct companies, such as Dell.com, face in retailing online?
9. Identify two key industry strategic factors and describe how they impact the viability of firms operating within an industry.
10. In analyzing the viability of a firm, what questions would you ask to determine how the firm is affected by the technology it uses?
11. Describe three unique challenges that online retailers face, compared to offline retailers.
12. Why is the service sector one of the most natural avenues for e-commerce?
13. Why has the mortgage industry been slower to move to online business models than other online financial services industries?
14. Define channel conflict and explain how it applies to the retail industry.
15. What is the most common use of real estate Web sites? What do most consumers do when they go to them?
16. What are two major trends currently affecting the online travel industry?

17. Describe three ways that social networking has affected the online recruitment industry.
18. In addition to matching job applicants with available positions, what larger function do online job sites fill? Explain how such sites can affect salaries and going rates.
19. Describe the business model of sharing economy companies.
20. Why are sharing economy companies viewed as being disruptive and controversial?

PROJECTS

1. Access the EDGAR archives at Sec.gov, where you can review 10-K filings for all public companies. Search for the 10-K report for the most recent completed fiscal year for two online retail companies of your choice (preferably ones operating in the same industry, such as Staples Inc. and Office Depot Inc., Amazon and Walmart, etc.). Prepare a presentation that compares the financial stability and prospects of the two businesses, focusing specifically on the performance of their respective e-commerce operations.

2. Find an example not mentioned in the text of each of the four types of online retailing business models. Prepare a short report describing each firm and why it is an example of the particular business model.

3. Drawing on material in the chapter and your own research, prepare a short paper describing your views on the major social and legal issues facing online retailers.

4. Choose a services industry not discussed in the chapter (such as legal services, medical services, accounting services, or another of your choosing). Prepare a 3- to 5-page report discussing recent trends affecting online provision of these services.

5. Together with a teammate, investigate the use of mobile apps in the online retail or financial services industries. Prepare a short joint presentation on your findings.

REFERENCES

Accenture. "The Digital Insurer: Accenture US Personal-Lines Insurance Consumer Survey." (April 23, 2013).

Amazon.com, Inc. Form 10-K for the fiscal year ended December 31, 2014, filed with the Securities and Exchange Commission (January 31, 2014a).

Amazon.com, Inc. Form 10-Q for the quarterly period ended June 30, 2014, filed with the Securities and Exchange Commission (July 25, 2014b).

Bardhan, Ashok. "The US Economy Grows, But Jobs Don't." Yale Global Online (March 13, 2014).

Brown, Jeffrey, and Austan Goolsbee. "Does the Internet Make Markets More Competitive? Evidence from the Life Insurance Industry." John F. Kennedy School of Government, Harvard University. Research Working Paper RWP00-007 (2000).

Bruene, Jim. "Metrics: Mobile Traffic at the 10 Largest U.S. Banks." Netbanker.com (March 27, 2013).

Brynjolfsson, Erik, Astrid Andrea Dick, and Michael D. Smith. "Search and Product Differentiation at an Internet Shopbot," Center for eBusiness@MIT (December, 2004).

Bureau of Economic Analysis, U.S. Department of Commerce. "Table 3: Gross Domestic Product and Related Measures: Level and Change from Preceding Period." www.bea.gov (accessed May 29, 2014).

Careerbuilder. "Number of Employees Passing on Applicants Due to Social Media Posts Continues to Rise." (June 26, 2014).

Chaudhuri, Saabira. "Lenders Place Their Bets on Mobile Banking." *Wall Street Journal* (April 9, 2014).

Compete.com. "Site Profiles: Fidelity.com, Sharebuilder, Scottrade, TDAmeritrade, E-Trade, Vanguard, Charles Schwab, Merrill Lynch, and Troweprice." (September 2014).

comScore. "Brokerage Trends." (January 24, 2014a).

comScore. "Digital Banking Trends and Observations." (2014b).

comScore. "2013 Online Auto Insurance Shopping Report." (October 18, 2013a).

De La Merced, Michael. "Zillow to Acquire Trulia for $3.5 Billion." *New York Times* (July 28, 2014).

Demos, Telis, and Matt Jarzemsky. "Alibaba IPO: A Big Deal, and, Backers Argue, a Real Steal." *Wall Street Journal* (September 11, 2014).

Dusto, Amy. "Dell Revamps Its Mobile Site." Internetretailer.com (September 19, 2012).

eMarketer, Inc. "US Retail Ecommerce Sales, 2012–2018." (April 2014a).

eMarketer, Inc. "US B2C Mcommerce Sales, 2012–2018." (April 2014b).

eMarketer, Inc. "US Mobile Buyers, by Device, 2012–2018." (April 1, 2014c).

eMarketer, Inc. (Bryan Yeager) "US Digital and Mobile Banking 2014: User Forecast, Key Trends and Market Opportunities." (August 2014d).

eMarketer, Inc. (Alison McCarthy) "Worldwide B2C Ecommerce: Q3 2014 Complete Forecast." (August 2014e).

eMarketer, Inc. (Jeremy Kressman). "Travel Purchases on the Go." (June 2014f).

eMarketer, Inc. "Mobile Devices Trending for UK Travel Researchers." (June 20, 2014g).

eMarketer, Inc. "Recruiters Rely More on Social Media for Talent." (February 26, 2013).

eMarketer, Inc. (Jeffrey Grau). "E-commerce in the US: Retail Trends." (May 2005)

Evans, Philip, and Thomas S. Wurster. *Blown to Bits: How the New Economics of Information Transforms Strategy*. Cambridge, MA: Harvard Business School Press (2000).

Friedman, Thomas L. "And Now for a Bit of Good News..." *New York Times* (July 19, 2014).

He, Ray C. "Introducing New Like and Share Buttons." Developers.facebook.com (November 6, 2013).

Internet Retailer. "Top 500 Guide 2014 Edition." (2014a).

Internet Retailer. "The Mobile 500 2015 Edition." (2014b).

Javelin Strategy & Research. "Javelin Identifies $1.5B in Mobile Banking Cost Savings by Leveraging Omnichannel Approach." (July 8, 2013).

Johnson, Lauren. "Macy's Partners with Spotify to Further Mobile Advertising Stride." Mobilecommercedaily.com (August 1, 2012).

Kats, Rimma. "Macy's Exec: Mobile Amplifies Multichannel, Multiscreen Marketing." Mobilecommercedaily.com (May 13, 2013).

Kepes, Ben. "Just How Big Is Amazon's Cloud Business? Latest Earnings Reports Question Analyst Estimates, Or Does It?" Forbes.com (July 29, 2014).

Kroll, Karen M. "The Favorite 50 2014." Nrf.com (September 3, 2014).

Lands' End, Inc. "About Lands' End." Landsend.com (accessed October 1, 2014).

LIMRA. "Disruptive Consumers Want More Mobile Services." (July 9, 2014a).

LIMRA. "Insurers' Use of Social Media Has Jumped More than 50 Percent Since 2010." (July 22, 2014b).

LIMRA and Life and Health Insurance Foundation for Education (LIFE). "2013 Insurance Barometer Study." (April 16, 2013).

Love, Jack. "News Analysis: Big Store Sales Are a Tale of Two Channels." Internetretailer.com (August 19, 2013).

Macy's. "Macy's Outlines New Omnichannel Strategy and Tech." Internetretailer.com (September 18, 2014).

McGrath, Maggie. "Amazon Falling Fast After Fourth Quarter Earnings Miss." Forbes.com (January 30, 2014).

McIntyre, Hugh. "Amazon's New Music Streaming Service Not Exactly Ready For 'Prime' Time." *Forbes* (June 13, 2014).

Mojiva. "Finance to Go: A Snapshot of Mobile's Role in the Lives of Financially Savvy American Consumers." (May 8, 2013).

Needleman, Sarah, and Angus Loten. "Startups Want to Be the Next Airbnb, Uber." *Wall Street Journal* (May 7, 2014).

Ovide, Shira. "Google, Amazon and Microsoft's Costly Spending War." Blogs.wsj.com (April 28, 2014).

Panzarino, Matthew. "Leaked Uber Numbers Point to Over $1B Gross, $213 Million Revenue." Techcrunch.com (December 4, 2013).

Perez, Sarah. "Amazon's Fire Phone Introduces Firefly, A Feature That Lets You Identify (And Buy!) Things You See In The Real World." Techcrunch (June 18, 2014).

Pilon, Anne. "LinkedIn Survey: More Than One Third of Job Hunters Use Networking Site." Atym.com (January 14, 2013).

Portillo, Ely. "Amazon to Open Distribution Center Near Concord Airport." *Charlotte Observer* (September 9, 2014).

Rosenberg, Tina. "It's Not Just Nice to Share, It's the Future." *New York Times* (June 5, 2013).

Rusli, Evelyn, and Douglas Macmillan. "Uber Gets an Uber-Valuation." *Wall Street Journal* (June 6, 2014).

Somaiya, Ravi. "Amazon to Stream Original HBO Content." *New York Times* (April 23, 2014).

Stone, Brad. "Why Redfin, Zillow, and Trulia Haven't Killed Off Real Estate Brokers." Businessweek.com (March 7, 2013).

U.S. Census Bureau. *Statistical Abstract of the United States 2012* (2012).

U.S. Department of Labor Bureau of Labor Statistics. "Industry Employment and Output Projections to 2022." *Monthly Labor Review* (December 2013).

Weil, Jonathon. "Securities Rules Help to Close the Earning Reports GAAP." *Wall Street Journal* (April 24, 2003).

Yodlee, Inc. "About Us." (accessed September 23, 2014).

CHAPTER 12

B2B E-commerce

LEARNING OBJECTIVES

After reading this chapter, you will be able to:

- Discuss the evolution and growth of B2B e-commerce, as well as its potential benefits and challenges.
- Understand how procurement and supply chains relate to B2B e-commerce.
- Identify major trends in supply chain management and collaborative commerce.
- Understand the different characteristics and types of Net marketplaces.
- Understand the objectives of private industrial networks, their role in supporting collaborative commerce, and the barriers to their implementation.

Alibaba:

China's E-commerce King

Alibaba is China's undisputed B2C and B2B e-commerce king. Founded in 1999 by Jack Ma, it began as a B2B exchange, enabling Chinese manufacturers to sell products such as circuit breakers and hydraulic cylinders to international traders and retailers. In the next decade, the Alibaba Group branched out, first into the C2C sector and then into the B2C sector, both of which also proved lucrative.

© paradox/Fotolia.com

Today, Alibaba has grown to a size that rivals or trumps many of the world's established tech giants. In 2014, the company made a splashy initial public offering on the New York Stock Exchange, starting at $68 per share and finishing its first day of trading up 38% at nearly $94. The IPO raised $21.8 billion for the e-commerce giant, whose market value of $168 billion was approximately as large as the entire American IPO market to that point in the year ($180 billion). Despite a slowdown in the Chinese economy, Alibaba announced a 54% increase in revenue and a 16% increase in profits in its first earnings report as a public company.

Alibaba operates eBay-like and Amazon-like businesses, and records more trade volume than those two companies combined! Alibaba does not hold inventory, manage warehouses, or perform fulfillment nor does it charge its users. Instead, Alibaba runs platforms that connect sellers and buyers and earns revenue from commissions and advertising. Alibaba is estimated to control somewhere between 45% to 80% of China's rapidly expanding e-commerce market. Yahoo owned 22% of Alibaba prior to selling $6 billion worth of stock during the IPO, while Japanese wireless carrier Softbank Corp holds 37% and Ma retains approximately 7.4%. The success of the company's IPO propelled Ma's net worth to well over $20 billion. Though some investors worry about Alibaba's lack of fulfillment facilities, most analysts expect the company to continue its strong upward trend going forward. Internet penetration in China lags behind that of many Western countries, offering more room for domestic growth in addition to any attempts the company makes to move into other markets.

The trajectory of Alibaba from its humbler beginnings to its current heights mirrors the coming of age and flourishing of Chinese e-commerce, a process that is ongoing. Chinese e-commerce surpassed the United States in 2014 and is on track to continue 32% average annual growth for the next two to three years. In all likelihood, by 2020,

SOURCES: "Why Alibaba Says Its Nothing Like Amazon," Pymnts. com, November 5, 2014; "Alibaba, Shrugging Off Slowdown in Chinese Economy, Reports Strong Earnings," by Paul Mozur, *New York Times,* November 4, 2014; "Yahoo's Alibaba IPO Riches: $6.3 Billion," by Scott Austin, Blogs.wsj. com, October 21, 2014; "A Soaring Debut for Alibaba," by Michael J. De La Merced, *New York Times,* September 19, 2014; "Atlantic Equities Initiates Coverage on Alibaba, Cites 80% Market Penetration," by John Seward, Benzinga.com, September 8, 2014; "As Giant U.S. IPO Nears, Alibaba's China E-Commerce Crown Slips," by Adam Jourdan, Reuters, July 14, 2014; "China Officially Passes the U.S. in E-Commerce," by Frank Tong, *Internet Retailer,* May 29, 2014; "Meet Alibaba, Yahoo's Chinese Secret Weapon," by Julianne Pepitone, Money.cnn.com, October 29, 2013; "Alibaba IPO Could Raise $18B–$25B on $110B Valuation, Company's Growth 'Meteoric'," by John Koetsier, Venturebeat.com, October 16, 2013; "Alibaba Nears Facebook Sales With Double the Profit," by Lulu Yilun Chen, Bloomberg.com, October 16, 2013; "Alibaba Is Just the Beginning: How B2B Market-places Will Thrive (for Real, This Time)," by Boris Wertz, Gigaom. com, June 30, 2013; "Alibaba Leads World in B2B Service," Usa.chinadaily.com.cn, June 20, 2013; "Why Alibaba's Future Looks Bright," by Willis Wee, Techinasia. com, May 21, 2013; "China's Alibaba Targets Unreliable Sellers with Increased Transparency on B2B Site Alibaba.com," by Jon Russell, Thenextweb.com/asia, November 26, 2012; "Alibaba.com Begins Refresh of B2B Site," by Justin King, Ecommerce-andb2b.com, October 19, 2012.

Chinese e-commerce will dwarf the United States, Great Britain, Japan, Germany, and France combined.

Like many early players, Alibaba.com used an aggregation of supply model to connect buyers in North America and Europe to many SME suppliers in China. It created a platform to which sellers would upload their products, businesses would upload their requirements, and supplier-buyer matches would be made. When demand for Chinese goods faltered during the global recession of 2009, Alibaba.com transitioned to recruiting sellers interested in marketing their goods to China, to Japan through its Japanese-language site (Alibaba.co.jp), and to India, where it had opened a branch.

Today, there are three B2B divisions. Alibaba.com remains the global sourcing solution on which business is conducted in English between importers and exporters from over 240 countries. The Chinese language site, 1688.com, is dedicated to domestic B2B transactions, and AliExpress.com serves small businesses, offering wholesale pricing without bulk buying requirements. By mid-2013, Alibaba.com claimed its 100 millionth customer, making it the largest B2B e-commerce provider in the world, and these numbers included a doubling over two years' time of the domestic customers on 1688.com.

Alibaba's site design emphasizes ease of use and consumer-friendliness. A User Guide outlines a simple process for using the site, and the core function is search, returning results with special attention to bargains and top global suppliers. Sellers found to have committed fraud are expelled, and when Alibaba intervention is required to resolve a dispute and sellers are found culpable, the seller's page receives a public warning. Seller pages also display recent complaints. In the early years of Chinese e-commerce, counterfeit products and resale of branded goods were rampant. Alibaba's policies were formed with this history in mind, aiming to protect its customers.

The second wave of B2B markets seeks to fulfill the promise of its predecessors which vaporized when the dot.com bubble deflated: cost savings and expanded markets from the virtual assembly of manufacturers, service providers, and their customers and the Web-based delivery of all supplier-customer transactions. Transaction transparency and trust will be key in making procurement and supply chain efficiency a reality for small and medium-sized businesses. While large companies were often able to build their own dedicated horizontal marketplaces, and vertical consortia for particular industries such as the automotive, chemical, and MRO-parts markets prospered, 90% of SMEs had few options. Unable to afford Electronic Data Interchange (EDI) or other automated procurement systems, they continued to rely on paper purchase orders and faxed RFQs. But as the rest of the world hatches new B2B startups to serve the Long Tail of the SME market, they will have to play catch-up with Alibaba, which has been providing procurement and supply chain efficiencies to small and mid-sized companies for 15 years. Like Alibaba, they must lower transaction costs and identify unique suppliers and products for their buyers by providing a robust store of suppliers, and using matching algorithms, personalization, and Big Data analytics to help buyers find the supplier with the best product to meet their needs.

The Alibaba case illustrates the exciting potential for B2B e-commerce to lower production costs, increase collaboration among firms, speed up new product delivery, and ultimately revolutionize both the manufacturing process inherited from the early twentieth century and the way industrial products are designed and manufactured. This case also introduces new themes in B2B commerce: sustainability, environmental impacts, and social justice. Alibaba is an example of just one type of B2B e-commerce, but there are many other equally promising efforts to use the Internet to change the relationships among manufacturers and their suppliers. In the fashion industry, the combination of high-speed value chains coupled with equally high-speed trendy design not only clears shelves (and reduces the likelihood of clearance sales), but increases profits by increasing value to consumers (Zarroli, 2013; Cachon and Swinney, 2011). In the automobile industry, for instance, the success of Volkswagen's Group Business Platform and similar networks operated by the major automobile firms in the world stands in contrast to an earlier industry-sponsored marketplace called Covisint. Founded in 1999 by five of the world's largest automakers (General Motors, Ford, Chrysler, Nissan, and Peugeot), Covisint hoped to provide a digital marketplace connecting thousands of suppliers to a few huge buyers using auctions and procurement services. While initially successful, Covisint was sold in June 2004, although it continues as a B2B services firm in a number of industries. Its auction business was sold to FreeMarkets, an early B2B auction company, which itself was sold to another B2B e-commerce firm called Ariba later in 2004. In 2014, Ariba survives as a successful software firm (now owned by SAP AG) focusing on the procurement process and the operation of a successful supplier trading platform and network.

The failure of Covisint (as well as Ford's AutoExchange) and the simultaneous growth in B2B e-commerce efforts such as Volkswagen's Group Business Platform illustrate the difficulties of achieving the broad visions established during the early days of e-commerce. From a high of 1,500 B2B exchanges in 2000, the number has dwindled to less than 200 survivors today (Rosenzweig et al., 2011). Like B2C commerce, the B2B marketplace has consolidated, evolved, and moved on to more attainable visions. Changes in information technology, from smartphones to cloud computing, have greatly reduced the cost of B2B trading systems. In the process, many B2B efforts have experienced extraordinary success. There are many failed efforts to consider as well; these provide important lessons to all managers.

In this chapter, we examine three different B2B e-commerce themes: procurement, supply chain management, and collaborative commerce. Each of these business processes has changed greatly with the evolution of B2B e-commerce systems. In Sections 12.1 and 12.2, we provide an overview of B2B e-commerce, the procurement process, and supply chains. In Section 12.3, we place B2B e-commerce in the context of trends in procurement, supply chain management, and collaborative commerce. The final two sections describe the two fundamental types of B2B e-commerce: Net marketplaces and private industrial networks.

Table 12.1 summarizes the leading trends in B2B e-commerce in the 2014–2015 period. Perhaps the most important themes are growing industry concern with supply chain risk and environmental impact, along with a growing public concern with the

TABLE 12.1	MAJOR TRENDS IN B2B E-COMMERCE, 2014–2015

BUSINESS

- B2B e-commerce growth continues to accelerate in 2014 to pre-recession levels as the global economy continues to recover from recession
- Risk management: Companies heighten their focus on risks in supply chains after being blindsided in recent years by a number of natural and man-made disasters.
- Regional manufacturing: risks of far-flung global networks lead to an increase in regional manufacturing and supply chains, moving production closer to market demand.
- Flexibility: growing emphasis on rapid-response and adaptive supply chains rather than lowest cost supply chains, which typically carry great risks.
- Supply chain visibility: growing calls for more real-time data that would allow managers to see across not only their production, but also see into the production and financial condition of their key suppliers.
- Social and mobile commerce and customer intimacy: buyers, like consumers, are tapping into their tablets, smartphones, and social network sites for purchasing, scheduling, exception handling, and deciding with their B2B customers and suppliers in order to manage supply chain risk.

TECHNOLOGY

- Big data: global trade and logistics systems are generating huge repositories of B2B data, swamping management understanding and controls.
- Business analytics: growing emphasis on use of business analytics software (business intelligence) to understand very large data sets.
- Cloud: migration of B2B hardware and software to cloud computing and cloud apps, away from individual corporate data centers, as a means of slowing rising technology costs. B2B systems move to cloud computing providers like IBM, Oracle, Amazon, Google, and HP as their core technology.
- Mobile platform: growing use of mobile platform for B2B systems (CRM, SCM, and enterprise), putting B2B commerce into managers' palms.
- Social networks: increasing use of social network platforms for feedback from customers, strengthening customer and supplier relationships, adjusting prices and orders, and enhancing decision making.
- Internet of Things: The number of Internet-connected sensors and other intelligent devices that measure and monitor data continues to grow exponentially and begins to impact how supply chains operate.

SOCIETY

- Accountability: growing demands for supply chain accountability and monitoring in developed countries driven by reports of poor working conditions in Asian factories.
- Sustainable supply chains: growing public demand for businesses to mitigate their environmental impact leads from local environmental optimization to consideration of the entire supply chain from design, production, customer service, and post-use disposal.
- Acceptance and growth of B2B platforms: Ariba, one of the largest Net marketplaces, has over 1 million connected businesses that participate in transactions with a value of over $500 billion a year.

accountability of supply chains—in particular, violations of developed-world expectations of working conditions in third-world factories that play a key role in the production of goods sold in more developed countries. What many firms have learned in the last decade is that supply chains can strengthen or weaken a company depending on a number of factors related to supply chain efficiency such as community engagement, labor relations, environmental protection, and sustainability. Yet many believe that all of these related factors are important to the long profitability of firms (Beard and Hornik, 2011). At the same time, in part because of the globalization of supply chains, B2B e-commerce systems are now used by nearly all of the U.S. S&P 500 firms, where over half of all revenues are produced offshore. Thousands of smaller firms are now able to participate in B2B systems as low-cost cloud-based computing and software-as-a-service (SaaS) become widely available. The cost of participating in B2B e-commerce systems has fallen significantly, allowing smaller firms to participate along with giant firms. Taking advantage of the exploding mobile platform, more companies are using smartphones and tablet computers to run their businesses from any location. There are hundreds of iPhone and Android apps available from enterprise B2B vendors like SAP, IBM, Oracle, and others that link to supply chain management systems (Enright, 2013; Bolukbasi, 2011; Melnyk, 2010). Social network tools are pushing into the B2B world as well as the consumer world. B2B managers are increasingly using public and private social network sites and technologies to enable long-term conversations with their customers and suppliers. Executives at firms large and small are coming to realize that they are competing not just with other firms but with those firms' supply chains as well. **Supply chain competition** refers to the fact that in some industries firms are able to differentiate their product or pricing, and achieve a competitive advantage, due to superior supply chain management. Arguably, firms with superior supply chains can produce better products, more quickly, and at a lower cost than those with simply adequate supply chains (Antai, 2011; Rice and Hoppe, 2001).

supply chain competition
differentiating a firm's products or prices on the basis of superior supply chain management

12.1 AN OVERVIEW OF B2B E-COMMERCE

The trade between business firms represents a huge marketplace. The total amount of B2B trade in the United States in 2014 is about $13.8 trillion, with B2B e-commerce contributing about $5.7 trillion of that amount (U.S. Census Bureau, 2014; authors' estimates). By 2018, B2B e-commerce is expected to grow to about $7.8 trillion in the United States. Worldwide, B2B e-commerce is estimated to be around €12.4 trillion.

The process of conducting trade among business firms is complex and requires significant human intervention, and therefore, consumes significant resources. Some firms estimate that each corporate purchase order for support products costs them, on average, at least $100 in administrative overhead. Administrative overhead includes processing paper, approving purchase decisions, spending time using the telephone and fax machines to search for products and arrange for purchases, arranging for shipping, and receiving the goods. Across the economy, this adds up to trillions of dollars annually being spent for procurement processes that could potentially be automated. If even just a portion of inter-firm trade were automated, and parts of the entire procurement process assisted by the Internet, then literally trillions of dollars might be released for more productive uses, consumer prices potentially would fall, productivity would increase, and the economic wealth of the nation would expand. This is the promise of B2B e-commerce. The challenge of B2B e-commerce is changing existing patterns and systems of procurement, and designing and implementing new digital B2B solutions.

SOME BASIC DEFINITIONS

B2B commerce
all types of inter-firm trade

B2B e-commerce (B2B digital commerce)
that portion of B2B commerce that is enabled by the Internet and mobile apps

supply chain
the links that connect business firms with one another to coordinate production

automated order entry systems
involve the use of telephone modems to send digital orders

seller-side solutions
seller-biased markets that are owned by, and show only goods from, a single seller

electronic data interchange (EDI)
a communications standard for sharing business documents and settlement information among a small number of firms

buyer-side solutions
buyer-biased markets that are owned by buyers and that aim to reduce the procurement costs of supplies for buyers

Before the Internet, business-to-business transactions were referred to simply as *trade* or the *procurement process*. We use the term **B2B commerce** to describe all types of inter-firm trade to exchange value across organizational boundaries. B2B commerce includes the following business processes: customer relationship management, demand management, order fulfillment, manufacturing management, procurement, product development, returns, logistics/transportation, and inventory management (Barlow, 2011). This definition of B2B commerce does not include transactions that occur within the boundaries of a single firm—for instance, the transfer of goods and value from one subsidiary to another, or the use of corporate intranets to manage the firm. We use the term **B2B e-commerce** (or **B2B digital commerce**) to describe specifically that portion of B2B commerce that is enabled by the Internet (including mobile apps) (Fauska, et al., 2013). The links that connect business firms in the production of goods and services are referred to as the supply chain. **Supply chains** are a complex system of organizations, people, business processes, technology, and information, all of which need to work together to produce products efficiently. Today's supply chains are often global, connecting the smartphones in New York to the shipyards in Los Angeles and Quindow, and to the Foxconn factories that produce the phones. They are also local and national in scope.

THE EVOLUTION OF B2B E-COMMERCE

B2B e-commerce has evolved over a 35-year period through several technology-driven stages (see **Figure 12.1**). The first step in the development of B2B e-commerce in the mid-1970s was **automated order entry systems** that involved the use of telephone modems to send digital orders to health care products companies such as Baxter Healthcare. Baxter, a diversified supplier of hospital supplies, placed telephone modems in its customers' procurement offices to automate reordering from Baxter's computerized inventory database (and to discourage reordering from competitors). This early technology was replaced by personal computers using private networks in the late 1980s, and by Internet workstations accessing electronic online catalogs in the late 1990s. Automated order entry systems are **seller-side solutions**. They are owned by the suppliers and are seller-biased markets—they show only goods from a single seller. Customers benefited from these systems because they reduced the costs of inventory replenishment and were paid for largely by the suppliers. Automated order entry systems continue to play an important role in B2B commerce.

By the late 1970s, a new form of computer-to-computer communication called **electronic data interchange (EDI)** emerged. We describe EDI in greater detail later in this chapter, but at this point, it is necessary only to know that EDI is a communications standard for sharing business documents such as invoices, purchase orders, shipping bills, product stocking numbers (SKUs), and settlement information among a small number of firms. Virtually all large firms have EDI systems, and most industry groups have industry standards for defining documents in that industry. EDI systems are owned by the buyers, hence they are **buyer-side solutions** and buyer-biased

| FIGURE 12.1 | **THE EVOLUTION OF THE USE OF TECHNOLOGY PLATFORMS IN B2B E-COMMERCE** |

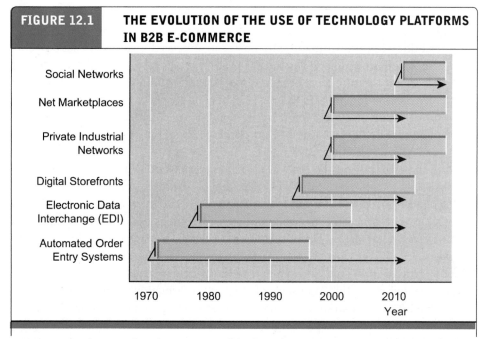

B2B e-commerce has gone through many stages of development since the 1970s. Each stage reflects a major change in technology platforms from mainframes to private dedicated networks, and finally to the Internet. In 2013, social networks—both private and public—were being used to coordinate decision-making in B2B commerce.

because they aim to reduce the procurement costs of supplies for the buyer. Of course, by automating the transaction, EDI systems also benefit the sellers through customer cost reduction. The topology of EDI systems is often referred to as a **hub-and-spoke system**, with the buyers in the center and the suppliers connected to the central hub via private dedicated networks.

EDI systems generally serve vertical markets. A **vertical market** is one that provides expertise and products for a specific industry, such as automobiles. In contrast, **horizontal markets** serve many different industries.

B2B e-commerce Web sites emerged in the mid-1990s along with the commercialization of the Internet. **B2B e-commerce Web sites** are perhaps the simplest and easiest form of B2B e-commerce to understand, because they are just online catalogs of products made available to the public marketplace by a single supplier. Owned by the supplier, they are seller-side solutions and seller-biased because they show only the products offered by a single supplier.

B2B e-commerce Web sites are a natural descendant of automated order entry systems, but there are two important differences: (1) the far less expensive and more universal Internet becomes the communication media and displaces private networks, and (2) B2B e-commerce Web sites tend to serve horizontal markets—they carry products that serve a wide variety of industries. Although B2B e-commerce Web sites emerged prior to Net marketplaces (described next), they are usually considered

hub-and-spoke system
suppliers connected to a central hub of buyers via private dedicated networks

vertical market
one that provides expertise and products for a specific industry

horizontal markets
markets that serve many different industries

B2B e-commerce Web site
online catalog of products made available to the public marketplace by a single supplier

a type of Net marketplace. Today, more and more B2B manufacturers, distributors, and suppliers are using B2B e-commerce Web sites to sell directly to B2B customers, who most often are procurement/purchasing agents, as discussed in Section 12.2.

Net marketplace
brings hundreds to thousands of suppliers and buyers into a single Internet-based environment to conduct trade

Net marketplaces emerged in the late 1990s as a natural extension and scaling-up of the electronic storefronts. There are many different kinds of Net marketplaces, which we describe in detail in Section 12.4, but the essential characteristic of a Net marketplace is that they bring hundreds to thousands of suppliers—each with a digital catalog and potentially thousands of purchasing firms—into a single Internet-based environment to conduct trade.

Net marketplaces can be organized under a variety of ownership models. Some are owned by independent third parties backed by venture capital, some are owned by established firms who are the main or only market players, and some are a mix of both. Net marketplaces establish the prices of the goods they offer in four primary ways—fixed catalog prices, or more dynamic pricing, such as negotiation, auction, or bid/ask ("exchange" model). Net marketplaces earn revenue in a number of ways, including transaction fees, subscription fees, service fees, software licensing fees, advertising and marketing, and sales of data and information. In the last few years, cloud-based B2B Net marketplaces have emerged, and generate revenue by selling access to their storage, software services, and communications facilities.

Although the primary benefits and biases of Net marketplaces have to be determined on a case-by-case basis depending on ownership and pricing mechanisms, it is often the case that Net marketplaces are biased against suppliers because they can force suppliers to reveal their prices and terms to other suppliers in the marketplace. Net marketplaces can also significantly extend the benefits of simple electronic storefronts by seeking to automate the procurement value chain of both selling and buying firms.

private industrial networks (private trading exchange, PTX)
Internet-based communication environments that extend far beyond procurement to encompass truly collaborative commerce

Private industrial networks also emerged in the last decade as natural extensions of EDI systems and the existing close relationships that developed between large industrial firms and their trusted suppliers. Described in more detail in Section 12.5, **private industrial networks** (sometimes also referred to as a *private trading exchange*, or *PTX*) are Internet-based communication environments that extend far beyond procurement to encompass supply chain efficiency enhancements and truly collaborative commerce. Private industrial networks permit buyer firms and their principal suppliers to share product design and development, marketing, inventory, production scheduling, and unstructured communications. Like EDI, private industrial networks are owned by the buyers and are buyer-side solutions with buyer biases. These systems are directly intended to improve the cost position and flexibility of large industrial firms (Yoo et al., 2011; Kumaran, 2002). These private industrial networks have a much higher survival rate than other Net marketplaces (Rosenzweig, 2011).

Naturally, private industrial networks have significant benefits for suppliers as well. Inclusion in the direct supply chain for a major industrial purchasing company can allow a supplier to increase both revenue and margins because the environment is not competitive—only a few suppliers are included in the private industrial network. These networks are the most prevalent form of B2B e-commerce, and this will continue into the foreseeable future.

| FIGURE 12.2 | **GROWTH OF B2B E-COMMERCE IN THE UNITED STATES 2009–2018** |

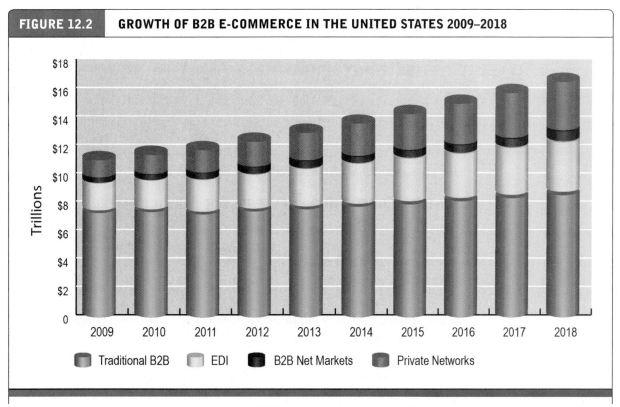

Private industrial networks are the fastest growing form of B2B e-commerce, which includes EDI, B2B Net marketplaces, and private industrial markets.

SOURCES: Based on data from U.S. Census Bureau, 2014; authors' estimates.

THE GROWTH OF B2B E-COMMERCE

Figure 12.2 illustrates the growth of B2B e-commerce, as well that of traditional B2B commerce, during the period 2009–2018. However, let's focus on the growth of B2B e-commerce during the period 2014–2018. During this time, B2B e-commerce is projected to grow from about $5.7 trillion in 2014 (about 41% of total B2B commerce in the United States) to $7.8 trillion (48% of total B2B commerce) in 2018. Several observations are important to note with respect to Figure 12.2. First, it shows that the initial belief that online marketplaces would become the dominant form of B2B e-commerce is not supported. Second, private industrial networks play a dominant role in B2B e-commerce, both now and in the future. Third, non-EDI B2B e-commerce is the most rapidly growing type of B2B e-commerce. However, EDI remains quite common and continues to be a workhorse of B2B commerce.

Not all industries will be similarly affected by B2B e-commerce, nor will all industries similarly benefit from B2B. Several factors influence the speed with which industries migrate to B2B e-commerce and the volume of transactions. Those industries in which there is already significant utilization of EDI (indicating concentration of buyers and suppliers) and large investments in information technology and Internet infrastructure can be expected to move first and fastest to B2B e-commerce utilization.

The aerospace and defense, computer, and industrial equipment industries meet these criteria. Where the marketplace is highly concentrated on either the purchasing or selling side, or both, conditions are also ripe for rapid B2B e-commerce growth, as in the energy and chemical industries. In the case of health care, the federal government, health care providers (doctors and hospitals), and major insurance companies are moving towards a national medical record system and the use of the Internet for managing medical payments. Coordinating the various players in the health care system is an extraordinary B2B challenge. Computer service firms like IBM and Microsoft, and B2B service firms like Covisint, are expanding the use of information ecosystems where health providers and insurers can share information.

POTENTIAL BENEFITS AND CHALLENGES OF B2B E-COMMERCE

Regardless of the specific type, B2B commerce as a whole promises many strategic benefits to participating firms—both buyers and sellers—and impressive gains for the economy. B2B e-commerce can:

- Lower administrative costs
- Lower search costs for buyers
- Reduce inventory costs by increasing competition among suppliers (increasing price transparency) and reducing inventory to the bare minimum
- Lower transaction costs by eliminating paperwork and automating parts of the procurement process
- Increase production flexibility by ensuring delivery of parts just at the right time (known as just in time production)
- Improve quality of products by increasing cooperation among buyers and sellers and reducing quality issues
- Decrease product cycle time by sharing designs and production schedules with suppliers
- Increase opportunities for collaborating with suppliers and distributors
- Create greater price transparency—the ability to see the actual buy and sell prices in a market
- Increase the visibility and real-time information sharing among all participants in the supply chain network.

B2B e-commerce offers potential first-mover strategic benefits for individual firms as well. Firms that move their procurement processes online first will experience impressive gains in productivity, cost reduction, and potentially much faster introduction of new, higher-quality products. While these gains may be imitated by other competing firms, it is also clear from the history of B2B e-commerce that firms making sustained investments in information technology and B2B e-commerce can adapt much faster to new technologies as they emerge, creating a string of first-mover advantages.

While there are many potential benefits to B2B e-commerce, there are also considerable risks and challenges. Often real-world supply chains fail to provide visibility into the supply chain because they lack real-time demand, production, and logistics data, and have inadequate financial data on suppliers. The result is unexpected supplier failure and disruption to the supply chain. Builders of B2B supply chains often had little concern for the environmental impacts of supply chains, the sensitivity of supply chains to natural events, fluctuating fuel and labor costs, or the impact of public values involving labor and environmental policies. The result in 2014 is that many Fortune 1000 supply chains are risky, vulnerable, and socially and environmentally unsustainable. Read *Insight on Society: Where's My iPad? Apple's Supply Chain Risks and Vulnerabilities* for a look at the impact the Tohoku earthquake in the prefecture of Fukushima, Japan, had on global supply chains, as well as the reputational risk posed by supply chains.

12.2 THE PROCUREMENT PROCESS AND SUPPLY CHAINS

The subject of B2B e-commerce can be complex because there are so many ways the Internet can be used to support the exchange of goods and payments among organizations, efficient supply chains, and collaboration. At the most basic level, B2B e-commerce is about changing the **procurement process** (how business firms purchase goods they need to produce goods they will ultimately sell to consumers) of thousands of firms across the world. In the procurement process, firms purchase goods from a set of suppliers, and they in turn purchase their inputs from a set of suppliers. The supply chain includes not just the firms themselves, but also the relationships among them and the processes that connect them.

procurement process
how firms purchase goods they need to produce goods for consumers

STEPS IN THE PROCUREMENT PROCESS

There are seven separate steps in the procurement process (see **Figure 12.3**). The first three steps involve the decision of who to buy from and what to pay: searching

| **FIGURE 12.3** | **THE PROCUREMENT PROCESS** |

1	2	3	4	5	6	7
Search	**Qualify**	**Negotiate**	**Purchase Order**	**Invoicing**	**Shipping**	**Remittance Payment**
Catalogs	Research	Price	Order product	Receive PO	Enter into shipper's tracking system	Receive goods
Internet	Credit history	Credit terms	Initiate purchase order (PO)	Enter into financial system	Ship goods	Enter shipping documents into warehouse system
Salespersons	Check with competitors	Escrow	Enter into system	Enter into production system	Deliver goods	Verify and correct invoice
Brochures	Telephone research	Quality	Mail PO	Send invoice	Enter into tracking system	Resend invoice
Telephone		Timing		Match with PO		Cut check
Fax				Internal review		Add corrected invoice to back office systems
				Enter into warehouse system		

The procurement process is a lengthy and complicated series of steps that involves the seller, buyer, and shipping companies in a series of connected transactions.

INSIGHT ON SOCIETY

WHERE'S MY IPAD? GLOBAL SUPPLY CHAIN RISK AND VULNERABILITY

On Friday, March 11, 2011, a magnitude 9.0 earthquake occurred offshore of northern Japan and the Oshika Peninsula of Tohoku. The Tohoku earthquake was the largest in recorded history and it immediately created a number of tsunami waves, some of which exceeded 100 feet in height and penetrated up to six miles inland. In their path were six coastal nuclear reactors in the Fukushima Prefecture near the town of Okuma, the largest nuclear power site in the world. The earthquake and tsunami combined to cut off the nuclear plant's electrical power, which caused the water pumps that keep the nuclear material from overheating and melting to stop. Backup diesel generators were swamped by the tsunami waves. Several of the nuclear reactors exploded and began leaking dangerous levels of radiation as fuel rods melted at temperatures exceeding 5,000 degrees. The government evacuated the entire population within a radius of 20 miles, and radiation levels rose throughout Japan, contaminating the surrounding countryside and ocean. Over 13,000 people lost their lives directly from the earthquake and tsunami, and the ultimate death and disease tolls from the nuclear disaster are still unknown.

The impact of the Tohoku earthquake on global supply chains was just as unexpected as the earthquake itself, although one wonders if either should have been unexpected. In fact, the earthquake exposed significant weaknesses and vulnerabilities in today's modern B2B supply chains. Technology, globalization of trade, and high levels of wage disparity between the developed and undeveloped worlds have led to a massive outsourcing of manufacturing around the world, mostly to low-wage countries but also

to countries with unusual expertise as well as low wages like Japan. Today, every component of every manufactured product is carefully examined by company engineers and financial managers with an eye to finding the lowest cost and highest quality manufacturer in the world. Production inevitably tends to concentrate at single firms that are given very high order volumes if they can meet the price. Large orders make lower prices easier to grant because of scale economies. Rather than spread production among multiple suppliers using small production runs, why not concentrate orders among one or two preferred global suppliers with huge production runs? The answer: when you concentrate production globally on a few suppliers, you also concentrate risk.

As a result, the world's manufacturing base is less redundant, flexible, and adaptive than older traditional supply chains. Interdependencies have grown into a tightly coupled machine that is quite fragile. Risk assessment in supply chains has been weak or nonexistent.

Computers, cell phones, Caterpillar earth movers, Boeing airplanes, and automobiles from Toyota, Ford, GM, and Honda are just a few of the complex manufactured goods that rely on parts and subassemblies made thousands of miles away from their assembly plants. Most of these manufacturers know who their first-tier suppliers are but don't have a clue as to who supplies their suppliers, and so on down the line of the industrial spider's web that constitutes the real world of supply chains. None of the firms above had considered the impact of an earthquake on their supply chains, or a nuclear meltdown, or even a financial collapse in the global banking system—all typical risks found in the real world.

Take the Apple iPad. IHS iSuppli is a market research firm that tears apart consumer electronic devices to discover how they are made, who makes the components, and where they are made, in order to obtain market intelligence on producer prices and profits. In its teardown of an iPad, it identified at least five major components sourced from Japanese suppliers, some of whom are located in northern Japan: NAND flash from Toshiba Corp., dynamic random access memory (DRAM) made by Elpida Memory Inc., an electronic compass from AKM Semiconductor, the touch screen overlay glass likely from Asahi Glass Co., and the system battery from Apple Japan Inc. Not all of these suppliers were directly impacted by the earthquake, but some were, and many have subsuppliers of various hard-to-replace small components that were directly impacted. The iPad and iPhone's unusually shaped lithium batteries used a crucial polymer made by Kureha, a Japanese firm in the nuclear contamination zone. Kureha controls 70% of the global production of this polymer. Apple was not the only consumer product manufacturer hit hard: computer chips are built on silicon wafers, and 25% of the world's supply is made by two Japanese manufacturers, both of which have shut down wafer production. A similar teardown by IHS of an iPad in 2014 shows that Apple still is using parts from many of the same firms whose production facilities are located in countries vulnerable to significant disruption for various reasons.

Apple is especially susceptible to supply chain disruptions because its new products often experience huge surges in demand, stressing its supply chains in normal times, and causing 2–4-week delays in meeting orders. Apple's iPhone 5s and 5c, which sold more than 9 million units in the first month of their introduction in September 2013, are no different from previous Apple products. Over 90% of the parts, and the final assembly, originate from China and Mongolia (for the rare earths used in the batteries). In the first month, Apple was out of stock of a popular gold model, with a several-week backlog.

Apple has made some changes in its supply chain sourcing in order to lessen the risk of disruption. UBM TechInsights took apart several iPads and found that many of the components were made by two or more manufacturers when comparing different iPads. The retina display, for instance, was produced by three different manufacturers (Samsung, LG, and a third company not identified). Still, many of the major components were made by the same Asian companies that ran into difficulties with nuclear accidents and Asian floods. It's unclear if using multiple suppliers all from the same region mitigates Apple's supply chain risk, or if it is an effort to extract lower prices from competing suppliers.

Apple was not the only manufacturer that learned a lesson in supply chain risk from the Japanese earthquake: Boeing was without carbon fiber airframe assemblies made in Japan; Ford and GM closed factories for lack of Japanese transmissions; and Caterpillar reduced production at its factories worldwide as it attempted to secure alternative suppliers.

Supply chain risk involves more than disruptions in production, as Apple and many other companies have discovered. Supply chains can produce reputational risks when key suppliers engage in labor and environmental policies and practices that are unacceptable to developed world audiences. For instance, for much of 2012, Apple was under attack in the United States and Europe after an audit by the Fair Labor Association found that workers at several assembly plants operated by Apple contractor Foxconn were exposed to toxic chemicals and forced to work over 60 hours a week under dangerous work conditions.

For instance, in November 2012, a fire in a clothing factory in Dhaka, Bangladesh, killed 117 workers, mostly women and children. Well-known brands from Europe and the United States, among them Walmart and Spanish giant Inditex, were producing clothing in this factory. Walmart claimed a subcontractor was using this factory

(continued)

without Walmart's knowledge. The fire cre-ated a worldwide protest, and has led to gov-ernment and industry efforts to certify factory safety in Bangladesh and hold firms responsible for working conditions.

One might think that in the so-called global and Internet economy, computer-based supply chains could quickly and effortlessly adjust to find new suppliers for just about any component or industrial material in a matter of minutes. Think again. New supply chains will need to be built that optimize not just cost but also survivability in the event of common disasters. They must also take into account efforts to reform labor and environ-mental practices of those involved in the supply chain.

SOURCES: "Apple Goes on Hiring Binge in Asia to Speed Product Releases," by Eva Dou, *Wall Street Journal*, March 3, 2014; "Teardown: Apple's Latest iPhones Are Not as Green as the Company Claims," by Roger Chang, Wired.com, September 20, 2013; "Gold iPhone 5S Backordered Online in US, Elsewhere," by Josh Lowensohn, Cnetnews.com, September 20, 2013; "Infographic Breaks Down Apple's iPhone Supply Chain," by Bryan Chaffin, MacOb-server.com, August 6, 2013; "Bangladesh Factory, Site of Fire That Trapped and Killed 7, Made European Brands," by Julfikar Ali Manik and Jim Yardley, *New York Times*, January 27, 2013; "Disruptions: Too Much Silence on Working Conditions," by Nick Bilton, *New York Times*, April 8, 2012; "Audit Faults Apple Supplier," by Jessica Vascellaro, *Wall Street Journal*, March 30, 2012; "Under the Hood of Apple's Tablet," by Don Clark, *Wall Street Journal*, March 16, 2012; "In China, Human Costs Are Built Into an iPad," by Charles Duhigg and David Barboza, *New York Times*, January 25, 2012; "Japan: The Business After Shocks," by Andrew Dowell, *Wall Street Journal*, March 25, 2011; "Some Worry the Success of Apple Is Tied to Japan," by Miguel Helft, *New York Times*, March 22, 2011; "Crisis Tests Supply Chain's Weak Links," by James Hookway and Aries Poon, *Wall Street Journal*, March 18, 2011; "Caterpillar Warns of Supply Problems From Quake," by Bob Tita, *Wall Street Journal*, March 18, 2011; "Lacking Parts, G.M. Will Close Plant," by Nick Bunkley, *New York Times*, March 17, 2011.

direct goods

goods directly involved in the production process

indirect goods

all other goods not directly involved in the production process

MRO goods

products for maintenance, repair, and operations

contract purchasing

involves long-term written agreements to purchase specified products, under agreed-upon terms and quality, for an extended period of time

spot purchasing

involves the purchase of goods based on immediate needs in larger marketplaces that involve many suppliers

for suppliers of specific products; qualifying both the seller and the products they sell; and negotiating prices, credit terms, escrow requirements, quality, and scheduling of delivery. Once a supplier is identified, purchase orders are issued, the buyer is sent an invoice, the goods are shipped, and the buyer sends a payment. Each of these steps in the procurement process is composed of many separate business processes and subactivities. Each of these activities must be recorded in the information systems of the seller, buyer, and shipper. Often, this data entry is not automatic and involves a great deal of manual labor, telephone calls, faxes, and e-mails.

TYPES OF PROCUREMENT

Two distinctions are important for understanding how B2B e-commerce can improve the procurement process. First, firms make purchases of two kinds of goods from suppliers: direct goods and indirect goods. **Direct goods** are goods integrally involved in the production process; for instance, when an automobile manufacturer purchases sheet steel for auto body production. **Indirect goods** are all other goods not directly involved in the production process, such as office supplies and maintenance products. Often these goods are called **MRO goods**—products for maintenance, repair, and operations.

Second, firms use two different methods for purchasing goods: contract purchas-ing and spot purchasing. **Contract purchasing** involves long-term written agreements to purchase specified products, with agreed-upon terms and quality, for an extended period of time. Generally, firms purchase direct goods using long-term contracts. **Spot purchasing** involves the purchase of goods based on immediate needs in larger marketplaces that involve many suppliers. Generally, firms use spot purchasing for indirect goods, although in some cases, firms also use spot purchasing for direct goods.

According to some estimates, about 65% of inter-firm trade involves contract purchasing of direct goods, and 35% involves spot purchasing of indirect goods (Ariba, 2014; Kaplan and Sawhney, 2000). This finding is significant for understanding B2B e-commerce.

Although the procurement process involves the purchasing of goods, it is extraordinarily information-intense, involving the movement of information among many existing corporate systems. The procurement process today is also very labor-intensive, directly involving millions of employees, not including those engaged in transportation, finance, insurance, or general office administration related to the process. The key players in the procurement process are the purchasing managers. They ultimately decide who to buy from, what to buy, and on what terms. Purchasing managers ("procurement managers" in the business press) are also the key decision makers for the adoption of B2B e-commerce solutions. As purchasing managers have become more familiar and comfortable with B2C e-commerce in their personal lives, they are increasingly coming to expect the same type of purchasing experience in the B2B arena. As a result, B2B manufacturers, suppliers, and distributors are finding that in order to effectively compete, they must pay more attention to the online customer experience, just as their B2C counterparts do. Features that B2B customers now expect include enhanced search functionality, up-to-date product pricing and availability information, product configurators, mobile support, online support forums, live customer service reps, and a database that contains their corporate purchasing history, shipping preferences, and payment data, and provides support for repeat orders.

MULTI-TIER SUPPLY CHAINS

Although Figure 12.3 captures some of the complexity of the procurement process, it is important to realize that firms purchase thousands of goods from thousands of suppliers. The suppliers, in turn, must purchase their inputs from their suppliers. Large manufacturers such as Ford Motor Company have over 20,000 suppliers of parts, packaging, and technology. The number of secondary and tertiary suppliers is at least as large. Together, this extended **multi-tier supply chain** (the chain of primary, secondary, and tertiary suppliers) constitutes a crucial aspect of the industrial infrastructure of the economy. **Figure 12.4** depicts a firm's multi-tier supply chain.

multi-tier supply chain
the chain of primary, secondary, and tertiary suppliers

The supply chain depicted in Figure 12.4 is a three-tier chain simplified for the sake of illustration. In fact, large Fortune 1000 firms have thousands of suppliers, who in turn have thousands of smaller suppliers. The complexity of the supply chain suggests a combinatorial explosion. Assuming a manufacturer has four primary suppliers and each one has three primary suppliers, and each of these has three primary suppliers, then the total number of suppliers in the chain (including the buying firm) rises to 53. This figure does not include the shippers, insurers, and financiers involved in the transactions.

Immediately, you can see from Figure 12.4 that the procurement process involves a very large number of suppliers, each of whom must be coordinated with the production needs of the ultimate purchaser—the buying firm. You can also understand how difficult it is to manage the supply chain, or obtain visibility into the supply chain simply because of its size and scope.

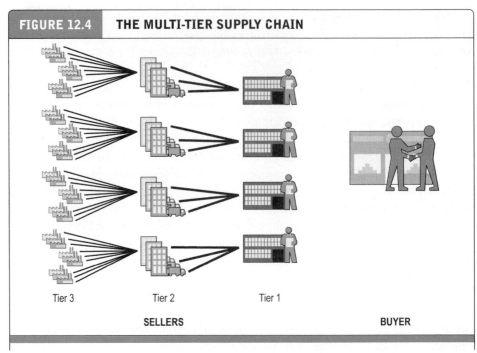

FIGURE 12.4 **THE MULTI-TIER SUPPLY CHAIN**

Tier 3   Tier 2   Tier 1

SELLERS   BUYER

The supply chain for every firm is composed of multiple tiers of suppliers.

VISIBILITY AND OTHER CONCEPTS IN SUPPLY CHAIN MANAGEMENT

The global, multi-tier nature of supply chains produces a number of challenges for supply chain mangers. A central concept of supply chains is supply chain visibility, which refers to the ability of a firm to monitor the output of its first and second tier suppliers, track and manage supplier orders, and manage transportation and logistics providers who are moving the products. A supply chain is visible when you know exactly what you have ordered from your suppliers and what their production schedule is, and when you can track the goods through shipping and trucking firms to your in-bound warehouse. With this knowledge, the firm's internal enterprise systems can produce production schedules and develop financial forecasts (Long, 2014; Cecere, 2014; Cecere, 2013.)

Other key concepts in supply chain management, and which are also central management challenges, are described in **Table 12.2**.

THE ROLE OF EXISTING LEGACY COMPUTER SYSTEMS AND ENTERPRISE SYSTEMS IN SUPPLY CHAINS

Complicating any efforts to coordinate the many firms in a supply chain is the fact that each firm generally has its own set of legacy computer systems, sometimes home-grown or customized, that cannot easily pass information to other systems. **Legacy computer systems** generally are older enterprise systems used to manage key business processes within a firm in a variety of functional areas from manufacturing, logistics, finance, and human resources. **Enterprise systems** are corporate-wide

legacy computer systems
older mainframe systems used to manage key business processes within a firm in a variety of functional areas

enterprise systems
corporate-wide systems that relate to all aspects of production, including finance, human resources, and procurement

TABLE 12.2	CONCEPTS AND CHALLENGES IN SUPPLY CHAIN MANAGEMENT
CONCEPT/CHALLENGE	DESCRIPTION
Visibility	Ability to monitor suppliers, orders, and logistics
Demand forecasting	Informing your suppliers of future demand
Production scheduling	Informing your suppliers of the production schedule
Order management	Keeping track of orders to your suppliers
Logistics management	Managing your logistics partners based on your production schedule

systems that relate to all aspects of production, including finance, human resources, and procurement. Many large Fortune 500 global firms have implemented global enterprise-wide systems from major vendors such as IBM, SAP, Oracle, and others. Generally enterprise systems have an inward focus on the firm's internal production processes, and only tangentially were concerned with suppliers. More contemporary cloud-based dedicated B2B software that can be integrated with existing enterprise systems are growing in importance. Firms like Oracle and SAP have made major purchases of B2B software firms in recent years, and are attempting to expand their offerings of cloud-based supply chain management systems that can work seamlessly with their legacy offerings.

12.3 TRENDS IN SUPPLY CHAIN MANAGEMENT AND COLLABORATIVE COMMERCE

It is impossible to comprehend the actual and potential contribution of B2B e-commerce, or the successes and failures of B2B e-commerce vendors and markets, without understanding ongoing efforts to improve the procurement process through a variety of supply chain management programs that long preceded the development of e-commerce.

Supply chain management (SCM) refers to a wide variety of activities that firms and industries use to coordinate the key players in their procurement process. For the most part, today's procurement managers still work with telephones, e-mail, fax machines, face-to-face conversations, and instinct, relying on trusted long-term suppliers for their strategic purchases of goods directly involved in the production process.

There have been a number of major developments in supply chain management over the last two decades that set the ground rules for understanding how B2B e-commerce works (or fails to work). These developments include just-in-time and lean production, supply chain simplification, adaptive supply chains, sustainable

supply chain management (SCM)
refers to a wide variety of activities that firms and industries use to coordinate the key players in their procurement process

supply chains, electronic data interchange (EDI), supply chain management systems, and collaborative commerce (Supply Chain Digest, 2012a).

JUST-IN-TIME AND LEAN PRODUCTION

One of the significant costs in any production process is the cost of in-process inventory: the parts and supplies needed to produce a product or service. **Just-in-time production** is a method of inventory cost management that seeks to reduce excess inventory to a bare minimum. In just-in-time production, the parts needed for, say, an automobile, arrive at the assembly factory a few hours or even minutes before they are attached to a car. Payment for the parts does not occur until the parts are attached to a vehicle on the production line. In the past, producers used to order enough parts for a week or even a month's worth of production, creating huge, costly buffers in the production process. These buffers assured that parts would almost always be available, but at a large cost. **Lean production** is a set of production methods and tools that focuses on the elimination of waste throughout the customer value chain. It is an extension of just-in-time beyond inventory management to the full range of activities that create customer value. Originally, just-in-time and lean methods were implemented with phones, faxes, and paper documents to coordinate the flow of parts in inventory. Supply chain management systems now have largely automated the process of acquiring inventory from suppliers, and made possible significant savings on a global basis. Arguably, contemporary supply chain systems are the foundation of today's global B2B production system.

SUPPLY CHAIN SIMPLIFICATION

Many manufacturing firms have spent the past two decades reducing the size of their supply chains and working more closely with a smaller group of strategic supplier firms to reduce both product costs and administrative costs, while improving quality, a trend known as **supply chain simplification**. Following the lead of Japanese industry, for instance, the automobile industry has systematically reduced the number of its suppliers by over 50%. Instead of open bidding for orders, large manufacturers have chosen to work with strategic partner supply firms under long-term contracts that guarantee the supplier business and also establish quality, cost, and timing goals. These strategic partnership programs are essential for just-in-time production models, and often involve joint product development and design, integration of computer systems, and tight coupling of the production processes of two or more companies. **Tight coupling** is a method for ensuring that suppliers precisely deliver the ordered parts at a specific time and to a particular location, ensuring the production process is not interrupted for lack of parts.

SUPPLY CHAIN BLACK SWANS: ADAPTIVE SUPPLY CHAINS

While firms have greatly simplified their supply chains in the last decade, they have also sought to centralize them by adopting a single, global supply chain system that integrates all the firm's vendor and logistics information into a single enterprise-wide system. Large software firms like Oracle, IBM, and SAP encourage firms to adopt a "one

just-in-time production
a method of inventory cost management that seeks to reduce excess inventory to a bare minimum

lean production
a set of production methods and tools that focuses on the elimination of waste throughout the customer value chain

supply chain simplification
involves reducing the size of the supply chain and working more closely with a smaller group of strategic supplier firms to reduce both product costs and administrative costs, while improving quality

tight coupling
a method for ensuring that suppliers precisely deliver the ordered parts, at a specific time and particular location, to ensure the production process is not interrupted for lack of parts

world, one firm, one database" enterprise-wide view of the world in order to achieve scale economies, simplicity, and to optimize global cost and value.

Beginning in earnest in 2000, managers in developed countries used these new technological capabilities to push manufacturing and production to the lowest cost labor regions of the world, specifically China and South East Asia. This movement of production to Asia was also enabled by the entrance of China into the World Trade Organization in September 2001. Suddenly, it was both technologically and politically possible to concentrate production wherever possible in the lowest cost region of the world. These developments were also supported by low-cost fuel, which made both transoceanic shipping and production inexpensive, and relative political stability in the region. By 2005, many economists believed a new world economic order had emerged based on cheap labor in Asia capable of producing inexpensive products for Western consumers, profits for global firms, and the opening of Asian markets to sophisticated Western goods and financial products.

As it turns out, there were many risks and costs to this strategy of concentrating production in China and Asia in a world of economic, financial, political, and even geological instability. Today, managers need to be more careful in balancing gains in efficiency from a highly centralized supply chain, with the risks inherent to such a strategy (Long, 2014). For instance, in the global financial crisis of 2007–2009, relying on suppliers in parts of Europe where currencies and interest rates fluctuated greatly exposed many firms to higher costs than anticipated. Suddenly, key suppliers could not obtain financing for their production or shipments. In March 2011, following the earthquake and tsunami in Japan, key suppliers in Japan were forced to shut down or slow production because of nuclear contamination of the entire Fukushima region where, as its turns out, major Japanese and American firms had automobile parts factories. As a result, General Motors could no longer obtain transmissions for its Volt electric car, and had to shut down a truck factory in Louisiana due to a lack of parts from Japan. Japanese and other global firms could not obtain batteries, switches, and axle assemblies. Production lead times in the automobile industry were very short, and inventories of parts were intentionally very lean, with only a few weeks' supply on hand. Texas Instruments shut down several of its Japanese plants, as did Toshiba, putting a crimp on the world supply of NAND flash memory chips used in smart-phones (Jolly, 2011; Bunkley, 2011). Caterpillar, Sony, Boeing, Volvo, and hundreds of other firms that are all part of a tightly coupled world supply chain also experienced supply chain disruptions. And then, in October of 2011, torrential rains in Thailand led to flooding of many of its key industrial regions, and the wiping out of a significant share of the world's electronics components from hard disk drives to automobile subsystems, cameras, and notebook PCs (Supply Chain Digest, 2012b; Hookway, 2012). In 2012 and 2013, the source of supply chain disruptions shifted to technology, with major disruptions due to failure of cloud-based services and cyberattacks (Gusman, 2013; Zurich Insurance, 2012).

The risks and costs of extended and concentrated supply chains have begun to change corporate strategies (Chopra and Sodhi, 2014). To cope with unpredictable world events, firms are taking steps to create **adaptive supply chains** that allow them to react to disruptions in the supply chain in a particular region by moving production

adaptive supply chain
allows companies to react to disruptions in the supply chain in a particular region by moving production to a different region

to a different region. Many companies are breaking up single global supply chain systems into regional or product-based supply chains and reducing the level of centralization. Using adaptive supply chains, firms can decide to locate some production of parts in Latin America, for instance, rather than having all their production or suppliers in a single country such as Japan. They will be able to move production around the world to temporary safe harbors. This may result in higher short-term costs, but provide substantial, longer-term risk protection in the event any single region is disrupted. Increasingly, supply chains are being built based on the assumption that global disruptions in supply are inevitable, but not predictable (Simchi-Levi et al., 2011; Malik et al., 2011). The focus in 2014 is on optimal-cost, not low-cost, supply chains, and more distributed manufacturing along with more flexible supply chains that can shift reliably from high-risk to low-risk areas. Regional manufacturing means shorter supply chains that can respond rapidly to changing consumer tastes and demand levels (Cachon and Swinney, 2011; Hewlett-Packard, 2013).

ACCOUNTABLE SUPPLY CHAINS: LABOR STANDARDS

accountable supply chain

one where the labor conditions in low-wage, underdeveloped producer countries are visible and morally acceptable to ultimate consumers in more developed industrial societies

Accountable supply chains are those where the labor conditions in low-wage, underdeveloped producer countries are visible and morally acceptable to ultimate consumers in more developed industrial societies. For much of the last century, American and European manufacturers with global supply chains with large offshore production facilities sought to hide the realities of their offshore factories from Western reporters and ordinary citizens. For global firms with long supply chains, visibility did not mean their consumers could understand how their products were made.

Beginning in 2000, and in part because of the growing power of the Internet to empower citizen reporters around the world, the realities of global supply chains have slowly become more transparent to the public. For instance, for much of the past decade, beginning in 1997, Nike, the world's largest manufacturer of sporting goods, has been under intense criticism for exploiting foreign workers, operating sweat shops, employing children, and allowing dangerous conditions in its subcontractor factories. As a result, Nike has introduced significant changes to its global supply chain.

With the emergence of truly global supply chains, and political changes at the World Trade Organization, which opened up European and American markets to Asian goods and services, many—if not most—of the electronics, toys, cosmetics, industrial supplies, footwear, apparel, and other goods consumed in the developed world are made by workers in factories in the less developed world, primarily in Asia and Latin America. Unfortunately, but quite understandably, the labor conditions in these factories in most cases do not meet the minimal labor standards of Europe or America even though these factories pay higher wages and offer better working conditions than other local jobs in the host country. In many cases, the cost for a worker of not having a job in what—to Western standards—are horrible working conditions is to sink deeper into poverty and even worse conditions. Many point out that labor conditions were brutal in the United States and Europe in the nineteenth and early twentieth century when these countries were building industrial economies, and therefore, whatever conditions exist in offshore factories in 2014 are no worse than developed countries in their early years of rapid industrialization.

The argument results in a painful ethical dilemma, a terrible trade-off: cheap manufactured goods that increase consumer welfare in developed countries seem to require human misery in less developed countries. Indeed, these jobs would never have been moved to less developed parts of world without exceptionally low, even survival level, wages.

Notwithstanding the argument that having a job is better than being unemployed in low-wage countries, or any country, there are some working conditions that are completely unacceptable to consumers and therefore to firms in developed countries. Among these unacceptable working conditions are slave or forced labor, child employment, routine exposure to toxic substances, more than 48 hours of work per week, harassment and abuse, sexual exploitation, and compensation beneath the minimal standard of living leaving no disposable income. These practices were, and are, in some cases typical, and certainly not atypical, in many low-wage countries.

A number of groups in the last decade have contributed to efforts to make global supply chains transparent to reporters and citizens, and to develop minimal standards of accountability. Among these groups are the National Consumers League, Human Rights First, the Maquilla Solidarity Network, the Global Fairness Initiative, the Clean Clothes Campaign, the International Labor Organization (UN), and the Fair Labor Association (FLA). The FLA is a coalition of business firms with offshore production and global supply chains, universities, and private organizations. For member firms, the FLA conducts interviews with workers, makes unannounced visits to factories to track progress, and investigates complaints. They are also one of the major international labor standard-setting organizations (Fair Labor Organization, 2012).

In March 2012, the FLA released its investigation of Hon Hai Precision Industry Company (a Taiwan-based company known as Foxconn), which is the assembler of nearly all iPhones and iPads in the world. Foxconn operates what is alleged to be the largest factory in the world in Longhua, Shenzhen, where over 250,000 workers assemble electronics goods. The audit of working conditions at Foxconn was authorized by Apple, a member of the FLA, and was based on 35,000 surveys of workers at the Longhua factory. The report found over 50 legal and code violations (sometimes in violation of Chinese laws) including requiring too many hours of work a week (over 60), failing to pay workers for overtime, and hazardous conditions that injured workers (Fair Labor Association, 2012).

SUSTAINABLE SUPPLY CHAINS: LEAN, MEAN, AND GREEN

Sustainable business is a call for business to take social and ecological interests, and not just corporate profits, into account in all their decision-making throughout the firm. No small request. Since the United Nations World Commission on Environment and Development (WCED) published the first comprehensive report on sustainable business in 1987, firms around the globe have struggled with these concepts and in some cases ignored or resisted them as simply a threat to sustained profitability. The commission's report (*Our Common Future*) argued for a balance of profits, social community development, and minimal impact on the world environment, including of course, the carbon footprint of business. By 2013, the consensus among major firms

sustainable supply chain

involves using the most efficient environment-regarding means of production, distribution, and logistics

in Europe, Asia, and the United States has become that in the long term, and through careful planning, sustainable business and **sustainable supply chains** are just good business because it means using the most efficient environment-regarding means of production, distribution, and logistics. These efficient methods create value for consumers, investors, and communities.

Notions of sustainable business have had a powerful impact on supply chain thinking. In part, these efforts are good risk management: all advanced countries have substantially strengthened their environmental regulations. It makes good business sense for firms to prepare methods and operations suitable to this new environment.

For instance, all the major textiles brands and retailers have announced plans for a more sustainable supply chain in textiles. One of the world's truly ancient industries, textiles supports millions of workers while consuming extraordinary resources: it takes 1,000 gallons of water to make one pound of finished cotton (your jeans, for instance). While growing cotton has its issues (fertilizer), the subsequent dying, finishing, and cleaning of cotton makes it the number one industrial polluter on Earth (cKinetics, 2010). It's not a small matter then that Walmart, Gap, Levi's, Nike, and other large players in the industry are taking steps to reduce the environmental impact of their operations by improving the efficiency of the entire supply and distribution chains.

With the help of IBM, SAP, and Oracle, other firms and entire industries are working to develop sustainable supply chains. McKesson, North America's largest distributor of drugs, uses IBM's Supply Chain Sustainability Management Solution (SCSM) to minimize carbon dioxide emissions throughout its supply chain, while lowering its distribution costs. SCSM (a business analytics package that works with IBM's B2B software) can determine low-cost refrigeration alternatives for certain medicines (such as insulin and vaccines), identify the environmentally least harmful way to bring new products into its distribution network, and determine the best way to transport pharmaceuticals to customers (IBM, 2011a).

ELECTRONIC DATA INTERCHANGE (EDI)

As noted in the previous section, B2B e-commerce did not originate with the Internet, but in fact has its roots in technologies such as EDI that were first developed in the mid-1970s and 1980s. EDI is a broadly defined communications protocol for exchanging documents among computers using technical standards developed by the American National Standards Institute (ANSI X12 standards) and international bodies such as the United Nations (EDIFACT standards).

EDI was developed to reduce the cost, delays, and errors inherent in the manual exchanges of documents such as purchase orders, shipping documents, price lists, payments, and customer data. EDI differs from an unstructured message because its messages are organized with distinct fields for each of the important pieces of information in a commercial transaction such as transaction date, product purchased, amount, sender's name, address, and recipient's name.

Each major industry in the United States and throughout much of the industrial world has EDI industry committees that define the structure and information fields of electronic documents for that industry. Estimates indicate that B2B e-commerce EDI transactions will total about $2.9 trillion in 2014, about 50% of all B2B e-commerce

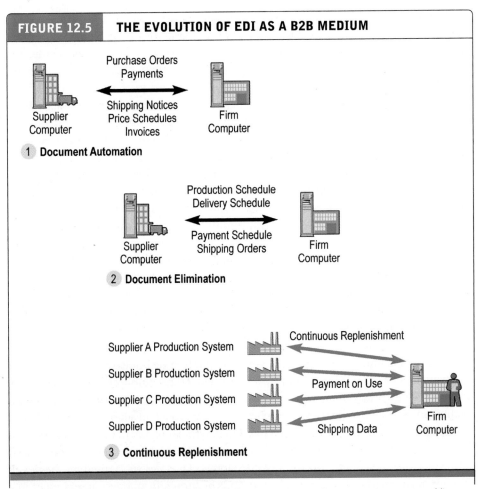

FIGURE 12.5   THE EVOLUTION OF EDI AS A B2B MEDIUM

EDI has evolved from a simple point-to-point digital communications medium to a many-to-one enabling tool for continuous inventory replenishment.

(U.S. Census Bureau, 2014; authors' estimates). In this sense, EDI remains very important in the development of B2B e-commerce (Cecere, 2014).

EDI has evolved significantly since the 1980s (see **Figure 12.5**). Initially, EDI focused on document automation (Stage 1). Procurement agents created purchase orders electronically and sent them to trading partners, who in turn shipped order fulfillment and shipping notices electronically back to the purchaser. Invoices, payments, and other documents followed. These early implementations replaced the postal system for document transmission, and resulted in same-day shipping of orders (rather than a week's delay caused by the postal system), reduced errors, and lower costs. The second stage of EDI development began in the early 1990s, driven largely by the automation of internal industrial processes and movement toward just-in time production and continuous production. New methods of production called for greater flexibility in scheduling, shipping, and financing of supplies. EDI evolved to become a tool for continuous inventory replenishment. EDI was used to eliminate purchase orders and other documents entirely, replacing them with production schedules and inventory balances. Supplier firms were sent monthly statements of production requirements and precise scheduled delivery times, and the orders would be fulfilled continuously, with inventory and payments being adjusted at the end of each month.

In the third stage of EDI, beginning in the mid-1990s, suppliers were given online access to selected parts of the purchasing firm's production and delivery schedules, and, under long-term contracts, were required to meet those schedules on their own without intervention by firm purchasing agents. Movement toward this continuous real-time access model of EDI was spurred in the 1990s by large manufacturing and process firms (such as oil and chemical companies) that were implementing enterprise systems. These systems required standardization of business processes and resulted in the automation of production, logistics, and many financial processes. These new processes required much closer relationships with suppliers and logistics partners (shipping and ground transporters), who were required to be more precise in delivery scheduling and more flexible in inventory management. This level of supplier precision could never be achieved economically by human purchasing agents. This third stage of EDI enabled the era of continuous replenishment. For instance, Walmart and Toys"R"Us provide their suppliers with access to their store inventories, and the suppliers are expected to keep the stock of items on the shelf within prespecified targets. Similar developments occurred in the grocery industry.

Today, EDI must be viewed as a general enabling technology that provides for the exchange of critical business information between computer applications supporting a wide variety of business processes. EDI is an important industrial network technology, suited to support communications among a small set of strategic partners in direct, long-term trading relationships. The technical platform of EDI has changed from mainframes to personal computers, from corporate data centers to cloud-based software-as-a-service platforms (described below). EDI is not well suited for the development of Net marketplaces, where thousands of suppliers and purchasers meet in a digital arena to negotiate prices. EDI supports direct bilateral communications among a small set of firms and does not permit the multilateral, dynamic relationships of a true marketplace. EDI does not provide for price transparency among a large number of suppliers, does not scale easily to include new participants, and is not a real-time communications environment. EDI does not have a rich communications environment that can simultaneously support e-mail messaging, video conferencing, sharing of graphic documents, network meetings, or user-friendly flexible database creation and management.

MOBILE B2B

Bring Your Own Device (BYOD) policy
employees use their personal smartphone, tablet, or laptop computer on the company's network

Just as with B2C commerce, mobile devices have become increasingly important in all aspects of B2B e-commerce, through all steps of the procurement process and throughout the supply chain. More and more companies have adopted a **Bring Your Own Device (BYOD) policy**, in which employees use their personal smartphone, tablet, or laptop computer on the company's network, which has helped contribute to their growing importance in B2B. Cisco estimates that by 2016, mobile traffic will represent over 25% of all business Internet traffic, up from less than 5% in 2011 (Forrester, 2013).

On the procurement front, B2B buyers are increasingly using mobile devices for all phases of the purchase process, from discovery to decision-making, to actual purchase. One study found that over 50% of B2B decision-makers surveyed used a mobile device to research products, equipment, services, and suppliers. B2B buyers want to be able to place orders using mobile devices just as they do in the B2C arena, and increasingly expect B2B e-commerce sites to be readily accessible from such devices, to be able to start an order from a device and finish it on their desktop and vice versa, and to be able to get online customer service on their mobile devices (eMarketer, Inc., 2014; Forrester, 2013).

On the supply chain front, many supply chain network and software providers are enhancing their offerings by providing support for mobile devices and applications. For instance, Elementum provides a variety of mobile apps running on a cloud platform to track various aspects of the supply chain and enable supply chain visibility. For instance, Elementum's Exposure App enables companies to identify and respond to risks in their supply chain, providing real-time alerts on events that may impact the supply, manufacture, or distribution of components of their products. Elementum's Perspective App helps companies monitor the health of their supply chain by providing a dashboard that provides real-time tracking of key performance indicators (KPIs) in the supply chain.

B2B IN THE CLOUD

In the traditional approach to B2B enterprise systems, firms build on their existing on-premise, enterprise production systems that keep track of their manufacturing and distribution processes to include new functionality connecting them to their suppliers' systems. This is a very expensive process that involves connecting suppliers one at a time, establishing the telecommunications channels, and managing the data quality issues, not to mention the cost of building the infrastructure of computers and telecommunications to support coordination of suppliers and B2B transactions. Cloud computing (described in Chapter 2) is increasingly being used to greatly reduce the cost of building and maintaining B2B systems.

In **cloud-based B2B systems**, much of the expense of B2B systems is shifted from the firm to a B2B network provider, sometimes called a data hub or B2B platform (see **Figure 12.6**). The cloud platform owner provides the computing and telecommunications capability; establishes connections with the firm's partners; provides software on-demand (software-as-a-service or SAAS) to connect the firm's systems to its partners' systems; performs data coordination and cleaning; and manages data quality for all members. Network effects apply here: the cost of these tasks and capabilities is spread over all members, reducing costs for all. B2B network providers also provide communication environments and file storage services that allow partners to work together more closely, and to collaborate on improving the flow of goods and transactions. B2B network providers charge customers on a demand basis, rather than on a percentage of their transactions' value, depending on their utilization of the network.

cloud-based B2B system
shifts much of the expense of B2B systems from the firm to a B2B network provider, sometimes called a data hub or B2B platform

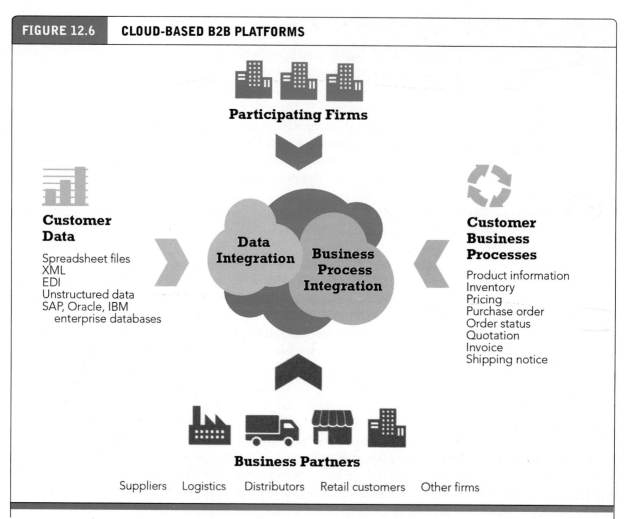

FIGURE 12.6 **CLOUD-BASED B2B PLATFORMS**

Participating Firms

Customer Data

Spreadsheet files
XML
EDI
Unstructured data
SAP, Oracle, IBM
  enterprise databases

Data Integration

Business Process Integration

Customer Business Processes

Product information
Inventory
Pricing
Purchase order
Order status
Quotation
Invoice
Shipping notice

Business Partners

Suppliers   Logistics   Distributors   Retail customers   Other firms

Cloud-based B2B platforms integrate a firm's customer data, business processes, and business partners into a cloud-based software system. Businesses are charged for the hardware and software platform on a utilization basis, reducing their costs significantly.

Suppliers of traditional on-premise B2B and supply chain management systems have responded by purchasing cloud-based B2B networks in the last few years. For instance, SAP purchased Ariba, one of the first and largest cloud-based B2B transaction networks, in 2012 for $4.6 billion. Ariba's global network automates more than $500 billion in commercial transactions, collaborations, and business intelligence among a wide range of suppliers, shipping, and logistics firms. SAP, the largest supplier of firm-base enterprise systems, supplies software that supports internal business processes. Other B2B network providers include E2Open and GT Nexus.

Unlike traditional firm-based B2B systems, cloud-based B2B data networks can be implemented in short periods of time to respond to corporate mergers and rapidly changing markets, as *Insight on Technology: Your Shoes Are in the Cloud* illustrates.

INSIGHT ON TECHNOLOGY

YOUR SHOES ARE IN THE CLOUD

Have you ever worn Keds, Hush Puppies, Merrells, Sebagos, Sperry Topsiders, or Sauconys? If so, you've had a product made by Wolverine World Wide Inc. on your feet. Although you may not be familiar with its name, Wolverine is one of the world's largest designers, manufacturers, and marketers of footwear for sports, casual wear, and work. The company's business is divided into three segments: its Lifestyle Group includes Sperry Topsider, Stride Rite, Hush Puppies and Keds. Its Performance Group includes Merrell, Saucony, Chaco, and Patagonia. The Heritage Group comprises brands such as Wolverine, Cat, Bates, Sebago, Harley-Davidson, and HyTest Safety. Wolverine was founded in Grand Rapids, Michigan, in 1883, and originally made the boots that built America's railroads, skyscrapers, and highways. Since then the company has expanded largely by purchasing well-known name brand manufacturers. The company sells its footwear through national retailers, catalog sales, and consumer direct businesses at various e-commerce Web sites.

In 2013, Wolverine generated $2.7 billion in revenue, up from $1.6 billion in 2012, a whopping 68% increase due in large part to acquisition of the popular Saucony and Keds brands. In 2012, it purchased a total of four brands that increased its revenue by $1 billion in a single year. The company has 7,200 employees worldwide. Today, Wolverine sources production of more than 100 million pairs of shoes from 110 factories located in 20 countries. The company's major competitors are Nike (the global giant with $25 billion in revenue) and Deckers (with $1.5 billion in revenue). The global footwear market is estimated to be $123 billion, with a 5.6% annual growth rate. Coming out of the 2008–2011 recession when sales were flat, strong global growth for footwear is predicted for the next five years.

Like many global consumer goods manufacturers, Wolverine has faced a number of challenges in managing its global supply chain with both the supply and retail fronts. In the early 2000s, Wolverine's supply chain management capability was based on SAP's BusinessSuite enterprise software. The SAP software centralized and consolidated its operations across all its brands and created an integrated system platform for managing the supply chain, customer relationships, orders, and financial reporting. However, the system could not recognize multiple currencies, languages, or global standards. Signing up new suppliers or retail outlets was an expensive and sometimes lengthy process. Out-of-stock situations were growing as the company could not respond to retailer demands for specific styles. Matching inventory to actual demand was becoming more difficult as fashions changed rapidly. Working with global retailers was difficult at times because the existing system could not work with different languages and currencies. Many of the company's largest global retailers were not comfortable transacting in dollars. In response, Wolverine expanded its SAP enterprise system by adopting the software firm's SAP Retail solutions. This new system had global capabilities that enable different languages and currencies to be used for transactions and communications. The new system also allowed Wolverine managers as well as their retail partners to gain increased, real-time visibility into consumer demand, supply chain, and store operations. As a result, stock outs have declined, and revenues at retail stores have increased 15 to 25% in various segments.

On the supplier side of its operations, Wolverine also faced significant challenges. Its 2012 acquisition of Saucony and Keds brought in an additional $1 billion worth of transactions to pro-

(continued)

cess, and might have quickly overwhelmed its domestic supply chain's systems. Its SAP enterprise system was a traditional on-premise, very large system that was designed to enhance Wolverine's supply chain, and not the entire ecosystem of manufacturing, logistics, and financial firms that work with Wolverine to manufacture and distribute shoes. Wolverine in fact had over 200 suppliers in 120 countries that had their own supply chain software, and integrating them into a single platform was unimaginable, costly, and time consuming. There was no easy (or inexpensive) way to scale up its existing supply chain system to include all its partners, and their millions of transactions. It was difficult for its global suppliers to sign up to Wolverine's domestic system, the payment system was outdated, and logistics and finance were not supported in the existing system.

For help Wolverine turned to GT Nexus, a provider of a cloud-based supply chain platform. GT Nexus is a network of supply chain networks that allows firms to tie their own supply chain systems into a global platform and communicate with their partners, who may be manufacturers,

shipping companies, finance firms, and retailers. Unlike with traditional enterprise software, Wolverine does not buy the package, or pay monthly rental costs, or host the software on its servers. Instead, GT Nexus provides an on-demand, pay-as-you-go, software-as-a-service model. Some of the services provided include supplier enablement, purchase-to-payment financial tracking, tracking of packing and shipping, financing of transactions, freight contracting, auditing, documentation and customs, and in-transit tracking. GT Nexus bills itself as an on-demand, cloud-based, global supply chain management platform. Currently, GT Nexus supports supply chain management at 25,000 companies, has over 100,000 users, and manages an estimated $100 billion in trades.

Using GT Nexus, Wolverine can provide its suppliers, retailers, logistics, and financial partners a single login to the global Wolverine supply chain. Wolverine managers and their supply partners can see the entire supply chain from suppliers of raw materials, to manufacturers, transporters, and ultimately retail store orders.

SOURCES: "Wolverine World Wide Achieving Business Clarity to Grow Retail Globally," SAP Transformation Study, SAP.com, May 6, 2014; "Powering the World's Most Responsive and Adaptive Supply Chain Networks," Gtnexus.com/about, May 2014; "Global Footwear Manufacturing: Market Research Report," IBISworld.com, March 2014; "SEC Form 10k for the fiscal year ended December 31, 2013," Wolverine World Wide, Inc., February 25, 2014; "Shoe Supply Chain Has Sole Version of Truth," by Jane Bird, *Financial Times*, January 29, 2014.

SUPPLY CHAIN MANAGEMENT SYSTEMS

supply chain management (SCM) systems

continuously link the activities of buying, making, and moving products from suppliers to purchasing firms, as well as integrating the demand side of the business equation by including the order entry system in the process

Supply chain simplification, just in time and lean production, focusing on strategic partners in the production process, enterprise systems, and continuous inventory replenishment are the foundation for contemporary supply chain management (SCM) systems. **Supply chain management systems** continuously link the activities of buying, making, and moving products from suppliers to purchasing firms, as well as integrating the demand side of the business equation by including the order entry system in the process. With an SCM system and continuous replenishment, inventory is greatly reduced and production begins only when an order is received (see **Figure 12.7**). These systems enable just-in-time and lean-production methods.

Hewlett-Packard (HP) is one of the largest technology companies in the world, with sales of $112 billion in 2013. With operations in 178 countries, sales in 43 currencies, and 15 languages, HP is truly a global firm with global supply chain issues that

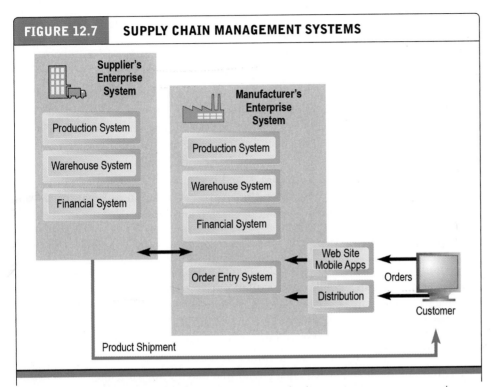

FIGURE 12.7 **SUPPLY CHAIN MANAGEMENT SYSTEMS**

SCM systems coordinate the activities of suppliers, shippers, and order entry systems to automate order entry through production, payment, and shipping business processes. Increasingly customers, as well as employees working throughout the supply chain, are using smartphones, tablets, and mobile apps to place and coordinate orders.

became even more complicated as HP expanded by making over 200 acquisitions in the last decade. In 2014 HP has the 9th largest supply chain in the world, and largest supply chain among technology manufacturers. HP has about 200,000 products and 100,000 suppliers. To cope with one of the most complex supply chains in the world, HP developed a real-time networked supply chain hub called KeyChain that handled over 500,000 transactions in 2013. HP's KeyChain system is a Web-based, order-driven supply chain management system that begins with either a customer placing an order online or the receipt of an order from a dealer. The order is forwarded from the order entry system to HP's production and delivery system. From there, the order is routed to one of several HP contractor supplier firms. One such firm is Synnex in Fremont, California. At Synnex, computers verify the order with HP and validate the ordered configuration to ensure the PC can be manufactured (e.g., will not have missing parts or fail a design specification set by HP). The order is then forwarded to a computer-based production control system that issues a bar-coded production ticket to factory assemblers. Simultaneously, a parts order is forwarded to Synnex's warehouse and inventory management system. A worker assembles the computer, and then the computer is boxed, tagged, and shipped to the customer. The delivery is monitored and tracked by HP's supply chain management system, which links directly to one of several overnight delivery systems operated by Airborne Express, Federal Express, and UPS. The elapsed time from order entry to shipping is 48 hours. With this system, Synnex and HP have eliminated the need to hold PCs in inventory, reduced cycle time from one week to 48 hours, and reduced errors. HP has extended this system to become a global B2B order tracking, reporting, and support system for large HP customers (Synnex Corporation, 2014; Hewlett-Packard, 2014).

It isn't just huge technology companies that use supply chain software. There's nothing quite so perishable as fashionable underwear given the rate of fashion change. Under Armour, which is the world's No. 1 performance athletic brand, uses software from SAP to predict sales, plan inventory, and coordinate suppliers (Gilmore, 2014; Booen, 2011). Prior to using these tools, Under Armour often missed sales because it did not produce enough of popular items, or overproduced items that were not selling.

COLLABORATIVE COMMERCE

collaborative commerce

the use of digital technologies to permit organizations to collaboratively design, develop, build, and manage products through their life cycles

Collaborative commerce is a direct extension of supply chain management systems, as well as supply chain simplification. **Collaborative commerce** is defined as the use of digital technologies to permit firms to collaboratively design, develop, build, market, and manage products through their life cycles. This is a much broader mission than EDI or simply managing the flow of information among organizations. Collaborative commerce involves a definitive move from a transaction focus to a relationship focus among the supply chain participants. Rather than having an arm's-length adversarial relationship with suppliers, collaborative commerce fosters sharing of sensitive internal information with suppliers and purchasers. Managing collaborative commerce requires knowing exactly what information to share with whom. Collaborative commerce extends beyond supply chain management activities to include the collaborative development of new products and services by multiple cooperating firms.

A good example of collaborative commerce is the long-term effort of P&G, the world's largest manufacturer of personal and health care products, from Crest toothpaste to Tide soap, to work with suppliers and even customers to develop 50% of its product line over time. In the past, for instance, P&G would design a bottle or product package in-house, and then turn to over 100 suppliers of packaging to find out what it would cost and try to bargain that down. Using Ariba's procurement network, P&G asks its suppliers to come up with innovative ideas for packaging and pricing. Taking it a step further, P&G's Web site, Pgconnectdevelop.com, solicits new product ideas from suppliers and customers. About 50% of P&G's new products originate with substantial input from its suppliers and customers (P&G, 2011; Vance, 2010). P&G is also collaborating with its biggest online customer, Amazon, by co-locating their operations (Ng, 2013). P&G sets aside warehouse space for P&G products purchased by Amazon customers. Amazon ships the products to its customers directly from the P&G warehouses rather than ship them first to Amazon warehouses, and then to the consumer. This collaboration results in Amazon reducing its costs of shipping and storing goods, becoming more competitive on price compared to Wal-Mart and Costco, and reducing the time it takes to arrive at consumers' homes. For P&G collaboration means savings on transportation costs incurred trucking products to Amazon warehouses, and Amazon's help in boosting online sales of P&G products. Other

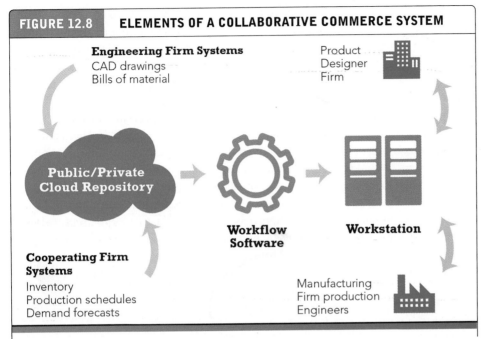

FIGURE 12.8 — **ELEMENTS OF A COLLABORATIVE COMMERCE SYSTEM**

A collaborative commerce application includes a cloud repository where employees at several different firms can store engineering drawings and other documents. Workflow software determines who can see this data and what rules will apply for displaying the data on individual workstations.

well-known companies using collaboration to develop and deliver products include Lego (DesignByMe), Harley Davidson, Starbucks, and GE's Ecomagination program (James, 2012; Esposito, 2012).

Although collaborative commerce can involve customers as well as suppliers in the development of products, for the most part, it is concerned with the development of a rich communications environment to enable inter-firm sharing of designs, production plans, inventory levels, delivery schedules, and the development of shared products (see **Figure 12.8**).

Collaborative commerce is very different from EDI, which is a technology for structured communications among firms. Collaborative commerce is more like an interactive teleconference among members of the supply chain. EDI and collaborative commerce share one characteristic: they are not open, competitive marketplaces, but instead are, technically, private industrial networks that connect strategic partners in a supply chain.

Collaboration 2.0: Cloud, Web, Social, and Mobile

The technology of collaborative commerce has changed greatly since its inception over thirty years ago with tools like Lotus Notes, which was used almost entirely within firms to establish an environment where employees could share ideas, notes, and ideas, and work on projects together. What's new about collaboration tools today is that the software and data are stored on cloud servers where it is less expensive, and easy to update; social tools like Facebook and Twitter are commonly used by employees in many firms, while other firms deploy their own social networking platform; the Web enables very inexpensive collaborative environments; and the hardware is mobile so collaboration can take place in many more places and times (Gohring, 2014). Collaboration technologies have expanded collaboration from a within-the-firm platform to a primary tool of inter-firm B2B collaboration.

Broadband video networks like Cisco's TelePresence Studios are beginning to play a role in enabling frequent, long-distance, collaboration among supply chain partners. TelePresence is one of several high-bandwidth video systems from different vendors that give users the impression they are sharing physical space with other participants who are in fact located remotely, sometimes on the other side of the globe. P&G has over forty TelePresence studios in its facilities around the world to encourage collaboration among its employees and suppliers (Cisco, 2013, 2011). Cisco's @CiscoLiveDesk's Twitter feed enhances the TelePresence experience by adding face-to-face support, scheduling assistance, and demos. Using Skype video conferencing, even tiny businesses can take advantage of very inexpensive collaborative platforms over the Web, or mobile platforms.

In Section 12.5, we discuss collaborative commerce in greater depth as a technology that enables private industrial networks.

SOCIAL NETWORKS AND B2B: THE EXTENDED SOCIAL ENTERPRISE

It's a short step from collaboration with vendors, suppliers, and customers, to a more personal relationship based on conversations with participants in the supply chain using social networks—both private and public. Here, the conversations and sharing of ideas are more unstructured, situational, and personal. Procurement officers, managers of supply chains, and logistics managers are people too, and they participate in the same social network culture provided by Facebook, Twitter, Tumblr, Instagram, and a host of other public social networks as we all do. Being able to respond to fast moving developments that affect supply chains requires something more than a Web site, e-mail, or telephone calls. Social networks can provide the intimate connections among customers, suppliers, and logistics partners that are needed to keep the supply chain functioning, and to make decisions based on current conditions (Red Prairie, 2012).

Participants in the supply chain network are tapping into their tablet computers, smartphones, and social network sites for purchasing, scheduling, exception handling, and deciding with their B2B customers and suppliers. In many cases, supply chain social networks are private—owned by the largest firm in the supply chain network. In other cases, firms develop Facebook pages to organize conversations among supply chain network members.

Some examples of social B2B include TradeSpace, a UK-based business social network where business people can share experiences and ideas, and buy and sell products. Cisco is using its Web site and Facebook pages to run new product campaigns for its business customers using social networks exclusively. Dell, like many businesses, uses its YouTube channel to engage suppliers and customers in conversations about existing products, and ideas for new products. Social networks are beginning to be common tools for managers engaged in B2B commerce. Public social network sites like Facebook and Twitter can be excellent for coordinating the flow of information among business partners through the supply chain.

12.4 NET MARKETPLACES

One of the most compelling visions of B2B e-commerce is that of an online market-place that would bring thousands of fragmented suppliers into contact with hundreds of major purchasers of industrial goods for the purpose of conducting frictionless commerce. The hope was that these suppliers would compete with one another on price, transactions would be automated and low cost, and as a result, the price of industrial supplies would fall. By extracting fees from buyers and sellers on each transaction, third-party intermediary market makers could earn significant revenues. These Net marketplaces could scale easily as volume increased by simply adding more computers and communications equipment.

In pursuit of this vision, well over 1,500 Net marketplaces sprang up in the early days of e-commerce. Unfortunately, many of them have since disappeared and the population is expected to stabilize at about 200. Still, many survive, and they are joined by other types of Net marketplaces—some private and some public—based on different assumptions that are quite successful.

CHARACTERISTICS OF NET MARKETPLACES

There is a confusing variety of Net marketplaces today, and several different ways to classify them. For instance, some writers classify Net marketplaces on the basis of their pricing mechanisms—auction, bid/ask, negotiated price, and fixed prices—while others classify markets based on characteristics of the markets they serve (vertical versus horizontal, or sell-side versus buy-side), or ownership (industry-owned consortia versus independent third-party intermediaries). **Table 12.3** describes some of the important characteristics of Net marketplaces.

TABLE 12.3	CHARACTERISTICS OF NET MARKETPLACES: A B2B VOCABULARY
CHARACTERISTIC	MEANING
Bias	Sell-side vs. buy-side vs. neutral. Whose interests are advantaged: buyers, sellers, or no bias?
Ownership	Industry vs. third party. Who owns the marketplace?
Pricing mechanism	Fixed-price catalogs, auctions, bid/ask, and RFPs/RFQs.
Scope/Focus	Horizontal vs. vertical markets.
Value creation	What benefits do they offer customers or suppliers?
Access to market	In public markets, any firm can enter, but in private markets, entry is by invitation only.

TYPES OF NET MARKETPLACES

Although each of these distinctions helps describe the phenomenon of Net market-places, they do not focus on the central business functionality provided, nor are they capable by themselves of describing the variety of Net marketplaces.

In **Figure 12.9**, we present a classification of Net marketplaces that focuses on their business functionality; that is, what these Net marketplaces provide for businesses seeking solutions. We use two dimensions of Net marketplaces to create a four-cell classification table. We differentiate Net marketplaces as providing either indirect goods (goods used to support production) or direct goods (goods used in production), and we distinguish markets as providing either contractual purchasing (where purchases take place over many years according to a contract between the firm and its vendor) or spot purchasing (where purchases are episodic and anonymous—vendors and buyers do not have an ongoing relationship and may not know one another). The intersection of these dimensions produces four main types of Net marketplaces that are relatively straightforward: e-distributors, e-procurement networks, exchanges, and industry consortia. Note, however, that in the real world, some Net marketplaces can

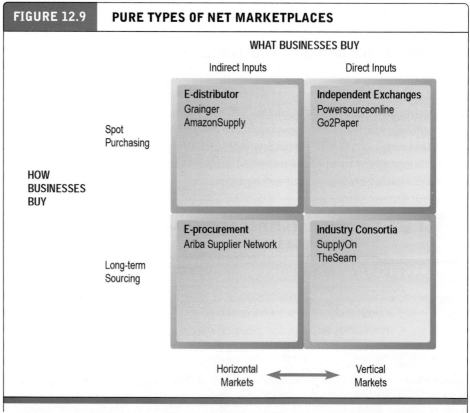

FIGURE 12.9 PURE TYPES OF NET MARKETPLACES

There are four main types of Net marketplaces based on the intersection of two dimensions: how businesses buy and what they buy. A third dimension—horizontal versus vertical markets—also distinguishes the different types of Net marketplaces.

FIGURE 12.10	E-DISTRIBUTORS

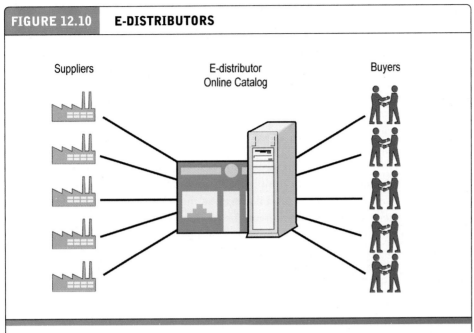

E-distributors are firms that bring the products of thousands of suppliers into a single online catalog for sale to thousands of buyer firms. E-distributors are sometimes referred to as one-to-many markets, one seller serving many firms.

be found in multiple parts of this figure as business models change and opportunities appear and disappear. Nevertheless, the discussion of "pure types" of Net marketplaces is a useful starting point.

Each of these Net marketplaces seeks to provide value to customers in different ways. We discuss each type of Net marketplace in more detail in the following sections.

E-distributors

E-distributors are the most common and most easily understood type of Net marketplace. An **e-distributor** provides an online catalog that represents the products of thousands of direct manufacturers (see **Figure 12.10**). E-distributors are independently owned intermediaries that offer industrial customers a single source from which to order indirect goods (often referred to as MRO) on a spot, as-needed basis. A significant percentage of corporate purchases cannot be satisfied under a company's existing contracts, and must be purchased on a spot basis. E-distributors make money by charging a markup on products they distribute.

Organizations and firms in all industries require MRO supplies. The MRO function maintains, repairs, and operates commercial buildings and maintains all the machinery of these buildings from heating, ventilating, and air conditioning systems to lighting fixtures.

E-distributors operate in horizontal markets because they serve many different industries with products from many different suppliers. E-distributors usually operate

e-distributor

provides an online catalog that represents the products of thousands of direct manufacturers

public markets in the sense that any firm can order from the catalog, as opposed to private markets, where membership is restricted to selected firms.

E-distributor prices are usually fixed, but large customers receive discounts and other incentives to purchase, such as credit, reporting on account activity, and limited forms of business purchasing rules (for instance, no purchases greater than $500 for a single item without a purchase order). The primary benefits offered to industrial customers are lower search costs, lower transaction costs, wide selection, rapid delivery, and low prices.

W.W. Grainger is probably the most frequently cited example of an e-distributor. Grainger is involved in long-term systematic sourcing as well as spot sourcing, but its emphasis is on spot sourcing. Grainger's business model is to become the world's leading source of MRO suppliers, and its revenue model is that of a typical retailer: it owns the products, and takes a markup on the products it sells to customers. Grainger's Web site and mobile apps provide users with a digital version of Grainger's famous seven-pound catalog, plus other parts not available in the catalog (adding up to around 900,000 parts), as well as a complete ordering and payment system. In 2013, Grainger recorded $3.1 billion in e-commerce revenues (one-third of its total sales), up 15% from 2012 (W.W. Grainger Inc., 2014). McMaster-Carr, a New Jersey-based industrial parts mecca for machinists and manufacturers around the world, is a similar e-distributor. In 2013, Amazon also entered the B2B distributor market with AmazonSupply, aiming to leverage its global B2C fulfillment infrastructure into the B2B arena. Other examples of e-distributors include B2Buy and NeweggBusiness.

E-procurement

e-procurement Net marketplace

independently owned intermediary that connects hundreds of online suppliers offering millions of maintenance and repair parts to business firms who pay fees to join the market

An **e-procurement Net marketplace** is an independently owned intermediary that connects hundreds of online suppliers offering millions of maintenance and repair parts to business firms who pay fees to join the market (see **Figure 12.11**). E-procurement Net marketplaces are typically used for long-term contractual purchasing of indirect goods (MRO); they create online horizontal markets, but they also provide for members' spot sourcing of MRO supplies. E-procurement companies make money by charging a percentage of each transaction, licensing consulting services and software, and assessing network use fees (Trkman and McCormack, 2010).

value chain management (VCM) services

include automation of a firm's entire procurement process on the buyer side and automation of the selling business processes on the seller side

E-procurement companies expand on the business model of simpler e-distributors by including the online catalogs of hundreds of suppliers and offering value chain management services to both buyers and sellers. **Value chain management (VCM) services** provided by e-procurement companies include automation of a firm's entire procurement process on the buyer side and automation of the selling business processes on the seller side. For purchasers, e-procurement companies automate purchase orders, requisitions, sourcing, business rules enforcement, invoicing, and payment. For suppliers, e-procurement companies provide catalog creation and content management, order management, fulfillment, invoicing, shipment, and settlement.

E-procurement Net marketplaces are sometimes referred to as many-to-many markets. They are mediated by an independent third party that purports to represent both buyers and sellers, and hence claim to be neutral. On the other hand, because

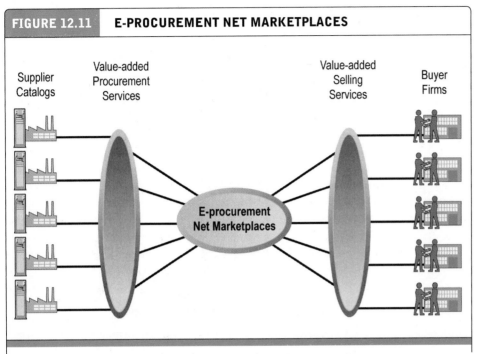

FIGURE 12.11   E-PROCUREMENT NET MARKETPLACES

E-procurement Net marketplaces aggregate hundreds of catalogs in a single marketplace and make them available to firms, often on a custom basis that reflects only the suppliers desired by the participating firms.

they may include the catalogs of both competing suppliers and competing e-distributors, they likely have a bias in favor of the buyers. Nevertheless, by aggregating huge buyer firms into their networks, they provide distinct marketing benefits for suppliers and reduce customer acquisition costs.

Ariba stands out as one of the poster children of the B2B age, a firm born before its time. Promising to revolutionize inter-firm trade, Ariba started out in 1996 hoping to build a global business network linking buyers and sellers—sort of an eBay for business. With little revenue, the stock shot past $1,000 a share by March 2000. But sellers and buyers did not join the network in large part because they did not understand the opportunity, were too wedded to their traditional procurement processes, and did not trust outsiders to control their purchasing and vendor relationship. In September 2001, Ariba's share price tanked to $2.20. Ariba survived largely by selling software that helped large firms understand their procurement processes and costs. Finally, by 2008, large and small firms had become more sophisticated in their purchasing and supply change management practices, and Ariba's original idea of a global network of suppliers and purchasers of a wide variety of industrial goods came back to life. In 2012, SAP, the largest enterprise software firm, purchased Ariba for $4.3 billion in an effort to strengthen its B2B e-commerce suite. Today, Ariba (now owned by SAP AG) is a leading provider of collaborative business commerce solutions that includes an e-procurement Net marketplace called the Ariba Supplier Network. Other players in

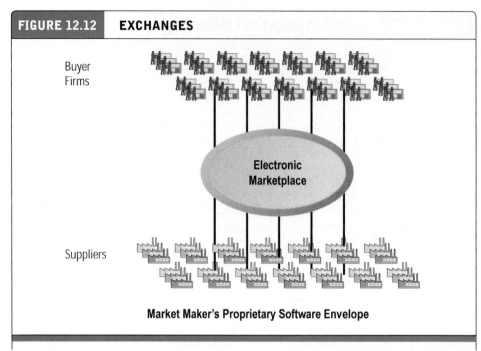

FIGURE 12.12 **EXCHANGES**

Buyer Firms

Electronic Marketplace

Suppliers

Market Maker's Proprietary Software Envelope

Independent exchanges bring potentially thousands of suppliers to a vertical (industry-specific) marketplace to sell their goods to potentially thousands of buyer firms. Exchanges are sometimes referred to as many-to-many markets because they have many suppliers serving many buyer firms.

this market segment include Perfect Commerce, BravoSolution, A.T. Kearney Procurement & Analytic Solutions, and Emptoris (purchased by IBM in 2012).

Exchanges

exchange

independently owned online marketplace that connects hundreds to potentially thousands of suppliers and buyers in a dynamic, real-time environment

An **exchange** is an independently owned online marketplace that connects hundreds to potentially thousands of suppliers and buyers in a dynamic, real-time environment (see **Figure 12.12**). Although there are exceptions, exchanges generally create vertical markets that focus on the spot-purchasing requirements of large firms in a single industry, such as computers and telecommunications, electronics, food, and industrial equipment. Exchanges were the prototype Internet-based marketplace in the early days of e-commerce; as noted previously, over 1,500 were created in this period, but most have failed.

Exchanges make money by charging a commission on the transaction. The pricing model can be through an online negotiation, auction, RFQ, or fixed buy-and-sell prices. The benefits offered to customers of exchanges include reduced search cost for parts and spare capacity. Other benefits include lower prices created by a global marketplace driven by competition among suppliers who would, presumably, sell goods at very low profit margins at one world-market price. The benefits offered suppliers are access to a global purchasing environment and the opportunity to unload production overruns (although at very competitive prices and low profit margins). Even though they are private intermediaries, exchanges are public in the sense of permitting any bona fide buyer or seller to participate.

Exchanges tend to be biased toward the buyer even though they are independently owned and presumably neutral. Suppliers are disadvantaged by the fact that exchanges put them in direct price competition with other similar suppliers around the globe, driving profit margins down. Exchanges have failed primarily because suppliers have refused to join them, and hence, the existing markets have very low liquidity, defeating the very purpose and benefits of an exchange. **Liquidity** is typically measured by the number of buyers and sellers in a market, the volume of transactions, and the size of transactions. You know a market is liquid when you can buy or sell just about any size order at just about any time you want. On all of these measures, many exchanges failed, resulting in a very small number of participants, few trades, and small trade value per transaction. The most common reason for not using exchanges is the absence of traditional, trusted suppliers.

While most exchanges tend to be vertical marketplaces offering direct supplies, some exchanges offer indirect inputs as well, such as electricity and power, transportation services (usually to the transportation industry), and professional services. **Table 12.4** lists a few examples of some current independent exchanges.

The following capsule descriptions of two exchanges provide insight into their origins and current functions.

Global Wine & Spirits (GWS) is unique among independent exchanges, not only as a start-up that has managed to survive, but also as a latecomer to the B2B e-commerce community. GWS opened in 1999, but did not begin to trade products online until May 2001. Based in Montreal, Quebec, GWS is operated by Mediagrif Interactive Technologies Inc., a Canadian company that operates a number of independent exchanges in a variety of industries. GWS offers a spot marketplace for wines, where wine and spirit producers offer wines for sale; a call for tenders market, where members make offers to purchase wines and spirits; a trade database with listings of thousands of industry professionals; and a wine and spirits catalog with over 35,000 products and 6,700 companies (Globalwinespirits.com, 2014).

Inventory Locator Service (ILS) has its roots as an offline intermediary, serving as a listing service for aftermarket parts in the aerospace industry. Upon opening in

liquidity
typically measured by the number of buyers and sellers in a market, the volume of transactions, and the size of transactions

TABLE 12.4	**EXAMPLES OF INDEPENDENT EXCHANGES**
EXCHANGE	FOCUS
PowerSource Online	Computer parts exchange
Converge	Electronic components
IronPlanet	Used heavy equipment
EquipNet	Used industrial equipment
IntercontinentalExchange	International online marketplace for over 600 commodities

1979, ILS initially provided a telephone and fax-based directory of aftermarket parts to airplane owners and mechanics, along with government procurement professionals. As early as 1984, ILS incorporated e-mail capabilities as part of its RFQ services, and by 1998, it had begun to conduct online auctions for hard-to-find parts. In 2014, ILS maintains an Internet-accessible database of over 85 million aerospace and marine industry parts, and has also developed an eRFQ feature that helps users streamline their sourcing processes. The network's 23,000 subscribers in 93 different countries access the site over 75,000 times a day (Inventory Locator Service, 2014).

Industry Consortia

industry consortium
industry-owned vertical market that enables buyers to purchase direct inputs (both goods and services) from a limited set of invited participants

An **industry consortium** is an industry-owned vertical market that enables buyers in the industry to purchase direct inputs (both goods and services) (see **Figure 12.13**). Industry consortia emphasize long-term contractual purchasing, the development of stable relationships (as opposed to merely an anonymous transaction emphasis), and the creation of industry-wide data standards and synchronization efforts. Industry consortia are more focused on optimizing long-term supply relationships than

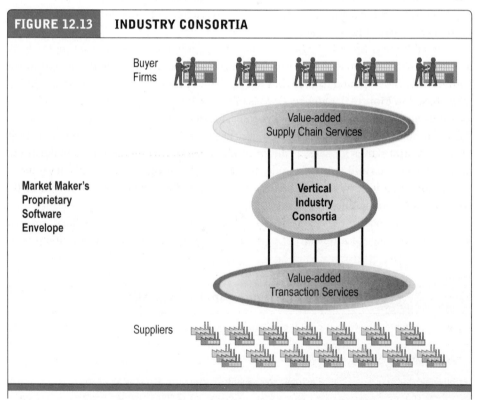

| FIGURE 12.13 | INDUSTRY CONSORTIA |

Industry consortia bring thousands of suppliers into direct contact with a smaller number of very large buyers. The market makers provide value-added software services for procurement, transaction management, shipping, and payment for both buyers and suppliers. Industry consortia are sometimes referred to as many-to-few markets, where many suppliers (albeit selected by the buyers) serve a few very large buyers, mediated by a variety of value-added services.

independent exchanges, which tend to focus more on short-term transactions. The ultimate objective of industry consortia is the unification of supply chains within entire industries, across many tiers, through common data definitions, network standards, and computing platforms.

Industry consortia sprang up in part as a reaction to the development of independently owned exchanges, which were viewed by large industries (such as the automotive and chemical industries) as market interlopers that would not directly serve the interests of large buyers, but would instead line their own pockets and those of their venture capital investors. Rather than "pay-to-play," large firms decided to "pay-to-own" their markets. Another concern of large firms was that Net marketplaces would work only if large suppliers and buyers participated, and only if there was liquidity. Independent exchanges were not attracting enough players to achieve liquidity. In addition, exchanges often failed to provide additional value-added services that would transform the value chain for the entire industry, including linking the new marketplaces to firms' ERP systems.

Industry consortia make money in a number of ways. Industry members usually pay for the creation of the consortia's capabilities and contribute initial operating capital. Then industry consortia charge buyer and seller firms transaction and subscription fees. Industry members—both buyers and sellers—are expected to reap benefits far greater than their contributions through the rationalization of the procurement process, competition among vendors, and closer relationships with vendors.

Industry consortia offer many different pricing mechanisms, ranging from auctions to fixed prices to RFQs, depending on the products and the situation. Prices can also be negotiated, and the environment, while competitive, is nevertheless restricted to a smaller number of buyers—selected, reliable, and long-term suppliers who are often viewed as strategic industry partners. The bias of industry consortia is clearly toward the large buyers who control access to this lucrative market channel and can benefit from competitive pricing offered by alternative suppliers. Benefits to suppliers come from access to large buyer firm procurement systems, long-term stable relationships, and large order sizes.

Industry consortia can force suppliers to use the consortia's networks and proprietary software as a condition of selling to the industry's members. Although exchanges failed for a lack of suppliers and liquidity, the market power of consortia members ensures suppliers will participate, so consortia may be able to avoid the fate of voluntary exchanges. Clearly, industry consortia are at an advantage when compared to independent exchanges because, unlike the venture-capital-backed exchanges, they have deep-pocket financial backing from the very start and guaranteed liquidity based on a steady flow of large firm orders. Yet industry consortia are a relatively new phenomenon, and the long-term profitability of these consortia, especially when several consortia exist for a single industry, has yet to be demonstrated. In fact, the number of firms that can be defined as purely industry consortia has declined since the early 2000s, with many firms broadening their mission to encompass more than one industry, or more commonly, being sold by the original industry founders to private investors. For example, GHX, originally founded in 2000 by companies in the pharmaceutical and medical supply industry, is now owned by a private equity firm.

TABLE 12.5	INDUSTRY CONSORTIA BY INDUSTRY
INDUSTRY	NAME OF INDUSTRY CONSORTIA
Agribusiness	The Seam (Cotton Consortium)
Automotive	SupplyOn
Chemical	Elemica
Food	Dairy.com
Hospitality	Avendra

E2open, originally founded by IBM, Seagate, and Hitachi as an industry consortium for companies in the high technology industries, has since become a public company and now provides a cloud-based B2B platform and services for a wide variety of industries.

However, a number of industry consortia do remain. One example is TheSeam, which was founded in 2000 by leading global agribusiness companies such as Cargill, Louis Dreyfus, and others. TheSeam focused initially on creating a cotton trading exchange, and has since added peanuts, grains, and excess USDA farm commodities. TheSeam has handled over $4 billion in transactions since inception and more than 90% of the cotton buyers in the United States are active participants in its Cotton Trading system. **Table 12.5** lists some additional examples.

12.5 PRIVATE INDUSTRIAL NETWORKS

Private industrial networks today form the largest part of B2B e-commerce, both on and off the Internet. Industry analysts estimate that in 2014, over 50% of B2B expenditures by large firms will be for the development of private industrial networks. Private industrial networks can be considered the foundation of the extended enterprise, allowing firms to extend their boundaries and their business processes to include supply chain and logistics partners.

As noted at the beginning of this chapter, private industrial networks are direct descendants of existing EDI networks, and they are closely tied to existing ERP systems used by large firms. A private industrial network (sometimes referred to as a private trading exchange, or PTX) is a Web-enabled network for the coordination of trans-organizational business processes (sometimes also called collaborative commerce). A **trans-organizational business process** requires at least two independent firms to perform (Laudon and Laudon, 2014). For the most part, these networks originate in and closely involve the manufacturing and related support industries, and therefore we refer to them as industrial networks, although in the future they could just as easily

trans-organizational business process

process that requires at least two independent firms to perform

FIGURE 12.14	**PROCTER & GAMBLE'S PRIVATE INDUSTRIAL NETWORK**

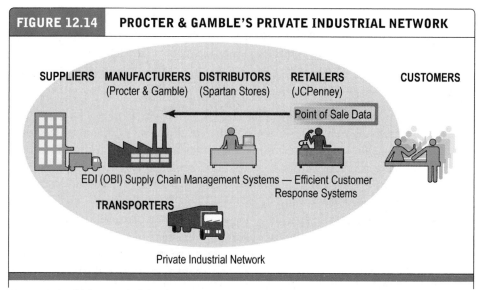

Procter & Gamble's private industrial network attempts to coordinate the trans-organizational business processes of the many firms it deals with in the consumer products industry.

apply to some services. Private industrial networks can be viewed as extended enterprises in the sense that they often begin as ERP systems in a single firm, and are then expanded to include (often using an extranet) the firm's major suppliers. **Figure 12.14** illustrates a private industrial network originally built by Procter & Gamble (P&G) in the United States to coordinate supply chains among its suppliers, distributors, truckers, and retailers.

In P&G's private industrial network shown in Figure 12.14, customer sales are captured at the cash register, which then initiates a flow of information back to distributors, P&G, and its suppliers. This tells P&G and its suppliers the exact level of demand for thousands of products. This information is then used to initiate production, supply, and transportation to replenish products at the distributors and retailers. This process is called an efficient customer response system (a demand-pull production model), and it relies on an equally efficient supply chain management system to coordinate the supply side.

GE, Dell, Cisco Systems, Microsoft, IBM, Nike, Coca-Cola, Walmart, Nokia, and Hewlett-Packard are among the firms operating successful private industrial networks.

OBJECTIVES OF PRIVATE INDUSTRIAL NETWORKS

The specific objectives of a private industrial network include:

- Developing efficient purchasing and selling business processes industry-wide
- Developing industry-wide resource planning to supplement enterprise-wide resource planning
- Increasing supply chain visibility—knowing the inventory levels of buyers and suppliers

- Achieving closer buyer-supplier relationships, including demand forecasting, communications, and conflict resolution
- Operating on a global scale—globalization
- Reducing risk by preventing imbalances of supply and demand, including developing financial derivatives, insurance, and futures markets

Private industrial networks serve different goals from Net marketplaces. Net marketplaces are primarily transaction-oriented, whereas private industrial networks focus on continuous business process coordination between companies. This can include much more than just supply chain management, such as product design, sourcing, demand forecasting, asset management, sales, and marketing. Private industrial networks do support transactions, but that is not their primary focus.

Private industrial networks usually focus on a single sponsoring company that "owns" the network, sets the rules, establishes governance (a structure of authority, rule enforcement, and control), and invites firms to participate at its sole discretion. Therefore, these networks are private. This sets them apart from industry consortia, which are usually owned by major firms collectively through equity participation. Whereas Net marketplaces have a strong focus on indirect goods and services, private industrial networks focus on strategic, direct goods and services.

For instance, True Value is one of the largest retailer-owned hardware cooperatives with operations in 54 countries, 4,600 plus stores, and 12 regional distribution centers. The logistics are staggering to consider: they routinely process over 60,000 domestic inbound loads, and over 600 million pounds of freight. True Value imports roughly 3,500 containers through 20 international ports and 10 domestic ports. The existing inbound supply chain system was fragmented, did not permit real-time tracking of packages, and when shipments were short or damaged, could not alert stores. The supply chain was "invisible": suppliers could not see store inventory levels, and stores could not see supplier shipments. Using a Web-based solution from Sterling Commerce (an IBM company), True Value created its own private industrial network to which all suppliers, shippers, and stores have access. The network focuses on three processes: domestic prepaid shipping, domestic collect, and international direct shipping. For each process the network tracks in real time the movement of goods from suppliers to shippers, warehouses, and stores. So far, the system has led to a 57% reduction in lead time needed for orders, a 10% increase in the fill rate of orders, and an 85% reduction in back orders. If goods are delayed, damaged, or unavailable, the system alerts all parties automatically (True Value, 2013; IBM, 2011b).

Perhaps no single firm better illustrates the benefits of developing private industrial networks than Walmart, described in *Insight on Business: Walmart Develops a Private Industrial Network*.

PRIVATE INDUSTRIAL NETWORKS AND COLLABORATIVE COMMERCE

Private industrial networks can do much more than just serve a supply chain and efficient customer response system. They can also include other activities of a single large manufacturing firm, such as design of products and engineering diagrams, as well as marketing plans and demand forecasting. Collaboration among businesses

INSIGHT ON BUSINESS

WALMART DEVELOPS A PRIVATE INDUSTRIAL NETWORK

Walmart is a well-known leader in the application of network technology to coordinate its supply chain. Walmart's supply chain is the secret sauce behind its claim of offering the lowest prices everyday. Walmart is able to make this promise because it has possibly the most efficient B2B supply chain in the world. It doesn't hurt to also be the largest purchaser of consumer goods in the world. With sales of $473 billion for the fiscal year ending January 2014, Walmart has been able to use information technology to achieve a decisive cost advantage over competitors. As you might imagine, the world's largest retailer also has the world's largest supply chain, with more than 100,000 suppliers worldwide. In the United States, Walmart has more than 4,800 retail stores (including Sam's Clubs). The larger stores stock as many as 200,000 different items. Internationally, Walmart has over 6,100 additional stores in 26 countries, giving it a total of almost 11,000 retail units.

In the late 1980s, Walmart developed the beginnings of collaborative commerce using an EDI-based SCM system that required its large suppliers to use Walmart's proprietary EDI network to respond to orders from Walmart purchasing managers. In 1991, Walmart expanded the capabilities of its EDI-based network by introducing Retail Link. This system connected Walmart's largest suppliers to Walmart's own inventory management system, and it required large suppliers to track actual sales by stores and to replenish supplies as dictated by demand and following rules imposed by Walmart. Walmart also introduced financial payment systems that ensure that Walmart does not own the goods until they arrive and are shelved.

In 1997, Walmart moved Retail Link to an extranet that allowed suppliers to directly link over the Internet into Walmart's inventory management system. In 2000, Walmart hired an outside firm to upgrade Retail Link from being a supply chain management tool toward a more collaborative forecasting, planning, and replenishment system. Using demand aggregation software provided by Atlas Technology Group, Walmart purchasing agents were now able to aggregate demand from all of Walmart's separate stores in the United States into a single RFQ from suppliers. This gave Walmart tremendous clout with even the largest suppliers. The Atlas software helps Walmart purchasing agents select a winning bid and negotiate final contracts.

In addition, suppliers can now immediately access information on inventories, purchase orders, invoice status, and sales forecasts, based on 104 weeks of data. Data is available by item, by store, and by hour. The system does not require smaller supplier firms to adopt expensive EDI software solutions. Instead, they can use standard browsers and PCs loaded with free software from Walmart.

In 2002, Walmart switched to an entirely Internet-based private network. Walmart adopted AS2, a software package from iSoft Corporation. AS2 implemented EDI-INT (an Internet-based standard version of EDI), and the result was a radical reduction in communications costs. In 2007, Walmart's rapid growth, especially global operations, forced it to go outside for its financial services operation systems. Walmart hired SAP, an enterprise software management firm, to build a global financial management system for Walmart. Walmart had finally started to outgrow its homegrown systems.

By 2014, Walmart's B2B supply chain management system had mastered on a global scale the following capabilities: cross docking, demand planning, forecasting, inventory management, strate-

(continued)

gic sourcing, and distribution management. Walmart is also focused on business analytics—working smarter—rather than just simply making the movement and tracking of goods more efficient. For instance, in 2012 Walmart purchased Quintiq Inc., a supply chain management tool for improving load assignment and dispatch of trucks for large retailers. Quintiq's software will enable Walmart's managers to optimize the loading of its trucks and to reduce the time required to supply its retail stores. In 2013, Walmart introduced SPARC, a mobile app that gives suppliers access to real-time data on their inventories in Walmart stores via iPhone and Android smartphones, allowing them to monitor their products' performance and make real-time stocking decisions.

Despite its success in building a world-class supply chain to support almost 11,000 stores, Walmart was not well prepared to deal with online sales, or to compete with the online champion, Amazon. From the beginning, Walmart separated out its fledgling e-commerce operation as a separate company with a much lower priority for investment than its physical stores. It was late to invest in an Internet supply chain because the separate companies could never agree on whether it was a good investment. Instead, Walmart's Internet supply chain is a work in progress, relying on employees at some of the stores to pick online orders and ship from the store, while other orders are handled by a few Internet order warehouses. Last year, Walmart had $10 billion in online sales (compared to Amazon's $68 billion), and this represented only about 2% of its $473 billion in sales. In 2013, Walmart began creating a new inventory and logistics system that will combine the inventory information from its 4,800 stores and 158 warehouses and then decide the most efficient way to pick and ship online orders.

Like other large global firms, Walmart's global supply chain has been criticized for exploiting labor in underdeveloped countries where it buys products and in home markets where it sells them, bribing officials to look the other way, destroying environments, and wasting energy. In response to critics, Walmart has taken a number of steps. Walmart has set a goal of reducing carbon emissions in its supply chain by 20 million metric tons by 2015, and a goal of 100% renewable energy use in the United States. Walmart has made less progress in its labor policies: In 2012, the ABP pension fund blacklisted Walmart for failing to comply with the United Nations' Global Compact principles that include a set of core values relating to human rights, labor standards, the environment, and anti-corruption efforts. In 2014, the National Labor Relations Board issued a complaint against Walmart claiming that it had illegally retaliated against workers who took part in protests about working conditions and a U.S. Department of Justice investigation into allegations that Walmart bribed Mexican officials to expand its stores and supply chain in Mexico remains ongoing.

Walmart's success spurred its competitors in the retail industry to develop industry-wide private industrial networks such as Global NetXchange (now Agentrics) in an effort to duplicate the success of Walmart. Walmart executives have said Walmart will not join these networks, or any industry-sponsored consortium or independent exchange, because doing so would only help its competitors achieve what Walmart has already accomplished with Retail Link.

SOURCES: "Wal-Mart Looks to Grow by Embracing Smaller Stores," by Shelly Banjo, *Wall Street Journal*, July 8, 2014; "Corporate & Financial Facts," Walmart.com, February 2014; "Biggest Lessons Listed for New Wal-Mart Suppliers," by Kim Souza, Thecitywire.com, November 20, 2013; "Walmart's SPARC initiative in Spotlight Again," Retailingtoday.com, October 10, 2013; "Wal-Mart's E-Stumble With Amazon," by Shelly Banso, *Wall Street Journal*, June 19, 2013; "The Trouble Lurking on Walmart's Empty Shelves," by Bill Saporito, *Time Business*, April 9, 2013; "Walmart's Secret Sauce: How the Largest Survives and Thrives," by Chris Petersen, Retailcustomerexperience.com, March 27, 2013; "Wal-Mart Toughens Supplier Policies," by Shelly Banjo, *Wall Street Journal*, January 21, 2013; "How Walmart is Changing Supplier Sustainability-Again," by Aran Rice, Renewablechoice.com, May 30, 2012; "Wal-Mart's Dirty Partners," by Josh Eidelson, Salon.com, July 6, 2012; "The Walmart Model and the Human Cost of Our Low Priced Goods," by Juan De Lara, *The Guardian*, July 25, 2012; "Supply Chain News: Walmart, Sustainability, and Troubles in Mexico," by Dan Gilmore, *Supply Chain Digest*, April 26, 2012; "Retail Giant Optimizes Supply Chain Processes With Quintiq Software," *Supply&Demand Chain Executive*, February 15, 2012; "Walmart Adds $7 Billion Through Acquisition in 2011," by Nate Holmes, InstoreTrends.com, May 11, 2012.

can take many forms and involve a wide range of activities—from simple supply chain management to coordinating market feedback to designers at supply firms (see **Figure 12.15**).

One form of collaboration—and perhaps the most profound—is industry-wide **collaborative resource planning, forecasting, and replenishment (CPFR)**, which involves working with network members to forecast demand, develop production plans, and coordinate shipping, warehousing, and stocking activities to ensure that retail and wholesale shelf space is replenished with just the right amount of goods. If this goal is achieved, hundreds of millions of dollars of excess inventory and capacity could be wrung out of an industry. This activity alone is likely to produce the largest benefits and justify the cost of developing private industrial networks.

A second area of collaboration is *demand chain visibility*. In the past, it was impossible to know where excess capacity or supplies existed in the supply and distribution chains. For instance, retailers might have significantly overstocked shelves, but suppliers and manufacturers—not knowing this—might be building excess capacity or supplies for even more production. These excess inventories would raise costs for the entire industry and create extraordinary pressures to discount merchandise, reducing profits for everyone.

collaborative resource planning, forecasting, and replenishment (CPFR)

involves working with network members to forecast demand, develop production plans, and coordinate shipping, warehousing, and stocking activities to ensure that retail and wholesale shelf space is replenished with just the right amount of goods

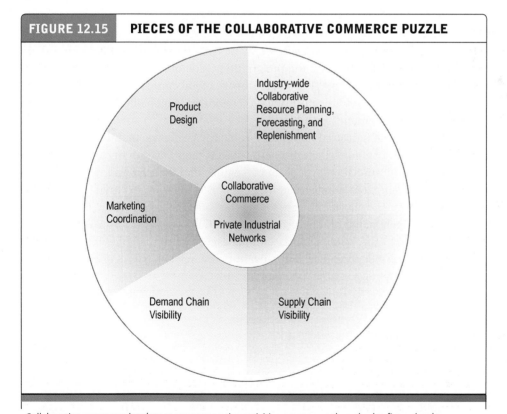

| FIGURE 12.15 | PIECES OF THE COLLABORATIVE COMMERCE PUZZLE |

Collaborative commerce involves many cooperative activities among supply and sales firms closely interacting with a single large firm through a private industrial network.

A third area of collaboration is *marketing coordination and product design*. Manufacturers that use or produce highly engineered parts use private industrial networks to coordinate both their internal design and marketing activities, as well as related activities of their supply and distribution chain partners. By involving their suppliers in product design and marketing initiatives, manufacturing firms can ensure that the parts produced actually fulfill the claims of marketers. On the reverse flow, feedback from customers can be used by marketers to speak directly to product designers at the firm and its suppliers. For the first time, closed loop marketing (customer feedback directly impacting design and production) can become a reality.

IMPLEMENTATION BARRIERS

Although private industrial networks represent a large part of the future of B2B, there are many barriers to its complete implementation. Participating firms are required to share sensitive data with their business partners, up and down the supply chain. What in the past was considered proprietary and secret must now be shared. In a digital environment, it can be difficult to control the limits of information sharing. Information a firm freely gives to its largest customer may end up being shared with its closest competitor.

Integrating private industrial networks into existing enterprise systems and EDI networks poses a significant investment of time and money. The leading providers of enterprise systems to Fortune 500 companies (Oracle, IBM, and SAP) do offer B2B modules, and supply chain management capabilities, that can be added to their existing software suites. Nevertheless, implementing these modules is a very expensive proposition in part because the procurement side of many Fortune 500 firms is so fragmented and out-of-date. For smaller firms, cloud computing and software as a service (SaaS) alternatives are appearing on the market, which offer far less-expensive supply chain management capabilities.

Adopting private industrial networks also requires a change in mindset and behavior for employees. Essentially, employees must shift their loyalties from the firm to the wider trans-organizational enterprise and recognize that their fate is intertwined with the fate of their suppliers and distributors. Suppliers in turn are required to change the way they manage and allocate their resources because their own production is tightly coupled with the demands of their private industrial network partners. All participants in the supply and distribution chains, with the exception of the large network owner, lose some of their independence, and must initiate large behavioral change programs in order to participate (Laudon and Laudon, 2014).

12.6   CASE STUDY

Elemica:
Cooperation, Collaboration, and Community

It may seem unusual to refer to an entire industry as a community, a word reserved typically for collections of people who more or less know one another. Trade associations are one example of an industrial community. Trade associations form in an effort to pursue the interests of all members in the community although usually they do not include customers in the community. Elemica is a B2B cloud-based, supply chain platform aiming to revolutionize the entire supply chain of the chemical, tire and rubber, energy, and other process industries worldwide. Elemica's purpose is not just to foster cooperation on a one-to-one inter-firm basis, or just to foster collaboration on multi-firm projects, but instead to lift all boats on an industry tide by providing an inter-firm platform for communicating B2B information, and thereby making all firms more efficient. Elemica is one of the few survivors of the early B2B e-commerce years. In 2014, Elemica connects over 6,500 companies to its network and clears over $250 billion in transactions a year. Clients include BASF, BP, Continental, The Dow Chemical Company, DuPont, The Goodyear Tire & Rubber Company, LANXESS, Michelin, Rhodia, Shell, Sumitomo Chemical, Yokohama, and Wacker.

Elemica was founded by 22 leading corporations in the chemical industry (including oil and industrial gases) to provide cloud-based order management and supply chain applications and services. A single platform provides one-stop shopping so that companies can buy and sell products to one another through their own enterprise systems or using a Web alternative. It also helps companies automate all of their business processes, creating efficiencies and economies of scale that lead to an improved bottom line.

How does Elemica achieve community among a diverse, global collection of firms where firms are often both customers and vendors to one another? It unites community members by linking together their enterprise systems. This is the "social glue" that sets Elemica apart. This "super platform" permits companies to communicate with one another and to conduct transactions, handle logistics, and keep the books. The Elemica commerce platform has effectively standardized industry business transactions for all network members regardless of the type of enterprise system they have, and it's leveled the playing field for trade partners who are less technically sophisticated. This neutral platform facilitates millions of transactions for industry suppliers, customers, and third-party providers. In this sense, Elemica is one of the most sophisticated technology platforms in the B2B space.

One of the largest investments for a company is its enterprise system. Despite these investments, intercompany relationships—the backbone of their supply chain—are often left to outdated and unreliable processes. These shortcomings cost billions in lost productivity, revenue, and profit. Elemica's eCommerce platform changes that. It helps its clients leverage their enterprise system investment by incorporating transactions to external trade partners. Elemica's QuickLink ERP connectivity enables companies to link their internal IT systems through a neutral platform so that information is moved into each company's database while maintaining confidentiality and security. The chemical and oil industries were among the first users of enterprise systems (referred to in the early years as manufacturing resource planning systems). These large-scale systems were developed by single firms in order to rationalize and control the manufacturing process. They achieved this objective by identifying the outputs, inputs, and processes involved in manufacturing and automating key elements including inventory control and planning, process control, warehousing and storage, and shipping/logistics. If a company needed to produce 10 tons of polyethylene plastic, its enterprise system could tell it precisely how many tons of petrochemical inputs were required, when they should be delivered to manufacturing, the machinery and labor force required to manufacture the product, how long it would take, where it would be stored, and sometimes how it would be shipped. The systems can estimate the cost at any stage.

Elemica facilitates transactions of all types including order processing and billing, and logistics management. However, unlike some other companies in the field, Elemica does not buy, sell, or own raw material products. Instead it acts as an intermediary, or network, linking companies together to automate confidential transactions. Like eBay or a credit card company, Elemica's revenue comes from charging transaction fees on a per-transaction basis. Its network of clients opens the door for companies to do business with all other connected buyers and sellers.

Elemica offers a variety of services for suppliers, customers, and logistic partners, enabling them to automate both their business processes and internal purchasing. A modular, cloud-based solution simplifies sales, procurement, and financial processes; integrates supply chain partners to diminish communication barriers; and reduces overhead and errors.

Elemica integrates information flow among global trading partners using a cloud-based business process network. This is often referred to as platform as a service (PaaS). Each client needs only a single connection to Elemica, and Elemica manages the connections to that company's external trade partners. That means a company needs only maintain one connection to Elemica (important when it's time for enterprise system maintenance or upgrade) rather than maintain a variable number of connections and infrastructure to all its trade partners. Once a company connects to Elemica, it can have access to thousands of other trading partners, including suppliers, customers, and logistics firms. Clients are charged for the service based on volume of usage. This is much more efficient than older EDI solutions to inter-company transactions. Elemica provides the platform for collaborative commerce through a fully automated integrated network of suppliers, customers, and third-party providers.

Elemica offers cloud-based solutions for four areas: Logistics Management, Customer Management, Supplier Management, and Sourcing Management. Using these solutions, companies can automate ordering, invoicing, shipment tracking, and day-to-day business operations. Companies can sign up for one or more solutions depending on their needs.

Here's an example of how Elemica works. Let's say you need to order vinyl acetate from one of your suppliers. You put the order into your internal enterprise system, the order is automatically routed to Elemica, Elemica routes the order to your supplier's internal enterprise system, and you get a confirmed receipt of the order. Elemica's QuickLink Network ensures the accuracy of the item number and purchase order number and sends an alert if there's an issue. Once an order is confirmed, Elemica's platform can be leveraged to plan and coordinate delivery and automatically send an invoice and submit payment. For small or medium firms that may not have an enterprise system, Elemica has a Web portal with online software that allows firms to participate in the community with suppliers and customers. The platform offers a closed-loop process, end to end, from the purchase order, to acknowledgments, load tenders and responses, carrier status updates, and dock scheduling. All of this takes place in a few seconds with little or no human intervention. Elemica has even developed a solution that allows a customer to send a purchase order via e-mail or a print driver (alleviating fax processes) that is then routed to Elemica. The company then routes it to the supplier in its preferred format, integrated with its enterprise system as though it were a true electronic order. This holistic approach to order management allows suppliers to automate the process with both strategic and core customers, without asking its customers to change their processes. It's a win-win situation for suppliers and customers. Elemica's QuickLink Network is sometimes referred to as Come as You Are network because it allows firms to use whatever communication tools they currently use, such as EDI, XML, and even e-mail, or formats associated with their enterprise systems.

Unlike the automobile industry or the airline industry, where a few companies dominate, the $5 trillion global chemical industry is made up of many companies of all sizes. In addition, unlike many other industries, chemical companies often buy the output from other chemical companies to use as raw materials for their products. Thus, chemical companies are often customers of one another as well as competitors.

Senior leaders at some of the larger chemical companies were aware of changes in technology that made the adoption of information technology and the tools of e-commerce more appealing. The questions were how to best use these advances to benefit their businesses and how to establish industry standards for electronic transactions to make them accessible and attainable for all. Leaders from companies such as Dow Chemical and DuPont began discussing this subject and determined that a cooperative alliance would be the most efficient way to move forward. They were met with initial skepticism by marketing and sales staff, worried that online procurement would negatively affect relationships. Further, senior corporate leadership wasn't sure that e-commerce would have any use in the chemical industry at all. And companies were cautious about the expense of investing in the infrastructure necessary for e-commerce.

However, there were compelling opportunities that were impossible to dismiss, including lowering costs, creating closer connections with customers and suppliers, and differentiating companies on something other than price. At the same time, new start-ups like e-Chemicals and PlasticsNet were making traditional chemical companies nervous. What would happen if their efforts to use information technology to streamline an inefficient supply chain helped them capture market share? In other words, if the more traditional companies didn't move forward, they might end up losing the revenue race.

When Dow began looking at start-ups that were using e-commerce and talking to their customers, they found that customers were concerned about making an investment to establish online connections with multiple firms. Dow and DuPont decided that the best and most economically efficient option was to offer customers the choice of a neutral one-to-one link. This would remove the obstacle of multiple connections. A strong, third-party network addressed the community concern about loss of control. The two companies decided to create and invest in a neutral e-commerce company, partnering with other companies to create the critical mass needed to make it viable.

In 1999, the corporate boards of Dow and DuPont agreed that there were major advantages to online transaction processing and additional online connections among buyers and sellers. Because time and cost considerations made multiple connections unattractive to customers, a hub concept was adopted. It was also decided that a neutral community was the best approach.

All participants shared the common goal of creating a neutral platform to facilitate inter-company transactions and enhance business processes. Dow and DuPont also reviewed the concept with the relevant regulatory agencies and received up-front approval. Ultimately, 22 global chemical companies were involved in the launch of Elemica.

When Elemica opened its doors in 1999, there were around 50 start-up B2B e-commerce companies in the chemical industry. Nearly all of these B2B companies were third-party-owned Net marketplaces suitable at best for short-term sourcing of some direct inputs. In 2014, only a handful of these Net marketplaces for the chemical industry remain. Elemica focuses on building longer-term business relationships by creating committed and contractual supply chains. The company acts only as a facilitator of business transactions and does not directly buy and sell chemical products.

Elemica's business model has been successful primarily because it addresses the needs of chemical, tire and rubber, energy, and selected process companies of all sizes. It does this by offering multiple options for connecting to its hub system, multiple products that can be used alone or in combination, and by ensuring that only one connection integrated with a client's enterprise system is needed for all transactions. Customers can use Elemica, and take advantage of the technology it offers, without purchasing an additional internal system.

With Elemica, companies benefit from improved operational efficiency, reduced costs due to elimination of redundant systems and excess inventory, and a much higher percentage of safe and reliable deliveries. The flexibility of Elemica's solutions and network combines simplification, standardization, and efficiency. And clients have increased their profitability and improved cash flow through faster payment.

A number of very large companies use Elemica's platform. In Europe, Shell Oil started using Elemica after recognizing that it had ongoing problems with the coordination of paperwork processing and deliveries. Truck drivers would arrive at delivery sites and wait up to two hours while paperwork was filled out. These delays were costing Shell money. Once Shell began using Elemica, things improved. Today, paperwork is processed 24 hours a day, and truck waiting time has been cut from an average of two hours to an average of 15 minutes. Given this success, Shell continues to expand its relationship with Elemica.

Dow Chemical began to transition to full procurement automation with Elemica in 2007. More than 300 of their MRO suppliers are now linked to Elemica's platform. Errors are down 75%, and Dow has achieved economies of scale that have led to meaningful financial savings. Elemica helped Dow unify multiple, disparate business processes, reduced the cost of getting contracted items from suppliers, and increased efficiency in procurement, operations, IT, and accounts payable.

Air Products & Chemicals, Inc. is a global provider of gases and chemicals with 22,000 employees worldwide, and $10 billion in revenue. A major customer asked them for online ordering, but the initial method proposed would have required considerable additional work for both parties. Because both companies were connected to Elemica, there was a better option—the Elemica Supply Chain Hosted Solution.

Elemica has also developed a sustainability program. In November 2011, Elemica received the Green Supply Chain Award from an industry group for incorporating sustainability goals into its supply chain services. Elemica says it has delivered more than 160 million messages since 2004, which equates to 1,666 cubic meters of landfill space, 18,160,002 liters of water saved in paper production, 17,434 trees, and 196,128 kilograms of CO_2 emissions. In February 2012, Elemica introduced a transportation management solution (ETM) powered by Oracle. Available as a cloud-based software-as-a-service (SaaS) on a subscription basis, ETM will enable Elemica member firms to optimize logistics and transportation business processes, resulting in supply chain savings and a reduction of carbon emissions.

In May 2013 Elemica introduced a new network platform that it calls a Supply Chain Operating Network (SCON), which has built-in social collaboration tools. The idea is to give clients the ability to discover, create, and build social business networks—just as Facebook provides its users the ability to build online social networks. SCON provides its clients with a cloud-based network for establishing business relationships and SaaS (software as a service) applications to carry on trading once the relationship is established. Instead of creating hundreds of one-to-one EDI connections with partners, and then building their own software applications, firms can now more easily just connect to the network and find all the tools they need to trade with many partners. And in May 2014, Elemica introduced its Process Control Tower, a graphical interface that offers a consolidated view of transactional data across all a customer's business partners. Based on the metaphor of an airport control tower, the idea is to give managers a near real-time view of their entire supply and logistics systems. In the past, and still in many firms today, this kind of supply chain information comes in many different forms, from faxes, to e-mails, spreadsheets, and EDI messages. The Control Tower eliminates these difficult-to-interpret messages, and greatly enhances supply chain visibility.

SOURCES: "Elemica Introduces New Supply Chain Process Control Tower," Elemica Corporation, May 7, 2014; "Top Ten Supply Chain Initiatives for 2014 That Are Reimagining How Companies Conduct Commerce," Elemica Corporation, January 13, 2014; "Elemica: Shifting From a Shared Services Bazaar to Platform 'PaaS' Standard," by Jason Busch, Spendmatters.com, November 18, 2013; "Elemica Announces Launch of New 'Delivery Schedule' Solution," Elemica Corporation, September 24, 2013; "The Social Side of Supply Chain Management," by Adrian Gonzalez, *Supply Chain Management Review*, August 2013; "Next Generation Supply Chain Networks Enable More Robust Collaborative Workflows Across Trading Partners to Increase Value," Becky Boyd, *Market Wired,* July 2, 2013; "Elemica Named to Inbound Logistics Top 100 Logistics IT Provider Awards," *Wall Street Journal*, April 24, 2013; "About Elemica," Elemica.com, August 31, 2013; "Elemica Introduces Transportation Management Solution," Elemica Corporation, February 16, 2012; "Elemica Wins 2011 SDCExec Green Supply Chain Award for Helping Clients Incorporate Sustainability Within Their Supply Chains," Elemica Corporation, November 29, 2011; "Elemica Procurement Case Study: Dow," Elemica Corporation, September 2010; "Elemica Order Management Case Study: BP," Elemica Corporation, September 2010; "Elemica Case Study: LanXess," Elemica Corporation, September 2010; "Elemica and Rubber-Network Merge," SDCExec.com, August 25, 2009; "Case Study: Elemica," http://www.ebusiness-watch.org/studies, August 25, 2009; "Once Elemica Tackled the Hard Part, the Rest Was Easy," SupplyChainBrain.com, August 5, 2009; "Elemica Merger with Rubber Network," Philly.com, August 3, 2009; "Elemica Automates B2B Transactions Between Trading Partners—Speeding Up Orders by 78%," Softwareag.com, January 2009; "Top Chemical Company Selects Elemica's Business Process Network to Automate Global Procurement," Redorbit.com, December 18, 2008.

Case Study Questions

1. If you were a small chemical company, what concerns would you have about joining Elemica?

2. Elemica provides a community for participants where they can transact, coordinate, and cooperate to produce products for less. Yet these firms also compete with one another when they sell chemicals to end-user firms in the automobile, airline, and manufacturing industries. How is this possible?

3. Review the concept of private industrial networks and describe how Elemica illustrates many of the features of such a network. In what ways is it different from a private industrial network?

12.7 REVIEW

KEY CONCEPTS

■ **Discuss the evolution and growth of B2B e-commerce, as well as its potential benefits and challenges.**

- Before the Internet, business-to-business transactions were referred to simply as *trade* or the *procurement process*. Today, we use the term *B2B commerce* to describe all types of inter-firm trade, and the term *B2B e-commerce* to describe specifically that portion of B2B commerce that is enabled by the Internet and mobile apps.
- In order to understand the evolution of B2B e-commerce, you must understand several key stages including:
  - *Automated order entry systems*, developed in the 1970s, involved the use of telephone modems to send digital orders.
  - *EDI* or *electronic data interchange*, developed in the late 1970s, is a communications standard for sharing various procurement documents including invoices, purchase orders, shipping bills, product stocking numbers (SKUs), and settlement information for an industry.
  - *B2B e-commerce Web sites* emerged in the 1990s along with the commercialization of the Internet. They are online catalogs containing the products that are made available to the general public by a single vendor.
  - *Net marketplaces* emerged in the late 1990s as a natural extension and scaling-up of the electronic storefront. The essential characteristic of all Net marketplaces is that they bring hundreds of suppliers, each with its own online catalog, together with potentially thousands of purchasing firms to form a single Internet-based marketplace.
  - *Private industrial networks* also emerged in the late 1990s with the commercialization of the Internet as a natural extension of EDI systems and the existing close relationships that developed between large industrial firms and their suppliers.
- Potential benefits of B2B e-commerce include lower administrative costs; lower search costs for buyers; reduced inventory costs; lower transaction costs; improved quality of products; decreased product cycle time; increased opportunities for collaborating with suppliers and distributors; greater price transparency; and increased visibility and real-time information sharing among all participants in the supply chain network.
- Potential risks and challenges include lack of real-time data, environmental impacts, natural disasters, labor concerns, and the impacts of economic, financial, and political instability.

■ **Understand how procurement and supply chains relate to B2B e-commerce.**

- The *procurement process* refers to the way business firms purchase the goods they need in order to produce the goods they will ultimately sell to consumers. Firms purchase goods from a set of suppliers who in turn purchase their inputs from a set of suppliers. These firms are linked in a series of connected transactions. The *supply chain* is the series of transactions that links sets of firms that do business with each other. It includes not only the firms themselves but also the relationships between them and the processes that connect them.
- There are two different types of procurements (purchases of direct goods and purchases of indirect goods) and two different methods of purchasing goods (contract purchases and spot purchases).
- The term *multi-tier supply chain* is used to describe the complex series of transactions that exists between a single firm with multiple primary suppliers, the secondary suppliers who do business with those primary suppliers, and the tertiary suppliers who do business with the secondary suppliers.

■ **Identify major trends in supply chain management and collaborative commerce.**

- *Supply chain management (SCM)* refers to a wide variety of activities that firms and industries use to coordinate the key players in their procurement process.
- *Just-in-time production* is a method of inventory cost management that seeks to eliminate excess inventory to a bare minimum.
- *Lean production* is a set of production methods and tools that focuses on the elimination of waste throughout the customer value chain.
- *Supply chain simplification* involves reducing the size of the supply chain and working more closely with a smaller group of strategic supplier firms to reduce both product costs and administrative costs, while improving quality
- *Adaptive supply chains* allow companies to react to disruptions in the supply chain in a particular region by moving production to a different region
- *Accountable supply chains* are those where the labor conditions in low-wage, underdeveloped producer countries are visible and morally acceptable to ultimate consumers in more developed industrial societies.
- *Sustainable supply chains* involve using the most efficient environment-regarding means of production, distribution, and logistics.
- EDI remains very important in the development of B2B e-commerce.
- Mobile B2B has become increasingly important in all aspects of B2B e-commerce, through all steps of the procurement process and throughout the supply chain.
- *Cloud-based B2B systems* shift much of the expense of B2B systems from the firm to a B2B network provider, sometimes called a data hub or B2B platform.
- Contemporary *supply chain management (SCM) systems* are based on supply chain simplification, just in time and lean production, focusing on strategic partners in the production process, enterprise systems, and continuous inventory replenishment.
- *Collaborative commerce* involves the use of digital technologies to permit firms to collaboratively design, develop, build, market, and manage products through their life cycles, and is a direct extension of supply chain management systems, as well as supply chain simplification. Collaborative commerce today involves cloud servers, social business tools, and mobile devices.
- Social networks are providing intimate connections among customers, suppliers, and logistics partners.

■ **Understand the different characteristics and types of Net marketplaces.**

- Characteristics of Net marketplaces include their bias (seller-side vs. buy-side vs. neutral), ownership (industry vs. third party), pricing mechanism (fixed priced catalogs, auctions, and RFPs/RFQs), scope/focus (horizontal vs. vertical), value creation (customers/suppliers), and access to markets (public vs. private).
- There are four main types of "pure" Net marketplaces:
  - *E-distributors* are independently owned intermediaries that offer industrial customers a single source from which to make spot purchases of indirect or MRO goods. E-distributors operate in a horizontal market that serves many different industries with products from many different suppliers.
  - *E-procurement Net marketplaces* are independently owned intermediaries connecting hundreds of online suppliers offering millions of MRO goods to business firms who pay a fee to join the market. E-procurement Net marketplaces operate in a horizontal market in which long-term contractual purchasing agreements are used to buy indirect goods.
  - *Exchanges* are independently owned online marketplaces that connect hundreds to thousands of suppliers and buyers in a dynamic real-time environment. They are typically vertical markets in which spot purchases can be made for direct inputs (both goods and services). Exchanges make money by charging a commission on each transaction.

- *Industry consortia* are industry-owned vertical markets where long-term contractual purchases of direct inputs can be made from a limited set of invited participants. Consortia serve to reduce supply chain inefficiencies by unifying the supply chain for an industry through a common network and computing platform.

■ **Understand the objectives of private industrial networks and their role in supporting collaborative commerce, and the barriers to their implementation.**

- Objectives of private industrial networks include developing efficient purchasing and selling business processes industry-wide; developing industry-wide resource planning to supplement enterprise-wide resource planning; increasing supply chain visibility; achieving closer buyer-supplier relationships; operating on a global scale; and reducing industry risk by preventing imbalances of supply and demand.
- Private industrial networks are transforming the supply chain by focusing on continuous business process coordination between companies. This coordination includes much more than just transaction support and supply chain management. Product design, demand forecasting, asset management, and sales and marketing plans can all be coordinated among network members. Some of the forms of collaboration used by private industrial networks include the following:
  - *CPFR* or *industry-wide collaborative resource planning, forecasting, and replenishment* involves working with network members to forecast demand, develop production plans, and coordinate shipping, warehousing, and stocking activities.
  - *Supply chain and distribution chain visibility* refers to the fact that, in the past, it was impossible to know where excess capacity existed in a supply or distribution chain. Eliminating excess inventories by halting the production of overstocked goods can raise the profit margins for all network members because products will no longer need to be discounted in order to move them off the shelves.
  - *Marketing and product design collaboration* can be used to involve a firm's suppliers in product design and marketing activities as well as in the related activities of their supply and distribution chain partners. This can ensure that the parts used to build a product live up to the claims of the marketers. Collaborative commerce applications used in a private industrial network can also make possible closed-loop marketing in which customer feedback will directly impact product design.

QUESTIONS

1. What factors influence the speed with which industries migrate to B2B e-commerce?
2. Describe the stages of evolution of EDI.
3. Describe three weaknesses of EDI in today's B2B e-commerce environment.
4. What types of ownership models and revenue models do Net marketplaces use?
5. Describe the steps in the procurement process. Which steps are least likely to benefit from automation and e-commerce technologies?
6. Define the term *supply chain* and explain what SCM systems attempt to do. What does supply chain simplification entail?
7. Explain the difference between a horizontal market and a vertical market.
8. Why do firms typically use spot purchasing for indirect goods and contractual purchasing for direct goods?
9. Explain the difference between just-in-time and lean production.
10. What are the risks involved in a global supply chain that pushes manufacturing and production to low-cost labor centers? How can these risks be mitigated?
11. Define sustainable business. What is the business value of a sustainable supply chain?
12. Describe three types of B2B collaboration enabled through private industrial networks.
13. What are the benefits for suppliers in a private industrial network?

14. How do the value chain management services provided by e-procurement companies benefit buyers? What services do they provide to suppliers?
15. What are the barriers to the complete implementation of private industrial networks?
16. What is a cloud-based B2B platform and what advantages does it offer?
17. What is the main reason why many of the independent exchanges developed in the early days of e-commerce failed?
18. How does collaborative commerce differ from EDI? How is it similar?
19. What does BYOD refer to?
20. How have social networks impacted B2B?

PROJECTS

1. Choose an industry and a B2B vertical market maker that interests you. Investigate the site and prepare a report that describes the size of the industry served, the type of Net marketplace provided, the benefits promised by the site for both suppliers and purchasers, and the history of the company. You might also investigate the bias (buyer versus seller), ownership (suppliers, buyers, independents), pricing mechanism(s), scope and focus, and access (public versus private) of the Net marketplace.

2. Examine the Web site of one of the e-distributors listed in Figure 12.9, and compare and contrast it to one of the Web sites listed for e-procurement Net marketplaces. If you were a business manager of a medium-sized firm, how would you decide where to purchase your indirect inputs—from an e-distributor or an e-procurement Net marketplace? Write a short report detailing your analysis.

3. Assume you are a procurement officer for an office furniture manufacturer of steel office equipment. You have a single factory located in the Midwest with 2,000 employees. You sell about 40% of your office furniture to retail-oriented catalog outlets such as Quill in response to specific customer orders, and the remainder of your output is sold to resellers under long-term contracts. You have a choice of purchasing raw steel inputs—mostly cold-rolled sheet steel—from an exchange and/or from an industry consortium. Which alternative would you choose and why? Prepare a presentation for management supporting your position.

4. You are involved in logistics management for your company, a national retailer of office furniture. In the last year the company has experienced a number of disruptions in its supply chain as vendors failed to deliver products on time, and the business has lost customers as a result. Your firm only has a limited IT department, and you would like to propose a cloud-based solution. Go to the web site of GT Nexus. Explore the Why GT Nexus tab, and the Solutions By Industry/Retail tab. Read several case studies on the site. Write a report to senior management why you believe that a cloud-based B2B solution is best for your firm.

REFERENCES

Antai, Imoh. "A Theory of the Competing Supply Chain: Alternatives for Development." *International Business Research* Vol 4, No. 1 (January 2011).

Ariba Inc., "Ariba-Spot-Buy-Powered-by-Ariba-Discovery." (May 13, 2014).

Barlow, Alexis. "Web Technologies and Supply Chains." Glasgow Calendonian University, Scotland. In *Supply Chain Management: New Perspectives*, edited by S. Renko. (2011).

Beard, Alison and Richard Hornik, "It's Hard to Be Good,"

Harvard Business Review Magazine, November 2011

Bunkley, Nick. "Lacking Parts, GM Will Close Plant." *New York Times* (March 17, 2011).

Bolukbasi, Hande. "Putting the Business in the Palm of Your Hand." SAPInsider.com (January 2011).

Booen, Brett. "The Under Armour Success Story: How SAP Improves the UA Supply Chain." SupplyChain-Digital.com (March 10, 2011).

Cachon, Gerard, and Robert Swinney, "The Value of Fast Fashion: Quick Response, Enhanced Design, and

Strategic Consumer Behavior." *Management Science* Vol. 57 778-795 (April 2011).

Cecere, Lora. "Supply Chain Visibility in Businss Networks." Supply Chain Insights, LLC (March 11, 2014).

Cecere, Lora. "EDI Workhorse of the Value Chain." Supply Chain Insights, LLC (November 20, 2013).

Chopra, Sunil and MamMohan Sodhi. "Reducing the risk of Supply Chain Disruptions." *MIT Sloan Management Review* (Spring 2014).

Cisco Systems, Inc. "Proctor & Gamble Revolutionize Collaboration With Cisco TelePresence." (March, 2011).

Cisco. "@CiscoLiveDesk." twitter.com/CiscoLiveDesk (accessed September 30, 2013).

Enright, Allison. "B2b E-commerce is Poised for Growth: More Than a Third of Business Buyers Plan to Spend More Online Next Year." InternetRetailer.com, May 31, 2013.

Esposito, Carl. "What Are the Best Examples of Crowdsourcing." Crowdsourcing.org (2012).

Fair Labor Association. "Independent Investigation of Apple Supplier, Foxconn Report Highlights." Fairlabor.org (March 30, 2012).

Fauska, Polina, Natalia Kryvinska, and Christine Strauss. "E-commerce and B2B Services Enterprises." 2013 International Conference on Advanced Information Networking and Application Workshops, IEEE (2013).

Gilmore, Dan. "Under Armour's Athletic Supply Chain." *Supply Chain Digest* (April 3, 2014).

Globalwinespirits.com. "About GWS." Globalwinespirts.com (September 2014).

Gohring, Nancy. "Collaboration 2.0: Old Meets New." *Computerworld* (April 10, 2014).

Gusman, Phil. "Most 2012 Supply-Chain Disruptions Were from Tech-Related Events, Not Weather." *Property Casualty Journal* (September 9, 2013).

Hewlett-Packard. "HP.com Business to Business." Hp.com (September 2014).

Hewlett-Packard. "Supply Chain Management For the Adaptive Enterprise." (2013).

IBM Corporation. "No Resting Place." (July 2011a).

IBM Corporation, "True Value Company: True Value Optimizes Their Inbound Supply Process with IBM Sterling Supply Chain Visibility." (July 2011b).

Inventory Locator Service LLC. ILSmart.com "About Us." (September 2014).

James, Henry. "Crowdsourcing Trends in 2012." Crowdsourcing.org (April 9, 2012).

Jolly, David. "Long Pause for Japanese Industry Raises Concerns About Supply Chain." *New York Times* (March 16, 2011).

Kaplan, Steven, and Mohanbir Sawhney. "E-Hubs: The New B2B Marketplaces." Harvard Business Review (May-June 2000).

Kumaran, S. "A Framework-Based Approach to Building Private Trading Exchanges." IBM Systems Journal (July 2002).

Laudon, Kenneth C. and Jane P. Laudon. *Management Information Systems: Managing the Digital Firm.* 13th edition. Upper Saddle River, NJ, Prentice Hall (2014).

Long, Gene, Jr. "Supply Chain Resiliency: From Insight to Foresight: Sustaining Shareholder Value by Hardening the Enterprise Against External Risks. *IHS Quarterly* (March 2014).

Melnyk, Steven, et al. "Supply Chain Management 2010 and Beyond." APICS Educational & Research Foundation (2010).

Red Prairie, Inc. "The B2B SoLoMo Imperative." (September 2012).

Rosenzweig, et al., "Through the service operations strategy looking glass: Influence of industrial sector, ownership, and service offerings on B2B e-marketplace failures." *Journal of Operations Management*, (29) (2011).

Supply Chain Digest. "Building the Supply Chain from the Shelf Back Research." (April 4, 2012a).

Supply Chain Digest. "Global Supply Chain: Toyota Taking Massive Effort to Reduce Its Supply Chain Risk in Japan." (March 7, 2012b).

Synnex Corporation. Form 10-K for the fiscal year ended November 30, 2013, filed with the Securities and Exchange Commission (January 27, 2014).

Trkman, P.; McCormack, K.; "Estimating the Benefits of Implementing E-Procurement," Engineering Management, IEEE Transaction, Volume 57, Issue 2 (May 2010).

True Value. Annual Report 2012. (March 2013).

U.S. Census Bureau. "eStats." (May 22, 2014).

Vance, Ashlee. "For an Online Marketplace, It's Better Late Than Never." *New York Times* (November 20, 2010).

W.W. Grainger. Inc. Form 10-K for the fiscal year ended December 31, 2013, filed with the Securities and Exchange Commission (February 27, 2014).

Yoo, Byungjoon; V. Choudray; and T. Mukhopadhyay. "Marketplaces or Web Service: Alternate Business Models for Electronic B2B Commerce." *Proceedings of the 44th Hawaii International Conference on System Sciences* (HICSS) (2011).

Zarroli, Jim. "In Trendy World Of Fast Fashion, Styles Aren't Made To Last." National Public Radio (March 11, 2013).

Zurich Insurance. "Outsourcing Failures Now in Top 3 as Causes of Supply Chain Disruption." *Insurance Journal* (November 8, 2012).

Index

A

a la carte revenue model, 611, 648, 659

abandonment rate, 413, 434, 436

Abdulmutallab, Umar Farouk, 245

ABP pension fund, 830

academic disciplines, concerned with e-commerce, 84–85

ACC files, 336

Accenture, 71, 757

acceptance testing, 191

access controls, 283

accessibility, 215, 216–217

account aggregation, 755

accountability, 531–533, 788

accountable supply chains, 804–805

ACI Worldwide, 298

ACLU (American Civil Liberties Union), 321, 691

ACPA (Anticybersquatting Consumer Protection Act), 572–573, 574

acquisition rate, 434, 435, 512

active content, 211–214

Active Server Pages. *See* ASP

ActiveX (Microsoft). *See* Microsoft ActiveX

Acxiom, 83, 410, 544

ad exchanges, 395–396

ad fraud, 396

ad targeting, 385–386

ad servers, 147, 200

ad-blocking software, 539–540

ad-supported business model, 358

ADA (Americans with Disabilities Act), 217, 690

adaptive supply chains, 802–804

Adap.tv, 707

adaptive Web design. *See* AWD

AdChoices, 555

add-to-cart rate, 443

ADEA (Age Discrimination in Employment Act), 690

Adidas, 421

administrative overhead, 789

Adobe, 213, 223, 254, 331, 707

Adobe Analytics, 331, 443

Adobe Dreamweaver CC, 142, 186

Adobe EchoSign, 258, 271

Adobe Flash, 142–143, 151, 224, 616
cookies, 425, 426
online marketing and, 390
security and, 247

Adobe Reader, 247, 261

ADT (company), 137

Advanced Encryption Standard. *See* AES

Advanced Research Projects Agency Network. *See* ARPANET

advertising (offline). *See also* online advertising; marketing; online marketing
effectiveness of online marketing compared with, 438–441
integrating online marketing with, 404–405
prior to e-commerce, 50–51
trust-building and, 380

advertising business model, 333

advertising networks, 394–395

advertising revenue model, 318, 322

adware, 250

AES (Advanced Encryption Standard), 269, 278

affiliate marketing, 331, 399–400

affiliate referral fees business model, B2C and, 333

affiliate revenue model, described, 319, 322

affinity communities, 688, 692

affinity group portal, 707, 708

Africa, 73, 139, 236, 368, 677

Age Discrimination in Employment Act. *See* ADEA

agency model, 645

Agentrics, 830

aggregators, 335, 762, 638–647

agribusiness, 826

AgoraCart, 202

AIM (AOL Instant Messenger), 148

air conditioning systems software, hackers and, 255–256

Air Products & Chemicals, 838

Airbnb, 47, 58, 296, 480, 769, 770, 771–772, 773
market creator business model and, 339, 340
RoR and, 214

Airborne Express, 814

Airbus, 343

aircraft industry, 797, 803

airline industry, 226–227, 323, 346. *See also* travel industry

Ajax, 214
Akamai, 331, 161–164, 193, 259
AKM Semiconductor, 797
Alando, 73
Alcatel, 133
Alexa, 86
algorithm(s)
    fake travel reviews and, 764
    link farms and, 389
    long tail marketing and, 421
    Page Rank, 624
    payment systems and, 294
    routing, 105
alias names, 243
Alibaba, 420, 712, 741, 785–786, 787
Alice (French ISP), 120
Alice Corporation v. CLS Bank International, 569
AliExpress.com, 786
AllSeen Alliance, 137
Altair desktop computer, 102
AltaVista, 149, 150
AlumniFinder, 329
Amazon, 734–743
    affiliate program, 399
    B2C e-commerce and, 58
    book reviews, 380
    business models and, 318, 319, 330, 333,
      644–645, 735–736
    classification of, as an e-tailer, 332
    cloud computing and, 336–337, 736, 737
    collaborative commerce and, 814–815
    digital media ecosystems and, 642–644
    financial analysis, 738–740
    first-mover advantage and, 324
    future prospects for, 79, 742–743
    history of the Internet and, 103
    as intermediary, 75
    one-click purchasing, 347, 351, 353
    online marketing and, 374, 405, 418–420
    original vision of, 734–735
    Pandora and, 358
    patents and, 565
    pricing debates and, 645
    ranked by online sales, 78
    recommender systems, 374
    security and, 274

    self-publishing and, 638
    strategic analysis, 740–742
    taxation and, 579, 742
    value chains and, 349
    value webs and, 350
    Walmart and, competition between, 830
    Weebly and, 189
    widgets and, 156, 214
    yield management and, 418
Amazon Appstore, 158, 403
Amazon Books Publishing, 620
Amazon Cloud Player, 735
Amazon EC2 (Elastic Compute Cloud), 188, 736, 737
Amazon Digital Music, 336–337
Amazon Fire phone, 229, 735, 740–741
Amazon Fire TV, 740
Amazon Instant Video, 736, 741, 742
Amazon Kindle, 318, 336, 590, 736, 740–741
    business models and, 645
    digital media ecosystems and, 642–644
    DRM and, 615
    sales numbers, 643
    Unlimited subscription service, 318, 319,
      646–647
Amazon Kindle Fire tablet, 336, 640, 643, 735, 740,
    742
Amazon Local, 403
Amazon Marketplace, 735
Amazon MP3, 154
Amazon Music (Cloud Player), 336, 337, 735, 736,
    741
Amazon Payments, 288, 289, 292
Amazon Prime, 659, 670, 740
Amazon Prime Music, 742
Amazon S3 (Simple Storage Service), 736
Amazon Services, 735
Amazon Stores, 184
Amazon Supply, 341, 820
Amazon Wallet, 736
Amazon Web Services (AWS), 111, 113, 188, 331, 736,
    737–738, 740
Amazon Webstore, 735
Amazon Widgets, 214
America Online. *See* AOL
American Airlines, 226
American Civil Liberties Union. *See* ACLU

American Express, 320, 299, 510

American Institute of Graphic Arts. *See* AIGA

American National Standards Institute. *See* ANSI

American Telephone & Telegraph. *See* AT&T

American Standard Code for Information Interchange. *See* ASCII

Americans with Disabilities Act. *See* ADA

Amobee, 368

amplification, 434, 436, 465, 472–473, 481, 487, 512

analytics. *See also* Web analytics, 136, 750, 788

    Adobe Analytics, 331, 443

    Amazon Web Services and, 737, 738

    Big Data and, 47, 136, 371, 543, 750

    business analytics, 47, 355, 371, 543, 750, 788, 806, 830

    Curalate, 488

    Dell and, 747

    ExchangeHunterJumper and, 517

    Facebook and, 474

    Fairmont Hotels and, 475

    Fireclick, 435

    Google Analytics, 202, 331, 426, 443, 474, 476, 517

    IBM Digital Analytics, 331, 443, 474

    mobile, 738, 747

    open source, 202

    Pinterest and, 488

    SCSM, 806

    Walmart and, 830

    Web analytics, 47, 435, 441–443

    Webtrends, 331, 197, 474

Ancestry.co.uk, 318, 319

Anderson, Chris, 358, 415, 420, 421

Andreessen, Marc, 103, 138, 359

Android (Google)

    Appery.io and, 222

    automobile industry and, 137

    B2B e-commerce and, 789

    BiznessApps and, 224

    cloud computing and, 336

    cross-platform apps and, 222

    HTML5 and, 143, 144

    IoT and, 137

    mobile apps and, 159

    Orbitz and, 227, 228, 229

    patents and, 566–568

payment systems, 302–303, 304

    privacy issues and, 539

    security and, 263, 264–265

    shift towards apps and, 65

angel investors, 327

AngelFire, 189

AngelList, 329

angle brackets (< >), 138, 142

Angry Birds, 263, 489, 665

annual media consumption statistics, 609–610

Anonymous (hacktivist group), 254

anonymous information, 536–537

anonymous profiles, 540–542

anonymous remailers, 557

anonymous surfing, 557

ANSI (American National Standards Institute), 806

Anticybersquatting Consumer Protection Act. *See* ACPA

Anti-Phishing Working Group. *See* APWG

anti-spyware, 250

anti-trust violations, 552, 645

anti-virus software, 281–282. *See also* viruses

AOL (America Online). *See also* portals

    AIM (AOL Instant Messenger), 148

    classification of, as a portal, 333, 335, 338, 683, 702–704

    customization of, 412

    display ads and, 390

    Do Not Track and, 427

    evolution of, 705-733

    Huffington Post and, 631

    mobile advertising and, 707

    original Web series and, 607, 706

    phishing and, 253

    programmatic ad platform and, 446, 706–707

    search engine, 149

    time spent on, 686

    transformation of, 705–707

    video content and, 607, 613, 706

Apache, 146, 194, 202, 430

APIs (application programming interfaces), 321

apparel industry, 77

Appbackr, 528

Appery.io, 222

applause ratio, 434, 436

Apple, 47, 157, 331

augmented reality and, 97
automobile industry and, 136–137
cloud computing and, 266, 300, 336–337, 652, 657, 660
desktop computers, invention of, 102
digital media ecosystems and, 642–644
disruptive technologies and, 356
entrepreneurs and, 47
Genius app and, 159
history of the Internet and, 103
HTML5 and, 143
intellectual property and, 48
labor practices and, 797, 805
online marketing and, 403
patents and, 566–568
payment systems, 299, 300, 304
privacy issues and, 544
promotional videos, 156
ranked by online sales, 78
retail stores, 75
security and, 264, 276, 281
surveillance and, 127, 245
widgets and, 156
Apple AirPlay, 137
Apple App Store, 64, 65, 158, 160, 359, 403, 637
Apple Calendar, 229
Apple CarPlay, 137
Apple Dashboard Widgets, 214
Apple FaceTime, 156
Apple Find My iPhone API, 266
Apple iAd, 403, 499, 500–502
Apple iBeacon, 508, 510–511, 744
Apple iBooks, 284, 643, 645, 649
Apple iBooks Author, 647
Apple iBooks Store, 284, 643, 645
Apple iBooks Textbooks, 647
Apple iCloud, 266, 300, 337, 652, 657, 660
Apple iPad. *See* iPad (Apple)
Apple iPhone. *See* iPhone (Apple)
Apple iPod. *See* iPod (Apple)
Apple iOS, 158
    cross-platform apps and, 222
    HTML5 and, 143, 144
    location-based marketing, 508
    mobile apps and, 160
    payment systems and, 302, 304

security and, 263, 264
Apple iTunes, 89, 614, 616, 630, 662
    business models and, 322, 324, 333, 358
    competitive advantage and, 324
    Match, 337
    overview of, 154
    Pandora and, 358
    security and, 263, 264
    television content and, 154–155
Apple Macintosh. *See* Macintosh (Apple)
Apple Newsstand, 640
Apple Passbook, 293
Apple Pay, 288, 293, 300–301, 303, 510
Apple Safari browser, 275, 552
Apple Siri. *See* Siri (Apple)
Apple Watch, 136
appliance servers, 207
application gateways, 279. *See* gateways
Application Layer, 106, 113, 114
application programming interfaces. *See* APIs
Applications layer, 116
apps. *See also* mobile apps
    cloud computing and, 112
    crowdfunding and, 328
    described, 49
    Facebook and, 683, 684–685
    Google Glass and, 96
    growth in the number of, 64–65
    HTML5 and, 144
    install ads, 367, 469, 479
    leading, 493–494
    location-based marketing and, 507
    security and, 263
    "smart", 65
    social networks and, 683, 684–685
    surveillance and, 127
Appstores.com, 368
APPY Award, 229
APWG (Anti-Phishing Working Group), 253
Arab Spring, 125
Arbor Networks, 259
Ariba, 787, 788, 821
    business models and, 342
    collaborative commerce and, 810
    Supplier, 341, 821
Armstrong, Tim, 705, 706

ARPANET (Advanced Research Projects Agency Network), 100, 102, 103

AS2 (iSoft Corporation), 829

Asahi Glass, 797

Ascension Island, 88

ASCII (American Standard Code for Information Interchange), 268

Asia-Pacific, 58, 59, 115, 681

Ask, 148, 149, 210, 333, 338, 686, 704

Aslin, Dagny Amber, 513–516

ASP (MicrosoftActive Server Pages), 198, 208, 212

ASP.NET, 212, 214

assets, definition of, 733

Associated Press, 262

astroturfing, 763

asymmetry, definition of, 324

A.T. Kearney Procurement & Analytic Solutions, 822

AT&T (American Telephone & Telegraph), 66, 103, 578, 584, 741, 617
  Internet backbone and, 118
  location-based marketing and, 508
  IoT and, 136, 137
  publishing industry and, 642
  security and, 264
  Wi-Fi Services, 133

Atlas Technology Group, 829

attachments (e-mail), 148, 248

Attaturk, Mustafa Kernal, 126

attrition rate, 434, 436

auction(s). *See* eBay, Priceline, online auctions

auction server, 200

AuctionWeb, 103. *See* eBay

audio/video servers, 200

augmented reality, 95–97. *See also* Google Glass

Australia, 72, 126, 139, 158, 203, 217, 239, 328, 368, 408, 459, 568, 604

Australian Communications and Media Authority, 126

Austria, 538

authentication, 258, 267, 278, 283

authenticity, 243, 244

authorization policies/management systems, 284

Authorize.net payment gateway, 291

Authors Guild, 592, 593, 594

automated order entry, 790, 791

automated response systems, 413

automobile industry, 574–575, 826
  business models and, 323, 343
  IoT and, 136–137
  online marketing and, 374, 385, 393, 397–398, 411, 416, 446
  regulation of, 79
  statistics, 77
  supply chain management and, 797, 799, 802, 803

Auxmoney, 329

availability, described, 244

Aviate, 709

AWD (adaptive Web design), 221, 222

AWS (Amazon Web Services). *See* Amazon Web Services (AWS)

Azmalo.pk, 72

B

B2B digital commerce. *See* B2B e-commerce

B2B (business-to-business) commerce, described, 790

B2B (business-to-business) e-commerce, 47, 776
  auctions, 694, 697, 699, 787
  business models and, 330, 341–354
  challenges of, 794–795
  collaborative commerce and, 784–843
  described, 58, 790
  evolution of, 790–791
  exchanges, 342–343, 348
  growth of, 60, 793–794
  leading trends in, 787–788
  major trends, 47
  mobile, 808–809
  online marketing and, 370
  origins of e-commerce and, 66
  overview, 789–795
  potential benefits of, 794–795
  security and, 258
  servers, 200
  service provider, statistics, 342
  social networks and, 688
  statistics, 58, 60, 61, 71, 788, 789, 793–794
  supply chain management and, 784–843
  trends, 788

Web sites, described, 791

B2Buy, 820

B2C (business-to-consumer) auctions, 694

B2C (business-to-consumer) e-commerce, 370, 759

    business models and, 330, 332–342

    described, 57, 58

    growth of, 59

    origins of e-commerce and, 66

    overview of, 57–58

    social networks and, 688

    statistics, 57, 59, 61, 66–67, 71, 74

backbone (Internet), 103, 104, 117–118, 249, 582

backend databases, 192, 194

backend layer, 194, 195

BackTweets, 481

Bad Piggies, 263

Baidu, 148

Bain & Company, 406

"baiting and switching" customers, 75

balance sheets, 733

bandwidth, 129–134, 259

    choices, 120

    described, 117

    fees, 670

    growth in, 99, 162

    limitations, 124

    music services and, 154

    rationing, 583

    standards, list of, 131

Bangladesh, 797, 798

Bank of America, 248, 253, 299, 722, 753

bank transfers, 288

banking industry. *See also* financial services; online banking

    ApplePay and, 299–301

    Bitcoin and, 295–296

    EBPP and, 294, 297, 298

    history of the Internet and, 103

    impact of e-commerce on, 752

    mobile platform and, 59, 262, 265, 293, 753

    online credit card transactions and, 290–291

    PayPal and, 292, 303

    security and, 241, 243, 248, 250–253

    venture capital investors and, 327

Bankoff, Jim, 634

banner ads, 385, 441, 628

advent of, 103

click-through rates, 438

cost of, 440

described, 390

dynamic page generation tools and, 198–199

first sales of, 66

mobile marketing and, 402–403

bar-coded production tickets, 813

bargaining power, 344, 346, 347

Barnes & Noble, 257, 332, 405, 565, 638

barriers to entry, 332, 344, 346, 347, 730

BASF, 833

batch requests, scaling techniques and, 207

Battelle, John, 410

batteries, 263, 797

Baumschlager, Stefan, 313, 315

Baxter Healthcare, 66, 790

Bazaarvoice, 331

BBB. *See* Better Business Bureau

BBC World News, 126

BBN Technologies, 102

BBVA, 753

BCD Travel, 761

beacons (Web bugs), 425, 427, 510–511

Beatguide, 313–315, 316

Becker, Gene, 96

Beers, Kim, 189

behavioral targeting (interest-based advertising), 70, 405–411, 540–542, 551

Bieber, Justin, 489

Benadryl, 690

Benassaya, Jonathan, 605

Bench, 340

benchmarking, 192

Benjamin Moore Color Capture, 160

Bentley-Walker, 121

Bergdorf Goodman, 485

Berliner Morgenpost, 315

Berners-Lee, Tim, 65, 103, 137, 138, 144

Bernina of America, Inc. v. Fashion Fabrics Int'l, Inc., 574

Best Buy, 78, 299, 300, 727

Better Business Bureau (BBB), 555

Betts, Tom, 171

Bezos, Jeff, 103, 617, 630, 734, 736, 741

bidding fee (penny) auction, 698

bid(s), in auctions, 700, 702. *See also* online auctions
Bid4Assets, 695
Big Data
    B2B e-commerce and, 788
    challenges of, 430–431
    described, 430
    online marketing and, 371, 425–431
    online retail and, 723
    predictive marketing and, 750–751
    technology trends and, 47
    White house report on, 543–544
bill payment systems. *See* EBPP (electronic billing
  presentment) systems
Bill of Rights, 553
billboards, 441
Bill Me Later. *See* BML
Bilski et al v. Kappos, 569
binary digits. *See* bits
Bing (Microsoft), 150, 151, 210, 333, 686, 709
    China and, 578
    data retention policies, 545.
    Facebook Graph Search and, 389, 467, 707
    Foursquare and, 320
    local search and, 403
    mobile search advertising and, 492
    social search, 151
    top portal/search engine, 338, 704
    trademarks and, 575
biometrics, 284, 293
Birchbox, 751
bit.ly (short URL service), 517
Bitar, Mohamad, 457
Bitcoins, 241, 294, 295–296, 588
BitLicense, 296
bits (binary digits), 105, 268
bits per second. *See* Bps
BitTorrent, 86, 87, 88
BiznessApps, 224
BizRate, 331
black hats, 254
Blackberry (RIM), 111, 158, 159, 264, 265
blacklisted Web sites, 125
blackmailing sites, 259
Blackwell, Brendon, 313
BLE (Bluetooth low energy), 508, 510–511
Blippar, 95–97

Blogger, 153
blogs (weblogs), 126, 628, 679
    described, 152
    online marketing and, 400, 402
    overview of, 152–153
Bloomingdale's, 299
Blue Nile, 332
Bluefly, 332, 333
Bluetooth, 133–134, 136, 263
Bluetooth low energy. *See* BLE
BMI Baby, 217
BML (Bill Me Later), 288, 289, 292, 711–712
BMW, 141, 343, 351, 382
Boeing, 797, 803
Boingo Wireless, 132
BoldChat, 331
book publishing. *See also* Apple iBooks; e-books;
  Google Books; publishing industry
    business models and, 318, 334–335
    book reviews, 380
    Google Books settlement and, 590–594
    intellectual property rights and, 558
    legislation and, 561
    media convergence and, 618–620
    one-click purchasing and, 565
    online marketing and, 380, 405, 417, 435
    online sales, 77
    printed versus e-book editions of, sales statistics
      for, 641
    pricing of, 75
Booking.com, 761
Bosch, 343
botnets, 239, 249–250, 251
bots (robots), 249
bounce-back rate, 434, 436
BP (British Petroleum), 833
Bps (bits per second), 117
Braintree, 296, 712
brand(s), 70, 219, 324
    online marketing, 465–466, 468–472, 481,
      486–487, 503, 513–518
    Web sites and, 383
brandjacking, 572–573
BravoSolution, 822
Brazil, 47, 459, 606, 681
bricks-and-clicks business model, 46, 74, 333,

743–744
bricks-and-mortar businesses, 70, 188, 332, 644
BrightRoll Platform, 365
Brin, Sergey, 150
Britain. *See* Great Britain, United Kingdom
Britannica, 56
broadband, 70, 122
 adoption levels, 373
 described, 120
 expansion of, 651–652
 online marketing and, 370, 373
 statistics, 370
 stimulus package for, 104
Broadband Data Improvement Act, 104
Broadband Technology Opportunities Program, 128
broadcast model (one-to-many), 55
Broadcom, IoT and, 137
Bronto Software, 331
Brown Bag Software v. Symantec Corp., 560
browse-to-buy ratio, 434, 435
browser(s)
 described, 100, 147
 growth in the number of apps and, 64–65
 HTML and, 138
 hypertext and, 139–141
 invention of, 103
 parasites, 250
 security and, 275, 276, 277
 tracking files and, 427
 URLs and, 108
 Web servers and, 146
BT (Italia), 120
BT (Plus Net), 120
budgets, e-commerce presence, 179–180
Buffet, Warren, 630
bugs. *See* beacons (Web bugs)
Bulgaria, 253
bundling, 417
Burberry, 407, 408
Buscemi, Steve, 706
Bush, Vannevar, 137–138
business
 analytics, 47, 71, 788
 basic concepts, 80
 concepts, overview of, 312–364
 objectives, identifying, 182–183

plan, described, 316
procedures, security and, 282–287
processes, 352
strategy, described, 350–354
business models. *See also* e-commerce business models
 Amazon, 579, 734, 735–738
 auctions and, 697
 categorizing, 330–331
 Dell, 75, 333, 746–747
 described, 316
 developing, when planning e-commerce presence, 174–175
 disruption, 354–356
 eight key elements of, 326
 e-book, 644–646
 e-tailing, 733–747
 eBay, 319, 322, 331, 333, 339, 347, 711
 EBPP, 297–298
 Elemica, 833–838
 e-procurement, 577
 Facebook, 320, 332–334
 gaming, 666
 Grainger, 820
 industry structural analysis and, 345–346
 LinkedIn, 333, 334
 Macy's, 743
 major B2B, 58, 341–354
 major B2C, 58, 332–341
 music industry and, 88–89, 657, 662–664
 Netflix, 318, 667–670
 newspapers, 621–632
 online content, 607
 online movie, 655–656
 OpenTable, 775, 777
 overview, 316–331
 Pandora, 358–359
 portals and, 708–709
 selecting, 174–175
 sharing economy, 46, 57, 769–770
 social networks and, 688, 692
 YouTube, 615
business-to-business e-commerce. *See* B2B e-commerce
business-to-consumer auctions. *See* B2C auctions
business-to-consumer e-commerce. *See* B2C

e-commerce
Buy.com, 292
Buy buttons, 723, 729, 646
buy-side servers, 199, 200
buyer-side solutions, described, 790
Buzzfeed, 622, 631, 632, 633
BYOD (Bring Your Own Device) policy, 808–809

C

C+ (high-level language), 158
C++ (high-level language), 158
C2C (consumer-to-consumer) auctions, 58–59, 694
C2C (consumer-to-consumer) e-commerce, 58–59, 61
Cabir, 263
Cable Communications Policy Act, 547
cable Internet, 120, 121, 122
cable modems, 106, 279. *See also* modems
cable television, 57, 614, 651–653, 669
cable video on demand, 656
caches, scaling techniques and, 207
Cadillac, 706
CakePHP, 213
CALEA (Communications Assistance for Law Enforcement Act), 260, 543
California Online Privacy Protection Act, 548
Cameron, David, 578
campaign IDs, 215
campus area networks. *See* CANs
CAN-SPAM Act, 286, 398, 399
Canada, 44, 109, 253, 328, 399, 408, 458, 459, 545, 587, 738, 774, 777
cannibalization, 610
Canon, 355
CANs (campus area networks), 118
cap pricing, 582
capital, raising, 326–327
Capital Factory, 327
Capital One, 753
carbon monoxide alarms, 136
carbon footprints, 805, 830, 838. *See also* sustainability
Carbonite, 333, 340
carding forums, 245
CareerBuilder, 765, 766, 768, 678

career services. *See* online career services.
Cargill, 826
Carnegie Mellon University, 261, 285, 538
Carrefour, 46
cart conversion rate, 434, 436
CAs (certification authorities), 274–276
Cascading Style Sheets. *See* CSS
Case, Steve, 705
case studies (listed by name)
    Akamai Technologies, 161–164
    eBay, 710–713
    Elemica, 833–838
    ExchangeHunterJumper.com (The Exchange), 513–518
    Google Books, 590–594
    mobile payment market, 299–304
    Netflix, 667–670
    Open Table, 774–778
    Orbitz Worldwide, 226–229
    Pandora, 357–360
    programmatic advertising, 444–447
    TPB (The Pirate Bay), 86–89
catalog display servers, 200
catalog merchant business model, 75, 333, 744–745
catalog sales, 78, 332
Caterpillar, 797, 803
CBS Inc., 619–620, 649
CCI (Center for Copyright Information), 564
CCMP authentication code protocol, 278
ccTLDs, 139
CD (compact disc) sales, 75, 661–665
CDA (Communications Decency Act), 585
CDMA (Code Division Multiple Access), 132
CDN (content delivery network), 163, 331
cell phones, 131. *See also* smartphones
cell towers, 508–509
Cendant, 762
censorship, 125
Center for Copyright Information. *See* CCI
Center for Democracy and Technology, 556
Center for Strategic and International Studies, 239
central processing units. See CPUs.
CenturyLink, 188
CEOs (chief executive officers), 256, 282, 300, 359
Cerf, Vint, 102
CERN (European Particle Physics Laboratory), 103,

137, 285, 287

CERT Coordination Center, 285

certification authorities. *See* CAs.

CGI (Common Gateway Interface), 192, 198, 211–212

Channel Advisor, 331

channel conflict, 746

channel management, 699–700

ChapStick, 689, 690

Charles Schwab, 722, 754

Charmin SitOrSquat Restroom Finder, 160

chat. *See also* SMS (Short Message Service) texting
    server, 200
    surveillance and, 245

CheapTickets, 346

Check (company), 297

checkout conversion rate, 434, 436

Checkpoint, 331

chemical industry, 826, 833–838

Chernobyl, 251

Chesky, Brian, 771

Chestnut, Ben, 359

chief executive officers. *See* CEOs

child labor, 805. *See also* labor practices

Child Pornography Prevention Act, 585

children. *See also* child labor; COPPA (Children's Online Privacy Protection Act)
    marketing to, 489–490
    protection of, 585–586

Children's Internet Protection Act. *See* CIPA

Children's Online Protection Act (COPA), 585

Chin, Denny, 593

China, 72, 190, 368, 606, 647
    Alibaba in, 420, 712, 741, 785–786
    Bitcoin and, 296
    governance issues and, 123
    Great Firewall of, 125, 578
    growth of e-commerce in, 47
    luxury spending and, 406
    mobile phones in, 111
    Puma in, 44, 45
    search engines in, 148
    social networks in, 677–678, 681
    supply chain management and, 411, 797, 803, 805
    surveillance in, 125–126, 577–578

    taxation in, 581

ChoicePoint, 544

Chorus, 635–636

Chronicle Forums, 692

Chrome. *See* Google Chrome

Chrysler, 397, 446, 690, 787

cigarettes, 586–587

CIO (chief information officers), 256, 282

CIO magazine, 335

CIPA (Children's Internet Protection Act), 585–586

cipher text, described, 267

CircleUp, 329

circuit-switched networks, 104

Cisco Systems
    @CiscoLiveDesk Twitter feed, 816
    B2B collaborative commerce and, 816
    certificate authority, 276
    GENI initiative and, 129
    Cisco TelePresence Studios, 156, 816
    Internet traffic statistics, 162
    Internet video statistics, 161
    IoT and, 137
    load balancing software, 208
    mobile traffic statistics, 808–809
    routers, 133
    private industrial network and, 827
    security statistics, 249, 264
    social networks and, 688, 692, 816
    surveillance and, 125
    WebEx and, 156

Citadel Trojan/botnet, 250, 251

Citibank, 252, 256

Citigroup, 299, 722, 753

Citysearch, 403

Civil Rights Act, 690

Civil War, 245

Clark, Jim, 103, 138

classified ads, 630

Clean Clothes Campaign, 805

clearinghouses, 290–291

click fraud, 390, 398

click-through rates. *See* CTR

Click-to-Call, 331

Clickability (company), 199

clickstream behavior, 377–378

client(s). *See also* client/server computing

described, 109
mobile platforms as the new, 111
network architecture limitations and, 124
thin, 110
security and, 281–282
client/server computing, 102, 115
described, 108–110
of corporate computing and, 81
the history of the Internet and, 100, 108–110
climate change. *See* sustainability
cloud computing, 652, 657, 660
Akamai and, 163–164
Amazon and, 336–337, 736, 737
AWD and, 221
B2B e-commerce and, 788, 809–810
business models and, 336–337
cloud streaming model, 336–337
co-location and, 188
collaborative commerce and, 811–812, 815–816, 833–838
described, 111
e-commerce enablers and, 331
Elemica and, 833–838
freemium strategy and, 358–359
growth in, 99
history of the Internet and, 104
IPXs and, 832
model, overview of, 111–113
online marketing and, 371, 476
security and, 266
server farms and, 191
technology trends and, 47
cloud servers, 57, 337
CloudLab, 129
CMS (content management systems), 44, 186, 199, 635
CNN (Cable News Network), 323, 333, 335
CNP (Cardholder Not Present) transactions, 289
coaxial (copper) cables, 124, 130
CoC (coding by convention), 214
Coca-Cola, 402, 504, 687, 827
COD (cash on delivery), 289
Code Division Multiple Access. *See* CDMA
CodeIgniter, 213
CodeRed, 251
Cogent, 118

cognitive energy, 52
ColdFusion, described, 213, 214
Colgate-Palmolive Max White Photo Recharger, 160
collaborative commerce
described, 814
overview of, 814–816
private industrial networks and, 828–832
trends in, 801–817
collaborative resource planning, forecasting and replenishment. *See* CPFR
collaborative shopping, 401
Collective Utilitarian principle, 534
colocation/co-location, 188, 191, 814
Comcast, 136, 583–584, 670
Xfinity, 582, 704
Commerce Department (United States), 122, 554
Commerce Server (Microsoft), 202
CommerceHub, 331
commercial transactions, defined, 49. *See also* transactions
Commission Junction, 400
commoditization, 351
Common Gateway Interface. *See* CGI
Communications Assistance for Law Enforcement Act. *See* CALEA
Communications Decency Act. *See* CDA
communities. *See also* social networks
of consumption, 69
creating the foundation for, 465
online marketing and, 219, 465, 472, 481, 487, 512
community effects, 373–374
community provider, 332–334
comparison engine feeds, 331
competition, 344, 347, 731, 741–742
B2B e-commerce and, 830
cost, strategy of, described, 352
the history of e-commerce and, 69
movie industry and, 660
competitive advantage, 323–324, 326, 347
competitive environment, 322–323, 326
complementarity, 610
complementary resources, described, 324
computer(s). *See also specific types*
-based training, 322, 323
chips, 797

sales, 77

scientists, 84

Computer Fraud and Abuse Act, 286

Computer Matching and Privacy Protection Act, 547

Computer Security Act, 547

Computer Security Enhancement Act, 286

Computer Software Copyright Act, 560

Compuware, 331

comScore, 396, 436, 447, 753, 754, 757, 762

confidentiality, 243, 244, 267

Conflicker worm, 248, 251

congestion, 124

congestion pricing, 582–583

Congress (United States), 79, 260. *See also* legislation

consolidator business model, 297–298

Constant Contact, 331

Constitution (United States), 545, 558, 578, 615. *See also* First Amendment

consumer(s). *See also* consumer behavior; customers

    apps and, 64–65

    big-ticket items and, 379

    intentional acts by, 379–380

    profiles, 370–375, 425–426

    small-ticket items and, 379

    trust, in auctions, 696, 701

    consumer behavior, 370–380

    in auctions, 701

    online financial, 752–753

Consumer Location Privacy Protection Act, 539

Consumer Privacy Bill of Rights, 553

Consumer Reports, 318, 322

consumer-to-consumer (C2C) auctions. *See* C2C auctions

consumer-to-consumer (C2C) e-commerce. *See* C2C e-commerce

content. *See also* online content

    convergence, 617–618

    determining the origins of, 176–177

    dynamic, 176–177

    farms, 389

    "is King" principle, 627–629

    static, 176–177

    types of, 176–177

content delivery networks. *See* CDN

content management systems. *See* CMS

content provider(s). *See also* content

    described, 334

    business model, described, 333

    overview of, 334–335

Continental Airlines, 343, 226, 833

contract purchasing, 798

Converge, 823

Conversant, 331

conversation rate, 436, 472, 481, 487

Converse Sampler, 160

conversion ratio, 434, 435

Cook, Timothy, 300

cookies

    described, 152

    personalization and, 215

    online marketing and, 405, 424–427

    privacy issues and, 537, 545, 546, 557

    security and, 277

    Super Cookies, 537

    supplementing transaction logs with, 424–425

    third-party, 540

COPA (Children's Online Protection Act), 585

COPPA (Children's Online Privacy Protection Act), 489–490, 547, 549, 555, 586

copper cable, 130

copyright(s), 47, 48, 532–533. *See also* intellectual property

    content providers and, 335

    described, 559

    music and, 86–89

    overview, 559–564

    special challenges related to, 81, 84

Copyright Act, 592, 615

Copyright Term Extension Act. *See* CTEA

core competencies, 731

Cornell University, 764

cost(s)

    competition, described, 353

    of the Internet, declining, 135–136

    transparency, described, 54

cost per action. *See* CPA

cost per click. *See* CPC

cost per thousand. *See* CPM

Costco, 78, 727, 814

coupons, 402, 403

Covisint, 787, 794

CPA (cost per action), 439–440

CPC Strategy, 331

CPC (cost per click), 439–440

CPFR (collaborative resource planning, forecasting and replenishment), 831

CPM (cost per thousand), 439–440

CPUs (central processing units), 208

crackers, described, 253

Craigslist, 58, 630

crawlers. *See* search engines

CrawlTrack, 202

credit bureaus, 544

credit card(s). *See also* credit card transaction(s)
    CVV codes, 255
    e-commerce enablers, 291
    fraud, 240, 257–258
    PayPal and, 711–712
    software, 202
    system architecture and, 194

credit card transaction(s). *See also* credit cards
    diagrams of, 246, 290
    overview, 289–291
    payment systems, 288–294
    SDLC and, 186
    shopping carts and, 201
    typical, vulnerable points in, 247

Critical Path, 712

CRM (customer relationship management), 331, 350, 431–433, 775

Croatia, 253

Crowdfunder, 329

crowdfunding, 327, 328–329

Crowdtilt, 328

Crowley, Dennis, 320, 321

CrowPeak Technology, 199

CryptoLocker, 249, 251

cryptography. *See also* encryption.
    public key, 269–273, 276
    symmetric key, 268–269

CS&C (Office of Cybersecurity and Communications), 285

CSNET (Computer Science Network), 102

CSS (Cascading Style Sheets), 143, 221, 222
    social marketing and, 517
    Weebly and, 189

CTEA (Copyright Term Extension Act), 559–560

CTR (click-through rates), 397, 433–438

current liabilities, 733

CurrentC system, 303–304

customer(s). *See also* consumers
    acquisition costs, 76
    co-production, 411–412
    establishing relationships with, through Web sites, 383–384
    experience, described, 383–384
    feedback, gathering, 219
    forums, e-commerce enablers and, 331
    ID, 215
    intimacy, described, 353
    loyalty, 376, 412, 434, 435, 443
    power of, 730
    profiles, described, 429
    retention, 360, 405–413
    reviews, e-commerce enablers and, 331
    satisfaction, 383
    service, overview of, 412–413
    sign-in, 220
    support, SDLC and, 183
    touchpoints, 431
    value chains and, 348

customer relationship management. *See* CRM

customization. *See also* personalization
    described, 54, 55, 345, 215
    ethical, social and political implications of, 529
    impact on business environment, 345, 353
    online marketing and, 411, 423
    online retailing and services and, 728, 752
    overview of, 411–412
    SDLC and, 183
    tools for, 215
    unique feature of e-commerce technology, 54, 55
    value proposition and, 317

CVAA (21st Century Communications and Video Accessibility Act), 216, 217

cyber black market, 240–241

Cyber Security Enhancement Act, 543

cybercrime
    cost of, 239, 240–241
    ethics and, 528
    increasing punishment for, 285

in Europe, 235–237

mobile apps and, 263

scope of, 239–242

cyberespionage, scope of, 239–242

cyberlockers, 564, 656–657

cyberpiracy, 572, 573–608

CyberSource, 291

Cyberspace Electronic Security Act, 286

cybersquatting, 572–573

cybervandalism, 254

D

Da Vinci, Leonardo, 268

Daraz.pk, 72

dark social, use of the term, 464

"Dark" Web. *See* Deep Web

data

repositories, 71

data breaches, 254–257, 285

data brokers, 440

described, 535

FTC and, 552–553

governments as among the largest users of, 544–545

information collection by, 535, 536–537

privacy issues and, 535

data capture, 146, 196

data mining, 425–431

described, 428–429

model-driven, 429

query-driven, 429

data warehouses, 425–431

Data Accountability and Trust Act

Data Encryption Standard. *See* DES

database(s)

CRM and, 432

deep Web and, 62

described, 428

dynamic page generation tools and, 198

music, 357

online marketing and, 410, 423–431, 476

security and, 248

servers, described, 147, 200

shopping cart, 423–424

software, 202

supply chain management and, 803

system architecture and, 194

Datalogix, 83

dating services, 318, 548

Davis, Tom, 44

DBMS (database management system), 428

DDoS (Distributed Denial of Service) attacks, 164, 259, 266

DEA (Drug Enforcement Agency), 127, 587

debit cards, 204, 288. *See also* payment systems

debt, long-term, 733

debugging, 192

deep linking, 575–576. *See also* linking

deep packet inspection, 126, 127, 537, 542

Deep Web, 62, 588

DeepFace, 542. *See also* facial recognition

Deezer, 603–606, 607

Defense Advanced Research Agency. *See* DARPA

Defense Department (United States), 100, 102, 149

delivery rate, 434, 436

Dell

Bitcoin and, 296

business models and, 75, 333, 746–747

as a e-commerce enabler, 331

IoT and, 137

public cloud provider, 111

private industrial network and, 827

ranked by online sales, 78, 727

social network and, 816

Web servers and, 146

Dell, Michael, 746

Delta Airlines, 226

Delta-Search, 148

demand curves, 413, 415

demand chain visibility, 831

demand forecasting, described, 801

demand-pull model, 746

Demandware, 44, 331, 203

democracy, 47, 125, 126, 420

demographic(s), 436, 626. *See also* consumers

advertising networks and, 394

consumer behavior and, 374–375

profiles, 372–373

Denial of Service attacks. *See* DoS attacks

Denmark, 88, 288, 296, 328, 581

Department of Homeland Security (United States),

256, 285

DeRodes, Bob, 256

DES (Data Encryption Standard), 269

desktop computer(s). *See also* PCs (personal computers); Apple Macintosh
    apps and, 64
    sales statistics, 131

Deutsche Telekom, 121

deviantArt, 683

DHL, 589

dial-up Internet access, 105, 106, 120, 122, 705, 707

differentiation, 345, 347, 351–352, 353, 411, 412, 422

Diffie, Whitfield, 269

diffserv (differentiated quality of service), 135

digital cash, described, 294

digital certificates, described, 274–275

digital commerce, as synonym for e-commerce, 49

"digital divide," 372

digital envelopes, 273

Digital Library Initiative, 149

Digital Millennium Copyright Act. *See* DMCA

digital newsstands, 639–640

digital photography, 355

Digital Reality Trust, 188

digital rights management. *See* DRM

digital signatures (e-signatures)
    described, 270
    legislation regarding, 257–258
    limitations of, 275–276
    public key cryptography with, 270–272

digital storefronts, 791

Digital Subscriber Line. *See* DSL

digital wallets, 537

digitally enabled transactions, described, 49. *See also* transactions

Digitas, 411

dilemmas, ethical, 533

dilution, 571

direct e-mail marketing, 397–398

direct goods, 798

direct mail, 397, 440, 441

Direct Marketing Association. *See* DMA

disabled individuals. *See* accessibility

Discover (company), 299

Dish Network, 296

disintermediation, 69, 74

Disney, 155, 299, 669

display ad marketing, 390–397

disruption
    business model, 354–356
    described, 354
    newspapers and, 632–633
    supply chain management and, 803–804

disruptive technologies, 354, 111

disruptors, described, 355–356

Distributed Denial of Service attacks. *See* DDoS attacks

distribution channels, deconstructing, 70

distributors
    history of e-commerce and, 69
    value chains and, 348

Django, 202, 213–214

DMA (Direct Marketing Association), 399

DMARC.org, 253

DMCA (Digital Millennium Copyright Act), 561–564

DNS (Domain Name System), 103, 108–109

DNS namespaces, 61

DNS servers, described, 109

"Do Not E-mail" registry, 398

"Do Not Track" mechanisms, 551–552, 557, 427

doctrine of fair use, 560–561, 563

document automation, 807. *See also* EDI (Electronic Data Interchange)

DocuSign, 258, 271

domain name(s), 61–62, 103, 104, 139. *See also* DNS (Domain Name System); URLs (Uniform Resource Locators)
    described, 108
    e-commerce enablers and, 331
    legislation, 331
    types of, 139
    registration, 331

Domain Name System. *See* DNS

Domain Names Act, 586

Domino's Pizza, online marketing and, 471

Donahoe, John, 710, 711

Doritos, 386

DoS (Denial of Service) attacks, 239, 259

DOS (Disk Operating System) prompt, 108

dot-com companies, 71, 223

Dotster, 331

"dotted quad" addressing scheme, 107

DoubleClick, 541, 546. *See* Google DoubleClick

Dove Real Beauty Sketches, 400

Dow Chemical, 833, 836, 838

Downadup worm, 249

download speeds, of types of Internet service, 122

DreamIt Ventures, 327

Dreamweaver CC (Adobe), 186

Dreamworks, 660

drive-by download, described, 248

Driver's Privacy Protection Act, 547

DRM (digital rights management), 164, 649
    described, 615
    HTML5 and, 144
    overview, 615–616
    privacy issues and, 537

Droga5, 43

drones, 134–135

Dropbox, 358–359, 266

Dropcam, 136

drug trade (illegal), 586, 587–588

Drug Enforcement Agency. *See* DEA

Drupal, 199

DRY (Don't Repeat Yourself) programming principle, 214

DSL (Digital Subscriber Line), 106, 120, 121, 122, 279

Duane Reade, 299

due process, 532

DuPont, 833, 835

duration of engagement, 434

Dutch Internet auction, 697–698, 700

DVDs (digital video discs) sales, 653, 658–660, 665, 667

Dwolla, 292, 293

dynamic content, 177, 183, 208, 224

dynamic page generation tools, 198–199, 212, 213

dynamic pricing, 51, 417–419, 694, 792

E

E. & J. Gallo Winery, 572–573

E2Open, 810, 826

earbuds, wireless, 134

early-to-market innovators, 76

ease of purchase, 210

ease of use, security and, 244–245

Easy2 Technologies, 331

eavesdropping programs. *See* sniffers

eBags, 143

eBay, 203, 331, 741. *See also* online auctions; PayPal
    affiliate program, 399–400
    auctions and, 694, 695, 696, 697, 700, 702
    Bill Me Later and, 288, 289, 292, 712
    business models and, 319, 322, 331, 333, 339, 347, 711
    Buy It Now, 696
    case study, 710–713
    competition and, 347
    dynamic page generation and, 198
    entrepreneurs and, 47
    evolution of, 679, 710–713
    as an example of C2C e-commerce, 58
    feedback forums, 380
    future of, 79
    long tail marketing and, 420
    market creators and, 339
    online marketing and, 499
    organizational development and, 325
    payment systems and, 291–292, 296, 302–303
    security and, 253, 252, 254
    small businesses and, 47
    transaction fees, 834
    Weebly and, 190
    widgets and, 156

eBid, 695

e-books. *See also* Apple iBooks; Kindle e-reader (Amazon); publishing industry
    business models, 644–646
    DRM and, 615
    interactive, 647
    overview, 638–647
    platforms, challenges of, 646–647
    readers, time spend on, statistics for, 612
    sales statistics, 641–642

EBPP (electronic billing presentment and payment) systems, 294–297

e-business, 49–50

e-Chemicals, 836

e-commerce
    academic disciplines concerned with, 84–485
    advent of, 103
    assessing, 71–76

behavioral approaches to, 84–85

Consolidation period, 66, 68, 70–71, 74

described, 49

different types of, relative size of, 61

e-business and, difference between, 49–50

enablers, list of, 331

failures, 71–76

first 70 seconds of, 48–49

growth of, 46, 66

history of, 48–49, 66–79

infrastructure, overview of, 94–169

Invention period, 67–70, 74

major trends, 46–48

organizing themes related to, 79–85

origins of, 66

platform providers, e-commerce enablers and, 331

precursors to, 66

predictions, 76–79

presence, cost estimates, 179–180

presence, building, 170–233

reasons to study, 50–51

Reinvention period, 68, 71, 74

revolution, 46–66

statistics, 46–48, 76–77

successes, 71–76

technical approaches to, 84

technology, eight unique features of, 51–55

types of, 57–60

e-commerce business models. *See* business models.

e-commerce merchant server software, 200–201

e-commerce presence. *See also* apps; mobile sites; Web sites

    building, systematic approach to, 180–193

    choosing the right technology for, 180–181

    factors to consider for, 181

    four kinds of, 178–179

    hardware choices, 204–208

    imagining your, 174–180

    map, developing, 178–179

    platforms, choosing, 203–204

    timeline, developing, 179

economic value, profit as, 351

economic viability, 730–733

economics, 374

ecosystem(s)

information," 794

"mobile app," 159–160

Edelman, Ben, 574

edge-caching services, 193

EDI (Electronic Data Interchange), 66, 802, 829

    collaborative commerce and, 814, 815

    described, 790

    Elemica and, 835, 838

    evolution of, 791, 807–808

    growth of B2B e-commerce and, 793

    hub-and-spoke systems and, 791

    IPXs and, 832

    overview of, 806–808

    private industrial networks and, 792

    stages of, 807–808

    statistics, 806–807

    supply chain management and, 829

    Walmart and, 829

e-distributor business model, 341, 342, 818, 819–820

education

    apps and, 64

    GENI initiative and, 129

    level, as demographic data, 372, 402

efficiency, 348

E-Government Act, 547

Egypt, 125, 459, 606, 720–721

eHarmony.co.uk, 318, 319

Ehrich, Timo, 313

Ek, Daniel, 603

Ektron, 199

Eldred v. Ashcroft, 559–560

electronic billing presentment and payment systems. See EBPP systems

Electronic Communications Privacy Act, 286, 542, 544, 547

Electronic Data Interchange. *See* EDI

Electronic Privacy Information Center. *See* EPC.

electronic sell-through. *See* EST

Electronic Signatures in Global and National Commerce Act. *See* E-Sign Law

Elementum, 809

Elemica, 833, 838

11 Main, 712

Ello, 694

Elpida Memory, 797

e-mail. *See also* spam

attachments, 148, 248

marketing, 397–398, 434

overview of, 147–148

privacy issues and, 557

protocols, 113

scam letters, 252–253

security and, 243, 248, 255, 263, 266

surveillance by, 126, 127, 245

time spent on, statistics for, 610

Web servers and, 196

wiretaps, 260

Email Privacy Act, 544

eMarketer, 131, 143

EMC Documentum, 199

Emptoris, 822

EMV smart credit cards, 299

Encarta, 56

encryption. *See also* cryptography

cloud services and, 266

copyrights and, 559

described, 267

e-commerce enablers and, 331

government efforts to regulate and control, 287

legislation, 548

limitations of, 275–276

OpenSSL encryption, 262

overview of, 267–268

privacy issues and, 557

surveillance and, 126

Target and, 255

terrorism and, 245

transactions and, 290

encyclopedias, 56, 347. *See also* Wikipedia

energy, cost of, 79

engagement, 465, 472, 481, 487, 512

England, 88, 105, 421, 545, 581, 721. *See also* Great Britain, United Kingdom

English auction, 697, 700

enterprise portal, 703

enterprise resource planning. *See* ERP

enterprise systems, 800–801

enterprise-wide computing, 81

entrepreneurs. *See also* start-ups

academic study of, 85

business models and, 355

the history of e-commerce and, 70, 74

raising capital and, 326–327

seed capital and, 327

entertainment industry. *See also* online entertainment industry

Amazon and, 741

copyright infringement and, 564

revenues, 611, 612, 613

Entrust, 331

environmental issues, 795–798, 805, 830. *See also* sustainability

eoVision, 96

EPIC, 556

Epinions, 380

e-procurement, 341, 342, 818, 820–822

Epsilon, 83

EPUB files, 615

EquipNet, 823

Erdogan, Recep Tayyip, 126

e-readers, 590

eRFQ feature, 824

ERP (enterprise resource planning), 344, 350

B2B e-commerce and, 834

industry consortia and, 825

private industrial networks and, 826, 827

errors

"404 Error: Page Does Not Exist" message, 197

EDI and, 806

future of the Internet and, 135

site management tools and, 196–197

typographical, 209

E-Sign Law, 257, 286

esignatures/e-signatures. *See* digital signatures

ESPN, 323, 333, 480

EST (electronic sell-through), 656

e-tailing business models, 330, 332, 333, 733–749

Ethernet, 102. *See also* Internet2 project®

ethics. *See also* labor practices

basic concepts, 531–533

described, 531

dilemmas related to, 533–534

intellectual property and, 558–577

issues, organizing, model for, 529–531

overview, 524–600

principles of, 534

ethnicity, 372. *See also* demographic profiles

eToys, 76

E*Trade, 76, 319, 322, 333, 722, 754
Etsy, 58, 189, 333, 485
EU-5, 677, 727, 730, 759
Europasat, 121
Europe, 235
    censorship and, 126, 127
    Facebook in, 82–83
    payment systems, 288, 293
    TPB and, 86
European Commission
    accessibility, 217
    Apple-Samsung patent dispute, 567
    crowdfunding, 327, 329
    data protection, 526, 554
    Google Books Project and, 590, 592
    identity fraud, 258
    safe harbor, 554
    taxation, 581
European Cybercrime Center (EC3), 235–237
European Parliament, 217
European Particle Physics Laboratory. *See* CERN
European Union (E.U.), 79, 87, 327, 567. *See also*
  specific countries
    cybercrime, 235–237
    Data Protection Directive, 553–554
    Google Books, 592
    illegal drugs in, 588
    InMobi in, 368
    privacy issues and, 525–528, 541, 545, 553–554
    taxation and, 579, 581, 582
    Spotify in, 604
    Web accessibility, 217
Europol, 235–237
Eve (company), 76
Evernote, 254
eWeek, 248
exchange(s)
    described, 342, 822
    industry consortia and, comparison of, 825
    overview of, 342–344, 822–824
    value chains and, 348
ExchangeHunterJumper.com (The Exchange),
  513–518
Expedia, 228, 296, 333, 346, 471, 475, 722, 761
Experian, 331, 544
expertise, offering, 210

exploit kits, described, 247, 261–262
Expression Web (Microsoft), 142
eXtensible Markup Language. *See* XML
eyeballs, 460, 609–615
    freemium strategy and, 359
    the history of e-commerce and, 70
    SEM and, 386
    Web 2.0 and, 57

F

Faberge, 406
Facebook. *See also* Facebook Likes; social networks
    ad revenue, 462, 686, 687
    apps and, 64, 467, 684–685
    as portal, 702, 707, 709
    B2B e-commerce and, 816–817
    Beacon program, 82
    Big Data and, 431
    brand pages, 468–469, 470
    business models and, 320, 332–334
    Buy button and, 729
    censorship and, 126
    Camera app, 685
    Chat, 148
    classification of, as a portal, 338
    commerce, use of the term, 59
    community-building tools, 332–334
    company/for companies, 210
    Connect, 83
    Connectivity Lab, 134–135
    Creative Labs, 684–685
    Credits, 294
    crowdfunding and, 329
    dangers of, 689–691
    drones and, 134–135
    entrepreneurs and, 47
    Exchange (FBX), 83, 470
    features, 466–470
    fiber optics and, 130
    Foursquare and, 320
    Friend search, 467
    future of, 79, 693–694
    games and, 664, 666
    Google and, 496
    Graph Search, 389, 467

Home Android app, 685
lawsuits filed against, 83
magazines and, 638
market dominance of, 463
marketing campaigns, starting, 470–471
marketing results, measuring, 472–474
marketing tools, 466–468
Messenger app, 148, 684, 685
mobile and, 469–470, 501, 680, 682–683, 687
native apps and, 144
News Feed, 467, 468, 469, 470, 628, 684
OKCupid and, 548
online marketing and, 374, 383, 397–398,
  400–403, 408, 431, 436, 446, 466–474
overview, 466–474
Open Graph, 467
Page Post Ads, 469, 470
Paper app, 684
Poke app, 685
privacy and, 82–83, 536, 538, 539, 548, 684, 690,
  691, 693
Profile, 467
purchase of WhatsApp by, 148, 683, 685
security and, 260, 277
Share button, 468
shift towards apps and, 65
sidebar ads, 469, 470
small businesses and, 47
Sponsored Stories, 82
statistics, 152, 680, 681–682, 683, 686
Status update, 467
steaming media and, 151
stock, 83
surveillance and, 127, 245
tagging, 467
target audience of, 175
Timeline, 467
Trending, 467
Web 2.0 and, 56
widgets and, 156
Facebook Likes, 60
classification of, as a widget, 156
described, 466–468, 470
online marketing and, 383, 389, 409, 408
privacy and, 82–83
security and, 262

target audiences and, 176
facial recognition programs, 82–83, 536, 538,
  541–542
FaceTime. *See* Apple FaceTime
factor markets, 352
Fair Credit Reporting Act, 547
fair information practices principles, 549–553
Fair Labor Association. *See* FLA
fair use doctrine. *See* doctrine of fair use
Fairmont Raffles Hotels International. *See* FRHI
fake offers, 262
falun (Chinese religious group), 125
Family Educational Rights and Privacy Act, 547
fan acquisition, 464–465, 472, 481, 487
Fanini, Chris, 189
FAQs (Frequently Asked Questions), 412
fashion industry, 406
"fast-follower" firms, 76
FastCGI, 212
Fastweb, 120
Fawry Payment Services, 720
fax server, 200
FBI (Federal Bureau of Investigation), 127, 260, 399
    ISPs and, 578
    ransomware and, 249
FCC (Federal Communications Commission), 509
    Open Internet Order, 583
    net neutrality and, 583, 584
    Netflix and, 670
    rationing bandwidth and, 583
FDA (Food and Drug Administration), 587, 588
Federal Bureau of Investigation. *See* FBI
Federal Circuit Court of Appeals, 561
Federal Communications Commission. *See* FCC
Federal Express. *See* FedEx
Federal Networking Council. *See* FNC
Federal Reserve, 275, 301
Federal Trade Commission. *See* FTC
Federal Trademark Dilution Act. *See* FTDA
FedEx, 587, 589, 745, 814
feedback forums, 380
FeedBurner, 516
Feedly, 153
Ferguson (Missouri), protests in, 125
Ferguson, Rik, 235
fiber-optic cable, 124, 128, 130

Fidelity, 754

Field v. Google, Inc., 561

Fig Card, 712

file swapping, 48, 532

File Transfer Protocol. *See* FTP

Filo, David, 149

financial analysis, 731–733, 738–740

Financial Conduct Authority, 329

financial models. *See* revenue models

Financial Modernization Act (Gramm-Leach-Bliley Act), 286

financial portals, 755

financial services. *See also* banking industry; online financial services

    business models and, 319

    cloud computing and, 112

    customer acquisition costs, 76

    the history of e-commerce and, 70

    online marketing and, 385

    service providers and, 340

    transaction brokers and, 338–339

    venture capital investors and, 327

Financial Times, 54, 144, 171–173, 175, 262, 547, 625

Find and Call app, 160

fingerprint sensors, 284

Finland, 88, 158, 288

FiOS (fiber-optic service), 120, 121, 130

FIP (fair information practice) principles, 549–553, 555

Fireclick, 435

FireEye, 255

Firefox browser (Mozilla), 88, 139, 147, 277. *See also* browsers

firewall(s), 279–280

    Akamai and, 164

    IP spoofing and, 258

firm value chains. *See* value chains

firm value webs. *See* value webs

First Amendment, 561, 578. *See also* Constitution (United States)

First Look Media, 631

first movers, 69, 74, 76, 324, 338

First Swedish Court, 87

first/last mile, of the Internet, 129–134

first-tier supplies, 796

FIS Global, 298

FISA (Foreign Intelligence Surveillance Act), 260

FISA Amendments Reauthorization Act, 260

Fiserv, 298

Fitbit, 136

Fitzgerald, F. Scott, 406

5Min Media, 706

fixed costs, 413

FLA (Fair Labor Association), 797, 805

Flash. *See* Adobe Flash

flash marketing, 403, 417, 419

flash pricing (sales), 75

Flexcoin, 296

Flickr, 56, 126, 416, 709

Flipboard, 631

flower industry, 77

Flurry (company), 64

FNC (Federal Networking Council), 101

focus/market niche strategy, 353

FogDog, 76

food and beverage industry, 77

Food and Drug Administration. *See* FDA

Food, Drug, and Cosmetics Act. *See* FDCA

Fool.com, 692

footwear industry, 806, 811–812

    labor practices and, 804

    online marketing and, 393, 409, 411

    sustainability and, 806

Ford, 480

    B2B e-commerce and, 787, 799

    online marketing and, 374, 383, 446

Ford Motor Co. v. Lapertosa, 573–574

Foreign Intelligence Surveillance Act. *See* FISA

forgotten, right to be, 527, 535, 554

Forrester Research, 144, 378, 404

Fortune 100 companies, 195, 768

Fortune 500 companies, 78, 163, 191, 214, 355, 540, 832

Fortune 1000 companies, 468, 795

Foursquare, 56, 222, 320–321, 383

Fourteenth Amendment, 545. *See also* Constitution (United States)

4G (Fourth Generation) cell phone technology, 132, 134, 287

Fourth Amendment, 545

Fox News, 262

Foxconn factories, 790, 805

framing, 573, 576

France, 139, 287. *See also* European Union
    crowdfunding in, 329
    cybercrime, 239
    government regulation, 126–127, 527, 656
    InMobi in, 368
    ISPs in, 120
    Minitel, 66
    mobile apps in, 158
    online banking in, 753
    Puma in, 44
    search engines in, 148, 386
    Spotify, 605
    The Pirate Bay in, 87, 88
    Viadeo in, 677–678

France Telecom, 66

Franco, James, 706

free, as pricing strategy, 415–416, 620–621

Free (French ISP), 120

Freedom of Information Act, 547

freedom of speech, 126, 561

FreeMarkets, 787

freemium strategy, 318, 334, 357–360, 415–416, 611

French Ministry of Economy and Finance, 329

Fresh Direct, 340

FRHI (Fairmont Raffles Hotels International), 475–476

friction-free commerce, 69

Fry, 331

FTC (Federal Trade Commission)
    COPPA and, 586
    fair information practices (FIP) principles, 549–553, 555
    new privacy framework of, 551–552
    online marketing and, 393, 394, 398, 489–490
    reporting data breaches to, 285
    Snapchat and, 539
    typosquatting and, 574

FTDA (Federal Trademark Dilution Act), 571

FTP (File Transfer Protocol), 106, 114, 146, 196

fuel costs, 79

FuelBand, 136

fulfillment
    Amazon and, 735, 739–742
    catalog merchants and, 744, 745
    costs of, in auctions, 696
    online retail and, 722, 724, 725, 726, 733, 734, 747, 748
    Macy's and, 743, 744
    manufacturer-direct and, 746
    providers, 331

Fujitsu, 188

Fukushima nuclear accident, 795, 796

Funding Circle, 329

furniture industry, 77

G

GAAP earnings, 732–733

gadgets, 156

gambling. *See* online gambling

Gap, 319, 322, 806

Gartner, 112, 136

gasoline, price of, 79

gateways. *See* proxy servers

Gbps (gigabits per second), 105, 117

GE (General Electric), 137, 815, 827

GEICO, 575

gender differences, 372. *See also* demographic profiles

General Motors, 411, 416, 446, 803

GENI (Global Environment for Network Innovations) initiative, 104, 129–130

general communities, 688, 692

general top-level domains. *See* gTLDs

general-purpose portal, 704, 707, 708

generalists, 325

Generalized Markup Language. *See* GML

Genetic Information Nondiscrimination Act. *See* GINA

geo-aware, 508

GeoCities, 189, 679

geographical boundaries, 50

Georgia Tech, 160

geo-search, 508

GeoTrust, 331

Germany, 44, 88, 126, 127, 148, 217, 239, 329, 368, 386, 545, 567, 568, 581, 681, 730, 753, 774, 777. *See also* European Union

GetJar, 403

GetThere, 761

GHX, 825

gift cards, 304

gift industry, 77

gigabit, 117

gigabits per second. *See* Gbps

Gilt Groupe, 419, 734, 748

GINA (Genetic Information Nondiscrimination Act), 690, 691

Girls Around Me app, 321

Glam Media, 360

Glaser, Will, 357

Global Fairness Initiative, 805

global positioning system. *See* GPS

global reach, 345, 529. *See also* reach
    described, 52, 55
    differentiation and, 352
    as one of the eight features of e-commerce technology, 51–55
    online marketing and, 423
    scope strategy and, 353

Global Environment for Network Innovations. *See* GENI

Global NetXchange, 830

globalization
    B2B e-commerce and, 796
    private industrial networks and, 828
    security and, 238

GlobalSign, 275

GML (Generalized Markup Language), 141

Go2Paper, 58, 341, 818

GoDaddy, 331

Golden Rule, 534

Gonzalez, Albert, 257

Goodyear Tire & Rubber, 833

Google
    AOL and, 706–707
    apps and, 64, 65, 112, 494
    automobile industry and, 136–137
    business models and, 333
    cloud computing and, 336–337, 112
    ContentID system, 563
    disruptive technologies and, 356
    dominance of, over mobile marketing, 496
    drones and, 134
    as a e-commerce enabler, 331
    entrepreneurs and, 47
    fiber optics and, 130
    Hummingbird algorithm, 385
    intellectual property and, 48
    intelligent assistant, 157
    Journalism Fellowships, 628–629
    keywording and, 575
    Knowledge Graph, 388
    as leading search engine/portal, 149–150, 704, 708–709
    legislation and, 563, 564
    mobile ad revenues, 687
    mobile apps and, 157, 159, 687
    NSA and, 543
    online marketing and, 387, 403, 438–439, 445, 446, 492
    ownership of YouTube by, 56
    Page Rank algorithm, 150, 570, 624
    Panda algorithm, 388, 389
    Penguin algorithm, 388
    prescription drug sales, 587
    privacy issues and, 525–527, 538–539, 541, 544, 552
    purchase of Nest by, 541
    search engine, 149, 150, 388, 624, 708, 712
    security and, 248, 253, 264, 265, 276
    service providers and, 340
    small businesses and, 47
    social networks and, 400, 410, 463, 494, 510, 541, 680, 681, 683, 686
    social search terms and, 151
    surveillance and, 126, 127, 245
    TPB and, 87
    unique URLs and, 62
    Web 2.0 and, 56
    widgets and, 156

Google AdMob, 403, 499, 501, 507

Google AdSense, 189, 386, 509

Google AdWords, 150, 386, 387, 507, 541, 575

Google Analytics, 202, 331, 426, 443, 475–476, 517

Google Android. *See* Android (Google)

Google Books Library Project, 561, 590–594

Google Buzz, 552

Google Checkout, 189

Google Chrome, 275, 276

Goggle Docs, service providers and, 340

Google DoubleClick, 395, 426, 445

Google Glass, 65, 96–97, 136

Google Gmail, 124, 340, 541
Google Maps, 403, 504, 505, 507, 509
 censorship and, 127
 mashups and, 214
 service providers and, 340
 surveillance and, 126
Google Music Manager, 337
Google News, 157
Google Now, 157
Google Places, 403
Google Play, 154, 337, 403, 637, 643, 662, 663
Google+ (Google Plus), 400, 410, 463, 494, 510, 541, 680, 683, 686
Google +1, 382, 389
Google Reader, 153
Google Search, 157
Google Sites, 186, 416
Google Sponsored Links, 387
Google Talk, 148
Google Wallet
 described, 292
 NFC and, 293, 299
 statistics, 288, 289
 Tap & Pay system, 300, 303
Goto (Overture), 150
governance. *See also* legislation
 described, 577
 issues overview, 530–531
 overview of, 122–124, 577–584
GPS (global positioning systems), 227, 264, 497, 502, 536, 539
 Foursquare and, 321
 location-based marketing and, 508, 509
 online marketing and, 393
Graham-Leach-Blilely Act. *See* Financial Modernization Act
Grainger. *See* W.W. Grainger
Grand Theft Auto, 665
graphical user interface. *See* GUI
Great Britain, 578, 786. *See also* European Union; United Kingdom
Great Depression, 732
Greece, TPB and, 88
Greenland, 88
Green Supply Chain Awards, 838
grey hats, described, 254

Grokster, 88
gross margin, 731–732
gross rating points, 434
GroupM (company), 88
Groupon, 299, 371, 403, 730
 described, 58
 Node.js and, 213
 payment systems and, 299–300
 RoR and, 214
groupware server, 200
Grozkster, 532
GT Nexus, 810, 812
gTLDs (general top-level domains), 139–140
Guardian, The, 543
Gucci, 407
GUI (graphical user interface), 138, 838
GWS (Global Wine & Spirits), 823

H

Hachette, 646, 647
hackers (hacking), 253–257. *See also* hacking
hacktivism, 254
Hadoop, 430–431
Hadopi (French law), 603, 656
Haiti, 263
H&M, 510
hardware
 e-commerce enablers and, 331
 industry, 77
 as a service, 111–113
hardware platforms
 choosing, 204
 demand size, 204–205
 described, 204
 right-sizing, 204–205, 207–208
 supply side, 207–208
Harley-Davidson, 175, 815
Harvard Business Review, 335
Harvard Business School, 574, 725
Harvard University, 591
hash digests, 270–272, 275
hash functions, 270, 272
hashtags, 83
 described, 477
 Pinterest and, 483

Hastings, Reed, 668
HathiTrust, 594
HauteLook, 419
HBO (Home Box Office), 653, 669–670
health care
    apps and, 64
    B2B e-commerce and, 790, 794
    cloud computing and, 112
    Internet2® project, 128
    online marketing and, 385, 393
    retail sales statistics, 77
    security and, 258
    service providers and, 340
    sustainability and, 806
Health Insurance Portability and Accountability Act.
  See HIPPA
Heartbleed bug, 238, 262
Heartland Payment Systems, 255
Hellman, Martin, 269
HENRYs (High Earnings, Not Yet Rich), 406–407
herd behavior, 701
Hertz, 133
Hewlett Packard. *See* HP
highway (toll) pricing, 583
Hilton Hyatt, 227
HIPPA (Health Insurance Portability and Account-
  ability Act), 286, 547
hit-and-run pricing, 75
Hitachi, 826
hits, 434, 435
hobby industry, 77
Hocking, Amanda, 638–639
Hollywood, 614, 653–657, 658–660, 668
    Akamai and, 163
home improvement industry, 77
Home Depot, 254, 256, 300, 433, 690
Homeaway, 772
Homekit (Apple), 136
Homeland Security Act, 285, 286, 543
Hon Hai Precision Industry Company, 805
HootSuite, 331
Hoover's, 621
horizontal marketplaces, 343
horizontal markets, 791, 818
horizontal portals, 338
horizontal scaling, 207

horizontal/general business model, 333
Horohorin, Vladislav ("BadB"), 240
hospitality industry, industry consortia and, 826
host computers (hosts), described, 98
HostGator, 331
hosting
    choices in, 186
    cost of, 191
    ISPS and, 191
    services, e-commerce enablers and, 331
    versus outsourcing, 188–189
Hostway, 331
hotel reservation systems. *See* reservation systems;
  travel industry
hotspots (Wi-Fi), 131, 132, 133
Hotwired, 66, 103
HouseTrip, 772
HP (Hewlett-Packard)
    cloud computing and, 111
    as a e-commerce enabler, 331
    GENI initiative and, 129
    KeyChain system, 813–814
    private industrial exchanges and, 827
    social network and, 692
    supply chain management and, 812–814
    video conferencing and, 156
    Web servers and, 146
HP Autonomy, 199
HSPA (W-CDMA), 132
HSPA +, 132
HTML (HyperText Markup Language), 68, 103, 560.
  See also HTML5
    ActiveX and, 213
    advent of, 138
    Appery.io and, 222
    blog and, 153
    CGI and, 212
    cookies and, 425
    described, 62, 99, 141
    dynamic page generation tools and, 198
    invention of, 103
    Java and, 212–213
    JavaScript and, 213
    JSP and, 213
    mobile Web sites and, 218–225
    Mosaic and, 138

overview of, 141–144
PHP and, 202
RWD tools and, 221
sample code, 141
scaling techniques and, 208
versions, 142
Web clients and, 147
Web servers and, 146, 194, 196
Weebly and, 189
widgets and, 214
wikis and, 154
HTML5, 224, 392, 747. *See also* HTML (HyperText Markup Language)
Canvas, 143
described, 65, 142
growth in the popularity of, 99
mobile apps and, 221, 222
online marketing and, 390
Orbitz and, 228
RWD tools and, 221
tracking files and, 426
HTTP (HyperText Transfer Protocol)
advent of, 138
described, 113
hypertext and, 139
security and, 262, 279
TCP/IP and, 106
URLS and, 108
versions, 113
Web servers and, 146, 196
hub-and-spoke systems, described, 791
Hubspot, 400, 480
Huffington, Arianna, 706
Huffington Post, 622, 631, 632, 636, 706
Huggies, 334
Hughes, 121
Hulu, 318, 583, 619–620
Human Rights First, 805
Hummingbird algorithm (Google), 388, 421
Hurricane Sandy, 418
hybrid apps, 144, 219
hybrid cloud, described, 112
hybrid pricing model, 439
HyperCard (Apple), 103
hyperlink(s). *See also* hypertext
dead, 197

described, 99
history of the Web and, 138
invention of, 103
hypertext. *See also* hyperlinks; URLs (Uniform Resource Locators)
described, 139
overview of, 139–141
HyperText Markup Language. *See* HTML
HyperText Transfer Protocol. *See* HTTP

I

IAB (Interactive Advertising Bureau), 123, 143, 390, 391, 392, 396
IANA (Internet Assigned Numbers Authority), 99, 122, 577
iBeacons. *See* Apple iBeacon
IBM (International Business Machines), 129, 199
B2B e-commerce and, 789, 794
Big Data and, 750
cloud computing and, 111
DB2, 428
desktop computers, invention of, 102
dynamic page generation tools and, 198
e-commerce/as a e-commerce enabler, 331
industry consortia and, 826
IoT and, 137
mainframe computers, 355
online marketing and, 368, 443
private industrial networks and, 827
social networks and, 688, 692
supply chain management and, 802
sustainability and, 806
Web servers, 194
IBM Digital Analytics, 331, 443, 474
IBM Global Services, 188
IBM WebSphere Commerce, 202
ICANN (Internet Corporation for Assigned Names and Numbers), 103, 104, 122, 139, 577, 586
Iceland, TPB and, 88
iControl, 137
IDC (company), 430
identity fraud
described, 258
phishing attacks and, 253
IDS (intrusion detection system), 281

IEEE 746.11 standard, 132

IEEE 746.11 a/b/g/n standard, 133

IEEE 746.11ac standard, 132, 133

IEEE 746.16 standard, 133, 134. *See also* WiMax

IESG (Internet Engineering Steering Group), 123

IETF (Internet Engineering Task Force), 122–123

IGF (Internet Governance Forum), 123

IHOP (company), 133

IIS (Microsoft Internet Information Server), 146, 195, 212

Ikea, 499

iKee.B worm, 263

Iliad (Homer), 249

ILS (Inventory Locator Service), 823–824

IM (instant messaging), 126, 148. *See also* SMS (Short Message Service) texting

IMAP (Internet Message Access Protocol), 113

IMG tags, 425

implementation, 191–192, 283, 832

impressions, 433, 434

Improving Critical Infrastructure Cybersecurity Executive Order, 286

IMPs (Interface Message Processors), 102

in-app ads, 493–494

in-app purchases, made by children, 490

Inbound Logistics, 352

inbound marketing, 400

income levels, 372, 406–408. *See also* demographic profiles

incubators, described, 327

independent exchanges, 818

India, 44, 47, 111, 115, 276, 367–368, 458–458, 587, 677, 743, 746

Indiegogo, 214, 327, 328

indirect goods, 798

Inditex, 797

Industrial Internet. *See* IoT (Internet of Things)

Industrial Internet Consortium, 137

industry consortia, 341, 343, 818, 824–826

industry convergence, 618–620

industry structure and dynamics, 344–347

industry value chain. *See* value chains

influencers, 400

information
    asymmetry, 50–51, 68
    density, 51–55, 345, 352, 423, 529
    goods, 412
    policy sets, 215
    requirements, identifying, 182–183
    rights, 530, 534–557
    value of stolen, 240–241

information privacy, 535. *See also* privacy

informed consent, 546

Infoseek, 66

initial public offerings. *See* IPOs

InMobi, 157, 367–369, 403

input fields, 143

insider attacks, 260–261

Instacart, 73

Instagram, 65, 463, 680, 682, 683, 685, 693
    B2B e-commerce and, 816–817
    described, 56

instant messaging. *See* IM

InstantService, 412

insurance services. *See* online insurance

integrity, described, 243, 244

Intel chips, 111, 137

intellectual property. *See also* copyrights; patents; trademarks
    protection, types of, 559
    rights, overview, 558–577

intelligent personal assistants, 156–157

interaction rate, 438, 472, 481, 487

interactivity, 345, 529
    described, 53, 55, 345
    differentiation and, 352
    as one of the eight features of e-commerce technology, 51–55
    online marketing and, 423
    tools, overview of, 211–214

IntercontinentalExchange, 823

interest-based advertising. *See* behavioral targeting

interest-based social network, 688, 692

intermediaries, 75

Interface Message Processors. *See* IMPs

Internal Revenue Service. *See* IRS

International Business Machines. *See* IBM

International Centre for Science in Drug Policy, 588

International Labor Organization (United Nations), 805

Internet
    access drones, 134–135

architecture of, 115–116, 124

audience, 370–380

Commercialization Phase, 100, 101, 103

communications, protecting, overview of, 266–267

costs, declining, 135–136

current limitations of, 124–128

current state of, 115–124

described, 49, 61, 98, 99, 101

evolution of, 100–101

evolution of corporate computing and, 81

features/services, 147–147

first/last mile of, 129–134

future, 135–137

governance overview of, 122–124

growth of, 61–65

history of, 61

hosts, described, 61–62

hourglass model of, 116

Innovation Phase, 100, 102

Institutionalization Phase, 100–103

key technology concepts, 101–110

Layer, described, 106

marketing technologies, 422–433

radio, 154

society, moral dimensions of, 530–531

size of, 61

statistics, 61–65, 80, 112, 161–162, 370–372

Systems Consortium, 61

technology background, 98–115

telephony, 155

"time," use of the term, 100

timeline, 102

traffic patterns, 370–374

usage scope, 371–372

"wired," limitations of, 124–125

Internet Assigned Numbers Authority. *See* IANA

Internet Association, 772

Internet Corporation for Assigned Names and Numbers. *See* ICANN

Internet Engineering Steering Group. *See* IESG

Internet Engineering Task Force. *See* IETF

Internet Exchange Points. *See* IXPs

Internet Explorer browser (Microsoft), 138–139, 213

Internet Governance Forum. *See* IGF

Internet Message Access Protocol. *See* IMAP

Internet of Things. *See* IoT

Internet Protocol. *See* IP

Internet Relay Chat. *See* IRC

Internet Research Task Force. *See* IRTF

Internet Retailer, 60, 143, 743

Internet Service Providers. *See* ISPs

Internet Society. *See* ISOC

Internet Tax Freedom Act, 579

Internet2® project, 103, 128, 129, 130

Internet video on demand (iVOD)

internetwork, use of the term, 99

Interpol, 587

interstitial ads, 391

intranet, 121–122

intrusion detection system. *See* IDS

intrusion prevention system. *See* IPS

Intuit Paytrust, 297

inventories, 183, 258

    B2B e-commerce and, 790, 794

    exchanges and, 823–824

    IPXs and, 830

    long tail marketing and, 420

    SDLC and, 186

    supply chain management and, 830

invoices, payment systems and, 288

I/O intensive, 205

IoT (Internet of Things), 99, 104, 134, 136–137, 788

IP (Internet Protocol). *See also* IP (Internet Protocol) addresses

    described, 106

    Internet2® project, 128

    security and, 278, 279

IP (Internet Protocol) addresses. *See also* IANA (Internet Assigned Numbers Authority)

    described, 106–108, 109

    Internet hosts and, 61

    online marketing and, 505

    resolving, 61–62

    security and, 279

    Web servers and, 146

IP spoofing. *See* spoofing

IP telephony, described, 155

iPad (Apple), 59, 159, 643

    Apple Siri and, 157

    BiznessApps and, 224

    client/server computing and, 111

online marketing and, 407
patents and, 566–568
payment systems, 301, 302
privacy issues and, 539
security and, 266
supply chain risk/ vulnerability and, 796–798
Wi-Fi and, 134
iPhone (Apple), 104, 508. *See also* m-commerce (mobile e-commerce)
advent of, 159
Apple Siri and, 157
B2B e-commerce and, 789
batteries, 797
biometrics and, 284
BiznessApps and, 224
cloud computing and, 265, 336, 337
eBay and, 712
encryption algorithms, 544
Flash and, 224
iOS, 111
labor practices and, 805
manufacture of, 790
Orbitz and, 228
patents and, 566–568
payment systems, 293, 300, 301
privacy issues and, 539, 544
security and, 263, 264, 266
supply chain management and, 797
synching, to automobile infotainment systems, 137
Wi-Fi and, 134
iPod (Apple)
Apple Siri and, 157
cloud computing and, 336
mobile apps and, 159
patents and, 566–568
podcasts and, 153
IPOs (initial public offerings), 72, 227, 369, 677, 678, 741, 776, 785
iProspect, 331
IPS (intrusion prevention system), 281
IPv4 (Internet Protocol version 4), 107
IPv6 (Internet Protocol version 6), 99, 104, 107, 136
Iran, 126, 577
Ireland, 88, 328, 459, 580, 582
IronPlanet, 823

IRC (Internet Relay Chat), 693
IRS (Internal Revenue Service), 249
IRTF (Internet Research Task Force), 123
ISOC (Internet Society), 104, 113, 123
iSoft Corporation, 829
ISPs (Internet Service Providers)
Akamai and, 163
bandwidth choices, 120
blogs and, 153
in China, 578
described, 118
FCC and, 583
the history of the Internet and, 104
hosting and, 191
IMAP and, 113
IXPs and, 118–120
legislation and, 562–563
Netflix and, 670
NOGs and, 123
overview of, 118–121
security and, 260, 278, 285
service levels, 120
spam and, 399
surveillance by, 126, 260
Web site maintenance and, 192
Israel, 296
iSuppli, 796–797
Italy, 88, 120, 288, 329, 568, 618, 777
iTunes. *See* Apple iTunes
iVillage, 334, 692
iVOD (Internet video on demand), 655–656
Ixiasoft, 199
IXPs (Internet Exchange Points), 118, 119–120, 123

J

Jabbar Internet Group, 719, 720
Jabong.com, 72, 73
Jackbox Games' You Don't Know Jack, 402
Jackson Hewitt, 471
Japan, 239, 408, 562,
earthquake, tsunami and Fukushima nuclear accident in, 795, 796, 803
InMobi in, 368
OpenTable in, 774, 777
payment systems in, 288–289

security and, 250
social networks in, 681
supply chains and, 795, 796, 803, 804
Jasmine Revolution, 125
Java
described, 212
mobile apps and, 158
online marketing and, 390
security and, 261
servlets, 213
smartphones and, 111
Java Database Connectivity. *See* JDBC
Java Server Pages. *See* JSP
Java Runtime Environment. *See* JRE
Java VM (Virtual Machine), 212
JavaScript, 212–213, 214
Appery.io and, 222
AWD and, 221
HTML5 and, 143
online marketing and, 390, 392
RoR and, 214
security and, 248
Javelin Strategy & Research, 288, 753
Jawbone Up, 136
JCPenny, 332, 389, 728
JDA Software, 331
JDBC (Java Database Connectivity), 198
Jeep, 397–398
jewelry industry, 77. *See also* luxury goods
Jobs, Steve, 143, 159, 590, 616, 645
JOBS (Jumpstart Our Business Startups) Act, 327, 329
Joomla, 199
Jordan, Jeff, 776
Joud Store, 721
Joyent, 188
JPMorgan Chase, 722, 753
jQuery Mobile, 222
JRE (Java Runtime Environment), 247
JSP (Java Server Pages), 198, 212–213
"juggernaut, taming the," 80–84
Jumia, 73
Juniper Networks, 125
Just Falafel, 457–459
just-in-time production, described, 802

Justice Department (United States), 249, 589, 590, 593, 645, 830

K

KAF, 721
Kahn, Bob, 102
Kaspersky, Eugene, 235
Kaspersky Labs, 235, 261, 264
Kayak, 228
Kazaa, 88, 346
Kbps (kilobits per second), 117
Kelinrock, Leonard, 105
Kellog, 396
Kelly v. Arriba Soft, 561
key (cipher), described, 267
keyloggers, 253
Keynote, 331
keywording, 573, 575
keywords, 210. *See also* metatags
advertising, 387
long tail marketing and, 421
online marketing and, 486
KFC (Kentucky Fried Chicken), 690
Kickstarter, 327, 328, 329
killer apps, 62, 102
kilobits, 117
kilobits per second. *See* Kbps
Kindle e-reader. *See* Amazon Kindle
Klein, Ezra, 635
Kleiner Perkins Caufield & Byers, 367
Kleinrock, Leonard, 102
Kmart, 292
Knowledge Graph (Google), 388
Kodak, 355
Korea. *See* North Korea, South Korea
Kozmo, 722
Kraft app, 159–160
Kureha, 797
KwikChex, 763

L

labor practices, 797, 804–805, 830. *See also* work conditions
Lady Gaga, 419

Lamoda.ru, 72

LAMP, 213, 214

Land Rover, 500–501

Land's End, 484, 485, 741, 744–745

Landweber, Lawrence, 102

LANs (local area networks), 67, 81, 102, 106

LANXESS, 833

Lapertosa, 573–574

laptops, increased sales of, 131

latency, 124, 135, 162

Latin America, 288, 368, 606, 677, 681, 804

Law of One Price, 413

Lawrence, Jennifer, 266

Layar, 95–97

Layton, Thomas, 776

Lazada, 73

lead generation marketing, 400

lean production, described, 802

least effort, path requiring the, 52

legacy computer systems, 800–801

legal decisions (U.S)

    Alice Corporation v. CLS Bank International, 569

    Bernina of America, Inc. v. Fashion Fabrics Int'l, Inc., 574

    Bilski et al v. Kappos, 569

    Brown Bag Software v. Symantec Corp., 560

    Eldred v. Ashcroft, 559–560

    Field v. Google, Inc., 561

    Ford Motor Co. v. Lapertosa, 573–574

    Kelly v. Arriba Soft, 561

    Metro-Goldwyn-Mayer Studios v. Grokster, et. al., 88, 532

    National Association of the Deaf, et al., v. Netflix, Inc., 217

    Nissan Motor Co., Ltd. v. Nissan Computer Corp, 574–575

    Paine Webber Inc. v. Fortuny, 574

    Perfect 10, In. v. Amazon.com, Inc. et. al., 561

    Playboy Enterprises, Inc. v. Global Site Designs, Inc., 574

    Playboy Enterprises, Inc. v. Netscape Communications, Inc., 575

    State Street Bank & Trust v. Signature Financial Group, Inc., 569

    Ticketmaster Corp. v. Tickets.com, 575–576

    Washington Post, et al. v. Total News, Inc., 576

legislation (U.S.), 79, 282–287

    Age Discrimination in Employment Act (ADEA), 690

    Americans with Disabilities Act (ADA), 216, 217

    Anticybersquatting Consumer Protection Act (ACPA), 572, 572–573, 574

    Broadband Data Improvement Act, 104

    Cable Communications Policy Act, 547

    California Online Privacy Protection Act, 548

    CAN-SPAM Act, 286, 398–399

    Child Pornography Prevention Act, 585

    Children's Internet Protection Act (CIPA), 585–586

    Children's Online Privacy Protection Act (COPPA), 489–490, 547–549, 555, 586

    Children's Online Protection Act (COPA), 585

    Civil Rights Act, 690

    Communications Assistance for Law Enforcement Act (CALEA), 260, 543

    Communications Decency Act (CDA), 585

    Computer Fraud and Abuse Act, 286

    Computer Matching and Privacy Protection Act, 547

    Computer Security Act, 547

    Computer Security Enhancement Act, 286

    Computer Software Copyright Act, 560

    Consumer Location Privacy Protection Act, 539

    Copyright Act, 592, 615

    Copyright Term Extension Act (CTEA), 559–560

    Cyber Security Enhancement Act, 543

    Cyberspace Electronic Security Act, 286

    Digital Millennium Copyright Act (DMCA), 561–564

    Domain Names Act, 586

    Driver's Privacy Protection Act, 547

    E-Government Act, 547

    Electronic Communications Privacy Act, 286, 542, 544, 547

    Email Privacy Act, 544

    Electronic Signatures in Global and National Commerce Act (E-Sign Law), 257, 286

    Fair Credit Reporting Act, 547

    Family Educational Rights and Privacy Act, 547

    Federal Trademark Dilution Act (FTDA), 571

    Financial Modernization Act (Gramm-Leach-

Bliley Act), 286

FISA Amendments Reauthorization Act, 260

Freedom of Information Act, 547

Genetic Information Nondiscrimination Act (GINA), 690, 691

Health Insurance Portability and Accountability Act (HIPPA), 286, 547

Homeland Security Act, 285, 286, 543

Internet Tax Freedom Act, 579

JOBS (Jumpstart Our Business Startups) Act, 327, 329

National Information Infrastructure Protection Act, 286

Prevent All Cigarette Trafficking Act, 589

Privacy Act, 547

Privacy Protection Act, 547

Rehabilitation Act, 217

Right to Financial Privacy Act, 547

Trademark Act, 571

21st Century Communications and Video Accessibility Act (CVAA), 216, 217

Unlawful Internet Gambling Enforcement Act, 589

U.S. SAFE WEB Act, 286

USA PATRIOT Act, 260, 285, 286, 543, 578

Video Privacy Protection Act, 547

Wire Act, 589

Lego, 815

Leighton, Tom, 162

Lenovo, 331

Level 3 Communications, 118, 163

leverage, 325

Levi's, 806

Lewin, Daniel, 162

LG Electronics, 480

LG (company), 136, 157, 331, 368

liability, 257, 532, 733

Liberty Global, 121

libraries, 591–592

Library of Congress, 431

licensing agreements, 320

Licklider, J. C. R., 102

Likes. *See* Facebook Likes

LillianVernon, 333

Lilly, 393

Limelight, 331

Limelight Networks, 163

Linden Dollars, 294

Linden Lab, 294

LINE, 681

link farms. *See* spam (junk) Web sites

link visitors, 633

links. *See* hyperlinks

link-side servers, 199, 200

LinkedIn, 680, 688, 767–768

business models and, 333, 334

community-building tools, 332–334

freemium strategy and, 358, 359, 687

market dominance of, 463

native apps and, 144

Node.js and, 213

security and, 260

statistics, 152, 683, 686, 687, 693

linking, 573, 575–576. *See also* hyperlinks

Linux

mobile, cross-platform apps and, 222

open source browsers for, 147

security and, 261, 262, 281

smartphones and, 111

Web clients and, 147

Web server software and, 194

liquidity, 343, 695, 696, 697, 823, 825

list server, 200

listserv, 151

Live Chat, 331

LiveJournal, 153

LivePerson, 331, 412

LivingSocial, 371, 403, 730

L.L. Bean, 78, 353, 741, 744–745

Akamai and, 163

business models and, 319, 322, 333

local advertising. *See* location-based marketing

local area networks. *See* LANS

local e-commerce, 47, 58, 60, 61, 211

local mobile marketing. *See* location-based marketing

local marketing. *See* location-based marketing

location-based marketing, 401–402.

attractiveness of, 509

growth of, 504–506

introduction to, 460–462

overview, 456–523

platforms, 506–507
results, measuring, 512
technologies, 507–509
tools, 509–511
location-based services, 504
logical design, described, 184
logistics management, described, 801
long tail marketing, 419–421
long-term sourcing, 818
"look and feel" copyrights, 560
Lord & Taylor, 296, 480
Lorentzon, Martin, 603
loser's lament, 701
L'Oreal, 396
Lotus Notes, 815
Louis Dreyfus (company), 826
loyalty, 434, 435
LTE (Long-Term Evolution), 132
Lufthansa, 221
LulzSec hacktivist group
Lundstrom, Carl, 88
luxury goods, 320, 406–409, 748
LVMH, 406
Lyft, 339, 769

M

Ma, Jack, 785–786
Macintosh (Apple), 103, 138
cloud computing and, 336, 337
open source browsers for, 147
security and, 261, 262, 266
video conferencing and, 156
Web clients and, 147
macro viruses, examples, 251
Macy's, 78, 299, 302, 511, 727, 743–744
madware, 263
MAEs (Metropolitan Area Exchanges), 118
magazine(s)
aggregators, 638–647
digital newstands and, 639–640
tablets and, 633–638
Magento, 331, 203
Magzter, 640
mail servers, 147, 200, 260, 280
MailChimp, 331, 359

Mailholt, Danielle, 690
mainframe computers, 61, 81, 355, 100, 110
maintenance and repair operations. *See* MRO
Maktoob, 719
Malaysia, 88, 157, 368
malicious code. *See* malware
malware
described, 247
IoT and, 137
overview of, 247–250
smartphones and, 263, 264–265
statistics, 239
"man in the middle" attacks, 296
management team, 326–327
management policies, 282–287
manufacturer-direct firms, 333, 745–747
many-to-many model of mass communication, 55
MapMyDogWalk app, 393
Maquilla Solidarity Network, 805
marginal costs, 413–414
marginal revenue, 414
Marhely, Daniel, 605
market
creator business model, 333, 339–340
entry costs, described, 53
liquidity, 343
middlemen, 69
opportunity, 322, 323, 326
segmentation, 198
size, 52
strategy, 325, 326
marketing (offline). *See also* advertising; online marketing
managers, 325
prior to e-commerce, 50–51
marketplace
characterizing, 175–176
described, 52
location-based marketing and, 511–512
management, e-commerce enablers and, 331
software training market and, 322, 323
ubiquity and, 55
Marketplace Fairness Act. *See* MFA
marketspace, 52, 55, 68, 322
markup languages, 141–147. *See also* HTML; XML
markup tags, 141–142, 145

Marriott, 227

mashups, described, 214

mass communication models, 55

MasterCard, 298–299, 689

MasterCard MasterPass, 292

MasterCard PayPass, 293

Mattel, business models and, 333

Mbps (megabits per second), 105, 117

McAfee, 235, 331, 281

McDonald's, 133, 299, 689–690

MCI, 103

McKesson, 806

m-commerce (mobile e-commerce). *See also* mobile
  marketing
    business models, 330
    collaborative commerce and, 815–816
    current state of, 488–495
    described, 58, 59
    growth of, 59, 491
    growth in mobile Internet access and, 63
    hardware platforms, e-commerce enablers and,
     331
    revenue by device, 494
    statistics, 59, 61
    ubiquity and, 52
    in United Kingdom, 47, 59

MCX (Merchant Customer Exchange), 303–304

MD4 hash function, 270

MD5 hash function, 270

media convergence, 617–620

media industry structure, 616–617

Media Player (Windows), 151

Media Rating Council, 396

MeetMe, 683

Meetup, 678, 683

mega data breaches, 240

megabit, 117

megabits per second. *See* Mbps

Megaupload, 657

Melissa, 251

menu costs, described, 51

Mercedes Benz, 407

Mercedes Reporter, 407

merchant accounts, described, 290

merchant server software packages (e-commerce
  software platforms), 201–204

"mesh" (sharing economy) business model, 57

message integrity, 267, 270, 277

MessageMe, 148

Metacafe, steaming media and, 151

Metaio, 97

metatagging, 573, 574–575

metatags, 210

Metcalfe, Bob, 102

Metcalfe's Law, 69

metered subscriptions, 629

Metropolitan Area Exchanges. *See* MAEs

Metro-Goldwyn-Mayer Studios v. Grokster, et. al., 88,
  532

Mexico, 277, 581, 587, 677, 774, 777, 830

Michelin, 833

Microsoft. *See also* ASP; Bing; MSN (Microsoft
  Network)
    AOL and, 706
    B2B e-commerce and, 794
    bundling of software by, 417
    CANs and, 118
    cloud computing and, 112, 188
    as a e-commerce enabler, 331
    Foursquare and, 320
    the history of the Web and, 138–139
    IoT and, 137
    privacy issues and, 545
    private industrial networks and, 827
    security and, 250, 253, 261, 269, 276, 281
    spam and, 399
    surveillance and, 125, 127, 245

Microsoft ActiveX, 213

Microsoft adCenter, 387

Microsoft Cortana, 157

Microsoft Expression Web, 142

Microsoft Internet Explorer browser, 138–139, 213

Microsoft Internet Information Server (IIS). *See* IIS

Microsoft Office, 355, 417

Microsoft .NET framework, 212

Microsoft SQL Server, 248, 737

Microsoft Visual Studio, 186

Microsoft Windows, 69, 108, 159
    ASP and, 212
    the history of the Web and, 138
    IIS and, 195
    open source browsers for, 147

Ping and, 114
security and, 247, 250, 276, 281
Web clients and, 147
Microsoft Windows Live, 112
Microsoft Windows Mobile, 111, 222
Microsoft Windows Phone, 143, 158, 222, 568
Microsoft Windows Vista, 108
Microsoft Xbox, 664, 666
middlemen, 339
Middleware Services layer, 116
milestones, developing, 179
military operations, 163. *See also* cyberwar
Military.com, 692
Mindshare, 500
minicomputers, 81
Minitel, 66
Miramax, 706
Mirror Image Internet, 163
mission statement, 174
MIT (Massachusetts Institute of Technology), 102, 162
Mitnick, Kevin, 252
mixed mode apps, 144
Mixi, 681
MLB (Major League Baseball), 248
MMAs (malicious mobile apps), 263
MMTG Labs, 368
mobile advertising, 64, 198–199, 367–369, 402–403. *See also* mobile marketing
mobile apps, 157–158. *See also* mobile devices; native apps
    building, 218–225
    cost of, 222–225
    cross-platform tools for, 222
    described, 218
    developing, 218–225
    development, platforms, 158
    ecosystem, 159–160
    Financial Times, 171–173
    major trends, 47
    marketplaces, 158–159
    native, 158
    online marketing and, 403
    online real estate services and, 758
    Orbitz Worldwide and, 226–229
    overview of, 157–160

performance of, 222–225
platforms, 158
statistics, 157–158, 159–150
technology trends and, 47
mobile browsers, 64, 157–158, 223, 469
mobile devices. *See also* mobile apps; m-commerce; mobile marketing
    features, 496–498
    how people actually use, 492–493
mobile e-commerce. *See* m-commerce
mobile first design, 221
mobile local marketing. *See* location-based marketing
mobile marketing, 402–403. *See also* mobile devices
    campaigns, selected, 499
    campaigns, starting, 499–502
    described, 382
    effect of the multi-screen environment on, 495
    features, 495–498
    firms, by revenue, 496–497
    introduction to, 460–462
    optimizing, 475–476
    overview, 456–523
    results, measuring, 503–503
    tools, 498–499
mobile payment systems, 293, 299–304
mobile platform(s)
    described, 62
    growth of, 61–65
    privacy issues and, 539–540
    security and, 262–263
mobile Web sites. *See also* Web sites
    cost of, 222–225
    described, 218
    design considerations, 220–385
    developing, 218–225
    performance of, 222–225
Mofuse, 222, 224
monetization features, 189
Mongolia, 797
monopolies, 69, 103, 111
Monsoon Commerce, 331
Monster, 333, 722, 765, 766, 767, 768
MoPub, 403, 499
Morgan Chase, 299
Morse, Samuel F. B., 569

Morse code, 569

mortgage services, 749

Mosaic browser, 103, 138, 359. *See also* browsers

MoPub (Twitter), 403, 499

MoSynch, 222

Motion Picture Association of America, *See* MPPA

Motley Fool, 334

MOTO (mail order/telephone order) sales, 289, 579, 724–725

Motorola, 136

Mouchawar, Ronaldo, 721

Movable Type, 153

movie industry. *See also* entertainment industry; Hollywood; Netflix
  business models and, 334–335
  industry, 653–657
  piracy and, 656

Mozilla, 147

Mozilla Firesheep, 277

MP3 files, 153, 336

MPPA (Motion Picture Association of America), 564

MRAID (mobile rich media and interface definitions), 392

MRO (maintenance, repair, and operations) supplies, 342, 350, 353, 798, 819, 820, 838

MSN (Microsoft Network), 75. *See also* portals
  Careerbuilder and, 766
  customization of, 412
  MSN Money, 755
  online entertainment distribution and, 649
  portal business model and, 333, 335, 702, 703, 704
  statistics, 683, 686, 702, 703, 704
  widgets, 156

Mt. Gox exchange, 296

multi-channel marketing, 404–405

multi-device platforms, 495

multi-tier architecture, 193, 194

multi-tier supply chains, 799–800

music industry
  business models and, 318, 324, 334, 336–337, 357–360
  changes in, 657–664
  cloud computing and, 336–337
  competitive advantage and, 324
  DRM and, 615–616

freemium strategy and, 357–360
  legislation and, 562–564
  long tail marketing and, 421
  network architecture limitations and, 124
  pricing and, 419
  revenues, 657–658
  sales statistics, 77
  services, overview of, 154–155

mutually assured destruction. *See* MAD

Myanmar, 214

Mydoom, 251

MyPoints, 319, 322

Myspace, 334, 683, 686

N

NAI (Network Advertising Initiative), 427, 555

Name Your Own Price auction (Priceline), 697, 698

NAND flash memory, 797, 803

NAPs (Network Access Points), 118

Napster, 346, 562, 661

narcotics trade, 587

narrowband, 120, 122

NAS, 721

Naspers, 720

National Association of Realtors, 758

National Association of the Deaf, et al., v. Netflix, Inc., 217

National Center for Supercomputing Applications. *See* NCSA

National Consumers League, 805

National Cybersecurity and Communications Integration Center. *See* NCCIC

National Cyber-Forensics & Training Alliance. *See* NCFTA

National Domestic Communications Assistance Center. *See* NDCAC

National Endowment for the Arts. *See* NEA

National Federation of the Blind. *See* NFB

National Information Infrastructure Protection Act, 286

National Infrastructure Protection Center. *See* NIPC

National Labor Relations Board. *See* NLRB

National Public Radio. *See* NPR

National Security Agency. *See* NSA

National Science Foundation. *See* NSF

National Telecommunications and Information Administration. *See* NTIA

native advertising, 371, 393–394

native app(s), 158, 143, 144, 218–225. *See also* mobile apps

NaturallyCurly, 194, 692

navigation, 209, 210

Nazi memorabilia, 127

NBCUniversal, 155

NCCIC (National Cybersecurity and Communications Integration Center), 285

NCFTA (National Cyber-Forensics & Training Alliance), 399

NCSA (National Center for Supercomputing Applications), 103, 138

NDCAC (National Domestic Communications Assistance Center), 127

NDN syndication service, 613

NDOT Technologies, 721

near field communication. *See* NFC

neighborhood effects, 373–374

Nelson, Ted, 138

Nest Labs, 136, 541

"net bombs," 161

net margin, 732

Net marketplaces. *See also* exchanges
B2B e-commerce and, 788
characteristics of, 817
described, 792
Elemica and, 836–837
evolution of, 791
goals of, 828
overview of, 817–826
types of, 818–826

net neutrality, 582–584

net value, 620–621

Net-a-Porter, 406, 407

Netcraft, 194, 214

Netflix, 161, 217, 583–584, 655, 658–659
business models and, 318
case study, 667–670
competition and, 660
market leadership of, 651
media convergence and, 619–620
ranked by online sales, 78
recommender system, 421

Netherlands, 567, 568, 606

Netscape Corporation, 103, 138–139, 359, 575

Netscape Navigator, 138

Netsky.P, 251

NetSuite, 331, 203

network(s). *See also* Internet; social networks; World Wide Web
100-Gbps, 128, 129
effects, 69, 809
externalities, 53, 338
keyword advertising (context advertising), 387
notification, described, 60, 401

Network Access Points. *See* NAPs

Network Advertising Initiative. *See* NAI

Network Interface Layer, 106

Network Perfect Commerce, 341

Network Service Providers. *See* NSPs

Network Solutions, 331, 103, 572

Network Technology Substrate layer, 116

Neustar, 259

New York Stock Exchange, 339. *See also* stock markets

New York Times, 393, 412, 415–416
archived content charges, 629
business models and, 625
Test (Perfect Information Rule), 534
versioning and, 416

New York University, 118

New Zealand, 134, 328, 564

news server, 200

News Corp, 155

Newegg, 570, 734

NeweggBusiness, 820

newspaper(s). *See also specific newspapers*
ads, 440
audience size and growth, 626–627
business models and, 333, 334–335, 621–622
digital ad revenue and, 627–628
evolution of, 623–626
framing and, 576
global reach and, 52
online marketing and, 393, 412, 440–441
overview, 621–633
profits and, 620
release of NSA documents to, 543
revenue models, 629–630

security and, 262

time spend on, statistics for, 612

Web presence of, overview of, 171–174

Next Issue Media, 640

NFC (near field communication) chips, 288, 293, 299–301, 303, 510

niche markets, 355, 210, 493

niche products, 419, 421

Nielsen, 436

Nigerian letter scam, 252–253

Nike, 411, 804, 806, 827

Nike+, 136

9flats, 771-772

Ning, 359–360

Ninja Sphere, 328

NIPC (National Infrastructure Protection Center)

Nissan, Uzi, 574–575

Nissan Motor Co., Ltd. v. Nissan Computer Corp, 574–575

NLRB (National Labor Relations Board), 830

No Free Lunch principle, 534

Node.js, 213

NOGs (Internet Network Operators Groups), 123

Nokia, 263, 827

nonrepudiation, 243, 244, 267

Nordstrom, 748

North Korea, 577

Northwest Airlines, 226

Norway, 288, 328

Notepad (Microsoft), 142

Nowness Web site, 406

NPR (National Public Radio), 262

NSA (National Security Agency), 535–536

DES and, 269

FISA and, 260

ISPs and, 578

PRISM program, 127, 269, 543

smartphones and, 265, 544

Snowden case and, 245–246, 260, 287, 543

terrorism and, 245–246

XKeyscore, 127, 260

NSF (National Science Foundation), 100, 103, 104. *See also* GENI initiative

NSFNET, 100, 103

NSPs (Network Service Providers), 117

NTIA (National Telecommunications and Informa-tion Administration), 122, 128

NTT Communications (Verio), 118

Nymex, 251

O

Obama, Barack, 104, 589

Obama administration, 286, 543, 553

Objective-C (programming language), 158

OBM Digital Analytics, 331

OC-3 standard, 131

OC-12 standard, 131

OC-48 standard, 131

OC-192 standard, 131

Occupy Wall Street, 125

Oculus Rift, 97, 329

Oculus VR, 96–97

ODBC (Open Database Connectivity), 198

OdeigO, 761

OECD (Organization for Economic Cooperation and Development), 287, 579

Oerting, Troels, 237

Office (Microsoft). *See* Microsoft Office

office equipment industry, 77

Office Depot, 78, 727

Office of Cybersecurity and Communications. *See* CS&C

OfficeMax, 78, 499, 727

offline marketing, 382, 404–405. *See also* advertising

offline service sector, 749–752

OKCupid, 548

OLAP (online analytical processing), 432

Oldandsold, 695

Omidyar, Pierre, 103, 325, 630–631, 710

omni-channel firms, 35–43, 726, 727, 729, 743–744

OmniUpdate, 199

1&1 (company), 331

one-click purchasing, 565

one-to-one marketing, 405–411. *See also* personalization

one-way irreversible mathematical function, 269–270

online advertising. *See also* online marketing

apps and, 64–65

concepts, 366–454

costs of, 439–440

described, 384–385
effectiveness of, 437–439
Facebook and, 82–83
formats, 498–499
the history of e-commerce and, 68
newspapers and, 627–628
payment systems and, 300
search engines and, 150, 386–390
statistics, 384–385
steaming media and, 151
strategies, 381–421
streaming video ads, 155
targeting, 385–386
tolerance for, 613–615
tools, 384–403
online analytical processing. See OLAP.
online auctions, 694–702. *See also* eBay; Priceline
    as business model, 339, 697
    as pricing mechanism, 418
    benefits and costs of, 695–697
    B2B e-commerce and, 787
    C2C e-commerce and, 58–59
    consumer-to-consumer (C2C) auctions, 694
    consumer trust in, 701
    factors to consider when choosing, 699–700
    fraud/abuse in, 701–702
    leading auction sites, 695
    methods of reducing risk, 702
    Name Your Own Price (Priceline)
    patent on, 570
    prices in, 700–701
    types/examples of, 697–698
    when to use (and for what), 698–700
online banking, 66, 753–754. *See also* financial services
online brokerages, 753–754. *See also* financial services
online career services, 765–769
online catalog(s)
    described, 200
    servers and, 200–201
    software, 202
online content
    revenue, 610–611
    audience/market, 609–615
    consumption, 612–613

    overview, 602–675
    profits, 620–621
    trends, 607–608
    revenue models, 611
online entertainment industry, 607, 609. *See also* entertainment industry
    audience size and growth, 650
    five major players in, 648
    overview, 648–670
online financial services, 752–759
online forum, 151
online gambling, 126, 586–587
online games, 318, 402–403, 610, 612, 664–666
online insurance services, 756–757
online lending services, 755–756
online marketing. *See also* social marketing; mobile marketing; online advertising
    automation, 431–433
    behavioral approaches and, 84–85
    browsers versus buyers and, 378–379
    collaborative commerce and, 831, 832
    concepts, 366–454
    costs and benefits of, 433–443
    history of e-commerce and, 67
    Internet technologies for, 422–433
    metrics, 433–437
    multi-channel, 404–405
    platforms, 462
    purchasing decisions and, 375–378
    results, measuring, 441–443
    statistics, 371
    strategies, 381–421
    technology, unique features of, 423
    tools, 384–403
online media. *See* online content
online mortgage services, 755–756, 757
Online Privacy Alliance. *See* OPA
online real estate services, 757–759
online recruitment. *See* online career services
online retail sector
    common themes in, 747–749
    firms, analyzing the viability of, 730–733
    growth of, 726–727
    overview, 718–731
    present state of, 726–730
    what's new in, 723

vision, 725–726
online service sector, 718–640, 749–752
online social network, 681. *See also* social networks
online stored value payment system, 291–292. *See also* PayPal
online video. *See also* YouTube
    business models and, 334–335
    e-commerce enablers and, 331
    overview, 651–653
    statistics, 161
    time spent watching, statistics for, 612
    top Web sites for, 614
ooVoo (company), 156
OPA (Online Privacy Alliance), 555, 556
"open architecture" networking, 102
Open Automotive Alliance, 136
Open Book Alliance, 592
Open Database Connectivity. *See* ODBC
Open Interconnect Consortium, 137
open rate, 434, 436
open source software, 147, 202
Open Web Analytics, 202
openness, era of, 82
OpenSSL encryption, 262
OpenTable, 157, 296, 774–778
OpenText, 199
OpenCMS, 199
operating margin, 732
operations management scientists, 84
opportunism, 380
Optimum Online, 132
Optimum WiFi, 132
opt-in model, 397, 398, 399, 546
opt-out model, 398, 546, 553
Opus Fresh, 328
Oracle, 112, 199
    B2B e-commerce and, 789
    dynamic page generation tools and, 198
    as a e-commerce enabler, 331
    Elemica and, 838
    security and, 247, 261
    supply chain management and, 802
    sustainability and, 806
Oracle ATG Web Commerce, 202
Orange, 120
Orbitz Worldwide, 226–229, 333, 761, 762

order fulfillment, 68, 331
order management, 331, 801
order processing, 186
organic search, 387
organizational development, 325, 326
Organization for Economic Cooperation and Development. *See* OECD
Orkut, 681
Orphan Works Project, 594
osCommerce , 202
OTT (over-the-top) entertainment services, 652
Our Common Future report (WCED), 805–806
outsourcing, 181, 184–186, 187–188, 191
Oxygen, 692
Overlay Media, 368
Overstock, 296
Overture, 150
Oyster, 318

P

P&G (Procter & Gamble), 341, 447, 746, 692, 814, 816, 827
P2P (peer-to-peer) networks, 87, 89, 358, 532, 615
PaaS (Platform as a Service), 342, 834
packet(s)
    described, 101
    filters, 279
    the history of the Internet and, 102
    latency and, 135
    routers and, 105
    surveillance by, 126
Packet InterNet Groper. *See* Ping
packet switching, 108
    described, 101, 105, 106
    the history of the Internet and, 102, 104
    overview of, 101–106
page
    delivery, 193
    generation speed, 193
    load times, 143
    views, described, 434, 435
Page, Larry, 150, 526, 527
Page Source command, 141
PageRank algorithm (Google), 150, 389
paid inclusion (sponsored link), 387

Paine Webber Inc. v. Fortuny, 574

Pakistan, 72, 125, 606

Panda Security, 247–248, 249

Pandora, 318, 337, 357–359, 403, 416, 620, 648, 649

PaperThin, 199

Pareto principle, 420

passwords
    data breaches and, 254
    cloud services and, 266
    Heartbleed hug and, 262
    phishing and, 252–253
    theft of, by a Russian crime ring, 257

Patch Properties, 403

patents, 564–570, 647

pay-as-you-go strategy, 112

pay-as-you-grow strategy, 112

Payleven, 73

payment service providers (payment gateways), 291

payment systems. *See also* credit card payment
  systems; PayPal; transactions
    alternative online, 291–293
    e-commerce enablers and, 331
    limitations of, 291
    major trends in, 288
    mobile, 293
    mobile, 299–304
    overview of, 287–294
    statistics, 288, 288–289
    Target and, 255–256

PayPal
    cigarette merchants and, 589
    described, 291–292
    eBay and, 697, 711–712
    e-commerce enabler, 331
    mobile payments and, 293, 299–303, 499, 711,
      712
    security and, 241, 252, 253
    statistics, 288, 289, 291–292, 303, 711
    Weebly and, 189

PayPal Here, 711

payroll systems, 192

Paytrust (Intuit), 297

paywall, 629

PCAST (President's Council of Advisors on Science
  and Technology), 544

PCs (personal computers)

apps and, 64
    client/server computing and, 110, 111
    cloud computing and, 336, 337
    evolution of corporate computing and, 81
    the history of e-commerce and, 67
    the history of the Web and, 138
    industry, disruption of, 355
    Intel chips and, 111
    invention of, 102
    Microsoft Office and, 355
    online marketing and, 371
    origins of e-commerce and, 66
    scaling techniques and, 208
    security and, 250, 261, 263
    statistics, 99, 110, 111
    technology trends and, 47

PDF (Portable Document Format), 162, 248, 615

Peapod, 340

peer-to-peer networks. *See* P2P networks

Penguin, 388

penny (bidding fee) auction, 698

Pepsico, 386

Perfect Commerce, 822

perfect competition model, 75

perfect markets, 74, 324–324

Perfect 10, In. v. Amazon.com, Inc. et. al., 561

Perl, 212

personal computers. *See* PCs

personal profiles, 541

personalization. *See also* customization
    described, 54, 55, 215, 345
    ethical, social and political implications of, 529
    HTML5 and, 144
    impact on business environment, 345, 352, 353
    online marketing and, 405, 411, 423, 438, 541
    online retailing and services and, 728, 752, 758
    SDLC and, 183
    tools for, 215
    unique feature of e-commerce technology and,
      54, 55
    value proposition and, 317

personally identifiable information. *See* PII

Peru, 88

Petsmart, 175

Pew Research Center, 372, 539

Pez dispensers, 325

PGP (Pretty Good Privacy), 275

pharmaceutical industry, 66

pharming, described, 258–259

Philatelicphantasies, 695

Phillips, 393

phishing, 240, 249, 252–253, 258, 262, 266, 399

PHP, 202, 213–214

physical design, 184

Pictela, 706

piggyback strategies, 414, 416

PII (personally identifiable information), 536–537, 548, 553–552

PIN codes, 253, 255, 284, 303

Ping (Packet InterNet Groper), 108, 114

Pinterest, 333, 680

    apps, 483

    community-building tools, 334

    described, 152, 481–488, 682

    future of, 79

    hashtags, 483

    magazines and, 638

    market dominance of, 463

    market strategy and, 325

    marketing tools, 482–484

    online marketing and, 481–488

    Pin It button, 483, 486, 487

    pins, 483

    Promoted Pins, 484

    statistics, 682, 686, 687, 693

    target audience of, 175

    widgets, 214, 483

piracy, 86–89, 656

Pirate Bay. *See* TPB (The Pirate Bay)

Piwik, 202

PKI (public key infrastructure), 274–276

Platform as a Service. *See* PaaS

Playboy Enterprises, Inc. v. Global Site Designs, Inc., 574

Playboy Enterprises, Inc. v. Netscape Communications, Inc., 575

plug-ins, 142, 143, 144, 151, 186, 214, 261, 275, 467

PocketGear, 403

podcasts, described, 153

PointRoll, 438

Poland, 263, 604, 606

political issues. *See also* governance; legislation

    organizing, model for, 529–531

    overview, 524–600

political movements, 125, 214

polymorphic malware, 240

Polyvore, 683

Ponemon Institute, 239, 261

POP (Post Office Protocol 3), 113

pop-up/under ads, 209, 250, 263, 386, 391, 398

pop-up blocking, 147, 557

pornography, 79, 126, 127, 398, 531, 578, 585–586

Porsche, 480

Portable Document Format. *See* PDF

portal(s). *See also* specific portals

    business model, described, 333, 708–709

    described, 335

    enterprise, 703–704

    financial, 755

    general-purpose, 704, 707–708

    growth/evolution of, 703–704

    overview of, 335–338, 702–709

    revenue sources, 709

    top, 338, 713

    vertical market, 704, 707–708

post-aggregation services, 335

Post Office Protocol. *See* POP

Postal Service (United States), 275

potentially unwanted programs. *See* PUPs

PowerReviews, 331

Powersourceonline, 818, 823

practice network, 688, 692

predictive marketing, 750–751

prescription drugs, 586–588

President's Council of Advisors on Science and Technology. *See* PCAST

Pretty Good Privacy. *See* PGP

Prevent All Cigarette Trafficking Act, 589

Priceline

    business model and, 333, 339

    Name Your Own Price auctions and, 570, 761, 698, 699

    OpenTable and, 778

    patents and, 570

    travel industry and, 226, 228, 323, 475, 761

price(s); pricing

    algorithms, 418

    auctions and, 694, 695, 696, 699, 700–701, 702

B2B e-commerce and, 792, 794
book publishing and, 645
described, 413
discrimination, 414
discovery, 53, 695
discrimination, 54, 199, 385, 414, 700
dispersion, 75
dynamic, 51, 417–419, 694, 792
exchanges and, 822–824
fixed, 414, 417, 696, 699, 700, 711, 817
highway (toll), 583
the history of e-commerce and, 68, 69
Net marketplaces and, 792
online advertising, 439–440
online marketing and, 413–419
purchasing decisions and, 375–378
strategies, 413–419
transparency, 54, 413, 696, 794
uniform, 698, 700
print advertising, 396
print media, 178–179, 439, 623–625
printing press, 53, 55
PRISM program, 127
privacy, 47, 542–545. *See also* surveillance
advocacy groups, list of, 556
cookies and, 426–427
decline in, 48
described, 243, 244, 535
European Union and, 525–528
evolution of computing and, 81
Facebook and, 82–83, 684, 690, 691, 694
Foursquare and, 321
information rights and, 534–557
Internet users' efforts to preserve, 539–540
legislation, 539, 543, 545–546
online marketing and, 490
payment systems and, 300
policies, 82–83, 215, 321, 548
private industry self-regulation and, 554–556
protection business, emerging, 556–557
"Right to be Forgotten" and, 527, 535, 554
social networks and, 684, 691
technological solutions, 557
Privacy Act, 547
Privacy.org, 556
private cloud, described, 112

Privacy Foundation, 426
Privacy Protection Act, 547
Privacy Rights Clearinghouse, 556
private industrial networks (PTX (private trading exchange))
evolution of B2B e-commerce and, 791
overview, 343–344, 792, 826–832.
Procter & Gamble. *See* P&G
procurement process. *See* B2B e-commerce
described, 795
purchasing managers and, 799
overview of, 795–801
steps, 795–796
product(s)
cycle time, 794
design, collaborative commerce and, 831, 832
substitute, existence of, 730
production scheduling, described, 801
profiling, 540–542, 550. *See* consumer profiling
profits
business strategies and, 350–351
described, 350
industry structure and, 344
Web 2.0 and, 57
programmatic advertising, 371, 395–396, 444–447, 706–707
Project Loon, 134
property rights, 530, 576–577
protocol(s), 106, 113–115
Providence Equity Partners, 155
proximity marketing, 507–508, 510–511
proxy servers (proxies), 126, 200, 279–280
psychology, 374
PTAT (Page Likes, People Talking About This), 474
PTX (private trading exchange). *See* private industrial network
public cloud, described, 111
public key cryptography
described, 269–270
digital envelopes and, 273
using digital signatures and hash digests, 270–272
public key infrastructure. *See* PKI
public policy. *See* legislation
public safety/welfare, 245–246, 584–586, 531
publishing, 77, 621–647. *See also* e-books; book pub-

lishing; newspapers; magazines
business models and, 318, 334–335
book reviews, 380
Google Books settlement and, 590–594
intellectual property rights and, 558
legislation and, 561
media convergence and, 618–620
one-click purchasing and, 565
online marketing and, 380, 405, 417, 435
online sales, 77
printed versus e-book editions, sales statistics
for, 641
pricing of, 75
self-publishing and, 638–639, 644
Pubslush, 328
Puma, 43–45
PUPs (potentially unwanted programs), 250–252
purchasing
decisions, 375–378
Web analytics, 441–443
Python, 214

Q

QoS (quality of service), 124
QQ, 681
QR (quick response) codes, 304, 402, 488, 511
Qualcomm, 137
QuickTime (Apple), 143, 151
Quintiq, 830
Qzone, 681

R

racial differences, 372. *See also* demographic profiles
Racersauction, 695
Rackspace, 188, 331
radio
ads, 437, 441
e-commerce presence maps and, 178–179
information richness and, 53
regulation of, 79
global reach and, 52
radio frequency identification. *See* RFID
railroad insutry, regulation of, 79
Rakuten, 144
Rakuten LinkShare, 331, 400

RAM (random access memory), 110, 208
Ramnit, 251
Randolph, Marc, 667–668
ransomware (scareware), 240, 249, 251
rare earths, 797
Ratesetter, 329
reach, 52, 53, 434, 435, 463, 468, 469, 472, 703, 704.
See also amplification; global reach
real-time bidding process. *See* RTB
real-time customer service chat systems, 412–413
Really Simple Syndication. *See* RSS
RealMedia Player, 151
RealPlayer, 143
Realtor (company), 406
recency, 434, 435
recessions, 406, 788, 803
recommender systems, 420–421
Red Bull, 489
Red Bull Amplifier, 315
Red Hat Linux (Apache), 331
Reddit, 631
RedLaser, 712
redundancy, 118, 208
Reed Elsevier, 417
referral fees, 319
registration forms, 422–424
registration requirements, 209
Rehabilitation Act, 217
REI, 332
relational databases, 428
RenRen, 681
rental car agencies, 226–229
repressive regimes, 47
Requests for Comment. *See* RFCs
Requests for Quotations. *See* RFQs
Resident Advisor, 314–315
responsibility, 531–533
responsive design. *See* RWD
responsive Web design. *See* RWD
restaurant reservations, 774–778
retailers
e-distributers and, 820
global market, overall statistics for, 67
history of the Internet and, 103
information richness and, 53
leading mobile, 492

online marketing and, 385
ranked by online sales, 78
revenue, online, by category, 77
sales, statistics, 76
statistics, 48
value chains and, 348
retargeting ads, 409
retention rate, 434, 436
return on investment. *See* ROI
Reventon, 251
revenue model(s), 174–175, 326, 611
described, 318–319
hybrid, 334
newspapers and, 629–630
overview of, 318–320
RFCs (Requests for Comment), 113
RFID (radio frequency identification), 136–137. *See also* IoT (Internet of Things)
RFID tags, 750
RFQs (requests for quotations), 822, 824, 825, 829
Rhapsody, 318, 333, 334, 336, 604, 615, 649, 663
Rhodia, 833
rich media
ads, 390–392
e-commerce enablers and, 331
history of e-commerce and, 70
mobile marketing and, 402–403
"Rich Boy, The" (Fitzgerald)
richness, 345, 529
described, 53, 55
differentiation and, 352
feature of e-commerce technology, 51–55
online marketing and, 423
RightMove.com, 97
"right to be forgotten", 527, 535, 554
Right to Financial Privacy Act, 547
RightSignature, 258
RightStart, 334
RIM (Research in Motion), 264. *See also* Blackberry (RIM)
Rinspeed, 96
risk assessment, 282
risk aversion, 534
rivalry, among competitors, 346, 347
RKG, 331
Roberts, Larry, 102

RocketHub, 328
Rocket Internet, 72–73, 771
RocketLawyer, 333, 340
ROI (return on investment), 69
Romania, 253
rootkit, 249
root servers, described, 109
Ropars, Olivier, 712
ROPO (research online, purchase offline), 374, 378
RoR (Ruby on Rails), 202, 213–214
Rosetta Stone, 575, 688
routers
described, 105
security and, 258, 279
routing algorithms, 105
Royal National Institute of the Blind (RNIB), 217
RSS (Really Simple Syndication), 153
RSS feeds, 516
RTB (real-time bidding process), 395–396, 445, 446
Rubicon Project, 369
Ruby on Rails. *See* RoR
Rue La La (company), 419, 499
Rusenko, David, 189
Russia, 44, 123, 368, 604
payment systems and, 296
security and, 236, 257
social networks in, 677, 681
surveillance by, 126
Rustock botnet, 250
RWD (responsive Web design), 221, 222

S

SaaS (Software as a Service), 199, 342, 775
B2B e-commerce and, 789, 809
Elemica and, 838
IPXs and, 832
merchant server software and, 203
overview of, 111–113
Sabre Corporation, 761
SAD (systems analysis and design), 219–220
Safari browser (Apple), 275, 552
safe harbor, 554, 563
Sailing Anarchy, 692
Sailnet, 333
Saint Maarten, 88

sales revenue model, 319, 322

sales persons, 53

sales tax, 579–582, 742. *See also* taxation

Salesforce, 112, 331

Sality.AE, 251

Samani, Raj, 235

Sam's Club, 694

Samsung, 136, 331, 566–568

Samwer, Alexander, 72–73

Samwer, Marc, 72–73

Samwer, Oliver, 72

sandboxes, 265

SAP, 112, 331

    B2B e-commerce and, 789

    collaborative commerce and, 810, 811

    dynamic page generation tools and, 198

    purchase of Ariba by, 821

    Retail solutions, 811

    supply chain management and, 802

    sustainability and, 806

    Walmart and, 829

    Wolverine and, 811–812

satellite service, cost/speed of, 120, 121

Saudi Arabia, 577, 606, 721,

SAY Media, 393

scalability, overview of, 207–208

scale economies, described, 342, 796

SCGI, 212

Schaeffler, 343

Schwab (Charles Schwab), 722, 754

SCA (Stored Communication Act), 692

SCM (supply chain management)

    described, 801, 812

    overview of, 812–814

    trends, 801–817

    Walmart and, 829

scope strategy, described, 353

"screen diversity" (multi-screen) environment, 495

Scribd, 318

SDLC (systems development life cycle)

    described, 182

    overview of, 182–191

Seagate, 826

search costs, 68

search engine(s). *See also* SEM (search engine marketing); SEO (search engine optimization)

advertising, 386–390, 409–410, 498, 686

campaigns, 70

described, 148

the history of e-commerce and, 70–71

history of, 148

overview of, 148–151

privacy issues and, 537, 545

top five, 149, 338

Web servers and, 146, 196

Web site optimization and, 210–211

search engine marketing. *See* SEM

search engine optimization. *See* SEO

Sears, 78, 292, 303, 333, 727

SEC (Securities and Exchange Commission), 62, 83, 327, 329, 174

Second Life, 294

Secret key cryptography, 268

Section 508, 217

Secure Electronic Transaction protocol. *See* SET protocol

secure negotiated session, 276–278

Secure Sockets Layer. *See* SSL

SecurID token, 284

Securities Act, 732

Securities and Exchange Commission. *See* SEC

security

    Akamai and, 164

    audits, described, 284

    breaches, disclosure of, 548

    business procedures, 282–287

    cameras, 136

    decline in overall, 47

    dimensions of, 243–244

    e-commerce enablers and, 331

    environment, 238–246

    the history of the Internet and, 104

    importance of, 242–243

    IoT and, 137

    legislation, 282–287

    management policies, 282–287

    organization, 283

    other values and, tension between, 244–246

    overview of, 234–310

    payment systems and, 296, 300–304

    plans, 284–284

    policies, described, 282

poorly designed software and, 261–262
protecting networks, 278–281
public safety and, tension between, 245–246
reports, 240
securing communication channels, 276–278
technology solutions, 266–282
threats, overview of, 246–266
token, described, 284
underground economy market and, 240–241
Web servers and, 146
seed capital, described, 327
SeedInvest, 329
Seed&Spark, 328
sell-side servers, 199, 200
seller-side solutions, 790
seller's lament, 701
Selvadurai, Naveen, 320
SEM (search engine marketing), 47, 150, 178, 331,
   370, 371, 377, 381, 382, 386–390
Senate Committee on Commerce, Science and
   Transportation, 104
sensors. *See* IoT (Internet of Things)
sensory input filtering, 392
sentiment analysis (buzz), 443
sentiment ratio, 434, 436
SEO (search engine optimization), 179, 202, 388,
   389
search costs, described, 53
Seriot, Nicolas, 264
Sertifi, 271
server(s). *See also* Web servers
   cloud computing and, 336
   described, 110
   dynamic page generation tools and, 198
   farms, 191
   security and, 277, 281–282
   software, e-commerce enablers and, 331
   surveillance and, 127
   URLS and, 108
service levels, guaranteed, 135
service provider(s), 333, 340–341
session keys, described, 277
SET (secure electronic transaction) protocol, 291
7-Eleven, 303
SGML (Standard Generalized Markup Language),
   138

Shadowcrew, 245
sharing economy (mesh economy), companies,
   339–340, 769–773
Shell Oil, 833, 837
Sherpalo Investments, 367
Shetty, Reema, 457
shipping costs, 75
shipyards, 790
shopBeacon, 511
Shopgoodwill, 695
Shopify, 189, 214
Shopkick, 511
shopping cart(s)
   abandoned, 412
   CGI and, 211
   databases, 423–424
   described, 201
   latency and, 162
   privacy issues and, 537
   SDLC and, 186
   servers, 200
   software, 202
   Web analytics and, 442–443
   Weebly and, 189
Shopwings, 73
Shopzilla, 335
Shrem, Charlie, 295
Siemens, 343
Signature Financial, 569
signed certificates, 275
Silanis e-SignLive, 258
silicon wafers, 797
Silk Road black market, 295, 588
Silverman, Ben, 605
SIM, 265
SIMILE Widgets, 214
Simple Mail Transfer Protocol. *See* SMTP
Sina Weibo, 681
Singapore, 368, 577, 772
Siri (Apple), 65, 157
site management tools, 196–197
Skinzo, 721
Sky Broadband, 120
Skype, 126, 148, 155, 415–416
Slammer worm, 248, 251
Slingshot, 683

Slippery Slope, 534

Small Business Administration (United States), 327

smart home platforms, 136

SmartBear, 331

smartphone(s). *See also specific devices*

    apps and, 64

    as disruptive technologies, 111, 355

    encryption algorithms and, 544

    history of e-commerce and, 71

    history of the Internet and, 104

    how people actually use, 492–493

    NFC–enabled, 293

    online marketing and, 371, 402, 460–462

    payment systems and, 293, 299–301

    privacy issues and, 535–537, 544

    security and, 263, 264–265

    statistics, 131, 223

    surveillance and, 127

    technology trends and, 47

smartwatches, 136

smishing attacks, 263

smoke detectors, 136

SMS (Short Message Service) texting. *See also* texting

    cost of, 148

    location-based marketing and, 506

    online marketing and, 403, 419

    pricing and, 419

    security and, 263

    spoofing, 263

SMTP (Simple Mail Transfer Protocol), 106, 113

Snapchat, 148, 464, 490, 539, 683, 685, 709, 711

Snapple, 383, 411

Snapshot, 683

sniffers, 260

Snowden, Edward, 127, 245–246, 260, 287, 543

social advertising, 47, 401–402. *See also* social marketing

social commerce. *See* social e-commerce

social contagion, in social networks, 373–374

Social Contract Rule, 534

social density, 466

social gaming, 664, 666

social e-commerce, 46, 728

    Buy buttons, 723, 729, 646

    described, 58, 59

    Facebook and, 58, 729

    overview of, 59–60, 729, 749

    statistics, 47, 61

social engineering, described, 252. *See also* phishing

social graph, 389, 410, 467

social issues. *See also* ethics

    organizing, model for, 529–531

    overview, 524–600

social media. *See also* social networks; social marketing

    e-commerce presence maps and, 178–179

    employee policies, 691

    online marketing and, 371

social marketing

    case study, 513–518

    described, 382

    downside of, 488

    e-commerce enablers and, 331

    expansion of, 371

    introduction to, 460–462

    metrics, 434

    optimizing, 475–476

    overview, 456–523

    players, 463–464

    process, 464–466

social network(s), 681, 679–694. *See also specific social networks*

    advertising revenue and, 686, 687

    apps and, 683, 684–685

    B2B e-commerce and, 788, 791, 816–817

    business models of, 686–688, 692

    collaborative commerce and, 815–816

    community effects and, 373–374

    corporate businesses and, 687–688

    dangers of, 689–692

    demographics and, 681, 685

    examples of, 683, 688

    features and technologies of, 692–693

    future of, 693–694

    growth of, 681–683, 686

    history and evolution of, 679–680

    history of e-commerce and, 71

    major trends, 46–48

    online marketing and, 389, 393, 441

    online recruitment trends and, 767–768

    outside United States, 681

    overview of, 152

mobile platform and, 680, 682, 683, 687
privacy issues and, 536, 538
professions and, 677–678
security and, 260, 262, 277
statistics and, 610, 680–683, 685, 693
top sites, 681, 682, 683
types of, 680
unique features of e-commerce technology and, 55
social search (recommendation), 389, 401
Social Security numbers, 274
social sign-on, 60, 401
social technologies, 345, 529
described, 55
as one of the eight features of e-commerce technology, 51–55
online marketing and, 423
user content generation and, 54–55
social TV, 651
SocialFlow, 331
social-mobile-local nexus, 403
sociology, 374
Softbank, 368, 785
Softlayer (IBM), 188
software. *See also specific software*
bundling, 417
choosing, 193–204
e-commerce enablers and, 331
poorly designed, 261–262
Software as a Service. *See SaaS*
Sohu Sogou, 148
SONET (Synchronous Optical Networks), 131
Sony, 249, 803
SoundCloud, 126, 313–314
Souq.com, 719–721, 722
South Korea, 120, 127, 157, 248, 368, 411, 568, 606
Spain, 148, 368, 386, 527, 581, 604, 681, 777
spam
botnets and, 250
described, 398
laws, 399
legislation, 398
persistence of, as a problem, 47
statistics, 398
spam (junk) Web sites, described, 258–259, 389
SPARC, 830

spear phishing, 240
speed tiers, 582
spiders. *See search engines*
spoken commands. *See voice commands*
sponsored communities, 688, 692
sponsored links, 150–151
sponsorships, 393, 439, 441
spoofing, described, 258–259
sports industry, 613, 634
business models and, 323, 333, 335
spot purchasing, 798, 818
Spotify, 318, 319, 603–606, 607, 620, 648, 649
Sprint, 66, 103, 118
Spurlock, Morgan, 706
SpyPhone, 264
spyware, 252, 537, 548, 557
SQL (Structured Query Language), 261, 428
SQL injection attacks, 261
SQL Server (Microsoft), 248
Square (company), 73, 299, 301–302
Square Reader, 301
Square Register, 302
Squarespace, 186, 189
SSL (Secure Sockets Layer), 146, 269
described, 276–278
Heartbleed hug and, 262
transactions and, 290
SSL/TLS (Secure Sockets Layer/Transport Layer Security), 114, 196
Stackshowers, 695
Standard Generalized Markup Language. *See SGML*
Stanford University, 102, 149, 150, 591
Staples, 78, 299, 332, 727
Starbucks, 133, 480, 815
app, 263
online marketing and, 499
payment systems, 302
security and, 263
Startupbootcamp, 73
start-ups. *See also entrepreneurs*
B2B e-commerce and, 836
business models and, 322, 327, 329
crowdfunding and, 327, 329
payment systems, 299
Web sites for, 188
Weebly and, 190

Starz cable network, 669

State Street Bank & Trust v. Signature Financial Group, Inc., 569

stateless, described, 204

Steinhafel, Gregg, 256

Sterling Commerce, 828

stickiness (duration), 434, 435

Stirling, Lindsey, 421

Stitcher, 606

Stitch Fix, 750–751

stock market, 83, 338–339, 406

Stored Communication Act (SCA). *See* SCA

Story Stream, 635–636

strategic analysis, 730–731, 740–742

strategic partners, 327

strategy of cost competition, 352

StreamCast, 88

streaming media, 151, 331

streaming music, 603–606

streaming video, 163, 175

strengths, building on your, 177–178

Stripe, 293

StudioNow, 706

Structured Query Language. *See* SQL

Subaru, 393

subscription revenue model, 318, 319, 322, 333, 611

substitute products, threat of, 344, 346, 347

substitution cipher, 268

Sukar.com, 720

Sumitomo Chemical, 833

Sun Solaris, 196

Sunde, Peter, 88

Sunoco, 303

SuperPages, 403

supply and demand, 419

supply chain(s)

    business models and, 343

    competition, 789

    described, 790

    procurement process and, overview of, 795–801

    simplification, 802

    value webs and, 350

    visibility and, 800

supply chain management. *See* SCM

supply-push model, 746

SupplyOn, 341, 343, 818

Supreme Court (United States), 569. *See also* legal decisions

"surface/visible" Web, 62

surge pricing, 418–419

surveillance, 47, 245–246

    the history of e-commerce and, 74

    overview of, 125–126

    privacy issues and, 542–545

    sniffers and, 260

sustainability, 788

    Elemica and, 838

    supply chain management and, 805–806

    Walmart and, 830

sustaining technologies, described, 355

sustainable supply chains, 806

Swarm app, 321

Swatch, 136

"sweat of the brow" theory, 568

Sweden, 87–88, 288, 328, 368, 581, 603

Swift, Taylor, 605

switching costs, 69, 353

SWOT analysis, 177–178

Sybase, 198

Symantec, 240, 254, 262

Symantec Norton AntiVirus, 281

Symbian, 222, 263

symmetric key cryptography, 268–269.

synchronous optical networks. *See* SONET

syndication, 335

synergies, 731

Synnex, 813, 814

Syria, 262

system architecture, 194, 208

system design specification, described, 184

System Doctor, 250

system functionality requirements, 182–183

system testing, 191

systems analysis/planning phase (SDLC), 182–183

systems development life cycle. *See* SDLC

T

21st Century Communications and Video Accessibility Act. *See* CVAA

T1 connections, 120–122, 131

T3 connections, 120, 121–122, 131
tabbed browsing, 147
tablet computers. *See also* m-commerce (mobile
 e-commerce)
  apps and, 64
  as disruptive technologies, 355
  growth in the number of, 99
  the history of e-commerce and, 71
  increased sales of, 131
  magazines and, 633–638
  online marketing and, 371, 402, 460–462
  as the preferred mobile shopping device,
   167–168
  security and, 265, 266
  statistics, 63
  technology trends and, 47
Tagged, 683
Taiwan, 157, 368, 606, 805
TalkTalk, 120
Target, 299, 300, 303, 728
  online marketing and, 471
  security and, 241, 254–256
target audience, understanding, 175
TaskRabbit, 296, 769
Tata Communications, 118
taxation, 48, 578–582. *See also* sales tax; VAT (value-
 added tax)
  Amazon and, 579, 742
  global nature of e-commerce and, 84
  increased acceptance of, for online purchases,
   47
  purchasing decisions and, 375
  value-added (VAT), 579, 582
TCP (Transmission Control Protocol), 262, 279
TCP/IP (Transmission Control Protocol/Internet
 Protocol), 100, 102
  architecture, 107
  described, 106
  FTP and, 114
  Internet architecture and, 116, 117
  intranets and, 121–122
  invention of, 102
  protocol suite, 107
  security and, 258, 277
TechCrunch, 706
technological convergence, 617

technologists, 68
technology, e-commerce
  eight unique features of, 345
  infrastructure, 79–80
  trends, 47
TechStars, 327
Telefonica, 121
telegraph wires, tapping of, 245
telephone(s)
  -based customer service, 413
  closed nature of, security and, 264
  the history of the Internet and, 100, 104
  as a one-to-one technology, 55
  sales, 75
  statistics, 370
  wireless Internet access, 131–133
  wiretapping of, 245
telepresence, overview of, 156
television, 396, 651–653
  advertising, 437, 439, 441, 478, 479, 480, 495
  business models and, 318, 334–335
  e-commerce presence maps and, 178–179
  global reach and, 52
  information richness and, 53
  interactivity and, 53
  iTunes Store and, 154–155
  regulation of, 79
  share of U.S. households achieved by, 62
  statistics, 370
  viewing statistics, 404
Teliris, 156
Telnet, 114
Tencent Soso, 148
terabits 128, 130
Terms of Use policies, 546
terrorism, 127, 245–246, 543. *See also* surveillance
Tesco, 46, 690
testing, overview of, 191–192
Texas Instruments, 803
texting. *See also* SMS (Short Message Service)
  cost of, 148
  location-based marketing and, 506
  mobile marketing and, 402–403, 419
  pricing and, 419
  security and, 263
  spoofing, 263

surveillance and, 127
Tewari, Naveen, 367–369
textile industry, 806
Thailand, 577, 803
Thawte, 331
The Iconic, 72
Theknot, 174, 175
thermostats, smart, 136
TheSeam, 341, 818, 826
3G (Third generation) technology, 132, 134, 505, 508
Thing Labs, 706
Tiananmen Square massacre, 125, 126
Tianji, 677–678
Ticketmaster Corp. v. Tickets.com, 575–576
Tiffany & Co., 160, 408, 748
Tiger Global Management, 720
tiger teams, 254
tight coupling, 802
Timberland, 411
time starvation, 340–341
Time Warner, 136, 137, 584, 705–706
TinyCo, 490
Tiscali, 120
Titan Aerospace, 134
TJX Companies, 255, 257
TLDs (top-level domains), 109, 139–141
TLS (Transport Layer Security), 146, 276–278, 290
T-Mobile, 132, 133
Tohuku earthquake, 795, 796, 803
Token Ring networks, TCP/IP and, 106
Tomlinson, Ray, 102
T-Online, 148
top-level domains. *See* TLD, 259
Tor network, 88, 241
Toshiba Corporation, 797, 803
totalitarian dictators, 125
TotalNews, 576
toy industry, 77
Toys "R" Us, 808
TPB (The Pirate Bay), 86–89
Tracert, described, 114
tracking codes, 425
tracking files, 424–427. *See also* mobile apps; beacons; cookies

Trademark Act, 571
trademarks, 571–576. *See also* intellectual property
TradeSpace, 816
transaction(s). *See also* credit card transactions; payment systems
    auctions and, 695, 696
    broker business model, described, 333
    brokers, 333, 338–340, 749
    costs, 68, 75, 794
    described, 49
    the eight unique features of e-commerce technology and, 51–55
    fee revenue model, described, 319, 322
    fees, 319, 333, 334, 834
    logs, 422–425, 537
    processing, 200
    SDLC and, 183
    security and, 246–266
    statistics, 48
    typical, 246
    vulnerable points in, 247
Transmission Control Protocol. *See* TCP
Transmission Control Protocol/Internet Protocol. *See* TCP/IP
trans-organization business process, 826–827
transparency, era of, 82
Transport Layer, 106, 114
Transport Layer Security. *See* TLS
Transport Services and Representation Standards layer, 116
Transportation Department (United States), 227
transposition cipher, 268
TransUnion Corporation, 544
travel industry, 54, 759–764
    aggregator sites, 762
    business models and, 323, 333
    C2C e-commerce and, 58
    the history of e-commerce and, 70
    industry, dynamics, 761–762
    industry structural analysis and, 346
    mobile Web sites/apps and, 226–229
    online marketing and, 385, 418–419, 475–476
    origins of e-commerce and, 66
    phony reviews and, 763–764
    pricing and, 75, 418, 419
Travelocity, 323, 333, 346, 228, 761

Trend Micro, 235, 263
TripAdvisor, 761, 762, 763–764
Trojan horses, 239, 249, 251
True Value (company), 828
trust, of consumers, 380
TRUSTe Internet privacy protection program, 555
Tuenti, 681
TUI AG, 761
Tumblr, 46, 153, 729, 680, 682, 686, 688, 693, 709
    B2B e-commerce and, 816–817
    described, 56–57, 463, 464, 682
    hashtags and, 83
    market dominance of, 463
    security and, 262
    social marketing and, 382, 463–465
Tunisia, 125, 606
tunneling, 278
Turkey, 126, 459, 606
24/7 RealMedia, 541
TweetDeck, 481
twisted-pair cable, 130
Twitalyzer, 481
Twitter, 46, 680, 688
    apps and, 64
    B2B e-commerce and, 816–817
    business models and, 320, 333, 334
    Buy button and, 729
    censorship and, 126
    collaborative commerce and, 816
    community-building tools, 332–334
    dangers of, 689–690
    features, 474–481
    followers, 477
    future of, 79
    hashtags and, 83, 477
    Lead Generation Cards, 478, 480
    links, 477
    magazines and, 638
    market strategy and, 325
    market dominance of, 463
    marketing campaigns, starting, 479–480
    marketing results, measuring, 480–481
    messages (DM), 477
    micro blogging text messaging service, 464
    mobile ads, 479
    online marketing and, 403, 474–481
    overview, 474–481
    replies, 477
    retweet, 477
    security and, 241, 262, 277
    statistics, 56, 152, 461, 681–683, 685–687, 693
    surveillance and, 127
    target audiences and, 176
    television ad retargeting, 478, 479, 480
    timeline, 477
    tweets, 477
    Web 2.0 and, 56
Twitter Amplify, 478, 479
Twitter Enhanced Profile Pages, 478, 479
Twitter MoPub, 403, 499
Twitter Promoted Accounts, 478, 479
Twitter Promoted Trends, 478, 479, 480
Twitter Promoted Tweets, 320, 477, 479
2001: A Space Odyssey (film), 156
two-tier architecture, 193, 194, 195
TypePad, 153
typosquatting, 574

U

Uber, 47, 58, 339–340, 769–773
    described, 57
    future of, 79
    payment systems and, 296, 299–300
    pricing and, 418–419
uBid, 695
ubiquity, 423, 529
    described, 52, 55, 345
    differentiation and, 352
    as one of the eight features of e-commerce
      technology, 51–55
    scope strategy and, 353
UBM TechInsights, 797
U.K. *See* United Kingdom
Ukash, 294
Ulbricht, Ross, 588
UltraViolet, 657
UMVs (unique monthly visitors), 176. *See also*
  unique visitors
Unbound Commerce, 331
Under Armour, 814

underground (shadow) economy market, 240–241
unfair competitive advantage, described, 324
unfit fitness, 355
Uniform Resource Locators. *See* URLs
unique visitors, 183, 196, 434, 435, 436, 460, 463, 503, 512, 632, 683, 703, 704
   adult Web sites, 585
   apps, 494
   BuzzFeed, 632
   Dell, 747
   Digg, 632
   eBay, 694
   Facebook, 401, 680
   job sites, 765
   Macys, 744
   New Yorker, 637
   online brokerages, 754
   online newspapers, 626, 627, 632, 635
   online video sites, 614
   Orbitz Worldwide, 226
   Pandora, 614
   Pinterest, 482, 682
   Priceline, 698
   pure digital news siites, 632
   Realtor.com, 758
   Reddit, 631
   Skittles, 468
   top portal/search engines, 683, 702
   top social networks, 683
   U.S. banking Web sites, 753
   Vice, 631
   YouTube, 154
   Weebly, 189
   Wikipedia, 154
unit testing, 191
United Airlines, 226
United Arab Emirates (UAE), 457–459, 606, 719, 721
United Kingdom (U.K). *See also* Great Britain; European Union
   crowdfunding in, 328–329
   cybercrime in, 235, 239, 253
   Just Falafel in, 458
   InMobi in, 368
   mobile device usage in, 157–159, 493, 730
   mobile e-commerce in, 47, 59, 494, 723, 730
   mobile marketing expenditures in, 495, 496

   online gambling, 589
   OpenTable in, 774, 777
   Puma in, 43
   regulation of encryption software, 287
   Spotify in, 604
   Tiffany in, 408
   time spent with media in, 404
   TripAdvisor in, 783
United Nations, 123, 217, 562, 805, 806, 830
United Parcel Service. *See* UPS
United States Patents and Trademarks Office. *See* USPTO
United States Postal Service. *See* USPS
universal computing, 138
universal standards, 51–55, 345, 353, 423, 529
universalism, 534
University of California, Berkeley, 149
University of Florida, 129
University of Illinois, 103
University of New Hampshire, 189
University of Utah, 102
Unix, 138, 194, 212, 281, 296
Unlawful Internet Gambling Enforcement Act, 589
unsubscribe rate, 434
UPS (United Parcel Service), 350, 373, 814, 589, 745
Urban Futbol, 489
Urbanspoon, 777
URLs (Uniform Resource Locators), 83, 486. *See also* domain names; hyperlinks
   dead, 197
   described, 108
   hypertext and, 139
   parts of, 108, 139
   search engines and, 150
   security and, 263, 275, 277
   sharing, 210
   unique, 62
US Ignite, 129
U.S. Patent Act, 564
U.S. SAFE WEB Act, 286
US-CERT (United States Computer Emergency Readiness Team), 285
USA PATRIOT Act, 260, 285, 286, 543, 578
Usablenet, 331
usage-based billing, 582
USDA farm commodities, 826

user profiles, online marketing and, 394
USPS (United States Postal Service), 350
USPTO (United States Patent and Trademark Office), 565, 567, 569, 571
utility programs, 113–41`29
UUnet, 103

V

value chain(s), 352, 354, 579, 787, 792, 802, 825
    firm, described, 349, 731
    industry, 348, 759
value chain management. *See* VCM
value proposition, 317–318, 326
value webs, 349–350
Valve, 97
variable costs, 413
VAT (value-added taxes), 579, 580–581, 582
VBScript (Microsoft), 213
VCM (value chain management), 342, 820–821
Veltri, Dan, 189
vendors, 379–380
venture capital
    freemium strategy and, 359
    industry consortia and, 825
    investors, described, 327
    privacy issues and, 556
Verio (NTT Communications), 118
VeriSign, 140, 276, 331
Verizon, 118, 188, 264, 396, 508, 578, 584, 617, 670, 704, 706
versioning, 416
vertical/specialized (vortal) business model, 333
vertical market portals, 704, 707–709
vertical marketplaces, 343
vertical markets, described, 791, 818
vertical scaling, described, 207
Vevo, 617, 683
Viacom, 563, 564
Viadeo, 677-678
ViaForensics, 263
Viber, 148
Vice, 631
video. *See* online video
video ads, 371
    costs, 441

described, 392–393
display ad marketing and, 391–393
Google and, 496
the history of e-commerce and, 70
video chat, overview of, 156
video conferencing, overview of, 156
video games, 318, 329. *See also* online games
Video Privacy Protection Act, 547
video servers, described, 147
video services, overview of, 154–155
View Source option, 425
view-through rate. *See* VTR
view-to-cart ratio, 434, 435
viewability, 396–397, 435
Viget, 44
Vine, 683
viral marketing, 71, 400
Virgin Media, 120
virtual currencies, 294, 295–296
virtual merchant business model, 333, 733–735
virtual private networks. *See* VPNs
virtual reality, 329. *See also* Oculus Rift; Google Glass
virtual scrapbooks. *See* Pinterest
Virtualstream, 188
virus(es), 235, 239
    backdoors and, 249
    described, 248
    examples, 251
    file-infecting, 251
    payloads, 248
Virut virus, 249
Visa, 299
Visa Checkout, 292
VisaNow, 333
vishing attacks, 263
visibility, 800, 801, 827
vision statement, 174
visioning process, 174
VisualRoute, 114, 115
Visual Studio (Microsoft), 186
VK, 681
Vodaphone, 118, 121
Voice Now (LG), 157
VoIP (Voice over Internet Protocol), 127, 155
Volvo, 66, 803

Vonage, 155
Vox Media, 631, 634–637
VPNs (virtual private networks), 241, 278
VTR (view-through rate), 434, 435
Vuforia, 97

W

W3 Innovations, 490
W3C (World Wide Web Consortium), 113, 123, 143, 144, 427
Walgreen's, 299
Wall Street Journal, 440
    business models and, 322, 334, 335, 625
walled garden, 615–616
Walmart, 727, 728, 808
    Big Data and, 751
    business models and, 333, 341
    classification of, as an e-tailer, 332
    collaborative commerce and, 814
    labor practices and, 797–798
    Node.js and, 213
    online marketing and, 408, 499
    payment systems and, 299, 300, 303
    private industrial networks and, 827, 828, 829–830
    ranked by online sales, 78
    Retail Link, 829
    revenue statistics, 66
    supply chain management and, 806
    sustainability and, 806
    widgets and, 156
Walt Disney Company. *See* Disney
Warg, Gottfrid Svartholm, 88
warrants, 127, 265
Washington Post, 576, 625, 630, 635
Washington Post, et al. v. Total News, Inc., 576
Washio, 73
Wayport. *See* AT&T Wi-Fi Services, 133
WCAG (Web Content Accessibility Guidelines), 216–217
WCED (United Nations World Commission on Environment and Development), 805
weakness, overcoming, 177–178
wearable devices, 136
Web (World Wide Web)
    advent of, 103, 137–138
    collaborative commerce and, 815–816
    crawler, 150, 387
    as "dead," proclamations of, 65
    described, 49, 62, 99
    evolution of corporate computing and, 81
    features/services, 147–147
    growth of, 61–65
    growth in the number of apps and, 64–65
    the history of e-commerce and, 66–79
    overview of, 137–147
    shift towards apps and, 64–65
    Wild West" character of, 70
Web 1.0, 56, 57
Web 2.0, 56–57, 152–157, 214, 340
Web analytics, 197, 435. *See also* analytics
    described, 441
    e-commerce enablers and, 331
    overview of, 441–443
    software, 202
Web application servers, 194, 199–200
Web apps, 156
Web beacons. *See* beacons
Web browsers. *See* browsers
Web bugs. *See* beacons (Web bugs)
Web clients, 145–147
Web Content Accessibility Guidelines. *See* WCAG
WebCrawler, 149
Web pages, 62, 99, 146. *See also* Web sites
    design, 221
    downloading, 121, 162
    dynamic, 198, 213
    early, 138, 193
    HTML and, 141–142, 143, 560
    HTTP and, 113, 139
    JSP and, 213
    proxy servers and, 280
    search engines and, 62, 148, 149, 150
    static, 205
Web performance management, 331
Web presence, 70–71, 218, 443, 745
Web Privacy Center, 426
Web server(s). *See also* servers
    basic functionality provider by, 196
    extension, 212
    HTML5 and, 143

open source software for, 202
overview of, 145–147
performance, degradation in, 206
software, 146, 194–199
Web Server Survey (Netcraft), 194
Web services, 46, 98, 99, 147, 156–157
Web site(s)
architecture, simple versus multi-tiered, 193–194
basic business considerations for, 209–210
cost, 179–180, 187
design, e-commerce enablers and, 331
e-commerce presence maps and, 178–179
features that annoy customers, 209
hosting your own, 188
implementation of, 191–192
interactivity tools, 211–214
logical design, 185
maintenance, 191–192
management tools, 196–197
online marketing and, 382, 383–384
optimization tools, 210–211
performance, degradation in, 206
performance, optimizing, 192–192
physical design, 185
SDLC, 182–191
security, available tools for, 267
software, choosing, 193–204
spoof, 275
successful, eight most important factors of, 210
templates, 189
testing, 191
tools for building, 186–187
Weebly and, 189–190
Web-based attacks, statistics, 239
WebChat, 126
WebCrawler, 149
WebEx (Cisco), 156
WebIntellects, 331
weblogs. *See* blogs (weblogs)
WebMD, 334, 393
Webroot, 263
Webtrends, 197, 331, 443, 474
WebTrust, 555
Webvan, 76, 722
WeChat, 464

Weebly, 186, 189–190
Weinstein Company, 660, 668
Well, The 334, 679
Wells Fargo, 299, 722, 753
WEP (Wired Equivalency Policy), 278
West Elm, 485
Westchester.gov, 692
Westergren, Tim, 357
WhatsApp, 65, 148, 464, 683, 685
WHERE, 712
white hats, 254
Whitman, Meg, 710
Whole Foods, 299, 485
wholesale model, 644–645
Wi-Fi. *See also* wireless networks
described, 132, 133
IoT and, 136
location-based marketing and, 508, 509, 510
network diagram, 133
Orbitz and, 227
security and, 263, 278
widgets, 156, 214
Wikimedia Foundation, 154
Wikipedia, 56, 95, 347, 154, 686
wikis, 154. *See also* Wikipedia
Wikitude, 95–97
"Wild West" character, of the Web, 70
Williams-Sonoma, 203
WiMax, 132, 133, 134
Wimdu, 771–772
Windows (Microsoft), 69, 108, 159
ASP and, 212
the history of the Web and, 138
IIS and, 195
open source browsers for, 147
Ping and, 114
security and, 247, 250, 276, 281
Web clients and, 147
Windows Live (Microsoft), 112
Windows Mobile (Microsoft), 111, 222
Windows Phone (Microsoft), 143, 158, 222, 568
Windows Vista (Microsoft), 108
"winner take all" market, 69, 421
winner's regret, 701
WIPO (World Intellectual Property Organization), 562–563, 571

Wired Magazine, 420

wireless access points. *See* hotspots

wireless Internet, 130–134. *See also* Wi-Fi

wireless local area networks. *See* WLANs

Wireless Markup Language. *See* WML

wiretapping, 245

Wix, 189, 190, 222, 224

WLANs (wireless local area networks), 131–132, 134

WML (Wireless Markup Language), 227

Wolfram Connected Devices Project, 137

Wolfram|Alpha Widgets, 214

Wolverine World Wide, 811

Woof Purr Studio, 189

WORA (Write Once Run Anywhere) programs, 212

Word (Microsoft), 142

WordPad (Microsoft), 142

WordPress, 153, 186, 188, 189, 199, 214

working capital, 733

working conditions, 788, 797–798, 804–805. *See also* labor practices

World Bank, 328

World Book encyclopedias, 347

World Intellectual Property Organization. *See* WIPO.

World Trade Center attack (1993), 245

World Trade Center attack (September 11, 2011), 245

World Trade Organization. See WTO

World War II, 268

World Wide Web. *See* Web; Web sites

worms, 248, 251, 239, 281

WPA2 (Wi-Fi Protected Access 2), 278

WTO (World Trade Organization), 803, 804

WUPay (Western Union), 292

W.W. Grainger, 78, 341, 342, 353, 818, 820

WYSIWYG editing, 199

X

Xanga, 153

Xbox. *See* Microsoft Xbox

X-cart, 202

Xerox, 532

XeroxParc Labs, 102

Xing, 681

XML (eXtensible Markup Language), 142, 145, 835

XSEDE (Extreme Science and Engineering Discovery Environment), 129

Y

Y&R Group, 500

Yahoo

   business models and, 322, 333, 702, 703, 708, 709

   classification of, as a portal, 335, 338

   issues facing, 709

   as a intermediary, 75

   legislation and, 563–564

   magazines and, 638

   NSA and, 543

   online marketing and, 410, 411, 444–446

   ownership of Tumblr by, 56, 682

   pricing and, 583

   privacy issues and, 539, 545, 546, 548, 555

   security and, 248, 253, 276

   sponsored links and, 150

   statistics, 683, 686

   surveillance and, 125

   top portal/search engine, 683, 686, 702, 704

   tracking files and, 427

Yahoo Directory, 210

Yahoo Local, 403

Yahoo Messenger, 148

Yahoo Sponsored Search, 387

Yahoo Stores Professional, 201–202

Yang, Jerry, 149

Y Combinator, 190, 327

Yelp, 403, 490, 763–764, 630

yield management, 418

Yodlee, 298

Yokohama, 833

Yousef, Ramzi, 245

YouTube, 46, 64

   described, 56

   B2B e-commerce and, 816

   censorship and, 126

   fiber optics and, 130

   market strategy and, 325

   movie rental service, 659–660

   online marketing and, 400, 408

   statistics, 161, 686

   steaming media and, 151

YP (Yellow Pages), 97, 403, 496, 507

Z

Zagat, 777
Zagura, 97
Zalando, 72, 96
Zalora, 72, 73
ZANO, 328
Zanui, 72
Zappos, 45, 393, 409
Zediva, 564
09 Droid developer, 265
Zen Cart, 202
zero-day vulnerability, 261–262
Zeus botnet, 249, 250, 251
Ziegfeld, Ziggy, 417

Zigbee, 136
Zimmerman, Phil, 275
Zinio, 638, 639–640
ZIP codes, 143, 163, 446
Zipjet, 73
Zong, 712
Zopa, 329
Zotob, 251
Zubie, 137
Zuccarini, John, 574
Zuckerberg, Mark, 72, 82, 684
Z-Wave, 136
Zynga, 539, 666

Credits

CHAPTER 1
p.43, Jumping Puma, © ngaga35/Fotolia.com; p.86, Pirate Bay, © Tommy (Louth)/Alamy.

CHAPTER 2
p.96, Augmented Reality, © fairoesh/Fotolia.com; Figure 2.10, © Visualware, Inc., 2012. Used with permission.

CHAPTER 3
p.171, HTML5, © Azimuth Interactive, Inc.; Figure 3.12, screenshot of WebTrends Analytics 10, © WebTrends, Inc., 2014. Used with permission.

CHAPTER 4
p.235, CyberAttack, © Rafal Olechowski/Fotolia; Figure 4.4, © keith morris/Alamy, p.302, PayPal, © Ian Dagnall/Alamy

CHAPTER 5
p.313, Electronic Music, © grasycho/Fotolia.com; p.357, Pandora.com, © NetPhotos/Alamy

CHAPTER 6
p.367, Mobile Advertising, © fotografiedk/Fotolia.com; Figure 6.1, adapted from Kotler and Armstrong, Principles of Marketing, 13e, 2009. Reprinted by permission of Pearson Education, Inc., Upper Saddle River, NJ; Figures 6.5 and 6.8, based on data from eMarketer, Inc.,© 2014, used with permission; Table 6.4, based on data from eMarketer, Inc., © 2014, used with permission.

CHAPTER 7
p.457, Social Media in Different Languages, © maigi/Fotolia.com; Figures 7.5, 7.8, 7.9, 7.10, 7.11, and 7.15, based on data from eMarketer, Inc., © 2014, used with permission; p.513, ExchangeHunterJumper.com, © 2014 Eohippus, LLC.

CHAPTER 8
p.525, Privacy Policy, © fotodo/Fotolia.com, p.590, Google books, © Cyberstock/Alamy.

CHAPTER 9
p.603, Globe with Headphones, © Kit Wai Chan/Fotolia.com; Figures 9.18 and 9.22, based on data from eMarketer, Inc., © 2014, used with permission; p. 667, © Digitallife/Alamy.

CHAPTER 10
p.677, Social Networks Around the World, © gigra/Fotolia.com; Figure 10.2, based on data from eMarketer, Inc., © 2014, used with permission; p.710, eBay, © Iain Masterton/Alamy.

CHAPTER 11
p.719, Globe with focus on Africa, Middle East, Europe, © Fenton/Fotolia.com; Figures 11.2 and 11.3, based on data from eMarketer, Inc., © 2014, used with permission; p. 774, OpenTable, © Justin Sullivan/Getty Images.

CHAPTER 12
p. 785, B2B, © paradox/Fotolia.com

Video Cases

CHAPTER 1 INTRODUCTION TO E-COMMERCE

1.1 The Future of E-commerce

CHAPTER 2 E-COMMERCE INFRASTRUCTURE

2.1 Google Data Center Efficiency Best Practices

2.2 NBA: Competing on Global Delivery

CHAPTER 3 BUILDING AN E-COMMERCE PRESENCE

3.1 ESPN Goes to eXtreme Scale

3.2 Data Warehousing at REI: Understanding the Customer

CHAPTER 4 E-COMMERCE SECURITY AND PAYMENT SYSTEMS

4.1 Cyberespionage: The Chinese Threat

4.2 Stuxnet and Cyberwarfare

4.3 IBM Zone Trusted Information Channel (ZTIC)

4.4 Open ID and Web Security

CHAPTER 5 E-COMMERCE BUSINESS STRATEGIES

5.1 Deals Galore at Groupon

5.2 Angel Investing

CHAPTER 6 E-COMMERCE MARKETING AND ADVERTISING

6.1 Nielsen Online Campaign Ratings

CHAPTER 7 SOCIAL, MOBILE, AND LOCAL MARKETING

7.1 The Power of Like

CHAPTER 8 ETHICS, LAW, AND E-COMMERCE

8.1 Facebook Privacy

8.2 What Net Neutrality Means for You

8.3 Lawrence Lessig on Net Neutrality

CHAPTER 9 ONLINE MEDIA

9.1 YouTube's 7th Birthday

CHAPTER 10 ONLINE COMMUNITIES

10.1 Mint Returns for Goodwill's eBay Auctions of Thrift-Store Finds

CHAPTER 11 E-COMMERCE RETAILING AND SERVICES

11.1 Etsy: A Marketplace and a Community

CHAPTER 12 B2B E-COMMERCE

12.1 Ford AutoXchange B2B Marketplace

12.2 Flextronics Uses Elementum's Cloud-based Mobile Supply Chain Apps

Learning Tracks

CHAPTER 1 INTRODUCTION TO E-COMMERCE

1.1 Global E-commerce Europe

1.2 Global E-commerce Latin America

1.3 Global E-commerce China

CHAPTER 6 E-COMMERCE MARKETING AND ADVERTISING

6.1 Basic Marketing Concepts

6.2 Consumer Behavior: Cultural, Social, and Psychological Background Factors

6.3 Social Media Marketing—Blogging

CHAPTER 7 SOCIAL, MOBILE, AND LOCAL MARKETING

7.1 Social Media Marketing: Facebook

7.2 Social Media Marketing: Twitter

E-commerce 2015 Companion Web Site